The Good
Food Guide
2004

D1465092

About the Editor

Andrew Turvil has been head of the research and inspection programme, as well as a member of the senior editorial team, for *The Good Food Guide* since the early '90s. He is the Guide's sixth Editor since its beginnings in 1951. He is also the Editor of *The Which? Pub Guide*.

The Good Food Guide 2004

Edited by
Andrew Turvil

Consultant Editor
Jim Ainsworth

WHICH?
BOOKS
CONSUMERS' ASSOCIATION

Which? Books are commissioned and researched by
Consumers' Association and published by
Which? Ltd, 2 Marylebone Road,
London NW1 4DF

Distributed by The Penguin Group:
Penguin Books Ltd, 80 Strand,
London WC2R 0RL

British Library Cataloguing in Publication Data
A catalogue record for this book is
available from the British Library

ISBN 0 85202 936 5

Senior contributing writers: Bill Evans, David Kenning, Susan Low, David Mabey
and Stuart Walton

Also warm thanks to: Margaret Atherton, Lynn Bressler, Linda Edge, John
Kenward, Hugh Morgan, Katharine Servant, Allen Stidwell and Richard John
Wheelwright

In-house editorial and production: Charlie Hardy, Kevin Leamy, Diane Tang,
Mary Tang and Alison Williams

For a full list of Which? books, please write to:
Which? Books, Castlemead, Gascoyne Way,
Hertford X, SG14 1LH
or access our web site at http://www.which.net

Photoset by Tradespools, Frome, Somerset
Printed in England by Clays Ltd, St Ives plc

Cover: Price Watkins Design Limited

Contents

The Good Food Guide voucher scheme £5

Again this year the Guide includes three £5 vouchers that readers will be able to redeem against the price of meals taken in participating restaurants. (Look for the £5 symbol at the very end of entries to locate those participating.) Only one voucher may be used per booked table, for a minimum of two people. Remember that your intention to use the voucher MUST be mentioned at the time of booking. Some restaurants may restrict use of the voucher at some sessions or for some menus (usually 'special offer' or lower-cost set meals); it is best to ask when booking. Actual vouchers (not photocopies) must be presented. The vouchers will be valid from 1 October 2003 to 30 September 2004, and may not be used in conjunction with any other offers.

The Guide online

Internet users can find *The Good Food Guide* online at the Which? Online website http://www.which.net. You will need to be a Which? Online subscriber to make full use of the Guide online. See the website for details.

How to use the Guide

FINDING A RESTAURANT

If you are seeking a restaurant in a particular area: *first go to the maps* at the centre of the book. Once you know the locality (or, for London, the restaurant name), go to the relevant section of the book to find the entry for the restaurant. The Guide's main entries are divided into seven sections: London, England, Scotland, Wales, Channel Islands, Northern Ireland, and Republic of Ireland. In the London section, restaurants are listed alphabetically by name; in all other sections, they are listed by locality (usually the name of the town or village).

In addition to the main entries are the Round-ups (a range of restaurants, cafés, bistros and pubs that are worth a visit but do not merit a full entry): those for London can be found just after the London main-entry section, and those for everywhere else are towards the back of the book just after the Republic of Ireland main-entry section.

If you know the name of the restaurant: *go to the index* at the back of the book, which lists both main and Round-up entries.

If you are seeking award-winning restaurants, those offering a particular cuisine, etc.: *make use of the lists* starting on page 10, which feature the top-rated restaurants, The Guide's longest-serving restaurants, restaurants with outstanding wine cellars, special awards for 2004, London restaurants by cuisine, and new entries.

HOW TO READ A GUIDE ENTRY

Please see inside front cover for explanation of symbols and cooking marks. At the top of each main entry you will find the restaurant's name, map number, address, telephone and fax numbers, its email address and website if it has these, as well as any symbols that may apply to the establishment. The cuisine style is also given; this is not meant to be a comprehensive assessment of cooking style, but rather to act as a helpful pointer and in many cases has been suggested by the restaurant itself. At the top of entries you will also find the mark, from 1 to 10, awarded by the editor for cooking, and the cost range for one person having a three-course meal including wine. The middle part of the entry describes food, wines, atmosphere and so on, while the final section gives a wealth of additional information, explained below.

Cost

The price range given is based on the cost of a three-course meal (lunch and/or dinner) for one person, including coffee, house wine, service and cover charge where applicable, according to information supplied by the restaurant. The lower figure is the least you are likely to pay, from either á la carte or set-price menus, and may apply only to lunch. The higher figure indicates a probable maximum cost, sometimes based on a set-price meal of more than three courses, if that is what is offered. This figure is inflated by 20 per cent to reflect the fact that some people may order more expensive wine, extra drinks and some higher-priced 'special' dishes, and that price rises may come into effect during the life-time of this edition of the Guide.

Meals

At the bottom of entries information on the types of meals offered is given, with any variations for lunch (L) and dinner (D), and details of availability. An á la carte menu is signified by the letters *alc*. This is followed by a range of prices for main courses, rounded up to the nearest 50p. *Set L* denotes a set-price lunch; *Set D* means set-price dinner. Set meals usually consist of three courses, but can include many more. If a set meal has fewer than three courses, this is stated. If there is a cover charge, this is also indicated. Brief details of other menus, such as light lunch or bar snacks, are also given. If there is a cover charge, that is also mentioned here.

Service

Net prices means that prices of food and wine are inclusive of service charge, and this is indicated clearly on the menu and bill; *not inc*, that service is not included and is left to the discretion of the customer; *10%*, that a fixed service charge of 10 per cent is automatically added to the bill; *10% (optional)*, that 10 per cent is added to the bill along with the word 'optional' or similar qualifier; and *none*, that no service charge is made or expected and that any money offered is refused. *Card slips closed* indicates that the total on the slips of credit cards is closed when handed over for signature.

Other details

Information is also given on *seating, outside seating* and *private parties*. We say *car park* if the restaurant provides free parking facilities for patrons (*small car park* if it has only a few spaces), and say *vegetarian meals* only if menus list at least one vegetarian option as a starter and one as a main course (if this is not noted, a restaurant may still be able to offer vegetarian options with prior notice – it is worth phoning to check).

Any restrictions on children are given, such as *no children* or *no children under 6 after 8pm*; otherwise, it can be assumed that children are welcome. In addition, *children's helpings* are noted if smaller portions are available at a reduced price; *jacket and tie* if it is compulsory for men to wear a jacket and tie to the restaurant; *no smoking* if smoking is not permitted in all eating areas (or other restrictions on smoking are explained); *wheelchair access* if the proprietor has confirmed that the entrance is at least 80cm wide and passages at least 120cm wide in accordance with the Royal Association for Disability and Rehabilitation (RADAR) recommendations, and *also WC* if the proprietor has assured us that toilet facilities are suitable for disabled people (*not WC* means these are not available or the proprietor is not sure). *Music* indicates that live or recorded music is usually played in the dining-room; *occasional music* that it sometimes is; *no music* that it never is. *No mobile phones* means the restaurant requests these are switched off.

Accommodation

For establishments offering overnight accommodation, the number of rooms, along with facilities provided in the rooms (e.g. bath/shower, TV, phone), is set out. Prices are given usually for bed and breakfast (*B&B*). *D,B&B* indicates that the price also includes dinner. The first figure given is the lowest price for one person in a single room, or single occupancy of a double, the second is the most expensive price for two people in a double room or suite. *Rooms for disabled* means the establishment has stated that its accommodation is suitable for wheelchair-users. Restrictions on children, and facilities for guests with babies, are indicated. *The Which? Guide to Good Hotels* means the establishment is also listed in the 2004 edition of our sister guide to around 1,000 hotels in Britain.

Miscellaneous information

At the end of London entries, the nearest Underground station is given after the symbol ⊖. For restaurants that have elected to participate in the *Good Food Guide* £5 voucher scheme, a (£5) symbol appears at the very end of entries (see page 6 for further details).

The top-rated restaurants

(See inside front cover for explanation of marking system.)

Mark **10** for cooking

London
Gordon Ramsay, SW3

Mark **9** for cooking

England
Fat Duck, Bray
Le Manoir aux Quat' Saisons, Great
    Milton
Waterside Inn, Bray
Winteringham Fields, Winteringham

Mark **8** for cooking

London
The Capital, SW3
Pied-à-Terre, W1
Square, W1
Tom Aikens, SW3

England
Le Champignon Sauvage, Cheltenham
Vineyard at Stockcross, Stockcross
Gidleigh Park, Chagford
Hibiscus, Ludlow
Merchant House, Ludlow

Mark **7** for cooking

London
Foliage, SW1
Le Gavroche, W1
Gordon Ramsay at Claridge's, W1
Lindsay House, W1
Pharmacy, W11
Sketch, W1

England
Castle House, La Rive, Hereford
Le Champignon Sauvage, Cheltenham
Clivedon, Waldo's, Taplow
Fischer's Baslow Hall, Baslow
Hambleton Hall, Hambleton
Harry's Place, Great Gonerby
Hibiscus, Ludlow
Juniper, Altrincham
Monsieur Max, Hampton Hill
Castle Hotel, Taunton
Castle House, La Rive, Hereford
Cliveden, Waldo's, Taplow

Fischer's Baslow Hall, Baslow
Grand Hotel, Mirabelle, Eastbourne
Gravetye Manor, East Grinstead
Greenway, Shurdington
Hambleton Hall, Upper Hambleton
Harry's Place, Great Gonerby
Juniper, Altrincham
McClements, Twickenham
Mr Underhill's, Ludlow
Pool Court at 42, Leeds
Whatley Manor, Easton Grey
Yorke Arms, Ramsgill

Scotland
The Creel, St Margaret's Hope

Wales
Tyddyn Llan, Llandrillo
Ynyshir Hall, Eglywsfach

The Guide's longest-serving restaurants

The Guide has seen many restaurants come and go. Some, however, have stayed the course with tenacity. (Qualification for this list is that the restaurant has been in each edition of the Guide subsequent to its first entry.)

Connaught, W1	51 years
Gay Hussar, W1	47 years
Gravetye Manor, East Grinstead	47 years
Porth Tocyn Hotel, Abersoch	47 years
Sharrow Bay, Ullswater	43 years
Walnut Tree Inn, Llandewi Skirrid	39 years
Black Bull Inn, Moulton	37 years
Rothay Manor, Ambleside	35 years
Le Gavroche, W1	34 years
Summer Isles Hotel, Achiltibuie	34 years
The Capital, SW3	33 years
Miller Howe, Windermere	33 years
Old Fire Engine House, Ely	32 years
Ubiquitous Chip, Glasgow	32 years
Druidstone, Broad Haven	31 years
Peat Inn, Peat Inn	31 years
Plumber Manor, Sturminster Newton	31 years
Waterside Inn, Bray	31 years
White Moss House, Grasmere	31 years
Carved Angel, Dartmouth	30 years
Isle of Eriska, Eriska	30 years
Airds, Port Appin	28 years
Farlam Hall, Brampton	27 years
Langan's Brasserie, W1	27 years
Corse Lawn House, Corse Lawn	26 years
Gidleigh Park, Chagford	26 years
White House, Williton	26 years
Hambleton Hall, Upper Hambleton	25 years
The Pier Hotel, Harbourside Restaurant, Harwich	25 years
Sabras, NW10	25 years
Brown's, Worcester	24 years
Grafton Manor, Bromsgrove	24 years
Magpie Café, Whitby	24 years
Champany Inn, Linlithgow	23 years
Drum and Monkey, Harrogate	23 years
Homewood Park, Hinton Charterhouse	23 years
Royal Crescent, Pimpernel's, Bath	23 years
RSJ, SE1	23 years
Seafood Restaurant, Padstow	23 years
Sir Charles Napier, Chinnor	23 years
Y Bistro, Llanberis	23 years
Le Caprice, SW3	22 years
Kalpna, Edinburgh	22 years
Little Barwick House, Little Barwick	22 years
Moss Nook, Manchester	22 years
Neal Street Restaurant, WC2	22 years
Sportsman's Arms, Wath-in-Nidderdale	22 years

Restaurants with outstanding wine cellars
Marked in the text with a ▮

London
Bibendum, SW3
Bleeding Heart, EC1
Chez Bruce, SW17
The Don, EC4
Enoteca Turi, SW15
Fifth Floor, SW1
Gordon Ramsay, SW3
Great Eastern Hotel, Aurora, EC2
Oxo Tower, SE1
Pied-à-Terre, W1
Le Pont de la Tour, SE1
Ransome's Dock, SW11
RSJ, SE1
Square, W1
Tate Britain Restaurant, SW1
La Trompette, W4
Zaika, W8

England
Birmingham, Hotel du Vin
Bolton Abbey, Devonshire Arms, Burlington Restaurant
Bowness-on-Windermere, Porthole Eating House
Bray, Fat Duck
Brighton, Hotel du Vin
Bristol, Hotel du Vin
Chagford, Gidleigh Park
Chester, Chester Grosvenor, Arkle
Chinnor, Sir Charles Napier
Corse Lawn, Corse Lawn House
East Grinstead, Gravetye Manor
Faversham, Read's
Grasmere, White Moss House
Great Milton, Le Manoir aux Quat' Saisons
Huntingdon, Old Bridge Hotel
Kew, Glasshouse
Leeds, Sous le Nez en Ville
Lewdown, Lewtrenchard Manor
Little Bedwyn, Harrow Inn
Lyndhurst, Le Poussin at Parkhill
Newton Longville, Crooked Billet
Oxford, Cherwell Boathouse
Padstow, Seafood Restaurant
Petersfield, JSW
Ross-on-Wye, Pheasant at Ross
Stockcross, Vineyard at Stockcross
Tunbridge Wells, Hotel du Vin
Ullswater, Sharrow Bay
Williton, White House
Winchester, Hotel du Vin

Scotland
Achiltibuie, Summer Isles Hotel
Anstruther, Cellar
Edinburgh, Forth Floor
Edinburgh, Valvona & Crolla Caffé Bar
Glasgow, Ubiquitous Chip
Gullane, Greywalls Hotel
Linlithgow, Champany Inn
Peat Inn, Peat Inn

Wales
Aberdovey, Penhelig Arms Hotel
Llandrillo, Tyddyn Llan
Llandudno, St Tudno Hotel, Garden Room Restaurant
Pwllheli, Plas Bodegroes
Reynoldston, Fairyhill

Republic of Ireland
Kenmare, Sheen Falls Lodge, La Cascade
Newport, Newport House

Channel Islands
St Saviour, Longueville Manor

Special awards 2004

This award does not necessarily go to the restaurants with the highest mark for cooking, but rather to ones which have shown particular merit or achievement during the year. It may go to an old favourite or to a new entry, but in either case the places listed below have been singled out because they have enhanced the eating-out experience in some special way.

London
Berkeley Square Café, W1 — *London newcomer of the year*
Tom Aikens, SW3 — *London restaurant of the year*

England
Auberge du Lac, Welwyn Garden City — *Hertfordshire commended*
L'Enclume, Cartmel — *Cumbria newcomer of the year*
Falcon Inn, Poulton — *Gloucestershire newcomer of the year*
Fisherman's Lodge, Newcastle upon Tyne — *Tyne & Wear commended*
Hibiscus, Ludlow — *Shropshire restaurant of the year*
Longridge Restaurant, Longride — *Lancashire commended*
Le Mont, Manchester — *Greater Manchester commended*
Ripley's, St Merryn — *Cornwall commended*
White Horse Inn, Bridge — *Kent newcomer of the year*
Willow Tree, Taunton — *Somerset newcomer of the year*

Scotland
Balmoral Number One, Edinburgh — *Scotland commended*
The Creel, St Margaret's Hope — *Scotland restaurant of the year*
La Potinière, Gullane — *Scotland newcomer of the year*

Wales
Hotel Portmeirion, Portmeirion — *Wales commended*
Tyddyn Llan, Llandrillo — *Wales restaurant of the year*

London restaurants by cuisine

Boundaries between some national cuisines – British, French and Italian particularly – are not as marked as they used to be. Therefore, the restaurants listed below are classified by the predominant influence, although there may be some crossover. The headings are in many cases more generalised than the brief cuisine descriptions given at the tops of the entries themselves

American
Christopher's, WC2

British
Brian Turner Mayfair, W1
Popeseye, W14
Quality Chop House, EC1
St John, EC1
Smiths of Smithfield, Top Floor, EC1
Tate Britain Restaurant, SW1
Wiltons, SW1

Chinese
Ecapital, W1
Four Seasons, W2
Fung Shing, WC2
Golden Dragon, W1
Hakkasan, W1
Mandarin Kitchen, W2
Mr Kong, WC2
New Diamond, WC2
Phoenix Palace, NW1
Royal China, W1

Danish
Lundum's, SW7

East European/ Eurasian
Baltic, SE1
Gay Hussar, W1
Potemkin, EC1

Fish/Seafood
Aquarium, E1
Back to Basics, W1
Bibendum Oyster Bar, SW3
Café Fish, SW1
Fish Hoek, W4
Fish Shop, EC1
Fishworks, W4
J. Sheekey, WC2
Lou Pescadou, SW5
One-O-One, SW1
Rasa Samudra, W1
Wheelers, SW1

French
Admiralty, WC2
Almeida, N1
Aubergine, SW10
Belair House, SE21
Bistro Aix, N8

Bleeding Heart, EC1
Brasserie Roux, SW1
Brasserie St Quentin, SW3
The Capital, SW3
Le Chardon, SE22
Chez Max, SW3
Chez Moi, W14
Club Gascon, EC1
Le Colombier, SW3
Le Coq d'Argent, EC2
Deca, W1
The Don, EC4
Drones, SW1
L'Escargot, Ground Floor, W1
L'Escargot, Picasso Room, W1
L'Estaminet, WC2
Fleur, SW1
Le Gavroche, W1
Gordon Ramsay, SW3
Gordon Ramsay at Claridge's, W1
Incognico, WC2
Mirabelle, W1
L'Oranger, SW1
Orrery, W1
Palais du Jardin, WC2
Pharmacy, W11
Pied-à-Terre , W1
La Poule au Pot, SW1
QC, WC1
Racine, SW3
Roussillon, SW1 RSJ, SE1
Savoy Grill, WC2
Sketch, W1
South, EC2
Square, W1
Swissôtel The Howard, Jaan, WC2
Tom Aikens, SW3
Les Trois Garçons, E1
La Trompette, W4
La Trouvaille, W1

Fusion
e&o, W11
Great Eastern Dining Room, EC2
Providores, W1
River Walk Restaurant, SE1
Sugar Club, W1

Greek
The Real Greek & Mezedopolio, N1
Real Greek Souvlaki and Bar, EC1

Indian/Pakistani
Babur Brasserie, SE23
Benares, W1
Café Spice Namaste, E1
Chutney Mary, SW10
Cinnamon Club, SW1
Ginger, W2
Haandi, SW3
New Tayyabs, E1
Parsee, N19
Raadha Krishna Bhavan, SW17
Rasa Samudra, W1
Rasa Travancore, N16
Red Fort, W1
Salloos, SW1
Sarkhel's, Sw1
Tamarind, W1
Yatra, W1
Zaika, W8

Indian vegetarian
Kastoori, SW17
Rasa, N16 and W1
Sabras, NW10

Indonesian/ Straits
Singapore Garden, NW6

Italian
Al Duca, SW1
Al San Vincenzo, W2
Alloro, W1
Arancia, SE16
Ark, W8
Assaggi, W2
Cecconi's, W1
Il Convivio, SW1
Eddalino, W1
Enoteca Turi, SW15
Fifteen, N1
Green Olive, W9
Isola, SW1
Locanda Locatelli, W1
Metrogusto Islington, N1
National Gallery, Crivelli's Garden, WC2
continued . . .

Neal Street Restaurant, WC2
Olivo, SW1
Paolo, W1
Passione, W1
Philpotts Mezzaluna, NW2
Quo Vadis, W1
Riva, SW13
River Café, W6
Rosmarino, NW8
Salusbury, NW6
Sardo, W1
Spiga, W1
Tentazioni, SE1
Timo, W8
West Street, WC2
Zafferano, SW1

Japanese/sushi bars

Café Japan, NW11
Itsu, SW3 and W1
K10, EC2
Kiku, W1
Kulu Kulu, W1
Matsuri High Holborn, WC1
Moshi Moshi Sushi, EC2,
    EC4 and E14
Nobu, W1
Sumosan, W1
Sushi-Say, NW2
Tsunami, SW4
Ubon, E14
Wagamama, WC1
Yokoso Sushi, EC4
Zuma, SW7

North African/ Middle Eastern

Adams Café, W12
Al Hamra, W1
Istanbul Iskembecisi, N16
Iznik, N5
Noura Brasserie, SW1
Original Tagines, W1

Tas, SE1

South American

Armadillo, E8
Fina Estampa, SE1

Spanish

Cambio de Tercio, SW5
Cigala, WC1
Fino, W1
Gaudí, EC1
Moro, EC1

Thai

Blue Elephant, SW6
Nahm, SW1
Thai Garden, E2

Vegetarian

Gate, NW3 and W6

Vietnamese

Huong-Viet, N1

New entries

These restaurants are new main entries in the Guide this year, although some may have appeared in previous years, or in the Round-ups last year.

London

Ark, W8
Armadillo, E8
Benares, W1
Berkeley Square Café, W1
Bistro Aix, N8
Boxwood Café, SW1
Brian Turner Mayfair, W1
Chez Max, SW3
Chez Moi, W14
Ealing Park Tavern, W5
Eddalino, W1
Fifteen, N1
Fino, W1
Fish Shop, EC1
Fishworks, W4
Flâneur, EC1
Fleur, SW1
The Green, SE22
The House, N1
Matsuri High Holborn, WC1
Mims, SW6
Mosaica @ the factory, N22
MVH, SW13
New Diamond, WC2
One Aldwych, Axis, WC2
Osia, SW1
Paolo, W1
Pharmacy, W11
Philpotts Mezzaluna, NW2
Potemkin, EC1
La Poule au Pot, SW1

Real Greek Souvlaki and Bar,
    EC1
River Walk Restaurant, SE1
Samphire, NW5
Savoy Grill, WC2
Sketch, W1
South, EC2
Sutton Arms Dining Room,
    EC1
Swissôtel The Howard, Jaan,
    WC2
Tom Aikens, SW3
Waterway, W9
Wheelers, SW1
Yokoso Sushi, EC4

England

Addingham, Fleece
Aldeburgh, 152 Aldeburgh
Ashwater, Blagdon Manor
Bagshot, Pennyhill Park,
    Latymer Restaurant
Berwick-upon-Tweed, No. 1
    Sallyport
Biddenden, West House
Blackpool, Kwizeen
Boughton Lees, Eastwell
    Manor
Bridge, White Horse Inn
Brighton, Hotel du Vin
Brighton, La Marinade
Bristol, Lords
Buxton, Columbine
Cambridge, Hotel Felix

Canterbury, Goods Shed
Cartmel, L'Enclume
Cavendish, George
Chigwell, Bluebell
Clifford's Mesne, Yew Tree
    Inn
Colwall Stone, Colwall Park
Cookham Dean, Inn on the
    Green
Corsley, Cross Keys
Cray's Pond, White Lion
Easton Grey, Whatley Manor
Emsworth, Fat Olives
Evesham, Wood Norton Hall,
    Le Duc's
Exford, Crown Hotel
Fawsley, Fawsley Hall, The
    Knightly Restaurant
Fernhurst, King's Arms
Fletching, Griffin Inn
Forton, Bay Horse Inn
Fowey, Marina Hotel, Nick
    Fisher at the Waterside
Galphay, Galphay Arms
Gateshead, McCoys at the
    Baltic, Rooftop Restaurant
Godalming, La Luna
Halifax, Shibden Mill Inn
Hathersage, George Hotel
Helston, Morley's
Hornby, Paul Reed's Dining
    Room, Castle Hotel
Huddersfield, Dining Rooms
    at Strawberry Fair
Instow, Decks

Ipswich, Bistro on the Quay
Kendal, Bridge House
Keswick, Swinside Lodge
Kingham, Mill House
Lamorna, Lamorna Cove
  Hotel
Leeds, No. 3 York Place
Leeds, Room
Leek, Number 64
Leigh-on-Sea, Boatyard
Liverpool, Other Place Bistro
Liverpool, Ziba at the
  Racquet Club
Lytham St Anne's, Dalmeny
  Hotel, Atrium
Manchester, Le Mont
Manchester, Watersreach at
  the Golden Tulip
Marlow, Vanilla Pod
Masham, Swinton Park
Monks Eleigh, Swan Inn
Newbury, Donnington Valley
  Hotel, Wine Press
Newcastle upon Tyne,
  Blackfriars Café Bar
Newcastle upon Tyne,
  Treacle Moon
Newcastle upon Tyne,
  Vermont Hotel, Blue Room
Norton, Vine Tree
Nottingham, Saltwater
Oakham, Nicks Restaurant,
  Lord Nelsons House
Padstow, The Ebb
Portscatho, Driftwood
Poulton, Falcon Inn
Reading, London Street
  Brasserie

Ripon, Restaurant Twenty
  Seven
Rockbeare, Jack in the
  Green
Romsey, Three Tuns
St Ives, Pickled Fish
St Mawes, Green Lantern
St Merryn, Ripley's
Saxmundham, Bell Hotel
Sheffield, Greenhead House
Sheffield, Slammers
Shurdington, Greenway
Southall, Madhu's
Southampton, Oxfords
Sowerby, Travellers Rest
Staithes, Endeavour
Stathern, Red Lion Inn
Taunton, Willow Tree
Teddington, Wharf
Thornbury, Thornbury Castle
Truro, Sevens
Twickenham, A Cena
Twickenham, Brula
Twickenham, Ma Cuisine
Wadhurst, Best Beech Inn
Whitstable, Wheelers Oyster
  Bar
Whittlesford, Tickell Arms
Winchcombe, 5 North Street
York, Rish

Scotland
Dufftown, La Faisanderie
Edinburgh, First Coast
Edinburgh, Forth Floor
Edinburgh, Rogue
Edinburgh, Witchery by the
  Castle

Glasgow, 78 St Vincent
Gullane, La Potinière
Inverness, Rocpool
Kilmacolm, Café Zola
Largoward, Inn at Lathones
Milngavie, Gavin's Mill
Pitlochry, Port-na-Craig Inn
St Monans, Seafood
  Restaurant

Wales
Aberaeron, Harbourmaster
  Hotel
Cardiff, Da Castaldo
Hay-on-Wye, Pear Tree
Newport, Chandlery
Penmaenpool, Penmaenu-
  chaf Hall
St Fagans, Old Post Office
Salem, Angel

Channel Islands
St Martin's, Auberge
St Pierre du Bois, Café du
  Moulin

Northern Ireland
Belfast, Rain City
Portstewart, Smyths

Republic of Ireland
Dublin, Bleu
Dublin, Dish
Dublin, Eden
Kilcolgan, Moran's Oyster
  Cottage

Introduction

The following 700 or so pages reflect the experiences of a group of people who have one thing in common: a passion for food – in particular, food that is cooked by someone else, eaten somewhere other than in their own home and, more often than not, enjoyed in the company of other people. The amazing thing is that so many of you are willing to share those experiences by writing to *The Good Food Guide*. The postbag and email inbox at the GFG offices are constantly bombarded with information, and we can't get enough of it. These stories of great meals, good meals, fair meals, and lousy meals are the foundations of what follows. The majority of reports we receive are telling us good things, not bad. There are complaints about prices and service even in some of the favourable letters, but the ringing endorsements outnumber the dressing-downs. The places that come in for most criticism don't make it into the Guide.

That is not to say that we don't have words of negativity within these pages. Those criticisms levelled at restaurants featured in the Guide are based on the experiences of readers – their customers – and Guide inspectors (also customers). The word 'inspector' sounds rather bureaucratic, I feel, though ours do not have clipboards to register a warm welcome (tick), cutlery correctly set (tick), or the right number of aperitifs behind the bar (tick). No, GFG inspectors are there to eat a meal – just like regular customers – although they have to write a detailed report. The food is the thing. This band of happy eaters includes ex-chefs, ex-restaurateurs, food and wine writers, and readers who have proven their mettle over time by providing informative, reliable feedback to the Guide – each with a palate, an eye for detail and an ability to communicate his or her opinions. They have *real* lives, and get no fee from us except reasonable reimbursement for their meal, visit anonymously and of course do not accept 'freebies' from restaurants. We currently have around 70 inspectors, who live all around the UK. We can get just about anywhere in the land at short notice to seek out the very best restaurants, cafés and pubs.

This is a Guide to be read. We could simply provide some addresses and symbols, but that wouldn't be half as much fun.

Restaurant culture?

We – the British public – are eating out in greater numbers than ever before, but where are we eating? Fast-food restaurants have had a bad year, by most reckonings, although they still account for a significant percentage of our total restaurant spend. All those mid-range, mid-market chain restaurants that swamp our high streets are responsible for another chunk (it would appear that every town has a requirement for a plethora of identikit restaurants offering the same kind of pizza/pasta/grill-type menu). These restaurants in most cases care more about the bottom line than the food on the plate, with the chefs not considered valued assets. We may be eating out a lot, but it seems much of the time we don't bother to seek out good-quality food.

With this Guide under your arm, you might find somewhere a lot more interesting just around the corner. The restaurants it features can be said to have the chains well and truly beaten on the quality of the product, but many 'good' restaurants (particularly outside the major cities) are often seen as special occasion venues – fine for a birthday or other celebration, but not for just when you feel like not cooking. The chains have got the measure of what people want when it comes to creating an informal atmosphere and pricing. To get a really blossoming restaurant culture, we need more quality places keeping it simple, pricing sensibly and making food the focus.

Long have we complained that we can go to France and drive into any village or town and find a decent, good-value restaurant. 'Now that's what I call a restaurant culture,' we cry, while here in the UK we are still a million miles from that. What you will find instead in every village or town is a pub. Take pot luck with the local inn and you're likely to be presented with food that has been taken from the freezer (careful not to drop it now), placed in the microwave (ping), and served with some lettuce, raw onion and un-ripe tomatoes – voila! A ray of light, however, is shed by the increasing number of pubs – many to be found within the pages of this Guide – that are taking food seriously, pushing it to the top of the agenda, and delivering really good meals at reasonable prices. These pubs are re-inventing themselves as the natural place to go for good value and cheerful informality. They're not all as competitively priced as one might hope, and some of them have taken gentrification to the extreme and ceased to be real pubs in all but name, but the thrust of what they are doing is certainly a move in the right direction.

Defining the times

Some fads and fashions in the restaurant scene, just as in the larger world, may well make the mark of those who invent or practise them, and are often based on sound ideas and deliver something of value, though they can lose their purity and purpose when subsumed in the mainstream. Nouvelle cuisine, for example, has now come to mean small portions and over-the-top presentation, though the movement was started in the early 1970s to encourage a straightforward and natural presentation of food. The mid-1990s saw the arrival of the fusion thing, and suddenly many chefs found their inner Eastern mysticism in a piece of lemongrass. Fashions such as these leave a legacy. Things are never quite the same again.

'New wave' Indian and Japanese restaurants are big right now, with sleek, contemporary-looking premises, and many in search of more authentic flavours. These big investments need a return, and guess who ends up paying for that? It is all very well providing an impressive dining room, but the cost has to be passed on to the customer. Too many of these restaurants focus so much on image that they forget about the food. That does not have to be the case – good design and good food fit very well together, and many have got the balance right, and are included in this edition.

The term 'molecular gastronomy' is one of the buzzwords right now, although the term is not new. Chefs like Ferran Adria near Barcelona and Pierre Gagnaire in Paris are applying science to cooking and eating. In the UK, Heston Blumenthal is the man most associated with this term (see Fat Duck, Bray). This exploration of what happens to food when it is cooked, and what happens in the mouth on tasting, leads to some amazing flavour combinations – as well as the questioning of established cooking techniques. The food at the Fat Duck is complex, not cheap, but has always proved good to eat. The humour and playfulness that it demonstrates hides some serious investigative work on the nature of cooking, but there is no sense of the customer being the guinea pig. As you go through the Guide you will find that these new ideas and new techniques are starting to spread, and are increasingly being taken up by others. To pull off this kind of innovative cooking is not easy, and takes skill and imagination.

Hold on, you might be thinking, I thought the idea was to keep things simple. Well, who doesn't want to be thrilled and excited by food from time to time? It's all about balance. If we want to keep developing and growing our restaurant culture, we need some zest and daring. Simplicity based on good ingredients treated well may lie at the foundation of a sound restaurant culture, but there should be something more, too. Maybe all I want today is a bowl of unadorned mussels, just as long as tomorrow I can choose to have a complex five-course extravaganza.

Theory of relativity

The scoring of restaurants in the Guide is not a science. The intention is to offer the reader an indication of the level of ambition and attainment of the cooking. The mark out of 10 has been the score since the 1996 edition and I have at present no plans to change it. Any reader familiar with the system will know that if a restaurant scores 1/10 there is no need for the chef to pack away his knives, turn off the gas and apply for a job elsewhere. We are dealing with the best restaurants in the country. A 1/10 in the GFG means that our readers and inspectors have put the restaurant in the top 1,000 in the UK.

To a certain extent, you can read between the lines. A restaurant serving fresh seafood straight from the sea and presenting it unadorned, but for the accompaniment of fresh chips and some bread from a local baker, is not going to score 8/10. It is still a great restaurant, it is exactly the kind of place our readers rave about, but it is going to score at the lower end of the scale. A slick city brasserie, meanwhile, offering a wide-ranging menu (confit duck, calf's liver, bit of sea bass, that sort of thing) isn't looking to be an 8 either. Shouldn't want to be. A 4/10 would suit that nicely (assuming what it delivers to the plate is all that it is chalked up to be). A smart dining room, however, with a brigade of chefs turning out a complex menu with legions of staff, might be considered to be under-performing if it scores only 4/10; hitting 6/10 might be more appropriate, especially if it charges accordingly. Anyone glancing at the Guide's top-rated restaurants (see page 10) will see a list of some seriously good establishments. These places have two things in common: the ingredients are impeccable, and the cooking skills top-notch. Some are very smart venues, others less so; some of the cooking very complex, some a little simpler. But you don't get near the top unless you consistently produce food that leads to rapturous letters dropping onto our doorstep – backed up by similarly rapturous responses from our inspectors.

John Kenward's article, 'In the spotlight', looks at the pressures on top chefs, and the extra burden of being judged. (See also our two other features: John Sergeant's affectionate look at political lunches, and Pam Roberts's adventures tracking down 'real food' in Los Angeles.)

Bulging postbag

Among the many issues cropping up in the letters we receive is, of course, smoking. For this edition, we have added an extra symbol to help explain the restrictions that restaurants tell us they have on smoking. Entries where a grey symbol appears at the top confirm that they have at least one no-smoking dining room on the premises (and therefore also at least one smoking room), or may restrict smoking to certain periods (e.g. until after 10pm); whereas the fully black symbol means that smoking is banned in all eating areas at all times.

As we go to press it looks as though the issue of smoking in public places is coming to the fore. The majority of feedback we get on the subject suggests that most readers prefer to eat in a smoke-free environment. It is currently the choice of restaurateurs whether any smoke-free areas are provided, but this decision may well be taken out of their hands before too long. These days we may be used to the sight of workers huddled outside doorways of offices for a smoke, and before too long that might be the case for restaurant-goers, too.

In the letters we receive value for money is perhaps the biggest issue of all. The tough times experienced by restaurants over the last few years haven't really led to an obvious drop in prices. There are some bargains to be had, though, particularly at lunch. Readers are reporting back that they've been able to get into some great restaurants at relatively short notice, and that set lunches are the way to try the top kitchens without breaking the bank. So – despite what you may hear – it is worth trying for that last-minute, 'impossible-to-book' table.

The pricing in restaurants is a complex subject, and we know by the large number that go bust each year that running a restaurant is not a licence to print money. A lot of places that don't make it out of the early stages, though, have failed for a more obvious reason: spending all the money on what the restaurant looks like and forgetting to concentrate on producing good food at a fair price. We all like a nice-looking dining room ('ooh, look, is that real leather?'), but we'd rather eat decent food. Most of the top-end restaurants in the book may be regarded as better value than mid-range ones that think they can charge the same price as the big boys without delivering the same quality. Restaurant prices are like football transfers or house prices: the highest price affects everything below. Wine mark-ups, high water charges and other incidentals are one way that restaurateurs bump up the final bill, but no customer likes to be surprised by a higher than expected cost of a meal out, and most probably won't return if they think they've been stung.

One thing spotted by eagle-eyed readers this year has been sommeliers tasting wine before delivering the bottle to the table. This is not wine that has been reported as oxidised or tainted in any way, so why the pre-emptive strike? I don't think the GFG office could cope with the increased level of postal deliveries and emails if this habit takes off in a big way. Another irritation among wine service is bottles kept off table. There are some places where wine glasses are topped up with effortless ease just before you think you might like some more, but restaurants without the sufficient level of staffing to do the job properly should just leave the bottle on the table.

Children, we are told, are still not given due consideration in restaurants. In the details at the bottom of entries we indicate places that offer children's helpings – small portions at a reduced price. The bespoke children's menu is also an opportunity for a little imagination, and I've spotted too few good and interesting ones this year (one that stands out can be found at Berkeley Square Café, London W1). The more frequently children eat out, the more relaxed they (and their parents) become, and before long they will be making demands for proper, fresh, well-prepared food. Which is as it should be. There is no reason why more of the restaurants in this Guide shouldn't make more effort *really* to welcome children.

So long, and thanks for all the fish

The following comes from the 1961 *Good Food Guide*: 'Things move too fast; neither I nor anyone else can paint a picture; nothing stands still long enough. Only a cine camera could cope. See how swiftly the chefs change. They whirl like dervishes.' On that note, a number of very fine restaurants have disappeared from the pages of the Guide this year. La Tante Claire has closed and we await the return of Pierre Koffman elsewhere as eagerly as we await the arrival of Marcus Wareing's Pètrus in the former Tante Claire premises. John Burton-Race's restaurant didn't survive his sabbatical in France (the TV show comes soon, I understand). Bristol has lost Markwicks and Harveys, and Romsey the Bregolis' Old Manor House. Kent is the poorer for the closure of the Sandgate Hotel. The Box Tree in Ilkley is not in the Guide at the request of the owner, Madame Avis, but is still going strong should you wish to visit.

The Good Food Guide *in the twenty-first century*

No sooner is the ink dry on this edition and we turn our attention to the next. It may seem a cliché, but this really is your Guide – produced from readers' feedback, for which we are grateful. Keep the letters and emails coming.

Raymond Postgate's idea back in an austere post-war Britain was to help those who wanted to track down half-decent food. Well, what is different now? We may have lots more choice, and lots more very decent restaurants, but we still need help to find them. This book should be uplifting; it should whet your appetite. We hope you go out and enjoy the restaurants featured in it, and that you'll find a moment to tell us about your experiences. I dare say you may find meals you don't enjoy – so tell us about those as well. This year we are working towards a stronger online presence, but news of that another time.

2003 saw the death of a long-time supporter of the Guide, David Wolfe, and I'd like to dedicate this edition to his memory.

Andrew Turvil

The food and drink of politics

John Sergeant, former political editor of ITN and chief political correspondent of the BBC, looks back at some memorable working lunches

When I reported politics for the BBC and later for ITV it was hard to avoid working at lunchtime. The French rather grandly call it *La Politique Gastronomique*, and knowing that you could add the name of a cabinet minister to your expenses meant the size of the bill was of little concern. How gastronomic the meal was crucially depended on how well you knew your guest and, putting this as delicately as possible, how much both of you could stomach. With Kenneth Clarke, for instance, the choices were relatively easy. Go to the Savoy Grill, start with oysters, followed by their roast of the day ('Perhaps, a little lamb, sir?'), and not a moment's hesitation when the desert trolley swayed into view. How could I possibly resist, and, far more important, why should I want to? For goodness' sake, we were both working, we had to eat somewhere, and he was the Chancellor of the Exchequer.

It is important, though, to know whom you have invited for lunch. I once arrived at the Savoy Grill and slipped in beside a cabinet minister only to be told that he had booked me for next week and would I mind going a few tables further along to where one of his colleagues was anxiously waiting. Everyone was charming, of course. What in other circumstances might be cause for considerable embarrassment was lightly brushed over. It was the sort of mistake, I was told, that anyone could make. On reflection, I could see the point. If you do have lots of cabinet ministers anxious to join you at lunch, and if there are moments when you temporarily lose control of some of the finer details of your diary, mistakes of this sort are bound to happen.

Forgetting entirely that a lunch has been arranged and a table booked can be a more difficult problem. I was once summoned from the press canteen at Westminster to be told that the Chief Secretary to the Treasury, William Waldegrave, had for some time been waiting for me at La Tante Claire in Chelsea and was wondering if he should start without me. I urged my taxi on, like Charlton Heston in the chariot scene from *Ben Hur*, but with considerably less effect. I arrived breathless twenty minutes later and, despite all my winsome charm, could not disguise the fact that a dreadful *faux pas* had been committed. I did try, though, not to aggravate the offence. Having apologised profusely, I manfully agreed that we should move on to other topics. Nothing is worse than a guest, or indeed the host, repeatedly saying how sorry he is for being late; and let us not forget La Tante Claire's reputation as one of the top restaurants in the country.

Beyond officialdom's dark hand

It is one of the paradoxes of political life that the higher you rise as a minister the more your life is controlled. Serving in government means giving up your time, and the civil service will make sure that a minister's diary is never empty. Douglas Hurd used to say when he was Home Secretary his life was cut up into half-an-hour segments. His officials would need to know what he was doing in any thirty-minute period during the day. When he became Foreign Secretary this was cut in half. He felt obliged to account for each quarter of an hour. Lunches, and other life-saving arrangements, have to be slotted in, but there is nothing casual about the way they are arranged. Once they are 'in the diary', the chances are that they will take place. The dark hand of officialdom is seldom absent. Officials, if requested, provide a background briefing on the journalists who are playing host. Thankfully, I have never seen what they wrote about me. (Probably along the lines: 'He's all right if he bothers to turn up.')

I would always try to arrange lunch alone with a minister. Sometimes one would try to invite a political adviser along as well. This had to be resisted on the straightforward, professional grounds that the job entails, where possible, the extraction of secrets. Having a potential witness hardly encourages the sort of reckless, career-threatening revelations, which we promised our editors these lunches were all about; and if, as was more likely, the lunch turned into a boring exposition of well-known facts why should I have my cover blown by some spotty, young political adviser? These occasions have a certain mystique about them and, I believed, it was our solemn duty to keep it that way.

Sometimes, though, I would resort to crude tactics in my search for journalistic scoops. I once had lunch with Jack Straw when, as home secretary, he had to decide whether the former dictator, General Pinochet, should be allowed to return to Chile or be extradited to Spain to face criminal charges. The decision would be announced by Mr Straw that afternoon. I picked up the wine list at the Savoy Grill and asked, with appropriately heavy emphasis: 'We could have a Spanish Rioja or we could go for a Cabernet Sauvignon from Chile: which way will you decide?' But Jack wouldn't play. 'No, John,' he replied, 'I really can't tell you: and you choose the wine.' To the dismay of Labour's left wing, an hour after our lunch it was revealed that the correct choice would have been the Cabernet Sauvignon. General Pinochet was allowed home. Did I get it wrong by choosing a Rioja? Of course not; I took a simple view that, as a drink, the Rioja might prove more reliable.

Stylish, restrained – and brave

Among the least revealing lunches, in my experience, can be those in Downing Street. If you reach the Prime Minister's inner sanctum at around lunch time you are likely to be given sandwiches and some bottled water, British of course. Tony Blair is not what you and I would describe as a drinker. I first had lunch with him when he was in the Shadow Cabinet. We went to Sir Terence Conran's Quaglinos, which had recently been opened; it was stylish and restrained, like me and Tony. As we made our way down the sweeping staircase into the restaurant, I could have sworn I heard someone say: 'Who's that bloke with John Sergeant?'

When I first started regularly taking politicians out to lunch I would invariably go with them to Mijanou in Ebury Street, in Victoria, now completely refurbished under new management as Il Convivio. It was Robin Cook who first recommended it to me and I was encouraged by the endorsement of *The Good Food Guide*. I rather liked the fact that Mijanou appeared from outside to be an ordinary terraced house and you had to ring to be let in. The problem with this small restaurant, though, was that the cabinet ministers' security men had difficulty in blending in to the background. They would sit within sight of our table, usually alone, always trying to look discreet, but never quite managing it.

I occasionally wondered what would happen if Tom King, or Sir Patrick Mayhew, were suddenly to be attacked by the IRA. I was anxious to know how I might fit in to the escape plan. The answer, it seemed, was not a lot. While waiting for the Northern Ireland secretary to arrive, one of the tough, but friendly, security men told me: 'Our job is to see that he is all right.' He pointed to where my guest would be sitting. 'We would get him out pronto.' I would presumably have been left to finish my meal.

It was at Mijanou that I first had lunch with John Major. He had recently been appointed foreign secretary and I did not know him well enough to realise that the wonderful menu served up by Neville and Sonia Blech would have been a little too ambitious for his taste. At the end of the meal he startled me my asking me for my advice as to how he should tackle the job of foreign secretary. 'Be brave,' I responded simply, not knowing just how brave he would have to be. A few hours later Nigel Lawson resigned as a result of a row with Margaret Thatcher and by six o'clock Mr Major had become Chancellor of the Exchequer. We both had a busy evening.

It's strange to look back on all those years of lunching and find myself playing down the experience, as if it didn't really matter. They were often extraordinary occasions, with some exceptional chefs doing their utmost to make them memorable. I worked my way across the best tables in London. But often the food could not be properly appreciated. Concentrating hard on what someone is saying, desperately trying to keep abreast of a whole range of subjects, is not good for the digestion. Now that I have left day-to-day political reporting, the pressure has eased. I don't have to come home so late. I don't have to know so much. It makes going out to lunch much more enjoyable.

Real food in Los Angeles

Pam Roberts, photographic historian, gastronome and long-time friend of the Guide, recounts her recent adventures on the West Coast tracking down the fabulously fresh and the exquisitely fishy

The Big Question was: would a keen, omnivorous cook and restaurant groupie but non-driver, working for three months in the ultimate motor city, be able to access good food, preferably organic, using only feet, public transport, the sporadic taxi and the occasional lift from disbelieving and ruefully head-shaking friends? Or would I frequently be reliant on a diet of double whoppers, chilli dogs, pizzas, subs, Cal-Mex takeout, or overly gloopy Italian, all replete with additives, sugar and fat? Or, might I even adopt the alternative Californian lifestyle, all jogging, rollerblading and working out on Muscle Beach with the boys, eating nothing but tofu, salads and sprouted grains, swilled down with freshly squeezed wheat grass?

Well, the answer was that Southern California has some of the best raw produce in the world and the nearer to its natural raw state it is eaten, the better it is. Good food in LA can easily be accessed by foot or bus, although a car is very useful for eating in restaurants later than 8.30pm when public transport, in some areas, ceases. Thus I failed to become a fast-food junkie – though did try one organic hamburger and one Polish chilli dog, and I do actually like wheat grass juice, and the tofu is terrific. I also indulged my passion for Japanese food and was able to wallow in vegetables and fruit.

The ultimate in fresh

While perhaps it is not quite in the same category as the first kiss, I will never forget the adrenalin rush from my first farmers' market experience during my initial visit to Santa Monica in 1991 (ten years after it had first opened). I had never seen anything like this before. It was to be six years before the first experimental farmers' market opened in the UK (in Bath in 1997).

The USA has taken farmers' markets to its heart, with over 20,000 farmers now selling directly through the 3,100-plus markets, 300 of which are in California, catering to around a million people per year. The greater Los Angeles area has over 60 farmers' markets a week, seven days a week, so long-distance joggers or those with cars (seemingly everybody in LA but me) need never go without their daily fresh arugula. Santa Monica has four Certified Farmers' Markets a week (i.e. the farmers supplying them have been certified as genuine growers of the produce offered), with 90 producers on Wednesday and 40 on Saturday travelling in from a 40-mile radius selling largely organic produce. And what terrific produce it is.

Bushes of mint, coriander, flat-leafed parsley, basil, dill and thyme, glinting with dew and so fresh they last for two weeks if properly stored: three giant bunches for $2 (£1.25). I thought, but only briefly, of those few yellowing stalks of organic coriander in plastic packs that British supermarkets sell for 95p that dissolve into khaki-coloured slimy mush in two days.

Bunches of beets in cardinal red, sunset orange, bullseye pink and white not only cooked in 20 minutes but provided a second vegetable with their squeaky fresh spinach-type leaves. Fennel the size of a football with a metre of silky green fronds and a buttery aniseed sweetness rarely got home from market un-nibbled. Tender asparagus, slender as a pencil or fat as a Mont Blanc pen. Citrus fruits – limes, oranges, grapefruits and lemons – with juice enough to give you all five portions a day in a few squeezes.

In search of the wobble

US farmers' markets generally do not sell meat, poultry or much fish, so my search for these continued. My first problem was stock. As an inveterate carcass-cooker, bone-boiler, stock-maker and risotto eater, I had initial problems finding an organic, free-range chicken that gave me the jellied chicken wobble I crave. After a few false starts ('farm fresh, cage-free and all natural' largely seemed to mean bland, tasteless, vapid and watery), I found Rosie's organic, cage-free as well as hormone-, antibiotic- and everything-else-free chickens at the Whole Foods and Wild Oats supermarket chains and never looked back.

These superior-flavoured chickens seem to have had rather an easy-armchair, feet-up-on-footstool-reading-Proust kind of life, given the copious amounts of fat that they produced and the silky tenderness of the drumstick meat. Nor did they have the deep livery, truffley, chewy punch of a Bresse chicken. They were born to be mild, and their stock wibbled rather than wobbled, but they were beak and shoulders above other chickens I tried.

Beef, pork and lamb I found disappointing, although hormone- and additive-free aged Piedmont beef was an occasional glorious exception. Duck, my usual beast of choice, was difficult to find and I was a long way from LA's various Chinatowns. (Although I understand that over in New York, duck is now the new chicken.) So I moved over to fish.

Fabulous even if finless

Santa Monica Seafood sells a wide range of fabulous fresh fish and prepared fishy comestibles, although Angelenos who have shopped here for any length of time can be forgiven for thinking that fish move effortlessly through the sea in fillets. I looked in vain for heads, tails and fins. The Japanese fishmongers at Santa Monica and Venice Beach Farmers' Markets also had great produce, and it was Japanese restaurants, two in particular, that provided my favourite fishy memories of Los Angeles.

I experienced three things there that will long be my foodie highlights. I ate local uni (sea urchin), from Santa Barbara, whenever I saw it on a menu, simply served with maybe thin slices of cucumber and a dribble of soy. At $12 (£7.50) a plate for a mix of sea, iodine and meltingly creamy texture on the tongue, it was very addictive and only surpassed by a new discovery . . . .

This was at Something's Fishy, the charmingly named Japanese shack restaurant on the Pacific Coast Highway. Avoid the Cal-Jap fusion stuff unless you like avocado sushi and strange tortured things done with vegetables in the name of tempura batter, and try instead the ankimo: monkfish (or frogfish) liver, also known as Japanese foie gras. The raw liver is salted, sakéd, de-veined, tightly wrapped in cling film and foil, steamed and served cold, sliced a centimetre thick with a little dash of citrus ponzu sauce to point up the flavour. The texture is dense, cool, creamy and silky but not fatty. The flavour is mildly livery but very deep.

From quick bite to wanton extravagance

Could it get better? Hard to believe but, in Los Angeles, all things are possible, even by foot. Takao is a tiny restaurant in Brentwood, and did not look, from the outside, capable of providing one of the best meals I have ever eaten. We dropped in there late one Saturday lunchtime for a quick bite of sushi and stayed for two hours, working our way through the delights on offer long after the restaurant had closed.

We had the undivided attention of the chef and owner himself, Takao Izumida, who, along with several members of his staff, previously worked with international top chef Nobuyuki Matsuhisa. The ankimo at Takao came with a teensy little dollop of caviar which changed the flavour and the overall mouth experience startlingly. It achieved its effect in much the same way that, though oysters are good and caviar is good, putting the two together allows the brine of the oysters to couple with the sweet smokiness of the caviar and create something quite different.

The uni sushi was amazing (and I was an afficionado by now after extensive practice). With a raw quail's egg yolk balanced on top, a trick we picked up from regulars at Something's Fishy but probably a trick too far and not necessary for a base product this good; nonetheless, it was a very Tampopo moment. The tuna tartare, mixed with a little minutely shredded spring onion and a dash of wasabi, again with caviar (the dollops got bigger as we kept on ordering and eating), was another sublime plateful.

We had blithely ordered ikura sushi (salmon roe) with yet another quail's egg yolk but Takao refused to serve it with any adornment saying it did not need it. I do so love a bossy chef, especially when he is right.

How can I describe something which had the flavour of cool, pure salmon sea and the texture of elusive liquid salmon air popping in the mouth? This ikura was fresh salmon roe, neither salted, pasteurised, preserved nor dyed orange but fresh from the fish that day, slowly and painstakingly extracted so as not to break the precious eggs, gently washed (doubtless by virgins riding unicorns) with a little saké. Nothing else. It was a pale rose champagne colour and the slightest tongue pressure released a flood of delicate flavour. The season is extremely short we were told. Around 28 March is the date to put in your diaries for 2004.

Takao then took over the rest of our meal and gave us Spanish mackerel tartare, carpaccio of halibut, eel, scallops sashimi with rice and tea to finish. Finally, a small blue glass bowl of ikura arrived, with a spoon. Beats petits fours and coffee in my book any day. And the price for this wanton extravagance and the death of a few hundred potential salmons? Around £78 for two. (A second visit three months later was, if possible, even better.)

I know that we should be very circumspect about eating endangered fish and, even more so about eating fish roe (and to add insult to injury, I was also treated to amazing shad roe at Michael's, a very chi-chi restaurant in Santa Monica, the roe flown in from the Hudson River that day). But, I will eat this sort of food maybe once a year or less. Having had the best, I won't be ordering inferior produce again and will be excessively choosy. I am now back on my usual diet eschewing fish eggs and fish livers. That is, until my next trip to Los Angeles.

Some useful addresses:

Santa Monica Farmers' Market
Arizona Ave (at 2nd & 3rd Streets)
Santa Monica CA 90401
Tel: (+1.310) 458 8712

Santa Monica Seafood
1205 Colorado Avenue
Santa Monica
CA 90401
And elsewhere

Takao Restaurant
11656 San Vicente Boulevard
Brentwood
CA 90049
Tel: (+1.310) 207 8636

Something's Fishy
18753 Pacific Coast Highway
Malibu
CA 90265
Tel: (+1.310) 456 0027

Michael's
1147 Third Street
Santa Monica
CA 90401
Tel: (+1.310) 451 0843

Whole Foods Market
11737 San Vicente Boulevard
Brentwood
CA 90049
And elsewhere

Wild Oats Market
1425 Montana Avenue
Santa Monica
CA 90401
And elsewhere

In the spotlight

John Kenward ran and cooked in his *Good Food Guide*-featured restaurant 'Kenwards' in Lewes, Sussex from 1980 to 1991. Nowadays, from the more relaxing perspective as customer, he recalls the real and imagined fears generated during those years in front of the stove

After I opened my restaurant and experienced my first few weeks at the cooker, I began to see that my 'performance' was not unlike that of an actor in the theatre. In both cases, the effort put in can seem quickly to become a quotidian chore: day after day you do your best to deliver the repertoire.

But for customers – members of the 'audience' – the occasion is usually thought of as a 'treat', one often coloured by unrealistic expectations. Anticipation as well as prejudice will have been generated by reviews in the daily paper and, for the restaurant, most probably in a respected food guide.

As in the case of the actor, for the cook the pressure as 'performance time' approaches each day creates anxiety as well as adrenalin flow. Preparedness is all: you know you can cook; you know your ingredients are first-class; you are ready for your customers. Yet.

What you are not ready for is the critic, whether a newspaper reviewer, anonymous food-guide inspector, or a customer who might write in to a food guide to complain about some peeve real or imagined. Unlike in an actor's case, where fears of public ridicule are focused on the judgement given after press night, restaurants are under scrutiny day in, day out. Any customer at any time could go public on the hollandaise that curdled, the distracted waiter who spilt the Sancerre, or the fish scale clinging to the otherwise pristine cutlery.

Not that any of those small disasters actually happened to me; but when you are running a high-profile place, you cannot help worrying.

End-of-year report

Before becoming a cook in a professional sense, I had been an enthusiastic reader of *The Good Food Guide*. My confidence in its reliability and readability extended to placing an annual order, which meant it arrived through the post bang on time (or thereabouts) every year. I anticipated the keen delight of opening a new Guide, to find then-Editor Christopher Driver's pen demoting or lifting a reputation in a single phrase, and loved the anonymous *frisson* of finding traces of reports I'd sent in on my eating-out experiences.

I had not realised at that point that the other side of a fence could be quite so different. Once I was a restaurateur, the pleasure of waiting for the Guide to arrive was transformed into a period of terror: for weeks, I feared that thud on the doormat. When the book did arrive, the rush to know overcame the fears and made for a fevered opening ceremony. The precept 'less haste, more speed' ignored completely, I ripped apart the packaging, no longer caring a hoot for format or cover or who was opening what exciting new venue. I went straight to the bone: me, my place, how had *I* been judged? My end-of-year report.

What were the worst fears? Not, oddly enough, to be cast out of the Guide totally: self-deludingly that could be explained as an error (blame the typesetters, proof-reader, dozy junior editor). Nor was it seeing a rather indifferent place in the locality gaining an unworthy entry, even if it received more praise than one's own efforts. That could be dismissed as a foolish error of judgement.

No. The worst fear focused on a little number. THE MARK. *The Good Food Guide* has seen many variations on the theme since Drew Smith introduced the pernicious (in my view) league table in 1985: it could be something out of 20, or the 1 to 5 that succeeded that (only to be succeeded by the 1 to 10 system currently).

The score I had achieved in any year instantly signalled either gratification or despair: no in-between. Prose assessment was out and the numbers game was in (or so it seemed). Peer comparison was so much simpler with numbers: while qualitative judgement can be questioned or is open to interpretation, one (almost) believes that numbers never lie.

Anyone could strike the blow

Being mildly paranoid is a trait most restaurateurs probably are born with – if they are serious restaurateurs. They cannot help but believe that each 'performance', each table of customers has the potential to prick one's hard-earned reputation, perhaps leave it in tatters. An experienced inspector from a guide would be bad enough, but for many a restaurateur what generates the most worry is the belief that *anyone* coming through the door could send off opinionated, inaccurate reports to a guide, and that these would (horror of horrors) affect THE MARK.

With this heightened awareness, all but the most regular and kindly customers become suspects. An unexplained absence of a regular triggers worries that something BIG has gone wrong. Or perhaps an event in a customer's private life – a marital matter, a road-rage incident, an impending case of the flu – could make him or her predisposed to spilling out a sharply critical note to a guide on whatever in the meal was perceived not to please.

In those days, there was a special place in my psyche for lawyers and dentists under the age of 30. No, I do not support prejudices nor harbour grudges. Yet, I could not help imagining them, glimpsed through the kitchen door, swirling their glasses of wine, as People Who Had Read Last Weekend's Colour Supplement, and as a result were now asking each other: 'What do you taste? Leather, cowpats . . . .' 'Grapes!', I invisibly prompted. 'Grapes!' I could imagine them running home to compose a ruinous report: 'Cowpats, followed by shambolic service and indifferent food.'

A new perspective

Well, those days are over. As an ex-restaurateur who maintains a passion for good food cooked well, I have now become a regular reporter on restaurants to a particular food guide: this one you are reading. If only my closer association with the Guide had come when it mattered, to set my mind at ease – but of course that's how things work. As long claimed, and as is true, incorruptibility and anonymity are the base line standards maintained by the GFG: chefs and restaurateurs can influence what's in its pages only by what they produce on the plate.

So, to all those anxious cooks still working hard, here's my dollop of advice: exorcise those fears of imagined dissatisfied and angry hordes of customers rushing away to their word processors with the sole aim of putting you out of business. If you are doing things right, most of them are rooting for you. The last thing they want to see is a decent place close its doors because its reputation has been unjustly damaged by, say, a dirty fork.

London

Adams Café £

map 12

77 Askew Road, W12 9AH
TEL/FAX: (020) 8743 0572

COOKING **3**
NORTH AFRICAN
£24–£28

This thoroughly Moroccan, buzzing little restaurant is as good an introduction to North African food as you'll find in the UK. Cheese cigars (filo filled with cheese and fresh herbs), and a pot of harissa – 'dangerous...needs to be applied with care!' – might start the robust but aromatic adventure. Couscous dishes, from meatballs to stuffed squid, and grills, give equal emphasis to meat and fish, while slow-cooked tagines demonstrate classic Moroccan combinations: chicken with pickled lemons, or with apricots and almonds, or lamb with prunes, almonds and sultanas. Vegetarian alternatives include pulses with spinach and rice, while desserts run to home-made lemon or almond tart. The wine list, though brief, starts at £9; Pouilly-Fuissé comes in at £16, with Château Musar at the top end only £19.

CHEF: Sofiene Chahed   PROPRIETORS: Abdel and Frances Boukraa   OPEN: Mon to Sat D only 7 to 11   CLOSED: 25 Dec to 1 Jan, bank hols   MEALS: Set D £10.50 (1 course) to £15.50   SERVICE: 10%, card slips closed   CARDS: Amex, Delta, MasterCard, Switch, Visa   DETAILS: 60 seats. Private parties: 24 private room. Vegetarian meals. Wheelchair access (not WC). Music ⊖ Ravenscourt Park £5

Admiral Codrington

map 14

17 Mossop Street, SW3 2LY
TEL: (020) 7581 0005   FAX: (020) 7589 2452

COOKING **4**
MODERN EUROPEAN
£32–£56

While the Admiral Codrington might look like your typical Victorian pub, the smart people spilling out and a bar with a wide range of wines and a prominent display of cocktail ingredients suggest otherwise. Plunge through the dark-floored bar and the mood changes dramatically; the mainly modern restaurant, with its pale oak floor and a nautical theme, has a sliding roof that transforms the conservatory into an al fresco dining space. Within a generally high level of achievement, highlights have included impeccable gazpacho dressing of intense flavour with a crab timbale, roast monkfish tail with a 'triumphant' combination of sweet potato and earthy celeriac in caramelised rösti, and perfectly executed butterscotch-topped banana Tatin with banana ice cream. Foie gras and chicken liver parfait has come with fig jam, and pink and juicy pan-fried duck breast with a blueberry jus and honey-roast vegetables. Service is cheerful and informal. The New World is the source for most of the sub-£20 wines on the short list, while more traditional bottles rule the upper end. Bottle prices are good, starting at £12, and all wines also come by the glass (from £3).

CHEFS: Kirsty Green and Mickey O'Connor   PROPRIETOR: Longshot plc   OPEN: all week 12 to 2.30 (3.30 Sat and Sun), 7 to 11 (10.30 Sun)   CLOSED: 24 to 26 Dec   MEALS: alc (main courses £9 to £15). Cover 50p. Bar L menu available   SERVICE: 12.5% (optional), card slips closed   CARDS: Amex, Delta, MasterCard, Switch, Visa   DETAILS: 54 seats. Private parties: 45 main room. Vegetarian meals. Children's helpings. Wheelchair access (not WC). Music. Air-conditioned ⊖ South Kensington

Admiralty ⅝✳

map 13

Somerset House, Strand, WC2R 1LA

COOKING 5

TEL: (020) 7845 4646   FAX: (020) 7845 4658

FRENCH

£37–£104

The setting, off the courtyard of Somerset House, is as grand as only the capital can provide. At night the expansive space is washed with floodlights, and spouts of water from the fountains dance in the breeze. If it isn't too breezy, bag a table on the terrace for the best views of the City and the river. Inside, the colour collisions take a little getting over, with turquoise banquettes set against a carrot backdrop, but attention is eventually focused quite rightly on Morgan Meunier's modern French menus.

Fine breads arrive in their own little wooden boats with first-class butter, giving an initial hint of the quality-consciousness that underscores the cooking. A serving of foie gras has been well seasoned and impeccably timed, sitting on thin strands of green beans, with a spicy apple chutney. Snails and garlic are a familiar enough partnership, but may well come parcelled up as ravioli, cooked in Chablis with artichokes, and sauced with red wine and lemon butter. Although presentations may look modern and minimalist, they deliver classic flavours, well judged in their combinations of delicacy and strength. A main-course pot-roast veal loin (for two) 'inspired and comforted in equal measure', the meat carefully timed, served with a citrus-spiked cannelloni of sweetbreads and pine nuts, all sauced with morels in a velouté of vin jaune. Among fish options, there might be monkfish served with a salsify beignet, glazed button onions and baby leeks in a red wine sauce.

Desserts show a welcome willingness to experiment with tart flavours: they have included a painstakingly made chocolate tuile basket containing a scoop of pale pink rhubarb ice cream, and an apple and lime soufflé with Granny Smith coulis and citrus sorbet. To add to it all, the place is awash with well-drilled, professional staff. The exclusively French wine list begins, refreshingly enough, with wines from the lesser-known corners, before proceeding on its trek to the summit of classed-growth Bordeaux. There are many halves, and a good selection by the glass, but not much below £20. House wines, a Grenache and a Terret, are £15.

CHEF: Morgan Meunier   PROPRIETOR: Restaurant Associates   OPEN: all week L 12 to 2.30, Mon to Sat D 6 to 10.30   CLOSED: 25 and 26 Dec, D Easter Mon   MEALS: Set L £21.50 (2 courses) to £25, Set D £28 (2 courses) to £42 (whole table only)   SERVICE: 12.5% (optional)   CARDS: Amex,

Delta, Diners, MasterCard, Switch, Visa DETAILS: 60 seats. Private parties: 60 main room, 15 to 30 private rooms. Vegetarian meals. No smoking in 1 dining room. Wheelchair access (also WC). Music ⊖ Temple, Covent Garden

Alastair Little

map 15

49 Frith Street, W1D 4SG
TEL: (020) 7734 5183 FAX: (020) 7734 5206

COOKING 4
MODERN EUROPEAN
£43–£59

The setting changes little: a long room with pastel-painted walls sporting framed photographs (for sale), simply set tables, wooden floors, and a bookshelf at the far end. Part of the appeal is the place's commitment to plainness and its lack of pretension, and the resolutely unflashy surroundings are matched by equally unshowy food. The eponymous Alastair is no longer a partner, but the team in the kitchen can still turn out generally bright, contemporary stuff, presented with some skill and care. A starter of grilled squid with lightly acidic sour cream and sharply sweet chilli jam is freshened up by coriander leaves, while a springtime main course of new season's lamb is decked out with kidney beans, couscous and a radish and lettuce salad.

This kitchen demonstrates that food needn't be elaborate to succeed, making a virtue of, for example, moist and well-flavoured chicken saltimbocca (wrapped in Parma ham and grilled), served with tasty rösti and wild mushrooms. Among desserts, a version of café liégeois combines coffee granita, vanilla ice cream and chocolate sauce, while a rich and satisfying dark and white chocolate truffle cake comes with a smooth, delicately flavoured ginger sauce. T-shirted service is friendly and engaging, and a roving wine list starts with house French Sauvignon Blanc and Mano's Primitivo from Puglia at £17.

CHEFS: Sue Lewis and Juliet Peston PROPRIETORS: Kirsten Tormod and Mercedes Andre-Vega OPEN: Mon to Fri L 12 to 3, Mon to Sat D 6 to 11.30 CLOSED: 24 to 26 Dec, bank hols MEALS: Set L £29, Set D £35 SERVICE: not inc CARDS: Amex, Diners, MasterCard, Switch, Visa DETAILS: 60 seats. Private parties: 25 main room. Wheelchair access (not WC). No music. Air-conditioned ⊖ Tottenham Court Road

Al Duca ♥

map 15

4–5 Duke of York Street, SW1Y 6LA
TEL: (020) 7839 3090 FAX: (020) 7839 4050
EMAIL: info@alduca-restaurant.co.uk
WEBSITE: www.alduca-restaurant.co.uk

COOKING 3
ITALIAN
£30–£67

In summer, windows are flung open to the street, in winter it can seem more introverted, but this handsomely furnished, contemporary Italian restaurant near Jermyn Street, with its frosted-glass panels, rounded pillars and wall of wine bottles, makes the most of its setting. The menus are a set price (note the pre- and post-theatre deals); although full of variety, they are sprinkled with quite a few distracting supplements. But good materials have included an open raviolo of scallops, tiger prawns and halibut in a mellow yet deeply flavoured shellfish-based sauce, and accurately timed halibut with delightfully crisp, salty, savoury skin, served with lentils.

Textures constitute part of the enjoyment in several dishes, including elongated cubes of crispy polenta that accompany pan-fried wild mushrooms and chicken livers. Presentation is straightforward and all the better for it: perhaps pink-cooked veal chop well supported by roast potatoes and a generous dollop of spinach tossed with pine nuts. Finish with above-average tiramisù, or perhaps a thickish biscuity pastry case with an almond-based cake-like filling topped with pieces of pear, served with cinnamon-impregnated cream. The wine list makes a thorough tour of Italy, picking up everything from classic Barolos to new-wave Sardinians on its travels. Just a handful come in under £20, but 11 wines by the glass offer the chance to sample some interesting flavours from £4.50 to £7.

CHEF: Antonio Cucchiara   PROPRIETOR: Cuisine Collection   OPEN: Mon to Sat 12 to 2.30 (12.30 to 3 Sat), 6 to 11   CLOSED: 25 and 26 Dec   MEALS: Set L £17.50 (2 courses) to £23.50, Set D Mon to Sat 6 to 7, Mon to Wed 10.30 to 11 £13.50 (2 courses) to £16.50, Set D Mon to Sat £20 (2 courses) to £28   SERVICE: 12.5% (optional), card slips closed   CARDS: Amex, Delta, Diners, MasterCard, Switch, Visa   DETAILS: 60 seats. Private parties: 60 main room. Vegetarian meals. Children's helpings. No cigars/pipes. Wheelchair access (not WC). No music. No mobile phones. Air-conditioned   ⊖ Piccadilly Circus (£5)

Al Hamra
map 15

31–33 Shepherd Market, W1Y 7PT
TEL: (020) 7493 1954   FAX: (020) 7493 1044
EMAIL: mail@alhamra.co.uk
WEBSITE: www.alhamrarestaurant.com

COOKING 4
LEBANESE
£43–£78

Al Hamra celebrates 20 years in 2004, and in all that time its reputation as London's foremost Lebanese restaurant has remained largely unchallenged (Noura, SW1, being the young pretender; see entry). It draws a lively crowd, and tables are packed into the large dining room. Weather permitting, you can also eat outside on the heated patio.

The unchanging menu runs to almost 100 items, around half of which are hot and cold meze, representing a fairly comprehensive trawl through the Lebanese repertoire – from tabbouleh, hummus and muhamara (fried mixed nuts with herbs and chilli) to kibbeh nayeh (spiced minced raw lamb with crushed wheat) and hummus kawarmah (diced lamb with pine nuts and hummus). Among main courses, the chargrill is king, producing the likes of shawarma (lamb marinated in vinegar and spices) and farruje meshwi (whole poussin with garlic sauce). There is also fish, such as baked trout with spicy vegetables, and a few token 'Continental' dishes. The wine list opens with a selection of Lebanese bottles, including Ch. Musar at £36. House French is £15, though the rest of the list – dominated by France – stays above £20.

CHEF: Mahir Abboud   PROPRIETOR: Hassan Fansa   OPEN: all week 12 to 11.30   CLOSED: 24 Dec to 2 Jan   MEALS: alc (main courses £14 to £22.50). Set L and D £30. Cover £2.50   SERVICE: not inc   CARDS: Amex, Delta, Diners, MasterCard, Switch, Visa   DETAILS: 65 seats. 24 seats outside. Private parties: 70 main room. Vegetarian meals. Children's helpings. Wheelchair access (not WC). Music. Air-conditioned   ⊖ Green Park (£5)

All entries, including Round-ups, are fully indexed at the back of the Guide.

Alloro ♥

map 15

19–20 Dover Street, W1S 4LU
TEL: (020) 7495 4768   FAX: (020) 7629 5348

COOKING 5
ITALIAN
£40–£60

A floor of large polished wooden squares, and flowers on the well-spaced, white-clothed tables, give this venue just off Piccadilly a comfortable feel. The menu, reminiscent of its sister Zafferano (see entry), makes a virtue of simplicity, offering warm grilled vegetables with olive oil and basil, or grilled asparagus with quails' eggs and Parmesan. Even main courses can be as straightforward as tuna steak with tomato and rocket salad, or rabbit saddle with purple sprouting broccoli and garlic confit, but the repertoire also entices with seared scallop in cep broth, and roast suckling pig with a spring salad. Fine materials underpin the menu, which show to good effect in uncomplicated starters such as fresh spinach leaves with goats' cheese and balsamic dressing. An occasional braise (such as osso buco served with Sardinian couscous and saffron) takes its place alongside the principal cooking techniques: pan-frying and chargrilling – of plaice with a basil crust, sea bass fillet with broad beans, or calf's liver with steamed vegetables. Tiramisù makes a predictable appearance, but there may also be Sicilian cannoli with buffalo ricotta and pistachio sauce, or a green apple strudel with Sambuca sorbet. The wine list is an all-Italian affair with a sure eye for good producers. Numerous legendary wines, many offered in a range of vintages, will impress, but value will not, with high prices generally and just the Sicilian house bottles under £20. A dozen options by the glass are £3.50 to £7.

CHEF: Marzio Zacchi   PROPRIETOR: A To Z Restaurants Ltd   OPEN: Mon to Fri L 12 to 2.30, Mon to Sat D 7 to 10.30   CLOSED: 24 Dec to 2 Jan, 3 days at Easter, bank hols   MEALS: Set L £22 (2 courses) to £25, Set D £27.50 (2 courses) to £35. Bar menu available Mon to Fri 12 to 3   SERVICE: 12.5% (optional), card slips closed   CARDS: Amex, Delta, Diners, MasterCard, Switch, Visa   DETAILS: 65 seats. Vegetarian meals. No cigars/pipes. Occasional music. Air-conditioned ⊖ Green Park

Almeida ♥

map 13

30 Almeida Street, N1 1AD
TEL: (020) 7354 4777   FAX: (020) 7354 2777
EMAIL: oliviere@conran-restaurants.co.uk
WEBSITE: www.almeida-restaurant.co.uk

COOKING 4
FRENCH BISTRO
£29–£71

Another arm of the Conran empire sprang up opposite Islington's Almeida Theatre in late 2001, and continues to develop. A year after opening, the place introduced a tapas menu, available in the bar from noon until 11pm. This mixes Spanish and southern French dishes in conveniently small portions: jamón Serrano, marinated provençale vegetables, pork belly with paprika oil, and so forth. The main restaurant, with its bentwood chairs, offers renditions of French bourgeois cooking that generally pass muster. A whole roasted sea bass with artichokes and mushrooms pleased one regular reporter, as did pâté de foie gras with toast, and a well-made crème brûlée. Scallops à la brochette, and turbot with hollandaise have also been well received, and much merriment is occasioned by the sashaying past of various trolleys, which bear charcuterie, pâtés, cheeses and tarts. Alternative puddings might be cherry soup, or prune and Armagnac parfait.

A mostly French selection of 18 wines by the glass (from £3), carafe or bottle features on the reverse of the menu, with enough of interest under £20, and sets the tone for the Franco-centric main list. Languedoc, the Loire and the south-west spice up the weighty collections of Burgundy and Bordeaux. There are three sherries, but otherwise Spain hasn't kept pace with the introduction of tapas. Punchy little selections from Italy and the New World round things off.

CHEF: Ian Wood   PROPRIETOR: Conran Restaurants   OPEN: all week 12 to 3, 6 to 11   CLOSED: 25 and 26 Dec, 1 Jan, Good Fri   MEALS: alc (main courses £11.50 to £20). Set L and D 6 to 7 and 10 to 11 £14.50 (2 courses) to £17.50   SERVICE: 12.5% (optional), card slips closed   CARDS: Amex, Delta, Diners, MasterCard, Switch, Visa   DETAILS: 90 seats. Private parties: 90 main room, 16 to 20 private rooms. No cigars/pipes. Wheelchair access (also WC). No music. Air-conditioned ⊖ Angel, Highbury & Islington (£5)

Al San Vincenzo   map 13

30 Connaught Street, W2 2AF   COOKING 2
TEL: (020) 7262 9623   ITALIAN
                                                       £50–£59

Al San Vincenzo is on a charming street off the buzzy southern reaches of the Edgware Road. Eight tables snuggle into the small, low-key room, with its plain wooden floor and parchment-coloured walls hung with framed black and white pictures of the old country. The food is home-style Italian, with minimal presentation skills: the plain white plates are not drizzled with herbed oils or decorated with artistic blobs and blotches. The handwritten, photocopied menu lists a half-dozen starters and main courses. After tucking into light and fluffy ciabatta-style bread, start, perhaps, with a well-judged dish of fresh pappardelle pasta with smoked haddock and broad beans before moving on to an earthy, subtly flavoured main course of fillet of gurnard dressed with sunblush tomatoes and olive oil, served with potato purée and lentils. To finish, savoury lovers may be tempted by Italian farmhouse cheese and the sweet-toothed by the likes of buffalo milk cheesecake with wild berry sauce. Service is pleasant and friendly, but waits for food can be long. The wine list is unexciting; bottle prices start at £16.

CHEF: Vincenzo Borgonzolo   PROPRIETORS: Elaine and Vincenzo Borgonzolo   OPEN: Mon to Fri L 12.30 to 1.30, Mon to Sat D 7 to 9.30   MEALS: Set L and D £28.50 (2 courses) to £34.50   SERVICE: not inc, 12.5% for parties of 5 or more   CARDS: Delta, MasterCard, Switch, Visa   DETAILS: 24 seats. Private parties: 20 main room. Vegetarian meals. No children under 12. No cigars/pipes. Music ⊖ Marble Arch

---

Anglesea Arms £   map 12

35 Wingate Road, W6 0UR   COOKING 2
TEL: (020) 8749 1291   FAX: (020) 8749 1254   MODERN EUROPEAN
                                                       £21–£42

Get there early, seems to be the message at this unpretentious, bustling, neighbourhood gastro-pub, or you'll be in for a long wait at the bar for a table (no bookings are accepted). The open layout takes in a dedicated dining area with vaulted glass skylight, ceiling fans and a no-frills bare-boards and brick-wall décor, together with a mish-mash of wooden furniture. The cooking is spiked by a mix of Mediterranean and more distant influences: perhaps Moroccan spiced chicken fillets, couscous, chickpeas, aubergine and Argan oil, or ravioli with ceps, tarragon, spinach and Parmesan to start. To follow, expect sautéed calf's liver, pancetta, savoury soft polenta, capers and rosemary, while desserts might include pear and frangipane tart with vanilla ice cream. The compact wine list is equally global, offering house bottles from £10.50 and 15 by the glass from £2.50.

CHEF: Jacky Lelièvre   PROPRIETOR: Fiona Evans   OPEN: all week 12.30 to 2.45 (Sun 1 to 3.30), 7 to 10.30 (10.15 Sun)   CLOSED: 24 to 30 Dec   MEALS: alc (main courses L £8 to £8.50, D £10 to £13). Set L £9.95 (2 courses) to £12.95   SERVICE: not inc, 12.5% for parties of 6 or more   CARDS: Delta, MasterCard, Switch, Visa   DETAILS: 36 seats. 20 seats outside. Private parties: 80 main room. Vegetarian meals. Children's helpings. No cigars. Wheelchair access (not WC). No music
⊖ Ravenscourt Park

Aquarium   map 13

Ivory House, St Katharine's Dock, E1W 1AT
TEL: (020) 7480 6116   FAX: (020) 7480 5973   COOKING 3
EMAIL: info@theaquarium.co.uk   INTERNATIONAL/SEAFOOD
WEBSITE: www.theaquarium.co.uk   £33–£95

Floor-to-ceiling windows make it easy to imagine how this fish restaurant got its name. Pillars in exposed brick or painted aubergine, a bar with zinc-coated sides, industrial-style spotlights and flooring, plus woven plastic sheeting concealing the ceiling gives the Aquarium an urban feel, and the waterside location, with shaded terrace and dockside views, certainly makes an impression.

Swedish chef/proprietor Christian Sandefeldt sells fish that come only from sustainable stocks, and – other restaurateurs please note – his menus still contain much of interest. Devon crab, Irish rock oysters, langoustines and native lobster are there for the those wanting a pure seafood hit; otherwise the kitchen can run to, among starters, carpaccio of tuna and veal with mint dressing, or smoked eel with truffled potato purée, wild mushrooms and quails' eggs. Main courses can be equally inventive: viz. tempura of Swedish perch with prawn and pork dumplings in miso broth, or roast fillet of black bream with roast tomato, onion gnocchi and chorizo. Seared foie gras marinated in orange and vanilla with a rhubarb tartlet, and suprême of English chicken with bread pudding and tarragon jus are the non-seafood options on one menu. Finish with, perhaps, pineapple tarte Tatin with coconut sorbet, pots of chocolate, crème brûlée du jour, or a selection of French cheeses. Close to 40 wines, listed by country, begin at £13.50, with seven by the glass.

CHEF: Christian Sandefeldt   PROPRIETORS: Christian and Kerstin Sandefeldt   OPEN: Mon to Sat L 12 to 3 (4 Sat), Tue to Sat D 6.30 to 11   CLOSED: Christmas and New Year   MEALS: alc (main courses £13.50 to £30). Set L Mon to Fri and D £17.50 (2 courses) to £20.50. Sat brunch menu available, also tapas/meze bar menu   SERVICE: 12.5% (optional), card slips closed   CARDS:

Amex, Diners, MasterCard, Switch, Visa   DETAILS: 65 seats. 50 seats outside. Private parties: 400 main room, 10 to 60 private rooms. No children under 8 on terrace. Wheelchair access (not WC). No music   ⊖ Tower Hill

Arancia £   map 13

52 Southwark Park Road, SE16 3RS   COOKING 2
TEL/FAX: (020) 7394 1751   ITALIAN
WEBSITE: www.arancia-london.co.uk   £18–£33

This neighbourhood Italian offers informal surroundings with a weekly-changing menu and prices that keep the locals coming back. Signature 'Arancini' – deep-fried risotto croquettes with mozzarella – and grilled squid with roast peppers and walnut salsa are typical of the output, which extends to main courses such as baked skate with chilli, garlic and anchovies, or braised rabbit and guinea fowl with fennel. Pasta crops up too, perhaps in the form of home-made zucchini and ricotta ravioli. Service is pleasant and informal. The exclusively Italian wine list gives some good-value drinking, with all but one bottle under £20. House Sicilian is £9.

CHEF/PROPRIETOR: C. O'Sullivan   OPEN: Tue to Sat 12.30 to 2.30, 7 to 11   CLOSED: 23 Dec to 3 Jan   MEALS: alc (main courses £9 to £10). Set L £7.50 (2 courses) to £10.50   SERVICE: not inc, card slips closed   CARDS: Delta, MasterCard, Switch, Visa   DETAILS: 40 seats. 10 seats outside. Private parties: 40 main room. Vegetarian meals. No cigars/pipes. Music. No mobile phones   ⊖ Bermondsey (£5)

Ark   NEW ENTRY   map 13

122 Palace Gardens Terrace, W8 4RT
TEL: (020) 7229 4024   FAX: (020) 7792 8787   COOKING 2
EMAIL: mail@thearkrestaurant.co.uk   ITALIAN
WEBSITE: www.thearkrestaurant.co.uk   £26–£61

The Ark has proved itself an enjoyable, unpretentious and popular neighbourhood venue. Beyond the patio set with tables is a bar area and small dining room decked out with a dark-wood floor, painted wooden panelling, and skylights and windows with sail-like Roman blinds. Expect straightforward, authentic and comforting Italian cuisine – rather than culinary fireworks – which pays due attention to seasonality and treats ingredients respectfully. The menu rolls out in traditional format, divided into antipasti, primi piatti, secondi piatti, contorni, and dolce. Try deep-fried courgette flowers generously stuffed with ricotta and basil, or risotto with champagne and wild asparagus, and then tender grilled veal chop in a Parmesan crust with roast baby vegetables, or seared scallops with capers, anchovies and Tuscan bread salad. Finish with a tartlet of raspberries, or grappa-laced pannacotta. Service is cordial, friendly and prompt, and some good producers show up on the all-Italian, well-chosen wine list. Prices are fair, with bottles starting at £12.50, and around a dozen are sold by the glass from £3.25.

CHEF: Enrico Perotti   PROPRIETOR: Louise Mayo   OPEN: Tue to Sun L 12 to 2.45, Mon to Sat D 6.30 to 10.45   CLOSED: bank hols   MEALS: alc (main courses £11 to £18). Set L £12.50 (2 courses) to £15   SERVICE: 12.5%, card slips closed   CARDS: Amex, Delta, MasterCard, Switch,

Visa   DETAILS: 50 seats. 12 seats outside. Private parties: 60 main room. Vegetarian meals. Children's helpings. Wheelchair access (not WC). Occasional music. Air-conditioned
⊖ Notting Hill Gate £5

Armadillo   NEW ENTRY   map 12

41 Broadway Market, E8 4PH   COOKING 2
TEL/FAX: (020) 7249 3633   SOUTH AMERICAN
WEBSITE: www.armadillorestaurant.co.uk   £27–£42

This aching-to-be-hip part of Hackney is home to one of the least hackneyed styles of cooking around: modern South American. The restaurant is plainly decorated with artefacts from that continent, and the weekly-changing menu features South American culinary creations seldom seen outside the region, such as humitas (steamed sweetcorn 'dumplings', here flavoured with cheese and Serrano ham) and llapingachos (Ecuadorian potato and cheese cake), served with peanut sauce. A more prosaic grilled Argentinian steak may be served with Jersey Royals and courgette and chipotle chilli. Good use of the chilli pepper as a flavouring is demonstrated in tostaditas turulas – small corn bases topped with dried shrimp, jalapeño and tomato. Service is charming, chatty and efficient, and the 'Latino' wine list – mostly Iberian and South American – offers good-value drinking, with house wines at £11 (£3.80 a glass).

CHEF/PROPRIETOR: Rogerio David   OPEN: all week D only 6.30 to 10.30 (10 Sun)   CLOSED: Christmas to New Year, last 2 weeks Aug   MEALS: alc (main courses £10 to £14.50)   SERVICE: not inc, card slips closed, 12.5% for parties of 5 or more   CARDS: Amex, Delta, Diners, MasterCard, Switch, Visa   DETAILS: 55 seats. 10 seats outside. Private parties: 30 main room, 10 to 25 private rooms. Vegetarian meals. No cigars/pipes. Music   ⊖ Bethnal Green

Assaggi   map 13

The Chepstow, 39 Chepstow Place, W2 4TS   COOKING 4
TEL: (020) 7792 5501   FAX: (020) 7792 9033   ITALIAN
                                                               £38–£71

The surroundings – a dining room above a pub (albeit in a fashionable neighbourhood) – may be 'no gastrodrome', but this unpretentious, small space is thoughtfully fitted out with varying textures of wood and Rothko-esque paintings. The atmosphere somehow manages to feel stylish and minimalist, but at the same time cheerful and laid back (thanks to beneficent Italian staff), although things can get noisy. The menu, written in Italian, centres on dishes in which fine ingredients are treated simply. At inspection a starter of scallops with saffron, pan-fried in butter and resting on crunchy pearl barley and finely diced vegetables, impressed with its impeccable freshness and flavour. Main courses may feature the likes of pan-fried guinea fowl and pancetta balanced atop intensely flavoured pea purée and offset with truffle oil and truffle shavings, or grilled turbot on a bed of deep-fried carrot and courgette with tiny cubes of steamed potato and a tomato and pepper sauce. Finish with 'moist and light' ricotta and amaretto cheesecake, or rich chocolate cake. The wine list is short and exclusively Italian, with good producers listed (those with deep pockets might like to check out the 'special vintages' section). Argiolas' red and white open proceedings at £13.95 (£3.25 a glass).

CHEF: Nino Sassu   PROPRIETORS: Nino Sassu and Pietro Fraccari   OPEN: Mon to Sat 12.30 (1 Sat) to 2.30, 7.30 to 11.30   CLOSED: 2 weeks Christmas, bank hols   MEALS: alc (main courses £11 to £20)   SERVICE: not inc, card slips closed   CARDS: Delta, Diners, MasterCard, Switch, Visa DETAILS: 35 seats. Vegetarian meals. Children's helpings. No music. Air-conditioned   ⊖ Notting Hill Gate

Atlantic Bar and Grill ♀   map 15

20 Glasshouse Street, W1B 5DJ
TEL: (020) 7734 4888   FAX: (020) 7734 5400
WEBSITE: www.atlanticbarandgrill.com

| NEW CHEF |
MODERN EUROPEAN
£35–£72

'A Fellini-esque experience' was how one reporter described a visit to this vibrant, fun and trendy restaurant. Décor in the huge, spacious dining room recreates the looks of a transatlantic liner, the focal point being the lively cocktail bar at the centre, where expert bartenders provide a touch of theatre with their shaking and stirring. As the Guide was going to press, another new chef was due to take over: Ben O'Donoghue, an Australian with previous experience in front of the camera as well as the stove, starts in early September 2003. Previous menus have offered an appealing assortment of fashionable flavours in a broadly European vein: crisp calamari salad with wasabi slaw and coriander oil, risotto Milanese, veal entrecôte with pancetta-wrapped asparagus, capers and lemon, chargrilled bluefin tuna niçoise salad, concluding with perhaps Atlantic chocolate bomb or pannacotta with blackberries. Reports on the new team, please. Wines are a smart international bunch. A serious approach to France extends to good bottles from Alsace and the Loire, while an impressive array of Australian reds tops the New World contributions. Wines by the glass (17 at £4.80–£11) might be the best option to follow a round of cocktails. House red and white are £14 but prices climb steeply.

CHEF: Ben O'Donoghue   PROPRIETORS: Oliver Peyton and Gruppo Ltd   OPEN: Mon to Sat D, Sun brunch 12 to 2   CLOSED: bank hols   MEALS: alc D (main courses £7.50 to £22.50). Bar menu available L   SERVICE: 12.5% (optional), card slips closed   CARDS: Amex, Delta, MasterCard, Switch, Visa   DETAILS: 160 seats. Private parties: 250 main room, 75 to 80 private rooms. Wheelchair access (not WC). Music. Air-conditioned   ⊖ Piccadilly Circus

Aubergine   map 14

11 Park Walk, SW10 0AJ
TEL: (020) 7352 3449   FAX: (020) 7351 1770

COOKING 6
MODERN FRENCH
£47–£126

Just off Fulham Road, Aubergine has the air of a neighbourhood restaurant, albeit in a smarter-than-average neighbourhood. Recently refurbished, it looks 'very 1980s' with its beige-coloured sponged walls, sploshy paintings and aubergine-themed cruets, cutlery and crockery. Seriousness of intent is apparent from the well-spaced tables, upholstered chairs, and a veritable cornucopia of fine materials. The food is modern, but not aggressively so; rather, its backbone of fairly conservative dishes is enlivened by a few surprise elements, such as beetroot with foie gras, and a galette of pig's head – a succulent, porky-flavoured, fishcake-sized fritter on piquantly dressed diced potato – accompanied by four sweet, briny langoustines.

Impressively, dishes are presented comparatively straightforwardly, there are no extraneous garnishes, and everything on the plate has a purpose. An exemplary starter of ravioli – coral-coloured pasta generously stuffed with chunks of lobster – is accompanied by no more than a clean, intensely flavoured basil purée and wilted greens. Dishes are fine-tuned to get the best out of ingredients, and the kitchen doesn't skimp on either quality or technique. Meats are pink and well flavoured, producing an early-summer treat of best end of lamb with braised peas, onions, lettuce and mint, and sauces are rich and concentrated yet not too heavily reduced.

A highlight among desserts has been a light, creamy lime parfait sandwiched between crisp brandy-snap biscuits, with little heaps of shredded, candied ginger and squiggles of intense, zippy lime and ginger sauces: 'a fantastic example of how to extract every last ounce of flavour and texture out of two simple ingredients'. Service is quite formal, and, thanks to an understanding and informative maître d', everything runs smoothly. With just two bottles under £25, the wine list is not for the faint of heart or thin of wallet. There's no faulting the selection, however, which concentrates on the very best of France but flourishes quality names at every turn.

CHEF: William Drabble   PROPRIETOR: A To Z Restaurants   OPEN: Mon to Fri L 12 to 2.30, Mon to Sat D 7 to 11   CLOSED: 2 weeks Christmas, bank hols   MEALS: Set L £32, Set D £50 to £70 (whole table)   SERVICE: 12.5% (optional), card slips closed   CARDS: Amex, Delta, Diners, MasterCard, Switch, Visa   DETAILS: 55 seats. Private parties: 60 main room. No cigars. Wheelchair access (not WC). No music. No mobile phones. Air-conditioned   ⊖ South Kensington, Gloucester Road

---

Avenue ▮ 🍴

7–9 St James's Street, SW1A 1EE

TEL: (020) 7321 2111   FAX: (020) 7321 2500

EMAIL: avenue@egami.co.uk

WEBSITE: www.theavenue.co.uk

map 15

COOKING 2

MODERN EUROPEAN

£33–£64

Plumb in the middle of well-heeled St James's, the Avenue is designed to exude the kind of opulence that is too lofty for anything as everyday as decoration. It is a big, entirely white but dimly lit space, with a long bar running down one side and staff who glide by unsmiling, as though to blend in with the ultra-cool ambience. The menu is in the same Greatest Hits mould as some of London's other big eateries, running the gamut from fish fingers and chips to ostrich with lentils and watercress. A first-course slice of meaty, full-flavoured rabbit terrine, served with onion marmalade, a rocket salad and toast, was a success at an inspection meal, as was a generous serving of lamb chops, accompanied by rosemary potatoes, to follow. Other vegetables are separately priced, but good. Given the cost of it all, there are a few too many reports of under-par dishes for comfort, and desserts in particular leave room for much improvement. A slick, modern wine list, arranged loosely by grape variety, has many Old and New World classics. Prices are high but start at £14.50, and around 30 by the glass range from the basics at £3.65 to a premium Australian red at £13.75.

CHEF: Ivan Mather   PROPRIETOR: Moving Image Restaurants plc   OPEN: all week 12 to 3, 5.45 to 12 (12.30 Fri and Sat)   CLOSED: 25 and 26 Dec, 1 Jan   MEALS: alc D (main courses £13.50 to £17.50). Set L and D 5.45 to 7.30 and 10.30 to 12 (12.30 Fri and Sat) £17.95 (2 courses) to £19.95.

Bar menu available   SERVICE: 12.5% (optional), card slips closed   CARDS: Amex, Delta, Diners, MasterCard, Switch, Visa   DETAILS: 180 seats. Private parties: 140 main room. Vegetarian meals. Wheelchair access (also WC). Music. Air-conditioned   ⊖ Green Park

Babur Brasserie £

map 12

119 Brockley Rise, SE23 1JP

COOKING 2

TEL: (020) 8291 2400   FAX: (020) 8291 4881

INDIAN

WEBSITE: www.babur-brasserie.com

£23–£49

The Babur Brasserie goes where most suburban high street Indian restaurants fear to tread, moving beyond the usual clichés into the regional specialities of India. The menu ranges far and wide, from Kerala, Goa, Gujerat to mid- and northern India; there is also a separate vegetarian menu. 'Celebrating spice' is Babur Brasserie's self-proclaimed *raison d'être*, and spicing, as well as timing and presentation, is generally well handled (although waits for food can be long). Lovage seeds, cumin and asafoetida may be used to flavour a dish of bananas, sweet potatoes, baby aubergines and shallots, while roasted star anise, fenugreek seeds, red chillies, coconut and cinnamon are used in a Goan dish of beef Xacuti. Breads are unusually good, as are rice dishes and, for desserts, own-made kulfi comes in unusual flavours. Prices on the brief wine list start at £9.25. Refurbishment is planned as we go to press.

CHEF: Enam Rahman   PROPRIETOR: Babur 1998 Ltd   OPEN: Sat to Thur L 12 to 2, all week D 6 to 11   CLOSED: 25 and 26 Dec   MEALS: alc (main courses £7.50 to £13). Set D £14.95   SERVICE: not inc   CARDS: Amex, Delta, Diners, MasterCard, Switch, Visa   DETAILS: 56 seats. Private parties: 40 main room. Vegetarian meals. Music. Air-conditioned   (£5)

Back to Basics ⁵⁄✳

map 15

21A Foley Street, W1W 6DS

TEL: (020) 7436 2181   FAX: (020) 7436 2180

COOKING 3

EMAIL: fishisthedish@aol.com

SEAFOOD

WEBSITE: www.backtobasics.uk.com

£29–£56

Billed as 'A Seafood Lover's Delight', this crowded, entertaining venue remains a Fitzrovia favourite. Tables outside are at a premium when the sun shines; otherwise sit indoors and amuse your eyes with the 'nautical miscellany'. The specials board headed 'Today's Catch' takes pride of place, although supplies depend on 'the weather, demands and fishermen's moods'. Items run out quickly, but you might encounter whole John Dory with asparagus, tomato and rosemary vinaigrette, or fillet of wild sea trout with lemon and a 'spritely mix' of samphire, sliced red onions, oyster mushrooms and flat-leaf parsley. Bread is recommended, and the standard menu is a familiar trawl through big bowls of fish soup, platters of smoked seafood and salads, plus a few meaty alternatives like duck breast with orange sauce. 'Boozy' desserts might include chocolate terrine with toffee and brandy sauce. House wines at £12.95 head the short list, although it's worth exploring the 'Alternative Cellar', which boasts some classy French vintages.

CHEF: Stefan Pflaumer   PROPRIETOR: Ursula Higgs   OPEN: Mon to Sat 12 to 3, 6 to 10.30   MEALS: alc (main courses £10 to £16.50)   SERVICE: 12.5% (optional)   CARDS: Amex, Delta, Diners, MasterCard, Switch, Visa   DETAILS: 40 seats. 40 seats outside. Private parties: 50 main room, 7 to 10 private rooms. Vegetarian meals. Children's helpings. No smoking in 1 dining room. Wheelchair access (not WC). Music   ⊖ Oxford Circus, Goodge Street   £5

Baltic

map 13

74 Blackfriars Road, SE1 8HA
TEL: (020) 7928 1111   FAX: (020) 7928 8487
EMAIL: info@balticrestaurant.co.uk
WEBSITE: www.balticrestaurant.co.uk

COOKING 2
EAST/NORTH EUROPEAN
£24–£55

A stone's throw from Southwark Tube station, and within ambling distance of Tate Modern, is this big, welcoming restaurant specialising in the food of what were once the Iron Curtain countries of north-east Europe. Menu choice is enticing, gathering in its widely cast net steamed mussels with bacon and beer, roast monkfish with kabanos sausage and potatoes, and beef zrazy (which is rolled with pickles and mustard and served with kasza and mushrooms). While there are occasional misses – overcooked pork chop served with dry red cabbage at one meal – it mostly satisfies. Less obviously Baltic dishes include salmon and haddock fishcakes with spinach and sorrel sauce. Finish with crème brûlée with sour cherries, or nalesniki (crêpes filled with sweet cheese, nuts and raisins). Wines are an inviting international bunch (although there are none, oddly, from Eastern Europe) at mostly manageable prices. House vins de pays are £11.50.

CHEF: Nick Pound   PROPRIETOR: Jan Woroniecki   OPEN: Sun to Fri L 12 to 3.30, all week D 6 to 11   MEALS: alc (main courses £9 to £14.50). Set L and D 6 to 7.30 £11.50 (2 courses) to £13.50   SERVICE: 12.5% (optional)   CARDS: Amex, Diners, MasterCard, Switch, Visa   DETAILS: 100 seats. 20 seats outside. Private parties: 100 main room, 10 to 35 private rooms. Vegetarian meals. Wheelchair access (also WC). Music. Air-conditioned   ⊖ Southwark, Waterloo   £5

Bank Aldwych ▼

map 13

1 Kingsway, Aldwych, WC2B 6XF
TEL: (020) 7379 9797   FAX: (020) 7240 7001
EMAIL: aldres@bankrestaurants.com
WEBSITE: www.bankrestaurants.com

COOKING 4
MODERN EUROPEAN
£26–£70

This stylish original Bank (see entry below for one of its off-shoots), with its glassy ceiling, wooden floors and cool waiting staff, doesn't show its age. It is now established as a brunch venue, but the long menu also lists breakfast, lunch and dinner dishes, all on one carte, brasserie-style. The cooking is technically sound, if not exactly inventive, though some reports suggest that value for money is not what it might be. The menu is pan-European, with a few Asian twists; expect the likes of Baltic herrings and new potatoes, tomato and mozzarella salad, and orange and miso baked salmon with pak choi. Fish figures large, as in a starter of haddock and ricotta tart, described as 'elegant and well balanced in seasoning'. Bank mixed grill and roast rump of lamb with provençale vegetables are suitably robust meat options. Desserts like cheesecake and sticky toffee pudding aim for comfort. The short wine list is packed with tasty stuff at prices you would expect to pay here. A short selection of prestige wines adds a flourish, and it's heartening to see Bank championing the excellent New Wave Wines from Tenterden. House wines are £12.95, and six whites and six reds come by the glass (£3.50 to £6.40).

CHEF: Peter Lloyd   PROPRIETOR: Bank Restaurant Group plc   OPEN: all week 12 to 2.45 (11.30 to 3 Sat and Sun), 5.30 to 11 (11.30 Sat, 10 Sun)   CLOSED: 25 and 26 Dec, 1 Jan   MEALS: alc (main courses £11.50 to £21.50). Set L £12.50 (2 courses) to £15. Set D 5.30 to 7 £12.50 (2 courses) to £15. Evening bar menu available   SERVICE: 12.5% (optional), card slips closed   CARDS: Amex, Delta, Diners, MasterCard, Switch, Visa   DETAILS: 220 seats. Private parties: 30 private room. Vegetarian meals. Children's helpings. Wheelchair access (also WC). Occasional music. Air-conditioned   ⊖ Holborn £5

Bank Westminster ♥

map 13

45 Buckingham Gate, SW1E 6BS
TEL: (020) 7379 9797   FAX: (020) 7379 5070
EMAIL: westres@bankrestaurants.com
WEBSITE: www.bankrestaurants.com

COOKING 3
MODERN EUROPEAN
£26–£79

Some see this as too noisy by half, others as a 'lively brasserie in the heart of Westminster'. Either way, it is a colourful modern conservatory-style dining room at the rear of the Crowne Plaza Hotel, tucked in behind the associated Zander Bar. It has blues, yellows, lots of glass and wooden floors, plus comfortable, purple Julyan Wickham armchairs surrounding white-dressed tables and staff in Mao-style garb. The menu remains as cosmopolitan as the original (see entry above) – steak and kidney pudding may jostle against seared marlin with wok-fried greens and lime sauce. An exuberantly seasoned but delicious starter of black pudding with foie gras, fried duck's egg and pancetta has impressed, and among main courses (with vegetables extra) might be three generous slices of monkfish wrapped in thin bacon. Poor mash has let down a dish of Cumberland sausages, but 'gloriously deep, rosy' summer pudding, bursting with seasonal berries and served with clotted cream has been a successful ending. The wine list is the same as for the original Bank Aldwych (see entry).

CHEF: Matt Dawson   PROPRIETOR: Bank Restaurant Group plc   OPEN: Mon to Fri L 12 to 2.45, Mon to Sat D 5.30 to 11   CLOSED: 25 and 26 Dec, 1 Jan   MEALS: alc (main courses £11.50 to £24.50). Set L £12.50 (2 courses) to £15, Set D 5.30 to 7 and 10 to 11 £12.50 (2 courses) to £15   SERVICE: 12.5% (optional), card slips closed   CARDS: Amex, Delta, Diners, MasterCard, Switch, Visa   DETAILS: 130 seats. 25 seats outside. Private parties: 50 main room; 20 to 40 private rooms. Vegetarian meals. Children's helpings. Wheelchair access (also WC). Occasional music. Air-conditioned   ⊖ St James's Park £5

Belair House

map 12

Gallery Road, Dulwich Village, SE21 7AB
TEL: (020) 8299 9788   FAX: (020) 8299 6793
EMAIL: info@belairhouse.co.uk
WEBSITE: www.belairhouse.co.uk

COOKING 2
MODERN FRENCH
£36–£56

Belair House is universally acclaimed by readers as a fantastic venue: a lovely period house in the middle of Dulwich parkland. One large dining room, with a bay-windowed area off to one side, has a particularly tranquil feel. Since last year there has been a change of ownership, and the interior has also been recently redecorated, making it a little more light and airy. The set-price menus can see some quite complicated dishes, and chef Zak Elhamdou seems keen on gutsy Mediterranean flavours. Provençale soup with aïoli makes a nice, if very rich, starter, and a vegetarian option might be a goats' cheese tartlet drizzled with pesto. Main course tournedos of Aberdeen Angus beef may come with spinach, ceps and truffled veal jus. Chocolate-based desserts, such as chocolate terrine with praline and crème anglaise, have gone down well. House wines from the international list start at £16 and rise quickly.

CHEF: Zak Elhamdou PROPRIETOR: Sam Hajaj OPEN: Tue to Sun L 12 to 2.30, Tue to Sat D 7 to 10.30 MEALS: Set L £18 (2 courses) to £22, Set D £32. Bar menu available Tue to Sat SERVICE: 12.5% (optional), card slips closed CARDS: Amex, Delta, Diners, MasterCard, Switch, Visa DETAILS: 85 seats. 30 seats outside. Private parties: 85 main room. Car park. Vegetarian meals. Children's helpings. Wheelchair access (also WC). Occasional music £5

Belvedere Marco Pierre White map 13

off Abbotsbury Road, W8 6LU
TEL: (020) 7602 1238 FAX: (020) 7610 4382
EMAIL: sales@whitestarline.org.uk
WEBSITE: www.whitestarline.org.uk

COOKING 4
MODERN BRITISH/MEDITERRANEAN
£34–£87

The beautiful dining room, with its mirrors, parquet floor, vaulted ceiling and handsome pots of enormous lilies, makes a fine setting, and views of the gardens from the terrace are stunning. One is never sure whether to take classical terms at face value, or assume they are a modern interpretation: witness the reporter who, on returning home, thumbed through his *Larousse Gastronomique* in a vain attempt to find out why his 'hors d'oeuvre à la bordelaise' meant 'snails'. Picking your way through mussels 'Maison Prunier', tartare of salmon 'à la russe', or omelette of langoustines 'Rothschild' needs some help, and waiting staff, at least at inspection, seemed to be short on the necessary enthusiasm.

That aside, there are some first-class dishes to be had, not least among seafood: a rich red mullet soup à la marseillaise, dressed crab à l'anglaise, Dover sole with a good tartare sauce, and grilled scallops and calamari with dabs of black squid ink. Other successes have included a deeply flavoured and perfectly cooked rib of well-hung Aberdeen Angus, with a row of oysters across it, accompanied by an intense jus, a crumbly pastry tart of chocolate with milk ice cream, and a refreshing dish of ripe red fruits in a not-too-firmly-set champagne jelly. Don't expect any bargains on the wine list; those who don't mind the mark-ups, however, can drink very well indeed. House Côtes du Rhône white is £19, Côte Roannaise red £21.50.

CHEF: Matthew Brown PROPRIETORS: Jimmy Lahoud and Marco Pierre White OPEN: all week 12 to 2.30 (3.30 Sun), 6 to 11 CLOSED: Sun D in winter MEALS: alc (main courses £15.50 to £25). Set L Mon to Sat £14.95 (2 courses) to £17.95, Set L Sun £19.50 SERVICE: 12.5% (optional), card slips closed CARDS: Amex, Delta, Diners, MasterCard, Switch, Visa DETAILS: 144 seats. 20 seats outside. Private parties: 144 main room, 24 to 60 private rooms. Occasional music. Air-conditioned ⊖ Holland Park, High Street Kensington

Benares ✳

	NEW ENTRY map 15

12 Berkeley Square, W1X 5HG
TEL: (020) 7629 8886   FAX: (020) 7491 8883

COOKING 3
MODERN INDIAN
£28–£66

This new Indian restaurant – named after the ancient city of Benares, considered one of the holiest sites in India (the city is now called Varanasi) – is certainly an elegant and stylish venue: the candlelit entrance lobby has a marble floor and a lily pond, though the dining room is somewhat stark by comparison. Chef-proprietor Atul Kochhar (formerly at Tamarind, see entry) offers a mix of new and old ideas in his cooking, with traditional dishes such as achari gosht alongside innovations such as John Dory with mint. Ingredients are well sourced and dishes are attractively presented, although technique is variable: highlights have included 'meltingly tender' tandoor-cooked chicken tikka, thick-textured dhal makhani, stir-fried cauliflower, broccoli and carrots with ginger, tomato and coriander, and baked fig and yoghurt pudding. Breads are also good, notably the roomali roti. The wine list is elaborate, and offers a fair choice of wines from around the world, at prices that are 'tolerable by Mayfair standards'.

CHEF/PROPRIETOR: Atul Kochhar   OPEN: Mon to Fri L 12 to 2.30, all week D 5.30 to 10.30   CLOSED: 24 to 31 Dec   MEALS: alc (main courses £12.50 to £19.50). Set L £11.50 (2 courses) to £13.50. Bar menu also available   SERVICE: 12.5% (optional), card slips closed   CARDS: Amex, MasterCard, Switch, Visa   DETAILS: 100 seats. Private parties: 90 main room, 6 to 26 private rooms. Vegetarian meals. No smoking. Wheelchair access (also WC). Occasional music. Air-conditioned   ⊖ Green Park

Berkeley Square Café

(LONDON OF THE YEAR NEWCOMER)

	NEW ENTRY map 15

7 Davies Street, W1K 3DD
TEL: (020) 7629 6993   FAX: (020) 7491 9719
EMAIL: info@berkeleysquarecafe.com
WEBSITE: www.berkeleysquarecafe.com

COOKING 6
MODERN FRENCH
£34–£72

Although just off the famous square, the café is near enough to claim its honorary title. It occupies two floors, with a small bar, a wine cellar (through a glass door marked 'Heaven'), and shades of mauve and purple on the walls, curtains and floors. Steven Black is clearly a gifted chef who learned much from his time with Michel Guérard in France, and his cooking seems very much at home in this comparatively intimate setting (hardly a café, though). Ingredients are classy, and the menu is appealing without trying to astonish. Even the soups sound interesting: chilled lettuce with pickled cucumber, and spinach with goats' cheese mousse and crispy bacon.

The quality of materials, accurate timing and attractive presentation have come together in a dish of plump, moist, carefully roasted scallops separated from lightly seared slivers of foie gras (resting on diced asparagus and girolles) by a decorative smear of parsnip purée. A similar configuration has been applied to slices of tender, braised belly pork and caramelised peach, with a line of creamy, flavourful cauliflower and truffle purée between them. Neal's Yard cheeses are kept in uniformly fine condition, and desserts have been singled out for special praise, taking in a sphere of apple and cinnamon crumble with a scoop of cinnamon ice cream, and an even more impressive chocolate mousse topped with an 'utterly perfect' lime sorbet. The only fault of any significance at inspection was poor bread, while worthy of particular celebration is the presence of the 'Young Gourmet's Menu': either two or three courses, with a good and interesting (and non-patronising) choice. Service is friendly and alert. Wines don't come cheap, but quality is dependable in all regions. Eight come by the glass for £3.80 to £6.50, and the dessert wine selection is interesting. Big spenders can turn straight to the fine wine selection for some top-class Bordeaux.

CHEF: Steven Black   PROPRIETORS: Vince Power and Steven Black   OPEN: Mon to Fri 12 to 2.30, 6 to 10   CLOSED: Christmas, last 2 weeks Aug, bank hols   MEALS: Set L £14.95 (2 courses) to £42.50, Set D £32.50 (2 courses) to £42.50   SERVICE: 12.5% (optional), card slips closed   CARDS: Amex, Delta, MasterCard, Switch, Visa   DETAILS: 75 seats. 14 seats outside. Private parties: 8 to 20 private rooms. Vegetarian meals. Children's helpings. No-smoking area. Occasional music. Air-conditioned

Bibendum 🍸 map 14

Michelin House, 81 Fulham Road, SW3 6RD
TEL: (020) 7581 5817   FAX: (020) 7823 7925
EMAIL: reservations@bibendum.co.uk
WEBSITE: www.bibendum.co.uk

COOKING 4
MODERN BRITISH
£41–£99

'One of the most beguiling dining rooms in London' is a popular verdict on what is still in many ways the Conran flagship, an expansive, comfortable first-floor room above the original Conran Shop and the Oyster Bar (see entry). The predominantly blue stained-glass windows, mosaic-tiled floor and the repeated Michelin Man logo form the backdrop to the modern brasserie cooking in which the kitchen has always traded.

At lunch, a good-value fixed-price menu is operated, while in the evenings a carte comprising around 15 to 20 choices of both starters and main courses comes into play. Among dishes that have pleased have been a simple serving of Serrano ham with figs; herrings coloured vivid red from a beetroot and horseradish marinade on a warm potato and sweet onion salad; and a warm salad of smoked eel on crushed Jersey Royals with bacon and hollandaise. At inspection, however, three overcooked and under-seasoned scallops let the side down (especially at £24.50), and main-course veal fillet was dry, though its accompanying tartlet of shallots in béarnaise was appealing enough. A much better dish has been 'tender and deeply tasty' roast pork loin with prunes and Armagnac. Desserts have hit some high notes too, in the form of a rich chocolate pithiviers, and tarte fine aux pommes with vanilla ice cream. Prices tend to excite comment, not helped by bread, olives and vegetables being charged extra. Service, at 12.5 per cent, could show itself more willing.

The majestic wine list, however, does not exclude those on smaller budgets and has a good range below and around £20. Pricing is fitful, sometimes offering better value than many lesser lists, though steep elsewhere. Names of the day – Wither Hills, Capçanes, Boekenhoutskloof and the like – push up the pulse rate, but the heart of the list is a profound collection of France's finest that stands aloof from the buzz of fashion. Italy, Australia and California lead the rest. Just six wines come by the glass (£4.25 to £4.95) or 450ml 'pot'.

CHEF: Matthew Harris PROPRIETORS: Graham Williams, Simon Hopkinson, Michael Hamlyn and Sir Terence Conran OPEN: all week 12 to 2.30 (3 Sat and Sun), 7 to 11.30 (10.15 Sun) CLOSED: 24 to 26 Dec D MEALS: alc D (main courses £16.50 to £24.50). Set L £25 SERVICE: 12.5% (optional), card slips closed CARDS: Amex, Delta, Diners, MasterCard, Switch, Visa DETAILS: 76 seats. Children's helpings. Wheelchair access (not WC). No music. No mobile phones. Air-conditioned ⊖ South Kensington

Bibendum Oyster Bar ✻

map 14

Michelin House, 81 Fulham Road, SW3 6RD
TEL: (020) 7581 5817 FAX: (020) 7823 7925
EMAIL: reservations@bibendum.co.uk
WEBSITE: www.bibendum.co.uk

COOKING 3
SEAFOOD
£32–£77

A place 'for trendy people, who see spareness as a fashion statement', thought one visitor to this establishment in the impressive Michelin building. In warmer weather, sit in the foyer, with marble tables, metal chairs and original mosaic floor; otherwise shelter from draughts in the small inner bar. Supremely fresh oysters on ice are the stars here, full of distinctive flavours: 'the Colchesters saltier, the Rocks sweeter'. Lobster is also a winner, beautifully presented on the plate with a pot of classic French mayonnaise. The rest of the menu is peppered with salad ideas: Szechuan chicken, or smoked duck breast with potato and spring onion, for example. There are also some specials like roast cod with peperonata, and meat gets a look-in with (cold) marinated lamb rump with Asian salad. Desserts might include rich, sweet crème brûlée and 'heavily spiced' poached pear with crème fraîche ice cream. The wine list tilts towards whites and champagnes, with house selections from £15.95.

CHEF: Matthew Harris PROPRIETORS: Sir Terence Conran and Simon Hopkinson OPEN: all week 12 to 2.30 (12.30 to 3 Sat and Sun), 7 to 11.30 (10.15 Sun) CLOSED: 24 to 26 Dec D MEALS: alc (main courses £16.50 to £24.50). Set L £25 SERVICE: 12.5% (optional), card slips closed CARDS: Amex, Delta, Diners, MasterCard, Switch, Visa DETAILS: 76 seats. Vegetarian meals. Children's helpings. No smoking in 1 dining room. Wheelchair access (not WC). No music. No mobile phones. Air-conditioned

Bistro Aix

NEW ENTRY map 12

54 Topsfield Parade, Tottenham Lane, N8 8PT
TEL/FAX: (020) 8340 6346
WEBSITE: www.bistroaix.co.uk

COOKING 3
FRENCH
£28–£54

This bistro established a reputation for honest, good cooking soon after it opened in mid-2002. Fans are impressed by its quirky, sympathetic decoration, while white tablecloths and napkins set the tone. First courses of prawns with Pernod in a buttery broth, and courgette ribbons with Parmesan, suggest that the kitchen knows how to keep things simple, while provençale authenticity is brought to bear on some main courses: tender pigeon with pungent blackberry sauce and a mushroom-filled pancake, and fish ragoût in a carefully judged saffron-infused stock, with crushed potatoes, aïoli and blobs of tapenade sharpening things up. Moist, cakey raspberry gratin, well partnered by a fine lime sauce, made a good finish for one reporter. Service is friendly, professional and accommodating, and the wine list, not surprisingly, is almost entirely French. House vins de pays are £11 a bottle, £3.50 a glass.

CHEF: Lynne Sanders   PROPRIETORS: Lynne Sanders and Andrew Schutt   OPEN: Tue to Sun 12 to 3, 6 to 10.30   MEALS: alc (main courses £9.50 to £15). Set L £11.50 (2 courses), Set D Sun £13.50 (2 courses) to £16.50   SERVICE: 12.5% (optional), card slips closed   CARDS: Amex, Delta, Diners, MasterCard, Switch, Visa   DETAILS: 44 seats. 20 seats outside. Private parties: 50 main room. Vegetarian meals. Children's helpings. No-smoking area. Wheelchair access (also WC). Music. Air-conditioned

Blandford Street

map 15

5–7 Blandford Street, W1U 3DB
TEL: (020) 7486 9696   FAX: (020) 7486 5067
EMAIL: bookings@blandford-street.co.uk
WEBSITE: www.blandford-street.co.uk

| NEW CHEF |
MODERN EUROPEAN
£32–£68

Smart, bright and cosmopolitan, and situated just off Marylebone High Street, Blandford Street strikes an upmarket pose, its white walls hung with bold modern artworks and mirrors, while white linen-dressed tables are set against wooden floors. The imaginative and appealing modern menu matches the décor. A new chef arrived in 2003, although the style that has produced a mille-feuille of foie gras with toasted almonds, caramelised onion and blueberry reduction, followed by roasted cannon of Welsh lamb 'moussaka' with feta cheese and Greek salad, is set to continue. Desserts have had a more familiar ring – perhaps a crumble of winter berries with cinnamon ice cream. The French-led wine list travels the globe for inspiration, offering eight house wines from £14 and ten by the glass from £4.

CHEF: Martin Moore   PROPRIETOR: Nicholas and Emmaline Lambert   OPEN: Mon to Fri L 12 to 2.30, Mon to Sat D 6.30 to 10.30   CLOSED: 25 Dec to 5 Jan, Easter weekend, bank hols   MEALS: alc (main courses £15 to £20). Set L and D 6.30 to 7 £15 (2 courses) to £20   SERVICE: 12.5% (optional), card slips closed   CARDS: Amex, Delta, Diners, MasterCard, Switch, Visa   DETAILS: 55 seats. 6 seats outside. Private parties: 55 main room. Vegetarian meals. Children's helpings. No-smoking area. No cigars/pipes. Wheelchair access (not WC). Occasional music. Air-conditioned   ⊖ Bond Street, Baker Street

Bleeding Heart

map 13

The Cellars, Bleeding Heart Yard,
Greville Street, EC1N 8SJ
TEL: (020) 7242 2056   FAX: (020) 7831 1402
EMAIL: bookings@bleedingheart.co.uk

COOKING 2
FRENCH
£36–£63

Bleeding Heart Yard has quite a history (read about it on the back of the menu) and was mentioned by Dickens in *Little Dorrit* (read the novel). In the cellars below the yard is this warm and welcoming two-roomed restaurant with wooden floors and walls. Starters and main courses are listed on the menu in French with English subtitles; among the former might be tortellini of 'fresh and vibrant' crab in a lobster broth, with wild mushroom and pearl barley risotto among the latter. Otherwise, you might find 'deliciously tasty' baked goats' cheese timbale with roast courgettes and grilled red peppers, or foie gras terrine with roast fig vinaigrette, followed by 'juicy and tender' fillet of sea bass on a bed of lobster risotto with truffled green beans and pea velouté, or fillet of beef with ceps, roast salsify, rösti and a Madeira jus. Mango soufflé with rum sauce is worth the 15-minute wait ('one of the most enjoyed puds I've ever had anywhere'), and chocolate terrine with a cappuccino sauce is equally well reported. The French staff are well trained but can need prompting, and, not surprisingly, France dominates the long wine list. New Zealand is at the head of an invigorating New World pack that breaks the traditional feel, with Australia and California at its heels. Sub-£20 bottles pop up here and there, and around 25 wines come by the glass for £3.75 to £6.55.

CHEF: Mat Burns   PROPRIETORS: Robert and Robyn Wilson   OPEN: Mon to Fri 12 to 2.30, 6 to 10.30   CLOSED: 1 week Christmas, bank hols   MEALS: alc (main courses £11 to £19)   SERVICE: 12.5% (optional), card slips closed   CARDS: Amex, Delta, Diners, MasterCard, Switch, Visa   DETAILS: 110 seats. 40 seats outside. Private parties: 105 main room, 35 to 50 private rooms. Vegetarian meals. No children. Wheelchair access (not WC). No music. Air-conditioned ⊖ Farringdon, Chancery Lane

---

Blue Elephant ✎

map 12

3–6 Fulham Broadway, SW6 1AA
TEL: (020) 7385 6595   FAX: (020) 7386 7665
EMAIL: london@blueelephant.com
WEBSITE: www.blueelephant.com

COOKING 1
THAI
£39–£75

Tropical plants, a pool with brightly coloured fish traversed by bridges, a waterfall – the scope of the main dining room is awesome, with several large areas separated by luxuriant foliage. If the air-conditioners had a 'steam' setting, this could almost be Thailand. The menu is broad in scope and quite appealing, with plenty of choice for vegetarians, from the ubiquitous pad thai, and roasted duck curry, to more unusual dishes, such as Thai chicken 'soufflé' steamed in a banana leaf. The spiciness of dishes is indicated by the number of elephants alongside the item on the menu, from zero to four. Prices are a distinct step up from the norm for this type of cuisine – well, someone has to water all those plants. Blue Elephant-labelled wines are from good producers in France, and there are reliable names from around the world throughout the list. As with the food, prices are on the high side, but a tasty drop well suited to Thai cuisine is not out of the question for under £20.

CHEF: Somphong Sae-Jew   PROPRIETOR: Blue Elephant International plc   OPEN: Sun to Fri L 12 to 2.30, all week D 7 (6 Fri and Sat) to 12   CLOSED: Christmas   MEALS: alc (main courses £9.50 to £28). Set L £10 to £15 (2 courses), Set D £33 to £37. Cover £1.50   SERVICE: not inc   CARDS: Amex, Delta, Diners, MasterCard, Switch, Visa   DETAILS: 250 seats. Vegetarian meals. Children's helpings. No music. Air-conditioned   ⊖ Fulham Broadway

---

'Somebody who may have been [the proprietor] handed the menus and wine lists out in the drawing room, giving a good impression of somebody running a half-marathon for a worthy charity.' (On eating in Sussex)

Blueprint Café

map 13

Design Museum, Butlers Wharf, SE1 2YD
TEL: (020) 7378 7031   FAX: (020) 7357 8810
EMAIL: blueprintcafe@conran-restaurants.co.uk
WEBSITE: www.conran.com

COOKING 3
MODERN EUROPEAN
£32–£61

The Conran stamp of relaxed Euro-modernity informs the unfussy furniture here as much as the no-nonsense approach to the food. The first-floor location helps elevate the waterside views to a different level, and the tables on the balcony remain in great demand. The menu reads robustly: starters include a plate of pickled herrings with beetroot and cucumber salads, or smoked haddock with lentils and mustard cream, or chicken and spinach terrine. Among main courses you might expect roast skate accompanied by horseradish, parsley and almonds, or roast pigeon with trevisse, shallots, balsamic and sage. A good selection of British cheeses and strong textural contrasts between a properly dry almond cake and the accompanying cardamom and pistachio ice cream rounded one couple's meal off nicely. Wines are universally interesting, with some high-quality bottles; prices start at £13 (£4 a glass).

CHEF: Jeremy Lee   PROPRIETOR: Conran Restaurants   OPEN: all week L 12 to 3, Mon to Sat D 6 to 11   CLOSED: 25 and 26 Dec, 1 and 2 Jan   MEALS: alc (main courses £12 to £17.50)   SERVICE: 12.5% (optional), card slips closed   CARDS: Amex, Diners, MasterCard, Switch, Visa   DETAILS: 110 seats. 30 seats outside. Private parties: 130 main room. Vegetarian meals. Children's helpings. Wheelchair access (not WC). No music   ⊖ Tower Hill, London Bridge

---

Boxwood Café

| NEW ENTRY | map 14

Berkeley Hotel, Wilton Place, SW1X 7RL
TEL: (020) 7235 1010   FAX: (020) 7235 1011
EMAIL: boxwoodcafe@gordonramsay.com
WEBSITE: www.gordonramsay.com

COOKING 3
MODERN BRITISH
£43–£66

Occupying the space in the Berkeley Hotel that formerly housed Vong, the Boxwood is Gordon Ramsay's homage to the cafés of New York. One well-travelled inspector felt that with its Art Deco styling and dramatic centrepiece staircase, it captured the New York mood very well, and piped jazz adds to the atmosphere. Only the cigarette smoke lacks authenticity. Menus have a retro vibe and a high comfort factor, with nettle and potato soup with poached quails' eggs, roast lobster with garlic butter and 'tremendous' chips, poached hake with parsley cream sauce, and braised lamb with carrots and dumplings. An inspection meal found a few dishes requiring more attention to detail, but hits included a generous slice of roast foie gras set off with a classy combination of peach, spring onion and ginger, and a salad of crab, squid, borlotti beans and baby artichokes. Desserts are updates of childhood favourites such as poppy seed knickerbocker glory with roasted apricots and pannacotta. The short, eclectic wine list majors in New World offerings. Mark-ups are on the high side and there are few bottles under £25.

CHEF: Stuart Gillies   PROPRIETOR: Gordon Ramsay   OPEN: all week 12 to 3 (4 Sat and Sun), 6 to 11   MEALS: alc (main courses £12.50 to £16)   SERVICE: not inc   CARDS: Amex, Delta, MasterCard, Switch, Visa   DETAILS: 130 seats. Private parties: 120 main room, 8 to 18 private rooms. Vegetarian meals. Children's helpings. No cigars/pipes. Wheelchair access (not WC). Music. Air-conditioned   ⊖ Knightsbridge

Bradleys ♥

25 Winchester Road, Swiss Cottage, NW3 3NR
TEL: (020) 7722 3457   FAX: (020) 7435 1392

map 13

COOKING 3
MODERN EUROPEAN
£28–£72

The look is easy on the eye and contemporary, with soft beige/cream tones complemented by wooden floors and colourful flower arrangements and paintings. The menu, too, is contemporary, with starters like rabbit and foie gras terrine with cornichons and pickled onions, or ricotta and lemon raviolo with asparagus, oyster mushrooms and 'agua verde'. Main courses are big on grilling, with chargrilled halibut, grilled entrecôte steak and seafood mixed grill putting in an appearance; vegetarians might favour tomato tarte Tatin with aubergine roulade and asparagus and pea flan. Sweets range from apricot and amaretto soufflé to lemon meringue pie. A set menu, with three choices per course, offers good value for lunch or early dinner. An inviting wine list, arranged by style, is not super-cheap but has a fair range under £20, interesting bottles above that, and a page of older vintages. There are eight by the glass (£3.50 to £5), plus seven dessert wines (£4.50 to £9.50).

CHEF: Simon Bradley   PROPRIETORS: Simon and Jolanta Bradley   OPEN: Sun to Fri L 12 to 3, all week D 6 to 11   CLOSED: 25 Dec to 4 Jan   MEALS: alc (main courses £13.50 to £19.50). Set L £12 (2 courses) to £16, Set D 6 to 7 £12 (2 courses) to £16   SERVICE: 12.5% (optional), card slips closed   CARDS: Amex, Delta, MasterCard, Switch, Visa   DETAILS: 65 seats. Private parties: 75 main room. Vegetarian meals. No cigars/pipes. Music. No mobile phones. Air-conditioned ⊖ Swiss Cottage (£5)

▲ Brasserie Roux

Sofitel St James Hotel, 8 Pall Mall, SW1Y 5NG
TEL: (020) 7968 2900   FAX: (020) 7747 2242
EMAIL: h3144-fb4@accor-hotels.com

map 15

COOKING 4
CLASSIC FRENCH
£24–£71

The brasserie is housed in a hotel on a Pall Mall corner but is run very much as a stand-alone business, so much so that it has two entrances: choose the hotel one if you want access to the bar before eating. Intentionally as French as can be, the décor evokes the majestic surroundings of large-scale Paris eateries, with a cockerel motif on the walls to rub the point home further. A long menu deals in precisely the kinds of dishes one expects, and the kitchen makes a good fist of most of them: bright red classic fish soup with croûtons, Gruyère and rouille all present, correct and bursting with flavour, roast duck à l'orange with bordelaise potatoes, and 'powerfully tasty' lemon tart added up to a fine spring lunch for one impressed reporter. Items such as pipérade with peppers and tomatoes, or boudin noir with an 'astringent' apple and sage compote, appear to be made according to sound Gallic principle, while the timing and overall balance of a main course of veal kidney served with tagliatelle and a grain mustard sauce were both exemplary. Time-warp desserts include rum baba and profiteroles, or there are French cheeses from specialists Vernier. Service is commended as 'impeccable'. Gallic chauvinism is notably absent from a likeable, good-value wine list that happily unites Chablis and Colchagua Valley under the banner of Chardonnay. A dozen table wines and three fizzes come by the glass (£3.50 to £6.50 and £6.50 to £7 respectively).

CHEFS: Albert Roux and Glen Watson   PROPRIETOR: Accor UK   OPEN: all week 12 to 3, 5.30 to 11.30 (10.30 Sun)   MEALS: alc (main courses £6.50 to £23.50). Set D 5.30 to 7 and 10.45 to 11.30 £15   SERVICE: 12.5% (optional), card slips closed   CARDS: Amex, Delta, Diners, MasterCard, Switch, Visa   DETAILS: 98 seats. Private parties: 100 main room, 2 to 12 private rooms. Vegetarian meals. Children's helpings. No-smoking area. Wheelchair access (also WC). Music. Air-conditioned   ACCOMMODATION: 186 rooms, all with bath/shower. TV. Phone. Room only £275 to £710. Rooms for disabled. Baby facilities   ⊖ Piccadilly Circus

Brasserie St Quentin   map 14

243 Brompton Road, SW3 2EP
TEL: (020) 7589 8005   FAX: (020) 7584 6064   COOKING 3
EMAIL: reservations@brasseriestquentin.co.uk   MODERN FRENCH
WEBSITE: www.brasseriestquentin.co.uk   £29–£75

Sitting in a window looking across to the Brompton Oratory made a pair of diners feel they had been transported to Paris, a feeling reinforced by the bustling atmosphere and archetypal brasserie menu: soupe de poissons with Gruyère and croûtons, confit of duck, and Dover sole meunière all make appearances. Broader influences are brought to bear with smoked Hereford duck breast with tabbouleh and French beans, or Dorset crab with toasted Poilâne bread to start, and Cranborne pork sausages with mash, 'superb' grilled calf's liver with bacon and sage mash, or boned quail stuffed with wild mushrooms on pea purée among main courses. Desserts include raspberry crème brûlée, and apple tart with Calvados and raisin ice cream. Service is polite and pleasant, although some reporters have commented on delays: gaps can be filled with one, or more, of the many good wines offered by the glass (three sherries and eleven wines for £3.50 to £4.80). The full list has plenty of affordable drinking from lesser-known regions and producers in France, as well as smarter bottles. Prices start at £14.

CHEF: Nana Akuffo   PROPRIETOR: Brasserie St Quentin 2002 Ltd   OPEN: all week 12 to 10.30 (10 Sun)   CLOSED: 24 to 29 Dec, 2 weeks Aug   MEALS: alc (main courses £9 to £23.50). Set L and D (exc after 7.30) £14.50 (2 courses) to £16.50   SERVICE: 12.5% (optional), card slips closed   CARDS: Amex, Delta, Diners, MasterCard, Switch, Visa   DETAILS: 80 seats. 6 seats outside. Private parties: 12 main room, 6 to 25 private rooms. Vegetarian meals. Wheelchair access (not WC). Occasional music. Air-conditioned   ⊖ Knightsbridge, South Kensington

Brian Turner Mayfair ▼   NEW ENTRY

Millenium Hotel, 44 Grosvenor Square, W1K 2HP   COOKING 3
TEL: (020) 7596 3444   FAX: (020) 7596 3443   ENGLISH
EMAIL: turner.mayfair@mill-cop.com   £37–£74

The opening of Brian Turner Mayfair sees the return of Brian Turner CBE to the restaurant kitchen, following the closure of Turner's in 2001. As might be expected from this chef, the cooking is very much based on British (one might even be more specific and say northern English) classics. 'Wholesome', 'simple' and 'satisfying' are words that have been used to describe the cooking. Starters might include 'moist and very tasty' smoked fillet of eel with streaky bacon served on warm potato salad. Meaty mains might feature steak and kidney 'plate pie' with oyster and kidney gravy, and the menu's 'grills & roasts' section lists the likes of rib of Aberdeen Angus with seasoned pudding and a shallot jus. Vegetarians aren't forgotten – leek and goats' cheese pie was enhanced by a well-judged parsley sauce – while desserts such as apple and pineapple crumble with clotted cream are decidedly old-fashioned. The wine list, however, is bang up to the minute and has a keen eye for quality in all regions. Australia and New Zealand are particular favourites. Mark-ups range from fair for Mayfair to high, with bottles starting at £17 and 11 by the glass from £4 to £6.

CHEFS: Brian Turner and Paul Bates   PROPRIETOR: Millennium and Copthorne Hotels   OPEN: Sun to Fri L 12.30 to 2.30, Mon to Sat D 6.30 to 11   MEALS: alc (main courses £11.50 to £18.50). Set L £19.50 (2 courses) to £21.50   SERVICE: 12.5% (optional), card slips closed   CARDS: Amex, Delta, Diners, MasterCard, Switch, Visa   DETAILS: 86 seats. 24 seats outside. Private parties: 24 to 40 private rooms. Vegetarian meals. No-smoking area. No pipes. Wheelchair access (also WC). Occasional music. Air-conditioned   ⊖ Bond Street, Green Park (£5)

Café du Jardin ♥

map 15

28 Wellington Street, WC2E 7BD
TEL: (020) 7836 8769 and 8760
FAX: (020) 7836 4123
WEBSITE: www.lecafedujardin.com

COOKING 1
MODERN BRITISH
£23–£55

Occupying a large corner site, the café has windows on to bustling Wellington Street and Covent Garden from its high-ceilinged, street-level room (there's a basement too). It's popular with pre- and post-theatre diners, and its small, tightly packed tables create a lively, buzzy atmosphere. The kitchen's modern carte is ambitiously lengthy, with some Mediterranean influences. Expect the likes of buffalo mozzarella with a herb and caper salad, salted anchovies and black olive dressing to start, followed by crisp-skinned fillet of sea bass with fennel slaw and gremolata. Classics find their place, too, with bouillabaisse of grilled fish with lobster ravioli, or perhaps veal cutlet milanese with lemon butter. Desserts follow a familiar route: sticky toffee pudding with vanilla ice cream and hot fudge sauce, or white and dark chocolate mousse. A sister restaurant, Le Deuxième, is in Long Acre (see entry).

The unassuming, closely typed wine list is actually a little gem, an international mix taking in oddities like Gaillac from the Técou co-op (£22.50), sought-after bottles such as 1995 Jim Barry Armagh Shiraz (£40) and enough under £20 to stifle any grumbles. A separate fine wine list handles the superleague. House vin de pays is £10.50, and a dozen by the 250ml glass are £3.50 to £6.35. The 15 per cent 'optional' service charge is hard to swallow.

CHEF: Tony Howorth   PROPRIETORS: Robert Seigler and Tony Howorth   OPEN: Mon to Sat 12 to 3, 5.30 to 12, Sun 12 to 11   CLOSED: 24 and 25 Dec   MEALS: alc (main courses £8.50 to £16). Set L and D Mon to Sat 5.30 to 7.30 and 10 to 12, Sun 12 to 11 £10.95 (2 courses) to £14.50

SERVICE: 15% (optional), card slips closed   CARDS: Amex, Delta, MasterCard, Switch, Visa
DETAILS: 100 seats. 20 seats outside. Private parties: 65 main room, 30 to 60 private rooms.
Vegetarian meals. Wheelchair access (not WC). Music. Air-conditioned   ⊖ Covent Garden

Café Fish

36–40 Rupert Street, W1V 6DW
TEL: (020) 7287 8989   FAX: (020) 7287 8400

map 15

COOKING 2
SEAFOOD
£31–£67

This cheeringly informal restaurant, with bare wood underfoot and Formica-topped tables, is as 'dependable as usual'. Fish, shellfish and crustaceans are the business of the menu (give or take the odd pudding to round things off), and summed up by one fan as 'fresh food, tastefully prepared, not elaborate, but attractively presented'. Begin with deep-fried Cajun whitebait with paprika mayonnaise, or tempura squid with satay and sweet chilli sauce, to ring the changes on a repertoire that otherwise deals in popular classic preparations. These include fish hotpot with tomato sauce and saffron rice, grilled lobster with garlic butter and chips, and seared salmon with mashed potato. Mostly white wines include oceans of Chardonnay, but relief is provided by Sauvignon, Muscadet and one or two unexpected bottles such as a white Corbières. Prices start at £10.50.

CHEF: Richard Gilbert   PROPRIETOR: Groupe Chez Gérard   OPEN: Sun 2 to 9, Mon to Sat 12 to 11.30   MEALS: alc (main courses £10.50 to £26). Set L and pre-theatre D £10 (2 courses)
SERVICE: 12.5%, card slips closed   CARDS: Amex, Delta, Diners, MasterCard, Switch, Visa
DETAILS: 170 seats. Private parties: 100 main room. Children's helpings. No-smoking area.
Wheelchair access (also WC). Music. Air-conditioned   ⊖ Piccadilly Circus, Leicester Square

Café Japan £

626 Finchley Road, NW11 7RR
TEL: (020) 8455 6854

map 13

COOKING 4
JAPANESE
£18–£47

The presence of plastic wisteria as decoration points up the lack of pretension about this 'simple but charming' restaurant. Two rows of no-nonsense lacquered pine tables are lined up against yellow-painted walls festooned with sushi charts, and a large number of staff are in perpetual motion. The menus major on sushi but also offer a variety of cooked dishes, such as crispy-fried salmon. Ordering is made easier with various set menus and combination platters of sushi and sashimi, but for some of the more exotic items it's best to ask for guidance from the owner, who keeps a watchful eye over proceedings. High standards were evident throughout an inspection meal that started with a sashimi platter of 'very fresh' salmon, sea bass and wedges of 'startlingly dark scarlet' tuna of impressive quality. Other successes have included 'rich and satisfying' toro sashimi, black cod with crisply seared skin, and vegetable sushi such as cooked gourd and soft, delicate avocado. Desserts are bought in, but green tea ice cream has been recommended nonetheless. Wines are limited to white or red at £8.50 a bottle, but there are also a couple of varieties of saké, Japanese plum wine and Japanese beers.

CHEF/PROPRIETOR: Koichi Konnai   OPEN: Sat and Sun L 12 to 2, Wed to Sun D 6 to 10 (9.30 Sun)
MEALS: alc (main courses L £1.50 to £10, D £5 to £16.50). Set L £6.90 (2 courses), Set D £12 (2 courses) to £16.50   SERVICE: not inc   CARDS: MasterCard, Switch, Visa   DETAILS: 39 seats. No smoking in 1 dining room. Music. Air-conditioned   ⊖ Golders Green

Café Spice Namaste

map 12 & 13

16 Prescot Street, E1 8AZ
TEL: (020) 7488 9242   FAX: (020) 7481 0508
WEBSITE: www.cafespice.co.uk

COOKING 3
INDIAN
£35–£61

This red-brick building was once a Magistrate's Court, but the Victorian exterior is deceptive; it now houses an imaginative Indian restaurant, and the interior is vivid with saffron, cinnamon and blue. Café Spice's Lavender Hill branch has closed, but the menu at the original E1 restaurant still holds many surprises, for this is not your average high-street 'curry house'. One of the appetisers is maatla nu paneer nay achar (fresh buffalo mozzarella – similar to a fresh buffalo-milk whey cheese made in Gujarat, says the menu) served with pickle and crackers. And the menu is strong on Parsee dishes, such as a the classic lamb dhansak, and Parsee-style chicken curry with nuts, coconut and Kashmiri chillies, but there are dishes from elsewhere on the Subcontinent, too, such as the Goan-style pork vindaloo, and even whole sea bass in Café Spice's own 'Indo-Szechwan-style' hot garlic sauce. 'Creative cooking and super service' characterised one recent visitor's experience here, and pin-point accuracy of timing marks the most successful dishes. Wines are listed by style and evidently chosen to complement the food. Bottle prices start at £12.95.

CHEFS: Cyrus Todiwala and Angelo Collaco   PROPRIETORS: Michael Gottlieb and Cyrus Todiwala
OPEN: Mon to Fri L 12 to 3, Mon to Sat D 6.15 to 10.30   CLOSED: 25 Dec to 1 Jan, bank hols
MEALS: alc (main courses £10 to £16). Set L and D £20 (2 courses) to £35   SERVICE: 12.5% (optional), card slips closed   CARDS: Amex, Delta, Diners, MasterCard, Switch, Visa   DETAILS: 140 seats. Private parties: 160 main room. Vegetarian meals. Wheelchair access (also WC). Music. Air-conditioned   ⊖ Tower Hill £5

Cambio de Tercio

map 14

163 Old Brompton Road, SW5 0LJ
TEL: (020) 7244 8970   FAX: (020) 7373 8817

COOKING 3
MODERN SPANISH
£36–£61

Described as 'authentically Spanish' by one visitor, Cambio de Tercio offers a number of surprises compared with the tapas that many British diners are used to. A plate of ham, or 'gambas fritas' – prawns fried with almonds and a garlic emulsion – are among the more familiar dishes, whereas fried cakes of Majorcan soft chorizo in white wine, or octopus with a light potato purée and sweet paprika really catch the eye. Main courses run to red mullet in sherry vinegar sauce with grilled asparagus and green peppers, and caramelised oxtail with a red wine jus and grilled potatoes. Traditional staples of lamb and suckling pig may also make an appearance. Finish with caramelised coconut bread cake with lemon ice cream, or a simpler infusion of red berries with yoghurt foam. Spanish cheeses are other possibilities, and the exclusively Spanish wine list helpfully arranges wines by style. Prices are on the high side, but the list provides a fascinating excursion through the country, and plenty by the glass includes a range of sherries. House wines open at £13.

CHEF: Javier Jimenez   PROPRIETOR: Abel Lusa   OPEN: all week 12 to 2.30, 7 to 9.30   CLOSED: 2 weeks Christmas   MEALS: alc (main courses £13.50 to £16.50)   SERVICE: not inc, 12.5% for parties of 6 or more   CARDS: Amex, Delta, MasterCard, Switch, Visa   DETAILS: 45 seats. 8 seats outside. Private parties: 80 main room, 15 to 20 private rooms. No-smoking area. Wheelchair access (not WC). Music. Air-conditioned   ⊖ Gloucester Road

Cantaloupe   map 13

35–42 Charlotte Road, EC2A 3PD
TEL: (020) 7613 4411   FAX: (020) 7613 4111   COOKING 3
EMAIL: info@cantaloupegroup.co.uk   IBERIAN/SOUTH AMERICAN
WEBSITE: www.cantaloupe.co.uk   £28–£47

Decibel levels in the two densely populated bars of this trendy Hoxton venue can be very high at peak times, according to disgruntled reporters who had been hoping for some peace and quiet in the adjoining dining area. Thankfully the food makes amends for any aural discomforts. The kitchen – open to view amid the throng – takes its cue from the Mediterranean borderlands for a menu of manageable proportions that might include roast rump of lamb with Umbrian lentils, chickpeas, morcilla and salsa verde, as well as roast sea bass with couscous salad, yoghurt, honey and tahini sauce. There are plates of Spanish 'deli' favourites to start, meze among the main courses, and desserts ranging from Cuban coffee brûlée to Framboise-marinated strawberries with lime and Tequila ice cream. A tapas menu is also available in the bar at lunchtimes (and for Sunday brunch). Bottles from the lively and geographically apposite wine list start at £11.50.

CHEF: Henry Brereton   PROPRIETORS: Richard Bigg and Nigel Foster   OPEN: Mon to Fri L 12 to 3, all week D 6 (7 Sat) to 11.30 (10.30 Sun)   MEALS: alc (main courses £9 to £13). Set L £10 (2 courses). Bar menu also available. Sun brunch 12 to 4   SERVICE: 12.5% (optional), card slips closed   CARDS: Amex, Delta, Diners, MasterCard, Switch, Visa   DETAILS: 66 seats. Private parties: 66 main room. Vegetarian meals. Wheelchair access (also WC). Music. Air-conditioned   ⊖ Old Street

▲ The Capital ♥   map 14

22–26 Basil Street, SW3 1AT
TEL: (020) 7589 5171   FAX: (020) 7225 0011   COOKING 8
EMAIL: reservations@capitalhotel.co.uk   FRENCH
WEBSITE: www.capitalhotel.co.uk   £44–£119

Semi-circular wooden sculptures – on mirrors reflecting the light of enormous chandeliers – stand out in an otherwise unremarkable setting. Wild mushrooms, truffles and foie gras might be expected in this location, but humbler items like saddle of rabbit balance them. Eric Chavot's refined and complex cooking is never too fussy, and materials are first-class: three langoustines 'of exemplary freshness, cooked to perfection', say, served on aïoli potato cubes, with deep-fried chorizo and pecorino bruschetta.

Modest cuts are adapted to a smart restaurant format, compiling varied yet integrated dishes. Veal sweetbread, for example, crustily encased in chopped nuts, comes with mushrooms and potato gnocchi in a well-judged, deep-flavoured, stock-based sauce; tiny piles of pig's ear and brain add further soft and crispy textures to a dish 'brilliantly conceived and executed'. Likewise the richness of a small piece of belly pork with a sweet honey glaze, plus a cube of trotter meat (breadcrumbed and deep-fried) and superb black pudding, is balanced by an 'inspired' towerlet of finely chopped celeriac topped with apple jelly.

Sometimes there's modest invention: a rich shellfish 'cassoulet' (Scottish lobster claw, large shelled prawn and a scallop – all 'fresh as can be' – plus the obligatory beans, some belly pork, and a small sausage of foie gras and truffle) over which the waiter ladles concentrated shellfish jus. But, even when there are no surprises, the cooking is accomplished, and the result typically indulgent – witness two bloody pigeon breasts, and two stuffed legs, plus a potato cake wrapped in flavourful Alsace bacon, all in a sauce headily aromatic with truffle. Desserts may not regularly match earlier dishes, but can reach the heights, as with a 'stunning' and refreshing strawberry and watermelon consommé with lime ice cream.

Service is polite, formal and accomplished. Bordeaux and Burgundy proudly dominate a notable list that digs deep into older vintages, and champagne is a speciality. Quality remains high elsewhere in Europe, and in the New World. Prices, too, are high, and £20 covers nothing but the four most basic options; nevertheless, a good range by the glass (£5.50–£12.50) offers the chance to sip something of appropriate calibre.

CHEF: Eric Chavot   PROPRIETOR: David Levin   OPEN: all week 12 to 2.30, 7 to 11   MEALS: Set L £28.50, Set D £48 (2 courses) to £68 (whole table)   SERVICE: 12.5% (optional), card slips closed   CARDS: Amex, Delta, Diners, MasterCard, Switch, Visa   DETAILS: 35 seats. Private parties: 35 main room, 24 private room. Vegetarian meals. Wheelchair access (not WC). No music. Air-conditioned   ACCOMMODATION: 48 rooms, all with bath/shower. TV. Phone. Room only £170 to £245. Baby facilities (*The Which? Guide to Good Hotels*)   ⊖ Knightsbridge £5

Le Caprice
map 15

Arlington House, Arlington Street, SW1A 1RT
TEL: (020) 7629 2239   FAX: (020) 7493 9040

COOKING 4
MODERN BRITISH
£36–£87

It looks fittingly discreet from the outside. Black and white is the dominant theme on entering, with walls, floor and ceiling all neatly echoed by monochrome photos of famous faces from the '60s. Excellent breads and basic starters such as Caesar salad and a well-flavoured mushroom tart may be followed by haddock in pleasingly light batter, chips just on the right side of crispy and good tartare sauce, or kidneys on a potato cake with mustard sauce – tried-and-tested combinations delivered in style. A gingery walnut parkin summoned childhood memories, served with vanilla-speckled custard. Vegans and vegetarians have their own menu. The wine list still manages to look fresh and runs to some very smart bottles, but never gets too big for its bistro boots. Prices can be a bit high, but start at just £11.75 and a dozen by the glass (£4.75 to £9.75) span the range effectively.

CHEF: Kevin Gratton   PROPRIETOR: Signature Restaurants plc   OPEN: all week 12 to 3 (3.30 Sun), 5.30 (6 Sun) to 12   CLOSED: 25 and 26 Dec, 1 Jan, Aug bank hol   MEALS: alc (main courses £10 to £23.50). Cover £1.50. Brunch menu Sun   SERVICE: not inc   CARDS: Amex, Delta, Diners, MasterCard, Switch, Visa   DETAILS: 80 seats. Private parties: 8 main room. Vegetarian meals. Wheelchair access (not WC). Music. No mobile phones. Air-conditioned   ⊖ Green Park

Cecconi's ▼ 🍷   map 15

5A Burlington Gardens, W1S 3EP	COOKING 6
TEL: (020) 7434 1500 FAX: (020) 7494 2440	ITALIAN
WEBSITE: www.cecconis.co.uk	£57–92

Right behind the Royal Academy in Mayfair, the 'extremely smart' first impression of Cecconi's is sustained throughout the interior, from the dark wood and plain walls to the striking paintings that cover them. The appointment of Stephen Terry (ex-Walnut Tree, Llandewi Skirrid, see entry, Wales) as executive chef and Mark Robertson as head chef has resulted in a giant leap forward, producing the best Italian meal one seasoned eater had had in the UK for a long while. The kitchen's understanding of the subtleties of Italian food was fully expressed for one reporter by carpaccio of monkfish with grilled zucchini, squid ink, lemon, capers and flat parsley – no gimmickry, everything perfectly fresh. Light potato gnocchi with chopped pancetta and sliced baby courgette, and tortelli (first-rate pasta) with ricotta, nettle leaves, lemon and pine nuts have been satisfying second courses. Welsh rack of lamb served on spinach with grilled aubergine was top-notch meat at inspection, while 'fresh and boldly flavoured' scallops came seasonally with peas, broad beans and asparagus.

'Worth the 20-minute wait', was the verdict of one visitor on a tiramisù soufflé, an excellent variation on a classic dessert. Service, by a veritable army of foot-soldiers, is generally well orchestrated, too. The wine list concentrates on a glorious range from all corners of Italy, with a smattering from elsewhere. Service is knowledgeable and quality is high, but so are prices. Nonetheless, a bit of digging, especially in the islands and the south, will turn up bottles under £20. There are very few half-bottles, but ten by the glass are £5 to £9.

CHEFS: Stephen Terry and Mark Robertson   PROPRIETOR: Hani Farsi   OPEN: Mon to Sat L 12 to 3, all week D 6.30 (7 Sat) to 11   MEALS: alc (main courses £16.50 to £28). Cover £1.50. Bar menu also available   SERVICE: 12.5% (optional)   CARDS: Amex, Delta, MasterCard, Switch, Visa   DETAILS: 86 seats. Private parties: 10 main room. Vegetarian meals. Occasional music. Air-conditioned   ⊖ Green Park, Piccadilly Circus

Chapter Two 🗱   map 12

43/45 Montpelier Vale, SE3 0TJ	
TEL: (020) 8333 2666 FAX: (020) 8355 8399	COOKING 4
EMAIL: chaptertwo@chaptersrestaurant.com	MODERN EUROPEAN
WEBSITE: www.chaptersrestaurant.co.uk	£30–£52

Chapter Two, in Blackheath, is sister to Chapter One in Farnborough, Kent (see entry). It occupies two floors – both are light and spacious, with light, crisp linen, smart upholstered chairs and boldly coloured art on the walls. The set menu (which varies in price, but not content, between lunch and dinner, and at weekends) is ambitious and modern. Start perhaps with velouté of Jerusalem artichokes with bacon dumplings, or roast scallops with white bean purée and ginger cream. Main courses can be as robust as assiette of Cambridge pork, potato and pancetta pie with an apple Tatin, or as soothing as roast cod with spinach and shellfish chowder. For vegetarians, herb ravioli of roast baby vegetables with a light herb infusion shows a desire to please. Desserts have mostly been well received: a hot chocolate fondant with a cornet of raspberry sorbet, or Grand Marnier parfait with mandarin compote and orange syrup. A straightforward wine list in price order offers around 60 wines with a leaning towards France and plenty at less than £25; half a dozen house wines start with vins de pays at £13.50.

CHEF: Lyndon Edwards   PROPRIETOR: Selective Restaurants Group   OPEN: all week 12 to 2.30 (3.30 Sun), 6.30 to 10.30 (11 Fri and Sat)   CLOSED: 2 and 3 Jan   MEALS: Set L £14.50 (2 courses) to £18.50, Set L Sun £14.50 (2 courses) to £16.50, Set D £16.50 (2 courses) to £22.50   SERVICE: 12.5% (optional), card slips closed   CARDS: Amex, Delta, Diners, MasterCard, Switch, Visa   DETAILS: 70 seats. Private parties: 50 main room. Vegetarian meals. Children's helpings. No smoking. Wheelchair access (also WC). Music. Air-conditioned

Le Chardon £

map 12

65 Lordship Lane, SE22 8EP
TEL: (020) 8299 1921   FAX: (020) 8693 0959

COOKING 1
FRENCH
£20–£50

The eponymous thistles can be spotted in patterned tiles adorning the walls of this former grocer's shop. The style here, decorative and culinary, is French brasserie, with dishes such as onion soup, moules marinière and snails. The menu undergoes a slight identity crisis with Thai fishcakes, but gets back on track with main courses of wild pigeon breasts with green peppercorn sauce, and pork shank with lentils and smoked bacon. If not all dishes have been flawless, the supporting act of pommes dauphinoise, 'disgracefully unctuous and very good', certainly has. Puddings have gone down well: for example, nougatine ice cream with crystallised fruits. Another slight detour from the Gallic is the Sunday roast lunch served until 5pm. A short, predominantly French list offers plenty of interest below £20, and seven house wines start at £9.95 (£2.80 a glass). The Green in East Dulwich Road is under the same ownership (see entry).

CHEFS: Didier Lemond and Didier Dixneuf   PROPRIETOR: Robert Benayer   OPEN: all week 12 to 11 CLOSED: 25 Dec D, bank hols   MEALS: alc (main courses £7.50 to £13.50). Set L Mon to Sat £6.95 to £9.95 (2 courses), Set L Sun £13.50   SERVICE: 10% (optional)   CARDS: Amex, Delta, MasterCard, Switch, Visa   DETAILS: 52 seats. 30 seats outside. Private parties: 60 main room. Vegetarian meals. Children's helpings. Music. Air-conditioned (£5)

All details are as accurate as possible at the time of going to press, but chefs and owners often change, and it is wise to check by telephone before making a special journey. Many readers have been disappointed when set-price bargain meals are no longer available. Ask when booking.

Chez Bruce 🍷 ⁵✖

map 12

2 Bellevue Road, SW17 7EG   COOKING **6**
TEL: (020) 8672 0114   FAX: (020) 8767 6648   MODERN BRITISH
£40–£77

Bright, comfortable and relaxing, Bruce Poole's Wandsworth restaurant overlooks the common and draws the crowds with an appealing modern menu. Upstairs (non-smoking) is small and intimate, while the ground floor's wood and white paint are offset by framed prints of classical art. With its generous choice (around eight options per course), the menu's sweep takes in an impressive range of materials and treatments, from a wedge of warm onion tart with Lancashire cheese and walnuts, to a vibrant-sounding sweet-and-sour squid salad with chilli, ginger, garlic and coriander, to roast skate with artichokes, duxelles and buttered kale.

Dishes don't try to be too clever, so the kitchen is not stretched beyond its capabilities. Some find the results a bit short on excitement, while others praise the 'effortless' cooking: a 'zingingly fresh' gazpacho, for example, or a 'textbook-quality' dish of rabbit. Offal plays a significant role in the repertoire, appearing in the form of an oxtail and pig's trotter croquette with sauce gribiche, and a main course of sautéed calves' kidneys and sweetbreads with garlic, parsley, and a potato galette. A sense of comfort and indulgence pervades the menu, exemplified by dishes such as smoked haddock with creamed leeks and a poached egg, grilled veal chop with béarnaise sauce, and most of the desserts: treacle tart with Jersey cream, and chocolate fondant with a poached pear and vanilla ice.

'Effortless' might also be the best word for the magnificent wine list that calmly cherry-picks the best in all regions and stays on top of trends such as the recent surge of interest in Austrian Grüner Veltliner. Around 40 table wines and 20 dessert wines are served by the glass, and the list of half-bottles is equally impressive. Prices are reasonable for the quality, but with just two wines under £20, don't expect bargains.

CHEF: Bruce Poole   PROPRIETORS: Nigel Platts-Martin and Bruce Poole   OPEN: Mon to Fri 12 to 1.55, 7 (6.30 Fri) to 10.25, Sat 12 to 2.55, 6.30 to 10.25, Sun 12.30 to 3.25, 7 to 10.25   MEALS: Set L Mon to Fri £18.50 (2 courses) to £23.50, Set L Sat £25, Set L Sun £27.50, Set D £30 to £40 SERVICE: 12.5% (optional), card slips closed   CARDS: Amex, Delta, Diners, MasterCard, Switch, Visa   DETAILS: 85 seats. Private parties: 70 main room, 10 to 16 private rooms. Children's helpings at L. No children at D. No smoking in 1 dining room. No cigars/pipes. Wheelchair access (not WC). No music. No mobile phones. Air-conditioned   ⊖ Balham

Chez Max

| NEW ENTRY | map 14

3 Yeoman's Row, SW3 2AL
TEL: (020) 7590 9999   FAX: (020) 7590 9900   COOKING **2**
EMAIL: sales@whitestarline.org.uk   FRENCH BRASSERIE
WEBSITE: www.whitestarline.org.uk   £29–£63

Max Renzland is no stranger to the Guide, seen most recently at Monsieur Max at Hampton Hill (see entry, although Max himself is no longer involved), and the latest version of Chez Max brings him into partnership with Marco Pierre White in what was once White's Parisienne Chophouse, occupying an airy basement off the Brompton Road. The French brasserie styling is laid on thickly: smoky mirrors, posters of exotic drinks, menus from famous French restaurants, and evocative menu items etched on glass screens. The menus bang home the bourgeois message with the likes of snails in garlic butter, salade niçoise, chateaubriand with béarnaise, and Dover sole meunière. Standards have been up and down, but at its best the kitchen has turned out 'expertly made' boudin blanc with pomme purée and charcuterie sauce, 'exemplary' roast sea bass with spinach in a saffron, leek and potato broth, 'robust yet balanced' roast loin of rabbit stuffed with its liver and kidney on boulangère potatoes, and 'densely rich and wicked' pot au chocolat with Williams pear sorbet. Wines are mostly but not exclusively French and cover a fair range of styles and prices, starting with vins de pays at £13.50.

CHEF: Max Renzland PROPRIETORS: Jimmy Lahoud, Marco Pierre White and Max Renzland OPEN: all week 12 to 3 (4 Sun), 6 to 11 (10 Sun and bank hols) MEALS: alc (main courses £10.50 to £18.50). Set L £13.50 (2 courses) to £16.50, Set D £16.50 SERVICE: 12.5% (optional), card slips closed CARDS: Amex, Delta, Diners, MasterCard, Switch, Visa DETAILS: 120 seats. Private parties: 10 main room, 10 to 26 private rooms. Vegetarian meals. Children's helpings. Music. Air-conditioned ⊖ Knightsbridge, South Kensington

Chez Moi

NEW ENTRY map 12

23 Richmond Way, W14 0AS COOKING 2
TEL: (020) 7602 6004 FAX: (020) 7602 8147 FRENCH
EMAIL: chezmoi_rest@hotmail.com £26–£56

Philippe Bruyer, once manager of Chez Moi in Holland Park, has bought the business and relocated it under the same name here (in what used to be Chinon). The move has resulted in a return to more traditional French roots: viz. salade of foie gras, French beans and quail's eggs and oven-baked snails with beurre d'escargot. Main courses have seen classic duck à l'orange, featuring a light jus, with roast potatoes and petit pois, and a medley of fish in a saffron nage. Desserts extend to 'well-judged' crêpes suzette, and tarte fine aux pommes. The interior is much more 'moderne', as is the young hospitable French staff. Wines are predominantly Gallic: prices are fair, with a reasonable range of half-bottles as well as eight selected wines by the glass from £4.25.

CHEF: Mark Stapley PROPRIETOR: Philippe Bruyer OPEN: Sun to Fri L 12 to 2.30 (3 Sun), Mon to Sat D 6.30 to 10.30 MEALS: alc (main courses £13 to £17). Set L Mon to Fri £12.50 (2 courses) to £14.50, Set L Sun £15.50 (2 courses) to £17.50 SERVICE: not inc CARDS: Amex, Delta, Diners, MasterCard, Switch, Visa DETAILS: 60 seats. 12 seats outside. Private parties: 10 main room, 10 to 25 private rooms. Children's helpings. No cigars/pipes. Wheelchair access (also WC). No music. Air-conditioned ⊖ Shepherd's Bush

'[It's] like having dinner in a cross between a stuffy gentleman's club and a bunker, except that you've got a pianist tinkling away in the background, poor woman.' (On eating in Cheshire)

Christopher's ♥

map 15

18 Wellington Street, WC2E 7DD
TEL: (020) 7240 4222
EMAIL: coventgarden@christophersgrill.com
WEBSITE: www.christophersgrill.com

COOKING 2
CONTEMPORARY AMERICAN
£28–£81

Refurbishment has left intact the impressive sweeping stone staircase that leads up to the first floor. In the main dining room, with its soft colours and modern lighting, large windows give views on to the street and over Waterloo Bridge. The style is based on the grand steak and lobster houses of America's eastern seaboard, although the menus extend well beyond grilled Maine lobster with garlic butter, and ribeye with slow-roast tomatoes, tobacco onions and Roquefort butter. Noteworthy successes have included tomato risotto given some oomph with chipotle and pieces of crispy mushroom, and well-timed roast fillets of sea bass on crushed roast potatoes with a contrasting sauce of tomato, pancetta and tarragon. Vegetables are 'exceptionally good', and puddings seem to end things on a high note, judging by reports of clean-flavoured raspberry, mango and lemon sorbets, and runny-centred, rich and intense warm sunken chocolate soufflé cake with espresso ice cream. Service is smart, friendly and attentive. Wines come under the headings of 'The Americas' and 'The Rest of the World', but even if California takes the lead, France is well represented and Australian and New Zealand whites stand out. While prices are on the high side, there's a fair selection under £20 and the option of a glass or 50cl pot on a dozen or so wines.

CHEF: Adrian Searing PROPRIETOR: Christopher Gilmour OPEN: all week L 12 to 3, Mon to Sat D 5 to 11.45 CLOSED: 25 and 26 Dec, Easter MEALS: alc (main courses £9.50 to £29). Set brunch Sat and Sun £11.95 (2 courses) to £16, Set D 5 to 7, 10 to 11.45 £13.50 (2 courses) to £17.50. Bar menu available Mon to Sat SERVICE: 12.5% (optional), card slips closed CARDS: Amex, Delta, Diners, MasterCard, Switch, Visa DETAILS: 110 seats. Private parties: 10 to 40 private rooms. Vegetarian meals. Children's helpings. Wheelchair access (also WC). No music. Air-conditioned
⊖ Covent Garden

Chutney Mary

map 12

535 King's Road, SW10 0SZ
TEL: (020) 7351 3113 FAX: (020) 7351 7694
EMAIL: mw@realindianfood.com
WEBSITE: www.realindianfood.com

COOKING 2
INDIAN
£30–£72

Chutney Mary's interior is redolent of India. The three sections of the downstairs dining room are brightened with silk cushions, a 'skylight' that changes the colour of the lighting in the dining room throughout the evening, and warm light supplied by candles and well-placed side lamps and ceiling spots. 'This being modern Indian, poppadoms are out, amuse-bouches in' – on one visit this was a cup of chicken and almond soup. From the main menu, one frequent visitor was pleased with the 'excellent flavours, freshness and spicing' in a main course of chicken stuffed with mashed fenugreek leaves with almond sauce. Starters may include inventive-sounding dishes such as Konkan-style prawns stir-fried with herbs and asparagus, or chandini (which translates as 'moonlight') chicken tikka, cooked using only 'white spices'. Well-conceived desserts may run to dark chocolate fondant with orange blossom lassi, or chilled rice pudding with a salsa of mango and chilli. Service gets mixed reports, from 'indifferent' to 'extremely attentive'. The wine list explains in some detail the principles of matching different styles with particular sections of the menu and offers enticing bottles with which to test these claims, new-wave Italians being a favourite. Prices have slid upwards since last year, with only a few bottles under £20 nowadays. Sixteen table wines come by the glass for £3.75 to £7.75.

CHEFS: Nagarajan Rubinath and Uday Salunkhe   PROPRIETORS: Namita and Camellia Panjabi, and Ranjit Mathrani   OPEN: Mon to Fri 6.30 to 11, Sat 12.30 to 2.30, 6.30 to 11, Sun 12.30 to 10.30   MEALS: alc exc Sun L (main courses £12.50 to £24). Set L Sat and Sun £16.50   SERVICE: 12.5% (optional), card slips closed   CARDS: Amex, Delta, Diners, MasterCard, Switch, Visa   DETAILS: 110 seats. Private parties: 110 main room, 10 to 30 private rooms. Vegetarian meals. No-smoking area. Occasional music. Air-conditioned   ⊖ Fulham Broadway

Cigala
map 13

54 Lamb's Conduit Street, WC1N 3LW
TEL: (020) 7405 1717   FAX: (020) 7242 9949
WEBSITE: www.cigala.co.uk

COOKING 3
SPANISH
£29–£53

Here Spanish food and wine is mercifully shorn of castanets, guitars and tatty bullfight posters and served amid clean lines, subdued colours and bare white walls. This no-nonsense approach, along with the fun atmosphere and 'earthy food', make Cigala stand out from the Iberian crowd. Things can kick off as simply as habas con jamon, the broad beans and ham lifted by the addition of mint, or the more unusual pan-fried squid accompanied by a good romescu sauce. The excellent timing of fish cookery was noted in a delicate collection of asparagus, broad beans and mint acting as the perfect foil for grilled halibut, while chunky roots and pulses in olla gitana contrasted nicely with the thin saffron broth. Finish with desserts like leche frita (deep-fried custard). Service is willing, cheerful but not necessarily knowledgeable. Sherries, aguardiente and a range of brandies complement a wine list, organised by grape variety, that provides an informed trip across Spain, with plenty under £20 in most regions. A dozen wines by the glass from £3.75 to £7 introduce some of the best and least known flavours. A tapas menu of around 30 dishes includes good meats (perhaps lomo, chorizo, and salchichon), mojama (wind-dried tuna), patatas bravas and tortilla espanola.

CHEF/PROPRIETOR: Jake Hodges   OPEN: all week 12 to 2.45, 6 to 10.45 (Sun 12.30 to 9.30)   CLOSED: 25 and 26 Dec, 1 Jan, Easter weekend   MEALS: alc (main courses £12.50 to £18.50). Set L Mon to Fri £15 (2 courses) to £18. Tapas menu available   SERVICE: 12.5% (optional), card slips closed   CARDS: Amex, Diners, MasterCard, Switch, Visa   DETAILS: 65 seats. 20 seats outside. Private parties: 70 main room. Vegetarian meals. Wheelchair access (not WC). No music. Air-conditioned   ⊖ Holborn

---

Some restaurants leave credit card slips open even though they also make a fixed (or 'optional') service charge. The Guide strongly disapproves of this practice as it may result in consumers unknowingly paying twice for service.

Cinnamon Club

map 13

Old Westminster Library, 30 Great Smith
Street, SW1P 3BU
TEL: (020) 7222 2555   FAX: (020) 7222 1333
EMAIL: info@cinnamonclub.com
WEBSITE: www.cinnamonclub.com

COOKING 4
MODERN INDIAN
£38–£89

Even if you're not the bookish sort and have never felt the urge to become a librarian, one must admit that the imposing space of the Old Westminster Library (a large number of books remain on display in the upstairs gallery) is a sight to behold. The Cinnamon Club is undeniably popular and the Guide receives a great deal of feedback about the restaurant, much positive (for the cooking in particular), some negative (service and pricing). Chef Vivek Singh presides over an inventive Indian-based menu that offers a number of quirks and turns. There is 'a real sense of excitement about the food', according to one visitor. A praiseworthy main course of black cod served in coconut and lemon sauce may be served with mustard greens, while tandoor-smoked lamb with masala spinach was proclaimed 'a sheer triumph' by one contented diner. Sweets, such as a trio of coconut desserts (coconut ice cream, coconut brûlée and a coconut and pastry roll) are 'beautifully presented'. They now offer a five-course gastronomic menu, each dish accompanied by a glass of wine. The wine list has Rieslings, Gewürztraminers, Sauvignons and lively reds aplenty to suit the food, as well as less useful selections of prestigious bottles. Prices start at £15 but mark-ups are high. Ten by the small (125ml) glass are £3.60 to £7.20 – a substantial hike on the bottle price.

CHEF: Vivek Singh   PROPRIETOR: Iqbal Wahhab   OPEN: Mon to Fri L 12 to 2.30, Mon to Sat D 6 to 11.45   CLOSED: bank hols   MEALS: alc (main courses L £11 to £22, D £11 to £31). Set L and D 6 to 7 £19 (2 courses) to £22, Set D £60 to £95 (inc wine, whole table)   SERVICE: 12.5% (optional), card slips closed   CARDS: Amex, Delta, Diners, MasterCard, Switch, Visa   DETAILS: 200 seats. Private parties: 150 main room, 30 to 50 private rooms. Vegetarian meals. Children's helpings. No music. Air-conditioned   ⊖ St James's Park, Westminster

Circus

map 15

1 Upper James Street, W1R 4BP
TEL: (020) 7534 4000   FAX: (020) 7534 4010
EMAIL: circus@egami.co.uk
WEBSITE: www.circusbar.co.uk

COOKING 3
MODERN EUROPEAN
£28–£68

Circus occupies a corner site just off Golden Square, so its large picture windows take in views over two Soho streets. The muted neutral colour scheme along with generous table size and spacing create a calming atmosphere (helped by the fact that the restaurant is free of Muzak). It can seem a bit dark, though, on a winter's evening. The good-value pre-theatre menu is appreciated by readers (booking is advisable).

An occasional Oriental flavour finds its way in the cooking: seared tuna with wakame, cucumber and soy dressing, perhaps, or Thai roast ostrich breast with red curry and jasmine rice. Europe, though, remains the menu's favoured stomping ground: witness beef medallions with mash and peppercorn sauce; globe artichoke risotto with asparagus, lemon oil and Parmesan; or a starter of roast quail with figs and gorgonzola. Desserts might include amaretto cheesecake or coffee chocolate pecan torte. The varietally organised wine list remains eclectic and appealing. House wine begins at £14.50, but otherwise choice below £20 is limited.

CHEF: Richard Lee PROPRIETOR: Mirror Image Restaurants OPEN: Mon to Fri L 12 to 3, Mon to Sat D 5.45 to 12 CLOSED: 25 and 26 Dec, 1 Jan, bank hols MEALS: alc (main courses £13.50 to £18). Set L £12.50 (2 courses) to £19.50, Set D 5.45 to 7.30 and 10.30 to 12 £12.50 (2 courses) to £15, Set D £17.50 (2 courses) to £19.50 SERVICE: 12.5% (optional), card slips closed CARDS: Amex, Delta, Diners, MasterCard, Switch, Visa DETAILS: 140 seats. Private parties: 190 main room, 12 to 25 private rooms. Vegetarian meals. Children's helpings. Wheelchair access (not WC). No music. Air-conditioned ⊖ Piccadilly Circus £5

Clarke's ♥   map 13

124 Kensington Church Street, W8 4BH
TEL: (020) 7221 9225   FAX: (020) 7229 4564   COOKING 4
EMAIL: restaurant@sallyclarke.com   MODERN BRITISH
WEBSITE: www.sallyclarke.com   £38–£66

In a row of expensive antique shops and estate agents, the dark green façade exudes an air of 'restrained elegance'. Of the two dining rooms, the basement one affords a view of the kitchen, which offers a no-choice menu at dinner (although each course is priced separately, so there is no need to eat all four), and around four items per course at lunch (which has the added benefit of a printed menu). Lack of choice is always a high-risk strategy, partly because it inhibits a bold approach, and partly because visitors expect something wonderful in return for giving up their right to choose; but it does enable the kitchen to focus attention where it is needed.

The approach has been characterised as 'domestic', offering, for example, thick slices of smoked salmon on a buckwheat blini the size of a small crumpet, surrounded by crème fraîche, with a lightly dressed salad. Ingredients are generally well sourced – the best organic salad leaves (from Wiltshire), and high-quality prawns, for example. Judgement of cooking times is accurate, as it should be in the circumstances, producing properly grilled and pink lamb cutlets, and pieces of carefully cooked and carved guinea fowl with lightly crisp skin, served with a scoop of soft polenta topped with Parmesan.

More demanding cooking skills tend to be reserved for ancillaries such as bread, pastry, biscuits and chocolate truffles, reflecting the fact that ambition is modest and that dishes are simply conceived and capably rendered without provoking any wild rush of adrenalin. Cheeses are kept in prime condition and served with fine oatmeal biscuits, while desserts have included a chilled lemon custard served with a dribble of raspberry sauce and a crisp, sugary, buttery palmier. Portion sizes are large, and service is professional and charming, although the cost is proving difficult for reporters to accept, given what else they can get in London for a similar price. The appealing wine list is strong in France and California, but shorter selections from Italy and the Antipodes show equal commitment to quality. Prices are not excessive, but diners with less than £20 to spend on wine will miss out on most of the fun – although half-bottles are a serious option. Six wines by the glass (£4 to £7.50) are complemented by sherries from Lustau.

CHEFS: Sally Clarke and Elizabeth Payne   PROPRIETOR: Sally Clarke   OPEN: Mon to Sat 12.30 (11 Sat) to 2, 7 to 10   CLOSED: 10 days Christmas, bank hols   MEALS: alc L (main courses £14). Set D £48   SERVICE: net prices, card slips closed   CARDS: Amex, Delta, Diners, MasterCard, Switch, Visa   DETAILS: 80 seats. No smoking Sat L, Mon to Sat D. Wheelchair access (not WC). No music. No mobile phones. Air-conditioned   ⊖ Notting Hill Gate

Clerkenwell Dining Room   map 13

69–73 St John Street, EC1M 4AN
TEL: (020) 7253 9000   FAX: (020) 7253 3322   COOKING 4
EMAIL: zak@theclerkenwell.com   MODERN EUROPEAN
WEBSITE: www.theclerkenwell.com   £28–£59

Cream walls and the occasional splash of vivid blue set the tone at this quietly civilised restaurant in what is now almost the north Smithfield restaurant quarter. The confident cooking of Andrew Thompson has a basis in favoured combinations: for example, scallops with black pudding and confit cabbage among starters, and smoked haddock, poached egg, pancetta and grain mustard among main courses. Velouté of parsley and quails' eggs shows a tendency towards comfort over cutting-edge experimentation, as does a main course of Bresse pigeon with a pithiviers of wild mushrooms and melted onion thyme jus. Hot chocolate fondant has received high praise, and details such as walnut bread, excellent pastrywork and decent cappuccino reinforce the impression of a kitchen that cares. Some reporters see service as 'a strong point', while others have found it wanting. The slick wine selection suits the mood and packs plenty of interest into a couple of unannotated pages. Prices start at £13, but soon move past £20 and then swiftly up into classy territory occupied by top French, Italian and Californian bottles. Six wines by the glass come from across the range.

CHEF: Andrew Thompson   PROPRIETORS: Zak Jones and Andrew Thompson   OPEN: Mon to Fri L 12.15 to 2.30, Mon to Sat D 6 (Sat 7) to 11.15   CLOSED: 25 Dec, 1 Jan   MEALS: alc (main courses £13 to £16). Set L £12.50 (2 courses) to £15.50, Set D 6 to 7 £12.50 (2 courses) to £15.50   SERVICE: 12.5% (optional), card slips closed   CARDS: Amex, Delta, Diners, MasterCard, Switch, Visa   DETAILS: 120 seats. Private parties: 80 main room, 1 to 50 private rooms. Children's helpings. No cigars/pipes. Music. Air-conditioned   ⊖ Farringdon

Club Gascon   map 13

57 West Smithfield, EC1A 9DS   COOKING 5
TEL: (020) 7796 0600   FAX: (020) 7796 0601   FRENCH
                                                                  £36–£85

This is 'an everybody-should-do-it-once sort of place', though it helps to be prepared for its underlying concept – otherwise first-timers may well find themselves quite at sea. Pascal Aussignac, who hails from France's south-west, has drawn on Gascon culinary tradition to construct an offbeat, modern menu as challenging as the food itself: a selection of three or four small-portion dishes is ordered from the menu's seven sections (hors d'oeuvres, vegetables, cold foie gras, hot foie gras, seafood, meats and game).

It is to the credit of this approach that many of the more unlikely-sounding ideas are among the most successful: a creamy stew of broad and white beans infused with lavender; grilled confit of salmon on frothy cauliflower cream; and a frosted tarragon and chocolate waffle have all been enthusiastically reported. Meats might be given more obvious treatments, such as the grilled veal sweetbreads that come with earthy, salty mousserons, or the braised capon with chestnuts and black truffle, while the terrine de foie gras, with its little piles of coarse salt and cracked black pepper, is straight out of the textbook. A dimly lit dining room with mirror panels and gigantic floral displays provides a suitable setting for the food, and staff are as willing with advice as they need to be. Wines – from Bordeaux, the south-west and Languedoc-Roussillon – run from Pic St Loup and basic Buzet to 1967 Cahors and serious 1980s/90s claret; prices start at £11, but mark-ups will push up the bill.

CHEF: Pascal Aussignac   PROPRIETORS: Vincent Labeyrie and Pascal Aussignac   OPEN: Mon to Fri 12 to 2, Mon to Sat 7 to 10 (10.30 Sat)   CLOSED: 21 Dec to 5 Jan, bank hols   MEALS: alc (for parties of 6 or less; main courses £9 to £15.50). Set L and D whole table only £35 to £55 (inc wine)   SERVICE: 12.5% (optional), card slips closed   CARDS: Amex, Delta, MasterCard, Switch, Visa   DETAILS: 50 seats. Private parties: 48 main room. Vegetarian meals. Music. Air-conditioned   ⊖ Barbican

Le Colombier
map 14

145 Dovehouse Street, SW3 6LB
TEL: (020) 7351 1155   FAX: (020) 7351 0077

COOKING 3
FRENCH
£32–£63

Didier Garnier's restaurant (in a former pub) is French through and through, from the blue awning over the front terrace (closely packed with woven chairs) to the crisp white napery and the mellow ambience inside. Feuilleté escargots with garlic cream, and oeufs en meurette – a classic Burgundian dish of poached eggs in red wine – are typical starters. Main ingredients in most cases are allowed to speak for themselves, as in perfectly cooked turbot with hollandaise, or 'meltingly tender' filet au poivre. Puddings might be tarte Tatin, crème brûlée or fondant au chocolat. The service is French and efficient. The wine list is French too and fairly priced, with a good range of half-bottles and some good-value (for London) classics from Bordeaux and Burgundy. House Vin de Pays d'Oc is £3.30 a glass.

CHEF: Bart Vancapellen   PROPRIETOR: Didier Garnier   OPEN: all week 12 to 3 (3.30 Sun), 6.30 to 11 (10.30 Sun)   MEALS: alc (main courses £10.50 to £20). Set L and D 6.30 to 7 £13 (2 courses), Set L and D Sun £15   SERVICE: 12.5% (optional), card slips closed   CARDS: Amex, Delta, MasterCard, Switch, Visa   DETAILS: 70 seats. 30 seats outside. Private parties: 12 main room, 10 to 30 private rooms. Vegetarian meals. Wheelchair access (not WC). No music. Air-conditioned   ⊖ South Kensington

---

'A young waitress with a tray came scurrying past me in the hallway, and as she did so, a couple of empty paper petits fours cases wafted to the floor. "Oh I hate this, I hate it," she exclaimed, [and when] I stopped to pick them up for her, she didn't thank me for it before scurrying on. Perhaps she thought I was new staff.' (On eating in Sussex)

▲ The Connaught, Angela Hartnett's Menu ♥ ✳

map 15

16 Carlos Place, W1K 2AL
TEL: (020) 7592 1222   FAX: (020) 7592 1223
EMAIL: reservations@gordonramsay.com
WEBSITE: www.the-connaught.co.uk

COOKING **6**
MODERN EUROPEAN
£43–£84

The 'shock' expressed by the old guard at an institution and formerly male bastion being rejuvenated by a woman chef has more or less worn off. As the dust settles we can see that Mr Ramsay and his team have done a fine job, and that their 'tactful reinvention' of a revered classic, while respectful of tradition, aims (as at Claridges and the Savoy) to make the place more accessible to a wider public. The set-up consists of two dining rooms: Menu, which is the old restaurant expanded and modernised (with dark wood panelling and well-spaced tables), and the more intimate and romantic, non-smoking Grill, decorated in shades of green (or pistachio if you're a designer). The food is the same in both, although there is also a selection of old Connaught favourites in the Grill, including Dover sole meunière and pear Belle Hélène.

Despite the occasional pasta dish, the food is not particularly Italian, although an Italian feel still pervades, thanks to the comparatively simple and direct presentation, particularly of main courses. After a wobbly start, some rather poor dishes have been balanced by (among others) a very fine cep risotto, black ink tagliatelle with crab, and 'probably the best pheasant dish I've eaten', combining a perfectly roasted bird with a sweetcorn purée that was 'ablaze with flavour'. Ingredients are second to none, and the cooking is now assured, measured and considered. Ham minestrone with mushroom tortellini, employing a dozen different spring vegetables in a classy consommé and perfumed with a little truffle oil, is a dish of 'stunning clarity', while a sensational first course of agnolotti pasta derives 'thrilling depth of flavour' from its pheasant, celery and rosemary jus.

At its best the food is capable of delivering a virtuoso performance, from medium-rare duck breast with balsamic onions and braised leeks, to pan-fried halibut 'so fresh and perfectly cooked it almost defied belief', enhanced with meat jus and balsamic. Desserts, meanwhile, run to a benchmark pannacotta with thyme syrup and a compote of blueberries, and a fine example of chocolate fondant, its richness cleverly complemented by an exotic orange blossom and basil ice cream. Among incidentals, bread and the appetiser plate of dried hams and meats come in for praise, and a tray of mini-sorbets and ice creams before dessert is generally welcomed, although a few service glitches have intruded into some reports. It is all very well trying to make the restaurant and its food more accessible, but nobody seems to have told the person who assembles the wine list. A number of reporters have justifiably grumbled about the prices even while praising the selection and the service. Italy gets top billing, with an impressive roll call of star producers – Jermann, Gaja, Antinori and their ilk – complemented by some less obvious names that at least give the option of drinking a bottle for under £25. France is also covered in some detail, but the rest of the world receives only cursory attention. Ten wines by the glass start at £5 and soar up to Sassicaia for £65. As the Guide went to press The Terrace at the Connaught joined the fray, offering Mediterranean-inspired dishes such as gazpacho, Tuscan bean soup, deep-fried calamari, and pan-fried skate with black butter sauce.

CHEF: Angela Hartnett   PROPRIETOR: Gordon Ramsay Holdings Ltd   OPEN: all week 12 to 2.45, 5.45 to 10.45   MEALS: Set L £25, Set D £45 to £55   SERVICE: not inc   CARDS: Amex, Delta, MasterCard, Switch, Visa   DETAILS: 100 seats. Private parties: 70 main room, 8 to 22 private rooms. No smoking in 1 dining room. Wheelchair access (also WC). No music. No mobile phones. Air-conditioned   ACCOMMODATION: 92 rooms, all with bath/shower. TV. Phone. Room only £129 to £598. Rooms for disabled. Baby facilities   ⊖ Bond Street, Green Park

Il Convivio
map 13

143 Ebury Street, SW1W 9QN	COOKING 2
TEL: (020) 7730 4099 FAX: (020) 7730 4103	ITALIAN
WEBSITE: www.etruscagroup.co.uk	£31–£72

A modern Italian restaurant with a German-born chef in the middle of plutocratic Belgravia, Il Convivio enjoys firm support among readers. Larger within than it looks from the outside, it is filled with natural light from a glass roof. A reporter who began with gently sauced potato and rosemary ravioli, before going on to fillet of salt marsh lamb with fava beans, reclining finally into soft-centred chocolate soufflé with raspberry coulis, emerged well satisfied. The freshest of fish was evidenced by a main-course dish of fillets of sea bass garnished with prawns and a julienne of celery, and turbot with clams and tomato. Finish perhaps with fine caramelised apple tart with apple ice cream. Wines are all Italian, with the exception of a list of champagnes, and provide lesser-known examples of a hugely diverse winemaking culture. Prices start from £4 for a generous glass.

CHEF: Lukas Pfaff   PROPRIETOR: Etrusca Group   OPEN: Mon to Sat 12 to 3, 7 to 11   CLOSED: bank hols   MEALS: alc L (main courses £10.50 to £14). Set L £15.50 (2 courses) to £19.50, Set D £26.50 (2 courses) to £38.50   SERVICE: 12.5% (optional), card slips closed   CARDS: Amex, Delta, Diners, MasterCard, Switch, Visa   DETAILS: 65 seats. Private parties: 80 main room, 6 to 14 private rooms. Vegetarian meals. Cigars/pipes in bar area only. Music. Air-conditioned   ⊖ Victoria, Sloane Square (£5)

Le Coq d'Argent ♥
map 13

No 1 Poultry, EC2R 8EJ	COOKING 2
TEL: (020) 7395 5000 FAX: (020) 7395 5050	FRENCH
WEBSITE: www.conran.com	£42–£79

Riding in the lift up to this roof-top dining room is 'a wonderfully uplifting experience', and at the top there are spectacular views over the City to the river. Dining here is a 'quintessentially Conranesque' experience, from efficient service by smartly dressed waiters, through to 'free for all' smoking. Menus have a very French character (accurate English translations are provided) and the monthly-changing six-course tasting menu focuses on specific French regions – the Normandy version, for example, features cream of Jerusalem artichoke soup, roasted halibut with leek and sorrel sauce, and loin of veal with roasted apples, Calvados and a cream sauce. Variable standards have led to disappointments for some reporters, but successes have included 'excellent and generous' seafood platters, crisply fried frogs' legs with garlic mash and herb oil dressing, attractively presented pigeon with foie gras and accurately cooked baby vegetables, and rhubarb Charlotte to finish. The swaggering wine list lays on reams of champagnes and top Burgundy and Bordeaux, while also showing a healthy interest in the Loire and Italian reds. New World selections are briefer, but come the end of the meal sweet wines and ports are well covered. Pricing is unrestrained and the number of bottles under £20 is statistically insignificant, although budget-conscious diners will find boltholes in the south of France, Chile and South Africa.

CHEF: Mickael Weiss   PROPRIETOR: Conran Restaurants   OPEN: Mon to Fri L 11.30 to 3, Sun brunch 12 to 3, Mon to Sat D 6 (6.30 Sat) to 10   CLOSED: 8 Nov, 25 and 26 Dec   MEALS: alc (main courses £11.50 to £22.50). Set L £25 (2 courses) to £29.50, Set D £45. Bar menu also available Mon to Fri   SERVICE: 12.5% (optional), card slips closed   CARDS: Amex, Delta, Diners, MasterCard, Switch, Visa   DETAILS: 148 seats. Private parties: 148 main room. Vegetarian meals. Wheelchair access (also WC). Occasional music. No mobile phones. Air-conditioned ⊖ Bank

---

Cotto
map 12

44 Blythe Road, W14 0HA
TEL: (020) 7602 9333   FAX: (020) 7602 5003
EMAIL: bookings@cottorestaurant.co.uk

COOKING 3
MODERN EUROPEAN
£26–£48

Tucked away close behind the Olympia Exhibition Centre, this corner-sited restaurant has large French windows open to the street on both sides, but the décor is resolutely low-key, with plank flooring, chrome-framed chairs and not much to look at on the walls. James Kirby has cooked in some pace-setting kitchens, evidenced by the kinds of dishes that turn up on his studiedly modern British menus. A bowl of pea, mint and morel soup in May was vibrant and colourful, and a well-made raviolo enfolding salty brandade with rainbow chard and chilli was a well-balanced assemblage at an autumn meal. The star main course at inspection was a nicely seared and juicy escalope of veal wrapped around purple sprouting broccoli on a bed of coolish mash, with a delicately anchovy-spiked hollandaise. Others have enjoyed roast rabbit stuffed with a brilliant 'ratatouille' of borlotti beans, tomatoes and basil. Fish dishes may not be quite as exciting: An inspector's grilled Dover sole was a generous portion, served with seasonal asparagus and Jersey Royals, but unsauced and lacking its advertised Parma ham garnish. Finish with the likes of 'smooth and light' blackberry parfait with apple and blackberry compote. Minimal staff manage to cope, and know their way around the menu. Wines are an up-to-date international mix, with six by the glass (£3.50 to £4.60) and bottles from £12.90.

CHEF: James Kirby   PROPRIETORS: James and Jane Kirby and Warren Barton   OPEN: Mon to Fr L 12 to 2.30, Mon to Sat D 7 to 10.30   CLOSED: Christmas, bank hols   MEALS: Set L £15, Set D £18 SERVICE: 12.5% (optional), card slips closed   CARDS: Amex, Delta, MasterCard, Switch, Visa DETAILS: 70 seats. 8 seats outside. Private parties: 40 main room, 12 to 35 private rooms. Vegetarian meals. Children's helpings. Wheelchair access (not WC). Music. Air-conditioned ⊖ Kensington Olympia

---

A list of London restaurants by cuisine can be found near the front of the book.

Cow Dining Room

map 13

89 Westbourne Park Road, W2 5QH
TEL: (020) 7221 0021   FAX: (020) 7727 8687
EMAIL: thecow@thecow.freeserve.co.uk

COOKING **4**
MODERN EUROPEAN
£38–£66

Formerly the Railway Tavern, this informal West London pub-restaurant reputedly earned its current name from the reputation of an erstwhile landlady. It combines the modes of pub and restaurant well. Downstairs is a traditional bar with a small dining area to the rear and a tiny galley kitchen, while upstairs is the slightly more formal dining room. 'Eat heartily and give the house a good name' is the slogan blazoned across the top of menus. The temptation to comply is strong, given an attention-grabbing menu that deals in bright, robust Mediterranean flavours: fish soup with rouille, Gruyère and croûtons, or duck confit and game terrine with onion marmalade and toasted brioche for starters, followed by green peppercorn-crusted roasted salt cod with barigoule sauce, mullet with cockles, clams, garlic and parsley, or braised lamb shank with confit garlic and shallots. The downstairs menu offers simpler stuff along the lines of braised oxtail with mash, Catalan fish stew, or kedgeree. Plenty of wines are available by the glass; bottle prices on the short, eclectic list start at £12.50.

CHEF: James Rix   PROPRIETOR: Tom Conran   OPEN: Sat and Sun L 12.30 to 3.30, all week D 7 to 10.30   CLOSED: 25 Dec, 1 Jan   MEALS: alc exc Sat L (main courses £13 to £19). Set L Sat only £21 (2 courses) to £26. Bar menu also available   SERVICE: 12.5% (optional) for parties of 5 or more   CARDS: Delta, MasterCard, Switch, Visa   DETAILS: 32 seats. 10 seats outside. Private parties: 32 main room. Vegetarian meals. No music   ⊖ Westbourne Park

---

Crowthers

map 12

481 Upper Richmond Road West, SW14 7PU
TEL/FAX: (020) 8876 6372
EMAIL: pacrowther@aol.com

COOKING **2**
MODERN BRITISH/FRENCH
£39–£47

The Crowthers have been faithfully serving the local population for over two decades, and while the restaurant has had a facelift – freshly painted cream walls and pretty lights – the menu continues to offer some old favourites while occasionally venturing into new territory. Seared scallops with a timbale of basmati rice and light curry dressing, and mushrooms in filo pastry with wild mushroom sauce have been successful starters, as have main courses of sautéed calf's liver with onions, sage and Madeira, and honey glazed breast of duck with shallot and Burgundy sauce. Finish off with an 'accurately judged' caramelised pineapple with home-made Kahlùa ice cream, or a more traditional lemon tart. Service is warm and genial and often by the chef himself. A well-thought-out and fairly priced wine list offers, unusually, a choice of sherries and Kirs by the glass, and an interesting red Gaillac and a Chenin Blanc as house wines at £12.50 (£3.50 glass).

CHEF: Philip Crowther   PROPRIETORS: Philip and Shirley Crowther   OPEN: Tue to Sat D 7 to 10.30 (other times by prior booking only)   CLOSED: 1 week Christmas, 2 weeks Aug   MEALS: Set L £17.50 (2 courses) to £21.50, Set D £21.50 (2 courses) to £26.50   SERVICE: not inc   CARDS: Delta, MasterCard, Switch, Visa   DETAILS: 35 seats. Private parties: 35 main room. Vegetarian meals. Children's helpings. Wheelchair access (not WC). No music. Air-conditioned ⊖ Richmond (£5)

Deca ✏

map 15

23 Conduit Street, W1S 2XS

COOKING **4**

TEL: (020) 7493 7070   FAX: (020) 7493 7090

MODERN EUROPEAN

£26–£82

Nico Ladenis may finally have fully retired and no longer has any personal involvement, but Deca still bears the Nico stamp – smart, a touch formal, and deeply tasteful. It is the menu, though, that most distinctly reflects his influence: many choices (16 apiece for starters and main courses), each simply described, and nearly every one a familiar French classic. Reports of slipping standards since the departure of chef Paul Rhodes were not really borne out at inspection, though portion sizes were not overgenerous. Dressed crab with that classic accompaniment, celeriac rémoulade, comes as a small cylinder of white meat topped with dark meat, while a main course of charcoal-grilled John Dory may be served simply, with a drizzle of thyme oil. Desserts are generally of a high quality; apple tart and vanilla ice cream comprises a little rectangle of fanned caramelised slices of apples on thin pastry, with a 'profoundly flavoursome' vanilla ice cream. By many accounts, though, service is not nearly as accomplished nor as polished as one would expect. Wines start at £15 and are £4–£9.50 a glass: no wine list was available at the time of going to press.

CHEF: Jeremy Brown   PROPRIETOR: Chez Nico Restaurants Ltd   OPEN: Mon to Sat 12 to 3, 5.30 to 11   CLOSED: 10 days Christmas, 4 days Easter, bank hols   MEALS: alc (main courses £13.50 to £19.50). Set L £12.50, Set D 5.30 to 7 £12.50   SERVICE: 12.5% (optional), card slips closed   CARDS: Amex, Diners, MasterCard, Switch, Visa   DETAILS: 80 seats. Private parties: 11 to 18 private rooms. No pipes. Wheelchair access (also WC). No music. Air-conditioned   ⊖ Oxford Circus

Delfina Studio Café

map 13

50 Bermondsey Street, SE1 3UD

TEL: (020) 7357 0244   FAX: (020) 7357 0250

EMAIL: book@delfina.org.uk

COOKING **4**

GLOBAL

WEBSITE: www.delfina.org.uk

£33–£49

Artists who share this converted factory, plus office workers and others in the know, flock to this airy dining room where high walls provide space for exhibiting resident painters. Maria Elia supervises imaginative global cooking with touches of humour; variants of greasy-spoon standbys (forget sausage, egg, chips and mushroom; how about polenta Parmesan chips, poached egg, chorizo and shiitake for a starter?) are found alongside originals like a strawberry, balsamic and radicchio risotto – which, despite sounding like a refugee from Marinetti's *Futurist Cookbook*, was very successful. While the deftness that creates a tottering column of fine feta, roasted courgettes and mint for a starter sometimes slips – as in a chicken salad heavy in peach and salted almonds – a coconut and lemon-grass soup was 'fragrant, sumptuous, light and balanced'. More substantial were main dishes of Asian brisket ('a nice meat stew'), or pancetta-wrapped king prawns with petit pois and Jersey Royals. Appearances are as good as tastes in a pavlova with muscatel-soaked strawberries, and a banana crème brûlée accompanied by a chocolate sorbet. The short, well-chosen wine list runs from tasty Spanish basics at £12.50 to a handful of French classics at around £50, with 11 choices by the glass from £3 to £5.20.

CHEF: Maria Elia   PROPRIETORS: Digby Squires and Bruce Watson   OPEN: Mon to Fri L only 12 to 3   CLOSED: 24 Dec to 5 Jan   MEALS: alc (main courses £9 to £13.50)   SERVICE: 12.5% (optional), card slips closed   CARDS: Amex, Delta, Diners, MasterCard, Switch, Visa   DETAILS: 100 seats. Private parties: 260 main room, 5 to 500 private rooms. Vegetarian meals. Wheelchair access (also WC). No music   ⊖ London Bridge £5

Le Deuxième ♥

map 15

65A Long Acre, WC2E 9JH
TEL: (020) 7379 0033   FAX: (020) 7379 0066
WEBSITE: www.ledeuxieme.com

COOKING 3
MODERN EUROPEAN
£23–£58

It would be harder to get much nearer to the Covent Garden opera house without actually sitting in the dress circle. This companion to the much older Café du Jardin nearby (see entry) is a pleasantly light and airy place with tiled floor, black pillars and slick French service. The cooking hitches its wagon to no particular style, roaming at will from 'tasty and light' tempura of freshwater shrimp with sweet Thai dressing, through tagliolini tossed with crab, roasted peppers, chilli oil and coriander, to correctly rendered coq au vin with its unctuous cooking liquor. Meats are generally well-timed, the duck cooked to just pink, accompanied perhaps by fondant potato and red onion confit. Side-dishes of vegetables are charged separately, but are again carefully timed, and meals end with the likes of warm rice pudding with apricot compote, two-tone chocolate mousse, or sticky toffee pudding. The wine list packs 150 bottles into four unannotated pages that cover France in depth, with Italy, the USA and Australia accounting for most of the balance. Eighteen wines are offered in 250ml glasses from £3.85 to £6.20, and 24 come in half-bottles. There's also a pricier fine wine list. Service is added to the bill at 15%.

CHEF: Geoff Adams   PROPRIETORS: Robert Seigler and Tony Howorth   OPEN: Mon to Fri 12 to 3, 5 to 12, Sat 12 to 12, Sun 12 to 11   CLOSED: 24 and 25 Dec   MEALS: alc (main courses £11.50 to £16.50). Set L and D £10.95 (2 courses) to £14.50 (not available 7 to 10)   SERVICE: 15% (optional), card slips closed   CARDS: Amex, Delta, MasterCard, Switch, Visa   DETAILS: 60 seats. Private parties: 60 main room. Vegetarian meals. Wheelchair access (not WC). No music. Air-conditioned   ⊖ Covent Garden

Ditto

map 12

55–57 East Hill, SW18 2QE
TEL: (020) 8877 0110   FAX: (020) 8875 0710
WEBSITE: www.doditto.co.uk

COOKING 3
MODERN EUROPEAN
£26–£64

Look for the striking deep-blue and orange façade to locate this neighbourhood restaurant, which stands where East Hill bifurcates into a one-way system. The traffic noise can be relentless, but the mood in the unfussy dining room is congenial and unpressurised: displays of modern art brighten up the wall space, and there are flamboyant floral arrangements dotted around. Easy-going staff in jeans add to the sense of 'unhurried calm'. The monthly-changing menu aims to please without taking too many risks, and the kitchen is generally on target:

starters of gazpacho with crème fraîche, and smoked haddock fishcake with chive beurre blanc rub shoulders with main courses of twice-cooked lamb shank with basil mash, and pan-fried rump of Buccleuch beef with wild mushrooms and Gorgonzola, while desserts might run to pannacotta with a compote of berries. Reporters who have plumped for one of the affordable fixed-price deals have also been impressed by escabèche of mackerel on a piece of crisp air-dried ciabatta, and 'classic' slow-cooked belly pork with braised lettuce and an 'understated' sweet-and-sour sauce. Bar menus are available throughout the week. The worldwide wine list promises sound, affordable drinking from £11.25. There is also a sister branch in Clapham – Ditto Grill, 169 Clapham High Street; tel: (020) 7622 8169.

CHEF: Calum Watson   PROPRIETORS: Christian Duffell and Giles Cooper   OPEN: all week 12 to 3, 7 to 11 (9 Sun)   CLOSED: 25 and 26 Dec, bank hol Suns and Mons   MEALS: alc (main courses £11 to £17). Set D £15.50 (2 courses) to £19.50. Bar menu available   SERVICE: 12.5% (optional), card slips closed   CARDS: Delta, MasterCard, Switch, Visa   DETAILS: 100 seats. Private parties: 80 main room, 1 to 23 private rooms. Vegetarian meals. Children's helpings. Wheelchair access (not WC). Music (£5)

The Don 🍾

map 13

The Courtyard, 20 St Swithin's Lane, EC4N 8AD
TEL: (020) 7626 2606   FAX: (020) 7626 2616
EMAIL: bookings@thedonrestaurant.co.uk
WEBSITE: www.thedonrestaurant.co.uk

COOKING 2
FRENCH
£37–£65

'Must be a City treasure,' said one visitor of this sibling of Bleeding Heart (see entry). The historic building once belonged to Sandeman's (of port and sherry fame), and in its characterful, colourful interior classically turned out French staff keep an eagle eye on well-spaced tables. The menu includes a sprinkling of dressed-up classics, such as warm asparagus salad with sauce mousseline, and a spot-on tournedos Rossini with foie gras, pommes Parisienne and a rich, zingy gravy. Other winners have included monkfish baked with cockles and mussels in a light shellfish reduction, while desserts 'with maximum presentation values' have featured a warm caramelised pear and ginger pudding with cardamom ice cream.

Interesting sherries, table wines and a vintage port du jour come by the glass – a tempting alternative to the fine bottle list dominated by traditional France (though smaller Italian, Spanish and New World ranges are from good producers too). This quality orientation doesn't make for low-price drinking, though. For bottles under £20, try some wines from Trinity Hill, the owners' vineyard in New Zealand.

CHEFS: Matt Burns and Sam Wakeman   PROPRIETORS: Robert and Robyn Wilson   OPEN: Mon to Fri 12 to 2.30, 6.30 to 10   CLOSED: 1 week Christmas/New Year, bank hols   MEALS: alc (main courses £12 to £22)   SERVICE: 12.5% (optional), card slips closed   CARDS: Amex, Diners, MasterCard, Visa   DETAILS: 45 seats. Private parties: 50 main room, 24 private room. Vegetarian meals. No children. No children under 13. No music. No mobile phones. Air-conditioned
⊖ Bank

To find a restaurant in a particular area use the maps at the centre of the book.

Drapers Arms

map 13

44 Barnsbury Street, N1 1ER
TEL: (020) 7619 0348   FAX: (020) 7619 0413

COOKING 3
MODERN BRITISH-PLUS
£32–£55

The first-floor dining room at this large pub, in the middle of a residential side street in Islington, singles out the Drapers Arms as no ordinary local. Downstairs there's a lived-in, homely feel, with sofas, easy chairs and wooden furniture, while upstairs aspires to more sophistication. The long, narrow, high-ceilinged room has large windows, brass chandeliers, a wooden floor and bare wooden tables. But it is via the appealing, well-thought-out modern menu that it really cuts its cloth, displaying due flair and a nod to the Mediterranean in dishes such as saltimbocca with silver-skin onions, spinach and Gorgonzola, and grilled polenta, or perhaps steamed monkfish, clams, mussels and baby squid with chorizo and chickpeas. Inspiration comes from much further afield, too: maize-fed chicken is partnered by stir-fried pak choi and sweet chilli jus, and spiced aubergine, bulgur pilaff and yoghurt are teamed with grilled lamb cutlets. Expect more homespun desserts along the lines of cherry Bakewell tart with clotted cream, or white chocolate cheesecake with stem ginger. The compact wine list travels the globe and offers 18 bottles under £20, all also available by the glass for £3.50 to £5.50.

CHEF: Mark Emberton   PROPRIETORS: Paul McElhinney and Mark Emberton   OPEN: Sun L 12 to 4, Mon to Sat D 7 to 10.30   CLOSED: 25 to 28 Dec, 1 Jan   MEALS: alc (main courses £9 to £15). Bar L menu available   SERVICE: 12.5% (optional), card slips closed   CARDS: Delta, MasterCard, Switch, Visa   DETAILS: 100 seats. 50 seats outside. Vegetarian meals. Children's helpings. No children in bar after 7.30pm. Music   ⊖ Highbury & Islington

Drones

map 14

1 Pont Street, SW1X 9EJ
TEL: (020) 7235 9555   FAX: (020) 7235 9566
EMAIL: sales@whitestarline.org.uk
WEBSITE: www.whitestarline.org.uk

COOKING 5
ANGLO-FRENCH
£33–£87

One of Marco Pierre White's specialities has been taking old London restaurants that may have seen their last glory days at the close of the 1970s and breathing new life into them. This has been done with a combination of chic interior styling and the formulaic but solidly dependable menus for which his empire has become noted. At Drones, the sleek monochrome look is enhanced by Cornel Lucas photographs of showbiz legends and by lighting designed to flatter you as much as it does the surroundings.

The kitchen works well to an admirably consistent standard, producing for one reporter 'simple but superb' dressed crab with flaky French toast, pinkish côte de veau with wild mushrooms and pomme purée, and a perfectly caramelised tarte Tatin. The occasional dish strays beyond the immediate shores of the English Channel, so that fillet of red mullet might unexpectedly come à la marocaine with couscous, but the franglais orientation is the main centre of gravity – bemusingly so in fine poulet noir à la broche with 'garnish anglaise', satisfyingly so in a starter that combines pig's trotter with black pudding and a dressing of sauce gribiche. Red fruit jelly with raspberry syrup, which exhibits both stunning clarity and beguiling flavour, gets good notices, or there may be glace nougatine with chocolate sauce, or a selection of excellent British cheeses. Service is praised for its 'splendid' friendliness. Wine prices are less friendly, with whites starting at £15 for a Spanish Sauvignon, reds at £16.50 for a vin de pays, and ascending to very nearly four figures. Glass prices open at £3.75 for a Provençal rosé.

CHEF: Joseph Croan   PROPRIETORS: Marco Pierre White and Jimmy Lahoud   OPEN: Sun to Fri L 12 to 2.30 (3.30 Sun), Mon to Sat D 6 to 11 (11.30 Sat)   CLOSED: bank hols   MEALS: alc exc Sun L (main courses £15 to £25). Set L Mon to Fri £14.95 (2 courses) to £17.95, Set L Sun £19.50   SERVICE: 12.5% (optional), card slips closed   CARDS: Amex, Delta, Diners, MasterCard, Switch, Visa   DETAILS: 90 seats. Private parties: 40 main room, 10 to 40 private rooms. Wheelchair access (not WC). Music. Air-conditioned   ⊖ Knightsbridge, Sloane Square

e&o £   map 13

14 Blenheim Crescent, W11 1NN   NEW CHEF
TEL: (020) 7229 5454   FAX: (020) 7229 5522   ASIAN/FUSION
WEBSITE: www.eando.nu   £30–£59

The letters stand for Eastern and Oriental, so the orientation of the food should come as no surprise on arrival at this glitzy, hugely successful Ladbroke Grove venue. The sparely decorated room with its dark wood floor has a refreshingly informal, laid-back atmosphere, and reporters give thanks for its 'surprisingly low prices'. A new chef arrived in the summer of 2003, but no changes have occurred to the menu. Starters and main courses are bypassed in favour of a flexible assortment of Asian favourites (mixed vegetable tempura; beef teriyaki) and well-conceived pan-Asian fusion ideas, which are divided up into categories like dim sum (coconut and pomelo bahn trang; prawn sesame rolls; chicken and snow pea dumplings), salads, a couple of curries (jungle monkfish with Cape gooseberry, for example), 'great' sashimi including albacore (longfin tuna) with soy, ginger and chilli, and BBQ/roasts like 'top-notch', Nobu-inspired black cod with sweet miso. The idea is for each table to share. Desserts might include chocolate pudding; banana parfait with tempura banana; milk chocolate ice; and ginger tiramisù. France and the New World account for most of the fashionable wine list; house vin de pays is £3.70 a glass, £11 a bottle, and there's not a lot under £20. Will Ricker has opened another restaurant, Eight Over Eight, at 392 King's Road, SW3; tel: (020) 7349 9934.

CHEF: Simon Treadway   PROPRIETOR: Will Ricker   OPEN: all week 12.15 to 2.45, 6.15 to 10.45   CLOSED: Dec 24 to 28   MEALS: alc (main courses £8.50 to £19.50). Set L and D £32. Bar menu available   SERVICE: 12.5% (optional), card slips closed   CARDS: Amex, Delta, Diners, MasterCard, Switch, Visa   DETAILS: 82 seats. Private parties: 12 to 18 private rooms. Vegetarian meals. No cigars/pipes. No music. Air-conditioned   ⊖ Ladbroke Grove

New main entries are listed near the front of the book. Some may have appeared in earlier years (though not in the previous edition) or as a Round-up entry last year.

Eagle £

map 13

159 Farringdon Road, EC1R 3AL
TEL: (020) 7837 1353   FAX: (020) 7689 5882

COOKING 2
MEDITERRANEAN
£22–£39

They don't take bookings – so arrive early, bag a table and wait until the menu boards appear. This seriously busy gastro-pub virtually defined the new genre when it opened, and it thrives on that now-familiar deconstructed look. The place can be an overcrowded victim of its own popularity, which leads to a scrum, but the food is nearly always interesting, and prices pretty fair. The concise list of 'stand-alone' dishes is shot through with Spanish/Italian influences: fusilli might be cooked with red bell peppers and almonds, sardines are grilled and served with corn peppers and olives, while roast carrots and Jerusalem artichokes with watercress salad accompany lamb chops. 'Bife ana' (marinated rump steak 'sandwich') is a fixture. Finish with Portuguese custard tarts or Sardinian ewe's milk cheese, crispy flatbread and a pear. Another blackboard lists a dozen wines from £2.50 a glass, £10.50 a bottle; otherwise drink beer.

CHEF: Tom Norrington Davies   PROPRIETOR: Michael Belben   OPEN: all week L 12.30 to 2.30 (3.30 Sat and Sun), Mon to Sat D 6.30 to 10.30   CLOSED: 1 week Christmas, Easter Sun, bank hol Mons,   MEALS: alc (main courses £5 to £12)   SERVICE: not inc, card slips closed   CARDS: Delta, MasterCard, Switch, Visa   DETAILS: 70 seats. Vegetarian meals. Wheelchair access (not WC). Music   ⊖ Farringdon

Ealing Park Tavern £

| NEW ENTRY | map 12

222 South Ealing Road, W5 4RL
TEL: (020) 8758 1879

COOKING 2
MODERN BRITISH
£26–£40

This big corner pub joined the gastro-pub revolution in September 2001 and has managed to get the eating/drinking balance just right. The kitchen is the centrepiece of the part-panelled dining room, a suitably informal environment for the upbeat food. A 'meltingly soft and punchy' Gorgonzola, piquillo pepper and wild mushroom tart, or 'flavourful' asparagus soup might be followed by main courses of robust confit of pork belly with roast butternut squash and lentils, or baked salmon with pepper and garlic couscous and a cucumber and tomato salsa. Portions are on the large side, though desserts are worth exploring: perhaps sticky banana pudding with toffee sauce, or a lighter-sounding frozen berry mousse with mint cream. There is also a tapas menu served in the bar from 5 to 10pm. Service is friendly enough, but complaints about delays are not unusual. Around 35 wines provide some good drinking, with plenty below £20 and 16 by the glass for £2.75 to £4.50.

CHEF: Vincent Morse   PROPRIETORS: Nicholas Sharpe and Vincent Morse   OPEN: Tue to Sun L 12 to 3 (4 Sun), all week D 6 to 10.30 (9.30 Sun)   CLOSED: 25 Dec, 1 Jan   MEALS: alc (main courses L £7.50 to £10.50, D £8 to £12.50). Tapas bar menu available D   SERVICE: not inc, card slips closed, 12.5% for parties of 5 or more   CARDS: Amex, Delta, MasterCard, Switch, Visa   DETAILS: 70 seats. 40 seats outside. Private parties: 50 main room. Vegetarian meals. Wheelchair access (not WC). Music

ECapital

map 15

8 Gerrard Street, W1D 5PJ
TEL: (020) 7434 3838

NEW CHEF
CHINESE
£22–£76

In a setting that is contemporary, but hardly 'designer', this rather small restaurant makes a bold attempt to de-mystify the cooking of China's gastronomically least-known region. The core of its long menu is the section devoted to the 'almost unique' cuisine of Shanghai, and it pays to be adventurous: here you will find 'cardboard paper-thin' seasoned beef and 'steamed little juicy buns', plus blanch-fried pig's kidney with coriander, braised yellow eel, shredded pork with pickled leaves and Chinese broad beans and much more besides. In more familiar territory, there's also a full complement of dishes from other regions including Peking-style grilled sea bass, Cantonese crispy-skin chicken, and aromatic duck with pak choi and mushrooms. To drink, choose from the quartet of 'unfermented' teas, or dip into the minimal wine list, which consists solely of vintage bottles imported directly from Burgundy: prices from £12 to £100. Chef David Tam left as the Guide was going to press.

CHEF: Mr Wong   PROPRIETOR: Mark Chan   OPEN: Mon to Fri 12 to 11, Fri and Sat 12 to 12
MEALS: alc (main courses £5 to £20). Set L £10, Set D £15 to £20   SERVICE: 12.5% (optional)
CARDS: Amex, Diners, MasterCard, Switch, Visa   DETAILS: 60 seats. Private parties: 20 main
room. Vegetarian meals. Music. Air-conditioned   ⊖ Leicester Square

Eddalino ▼

NEW ENTRY   map 15

8–10 Wigmore Street, W1U 2RD
TEL: (020) 7637 0789   FAX: (020) 7637 2163
EMAIL: reservations@eddalino.co.uk
WEBSITE: www.eddalino.co.uk

COOKING 3
ITALIAN
£50–£83

Eddalino is an impressive newcomer to London's Italian scene. The décor divides people, some finding that the arcaded brick room divider and Italianate urns make the room 'small and intimate', while others note a similarity to a '1970s-style trat'. The menu, however, is imaginative and intriguing, and far more exciting than the surroundings might suggest. The kitchen doesn't adhere to tried-and-true techniques but seems willing to give unusual combinations a whirl: a main course ravioli was stuffed with John Dory and wild mushrooms, the fish and mushrooms finely minced, the mixture then wrapped in light pasta discs and served with a simple sage and butter sauce – all to 'stunning' effect. Starters may include subtly flavoured ricotta dumplings with broad beans and pancetta, or fettuccine with peas and dried tomatoes ('excellent, the way that truly simple Italian cooking should be'). Desserts are a cut or two above the Italian norm, and service, on the whole, is professional and friendly. The wine list reads like a roll call of leading, if not cutting-edge, Italian producers. There's reasonable choice under £20, and whites stay mostly under £30, while reds cruise smoothly into the three-figure world of Gaja and the top Super-Tuscans. Ten come by the glass for £4.50 to £7.50.

CHEF: Francesco Pesce   PROPRIETOR: Piero Zanelli   OPEN: Mon to Fri L 12 to 3, Mon to Sat D 6.30 to 10.30   MEALS: Set L and D £25 (2 courses) to £36   SERVICE: 12.5% (optional), card slips closed   CARDS: Amex, MasterCard, Switch, Visa   DETAILS: 70 seats. 6 seats outside. Private parties: 70 main room. Vegetarian meals. No-smoking area. Wheelchair access (not WC). Music. Air-conditioned   ⊖ Oxford Circus, Bond Street

Electric Brasserie

map 13

191 Portobello Road, W11 2ED
TEL: (020) 7908 9696   FAX: (020) 7908 9595
WEBSITE: www.the-electric.co.uk

| NEW CHEF |
BRASSERIE
£28–£68

The Electric Brasserie, part of the Electric Cinema complex, which sits smack in the middle of Portobello Road, is a mix of fashionable watering hole and French-style brasserie. It's very lively, 'full of trendy Notting Hill denizens'. The carte is divided into sections – starters, mains, 'trolley', 'for two', and so on – offering the likes of potted ham or lobster bisque, and even caviar, followed by duck cottage pie or, in summer, chargrilled salmon with broad beans, peas and dill mayonnaise. A new chef, Duncan Impey, had been brought on board as the Guide was going to press, although the menu looks set to remain much the same. Wines are mostly French, with prices starting at £13 for Vin de Pays d'Oc. Around a dozen are also sold by the glass (from £3.50) and 50cl carafe (from £8.75).

CHEF: Duncan Impey   PROPRIETOR: Nick Jones   OPEN: all week 12 to 5, 5 to 11   CLOSED: 24 and 25 Aug   MEALS: alc (main courses £12 to £20). Set L Mon to Fri £12 (2 courses) to £15, Set D £24 (2 courses) to £28   SERVICE: 12.5%, card slips closed   CARDS: Amex, Delta, MasterCard, Switch, Visa   DETAILS: 130 seats. 14 seats outside. Private parties: 3 main room. Vegetarian meals. Wheelchair access (also WC). Music. Air-conditioned   ⊖ Notting Hill Gate, Ladbroke Grove

Embassy

29–30 Old Burlington Street, W1S 3AN
TEL: (020) 7851 0956/7   FAX: (020) 7734 3224
EMAIL: embassy@embassylondon.com
WEBSITE: www.embassylondon.com

COOKING 6
MODERN BRITISH
£33–£80

'Upstairs, Downstairs' could be the catch phrase here: upstairs (well, the ground floor) is a serious restaurant, while downstairs is a thriving private members' club. Apart from the gold wallpaper, the restaurant's interior is rather understated, beige and dimly lit, but the dressed-up clientele who dine here before heading downstairs to revel are probably decoration enough ('I've not seen so many pairs of stilettos in one restaurant before,' mused a visitor). The thumping bass-line from the nightclub can penetrate the restaurant from time to time, but the food on the plate manages to outperform even this distraction: 'Embassy serves really excellent food.'

Reinvention of classic dishes is one of chef Garry Hollihead's strengths, so turbot véronique may feature – a thickish tranche of fish, lightly crusted outside but moist inside, with the expected grapes and a buttery unctuous sauce – or venison Wellington so tender that 'the knife drifted through it'. A starter of beef tartare may come with potato 'carpaccio' and Poilâne bread. For vegetarians, dishes such as tomato and aubergine tart with red onion marmalade and wild rocket beignets are worthy of attention. Summertime desserts may feature berry pavlova, or blueberry soufflé with lemon curd ice cream. Service has been variously described as 'competent and pleasant' and 'courteous and friendly'. Apart from house Vin de Pays d'Oc at £16.50 (£4.50 a glass), there's nothing on the wine list below £20, and not a lot under £30. The Hollihead/Fuller partnership now extends into Berkshire, with the refurbished of the Inn on the Green in Cookham Dean (see entry).

CHEF: Garry Hollihead   PROPRIETORS: Mark Fuller and Garry Hollihead   OPEN: Tue to Fri L 12 to 3, Tue to Sat D 6 to 11.30   CLOSED: 25 Dec   MEALS: alc (main courses £15 to £22). Set L £14.95 (2 courses) to £17.95, Set D exc Sat 8.30 to 11.30 £14.95 (2 courses) to £17.95   SERVICE: 12.5%, card slips closed   CARDS: Amex, Delta, MasterCard, Switch, Visa   DETAILS: 110 seats. 30 seats outside. Private parties: 110 main room, 20 to 500 private rooms. Vegetarian meals. Wheelchair access (not WC). Music. Air-conditioned   ⊖ Green Park, Piccadilly Circus (£5)

English Garden ⚡

map 14

10 Lincoln Street, SW3 2TS
TEL: (020) 7584 7272   FAX: (020) 75841961
EMAIL: english.garden@ukgateway.net
WEBSITE: www.lindsayhouse.co.uk

NEW CHEF
ANGLO-FRENCH
£38–£68

This Victorian house occupies a quiet spot just off the bustling King's Road. A long narrow interior in creamy muted colours with some banquette seating offers what one visitor described as a 'clubby' feel. A new chef arrived from sister restaurant Lindsay House (see entry) in summer 2003. No changes are expected to a style that has previously delivered escabèche of red mullet with warm salad of broad beans, or rillettes of guinea fowl and foie gras with confit cabbage among starters. Breast of organic chicken with white asparagus and girolles, or black bream with pea purée and pancetta are typical main courses. Expect desserts such as crème brûlée and sorbets. Service is charming, discreet and helpful. The wine list divides a good selection of wines by region and grape variety. Prices are on the weightier side, with French house wine at £16.

CHEF: Michael Lynch   PROPRIETOR: Searcys/Corrigan Ltd   OPEN: Tue to Sun L 12 to 2.30, all week D 6.30 to 11   CLOSED: Christmas, 1 week Aug   MEALS: Set L £19.50 (2 courses) to £23.50, Set D £29   SERVICE: 12.5% (optional), card slips closed   CARDS: Amex, Delta, Diners, MasterCard, Switch, Visa   DETAILS: 45 seats. Private parties: 6 to 35 main room, 6 to 35 private rooms. Children's helpings. Vegetarian meals. No smoking in 1 dining room. Wheelchair access (not WC). Music. No mobile phones. Air-conditioned   ⊖ Sloane Square (£5)

Enoteca Turi 🍾 ⚡

map 12

28 Putney High Street, SW15 1SQ
TEL: (020) 8785 4449   FAX: (020) 8780 5409

COOKING 3
ITALIAN
£32–£61

Many restaurants aspire to Italian ways of cooking, but this one really is a little piece of the mother country broken off and replanted in south-west London, not far from Putney Bridge. Pasta is made in-house, other ingredients are flown in from Italy, and the menus derive their inspiration from some of the lesser-known regional cuisines such as those of Puglia, Sardinia and Umbria. Neatly dressed tables and equally trim waiting staff set the tone for dishes such as breast of corn-fed chicken crusted with basil, pine nuts and pecorino, served with aubergine and mushrooms, or a main-course serving of seared scallops with scarola and lentil salad dressed in chilli and lemon thyme. Unusual antipasti preparations have included a Parmesan-coated deep-fried egg served with grilled asparagus, and there is the traditional option of a second-course pasta dish, perhaps pappardelle with duck simmered in red wine and herbs. Finish in classically sticky style with the likes of blood orange tart with chocolate 'salami', or Venetian chocolate torta with mint ice cream.

Every item on the menu is marked with a suggested bin from the fine and long list of wines that opens with a good range of affordable Italian reds and whites before launching into a catalogue of top producers, mostly from Italy but with a showing of French, Spanish and New World stars, all bearing hefty price tags. Super-Tuscans, Brunellos and especially Barolos are covered in depth. Five whites and five reds by the glass cost £3.50 to £7.25.

CHEF: Luca Lamari   PROPRIETOR: Giuseppe Turi   OPEN: Mon to Sat 12 to 2.30, 7 to 11   MEALS: alc (main courses L £8.50 to £10, D £11.50 to £16.50)   SERVICE: 12.5% (optional), card slips closed   CARDS: Amex, Delta, Diners, MasterCard, Switch, Visa   DETAILS: 80 seats. Private parties: 50 main room. Vegetarian meals. Children's helpings. No smoking in 1 dining room. Wheelchair access (also WC). No music. Air-conditioned   ⊖ Putney Bridge

L'Escargot, Ground Floor 🍷 map 15

48 Greek Street, W1 4EF
TEL: (020) 7439 7474   FAX: (020) 7437 0790
EMAIL: sales@whitestarline.org.uk
WEBSITE: www.whitestarline.org.uk

COOKING 4
MODERN FRENCH
£31–£61

Some serious paintings – including works by Chagall, Matisse and Miró – adorn the walls of this elegant, wooden-floored dining room, whose other wall is occupied by a large mirror. The ground floor takes more of a brasserie approach to its food than the Picasso Room above (see entry below), producing a carte of old favourites such as omelette Arnold Bennett, escargots bordelaise, smoked salmon blinis, and daube of beef. Dominic Teague has breathed some new life into the cooking, subjecting fine ingredients to generally capable treatments, including a moist, full-flavoured breast of Landes chicken in a prettily presented 'nest' of salsify batons, with peas and trompettes, and (in May) an escalope of salmon on a bed of sliced potatoes surrounded by a ring of truffle-scented broad bean sauce.

Starters have included a langoustine bisque with plenty of the main ingredient imparting strong flavour, and judicious use of cream giving it a silky texture, while desserts typically take in a hot chocolate fondant, and perhaps a coffee cup of semi-freddo incorporating a layer of mousse topped with liquid mocha, surmounted by frothy milk. Cheese comes ready plated (which does it no favours), bread is poor, and service at inspection was 'laughable', or would have been were it not for the charge levied. There's nothing laughable about the wine list, though, which is a serious heavyweight shared by the Picasso Room upstairs and perhaps better suited to that venue in its upper reaches: 1961 Bordeaux first growths, le Pin, Pétrus, old bottles of Grange and the like.

Ordinary folk can glug the house wine for £14, but otherwise the entry fee is £20. Best buy? Corbières from la Voulte-Gasparets at £20.50. Ten wines come by the glass for £4 to £6.

CHEFS: Jeff Galvin and Dominic Teague   PROPRIETORS: Jimmy Lahoud and Marco Pierre White
OPEN: Mon to Fri L 12 to 2.15, Mon to Sat D 6 to 11   CLOSED: 25 and 26 Dec, 1 Jan   MEALS: alc
(main courses £13). Set L and D 6 to 7 £14.95 (2 courses) to £17.95   SERVICE: 12.5% (optional),
card slips closed   CARDS: Amex, Delta, Diners, MasterCard, Switch, Visa   DETAILS: 80 seats.
Private parties: 80 main room, 10 to 60 private rooms. No cigars/pipes. Wheelchair access (not
WC). Music. Air-conditioned   ⊖ Tottenham Court Road, Leicester Square

L'Escargot, Picasso Room ♥   map 15

48 Greek Street, W1D 4EF
TEL: (020) 7439 7474   FAX: (020) 7437 0790   COOKING 6
EMAIL: sales@whitestarline.org.uk   MODERN FRENCH
WEBSITE: www.whitestarline.org.uk   £37–£94

More formal and refined than the Ground Floor (see entry above), the upstairs Picasso Room is larger, with pictures, sketches, prints and sculptures by the Great Man. Nevertheless, it is still a relaxed and friendly place. Although it offers poached oysters, pot-roast lobster, and salmon barigoule with sauce vierge, this is predominantly a hefty, rich and meaty menu, featuring a mosaic of rabbit and foie gras with sauce gribiche, wood pigeon pithiviers with roast chestnuts, and braised pig's trotter with essence of morels.

The kitchen's French credentials are evident in the sourcing as much as the treatments: milk-fed Pyrenean lamb, Landes chicken with broad beans and sauce Albufeira, and Bresse pigeon en vessie with Savoy cabbage. But it seems equally adept in all departments, producing a fine langoustine raviolo in a clean-flavoured fennel sauce, and excellent roast cod in a Sauternes jus served with a few girolles, green beans, and a scallop resting on parsley purée. That goes for desserts, too, including an apple tarte fine, and a freestanding coconut crème brûlée surrounded by coconut froth topped with a scoop of vanilla ice cream. Alternatively, there is a small but perfectly formed cheeseboard. Extras, from an appetiser of langoustine bisque to a plate of fine petits fours, add to enjoyment. The wine list is the same as for Ground Floor.

CHEF: Jeff Galvin   PROPRIETORS: Jimmy Lahoud and Marco Pierre White   OPEN: Tue to Fri L 12 to
2.15, Tue to Sat D 7 to 11   CLOSED: 25 and 26 Dec, 1 Jan, Aug   MEALS: Set L £20.50 (2 courses)
to £42, Set D £42   SERVICE: 15% (optional), card slips closed   CARDS: Amex, Delta, Diners,
MasterCard, Switch, Visa   DETAILS: 45 seats. Private parties: 45 main room, 10 to 60 private
rooms. Occasional music. No mobile phones. Air-conditioned   ⊖ Tottenham Court Road,
Leicester Square

L'Estaminet   map 15

14 Garrick Street, WC2E 9BJ   COOKING 2
TEL: (020) 7379 1432   FAX: (020) 7379 1530   FRENCH
     £26–£59

Serving theatreland for more than ten years, this is the kind of smart bistro-style restaurant you would want in your neighbourhood. L'Estaminet offers simple

French cooking: a 'superb and beautifully balanced' salade landaise with a generous portion of foie gras was followed by 'excellent' chateaubriand for one couple. Equally well reported have been brochette of langoustines à l'oriental, marmite de la mer (a substantial selection of cod, halibut, scallops, salmon, prawns and squid in a rich, creamy sauce), and a generous portion of 'tasty and tender' knuckle of lamb in honey and rosemary sauce on a bed of spinach with sautéed potatoes. Fruit tarts – perhaps poire or pomme – are in abundance for dessert, as is a French cheeseboard boasting over 20 varieties. The short wine list is exclusively French, with house wine £11.50.

CHEF: Philippe Tamet   PROPRIETOR: Maria Bellone   OPEN: Mon to Fri L 12 to 2.30, Mon to Sat D 5.45 to 11   CLOSED: bank hols   MEALS: alc (main courses £13 to £17). Set D 5.45 to 7.30 £13.99 (2 courses) to £15.50   SERVICE: 12.5%, card slips closed   CARDS: Amex, Delta, MasterCard, Switch, Visa   DETAILS: 55 seats. Private parties: 12 to 16 private rooms. No pipes . Music. Air-conditioned   ⊖ Leicester Square, Covent Garden

Eyre Brothers ♥

map 13

70 Leonard Street, EC2A 4BP

TEL: (020) 7613 5346   FAX: (020) 7739 8199

WEBSITE: www.eyrebrothers.co.uk

COOKING 3
MEDITERRANEAN
£35–£68

Regeneration may still have a little way to go in the neighbourhood, but the restaurant is smart enough with its frosted glass, backlit partitions and view of the kitchen. Spanish and Portuguese regional cooking forms the backbone of the menu (perhaps chickpea and salt cod soup), although other Mediterranean countries are also raided for ideas. It can be a robust style of cooking, with good ingredients at the heart of it, including fried scallops with sugar-snap peas and pancetta, and scrambled eggs with wild mushrooms on toasted sourdough. Other recommendable dishes have included Ibérico pork fillet, marinated with paprika and thyme, grilled 'surprisingly rare' and served with sliced potato cooked simply with garlic and oil. Desserts are less well reported. Madeiras and sherries count among the aperitifs, and 16 wines come by the glass (£3 to £7). The main selection skips lightly round the world, picking up good producers like Telmo Rodriguez in Spain and Dean Hewitson in Australia. Options under £20 are limited.

CHEFS: David Eyre and Jose Pizarro   PROPRIETORS: David and Robert Eyre   OPEN: Mon to Fri L 12 to 3, Mon to Sat D 6.30 to 11   CLOSED: 25 Dec and 1 Jan   MEALS: alc (main courses £13.50 to £25). Set L and D £19 (2 courses)   SERVICE: 12.5% (optional), card slips closed   CARDS: Amex, Delta, Diners, MasterCard, Switch, Visa   DETAILS: 95 seats. Private parties: 95 main room. Vegetarian meals. Children's helpings. No-smoking area. Wheelchair access (also WC). Occasional music. Air-conditioned   ⊖ Old Street £5

Fifteen ⚡

NEW ENTRY   map 13

15 Westland Place, N1 7LP

TEL: (020) 7251 1515   FAX: (020) 7251 2749

WEBSITE: www.fifteenrestaurant.com

COOKING 4
MODERN EUROPEAN
£56–£81

After years of working his way into our hearts through his TV appearances, everyone's favourite cheeky, chirpy Essex boy-chef has finally opened his own restaurant, and the suitably utilitarian and urban warehouse setting is as bright and breezy as his TV persona. On the ground floor is a deli and a retro-styled cocktail bar, while the main dining room is below and has a '60s/'70s kitsch vibe, with a lively mural on one wall and a view into the open-plan kitchen.

Enthusiastic dish descriptions detail the provenance of ingredients, and there is no doubt that quality in this respect is extremely high: as in a summery salad of grilled Sicilian peaches, buffalo mozzarella and Parma ham with basil, mint and balsamic dressing; and four rare grilled lamb cutlets on smooth and creamy mash with copious chanterelles and a 'sharp, zesty' vivid green salsa verde. The modern Italian cooking style – heavily influence by the River Café, as you might expect – has also produced bresaola with marinated artichokes, Amalfi lemons, thyme, toasted almonds and honey; seafood risotto with samphire, lemon and parsley; and pancetta-wrapped monkfish tail with lentils and a samphire and fennel salad. Not all dishes have lived up to their self-proclaimed 'fantastic' or 'amazing' promise, and prices (same for lunch and dinner) are high – if it's any consolation, all profits from the restaurant go to a charity to support budding young Jamies of the future. Service is appropriately relaxed and informal. Wines are undoubtedly well chosen but you'll have to search hard for much under £20.

CHEFS: Jamie Oliver, Tobie Puttock and Eamon Fullalove   PROPRIETORS: Jamie Oliver/Cheeky Chops Charity   OPEN: all week L 12 to 2.30, Mon to Sat D 6.30 to 11   CLOSED: bank hols MEALS: alc (main courses £22 to £27)   SERVICE: 12.5% (optional)   CARDS: Amex, Delta, MasterCard, Switch, Visa   DETAILS: 70 seats. Private parties: 70 main room. Vegetarian meals. Children's helpings. No smoking. Wheelchair access (not WC). Music. Air-conditioned   ⊖ Old Street

---

Fifth Floor 🍸

map 14

Harvey Nichols, 109–125 Knightsbridge,
SW1X 7RJ

COOKING 4

TEL: (020) 7235 5250

MODERN BRITISH

WEBSITE: www.harveynichols.com

£38–£77

Sharing the store's culinary focused top floor with the bustling food hall, wine shop, sushi bar, café and refurbished bar, the Fifth Floor restaurant, high above Knightsbridge, has been dealt the sleekest of twenty-first-century makeovers. Now oval shaped, the dining room is cloaked in a domed, faux-skylight ceiling and walls lined in glass tubes filled with fibre-optic lighting that change colour to enhance the mood. A striking backdrop for Mies van der Rohe chairs, impeccable table settings and a polished wood floor. The food, under head chef Simon Shaw, is as up to the minute as the décor. A starter of cannelloni of Cornish crab, for instance, is teamed with shellfish caramel and grapefruit jelly, while roasted scallop and langoustine is delivered with a boudin noir, chicken faggots and Jerusalem artichoke velouté. Main courses may take off on culinary sojourns for inspiration, from pan-fried loin of lamb flavoured with curry spices and finished with roasting juices and watermelon, to roasted monkfish wrapped in pancetta with clam minestrone, cavolo nero and black olive oil. Expect banana crème brûlée or 'first-rate' coconut tart with roasted pineapple to finish. A selection of 12 wines by the glass, £3.50–£10, is available from a 'pleasingly varied' list starting at £13.50. Said list arrived in the office just as the Guide went to press. Suffice to say, we're impressed.

CHEF: Simon Shaw   PROPRIETORS: Dickson Poon and Harvey Nichols   OPEN: all week 12 to 3 (3.30 Sat and Sun), 6.30 (6 Sun) to 11   MEALS: alc D (main courses £15 to £23.50). Set L £22 (2 courses) to £25   SERVICE: 10%, card slips closed   CARDS: Amex, Delta, Diners, MasterCard, Switch, Visa   DETAILS: 114 seats. Private parties: 114 main room. Vegetarian meals. Wheelchair access (also WC). No music. Air-conditioned   ⊖ Knightsbridge

Fina Estampa

map 13

150–152 Tooley Street, SE1 2TU
TEL/FAX: (020) 7403 1342
WEBSITE: www.finaestampa.co.uk

COOKING 2
PERUVIAN
£28–£51

'Inspired by memories of a holiday in Peru, we were very impressed by the authentic tastes,' commented one couple after eating here, where, thanks to rebuilding work, there's now a 'fabulous view' of Tower Bridge from the dining room. Native Peruvian Muzak sets the tone and the food is hearty, peasant style, with some refined touches. Potatoes play a central role in the cuisine – perhaps jazzed up with a sauce of fromage frais and mild yellow chilli, or dried and used in classic carapulcra. Alternatively, you might try seco (lamb or chicken in coriander sauce with Peruvian-style beans and salsa criolla), or king prawns with red onions, red peppers and herbs. The short wine list has some quaffable bottles from Chile and Argentina; prices are from £13.50.

CHEF: Bianca Jones   PROPRIETORS: Bianca and Richard Jones   OPEN: Mon to Fri L 12 to 2.30, Mon to Sat D 6.30 to 10.30   MEALS: alc (main courses £7.50 to £16)   SERVICE: 10% (optional)   CARDS: Amex, Delta, Diners, MasterCard, Switch, Visa   DETAILS: 70 seats. Private parties: 30 to 80 private rooms. Vegetarian meals. Children's helpings. Music   ⊖ London Bridge   (£5)

Fino

NEW ENTRY   map 15

33 Charlotte Street (entrance on Rathbone
Street), W1T 1RR
TEL: (020) 7813 8010   FAX: (020) 7813 8011
EMAIL: info@finorestaurant.com
WEBSITE: www.finorestaurant.com

COOKING 3
SPANISH
£29–£76

It is all too obvious from the moment the doorman ushers you down the oak staircase into the bright and 'energetic' dining room and bar that this is no ordinary tapas restaurant. The Hart brothers clearly understand the merits of attention to detail, and that is no surprise given their lineage in the restaurant business (see Hambleton Hall, Upper Hambleton). This bright and surprisingly airy basement has had a thorough contemporary makeover, with blond wood, frosted glass and rich reds helping to generate a smart-yet-relaxed, lively-but-serious atmosphere. A mezzanine bar area overlooks the restaurant. Service is well drilled, friendly and helpful. Order between four and six tapas per person, and these in due course will come out of the kitchen in 'waves'. There might be 'sensationally succulent' milk-fed lamb cutlets, or langoustines, diver-caught scallops or sardines from the plancha (chargrilled). Crisp fried shrimps and clams with sherry and ham are joined by tortilla, croquetas and jamon de Jabugo. Desserts (disappointing at inspection) include crema catalana and chocolate fondant. Wines are not confined to Spain (prices start at £12.50), and sherry is given due attention.

CHEF: Jean Philippe Patruno   PROPRIETORS: Sam and Eddie Hart   OPEN: Mon to Fr L 12 to 2.30,
Mon to Sat D 6 to 10.30   CLOSED: 25 Dec, bank hols   MEALS: alc (main courses £3.50 to £13.50).
Set L £17.95 to £28 (all min 2). Bar menu available   SERVICE: 12.5% (optional), card slips closed
CARDS: Amex, Delta, Diners, MasterCard, Switch, Visa   DETAILS: 75 seats. Private parties: 75
main room. Vegetarian meals. No cigars/pipes. Wheelchair access (also WC). No music. Air-
conditioned   ⊖ Goodge Street, Tottenham Court Road

First Floor   map 13

186 Portobello Road, W11 1LA   COOKING 2
TEL: (020) 7243 0072   FAX: (020) 7221 9440   MODERN BRITISH
                                                                           £24–£53

Like 'a wander into the film set of Notting Hill' was one visitor's impression to
this upstairs room of a pub overlooking the Portobello Road – a feeling brought
about by the 'impressive theatrical décor', including outsize wooden containers
of dried flowers and wax-encrusted candelabra. The menu deals in
contemporary food such as red onion and goats' cheese tarte Tatin, or 'smooth,
generous' foie gras parfait with onion and chilli marmalade. 'Comforting' main
courses have included ribeye steak with roast garlic and red wine sauce, and
baked hake fillet wrapped in pancetta with sage mash and minted pea broth.
There have been disappointments among the puddings, but 'rather delicious'
stem ginger ice cream has hit the spot. Service is friendly if a little too relaxed at
times, and the wine list is short and straightforward, offering interest at
affordable prices. It starts with French house at £11, and a third of the wines are
available by the glass.

CHEF: Alex Howard   PROPRIETOR: Anthony Harris   OPEN: all week L 12 to 3, Mon to Sat D 7 to
11.30   MEALS: alc (main courses L £7 to £10, D £10.50 to £15.50). Set L £10.50 (2 courses) to
£14, Set D £19.95 to £25.95. Bar menu available   SERVICE: 12.5% (optional), card slips closed
CARDS: Amex, Delta, Diners, MasterCard, Switch, Visa   DETAILS: 50 seats. Private parties: 28
main room, 15 to 60 private rooms. Vegetarian meals. Occasional music   ⊖ Ladbroke
Grove £5

Fish Hoek   map 12

8 Elliott Road, W4 1PE   COOKING 3
TEL: (020) 8742 0766   FAX: (020) 8742 3374   SEAFOOD/SOUTH AFRICAN
EMAIL: info@fishhoek.co.uk   £26–£83

This restaurant is all about seafood, served in a variety of often imaginative
ways, and South African-inspired. In case diners are in any doubt of that fact, a
collection of black and white photographs of fish are on hand to remind them.
Otherwise, the 'pleasantly designed' restaurant takes on a 'minimalist and
modern' tone. It is indisputably popular and busy, peopled with a 'well-heeled,
moneyed Chiswick clientele' who 'fit in perfectly among dramatic flower
displays, classic white tablecloths and handsome waiting staff'. Much of the fish
comes from South Africa (False Bay stump-nose fillets, Hout Bay yellowfin tuna,
Transkei red drum and so on) and is served in a number of imaginative ways.
Sautéed Mozambique pink prawn tails may come with roast bananas, coriander
and roasted red peppers, while smoked Atlantic snoek pâté might be served
with Cape seed loaf and apricot chutney. Generally, the lively, eclectic style

comes together well. Service is brisk and well drilled, while the all-South African wine list focuses on whites from £13.

CHEFS: Pete Gottgens and Michael Matheson   PROPRIETOR: Pete Gottgens   OPEN: Tue to Sun 12 to 2.30, 6 to 10.30 (11 Fri and Sat)   CLOSED: 22 Dec to 7 Jan   MEALS: alc (main courses £9 to £34). Set L and D 6 to 8 £9.95 (2 courses) to £14.95   SERVICE: not inc, 12.5% for parties of 6 or more   CARDS: Delta, MasterCard, Switch, Visa   DETAILS: 52 seats. Private parties: 50 main room. No-smoking area. Wheelchair access (also WC). Music. Air-conditioned   ⊖ Turnham Green

Fish Shop ⁵⨯   NEW ENTRY   map 13

360–362 St John Street, EC1V 4NR
TEL: (020) 7837 1199   FAX: (020) 7837 3399   COOKING 2
EMAIL: info@thefishshop.net   SEAFOOD
WEBSITE: www.thefishshop.net   £28–£80

Behind a black, large-windowed shopfront is a modern restaurant with yellow walls, grey carpets, white-clothed tables and wooden chairs. Seafood is the main business, with daily deliveries from Billingsgate and simple treatments bringing out of the best of top-quality raw materials: prawns with garlic mayonnaise, say, or smoked haddock soup, followed by grilled whole mackerel with tomato compote and a mixed-leaf salad, or pan-fried Dover sole with samphire, new potatoes and parsley butter. Deep-fried (either in batter or egg and matzo meal) cod with chips has been praised for its freshness and timing, and successful starters have included mussels marinière, and a firm, thin potato pancake topped with 'excellent' smoked salmon and salmon 'caviar', accompanied by crème fraîche and a drizzle of pesto. Desserts don't disappoint either: 'simple but effective' treacle tart with whisky-flavoured clotted cream, or – a highlight of dinner for one reporter – chocolate and almond fondant with warm chocolate sauce and crunchy praline ice cream. Service is smart and cheerful, and wines are mostly white, obviously enough, with a lively global range starting at £13.25 and eight by the glass (£3.75 to £6.25).

CHEF: David Nolan   PROPRIETORS: John Moyle, and Alan and Olga Conway   OPEN: Tue to Sat 12 to 3, 5.30 to 10.30   CLOSED: 24 Dec to 5 Jan, 6 to 13 Apr, Tue after bank hols   MEALS: alc (main courses £11 to £24.50). Set L and D 5.30 to 7 £13.50 (2 courses) to £17   SERVICE: 12.5% (optional), card slips closed   CARDS: Amex, Delta, Diners, MasterCard, Switch, Visa   DETAILS: 80 seats. 12 seats outside. Private parties: 80 main room, 12 to 80 private rooms. Vegetarian meals. Children's helpings. No smoking in 1 dining room. Wheelchair access (also WC). No music   (£5)

FishWorks ⁵⨯   NEW ENTRY   map 12

6 Turnham Green Terrace, W4 1QP   COOKING 2
TEL: (020) 8994 0086   SEAFOOD
WEBSITE: www.fishworks.co.uk   £33–£61

With a fishmonger's on the street and behind it a coolly stylish dining room, this is a welcome addition to the Chiswick scene. No frills or frippery (abstract art on the walls, cloth-less tables, wooden floors), and a relaxed and warm attitude towards service, point to the fact that the focus is where it should be – on the seafood. Here – and at sister establishments in Bath, Bristol and Christchurch (see entries) – menu and specials blackboards list the fresh seafood (delivered daily from UK and foreign ports) simply prepared. Three slices of smoked salmon with a wedge of lemon impressed for quality alone; then a grilled whole bass delicately scented with rosemary spiked into the flesh was 'a straightforward delight'. Another starter of crab salad with tarragon mayonnaise was excellent, bar an over-acidulated dressing on lettuce. Desserts include a rich baked chocolate pudding, and a decent lemon tart with thin, crisp pastry. The white-weighted wine list (which does include three 'good reds with fish') offers seven by the glass (£3.25 to £7.95) and, starting with £12.50 Chilean Chardonnay, rises to a £60 Burgundy, via intriguing old vintages of Muscadet.

CHEF: Jack Scarterfield   PROPRIETOR: FishWorks Plc   OPEN: Tue to Sat 12 to 3, 6 to 10.30
CLOSED: 25 Dec, each bank hol Mon and following Tue   MEALS: alc (main courses £9 to £22)
SERVICE: not inc   CARDS: Amex, Delta, MasterCard, Switch, Visa   DETAILS: 48 seats. 22 seats outside. Vegetarian meals. Children's helpings. No smoking. Wheelchair access (not WC). Music. Air-conditioned   ⊖ Turnham Green

Flâneur ⚡✳

NEW ENTRY   map 13

41 Farringdon Road, EC1M 3JB   COOKING 3
TEL: (020) 7404 4422   FAX: (020) 7831 4532   MODERN EUROPEAN-PLUS
EMAIL: mail@flaneur.com   £33–£47

Among the corporate, urban jungle of the City's northwest fringes, Flâneur – an upmarket grocery-cum-neighbourhood deli and restaurant – is an eye-catching oasis of good taste. 'Ogling the stock at Flâneur is a joy for anyone interested in food'; hardwood shelves stretch from floor to ceiling laden with a kaleidoscope of foodstuffs. There's no dining room to speak of: tables are scattered in small clusters between counters and shelves, the high-backed, wooden chairs and wooden tables looking both rustic and modern. Flâneur's well-endowed larder, based around small suppliers, drives both kitchen and food hall alike. Daily-changing menus display 'commendable seasonal focus', and extras like bread – moist slices of Maître Poilâne's finest – show quality from the off. Start with pan-fried buffalo ricotta with peas, asparagus, mint and basil, and follow perhaps with wild boar scaloppini with sage, lemon butter and handmade tagliatelle, or crispy-skin fillet of red mullet, spinach and sauce vierge. Finish with generous desserts, maybe a Guanaja chocolate cake with marinated cherries. Service is 'laid back but thoroughly professional', while the appealing wine list offers house at £10.90 (£2.90 by the glass).

CHEF: Jerome Hoban   PROPRIETOR: Gavin Monk   OPEN: all week L 12 to 3, Mon to Sat D 6 to 10
CLOSED: 25 and 26 Dec, 1 Jan   MEALS: alc (main courses £10 to £12). Brunch 9 to 4 Sat, Sun and bank hols   SERVICE: 12.5% (optional), 12.5% for parties of 6 or more, card slips closed   CARDS: Amex, Delta, Diners, MasterCard, Switch, Visa   DETAILS: 55 seats. Private parties: 100 main room. Vegetarian meals. Children's helpings. No smoking. Wheelchair access (not WC). No music. Air-conditioned   ⊖ Farringdon

---

'Roast leg of lamb [was served] medium only [because] ''we get a lot of old people''. . . .'
(On eating in Devon)

Fleur ☕

NEW ENTRY   map 14

33 St James's Street, SW1A 1HD
TEL: (020) 7930 4272   FAX: (020) 7930 9702
EMAIL: reservations@gordonramsay.com
WEBSITE: www.gordonramsay.com

COOKING 4
FRENCH
£37–£63

Following the relocation of Marcus Wareing and Pétrus to the Berkeley Hotel (sadly too late to be included in this edition), the site that was Pétrus has been relaunched as a more casual version of its former self. In other words, tables are slightly smaller and closer together, comfortable chairs have been replaced with red leather banquettes, and there's a little less formality and ceremony (but no less polish) to the service. Chef David Collard has broadened the cooking to bring in a few more exotic influences to the contemporary French style. Dishes tend to be complex, as in starters of 'beautifully light' boudin of chicken and veal shin with onion and potato sauté and veal truffle jus, or ravioli of crab and salmon with pink grapefruit, pak choi, basil purée and lemongrass bisque; and main courses of caramelised breast of Gressingham duck on glazed apple, spring onion, foie gras and honey-roasted duck jus, or 'perfectly roasted' lobster in its shell with another ravioli and braised cabbage on a 'top notch' lobster and port jus. Desserts appear not to be a strong point, although chocolate mille-feuille with griottine cherries and cherry sauce has made a good impression. Those with deep pockets will be able to have some fun indulging in the top-class Burgundies that litter the blue-blooded wine list, which includes a page devoted to the restaurant's namesake Ch. La Fleur-Pétrus. Prices start at £16.

CHEF: David Collard   PROPRIETOR: Gordon Ramsay   OPEN: all week 12 to 3, 6 to 11   MEALS: alc (main courses £11 to £18). Set L £21   SERVICE: not inc   CARDS: Amex, Delta, MasterCard, Switch, Visa   DETAILS: 60 seats. Private parties: 60 main room. Vegetarian meals. No cigars/pipes . Music. Air-conditioned   ⊖ Green Park

---

▲ Foliage ▼

map 14

Mandarin Oriental Hyde Park, 66 Knightsbridge,
SW1X 7LA
TEL: (020) 7235 2000   FAX: (020) 7201 2001
WEBSITE: www.mandarinoriental.com

COOKING 7
MODERN EUROPEAN
£50–£91

The high-ceilinged, white- and cream-painted room itself may not be particularly glamorous, but the view of Hyde Park lends a sense of space, light and animation. Service is deft and professional, and this posh place lives up to expectations; one diner had his 'best dinner of the year' here. The food is appealing, without indulging in fashionable excesses: scallops, for example, have appeared to good effect with crisp pancetta and smooth pea purée, as well as being paired with a cauliflower beignet and matching pannacotta. The menu takes its cue from classical ideas, yet brings freshness to the repertoire – witness turbot raviolo with pork, langoustine and horseradish cream, or roast saddle of venison with a fricassée of Jerusalem artichoke and chocolate sauce.

This is a kitchen dedicated to fine workmanship. Labour-intensive dishes abound on its set-price menus – from a brandade of frogs' legs raviolo with poached langoustine and shallot tempura, to roast sweetbread mille-feuille with onion compote, garlic caramel and potato gnocchi – all of them 'impeccable, perfectly seasoned and exquisite to look at'. Lunch, with around three choices per course, is unstinting of both skills and quality of materials, offering perhaps a duo of foie gras with caramelised endive Tatin, roast fillet of Limousin beef with provençale escargot confit, and a hot Cuban chocolate fondant with black cherry ice cream. Desserts, indeed, are as carefully considered as the rest, taking in a banana crème brûlée with sea salt caramel ice cream, and a raspberry ice cream with orange chibouste gratinée. The wine list has the grandeur to suit the surroundings and is priced accordingly. In France Bordeaux and Burgundy show their finest, and the Loire and Alsace have some treats. Vega Sicilia dominates Spain, and Australia and California are equally smart. The lunchtime wine offer of two glasses for £7 is the best bet for eaters on a budget, as almost the only bottles under £20 are two of the house wines at £19.50.

CHEF: Chris Staines   PROPRIETOR: Mandarin Oriental Hotel Group   OPEN: all week 12 to 2.30, 7 to 10.30   MEALS: Set L £25 to £32, Set D £42.50 to £55   SERVICE: 12.5% (optional)   CARDS: Amex, Diners, MasterCard, Switch, Visa   DETAILS: 46 seats. Vegetarian meals. Children's helpings. Wheelchair access (also WC). Music. Air-conditioned   ACCOMMODATION: 200 rooms, all with bath/shower. TV. Phone. Room only £255 to £4,500. Rooms for disabled. Baby facilities (*The Which? Guide to Good Hotels*)   ⊖ Knightsbridge

Four Seasons £

map 13

84 Queensway, W2 3RL
TEL: (020) 7229 4320

COOKING **3**
CANTONESE
£20–£64

The sight of roast duck, pork and other meats hanging in the window seems to do the trick of drawing in the crowds to this basic dining room on bustling Queensway, judging by the fact that it is always busy. It is a thoroughly unpretentious place, with all efforts focused on the simple aim of serving food rapidly enough to ensure that the queues don't end up stretching too far down the road. You may not be actively encouraged to hurry your meal, but don't expect long waits between courses.

What makes the place so popular is bona fide Cantonese cooking of the first order. Those roast meats are as good as they look: an inspector praised evenly cooked and excellently flavoured aromatic crispy duck, and 'very tender' double-cooked belly pork with yam, the vegetable soaking up the plentiful meat juices. Seafood and vegetables are handled in equally assured fashion: well-timed prawns with crunchy cashew nuts, mushrooms, ginger and carrots, for example, and lightly steamed gai lan (Chinese broccoli) with garlic. Two dozen wines include house vins de pays at £9.

CHEF: Mr Tong   PROPRIETOR: Four Seasons (Queensway) Ltd   OPEN: all week 12 to 11.15 (10.45 Sun)   MEALS: alc (main courses £5.50 to £20). Set L and D £12.50 to £17 (all min 2 or more)   SERVICE: 12.5%   CARDS: Amex, Delta, MasterCard, Switch, Visa   DETAILS: 70 seats. Private parties: 80 main room. Vegetarian meals. Music. Air-conditioned   ⊖ Bayswater, Queensway

The Guide is totally independent, accepts no free hospitality, and survives on the number of copies sold each year.

Fox Dining Room £

map 13

28 Paul Street, EC2A 4LB
TEL: (020) 7729 5708   FAX: (020) 7729 5808

COOKING 2
MODERN EUROPEAN
£29–£35

To get to the upstairs dining room at the Fox, one must first run the gauntlet of determined drinkers in the downstairs pub. The self-proclaimed 'rough edges' (according to a beer mat) are somewhat smoother in the upstairs room, the wooden floors softened with Turkish carpets, the ceiling and walls nicotine-influenced and the 'auction variety' tables and chairs comfortable enough. The Fox is sister to the Eagle (see entry) and a similar style of unfussy food (much of it Mediterranean-influenced) characterises the repertoire. The short menu features the likes of pigeon and duck gizzard salad, or pumpkin and almond soup, followed by semolina gnocchi and mushrooms, or pot-roast partridge and mash. No-frills desserts may include treacle tart or chocolate cake. Most of the food passes muster, but seasoning isn't always spot-on. The dozen-plus wines are gutsy and well chosen; all are available by the glass, from £2.50.

CHEF: Trish Hilferty   PROPRIETOR: Michael Belben   OPEN: Mon to Fri 12.30 to 3, 6.30 to 10
CLOSED: 10 days at Christmas, bank hols   MEALS: Set L and D £14 (2 courses) to £18.75. Bar menu available   SERVICE: not inc, card slips closed   CARDS: MasterCard, Switch, Visa
DETAILS: 36 seats. 20 seats outside. Private parties: 100 main room. Vegetarian meals. Children's helpings. No music   ⊖ Old Street, Liverpool Street

Fung Shing 🍞

map 15

15 Lisle Street, WC2H 7BE
TEL: (020) 7437 1539   FAX: (020) 7734 0284
WEBSITE: www.fungshing.co.uk

COOKING 3
CHINESE
£28–£72

'Seafood and exotic dishes are our speciality,' say the owners of this big-name restaurant in the heart of Chinatown. At its best, Fung Shing can perform as well as most of its rivals in the capital: one regular of ten years' standing found it 'very satisfying to eat such good-quality food' and singled out stuffed baby squid and 'very delicate' lamb with leeks from the inspiring list of chef's specials, which extends to sizzling beef with peppercorns, lime leaves and lemongrass, stir-fried crispy pigeon, and ostrich with ginger and spring onions. The kitchen also handles the standard Cantonese repertoire impressively: witness spicy prawns with chilli and garlic, lightly steamed sea bass, and 'superb' lemon chicken. However, there have been some worrying gripes from reporters in recent months concerning 'lukewarm' food, long gaps between dishes, and shambolic service; it is hoped that these are the result of a temporary blip rather than a sign of something 'more structurally unsound'. The wine list is a serious slate, including directly imported Bordeaux, although prices are on the high side. House wine is the most affordable option at £13.50.

CHEF: Chun Fat Cheung   PROPRIETOR: Fung Shing Partnership   OPEN: all week 12 to 11.15
CLOSED: 24 to 26 Dec, bank hol L   MEALS: alc (main courses £6.50 to £19). Set L £17, Set D £17 to £30 (all min 2 or more)   SERVICE: 10%, card slips closed   CARDS: Amex, Delta, Diners, MasterCard, Switch, Visa   DETAILS: 106 seats. Private parties: 50 main room, 20 to 50 private rooms. Vegetarian meals. Music. Air-conditioned   ⊖ Leicester Square

Gate

72 Belsize Lane, NW3 5BJ
TEL: (020) 7435 7733
EMAIL: belsize@gateveg.co.uk
51 Queen Caroline Street, W6 9QL
TEL: (020) 8748 6932
EMAIL: hammersmith@gateveg.co.uk
WEBSITE: www.gateveg.co.uk

NEW CHEF
VEGETARIAN
£24–£39

'The dishes are so good you don't realise the meat is missing,' was the reaction of one meat eater to the Gate experience. At the Belsize Park branch the two floors have long, narrow spaces, fairy lights, wood furniture and colourful abstracts on the walls – no earthenware, hair-shirt approach here – while the Hammersmith original is in a converted artists' studio and provides an appealing courtyard for outside eating. There was a game of 'musical kitchens' this year, which saw the two head chefs swapping over. The menus are similar, each demonstrating distinctly global leanings. Freshly baked bread with delicate olive oil has been a hit, and first courses of rich, eggy goats' cheese tart, or involtini of fried aubergine wrapping creamy cheese with herbs, show how simple formulae supported by good buying and intelligently applied skills can work well. Consistent risotto, sampled twice by the same diner within days, was 'unbelievably good, rich not cloying'; while cashew nut korma might be an alternative. Chocolate and chilli crème brûlée, with its separate yet complementary flavours and nicely glazed topping, was a real hit. Service is charmingly polite and attentive. Wines, a succinct European collection, start at £10.50 (£3 a glass), stay largely below £20, and include several organic bottles.

CHEFS: Martin Janicki (Belsize Park) and Joseph Tyrrell (Hammersmith)   PROPRIETORS: Adrian and Michael Daniel   OPEN: Belsize Sat and Sun L 12 to 2.45, all week D 6 to 10.45; Hammersmith Mon to Sat L 12 to 2.45, Mon to Fri D 6 to 10.45   CLOSED: 25 Dec, bank hols   MEALS: alc (main courses £8 to £11)   SERVICE: not inc, 12.5% for parties of 6 or more   CARDS: Amex, Delta, MasterCard, Switch, Visa   DETAILS: 55 seats. 6 outside. Private parties: main room 60 (Belsize); 50 seats. 25 outside. Private parties: main room 50 (Hammersmith). Vegetarian meals. Music   ⊖ Belsize Park, Hammersmith

---

Gaudí

map 13

63 Clerkenwell Road, EC1M 5NP
TEL: (020) 7608 3220   FAX: (020) 7250 1057
EMAIL: gaudi@turnmills.co.uk
WEBSITE: www.turnmills.co.uk/gaudi

COOKING 3
MODERN SPANISH
£27–£66

On a corner in bustling Clerkenwell, above Turnmills nightclub, this Spanish restaurant is a homage to the avant-garde architect. An open-plan kitchen overlooks the spacious, tiled-floored, brick-walled dining room, where ornamental displays of twisted branches are sprayed gold. The cooking follows a modern Spanish approach, with prolix bilingual menus offering baby artichokes with black truffle on a thyme-scented confit of ceps to start, followed by one of the invariably complex-sounding main courses such as baked sea bream with cod mousse, piquillo peppers and griddled squid wrapped in bacon in an ink sauce; or venison loin with tetilla (a Galician soft cheese), steamed green beans and baby vegetables, and a potato and onion tart, all sauced with red Rioja. Despite the pile-ups of ingredients, dishes appear to achieve both balance and restraint in terms of their contrasting flavours, an impression that also characterises the desserts, which are generally as impeccably Spanish as the rest of the menu. Turrón soufflé with sherry ice cream, a sauce of Patxaran and garnishes of preserved pomegranate and lime, seasoned with rosemary, is but one possible option. The exclusively Spanish wine list represents an opportunity to explore some of the lesser-known regions, opening with five by the glass from £3.50, or from £12.50 a bottle.

CHEF: Josep Carbonell   PROPRIETOR: Magda Newman   OPEN: Mon to Fri L 12 to 2.30, Mon to Sat D 7 to 10.30   CLOSED: Christmas, bank hols   MEALS: alc (main courses £12 to £22). Set L £12.50 (2 courses) to £15, Set D £35   SERVICE: 12.5% (optional)   CARDS: Amex, Delta, Diners, MasterCard, Switch, Visa   DETAILS: 35 seats. Private parties: 45 main room. Vegetarian meals. Music. Air-conditioned   ⊖ Farringdon

Le Gavroche ♀

map 15

43 Upper Brook Street, W1K 7QR
TEL: (020) 7408 0881   FAX: (020) 7491 4387
EMAIL: bookings@le-gavroche.com
WEBSITE: www.le-gavroche.co.uk

COOKING 7
FRENCH
£48–£152

'I have always been of the opinion that if you want to spend serious money in London, then there is no better place than here,' wrote one visitor. No doubt royalty would agree. 'The King of Swaziland and his entourage entered the restaurant just after we arrived. They occupied several large tables and even the chauffeurs and maids had a table of their own.' This has been one of the finest restaurants in the country ever since it opened some 35 years ago, and still acts as a beacon for those aspiring to haute cuisine. With so many other establishment restaurants getting the makeover treatment, often to the consternation of their traditionally inclined customers, Le Gavroche sails on, riding out the trends, providing a club-like shelter for its wealthy clientele, with the reassurance that nothing much needs to change. Perhaps the low ceiling and subdued lighting, in a windowless basement, add to this impression, although any solemnity is dispersed by the flowers, street urchin motif, and silver birds and animals that decorate the tables.

The food is not about surprise or innovation, although there are some fairly modern dishes, but it is about luxury, precision, comfort and indulgence: perhaps in a lobster mousse with caviar and champagne butter sauce, or in a dish of globe artichokes filled with velvety smooth foie gras and chicken mousse, and packed with black truffle. Although occasional lapses seem to thwart its high ambition, the food can come close to perfection, for example in the case of succulent langoustines and earthy morels in a deeply flavoured Madeira sauce. The range is impressive too, taking in game (pink loin of venison with caramelised root vegetables, wild mushrooms, cranberry sauce and a dark, intense, demi-glace) as well as lighter, more Mediterranean dishes such as a tender rib of veal accompanied by a polenta cake topped with 'outstanding' vegetables, and by a warm tomato, garlic, basil and olive oil sauce.

Pastry regularly comes in for praise, for example in a warm wild duck pie to start, and in a fine apple Tatin with 'perfectly caramelised' apples to finish. Soufflés in various forms are also a great success, from the unchanging cheese soufflé suissesse, and the fluffy omelette Rothschild with its well-judged apricot sauce, to a hot passion-fruit soufflé with a silky white chocolate ice cream. World-class service, ably headed by Silvano Giraldin, is 'as close to a perfect ballet performance as you could hope for'. Ninety-nine champagnes open a celebration of the finest wines of France, where a range of vintages is the norm rather than an exception. Bordeaux and Burgundy are in a class of their own, other regions impressive, and top Super-Tuscans and a handful of leading Californians keep the first growths company. Regional selections are the places for more affordable options. Sobering prices climb swiftly from £20, and nine wines come by the glass for £4 to £10.

CHEF: Michel Roux   PROPRIETOR: Le Gavroche Ltd   OPEN: Mon to Fri L 12 to 2, Mon to Sat D 7 to 11   CLOSED: Christmas, New Year, bank hols   MEALS: alc (main courses £28.50 to £41). Set L £42, Set D £80 (whole table)   SERVICE: 12.5% (optional), card slips closed   CARDS: Amex, Delta, Diners, MasterCard, Switch, Visa   DETAILS: 60 seats. Vegetarian meals. Jacket. No cigars/pipes in dining room. No music. Air-conditioned   ⊖ Marble Arch

---

Gay Hussar

2 Greek Street, W1D 4NB
TEL: (020) 7437 0973   FAX: (020) 7437 4631
EMAIL: gayhussar@corushotels.com

COOKING 1
HUNGARIAN
£30–£54

Born in 1953, this 'happy' Soho legend currently ranks second in the Guide's list of 'longest serving restaurants'. Little changes, although one visitor – returning after an absence of 25 years – noticed that the seats are now beige and that conversation is now accompanied by piped Hungarian folk music. Even so, the narrow downstairs dining room still feels like an antique 'railway carriage', high rankers from the political old guard continue to lunch here, and the food remains resolutely traditional. Regulars and tourists work their way through the classics – slabs of fish terrine with beetroot sauce and cucumber salad, full-bodied pancakes stuffed with veal goulash and mighty helpings of sautéed calf's liver with onions, bacon and paprika. Desserts are ever-popular chestnut purée, poppy-seed strudel and dobos torta. Drink Bull's Blood, Tokaji or the Hungarian house wines (from £10.75).

CHEF: Carlos Mendonca   PROPRIETOR: Restaurant Partnership plc   OPEN: Mon to Sat 12.15 to 2.30, 5.30 to 10.45   CLOSED: 25 and 26 Dec, bank hols   MEALS: alc (main courses £9.50 to £16.50). Set L £15.50 (2 courses) to £18.50   SERVICE: 12.5% (optional), card slips closed   CARDS: Amex, Delta, Diners, MasterCard, Switch, Visa   DETAILS: 70 seats. Private parties: 40 main room, 12 to 24 private rooms. Vegetarian meals. Children's helpings. No pipes. Wheelchair access (not WC). No music. Air-conditioned   ⊖ Tottenham Court Road   £5

'The owner brought in my drink with an accompanying bowl of crisps. He apologised, saying ''We weren't expecting any callers. My wife ate the rest of the canapés.'''
(On eating in Scotland)

Ginger

map 13

115 Westbourne Grove, W2 4UP
TEL: (020) 7908 1990   FAX: (020) 7908 1991
EMAIL: info@gingerrestaurant.co.uk
WEBSITE: www.gingerrestaurant.co.uk

NEW CHEF
BANGLADESHI
£30–£56

The aim of this vividly decorated restaurant is to serve authentic dishes inspired by the traditional home cooking of Bangladesh. Every corner of the Bengal region is explored, and it is not surprising that fish looms large on the menu: crab patties, and stuffed squid tandoori show up among starters, while main courses might feature whole sea bass with a light spicy broth, and dab chingri (apparently a 'special occasion' family treat involving king prawns, coconut milk and saffron served in a green coconut) – not to mention classic fish biryani. Elsewhere, expect duck and mango curry, lamb with green papaya, and a version of that ersatz curry house favourite, chicken tikka masala. Green bananas and red pumpkin add colour to the line-up of vegetables, and there's mango sorbet to finish. House wine at £12 heads the short, respectable list. A new chef was appointed after our inspection.

CHEF: Cruz Gomes   PROPRIETORS: Ollie Rahman and Abdul Kadir   OPEN: all week 12 to 5.30, 6 to 11 (12 Fri and Sat)   CLOSED: 25 and 26 Dec   MEALS: alc (main courses £7.50 to £14). Set L £7.50 (2 courses)   SERVICE: 12.5% (optional)   CARDS: Amex, Delta, MasterCard, Switch, Visa   DETAILS: 100 seats. Private parties: 70 main room, 15 to 40 private rooms. Vegetarian meals. Children's helpings. No-smoking area. Music. Air-conditioned   ⊖ Notting Hill Gate (£5)

Golden Dragon £

map 15

28–29 Gerrard Street, W1V 7LP
TEL: (020) 7734 2763   FAX: (020) 7734 1073

COOKING 2
CHINESE
£27–£58

A smart pair of eponymous dragons sit supremely against the back wall, overlooking three ancient statues of Confucian gentlemen in this colourful Chinatown address. Service has improved of late, and the kitchen seems to have regained its form, according to one who knows the place. Lunchtime dim sum feature an array of delights such as taro (yam) croquette, 'four delicacies' dumplings (including shiitake mushrooms wrapped in a layer of glass noodles), and lobster dumplings with 'salad cream'. Roast meats hang in the window and – at their best – are authentically sweet and succulent. Elsewhere, the full menu is mainly Cantonese, but without some of the exotica seen in other establishments. Reporters have enjoyed a 'handsome' hotpot of crab, glass noodles and chillies in an 'earthy' sauce, as well as turbot with ginger and spring onions, and a spot-on version of Chinese broccoli with oyster sauce. House wines are £9.

CHEF: Mr Wong   PROPRIETOR: Grandpord Ltd   OPEN: Mon to Sat 12 to 11.15 (11.45 Fri and Sat), Sun 11 to 10.45   CLOSED: 25 Dec   MEALS: alc (main courses £6.50 to £18). Set L and D £12.50 (2 courses) to £22.80 (all min 2 or more)   SERVICE: 10%   CARDS: Amex, Delta, Diners, MasterCard, Switch, Visa   DETAILS: 200 seats. Private parties: 200 main room, 10 to 40 private rooms. Vegetarian meals. Music. Air-conditioned   ⊖ Leicester Square, Piccadilly Circus

Gordon Ramsay ▮

map 14

68–69 Royal Hospital Road, SW3 4HP

COOKING **10**

TEL: (020) 7352 4441   FAX: (020) 7352 3334

FRENCH

WEBSITE: www.gordonramsay.com

£54–£124

No flags or bunting, no doormen in top hats, announce Britain's best restaurant. The place just exudes quiet confidence, its trademark aubergine colour used discreetly, its small, smart, understated dining room decorated with a few Murano-style glass baubles, and its relaxed customers arranged at crisply covered tables around a central mirrored pillar. Some tables may be a bit small, and the impeccable service can appear a mite fussy to some ('it can get a bit spooky when you are escorted to the loo'), but there is no question that the food is 'as good as it gets'. Despite all Gordon Ramsay's other restaurant openings and business activities, standards remain stratospherically high; only the Menu Prestige seems to suffer from an occasional lack of wizardry, although it has also provided one couple with 'the finest dinner we've ever had'.

Menu options are generous: the Menu Prestige at £80, a main menu with oodles of choice and, at lunch, two simple interchangeable set menus at a very reasonable price. What is remarkable about the food is that it has a freshly minted or 'just-painted' feel about it. Dishes are honed and practised, of course, but not set in aspic; they have a dynamic quality about them which is refreshing. A refined version of pig's trotter stuffed with sweetbreads, for example, downplays the gelatinous component, replacing it with richness from a lump of seared foie gras (surmounted by a fried quail's egg), and counterpointed by a very fine celeriac rémoulade. 'It was difficult to see how this could be bettered,' reported its eater, a sentiment that could equally apply to a tranche of dark red turbot fillet ('one of the best ever') looking more like a piece of beef from its contact with red wine, accompanied by a gently flavoured courgette and celeriac risotto, over which the waiter ladled a rich, dark, perfectly judged mahogany-coloured red wine and shallot sauce.

Excellence in quality of materials and cooking techniques is repeated in a first-rate piece of pink Cornish lamb carved into slices, with wonderful flavour, set for contrast on a confit of shoulder meat, splashed with a pleasingly thin, thyme-flavoured jus. There are, of course, lots of little additions to each dish – a few tiny mushrooms, the odd asparagus spear, a couple of halved tomatoes and so on – which add flavour and texture but which don't intrude on the main components.

Cheeses – an impressive variety – are kept in prime condition, and desserts are no less a highlight than the rest of the operation, taking in a large, immaculately judged ball of orange parfait balancing sweetness and zestiness, covered in crushed almonds, with a pool of warm chocolate and Grand Marnier sauce, accompanied by a couple of plump yet light chocolate madeleines. Service is hierarchical, unhurried, polished and precisely choreographed, from a team headed by Jean-Claude Breton, who is almost a caricature of himself: 'he first established that I had been before, by asking me, and then treated me like an old friend.' The sommelier is particularly helpful with the wine list, a mighty beast bristling with big names and steep prices. Bordeaux, for example, is dominated by multiple vintages of the first growths and Pétrus. But there are interesting quieter corners in the Loire, regional France, Germany and Italian whites.

France is the mainstay, with the rest of Europe giving strong support, while New World selections are brief, apart from a flurry of prestige bottles from Australia and California. House wines start the ball rolling at £18, seven come by the glass from £5 to £14, and there are loads of half-bottles.

CHEF/PROPRIETOR: Gordon Ramsay OPEN: Mon to Fri 12 to 2.30, 6.45 to 11 CLOSED: Christmas, bank hols MEALS: Set L £35, Set D £65 to £80 SERVICE: not inc CARDS: Amex, Delta, Diners, MasterCard, Switch, Visa DETAILS: 45 seats. Private parties: 45 main room. Vegetarian meals. No cigars in dining room. Wheelchair access (not WC). No music. No mobile phones. Air-conditioned ⊖ Sloane Square

Gordon Ramsay at Claridge's ▼   map 13

Brook Street, W1A 2JQ
TEL: (020) 7499 0099 FAX: (020) 7499 3099   COOKING 7
EMAIL: gordonramsay@claridges.co.uk   FRENCH
WEBSITE: www.gordonramsay.com   £42–£97

The dining room is a grand, high-ceilinged affair, with a few vestigial Art Deco mirrors, and lights that attract attention for their orange shades and fur trims. Tables are quite close together but smartly dressed, as indeed are the friendly, well-trained staff, who tend not to let things slow to a leisurely pace if they can help it. Mark Sargeant's beguiling modern cooking has a strong classical foundation, so it doesn't take too many risks, but it does produce sound dishes ranging from a soup bowl containing three crab tortellini (on shredded cabbage, carrot and rocket) over which the waiter pours a powerful fishy-flavoured consommé, to 'terrifically fresh' and accurately grilled red mullet on aubergine caviar with peas and tomato consommé.

Balance is a key component, evident in five accurately seared, hand-dived scallops, each topped with a sliver of black truffle, on a base of Jerusalem artichoke risotto, all surrounded by more artichoke (purée and crisps), but so well judged in terms of proportion that they didn't overshadow the delicate sweetness of the scallops. Whatever the food may lack in terms of adventure it more than makes up for in terms of sheer comfort and reassurance: perhaps 'sublime' roast turbot with 'immaculate' vegetables (spinach, baby asparagus and chicory) and a fine chicken velouté, or a black-leg chicken breast, poached then grilled, served on potato purée, surrounded by a fricassee of peas and tiny broad beans with a velouté of morels.

Cheeses are kept in good condition, and desserts have included an orange tart with a smooth-textured, full-blooded orange sorbet, and a rich-tasting banana parfait resting on a disc of hazelnut biscuit, topped with a scoop of first-class, rich, dark chocolate sorbet. Extras, including an appetiser and pre-dessert, are first-class, as are the vast majority of the wines on an imposing list centred on France. Bordeaux and Burgundy are monumental, crowned by vintages that are not just old but antique (and commanding five-figure prices), while the rest of France is more variable: the Loire is impeccable but Alsace lacks star names. Over £30 a bottle is the norm here, with just seven options under £20. Ten wines come by the glass from £5 (to £48).

CHEF: Mark Sargeant   PROPRIETOR: Gordon Ramsay Holdings Ltd   OPEN: all week 12 to 3, 5.45 to 11   MEALS: Set L £25, Set D £50 to £60   SERVICE: not inc   CARDS: Amex, Delta, MasterCard, Switch, Visa   DETAILS: 75 seats. Private parties: 75 main room, 8 to 32 private rooms. No cigars/pipes. Wheelchair access (also WC). No music. No mobile phones. Air-conditioned   ⊖ Bond Street

Great Eastern Dining Room £   map 13

54–56 Great Eastern Street, EC2A 3QR
TEL: (020) 7613 4545   FAX: (020) 7613 4137
EMAIL: kevin@thediningrooms.com
WEBSITE: www.greateasterndining.co.uk

COOKING 3
PAN-ASIAN
£29–£51

This popular, lively and noisy bar and dining room in a one-time fabric warehouse is the creation of Melbourne-born Will Ricker. The dining room is decked out in minimalist style, with dark wood and a Chinese-red wall, black and brown banquettes, eye-catching chandeliers and large windows. The presentation of dishes is striking, and the kitchen uses first-class ingredients and integrates different oriental traditions into them. The user-friendly menu divides neatly into dim sum (perhaps featuring edamame with chilli, soy and mirin, or water chestnut and mushroom dumplings flavoured with green tea with a sweet and spicy dipping sauce); sushi/sashimi (tuna or a mixed plate); tempura (tiger prawns with oba leaf); salads (duck, watermelon and cashew nut, for example); and 'house dishes' (maybe spicy barbecued chicken with nam prik, or beef nabe). On the reverse is a useful Asian food glossary, while desserts are European classics with an Eastern twist, among them ginger tiramisù. Staff are accomplished and knowledgeable. The New World has a strong influence on the wine list. Around a dozen bottles also come by the glass, with house French opening proceedings at £11.

CHEF: Andrew Keegan   PROPRIETOR: Will Ricker   OPEN: Mon to Sat 12 to 3, 6 to 11   CLOSED: Christmas, bank hol Mons   MEALS: alc (main courses £8 to £14). Set L and D £22.50 (2 courses) to £27. Bar menu available 12 (6 Sat) to 10.30   SERVICE: 12.5% (optional), card slips closed   CARDS: Amex, Delta, Diners, MasterCard, Switch, Visa   DETAILS: 65 seats. Private parties: 80 main room, 200 private room. Vegetarian meals. Wheelchair access (not WC). No music. Air-conditioned   ⊖ Old Street

▲ Great Eastern Hotel, Aurora ▮   map 13

Liverpool Street, EC2M 7QN
TEL: (020) 7618 7000   FAX: (020) 7618 7001
EMAIL: restaurantres@great-eastern-hotel.co.uk
WEBSITE: www.aurora-restaurant.co.uk

COOKING 4
MODERN EUROPEAN
£44–£86

The sympathetic restoration of this historic hotel is the result of a joint effort between Wyndham International and the Conran Group; the fine-dining restaurant Aurora is the jewel in the crown. 'This is indeed a very grand dining room,' said one reporter, struck by the spectacular domed roof and large supporting columns, the six modern chandeliers, the marble flooring and several large mirrors. Service is generally 'absolutely first-rate' and efforts are made to keep things moving at busy lunchtimes, when the City eats.

The menu certainly seems designed to appeal to expense-account clientele, with 'posh' offerings such as foie gras, lobster, Anjou pigeon and pata negra pork. Yet Warren Geraghty's cooking is actually more adventurous than the menu implies. The kitchen is willing to experiment: so that foie gras may feature in a starter with apple and goats' cheese as part of a terrine, for instance. Among dishes that have impressed reporters are sautéed sea scallops with a velvety, slightly smoky squid ink sauce; an imaginative 'Label Rouge' guinea fowl with lime and redcurrants; and a nicely textured pistachio soufflé with pistachio ice cream. The wine list rises to the grandeur of its surroundings with an impressive collection of Bordeaux and Burgundy, while making pretty much everywhere look like a specialism, from the Loire and the Rhône to Italy, Spain and the New World. Prices are mostly steep, but the cheapest bottles, such as the Spanish house red and white by Telmo Rodriguez (£15), are reasonable value and good quality. Fifteen come by the glass from £3.75 to £13.50.

CHEF: Warren Geraghty PROPRIETORS: Conran Holdings and Wyndham International OPEN: Mon to Fri 12 to 3, 6.45 to 10 MEALS: alc (main courses £16.50 to £31.50). Set L £28, Set D 6.45 to 9 £45 to £65 (inc wine, whole table) SERVICE: 12.5% (optional) CARDS: Amex, Delta, Diners, MasterCard, Switch, Visa DETAILS: 100 seats. Private parties: 100 main room. Vegetarian meals. Wheelchair access (also WC). Music. Air-conditioned ACCOMMODATION: 267 rooms, all with bath/shower. TV. Phone. Room only £225 to £495. Rooms for disabled ⊖ Liverpool Street

The Green £ | **NEW ENTRY** | map 12

58–60 East Dulwich Road, SE22 9AX
TEL: (020) 7732 7575   FAX: (020) 8693 0959
EMAIL: info@greenbar.co.uk
WEBSITE: www.greenbar.co.uk

COOKING **2**
MODERN EUROPEAN
£22–£47

This former supermarket (an offshoot of Le Chardon round the corner; see entry) opened in June 2002, and provides a buzzy bar at the front and dining room behind. A modern feel is created by the usual suspects of wooden floor, sharp lighting, bare wood tables, contemporary art, and, erm, a grand piano (that would be for Tuesday and Thursday night jazz). Smartly dressed francophone waiters are friendly, efficient and willing, though linguistic misunderstandings can occur. The menu is less overtly French than the sister establishment, taking in moules marinière, and foie gras ballottine with sharp onion jam to cut its richness, plus fishcakes with Thai chilli jam. The kitchen has roasted sea bream fillets and served them with champagne, chives and cream sauce, and slow-cooked a 'really excellent, hearty' shank of pork, darkened and tenderised in a rich sauce. Vegetables are well prepared though served in a match-all selection that sits uneasily with some dishes. A satisfyingly rich bitter chocolate mousse is one way to finish. House wines at £9.90 begin a succinct, knowledgeable list that has much below £20.

CHEF: Damien Gillespie PROPRIETOR: Robert Benyayer OPEN: all week 12 to 4 (5 Sun), 6 to 11 MEALS: alc (main courses £8 to £12). Set L £7.95 (2 courses), Set L Sun £13.95. Bar menu available SERVICE: 10% (optional) CARDS: Amex, Delta, MasterCard, Switch, Visa DETAILS: 120 seats. 40 seats outside. Private parties: 100 main room, 15 to 40 private rooms. Vegetarian meals. Children's helpings. Wheelchair access (also WC). Music. Air-conditioned (£5)

Greenhouse ▼

map 15

27A Hays Mews, W1X 7RJ   COOKING **5**
TEL: (020) 7499 3331   FAX: (020) 7499 5368   GLOBAL
EMAIL: reservations@greenhouserestaurant.co.uk   £40–£142

After a change of ownership, the Raffles-like air engendered by louvred screens and ceiling fans has been replaced by a smart green colour scheme, comfortably upholstered chairs, big floral displays, and generously spaced and crisply dressed tables. Just about everything on the long menu sounds fascinating, the combinations unusual but sensible, the pile-ups of ingredients irresistible: from Devon crab mayonnaise, via truffle risotto, to a casserole of duck liver, snails and pork confit with red onion jelly, foie gras, and garlic butter ravioli.

The kitchen can deliver some real treats: for example, a terrine made from pale pink foie gras and rosy-red leg and white saddle of rabbit, partnered by a disc of translucent pale green jelly tasting of tart Bramley apple, topped with a tiny quenelle of celeriac and mustard rémoulade, the whole thing 'a triumph in every way'. At its best, this is satisfying food, exemplified by a breast of guinea fowl rolled around a light herby cornbread stuffing, partnered by a domed pie of glazed puff pastry filled with chunks of truffled leg and rich smoked sausage 'rippling with flavour'.

Although not all dishes are equally adept or exciting, cheeses are well chosen and well kept, and desserts might feature blood orange espuma with rhubarb sorbet, or chocolate fondant with peanut butter ice cream. Use of mobile phones has irritated, and service comes in for some stick. The wine list is startlingly good and arranged by grape variety – so the fine selection of clarets is split between the Cabernet and Merlot sections. The occasional bottle limbos under the £20 barrier, and an excellent selection of 18 wines is offered by the glass (£3.50 to £12.50).

CHEF: Paul Merrett   PROPRIETOR: Marlon Abela   OPEN: Mon to Fri L 12 to 2.30, Mon to Sat D 6.30 to 11   MEALS: alc (main courses £15.50 to £26). Set L £20 (2 courses) to £25, Set D £55 to £105 (inc wine)   SERVICE: 12.5% (optional), card slips closed   CARDS: Amex, Delta, Diners, MasterCard, Switch, Visa   DETAILS: 70 seats. Private parties: 70 main room. Vegetarian meals. No cigars in dining room. Wheelchair access (not WC). No music. Air-conditioned   ⊖ Green Park

Green Olive 🦪

map 13

5 Warwick Place, W9 2PX   COOKING **2**
TEL/FAX: (020) 7289 2469   ITALIAN
                                                         £36–£69

Fittingly green-painted outside, Green Olive (part of the group that also includes Red Pepper and Crivelli's Garden at the National Gallery; see London Round-up and main entry sections respectively) is beside a busy pub in a line of shop-fronts. Inside, natural brickwork and cream walls are hung with gilt-framed mirrors and sepia prints (Italian themes), and tables are small and close-set. The two-to-four-course fixed-price menu is in Italian, translated (somewhat creatively) into English. Start, perhaps, with vitello tonnato and green beans (the meat well-textured, the tuna sauce very authentic), then – if you've the capacity – one of the 'primi piatti': watercress and gorgonzola risotto, say, or prawn ravioli. Main courses run to pan-fried cod with olive oil mash and braised red onions, or grilled ribeye with globe artichokes, and desserts are a high point; coffee semifreddo with almond sauce stands out, as does good, strong espresso. The all-Italian wine list has some high-quality bottles from good producers, but prices (from £14) are highish for a neighbourhood-style restaurant. Nine by the glass (plus four sweeties) are £4 to £9.

CHEF: Stefano Stecca   PROPRIETOR: Red Pepper Group   OPEN: all week 12.30 to 2.30, 7 to 10.30 CLOSED: 25 Dec, 1 Jan, bank hols   MEALS: Set L £18 (2 courses) to £26, Set D £21.50 (2 courses) to £30   SERVICE: 12.5% (optional), card slips closed   CARDS: Amex, Delta, MasterCard, Switch, Visa   DETAILS: 60 seats. Private parties: 30 main room. Children's helpings. No cigars. Wheelchair access (not WC). Music. Air-conditioned   ⊖ Warwick Avenue

Haandi
map 14

136 Brompton Road, Knightsbridge, SW3 1HY	COOKING 4
TEL: (020) 7823 7373 FAX: (020) 7823 9696	INDIAN
WEBSITE: www.haandi-restaurants.com	£35–£71

Haandi's somewhat unexciting yellow-brown-orange tones may not win design and décor awards, but – proving that you shouldn't judge a restaurant by its colour swatches – it nonetheless serves top-notch Indian food. Cooking from the North-west Frontier (and thus the tandoor) features large on the extensive menu, but there are dishes from throughout India. Those impressing reporters include aloo ki chaat (Bombay-style sweet-and-sour potatoes, with 'a tangy tamarind taste'); pindi channa masala (Punjabi-style spiced chickpea curry); gosht-ki-haandi (spiced lamb curry with tomato); and murgh daranpur (chicken in cumin masala). Breads, such as parathas, are excellent. Even such frequently encountered dishes as chicken tikka are done with unusual skill. Portion sizes are generous, and prices are fair for a Knightsbridge address, making this 'excellent value for money'. Service, though, can be untutored, if willing. The wine list makes a fair stab at recommending bottles to drink with various dishes; house Italian starts at £10.95. Downstairs from the restaurant is the Black Saffron Lounge, open for lighter bites and drinks.

CHEF: Ratan Singh   PROPRIETOR: Haandi Restaurants Ltd   OPEN: all week 12 to 3, 6 to 11 (11.30 Fri and Sat)   CLOSED: 25 Dec   MEALS: alc (main courses £6 to £13). Set L £7.95 to £13.95. Bar menu available   SERVICE: 12.5% (optional)   CARDS: Amex, Delta, Diners, MasterCard, Switch, Visa   DETAILS: 80 seats. 8 seats outside. Vegetarian meals. Music. Air-conditioned ⊖ Knightsbridge   £5

Hakkasan
map 15

8 Hanway Place, W1P 7DH	COOKING 5
TEL: (020) 7927 7000 FAX: (020) 7907 1889	CHINESE
	£47–£112

Few other restaurants manage such a Jekyll and Hyde persona. This is a celebrity hang-out in the evening and a place for great dim sum at lunchtime. Dark colours certainly contribute to the expensive nightclub feel; one couple turned up at 11.30pm, imagining the place might be winding down only to find it buzzing. If it looks like 'the epitome of modern chic', then the food matches it:

clean-tasting and light, with lots of fresh and zingy flavours. It seems to combine the freshness of Thai food, and Japanese attention to detail, with other elements from Malaysia, and even India.

The expanded range of lunchtime dim sum seems to have improved dramatically. Considered variously 'faultless', 'sublime' and 'exquisite', they are made with a combination of the freshest ingredients and immense skill. Among recommendations are the well-filled dumplings (prawn and enoki, scallop, bamboo with celery and wood ear), Alaskan snow crab wrapped in deep-fried vermicelli in XO sauce, scallop mei-roll, and baked venison puff. There are many unusual dishes not seen elsewhere, including a 'close-to-perfection' crispy duck and water chestnut puff with cardamom and fennel seed.

Standards of the repertoire are equally impressive, including prawn cheung fun (feather-light slippery noodles stuffed with four big fat juicy prawns apiece), and a revelatory light and fluffy dish of shredded turnip paste, crisp and golden outside, scattered through with little nuggets of char siu pork, garlic, ginger, onion and coriander. On the extensive carte, Pi pa duck is also a winner, with its thick, dense, livery breast meat and crisp, caramel-toffee skin, while salted fish and salted egg rice 'smelled of all the rotting fish in all the world but tasted divine'. Desserts are European and not up to the same standard, French and Chinese staff cope well, and there are some first-class wines but mark-ups are stiff, with nothing under £20. Eight wines by the glass (four of each) cost from £5.10 to £6.80 (£22 to £27 a bottle).

CHEF: Tong Chee Hwee   PROPRIETORS: Alan Yau and Partners   OPEN: all week 12 to 3.15 (4.30 Sat, Sun and bank hols), 6 to 11.30 (12 Thur to Sat)   MEALS: alc (main courses £8.50 to £55) SERVICE: 13%   CARDS: Amex, Delta, Diners, MasterCard, Switch, Visa   DETAILS: 190 seats. Vegetarian meals. Wheelchair access (also WC). Music. Air-conditioned

Highgate £

79 Highgate Road, NW5 1TL	COOKING 3
TEL: (020) 7485 8442 FAX: (020) 7482 0357	MODERN EUROPEAN
EMAIL: thehighgatebar@aol.com	£27–£48

The Highgate occupies what designers might call a 'difficult space' – a large converted warehouse with a busy bar and brasserie at ground level and a low-ceilinged restaurant downstairs. Some find the décor 'relaxing', others think it looks as though it was constructed from a flat-pack. Whatever, the food and the modest prices are generally of more interest to diners. The menus change weekly and may include starters such as a rustic-sounding terrine of smoked ham hock and confit chicken with pear and fig chutney, or a plate of Spanish charcuterie. Main courses tend to be straightforward, such as grilled organic sirloin steak with café de Paris butter, green beans and chips, or roast gilt-head bream with fennel, saffron and tomato. Desserts of bread-and-butter pudding and chocolate tart with vanilla ice cream are best described as classics. The short wine list is as modern and easy-going as the surroundings. House wines are £10.50, and the majority of bottles stay under £20, with a dozen sold in big 250ml glasses for £3.70 to £5.45.

CHEF: Jamie Polito   PROPRIETORS: James McDowell, Mark Slade, Nick Rouse and Jamie Polito OPEN: Mon to Fri L 12.30 to 3, Mon to Sat D 6.30 to 10.30   CLOSED: 25 to 27 Dec, 1 Jan   MEALS: alc (main courses £8.50 to £15.50). Bar menu available all week   SERVICE: 12.5% (optional), card slips closed   CARDS: Delta, MasterCard, Switch, Visa   DETAILS: 62 seats. 20 seats outside. Vegetarian meals. Children's helpings. No children after 8pm. No pipes. Music. Air-conditioned ⊖ Kentish Town (£5)

The House

NEW ENTRY

63–69 Canonbury Road, N1 2DG
TEL: (020) 7704 7410   FAX: (020) 7704 9388
EMAIL: info@inthehouse.biz
WEBSITE: www.inthehouse.biz

COOKING 2
MODERN EUROPEAN
£25–£61

On a corner in a quiet, leafy part of Canonbury, this popular gastro-pub is the haunt of a prosperous Islington crowd. The dining room at the back is a simple, cream-painted room, with modern prints, ceiling fans and wooden tables, with a hatch to the kitchen. The specials board and carte strike out on a modern, crowd-pleasing path that could pitch chargrilled rib of Buccleuch beef with a shallot crust, gratin dauphinois, green beans and jus gras alongside shepherd's pie. Parfait of foie gras and chicken livers with Armagnac and toasted brioche might precede sautéed cod with garlic and parsley mash and chorizo and saffron velouté. Valrhona hot chocolate pudding with coffee ice cream could head up desserts. The unorthodoxly laid out wine list has around ten by the glass (£2.60 to £4.75). Bottle prices open at £12.50.

CHEF: Jeremy Hollingsworth   PROPRIETOR: Barnaby Meredith   OPEN: Tue to Sun L 12 to 3.30, all week D 5.30 to 10.30 (9.30 Sun)   CLOSED: 24 to 27 Dec   MEALS: alc exc Sat and Sun L (main courses £9.50 to £20). Set L Sat and Sun £12.95 (2 courses) to £14.95, Set D Tue to Fri 5.30 to 7 £12.95 (2 courses) to £14.95   SERVICE: 12.5% (optional), card slips closed   CARDS: Delta, MasterCard, Switch, Visa   DETAILS: 100 seats. 100 seats outside. Private parties: 150 main room. Vegetarian meals. Children's helpings. No-smoking area. Wheelchair access (also WC). Music   ⊖ Highbury & Islington

Huong-Viet £

map 13

An-Viet House, 12–14 Englefield Road, N1 4LS
TEL: (020) 7249 0877

COOKING 1
VIETNAMESE
£23–£42

The premises are a Vietnamese Community Centre and home to this modest and very affordable canteen. Most of the staples of the native cuisine appear on the lengthy, 80-dish menu, including versions of canh and pho (traditional soups), wok-fried rice noodles, and 'wood charcoal BBQ dishes' (anything from tuna or kingfish in banana leaf to lamb with galangal). Appetisers range from fresh rolls with herbs in rice paper to pancakes with tofu; seafood might include tilapia and catfish, and there are a handful of desserts such as longans in syrup. The restaurant is now licensed, with house wine at £7.95; non-alcoholic alternatives include Vietnamese 'hot' coffee, jasmine tea and home-made lemonade.

CHEF: Thanh Vu   PROPRIETOR: Huong-Viet Ltd   OPEN: Mon to Sat 12 to 3.30 (4 Sat), 5.30 to 11   MEALS: alc (main courses £5 to £7). Set L £6 (2 courses), Set D £13 (min 4)   SERVICE: not inc L, 10% D, 12% for parties of 5 or more   CARDS: Delta, MasterCard, Switch, Visa   DETAILS: 60 seats. Private parties: 30 private room. Vegetarian meals. Children's helpings. Wheelchair access (also women's WC). Occasional music   ⊖ Angel, Liverpool Street

Incognico 🍞

map 15

117 Shaftesbury Avenue, WC2H 8AD
TEL: (020) 7836 8866   FAX: (020) 7240 9525

COOKING 4
FRENCH
£26–£87

The legendary chef Nico Ladenis may have fully retired from Incognico and Deca (see entry), but his legacy lives on in the restaurant's punning title. The style of cooking continues in the same vein, which is perhaps best described as classic French brasserie style. The venue has a degree of sombreness, all businesslike brown tones and dimmed lighting. Meals are likely to start with tapenade and crostini, and from there diners may move on to starters such as mille-feuille of cod brandade, served warm and properly fibrous, enhanced by the buttery flavour of the pastry. Foie gras may be served two ways: either in a terrine or as a lightly sautéed escalope, tenderly pink, topped with segments of caramelised orange. Dutch veal cutlet, served 'à la crème' with a thick, mushroomy, 'unutterably delicious' sauce, and confit of duck and a sweet stock-reduced sauce and lentils are typical of main courses. Timings are generally correct, and a fairly formidable degree of proficiency is in evidence in most dishes, although, at inspection, desserts were not as successful as previous courses. Although prices are by no means low, the set-price pre-theatre menu has been described as excellent value. Service is 'attentive and charming', and wines, mostly French, tend to be pricey. The cheapest is £15.50, and most bottles are over £20.

CHEF: Kirk Kirton   PROPRIETOR: Chez Nico Restaurants Ltd   OPEN: Mon to Sat 12 to 3, 5.30 to 12   CLOSED: 10 days Christmas, 4 days Easter, bank hol Mons   MEALS: alc (main courses £13.50 to £19.50). Set L and D 5.30 to 7 £12.50   SERVICE: 12.5% (optional), card slips closed   CARDS: Amex, Delta, Diners, MasterCard, Switch, Visa   DETAILS: 80 seats. Vegetarian meals. No pipes in dining room. Music. Air-conditioned   ⊖ Leicester Square

▲ InterContinental, Le Soufflé

map 14

1 Hamilton Place, W1V 0QY
TEL: (020) 7409 3131   FAX: (020) 7491 0926
WEBSITE: www.london.interconti.com

COOKING 5
MODERN EUROPEAN
£44–£94

Despite being located in a rather dim, windowless room, the ambience at Le Soufflé is surprisingly soothing. There's a white piano (which is played and sung along to with varying degrees of success), a plethora of mirrors and, on the white-clothed tables, a large assortment of posh silver cutlery and large glasses. The kitchen takes its duties seriously and menus have a fair number of luxury ingredients. Two menus – set-price and à la carte – operate in tandem. The former may feature a starter of seared foie gras with asparagus and girolles served in a tower, with a drizzle of creamy sauce. From the carte, a main course of herb-crusted lamb has been topped with a foie gras raviolo and surrounded by petits legumes – carrots, mini turnips, peas and celery in a foaming jus. 'Signature dishes' include roast 'osso buco' of monkfish served with caramelised button onions and salsify purée, and cumin roasted scallops and languoustines with cauliflower purée and thyme beurre blanc. A dedicated soufflé chef turns out savoury and sweet varieties, such as soufflé Grand Marnier or 'soufflés of the day' such as peach. Service is excellent, without being overly formal. France is the mainstay of the wine list, lining up rare bottles against more realistic options. Selections elsewhere are rather unadventurous and prices are high. Fourteen by the glass are £6 to £8.50.

CHEF: Michael Coaker PROPRIETOR: Intercontinental Hotels Group OPEN: Wed to Fri and Sun L 12.30 to 3, Wed to Sat D 7 to 10.30 (11.15 Sat) CLOSED: 26 to 30 Dec, bank hols MEALS: alc D (main courses £19.50 to £28). Set L £21.50 (2 courses) to £33.50, Set L Sun £33.50. Set D £40 to £47 SERVICE: not inc CARDS: Amex, Delta, Diners, MasterCard, Switch, Visa DETAILS: 70 seats. Private parties: 70 main room. Vegetarian meals. Children's helpings. No-smoking area. Wheelchair access (also WC). Music. No mobile phones. Air-conditioned ACCOMMODATION: 458 rooms, all with bath/shower. TV. Phone. Room only £129 to £320. Rooms for disabled. Baby facilities ⊖ Hyde Park Corner (£5)

Isola ♥ 🍴

145 Knightsbridge, SW1X 7PA
TEL: (020) 7838 1044 FAX: (020) 7838 1099

map 14

COOKING 4
ITALIAN
£29–£69

The impressive glass frontage of this shiny Knightsbridge restaurant gives way to an interior that's stylishly decked out in retro-1950s style, all chrome, black marble and spaciously arranged wooden tables. It's an atmospheric place, with industrious waiting staff resplendent in beige Nehru-style jackets and black trousers. New chef Mark Broadbent joined in June 2003, but the restaurant retains its Italian aspect, although what turns up on the plate may actually be more akin to modern European cooking. British ingredients such as Longhorn beef and Gloucester Old Spot pork pepper the menu, the latter perhaps turning up in a main course of pork confit with soft polenta and mostarda di frutta. Fish is handled well, as in carefully timed roast sea bass with wood-roast fennel and crushed olives, while starters might include an expertly made 'minestrone' of seafood, or a colourful, well-tuned dish of seared yellowfin tuna with parsley salad, vine tomato and fennel. Desserts such as wickedly dark Valrhona chocolate fondant with hazelnut fudge and mascarpone are followed by excellent cappuccino ('just like the best in Italy,' according to one visitor). The all-Italian wine list is a roll call of top producers and has a weakness for their premium offerings, managing to make even the south look pricey. A range of 30 by the glass (£3.40–£15.50) goes more than a little way to compensate, and 'taster trays' of five small glasses of white or red (£14 or £19) are a tempting option.

CHEF: Mark Broadbent PROPRIETOR: Oliver Peyton OPEN: Mon to Sat 12 to 2.45, 6 to 10.45 MEALS: alc D (main courses £9.50 to £22.50). Set L £15 (2 courses) to £18.50, Set D 6 to 7 £14 (2 courses) to £16.50. Bar menu available SERVICE: 12.5% (optional), card slips closed CARDS: Amex, Delta, MasterCard, Switch, Visa DETAILS: 144 seats. Private parties: 200 main room. Vegetarian meals. No-smoking area. Wheelchair access (also WC). Music. Air-conditioned ⊖ Knightsbridge

---

Dining rooms where music, either live or recorded, is never played are signalled by No music *in the details at the end of an entry.*

Istanbul Iskembecisi ✻ £

map 12

9 Stoke Newington Road, N16 8BH
TEL: (020) 7254 7291

COOKING 2
TURKISH
£15–£34

'Iskembe' is a traditional tripe soup to which you add salt, vinegar, lemon juice and pepper to suit your taste. It's just one of the gutsy Turkish delights that keeps customers thronging to this Stoke Newington neighbourhood restaurant till the early hours of the morning. The menu also has its quota of meze, from cacik (diced cucumber with yoghurt, garlic and mint) to kalamar (deep-fried squid 'served with its white sauce'), as well as a few gatecrashers such as prawn cocktail and avocado topped with cod roe purée. Kebabs, grills, slow-cooked stews and casseroles dominate the main courses (chicken iskender is 'bedded on pitta bread' with tomato sauce, yoghurt and parsley), and there's plenty for vegetarians. Zoom in on Buzbag and other Turkish wines for real authenticity; prices from £8.50.

CHEF: Murat Demir   PROPRIETOR: Ali Demir   OPEN: all week noon to 5am   MEALS: alc (main courses £6.50 to £10). Set L £5 (2 courses) to £7.50   SERVICE: not inc, card slips closed   CARDS: Delta, MasterCard, Switch, Visa   DETAILS: 95 seats. Private parties: 95 main room. Vegetarian meals. Children's helpings. No smoking in 1 dining room. Wheelchair access (not WC). Music. Air-conditioned   ⊖ Highbury & Islington (£5)

Itsu/Itsu (Soho) 🍞 ✻

118 Draycott Avenue, SW3 3AE
TEL: (020) 7590 2400   FAX: (020) 7590 2403
103 Wardour Street, W1V 3TD
TEL: (020) 7479 4790   FAX: (020) 4794795
WEBSITE: www.itsu.co.uk

COOKING 3
JAPANESE
£29–£41

Fashionable, up-to-the-minute and totally informal – no wonder these two siblings have lost none of their vigour or appeal. Music booms out, turnover is fast, and the whole set-up runs like clockwork. Kaitens (conveyor belts) hold centre stage and customers simply pick and choose from the colour-coded plates that pass by with relentless regularity. Japan may have inspired the concept, but the menu moves rapidly from classic sushi and sashimi based on salmon, tuna and eel into the eclectic world of chicken, coconut and galangal soup, Chinese broccoli salad with oyster dressing, and seared fillet of beef with shallot sauce. Other dishes are made to order: use your red button if you fancy chicken teriyaki, grilled tiger prawns with chilli salmon, or crispy handrolls. By contrast, desserts are unashamedly European – Valrhona chocolate mousse or crème brûlée, for example. Drink saké or a 'smart' beverage such as Moondance (fresh lemonade with iced ginger tea); there's also a minimal wine list from £12.95. A third branch is at Cabot Place East, Canary Wharf; tel: (020) 7512 9911.

CHEFS: Roberto Campana (Draycott) Angela Baird (Soho)   PROPRIETORS: Clive Schlee and Julian Metcalfe   OPEN: all week 12 to 11 (10 Sun)   CLOSED: 25 Dec and 1 Jan (Soho only)   MEALS: alc (sushi £2.50 to £3.75; take-away boxes £2.95 to £9.95; sashimi selections £9.95)   SERVICE: not inc, card slips closed   CARDS: Amex, Delta (exc Soho), MasterCard, Switch, Visa   DETAILS: 67

seats. Private parties: 50 main room (Draycott); 80 seats. Private parties: 100 main room (Soho). Vegetarian meals. No smoking in dining room. Wheelchair access (not WC). Music. Air-conditioned   ⊖ South Kensington (Draycott), Piccadilly Circus (Soho)

Ivy   map 15

1–5 West Street, WC2H 9NQ	COOKING 4
TEL: (020) 7836 4751 FAX: (020) 7240 9333	MODERN BRITISH
	£31–£93

You will already have heard that the legendary Ivy is a stargazing paradise, full of staff catering to luminaries of the stage, screen and dispatch box, but 'be assured' (offers a regular reporter) 'that mere mortals can book tables here too' – although you will have to wait in a telephone queuing system in order to do so. Expect rapidly turned tables, which chase the opening times of surrounding theatres, and unsentimentally brisk, efficient service.

The food has to vie for attention amid the throng, and the kitchen is able to satisfy without ever reaching the stars. A simple tart of leeks and girolles has plenty of flavour and bite, a sauté of Tuscan porcini with wild garlic on puntalette pasta is rich and savoury, and dressed in good olive oil, and late spring brings asparagus treated to nothing other than vinaigrette. The right mix of culinary styles among main courses introduces Thai-style sea bass with fragrant rice and a soy dip, the fish still wrapped in its banana leaf, or roast poulet des Landes with truffled jus and dauphinois potatoes. It is undoubtedly the quality of the raw materials that elevates these dishes above their inherent simplicity, an impression made again in the form of an oozingly rich date-studded sticky toffee pudding, or a savoury finisher such as crumbled creamy dolcelatte with pickled plum tomatoes. The French-led wine list provides some sound drinking at inevitably West End prices. A dozen sold by the glass start at £4.75, with bottle prices opening at £11.75.

CHEFS: Alan Bird and Tim Hughes   PROPRIETOR: Signature Restaurants plc   OPEN: all week 12 to 3 (3.30 Sun), 5.30 to 12   CLOSED: 25 and 26 Dec, 1 Jan, Aug bank hol   MEALS: alc (main courses £9.50 to £29.50). Set L Sat and Sun £18.50. Cover £1.50   SERVICE: not inc   CARDS: Amex, Delta, Diners, MasterCard, Switch, Visa   DETAILS: 100 seats. Private parties: 25 to 60 private rooms. Vegetarian meals. Wheelchair access (not WC). No music. Air-conditioned   ⊖ Leicester Square

Iznik £   map 13

19 Highbury Park, N5 1QJ	COOKING 2
TEL: (020) 7704 8099 FAX: (020) 7354 5697	TURKISH
	£21–£32

'Still as atmospheric and stylish as ever,' noted a regular visitor to the Oners' enchanting and welcoming Turkish restaurant, with its array of artefacts and tiny lamps flickering in the dining room. For sustaining daytime nourishment, the same reporter recommends an enormous dish of rich, filling soup (often lentil) served in 'a pint pot' with olive oil swirled on the surface and warm pitta bread on the side. Everything is remarkable value, and you can feast happily on the selection of meze, which includes patlikan salata (mashed aubergines with yoghurt and garlic), diced liver fried with paprika, and much more. Kebabs and slow-cooked stews based on lamb and chicken dominate main courses, but there are fish and vegetarian options too. Bramble mousse is the restaurant's signature dessert; otherwise look for traditional delights like revani (semolina cake drenched in syrup). Turkish house wine is £9.95.

CHEFS/PROPRIETORS: Adem and Pirlanta Oner OPEN: all week 10 to 3, 6.30 to 11 MEALS: alc (main courses £6.50 to £9.50) SERVICE: 10% CARDS: Delta, MasterCard, Switch, Visa DETAILS: 72 seats. Private parties: 72 main room. Vegetarian meals. Wheelchair access (not WC). Music ⊖ Highbury & Islington

J. Sheekey

map 15

28–32 St Martin's Court, WC2N 4AL
TEL: (020) 7240 2565 FAX: (020) 7240 8114

COOKING 4
BRITISH/SEAFOOD
£31–£105

J. Sheekey is one of those places that divides opinion. While some reporters rave about the restaurant's 'all-round excellence', others are less enthralled. All agree, however, that the entrance to the restaurant – a favoured celeb-spotting venue, for what it's worth – is more than a little bit gloomy, but that, once inside, the labyrinthine rooms and the 'general feeling of comfort' mean all that is forgotten. The carte has a bistro-like appearance, as do many of the dishes, such as salmon fishcake with sorrel sauce, and fish pie. In addition to British fishy staples such as jellied eels, oysters (two sorts) and, for the deep-pocketed, beluga caviar with blinis and sour cream, several daily specials may include grilled Cornish turbot with béarnaise sauce, or fillet of wild halibut with smoked salmon, cabbage and girolles.

'Meat dishes also available' notes the carte, and there is a separate vegan and vegetarian menu (including dishes such as Sicilian tomatoes with shredded fennel). Desserts may range from old-fashioned English (as in spotted dick) to old-fashioned American (chocolate cookies and brownies). Service, by a 'well-drilled team', headed up by an 'old-style maître d'', knows when to flatter with attention and when to play it cool. Wines, mostly French, are pretty pricey, starting at £12.75 for Trebbiano and moving up swiftly to three figures.

CHEFS: Elliot Ketley and Tim Hughes PROPRIETOR: Signature Group plc OPEN: all week 12 to 3 (3.30 Sun), 5.30 to 12 CLOSED: bank hols MEALS: alc (main courses £10 to £30). Set L Sat and Sun £14.75 (2 courses) to £18.50. Cover £1.50 SERVICE: not inc CARDS: Amex, Delta, Diners, MasterCard, Switch, Visa DETAILS: 105 seats. Vegetarian meals. No cigars/pipes in dining room. Wheelchair access (not WC). No music. No mobile phones. Air-conditioned ⊖ Leicester Square

K10 ⁵⁄✳ £

map 13

20 Copthall Avenue, EC2R 7DN
TEL: (020) 7562 8510 FAX: (020) 7562 8515
WEBSITE: www.k10.net

COOKING 2
JAPANESE
£19–£34

The name is a pun on 'kaiten', the conveyor belt that snakes around the long, slim rectangular basement room bearing colourful plates of sushi and sashimi. They are in stark contrast to the Spartan décor, but the atmosphere is animated enough and service cheerful and helpful. Overall, standards are high and value good compared with similar establishments in the City. Our inspector enjoyed a range of traditional dishes, including 'very fresh' salmon sashimi, crisp-skinned eel nigiri and crisp tempura prawns. Some of the more inventive items have not been so successful, but seared tuna with miso and mustard vinaigrette has been a hit, along with seared swordfish in spicy garlic and soy dressing with caramelised orange zest. Drink green tea, Japanese beer, saké, or one of the handful of wines (from £12.50 a bottle).

CHEF: Miguel Choy   PROPRIETOR: Christopher Kemper   OPEN: Mon to Fri 11.30 to 2.45, 5 to 9.45 CLOSED: Christmas, bank hols   MEALS: alc (main courses £2.50 to £4.50)   SERVICE: not inc, card slips closed   CARDS: Amex, Delta, Diners, MasterCard, Switch, Visa   DETAILS: 65 seats. Private parties: 100 main room. Vegetarian meals. No smoking. Music. Air-conditioned   ⊖ Moorgate, Liverpool Street

Kastoori £ map 12

188 Upper Tooting Road, SW17 7EJ
TEL: (020) 8767 7027

COOKING 3
GUJARATI VEGETARIAN
£19–£30

A Tooting stalwart since 1987, the excellent Gujarati cooking at Kastoori goes from strength to strength. The all-vegetarian menu also shows some East African influences, highlighted in the list of 'Thanki family specials' that date back to the time the family spent in Uganda. Starters include such dishes as bhel puri, bite-sized flavour bombs, combining puffed rice, potatoes, sev and onions with a tangy sweet-and-sour sauce. Curries, such as potato, chickpea and mung bean, are characterised by spicing that is of the clear, distinct kind that you only get through the use of freshly ground spices. These are complemented by fine bhatura bread, served puffed into a sphere, and plain and pilau rice. Care and attention is shown in the home-made chutneys. Kastoori is also one of the few places in the capital to serve shrikand as a dessert; their well-textured version of the curd cheese-based sweet has a rich flavour enhanced by cardamom, nutmeg and saffron and is topped with pistachios. The respectable and fairly priced wine list (prices start at £7.95) has a range of 24 bottles, including Omar Khayyam sparkling wine from India.

CHEF: Manoj Thanki   PROPRIETOR: Dinesh Thanki   OPEN: Wed to Sun L 12.30 to 2.30, all week D 6 to 10.30   CLOSED: 25 and 26 Dec, 1 week mid Jan   MEALS: alc (main courses £4.75 to £6). Thalis £8.50 to £16.25   SERVICE: not inc, card slips closed   CARDS: Delta, MasterCard, Visa DETAILS: 82 seats. Private parties: 20 main room. Vegetarian meals. Children's helpings. Wheelchair access (not WC). Music. No mobile phones. Air-conditioned   ⊖ Tooting Broadway

Kensington Place ▼ map 13

201 Kensington Church Street, W8 7LX
TEL: (020) 7727 3184   FAX: (020) 7229 2025
EMAIL: kpr@place-restaurants.co.uk
WEBSITE: www.egami.co.uk

COOKING 5
MODERN BRITISH
£30–£77

A Kensington landmark since the 1980s, Rowley Leigh's pace-setting restaurant has never lacked for enthusiastic, solid support. That is partly what lends it its air of confidence and assurance – that, and having been at the cutting-edge of metropolitan food fashion from the very moment of its inception. The space may not be to everyone's taste – it is a booming warehouse of a place decorated in industrial kitsch – but the service can be warmer than its reputation suggests, the menu is never less than enticing, and the wine list is a delight.

All this was confirmed again at inspection. A daily special that consisted of strips of raw salmon marinated in Japanese soy sauce with shallots, ginger and garlic represented a finely balanced intermingling of flavours. Fish main courses are well handled, too: a piece of good hake fillet is teamed with Puy lentils in lemon cream on a bed of spinach, all the components pulling together into an expressive whole. Lightness and directness continue to be the watchwords, delivering a simple fixed-price lunch dish of veal escalope with mousserons, sautéed with garlic and parsley. Vegetarian options might include artichokes and courgettes stuffed with ricotta, basil and lemon. An enterprising dessert made up of strips of grilled pineapple in a sauce of star anise and chilli, including cooked chilli slices, was a resounding triumph, the heat of the sauce offset by outstandingly fresh coconut ice cream. The wine list is an equally assured leader of the modern style, arranged by style and variety with minimum fuss. Quality is high, pricing not too bad and a few mature vintages add weight to the modish range. House bottles are around £14, and over 20 tempting options come by the glass (£4 to £11.25), plus a range of sherries.

CHEF: Rowley Leigh   PROPRIETORS: Moving Image Restaurants and Rowley Leigh   OPEN: all week 12 to 3.30, 6.30 to 11.45 (10.15 Sun)   MEALS: alc (main courses £13.50 to £19.50). Set L Mon to Fri £16.50, Set L Sun £18.50, Set D Mon to Fri £24.50 to £39.50 (inc wine)   SERVICE: 12.5% (optional), card slips closed   CARDS: Amex, MasterCard, Switch, Visa   DETAILS: 150 seats. Private parties: 120 main room, 12 to 45 private rooms. Vegetarian meals. Children's helpings. Wheelchair access (also WC). No music. Air-conditioned   ⊖ Notting Hill Gate   (£5)

Kiku
map 15

17 Half Moon Street, W1J 7BE
TEL: (020) 7499 4208   FAX: (020) 7409 3259

COOKING 3
JAPANESE
£23–£88

Stylistic simplicity is the watchword at this spacious Mayfair Japanese restaurant. Think chrome, stone, bamboo, blond wood and blinds. Service is smiling and willing to guide diners around the menu, which focuses on set meals and noodle dishes at lunchtimes but covers a broader range in the evenings. The dinner menu lists a wide selection of sushi, 'which will not disappoint', as well as sashimi, grilled and fried dishes, casseroles and soups, plus set dinners of ten to twelve courses. From the carte, agedashi tofu (deep-fried cubes of bean curd in a soy-based sauce) is accompanied by 'a healthy serving of grated daikon', and shabu-shabu – lean and tender Scottish beef fillet cooked in traditional 'steamboat' style – has been described as 'slow food at its best', served with Chinese leaves, shiitake mushrooms and baby turnips: 'an excellent version'. Wines tend towards pricey red Bordeaux and white Burgundy, but house wines are £12.50.

CHEFS: Y. Hattori, H. Yamauchi and T. Nishimura   PROPRIETORS: Hisashi and Mariko Taoka   OPEN: Mon to Sat L 12 to 2.30, all week D 6 to 10.15 (5.30 to 9.45 Sun and bank hols)   CLOSED: 25 and 26 Dec, 1 Jan   MEALS: alc (main courses £15 to £32). Set L £12 to £23, Set D £42 to £60

SERVICE: 12.5% (optional), card slips closed   CARDS: Amex, Diners, MasterCard, Switch, Visa
DETAILS: 96 seats. Private parties: 8 to 10 private rooms. Vegetarian meals. Wheelchair access
(also WC). Music. Air-conditioned   ⊖ Green Park £5

Kulu Kulu Sushi £   map 15

76 Brewer Street, W1F 9TX   COOKING 2
TEL: (020) 7734 7316   FAX: (020) 7734 6507   JAPANESE
                                                            £21–£39

Kulu Kulu remains a trusted place for decent sushi, delivered by conveyor belt.
Don't expect the most creative and contemporary take on Japanese cooking, and
ignore the slightly tired décor of the compact dining room, but enjoy the good-
quality traditional sushi and sashimi, as well as a decent range of
straightforward cooked dishes. Uniformly good nigiri include squid, mackerel,
octopus, eel, scallops, turbot and salmon roe; chilli tuna roll is a riot of colour;
deep-fried salmon is crisp on the outside, moist within; and a handroll of
salmon, avocado and tempura prawn has been a highlight. Help yourself to free
green tea; there is also a small selection of soft drinks, beers and saké, with house
wine £3.60 a glass, £12 a bottle. The second branch at 39 Thurloe Place, SW7, tel.
(020) 7589 2225, is to be joined by a third at 51–53 Shelton Street, WC2.

CHEF: Mr S. Kandsamy   PROPRIETOR: Mr K. Toyama   OPEN: Mon to Sat 12 to 2.30 (3.30 Sat), 5 to
10   CLOSED: bank hols   MEALS: alc (sushi £1.20 to £13)   SERVICE: not inc   CARDS: Delta,
MasterCard, Switch, Visa   DETAILS: 30 seats. Music. Air-conditioned   ⊖ Piccadilly Circus

Langan's Brasserie   map 15

Stratton Street, W1J 8LB   COOKING 1
TEL: (020) 7491 8822   FAX: (020) 7493 8309   ANGLO-FRENCH
WEBSITE: www.langansrestaurants.co.uk   £42–£73

The legendary Langan's is still full almost every night, and though the big stars
have moved on to more fashionable haunts there's always a happy buzz in the
air. Despite being packed in, tables are well spaced and set with crisp napery
and sparkling glasses, while service is highly polished. Spinach soufflé, bubble
and squeak, bangers and mash, and roast duck with sage and onion stuffing are
at the heart of the extensive repertoire of old-fashioned British brasserie fare.
Praise has come in for 'wholesome and tasty' mushrooms with Cheddar cheese,
pitta bread stuffed with grilled lamb, fillet steak with rösti, sea bass fillet in a
creamy sauce with mash and spinach, and 'excellent quality' lamb chops with a
light mint sauce, though some reporters have noted variable standards. Decent
house wines at £14 head up a concise list.

CHEFS: Ken Whitehead, Roy Smith and Dennis Mynott   PROPRIETOR: Richard Shepherd   OPEN:
Mon to Fri 12.15 to 11.45, Sat D only 7 to 12   CLOSED: bank hols   MEALS: alc (main courses
£13.50 to £18.50). Cover £1.50   SERVICE: 12.5% (optional)   CARDS: Amex, Delta, Diners,
MasterCard, Switch, Visa   DETAILS: 240 seats. Vegetarian meals. Children's helpings.
Wheelchair access (not WC). Music. Air-conditioned   ⊖ Green Park

✳ indicates there are some restrictions on smoking, though it is not banned altogether.

Lansdowne

map 13

90 Gloucester Avenue, NW1 8HX
TEL: (020) 7483 0409

COOKING 2
MODERN BRITISH
£33–£55

The Lansdowne, an infectiously buzzy hostelry in well-to-do Primrose Hill, was among the first of London's gastro-pubs. You eat either in the spacious ground-floor bar amid mismatched furniture and the drinks-only crowd, with the menu chalked above the bar, or upstairs in a slightly more formal atmosphere. Modern European culinary modes take in pizzette topped with bresaola, ricotta, parsley and truffle oil, and ravioli of pork, capers and herbs in lemon and rocket broth, but the menu – which changes daily – also finds room for 'succulent' grilled Welsh ribeye with chips and tartare sauce, and baked salmon with fennel, albeit seasoned with garlic, chilli and star anise. Finish with chocolate and pecan brownie or Greek yoghurt bavarois. Service, it is reported, can be chilly and unconcerned, which doesn't seem in keeping at all. The short wine list opens at £11.50 for a white Sicilian blend (£2.90 a glass).

CHEF: James Knight   PROPRIETOR: Amanda Pritchett   OPEN: Sun L 1 to 3, Tue to Sat D 7 to 10
CLOSED: 24 Dec to 3 Jan   MEALS: alc (main courses L £9.50 to £13.50, D £9.50 to £16). Bar menu
also available   SERVICE: 12.5%, card slips closed   CARDS: Delta, MasterCard, Switch, Visa
DETAILS: 55 seats. Private parties: 60 main room. Vegetarian meals. Music. No mobile phones
⊖ Chalk Farm

Launceston Place ▾

map 14

1A Launceston Place, W8 5RL
TEL: (020) 7937 6912   FAX: (020) 7938 2412

COOKING 2
MODERN BRITISH
£33–£64

Situated in a quiet side street in a well-to-do part of town, Launceston Place has an air of understated exclusivity, thanks to its atmospheric series of small linked rooms, and linen-clothed tables set with flowers and quality glassware. It is very popular with the locals. Cooking is typically modern British, in that it blends old ideas with new and takes inspiration from here, there and everywhere. Expect starters ranging from twice-baked goats' cheese soufflé with poached plums to grilled spicy squid with Thai salad. To follow, there may be pan-fried lemon sole on a mound of spinach with tartare sauce and matchstick chips, or crisp-skinned confit duck leg with spring onions and coriander-flecked potatoes, and to finish, classic tarte Tatin with prune and Armagnac ice cream, or chocolate pudding with clotted cream. Service is pleasant and courteous. The succinct wine list sticks to mainstream grape varieties and concentrates on quality. Whites are mostly Chardonnay (Burgundy complemented by a round-up of notable New World examples) and Sauvignon Blanc, while Bordeaux styles lead the reds. Prices are not the cheapest: bottles start at £15 and seven by the glass are £4.95–£6.95.

CHEF: Philip Reed   PROPRIETOR: Moving Image Ltd   OPEN: Sun to Fri L 12.30 to 2.30, all week D 7
to 11.30 (10 Sun)   CLOSED: 24 to 26 Dec, 1 Jan, Easter   MEALS: alc (main courses £15 to £18).
Set L £15.50 (2 courses) to £18.50   SERVICE: 12.5% (optional), card slips closed   CARDS: Amex,

Delta, Diners, MasterCard, Switch, Visa   DETAILS: 85 seats. Private parties: 30 main room, 2 to 14 private rooms. Vegetarian meals. No pipes. Wheelchair access (not WC). No music. Air-conditioned   ⊖ Gloucester Road

Light House   map 12

75–77 Ridgway, Wimbledon, SW19 4ST   COOKING 3
TEL: (020) 8944 6338   FAX: (020) 8946 4440   MODERN EUROPEAN
                                                                  £29–£57

It may not be a lighthouse, but it sure is a light house: enormous windows let the rays flood in, and pale wood and walls add to the airy atmosphere. The menu, set out in the Italian style – antipasti, primi and so on – demonstrates influences from further afield as well as some serious ambition in the kitchen. Black-bean marinated mozzarella with pickled carrots and Thai salad, and roast quail with aubergine and Parmesan patty are two ways to kick off a meal. Main courses might, at first glance, seem a little more familiar: pan-fried sea bass with tabbouleh, for example, but the accompanying watermelon rind pickle shows invention – likewise Aberdeen Angus pavé with pancetta and fonseca plums. At dessert stage, 'too heavy' panettone bread and butter pudding was a disappointment, but almond cantucci dunked in a glass of Vin Santo might just hit the spot. The short wine list takes a trip around the globe with little of interest below £25, although there are ten wines on offer by the glass. Bottle prices start at £13, £3.50 a glass.

CHEF: Michael Mannion   PROPRIETORS: Bob Finch and Ian Taylor   OPEN: all week 12 to 2.30 (3 Sun), Mon to Sat D 6.30 to 10.30   CLOSED: Christmas, Easter   MEALS: alc (main courses £10 to £16). Set L 12.50 (2 courses), Set L Sun £17 (2 courses)   SERVICE: 12.5%, card slips closed CARDS: Amex, Delta, Diners, MasterCard, Switch, Visa   DETAILS: 75 seats. Private parties: 75 main room. Vegetarian meals. No-smoking area. Wheelchair access (also WC). Occasional music. No mobile phones   ⊖ Wimbledon

Lightship Ten   map 13

5A St Katharine's Way,
St Katharine Docks, E1W 1LP
TEL: (020) 7481 3123   FAX: (020) 7702 0338   NEW CHEF
EMAIL: info@lightshipx.com   MODERN EUROPEAN
WEBSITE: www.lightshipx.com   £34–£62

This nineteenth-century sailing vessel, now docked at the gentrified wharves of St Katherine Docks, is certainly an unusual venue. There's a bar upstairs, while the dining room, all varnished wood enhanced by white linen tablecloths, is below decks. As this edition of the Guide was going to press, Jean Pierre Venturini, formerly the sous-chef, was in the process of taking over as head chef. As he's been on board, so to speak, for some time, it may be that the Scandinavian-inflected modern European approach to cooking will continue, but, assuming all goes well, we will have more to report in next year's edition. House wines start at £12.50.

CHEF: Jean Pierre Venturini   PROPRIETOR: Lightship Restaurant Ltd   OPEN: all week 12 to 10 (7 Sun)   CLOSED: Christmas and New Year   MEALS: alc (main courses £10 to £18). Bar menu also available   SERVICE: 12.5% (optional), card slips closed   CARDS: Amex, Delta, MasterCard, Switch, Visa   DETAILS: 60 seats. 60 outside. Private parties: 60 main room. Vegetarian meals. No children under 5. Music. Air-conditioned   ⊖ Tower Hill (£5)

Lindsay House

map 15

21 Romilly Street, W1D 5AF

TEL: (020) 7439 0450   FAX: (020) 7437 7349

WEBSITE: www.lindsayhouse.co.uk

COOKING **7**

MODERN BRITISH

£41–£83

Old fireplaces and original cornices combine with rough wooden floors, fabric blinds, cream walls and a few big paintings to achieve 'a country-house feel in the middle of London'. There are two dining rooms, one above the other, where a seven-course no-choice tasting menu vies for attention with a generous three-course one (there are cheaper versions for lunch and pre-theatre). Descriptions are straightforward, and there is lots to tempt.

Seasonality is a characteristic of the output, taking in grouse and partridge in autumn, and in spring a plate of three tiny white asparagus spears accompanied by morels, langoustines, and a deeply flavoured shellfish sauce. Fish is well treated too, judging by fresh, moist, accurately timed line-caught sea bass at inspection, accompanied by a fine lobster raviolo and pieces of chicken with a bone handle poked in, looking like 'chicken lollipops'. The food may not have quite the direct and earthy appeal of its earlier days, but such skilful cooking as this, applied to fine materials, ensures a high success rate. A portion of well-timed creamy cauliflower risotto is topped with wafer-thin slices of crunchy cauliflower and first-class crisply-fried pancetta; this may not be particularly original, but it is certainly well executed, just like another contemporary favourite, scallops with pork belly, in this case employing three fat, juicy scallops, a little oriental spicing and a splurge of carrot purée.

Desserts are a positive delight too, taking in thin slivers of pineapple moulded around a ball of tapioca, with a scoop of coconut sorbet and an upbeat mint and chilli syrup; and triangles of dark chocolate 'biscuit' with a light orange flavour, jammed together like a sandwich with the aid of a thick chocolate cream, served with a pure white ball of buttermilk ice cream and cracked pistachio. Service has been eccentric, while house wine starts at £23, or £7.50 a glass (no wine list was provided). First-timers note you must ring the doorbell to get into the place.

CHEF: Richard Corrigan   PROPRIETOR: Corrigan Restaurants Ltd   OPEN: Mon to Fri L 12 to 2.30, Mon to Sat D 6 to 11   CLOSED: 1 week Christmas, 2 weeks summer   MEALS: alc (main courses £21 to £25). Set L £23, Set pre-theatre D 6 to 7.15 £24.50 (2 courses) to £29.50, Set D £48 to £56 (whole table only)   SERVICE: 12.5% (optional), card slips closed   CARDS: Amex, Delta, Diners, MasterCard, Switch, Visa   DETAILS: 120 seats. Private parties: 35 main room, 4 to 35 private rooms. Vegetarian meals. Children's helpings. No-smoking area. No music. No mobile phones. Air-conditioned   ⊖ Leicester Square, Piccadilly Circus

---

If a restaurant is new to the Guide this year (did not appear as a main entry in the last edition), **NEW ENTRY** *appears opposite its name.*

Locanda Locatelli ▼

map 15

8 Seymour Street, W1H 7JZ
TEL: (020) 7935 9088   FAX: (020) 7935 1149
EMAIL: info@locandalocatelli.com
WEBSITE: www.locandalocatelli.com

COOKING **6**
ITALIAN
£49–£87

This fashionable Italian restaurant may lack the simple rustic charm that characterised Giorgio Locatelli's previous enterprise Zafferano, but it is hard to complain about the level of comfort or quality of the décor. Stylish and elegant, 'retro yet contemporary', the handsome and spacious dining room is done out in neutral coffee colours, shielded from the outside world by lattice screens, with room dividers to break up the space, and with large concave mirrors providing a distorted bird's eye view of everything. Not all experiences are equally happy – both food and service lapse from time to time, and the chaotic booking system endears itself to no one. The best dishes, though, are outstanding. Supremely fresh seafood is a hallmark, taking in juicy scallops simply paired with potato purée and 'lashings of saffron'; chunky brill with green olives and tomatoes; and roast Dover sole on the bone, accompanied by a mirepoix of peas, Risina beans, green beans and pearl barley, enlivened with an invigorating, benchmark pesto. This is simple, ingredient-led cooking of a high order. Preparation and seasoning of pasta dishes at inspection left something to be desired, but meat dishes have included roast rabbit with Parma ham and polenta, and a fine piece of dense, dark, flavourful chargrilled steak (correctly timed) served with onions, turnip tops and 'sublime' crisply fried baby artichoke.

Desserts are impressively rendered: a harmonious combination of almond fondant with pistachio, chestnut ice cream and apricot compote, for example, or a distinctive 'soup' of chocolate milkshake elevated by an ingenious combination of honeycomb and hazelnut praline. The bread selection is first-class, and service from well-dressed waiters is discreet, courteous and generally efficient and professional. The all-Italian wine list picks up a few simple bottles here, a few stars there, but saves its passions for Piedmont and Tuscany, where it rolls out multiple vintages of top Barolos, Barbarescos and Super-Tuscans. Just a handful come in under £20, and 15 by the glass are £4.50–£13. Grappa is another speciality, with 15 by the glass.

CHEFS: Giorgio Locatelli and Federico Sali   PROPRIETORS: Giorgio and Plaxy Locatelli   OPEN: Mon to Sat 12 to 3 (3.30 Sat), 7 to 11 (11.30 Fri and Sat)   MEALS: alc (main courses £18 to £27.50)   SERVICE: not inc, card slips closed   CARDS: Amex, Delta, MasterCard, Switch, Visa   DETAILS: 84 seats. Vegetarian meals. Children's helpings. No cigars/pipes. Wheelchair access (also WC). Occasional music. Air-conditioned   ⊖ Marble Arch

---

Lola's ▼ 🍞

map 13

The Mall, 359 Upper Street, N1 0PD
TEL: (020) 7359 1932   FAX: (020) 7359 2209
EMAIL: lolas@lolas.co.uk

COOKING **5**
MODERN EUROPEAN
£30–£63

At the heart of Islington, on the upper level of a converted tram shed, now an antiques market, Lola's has a relaxed atmosphere. Simple décor is enlivened with bright touches including a Moorish mosaic, and tables are widely spaced and smartly dressed with white cloths and single candles in glass holders. A period of flux in the kitchen has seen chefs come and go in rapid succession; currently at the helm is Elisha Carter, who has previously worked at Foliage and Putney Bridge (see entries). The changes seem to have occasioned a few slips in the otherwise clockwork operation, but the kitchen has maintained high standards, as an inspection meal demonstrated, opening with a tangy appetiser of tomato consommé with feta and basil. Though dishes tend to be more complex than the menu may lead you to expect, the cooking is generally characterised by lightness and delicacy, and flavours are well balanced, as in a starter of morel mushrooms stuffed with creamy chicken mousse and placed on a frothy morel-flavoured broth with asparagus tips and broad beans. This might be followed by poached turbot on a bed of tortellini with smoked salmon mousse and warm cucumber, plus warm smoked salmon topped with slivers of scallop, or perhaps veal fillet with its kidneys and sweetbreads, topped with strongly spiced chorizo, wild mushrooms, leeks and another frothy broth. A pre-dessert of smooth basil crème with raspberry jelly might precede lavender-infused strawberry soup with goats' cheese pannacotta – a refreshing way to end a meal.

If you fancy yourself as an expert wine taster, try the 'Flight of Tiresius' (£8.75) – three wines are served 'blind' and if you are 50 per cent right when you guess the grapes and the regions, you win a bottle to take home. Fun and experimentation are the forces that drive this eclectic list, with 16 choices by the glass (£3–£8.50), good sherries, a page of 'offbeat' bottles and, at its heart, an exciting and individual international range.

CHEF: Elisha Carter   PROPRIETOR: Morfudd Richards   OPEN: all week 12 to 2.30 (3 Sat and Sun), 6 to 11 (7 to 10 Sun)   CLOSED: 25 and 26 Dec, bank hols   MEALS: alc (main courses £13 to £19.50). Set L £15 (2 courses) to £18.25. Cover £1   SERVICE: not inc, 12.5% (optional) for parties of 5 or more   CARDS: Amex, Delta, Diners, MasterCard, Switch, Visa   DETAILS: 70 seats. Private parties: 8 to 14 private rooms. Vegetarian meals. No music. Air-conditioned   ⊖ Angel

Lou Pescadou

map 13

241 Old Brompton Road, SW5 9HP
TEL: (020) 7370 1057   FAX: (020) 7244 7545

COOKING 3
SEAFOOD
£21–£51

This long-established French seafood restaurant has had a facelift. Once awash with nautical bric-à-brac and fishing nets, it is now given over to contemporary understatement, with a few colourful prints of French scenes on the pale yellow walls. The famous porthole window, however, has been retained. Fruits de mer are the order of the day, every day, perhaps best sampled in the form of a generously plentiful first-course plateau bearing a whole crab in the shell, fat langoustines, brown shrimps, whelks, clams and oysters, 'all utterly fresh and singing of the sea'. Fried crumb-coated calamari are sweet and succulent, and come with fine home-made tartare sauce. There are meat main courses for those who fancy getting their teeth into a daube of venison, or duck pot-roasted with raspberry vinegar, but stars of the show are undoubtedly the fish specials, such as a whole roasted grey bream, cooked so that it slides readily off the bone, and served with a provençale sauce of tomatoes, onions and anchoïade that doesn't in the slightest overwhelm the fish itself. To finish, there may be croustillant aux fruits rouges, a light filo tart heaped up with strawberries, raspberries and whipped cream. A short wine list opens with house French at £11.50 (£3 a glass).

CHEF: Laurent David   PROPRIETORS: Daniel Chobert and Laurent David   OPEN: all week 12 to 3, 7 to 12   CLOSED: 1 week at Christmas   MEALS: alc (main courses £5.50 to £15). Set L Mon to Fri £10.90, Set L Sat and Sun, Set D Sat 6.30 to 7.45 and Set D Sun £14.50. Cover £1.50   SERVICE: 15% (optional), card slips closed   CARDS: Amex, Delta, Diners, MasterCard, Switch, Visa   DETAILS: 60 seats. 20 seats outside. Private parties: 50 main room, 15 to 50 private rooms. Vegetarian meals. Children's helpings. Wheelchair access (not WC). No music. Air-conditioned
⊖ Earls Court

Lundum's   map 14

119 Old Brompton Road, SW7 3RN	COOKING 4
TEL: (020) 7373 7774 FAX: (020) 7373 4472	DANISH
	£28–£69

This Kensington stalwart, a family-run Danish restaurant with stylish contemporary looks and a laid-back mood, is set for expansion, including a new bar area and private rooms. Kay Lundum still oversees operations, and although a new head chef is due to be appointed, it is unlikely that there will be any drastic changes to the cooking. Lunch menus offer traditional favourites from the Danish kitchen, from home-made marinated herrings with aquavit to meatballs with butter sauce. Dinner is more ambitious, giving modern Danish cuisine a French twist to produce white tomato mousse with spinach, tomato confit and balsamic, milk-poached halibut with chive and asparagus fricassee, and duck cured for 52 hours then roasted and served with new potatoes and horseradish sauce. Sunday brunch is a traditional buffet. An extensive and well-chosen wine list focuses on France and features some classy names from the major regions with hefty price tags. House wines are £13.25, but there's precious little else under £20.

CHEF: Kay Lundum   PROPRIETOR: the Lundum family   OPEN: all week L 12 to 3 (4 Sun), Mon to Sat 6 to 11   CLOSED: 23 Dec to 5 Jan   MEALS: alc (main courses £7.75 to £18.50). Set L £12.50 (2 courses) to £15.50, Sun brunch £17.50, Set D £17.25 (2 courses) to £21.50   SERVICE: 13.5% (optional), card slips closed   CARDS: Amex, Delta, Diners, MasterCard, Switch, Visa   DETAILS: 62 seats. 18 seats outside. Private parties: 12 main room, 4 to 20 private rooms. Vegetarian meals. Children's helpings. Wheelchair access (also WC). Music. Air-conditioned
⊖ Gloucester Road, South Kensington

Mandarin Kitchen £   map 13

14–16 Queensway, W2 3RX	COOKING 1
TEL: (020) 7727 9012 FAX: (020) 7727 9468	CHINESE
	£27–£79

Mandarin Kitchen has been plying its trade in Queensway's mini-Chinatown for almost two decades and it stays with a 'tried-and-true' formula. Seafood is the main theme, the cooking is mostly Cantonese and the menu aims to please all-comers. Some reporters have been well satisfied with crispy fried seaweed, prawn toasts and sizzling fillet steak, while others who have explored the repertoire have been impressed by deep-fried asparagus with garlic and peppercorn salt and a 'manifestly fresh', rich hotpot of crab with bean noodles in a sauce spiked with chillies, dried shrimps and ginger. Lobsters come six ways (including 'sashimi'), Dover sole is cooked with dried chilli and onion, and fried rice arrives generously embellished with all manner of goodies including Chinese sausage. Service is swift and the wine list is a fair selection, with eight house selections from £10.50.

CHEF: Paul Ngo   PROPRIETOR: Steven Cheung   OPEN: all week 12 to 11.30   MEALS: alc (main courses £6 to £28). Set L and D £10.90 (2 courses) to £20   SERVICE: not inc, card slips closed   CARDS: Amex, Delta, Diners, MasterCard, Switch, Visa   DETAILS: 100 seats. Private parties: 100 main room. Vegetarian meals. Wheelchair access (not WC). No music. Air-conditioned ⊖ Queensway

Mash 🍴

map 15

19–21 Great Portland Street, W1W 8QB
TEL: (020) 7637 5555   FAX: (020) 7637 7333
EMAIL: mash@gruppo.co.uk

COOKING 2
MODERN EUROPEAN
£31–£60

A round orange sign hangs outside this 'cool' but noisy bar/restaurant, and huge orange beer tanks can be seen behind a glass wall. Drinks and decibels set the mood on the ground floor, while the striking upstairs dining room is a visual stunner. New chef Simon Wadham is carrying on where Maddalena Bonino left off, so expect plenty of pizzas from the wood-fired ovens, other Italian staples and tweaked-up modern bistro ideas (mussels cooked in Mash wheat beer with garlic and herbs, for example). Best bets, however, are the daily specials: salmon and halibut tartare ('a lively and refreshing starter') and a 'clever' Middle Eastern-inspired dish of baby squid stuffed with barley and harissa have been heartily endorsed. Order hot Campaillou bread with olives to start, and finish with pannacotta with slices of pear. Service is 'professional and competent, but amicable too'. As well as the home-brewed beers and glamorous cocktails, a short, upbeat wine list, loosely arranged by grape variety, offers quality drinking from £13.50, but mostly over £20. A dozen by the glass are £4.50 to £8.50.

CHEF: Simon Wadham   PROPRIETOR: Oliver Peyton   OPEN: Mon to Sat 12 to 3, 6 to 10.30   CLOSED: bank hols   MEALS: alc (main courses L £10 to £14, D £9 to £17.50). Set L and D 6 to 7.30 and 10 to 10.30 £12 (2 courses) to £15   SERVICE: 12.5% (optional), card slips closed   CARDS: Amex, Delta, MasterCard, Switch, Visa   DETAILS: 160 seats. Private parties: 28 private room. Vegetarian meals. Wheelchair access (also WC). Music   ⊖ Oxford Circus

Matsuri High Holborn

NEW ENTRY   map 13

Mid City Place, 71 High Holborn, WC1V 6EA
TEL: (020) 7430 1970   FAX: (020) 7430 1971
EMAIL: eat@matsuri-restaurant.com
WEBSITE: www.matsuri-restaurant.com

COOKING 4
JAPANESE
£23–£88

Austere is an understatement when it comes to describing décor at this Japanese restaurant occupying a corner site on bustling High Holborn. With its fully glazed frontage, high ceilings, unadorned white walls and a single plant in a white concrete pot, it can feel like sitting in a goldfish bowl. Menus are long and cover a wide range of mostly straightforward authentic traditional Japanese cooking, although there are a few novelties, such as miso mozzarella sushi.

One of the stated aims of the restaurant is to demystify Japanese food for the benefit of Westerners, to which end detailed explanations of dishes are provided. But even an experienced inspector was impressed by the craftsmanship behind prawn tempura in crisp, feather-light batter; grilled blackened white fish with spicy namban sauce and a small deep-fried aubergine; and a three-part tokkurimushi pot comprising thin ponzu dipping sauce, grated daikon radish with red chilli, and a delicately flavoured dashi-based soup containing tofu, chicken and prawns. Among sushi, 'luscious, meaty' eel, fat scallops with fresh wasabi and 'rich, oily' sea urchin have been praised. Drinks include a good variety of sakés, sold by the glass, wooden box or flask, as well as a decent selection of lyrically described wines, priced from £13.50. The original branch of Matsuri is located at 15 Bury Street, SW1; tel: (020) 7839 1101.

CHEF: Hiroshi Sudo PROPRIETOR: JRK UK Ltd OPEN: Mon to Sat 12 to 3, 6 to 10 (9 Sat) CLOSED: bank hols MEALS: alc (main courses £8 to £25). Set L £8.50 (2 courses) to £80, Set D £25 to £80 SERVICE: 12.5% (optional) CARDS: Amex, Delta, Diners, MasterCard, Switch, Visa DETAILS: 120 seats. Private parties: 10 to 50 private rooms. Vegetarian meals. No cigars/pipes in sushi bar. Wheelchair access (also WC). Music. Air-conditioned ⊖ Holborn, Chancery Lane

Metrogusto Islington ▼ map 13

13 Theberton Street, N1 0QY COOKING 3
TEL/FAX: (020) 7226 9400 MODERN ITALIAN
WEBSITE: www.metrogusto.co.uk £32–£50

The 'rather groovy' interior of Metrogusto has rough concrete walls, clean-lined architectural wooden chairs and quirky, faux-primitive paintings on the wall – cool, pleasant and modern. There is a Sicilian slant to the menu, with dishes such as salad alla Siciliana of sweet-and-sour aubergine, served with rounds of toast and hints of chilli and mint, and grilled baby stuffed squid that come with deep-fried cherry tomatoes and a sweet, rich, red tomato-based sauce. Pasta dishes may include potato gnocchi with mozzarella, tomato and basil. Main courses lean toward the meaty, as in involtini of veal with artichokes and Gruyère with zucchini tempura. Desserts range from the trendy (apple tart with Parmesan ice cream) to the trad (tiramisù). Timings are not always as spot-on as they could be and the quality of service seems to vary according to how busy the place gets. The all-Italian wine list concentrates on good producers, ranging from £14.50 (£3.75 a glass) for Sardinian white from Sella e Mosca and climbs in gentle increments to top wines from Tuscan and Piemontese stars such as Isole e Olena and Michele Chiarlo.

CHEF: Antonio Di Salvo PROPRIETORS: Ambro and Susi Ianeselli OPEN: Fri and Sat 12 to 2.30, 6.30 to 11, Sun 12.30 to 3, 7 to 10, Mon to Thur D only 6.30 to 10.30 CLOSED: bank hols MEALS: alc D (main courses £9.50 to £15.50). Set L £14.50 (2 courses) to £18.50, Set D £22.50 SERVICE: 12.5% (optional), card slips closed CARDS: Amex, Delta, MasterCard, Switch, Visa DETAILS: 56 seats. Private parties: 24 main room, 20 to 24 private rooms. Vegetarian meals. No smoking in 1 dining room. No pipes/cigars. Wheelchair access (not WC). Music. Air-conditioned ⊖ Angel, Highbury & Islington (£5)

Mims

NEW ENTRY | map 12

541A King's Road, SW6 2EB
TEL/FAX: (020) 7751 0010
EMAIL: al-sersy@mimsrestaurant.co.uk

COOKING 3
MODERN EUROPEAN
£25–£37

Ali Al-Sersy has upped sticks and relocated from the relative obscurity of Barnet to a particularly bustling stretch of the King's Road. His aim remains the same as ever: to provide accomplished modern European cooking at remarkably low prices, and some reporters, including regulars at Barnet, have found everything up to the standards they have come to expect. Others, however, have been disappointed by the cheerless décor, indifferent service and some rather patchy cooking. There is undoubted talent in the kitchen, and at its best it can still turn out respectable results: ravioli with a mousse-like crab filling and seared salmon on basil jus; squid with black noodles; deep-fried cod in 'gossamer light' batter; pan-fried calf's liver; and roast duck with roasted vegetables and tasty cooking juices. 'Intense' caramelised lemon tart with jellied strawberries, and pear and almond tart with light pastry and distinct flavours have ended meals on a high note. The bring-your-own wine policy has been abandoned, so diners are now restricted to choosing from the lacklustre but good-value house list. Prices start at £9.50.

CHEF/PROPRIETOR: Ali Al-Sersy   OPEN: Tue to Sun 12.30 to 11   MEALS: Set L £7.50 (1 course) to £15, Set D £11 (1 course) to £18.50   SERVICE: 10%   CARDS: MasterCard, Switch, Visa   DETAILS: 45 seats. Private parties: 55 main room. No-smoking area. Wheelchair access (not WC). Music ⊖ Fulham Broadway (£5)

Mirabelle ♥

map 15

56 Curzon Street, W1J 8PA
TEL: (020) 7499 4636   FAX: (020) 7499 5449
EMAIL: sales@whitestarline.org.uk
WEBSITE: www.whitestarline.org.uk

COOKING 6
FRENCH
£37–£95

The raffish, other-worldly atmosphere of the Mirabelle continues to delight. For many it is the jewel in the Marco Pierre White crown, both for ambience and for the quality-consciousness and precision of Phil Cooper's cooking. The dining room is a brown study, dappled with reflections from a mirror-ball, gently wafted over by lazily turning ceiling fans. A bevy of staff helps maintain a high degree of efficiency, necessary when there is a time limit on tables. Few complain of feeling rushed, though, and if you want to linger over coffee and liqueurs there's always the lounge-bar.

Extensive menu choice runs from creamy-sauced asparagus to sevruga caviar and blinis among starters, and then cod à la niçoise to roast partridge for mains. Everything is brought off with consummate aplomb, looks neat on the plate and delivers the kinds of concentrated flavours that speak of careful buying and due diligence in preparation. Not all the dishes are as franglais in their outlook as gratinée of salmon à la viennoise that comes with a sabayon de champagne. It is possible to have red mullet in the Moroccan style with couscous and a cumin-scented sauce, or rump of lamb with clams. The principal orientation, though, is French, and you may feel that you are taking a lightning tour of *Larousse*

Gastronomique before concluding in satisfaction with tarte Tatin of pears à la vanille, or fine French farmhouse cheeses.

This is a restaurant that holds a £30,000 bottle of 1847 Ch. d'Yquem in its cellars, yet it comes as a pleasant surprise to open the wine list and find drinkable bottles under £20. Not many, admittedly, but they are one of the signs that this list is more about offering wines to enjoy with the food than laying on a roll call of famous names at credit-limit-busting prices. Alsace and the refined rather than blockbusting Australian selection are other signs, but of course the list's heart is in Bordeaux and Burgundy. A dozen wines in the 'Sommelier Selection' also come by the glass (£4.20 to £8), and there's an extensive fine wine list.

CHEF: Phil Cooper   PROPRIETOR: Marco Pierre White   OPEN: all week 12 to 2.30 (3 Sat and Sun), 6 to 11.15 (10.30 Sun)   MEALS: alc (main courses £14.50 to £28.50). Set L Mon to Sat £16.50 (2 courses) to £19.95, Set L Sun £19.50   SERVICE: 12.5%, card slips closed   CARDS: Amex, Delta, Diners, MasterCard, Switch, Visa   DETAILS: 120 seats. 40 seats outside. Private parties: 120 main room, 33 to 48 private rooms. Music. Air-conditioned   ⊖ Green Park

Mr Kong   map 15

21 Lisle Street, WC2H 7BA	COOKING 3
TEL: (020) 7437 7341 FAX: (020) 7437 7923	CHINESE
	£23–£54

Over the years, Mr Kong and family have turned this Lisle Street address into a bastion of reliable Cantonese cooking, and it remains 'a very decent alternative to more pricey restaurants in Chinatown', according to one correspondent. Not content with ploughing a well-worn, familiar furrow, chef/owner Mr K is always trying out new ideas: in 2002 he teamed glass noodles with steamed scallops, and in 2003 introduced the Sand Storm lobster and its crab and 'superior prawn' variations. Otherwise the list of specials and 'manager's recommendations' might run to spiced pig's knuckle with jellyfish, or stuffed fish maw with baby clams and prawn paste. In more familiar territory, the kitchen also delivers splendid hotpots (spicy bean curd with monks' vegetables has been endorsed), stuffed king prawns, and shredded lamb with ginger. Service is on the ball and pink tablecloths are part of the jolly, upbeat atmosphere in the small ground-floor dining room (more seating in the basement). The wine list is basic (house vin de pays is £7.80), or drink beer or tea.

CHEFS: K. Kong and Y.W. Lo   PROPRIETORS: K. Kong, Y.W. Lo, M.T. Lee, C.Y. Chau and Mrs S.Y. Liu   OPEN: all week noon to 2.45am (1.45 Sun)   CLOSED: 2 to 4 days Christmas   MEALS: alc (main courses £6 to £28). Set L and D £9.30 (2 courses) to £22   SERVICE: 10%   CARDS: Amex, Delta, Diners, MasterCard, Switch, Visa   DETAILS: 110 seats. Private parties: 40 main room. Vegetarian meals. Music. Air-conditioned   ⊖ Leicester Square

---

'They seem to take a very liberal view about what the staff put on their name badges. There was one called "Cartoon" a few years ago and today I noticed "Road Runner". Happily he didn't go "Meep, meep!" and zip around the place.' (On eating in Manchester)

▲ Mju 🍷

map 14

Millenium Hotel, 17 Sloane Street, SW1X 9NU
TEL: (020) 7201 6330   FAX: (020) 7201 6302
EMAIL: mju@mill-cop.com

COOKING **5**
GLOBAL
£32–£75

This spacious dining room is based around a large atrium on the first floor of the Millennium Hotel. After a parting of ways with consultant chef Tetsuya Waduka, the kitchen is now under the sole command of Paul Peters, who has tweaked the cooking style to give the Japanese-centred fusion ideas more of a European, specifically French, slant. The menu format has changed too, offering at dinner a three-course carte and six- or nine-course degustation menus, while lunch has a pick and mix of small dishes as before, plus a short menu du jour. Either way, there is still plenty to grab the attention. Among starters, ceviche of sea bass and scallop is from the more mainstream end of the repertoire, but there might also be mushroom and truffle glass noodles with mange-tout. Pan-fried foie gras comes with balsamic, honey and apple, and sugar-cured salmon with tobiko, cucumber and caviar. Main courses might include lobster udon with tarragon, chives and lobster oil; glazed duck breast with shiitake mushrooms, Asian greens and mugi miso sauce; and pan-fried monkfish with pea purée and courgette flower stuffed with osso bucco. For dessert you might try floating islands, or 'hand picked' cheeses.

Mju is justifiably proud of its impressive array of Australian red wines, but also lays on some top-class French bottles and a good showing from Alsace. Prices in general are not cheap, but there are some good-value bottles here, such as Alain Graillot's Crozes-Hermitage at £21. Chilean house is £15, and eight by the glass range from £5 to £10.

CHEF: Paul Peters   PROPRIETOR: Millennium & Copthorne   OPEN: Mon to Sat 12 to 2.30, 6 to 10.30   CLOSED: bank hols   MEALS: alc (main courses L £3.50 to £12.50, D £13 to £22). Set L £19.95 (2 courses) to £24.95 (both inc wine), Set D £40 to £60 (inc wine), Set D £60 to £90 (inc wine, whole table only). Bar menu also available   SERVICE: 12.5% (optional), card slips closed   CARDS: Amex, Delta, Diners, MasterCard, Switch, Visa   DETAILS: 110 seats. Private parties: 160 main room, 10 to 110 private rooms. Vegetarian meals. Children's helpings. No-smoking area. Wheelchair access (not WC). Music. No mobile phones. Air-conditioned   ACCOMMODATION: 222 rooms, all with bath/shower. TV. Phone. B&B £116 to £270. Rooms for disabled ⊖ Knightsbridge (£5)

▲ Montcalm Hotel, Crescent Restaurant

map 15

34–40, Great Cumberland Place, W1H 7TW
TEL: (020) 7402 4288   FAX: (020) 7724 9180
EMAIL: montcalm@montcalm.co.uk
WEBSITE: www.montcalm.co.uk

COOKING **3**
MODERN BRITISH
£31–£63

Just a short stroll from Marble Arch, the Montcalm has an appropriate air of calm, as does its Crescent restaurant. The dining room, overlooking the eponymous crescent, has light-coloured wood dado panelling, a 'country garden' mural on one wall, tables smartly dressed in white linen, chairs that are armed and comfortable, and waiting staff who are formally dressed and efficient. The fixed-price menu includes a half-bottle of house wine per person, and runs to a well-balanced starter of soft-shell crab and sweetcorn chowder garnished with garden herbs and a mousse-like butternut subric. Pan-fried veal chop on a bed of spinach with dauphine potatoes and a garnish of summer morel mushroom, broad beans and peas, crème fraîche and basil was a simply presented and well-rendered dish belying the complex-sounding description. To finish, a selection of Continental cheeses or, for sweet-lovers, desserts such as dark chocolate pot filled with summer fruit compote with praline ice cream may be just the ticket. For those venturing beyond the prix fixe half-bottles, the main wine list has some decent by-the-glass selections from £4. Bottle prices start at £17, but there's not much under £20.

CHEF: Ian Medas   PROPRIETOR: Nikko Hotels (UK) Ltd   OPEN: Mon to Fri L 12.30 to 2.30, all week D 6.30 to 10.30   CLOSED: bank hols L   MEALS: Set L and D £20 (2 courses) to £25 inc wine. Bar menu available   SERVICE: not inc   CARDS: Amex, Diners, MasterCard, Switch, Visa   DETAILS: 50 seats. Private parties: 60 main room, 20 private rooms. Vegetarian meals. Children's helpings. No-smoking area. Wheelchair access (also WC). No music. Air-conditioned   ACCOMMODATION: 120 rooms, all with bath/shower. TV. Phone. Room only £130 to £300. Rooms for disabled. Baby facilities   ⊖ Marble Arch (£5)

Moro   map 13

34–36 Exmouth Market, EC1R 4QE
TEL: (020) 7833 8336   FAX: (020) 7833 9338   COOKING 5
EMAIL: info@moro.co.uk   SPANISH/NORTH AFRICAN
WEBSITE: www.moro.co.uk   £32–£48

This bit of London has matured beyond its up-and-coming status and is now well and truly on the map. Likewise, Moro's take on Spanish/North African cooking may not raise as many eyebrows as it once did, but Sam and Sam Clark's restaurant still stands out from the crowd. 'I just think this place is fantastic,' said one enthusiastic regular. The dining room is large and simply decorated, with a zinc bar on one side and the kitchen, with its much-used chargrill and wood-fired oven, open for all to see. Tapas are served throughout the day at the bar, but at lunchtime and in the evening the place is 'a frenzy of activity'.

The menu changes, we are told, every two weeks. Braised cabbage with smoked Spanish paprika has met with praise, as has a main course of wood-roast pork with 'divine' mashed potato, sprouting broccoli and a Pedro Ximénez sauce. Pan-fried morcilla might come with garlic shoots, broad beans and toast in a summer starter, while the wood-fired oven is used to good effect for sardines, served with preserved lemons, coriander and warm potato salad. Staff, dressed in cool black, are friendly and helpful with explanations on the trickier bits of the menu. One visitor commented on 'fresh-tasting, unusual puddings', perhaps referring to the Málaga raisin ice cream, or yoghurt and pistachio cake. The well-conceived wine list holds some pleasant surprises, including seven sherries, five served by the glass. Most bottles originate in Spain, with prices starting at £11.

CHEFS: Samuel and Samantha Clark   PROPRIETORS: Mark Sainsbury, and Samuel and Samantha Clark   OPEN: Mon to Fri L 12.30 to 2.30, Mon to Sat D 7 to 10.30   CLOSED: Christmas, bank hols MEALS: alc (main courses £12.50 to £16.50). Tapas menu available Mon to Fri 12.30 to 10.30, Sat 6.30 to 10.30   SERVICE: not inc, 12.5% for parties of 6 or more   CARDS: Amex, Delta, Diners,

MasterCard, Switch, Visa   DETAILS: 90 seats. 15 seats outside. Private parties: 120 main room. Vegetarian meals. No cigars/pipes. Wheelchair access (also WC). No music. Air-conditioned
⊖ Farringdon

Mosaica @ the factory   NEW ENTRY   map 12

Unit C005, Building C, The Chocolate Factory,
Clarendon Road, N22 6XJ   COOKING 3
TEL: (020) 8889 2400   FAX: (020) 8889 1226   MODERN EUROPEAN
EMAIL: johnniemountain@hotmail.com   £24–£58

It's quite a thrill to find two cooks of pedigree in an industrial estate off Coburg Road in Wood Green. Since 2000, locals and émigrés from Hornsey and Highgate have enjoyed this huge, funky, noisy room with its worn painted floor and candle lighting – and food that takes in excellent home-made foccacia and utterly correct crème brûlée with unsweetened stewed rhubarb lurking at the bottom. The kitchen squeezes maximum flavour from basic ingredients: starting with a single, VERY big, expertly cooked prawn with an excellent buttery, lemony, shalloty, wine sauce; or a clear broth, full of flageolets, celery, carrots and courgettes. Main courses might include spicy crab pasta with thin al dente linguini, and crunchy chips accompanying a juicily tender rump steak; other possibilities might be sun-dried tomato and artichoke ravioli, or pink duck with mustard mash and red cabbage. Helpful and jolly young staff are just right for the quirky informality of this place. Fourteen decent-value wines start at £11.95, with three by the glass, and there's a second list of smarter bottles.

CHEFS/PROPRIETORS: John Mountain and David Orlowski   OPEN: Tue to Fri and Sun L 12 to 2, Tue to Sun D 7 to 10   CLOSED: bank hols Mon and Tue   MEALS: alc (main courses L £5.50 to £14, D £12 to £16)   CARDS: Amex, Delta, MasterCard, Switch, Visa   DETAILS: 120 seats. 70 seats outside. Private parties: 150 to 200 main room, 80 to 150 private rooms. Car park. Vegetarian meals. Children's helpings. No-smoking area. Wheelchair access (also WC). Music. No mobile phones. Air-conditioned   ⊖ Wood Green

Moshi Moshi Sushi 🌶✳ £   maps 12 and 13

24 Upper Level, Liverpool Street Station,
Broadgate EC2M 7QH
TEL/FAX: (020) 7247 3227
7–8 Limeburner Lane, EC4M 7HY
TEL: (020) 7248 1808   FAX: (020) 7248 1807
Level 2, Canada Place, E14 4QT   COOKING 2
TEL: (020) 7512 9201   FAX: (020) 7512 9685   JAPANESE
WEBSITE: www.moshimoshi.co.uk   £18–£39

The conveyor belt defines proceedings in this elite mini-chain of casual Japanese eating places. Opened in 1994, the branch above Liverpool Street Station set the wheels in motion, and there are now four outlets, including one in Brighton (see Round-ups). All have the same design concept, menu format and commitment to low prices. Sit at the counter and take your pick from colour-coded plates as they pass by. Nigiri sushi, maki, and sashimi are the main attraction, and 'geta' sushi sets (served on traditional wooden platters) are also served at tables. If you fancy something different, delve into the list of Japanese 'tapas' (prawn and grey mullet tempura, for example) or request a temaki handroll. Desserts range from poached pears with mascarpone to moshi (rice cakes filled with aduki bean, white bean and peanut paste). Tea, beers and juices suit the food; otherwise there is a handful of wines from £11.50.

CHEF: Enrico Venzon   PROPRIETOR: Caroline Bennett   OPEN: Broadgate: Mon to Fri 11.30 to 9.30; Limeburner Lane: Mon to Fri 11.30 to 3.30; Canada Place: all week 11 to 8 (7 Sat, 5 Sun) CLOSED: Christmas, bank hols   MEALS: alc (plates and sushi sets £1.50 to £14.50). Set L £5.90 to £12.50 (1 course), Set D £10.50 to £18 (2 courses). Cover 50p   SERVICE: none, card slips closed CARDS: Delta, Diners, MasterCard, Switch, Visa   DETAILS: 70 seats (Canada Place: 20 seats). Private parties: 70 main room. Vegetarian meals. No smoking. Wheelchair access (not WC). Music   ⊖ Liverpool Street, St Paul's, Canary Wharf

MVH

| NEW ENTRY | map 12 |

5 White Hart Lane, SW13   COOKING 4
TEL: (020) 8392 1111   'ECLECTIC'
£38–£59

Michael Von Hruschka is a chef with a great sense of theatre, and fans of his style (seen most recently at the Birdcage) won't be disappointed with his latest venture. Design is 'quirky, fun and wildly original', which is apparent before you even enter the building – a pair of giant antlers and a chessboard are stuck on the roof. Inside, the restaurant is divided into two parts: upstairs is Hell, a bar in floor-to-ceiling red and crammed with intriguing junk, while on the ground floor is the dining room, dubbed Heaven, all in white with features including an antlered tailor's dummy and fancy glass chandeliers.

But what about the food? Well, to call it elaborate doesn't do it justice. Meals begin with a succession of bizarre appetisers, including a set of test tubes presented in a box of sugar, each containing a vivid green and very refreshing cucumber, lime and mint flavoured liquid. Among starters proper have been delicate salmon mousse wrapped in a courgette flower, and rich rabbit rillettes in crunchy filo pastry, served with a complementary kumquat 'gunge'. Certain dishes, while 'wow' to look at, have proved to be more 'ho hum' in the eating, but roasted lemon sole with an intensely flavoured beetroot purée has impressed, as has a stew of tender, slow-cooked lamb with a richly spiced jus. After another parade of savouries and pre-desserts, meals might end with champagne and elderflower 'soup' served in a goblet with a light, frothy 'head', or rhubarb crème brûlée adorned with a shaving of dried rhubarb. With all the extras thrown in, dinner is considered excellent value for money, though mark-ups on the surprisingly prosaic wine list are rather hefty. House Chardonnay and Merlot are £17.

CHEF/PROPRIETOR: Michael Von Hruschka   OPEN: Thur to Sun L 12 to 2.30, all week D 6 to 10.30 CLOSED: 2 weeks Jan   MEALS: alc (main courses £8 to £14). Set L £19 (2 courses) to £22, Set D £26 (2 courses) to £29   SERVICE: 12.5% (optional), card slips closed   CARDS: Amex, Delta, MasterCard, Switch, Visa   DETAILS: 29 seats. 12 seats outside. Private parties: 35 main room, 12 to 25 private rooms. Vegetarian meals. Children's helpings. Music. Air-conditioned

---

⊱✖ *indicates that smoking is banned in all eating areas.*

▲ Nahm

map 14

Halkin Hotel, 5 Halkin Street, SW1X 7DJ
TEL: (020) 7333 1234   FAX: (020) 7333 1100   COOKING 4
EMAIL: christinag@halkin.co.uk   THAI
WEBSITE: www.halkin.co.uk   £44–£85

In 2001 the Halkin, a stalwart of the Guide, underwent a Far Eastern transformation. The stone Khmer Buddha in the lobby gives some indication of that orientation, and David Thompson's Thai-inspired restaurant forms the nerve centre. Don't expect an undiluted version of Thai cooking, though. This is Bangkok by way of Sydney, where Thompson first successfully established this genre.

The format is familiar enough. You opt either to choose from the carte or to go for the eight-course tasting menu, which is arranged according to cooking method. Outstanding dishes at inspection included ma hor (minced prawns and chicken simmered in palm sugar with deep-fried shallots, peanuts and garlic, garnished with mandarin segments and pineapple); grilled pork and clam salad with peppers and aubergines dressed with smoked fish flakes and coconut cream; and minced prawns with shrimp paste accompanied by chicken livers, cucumber, white turmeric, fennel, watercress and Thai basil. Coconut and galangal soup, with wild mushrooms, onion threads, blackened chilli pods and coriander, produced a world of creamy-hot satisfaction (you will be warned by the staff that the chillies are hotter than July. They mean it). The so-called 'Thai dessert' selection incorporates fresh fruit, such as mango, lychee, nashi pear and papaya, with sweetened sticky rice, coconut cream jelly, fried coconut and sesame seeds. Prices are as high as the labour-intensiveness of the food would lead you to anticipate, and occasionally a dish will fail to hang together, or seem a little underwhelming. The house wine selections, which start at £18.50, are an imaginative bunch, and there is a handful of half-bottles.

CHEF: David Thompson   PROPRIETOR: Christina Ong   OPEN: Mon to Fri L 12 to 2.30, all week D 7 to 11 (10 Sun)   MEALS: alc (main courses £15 to £25). Set L £18 (2 courses) to £26, Set D £47   SERVICE: 12.5% (optional)   CARDS: Amex, MasterCard, Switch, Visa   DETAILS: 75 seats. Private parties: 100 main room. No cigars. Wheelchair access (also WC). Music. Air-conditioned   ACCOMMODATION: 41 rooms, all with bath/shower. TV. Phone. Room only £280 to £390 (double room). Rooms for disabled. Baby facilities   ⊖ Hyde Park Corner (*The Which? Guide to Good Hotels*)

National Gallery, Crivelli's Garden ⁵⁄*

map 15

Trafalgar Square, WC2N 5DN
TEL: (020) 7747 2869
EMAIL: crivelli's.garden@nationalgallery.co.uk   COOKING 3
WEBSITE: www.nationalgallery.org.uk/plan/cafe/   ITALIAN
restaurant.htm   £25–£51

'If you can, bag a table by the window,' is one reporter's advice to those who would like to enjoy the fantastic views over Trafalgar Square offered here. Crivelli's Garden, housed on the first floor in the Sainsbury Wing of the National Gallery, is an ideal place to rest weary limbs after an edifying tour. The modern, minimalist décor is relieved by a profusion of large palms and murals. The menu is fairly short, moving briskly from such classic Italian pairings as Parma ham and melon, or more enterprising dishes such as roasted veal with pineapple and watercress salad, then on to pasta dishes such as own-made tagliolini with squid, crab, parsley and peas. Main courses may take in a grilled veal paillard with roasted peppers, or salmon fishcake with mango sauce. For desserts, classicists might hanker after a 'delectable' tiramisù. Ingredients are fresh, but timings can sometimes go astray. Service has ranged from 'laid-back' to 'efficient'. The short, all-Italian wine list is pedestrian, with house rosso and bianco starting at £10.95.

CHEF: Paolo Zanca   PROPRIETOR: Red Pepper Group   OPEN: all week L 11.30 to 4, Wed D 5.30 to 7.45   CLOSED: 25 Dec, Good Fri   MEALS: alc (main courses £10.50 to £13.50). Set L £12.50 (2 courses) to £15, Set D £15 (2 courses) to £17   SERVICE: 12.5% (optional), card slips closed   CARDS: Amex, Delta, MasterCard, Switch, Visa   DETAILS: 200 seats. Vegetarian meals. No smoking. Wheelchair access (also WC). No music. No mobile phones. Air-conditioned
⊖ Charing Cross

National Portrait Gallery, Portrait Restaurant ⁵⋇

map 15

Orange Street, WC2H 0HE
TEL: (020) 7312 2490   FAX: (020) 7925 0244
EMAIL: portrait.restaurant@searcys.co.uk
WEBSITE: www.searcys.co.uk

COOKING 3
MODERN BRITISH
£30–£59

Portrait Restaurant, with its beguiling rooftop views, is a vibrant, stylish 'designer-led' dining room. Chrome, blond-wood flooring, a dark grey and black colour scheme, and a huge expanse of window set the trendy tone. The menu is more traditional than you might expect – 'modern, bistro-style cuisine', as one reporter put it. Chicken liver and foie gras parfait may be served with 'a deliciously sour-sweet fig and orange chutney', while confit duck leg, with Savoy cabbage and turnip, comes with 'a perfect, crackling-like skin'. The cooking is based on good-quality ingredients, as in main courses of 'good, tender' shoulder of pork with rösti, or roast rump of lamb with tapenade. Desserts, such as poached spring fruit with star anise cream and a polenta biscuit, or strawberry semifreddo with mixed berry nougat, are well conceived. Service can be chaotic, if generally willing, tables are closely packed, and all those hard surfaces can lead to quite a clatter, but, as one reporter said: 'for these views I could just about forgive anything.' The concise wine list has plenty by the glass. Bottle prices begin at £14.75 (£3.75 a glass).

CHEF: Brendan Fyldes   PROPRIETOR: Searcy Tansley & Co Ltd   OPEN: all week L 11.45 to 2.45 (11.30 to 3 Sat and Sun), Thur and Fri D 5.30 to 8.30   CLOSED: 25 and 26 Dec, Good Fri   MEALS: alc (main courses £11 to £19). Set L Mon to Fri £22.50 (2 courses) to £27.50, Set L Sat and Sun £19.50 (2 courses) to £24.50, Set D Thur and Fri 5.30 to 6.30 £13.95 (2 courses) to £16.95. Light L menu available Mon to Fri 11.30 to 5, bar menu available Thur and Fri 5 to 9   SERVICE: 12.5% (optional), card slips closed   CARDS: Amex, Delta, MasterCard, Switch, Visa   DETAILS: 120 seats. Private parties: 250 main room. Vegetarian meals. No smoking in 1 dining room. Wheelchair access (also WC). No music. Air-conditioned   ⊖ Leicester Square

The Guide's top-rated restaurants are listed near the front of the book.

Neal Street Restaurant

map 15

26 Neal Street, WC2H 9PS	COOKING 2
TEL: (020) 7836 8368 FAX: (020) 7240 3964	ITALIAN
EMAIL: reserve@nealstreet.co.uk	£44–£79

Over the past 32 years, Antonio Carluccio's original restaurant, just a stone's throw from Covent Garden, has become something of a landmark for lovers of Italian food. Original Hockneys share white brick and mirrored walls with walking sticks carved by Carluccio himself, while terracotta floor tiles and tubular-steel chairs feature alongside. The style of cooking is simple, utilising quality ingredients for maximum flavour. The menu is classic Carluccio, not just featuring a love of mushrooms – perhaps a seasonal mixed sauté – but also speciality pasta, the likes of hand-cut ribbons with black truffle sauce and black truffle shavings. Expect main courses of salt-cod baked with potatoes and porcini mushrooms, or venison fillet with morel sauce and chestnuts, and finish with tiramisù, or poached pear with zabaglione sauce. A predominantly Italian wine list kicks in at £14.50, with ten offered by the glass from £3.75, but there are precious few bottles under £20. Carluccio's Caffés are popping up all over (see Round-up entry, London).

CHEF: Andrea Cavaliere   PROPRIETORS: Antonio and Priscilla Carluccio   OPEN: Mon to Sat 12.30 to 2.30, 6 to 11   CLOSED: bank hols exc Good Fri   MEALS: alc (main courses £13.50 to £22)   SERVICE: 12.5% (optional), card slips closed   CARDS: Amex, Diners, MasterCard, Switch, Visa   DETAILS: 65 seats. Private parties: 10 to 24 private rooms. Vegetarian meals. Children's helpings. Wheelchair access (not WC). No music. Air-conditioned   ⊖ Covent Garden

New Diamond £

NEW ENTRY

23 Lisle Street, WC2H 7BA	COOKING 2
TEL: (020) 7437 2517 and 7221	CANTONESE
FAX: (020) 7437 7221	£26–£53

'Authentic Cantonese-style dishes at competitive prices' is the name of the game at this Chinatown address, where a 'nice bunch' of polite young staff help to lift the jovial, chatty atmosphere in the neat, fresh-looking dining room. A soup of winter melon and mixed meat has been pronounced 'first-class', and the menu lists a fair showing of exotica such as boiled geoduck (a bivalve, also known as the 'elephant trunk clam') with jellyfish, and stewed fish head with bean curd; also note the trio of pigeon dishes and additional chef's specials such as venison with asparagus in XO sauce. Those looking for something less challenging needn't feel intimidated, because the kitchen can also deliver fine versions of deep-fried prawns with sweet-and-sour sauce, and velvety steamed chicken with Chinese mushrooms ('a simple dish, but done so well,' thought one reporter). The short, predominantly French wine list has house wines at £7.80.

CHEF: Phat Van Ly   PROPRIETORS: Wai Cheung Lam and Kwai Lin Ku   OPEN: all week 12 to 5, 5 to 2.40   CLOSED: 25 Dec, 1 Jan   MEALS: alc (main courses £6 to £20). Set D £9.50 to £25 (all min 2 or more)   SERVICE: 10%   CARDS: Amex, Delta, Diners, MasterCard, Switch, Visa   DETAILS: 80 seats. Vegetarian meals. No children under 3. Music. Air-conditioned

New Tayyabs ✱ £   map 12

83 Fieldgate Street, E1 1JU
TEL: (020) 7247 9543/6400   COOKING 2
EMAIL: info@tayyabs.co.uk   PAKISTANI
WEBSITE: www.tayyabs.co.uk   £14–£30

Crowds continue to descend on this revamped Whitechapel café, now looking noticeably chic. The décor is very much in vogue, with its modern chairs, designer lights and semi-abstract artwork, but the cooking has stayed true to its Pakistani Punjabi roots. Portions are big and prices are low. The bulk of the menu comprises an extensive selection of karahi dishes ranging from sag gosht and Karahi batera (quails) to dhal with karela (bitter melon); customers are even invited to create their own, using all the essential components. Each day the kitchen also prepares limited quantities of one or two specials: Sunday brings chicken biryani, and tinda (ivy gourd) masala. Start with mutton tikka or masala fish and finish with kheer or kulfi. The restaurant is unlicensed, but you can bring your own, or else drink lassi.

CHEFS: Mohammed Tayyab and M.S. Tayyab   PROPRIETOR: Mohammed Tayyab   OPEN: all week D only 5 to 11.30   MEALS: alc (main courses £3.50 to £10). BYO   SERVICE: not inc   CARDS: Amex, Delta, MasterCard, Switch, Visa   DETAILS: 120 seats. 16 seats outside. Private parties: 100 main room, 10 to 30 private rooms. No smoking in 1 dining room. Wheelchair access (not WC). Music. Air-conditioned   ⊖ Whitechapel, Aldgate East

Nicole's   map 15

158 New Bond Street, W1S 2UB   COOKING 3
TEL: (020) 7499 8408   FAX: (020) 7409 0381   MODERN EUROPEAN
      £51–£78

The basement dining area doesn't feel like anything other than a stand-alone restaurant – and a comfortable, modern one at that – so don't worry about getting in the way of the sales staff at Farhi's flagship London store. You can drop in for breakfast or afternoon tea, a mid-shopping lunch, or a full-on dinner.

The bread basket might yield focaccia, ciabatta and maybe a fruit and nut or sun-dried tomato variety, and starters run to soup, pasta or risotto of the day and, perhaps, lobster, artichoke and citrus salad. Take your pick from fish or meat main courses – five of each – with braised sea bream and clams with Spanish chickpea and chorizo stew, alongside Eastern-influenced cardamom and ginger braised lamb shank with almond and sultana pilau. Vanilla cheesecake has been praised as creamy yet light, or try bitter chocolate and apricot tart. Note the £1 cover charge and added 15 per cent service. Forty-plus wines from Old and New Worlds begin at £14.25, with many available by the glass.

CHEF: Annie Wayte   PROPRIETOR: Stephen Marks   OPEN: Mon to Sat L 12 to 3.30 (4 Sat), Mon to Fri D 6.30 to 10.45   CLOSED: 25 and 26 Dec, bank hols   MEALS: alc (main courses £18 to £21). Cover £1. Breakfast and bar menu available   SERVICE: 15% (optional)   CARDS: Amex, Delta, Diners, MasterCard, Switch, Visa   DETAILS: 95 seats. Private parties: 95 main room. Vegetarian meals. No-smoking area. Music. Air-conditioned   ⊖ Green Park

The Guide's longest-serving restaurants are listed near the front of the book.

Noble Rot

map 15

3–5 Mill Street, W1S 2AU
TEL: (020) 7629 8877 FAX: (020) 7629 8878
EMAIL: reception@noblerot.com
WEBSITE: www.noblerot.com

COOKING 4
MODERN EUROPEAN
£33–£75

Smartly located in Mayfair's fashion nirvana – near Savile Row and New Bond Street – Noble Rot is as well turned out as its clientele. On the ground floor is a restaurant with a light, cool atmosphere, the huge windows hung with blinds. Downstairs is a members' club. 'Mixing and matching not only the ingredients but also the flavours, textures and temperatures' is what the kitchen aims to do, and seems like a fair summary. To this end, the menu may kick off with roast bone marrow with cauliflower purée and Avruga caviar, or hot and cold foie gras (a cold piece with quince terrine, a seared piece with rose-scented jus). Main courses follow the theme, with the likes of fillet of veal with a piquillo polenta cake, pâtisson squash, grilled artichoke and a lemon reduction, or roast sea bass with courgette flowers, asparagus, fennel and vanilla-scented cream. Desserts such as tarte Tatin with thick slices of apple let the flavour of the ingredients show through. Presentation of dishes is smart. At lunchtime there is a good-value set menu, but that still leaves some stiff prices on the wine list to contend with. Quality is high on the four closely printed pages, one of which is devoted to sweet wines (naturally enough, given the name of the establishment), and six house wines at £15.75 to £19.50 (£5.50 to £6.50 a glass) are reliably tasty options.

CHEF: Julian Owen-Mold PROPRIETOR: Jessen & Co Restaurants OPEN: Mon to Fri L 12 to 3, Mon to Sat D 6 to 11 CLOSED: bank hols MEALS: alc (main courses £16 to £22). Set L £15.95 (2 courses) to £19.50 SERVICE: 12.5% (optional), card slips closed CARDS: Amex, Diners, MasterCard, Switch, Visa DETAILS: 65 seats. 20 seats outside. Private parties: 130 main room, 120 private room. Vegetarian meals. Children's helpings. Music. Air-conditioned ⊖ Oxford Circus £5

Nobu

map 15

19 Old Park Lane, W1Y 4LB
TEL: (020) 7447 4747 FAX: (020) 7447 4749
WEBSITE: www.noburestaurants.com

COOKING 5
MODERN JAPANESE
£36–£99

Few restaurants can remain fashionable for more than a couple of years, which makes Nobu's enduring popularity all the more impressive. Although it still draws its share of celebrities, most of the clientele that pack the huge, bare dining room for two sittings every evening are hotel guests and well-heeled locals. And you do need to be well heeled to eat here – prices reflect the going rate for an A-list international chef (Nobuyuki Matsuhisa has restaurants that range from New York via Beverly Hills to Tokyo), even if the actual cooking here is by the very capable Mark Edwards.

Menus are long and divided into many sections, but for those not familiar with Japanese cooking there is a team of well-drilled waitresses on hand to dispense advice in a friendly and non-patronising manner. Most of the repertoire is fairly straightforward and traditional and makes a good impression thanks to the first-rate quality of materials – notably in raw dishes such as 'firm, bouncy and very fresh-tasting' yellowtail sashimi that are given a hint of piquancy with slivers of jalapeño; or wafer-thin slices of scallop that 'melted in the mouth like ice cream', in a subtle ginger soy dressing. A bowl of simply steamed percebes (Spanish barnacles) with a zingy citrussy dipping sauce was a hit at inspection and 'great fun' to eat, while sizzling toban yaki beef featured 'strong tasting and incredibly tender' meat in a sticky savoury sauce. The kitchen does have its occasional off day, but the vast majority of reporters have left feeling very content. The wine list is aimed squarely at high rollers, but does include a few relatively modest bottles – prices start at £19 – and there is an impressive selection of saké.

CHEFS: Mark Edwards and Nobuyuki Matsuhisa   PROPRIETORS: Nobuyuki Matsuhisa, Robert De Niro and Drew Nieporent   OPEN: Mon to Fri L 12 to 2.15, Mon to Sun D 6 to 10.15 (11.15 Sat, 9.45 Sun)   MEALS: alc (main courses £14 to £29.50). Set L £24.50 to £50, Set D to £70   SERVICE: 15% (optional), card slips closed   CARDS: Amex, Delta, Diners, MasterCard, Switch, Visa   DETAILS: 150 seats. Vegetarian meals. No smoking in 1 dining room. Wheelchair access (also WC). Music. Air-conditioned   ⊖ Hyde Park, Green Park

Noura Brasserie

map 13

16 Hobart Place, SW1W 0HH
TEL: (020) 7235 9444   FAX: (020) 7235 9244
WEBSITE: www.noura-brasserie.co.uk

COOKING 5
LEBANESE
£35–£59

'What an unexpected treat!' enthused one reporter, whose expectations were greatly exceeded by the food served at this upmarket Middle Eastern restaurant. Despite being housed in part of a vast office block, the cool colours, dim lighting and spaciousness render it surprisingly elegant. The extensive menu, divided into long lists of 'platters', cold and hot meze and main courses, may raise doubts as to whether so many dishes can be freshly and carefully prepared, but experience suggests that indeed they can.

There is a light hand with spicing, and a delicacy and sensitivity of palate that marks the food served here. Cold meze such as silky smooth hummus, smoky moutabbal (aubergine purée) and tender stuffed vine leaves may precede hot meze such as tangy-sharp fatayer (baked spinach in pastry parcels). Main courses are mostly grilled or roasted. On inspection, the grilled minced lamb skewers, flavoured with parsley, pine nuts and onions, were a standout. Finally, resist if you can the home-made ice creams, the rosewater version of which has been described as 'velvety' and 'seductive'. Formally dressed staff are professional, proficient and solicitous. The drinks list is thick with the best names in champagne, Burgundy and Bordeaux – plus provides a selection of araks. Bottle prices start at £18 for house French white.

CHEF: Tony Esper   PROPRIETOR: Nader Bou Antoun   OPEN: all week 11.30am to 11.45pm   MEALS: alc (main courses £10 to £18). Set L 11.30 to 6 exc Sun £14 (2 courses), Set D £23 to £31 (all min 2)   SERVICE: not inc   CARDS: Amex, Delta, Diners, MasterCard, Switch, Visa   DETAILS: 100+ seats. Private parties: 125 main room. Vegetarian meals. Wheelchair access (also WC). Music. Air-conditioned   ⊖ Victoria

'Lighting is crepuscular, but in a churchy rather than sexy way. As we were ushered to our corner table, a standard lamp in the corner of the room by us was tenderly switched off, reducing the level by another few lumens.' (On eating in Sussex)

No. 6 George Street ✱ £

map 15

6 George Street, W1U 3QX
TEL: (020) 7935 1910   FAX: (020) 7935 6036

COOKING 2
MODERN BRITISH
£30–£52

This delicatessen-cum-restaurant in the beating heart of Marylebone exudes homely charm. At the front is a wonderfully old-fashioned shop selling a selection of jams, jellies and preserves, as well as fruit and vegetables, meats and cheeses. Towards the back is the dining room, a simply furnished space with white walls, plenty of scrubbed wood and not much else. The daily-changing menu has a strong seasonal element, but there's always at least a trace of the Mediterranean in some of the dishes. Good ingredients are simply prepared and simply served. Artichoke and buffalo mozzarella salad with pesto might make a summer starter, while field mushroom risotto with crème fraîche and chives might feature as a wintry main course. Salads are imaginatively put together and charcuterie is likely to figure somewhere on the menu. The wine list is short, with some interesting bottles; prices are modest, starting at £12.50.

CHEF: Emma Miller   PROPRIETORS: the Miller family   OPEN: Mon to Fri L only 12 to 3. Also open for breakfast and afternoon tea   CLOSED: 2 weeks Aug, bank hols   MEALS: alc (main courses £9.50 to £16)   SERVICE: not inc   CARDS: MasterCard, Switch, Visa   DETAILS: 32 seats. Private parties: 32 main room. Vegetarian meals. Children's helpings. No smoking. No music. Air-conditioned ⊖ Bond Street, Baker Street

Odette's �-

map 13

130 Regent's Park Road, NW1 8XL
TEL: (020) 7586 5486   FAX: (020) 7722 5388

COOKING 4
MODERN BRITISH
£26–£69

This popular, well-established neighbourhood restaurant in Primrose Hill underwent extensive refurbishment in the summer of 2003. There has also been a change of ownership, with Simon Bradley taking on proprietorial duties alongside those of head chef. The wine bar is no more and a brand new kitchen has been installed. The cooking shows a bold approach: witness a starter of crisp duck leg with tiger prawns tempura, lobster ice cream and a watermelon, mint and chilli salad – a dish whose combination of textures and flavours showed skilful handling. Simpler tastes might prefer roasted scallops with grilled asparagus and marinated ceps. Main courses are no less inventive, taking in slow-roast Gressingham duck breast with kohlrabi, apple and watercress salad, grilled veal chop with lemons, potato purée and battered onion rings, and grilled halibut with petits pois, crab mayonnaise and a balsamic reduction. For dessert, chocolate fondant has proved a superior version.

France tops the food-friendly wine list, with support from short, well-chosen ranges in other regions. Ordering by the glass to suit the different stages of a meal is a realistic option, with 17 table wines and a tempting selection of sweeties and sherries in all styles to choose from (all glasses £4 to £6). Eight house wines are £12 to £15, and the excitement starts around £20.

CHEF: Simon Bradley   PROPRIETORS: Simon Bradley and Richard Boulert   OPEN: all week L 12.30 to 2.30, Mon to Sat D 7 to 11   CLOSED: bank hols   MEALS: alc (main courses £14 to £24). Set L Sun to Fri £14.50   SERVICE: 12.5% (optional), card slips closed   CARDS: Amex, Delta, MasterCard, Switch, Visa   DETAILS: 60 seats. 8 seats outside. Private parties: 30 main room, 6 to 10 private rooms. Vegetarian meals. Children's helpings. Wheelchair access (not WC). No music ⊖ Chalk Farm

---

Olivo ·   map 13

---

21 Eccleston Street, SW1W 9LX	COOKING 2
TEL: (020) 7730 2505 FAX: (020) 7823 5377	ITALIAN/SARDINIAN
	£29–£54

A warm welcome for everyone is one good reason for choosing this close-packed Italian neighbourhood eatery. Another is its emphasis on Sardinian food, which brings unusual specialities like spaghetti alla bottariga: excellent pasta with grated grey mullet roe creating a burst of sea saltiness. Sweetbreads have been succulent here, and, along with well-timed fish – perhaps grilled sea bass (filleted if you wish) – has shown the kitchen can handle tricky dishes even when rushed. An interesting meat main course might be braised oxtail with red wine and polenta. At inspection, good Sardinian cheeses served with olive oil and walnuts outgunned poached pears with mascarpone and amaretti. Wines also set Olivo apart from standard Anglo-Italians. Everything is from north and central Italy or Sardinia, and three Sardinian dessert wines are available by the glass. Prices start at £14, and Barolo, Barbera and Turriga (Sardinian) are there for wealthy enthusiasts.

CHEF: Marco Melis   PROPRIETOR: Mauro Sanna   OPEN: Mon to Fri L 12 to 2.30, all week 7 to 11 CLOSED: 25 and 26 Dec, Good Fri, Easter Sun, bank hols   MEALS: alc D (main courses £10.50 to £14). Set L £15.50 (2 courses) to £17.50. Cover £1.50   SERVICE: not inc   CARDS: Amex, Delta, MasterCard, Switch, Visa   DETAILS: 40 seats. Private parties: 10 main room. Vegetarian meals. No music. Air-conditioned   ⊖ Victoria

---

▲ One Aldwych, Axis   NEW ENTRY   map 13

Aldwych, WC2B 4RH	
TEL: (020) 7300 0300 FAX: (020) 7300 0301	COOKING 4
EMAIL: axis@onealdwych.com	MODERN EUROPEAN
WEBSITE: www.onealdwych.com	£35–£74

Located in the basement of the chic, sophisticated One Aldwych Hotel, Axis has its own entrance on Aldwych and occupies a striking double-height space with soaring pillars and a vast mural depicting skyscraper buildings drawn with dramatic perspective. It's very urban-chic and cosmopolitan, modern and minimalist, with a pale-tiled floor, black leather chairs and banquettes and white linen-dressed tables.

The menu is an appealing modern European repertoire of light, well-executed dishes based on stylish, quality ingredients. An accomplished starter of smoked ham hock ravioli with vegetable rémoulade and apple and mustard dressing has been followed by a top-quality, squeaky-fresh halibut fillet topped with artichoke barigoule, frothy sweet pepper aïoli and rich lobster sauce. Sweet and savoury soufflés feature; a dessert-course pistachio soufflé may be accompanied by rich, dark chocolate sauce poured through the centre. Service is professional, knowledgeable and personable. The 16-page wine list is divided between France and the 'New World' (which, curiously, includes Italy, Spain and Portugal), with bottle prices starting at £16.50. Post- and pre-theatre menus are available.

Axis' sister restaurant, Indigo, overlooks the slick Lobby Bar, and offers brunch and pre- and post-theatre menus, alongside a full menu that runs to carpaccio of tuna and crab cakes with sweetcorn and coriander relish, to main courses like roast rump of lamb with honeyed courgettes, portabella mushrooms and rocket. Pasta, risotto and salads come in two sizes.

CHEF: Mark Gregory   PROPRIETOR: Gordon Campbell Gray   OPEN: Mon to Fri L 12 to 2.45, Mon to Sat D 5.45 to 10.45 (11.30 Sat)   CLOSED: 23 Dec to 6 Jan, bank hols   MEALS: alc (main courses £12 to £22). Set L and D 5.45 to 7.15, 10 to 10.45 £16.75 (2 courses) to £19.75   SERVICE: 12.5% (optional)   CARDS: Amex, Delta, Diners, MasterCard, Switch, Visa   DETAILS: 120 seats. Private parties: 120 main room. Vegetarian meals. Children's helpings. No cigars/pipes. Wheelchair access (also WC). Music. Air-conditioned   ACCOMMODATION: 105 rooms, all with bath/shower. TV. Phone. Room only £179 to £390. Rooms for disabled. Baby facilities. Swimming pool (*The Which? Guide to Good Hotels*)   ⊖ Charing Cross, Covent Garden, Temple

---

1 Lombard Street ♥   map 13

1 Lombard Street, EC3V 9AA
TEL: (020) 7929 6611   FAX: (020) 7929 6622   COOKING 6
EMAIL: reception@1lombardstreet.com   MODERN EUROPEAN
WEBSITE: www.1lombardstreet.com   £54–£98

1 Lombard Street is a former bank from the days when banks were opulent buildings. A magnificent dome rises above the huge brasserie, beyond which is the restaurant, another large and classically spacious room with a high ceiling and typically vast Georgian windows. The restaurant tables are laid with crisp starched napery, Reidel glasses and individual floating orchids, and 'precise' service is from a team dressed in coffee-coloured waistcoats or suits, according to rank.

Herbert Berger's classical French cooking is enhanced with numerous eclectic touches and novel flavour combinations, as in a salad of hare with celeriac and apple rémoulade, sweet-and-sour chestnut purée and juniper oil, or saddle of venison with caramelised pears, celeriac mousseline and game jus with spiced bread and port. Several dishes at inspection showed off some impressive technique, including half a lobster lightly grilled in its shell and laced with an intensely flavoured lobster and Sauternes jus, served with plump scallops 'oozing sweet fresh flavour' and 'zippy' lime-spiced carrot tagliatelle; and a trio of duck, comprising 'ultra tender, juicy and pink' breast topped with foie gras, a rissole of melting confit with braised apple on bubble and squeak, and a rolled leg with a duck liver stuffing, the whole providing a deeply satisfying range of flavours and textures. Presentation has characterised desserts – an Aztec-style pyramid of Ecuadorian bitter chocolate with a cup of contrastingly light almond milk granité. The Brasserie menu might offer a starter of warm salad of quail and its confit with aubergine caviar and rosemary jus, and a main of griddled salmon with sesame crust, wasabi and ginger beurre blanc.

The wine list favours short round-ups from most regions, with excursions into expense-account bottles in Italy and the USA. The 'Lombard Vault' holds – presumably very securely – a collection of fine clarets going back to a 1950 Pétrus for £1,500. Few bottles are under £20, but they are of decent quality, and house wines start at just £14, with 16 by the glass from £3.50 to £13.

CHEF: Herbert Berger   PROPRIETOR: Jessen & Co Restaurants   OPEN: Mon to Fri 12 to 2.30, 6 to 10   CLOSED: 25 and 26 Dec, 1 Jan, Easter, bank hols   MEALS: alc (main courses £28.50 to £29.50). Set L £32 (2 courses) to £38, Set D £34. Brasserie menu also available   SERVICE: 12.5% (optional), card slips closed   CARDS: Amex, Delta, Diners, MasterCard, Switch, Visa   DETAILS: 40 seats. Private parties: 220 main room, 100 private room. Vegetarian meals. Wheelchair access (also WC). Occasional music. Air-conditioned   ⊖ Bank (£5)

192

map 13

192 Kensington Park Road, W11 2ES	COOKING 1
TEL: (020) 7229 0482 FAX: (020) 7229 3300	MODERN BRITISH
	£29–£62

This perennially buzzy bar-cum-restaurant manages to be a magnet both for drinkers (who stick to the front bar) and for those seeking more substantial forms of sustenance. Seasonality is one of the kitchen's strong points, with the likes of courgette flowers, peas and broad beans turning up on a June menu. Combinations of flavours (many with an Italian inspiration) are generally straightforward and well judged, as in a starter of beef carpaccio with pickled cep and rocket, or pan-fried scallops with crispy courgettes, or a main course of monkfish wrapped in Parma ham with mozzarella and rocket. The wine list is notable both for its large selection by the glass and the number of bottles from trendy producers. Bottle prices start at £12.

CHEF: Stuart Kennedy   PROPRIETOR: Tom Byng   OPEN: all week 12.30 to 3 (3.30 Sat and Sun), 7 to 11.30 (11 Sun)   CLOSED: 25 Dec and 1 Jan   MEALS: alc (main courses £12 to £17). Set L £15 (2 courses) to £18   SERVICE: 12.5%, card slips closed   CARDS: MasterCard, Switch, Visa   DETAILS: 84 seats. Private parties: 8 main room. Vegetarian meals. No cigars/pipes. Wheelchair access (not WC). Music   ⊖ Ladbroke Grove, Notting Hill Gate

▲ One-O-One ⅝✳

map 14

101 Knightsbridge, SW1X 7RN	COOKING 5
TEL: (020) 7290 7101 FAX: (020) 7201 7884	SEAFOOD
EMAIL: oneoone@luxurycollection.com	£44–£97

Although the restaurant functions very much in its own right, it is actually on the ground floor of the Sheraton Park Tower Hotel, discreetly camouflaged behind an expansive glass frontage. The marine sculpture and the many seafood prints hung about the walls are clear signals that the central interest of Pascal Proyart's kitchen lies under water. This is very much la cuisine de la mer.

From the moment the amuse-bouche arrives – perhaps a stimulating piece of marinated salmon – it is clear that attention to detail, freshness and quality are all at a premium. Proyart grew up in a fishing village on the Breton coast, and his culinary obsession remains intact even amid the corporate luxe of a grand hotel. An exceptional first course of seared scallops with duck foie gras, a fricassee of ceps and diced tomato is indicative of a willingness to pair fish and meat, which is also on display in a main course of paella that teams up giant tiger prawns with chorizo. Timing is all with fish cookery, and dishes do not lack for polish in that department either: in a portion of roasted sea bass cooked 'just right', gaining depth from a garnish of tapenade and accompaniments of sautéed artichokes and potatoes crushed with basil. Roasted peppered lobster is expertly freed from the shell, although served in it, and arrives with tomato confit, potato 'mousseline thermidor' and a sauce of lobster-flavoured béarnaise. With oyster specialities and king crab legs from the Barents Sea, it is easy to get carried away, although expect to be brought back to terra firma with a bump when the Knightsbridge-sized bill arrives. If there's anything left in the bank, finish with chocolate and caramel tart with blood-orange sorbet, or mango carpaccio with lychee coulis. You won't seriously be expecting bargain wine prices, and nor will you be wrong. There is a decent selection by the glass from £5.25 for a Chilean Sauvignon Blanc (which comes in at £22 a bottle), but the bottle mark-ups soon leave £30 far behind.

CHEF: Pascal Proyart   PROPRIETOR: Sheraton Park Tower   OPEN: all week 12 to 2.30, 7 to 10.15
MEALS: alc (main courses £19 to £28). Set L £25, Set D £45   SERVICE: not inc   CARDS: Amex,
Delta, Diners, MasterCard, Switch, Visa   DETAILS: 68 seats. Private parties: 80 main room.
Children's helpings. No smoking in 1 dining room. Wheelchair access (not WC). Music. No
mobile phones. Air-conditioned   ACCOMMODATION: 280 rooms, all with bath/shower. TV. Phone.
Room only £228 to £400. Rooms for disabled. Baby facilities. Swimming pool
⊖ Knightsbridge

L'Oranger 🍴

map 15

5 St James's Street, SW1A 1EF
TEL: (020) 7839 3774   FAX: (020) 7839 4330

COOKING 4
FRENCH/MEDITERRANEAN
£45–£123

In surroundings of boutiques for gentlemen and cigar emporiums, which are reminiscent of a bygone era and seem to represent a peculiar type of Englishness, L'Oranger is by contrast a typically French restaurant. Its long rectangular dining room looks rather timeworn and the atmosphere is somewhat dreary, but service compensates with its charming and good-natured manner, as well as its efficiency.

The cooking is not the most adventurous around but its scope is broad, taking in contemporary ideas (such as chickpea compote with salted cod and crispy bread) alongside more traditional treatments (ribeye of beef with pan-fried foie gras); and several rustic dishes (split pea and smoked bacon soup) as well as some fairly luxurious creations (roasted Bresse chicken with black truffle). Despite a couple of serious disappointments – soggy tempura and severely overcooked John Dory – standards at a recent inspection meal were generally high, starting with a perfectly poached egg on thinly sliced waxy potatoes in vinaigrette and topped with caviar, followed by 'firm, just cooked' grilled Dover sole with a 'punchy' crab sauce, and well-timed roast duck, meticulously fanned out and served on baby artichokes. The highlight, however, was a well-risen, velvety textured hazelnut soufflé with a buttery almond sauce.

Anyone looking to counter the effect of the numerous menu supplements by choosing something modest from the wine list faces a difficult task – there is nothing under £24. However, those for whom money is no object will enjoy choosing from the superb selection of great French wines.

CHEF: Thierry Laborde   PROPRIETOR: A To Z Restaurants   OPEN: Mon to Fri L 12 to 2.30, Mon to Sat D 6.30 to 10.45   CLOSED: 25 to 31 Dec, bank hols   MEALS: Set L £22 (2 courses) to £26, Set D £39 (2 courses) to £45   SERVICE: 12.5% (optional), card slips closed   CARDS: Amex, Delta, Diners, MasterCard, Switch, Visa   DETAILS: 45 seats. 12 seats outside. Private parties: 24 main room. Vegetarian meals. Wheelchair access (not WC). No music. Air-conditioned   ⊖ Green Park

Original Tagines £   map 15

7A Dorset Street, W1U 6QN
TEL/FAX: (020) 7935 1545   COOKING 2
EMAIL: info@originaltagines.com   MOROCCAN
WEBSITE: www.originaltagines.com   £21–£54

The modest shop-front gives way to a simple dining room with a relaxed atmosphere, making a straightforward setting for some straightforward, and pretty authentic, Moroccan peasant cooking. Meals might begin in traditional fashion with harira soup and a choice of salads – say, broad bean, red pepper or lentil – before continuing with a selection of tagines: lamb with prunes, almonds and egg, or even a 'Berber' vegetarian version. Accompanying these are cracked wheat in tomato sauce, salad and bread. Alternatively, numerous couscous dishes are listed along with grilled chicken or lamb. To finish, choose from a selection of pastries or rice pudding with orange blossom, all rounded off with Moroccan coffee. Value is notable, which just adds to the reasons behind this restaurant's popularity – booking is advised. House wines start at £10.50, or £2.85 a glass.

CHEF: Serif Sepet   PROPRIETOR: Kenan Duran   OPEN: Mon to Fri L 12 to 3, Mon to Sat D 6 to 11   MEALS: alc (main courses £6.50 to £12). Set L £7.50 (2 courses), Set D £12.50 (2 courses)   SERVICE: not inc   CARDS: Amex, Delta, MasterCard, Switch, Visa   DETAILS: 36 seats. 12 seats outside. Private parties: 40 main room. Vegetarian meals. Wheelchair access (not WC). Music. No mobile phones. Air-conditioned   ⊖ Baker Street

Orrery ⌂   map 15

55–57 Marylebone High Street, W1M 3AE
TEL: (020) 7616 8000   FAX: (020) 7616 8080   COOKING 6
EMAIL: orreryreservations@conran.restaurants.co.uk   FRENCH
WEBSITE: www.orrery.co.uk   £37–£112

Above the furniture shop and épicerie, Orrery encapsulates the Conran design philosophy of sophisticated simplicity: a long, narrow, airy room with banquette seats down one side, windows overlooking the churchyard, and a passageway down the middle patrolled by staff. Despite a different chef, the repertoire has not completely changed – seared scallops ('wonderfully fresh and brilliantly timed'), for example, are still paired with fatty belly pork and an artistic swirl of cauliflower purée – and well-sourced raw materials remain the foundation, evident in a 'breathtakingly simple, but amazing' starter of smoked salmon with a poached egg and artichoke heart, and in a well-judged, three-part layered terrine made from chicken, celeriac and smooth, flavourful foie gras, with a sticky vinaigrette to pull it all together.

Although the food might lack a bit of soul, there is no doubting its technical accomplishment: a simple main course of roast veal sweetbread comes with bittersweet endive and a fine truffled potato purée, and tagine of pigeon – two pink breasts on a pile of saffron couscous – with a small, dark, sweet pastilla parcel and a theatrically served but decidedly un-fiery harissa sauce. The cheese trolley 'can be smelled from a few feet away' and bears an impressive collection of well-kept, mainly French unpasteurised examples, while desserts have included a well-risen apricot soufflé served with chocolate sauce and vanilla ice cream.

Staff are plentiful, 'overattentive' and busy (they 'fuss around' while neglecting more important matters); wines were tasted by two members of staff before our inspector was allowed a sniff, for what purpose was not made clear. On the other hand, one reporter had nothing but praise for the knowledgeable sommelier. This is a fascinating list – mostly French, with nothing but excellence in Bordeaux, Burgundy and the Rhône, a serious approach to the Loire and Alsace and notable depth in the south and south-west – but prices are a problem. House basics at £12 and £14 are the sops to diners on small budgets. Fifteen wines by the glass are £3.25–£13.50.

CHEF: André Garrett   PROPRIETOR: Conran Restaurants   OPEN: all week 12 to 3 (2.30 Sun), 7 to 11 (10.30 Sun)   CLOSED: 25 and 25 Dec, Good Fri   MEALS: alc (main courses £14.50 to £28). Set L £23.50, Set D Mon to Sat £50 to £80 (inc wine), Set D Sun £30 to £80 (inc wine). Bar menu available   SERVICE: 12.5% (optional), card slips closed   CARDS: Amex, Delta, Diners, MasterCard, Switch, Visa   DETAILS: 80 seats. 35 seats outside. Private parties: 80 main room. Vegetarian meals. No pipes. Wheelchair access (also WC). No music   ⊖ Baker Street, Regent's Park

Osia   NEW ENTRY

11 Haymarket (entrance in Orange Street),
SW1Y 4BP
TEL: (020) 7976 1313   FAX: (020) 7976 1919
EMAIL: nadir@osiarestaurant.com
WEBSITE: www.osiarestaurant.com

COOKING 4
CONTEMPORARY AUSTRALIAN
£39–£70

'Australian nouvelle?' 'Modern Australian?' 'British ingredients with Australian "bush" spices?' Whatever you might call it, the cooking at this central London newcomer puts an emphasis on provenance, sourcing quality British ingredients and adding Australian flourishes, such as warrigal greens, kumera and myrtle mayonnaise. The restaurant is cool and stylish, with tables laid out as a series of alcoves, the seats covered in olive-coloured leather. The menu is divided into 'food cocktails and ceviches' (such as the luscious, refreshing Pacific tuna ceviche with chilli, avocado purée and pickled pepper), then 'appetizers' and main courses. A starter of hand-dived scallops with wilted warrigal greens and coriander butter had big juicy scallops, nicely browned, and a main course of tender Dorrigo herbed rack of lamb with wilted pea shoots and kumera squash was dramatically presented on a round white plate, with a salty, caramelly sauce poured over the meat at the table. Inventive desserts such as baked rosella flower pudding with raspberry sorbet and rhubarb compote, and meringue pavlova drive home the Australian theme to good effect. What to drink in such a place? Cocktails or rather pricey wines seem to be the answer.

CHEF: Scott Webster   PROPRIETORS: Raymond De Fazio and Scott Webster   OPEN: Mon to Sat; 12 to 3, 5.30 to 10.45   CLOSED: 25 Dec, 1 Jan, bank hols   MEALS: alc (main courses £15 to £20). Set L £19 (2 courses) to £23   SERVICE: 12.5% (optional), card slips closed   CARDS: Amex, Delta, MasterCard, Switch, Visa   DETAILS: 70 seats. Vegetarian meals. Wheelchair access (also WC). Music. Air-conditioned   ⊖ Piccadilly, Leicester Square

Oxo Tower ▮   map 13

Oxo Tower Wharf, Barge House Street, SE1 9PH
TEL: (020) 7803 3888   FAX: (020) 7803 3838   COOKING 3
EMAIL: oxo.reservations@harveynichols.co.uk   MODERN BRITISH
WEBSITE: www.harveynichols.co.uk   £42–£84

As the title of a Channel 4 series has it, location, location, location is what's it about, and there are few more enviably sited restaurants in the capital than this. Take the express lift to the eighth floor of the red-brick building on the South Bank of the Thames and drink in the day or night views. Dave Miney's menus cut and paste the modes of the moment into an invigorating range of choice. Japanese notes surface regularly, presenting sea bass saikyo-style with pickled ginger, or partnering main-course turbot fillet with edamame (soy bean pods) and yuzu butter. Then there is the French paysan approach (braised pig's trotter galantine with sauce gribiche), the North African (vegetable tagine with couscous and spiced chickpea salsa), and even a spot of old English, as in loin of lamb with peas and broad beans. The descriptions are fun to decipher – 'pineapple parcel with coconut foam' sounds like something damaged in the post – and, most important, the food delivers on the palate. Crab mayonnaise with wilted pak choi and sweet chilli dressing, and a main course of pan-fried salmon with niçoise salad both satisfied one reporter. Service copes well with the press of business.

The house selection of around 50 wines, with up to a dozen by the glass (£3.75 to £8.40), makes a well-rounded list in itself, swooshing as effortlessly as the express lift from £14 to £60. But for real depth there's the 'Big List' that brings together hundreds of good, great and cultish wines from Old and New Worlds without forgetting that some of us have a budget to watch.

CHEF: Dave Miney   PROPRIETOR: Harvey Nichols & Co Ltd   OPEN: all week 12 to 3, 6 to 11 CLOSED: 25 and 26 Dec   MEALS: alc D (main courses £16 to £26.50). Set L £28.50   SERVICE: 12.5%, card slips closed   CARDS: Amex, Delta, Diners, MasterCard, Switch, Visa   DETAILS: 130 seats. 25 seats outside. Private parties: 8 main room. Vegetarian meals. Wheelchair access (also WC). No music. Air-conditioned   ⊖ Blackfriars, Waterloo

Palais du Jardin   map 15

136 Long Acre, WC2E 9AD   COOKING 2
TEL: (020) 7379 5353   FAX: (020) 7379 1846   FRENCH-PLUS
                                                                     £39–£70

This big brute of a place is especially useful in Covent Garden, with its bewildering mass of restaurants. Good-quality ingredients generally show up well in mainly classic French combinations: grilled fillets of sole filled with prawn mousse on boulangère potatoes in a champagne cream sauce, for example. But borrowings from further afield might include tempura of tuna with pickled cabbage and sweet pepper sauce, or crisp-fried duck breast with caramelised pineapple and pak choi. The professionalism and style of the waiting staff impress reliably. An 'afternoon menu', served between lunch and dinner, brings on smoked salmon on a potato and olive cake with grain mustard cream, and then maybe fillet steak or lobster salad. House wines are £12.50, but thereafter few bottles can be found under £20 from the predominantly French list.

CHEF: Jamie Scorer   PROPRIETOR: Le Palais du Jardin Ltd   OPEN: all week 12 to 3.15, 5.30 to 11.30; 'afternoon menu' 3.15 to 5.30   CLOSED: 25 and 26 Dec   MEALS: alc (main courses £14.50 to £23)   SERVICE: 12.5% (optional)   CARDS: Amex, Delta, Diners, MasterCard, Switch, Visa   DETAILS: 250 seats. 15 seats outside. Private parties: 250 main room, 80 to 100 private rooms. Vegetarian meals. No-smoking area. No cigars. Music. Air-conditioned   ⊖ Covent Garden, Leicester Square

Paolo   NEW ENTRY   map 15

16 Percy Street, W1T 1DT
TEL: (020) 7637 9900   FAX: (020) 7637 9696   COOKING 2
EMAIL: info@paolorestaurants.com   ITALIAN
WEBSITE: www.paolorestaurants.com   £29–£54

On the edges of Fitzrovia and Bloomsbury, Paolo has a simple, airy and unaffected décor. The menu, on which pasta figures large, might start with a seasonal soup, based on sweet, fresh peas, served in a large white bowl with a spoonful of fresh ricotta. Pasta is clearly a strength of chef Maurizio Morelli, formerly of Ibla (closed, sadly), and is served in a variety of ways: lemon-flavoured ravioli may be stuffed with buffalo ricotta and accompanied by a sauce made from vine-ripened pomodorini tomatoes, while strands of tagliolini may come with artichokes and salted ricotta. Inventive main courses may feature roast breast of duck with bittersweet braised chicory, discs of prickly pear and limoncello sauce. A 'divine' dessert of warm chocolate, almond and amaretto cake was 'less savoured than devoured' by one visitor. Service is friendly and professional. The all-Italian wine list opens with budget options from the south at £11.50 (£2.95 a glass) and cruises through to some very serious bottles.

CHEF: Maurizio Morelli   PROPRIETOR: Paolo Boschi   OPEN: Mon to Sat 12 to 3, 6 to 11   CLOSED: 25 and 26 Dec, 1 Jan   MEALS: alc (main courses £10 to £15). Set L £14.50 (2 courses) to £17.50   SERVICE: 12.5% (optional), card slips closed   CARDS: Amex, Delta, Diners, MasterCard, Switch, Visa   DETAILS: 65 seats. 6 seats outside. Private parties: 70 main room. Vegetarian meals. Children's helpings. Wheelchair access (not WC). Music. Air-conditioned   ⊖ Tottenham Court Road, Goodge Street   £5

'The resident ginger cat was more interested in my meal than [were] the staff'.
(On eating in Wiltshire)

Parsee ✱ £

map 12

34 Highgate Hill, N19 5NL
TEL: (020) 7272 9091   FAX: (020) 7687 1139
EMAIL: dining@theparsee.com
WEBSITE: www.theparsee.com

COOKING 3
PARSEE
£26–£48

Cyrus Todiwala of Café Spice Namaste (see entry) is the driving force and guiding light behind this restaurant, which celebrates the cooking of India's Parsee community. The décor reinforces the cultural message, although one correspondent thought the dining room 'inconspicuous and comfortably plain' despite the eye-catching colour scheme and walls dotted with sepia photographs and old portraits of famous Parsees.

The signature dish is dhansak, although this rendition is a world away from most curry-house versions: the sauce is almost dry, it includes meatballs for good measure, and it is accompanied by a browned onion and star anise-flavoured pilau rice. Starters include the intriguingly titled 'mumbai no frankie' – a Bombay snack of diced lamb packed into an 'egged' chapati. The menu also lists a quartet of chargrills, including marinated venison haunch and fiercely spiced Loch Fyne salmon; you might also find stuffed sea bass steamed in a banana leaf and – from Goa – pork vindaloo. Apricot toffee ice cream is a recommended dessert. Service receives plenty of praise, and the short wine list suits the food admirably. House French is £12.90.

CHEF/PROPRIETOR: Cyrus Todiwala   OPEN: Mon to Sat D only 6 to 10.45   CLOSED: Christmas, bank hols   MEALS: alc (main courses £10 to £13). Set D £20 to £30   SERVICE: 10% (optional), card slips closed   CARDS: Amex, Delta, Diners, MasterCard, Switch, Visa   DETAILS: 50 seats. Private parties: 30 main room, 10 to 18 private rooms. Vegetarian meals. Children's helpings. No smoking in 1 dining room. Wheelchair access (not WC). Music. Air-conditioned   ⊖ Archway

---

Passione

map 15

10 Charlotte Street, W1T 2LT
TEL: (020) 7636 2833   FAX: (020) 7636 2889
WEBSITE: www.passione.co.uk

COOKING 4
MODERN ITALIAN
£37–£66

You may not notice Passione's unassuming orange exterior until you're right upon it. Once you've arrived, though, there's a hustle and bustle that gives it a real sense of atmosphere. Service is 'attentive and helpful without being obtrusive', and everything seems to happen at a relaxed pace. Well-rendered rusticity and good timing are notable traits of the kitchen and, in the southern Italian tradition (from where chef Gennaro Contaldo hails), portions tend to be large. A reporter gave the thumbs-up to a healthy-sized starter of anchovy and orange salad, in which 'the pungent taste of the fish worked well against the freshness of the orange'. There's always a selection of pasta and rice dishes on hand – agnolini filled with mixed game and truffle sauce, perhaps, or risotto with wild sorrel – and main courses are equally balanced between fish (perhaps king prawns served atop chargrilled vegetables) and meat. For afters, good espresso follows on from sweets such as refreshing green apple sorbet. Wines – a short selection of smart bottles from Italy – start with a couple of basics at £13.50, or £3.50 a glass.

CHEF: Gennaro Contaldo PROPRIETORS: Gennaro Contaldo, Gennaro D'Urso and Liz Przybylski
OPEN: Mon to Fr L 12.30 to 2.15, Mon to Sat D 7 to 10.15 MEALS: alc (main courses £11 to
£19.50) SERVICE: 12.5% (optional), card slips closed CARDS: Amex, Delta, Diners,
MasterCard, Switch, Visa DETAILS: 50 seats. 8 seats outside. Private parties: 43 main room,
10 to 18 private rooms. Vegetarian meals. Wheelchair access (not WC). No music. Air-
conditioned ⊖ Goodge Street

Pharmacy   NEW ENTRY   map 13

150 Notting Hill Gate, W11 3QG
TEL: (020) 7221 2442   FAX: (020) 7243 2345   COOKING 7
EMAIL: mail@pharmacylondon.com   MODERN FRENCH
WEBSITE: www.pharmacy.london.com   £36–£85

After the initial flurry of interest that surrounded its opening, Pharmacy seemed
to settle into the role of a fashionable but gastronomically mediocre canteen for
the Notting Hill set. But following the appointment of Hywell Jones as chef, the
medically themed bar and brasserie is once more intent on making waves in the
London dining scene.

Jones has a respectable track record, having previously made a great
impression at Foliage (see entry) in recent years. He shows great technical skill
and a creative streak to conjure up original ideas such as the amuse-gueule of
savoury sweetcorn pannacotta with tiny red pepper dice that got an inspection
meal off to a fine start. Far more impressive, however, was a starter of very rare
seared bluefin tuna, served in a line of little squares, bookended with cones of
piquillo pepper stuffed with salt cod brandade and pesto, and set on a bed of
earthy and lightly spiced lentils. Other high points have included a creamy,
frothy velouté of butternut squash, poured at the table over a bowl of earthy ceps
and slices of aged Parmesan; line-caught sea bass 'cooked to perfection' and
served on a well-made shellfish lasagne in a pool of mushroom cappuccino with
cubes of warm cucumber; and chicken breast wrapped in bacon with peas and
chanterelle mushrooms. To finish, there is an excellent cheeseboard though
more serious temptation is offered in the shape of lemon tart with fine pastry and
a well-balanced filling, partnered with a delicate lemon sorbet and a gelée of
lemon, grapefruit and orange. The French-centred wine list offers plenty of
quality but few bargains. Prices start at £20.

CHEF: Hywell Jones PROPRIETOR: Hartford Plc OPEN: Mon to Fri L 12 to 2.30, Mon to Sat D 7 to
10.30 (11 Fri and Sat) MEALS: alc (main courses £14 to £26). Set L £16.50 (2 courses) to £18.50
SERVICE: 12.5% (optional), card slips closed CARDS: Amex, Delta, MasterCard, Switch, Visa
DETAILS: 90 seats. Private parties: 100 main room. Vegetarian meals. No music. Air-conditioned
⊖ Notting Hill Gate

Philpotts Mezzaluna   NEW ENTRY   map 13

424 Finchley Road, NW2 2HY   COOKING 2
TEL: (020) 7794 0455   FAX: (020) 7794 0452   ITALIAN
WEBSITE: www.philpotts-mezzaluna.com   £31–£42

David Philpott has been cooking Italian at his own Finchley Road address for
the past three years, and if the restaurant has a slightly provincial air (a not
surprising moon theme throughout), there is nothing parochial about the menu.

A straightforward pricing policy offering one to five courses might start with a complimentary cupful of asparagus soup followed perhaps by grilled asparagus with pea rémoulade, or stuffed artichoke with anchovy, ciabatta, garlic and parsley. Follow up with a 'subtle and flavourful' risotto verde or spinach and ricotta ravioli. Main courses such as fillet of lamb with canellini beans and olives, and parsley crusted cod with saffron mash have come in for praise along with desserts such as an 'aromatic' hot strawberry tart with lemongrass sorbet, and 'light and subtle' white chocolate pannacotta. Service, too, is skilled and attentive. Wine takes a trip around the world with a predictable emphasis on Italy, and plenty of interest below £25. House wine is a northern Italian duo at £14.50.

CHEF: David Philpott   PROPRIETORS: David Philpott and Alex Ross   OPEN: Tue to Fri L 12 to 2.30, Sun L 12 to 3, Tue to Sun D 7 to 11   CLOSED: 25 and 26 Dec, 1 Jan   MEALS: Set L £10 (1 course) to £25, Set D £20 (2 courses) to £33   SERVICE: not inc, 12.5% (optional) for parties of 6 or more   CARDS: Amex, MasterCard, Switch, Visa   DETAILS: 60 seats. Private parties: 60 main room. Vegetarian meals. Children's helpings. No cigars/pipes. Wheelchair access (not WC). Occasional music. Air-conditioned   ⊖ Golders Green £5

Phoenix 🌟

162–164 Lower Richmond Road, SW15 1LY
TEL: (020) 8780 3131   FAX: (020) 8780 1114
EMAIL: phoenix@sonnys.co.uk

COOKING 3
MODERN EUROPEAN
£27–£60

The Phoenix is a jumping, vibrant neighbourhood restaurant with white walls and hardwood floors, the interiors enlivened with changing displays of contemporary art, while an outside terrace with three huge parasols is enclosed by bamboo, clematis and rosemary plants. Franco Taruschio's tenure as consultant chef continues, bringing on to the menus impeccably recherché Italian touches. Quail egg and lentil crostini with slow-roast tomatoes; courgette risotto with pecorino; and braised oxtail with button onions and mash are joined by an eighteenth-century signature dish of abiding popularity, vincisgrassi maceratesi (a luxuriously creamy, truffly lasagne). Fruity desserts include a sorbet of 'blood peach', as well as vanilla bavarois with a salad of blood oranges. Service is sufficiently helpful to advise on menu choices if you feel a little lost. A good choice of wines by the glass supplements the main list, which in itself is fine but pricey. House French is £10.95.

CHEFS: Chris Parkinson and Franco Taruschio   PROPRIETOR: Rebecca Mascarenhas   OPEN: all week 12.30 to 2.30 (3 Sun), 7 to 11 (11.30 Fri and Sat)   CLOSED: bank hols   MEALS: alc (main courses £10.50 to £17). Set L £13.50 (2 courses) to £16.50, Set L Sun £19.50, Set D (not Fri/Sat) £13.50 (2 courses) to £16.50. Bar menu available (not Fri/Sat evenings)   SERVICE: 12.5% (optional), card slips closed   CARDS: Amex, Delta, Diners, MasterCard, Switch, Visa   DETAILS: 100 seats. 40 seats outside. Private parties: 100 main room. Vegetarian meals. Children's helpings. No smoking in 1 dining room. No pipes. Wheelchair access (also WC). Music. Air-conditioned   ⊖ Putney Bridge £5

🐦 *indicates that there has been a change of chef since last year's Guide, and the Editor has judged that the change is of sufficient interest to merit the reader's attention.*

Phoenix Palace £

map 13

3–5 Glentworth Street, NW1 5PG
TEL: (020) 7486 3515   FAX: (020) 7486 3401

COOKING 2
CHINESE
£24–£65

'Rather a surprise to find a Chinese this good away from the usual locations,' commented a visitor to this restaurant on the ground floor of a block of flats. Inside is a cavernous dining room that 'makes you feel that you are in Hong Kong' with its flowing water display, elegant redwood chairs and all manner of screens. The huge menu is primarily Cantonese – with a few regional detours – and seafood is a strength: eel has been strongly recommended, perhaps stir-fried with garlic and tangerine peel or given sweet-and-sour treatment and wrapped in lotus leaves. Other successes have included shark's lips and shredded duck soup, and a hotpot with stuffed bean curd and mixed meats, while staples such as chicken with cashew nuts don't let the side down. At lunchtime there are dim sum, plus a fascinating menu of one-plate dishes ranging from Japanese udon noodles in bean paste soup with butterfly prawns to fried rice with dried scallops and egg white. Service is 'very accommodating'. House French is £9.80.

CHEF: Kwok Wah Lam   PROPRIETOR: Nanon Ltd   OPEN: all week 12 (11 Sun) to 11.30 (10.30 Sun)
CLOSED: 25 and 26 Dec   MEALS: alc (main courses £5.50 to £22). Set L £5.50 (2 courses) to £8.80,
Set D £9.80 (2 courses) to £19.80 (all min 2)   SERVICE: 12.5%   CARDS: Delta, MasterCard,
Switch, Visa   DETAILS: 200 seats. Private parties: 160 main room, 10 to 30 private rooms.
Vegetarian meals. Occasional music. Air-conditioned   ⊖ Baker Street

Pied-à-Terre ▮ ✳

map 15

34 Charlotte Street, W1T 2NH
TEL: (020) 7636 1178   FAX: (020) 7916 1171
WEBSITE: www.pied.a.terre.co.uk

COOKING 8
FRENCH
£44–£85

In a street packed with attention-seeking restaurants, this one is reassuringly unobtrusive. It is not everybody's favourite in terms of design – some reporters still find the place comparatively 'drab' and 'sombre' – but the overall feel is of a smart, discreet space whose careful use of dark earthy colours, subtle lighting and stylish crockery add up to a comfortable, contemporary setting. As for the food, it falls into the 'expensive but worth it' category, offering varying amounts of choice on set-price menus with a couple of price supplements. 'A comprehensively fine meal with every dish technically perfect' is a fair summing up of the majority experience.

Shane Osborn combines sure-handed technique with clear, sometimes robust flavours, yet dishes are always well balanced: thin, nearly translucent pasta is filled to bursting with shredded oxtail meat and finely chopped mushrooms, and topped with slices of firm but yielding baby turnip to absorb the luxurious lentil purée and intense red wine sauce. Even soups come in for plaudits, typical being a foaming velouté of white beans with cubes of smoky pancetta and a large slice of black truffle: a modern comfort dish if ever there was. Spot-on timing, fine judgement and high quality materials characterise the output, and dishes are well focused, with just the right degree of complexity, as in a large skinless fillet of moist, seared salmon ('the most perfectly cooked piece of salmon I've ever seen') occupying centre stage, attended by a sticky, caramelised shallot, a ragout of mushrooms in a wine-based reduction, a dash of light hollandaise and a crisp pastry biscuit.

It may be fiddly stuff, especially with all the excellent pre-, mid- and post-meal freebies, but dishes never lose sight of their main purpose. Plum tarte fine is a winner, consisting of supremely thin slices of plum on a light, buttery puff pastry base, with a soft cinnamon ice cream, while creamed mango rice pudding with pineapple sorbet is 'one of the best puddings...ever'. Predominantly French staff are keen and well trained, and service is normally friendly and efficient, although it does vary. Burgundy is emphatically the main interest of the long wine list, with multiple vintages of fine bottles. Bordeaux is strong too, but other regions of France are sketchy by comparison. California leads the New World, while a serious approach to Austria is an unusual twist. Bottles under £20 turn up in a fair number of regions but mark-ups are high. A number of reporters have enjoyed the option of a recommended wine by the glass with each course.

CHEF: Shane Osborn   PROPRIETOR: David Moore   OPEN: Tue to Fri L 12 to 2.30, Mon to Sat D 6.30 to 11   CLOSED: Last week Dec, first week Jan   MEALS: Set L £20.50 (2 courses) to £39.50 (2 courses), Set D £39.50 (2 courses) to £65   SERVICE: 12.5% (optional), card slips closed   CARDS: Amex, Delta, MasterCard, Switch, Visa   DETAILS: 49 seats. Private parties: 7 main room, 6 to 14 private rooms. No smoking in 1 dining room. Wheelchair access (not WC). No music. Air-conditioned   ⊖ Goodge Street

---

Le Pont de la Tour

36D Shad Thames, SE1 2YE
TEL: (020) 7403 8403   FAX: (020) 7403 0267
WEBSITE: www.conran.com

map 13

COOKING 4
MODERN EUROPEAN
£45–£96

Here, at one of the most glamorously sited Conran restaurants, you eat overlooking a fairy-lit stretch of the Thames, with the (almost) eponymous bridge rising majestically before you. On a summer's evening a table on the terrace is a treat indeed, even if rather undersized for its purpose.

Martin Caws, who left Marco Pierre White's Mirabelle (see entry) for a south Asian sabbatical, took over the kitchen here in April 2003. Good ingredients are sympathetically handled, as in a straightforward starter of salmon tartare, vividly accompanied by confit tomatoes and basil, or a high-intensity main course of lamb rump, cooked pink, and successfully partnered with the roasted sweetbreads, potato gratin and morels. Richness for its own sake is carefully avoided, allowing a roast breast and confit leg of Landais duck to be served with an earthy salad of haricot beans and walnuts, or an iced mandarin soufflé to be teamed with dark chocolate sorbet. An inspection included an over-thickened velouté sauce with grilled scallops, and a flavourless tomato salad at £6.50 (vegetables are charged extra), but concluded on an upbeat note with fine nougatine parfait brilliantly accompanied by a red wine syrup. The turning round of tables is practised so diligently that you may be asked to get out before you've even seen the bill, which may just be mistaken as an act of charity by somebody not aware of the schedule.

The wine list shimmers with class and convinces in all regions. In France, Burgundy and Bordeaux are complemented by a great range from the Loire and some Rhône heavyweights. Elsewhere Italy and Australia shine brightest. Wines under £25 aren't too hard to find and promise good flavours. The 14 sold by the glass (£5.50–£12.75) are a cut or two above most ranges.

CHEF: Martin Caws   PROPRIETOR: Conran Restaurants   OPEN: Sun to Fri L 12 to 2.30, all week D 6 to 11 (10.30 Sun)   MEALS: alc (main courses £16.50 to £26). Set L £29.50. Bar menu available Mon to Sat   SERVICE: 12.5% (optional)   CARDS: Amex, MasterCard, Switch, Visa   DETAILS: 120 seats. 65 seats outside. Private parties: 5 to 20 private rooms. Vegetarian meals. Wheelchair access (not WC). Music. Air-conditioned   ⊖ London Bridge

Popeseye £

map 12

108 Blythe Road, W14 0HD
TEL: (020) 7610 4578

COOKING 1
STEAK AND GRILLS
£24–£78

This is as simple a formula as it gets. The menu consists only of steaks – sirloin, fillet or rump – served with chips, with an option of a side salad. That's it – except that the steaks are superb, grass-fed Aberdeen Angus delivered each day from the Scottish Highlands and hung for a minimum of a fortnight to maximise flavour. The smallest is a dainty six ounces, while for the robust of appetite they go up to just under two pounds. If you need more, there are a few puddings, ices or cheeses to finish. A good list of mostly red wines includes a fine run of clarets back to 1978. Another branch is at 277 Upper Richmond Road, London SW15, tel: (020) 8788 7733.

CHEF/PROPRIETOR: Ian Hutchison   OPEN: Mon to Sat D only 6.45 to 10.15   MEALS: alc (main courses £9.50 to £45.50)   SERVICE: 12.5% (optional)   CARDS: none   DETAILS: 34 seats. No cigars. Wheelchair access (not WC). Occasional music   ⊖ Olympia (£5)

Potemkin

NEW ENTRY   map 13

144 Clerkenwell Road, EC1R 5DP
TEL: (020) 7278 6661   FAX: (020) 7278 5551
EMAIL: reserve@potemkin.co.uk
WEBSITE: www.potemkin.co.uk

COOKING 4
RUSSIAN
£24–£63

From an exotic-looking vodka bar on a City street corner, narrow stairs lead down to a dark, intimate dining room. Caviar, Siberian dumplings, borscht and stuffed cabbage are all here, and zakuski (starters) include herring cake, smoked salmon and blini, and Kamchatka crab (in a mildly spicy mayonnaise on shredded lettuce). Sturgeon appears in several guises: in a soup, fried with asparagus and new potatoes, or slow-cooked in herb bouillon, then chilled, thinly sliced and juiced with lemon. Flavours are generally intriguing – marinated, pan-fried pork fillet, for example, served with red and yellow peppers and a sweet-sour tomato sauce – and dishes are well balanced, including good-quality red snapper on a grated vegetable salsa with a shallot and mustard sauce. Among desserts (not a forte), unfamiliar names may conceal dishes like strawberry cake, or a pancake filled with pleasantly sharp cherry compote. Meals can be accompanied by a plate of pickles and a glass of vodka from a list of about a hundred, starting with Cristall Superlux (£2.50 a 25ml shot) and including versions flavoured with cranberries, banana, lemon, herbs, spices, and (headed 'unusual') butterscotch, chocolate, coconut and cannabis. A token wine list starts with French white and Spanish red (£12) and includes Georgian bottles.

CHEF: Elena Fisher   PROPRIETOR: Southside Ltd   OPEN: Mon to Fri L 12 to 2.30, Mon to Sat D 6 to 10.30   CLOSED: Bank hols   MEALS: alc (main courses £9.50 to £18). Set L £5.99 (1 course) to £10 (2 courses)   SERVICE: 12.5% (optional), card slips closed   CARDS: Amex, Delta, Diners, MasterCard, Switch, Visa   DETAILS: 36 seats. Private parties: 36 main room. Vegetarian meals. No children. No cigars/pipes. Music. Air-conditioned (£5)

La Poule au Pot

| NEW ENTRY | map 14

231 Ebury Street, SW1W 8UT   COOKING 3
TEL: (020) 7730 7763   FAX: (020) 7259 9651   FRENCH
                                                          £28–£72

'If you cannot travel to France, travel to Ebury Street', advised one visitor to this much-frequented neighbourhood French restaurant, with its closely packed tables (booking essential). 'Rustic classical French cuisine' is how the proprietors describe the cooking, and the ambience, food and wines are absolutely, unequivocally French. Wooden floorboards, stone walls and large windows draped in lace add to the Gallic feel, the cooking is underpinned by classical techniques, but pleasantly devoid of fashion and pretension, served in more than generous portions. A French grandmère may be impressed by starters such as soupe de poisson, served in a deep pot and heartily festooned with mussels, scallops, a langoustine, white fish and red mullet, all in a good stock and offset by spicy rouille. Another classic, lapin à la moutarde, features tender, earthy meat, neatly jointed, complemented by a creamy but not over-rich mustard sauce. Desserts? Think mousse au chocolat, tarte Tatin and crème brûlée. Service is friendly, but can get haphazard when the place is in full swing. Wines are French, mostly Bordeaux and Burgundy; bottle prices kick in at £14.50 but rise quickly.

CHEF: Andrew Cafferkey   PROPRIETOR: Peter Frankel   OPEN: all week 12.30 to 2.30 (3.30 Sun), 7 to 11 (10 Sun)   CLOSED: 25 and 26 Dec   MEALS: alc (main courses £13 to £20). Set L £14.50 (2 courses) to £16   SERVICE: 12.5% (optional), card slips closed   CARDS: Amex, Delta, Diners, MasterCard, Switch, Visa   DETAILS: 70 seats. 40 seats outside. Private parties: 20 main room, 16 to 20 private rooms. Vegetarian meals. Wheelchair access (not WC). No music. Air-conditioned ⊖ Sloane Square

Providores ✸✖

map 15

109 Marylebone High Street, W1U 4RX   COOKING 5
TEL: (020) 7935 6175   FAX: (020) 7935 6877   FUSION
WEBSITE: www.theprovidores.co.uk   £39–£69

Beyond the bow-windowed front of what looks like an old London inn lies a high-ceilinged room that operates variously as a wine and tapas bar, café and meeting place. At the back, a flight of dark wooden steps leads to the airy and simply decorated first-floor dining room that is the Providores. Peter Gordon does fusion food like no one else, combining Spanish ideas and materials with some from his native New Zealand, and plenty more besides. Take your pick from a roasted sweet potato, celeriac and tahini soup with yuzu sesame yoghurt, or grilled ox tongue on aubergine and cumin relish with quinoa flat bread. And that's just for starters.

But don't be put off if it all sounds complicated. Straightforward roasting and pan-frying are at the heart of cooking techniques, and the kitchen's sound culinary sense keeps everything on track. Some dishes are comparatively restrained, such as roast rack of New Zealand venison with spiced red cabbage, roast Jerusalem artichokes and chestnut jus, but it is when boundaries are crossed that the whole thing really starts to fizz, taking in roast chump of lamb on braised chard with deep-fried horseradish polenta and tomato chilli jam, and pan-fried sea bass on nigella-roast butternut squash with curried lentils and spinach, and coconut and coriander labneh.

Desserts, by contrast, can seem positively homely, running from apple and gooseberry crumble with five-spice ice cream to a steamed chocolate and hazelnut pudding with chestnut and brandy parfait. Cocktails kick off the wine list, which majors on New Zealand (with quite a few by the glass) but has a small and lively selection from elsewhere. Aotea house red and white are £16.50.

CHEFS: Peter Gordon and Anna Hansen   PROPRIETORS: Peter Gordon, Anna Hansen, Michael McGrath and Jeremy Leeming   OPEN: Providores: all week 12 to 2.45, 6 to 10.45. Tapa Room: all week 9 to 10.30pm   CLOSED: 25, 26 and 31 Dec, 1 Jan   MEALS: alc (main courses £13.50 to £20). Tapas menu available   SERVICE: 12.5% (optional), card slips closed   CARDS: Amex, Delta, MasterCard, Switch, Visa   DETAILS: 40 seats. 6 seats outside. Private parties: 38 main room. Vegetarian meals. No smoking. Music. Air-conditioned   ⊖ Baker Street, Bond Street

Putney Bridge Restaurant   map 12

Embankment, SW15 1LB
TEL: (020) 8780 1811   FAX: (020) 8780 1211   COOKING 6
EMAIL: reservations@putneybridgerestaurant.com   MODERN FRENCH
WEBSITE: www.putneybridgerestaurant.com   £34–£86

It's hard not to notice the large wedge-shaped building that stands close by Putney Bridge, and it's no surprise that it has won a number of architectural awards. Topped with a distinctive copper roof, the ground floor is rendered in reddish-brown concrete, while the upper storey is completely transparent, giving diners great views over the Thames.

Anthony Demetre aims to make just as strong an impression with his cooking. To achieve this, he relies on clever techniques and the artful composition of dishes, layering on flavours and textures. A scallop starter, for example, features the shellfish roasted and partnered with chorizo, salsify and Savoy cabbage cream, while foie gras is sautéed and served on a spiced bread emulsion with Granny Smith apple and a black treacle vinaigrette. Culinary inspiration comes from far and wide, so main courses range from slow-cooked Aberdeen Angus fillet with pont neuf potatoes and a red wine and shallot sauce, to squab pigeon with warm spiced bulgur, a Maghreb-style pastilla, squash with argan oil, and a juice flavoured with hydromel and figs. 'The details are fascinating,' thought one reporter, citing the excellent home-baked breads, though some of the trickier touches (between-course incidentals, for example) are too gimmicky for some readers. French waiters are attentive and good-natured, and a passable choice of wines by the glass opens an extensive but fairly pricey wine list, with little under £20.

CHEF: Anthony Demetre   PROPRIETOR: Gerald Davidson   OPEN: all week L 12 to 2 (2.30 Sat, 3 Sun), Mon to Sat 7 (6.30 Fri and Sat) to 10.30   CLOSED: 25 and 26 Dec   MEALS: alc exc Sun L (main courses L £10, D £15.50 to £24.50). Set L £15.50 (2 courses) to £19.50, Set L Sun £22.50, Set D £49 (whole table only). Bar menu available   SERVICE: 12.5% (optional), card slips closed   CARDS: Amex, Delta, Diners, MasterCard, Switch, Visa   DETAILS: 90 seats. Private parties: 16 main room. Vegetarian meals. Children's helpings at Sun L. No children under 7 for D. No cigars/pipes. Wheelchair access (also WC). No music. Air-conditioned   ⊖ Putney Bridge (£5)

▲ QC

map 13

252 High Holborn, WC1V 7EN

COOKING **5**

TEL: (020) 7829 7000   FAX: (020) 7829 9889

MODERN FRENCH

WEBSITE: www.qcrestaurant.co.uk

£39–£73

As the restaurant and bar of the sumptuous Renaissance Chancery Court Hotel, the aptly named QC cuts an equally opulent pose in what was the former banking hall of the Pearl Assurance Company. Marble columns and walls, clean lines, Art Deco-style lighting, contemporary dark-wood furniture and immaculate table settings fill the huge space to create a grand dining experience; Conran meets the Edwardians, thought one reader. Chef Jun Tanaka trained with both Marco Pierre White and Nico Ladenis, and this pedigree shines through in a repertoire of modern, classical-based cuisine, fashioned around seasonality and quality ingredients. The style is both light and enticing, dishes are well balanced and presented, the imaginative carte dotted with luxury items. Therefore, expect a tartare of tuna with Oscietre caviar and warm cauliflower purée, or nage of caramelised scallop and langoustine with cucumber and ginger to start. A cannelloni of sweetbreads, fricassee of morels and broad beans makes an appealing partnership for roast veal cutlet, while buttered braised turbot is intriguingly teamed with a potage of shellfish and lentils, crispy shallots and garlic chips.

There's no let-up at dessert, where home-made pear and almond pithiviers with chestnut ice cream, or orange and chocolate soufflé, round things off in typical style. The wine list makes a good case for France without lingering too long and neatly summarises the rest of the world. Prices are high and just a few bottles slide in below £20. Fourteen by the glass start at £4.50 (although the cheapest red is £5.70).

CHEF: Jun Tanaka   PROPRIETOR: Renaissance Hotels   OPEN: Mon to Sat 12 to 3, 5 to 10.30   MEALS: alc D after 7 (main courses £16.50 to £22.50). Set L and D 5 to 7 £18.50 (2 courses) to £21.50   SERVICE: 12.5% (optional)   CARDS: Amex, Delta, Diners, MasterCard, Switch, Visa   DETAILS: 120 seats. Vegetarian meals. Children's helpings. No-smoking area. Wheelchair access (not WC). Occasional music. Air-conditioned   ACCOMMODATION: 356 rooms, all with bath/shower. TV. Phone. Room only £195 to £645. Rooms for disabled. Baby facilities   ⊖ Holborn

---

Card slips closed in the details at the end of an entry indicates that the total on the slips of credit cards is closed when handed over for signature.

Quality Chop House £ map 13

92–94 Farringdon Road, EC1R 3EA
TEL: (020) 7837 5093 FAX: (020) 7833 8748
EMAIL: qualitychophouse@clara.co.uk

COOKING 2
BRITISH
£27–£62

Hard wooden benches, paper napkins and straightforward 'traditional' cookery are back-to-basics hallmarks of this popular place. With jellied eels and sevruga caviar among starters, and mains of eggs, bacon and chips, Toulouse sausage and mash, or sea bass with fennel, it draws on a curious past – more rose-tinted trad-fusion than authentic heritage – but pleases nonetheless. Highlights can be a bowl of chips (vegetables come extra, but these are a meal in themselves) accompanying salmon fishcakes with strong sorrel sauce, or a refreshingly simple creamed rice pudding. Such essentially uncomplicated cookery requires spot-on ingredients, though, and an avocado and prawn salad was undermined by under-ripe avocado. It's quirky, generous with portions, and a touch numbing on the backside (probably not the place for leisurely dinners). With many beers and decent wines at fair prices, and plenty of quite modestly priced dishes, it's a cheery and fair-value venue.

CHEF/PROPRIETOR: Charles Fontaine OPEN: Sun to Fri L 12 to 3 (4 Sun), all week D 6.30 (7 Sun) to 11.30 CLOSED: 24 Dec to 3 Jan MEALS: alc (main courses £6.75 to £16.75). Sun brunch menu available SERVICE: not inc CARDS: Amex, Delta, MasterCard, Switch, Visa DETAILS: 65 seats. Private parties: 10 main room. Vegetarian meals. Children's helpings. No smoking in 1 dining room. No music. Air-conditioned ⊖ Farringdon

Quo Vadis map 15

26–29 Dean Street, W1V 6LL
TEL: (020) 7437 9585 FAX: (020) 7734 7593
EMAIL: sales@whitestarline.org.uk
WEBSITE: www.whitestarline.org.uk

COOKING 4
ITALIAN/MEDITERRANEAN
£33–£69

Quo Vadis' stained glass-windowed exterior gives way to something altogether more eccentric inside. Iguana skeletons crawl across the ceiling, snake skeletons are framed on the walls, and butterflies are arranged in spirals in display cases. Somehow, these artefacts are not out of keeping with the original windows, wood panelling and parquet flooring. The blend of traditional and modern is equally apparent on the menu. The food is distinctly Italian and the à la carte offers a number of trattoria classics such as vitello tonnato, cannelloni and fritto misto, plus some braises and casseroles. Flavours, however, tend to be every bit as bold as the interior suggests. A starter of aubergine and zucchini fritters may be set on an elaborate crisscross pattern of colourful purées with pure, concentrated flavours, while accurately cooked roast fillet of pork may be enlivened by a rosemary-scented balsamic gravy. Desserts cover much ground, from Italy (such as tiramisù) to beyond (a good old British steamed ginger pudding, served with lime ice cream). Service, though efficient, can seem impersonal. There are plenty of good bottles on the wine list, but little for those with modest wallets; prices start at £15 and quickly head north.

CHEF: Luca Siladi   PROPRIETORS: Marco Pierre White and Jimmy Lahoud   OPEN: Mon to Fri L 12 to 2.30, Mon to Sat D 5.30 to 11.30   CLOSED: 25 and 26 Dec, 1 Jan, bank hols   MEALS: alc (main courses £11 to £18). Set L and D 5.30 to 6.45 £14.95 (2 courses) to £19.95   SERVICE: 12.5% (optional), card slips closed   CARDS: Amex, Delta, Diners, MasterCard, Switch, Visa   DETAILS: 80 seats. Private parties: 80 main room, 10 to 90 private rooms. Vegetarian meals. Wheelchair access (not WC). No music. Air-conditioned   ⊖ Leicester Square, Tottenham Court Road

---

Racine £   map 14

239 Brompton Road, SW3 2EP   COOKING 4
TEL: (020) 7584 4477   RUSTIC FRENCH
                                                      £25–£54

With its browns, mustardy yellows and mirrors, Racine is comfortable (rather than ritzy) in a provincial style. Attractions of the refreshingly affordable (for Brompton Road) repertoire include a luxuriously smooth-textured, wobbly saffron mousse, served with fresh and bouncy mussels in a herb-flecked, buttery sauce – simple but skilful. Flavours are direct and enjoyable, textures 'completely correct', whether thick, creamy green pea and ham soup, or unctuous and deeply flavoured marmite Dieppoise containing pieces of cod, plaice, cockles and mussels.

A busy salade Lyonnaise represents the gutsier end of the spectrum, its frisée leaves beneath a mound of chicken livers, some delightfully soft and gelatinous pig's ear and shredded pork, and tête de veau (including cheek and lightly vinegared poached brain) sitting in the cooking liquor, with a simple, effectively rendered and lightly piquant ravigote sauce. Smooth, creamy textures extend to, for example, a bowl of warm rice pudding enterprisingly accompanied by a blob of beetroot jam. No pretensions here, or unnecessary garnishes, and only the bread disappoints. Service is friendly, accommodating and professional, and the predominantly French wine list has plenty under £20, plus some well-sourced Burgundies for deeper pockets. Prices start at £12.50, or £3.20 a glass.

CHEF: Henry Harris   PROPRIETORS: Eric Garnier and Henry Harris   OPEN: all week 12 to 3 (3.30 Sat and Sun), 6 to 10.30 (10 Sun)   CLOSED: 24 and 26 Dec   MEALS: alc (main courses £9 to £17.50). Set L £14.50 (2 courses) to £16.50, Set D 6 to 7.30 £14.50 (2 courses) to £16.50   SERVICE: 12.5% (optional), card slips closed   CARDS: Amex, Delta, MasterCard, Switch, Visa   DETAILS: 70 seats. 8 seats outside. Vegetarian meals. Wheelchair access (not WC). No music. Air-conditioned   ⊖ South Kensington

---

Radha Krishna Bhavan £   map 12

86 Tooting High Street, SW17 0RN
TEL: (020) 8682 0969   COOKING 2
EMAIL: tharidas@aol.com   SOUTH INDIAN
WEBSITE: www.mcdosa.com   £18–£38

With its huge, wall-length murals of palm-fringed beaches and colourful Hindu statuary, Radha Krishna Bhavan certainly conjures up strong images of South India's Kerala (which the owners refer to as 'one of the ten paradises on earth'). The menu, however, stretches well beyond Kerala to include a large collection of fairly ordinary 'Indian' dishes that are easily found elsewhere. What sets Radha

Krishna Bhavan apart are the well-executed South Indian specialities, such as steamed idli – savoury little cakes made from rice and black gram flour, served with sambar and chutney – or main courses such as kalan (mango) curry. Thoran vegetables (dry stir-fries) such as beetroot and cabbage are well handled, as are rice (including lemon and coconut) and breads. For drinks, however, it's perhaps best to stick to juices, lassi (sweet or salted) or beer: Cobra and Kingfisher cost £3.90 for a 650ml bottle.

CHEFS: Mr Salam and Mr Yusuf   PROPRIETORS: T. Haridas and family   OPEN: all week 12 to 3, 6 to 11 (12 Fri and Sat)   CLOSED: 25 and 26 Dec   MEALS: alc (main courses £2.50 to £7)   SERVICE: 10%, card slips closed   CARDS: Amex, Delta, Diners, MasterCard, Switch, Visa   DETAILS: 50 seats. Private parties: 60 main room. Vegetarian meals. Children's helpings. Wheelchair access (also WC). Occasional music. Air-conditioned   ⊖ Tooting Broadway ⟨£5⟩

Ransome's Dock 🍾

map 12

35–37 Parkgate Road, SW11 4NP
TEL: (020) 7223 1611   FAX: (020) 7924 2614
EMAIL: enquiries@ransomesdock.co.uk
WEBSITE: www.ransomesdock.co.uk

COOKING 4
MODERN EUROPEAN
£35–£71

This place lies between Albert and Battersea bridges, its outside tables fringing a small canal. After the slight slackening noted last year a re-energised kitchen produces interesting, carefully sourced ingredients prepared to unpretentious formulae. Smoked eel, 'simply divine' with a perfect buckwheat pancake, and supremely simple diver-caught scallops with roast red and orange beetroot, exemplify character and intention. Among main courses, tender lamb with a tarragon jus has brought out the liveliness of young vegetables, and accurately rendered turbot with a delicate crab sauce and al dente pasta made a fine balance. Standards are maintained to the end, with a benchmark textured soufflé of prunes not laced but inundated with Armagnac, or the perfect partnering of a lemony pannacotta on a crumbly sablé base with morellos, followed by very good coffee and 'wickedly' dark chocolates. Notwithstanding the odd booking error, service keeps up an informed good humour.

Passionate commitment to 'drinking pleasure and enjoyment' drives an exciting, ever-evolving wine list that draws mostly on Australia, California and France. Prices start around £14, and the changing 'Ransome's Dock Selection' offers a shortcut to good quality below and around £20; wines by the glass are serious choices (£4.50–£5.75), and Lustau almacenista sherries are an extra treat.

CHEFS/PROPRIETORS: Martin and Vanessa Lam   OPEN: Mon to Sat L and D 12 to 11, Sun L 12 to 3.30   CLOSED: Christmas, Aug bank hol   MEALS: alc exc Sat and Sun L (main courses £10.50 to £20). Set L exc Sat and Sun L (2 courses) £14.25. Sat and Sun brunch menu available   SERVICE: 12.5% (optional), card slips closed   CARDS: Amex, Delta, Diners, MasterCard, Switch, Visa   DETAILS: 55 seats. 20 seats outside. Private parties: 40 main room. Car park (evenings and weekends only). Vegetarian meals. Children's helpings. No pipes. Wheelchair access (also WC). Music   ⊖ Sloane Square

London Round-ups listing additional restaurants that may be worth a visit can be found after the main London section.

Rasa /Rasa W1

map 12 and 15

55 Stoke Newington Church Street, N16 0AR
TEL: (020) 7241 0344
Derring Street, W1S 1AD
TEL: (020) 7629 1346
WEBSITE: www.rasarestaurants.com

COOKING **2**
INDIAN/INDIAN VEGETARIAN
£27–£40

When it first opened, the original Stoke Newington branch of Rasa, which celebrates its tenth anniversary in 2004, was one of a small number of restaurants in the UK that offered genuine home-cooked regional Indian food, concentrating on the vegetarian cuisine of Kerala. Since then, it has in some respects been overtaken by the new breed of fashionable modern Indian restaurants, but still offers an attractive alternative to the average curry house. Starters are mostly snacks such as sliced aubergines in chilli and coriander batter, or plantain fritters in rice batter, while main dishes include filled dosas (pancakes) served with sambhar and coconut chutney, and various curries, including beetroot and spinach with yoghurt and coconut, paneer with garlic, peppers and tomato, and a sweet-sour mango and banana version with chilli and ginger. The menu at the central London branch, Rasa W1, is very similar, though prices are a little higher, and both offer a decent choice of wines priced from £8.95 (Rasa N16) and £10.95 (Rasa W1). Other branches are Rasa Samudra and Rasa Travancore (see entries), and a couple of Rasa Express outlets.

CHEFS: Rajan Karattin (Rasa N16); Sivaprasad Nair (Rasa W1) PROPRIETOR: Das Sreedharan
OPEN: Rasa N16 Sat and Sun L 12 to 2.45, all week D 6 to 10.45 (11.45 Fri and Sat); Rasa W1 Mon to Sat L 12 to 2.30, all week D 6 to 10.30 CLOSED: several days over Christmas MEALS: Rasa N16 alc (main courses £3.50 to £5). Set L and D £15.50. Rasa W1 alc (main courses £6 to £10). Set L and D £19.50 (veg) to £25 SERVICE: 12.5% (optional), card slips closed CARDS: Amex, Delta, Diners (exc Rasa), MasterCard, Switch, Visa DETAILS: 45 seats Rasa N16, 80 seats Rasa W1. Private parties: 45 Rasa N16, 100 Rasa W1. Vegetarian meals. No smoking Rasa N16. No-smoking area Rasa W1. Music. Air-conditioned ⊖ Bond Street (Rasa W1)

Rasa Samudra 🍴 ✻

map 15

5 Charlotte Street, W1T 1RE
TEL: (020) 7637 0222   FAX: (020) 7637 0224
WEBSITE: www.rasarestaurants.com

COOKING **3**
INDIAN SEAFOOD/VEGETARIAN
£33–£53

The bright pink façade of this Keralan fish restaurant stands out from the crowd, even in the restaurant-rich environs of Charlotte Street. Inside, Indian carvings abound and colourful saris hang in swathes from the ceilings. Generally, though, it's the buzz and conversation of people that provides the ambience. A few dishes here are found throughout southern India, but most of the fish dishes you won't find elsewhere in London – or outside Kerala for that matter. Although the kitchen is evidently capable of portraying the vibrancy and complexity of this region, not all dishes hit the heights. Recommended is the selection of crunchy pre-meal snacks, served with a variety of own-made pickles and chutneys – garlic and lemon have been singled out by reporters as particular favourites. Start, perhaps, with a light, well-spiced crab thoran (a dry-fried dish) spiked with ginger and chilli and served in a crab shell. On inspection, 'home-style tilapia' in an intriguingly flavoured sauce was pronounced 'complex, sophisticated, satisfying'. Desserts might range from a toffee-like mango kulfi to uninspiring banana ice cream. Service, though willing, lacks polish. The wine list is unexciting but prices are sensible, starting at £10.50.

CHEF: Prasad Mahadevan   PROPRIETOR: Das Sreedharan   OPEN: Mon to Sat L 12 to 2.30, all week D 6 to 10.30   CLOSED: 24 to 30 Dec, 1 Jan   MEALS: alc (main courses £6.50 to £12.50). Set L and D £22.50 (vegetarian) to £30 (seafood)   SERVICE: 12.5% (optional), card slips closed   CARDS: Amex, Delta, Diners, MasterCard, Switch, Visa   DETAILS: 90 seats. 4 seats outside. Private parties: 40 main room, 35 to 60 private rooms. Vegetarian meals. No smoking in 1 dining room. Wheelchair access (not WC). Music. No mobile phones   ⊖ Goodge Street, Tottenham Court Road

Rasa Travancore ⚡✳ £   map 12

56 Stoke Newington Church Street, N16 0NB
TEL: (020) 7249 1340   FAX: (020) 7637 0224
EMAIL: dasrasa@hotmail.com
WEBSITE: www.rasarestaurants.com

COOKING 1
INDIAN
£24–£39

Like its relatives (see entries above), this branch of Rasa opposite the original sports the now-familiar house colours and Keralan-inspired décor. The difference is in the menu, which focuses on regional Syrian Christian cooking – including meat as well as vegetarian and fish dishes. Pre-meal nibbles with inimitable home-made pickles and chutneys start things off in familiar style, but what follows is an intriguing blend of native tea shop snacks, festive specialities and even recipes from individual villages. Despite its prosaic title, 'lamb stew' (traditionally served after Easter fasting with appams) is complex, creamy and well balanced, while kappayum meenum vevichathu brings together tamarind-spiced kingfish with steamed tapioca. On the vegetarian front, reporters have also enjoyed kathrikka (sliced aubergines in batter with tomato chutney) and mysore bonda (potato balls with coconut chutney). House wine is £9.50.

CHEF: Anil Kumar Bhasi   PROPRIETOR: Das Sreedharan   OPEN: all week D only 6 to 10.45 (11.30 Fri and Sat)   MEALS: alc (main courses £4 to £8). Set D £20   SERVICE: 12.5%, card slips closed   CARDS: Amex, Delta, MasterCard, Switch, Visa   DETAILS: 40 seats. Private parties: 40 main room. Vegetarian meals. No smoking. Music. Air-conditioned   ⊖ Finsbury Park £5

The Real Greek & Mezedopolio   map 13

15 Hoxton Market, N1 6HG
TEL: (020) 7739 8212   FAX: (020) 7739 4910
WEBSITE: www.therealgreek.co.uk

COOKING 4
GREEK
£24–£59

The décor, the menu and the style of presentation and table setting are all reminiscent of Greece, but the clientele here are rather different – it's tucked behind ultra-trendy Hoxton Square, so attracts hip City kids and youthful throngs. Servers, too, take their trendy credentials seriously – there's lots of spiky gelled hair-dos and bare midriffs. Although there are the inevitable dissenters, most who come here are convinced by the skill of the kitchen and the quality of the ingredients, much of which is sourced direct from Greece. Mezedes might include oven-cooked gigandes, avgotaraho (cured grey mullet roe) and pan-fried kefalotiri (a Greek cow's milk cheese). For main courses, there might be roast rabbit with artichokes in a herby white wine sauce and 'super' ice creams such as Metaxa brandy and sultana or pineapple and lemongrass for afters. The Mezedopolio section of the operation, which serves purely mezedes, is louder and less secluded than the main restaurant. Vegetarian dishes might feature horta (a warm salad of seasonal leaves) while meat dishes might turn up preserved chicken with walnuts. The all-Greek wine list will challenge pronunciation capabilities and is well worth a close look. Bottle prices start at £12.25.

CHEFS: Theodore Kyriakou and Ian Madine PROPRIETORS: Paloma Campbell and Theodore Kyriakou OPEN: Mon to Sat 12 to 3, 5.30 to 10.30 MEALS: alc (main courses £15.30 to £17). Set L and D 5.30 to 7 £10 (2 courses) to £13.50 SERVICE: not inc, 12.5% (optional) for tables of 6 or more CARDS: Delta, MasterCard, Switch, Visa DETAILS: 75 seats. 20 seats outside. Private parties: 75 main room, 8 to 20 private rooms. Vegetarian meals. Children's helpings. No cigars/pipes. Wheelchair access (also WC). No music ⊖ Old Street

Real Greek Souvlaki and Bar £ NEW ENTRY map 13

140–142 St John Street, EC1V 4UA
TEL: (020) 7253 7234 FAX: (020) 7253 7235
EMAIL: admin@souvlaki.demon.co.uk
WEBSITE: www.therealgreek.co.uk

COOKING 2
GREEK
£24–£46

This new outpost of The Real Greek (see entry above) promises all-day Greek street food in a setting that is 'industrial chic'. Perch on a high stool or grab a table if you fancy lingering. Breakfast (till noon) is the genuine article: frittata with honey, eggs with prosciutto, and so on. Mezedes are the stars at lunchtime: gigandes plaki (oven-baked giant beans from Kastoria) is a showstopper, likewise htipiti (puréed matured cheeses, peppers, roasted onions and olive oil) and even taramasalata is in a class of its own. Skewered souvlaki varies seasonally (pork from November to May, lamb at other times), and it looks the part with its wrapping of warm sourdough bread and a paper sleeve. The dedication to authentic ingredients also shows in grilled smoked sausage from Evritania, and seared scallops with Santorinian fava and caper leaves. Desserts couldn't be simpler, say slices of walnut cake or poached pears. To drink, there are Greek beers, cocktails laced with ouzo and a handful of native wines from £11.

CHEFS: Theodore Kyriakou and Ian Madine PROPRIETORS: Theodore Kyriakou and Paloma Campbell OPEN: Mon to Sat 10 to 11 CLOSED: 25 and 26 Dec, bank hols MEALS: alc (main courses £5 to £12). Breakfast menu also available SERVICE: not inc CARDS: Delta, Diners, MasterCard, Switch, Visa DETAILS: 82 seats. Private parties: 100 main room, 15 to 30 private rooms. Vegetarian meals. No cigars. Wheelchair access (not WC). Music. Air-conditioned ⊖ Farringdon

'The young head waiter gives a highly animated performance full of gesticulations, but is strangely detached. It is as if he is practising in the mirror the routine he will use on the girl he fancies at the office.' (On eating in Cambridgeshire)

Red Fort ✳

map 15

77 Dean Street, W1D 3SH
TEL: (020) 7437 2525   FAX: (020) 7434 0721
EMAIL: info@redfort.co.uk
WEBSITE: www.redfort.co.uk

COOKING 4
NEW-WAVE INDIAN
£32–£74

The reincarnation of this long-standing Soho Indian restaurant has worked well, and the refurbishment continues to garner favour. In addition to the plush, atmospheric décor, service, from waiters dressed uniformly in black trousers and mushroom-coloured shirts, is most impressive. The food, too, impresses. Although best described as 'modern Indian', it is less experimental than that served at several other modern Indian restaurants in the capital. The starting point is Mughal Court cooking, of which chef Mohammed Rais (formerly of the Maurya Sheraton in Delhi) is a leading exponent. Specialities include the likes of sabz biryani – basmati rice, vegetables and spices cooked by the 'dum pukht' method (that is, 'steamed' in a sealed pot). One reporter was impressed by tandoori salmon, 'moist and suffused with the charcoal smell of the tandoor'. Expect spices such as nutmeg, star anise, dill, poppy seeds and mace to enliven the dishes here. The bread selection is very good, and desserts such as eggless Alphonso mango ice cream are more than a cut above the average. Wines, though expensive (house wines start at £16), are carefully selected to match the food.

CHEF: Mohammed Rais   PROPRIETOR: Amin Ali   OPEN: Mon to Fri L 12 to 2.15, Mon to Sat D 5.45 to 11.15   MEALS: alc (main courses £12 to £28). Set L £12 (2 courses), Set D 5.45 to 7 £16 (2 courses)   SERVICE: 12.5% (optional)   CARDS: Amex, Delta, Diners, MasterCard, Switch, Visa   DETAILS: 77 seats. Private parties: 100 main room. Vegetarian meals. No smoking in 1 dining room. Wheelchair access (also WC). Music. Air-conditioned   ⊖ Tottenham Court Road

Redmond's ♥

map 12

170 Upper Richmond Road West, SW14 8AW
TEL: (020) 8878 1922   FAX: (020) 8878 1133

COOKING 5
MODERN BRITISH
£32–£50

A south-west London favourite, Redmond's continues to deliver the goods in its slick, professional style. The dining room, shielded from the passing traffic by clever glazing, feels enticingly comfortable, despite its modern décor and strong colours.

Although the cuisine is nominally modern British in style, there's a strong undercurrent of influences from across the Channel – for example in a starter of ballottine of quail and foie gras mousse with mushroom and green bean salad. The menu is quite short and, although chef Redmond Hayward generally steers a course towards tried and tested flavours, as in roast rump of lamb with gratin dauphinois and Madeira jus, that's not to say there's no experimentation; roast fillet of smoked haddock, for instance, may be enlivened with curry oil and, at the dessert course, bitter chocolate tart has been served with rosemary and caramel ice cream. Service, supervised by Pippa Hayward, is 'on the ball' and 'helpful without interfering'. The likeable modern wine list opts for brief and insightful selections, arranged by grape variety, style or region and held together by a bantering commentary. Four house wines are £14–£15 (£4–£4.25 a glass), and a good range of half-bottles includes treats such as Cuilleron's Condrieu (£25).

CHEF: Redmond Hayward   PROPRIETORS: Redmond and Pippa Hayward   OPEN: Sun L 12 to 2.30, Mon to Sat D 7 to 10.30   MEALS: Set L Sun £17.50 (2 courses) to £21, Set D £25 (2 courses) to £28.50   SERVICE: not inc, 10% (optional) for parties of 6 or more   CARDS: Delta, MasterCard, Switch, Visa   DETAILS: 48 seats. Private parties: 48 main room. Vegetarian meals. Children's helpings. No cigars/pipes; no-smoking area. Wheelchair access (not WC). No music. Air-conditioned

▲ Ritz ◁   map 15

150 Piccadilly, W1J 9BR
TEL: (020) 7493 8181   FAX: (020) 7493 2687   COOKING 4
EMAIL: ritzrestaurant@theritzlondon.com   FRENCH/ENGLISH
WEBSITE: www.theritzlondon.com   £72–£163

The dining room at the Ritz is a vast, impressive place, with a vaulting ceiling and lavish décor. The walls themselves seem to be made of marble, with one wall dominated by a vast trompe l'oeil mural of a summer scene. Tail-coated waiters tread thick carpets, chandeliers hang in profusion from the painted ceiling, and the effect is gloriously old-fashioned. The menu, too, appears like something from the past.

There's a certain theatricality about eating here, added to the spectacle of at-table assemblies (a section of the menu is dedicated to dishes 'prepared at your table'). One such, Caesar salad, is based on very fresh cos lettuce, the mustard and garlic dressing being vigorously beaten by the waiter before it is added to the other ingredients. Other starters may include well-made asparagus risotto, and among main courses may be grilled Dover sole with properly made béarnaise, or flavoursome breast of guinea fowl with 'excellent' creamed wild mushrooms. Vegetables, including mange-tout, broccoli, and spinach, are ordered separately and are reported as being 'very good'. One visitor expressed dismay at the quality of the cheeseboard – 'four unidentified cheeses' in 'tolerable condition' – but matters improved with the arrival of an assiette of chocolate: rich-tasting ice cream, 'excellent' bitter sorbet, a moist cake, and a brownie. Make sure your wallet is fat, because '1950s food at 2050s prices' is the name of the game. The wine list doesn't help either, with steep mark-ups. Two house wines come in at £24. Note the jacket and tie policy or suffer the 'fashion nightmare' of a loan from the staff.

CHEF: Dominique Blais   PROPRIETOR: Ellerman Investments   OPEN: all week 12.30 to 2.30, 6 to 11.15 (6.30 to 10 Sun)   MEALS: alc (main courses £25 to £40). Set L £37 to £55, Set D £43 to £65   SERVICE: net prices, card slips closed   CARDS: Amex, Delta, Diners, MasterCard, Switch, Visa   DETAILS: 110 seats. 25 seats outside. Private parties: 55 main room, 20 to 55 private rooms. Vegetarian meals. Children's helpings. Jacket and tie. Wheelchair access (also WC). Occasional music. No mobile phones. Air-conditioned   ACCOMMODATION: 133 rooms, all with bath/shower. TV. Phone. Room only £259 to £511. Rooms for disabled. Baby facilities   ⊖ Green Park

The Guide always appreciates hearing about changes of chef or owner.

Riva

map 12

169 Church Road, SW13 9HR
TEL: (020) 8748 0434

COOKING **3**
NORTH ITALIAN
£36–£64

Riva continues to enjoy faithful support among the denizens of Barnes for its blend of unpretentious, comforting atmosphere and simply prepared northern Italian food. Francesco Zanchetta orders a fair amount of the kitchen's supplies direct from Italy, guaranteeing a reassuring degree of authenticity in what is served, and the wide menu choice is extended by means of the daily specials that are always on offer. Saffron-yellow brodetta (a properly chunky fish soup), or perhaps a generous starter plate for two comprising langoustines, baccala with polenta, eel and lentils, mussels in red pesto and grilled oysters might precede an intermediate dish such as risotto alla valtellinese, which comes with Luganega sausage and radicchio. Main courses are rich and filling, dressing tuna steak with capers and green peppercorns, tomatoes and parsnips, or adding roast potatoes, peperonata and pecorino to best end of lamb in mustard and mint sauce. Look forward to versions of Italian favourites at dessert stage, from pannacotta with mixed berries to zabaglione with poached pears, vanilla ice cream and Frangelico liqueur. The short wine list kicks off with Pinot Bianco and Merlot from the Veneto at £12.50, but includes some of the fine new-wave Italian wines too – at a price.

CHEF: Francesco Zanchetta   PROPRIETOR: Andrea Riva   OPEN: Sun to Fri L 12 to 2.30, all week D 7 to 11 (9.30 Sun)   MEALS: alc (main courses £11.50 to £18.50)   SERVICE: 12.5%, card slips closed   CARDS: Amex, Delta, MasterCard, Switch, Visa   DETAILS: 45 seats. 8 seats outside. Private parties: 40 main room. Vegetarian meals. Children's helpings. No cigars/pipes. Wheelchair access (not WC). No music. No mobile phones. Air-conditioned   ⊖ Hammersmith

River Café ▼

map 12

Thames Wharf Studios, Rainville Road, W6 9HA
TEL: (020) 7386 4200   FAX: (020) 7386 4201
EMAIL: info@rivercafe.co.uk

COOKING **6**
ITALIAN
£36–£77

·Given the pressure on tables, a rather glitzy bar makes a useful holding area for those waiting their turn in the large and predominantly white dining room. Food and drink preparation take place behind a long, reflective steel and glass counter, windows give on to a grassy square opposite, and, in what is otherwise a sharp and cosmopolitan operation, a wood-burning oven adds an agreeably rustic feel: flames lick round the inside, and pans and trays are thrust into it now and again, perhaps bearing a Scottish grouse stuffed with thyme and garlic, or a thick, crisp-skinned sea bass fillet served with Castelluccio lentils. The food follows the seasons (Italy's rather than Britain's) and an essential simplicity rules the roost, producing for example a starter of buffalo mozzarella with figs, mint, basil and rocket, or half-a-dozen delicate parcels of pasta filled with wild greens and ricotta, sprinkled with grated pecorino, and bathed in a buttery sauce. Output may be variable, but for every dish that is below par there seems to be one that reaches well above the norm: at inspection a textbook black truffle risotto, acidulated with champagne, given depth from chicken stock, and lightly seasoned with Parmesan.

Dishes may be straightforward, but every item counts: a pleasantly sloppy dollop of polenta providing a neutral background for its savoury shelled prawns and tiny clams, or a mint-based salsa verde, and a fennel and potato bake, helping to point up neat, square-cut chunks of chargrilled, marinated leg of organic Highgrove lamb. Other highlights have included the accompaniment to a whole roast Anjou pigeon: a piece of soggy, deep mahogany-coloured bread that had been drenched in an Amarone-based sauce of incomparable depth and winey-gamey flavour. Chocolate Nemesis, just melting in the centre, continues to hold its own among desserts, although a lemon tart with wonderfully light pastry and a curdy filling is on a par. Staff are relaxed yet on the ball (they know who ordered what), and service is both amiable and efficient. The all-Italian wine list is bursting with good names from Tuscany and the north, although the full potential of the south has yet to be mined. Prices are about right for the quality, with basics at £10.50 and some good flavours among the 15 bottles under £20. A dozen by the glass are £3–£10.50.

CHEFS: Rose Gray, Ruth Rogers and Theo Randall PROPRIETORS: Rose Gray and Ruth Rogers OPEN: all week L 12.30 to 3, Mon to Sat D 7 to 9.15 CLOSED: 10 days at Christmas, bank hols MEALS: alc (main courses L £18 to £29, D £20 to £29). Set L Mon to Fri £19.50 (2 courses) SERVICE: 12.5% (optional), card slips closed CARDS: Amex, Delta, Diners, MasterCard, Switch, Visa DETAILS: 108 seats. 50 seats outside. Car park. Children's helpings. No cigars/pipes. Wheelchair access (also WC). No music ⊖ Hammersmith

River Walk Restaurant [NEW ENTRY] map 13

Oxo Tower Wharf, Barge House Street, SE1 9PH
TEL: (020) 7928 2884 FAX: (020) 7928 2868
EMAIL: reservations@riverwalk.co.uk
WEBSITE: www.riverwalk.co.uk

COOKING 5
PACIFIC RIM
£36–£64

Huge glass windows looking out over the Thames are a major talking point at this restaurant, where soothing mauve tones on walls and chairs (and banquettes) strike a contemporary note. The kitchen undertook a change of direction a few months after opening, taking in a decided swing to the east. The menu, with its focus on pan-Asian cooking is, according to one, 'imaginative and extremely unusual'. A guiding hand – willingly offered by servers – is needed to determine how many dishes are required: there are no straightforward first and second courses here, and plates are designed to be shared.

'Colourful, pleasingly crunchy and ablaze with flavour' is how one visitor described a dish of Thai vegetable salad, which combined true Thai flavours to winning effect. Fish dishes might include the likes of mirin-steeped sea bass with crispy rice noodles and spring onions, while meat may take the form of a complex dish of hoi sin duck breast with crunchy tofu. Desserts, not normally a high point in Asian restaurants, are equally vivid: think pineapple spring rolls, wrapped in a bright green leaf and served with ginger dipping sauce, or smooth lychee sorbet served with plum wine jelly. Servers are able to make sensible recommendations from the carefully chosen drinks list, which includes three infused sakés and a trio of sherries in addition to modern, food-friendly wines from around the world. Bottles start at £12 but are mostly a bit pricey. Fourteen by the glass are £3 to £8.

CHEFS: Richard Sawyer and Anthony North   PROPRIETORS: Richard Sawyer and Marc Whitley OPEN: Tue to Fri 12 to 3, Tue to Sat D 6 to 10.30   MEALS: alc (main courses £10 to £19.50). Set L £12.50 (2 courses) to £15. Bar and grill menu also available   SERVICE: 12.5% (optional), card slips closed   CARDS: Amex, Delta, Diners, MasterCard, Switch, Visa   DETAILS: 120 seats. 10 seats outside. Private parties: 120 main room. Vegetarian meals. Children's helpings. Wheelchair access (also WC). Music. Air-conditioned   ⊖ Waterloo, Blackfriars, Embankment, Southwark (£5)

Rosmarino ♥ map 13

1 Blenheim Terrace, NW8 0EH   COOKING 3
TEL: (020) 7328 5014   FAX: (020) 7625 2639   MODERN ITALIAN
£42–£67

The genteel, elegant setting of an Edwardian terrace in north-west London provides a fittingly classical setting for this Italian restaurant. As with other restaurants in the A To Z stable, ethnicity of the dishes speaks out loud and clear. A good example is the Sardinian-inspired squid-ink ravioli, gleaming black and stuffed with sea bass, topped with white bean sauce and dusted with grated bottarga (pressed grey mullet roe). Starters tend to be simple – goats' cheese salad with green beans and red onion marmalade, for example, or chargrilled asparagus with poached quail's eggs. Chargrilling is also used for fillet of sea bass (with potato sauce and spinach) and tuna steak (served with rocket and tomato). Carnivores, meanwhile, might be tempted by milk-fed baby lamb, pink and tender, served with artichokes, baby potatoes and a light jus. Consistency in the kitchen can be variable, particularly at busy times. The all-Italian wine list tours the country from top to toe, setting established classics alongside exciting newcomers, particularly from the south and the islands – although nine by the glass (£4.50–£10) stick mostly to the north. Bottle prices start at £15.

CHEF: Santino Busgiglio   PROPRIETOR: A To Z Restaurants   OPEN: all week 12 to 2.30, 7 to 10.30 (10.45 Fri and Sat)   CLOSED: 3 days at Christmas   MEALS: Set L £19.50 (2 courses) to £28, Set D £23.50 (2 courses) to £33   SERVICE: 12.5% (optional), card slips closed   CARDS: Amex, Delta, Diners, MasterCard, Switch, Visa   DETAILS: 70 seats. 30 seats outside. Private parties: 50 main room, 10 to 20 private rooms. Vegetarian meals. No-smoking area. Occasional music. Air-conditioned   ⊖ St John's Wood

Roussillon ♥ map 14

16 St Barnabas Street, SW1W 8PE
TEL: (020) 7730 5550   FAX: (020) 7824 8617   COOKING 5
EMAIL: reservations@roussillon.co.uk   MODERN FRENCH
WEBSITE: www.roussillon.co.uk   £37–£95

'What a treat!' exclaimed one visitor, charmed in equal measure by the food, wine and service. Behind the bow-fronted window, in a network of streets near Chelsea Barracks, the décor is 'calmly unobtrusive', and the menus full of difficult choices, including a seven-course vegetarian extravaganza (£50) and a seasonal tasting menu (£60) put together from the generous carte. Portions are small, although 'you don't feel short-changed'. Soups come highly recommended, from Mrs Beeton's Prince of Wales soup (a simple but rich-tasting veal consommé) to a pile of morels over which the waitress pours an intense beef reduction. Dublin Bay prawns have drawn applause too: caramelised, with a fondant artichoke and a smear of shellfish sauce, or simply served with an intense veal reduction. In May, seasonal vivid green risotto came with peas and asparagus, while the game repertoire has produced a tender fillet of Highland venison with caramelised pumpkin, Comice pear and a truffled celeriac purée.

Sourcing is heart-on-sleeve, from Donald Russell Angus beef and Gloucester Old Spot pork, via Isle of Wight garlic leaves (accompanying grilled halibut and steamed clams), to Red Torfrey Farm chicken. Unusual items might be a starter of roast beetroot and bone marrow, and desserts such as a spicy soufflé of organic goose egg with gingerbread soldiers and a maple infusion. Cheeses are 'full of character and in good condition', and bread is a highlight. France, notably the Roussillon region and its southern French cohorts, is the powerhouse of the wine list, with bottles from £16, but prices are high overall. An excellent range of 20 wines by the glass are £4–£10.50.

CHEF: Alexis Gauthier   PROPRIETORS: James and Andrew Palmer and Alexis Gauthier   OPEN: Wed to Fri L 12 to 2.30, Mon to Sat D 6.30 to 10.30   MEALS: Set L £24.50, Set D £39 to £60   SERVICE: 12.5% (optional), card slips closed   CARDS: Amex, Delta, MasterCard, Switch, Visa   DETAILS: 46 seats. Private parties: 60 main room, 8 to 28 private rooms. Vegetarian meals. No children under 8. No-smoking area. No cigars/pipes. Wheelchair access (not WC). No music. No mobile phones. Air-conditioned   ⊖ Sloane Square £5

Royal China £   map 15

40 Baker Street, W1V 7AJ
TEL: (020) 7487 4688   FAX: (020) 7935 7893
13 Queensway, W2 4QJ
TEL: (020) 7221 2535   FAX: (020) 7792 5752
68 Queen's Grove, NW8 6ER
TEL: (020) 7586 4280   FAX: (020) 7722 4750   COOKING 4
30 West Ferry Circus, E14   CHINESE
TEL: (020) 7719 0888   FAX: (020) 7719 0889   £20–£85

Four restaurants straddling the capital from W1 to E14, all defined by black and gold lacquered walls, bird motifs and silver flourishes. Queensway still engenders the most reports and it remains 'one of the busiest restaurants around', according to a regular. Service is often 'brusque' and you may have to queue even if you have booked, but the kitchen seldom falters in any department.

Dim sum are praised to the skies, and at lunchtime the kitchen also produces 'the most crispy example' of honey-roast suckling pig with jellyfish. Steamed pork and chilli dumplings are given a 'slight vinegar edge', while black bean sauce provides an 'earthy foil' to immaculately steamed sea bass. The litany of enthusiastically approved dishes continues with hot-and-spicy veal and roast chicken with 'a hint of fermented bean curd', while stewed belly pork with vegetables has been 'robust enough to take away some of the chill on a cold November evening'. 'Gai lan' (Chinese broccoli) are reckoned to be 'some of the most perfect vegetables one could imagine'; lotus leaf fried rice and Singapore noodles provide impressive backup, and the fresh fruit platter makes a refreshing finale. House wine is £12.

CHEFS: Man Yuk Leung (exec chef), Mr Wong and Mr Yeung   PROPRIETOR: Royal China Restaurant Group   OPEN: all week 12 (11 Sun) to 11 (11.30 Fri and Sat, 10 Sun)   CLOSED: 3 days at Christmas   MEALS: alc (main courses £7 to £25). Set L Mon to Fri £9 (2 courses) to £11, Set D £28 to £36   SERVICE: 12.5%   CARDS: Amex, Delta, MasterCard, Switch, Visa   DETAILS: 110 seats. Private parties: 130 main room, 10 to 15 private rooms. Vegetarian meals. Wheelchair access (also WC). Music. Air-conditioned   ⊖ Baker Street, Queensway, St John's Wood, Canary Wharf (DLR)

RSJ ▮   map 13

33 Coin Street, SE1 9NR   COOKING 3
TEL: (020) 7928 4554   MODERN FRENCH
EMAIL: sally.webber@rsj.uk.com   £30–£57

The area around the National Theatre is undergoing a period of revival, thanks to the development of the Coin Street Housing co-op and the increasing fortunes of the South Bank. Located in a delightfully understated nineteenth-century building (in what looks like a former shopfront), RSJ looks set to remain an integral part of the area's street scene. 'Clean, comfortable, light and airy' is how one visitor described the ambience, and service, too, has come in for commendation: 'the joy of eating at RSJ is that the style of service ensures that you can relax and enjoy yourself.' Although there are occasional misfires, the kitchen's considerable technical and aesthetic abilities are generally likely to impress. Dishes that have earned the thumbs-up from reporters include a falling-away-from-the-bone tender lamb shank with black and white pudding and flageolet beans, and smoked haddock soup with baby spinach and crème fraîche. A summer dessert might feature summer pudding with clotted cream. Prices are fair and the superb list of Loire wines – a region rarely explored in any depth in the UK – has long been a draw for wine lovers. Very fair prices encourage experimentation, helped along by a thorough introduction to the grape varieties and vintages, and a long list of dessert wines from both Vouvray and the Layon provides additional temptation. Other parts of the world feature briefly at the end of the list. Ten wines are offered by the glass for £2.95–£6.95.

CHEF: Ian Stabler   PROPRIETOR: Nigel Wilkinson   OPEN: Mon to Fri L 12 to 2.15, Mon to Sat D 5.30 to 11   MEALS: alc (main courses £11 to £18). Set L and D £15.95 (2 courses) to £16.95   SERVICE: 12.5% (optional), card slips closed   CARDS: Amex, Delta, Diners, MasterCard, Switch, Visa   DETAILS: 90 seats. Private parties: 8 main room, 12 to 50 private rooms. Vegetarian meals. Children's helpings. No-smoking area. No cigars/pipes. No music. Air-conditioned ⊖ Waterloo £5

Sabras £   map 12

263 High Road, Willesen Green, NW10 2RX   COOKING 4
TEL: (020) 8459 0340   FAX: (020) 8459 0541   INDIAN VEGETARIAN
                                                                               £28–£45

The Desai family have owned and nurtured Sabras for 30 years. This ultra-reliable restaurant, dedicated to vegetarian cooking, happily caters for Jains, vegans and observant Hindus. Gujarati cooking is the star of the show, with cooking from other regions, such as Delhi, Hyderabad and the Indian Punjab. Gujarati farshaan, served with apple and onion chutney and capsicum and cumin chutney, make a good place to start, perhaps with patish (balls of chickpea flour, fresh coconut, coriander, pomegranate, sesame seeds, poppy seeds, seasoned and coated in mashed potato, then deep-fried). Regional variations on South Indian masala dosas figure large on the menu; the Hyderabadi version may feature a 'feather-light, crispy' pancake, stuffed with 'a spicy, well-balanced' filling, topped with cashews. Dhals may be seasoned with tamarind or jaggery (unrefined cane or palm sugar), and breads, such as chapatis and stuffed parathas, are fresh, without a trace of greasiness. Desserts may include the Gujarati speciality basuri (milk cooked until thick, then enriched with sugar, ground almonds, pistachios and cardamom), or a choice of kulfi. For drinks, a variety of lassis and fruit juices vie with the short but well-priced wine list.

CHEF: Nalinee Desai   PROPRIETOR: Hemant Desai   OPEN: Tue to Sun D only 6.45 to 10.15 CLOSED: 25 and 26 Dec, bank hols   MEALS: alc (main courses £5 to £7.50). Set D 6.45 to 7.30 £6.50 (1 course) to £16.50. Cover 60p   SERVICE: 12.5% (optional), card slips closed   CARDS: Delta, MasterCard, Switch, Visa   DETAILS: 32 seats. Private parties: 20 main room. Vegetarian meals. No-smoking area. No cigars/pipes. Wheelchair access (not WC). Music. No mobile phones   ⊖ Dollis Hill   £5

St John
map 13

26 St John Street, EC1M 4AY
TEL: (020) 7251 0848   FAX: (020) 7251 4090
EMAIL: reservations@stjohnrestaurant.co.uk
WEBSITE: www.stjohnrestaurant.co.uk

COOKING 5
BRITISH
£42–£64

The uncompromisingly spartan interior of this former smokehouse – plain white walls pared back to the barest essentials and given no adornment – is a statement in itself. This minimal approach applies to the menu too. Descriptions may seem terse: 'snails in bacon' or 'roast bone marrow and parsley salad' (a signature dish) are listed as starters, for instance, but the menu speaks wholeheartedly of simplicity. This is bold and serious cooking, and St John ranks highly in the list of must-be-tried restaurants in London. These are dishes you'll struggle to find anywhere else. 'Items such as ox heart with swede are enough to shock even the most robust diner,' said one reporter, who nonetheless settled on a main course of suckling kid, 'a huge portion served with a fine compote of fennel'. Chitterlings served with dandelion and mustard sit alongside more gentle sounding lemon sole with tartare sauce, but vegetarians might be advised to sit this one out, despite the presence of baked leeks and salsify. The cooking, under the guidance of Fergus Henderson, is 'totally dependable', underscored by an admirable transparency and honesty. It's a 'true original', in the words of one fan. Service is 'young, energetic, knowledgeable and friendly'. Wines (served in ridiculously small glasses), from an all-French list, are decent value.

CHEFS: Fergus Henderson and Ed Lewis   PROPRIETORS: Trevor Gulliver and Fergus Henderson OPEN: Mon to Fri L 12 to 2.30, Mon to Sat D 6 to 11   CLOSED: Christmas and New Year, Easter bank hol   MEALS: alc (main courses £13.50 to £18). Bar menu also available   SERVICE: not inc,

12.5% (optional) for parties of 6 or more CARDS: Amex, Delta, Diners, MasterCard, Switch, Visa DETAILS: 100 seats. Private parties: 130 main room, 1 to 18 private rooms. No music. No mobile phones. Air-conditioned ⊖ Farringdon

Salisbury Tavern

map 12

21 Sherbrooke Road, SW6 7HX
TEL: (020) 7381 4005   FAX: (020) 7381 1002
EMAIL: thesalisburytavern@longshotplc.com

COOKING 3
MODERN EUROPEAN
£18–£55

The Salisbury is an upmarket Fulham pub, feeling spacious and open-plan inside (though there is some booth seating), and not above offering its patrons some televised sport on a large drop-down screen to go with the bar food menu. If that doesn't grab your attention, proceed through to the restaurant area, where clothless tables await in an uplifting skylit room – a particularly fine venue for a summer lunch. The kitchen caters throughout the day, from three-course breakfasts to early dining, and then the full-dress dinner menu, which brings a certain amount of dash to what are essentially simple classic dishes. Start perhaps with foie gras and chicken liver parfait with apple and pear chutney, or wild mushrooms on toasted brioche with hollandaise, before going on to a robust fish dish such as roasted monkfish with Parma ham and sweet potato purée. Main dishes are sparingly garnished, as the expectation is that you will spend a little more on a vegetable order (duck leg confit comes with parsnip purée and apple crisps), or alternatively leave room for one of the crowd-pleasing puddings, such as fresh fruit crumble with Cornish clotted cream. Vegetarians have their own menu to choose from. The short wine list could teach other gastro-pubs a thing or two, managing to cover most bases in around 30 bottles and offering everything from the £12 house wine to the £40 top bottles by the glass (£3–£10). It's a sibling of Admiral Codrington (see entry).

CHEF: Micky O'Connor   PROPRIETOR: Joel Cadbury   OPEN: all week 12 to 2.30 (3.30 Sat and Sun), 7 to 11 (10.30 Sun). Brunch Sat 10 to 12   CLOSED: 25 and 26 Dec, 31 Dec D   MEALS: alc (main courses £10 to £14.50). Set L Mon to Sat £12.50 (2 courses) to £15, Set D Mon to Fri before 7.30 £12.50 (2 courses) to £18. Cover £1. Bar menu available all week L   SERVICE: 12.5% (optional), card slips closed   CARDS: Amex, Delta, MasterCard, Switch, Visa   DETAILS: 75 seats. Private parties: 90 main room. Vegetarian meals. Children's helpings. Wheelchair access (also WC). Music. Air-conditioned   ⊖ Fulham Broadway, Parsons Green

Salloos

map 14

62–64 Kinnerton Street, SW1X 8ER
TEL: (020) 7235 4444

COOKING 3
PAKISTANI
£32–£62

Tucked away in a secluded Knightsbridge back street, Salloos has been feeding the local community and well-heeled visitors since 1977. 'It seems impervious to fashion,' noted one visitor – although the dining room was due to undergo renovation as the Guide went to press. The restaurant's aim has always been to serve the kind of authentic dishes that might be eaten in Pakistani homes; the charcoal tandoor ('no pesky modern gas version here', noted one aficionado) is used to good effect for king prawns, moist chicken tikka 'on the bone', quails and lamb chops. Spices are deployed emphatically as flavour-boosters – witness chicken karahi with its lively, well-balanced sauce – and a few unexpected items are tucked in among the biryanis and kormas: haleem akbari comprises shredded lamb with wheatgerm and lentils, while gurda masala makes use of chopped lambs' kidneys. Breads, including 'textbook' naan and impressively grease-free parathas, are a high point and genuine home-made kulfi is a creditable example. Service is 'eccentric but attentive'. Like the menu, the Corney & Barrow wine list is a pricey affair; house wine is £12.50.

CHEF: Abdul Aziz   PROPRIETOR: Muhammad Salahuddin   OPEN: Mon to Sat 12 to 2.30, 7 to 11.15 CLOSED: bank hols   MEALS: alc (main courses £11 to £15). Set L £16 (2 courses) to £21. Cover £1.50   SERVICE: 12.5% (optional), card slips closed   CARDS: Amex, Delta, Diners, MasterCard, Switch, Visa   DETAILS: 65 seats. Private parties: 65 main room. Vegetarian meals. No children under 8. No music. Air-conditioned   ⊖ Knightsbridge

Salusbury £

map 13

50–52 Salusbury Road, Queen's Park, NW6 6NN
TEL: (020) 7328 3286   FAX: (020) 7604 3300

COOKING 3
ITALIAN
£23–£44

Gastro-pub is definitely the word for this informal pub-cum-dining-room, where the menu gravitates towards Italy and the kitchen demonstrates a degree of skill and imagination. Fusilli with Italian sausage and turnip tops, pappardelle with artichoke and walnut cream, and Swiss chard and taleggio ravioli show a keen eye for rustic combinations and are a million miles from the old-school trattoria repertoire. Main courses return, in part, to the more familiar and home-grown, with evidence of well-sourced ingredients: Gloucester Old Spot fillet with liver and brussel tops, or Scottish ribeye steak with red wine and potato cake, alongside Welsh leg of lamb broth with potatoes, pecorino and leeks. Desserts return to Italy, with pannacotta and raspberries, or perhaps diplomatico: a mascarpone, chocolate and rum mousse. The wine list, too, is diplomatic enough, offering some 100 wines from around the world, arranged by style, with well over half the list under £25. Vins de pays starts the list at £10 (£2.60/£3.80 a glass).

CHEF: Enrico Sartor   PROPRIETORS: Nick Mash and Rod Claassen   OPEN: Tue to Sun L 12.30 to 3.15, all week D 7 to 10.15   CLOSED: 25, 26 and 31 Dec, 1 Jan   MEALS: alc (main courses £9 to £15). Set L Mon to Fri £5 (1 course). Set L Sun £12 (2 courses) to £15   SERVICE: not inc, 12.5% for parties of 7 or more   CARDS: Delta, MasterCard, Switch, Visa   DETAILS: 55 seats. 24 seats outside. Vegetarian meals. No children under 18 after 7pm. No music   ⊖ Queens Park

Samphire

NEW ENTRY   map 13

135 Fortess Road, NW5 2HR
TEL: (020) 7482 4855   FAX: (020) 7482 4856
WEBSITE: www.samphire-nw5.co.uk

COOKING 3
MODERN EUROPEAN
£25–£47

The addition of Samphire to the Tufnell Park scene will help no end in raising the glamour stakes of this low-profile neighbourhood. With an elegant 'S' etched into the glass door, what was once a small shop has had a second floor squeezed in, and has been fitted out in soft greys, varnished wood and subdued lighting. It wears its sophistication lightly: expect an enthusiastic reception and a buzzy atmosphere. Starters of smoked salmon with blini and chive crème fraîche, or a vegetarian tart of caramelised onion, thyme, black olives and goats' cheese, are typical of the kitchen's modern and unthreatening European repertoire. Main courses might include excellent calf's liver with a dolcelatte sauce of surprising delicacy, good oily spinach and a decent, neutral polenta; or 'perfectly prepared' chargrilled swordfish loin with Piedmont peppers and spinach. Puddings tend to be calorie-rich, taking in a chocolate tart ('rich and chocolatey without being too decadent') and a 'magical' cherry tarte Tatin. Staff exude a genuine friendliness, contributing to the impression of a place that works within sensible ambition and remains totally unpretentious. A succinct wine list with house wines at £11.50 includes serious Italian bottles, but prices throughout are fair, with most well below £20.

CHEFS: Dirceu Pozzebon and John O'Riordan   PROPRIETORS: Gordon Griffiths and Dirceu Pozzebon   OPEN: Sun L and D 12 to 9, Mon to Sat D 6.30 to 10.30   CLOSED: 25 and 26 Dec   MEALS: alc (main courses £9 to £13). Set L Sun £12.95 (2 courses) to £14.95   SERVICE: 12.5% (optional), card slips closed   CARDS: Delta, MasterCard, Switch, Visa   DETAILS: 54 seats. Private parties: 20 main room. Vegetarian meals. Children's helpings. Wheelchair access (not WC). Occasional music. Air-conditioned

Sardo ⁵⟨※⟩

map 15

45 Grafton Way, W1T 5DQ
TEL: (020) 7387 2521   FAX: (020) 7387 2559
EMAIL: info@sardo-restaurant.com
WEBSITE: www.sardo-restaurant.com

COOKING 3
SARDINIAN
£42–£65

Considering that Italy stretches from mountainous north to sun-baked south, it should be no surprise that the cooking varies markedly from region to region. Sardo – a cool, airy, modern-looking venue – focuses on the specialities of the Mediterranean island of Sardinia, which uses lots of seafood and, though simple, can seem quite exotic. Grilled baby squid with an aromatic herby stuffing and tomato sauce, and thinly sliced sun-dried tuna fillet on French beans and sun-dried tomatoes are typical starters. Like the rest of Italy, Sardinia has its own pasta specialities, including malloreddus, served here with tomato and sausage sauce. Main courses feature a few meaty options such as grilled Scotch beef steak with a Sardinian blue cheese topping, or marinated lamb steak with endive and potatoes. Bread, olives and olive oil are charged for (£1.50 per person). Authentic Sardinian food deserves authentic Sardinian wines: there are around 30 on the helpfully annotated list, along with the same number from the rest of Italy, and a few from France. Prices start at £14.

CHEF: Roberto Sardu   PROPRIETOR: Romolo Mudu   OPEN: Mon to Fri L 12 to 2.30, Mon to Sat D 6 to 10.30   CLOSED: Christmas, bank hols   MEALS: alc (main courses £11.50 to £20), Cover £1.50 (per person)   SERVICE: 12.5% (optional), card slips closed   CARDS: Amex, Delta, Diners, MasterCard, Switch, Visa   DETAILS: 60 seats. 9 seats outside. Private parties: 20 to 30 private rooms. No smoking in 1 dining room. Occasional music. Air-conditioned   ⊖ Warren Street

The nearest Underground station is indicated at the end of London entries.

Sarkhel's

map 12

199 Replingham Road, SW18 5LY
TEL: (020) 8870 1483
WEBSITE: www.sarkhels.com

COOKING 3
INDIAN
£19–£52

In recent years Sarkhel's has been following a steady upward trajectory, building on a foundation of unshowy but accomplished Indian cooking, with a menu that darts around the Subcontinent, picking out dishes that display the individual character of the regions. Starters tend to be snacky items like medu-vada sambar (lentil dumplings with coconut chutney), and murg ke chaap 'sixer' (spicy chicken drumsticks with a 'superb' fiery tamarind sauce). Equally noteworthy have been main courses of 'pleasingly complex' galinha cafreal (a Goan dish of pan-fried chicken and potatoes), tilapia in a 'deliciously savoury' curry sauce, and 'tender and dry' okra. Rice and breads are also well made. Drink traditional lassi or go for something from the short but well-chosen wine list. House South African red and white are £10.90 a bottle, £2.95 a glass.

CHEF: Udit Sarkhel PROPRIETORS: Veronica and Udit Sarkhel OPEN: Tue to Sun 12 to 2.30, 6 to 10.30 (11 Fri and Sat) CLOSED: 25 and 26 Dec MEALS: alc (main courses £7 to £12). Set L £5 (2 courses) to £9.95, Set D 6 to 8 £9.95 (thali) SERVICE: not inc CARDS: MasterCard, Switch, Visa DETAILS: 88 seats. Private parties: 110 main room. Vegetarian meals. Children's helpings. No-smoking area. Wheelchair access (also women's WC). Music. Air-conditioned
⊖ Southfields (£5)

Savoy Grill

NEW ENTRY   map 15

Strand, WC2R 0EU
EMAIL: savoygrill@marcuswareing.com
WEBSITE: www.marcuswareing.com

COOKING 4
MODERN FRENCH-PLUS
£44–£80

Following the Ramsay revolution at Claridge's and the Connaught, Marcus Wareing has taken his turn to inject life into another bastion of the old guard, bringing the centenarian Savoy Grill bang up to date. Decorative changes are subtle: upholstery of the banquette seating has been swapped for a more modern striped design, the colour of the panelled walls has been lightened, fixtures and fittings are stylish and suitably Art Deco, and the 'booth-like' privacy of the tables has been maintained. The restaurant is, in fact, labelled Marcus Wareing at the Savoy Grill, but we've placed it under 'S' to make it easier to locate in the Guide.

Wareing has shown respect for tradition (especially at lunchtime) by retaining a few menu fixtures such as omelette Arnold Bennett ('delicious, light and creamy') and steak and kidney pudding. At the same time, he has introduced dishes from his own repertoire of upmarket, inventive modern French cooking. Velvet-textured velouté of baby navet with roasted Scottish langoustines and baby gem lettuce made a classy start to an inspection meal, and was followed with a 'rich yet balanced' combination of roast Anjou pigeon with sautéed cep, pommes Anna, pan-fried foie gras and Madeira jus. Timing of fish cookery has been hit-and-miss: braised fillet of brill with braised fennel hearts, sautéed baby squid in chervil vinaigrette and fennel velouté has had mixed reports. The à la carte desserts may be a better option than something off the trolley. The cooking can undoubtedly reach great heights, but standards generally seem variable and several reporters have registered disappointments. Service is copious in number and mixed in ability. The wine list is huge and filled mainly with French wines, including some real blockbusters. There are no bargains to be had – mark-ups are severe – but a few wines by the glass and a dozen half-bottles reduce the pain. Prices start at £18.

CHEF: Joshua Emmett   PROPRIETOR: Marcus Wareing   OPEN: all week 12 to 2.30, 5.45 to 11   MEALS: Set L £25, Set D pre-theatre 5.45 to 6.45 £30, Set D £40 to £50   SERVICE: not inc   CARDS: Amex, Delta, MasterCard, Switch, Visa   DETAILS: 104 seats. Private parties: 100 main room, 20 to 40 private rooms. Vegetarian meals. Children's helpings. No cigars/pipes. No music. Air-conditioned   ⊖ Charing Cross

Searcy's 🍴

map 13

Level 2, Barbican Centre, Silk Street, EC2Y 8DS
TEL: (020) 7588 3008   FAX: (020) 7382 7247
EMAIL: searcy's-reservations@barbican.org.uk
WEBSITE: www.barbican.org.uk

COOKING 2
MODERN BRITISH
£39–£70

There is a, perhaps not surprisingly, vaguely corporate feel to this Barbican Centre restaurant dining room. The big L-shaped room has a bar at one end with squishy black armchairs and panels of brushed steel and pale wood; the room is somewhat enlivened by the odd splashes of colour from the abstract canvases dotted along the walls. Since last year, executive chef Michael James has taken over in the kitchen, and the restaurant also seems to have streamlined operations somewhat, dropping appetisers and pre-desserts and such. The short menu has a distinctly French feel to it, with frogs' legs here, poulet noir there. On inspection, the lamb in a main course of braised lamb shank with broad beans, bacon and sage was served falling-off-the-bone tender, into a good, sticky gravy, while a starter of moist, flavoursome pigeon faggot was served on a potato cake with a good mustard butter sauce. The wine list is divided into New and Old Worlds and there's plenty by the glass, with bottle prices starting at £17.

CHEF: Michael James   PROPRIETOR: Searcy's   OPEN: Mon to Fri L 12 to 2.30, Mon to Sat D 5 to 10   CLOSED: 24 and 25 Dec   MEALS: alc exc 5 to 7.30 (main courses £15 to £20). Set L and D £21 (2 courses) to £24. Bar menu also available   SERVICE: 12.5% (optional), card slips closed   CARDS: Amex, Diners, MasterCard, Switch, Visa   DETAILS: 86 seats. Private parties: 18 main room. Vegetarian meals. No-smoking area. Wheelchair access (also WC). Occasional music. Air-conditioned   ⊖ Barbican, Moorgate £5

Singapore Garden

map 13

83–83A Fairfax Road, NW6 4DY
TEL: (020) 7328 5314   FAX: (020) 7624 0656

COOKING 2
SINGAPOREAN
£18–£64

Bright paintings hang on the cream-coloured walls of this bustling neighbourhood restaurant in a parade of smart shops. There are classic Cantonese dishes on the menu, but the kitchen prides itself on its Singaporean and Malaysian repertoire, stinting neither the authenticity of ingredients nor the heat of spices. Teo chow braised pig's trotter, monkfish cooked in Assam curry spices with okra, and the more familiar beef rendang are among the notable menu options, while seafood specials and lobster served on a bed of chilli noodles are customer favourites. Crispy meatballs of pork and water chestnuts – delicately spiced, wrapped in a tofu skin and deep-fried – are a lesson in textural contrasts. Finish with sweetly coconutty sago melaka, or a fresh fruit platter. An absorbing wine list rises quite swiftly from £13.50, and its upper reaches include claret back to the 1970s – or there is saké, or Singaporean Tiger beer.

CHEF: Mrs Siam Kiang Lim   PROPRIETORS: the Lim family   OPEN: all week 12 to 2.45, 6 to 10.45 (11.15 Fri and Sat)   CLOSED: 4 days Christmas   MEALS: alc (main courses £6 to £15). Set L Mon to Fri £7 (2 courses) to £8.50, Set D £20 (min 2) to £25 (min 3)   SERVICE: 12.5% (optional), card slips closed   CARDS: Amex, Delta, Diners, MasterCard, Switch, Visa   DETAILS: 100 seats. 12 seats outside. Private parties: 60 main room, 6 private room. Vegetarian meals. No cigars. Music. Air-conditioned   ⊖ Swiss Cottage

Sketch

NEW ENTRY   map 15

9 Conduit Street, W1S 2YZ
TEL: 0870 777 4488   FAX: 0870 777 4400
EMAIL: res@sketch.uk.com

COOKING 7
MODERN FRENCH
£73–£242

This overblown £10 million conversion of the former headquarters of RIBA has had more column inches written about its jewel-encrusted toilets than most other restaurants get devoted to their food. Dinner in the Lecture Room restaurant has already earned notoriety for its extremely high prices – but what you get for your money is a truly unique experience that is always unpredictable, often exhilarating and occasionally frustrating. On a technical level, the cooking, overseen by Parisian superstar chef Pierre Gagnaire, is fastidiously well executed. The scale of the effort that goes into producing the highly wrought dishes is breathtaking, and flotillas of appetisers and between-course treats keep the kitchen on its toes. Some of the experimental combinations work well, others fail abjectly, but when it comes off the results are little short of sensational: langoustines cooked three ways, for example – including two 'melt in the mouth' langoustines on walnut shortcake with shredded caramelised pomegranate, and a tartare enlivened with green mango, pressed grapefruit and ginger – while another multipart starter simply labelled 'Vegetables' has featured an intensely flavoured turnip and cider broth containing tender pieces of turnip and celeriac and wilted chard.

A main course of Peking duck was the highlight of an inspection meal, comprising three pieces of pink duck breast and a further three stuffed with truffle and foie gras, served with a faultless glistening demi-glace sauce, plus red cabbage with blackcurrants, quetsch plums with walnuts, and a fine potato and spring onion cake containing cured wild boar ham. A turbot fillet, itself carefully cooked, was let down by its accompanying shrimp and prawn infusion with wilted cabbage (more like an insipid sauerkraut), pearl barley risotto and incandescent cucumber gelée with crème fraîche – but such are the risks of eating here. The consensus of reporters seems to be that if you can afford it, it's worth trying at least once. The wine list focuses squarely on France, giving only cursory acknowledgement to other countries. Even so, it manages to be an esoteric collection, missing out many of the big names. Mark-ups are high, but maybe not as high as you would expect, although there is scarcely anything under £40. Sketch also consists of the Gallery, West Bar, and Parlour, but we've spent long enough here.

CHEF: Pierre Gagnaire   PROPRIETOR: Mourad Mazouz   OPEN: Tue to Fri L 12 to 2, Tue to Sat D 7 to 10   CLOSED: 10 to 26 Aug   MEALS: alc (main courses £35 to £65). Set L £42 (2 courses) to £48   SERVICE: 12.5% (optional)   CARDS: Amex, Delta, Diners, MasterCard, Switch, Visa   DETAILS: 40 seats. Private parties: 40 main room. Vegetarian meals. Music. Air-conditioned   ⊖ Oxford Circus

Smiths of Smithfield, Top Floor ▼   map 13

67–77 Charterhouse Street, EC1M 6HJ
TEL: (020) 7251 7950   FAX: (020) 7236 5666
EMAIL: reservations@smithsofsmithfield.co.uk
WEBSITE: www.smithsofsmithfield.co.uk

COOKING 4
MODERN BRITISH
£35–£74

The fourth-floor restaurant at this converted warehouse has a long side-window overlooking the Barbican and St Paul's. There is plenty of other eating and drinking going on on the floors below you, but as long as the doorman is persuaded you are not any sort of impostor, you will be swiftly conveyed to the top by a lift that feels like a brightly coloured mobile padded cell. Given that the Smithfield meat market is just adjacent, it comes as no surprise to find that the centrepiece of the menu is a listing of rare-breed beef, such as Longhorn rump, Welsh Black fillet and Islay côte de boeuf for two. These are sensitively cooked and sauced, although the butchering at inspection seemed just a shade rough-and-ready. Meats are not all the kitchen can do, though. A large, precision-timed Dover sole was a good main course, served with shrimp butter and a plethora of tiny brown whiskery shrimps. To prime the appetite, first courses are built around stimulating flavours, such as the Jerusalem artichoke purée, capers and lemon that supported a pair of plump, fresh scallops, or the rare-breed beef carpaccio bravely served with a blue cheese dressing. Even vegetarians, who might well feel out on a limb in this vicinity, are catered for. Meals end with such indulgences as chocolate fondant made with Valrhona, served with orange ice cream topped with hot strips of candied peel. Service is 'efficient, helpful and fast'.

The wine list is as modern in conception as it is in presentation, with short, well-polished selections from under £20 to well over £100 in key French and New World regions and from forward-looking Italian and Spanish producers. Prices are on the high side. Bottles start at £15 and 14 wines come by the glass (£4.60–£8.50).

CHEF: Tony Moysie   PROPRIETOR: John Torode   OPEN: Sun to Fri L 12 to 2.45, all week D 6 to 12   MEALS: alc exc Sun L (main courses £10 to £28). Set L Sun £25   SERVICE: 12.5% (optional), card slips closed   CARDS: Amex, Delta, Diners, MasterCard, Switch, Visa   DETAILS: 28 seats seats. 36 seats outside. Private parties: 200 main room, 10 to 50 private rooms. Vegetarian meals. Children's helpings. No-smoking area. No cigars/pipes L before 2, D before 10. Wheelchair access (also WC). Music. Air-conditioned   ⊖ Farringdon

If 'The Which? Guide to Good Hotels' is noted at the end of an entry, this means that the establishment is also in the 2004 edition of our sister guide, published in September 2003.

Snows on the Green

map 12

166 Shepherd's Bush Road, W6 7PB
TEL: (020) 7603 2142   FAX: (020) 7602 7553
EMAIL: sebastian@snowsonthegreen.
freeserve.co.uk
WEBSITE: www.snowsonthegreen.co.uk

COOKING 3
MODERN BRITISH/MEDITERRANEAN
£26–£52

Sebastian Snow's chic, proficiently run restaurant opposite Brook Green is in its second decade of serving this part of west London. The ambience is warm, with concealed soft lighting, damask-covered tables, and a collection of art photos on the walls. The menus trawl regional Europe for inspiration, coming up with seared scallops and truffled leeks to partner a stuffed globe artichoke, adding asparagus, herbs and champagne to risotto, and blending Mediterranean vegetables and couscous to accompany a griddled sea bream sauced with salsa rossa. While it may all sound pretty robust in the description, the cumulative impact of the food is surprisingly gentle, even if you opt for something like peppered fillet of venison with bubble and squeak, bacon and beetroot. Meals end with light, fruity desserts such as raspberry and nougatine parfait, but for those with the capacity there may be sticky toffee and date pudding with clotted cream and caramel sauce. France, Italy and the southern hemisphere comprise the bulk of the expertly chosen wine list, and prices are mostly fairly restrained. Fourteen are available by the glass, from £3, and house Chardonnay and Cabernet Sauvignon are £11.50 a bottle.

CHEFS: Sebastian Snow and Paul Crescente   PROPRIETOR: Sebastian Snow   OPEN: Sun to Fri L 12 to 3, Mon to Sat D 6 to 11   MEALS: alc exc Sun L (main courses £11 to £16). Set L and D £11.50 (2 courses) to £15. Cover 95p   SERVICE: not inc, 12.5% for parties of 6 or more   CARDS: Amex, Delta, Diners, MasterCard, Switch, Visa   DETAILS: 80 seats. 10 seats outside. Private parties: 26 main room, 1 to 16 private rooms. Vegetarian meals. Children's helpings. No-smoking area. Wheelchair access (not WC). Music. No mobile phones. Air-conditioned   ⊖ Hammersmith

Sonny's

map 12

94 Church Road, SW13 0DQ
TEL: (020) 8748 0393   FAX: (020) 8748 2698

COOKING 5
MODERN EUROPEAN
£26–£61

The dining room at this long-standing neighbourhood restaurant is bigger than it looks from the outside, aided by good use of light and frosted glass. Service is breezy and friendly, and no attempt is made at formality. The menu is a sensible length, with about eight choices at each course, with extra vegetables including chips described by one as 'lightly fried, perfectly seasoned, the sort of chips that almost no one seems capable of making'. Since last year, a new chef, Helena Poulakka, has been appointed. She was previously head chef at La Tante Claire and has also worked at L'Oranger and Aubergine (see entries). Her arrival has made an impact here, elevating the level of cooking, as well as the presentation of dishes. One meal began with a courgette flower steamed and stuffed with generously flavoured lobster mousse and surrounded by a creamy lobster bisque, followed by a main course of monkfish niçoise, the fish served with a neat little pile of beans and a few cooked cherry tomatoes, plus slices of new potato, onion, black olives and two baked cloves of garlic. Slow-braised shoulder of lamb comes with kidney, couscous and merguez, while pistachio soufflé was the best of the desserts at inspection. Cheeses feature half a dozen well-kept British and French varieties. The wine list throws together a stimulating international bunch at refreshingly ungreedy prices, with 16 by the glass (£2.95–£8.50).

CHEF: Helena Poulakka   PROPRIETOR: Rebecca Mascarenhas   OPEN: all week L 12.30 to 2.30 (3 Sun), Mon to Sat D 7.30 to 10.45   CLOSED: bank hols   MEALS: alc (main courses £11 to £16). Set L £13 (2 courses) to £16, Set D Mon to Thur £16 (2 courses) to £19.50. Café menu available 12 to 4   SERVICE: 12.5% (optional), card slips closed   CARDS: Amex, MasterCard, Switch, Visa DETAILS: 105 seats. Private parties: 10 to 24 private rooms. Vegetarian meals. Children's helpings. No smoking in 1 dining room. Wheelchair access (not WC). No music. Air-conditioned ⊖ Hammersmith

South | NEW ENTRY | map 13

128 Curtain Road, EC2A 3AQ   COOKING 2
TEL: (020) 7729 4452   FRENCH
EMAIL: southrestaurant@aol.com   £24–£51

South occupies a corner site on Curtain Road, in the heart of Hoxton. The kitchen – and the chef's activities – are on view on one side of the room, which is done out in the minimal/modernist style that's *de rigueur* in this part of London. The 'good-looking carte', which changes daily, is influenced by the cooking of south-west France. There is likely to be foie gras in some form, perhaps with duck gizzard and an earthy lentil salad, and maybe grilled quails with spring onion and Camargue rice, or deep-fried baby squid and cuttlefish with tartare sauce. Desserts are fairly simple affairs, such as cherry clafoutis and chocolate mousse. 'Essentially Mediterranean cooking from a kitchen that shows intelligence and skill', is how one reporter summed it up. There's a good-value, no-choice prix fixe lunch, and the short wine list is 'gloriously French', mostly from the south-west of the country, and not too demanding on the wallet.

CHEFS: Cathy Bolton and John Watt   PROPRIETORS: Cathy Bolton and Jonathan Mortimer   OPEN: all week L 12 to 3, Mon to Sat D 6 to 10.30   CLOSED: 24 Dec 24 to 2 Jan, bank hols   MEALS: alc (main courses £9.50 to £14). Set L £12.95   SERVICE: 12.5% (optional), card slips closed   CARDS: Amex, Delta, MasterCard, Switch, Visa   DETAILS: 45 seats. 8 seats outside. Private parties: 20 main room. Vegetarian meals. Children's helpings. No-smoking area. Wheelchair access (also WC). Music   ⊖ Old Street

Spiga 🍴   map 15

84–86 Wardour Street, W1V 0TA   COOKING 1
TEL: (020) 7734 3444   FAX: (020) 7734 3332   ITALIAN
                                                              £31–£49

Spiga's clean and modern earth-toned dining room (a little stark for some), has a lively, Soho atmosphere, and the kitchen and its wood-fired brick oven open to view, allowing diners to spy on the proceedings through a pane of glass. Watch as the pizzas for which the restaurant is noted fly in and out of the oven at an impressive rate. Although pizza capricciosa was a bit of a let-down at inspection, with an unevenly cooked base and a tomato sauce that lacked its usual zing, reginette with duck and wild mushrooms was enjoyed. Bread is a strong point and a good dessert has been a subtle pannacotta with ginger. Service, from smart, clean-cut staff is good-humoured, and there's a decent choice by the glass on the wine list; prices start at £12 a bottle.

CHEF: Marzio Zacchi   PROPRIETOR: A To Z Restaurants   OPEN: all week 12 to 3, 6 to 12 (11 Sun, Mon and Tue)   CLOSED: 25, 26 and 31 Dec   MEALS: alc (main courses £12 to £14)   SERVICE: 12.5% (optional), card slips closed   CARDS: Amex, Diners, MasterCard, Switch, Visa   DETAILS: 100 seats. Private parties: 120 main room. Vegetarian meals. Children's helpings. Wheelchair access (also WC). Music. Air-conditioned   ⊖ Piccadilly Circus, Tottenham Court Road

Square 🍷   map 15

6–10 Bruton Street, W1J 6PU
TEL: (020) 7495 7100   FAX: (020) 7495 7150   COOKING 8
EMAIL: info@squarerestaurant.com   MODERN FRENCH
WEBSITE: www.squarerestaurant.com   £49–£120

A huge window looks on to the street, but most attention is focused on the spacious, high-ceilinged dining room itself, which crackles with energy and enjoyment (or simply 'noise', as some call it). The lighting is subtle, the paintings abstract and vibrant, and tables are covered with 'white starchery' and a large, decorative, space-devouring egg. For one visitor at least, this offers 'the best all-round dining experience in London'. The food pampers with luxury and soft textures, including a summer salad of 'perfectly cooked and exuberantly fresh' green asparagus anointed with a lush and pungent truffle cream (attended by other green vegetables, potatoes, and slices of hard-boiled, pale yellow duck egg), while a lasagne 'that could not have been improved in any way' consists of mostly white crabmeat mixed with chervil, wrapped in a thin and eggy pasta skin, and bathed in an intense, earthy, pinky-beige shellfish froth.

The food is notably creamy and comforting, be it a 'sandwich' of Old Spot belly pork filled with onions in a cream sauce (on a base of lentils, luxuriously topped with shelled langoustines), or roast scallops on truffle gnocchi, with a baby leek and rich, creamed, white onion purée. There is some very fine cooking, but equally quite a few dishes have failed to excite with their customary pop and crackle. Seafood, however, is particularly well handled, from a huge, fresh and perfectly timed fillet of turbot on a 'bourguignonne' risotto, to a juicy chunk of 'achingly fresh' sea bass, rather salty but accurately timed, with gnocchi, girolles and a creamy, intense, mushroomy froth (some dishes come without froth, by the way, but not many).

Desserts, like everything else, have delivered patchy success, from an under-par crème caramel (simply 'not an option' at these prices), to a light, refreshing and technically impressive mille-feuille of marinated pear, peeled white grapes and prune, separated by wafer-thin strips of brandy-snap. There is much praise for appetisers and for the pre-dessert of yoghurt, fruit purée and beignet. 'Wonderful' staff are knowledgeable, humorous, deft, friendly and efficient, able to do gravity or chirpy as necessary, and the sommelier is notably helpful – his assured guidance through the 'biblical' list having been appreciated by more than one reporter. Burgundy and Germany are the main focus for whites, while reds spread their net wider to take in extensive ranges from Bordeaux, Burgundy, the Rhône, Italy, the USA and Australia. Smaller, cherry-picked selections from other regions offer some of the best value, with worthwhile options under and around £20. Thirteen table wines and an interesting selection of sherries come by the glass – good champagnes and dessert wines, too, from long, classy lists – and there are half-bottles in abundance.

CHEF: Philip Howard   PROPRIETORS: Nigel Platts-Martin and Philip Howard   OPEN: Mon to Fri L 12 to 3, all week D 6.30 to 10.45 (10 Sun)   CLOSED: 24 to 26 Dec, L bank hols   MEALS: Set L £25 (2 courses) to £75, Set D £55 to £75   SERVICE: 12.5% (optional), card slips closed   CARDS: Amex, Delta, Diners, MasterCard, Switch, Visa   DETAILS: 75 seats. Private parties: 95 main room, 8 to 18 private rooms. Vegetarian meals. Children's helpings. Wheelchair access (also WC). No music. No mobile phones. Air-conditioned   ⊖ Green Park

Stepping Stone ♥   map 12

123 Queenstown Road SW8 3RH
TEL: (020) 7622 0555   FAX: (020) 7622 4230   COOKING 4
EMAIL: thesteppingstone@aol.com   MODERN BRITISH
WEBSITE: www.thesteppingstone.co.uk   £30–£52

Stepping Stone is the kind of neighbourhood restaurant that can give a neighbourhood a good name. The double-fronted premises has a modern interior, enriched with the use of 'vibrant' colours ('bright primrose yellow, duck egg blue, Florida lime, thunderstorm purple'), and prices that are designed to encourage repeat business. Chef Richard Harrison shows high culinary ambition, and equal vibrancy: Serrano ham and black pudding with eggs Benedict, or pink-cooked quail set off by the green of rocket and hints of brown-pink from a fried potato and Jerusalem artichoke salad – both looked as bright as their tastes were harmonious. Textural contrasts also star: rare ribeye with soft, deeply flavoured haggis ravioli, plus al dente green beans, and fennel deep-fried in breadcrumbs and Parmesan to add crispness. Uncharacteristically, a banana Tatin stopped short of golden jamminess, but good pastry, silky ice cream and fine espresso finished a meal well. 'Be adventurous' exhorts a wine list that offers plenty of scope for experimentation without breaking the bank. Flavours are well suited to support, rather than compete with, the culinary complexity. Prices start at £12.50, and four daily choices are offered by the glass.

CHEF: Richard Harrison   PROPRIETORS: Gary and Emer Levy   OPEN: Mon to Fri L 12 to 2.30, Mon to Sat D 7 to 11   CLOSED: 5 days Christmas, bank hols   MEALS: alc (main courses £8.75 to £15) SERVICE: 12.5% (optional), card slips closed   CARDS: Delta, MasterCard, Switch, Visa   DETAILS: 70 seats. Private parties: 70 main room. Vegetarian meals. Children's helpings. Wheelchair access (not WC). No music. No mobile phones. Air-conditioned   ⊖ Clapham Common (£5)

Sugar Club ⁵⊁   map 15

21 Warwick Street, W1R 5RB
TEL: (020) 7437 7776   FAX: (020) 7437 7778   COOKING 5
EMAIL: reservations@thesugarclub.co.uk   FUSION
WEBSITE: www.thesugarclub.co.uk   £35–£81

The décor at The Sugar Club – large windows, dark wood and pale, textured walls – has the kind of subtle, understated chic that allows the quality of the food to claim star status. Australian-born chef David Selex has made his mark here and has proved a worthy successor to Peter Gordon, the restaurant's famed founding chef (see entry, Providores); he too seems to be able to mingle the right flavours without turning fusion cooking into mere confusion. The menu is a long, tantalising list of dishes with flavours and ingredients drawn from around the Pacific. Novel twists and turns can be found in starters such as seared scallops with lemon miso vinaigrette, wasabi Tobiko and rose-petal sambal, or main courses such as grilled swordfish with cassava chips, aji amarillo chilli, yuzu guacamole and avruga caviar. The quality of most ingredients is high, offset by careful balancing of flavours. Desserts follow in the same vein, perhaps taking in dragon fruit with tutti-frutti sorbet, or honey, lemon and ginger crème brûlée with banana. Young, intelligent, largely Antipodean staff keep the pace moving while retaining a friendly attitude. The wine list is arranged mostly by grape, occasionally by style or country, whichever works best to present like with like from the large, modern range. A few bottles squeeze under £20, but don't expect any bargains. Only the house-label red and white from New Zealand come by the glass, for £5.90.

CHEF: David Selex   PROPRIETORS: Ashley Sumner and Vivienne Hayman   OPEN: Tue to Fr L 12 to 3, all week D 5.30 to 11 (6 to 10.30 Sun)   MEALS: alc (main courses £14 to £23.50). Set L £15.50 (2 courses) to £19.50, Set D 5.30 to 6.30 £15.50 (2 courses) to £19.50. Bar menu also available   SERVICE: 12.5% (optional)   CARDS: Amex, Diners, MasterCard, Switch, Visa   DETAILS: 120 seats. Private parties: 60 main room, 10 to 55 private rooms. Vegetarian meals. No smoking in 1 dining room. Wheelchair access (not WC). No music. Air-conditioned   ⊖ Oxford Circus, Piccadilly Circus

Sumosan

map 15

26 Albemarle Street, W1S 4HY
TEL: (020) 7495 5999   FAX: (020) 7355 1247
EMAIL: info@sumosan.com

COOKING 2
MODERN JAPANESE
£84–£128

Sumosan is one of a clutch of 'modern Japanese' restaurants in the capital that are riding the wave of interest in Japanese food. The restaurant is a big open space with shiny tables and a beige colour palette running to purple tones for effect. The menu is long, taking in salads, soup and udon, fish, meat and vegetarian dishes plus teppan yaki, tempura and, of course, 'deliciously fresh' sushi and sashimi. Ingredients such as natto (fermented soy beans) and shiso leaf, found in most Japanese restaurants, are absent here, but, unusually, lamb is served three ways and fried rice is served five ways. Appetisers include such trendy-sounding dishes as rock shrimp tempura with a creamy, spicy sauce, or oysters with ponzu dressing. Service is knowledgeable, and wines take a short zoom around the winemaking world, with bottle prices staring at £15 and rising quickly.

CHEF: B. Belkhit   PROPRIETOR: Janina Wolkow   OPEN: Mon to Fri L 12 to 2.45, all week D 6 to 11.30   MEALS: alc D (main courses £11.50 to £45). Set L £19.50 to £45, Set D £27.50 (6 to 7, min 2 people) to £65   SERVICE: 12.5%, card slips closed   CARDS: Amex, Delta, Diners, MasterCard, Switch, Visa   DETAILS: 120 seats. Private parties: 50 private room. No-smoking area. Wheelchair access (also WC). Music. Air-conditioned   ⊖ Green Park

See inside the front cover for an explanation of the symbols used at the tops of entries.

Sushi-Say ✻ £

map 12

33B Walm Lane, NW2 5SH

TEL: (020) 8459 2971 and 7512

FAX: (020) 8907 3229

COOKING 3

JAPANESE

£18–£73

Those in the know consider dinner at this small, homely family-run Japanese restaurant to be 'nearly as good as going to Japan', offering cooking that easily matches most of the big City places aimed at businessmen and at a fraction of the cost. No wonder it is such a popular venue, busy every night of the week. The only slight let-down at inspection was the sushi, which was 'acceptable but not stunning', but everything else was 'dead right', including nicely charred yakitori kebabs with a pungent sweet and salty sauce, chawan mushi egg soup, and attractively presented tempura prawns and vegetables. All of those dishes came from a set menu, while hits from the carte and dishes of the day have included 'soft, sweet and melting' simmered pumpkin in dashi, crisp deep-fried pancakes filled with gooey natto (fermented soya bean), and breaded deep-fried scallops on shredded cabbage and carrot. As well as a good selection of wines, all under £25, the drinks list includes flasks of hot or cold saké, beers, whiskies and shotchu, a Japanese spirit.

CHEF: Katsuhara Shimizu   PROPRIETORS: Katsuhara and Yuko Shimizu   OPEN: Sat and Sun L 1 to 3.15, Tue to Sun D 6.30 to 10.30 (11 Sat, 10 Sun)   MEALS: alc (main courses £6.50 to £19). Set L £7.90 to £12.50 (all 1 or 2 courses), Set D £18.20 to £28.60   SERVICE: not inc   CARDS: Amex, Delta, MasterCard, Switch, Visa   DETAILS: 36 seats. Private parties: 20 main room. Vegetarian meals. No smoking. Wheelchair access (also WC). No music. Air-conditioned   ⊖ Willesden Green

Sutton Arms Dining Room

NEW ENTRY   map 13

4 Carthusian Street, EC1M 6EB

TEL: (020) 7253 0723

COOKING 3

MODERN EUROPEAN

£25–£45

Just across the road from the Barbican Tube station, the Sutton – reputedly one of the most haunted pubs in London – attracts a down-to-earth, modern-day City crowd. The first-floor dining room, over the traditional bar, offers plenty of natural light, is unfussy and simply adorned, suggesting 'that the food itself is the sole priority' here. Chef Rosie Sykes, also a food writer for *The Guardian*, is at the helm in the kitchen, offering a short, daily-changing carte. Dishes display clarity, deliver simple yet imaginative pairings of good raw materials, and offer seasonal focus and generous portioning. A starter of lambs' sweetbreads braised with peas and mint 'knocked the socks off' one reporter, the peas 'astoundingly fresh, and sweetbreads tender and accurately cooked'. A robust main dish of veal chop with celeriac and leek and morel sauce also came 'bursting with flavour'. Though desserts also prove a strength (perhaps chocolate tart with crème fraîche, or pistachio and almond cake with yoghurt ice cream), service can be slow and nonchalant. The sympathetically compact, global wine list, arranged by price, offers ample drinking under £20, with house bottles from £11 and 18 by the glass from £2.80.

CHEFS: Rosie Sykes and Tim Dillon   PROPRIETORS: Jon Flitney and Rosie Sykes   OPEN: Tue to Fri L 12.30 to 2, Mon to Fri D 6 to 10   CLOSED: 2 weeks at Christmas, bank hols   MEALS: alc (main courses £10 to £15). Set L £12.50 (2 courses) to £15.50   SERVICE: not inc   CARDS: Amex, Delta, MasterCard, Switch, Visa   DETAILS: 26 seats. Private parties: 28 main room. Vegetarian meals. No children. No music   ⊖ Barbican

---

▲ Swissôtel The Howard, Jaan [NEW ENTRY]   map 13

Temple Place, WC2R 2PR
TEL: (020) 7836 3555   FAX: (020) 7379 4547
EMAIL: reservations.london@swissotel.com
WEBSITE: www.swissotel.com

COOKING 3
MODERN FRENCH/
SOUTH-EAST ASIAN
£36–£107

Jaan is housed in a newly refurbished business hotel close to the Embankment. Tables in the luxuriously appointed dining room come with plenty of elbow room, and full-height windows give a view over a courtyard garden, which is used for al fresco dining. The ambitious cooking is described as French-Khmer, which essentially means a fusion of European and South-east Asian flavours. A starter of tuna carpaccio with lumpfish caviar, wasabi ice cream and sesame vinaigrette failed to make the desired impact at inspection but nonetheless was a riot of colour and featured 'sparklingly fresh' fish. Main courses have been more successful, including 'waxy, translucent and devastatingly fresh' baked turbot with ceps, courgettes and spiced chicken jus, and 'rare, succulent' grilled beef fillet with braised veal tongue, okra tempura and pepper vinegar sauce. An expertly made mango and jackfruit soufflé, with mango sorbet, has made a good impression among desserts. Service wins plaudits for its effortless grace, but there is nothing gracious about the wine list. Quality may be good but prices are stiff, with just two bottles squeezing in under £20. Wines by the glass (from £5 to £12) are a class act, and prestige bottles with three-figure prices abound.

CHEF: Nam Nguyen   PROPRIETOR: Raffles International   OPEN: Mon to Fri L 12 to 2.30, all week D 5.30 to 10.30   MEALS: alc (main courses £16 to £23). Set L £16.50 (2 courses) to £19.50, Set D 5.30 to 7.15 £19 (2 courses) to £22, Set D £45 to £75 (inc. wine). Bar menu available   SERVICE: 12.5%, card slips closed   CARDS: Amex, Delta, Diners, MasterCard, Switch, Visa   DETAILS: 55 seats. 40 seats outside. Private parties: 100 main room, 5 to 120 private rooms. Car park. Vegetarian meals. Children's helpings. No-smoking area. Wheelchair access (also WC). Music. Air-conditioned   ACCOMMODATION: 189 rooms, all with bath/shower. TV. Phone. Room only £295 to £650. Baby facilities

---

Tamarind ✎   map 15

20 Queen Street, W1J 5PR
TEL: (020) 7629 3561   FAX: (020) 7499 5034
EMAIL: tamarind.restaurant@virgin.net
WEBSITE: www.tamarindrestaurant.com

COOKING 3
MODERN INDIAN
£30–£79

In August 2002 former chef Atul Kochhar left Tamarind to strike out on his own with Benares (see entry). Since then, former sous-chef Alfred Prasad has taken over the stoves and seems to have had no difficulty in adjusting to his new role. The refurbished basement dining room is smartly decorated: taupe-coloured walls are hung with mirrors, and two bronzed pillars dominate the centre of the room. The menu offers dishes from throughout the Subcontinent, although the cooking of the North-west dominates. Poppadoms precede starters such as murgh achari tikka: tender, succulent pieces of chicken marinated in pickling spices and mint then cooked in the tandoor. In fact, much use is made of the tandoor, for Peshawari-style lamb chops to marinated monkfish. At inspection, main-course achari prawns were the stars of the show, the prawns cooked until just tender with tomatoes and spices. Vegetables can be a bit hit and miss, but rice is fine and bread includes 'fresh and thin' roomali roti, seldom found outside India. Desserts such as pistachio kulfi and carrot halva are properly flavoured. Service is impressive, and wines are good but pricey and don't go that far towards their stated aim of matching the food. The house selection of ten bottles, all available by the glass, starts at £14.50.

CHEF: Alfred Prasad   PROPRIETOR: Indian Cuisine Ltd   OPEN: Sun to Fri L 12 to 2.45, all week D 6 to 11.30 (10.30 Sun)   CLOSED: 25 to 28 Dec, L bank hols   MEALS: alc (main courses £13.50 to £26). Set L £14.50 (2 courses) to £16.50, Set D £34.50 to £48 (D all min 6 people)   SERVICE: 12.5% (optional), card slips closed   CARDS: Amex, Delta, Diners, MasterCard, Switch, Visa   DETAILS: 90 seats. Private parties: 100 main room. Vegetarian meals. No children under 10. Music. No mobile phones. Air-conditioned   ⊖ Green Park

---

Tas £   map 13

---

33 The Cut, SE1 8LF   COOKING 2
TEL: (020) 7928 1444   FAX: (020) 7633 9686   TURKISH
WEBSITE: www.tasrestaurant.com   £19–£44

Great value, excellent service, bags of atmosphere and live music are the prime ingredients in this stylish Turkish brasserie close to the Old Vic and the Festival Hall. No wonder the place is 'understandably always full'. The array of hot and cold meze continues to win votes, especially börek (filo pastry filled with feta cheese and spinach), and warm aubergines with peppers and cool, fresh yoghurt; otherwise, try midye corbasi (mussel soup spiced with coriander and ginger) as a starter. To follow there are grills aplenty (lambs' kidneys with oregano and cumin has hit the button), and casseroled lamb, moussaka and 'foil-baked' halibut have been praised. Vegetarians are offered plenty of choice, and desserts include traditional recipes such as kunefe ('shredded wheat' with unsalted white cheese and honey syrup). 'Freebie bread and hummus' is much appreciated, while a few gutsy Turkish wines complement the food; house Villa Doluca is £10.95.

CHEF/PROPRIETOR: Onder Sahan   OPEN: all week 12 to 11.30 (Sun 12 to 10.30)   MEALS: alc (main courses £5 to £15). Set L and D £7.25 (2 courses) to £18.50   SERVICE: 10%   CARDS: Amex, Delta, MasterCard, Switch, Visa   DETAILS: 140 seats. 8 seats outside. Private parties: 50 main room. Vegetarian meals. No-smoking area. No cigars/pipes. Wheelchair access (also WC). Music. Air-conditioned   ⊖ Southwark

---

Several sharp operators have tried to extort money from restaurateurs on the promise of an entry in a guidebook that has never appeared. **The Good Food Guide** *makes no charge for inclusion.*

Tate Britain Restaurant 📍   map 13

Millbank, SW1P 4RG   COOKING 3
TEL: (020) 7887 8825   FAX: (020) 7887 8902   MODERN BRITISH
WEBSITE: www.tate.org.uk   £33–£69

The Tate Britain Restaurant offers a good excuse to visit the gallery, even if you aren't interested in paint on canvas. It is, as one visitor put it, an 'ideal venue at which to meet with friends', with 'interesting food and excellent wines'. The à la carte and (rather short) set menus feature plenty of seasonal ingredients and attractive combinations. Dishes that have met with approval include a starter of dressed crab, 'nicely fresh and accurately seasoned', with 'a good swirl of brown meat', a salad of baby squid, chorizo and white beans, and a slow-roasted shoulder of lamb in honey and rosemary. The 'well-matured, highly tasty' Glen Fyne rump steak served with crunchy chips has also been given a thumbs-up. Staff are 'friendly and knowledgeable about Rex Whistler and the history behind his wonderful mural', which is a major talking point of the restaurant.

Everyone raves about the wine list. Half-bottles are a major feature of the profound and civilised selection, packed with great names and properly matured wines. Wine buyer Hamish Anderson's knowledge is allied to great enthusiasm and the list is anything but hidebound – even classic regions are fizzing with cutting-edge finds, and the helpful notes make this a great place for new discoveries, starting with the adventurous range of 16 by the glass (£3.95–£9.20).

CHEF: Chris Dines   PROPRIETOR: Tate Catering   OPEN: all week L only 12 to 3   MEALS: alc (main courses £10.50 to £18). Set L £16.95 (2 courses) to £19.50   SERVICE: not inc, card slips closed CARDS: Amex, Delta, Diners, MasterCard, Switch, Visa   DETAILS: 100 seats. 20 seats outside. Private parties: 40 main room. Vegetarian meals. Children's helpings. No-smoking area. Wheelchair access (also WC). No music. Air-conditioned   ⊖ Pimlico

Tentazioni   map 13

2 Mill Street, SE1 2BD
TEL/FAX: (020) 7237 1100   COOKING 3
EMAIL: tentazioni@aol.com   MODERN ITALIAN
WEBSITE: www.tentazioni.co.uk   £32–£61

This very Italian place seeks to contribute to the sophistication that has succeeded the stevedores in this part of town. Big, generously spaced tables on tiled floors generate a feeling of Mediterranean relaxation, and things start well with excellent breads. First courses combine assertive flavourings – pink gnochetti with basil sauce and an elegant confit of smoked ricotta and sun-dried tomato, for instance – or are visually stunning, as in a vibrant assemblage of squid-ink lasagne. A main-course parmigiana of courgettes and tomato has come with a good, tangy goats' cheese pudding, while breast of guinea fowl was partnered by juniper, potatoes and pumpkin cake. Chocolate cannelloni pastries with a chocolate cream filling served with a Grand Marnier and pineapple sorbet was a high point at inspection. Pleasant and friendly service could do better. The wine list is all-Italian, with some good choices from the south around £20, and some top names adding a touch of glamour. Prices start at £14 for basics, and eight come by the glass for £4–£6.

CHEF: Riccardo Giacomini   PROPRIETORS: Christian di Pierro and Maurizio Rimerici   OPEN: Tue to Fri L 12 to 2.30, Mon to Sat D 7 to 11   MEALS: alc (main courses £12 to £18). Set L £15 (2 courses) to £19. Set D £26 to £36   SERVICE: 12.5% (optional), card slips closed   CARDS: Amex, Delta, Diners, MasterCard, Switch, Visa   DETAILS: 50 seats. Private parties: 40 main room, 20 to 30 private rooms. Vegetarian meals. Children's helpings. Music   ⊖ London Bridge (£5)

Thai Garden ⅍ £

map 12

249 Globe Road, E2 0JD
TEL: (020) 8981 5748
EMAIL: thaigarden@hotmail.com
WEBSITE: www.thethaigarden.co.uk

COOKING 1
THAI SEAFOOD/VEGETARIAN
£17–£42

From the outside, Thai Garden looks like a basic East End café, but it's a café with a difference: it serves proper home-style Thai food – and although it styles itself a 'vegetarian restaurant', it serves seafood as well. Dishes go beyond the usual red, green and yellow coconut-milk-based sauces, featuring the likes of mushroom 'larb' (a northern Thai dish), gaeng som (a sour curry of prawns, French beans, Chinese leaves and cabbage) and 'su ki ya ki', a Thai take on Japanese sukiyaki. At its best, the Thai Garden offers simple cooking and fresh ingredients, correctly seasoned, resulting in 'true' Thai flavours, though flavourings can be a touch timid on occasion. Overall, this is a good neighbourhood restaurant serving authentic Thai cooking. House wines sell for a modest £7.50, and only the £17 champagne tops £15.

CHEF: Suthinee Hufton Singhara   PROPRIETORS: Suthinee and Jack Hufton   OPEN: Mon to Fri L 12 to 2.30, all week D 6 to 10.30   CLOSED: bank hols   MEALS: alc (main courses £4.50 to £7). Set L (min 2) £7.50 to £8.50, Set D (min 2) £16 to £20   SERVICE: 10%, card slips closed   CARDS: Delta, MasterCard, Switch, Visa   DETAILS: 32 seats. Private parties: 20 main room, 12 to 14 private rooms. Vegetarian meals. No smoking in 1 dining room. Wheelchair access (not WC). Music   ⊖ Bethnal Green (£5)

Thyme ⅍

map 12

14 Clapham Park Road, SW4 7BB
TEL: (020) 7627 2468   FAX: (020) 7627 2424
EMAIL: adam@thymeandspace.com
WEBSITE: www.thymeandspace.com

COOKING 4
MODERN EUROPEAN
£37–£69

Just around the corner from Clapham Common tube, Adam Byatt and Adam Oates – both formerly at Claridge's and Square (see entries) – have created an innovative, much-discussed neighbourhood dining room. The simple space – wood floor, cream walls hung with abstracts, Venetian blinds, a red bar, and white linen-dressed tables in three rows – is generally 'bustling with thirty-somethings'. Thyme has marched on, changing its original menu format; there's still no carte, and now everything revolves around three tasting menus (at D £25, £30 and £40), plus a vegetarian menu at £22.50. Wines by the glass can come individually matched to each course for an additional fixed price. Dishes certainly aim high and the ambition is evident in the six-course line-up at £40

(£70 with matched wines): roast foie gras on toast, quail consommé, muscat grapes; garlic-roast langoustines, langoustine cannelloni, langoustine velouté; ballottine of sole, truffled cauliflower, baby gem; pot roast rump of beef, red onion Tatin, braised beef rib, red wine, girolles; fondue of Fourme d'Ambert; assiette of Arabic coffee. Portions, by the way, are starter size and dishes can be swapped from menu to menu. Staff are 'sunny, attentive' and capable, the maitre d' observant and 'switched on', while the French-led, global list offers house at £17.50, though prices soon escalate (an admirable selection by the glass from £4.50 could compensate).

CHEFS/PROPRIETORS: Adam Byatt and Adam Oates OPEN: Tue to Sat 12.30 to 2, 6.30 to 11 CLOSED: Christmas MEALS: Set L £12.50 (2 courses) to £40 (inc wine), Set D £25 to £70 (inc wine) SERVICE: 12.5% (optional), card slips closed CARDS: Amex, Delta, MasterCard, Switch, Visa DETAILS: 45 seats. Private parties: 50 main room. Vegetarian meals. No-smoking area. Wheelchair access (not WC). No music. Air-conditioned ⊖ Clapham Common

Timo ⅝✳

343 Kensington High Street, W8 6NW
TEL: (020) 7603 3888 FAX: (020) 7603 8111

map 13

COOKING 4
ITALIAN
£37–£47

There's a feeling of modernity and style to this relative newcomer to the Kensington scene. The long, narrow room has lots of pale wood and glass, the tables set with shining glasses and gleaming cutlery. The cooking is 'very simple contemporary Italian' and one visitor has noted a similarity to the style of Zafferano (see entry), which is part of the same group. Choose two, three or four courses for a set price, with supplements for some dishes. Starters such as wild boar ham with rocket, celeriac and mayonnaise, or carpaccio of smoked fish with fennel and chives, rely heavily on assemblies. Pasta dishes that have won approval include a simple tagliatelle with black truffle and flavourful ravioli of oxtail. Main courses extend to monkfish with spinach and capers, and roast veal kidney with green lentils and parsley sauce. Desserts include Italian staples such as gelato and pannacotta. Service is generally polished, although there have been reports of indifference and inflexibility. Wines (apart from a few champagnes) come exclusively from Italy and, though carefully chosen, offer little choice, at around the £20 mark.

CHEF: Valerio Naros PROPRIETOR: A To Z Restaurants OPEN: all week 12 to 3, 7 to 11 (10.30 Sun) CLOSED: L bank hols, Dec 25 MEALS: Set L £11 (1 course) to £19.50, Set D £19.50 (2 courses) to £29.50 SERVICE: 12.5% (optional), card slips closed CARDS: Amex, Delta, MasterCard, Switch, Visa DETAILS: 55 seats. Vegetarian meals. No smoking in 1 dining room. No cigars throughout. Wheelchair access (not WC). No music. Air-conditioned ⊖ High Street Kensington

Occasional music *in the details at the end of an entry means live or recorded music is played in the dining room only rarely or for special events.* No music *means it is never played.*

Tom Aikens

LONDON OF THE YEAR RESTAURANT

NEW ENTRY map 14

43 Elystan Street, SW3 3NT
TEL: (020) 7584 2003
FAX: (020) 7584 2001
EMAIL: info@tomaikens.co.uk
WEBSITE: www.tomaikens.co.uk

COOKING **8**
MODERN FRENCH
£38–£92

Tom Aikens gained his reputation at Pied-à-Terre (see entry), left to cook privately, and has now returned to the public arena. His smart new Chelsea restaurant has little colour: black leather chairs, screened windows and white-painted walls, relieved only by a few modern paintings. And the uncluttered menu lists dishes by their main component, plus a simple description; 'rabbit' is a confit with carrot and tarragon salad and Sauternes jelly; 'lobster' comes with Jabugo ham, rosemary and apple juice. Invention hasn't been simplified away, though: one starter combines potato soup and duck consommé with a salad of duck tongues. Underlying everything are notably fresh and well-sourced materials.

Tom's cooking used to be characterised by complexity and elaborate technique; now it is more assured and coherent, less showy. There is entertainment for both eyes and taste buds, though: viz. perfectly roast langoustines on slivers of braised pork belly, each topped with a raviolo of black truffle, a smear of rich artichoke purée surrounding the whole. Chicken, organic and flavoursome, may appear as pieces of poached breast interleaved with boned leg stuffed with chicken mousse and leek, accompanied by 'stunning' tubes of truffle-scented macaroni and topped with cheese gratin, all in a pool of delicate artichoke sauce. Well-timed John Dory fillets in a sparse red wine sauce, have come with two 'utterly divine langoustine tempura'.

Desserts, not quite so starry, have included apple torpedoes between leaves of filo pastry with almonds, topped with a scoop of silky-textured apple sorbet; and a pineapple slice, roasted with vanilla and rum, with pineapple jelly and 'one of the most delicate [pineapple sorbets] I have ever tasted'. Cheeses are in good condition, but bread and coffee could do with a fillip (the latter comes with excellent chocolates, a toast-rack of flavoured tuiles, and a basket of 'sublime' madeleines). Service, under Laura Aikens, is first-class. The Rhône, Burgundy, Bordeaux and southern France underpin the heavyweight wine list, and briefer selections from elsewhere in France and abroad are more than respectable. Prices start just under £20, but above £30 the options open up; otherwise, choose from the dozen by the glass for £6–£14.

CHEF: Tom Aikens   PROPRIETOR: T & L Ltd   OPEN: Mon to Fri 12 to 2.30, 7 to 11   CLOSED: 2 weeks at Christmas, bank hols   MEALS: Set L £24.50, Set D £49, Set L and D for whole table only £59   SERVICE: 12.5% (optional), card slips closed   CARDS: Amex, Delta, MasterCard, Switch, Visa   DETAILS: 60 seats. Children's helpings. No cigars. Wheelchair access (also WC). No music. No mobile phones. Air-conditioned

---

£ *means that it is possible to have a three-course meal, including coffee, half a bottle of house wine and service for £30 or less per person, at any time the restaurant is open, i.e. at dinner as well as lunch. It may be possible to spend considerably more than this, but by choosing carefully you should find £30 or less achievable.*

Les Trois Garçons

map 13

1 Club Row, E1 6JX   COOKING 4
TEL: (020) 7613 1924   FAX: (020) 7613 3067   FRENCH
WEBSITE: www.lestroisgarcons.com   £41–£79

'Astonishing', 'outstanding', 'totally eccentric', even 'bejewelled taxidermy', say reporters striving to characterise the beguiling interior of this former East End pub. The décor is the OTT opposite of the currently fashionable stripped-down, spare minimalism: the room is bedecked with chandeliers, handbags, costume jewellery, stuffed creatures and much, much more. Waiters clad in black, French-style, add a fitting formality to the theatricality.

The cooking is rather more conservative than the surroundings, French with a pleasing, underlying intensity. Start with, say, sautéed tiger prawns served with crushed herbs, Jersey potatoes and a garlic sauce with added coconut, or a foie gras terrine layered with black truffles accompanied by a plum compote. A winter main course of chestnut-stuffed roast guinea fowl comes with cocotte potatoes, Brussels sprouts, plus merguez sausage, bacon and a tarragon sauce; summer could bring grilled Dover sole with samphire and globe artichokes, and the extra vegetables include gratin dauphinois. Desserts such as tarte Tatin, crème brûlée and lemon tart are high on tradition, or there might be a honeycomb parfait with whisky fudge cake. Classical French regions dominate the wine list, of course, but there are token forays into New World territory, too. Prices start at £19.50 and move swiftly upwards.

CHEF: Ade Adigun   PROPRIETORS: Michel Lasserre, Stefan Karlson and Hassan Abdullah   OPEN: Mon to Sat D only 7 to 10.30 (11 Thur to Sat)   CLOSED: 23 Dec to 4 Jan   MEALS: alc D (main courses £12.50 to £22). Set D Thur to Sat £20 (2 courses) to £42   SERVICE: 12.5% (optional) CARDS: Amex, Delta, Diners, MasterCard, Switch, Visa   DETAILS: 85 seats. Private parties: 85 main room, 4 to 16 private rooms. Vegetarian meals. Wheelchair access (not WC). Music. Air-conditioned   ⊖ Liverpool Street

La Trompette 🍾

map 12

5–7 Devonshire Road, Chiswick, W4 2EU   COOKING 6
TEL: (020) 8747 1836   FAX: (020) 8995 8097   FRENCH
    £36–£68

This 'smart, friendly neighbourhood restaurant' is a study in brown, its close-together tables producing a sense of intimacy. Start, maybe, with 'benchmark pasta' like crab and scallop tortelloni with a creamy cauliflower velouté, or try two wooden skewers threaded with flattened, grilled duck hearts, served with four fat chips and tartare sauce. The confident cooking has produced succulent, well-timed, free-range chicken with peas and cocotte potatoes, and a large piece of pink but not particularly well trimmed veal with ceps, snails, and 'knockout' potato purée reeking of truffle. Offal-fanciers might pick a plate of grilled calf's liver and kidney (both cooked pink), served with a piece of deep-fried, breadcrumb-coated brain and a section of stuffed pig's trotter with 'exceptional depth of flavour', all on a layer of well-made white onion risotto. Desserts may sometimes lack sparkle, but they have included a classic, dark, moist, sticky toffee pudding with a strongly flavoured caramel sauce, or a trifle involving pineapple, mango, paw paw and a passion fruit-flavoured custard, served with banana beignets. Service can be pushed at busy times, but staff are perceptive and efficient. Exciting wines by the glass (£3.70–£10.50) introduce a confident wine list on song in all regions, although France, Italy, Australia and New Zealand stand out. With prices from £14.50, diners on a budget aren't excluded, but the action really starts above £20.

CHEF: Ollie Couillaud   PROPRIETORS: Nigel Platts-Martin and Bruce Poole   OPEN: all week 12 to 2.30 (3 Sun), 6.30 to 10.30 (7 to 10 Sun)   CLOSED: 24 to 26 Dec   MEALS: Set L £15 (1 course) to £21.50, Set D £17.50 (1 course) to £30   SERVICE: 12.5% (optional), card slips closed   CARDS: Amex, Delta, MasterCard, Switch, Visa   DETAILS: 75 seats. 16 seats outside. Children's helpings. No cigars/pipes. Wheelchair access (also WC). No music. Air-conditioned ⊖ Turnham Green

La Trouvaille

map 15

12A Newburgh Street, W1F 7RR
TEL: (020) 7287 8488   FAX: (020) 7434 0170

COOKING 3
PROVINCIAL FRENCH
£25–£67

La Trouvaille, tucked away in Soho, has a bistro feel; small interconnecting rooms, closely spaced wooden tables, a church pew and large mirrors make for a 'curious yet successful mix'. The menu's emphasis is on unconventional regional French cooking, such as skewered mussels with wild boar pancetta, smoked monkfish cheeks with mango, and the slightly more conventional apple and black pudding tart, or green bean salad with a soft-boiled duck egg. Main courses show a dedication to sourcing organic and free-range ingredients: skirt of Galloway beef with crayfish and liquorice bisque, for instance, or Herdwick mutton fillet with a lavender sauce. Puddings such as mousse au chocolat ('the real stuff', according to the menu), pistachio crème brûlée, or goats' cheese yoghurt provide Gallic flavour to the end. The short wine list sticks to southern French regions, from basic vins de pays at £13.50 (£3.50 a glass) to Languedoc classics such as l'Hortus (£41) and Mas de Daumas Gassac (£52). A sister restaurant, Brasserie La Trouvaille, can be found at 353 Upper Street, N1; tel: (020) 7704 8323.

CHEF: Sebastian Gagnebé   PROPRIETOR: Thierry Bouteloup   OPEN: Mon to Sat 12 to 3, 6 to 11   CLOSED: Christmas, bank hols   MEALS: alc D (main courses £12.50 to £18). Set L £16.95 (2 courses) to £19.75, Set D 6 to 6.45 £10.95 (2 courses) to £13.75   SERVICE: 12.5% (optional), card slips closed   CARDS: Amex, Delta, Diners, MasterCard, Switch, Visa   DETAILS: 33 seats. 15 seats outside. Private parties: 8 main room, 8 to 18 private rooms. No cigars/pipes. No music ⊖ Oxford Circus

Tsunami

map 12

Unit 3, 1–7 Voltaire Road, SW4 6DQ
TEL: (020) 7978 1610   FAX: (020) 7978 1591

COOKING 2
JAPANESE
£34–£59

The railway sidings and rows of modest shops found in this still-gentrifying part of Clapham may seem an unlikely setting for a modern Japanese restaurant, but that's just one of the surprises this place can spring. The spacious interior, all cool, dark wood and off-white walls, attracts a trendy crowd. Other surprises lie in wait on the menu, which may be 'a revelation to people whose experience is limited to sushi bars'. Seasonal specials might include pan-fried ginger-honey quail with black truffle sauce, or (from the list of appetisers) sea urchin tempura with shiso leaf, or grilled scallops with smelt eggs and creamy spicy sauce. Sushi can seem uninspired in comparison, but the 'delicacy, flavour and freshness' of the rest of the menu tend to make up for it. Black-clad servers are charming and accommodating. Wines are not very exciting but mostly under £25.

CHEFS/PROPRIETORS: Ni Lennette and Ken Sam OPEN: Sat 12.30 to 11, Mon to Sat D 6 to 11 CLOSED: 22 Dec to 2 Jan MEALS: alc (main courses £10 to £14) SERVICE: 12.5% (optional), card slips closed CARDS: Delta, MasterCard, Switch, Visa DETAILS: 100 seats. Private parties: 130 main room. Vegetarian meals. Children's helpings. No music. Air-conditioned

Ubon

map 12

34 Westferry Circus, Canary Wharf, E14 8RR

TEL: (020) 7719 7800   FAX: (020) 7719 7801

COOKING 5
JAPANESE
£56–£142

The sister restaurant to the West End's Nobu (see entry) is next to the Four Seasons Hotel at Canary Wharf. First-timers may discover that half the fun of visiting it is in working out how to get through an assault course of apparently locked gates and doors, but persevere and take the lift to the fourth floor: a high-ceilinged dining room offers panoramic views down the river. As at Nobu, the menu deals in exquisitely presented Japanese dishes, with splashes of Western technique counterpointing the fresh, simple flavours. Staff, dressed in neutral black, are not too cool to help, and the food arrives in a logical order, a succession of small dishes, divided into appetisers, sashimi, soup, rice, noodles, salads and sushi rolls.

Salmon tiradito is a highlight, wafer-thin slices of immaculately fresh fish with an optional caviar garnish, coriander leaves and a ceviche-like dressing strong on lime. Toro sashimi wrapped in a shiso leaf is succulent and subtle, while the cooked shrimp sushi slightly outshines a version based on freshwater eel. Black cod with miso has deservedly become a signature dish, the miso paste cleverly charred on to the surface of the fish, delivering layers of savoury complexity. Wagyu beef should not be missed, either: it comes with spicy Peruvian anti-cucho sauce and a dip flavoured with mustard and honey, but it is the miraculous tenderness and subtlety of the meat that really shines, 'as though you had never had beef before'. Finish with a bento box containing perhaps a cake of warm chocolate fondant alongside a subtle, creamy green tea ice cream, or with banana and red bean harumaki with five-spice ice cream. The cost will be anything from stiff to astronomical. Wines play their part in pumping up that bill. The Matsuhisa-branded house wines, a Chardonnay and a Cabernet Sauvignon from California, are £50 a bottle, although prices start at £26 and half a dozen are served by the glass from £5.50.

CHEF: Mark Edwards PROPRIETOR: Nobu Matsuhisa OPEN: Mon to Fri L 12 to 2.30, Mon to Sat D 6 to 10.15 MEALS: alc (main courses £13.50 to £28). Set L £24.50 to £50, Set D £50 to £90 (min 12) SERVICE: 12.5% (optional), card slips closed CARDS: Amex, Delta, Diners, MasterCard, Switch, Visa DETAILS: 120 seats. Private parties: 150 main room. Vegetarian meals. No-smoking area. No cigars/pipes. Wheelchair access (also WC). Music. Air-conditioned
⊖ Canary Wharf, Westferry (DLR)

The Vale

map 13

99 Chippenham Road, W9 2AB
TEL: (020) 7266 0990 FAX: (020) 7286 7224

COOKING **2**
MODERN BRITISH
£21–£46

Consisting largely of blue-painted lean-to conservatories, this smart brick building on a corner site has a friendly and relaxed feel, and puts good cooking high on its agenda. It has produced dense, well-flavoured breads; fine salade niçoise; a rich and tender roast chicken dish with finely puréed, olive oil mash and spinach; and rhubarb fool (pleasant though under-fruited) – all this part of an excellent-value set meal. From the à la carte menu, a well-textured squid stuffed with ratatouille preceded moist, flaky pan-fried halibut with 'gutsy' creamed leeks, mussels and an intense crab jus, lightened by Jersey Royals. Salads and pasta dishes come in two sizes. More than half the bottles on the suitably modern wine list are under £20, and ten of them come by the glass (£2.75–£4). An unusually good range of sweet wines by the glass could accompany or substitute for dessert.

CHEF: Robin Tarver PROPRIETORS: Francesca Melman and Robin Tarver OPEN: Tue to Fri L 12.30 to 2.30, Sun L 11 to 4, Mon to Sat D 7 to 11 MEALS: alc (main courses £9 to £14). Set L Tue to Fri £9.50 (2 courses) to £18.50, Sun brunch £18.50, Set D £12 (2 courses) to £15 SERVICE: 12.5% (optional), card slips closed CARDS: Delta, Diners, MasterCard, Switch, Visa DETAILS: 70 seats. Private parties: 30 main room, 14 to 40 private rooms. Vegetarian meals. Children's helpings. No smoking in 1 dining room. Wheelchair access (not WC). Occasional music. Air-conditioned ⊖ Maida Vale (£5)

Villandry Dining Room ⁵⅟✳

map 15

170 Great Portland Street, W1W 5QB
TEL: (020) 7631 3131 FAX: (020) 7631 3030
WEBSITE: www.villandry.com

COOKING **2**
MODERN EUROPEAN
£31–£68

A wander through Villandry's irresistible food emporium certainly whets the appetite, and the appealing cheese and charcuterie counters supply both the bar and restaurant. The latter is a bustling, noisy room where the daily-changing menu aims for simple, high-quality food, using whatever is fresh in the market. In May, roast pigeon has come with green beans, lardons and a well-dressed salad, followed by large, juicy nuggets of monkfish on tender, wilted cavolo nero with perfectly roasted fennel and creamy, lemony beurre blanc. Timing is not always spot-on, though, and some readers have noted cold or overcooked food. Starters like mackerel pâté with watercress and new potato salad have been praised for their robust simplicity, and desserts including moist chocolate cake and lemon tart have satisfied. Service can vary depending on the pressure on staff (it can get very busy). A wine list was not provided, though we understand house wine is £12.50 and around 20 wines are available by the glass, from £3.50 to £6.50.

CHEFS: Steve Evernett-Watts and Sara Berg PROPRIETORS: Martha Greene and Jeremy Sinclair OPEN: all week L 12 to 3.30, Mon to Sat D 6 to 10.30 CLOSED: 10 days at Christmas MEALS: alc (main courses £11 to £21). Set D 6 to 7 £15.50 (2 courses) to £18.50. Bar menu available SERVICE: 12.5% (optional), net prices, card slips closed CARDS: Amex, Delta, MasterCard,

Switch, Visa DETAILS: 100 seats. 20 seats outside. Private parties: 120 main room, 10 to 120 private rooms. Vegetarian meals. No smoking. Wheelchair access (not WC). No music. Air-conditioned ⊖ Great Portland Street

Wagamama 🍴 £

map 15

4A Streatham Street, WC1A 1JB
TEL: (020) 7323 9223
WEBSITE: www.wagamama.com

COOKING 1
JAPANESE-STYLE
£19–£30

'Positive eating for positive living' is Wagamama's message. What it offers is lifestyle nutrition grafted on to the concept of traditional Japanese ramen shops; there are no bookings and customers eat communally at canteen-style benches. Mainstays on the menu are three sorts of noodles – soba, udon and ramen – that might be teppan-fried or added to soups with, say, honey-roast pork or chargrilled salmon; there are also well-reported 'katsu' curries and various side dishes such as edamame and yakitori. Despite the restaurant's computer-ordering system, meals do not always move on apace: 'only in the UK do we take a fast food idea and slow it down,' observed one reporter. Raw juices and green tea are the food's ideological bedfellows, although you can opt for saké, Japanese beer or wine (house French is £10.35). Streatham Street is the godfather, but there are now some 20 outlets throughout the UK plus franchises abroad.

CHEFS: Adrian McCormack and Paul Meyer PROPRIETOR: Paul O'Farrell OPEN: Mon to Sat 12 to 11, Sun 12.30 to 10 MEALS: alc (main courses £6 to £8.50) SERVICE: not inc, card slips closed CARDS: Amex, Delta, Diners, MasterCard, Switch, Visa DETAILS: 130 seats. Vegetarian meals. No smoking. Wheelchair access (also WC). No music. Air-conditioned ⊖ Tottenham Court Road

Wapping Food

map 12

Wapping Hydraulic Power Station,
Wapping Wall, E1W 3ST
TEL: (020) 7680 2080
EMAIL: jules@wapping-wpt.com

COOKING 3
MODERN EUROPEAN/MEDITERRANEAN
£38–£59

'Fun' is a favourite description of this extraordinary restaurant-cum-gallery housed in a defunct hydraulic power station. The vast interior is now 'funky Orwellian' – a reference to the original ironwork and preserved mechanical paraphernalia, as well as the contemporary multimedia 'installations' that now form part of the show. Trendy ingredients are given full rein in the kitchen: preserved lemons appear in chickpea soup, piquillo pepper salsa partners grilled red snapper, and smoked ricotta turns up in a dish of orrechiette with roast Jerusalem artichokes. At its best the cooking is exact and impressive – witness seared scallops with roasted peppers, rocket and vinaigrette Nero, slow-roast Middlewhite pork with chorizo and mussels, plus sublime fig and blackcurrant pannacotta. 'Sweet-natured and pretty professional' service wins the place a lot of friends. A list of around 20 globetrotting wines are fairly priced from £14.75.

CHEF: James Robson   PROPRIETOR: Wapping Restaurants Ltd   OPEN: all week L 12 to 3, Mon to Sat D 6.30 to 11   MEALS: alc (main courses £10 to £17)   SERVICE: not inc, 12.5% (optional) for parties of 6 or more   CARDS: Amex, Delta, Diners, MasterCard, Switch, Visa   DETAILS: 100 seats. 30 seats outside. Private parties: 75 main room. Car park. Vegetarian meals. Wheelchair access (also WC). Music   ⊖ Wapping £5

Waterloo Bar and Kitchen £   map 13

131 Waterloo Road, SE1 8UR   COOKING 2
TEL: (020) 7928 5086   FAX: (020) 7928 1880   GLOBAL
                                                                £23–£41

This basic, large space, with utilitarian furniture, open-plan kitchen and well-worn décor is near the Old Vic and handy for post-work gatherings or pre-theatre suppers. The relaxed atmosphere offers a good alternative to the pub. And then there is the food: substantial portions of everything is usual. Start with pork and pepper pâté, or avocado Caesar salad, and move on to main courses like two hefty pieces of decent-quality calf's liver, nicely pink, or a large chunk of monkfish with diced chorizo. There are three vegetarian pastas available. 'A Matterhorn of coffee cream on a thin slice of sponge cake topped with crunchy coffee beans', although not authentic tiramisù, was 'rich, silky, sumptuous'. Service is friendly and helpful. Around 30 well-chosen wines start at £9.50 (just one tops £20), and ten come by the glass.

CHEF: Bruce Miller   PROPRIETOR: Clive Watson   OPEN: Mon to Fri L 12 to 2.45, Mon to Sat D 5.30 to 10.30   CLOSED: Christmas, bank hols   MEALS: alc (main courses L £5 to £10, D £8 to £14). Set D £12.95 (2 courses)   SERVICE: not inc, 10% for parties of 6 or more   CARDS: Amex, Delta, Diners, MasterCard, Switch, Visa   DETAILS: 60 seats. 12 seats outside. Private parties: 60 main room. Vegetarian meals. Music   ⊖ Waterloo

Waterway   [NEW ENTRY]   map 13

54 Formosa Street, W9 2JU   COOKING 2
TEL: (020) 7266 3557   FAX: (020) 7266 3547   MODERN EUROPEAN
WEBSITE: www.thewaterway.co.uk   £24–£55

In this smart, cool, red-leather-and-dark-wood gastro-pub beside the Grand Union Canal, Michael Nadra shows that his previous experience in good kitchens certainly prepared him for quick-fire brasserie cooking. Dense, chewy bread, accurately timed meat and fish (lightly steamed mussels with ham hock showed well-judged flavouring too – saltiness moderated by fresh tarragon and a splash of Pernod), careful vegetable cooking, and 'brilliant lemon tart with rich, crisp pastry', identify this is as an adept kitchen that pitches its ambition at the appropriate level. Well-executed, neatly conceived, unelaborate combinations include grilled calf's kidneys with 'smooth, creamy mash' and fresh spinach cutting the richness of the kidneys, or marinated squid with sea bass and a fondue of root vegetables. Cocktails and bottled (rather than draught) beers indicate the age (and noise tolerance!) of expected customers, but the wines, starting at £10.50 are decent and fairly priced.

CHEF: Michael Nadra   PROPRIETOR: Tom Etridge   OPEN: all week 12.30 to 3, 6.30 (7 Sat and Sun) to 10.15 (10.30 Fri and Sat, 9.45 Sun)   CLOSED: 25 Dec   MEALS: alc (main courses £10.50 to £17.50). Set L £12.50 (2 courses) to £15, Set D £20 (2 courses) to £25. Bar menu available

SERVICE: 12.5% (optional)   CARDS: Amex, Delta, MasterCard, Switch, Visa   DETAILS: 66 seats. 40 seats outside. Private parties: 120 main room. Car park. Vegetarian meals. No cigars. Music. Air-conditioned   ⊖ Warwick Avenue

▲ West Street ♥ map 15

13–15 West Street, WC2H 9NE
TEL: (020) 7010 8600   FAX: (020) 7010 8601   COOKING 4
EMAIL: weststreet@egami.co.uk   ITALIAN
WEBSITE: www.egami.co.uk   £28–£67

Behind West Street's glass frontage are a basement bar, two table-clothed dining rooms – one on the ground floor and another on the first – and right at the top three rooms offering overnight accommodation. The same menus now apply throughout – no longer do you need to choose the ground floor to eat your wood-fired pizza. The rest of the menu is fairly long and draws on influences from around the globe, but without dabbling in any kind of 'fusion'. A starter of Vietnamese crab and papaya salad with prawn chips may be followed by a West Street cheese and bacon burger with chips, for example, yet there's a strong Italian undercurrent running through, too, with pasta (mushroom and ricotta tortelloni with mousserons, broad beans and sage, for example), the likes of Parmesan chicken with cherry vine tomatoes, and desserts such as Moscato zabaglione. 'Enjoyable food, not too ambitious, that delivers what it sets out to do' is how an inspector summed up West Street. Service is efficient and accommodating. That Italian current surfaces again on the wine list, which has a special focus on the country's wines and varieties in an international mix grouped by grape. There's plenty of choice under £20, and two dozen by the glass (£3.50–£9.25) offer a chance to broach some of the better bottles without breaking the bank.

CHEF: Lawrence Keogh   PROPRIETOR: Chris Booker   OPEN: Mon to Sat 12 to 3, 5.30 to 12   CLOSED: Christmas   MEALS: alc D only (main courses £14 to £19.50). Set L £15.95 (2 courses) to £17.95, Set D 5.30 to 7.15, 10.15 to 12 £13 (2 courses) to £15.50. Bar menu also available   SERVICE: 12.5% (optional), card slips closed   CARDS: Amex, Delta, Diners, MasterCard, Switch, Visa   DETAILS: 160 seats. Private parties: 100 main room, 1 to 32 private rooms. Vegetarian meals. Wheelchair access (also WC). Music. Air-conditioned   ACCOMMODATION: 3 rooms, all with bath/shower. TV. Phone. B&B £250 to £450 plus VAT. Rooms for disabled (*The Which? Guide to Good Hotels*)   ⊖ Leicester Square

Wheelers | NEW ENTRY | map 15

12A Duke of York Street, SW1 6LB   COOKING 2
TEL: (020) 7930 2460   FAX: (020) 7839 2394   SEAFOOD
                                                               £50–£95

Wheeler's has been located in this charming little building, clinging limpet-like to its larger neighbour, since 1856. A lot of oysters have been consumed in that time, but now it is owned by one of the restaurant world's big fish – Marco Pierre White. Small and narrow outside, it is slim and corridor-like within. Above the oyster bar, up narrow stairs, the long, thin dining rooms on two floors have maintained a traditional air, with leather banquettes, close-set tables, dark parquet floors and moulded-plaster ceilings. It is a smart, club-like space.

Mingling the English and French languages, the very traditional menu lists the likes of Dover sole in various guises, fish pie, dressed crab, and omelette Arnold Bennett. The last, in its own heavy copper pan, features undyed smoked haddock – rich, comforting stuff. Main courses like pan-fried skate with clams and jus à la Parisienne may feature a mid-sized wing scattered with capers to add welcome piquancy; vegetables are extra. Desserts, such as lemon tart, are adequate, and the conservative wine list sticks mostly to France; house bottles cost £18.50.

CHEF: Lee Bunting   PROPRIETOR: Marco Pierre White   OPEN: Mon to Fri L 12 to 2.30, Mon to Sat D 5.30 to 11   MEALS: alc (main courses £12.50 to £27)   SERVICE: 12.5% (optional), card slips closed   CARDS: Amex, Diners, MasterCard, Switch, Visa   DETAILS: 44 seats. Private parties: 18 main room, 1 to 4 private rooms. Vegetarian meals. Children's helpings. No music. Air-conditioned   ⊖ Piccadilly Circus, Green Park

William IV 🍸 £   map 12

786 Harrow Road, NW2 5JX   COOKING 2
TEL: (020) 8969 5944   FAX: (020) 8964 9218   MODERN EUROPEAN
WEBSITE: www.william-iv.co.uk   £26–£50

It may still remind some visitors of a Victorian boozer, but this watering hole on the Harrow Road is now a twenty-first-century gastro-pub in all but name. New chef Rino Scalco has followed on where his predecessor left off and his menu is a no-nonsense affair with strong Italian leanings. A meal might start with sauté chicken livers with spaghetti, parsley and capers or baby vegetable tempura with sweet chilli jam, and move on to main courses such as roast chump of lamb with fondant potatoes and cauliflower purée, or whole grilled royal bream with braised Puy lentils and salsa verde. For dessert there might be tarte Tatin with toffee sauce. At lunchtime, there's also a one-course, fixed-price deal including a glass of wine or a pint of beer. The wine list is grouped according to style ('fruit driven and texture', for example); prices start at £10.90.

CHEF: Rino Scalco   PROPRIETOR: Megamade Ltd   OPEN: all week 12 to 3 (4 Sat and Sun), 6 (7 Sat) to 11 (9.30 Sun)   MEALS: alc (main courses L £8 to £15, D £8 to £18). Set L £7.50 (1 course)   SERVICE: not inc, 10% (optional) for tables of 5 or more   CARDS: Amex, Delta, MasterCard, Switch, Visa   DETAILS: 80 seats. 70 seats outside. Private parties: 40 main room, 20 to 40 private rooms. Vegetarian meals. No cigars/pipes. Occasional music. No mobile phones   ⊖ Kensal Green

Wiltons   map 15

55 Jermyn Street, SW1Y 6LX
TEL: (020) 7629 9955   FAX: (020) 7495 6233   COOKING 5
EMAIL: wiltons@wiltons.co.uk   TRADITIONAL ENGLISH
WEBSITE: www.wiltons.co.uk   £43–£111

Most restaurants take the opportunity of refurbishment to present a newer image. Not so Wiltons, whose refit has been carried out with as little disturbance to the status quo as possible: beyond the seafood bar lies a series of rooms kitted out with 'Pullman' dining booths, green banquettes, a Victorian chandelier, and hunting and fishing prints. Firmly wedded to tradition, it has been serving oysters, lobsters and grills to toffs for generations, a style to which Jerome Ponchelle has taken like a duck to orange sauce; but then he did come from that other (former) bastion of tradition, the Connaught (see entry), when Michel Bourdin left.

The haven that Wiltons provides from the constant innovation and novelty all around it can be found in its Morecambe Bay potted shrimps, omelette Arnold Bennett, and avocado pear ('in perfect condition') with white crabmeat, not to mention its many grills, from Dover sole to Angus fillet steak and lambs' kidneys. The food may be simple, but materials are first-class, and the skilful cooking has taken in accurately seared scallops with apple and walnuts, a terrine of duck, pork and foie gras that pays homage to Michel Bourdin, and a saddle of rabbit wrapped in spinach and served with salsify. Sherry trifle and bread-and-butter pudding naturally turn up among desserts, alongside an excellently crafted raspberry crème brûlée. Staff and wines are mostly French, the latter uncomfortably priced for ordinary mortals. House wines are a minor claret at £36 and Durup Chablis at £38.

CHEF: Jerome Ponchelle   PROPRIETORS: the Hambro family   OPEN: all week L 12.15 to 2.30, Mon to Sat D 6.30 to 10.30   MEALS: alc (main courses £12 to £34). Set L Mon to Sat £26.50   SERVICE: not inc   CARDS: Amex, Delta, Diners, MasterCard, Switch, Visa   DETAILS: 75 seats. Private parties: 10 main room, 4 to 20 private rooms. Jacket and tie. Wheelchair access (also WC). No music. No mobile phones. Air-conditioned   ⊖ Green Park (£5)

Yatra   map 15

34 Dover Street, W1S 4NF
TEL: (020) 7493 0200   FAX: (020) 7493 4228   COOKING 3
EMAIL: yatra@lineone.net   INDIAN
WEBSITE: www.yatra.co.uk   £47–£68

Yatra is emblematic of the capital's burgeoning new wave of modern Indian restaurants. The look, with plenty of black tiling and bespoke lighting, is certainly right; an area of low seating gives the restaurant an oddly Japanese feel. The modern Indian cooking, though, is the real story. The menu combines dishes from throughout the Subcontinent, such as raan e Kandahar (yoghurt-marinated lamb cooked in the tandoor) from the far north-east, and Bengal fish curry from Calcutta. It also mingles classic (chicken molee) with contemporary (steamed rock lobster with ginger and lime); some dishes attempt, with varying degrees of success, to 'fuse' Asian and European flavours on the same plate. Most dishes get it right, though, the tandoori dishes having an attractive whiff of charcoal from the tandoor, and staples such as fluffy basmati rice and naan bread getting the thumbs-up. Vegetable dishes such as aloo jeera (potatoes cooked with cumin seeds and turmeric), and gobi mater (cauliflower and green peas cooked in a tomato and onion sauce flavoured with fenugreek), are well executed. The wine list is organised by style and tends toward the New World, with a few Indian wines, too. French house wine starts at £14 a bottle.

CHEF: Krishnapal Negi   PROPRIETOR: Sonu Lalvani   OPEN: Mon to Fri L 12 to 3, all week D 6 to 11 (11.30 Thur to Sat)   CLOSED: 25 Dec   MEALS: alc (main courses £13.50 to £18.50). Bar menu also available   SERVICE: 12.5% (optional), card slips closed   CARDS: Amex, Delta, MasterCard, Switch, Visa   DETAILS: 155 seats. Vegetarian meals. Wheelchair access (also WC). Music. Air-conditioned   ⊖ Green Park (£5)

Yokoso Sushi £

NEW ENTRY   map 13

40 Whitefriars Street, EC4Y 8BH
TEL: (020) 7583 9656   FAX: (020) 7583 9657

COOKING 3
JAPANESE
£16–£38

Yokoso Sushi is a well-hidden treasure, but you'd never guess it from the surroundings – down a rather unprepossessing staircase and across the hall from a betting shop. It is a brightly lit place, mostly smart although some remedial decoration could be in order. Dominating the centre of the room is a large conveyor belt, upon which the sparkling fresh food passes from chefs to diners. The service is solicitous, and the food is prepared with obvious care, maintaining a 'home-made taste'. Standards such as gyoza (steamed and fried pork dumplings), vegetable tempura, miso soup and chicken katsu (a breaded, fried cutlet) have a seldom-found delicacy. Sushi, such as sake (salmon) and toro (fatty tuna) are of good quality, succulent and prepared with good rice. Yokoso is a favoured lunchtime haunt for time-stretched City types, and offers very good value, too – but note that it closes early in the evening. House wine is a very reasonable £9.

CHEF: Mr Raveenvran   PROPRIETOR: R. Galamanathan   OPEN: Mon to Fri 11.30 to 7.30   MEALS: alc (main courses £2.50 to £12). Set L and D £6.50 (2 courses)   SERVICE: not inc   CARDS: Amex, MasterCard, Switch, Visa   DETAILS: 53 seats. Private parties: 58 main room. Vegetarian meals. Children's helpings. Music. Air-conditioned   ⊖ Blackfriars

---

Zafferano

map 14

15–16 Lowndes Street, SW1X 9EY
TEL: (020) 7235 5800   FAX: (020) 7235 1971

COOKING 6
ITALIAN
£40–£85

Two interconnecting, awkwardly shaped small rooms constitute what is still 'one of the best Italian restaurants in town'. With tiled floor, bare brick walls and small tables, it is comfortable enough, but what sustains it is a consistently high standard of cooking, matched by efficient and friendly service. Befitting the location, the food is sophisticated, rather than rustic, but has a genuinely Italian feel – from a 'benchmark' dish of mozzarella with grilled aubergine and salad, to delicate pappardelle folded around fine porcini, or earthy, creamy chestnut tagliatelle with wild mushrooms.

Such direct and easy appeal rests on a larder of first-class materials and some 'very classy cooking indeed'. Fish is characteristically impressive, from a 'simple yet intelligent combination' of accurately pan-fried brill with lentils and parsley (the flavour lifted by a little ginger) to 'beautifully cooked' monkfish with aubergine and sweet chilli, a dash of tangy lime emphasising its clean flavours. Meat dishes are no less successful: witness robust and flavoursome medallions of venison artfully paired with chicory, or pink and tender pigeon, off the bone, served on a bed of spinach with a garlic purée. Beyond tiramisù on the dessert menu might be warm fig tart with vanilla ice cream, or ricotta and lemon cake with rum and raisin ice cream. An impressive collection of Italian wines doesn't come cheap, particularly not those from the Riserve Toscana and Riserve

Piemonte sections, but there are about a dozen under £20, including house
Rosso Piceno and Bianco di Santa Barbara at £14.50.

CHEF: Andy Needham   PROPRIETOR: A To Z Restaurants   OPEN: all week 12 to 2.30, 7 to 11
(10.30 Sun)   CLOSED: 25 Dec, Easter bank hol   MEALS: Set L £21.50 (2 courses) to £30.50, Set D
£29.50 (2 courses) to £41.50   SERVICE: not inc   CARDS: Amex, Delta, Diners, MasterCard,
Switch, Visa   DETAILS: 45 seats. Vegetarian meals. Children's helpings. No cigars/pipes.
Wheelchair access (not WC). Music. No mobile phones. Air-conditioned   ⊖ Knightsbridge

Zaika ▮   map 13

1 Kensington High Street, W8 5NP
TEL: (020) 7795 6533   FAX: (020) 7937 8854   COOKING 5
EMAIL: info@zaika-restaurant.co.uk   MODERN INDIAN
WEBSITE: www.zaika-restaurant.co.uk   £28–£89

The makeover of this big, airy banking hall has been managed with what seems
like the minimum of resources – just a few baroque wooden statues of elephants
and some drapes of material – but a number of things help to make Zaika stand
out from the crowd: its prices (which don't seem to faze the lively, rich-looking
clientele), some of the ingredients, and the generally confident treatment that
helps the food transcend culinary boundaries.

  Although much of the menu is as familiar as lamb rogan josh or chicken
masala, more unusual items (for an Indian restaurant) include salmon and cod
fishcakes, scallops done three ways, and a skewer of accurately grilled pheasant
breast given the masala treatment and served with a mound of dryish sago.
Seafood is generally well rendered, be it home-smoked salmon marinated in
mustard and dill and given the tandoor treatment, or crispy softshell crab (one
only, gone in a couple of mouthfuls), served with rice cakes and lentils. Trios are
a favoured vehicle, successfully applied to vegetables (spinach purée with cubes
of paneer, chunks of potato in a spicy sauce, and a simple but flavourful dhal
with a deeply smoky undertone); and to duck (ungreasy samosa with a mango-
flavoured dressing; a fine skewer of minced duck combined with pepper and
spring onion; and a salad of breast meat). Spicing is generally fresh and vibrant,
and Western presentation extends to a small tower of pancakes separated by
layers of stewed fruit, with fresh fruit around the edge, a brandy-snap basket,
and a small scoop of flavour-packed ice cream. A cover charge is applied (small
poppadoms arrive with first-rate chutneys and without asking), there is only
one beer (Cobra), but as if to underline the break with standard Indian food, a
list of over 350 wines includes massive selections of the cream of France and
Italy and some very fine dessert wines. Fifteen come by the glass from £5 to £7.50
and there's a tolerable choice under £20.

CHEF: Vineet Bhatia   PROPRIETORS: Cuisine Collection and Vineet Bhatia   OPEN: Sun to Fri L 12
to 2.45, all week D 6.30 to 10.45 (9.45 Sun)   CLOSED: 24 and 25 Dec, bank hols   MEALS: alc (main
courses £12.50 to £26). Set L £11.95 (2 courses) to £13.95, Set D £33.50 to £50. Cover £1.50
SERVICE: 12.5% (optional), card slips closed   CARDS: Amex, Delta, Diners, MasterCard, Switch,
Visa   DETAILS: 80 seats. Private parties: 100 main room. Vegetarian meals. Children's helpings.
No cigars/pipes. Wheelchair access (not WC). Music. No mobile phones. Air-conditioned
⊖ Kensington High Street (£5)

Zuma ▼

map 14

5 Raphael Street, SW7 1DL
TEL: (020) 7584 1010   FAX: (020) 7584 5005
EMAIL: info@zumarestaurant.com
WEBSITE: www.zumarestaurant.com

COOKING 5
MODERN JAPANESE
£38–£92

Zuma proves the point that you can't judge a restaurant by its exterior. It occupies the ground floor of a modern office block, but the interior is a large space done up in tasteful, contemporary style, with lots of polished wood and stone surfaces. The large bar area (where some interesting saké-based cocktails are served) is a home away from home for the young, glamorous set. Zuma's trendiness inevitably draws comparisons with Nobu (see entry, London), as does the modern Japanese menu. Despite the length and detail of the menu, the staff know their stuff and do their best to arrange the various selections of 'small dishes and salads', vegetables, meat, seafood, tempura, etc. in a sensible order.

'Small dishes' take in the likes of green beans with tofu and miso sauce, and crispy fried squid with green chilli salt. The fish for the wide selection of sushi, such as hamachi (yellowtail) and o-toro (best-quality fatty tuna) is sea-fresh, and there are inventive maki (rolled sushi) based on roast duck with red miso, or prawn tempura, as well. A main course of 'very tender' tiger prawn has been 'served in its shell, but carefully removed and reassembled', according to one visitor, who also enjoyed 'very lightly handled' vegetable tempura. From the large, open robata grill may come barbecued seasoned rice, wagyu beef with soy and wasabi, and minced chicken skewers with sansho pepper. For dessert, the recipient of a hot chocolate fondant with a passion-fruit centre was pleased with his choice. The first page of the wine list is devoted to saké, with useful tasting notes for the uninitiated. Wines are well chosen but pricey, starting at £18. The New World is dominated by Australia, while Alsace and German whites feature in a food-friendly Old World line-up. Ten wines by the glass are £4.75 to £8.50.

CHEFS: Rainer Becker and Colin Clague   PROPRIETORS: Arjun Waney and Rainer Becker   OPEN: all week 12 to 2.30, 6 to 11.30 (10.30 Sun)   CLOSED: 25 and 26 Dec   MEALS: alc (main courses £8.50 to £44). Set L £8.50 to £14.80. Light L and bar menus available   SERVICE: 12.5% (optional), card slips closed   CARDS: Amex, Diners, MasterCard, Switch, Visa   DETAILS: 140 seats. Private parties: 8 to 14 private rooms. Vegetarian meals. No-smoking area. Wheelchair access (also WC). Music. Air-conditioned   ⊖ Knightsbridge

London round-ups

With so many venues vying for attention, finding a place to eat out in London that offers the right blend of food, location, style and price to suit the occasion can often be very much down to potluck. This section aims to make choosing easier by providing details of a broad range of restaurants, bistros, cafés, hotel dining rooms, and so on, that are deserving of attention, though they do not merit a full entry. There are also one or two rising stars, well worth keeping an eye on, and in some cases establishments have been included here rather than in the main entries because of significant late changes or a lack of positive feedback. Reports on these places are particularly welcome. Brief details of opening times and prices are given in each entry where available.

Asakusa NW1
265 Eversholt Street   map 13
(020) 7388 8399
A genuine neighbourhood Japanese restaurant just a few hundred yards from Euston station. Commuters in need of revival rub shoulders with locals in a simple dining room where the walls are hung with posters listing untranslated specialities. The menu runs from nigiri sushi (£8.80) and sashimi moriawase to unagi kabayaki (grilled eel with 'special sauce', £7.30) and agedashi-nasu (deep-fried aubergines and prawns). For the less adventurous, there are also very affordable set dinners (£6–£10) based around tempura, teriyaki and the like. Open Mon to Sat D only.

L'Auberge SW15
22 Upper Richmond Road   map 12
(020) 8874 3593
The location may be East Putney, but Pascal Ardilly's restaurant succeeds in living up to its Gallic name with food that is as French as the 'tricolor'. Robust peasant dishes share the billing with some bourgeois and classically inclined specialities: begin with grilled honeyed goats' cheese salad (£4.80) or red pepper bavarois before marinated civet of pork (£11.95). M. Ardilly is a trained patissier, and his desserts might include lavender-scented crème brûlée (£4.25) or crêpe des îles. House wine at £10.50 tops the short, totally French list. Open Tue to Sat D only.

Azou W6
375 King Street   map 12
(020) 8563 7266
Couscous and tagine in various guises (from £9.50–£12.50) dominate the short menu in this bright little restaurant, which garners ideas from Morocco, Algeria and Tunisia. Start with bourek (crisp pastries with different fillings, from £4) or falafel, and finish with farka (couscous sweetened with dried fruit and nuts). In between, there are also a few grills and specials like mechui (roast lamb shank) and duck with harissa and saffron. Drink Casablanca Moroccan lager or something from the minuscule wine list (prices from £9.90). Closed Sat and Sun L.

The Barnsbury N1
209–211 Liverpool Road   map 13
(020) 7607 5519
'Chandeliers' constructed from inverted wine glasses and regular art exhibitions catch the eye in this Islington pub; otherwise it still looks very much like a local boozer. Choose between excellent-value set lunches (£6.50–£9) and the printed menu, which drifts from Med-inspired ideas like chorizo and butterbean salad (£5.25) and roast chicken breast with pesto and sun-dried tomatoes (£8.50) to pan-fried swordfish with mango and red onion salsa. Finish with something sweet like warm chocolate cake with caramelised oranges (£4). Real ales, Belgian beers and plenty of organic

wines on the list; prices from £11. Open all week.

Bertorelli's WC2

44A Floral Street map 15
(020) 7836 3969

'Interesting and most useful in the area' was one couple's assessment of this lively Covent Garden Italian, a popular pre-, post- and instead-of-theatre venue. Classic dishes such as 'superb spaghetti bolognese' (£7.95) get the thumbs-up, while more adventurous diners could choose chargrilled swordfish with black olive, fennel and dandelion salad (£13.95). For the full works start with seafood and rocket salad, factor in a small plate of pasta and a main, then finish up with well-liked ice creams. Closed Sun. Other branches are at 19 Charlotte Street, W1, tel: (020) 7636 4174, and 11 Frith Street, W1, tel: (020) 7494 3491.

Bluebird SW3

350 King's Road map 14
(020) 7559 1000

The food shop is now run by Sainsbury's, but this Conran gastro-complex still retains its bustling restaurant. Punters are faced with a huge choice on the menu, from prawn cocktail (£8.95) and foie gras terrine with roasted peaches to Dover sole with caper butter (£25.25) and 'poulet noir' with girolles and tomato confit – plus numerous crustacea. Brunch is the big draw at weekends: gnocchi roast pumpkin and thyme (£11.25) has been applauded and children can enjoy proper fish and chips. House wines (£13.50) are the most affordable bets on the long list. Open all week.

Boisdale SW1

15 Eccleston Street map 13
(020) 7730 6922

Live jazz, Cuban cigars, whiskies galore and an upper-crust 250-bin wine list (from £12.90) are just part of the package in this clubby Belgravia venue. The kitchen shows its allegiance to top-drawer Scottish produce, particularly in the fixed-price dinner menu headed '1745' (that's

the price as well as the date): here you will find marinated salmon with pickled cucumber, roast haggis with 'bashed neeps', and Perthshire rabbit with home-made noodles and Pommery mustard sauce. Desserts (£5.50) also have a Scots accent. Open Mon to Sat L and D. There is a second branch at 202 Bishopsgate, Swedeland Court, EC2, tel: (020) 7283 1763.

Brady's SW18

513 Old York Road map 12
(020) 8877 9599

Fish 'n chips has been the focus of this no-frills Wandsworth favourite for well over a decade – the only change has been to reflect the shift in customers' tastes from battered to grilled fish. Haddock, skate, bream, sole, tuna and more are listed on the blackboards daily at £6.35–£8.95, with mushy peas and gherkins on the side. Simple starters like potted shrimps and prawn cocktail from £2 and comforting desserts at £1.95. Tiny but inexpensive wine list. Open Mon to Sat D only.

Café Portugal SW8

6A Victoria House map 13
(020) 7587 1962

'Cross the threshold and you are in downtown Lisbon,' notes a convert to this popular neighbourhood venue. It can get jam-packed with 'happily noshing families', although an easy-going, laid-back atmosphere prevails. Sit in the café/bar and graze on tapas-style dishes ranging from oysters (95p each) to grilled sardines, chicken gizzards and chorizo in red wine; there's also bitoque ('bashed steak' with a fried egg on top). The full works in the adjoining restaurant extends to paella three ways (around £10), various takes on salt-cod, and grilled baby chicken in chilli sauce. Patriotically Portuguese beers and wines. Open all week.

Carluccio's Caffe W1

8 Market Place map 15
(020) 7636 2228

The chain continues to expand, with 11 café-delis in and around London currently serving up the same formula of affordable, variably authentic Italian fare in a clattering canteen environment. Breads and coffees come in for most praise while main dishes are 'average' to 'appetising' (£5–£10.50). Service fell down for one business lunch, but a party of 12 sang its praises for a 'riotously satisfying' pre-theatre dinner that made good use of the children's menu and ice creams. Short Italian wine list all under £20. Open all week.

Champor-Champor   SE1
62 Weston Street   map 13
(020) 7403 4600

Tucked away in the back streets of London Bridge is an explosion of Asian colour packed into a tiny dining room. The mix-and-match Asian cooking is loosely Malay, offered as a 'thrilling' two- or three-course set menu (£19.90/£24.50) that might include catfish and crispy sun-dried stingray salad followed by pan-fried seabass with edamame and coconut purée, or for vegetarians wild mushroom won ton with jasmine tea soup, burnt coconut salad and cashew rice. Charming service, a dozen Asian beers and an eclectic, affordable wine list seal the deal. Reports please. Open Tue to Sat D (L bookings only).

Chapel   NW1
48 Chapel Street   map 13
(020) 7402 9220

A lively crowd packs into this cheery, workmanlike pub, where much of the attraction is focused on the blackboard menu. Starters (from £3.50–£6) always include a soup (perhaps sweet potato, tomato and rocket) and modern ideas like a salad of pan-fried sea bass with teriyaki sauce. Main courses (from £10) tend towards hefty portions of chargrilled protein like organic rib of beef with béarnaise sauce or tuna steak with mash, while a dessert (£3.50) such as raspberry bavarois might close the show. Around 30 global wines are also listed on a blackboard. Open all week, L and D.

Chor Bizarre   W1
16 Albemarle Street   map 15
(020) 7629 9802 and 8542

The name is a pun on 'Chor Bazaar' (a thieves' market) and this eclectic Indian restaurant is kitted out like an eccentric bric-a-brac shop with plenty of gimmicky gestures to boot. The menu is a boldly ambitious affair that treks its way around the regions of the Subcontinent. Thalis and tiffins arrive on metal platters or banana leaves. Prices throughout are not 'cheap' (mains £13 – £18), but service is 'capable and friendly' and the wine list is a 'delightful' collection chosen by Charles Metcalfe. Open all week.

Chuen Cheng Ku   W1
17 Wardour Street   map 15
(020) 7734 3281 and 3509

'It makes Chinatown part of what it is,' observed a regular who has been frequenting this old campaigner for years. The restaurant is an atmospheric three-storey giant noted for its dim sum, which are dispensed from a cavalcade of heated trolleys. A few new morsels have been added to the long repertoire of late: scallop chueng fun has been singled out, but legions of 'first-rate' trolley girls also tout all manner of dumplings, deep-fried items and bowls of soup noodles. Dishes on the full Cantonese menu have been praised for their authentic flavours. Drink tea, beer or wine. Open all week.

Cru   N1
2–4 Rufus Street   map 13
(020) 7729 5252

Behind the White Cube gallery, just off trendy Hoxton Square, Cru is a 'delightful urban restaurant' in a converted warehouse that provides a spacious, sociable environment. Cheerful young staff serve stylish food, firmly rooted in the Mediterranean, from a short, daily-changing menu (main courses £8–£15). A chef change just as we went to press prevented a main entry for this edition. Expect confit tuna with fennel and tomato, pan-fried monkfish on chive mash, or baked chicken with spiced

Moroccan tabbouleh. Wind up, perhaps with passion-fruit crème brûlée. Open all week.

Del Buongustaio   SW15
283–285 Putney Bridge Road   map 12
(020) 8780 9361

Putney locals generate a lively buzz in this discreet, rustically designed Italian restaurant. Its flexible, regularly changing menus are based on sound ingredients and the repertoire is a promising mix of classic recipes and regional specialities jazzed up with a few voguish flourishes. Scallops on stewed Catellucio lentils, pigeon breast with Italian 'mustard fruits' and rotolini of veal with tomatoes and wine show the style (main courses £10–£16). A 'lounge menu' is served in the adjoining Pasticceria. Four house selections top the all-Italian wine list. Open all week L and Mon to Sat D.

Diwana Bhel Poori   NW1
121 Drummond Street   map 13
(020) 7387 5556

The frontrunner for vegetarian food in Drummond Street's 'Little India' – a fascinating enclave within earshot of Euston station. Eponymous bhel pooris are firm favourites, closely followed by other street snacks like aloo papri chat; the menu also features a decent contingent of curries, including well-reported channa masala and mattar paneer. Thalis are a nifty way of having a complete meal assembled for you on a metal tray, and lunchtime buffets (around £6) always bring in the crowds. Unlicensed, but lassi is a top-drawer version. Open all week.

Ebury Wine Bar   SW1
139 Ebury Street   map 13
(020) 7730 5447

A pedigree wine list helps to explain the enduring reputation of this venerable Belgravia bolt-hole: no fewer than 38 are available by the glass (from £3.20), and monthly promotions provide even more oenophilic possibilities. The menu keeps pace in modern style with chicken and Thai noodle salad (£5), pan-fried skate

with samphire (£14.50), or pork and leek sausages with pomegranate and onion jus, while desserts like passion-fruit and white chocolate brulée (£5.25) maintain the momentum. Set lunches are a bargain at £12.50 and bar snacks are served throughout the day. Open all week.

Efes Kebab House   W1
80 Great Titchfield Street   map 15
(020) 7636 1953

'Hard to beat and I am sure the portions get bigger each time I visit' is one reporter's view of the 'reliable', reasonably priced Turkish food served in this long-established venue. Since 1975, the kitchen has been keeping the customers satisfied with a creditable assortment of familiar meze (tarama and hummus are 'as good as ever'), backed up by high-protein kebabs and grills (shish kofta, kidney, lemon chicken, lamb chops, chicken cutlets, lamb doner), which are generally served with rice and salad. Around 30 wines include some Turkish. Closed Sun. Efes II is just around the corner at 175 Great Portland Street, W1, tel: (020) 7436 0600, and is open all week.

Emile's   SW15
96 Felsham Road   map 12
(020) 8789 3323

A genuine 'neighbourhood' restaurant of some 15 years' standing, with food that 'seems to exemplify all the best of multicultural Britain'. Individual beef Wellington is the signature dish, but fixed-price blackboard menus (two courses £17.50, three courses £19.95) quickly embrace everything from Indian-influenced fishcake with dhal and a tomato and coriander salsa to Greek yoghurt terrine with mango salad. In between, you might expect calf's liver with bacon and onion mash or pigeon breasts with beetroot. Emile leads an efficient team out front, and the value-for-money extends to an affordable wine list. Closed Sun.

L'Etranger   SW7
36 Gloucester Road   map 14
(020) 7584 1118
Chef Jerome Tauvron (formerly of Ozer –
see entry below) is now based at this
modernist study in greys and mauves set
on a Kensington corner. The menu, in
French with English translations, also
draws on oriental influences, either
directly, as in a starter of crispy black
peppered squid with sweet chilli (£8.50)
or in fusions such as 'Le Wok', combining
prawns, snails, fennel and lemongrass
(£16.50). Desserts (£6.50) pursue the
theme – perhaps chocolate spring roll with
shizo leaves. Simpler set meals served at
lunch and early evening are £14.50–
£16.50. Excellent, serious wine list. Closed
Sat L.

fish!   SE1
Cathedral Street   map 13
(020) 7407 3803
The original fish! (still going strong) stands
out amid the Victorian ironwork of
Borough Market, and the large, bright and
modern venue 'continues to do simple
things well'. That translates as a selection
of fresh fish of the day, steamed or grilled
with a choice of five sauces (£10–£19.50),
plus a regular menu featuring oysters, crab
cakes, tuna burgers and fish pie. Short,
fish-friendly wine list from £12.95. Open
all week.

La Galette   W1
56 Paddington Street   map 15
(020) 7935 1554
The simple Breton tradition of the well-
made pancake survives transplantation to
Marylebone in a minimally furnished
space warmed by a bare brick wall and
orangey lighting. La Galette takes its name
from the version made with buckwheat
flour, offered here with 15 choices of
filling (£5.60–£8.50) – comforting stuff
like smoked bacon with creamed leeks and
parsley or ratatouille. Starters span
France, while crêpes do the honours for
dessert. Open daily from breakfast, it's
equally suited to a snack or a three-course
dinner. Drink Normandy and Breton

ciders served in traditional porcelain cups.
Open all week.

Gilbeys   W5
77 The Grove   map 12
(020) 8840 7568
The bright conservatory and secluded
garden are the places to enjoy imaginative
bistro food and wines from the extensive
French range traded by the Gilbeys Group.
Two-course set menus at L £7.50 and D
£11.50 offer excellent value, while the
carte extends into chicken, bacon and foie
gras terrine (£5.95), then grilled fillet of
kingfish with mixed bean and tomato
salad (£13.95). The attractively priced
wines start at £9.50. Open Tue to Sun L
and Tue to Sat D.

Golborne House   W10
36 Golborne Road   map 13
(020) 8960 6260
This re-invented local boozer close to
Westbourne Park Tube now plies its trade
as an urban gastro-pub. Friendly service
helps things along, and the menu puts on
a convincing worldwide show. Thai duck
salad with coriander and mint (£7.25)
should wake up the taste buds, while main
courses might range from lamb shank
with roast celeriac mash (£12.50) to crispy
sea bass with leeks, broad beans and salsa
verde. Mango and passion-fruit pavlova
(£3.95) is a typically eclectic dessert.
Worth considering for a late lunch (last
food orders 3.45pm). Zippy cocktails and a
fairly priced wine list from £10.50. Open
all week L and D.

Grand Union   W9
45 Woodfield Road   map 13
(020)72861886
The Grand Union Canal passes the garden
at the back, hence the name of this relaxed
pub-diner – just ignore the concrete
monstrosity of the Westway. Bare boards,
mix-and-match wooden furniture and the
obligatory big leather sofa set the scene,
with menus casually laid on all tables and
chalked up in the areas more clearly
focused on food. Inventive pies – maybe
beef, potato and horseradish (£7.50) – are

the speciality on a menu of modernised but comfortingly hearty pub grub. Informed and upbeat service. Adnams beers and 11 wines by the glass from a short list. Open all week.

Great Nepalese   NW1
48 Eversholt Street   map 13
(020) 7388 6737

'I shall endeavour to visit whenever I have got a 7 o'clock train to catch,' admits a fan of this eminently likeable restaurant within earshot of Euston. Service is speedy and the place wears its true Nepalese colours on its sleeve. Starters such as masco bara (deep-fried lentil pancakes) and kalezo ra chyau (spiced chicken livers) precede bhutuwa chicken with green herbs, dumba (mutton) curry and some fascinating vegetable dishes like aloo bodi tama (potatoes with bamboo shoots and black-eyed beans). Standard curry house favourites play a supporting role. Three-course business lunches are a snip; drink mango lassi, beer or house wine. Open all week.

Havelock Tavern   W14
57 Masbro Road   map 12
(020) 7603 5374

The corner-sited Havelock, set amid the residential houses of Brook Green, is a real pub making real efforts to serve good food. The open-plan bar has minimum frills, tables are rough-and-ready, and real ales are on tap. The kitchen is a serious operation, producing mostly Mediterranean-focused food that suits the relaxed informality of the setting. Start with monkfish wrapped in Parma ham with sun-dried tomato relish (£6), and move on to confit of duck with mash and a rich red wine sauce (£10.50). One course, two courses, three courses – anything goes. Service is friendly and delivery to table suitably robust. Open all week.

The Hempel   W2
31–35 Craven Hill Gardens   map 13
(020) 7298 9000

Nothing but a discrete 'H' logo marks the entrance to this exercise in minimalism. A frosted glass staircase leads down from the all-white hotel reception to the angular black-and-white lines of the I-Thai restaurant – a punning marriage of Japanese and Italian cusines, meaning perhaps linguine of clams with garlic, mizuna and chilli oil (£12), then roast rump of lamb with pea and wasabi mashed potatoes (£24.50). Lunchtime bento boxes (£15.50–£24.50) offer better value. Designer-clad staff provide 'hospitable' and 'engaging' service to a casually wealthy clientele. Wines, from £20.50, are mostly Italian and New World. Open all week (phone to confirm Sun).

Joe Allen   WC2
13 Exeter Street   map 15
(020) 7836 0651

Since the late '70s, this vibrant Convent Garden joint has been an ambassador for transatlantic cooking – and it shows no sign of waning. Pecan-crusted goats' cheese with sweet chilli jelly is a typically patriotic opener (£6.50), although heavy-duty mains (around £14) span the globe: bestselling burgers, spicy potato enchilada and chilli sit alongside steamed John Dory with pak choi and Thai curry sauce, and grilled lamb rump with couscous. Sweets include all-American favourites like cheesecake and brownies (£5.50), and plenty of flag-waving US wines appear on the list; prices from £14. Open all week.

Kasturi   EC3
57 Aldgate High Street   map 13
(020) 7480 7402

Smart design touches, from the sign projected on the pavement outside to the high-quality china, announce that Kasturi is aiming a notch or two above the average tandoori, and lunchtime crowds attest to its popularity. Spicing is powerful and direct. Prawn malabari presented in a coconut shell (£11.95) and aloo annardhana (potato with spices and pomegranate seeds £2.75) have been highlights, and naans are good. A low-fat ethos sometimes translates into small portions. Indian lagers and New World wines. Closed Sat L and all day Sun.

Lahore Kebab House   E1

2 Umberston Street   map 13
(020) 7488 2551

This basic Punjabi kebab house off the Commercial Road has been satisfying its customers with the same short menu for decades – the sort of history that gives it the right to append 'original' to its name. Grilled lamb chops are the house speciality, with a karahi version (served in sauce in a metal bowl) on Fridays. Chicken, prawns and fish are the regular karahi options while other specials are on a board. Main courses around £6. A range of dhals, samosas and vegetable dishes round out a meal. BYO drinks. Open all week.

Lemonia   NW1

89 Regents Park Road   map 13
(020) 7586 7454

Mr and Mrs Evangelou's Greek-Cypriot restaurant has been pleasing Primrose Hill locals and others since 1979 and it continues unabated. Ultra-cheap set menus (two courses £7.25) are unbeatable value at lunchtime, but the full menu is an equally affordable prospect. Meze (mostly around £3.50) contain all the usual favourites, from tahini and tabbouleh to deep-fried kalamari and loukanika (spiced Greek sausages). Otherwise expect a comprehensive tour taking in dolmades (£8.50), lemonado (lamb with herbs in lemon sauce) and chargrills ranging from veal cutlets to ordikia (quails). House wine is £12.75. Closed Sat L and Sun D.

Little Georgia   E8

2 Broadway Market   map 12
(020) 7249 9070

Café by day and restaurant by night, this converted pub close to Regent's Park Canal makes an unexpected setting for traditional Georgian cooking. Two new chefs were due to arrive from the homeland as the Guide went to press; meanwhile, the short evening menu ploughs a rustic furrow with a 'really fine' selection of mostly vegetarian meze (£12.50 for two), 'rich, moreish' breads and a few more substantial items like summer tolma (stuffed cabbage rolls with yoghurt sauce, £12) and lobio (green beans baked with egg). Service is 'sweet', and gutsy Old Tblisi wine (£13) is the thing to drink. Open Tue to Sun D.

Livebait   SE1

43–45 The Cut   map 13
(020) 7928 7211

The original of a mini-chain that now has a handful of branches in London and outlets elsewhere (see index). This livewire place close to the Old Vic is hardly the most comfortable in town and service can be 'perfunctory', but crowds still flock in for seafood platters, moules marinière (£5.75) and dishes ranging from cod 'n chips (£13.75) to roasted sea bass with broad beans, asparagus and beurre blanc. Finish with praiseworthy sweets like rhubarb crème brûlée (£4.75) or farmhouse cheeses. Whites outnumber reds on the wine list, which starts at £10.95. Closed Sun.

Lobster Pot   SE11

3 Kennington Lane   map 13
(020) 7582 5556

Decked out like a trawler cabin (complete with portholes, nets and lifebelts), Hervé Régent's idiosyncratic seafood restaurant still offers high-quality fish, and you can delve into the full piscine repertoire by ordering a large 'plateau de fruits de mer' (£22.50). M. Régent also turns his hand to skate with brown butter and capers (£14.50), monkfish with wild mushrooms and Pernod, and meaty items like calves' kidneys with port sauce. Breton crêpes (£5.30) are a sound bet for dessert. The short Gallic list has house wines at £10.50. Open Tue to Sat L and D.

Lomo   SW10

222 Fulham Road   map 14
(020) 7349 8848

Classic tapas in a modern and informal setting. The glass frontage opens on to the street on warm days, so perch on high stools to see and be seen on this busy strip of the Fulham Road. A traditional range of tapas starts at £2.95 while bigger raciones take in pork loin (the eponymous lomo) in various guises up to the special lomo Iberico at £7.50. Beers and wines (lots by the glass, including a slate of sherries) are mainly Spanish. Nightly live music (not too loud), Spanish football on Saturdays and films on Sundays make this a mini cultural centre. Open Sat L and all week D.

Lucky Seven   W2
127 Westbourne Park Road   map 13
(020) 7727 6771
There are no bookings, so expect to share a booth in this diminutive version of an American diner. Breakfast brings eggs 'any style', hash browns, buttermilk pancakes, home-made sausages and more. Later, there are bowls of 'exterminator' chilli (£4.95) and 'Garden of Eden' salads, not to mention 100 per cent organic burgers ranging from 'classic' (£4.25) to 'high roller double-decker fully loaded'. Fairy cakes (£1.60 each) and banana splits add a sweet touch. To drink, choose between shakes, malts, floats, root beer and a couple of wines (from £13.50). Open all week.

Mango Tree   SW1
46 Grosvenor Place   map 14
(020) 7823 1888
An auspicious Belgravia address and an upper-crust location behind Buckingham Palace are suitably fashionable trappings for this calm and stylishly appointed Thai restaurant. The menu jogs its way around the mainstays of the cuisine, stopping off for classic hot-and-sour salads like som tum (green papaya) and appetisers including shrimp spring rolls (£6.25), as well as soups, curries (monkfish with scallops, for example), stir-fries and grills (sea bass wrapped in banana leaves £15.50). Like the menu, the wine list is aimed at those with deep pockets; prices start at £19. Open all week.

Manzi's   WC2
1–2 Leicester Street   map 15
(020) 7734 0224
Owned by the Manzi family since 1928, this old West End campaigner isn't about

to become a follower of fashion. Classical seafood cookery is the order of the day in the 'eccentric and rather idiosyncratic' downstairs dining room: grilled sardines (£3.95) is a well-reported starter, while grilled swordfish and halibut steak (£18.95) with 'very crisp chips' have also received plaudits. Puddings are well-respected creations like strawberries Romanoff (£3.95). Staff – young and old – are full of smiles. Handy for the theatres; accommodation available. House wine is £10.50. Closed Sun L.

Masala Zone   W1
9 Marshall Street   map 15
(020) 7287 9966
West End shoppers and the office crowd frequent this busy Indian canteen close to Carnaby Street. Find a seat at one of the refectory tables and check out the menu: here are street snacks like sev puri (from £2.75), chana dabalroti (chickpeas and lotus roots with hunks of bread), noodle dishes (around £5.50), curries such as green lamb masala, and thalis (£6.25–£11), while 'sandwiches' (chicken tikka on ciabatta, for example) are handy for a take-out. Wines from £9.75, otherwise drink lassi or Tiger beer. Open all week. A second branch is at 80 Upper Street, N1 tel: (020) 7359 3399.

Mela   WC2
152–156 Shaftesbury Avenue   map 15
(020) 7836 8635
'A celebration of Indian cuisine country-style' is how the owners describe their re-vamped menu in this contemporary restaurant. Some 'really unusual dishes' share the stage with old favourites. The repertoire spans everything from 'vibrant' Indian street food to stir-fries and tandooris, taking in pot-roast quails with tomato masala and crushed dried mango (£4.95), ragda patties with white peas, and Malabari seafood stew (£11.95). Cut-price, three-dish lunches are £4.95. Drink Kingfisher beer or house wine (£10.90). Open all week. A sister restaurant, Chowki, is in Denman Street, Soho.

MemSaheb on Thames   E14
65–67 Amsterdam Road   map 15
(020) 7538 3008

Looking across the river from the Isle of Dogs to the Dome, Memsaheb is an up-to-date Indian restaurant sporting bright white walls and red plush chairs in a colour theme repeated on the ultra-clear menu. Interesting options include kabuli salad (chickpeas and egg with green chilli, coriander, mustard oil and tamarind), Rajasthani karghosh (rabbit in a mild sauce with garlic sautéed spinach and carrots), and the special 'kitchen curry' of the day, as eaten by the staff. Starters are mostly £3–£4, mains from £6.95. Closed Sat and Sun L.

Mezzanine   SE1
National Theatre   map 13
(020) 7452 3600

'Top marks for speed and efficiency', noted a couple of theatregoers after a quick repast in this buzzy venue attached to the National. Menus are fixed price (two courses for £17.95 and three for £19.95), and reviewers have praised spinach mousse with a three-cheese sauce as well as calf's liver with smoked bacon, roasted red onions and Pommery mustard sauce. Fish also gets plenty of applause – dorade fillet on minted pea purée with crisp chorizo, for example – while approved desserts have included Cointreau oranges with crème fraîche. The short wine list starts at £12.95 (£3.40 a glass). Open Mon to Sat D.

Mirch Masala   SW16
1416 London Road   map 12
(020) 8679 1828

Only prawn dishes cost more than £6 in this casual suburban Indian – which may explain the regular queues. The menu opens with 'warmers' (starters) such as chilli bhajias, tandoori chicken wings and garlic mussels before a big contingent of 'steamers' (main dishes), including karahis (everything from mushrooms to ginger chicken), 'deigi' specials and familiar curries. 'Coolers' in the shape of rice, breads and sweets form the back up.

Unlicensed, so BYO or drink lassi. Open all week. There's a second outlet at 213 Upper Tooting Road, SW17, tel: (020) 8672 7500 and a third is planned in Southall.

Miyama   W1
38 Clarges Street   map 15
(020) 7499 2443

Mr Miyama's eponymous Japanese restaurant has been in business for over 20 years, sitting in a prime Mayfair site but still charging prices to please all-comers. The menu spans all aspects of Japanese cuisine – sushi, sashimi, noodles and soups are complemented by a good range of starters. Set lunches (£8.50–£22) range from single dishes with rice, pickles, miso and dessert to a four-course blow-out. Short, good-value wine list. Closed Sat and Sun L.

Momo   W1
25 Heddon Street   map 15
(020) 7434 4040

The flamboyant Moroccan style draws a fairly young crowd, but is by no means mere window dressing. Authentic couscous dishes and tagines (£15) – perhaps lamb with quince and almonds or chicken with preserved lemon confit – fulfil the promised North African excursion. Start with Zaalouk, a compote of aubergines, tomatoes and shallots (£6.50) and leave space for Maghrebi pastries (£5.50). Mô next door serves teas and light meals. Closed Sun L.

Mon Plaisir   WC2
21 Monmouth Street   map 15
(020) 7836 7243

'Nothing much changes' at this unreservedly French West End institution. Classic bistro décor of bare boards and posters, white-draped tables packed in tight, reliable food and brisk, heavily accented service keep francophile regulars coming back year after year. Oysters or foie gras precede fish or meat mains at £14–£17: perhaps filet de chevreuil aux trésors des bois (venison with wild mushrooms). The set 'menu Parisien' at £23.50 has two starters then no choice. Pre- and post-theatre menus are a good-value £12.40 for two courses with wine and coffee. The French wine list features four Loire reds for an authentic Parisian experience. Closed Sat L and Sun.

New World   W1
1 Gerrard Place   map 15
(020) 7434 2508
A Chinatown institution, this huge, no-frills Cantonese restaurant buzzes when busy and continues to impress with lunchtime dim sum and a wide range of set meals, from two courses (£7.80) to a ten-course feast (£40). Monthly-changing chef's specials such as soft shell crab with chilli and salt, and stuffed duck with mashed prawn, make tempting additions to the menu. Open all week.

Numidie   SE19
48 Westow Hill   map 12
(020) 8766 6166
A simple blue awning and flower baskets colourfully announce this Mediterranean bistro, named after an ancient North African civilisation. A poster of French-Algerian football star Zinedine Zidane is an appropriate emblematic presence. Tagines feature in lamb, poussin, bream and vegetarian versions (£7.50–£12.50), while fragrant mains include duck breast with lavender honey (£10.50). Salads and seafood dominate the starters, perhaps fried baby squid with crab or the house special salad of artichoke heart, sun-dried tomatoes, olives, chekchouka (spiced tomato and pepper) and feta cheese. Short wine list from £9.50. Open Tue to Sun D only.

The Oak   W2
137 Westbourne Park Road   map 13
(020) 7221 3355
The restaurant above this West London gastro-pub closed at Easter 2003 and was due to re-open in September as a 'member's lounge dining club'. The ground-floor bar carries on regardless, with queues for tables by 8 in the evening. Pizzas from the wood-fired oven (£7.50–£12.50) hold centre-stage – and 'very

good' they are, too. The rest of the short daily menu is a high-speed Mediterranean hop from gazpacho (£5.50) and roasted beetroot with baked tomatoes and rocket to poached rhubarb with strawberry gelato (£5), and chocolate tiramisù. Affordable European wines from £11.50. Closed Mon L.

Old Delhi   W2
48 Kendal Street   map 13
(020) 7723 3335
With a harpist playing every Wednesday and Saturday, this is no high-street curry house, but an upmarket restaurant decked out in marble and wood with a smart dress code. The long menu takes India beyond the standards, but the name Old Delhi is something of a misnomer because the real excitement lies in discovering the Persian specialities: maybe mirza-ghasemi – a mash of aubergine and egg with garlic and spices – from a range of starters at around £5, then fesenjune (£13.65), a duck dish flavoured with walnut and pomegranate. The modern wine list includes some prestige bottles at crazy prices. Open all week.

Ole Tapas Restaurant   SW6
Broadway Chambers   map 12
(020) 7610 2010
This feisty little tapas bar opposite the Tube station makes a welcome new option in Fulham Broadway. Minimalist décor throws attention on the centrepiece mirror with modernist stained glass surround. A long, seasonally changing list of tapas (£3.30–£6.35) pushes well beyond the norms with five different versions of tortilla or the more complex prawn ravioli and scallops dressed with seafood essence and risotto. Short, all-Spanish wine list and upbeat service from convivial staff. Putney branch promised for November 2003. Closed Sun.

Ozer   W1
5 Langham Place   map 15
(020) 7323 0505

This throbbing West End restaurant and bar belongs to the Sofra chain (see London Round-up entry), and the food is a broad sweep through the Turkish repertoire with a few Anatolian extras. Meze (£3.45) are a great favourite and the menu also features classic grills (from £7.50) plus dishes like 'oven-cooked' chicken tandir with potatoes and chickpeas, or spicy meatballs with tomato sauce and potatoes. Turkish house wines £12.50. Open all week.

The Perseverance   WC1
63 Lamb's Conduit Street   map 13
(020) 7405 8278

Downstairs is exactly what you might expect from a flock-wallpapered city pub, but the bright first-floor dining room paints a more contemporary picture. A new team is now installed in the kitchen, but the menu follows the same eclectic path as before: classic salad niçoise is a trendy rendition with tataki tuna and a tuna confit (£6.75), while more substantial items might range from braised rabbit with rösti, broad beans and tarragon jus (£11.95) to roast cod with mussel and clam sauce. Puddings (around £5) are the likes of strawberry and thyme soup with white peach sorbet. House French is £10.90. Closed Sun L.

Porte des Indes   W1
32 Bryanston Street   map 13
(020) 7224 0055

Bollywood meets Disney World in this grandiose Indian restaurant complete with giant palms, paintings and a wall of water by the staircase. The menu promises plenty of familiar dishes (crab Malabar, rogan josh) – although they may hide behind curious names – and there's a sizeable contingent from 'Les Indes Françaises' (cassoulet de fruits de mer in 'local vindai spices', for example). Decent choice for vegetarians. Mains £9.90 to £17, and set L and D menus available. The wide-ranging wine list includes

representatives from Canada and India. Closed Sat L.

Prospect Grill   WC2
4–6 Garrick Street   map 15
(020) 7379 0412

A discreet Covent Garden bolt-hole with low lights and a distinctly clubby, although not staid, atmosphere. Chargrilling is the name of the game and it is applied to everything from burgers (including a tuna version with fried green chilli salsa, £14.95) to halloumi cheese and squid (served with rocket and cherry tomato salad). Alternatively, you might consider sea bass fillet with roasted fennel or herbed vegetarian sausages with crushed potatoes (£10.95). Set meals are available (£14.95 for two courses, £16.95 for three) from noon to 7.30. Jazzy cocktails and aperitifs, plus a laudable choice of keenly selected wines from £13.95. Closed Sun.

Quaglino's   SW1
16 Bury Street   map 15
(020) 7930 6767

The sheer scale of the place can take its toll, both in the kitchen and out front, but the modern brasserie-style cooking still inspires some favourable feedback: traditional fish soup (£7.50) is a 'pleasing' brew and tuna has been 'delicately' seared, while main courses might run to roast rabbit with sorrel sauce (£16.50); to close the show there are classic desserts such as chocolate St Emilion (£6.50). House French is £13.50. Open all week.

Ragam   W1
57 Cleveland Street   map 15
(020) 7636 9098

Among the first to promote South Indian and Keralan cooking in the capital, this utilitarian, family-owned restaurant still offers authentic dishes at very affordable prices. Highlights on the menu are 'ever popular specialities' (from £2–£4.50) like masala dosai, iddly (steamed cakes of rice and black 'gram') and poori masala (puffed-up fried bread with spiced potato), plus distinctively flavoured vegetable dishes like cabbage thoran and French beans with coconut. The kitchen also has its own way with curry-house stalwarts like lamb dhansak and prawn korma (all £4.50). Wines from £9. Open all week.

Randall & Aubin   W1
16 Brewer Street   map 15
(020) 7287 4447

Hooks hanging from the ceiling and original tiled walls are reminders that this lively, trendy, Soho 'canteen' was once a butcher's shop. Displays of seafood fill the window and a rotisserie turns out spit roasts (£10.50), but you can order anything from a goats' cheese baguette (£6.50) to a pot of caviar with blinis; alternatively, choose moules marinière, eggs Benedict, or steak with frites. House wines start at £10.50. Closed Sun L. There is a branch at 329–331 Fulham Road, SW10, tel: (020) 782 3515.

Rani   N3
7 Long Lane   map 12
(020) 8349 4386

Since 1984, the Pattni family has been flying the flag for Indian vegetarian cooking and they remain true to their dietary principles. A 60-dish menu built around regional Gujarati cuisine is bolstered by fascinating weekly specials: bhindi khadi is yoghurt soup with okra rings, dudhi chana comprises white marrow and chickpeas flavoured with dill. The regular selection takes in starters (aloo papri chat, spinach bhajias, etc), slow-cooked 'sak' curries (e.g. banana methi), breads and rice. Most dishes are £3–£6, with thalis from £7.80 per head. Wine is £9.70; otherwise opt for lassi, beer or juice. Open all week D only.

Rebato's   SW8
169 South Lambeth Road   map 12
(020) 7735 6388

An Iberian institution, the dark front bar is dedicated to menus of tapas and more tapas (the vegetarian options). Here you can snack on grilled sardines, Serrano ham, Welsh lamb cutlets or oyster mushrooms with garlic and peppers at £2.25–£6 per dish. Behind is a well-lit restaurant with tiled floor, skylights and plants hinting at a courtyard feel, where a fixed price of £16.95 gets you a broad choice of starters and mains – perhaps fried calamares followed by kidneys sautéed in sherry with mushroom and bacon. Closed Sat L and Sun.

Red Pepper   W9
8 Formosa Street   map13
(020) 7266 2708

This buzzing Italian favourite in Maida Vale is still packing in the crowds for a classic old-school menu of pizzas (£6–£9) and pastas (£8–£10) with a few twists, as in a starter of lemon marinated salmon with rocket, pear and pecorino cheese. Then tuck into pappardelle with lamb sauce, black olives and aubergine; risotto with prawns and broccoli cream; or a fiery 'rossi' pizza (with red peppers, roasted garlic and chilli oil). Finish with tiramisù. Queues possible at peak times. Workmanlike Italian wine list. Open Sat and Sun L, all week D.

Rules   WC2
35 Maiden Lane   map 15
(020) 7836 5314

For more than 200 years Rules has been championing the cause of 'Bulldog British' traditional cooking in a remarkable setting that still wins converts with its 'lively, yet reassuringly comfortable atmosphere'. Visitors come here for generous helpings of steak and kidney pie with mash (£14.95), jugged hare, near-legendary roasts and 'famous grouse'. There are starters ranging from Stilton and walnut tart with pear chutney (£6.95) to rabbit and foie gras terrine, while desserts (all £6.50) fly the flag for summer pudding and raspberry syllabub trifle. French house wines come by the glass, jug or bottle (£13.95). Open all week L and D.

Sofra   WC2
36 Tavistock Street   map 15
(020) 7240 3773

'Big, strong flavours and textures' give the food its kick in this bright and buzzy

Turkish rendezvous deep in Covent Garden tourist land. The huge menu has plenty to keep vegetarians interested, but also satisfies carnivores with its array of hot and cold meze, chargrills and casseroles. Main courses (£6–£13) run to grilled marinated chicken, lamb kofte, gently stewed lamb, and cod with coriander. Turkish house wines are £2.95 a glass, £11.50 a bottle. Open all week. This is an international chain with outlets abroad and a growing number of branches dotted around London.

Soho Spice   W1
124–126 Wardour Street   map 15
(020) 7434 0808

Contemporary décor in orange, purple and gold contributes to a comfortably smart but informal atmosphere. A sensibly short menu, with starters at £3–£5 and mains at £8.50–£13, sets old favourites like seekh kebab and rogan josh against eye-catching options such as mirch baingan (baby aubergine and bullet chillies cooked with yoghurt, sesame, fennel and poppy seeds). 'Selections' are basically thalis, offering an introduction to the range of dishes. Set menu, £6 for two courses, before 6.30pm. Draught Kingfisher, bottled beers and a handful of decent wines. Open all week.

La Spighetta   W1
43 Blandford Street   map 15
(020) 7486 7340

Dive off Baker Street to find this slick Italian in a basement dining room with a wood-fired pizza oven lending a rustic glow. Toppings are classical, but not always standard, with daily specials bringing combinations like Gorgonzola, radicchio and Parmesan (£8.50). Pastas (£7–£9) follow a similar pattern, and a weekly-changing risotto is cooked to order, while chargrilling and pan-frying are favoured for mains such as fillet of cod with lentils and basil sauce (£12.90). Closed Sat and Sun L.

Spread Eagle   SE10
1–2 Stockwell Street   map 12
(020) 8853 2333

The history lives on, although this atmospheric seventeenth-century Greenwich inn now functions as a restaurant rather than a pub. The 'francophone' menu shows concessions to global modernity (grilled polenta with pepper oil and baby spinach, for example). Fish is a good choice (sea bream with wilted vegetables and a grape and white wine sauce has impressed), Gallic cheeses are out of the top drawer, and skilfully wrought desserts might include chocolate marquise and spiced crème brûlée with 'a perfect thin skating rink topping'. House wine is priced at £15.50 (£3.50 a glass). Closed Mon L.

Star of India   SW5
154 Old Brompton Road   map 14
(020) 7373 2901

A local Indian only if you consider that Kensington is the locality, the smart Star shuns standard dishes or at the very least reinvents them. Samosas come southern-style filled with crab, curry leaves and coconut; chicken tikka is 'enriched' with sun-dried fenugreek leaves. Complex house specials include bharwan bateyr (£12.50): boned quail stuffed with spiced chicken mince, quails' eggs, pine nuts and sunflower seeds and served with a Kashmiri sauce. Intriguing vegetable and rice dishes keep the interest up. Open all week.

Swag & Tails   SW7
10–11 Fairholt Street   map 14
(020) 7584 6926

Impeccably turned out and festooned with flowers, this bar/restaurant in a quiet mews is a boon for footsore Knightsbridge shoppers. The menu changes during each session ('everything is constantly on the move'), and it's a roll-call of busy dishes with a keen international edge: pan-seared foie gras with rhubarb jam and sherry vinegar caramel (£8.95) alongside hummus; sauté chicken livers with chorizo on saffron and spring onion rice

(£12.50); as well as red curry prawn samosas. Desserts could take in warm vanilla rice pudding with honey-glazed peaches (£5.50). Interesting wines from £2.95 a glass, £10.95 a bottle. Open Mon to Fri L and D.

Tate Modern SE1
Bankside map 13
(020) 7401 5020
Views over the Thames to St Paul's from Tate Modern's Bankside location are exploited to the full from this vantage point on the seventh floor. Breakfast pastries and sweet or savoury afternoon snacks keep the café ticking all day, but lunch is the main focus and it is worth reserving to avoid the queue. Ricotta, rocket and tomato tart (£5.50) might precede corn-fed chicken breast with pearl barley, lemon thyme and leeks (£9.50). Lighter options include imaginative sandwiches such as roast suckling pig with fennel and spiced apple (£6.50). Short but smart wine list from £13. Open all week L and D.

Thai Bistro W4
99 Chiswick High Road map 12
(020) 8995 5774
'Reliable as ever', confirms a long-time supporter of this Chiswick neighbourhood restaurant. Ingredients are authentic, the cooking shows plenty of skill and staple dishes from the menu continue to receive endorsements: tom yum goong soup ('a rich mix of correctly balanced flavours') and papaya salad 'suffused with a robust chilli flavour' come top of the class, although other items are competently handled – red chicken curry, spicy prawns, potatoes with mushrooms and ginger, and pad thai noodles, for example. Service is friendly and exceedingly courteous. Six house wines are £10.50 each. Open all week L and D.

3 Monkeys SE24
136–140 Herne Hill map 12
(020) 7738 5500
There's a lot going on at this modern Indian restaurant: a show kitchen allows chefs to prepare specialities on stage, there's live jazz Sunday evenings and the place even has its own wine shop. The menu is a trip round the Subcontinent for starters like zinga shorba (chilled yoghurt and shrimp soup, £5.25), tandooris, and main dishes like chicken nilgiri with cashews, tamarind and coconut milk (£9.50). Good selection of vegetables, rice and breads. Forty wines from £13.50. Open all week D only.

Tokyo Diner WC2
2 Newport Place map 15
(020) 7287 8777
The street-corner location is hardly glamorous, but this café continues to provide a breath of Japanese fresh air. It is still 'amazingly good value', and there are discounts if you call in during the afternoon session. Single-course donburi meals (from £6), bento boxes, soup noodles, and 'katsu' curries (from £4.10) are the kitchen's stock in trade, although you can also get lunchtime 'sets' such as cold aubergine agé bitashi and salmon shio grill (£8.20). Service is 'young, enthusiastic and cool'; no bookings, no tips, no cheques. Tea is free, house wine is around £7. Open all week.

Truc Vert W1
42 North Audley Street map 15
(020) 7491 9988
A few steps from the crush of Oxford Street, this combined delicatessen and restaurant pulls together ideas from north, south and east of the Mediterranean. All-Italian buffalo mozzarella with roast tomato, avocado, rocket and pesto (£7.50) might be followed by grilled chicken breast with spiced vegetable couscous, butter beans and rose harissa (£13). Soups and starters could make a satisfying lunch. Cheeses and charcuterie are priced by weight. Closed Sat and Sun D.

Two Brothers N3
297–303 Regents Park Road map 12
(020) 8346 0469
The Manzi brothers' popular fish and chip restaurant focuses firmly on what really

counts – the freshness of the fish and the lightness of the batter. The smart, maritime-themed interior with heavy white linen tablecloths feels as timeless as the unchanging menu, where starters including cod's roe in batter and jellied eels precede a broad range of fish fried in batter or, on request, matzo meal, or steamed or grilled (£8–£18). Side dishes are an unblinkingly traditional line-up of pickled onions, gherkins and mushy peas. Bottled beers and a short fish-friendly wine list. Open Tue to Sat L and D.

Vama   SW10
438 Kings Road   map 13
(020) 7565 8500

Overlooking swanky King's Road, this modern Indian keeps pace with its fashionable Chelsea setting. Outside is a small terrace for al fresco meals and the dining room looks the part with its tiled floor, artefacts and lanterns. The cooking is described as rustic North Indian and much use is made of wood- and charcoal-fired clay ovens. Among the list of unusual starters are pasanda ke tukre (smoked lamb kebabs with papaya and spices, £11), while mains range from aloo anda (potato and organic egg curry, £6.50) to whole lobster tandoori masala (£26). House French is £13. Open all week.

Vasco & Piero's Pavilion   W1
15 Poland Street   map 15
(020) 7437 8774

'Friendly service and good cooking' are the watchwords at this long-running Soho restaurant, concluded one satisfied visitor, while regulars of 25 years' standing note a new lease of life, bringing an energetic bustle to dinner at the close-packed tables. Menus drawing on Umbrian cuisine change twice daily, but 'superb' calf's liver in various guises is a regular feature, and pasta consistently pleases. Well-received innovations include sea bass fillets wrapped in 'wafer-thin' aubergine slices served on wilted spinach. Dinner is £19.50 for two courses, £23.50 for three. All Italian wine list. Closed Sat L and Sun.

The Victoria   SW14
10 West Temple Sheen   map 12
(020) 8876 4238

To search out this popular gastro-pub, weave through the back streets off the Upper Richmond Road and look for the profile of a young Victoria with Union Jacks rampant. One large room with bare boards, open fire and leather chairs leads through to an airy conservatory overlooking a children's play area. A one-page weekly-changing menu follows the seasons and roves around Europe for inspiration. Soups (such as roast Tuscan chestnut and pancetta) and a tapas plate are regular starters (£4–£9) and mains at £10–£16 might include duck confit with Puy lentils, cider and bacon sauce. Good, short wine list. Accommodation available. Open all week.

Vrisaki   N22
73 Myddleton Road   map 13
(020) 8889 8760

Mezes are the thing to go for at this Greek stalwart near Alexandra Palace – £32 buys a meal's worth for two. Otherwise, Greek starters are followed by a range of fish at around £16 or charcoal-grilled kebabs at £10. Kleftiko, souvla, moussaka and dolmades complete the authentic line-up, and are matched by an old-fashioned list of Greek wines or Keo beer; plus Metaxa brandy or ouzo to follow desserts from the trolley. Open Mon to Sat L and D.

Yoshino   W1
3 Piccadilly Place   map 15
(020) 7434 3616

This discreet restaurant is worth considering if you are in Piccadilly and fancy some authentic Japanese food. According to one devotee, it boasts 'the best sashimi in London', as well as 'stunning' tuna tatake with ginger and spring onion. The home-made tofu also comes in for high praise, and the kitchen's prowess extends to sushi, hotpots and other well-tried classics. Lunchtime specials are decent value. Esoteric vodkas and sakés line up alongside beers, tea comes free, and there's also a modest selection of wines. Closed Sun.

England

Stephan Langton Inn ✹ £

Friday Street, Abinger Common RH5 6JR
TEL: (01306) 730775
from A25 Dorking to Guildford road after Wotton
take Hollow Lane signed Friday Street, then
sharp left (also signed Friday Street), follow very   COOKING **3**
narrow road, turn right at pond; pub is after   MODERN BRITISH
cottages   £27–£38

Down country lanes, with only a few cottages nearby, the red-brick pub seems
little changed in decades. Tables with umbrellas sit outside, the bar is open to
drinkers (for whom there's a bar menu at lunchtime), and the yellow dining
room with 'ethnic carpets' on the walls offers bare wooden tables without side
plates for the excellent bread. Portions are generous, materials of noteworthy
quality, and ideas interesting without being outlandish. Meals might start with
pasta – perhaps ribbons of pappardelle with crunchy broccoli florets in a well-
flavoured pesto – and well-handled fish encompasses flakes of fried cod with a
wedge of roast pumpkin, or springy-textured chargrilled sea bream with tomato
and artichoke risotto. Equally successful meat dishes range from pink duck
magret, thickly sliced, to flavourful, slow-roast pork that 'more or less fell apart',
served with crisp crackling, cannellini beans and chorizo. Vanilla and Bourbon
crème brûlée is 'Croesus-rich and the size of a skating rink', while plump,
alcoholic prunes are topped with equally inebriating Armagnac ice cream.
Service is friendly and efficient, and a short wine list, pivoting around the £20
mark, offers curiosities like Irouléguy Blanc and includes half a dozen by the
glass. House French is £9.

CHEF: Jonathan Coomb   PROPRIETORS: Jonathan Coomb and Cynthia Rajabally   OPEN: Sun L
12.30 to 3, Tue to Sat D 7 to 10   CLOSED: 24 Dec D, 31 Dec D, 1 Jan D   MEALS: alc (main courses
£11 to £13). Bar menu available Mon to Sat L   SERVICE: not inc, card slips closed   CARDS: Delta,
MasterCard, Switch, Visa   DETAILS: 50 seats. 50 seats outside. Private parties: 50 main room.
Car park. Children's helpings. No smoking. Wheelchair access (not WC). Music £5

'The pastry [of my tarte Tatin] was completely white, completely soft . . . . I ate the apple
chunks off it, and then rolled up the pastry (it rolled up as easily as a blanket), to try to make it
look as if I'd left a bit less than I actually had.' (On eating in Gloucestershire.)

ABINGER HAMMER Surrey

map 3

Drakes on the Pond

Dorking Road, Abinger Hammer RH5 6SA

TEL/FAX: (01306) 731174

WEBSITE: www.drakesonthepond.com

COOKING 6

MODERN EUROPEAN

£31–£60

Not so much on a pond as beside the A25 in this divertingly named and attractive Surrey village, Drakes is a winningly simple but highly polished operation. The small restaurant is done out in vivid yellow, with comfortable chairs, good napery and a straightforwardly written menu. Lunch seems a consistently popular option, with just a pair of choices at each stage, but offering demonstrably good value. Main courses of sea bass with spinach and vermouth sauce and roast partridge with a sauce of elderberry pleased, with light cooking and accurate seasoning bringing the best out of both bird and fish. In the evenings, the choice widens and dishes become more complex, with starters such as sautéed foie gras with carrot and cardamom cream, being followed perhaps by breast of Gressingham duck with creamed leeks, shallots and balsamic vinegar, or a vegetarian option consisting of a marinated potato wrapped in spinach accompanied by casseroled ceps. Desserts have included intensely rich chocolate marquise, served maybe with cherries or vanilla and orange ice creams, and a dish of Malibu-roasted pineapple with coconut ice. Even a simple mandarin sorbet is pronounced excellent.

Some have felt the place lacks atmosphere, in that staff don't have much to say, but that may come as a refreshing alternative to 'Enjoy!' every few minutes. The wine list is a commendable selection, broad in scope. Eight house wines plus champagne may be taken by the glass from £3.75 or from £16 a bottle, but mark-ups otherwise are very Home Counties.

CHEF: Steve Drake   PROPRIETORS: Tracey Honeysett and John Morris   OPEN: Tue to Fri L 12 to 1.30, Tue to Sat D 6.45 to 9.30   CLOSED: Christmas, New Year, 2 weeks Aug/Sept   MEALS: Set L £17 (2 courses) to £21, Set D £29.50 (2 courses) to £34.50   SERVICE: not inc   CARDS: MasterCard, Switch, Visa   DETAILS: 32 seats. Private parties: 30 main room. Car park. No children under 10. No smoking before 9.30pm; no cigars/pipes. Wheelchair access (not WC). No music. Air-conditioned

ADDINGHAM West Yorkshire

map 8

Fleece ⅝⊁ £

NEW ENTRY

154 Main Street, Addingham LS29 0LY

TEL: (01943) 830491

COOKING 3

MODERN BRITISH

£20–£45

At first glance, this is a 'proper' pub where beer, bar games and food jostle happily, though on closer examination the food really grabs your attention. Seasonal supplies are the menu's foundation, with local farmers, cheese-makers, moorland shoots and Whitby fishermen providing quality. Dishes are chalked up on blackboards, so choosing can involve a bit of legwork, but once decisions are made, the friendly service follows restaurant routines. The touch is usually light, as with pigeon breast in a starter, superbly pink and tender among leaves and asparagus, the dish brought together with a well-balanced balsamic reduction. A main course of perfect pan-fried monkfish on a mustard mash showed deft technique, and unpeeled chunky chips with excellent thinly battered halibut were 'too moreish!' Great-tasting rice pudding in a substantial portion outfaced one happy eater; alternatively, there are interesting, well-kept cheeses. Decent growers abound on the short wine list; prices start at £11.50, and, with 11 wines available in two different glass sizes from £2.50, there's some tasting fun to be had.

CHEF: Matthew Brown   PROPRIETOR: Chris Monkman   OPEN: Mon to Sat 12 to 2.30, 6 to 9.30, Sun 12 to 8   MEALS: alc (main courses £6 to £14). Set L Sun £11.95. Bar menu available L and D   SERVICE: not inc, card slips closed   CARDS: Delta, MasterCard, Switch, Visa   DETAILS: 60 seats. 40 seats outside. Car park. Vegetarian meals. Children's helpings. No smoking in 1 dining room. Wheelchair access (not WC). No music

---

ALDEBURGH Suffolk   **map 6**

Lighthouse 💥 £

77 High Street, Aldeburgh IP15 5AU   COOKING 3
TEL/FAX: (01728) 453377   MODERN BRITISH-PLUS
                                                                          £23–£46

The Lighthouse's Suffolk coast mini-empire continues to grow. In addition to the Aldeburgh Cookery School, co-run by Sara Fox, the team have opened a new café/sandwich bar called Munchies, run by Sara Fox's and Peter Hill's daughter, Susie Clarke. The Lighthouse itself remains very lively and busy, and booking is advisable. Fish, not surprisingly given the location, figures largely on the daily-changing menu. A well-flavoured stock forms the basis of a flavourful fish soup, while freshly dressed Cromer crab may have the absolute minimum done to it, relying solely on the high quality of the crustacean itself. Main courses might take in 'beautifully cooked' skate wing with black butter and capers, and meat eaters may be tempted by the likes of fillet steak with shallot gravy and chunky chips. Puddings tend towards simplicity and comfort, as in a creamy lemon posset, or a warm walnut tart with vanilla ice cream. Service, headed by Peter Hill, sometimes struggles to keep up with the pace. The well-rounded wine list is refreshingly good value, with prices opening at around £11.

CHEFS: Sara Fox, Guy Welsh and Leon Manthorpe   PROPRIETORS: Sara Fox and Peter Hill   OPEN: all week 12 to 2 (2.30 Sat and Sun), 6.30 to 10   CLOSED: 1 week Oct, 2 weeks Jan   MEALS: alc L (main courses £6.50 to £12). Set D £14.25 (2 courses) to £21.50   SERVICE: not inc, card slips closed   CARDS: Amex, Delta, MasterCard, Switch, Visa   DETAILS: 95 seats. 25 seats outside. Private parties: 45 main room, 14 to 25 private rooms. Vegetarian meals. No smoking in 1 dining room. No cigars/pipes. Wheelchair access (also WC). No music. No mobile phones. Air-conditioned (£5)

All details are as accurate as possible at the time of going to press, but chefs and owners often change, and it is wise to check by telephone before making a special journey. Many readers have been disappointed when set-price bargain meals are no longer available. Ask when booking.

---

152 Aldeburgh

NEW ENTRY

152 High Street, Aldeburgh IP15 5AX
TEL: (01728) 454594
EMAIL: info@152aldeburgh.co.uk
WEBSITE: www.152aldeburgh.co.uk

COOKING 2
MODERN EUROPEAN
£21–£45

New owners have taken Café 152, renamed and revamped it impressively and professionally. Light, airy, wooden-floored with well-spaced tables, it is open all day, and service is friendly and efficient. Caesar salad with proper lardons, crispy croûtons and creamy vinaigrette, or mushroom and potato soup (creamy, mushroomy, with a swirl of truffle oil) show attention to detail. Winning fish and chips – top-class cod with crisp batter, chunky, grease-free chips, and tangy, capery tartare sauce – and confit duck leg with white bean and chorizo cassoulet have been successful main courses. A substantial plate of sorbets on a meringue base includes sweet pear, refreshing kiwi fruit and full-flavoured apricot, with an exemplary raspberry coulis. British cheeses and coffee are good too, while wines are a tasty bunch at good prices, including seven by the glass (£2.75 to £3.55). Everything is under £20, bar the fizz and four aptly described 'wines of interest'.

CHEF: Garry Cook   PROPRIETORS: Andrew Lister and Garry Cook   OPEN: all week 12 to 2.30, 6 to 10.30   MEALS: alc exc Sun L (main courses L £5 to £15, D £10.50 to £14). Set L £11 (1 course) to £18   SERVICE: not inc   CARDS: Amex, Delta, MasterCard, Switch, Visa   DETAILS: 52 seats. 10 seats outside. Private parties: 30 main room. Vegetarian meals. Music £5

Regatta ✶ £

171 High Street, Aldeburgh IP15 5AN
TEL: (01728) 452011   FAX: (01728) 453324
WEBSITE: www.regattaaldeburgh.com

COOKING 1
SEAFOOD/EUROPEAN
£23–£41

A cheerful-looking, well-kept restaurant in the centre of town, Regatta is as nautically themed as its name indicates. Simple, rustic furniture and a bare-boarded floor announce that there is nothing pretentious about the approach, and the cooking reinforces that. Among the noteworthy dishes reported by readers have been smooth and creamy leek and potato soup swirled with herb oil, home-smoked salmon with sweet tomato chutney, griddled breast of duck with wild mushroom sauce and good chips, and homely steak-and-kidney pie. Finish with bread-and-butter pudding with butterscotch sauce, or lime and yoghurt sorbet. Service is friendly and informal but efficient. With the exception of champagne, every bottle on the wine list is under £20, beginning with house French at £10.50 (£2.50 a glass).

CHEF: Robert Mabey   PROPRIETORS: Robert and Johanna Mabey   OPEN: all week 12 to 2, 6 to 10 (later from June to Aug)   CLOSED: Mon to Tue and Sun D during Nov to Mar   MEALS: alc (main courses £7.50 to £12)   SERVICE: not inc, card slips closed   CARDS: Amex, Delta, MasterCard, Switch, Visa   DETAILS: 90 seats. Private parties: 30 main room, 10 to 30 private rooms. Vegetarian meals. Children's helpings. No smoking in 1 dining room. Wheelchair access (also WC). No music. Air-conditioned £5

Juniper ⅚✳

21 The Downs, Altrincham WA14 2QD

TEL: (0161) 929 4008   FAX: (0161) 929 4009

EMAIL: reservations@juniper-restaurant.co.uk

COOKING **7**

MODERN FRENCH

£35–£78

A row of suburban shops and businesses may be an unusual location for a fine restaurant, but then little about Juniper is conventional. The basement bar is smart and comfortable, with armchairs and low tables, while the dining room's greeny-blue glow from back-lit glass bricks and its huge Uccello mural are more striking. Meals begin quite normally – moist fresh bread arrives with unsalted butter – but it isn't long before things begin to appear surreal. You like scallops? How do you fancy them with carrot julienne, saffron piccalilli, macaroni cheese purée, beetroot jelly, dried banana powder and fruitcake sauce? An alternative starter applies liquorice glaze, meringue dust and fruit shoelaces to a slow-cooked fillet of beef, while poached fillet of sea bass is served 'à la grecque', which is to say with leek-wrapped black olives, cornichon, bacon, pink fig purée, four Mediterranean vegetable purées and a beetroot cream assiette.

Innovation is unrelenting, but the food is invariably tasty and immaculately presented: from perfectly cooked turbot pieces served with chocolate brazils, peas (six in total), and splodges of sauce resembling fried eggs, to a substantial fillet of moist trout coated with warm olive oil and a sparse horseradish sauce, served with garlic beignets, some artfully arranged capers, and slicks of red peanut sauce sculpted in the shape of a fish's backbone – an 'inspired' main course. Dishes can seem 'jewel-like' in their size and brilliance: a marshmallow submerged in a frothy pea soup; or a piece of fresh, moist cod discreetly seasoned with curry, topped by a perfectly timed scallop and set about with dots of beetroot mayonnaise, a dab of yoghurt, puddles of yeast cream and a velvet 'kipper sauce' adding a robust smoky depth to it all.

It may sound gimmicky, but there is no doubting Paul Kitching's mastery of all the important techniques required to produce first-class food, together with a lively sense of humour. Desserts tend to be more conventional, which in this context might mean a hot cross bun soufflé with Cheddar cheese ice cream, or chocolate four ways: a Snickers crème brûlée, creamy hot chocolate, chocolate tart with Refresher Dust, and layered chocolate sorbets. Kate O'Brien leads a well-drilled young team of staff, and the high-quality wine list is full of interest, although there is little for bargain hunters. There are no house wines, just two reds and two whites available by the glass at £3.50.

CHEF/PROPRIETOR: Paul Kitching   OPEN: Tue to Fri L 12 to 2.15, Tue to Sat D 7 to 10   CLOSED: 1 week Feb, 2 weeks Sept   MEALS: alc (main courses £17 to £22). Set L £17.50 (2 courses) to £21.50, Set D £32.50   SERVICE: not inc, card slips closed   CARDS: Amex, Delta, MasterCard, Switch, Visa   DETAILS: 34 seats. Private parties: 32 main room. No smoking in 1 dining room. Music. Air-conditioned

---

Prices quoted in the Guide are based on information supplied by restaurateurs. The prices quoted at the top of each entry represent a range, from the lowest price of a three-course meal with service and wine to the highest; the latter is inflated by 20 per cent to take account of likely price rises during the year of the Guide.

AMBLESIDE Cumbria
map 8

Glass House ⅝✷

Rydal Road, Ambleside LA22 9AN
TEL: (015394) 32137   FAX: (015394) 33384
EMAIL: enquiries@theglasshouserestaurant.co.uk
WEBSITE: www.theglasshouse restaurant.co.uk

COOKING 3
MODERN EUROPEAN
£29–£58

Glass House, all three floors of it, is housed in what was a former mill (along with a glass studio and a still functioning watermill). Although some of the chains and pulleys remain to remind diners of the building's former life, the interior aims to emphasise the restaurant's contemporary credentials. Sandwiches, such as Cumberland ham with wholegrain mustard, are a popular choice with families at lunchtime, when menus also offer a selection of generally good-value, simple dishes, such as beef à la bourguignonne with mashed potato. At dinner, the focus changes somewhat, with a more serious menu featuring perhaps locally sourced Herdwick lamb or Lakeland confit duck leg, as well as dishes evoking Continental influences: antipasto as a starter, for instance, or a main course of pan-fried sea bass with pistou dressing. For afters, there are farmhouse cheeses or such simple pleasures as chocolate and hazelnut fudge cake or home-made ice creams. Wines are fairly priced and well chosen, and the list of bin ends and specials turns up some star bottles. House wines start at £11.75 (£2.85 a glass), and there is a huge collection of vintage Armagnac going back to 1900.

CHEF: Richard Collins   PROPRIETOR: Neil Farrell   OPEN: Wed to Mon 12 to 3, 6.30 to 9.30 (10 Sat, 9 Sun)   CLOSED: 24 to 26 Dec, 5 to 28 Jan   MEALS: alc (main courses £11.50 to £17). Set D £15 (2 courses) to £18. Light L available 12 to 5   SERVICE: not inc   CARDS: Delta, MasterCard, Switch, Visa   DETAILS: 100 seats. 40 seats outside. Private parties: 40 main room. Vegetarian meals. Children's helpings. No children under 5 at D. No smoking. Wheelchair access (not WC). Music (£5)

▲ Rothay Manor ¶ ⅝✷

Rothay Bridge, Ambleside LA22 0EH
TEL: (015394) 33605   FAX: (015394) 33607
EMAIL: hotel@rothaymanor.co.uk
WEBSITE: www.rothaymanor.co.uk
off A593 to Coniston, ¼m W of Ambleside

COOKING 3
MODERN BRITISH
£26–£52

Once owned by a well-to-do Liverpool merchant, this is an elegant, white-fronted, balconied building in lush, landscaped gardens. The interior has an aura of bygone days, and the atmosphere of unflustered gentility is appreciated – along with some rather enjoyable cooking. Cumberland sauce crops up on the set-price dinner menu in a terrine of wood pigeon, guinea fowl and pork, or there may be Cartmel Valley smoked salmon served straight with bread and butter. After a choice of soup or sorbet, it's on to main courses built around other regional ingredients, perhaps local pheasant served with sweet potato and spring onion mash and whisky sauce, or, when available, char from Lake Windermere. Desserts continue the traditional theme, and might well include egg custard tart adorned with rum and raisin ice cream, but pannacotta scented with lemongrass appears too. Informal service helps everyone to feel at home.

The wine selection covers classic regions, including Germany, but also takes in newer areas with discoveries from the Languedoc, slick modern throat-charmers from Kanu in South Africa, and restrained, stylish Dromana Estate wines from Victoria. Five come by the glass for £3 and it is possible to order half the contents of any bottle on the list.

CHEFS: Jane Binns and Colette Nixon PROPRIETOR: Nigel and Stephen Nixon OPEN: all week 12.30 to 2 (12.45 to 1.30 Sun), 7.30 to 9 CLOSED: 3 Jan to 6 Feb MEALS: alc L (main course £9.50). Set L £16, Set L Sun £18.50, Set D £30 to £33. Light L menu available Mon to Sat SERVICE: not inc, card slips closed CARDS: Amex, Delta, Diners, MasterCard, Switch, Visa DETAILS: 65 seats. Private parties: 34 main room. Car park. Vegetarian meals. Children's helpings. No children under 7 at D. No smoking. Wheelchair access (also WC). No music. Air-conditioned ACCOMMODATION: 17 rooms, all with bath/shower. TV. Phone. B&B £72 to £155. Rooms for disabled. Baby facilities (*The Which? Guide to Good Hotels*) £5

APPLETHWAITE Cumbria   map 10

▲ Underscar Manor ⅝✳

Applethwaite CA12 4PH	COOKING 6
TEL: (017687) 75000 FAX: (017687) 74904	ANGLO-FRENCH
off A66, ½m N of Keswick	£40–£71

This impressive Italianate pile on the lower slopes of Skiddaw was built in Victorian times and has a serene atmosphere and striking views over Derwent Water. Red squirrels gather on the lawn, and the house is attractively furnished, with a flamboyant display of price-tagged teddy bears in the lounge and an airy conservatory dining room. Despite the rather formal ceremony of dome-lifting, it is a friendly and unsnobbish place, with a wordy but nonetheless enticing menu that displays its credentials in the form of local venison saddle, or 'diver-harvested king sea scallops', perhaps accompanied by a scallop mousse in filo and a gingery white wine and butter sauce.

Ideas range from a comparatively straightforward cheese soufflé, to a rather more involved dish of roast rack of lamb that comes with two gâteaux (one of lamb hotpot, another of Puy lentil and red pepper) as well as beans in filo, roast garlic and a grain mustard sauce. A sense of balance, however, keeps the combinations reasonable yet appealing, taking in beer-battered Scottish scampi with herb risotto and a sweet-and-sour sauce, and an open raviolo of wild mushrooms with summer truffle and chargrilled asparagus. The kitchen is also accommodating, to the extent of offering beef fillet with or without its oxtail accompaniment, and serving its fish dishes as either a first or main course.

This is a busy kitchen whose work doesn't let up at dessert stage, as it turns out an individual strawberry and apple pie (with vanilla ice cream and crème anglaise), a dark chocolate and orange tart (with orange sauce and pistachio ice cream), and a soufflé of the day. A French-dominated wine list parades its share of prestige bottles, although there is some relief for the price-conscious, including an Entre-Deux-Mers white and Côtes du Rhone red at £16.

CHEF: Robert Thornton PROPRIETORS: Pauline and Derek Harrison, and Gordon Evans OPEN: all week 12 to 1, 7 to 8.30 (9 Sat) CLOSED: 2 or 3 days after New Year MEALS: alc (main courses £14 to £21). Set L £28, Set D £38 SERVICE: not inc, card slips closed CARDS: Amex,

MasterCard, Switch, Visa   DETAILS: 50 seats. 16 seats outside. Private parties: 30 main room, 20 private room. Car park. Vegetarian meals. No children under 12. Jacket and tie. No smoking. Occasional music. No mobile phones   ACCOMMODATION: 11 rooms, all with bath/shower. TV. Phone. D,B&B £120 to £250. No children under 12. Swimming pool (*The Which? Guide to Good Hotels*)

ARDINGTON Oxfordshire
map 2

▲ Boar's Head 🌠

Church Street, Ardington OX14 8QA

TEL/FAX: (01235) 833254

EMAIL: brucebuchan@theboarshead.freeserve.co.uk

off A417, 2½m E of Wantage

COOKING 3

MODERN EUROPEAN

£27–£57

Well-maintained and new-looking, black-timbered with pebble-dash infill, the Boar's Head's exterior belies its ancient origins. Inside, both bar areas are suitably bare and basic, while the restaurant, with wine maps on its walls, has more refinement. Chef Bruce Buchan espouses British cuisine with French and Spanish overtones. Fish is a strong suit: Cornish scallops with black pudding and bacon, or tartare of salmon with deep-fried oysters, feature among starters – though you could also choose, say, pan-fried foie gras with grapes in Montbazillac. Of around six main courses half are also fish – fillet of turbot with rösti, spinach and hollandaise for example – while meat options might take in rump of salt marsh lamb with toasted ratatouille and pesto mashed potato. To finish are farmhouse cheeses with sticky malt bread fresh from the oven, or hot Grand Marnier soufflé with iced chocolate ice cream. A wide-ranging wine list opens at £10.50 and is particularly strong on claret (from Côtes de Castillon to Ch. Pétrus, purse permitting).

CHEF: Bruce Buchan   PROPRIETORS: Bruce Buchan, Terry Chipperfield and Richard Douglas   OPEN: all week 12 to 2.15, 7 to 9.30   MEALS: alc (main courses £13.50 to £18.50). Set L Sun £16.95. Bar menu available except Sat D and Sun L   SERVICE: not inc   CARDS: Amex, Delta, MasterCard, Switch, Visa   DETAILS: 38 seats. 18 seats outside. Private parties: 26 main room, 10 to 16 private rooms. Car park. Children's helpings. No smoking in 1 dining room. Occasional music. No mobile phones   ACCOMMODATION: 3 rooms, all with bath/shower. TV. Phone. B&B £75 to £120. Baby facilities (*The Which? Guide to Good Hotels*) (£5)

ARLINGHAM Gloucestershire
map 2

▲ Old Passage Inn 🌠 £

Passage Road, Arlingham GL2 7JR

TEL: (01452) 740547   FAX: (01452) 741871

EMAIL: oldpassage@ukonline.co.uk

WEBSITE: www.fishattheoldpassageinn.co.uk

from A38 8m SW of Gloucester, turn NW; go through Arlingham to river bank

COOKING 4

SEAFOOD

£29–£57

A relaxed, stylish brasserie-like seafood restaurant is the surprise inside this Victorian pub, painted a deep forest green with bright red columns supporting a pediment over the porch. Such stunning isolation by the River Severn is not where you'd expect to find a Roux brothers émigré, but Patrick Le Mesurier's classical training shows through the essentially simple treatment of superb fish and shellfish (meat-eaters are offered a token Aberdeen Angus steak). Five varieties of English oyster head the menu; these can be ordered in multiples of three, and mixing and matching is encouraged. The deeply flavoured liquor in a bouillabaisse impressed more than its haddock, bass and salmon, but utterly basic mushy peas and a mustard mash both retained bite; their straightforward tastes delighted, and the Caesar salad that preceded it was correct, with copious shavings of Parmesan. Following fish restaurant tradition, puddings are on the simple side: perhaps almond tart, or a basic crème brûlée. Service is informal but informed. An intelligently chosen short wine list tours the world with reasonable prices starting at £10.40.

CHEFS: Patrick Le Mesurier and Raoul Moore   PROPRIETORS: the Moore family   OPEN: Tue to Sun L 12 to 2, Tue to Sat D 7 to 9 (6.45 to 9.30 Fri and Sat)   CLOSED: 1 week at Christmas   MEALS: alc (main courses £10.50 to £32). Set L and D £38   SERVICE: not inc   CARDS: Amex, Delta, MasterCard, Switch, Visa   DETAILS: 70 seats. 20 seats outside. Private parties: 70 main room, 5 to 12 private rooms. Car park. Vegetarian meals. Children's helpings. No smoking in dining room; separate smoking room. Wheelchair access (also WC). Music. Air-conditioned ACCOMMODATION: 3 rooms, all with bath/shower. TV. Phone. B&B £50 to £90 (*The Which? Guide to Good Hotels*)

ARNCLIFFE North Yorkshire   map 8

▲ Amerdale House ⅗✶

Arncliffe, Littondale BD23 5QE   COOKING 4
TEL: (01756) 770250   FAX: (01756) 770266   MODERN EUROPEAN
WEBSITE: www.amerdalehouse.co.uk   £45–£54

'The great thing about Amerdale House is that everything is done very well,' commented one guest, a sentiment back up by others. The 'lovely stone house' in a remote Yorkshire Dale is peaceful and elegant, with a dining room of polished wooden tables and immaculate cutlery and glassware. The four-course dinner menu, with limited choice, presents simply cooked food: a starter of herb omelette with roasted cherry tomatoes might lead to an intermediate course of smoked haddock kedgeree and then a main dish of roast loin of Gloucester Old Spot pork with caramelised apples and a red wine jus, or baked fillet of salmon with prawns and lemon butter sauce. If neither dessert – maybe raspberry and apple crème brûlée, or chocolate tart with vanilla ice cream - takes your fancy, there is always a platter of local cheeses with home-made oatcakes as an alternative. France and the southern hemisphere are the focus of the wine list, which offers around 30 half-bottles and a couple by the glass. Prices open at just above the £12 mark.

CHEF: Nigel Crapper   PROPRIETORS: Nigel and Paula Crapper   OPEN: all week D only 7.30 to 8 CLOSED: mid-Nov to mid-Mar   MEALS: Set D £34.50   SERVICE: not inc, card slips closed   CARDS: MasterCard, Switch, Visa   DETAILS: 24 seats. Car park. No smoking. No music ACCOMMODATION: 11 rooms, all with bath/shower. TV. Phone. D,B&B £158 to £162 (for 2 in a double room). Baby facilities (*The Which? Guide to Good Hotels*)

The Guide is totally independent, accepts no free hospitality, and survives on the number of copies sold each year.

▲ Crab & Lobster ⁵✳

Dishforth Road, Asenby YO7 3QL
TEL: (01845) 577286 FAX: (01845) 577109
EMAIL: reservations@crabandlobster.co.uk
WEBSITE: www.crabandlobster.co.uk
off A168, between A19 and A1

COOKING 2
FISH/MODERN EUROPEAN
£37–£79

While many pubs are happy to clutter up their interiors with bric-à-brac, the Crab & Lobster goes one better and has an outside that is just as busily decorated – including a rocking horse on the roof. Inside...well, several reporters have used the word 'eccentric' in their descriptions of the atmospheric main bar. The cooking is as eclectic as the décor and grabs the attention with some boldly modern ideas. Starters have included twice-baked soufflé with feta, spinach and roasted cherry tomatoes, and seared scallops with ginger and vanilla couscous and a balsamic and raspberry dressing, while main courses take in everything from beef fillet with oxtail ravioli, roast shallots, truffle mash and a red wine glaze, to loin of rabbit with sage and onion risotto, and fish and chips with minted mushy peas. Dessert might be Baileys crème brûlée with espresso ice cream and ginger shortbread. A bright list of fairly priced wines opens with eight house selections from £15 to £17. Accommodation is in the nearby Crab Manor.

CHEF: Steve Dean PROPRIETOR: Vimac Trading Ltd OPEN: all week 12 to 2.30, 7 to 9.30 MEALS: alc (main courses £13.50 to £29) SERVICE: not inc CARDS: Amex, Delta, MasterCard, Switch, Visa DETAILS: 150 seats. 50 seats outside. Private parties: 55 main room, 10 to 20 private rooms. Car park. Vegetarian meals. No smoking. Wheelchair access (also WC). Occasional music ACCOMMODATION: 11 rooms, all with bath/shower. TV. Phone. B&B £130 to £160 (double room). Rooms for disabled. Baby facilities

▲ Callow Hall ♟ ⁵✳

Mappleton, Ashbourne DE6 2AA
TEL: (01335) 300900 FAX: (01335) 300512
EMAIL: reservations@callowhall.co.uk
WEBSITE: www.callowhall.co.uk
from Ashbourne market place take A515, at top
of hill turn W at crossroads with Bowling Green
pub on left, Mappleton road is first on right after
bridge

COOKING 3
MODERN BRITISH-PLUS
£32–£61

This stone-built high-ceilinged mansion exudes the 'comfortable and relaxed' atmosphere created by generations of Spencers. The menu has a traditional foundation while venturing into more modern areas with considerable success, pairing fillet of lemon sole simply baked with lemon and parsley butter, Welsh lamb with maybe fig Tatin, honey and mint jus, or Scottish beef with a croûte of chicken liver pâté, wild mushrooms and red wine jus. Desserts range from rhubarb soufflé with rhubarb and ginger syrup, via baked Alaska with cherries marinated in Kirsch, to an appealing range of ice creams. The smoked salmon, breads and petits fours are all made in-house. Separate pricing of dishes offers an alternative to the extravagant but good-value set dinner. The wine list opens with a strong showing from the traditional regions of France and solid ranges from Italy and Spain, but the excitement comes with the more modern selections from Australia, New Zealand and Argentina. House wines start at £11.95 and a dozen are offered by the glass from £4.50 to £5.75. The ports and dessert wines are worth a look, too.

CHEFS: Anthony and David Spencer PROPRIETORS: David, Anthony, Dorothy and Emma Spencer OPEN: Sun L 12.30 to 1.30, Mon to Sat D 7.30 to 9.30 (Sun D residents only) CLOSED: 25 and 26 Dec MEALS: alc D (main courses £16.50 to £19.75). Set L Sun £22.50, Set D £38 SERVICE: not inc CARDS: Amex, Diners, MasterCard, Switch, Visa DETAILS: 80 seats. Private parties: 40 main room, 25 to 40 private rooms. Car park. Vegetarian meals. Children's helpings. No smoking. Wheelchair access (not WC). No music. No mobile phones ACCOMMODATION: 16 rooms, all with bath/shower. TV. Phone. B&B £90 to £175. Rooms for disabled. Baby facilities. Fishing (*The Which? Guide to Good Hotels*) £5

ASHBURTON Devon   map 1

Agaric ✸

30 North Street, Ashburton TQ13 7QD
TEL: (01364) 654478   COOKING 4
EMAIL: eat@agaricrestaurant.co.uk   MODERN BRITISH-PLUS
WEBSITE: www.agaricrestaurant.co.uk   £33–£56

Behind the unprepossessing dark shopfront is a single-roomed restaurant with a bistro-like atmosphere. It effectively combines ancient and modern, with smart, bare wooden tables, a stone fireplace containing a giant wooden mushroom, and a couple of shelves of bottles and jars of preserves for sale. Simplicity is one of the keynotes here, with first courses making use of simple assemblies and minimal cooking: crab salad with a smoky-flavoured mayonnaise, slices of honey-roast mutton ham with potato salad, or a round of Ticklemore goats' cheese on toasted brioche, with marinated peppers and olives contributing much-needed moisture.

Small local suppliers, some of them organic, play a role, especially in the superior quality of main courses. Among successes have been pink-roast, sweet-tasting loin of spring lamb on a bed of Puy lentils, beside a pile of 'excellent' chopped squash and sweet potato, and full-flavoured, free-range Dittisham chicken in a cream sauce gently infused with tarragon and brandy. Desserts have ranged from a very ordinary rhubarb and ginger crumble with a jug of double cream, to a first-class oeufs à la neige, the soft meringue encased in crisp caramel to give it just the textural contrast that most versions of this classic sadly lack. Although service has not always been up to the mark, it has also been friendly and easy-going. A short, enthusiastic wine list offers bright modern flavours at fair prices.

CHEF: Nick Coiley PROPRIETORS: Nick and Sophie Coiley OPEN: Wed to Sun L 12 to 2.30, Wed to Sat D 7 to 9 CLOSED: Christmas, first 2 weeks Feb, first 2 weeks Oct MEALS: alc (main courses £13 to £17). Set L £11.50 (2 courses) SERVICE: not inc, card slips closed CARDS: Delta, MasterCard, Switch, Visa DETAILS: 30 seats. 20 seats outside. Private parties: 30 main room. Vegetarian meals. Children's helpings. No smoking. Wheelchair access (also WC). No music

ASHFORD Derbyshire
map 9

▲ Riverside House ⁵⁄₄✳

Ashford in the Water DE45 1QF
TEL: (01629) 814275   FAX: (01629) 812873
EMAIL: riversidehouse@enta.net
WEBSITE: www.riversidehousehotel.co.uk

COOKING **4**
FRENCH-PLUS
£59–£64

A small stretch of duck-patrolled river full of brown trout separates this small, elegant, country-house hotel from the main road. It is creeper covered, with a welcoming bar, a comfortable lounge, a small conservatory, and a couple of dining rooms with polished wooden tables. Quite a few luxury materials are deployed – in a lobster and salmon ravioli with truffled leeks, for example – but there may also be slow-cooked leg of mutton, or a starter of vine tomato stuffed with mildly flavoured couscous. Scallops are particularly well reported: in one case four fresh, just-seared, juicy discs arranged around a pile of leaves, with a lively tomato, lemon and coriander salsa.

The set-price lunch receives its share of plaudits: perhaps scallops followed by loin of French rabbit stuffed with a light herb mousse (served with a risotto and Puy lentil gravy), then a light chocolate 'surprise' incorporating a scroll of fine biscuit, an ice cream on chopped orange flesh, and intensely flavoured chocolate and vanilla creams. Indeed, desserts are a highlight, judging by a first-class thin pastry case filled with cherries with an almondy topping. Service is friendly and professional, and although some of the wines on the wide-ranging list (sorry, 'directory') are short on detail (like the producer's name), prices are generally fair and interest is high. There are 30 house wines (15 of each) between £15.95 and £20.95 (£2.50 to £2.90 a glass).

CHEF: John Whelan   PROPRIETOR: Penelope Thornton   OPEN: all week 12 to 2.30, 7 to 9.30
MEALS: Set L £26.95, Set D £39.95. Brasserie menu available   SERVICE: not inc   CARDS: Amex, Delta, Diners, MasterCard, Switch, Visa   DETAILS: 50 seats. 40 seats outside. Private parties: 50 main room, 12 to 16 private rooms. Car park. Vegetarian meals. No children under 12. No smoking. Wheelchair access (also WC). No music. No mobile phones   ACCOMMODATION: 15 rooms, all with bath/shower. TV. Phone. B&B £85 to £155. Rooms for disabled. No children under 12   (£5)

ASHWATER Devon
map 1

▲ Blagdon Manor ⁵⁄₄✳
NEW ENTRY

Ashwater EX21 5DF
TEL: (01409) 211224   FAX: (01409) 211634
EMAIL: stay@blagdon.com
WEBSITE: www.blagdon.com
off A388, 9m N of Launceston

COOKING **1**
ENGLISH/MEDITERRANEAN
£24–£43

This pleasant, unassuming, isolated small hotel is a peaceful place set amid acres of rural pastures. A homely atmosphere pervades, with family photos and shelves of books in the lounge, while the plum-coloured dining room is decked out with flowers and fat candles on the fireplace. Cooking uses good raw materials, as in a starter of accurately timed scallops served with a chilli dressing, while main courses might be rack of new season's lamb with a mustard and herb crust, or pan-fried monkfish tail with smoked bacon and baby onions in a red wine and shallot butter sauce. Vegetarians are well represented with a separate menu. Round things off with chocolate fondant and poached pears, or a 'faultless' hot passion-fruit soufflé with vanilla ice cream, each intensely flavoured and beautifully balanced. Service, headed by Liz Morey, is committed, genuine and knowledgeable. The short wine list has decent bottles at £9.50, and, with markers like Sancerre at only £15.50 and a Rioja for £15.95, the pricing will please.

CHEF: Steve Morey   PROPRIETORS: Steve and Liz Morey   OPEN: Wed to Sun L 12 to 2, Tue to Sat D 7 to 9 (Mon and Sun D residents only)   CLOSED: 2 weeks Jan/Feb, 1 week May, 2 weeks Oct/Nov   MEALS: Set L £11 to £14 (both 2 courses), Set L Sun £17.50, Set D £21 (2 courses) to £25   SERVICE: not inc   CARDS: Delta, MasterCard, Switch, Visa   DETAILS: 24 seats. Private parties: 16 main room, 8 to 10 private rooms. Car park. Vegetarian meals. No children under 12. No smoking. Wheelchair access (not WC). No music   ACCOMMODATION: 7 rooms. TV. Phone. B&B £72 to £90. No children under 12 (*The Which? Guide to Good Hotels*)

AYCLIFFE Co Durham   map 10

County

13 The Green, Aycliffe Village DL5 6LX
TEL: (01325) 312273   FAX: (01325) 308780
WEBSITE: www.the-county.co.uk
from A1(M) junction 59, take A167 N for Newton   COOKING 3
Aycliffe; at 1st roundabout turn right; take   MODERN EUROPEAN
second right, then first right   £27–£51

The management describe this green-shuttered Georgian/Victorian building on the village green as 'a bistro-style restaurant', and it functions as such, with just a dash of pub about it too – note bar stools and a good selection of real ales. The interior is clean and bare, even a bit urban. Food ranges from simple steaks with fries and a salad to modern British dishes like slow-cooked confit of pork with bean and vegetable cassoulet, or starters of ham and honey mustard terrine with pease pudding, or 'home-smoked' salmon with lemon dressing. There's a mild Asian influence here, too: witness main courses like lime- and garlic-marinated chicken with coconut and lemongrass froth, pak choi and savoury rice, or (for a starter) chilli and lime king prawns. Desserts are fairly traditional, with apple tart Tatin, or raspberry cranachan with whisky. Besides several real ales, there is a mainly New World wine list offering good value, starting at £12.95 and sticking mostly under £20.

CHEF: Andrew Brown   PROPRIETORS: Andrew and Deborah Brown   OPEN: All week L 12 to 2 (3 Sun), Mon to Sat D 6 (6.45 Sat) to 9.30   CLOSED: 25 and 26 Dec, 1 Jan   MEALS: alc Mon to Sat (main courses £7 to £17). Set L £18.95 (2 courses) to £23.50. Bar L and early D (6 to 7) menu available Mon to Fri   SERVICE: not inc, card slips closed   CARDS: Amex, Delta, MasterCard, Switch, Visa   DETAILS: 80 seats. Private parties: 25 main room. Car park. Vegetarian meals. Children's helpings. Music. No mobile phones. Air-conditioned

Card slips closed *in the details at the end of an entry indicates that the total on the slips of credit cards is closed when handed over for signature.*

AYLESBURY Buckinghamshire   map 3

▲ Hartwell House ⁵⅟✳

Oxford Road, Aylesbury HP17 8NL
TEL: (01296) 747444   FAX: (01296) 747450
EMAIL: info@hartwell-house.com   COOKING **5**
WEBSITE: www.hartwell-house.com   BRITISH
on A418, 2m from Aylesbury towards Oxford   £22–£64

Perhaps it is the grandeur of the setting that causes some reporters to find the unpretentious, friendly and laid-back atmosphere surprising. Even the jacket and tie policy has been relaxed (it's 'jacket only' at dinner), but the ancient and 'very posh' Grade I listed mansion set in acres of landscaped parkland still looks much the sort of place where you might bump into an exiled king.

Chef Daniel Richardson cooks in an elegant and luxurious but unfussy modern British style. Dinner menus offer plenty of choice, starters ranging from confit of salmon with sevruga caviar, blinis, pickled cucumber and radish to pan-fried goats' cheese and toasted walnuts with a cranberry and mulled wine compote, via home-smoked pheasant and wild mushroom sausage with sage-flavoured potatoes. To follow, there might be roast breast of wild duck on Brussels leaves with anise-flavoured swede purée and fondant potato, pan-fried sea bass on dauphinoise potato, buttered spinach and a port and truffle sauce, or Aylesbury lamb noisettes with creamed rosemary potatoes, onion confit and forest mushrooms. A fine cheeseboard is a tempting alternative to desserts such as lemon mascarpone cheesecake with lemon ice cream, or mango mousse with pineapple crisps.

Many of the major names of Burgundy and Bordeaux are represented on the extensive wine list, but there is plenty to suit all pockets, with house wines starting at £14.90. There is also a good selection by the glass.

CHEF: Daniel Richardson   PROPRIETOR: Historic House Hotels Ltd   OPEN: all week 12.30 to 1.45, 7.30 to 9.45   CLOSED: 25 Dec and 1 Jan exc for residents   MEALS: Set L £22 to £29, Set D £32 to £46   SERVICE: net prices, card slips closed   CARDS: Amex, MasterCard, Switch, Visa   DETAILS: 60 seats. 25 seats outside. Private parties: 60 main room, 12 to 60 private rooms. Car park. Vegetarian meals. No children under 8. Jacket at D. No smoking. Wheelchair access (also WC). Occasional music. No mobile phones   ACCOMMODATION: 46 rooms, all with bath/shower. TV. Phone. Room only £145 to £245. Rooms for disabled. No children under 8. Swimming pool. Fishing (*The Which? Guide to Good Hotels*)

BAGSHOT Surrey   map 3

▲ Pennyhill Park, Latymer Restaurant NEW ENTRY

London Road, Bagshot GU19 5EU   COOKING **6**
TEL: (01276) 471774   FAX: (01276) 473217   MODERN EUROPEAN
WEBSITE: www.exclusivehotels.co.uk   £44–£79

Approach via a long driveway through lush grounds and make your way past decorative lions guarding the entrance, before being led into a sumptuous lounge for pre-dinner drinks amid oil paintings, tapestries and carved gargoyles. Luxury and comfort are the watchwords at this modern country club and hotel, and service is efficient, well polished and good-humoured. There are two dining options: the less formal St James Restaurant, or the haute cuisine experience of the Latymer Restaurant.

Menus in the latter present a repertoire of highly ambitious and intricately constructed dishes, but chef Marc Wilkinson handles it all with great aplomb to produce harmonious flavours and textures: in, for example, a starter of sweetbread and truffle fritter, its crisp crust yielding to a creamy middle, set on a disc of black pudding, topped with wild rocket and a shaving of black truffle and finished with a light apple purée and an aromatic bay leaf sauce. Main courses raise the game to another level: a two-part 'collection' of rabbit at inspection provided a 'masterful amalgam of textures and flavours' – the first part comprising slices of saddle on a risotto with a herby, milky flavour, along with a 'cannelloni', made with a sheet of calamari and containing minced rabbit, finished with a thread of light stock and wine based sauce; while the second stage combined the liver and kidney in a salad with a sweet, refreshing sauce. To finish, creamy fromage blanc mousse with delicate mango jelly and intense passion-fruit sorbet, or an elaborately crafted 'taste of rhubarb' platter featuring, among other things, a granita, a bavarois-style cream, a mint-infused rhubarb and melon drink and dainty triangles of pain d'épice.

The wine list is about as humble as you'd expect in the setting – in other words, not at all. It is well chosen, with interests in newer as well as classic regions, but wines under £30 are in a distinct minority. Wines by the glass, usually half a dozen, are selected on a daily basis.

CHEF: Marc Wilkinson   PROPRIETOR: Exclusive Hotels   OPEN: Tue to Sun 12 to 2, 7 to 9.30   MEALS: Set L £20 (2 courses) to £25, Set D £50   SERVICE: not inc   CARDS: MasterCard, Switch, Visa   DETAILS: 32 seats. 20 seats outside. Private parties: 32 main room. Car park. Vegetarian meals. No children. Wheelchair access (also WC). No music   ACCOMMODATION: 123 rooms, all with bath/shower. TV. Phone. Room only £175 to £180. Rooms for disabled. Baby facilities. Swimming pool

BAKEWELL Derbyshire   map 8

Renaissance ⁵✳

Bath Street, Bakewell DE45 1BX	COOKING 4
TEL: (01629) 812687	FRENCH
WEBSITE: www.renaissance-restaurant.com	£23–£50

Renaissance occupies a large stone and timber-clad building in the busy market town of Bakewell. The 'charming' dining room offers a light and bright feel with the use of soft beige and lemon colours next to pale oak beams. The menu offers classic French dishes, with consistency and good value being key features. The carte offers a degree of sophistication in the form of lemon sole and foie gras terrine served with a shiitake and Chablis sauce, or, more traditionally, confit of duck with apple chutney. Main courses might include pork fillet roulade with black pudding and bacon and a rich red wine sauce, or a trio of seafood: a prawn and scallop sausage, and fillets of red mullet and bream on a glazed curry sauce. Finish with chocolate and caramel gâteau on white chocolate sauce, or crêpes suzette. The cheaper set-price menu offers good value, as does the lunchtime Bistro menu. Service has received praise for the combination of its efficiency and informality. The wine list is predictably dominated by France, with some quality offerings from elsewhere. Prices are wide ranging, starting with three French house wines at £10.99.

CHEFS: Eric Piedaniel and J. Gibbard   PROPRIETORS: Mr and Mrs Eric Piedaniel, S. and D. Béraud
OPEN: Tue to Sat and first and second Sun of month L 12 to 1.30, Tue to Sat D 7 to 9.30   CLOSED: 2 weeks Christmas, first two weeks Aug   MEALS: Set L Tue to Sat £14.95 to £23.95, Set L Sun £15.95, Set D Tue to Thur £14.95 to £23.95, Set D Fri and Sat £23.95. Bistro menu available Tue to Sat L   SERVICE: not inc   CARDS: Amex, Delta, MasterCard, Switch, Visa   DETAILS: 65 seats. Private parties: 70 main room, 1 to 25 private rooms. Vegetarian meals. Children's helpings. No smoking. Wheelchair access (not WC). Music

BARNSLEY Gloucestershire   map 2

▲ Village Pub 🍷 ⁕

Barnsley GL7 5EF
TEL: (01285) 740421   FAX: (01285) 740142   COOKING 2
EMAIL: info@thevillagepub.co.uk   MODERN BRITISH
WEBSITE: www.thevillagepub.co.uk   £29–£47

This ancient grey Cotswold stone pub is set right on the main road that snakes through the village, with an attractive brick-paved courtyard to the rear. The name tells you nothing more nor less than you need to know about the place, though the décor of the open-plan bar is a rather cosmopolitan version of rural, with grouped series of prints on two-tone walls. Menus are rather more cutting-edge than you might expect to find in a traditional country inn. Starters of John Dory with red pepper salsa and mizuna, or pan-fried squid with chorizo and new potatoes, might be followed with duck breast on roast beetroot, baby red chard and horseradish, or whole grilled mackerel with roast tomato, anchovy and parsley salad. And to finish there may be hazelnut and chocolate torte. Despite being given assurances to the contrary, our inspector found that smoking seems to be tolerated throughout. The modern wine list (with an appetising Italian twist) is exactly right for the job – unfussy, arranged by style, mainly under £20, with 17 wines in two glass sizes (mostly £3.50 for 175ml).

As the Guide was going to press the owners opened Barnsley House, a country-house hotel whose kitchen is under the supervision of Franco Taruschio; tel: (01285) 740000.

CHEF: Michael Carr   PROPRIETORS: Tim Haigh and Rupert Pendered   OPEN: all week 12 to 2.30 (3 Sat and Sun), 7 to 9.30 (10 Fri and Sat)   MEALS: alc (main courses £10.50 to £16.50)   SERVICE: not inc   CARDS: MasterCard, Switch, Visa   DETAILS: 100 seats. 50 seats outside. Private parties: 30 main room. Car park. Vegetarian meals. Children's helpings. No smoking in 1 dining room. No music   ACCOMMODATION: 6 rooms, all with bath/shower. TV. Phone. B&B £65 to £125

The Guide is totally independent, accepts no free hospitality, and survives on the number of copies sold each year.

The text of entries is based on unsolicited reports sent in by readers, backed up by inspections conducted anonymously. The factual details under the text are from questionnaires the Guide sends to all restaurants that feature in the book.

BARWICK Somerset   map 2

▲ Little Barwick House ♥ ⁵✲

Barwick BA22 9TD
TEL: (01935) 423902   FAX: (01935) 420908
EMAIL: reservations@barwick7.fsnet.co.uk
WEBSITE: www.littlebarwickhouse.co.uk   COOKING **6**
take exit off A37 at roundabout 1m S of Yeovil;   MODERN ENGLISH
Little Barwick House ¼m on left   £29–£55

Just outside the village, Little Barwick House is a tall white Georgian building facing its own steeply sloping lawn. The garden, with its giant old trees, is a magical place to be on a warm summer's evening. Inside, the feel is distinctly English country house, although the dining room has a sparer look, with neutral colours, bare floorboards and well-spaced tables. Service, headed by Emma Ford, is professional and polished, conducted (almost soundlessly) by young women in floor-length designer outfits.

Tom Ford is in charge of the kitchen, which seems to centre on two styles: 'modern versions of Mediterranean classics' and British/northern European dishes. A starter of grilled fillets of red mullet with pan-fried polenta and wild rocket salad is an example of the former, and pink-roast breast of wild pigeon with black pudding and beetroot dressing of the latter. 'All but a work of art' is how one visitor described the presentation of a warm starter salad of pan-fried scallops with tomato compote, the ingredients arranged on a long rectangular dish, while fillet of local beef ('always beautifully tender and tasty') might turn up as a main course in a herb crust with red wine sauce. Vegetables, served on a side plate, get more than cursory treatment: courgette beignets ('fresh and perfect' long strips deep-fried in a very light beer batter), broccoli hollandaise and gratin dauphinois all gained favour at inspection. Desserts such as iced honey and saffron parfait with lavender sauce, with its 'stunning simplicity and clear yet subtle flavours', are a high point.

The wine list, arranged by style, makes interesting comparisons at all price levels – three well-reputed Pinot Noirs from New Zealand, Sancerre and Burgundy at around £23, for example. In the upper reaches, Bordeaux digs back to some old vintages, Burgundies are good and Australia soars all the way to the top. There are loads of half-bottles, and the eminently affordable house white and red (£12.75 a bottle, £4 a glass) find plenty of company under £20.

CHEFS: Tim Ford, Maxine Perrier and Trudi Gladman   PROPRIETORS: Tim and Emma Ford   OPEN: Wed to Sun L 12 to 2, Tue to Sat D 7 to 9   CLOSED: 2 weeks Christmas   MEALS: Set L Wed to Sat £15.50 (2 courses) to £17.50, Set L Sun £19.50, Set D £28.50 (2 courses) to £32.50   SERVICE: not inc, card slips closed   CARDS: Amex, MasterCard, Switch, Visa   DETAILS: 56 seats. 12 seats outside. Private parties: 30 main room, 18 private room. Car park. Children's helpings. No smoking. No music. No mobile phones. Air-conditioned   ACCOMMODATION: 6 rooms, all with bath/shower. TV. Phone. B&B £65 to £108. Baby facilities (*The Which? Guide to Good Hotels*)

Net prices *in the details at the end of an entry indicates that the prices given on a menu and on a bill are inclusive of VAT and service charge, and that this practice is clearly stated on menu and bill.*

▲ Cavendish Hotel, Gallery Restaurant 🍴

Church Lane, Baslow DE45 1SP
TEL: (01246) 582311   FAX: (01246) 582312   COOKING 3
EMAIL: info@cavendish-hotel.net   MODERN EUROPEAN
WEBSITE: www.cavendish-hotel.net   £45–£68

High ceilings, oil paintings galore, and large floral displays provide an impressive backdrop for Chris Allison's contemporary cooking. He seems good-natured, happy to alter dishes to suit individual tastes, although there is plenty that appeals off the peg – from a starter of aromatic confit of belly pork with braised wild rice, to seared dived scallops with hot fennel coleslaw and lobster oil as a main course. Treatments are straightforward but far from mundane: viz. a baked gâteau of goats' cheese with cardamom butter sauce, or a trio of salmon (Redwood smoked; fresh, encased in a crisp tempura batter; and a mix of fresh and smoked combined with herbs and potted in butter). Accurate timing shows in, for example, a suprême of pan-roast halibut, simply but effectively served on a bed of crisp rösti and shredded leeks, surrounded by a pea purée, with a drizzle of light, grain mustard sauce. Desserts have included a honey and walnut variation on bread-and-butter pudding, with a honey ice cream. 'Breads are worth a mention', and 'staff remain the nicest of any hotel we have stayed in'. Wines, arranged by style, are reasonably priced, and the bin ends are always worth a look. House French Chardonnay and Merlot are £13.95.

CHEF: Chris Allison   PROPRIETOR: Eric Marsh   OPEN: all week 12 to 2, 6 to 10   MEALS: alc (main courses £17 to £20)   SERVICE: not inc   CARDS: Amex, Delta, Diners, MasterCard, Switch, Visa DETAILS: 50 seats. Private parties: 50 main room, 16 private room. Car park. Children's helpings. No smoking. Occasional music   ACCOMMODATION: 23 rooms, all with bath/shower. TV. Phone. Room only £100 to £160. Fishing (*The Which? Guide to Good Hotels*)

▲ Fischer's Baslow Hall 🍷 🍴

Calver Road, Baslow DE45 1RR
TEL: (01246) 583259   FAX: (01246) 583818   COOKING 7
EMAIL: m.s@fischers-baslowhall.co.uk   MODERN EUROPEAN
WEBSITE: www.fischers-baslowhall.co.uk   £38–£94

Set back from the road in a stand of mature trees, Baslow is an inviting and comfortable place, where mullioned windows and weathered stone conspire to make it look older than its 97 years. There have been changes over the past 12 months: the dining room has been redecorated, with a lighter feel, and a new head chef has been appointed. Rupert Rowley, in his mid-twenties, lists some prestigious names on his CV (including Raymond Blanc, John Burton-Race and Gordon Ramsay), and the conclusion is that the cooking 'seems to be in safe hands'. Max Fischer has assumed the role of Kitchen Director, and continues day-to-day involvement.

Sourcing of raw materials (helped by a kitchen garden) is taken as seriously as before: a crab risotto with a soupy sauce 'bursting with robust crab flavour', for example, or two cylinders of pink, juicy, roast saddle of lamb accompanied by a panaché of beans (haricot, green, and peeled baby broad beans) in a tomato and thyme jus with 'real depth of flavour'. Luxuries are not allowed to swamp the menus, which consist of a three-course version plus a six-course 'Prestige' offering, and whose prices now match many of London's finest. Tripartite dishes remain a favoured vehicle, including an excellent one of foie gras incorporating sweet-tasting terrine with an intense mango sauce ('a perfect pairing'), a crisp and ungreasy deep-fried beignet, and an accurately pan-fried lobe coated in chopped hazelnuts ('a remarkably successful contrast of texture and flavour').

Desserts are no less impressive, taking in a variation on summer pudding, with bread and fruit compote arranged in layers, simply accompanied by a dollop of crème fraîche, and a passion-fruit soufflé of just the right texture, cooked in a dish coated with grated chocolate. Service may not be notably warm, but it is efficient and knowledgeable. The manageable size of the wine list is another bonus – for example, succinctly summing up Italian whites with three well-priced bottles – but it comes at the cost of depth: there's more to Australia and New Zealand than the Chardonnays and Sauvignons offered here. Bordeaux and Burgundy fare better and show where the list's heart lies. House wines start at £15, or £3.75 a glass.

CHEFS: Max Fischer and Rupert Rowley   PROPRIETORS: Max and Susan Fischer   OPEN: Tue to Sun L 12 to 1.30, Mon to Sat D 7 to 9.30 (Sun D residents only)   CLOSED: 25 and 26 Dec   MEALS: Set L Tue to Sat £20 (2 courses) to £24, Set L Sun £30, Set D Mon to Fri £25 (2 courses) to £30, Set D all week £54 to £64   SERVICE: not inc   CARDS: Amex, Delta, Diners, MasterCard, Switch, Visa   DETAILS: 68 seats. Private parties: 40 main room, 4 to 16 private rooms. Car park. Children's helpings. No children under 12 after 7pm. No smoking. Wheelchair access (not WC). No music. No mobile phones   ACCOMMODATION: 11 rooms, all with bath/shower. TV. Phone. B&B £100 to £180. Baby facilities (*The Which? Guide to Good Hotels*)

BATH Bath & N. E. Somerset   map 2

▲ Bath Priory ⅚✳

Weston Road, Bath BA1 2XT
TEL: (01225) 331922   FAX: (01225) 448276   COOKING 6
EMAIL: bathprioryhotel@compuserve.com   MODERN FRENCH
WEBSITE: www.thebathpriory.coo.uk   £40–£78

The elegant Georgian building struck one visitor as 'the perfect setting for a Hercule Poirot mystery', with its swimming pool looking like the Roman baths, formal garden, and ornate Victorian-style dining room. The food, though, is unmistakably modern, set about with items such as ravioli of rabbit and morels and crab risotto with a basil foam. A big plus is that the cooking is no more elaborate than it needs to be; main materials are kept centre stage, and accompaniments work harmoniously.

Shellfish typically features among first courses, perhaps appearing as caramelised diver caught scallops with creamed leeks and Parmesan crackling, or as roast langoustines with pappardelle, fennel and artichokes (though the latter attracts a supplement). The food comforts, in the shape of roast wood pigeon with truffled creamed potato for example, although clichés are generally conspicuous by their absence, as the kitchen opts for braised shin of veal in port with Savoy cabbage, alongside venison, for its main course meat selection. Vegetarians get their own menu (taking in anything from wild mushroom tart to goat cheese pithiviers), and desserts are indulgent without being too rich:

perhaps vanilla pannacotta with passion-fruit sorbet. Service is 'grand style, but very friendly and helpful', and wines are pretty grand too – between £20 and £30 for some very decent drinking, including a range of Italian and antipodean whites. House wine is £16.

CHEF: Robert Clayton PROPRIETOR: Andrew Brownsword OPEN: all week 12 to 1.45, 7 to 9 (9.30 Fri and Sat) MEALS: Set L £20 (2 courses) to £25, Set D £47.50 SERVICE: not inc CARDS: Amex, Delta, Diners, MasterCard, Switch, Visa DETAILS: 64 seats. Private parties: 64 main room, 6 to 16 private rooms. Car park. Vegetarian meals. Children's helpings. Jacket and tie. No smoking. Wheelchair access (also WC). Occasional music. No mobile phones ACCOMMODATION: 28 rooms, all with bath/shower. TV. Phone. B&B £145 to £400. Rooms for disabled. Baby facilities. Swimming pool (*The Which? Guide to Good Hotels*)

FishWorks ✂

6 Green Street, Bath BA1 2JY	COOKING 3
TEL: (01225) 448707	SEAFOOD
WEBSITE: www.fishworks.co.uk	£33–£61

You can't miss the Green Street entrance: everything, including the awning, is blue, a colour theme continued inside. Downstairs there's a fishmonger and an informal café with counters and stools; upstairs, in two rooms with small wooden tables and chairs, they serve, as one diner put it, 'great fresh fish, simply cooked'. This is the philosophy of the FishWorks group (see entries under Bristol, Christchurch and London), and it strikes a chord with our reporters. Besides the Classic and Shellfish menus, a specials board lists items from the daily landings. Many dishes can be starters or mains, and classic offerings include spaghetti with clams, chilli, garlic and parsley; skate with black butter; or Dartmouth crab salad with tarragon mayonnaise. It says something for the raw materials that 'melt-in-the-mouth-textured and packed-with-flavour' tuna convinced two members of a party that they did like tuna after all. Amongst shellfish expect Palourde clams, River Fowey mussels, Cornish winkles and harbour prawns. Among vegetables (extra) are slow-roast tomatoes with pesto, and fennel, chilli and herb salad. For dessert the usual suspects: lemon tart, crème brûlée, toffee pudding, etc. White wines begin at £12.50, with a handful of reds and a sherry completing the list.

CHEFS: Garry Rosser and Nick Martin PROPRIETOR: FishWorks plc OPEN: Tue to Sat 12 to 3, 6 to 10.30 CLOSED: 25 Dec, Tue after each bank hol Mon MEALS: alc (main courses £9 to £22) SERVICE: not inc CARDS: Amex, Delta, MasterCard, Switch, Visa DETAILS: 52 seats. 16 seats outside. Vegetarian meals. Children's helpings. No smoking. Wheelchair access (not WC). Music. No mobile phones. Air-conditioned

Moody Goose ✂

7A Kingsmead Square, Bath BA1 2AB	
TEL/FAX: (01225) 466688	COOKING 5
EMAIL: enquiries@moody-goose.com	ENGLISH
WEBSITE: www.moody-goose.com	£29–£63

A big blue sign near the Theatre Royal announces this cool, quiet, well-lit basement dining room, with its French watercolours, green slate floor and comfortable seating. Stephen Shore's cooking tends to be intricate ('very Bath' in one estimation) but is founded on generally sound ingredients, some local and seasonal – for example, a game terrine en croûte with home-made piccalilli – and some from further afield: perhaps a parfait of foie gras with celeriac rémoulade and Muscat jelly. West Country materials play a part, not least Cornish seafood, in the form of scallops with parsnip purée, and skate with chargrilled polenta and ratatouille.

Good judgement is evident in, for example, an appetite-enhancing mini quail pie that was 'rich, well flavoured and moist', and innovation extends to a starter of tender squid served with a pannacotta of mint and peppers. Although portion sizes seem to vary, quality is generally high, as in a plate of tiny heaps of belly pork, black pudding and faggot, or a dish of partridge that 'fed me, my husband, and there was some left over'. Among desserts, Bramley apple délices with apple fritters and Somerset cider sorbet ring the regional bell. Set-price meals are considered reasonable value, and the whole is backed up by friendly, helpful and personal service. Wines are well chosen across the board, starting with a page of house recommendations up to £17.50 (£4.20 a glass).

CHEF: Stephen Shore   PROPRIETORS: Stephen and Victoria Shore   OPEN: Mon to Sat 12 to 1.30, 6 to 9.30 (10 Sat)   CLOSED: Christmas, bank hols exc Good Fri   MEALS: alc D (main courses £18 to £20). Set L and D 6 to 7 £13 (2 courses) to £17.50, Set D £25   SERVICE: not inc   CARDS: Amex, Delta, Diners, MasterCard, Switch, Visa   DETAILS: 35 seats. Private parties: 22 main room, 8 private room. Children's helpings. No children under 8. No smoking in dining room, smoking permitted in bar. Music

▲ Queensberry Hotel ♥ ⅝✳

Russel Street, Bath BA1 2QF
TEL: (01225) 447928   FAX: (01225) 446065   COOKING 4
EMAIL: enquiries@bathqueensberry.com   ANGLO-FRENCH-PLUS
WEBSITE: www.bathqueensberry.com   £27–£60

Despite a change of ownership for this hotel in a secluded Georgian terrace, its Olive Tree restaurant is maintaining steady progress under chef Jason Horne. The 'large and handsome' split-level dining room has simple artistic décor with bright foodie prints on mushroom coloured walls, and service is well informed and friendly.

Jason Horne's cooking style has struck more than one reporter as reminiscent of 'the heyday of Elizabeth David' – in other words, 'classical Mediterranean'. So there may be seared scallops with sauté cauliflower and chard in a freshly spiced curried dressing, cream of mushroom soup with crisp croutons, or 'smooth, soft' boudin blanc with Madeira sauce and a confit of prunes and roasted shallots, followed by 'spankingly fresh' baked Cornish hake with squid, chorizo and haricot beans in a buttery red wine sauce, pan-fried beef fillet with oxtail and vegetable broth, or Gressingham duck breast with potato rösti and winter greens. The standard choice of accompaniment is new potatoes or old-fashioned creamy gratin dauphinoise. To finish, a hollowed-out roasted 'queen' pineapple containing a scoop of lime-flavoured vodka sorbet has made a favourable impression.

The wine list offers up plenty of modestly priced easy drinking before pushing into smarter bottles in Burgundy, Bordeaux, the Rhône and Italy. New World wines are well chosen. Six by the glass are £3.75/£4.75.

CHEF: Jason Horne PROPRIETORS: Mr and Mrs Lawrence Beere OPEN: Mon to Sat L 12 to 2, all week D 7 to 10 CLOSED: 4 days Christmas MEALS: alc (main courses £11 to £19). Set L £13.50 (2 courses) to £15.50, Set D Sun to Fri £26 SERVICE: not inc CARDS: Delta, MasterCard, Switch, Visa DETAILS: 65 seats. Private parties: 25 main room. Vegetarian meals. Children's helpings. No smoking. Wheelchair access (also WC). Music. Air-conditioned ACCOMMODATION: 29 rooms, all with bath/shower. TV. Phone. B&B £90 to £225. Rooms for disabled. Baby facilities (*The Which? Guide to Good Hotels*)

▲ Royal Crescent, Pimpernel's ▼ ⚹✳

16 Royal Crescent, Bath BA1 2LS

TEL: (01225) 823333 FAX: (01225) 339401

EMAIL: reservations@royalcrescent.co.uk

WEBSITE: www.royalcrescent.co.uk

COOKING 4

MODERN BRITISH

£40–£85

Turn up at the discreet front door and find yourself ushered into the elegant hallway, then across a pretty garden to the dower house where Pimpernel's is located. 'Victorian country house' is how it struck one visitor, the décor restrained despite murals of trees and a display of tiger lilies, and the tone formal, complete with roast beef wheeled out on a silver trolley. The carte has gone, and lunch and dinner now both offer a set-price meal, liberally sprinkled with the sort of fine materials you might expect for the price: smoked and wild salmon, beef tournedos, scallops, and blue-fin tuna among them.

Oriental leanings seem to have diminished, while classic combinations run from twice-baked goats' cheese soufflé to a tender rump of lamb ('beyond reproach') with a garlicky quenelle of bean purée on top, a glossy, golden lyonnaise potato cake, and a heap of lightly cooked spinach. Although dishes may not always have their hoped-for impact, ingredients are good and technique is generally sound, producing a 'delicate but distinctive' starter of thin, supple ravioli with a generous langoustine filling, and desserts such as a light, wobbly, perfectly risen and intensely flavoured amaretti soufflé. Extras are kept to a minimum (just bread, and chocolates with coffee), and service is efficient and mainly French. An ambitious, food-orientated range of 15 wines by the glass (£4 to £8.50) opens a list that is long on style if a bit too short on value (just three bottles are under £20). The main selection is arranged by wine style, with the really smart bottles reserved for the 'classic' category.

CHEF: Steven Blake PROPRIETOR: Von Essen Hotels OPEN: all week 12.30 to 2, 7 to 10 MEALS: Set L £14 (2 courses) to £25, Set D £35 (vegetarian) to £45 SERVICE: not inc CARDS: Amex, Delta, Diners, MasterCard, Switch, Visa DETAILS: 60 seats. 45 seats outside. Private parties: 40 main room, 40 to 100 private rooms. Car park. Vegetarian meals. Children's helpings. No smoking. Wheelchair access (not WC). Occasional music. Air-conditioned ACCOMMODATION: 45 rooms, all with bath/shower. TV. Phone. Room only £170 to £800. Rooms for disabled. Baby facilities. Swimming pool (*The Which? Guide to Good Hotels*)

If 'vegetarian meals' is noted in the details at the end of an entry, this means that a restaurant routinely lists at least one vegetarian starter and main course on menus. Other restaurants, however, may offer good vegetarian choices if you let them know in advance, so it is worthwhile phoning to enquire.

BATTLE East Sussex
map 3

Pilgrims ✻

1 High Street, Battle TN33 0AE
TEL: (01424) 772314 FAX: (01424) 775950
WEBSITE: www.foodrooms.co.uk

COOKING 2
MODERN EUROPEAN
£17–£52

Sitting literally in the shadow of the abbey, the building that houses the restaurant (as well as 'Food Rooms' for private functions) dates from the 1400s, when it was a rest-house for pilgrims. Enter through the low doorway and make your way through the high, timbered hall to the comfortable dining area with its large, well-spaced, white-clothed tables. The over-elaboration of menus mentioned last year has been pruned, and a useful addition made in an all-day 'Hall Menu' of confidently upmarket tea room, savoury snack and high-tea dishes like spiced garlic herring roes on toast, or warm Belgian chocolate tart. Ingredients come from over a hundred local suppliers, and 10 per cent of profits goes to charity (appropriate in this fine and ancient building that once sheltered pilgrims visiting the abbey over the road). Sound culinary traditions are followed (whole Dover sole meunière), sometimes with adaptations (calf's liver, Hollingrove bacon, red onion mash and crème de cassis). House wines from Languedoc and Bordeaux range from £10.50 to £12.65 (£2.95 to £3.50 a glass); a page of mainly French under-£15 bottles balances some higher-cost, if youngish, classics elsewhere.

CHEF: Glenn Keen PROPRIETORS: Toby and Rebecca Peters OPEN: all week L 12 to 3, Mon to Sat D 7 to 9.30 CLOSED: 25 Dec MEALS: alc (main courses L £6.50 to £18.50, D £10.50 to £19). Set L £14.75 (2 courses) to £19.50. Set D Mon to Thur £14.75 (2 courses) to £19.50. Hall menu and tapas menu available SERVICE: 12.5% (optional), card slips closed CARDS: Amex, MasterCard, Switch, Visa DETAILS: 50 seats. 50 seats outside. Private parties: 70 main room, 14 private room. Vegetarian meals. Children's helpings. No smoking in 1 dining room. Wheelchair access (not WC). No music £5

BEESTON Nottinghamshire
map 5

La Toque

61 Wollaton Road, Beeston NG9 2NG
TEL: (0115) 922 2268 FAX: (0115) 922 7979

COOKING 3
FRENCH
£29–£64

Don't ask why a restaurant so totally French should appear in a Nottingham suburb – just be grateful. Elegant outside, it is warm and intimate inside, where multicultural luxury pervades: foie gras, Parma ham and Cornish lobster are common ingredients on the menu. Humbler materials are not ignored, though appearing with flashy partners – skate with red mullet, rabbit with Agen prunes in a pithiviers with morels, and pigeon with foie gras. First courses such as large scallops complemented in texture and taste by slivers of fried Parma ham and a purée of broad beans, and a bold combination of asparagus soup with sautéed chicken livers, have won praise for imaginative flavouring and accurate timing. Intricate main-course combinations have descriptions running to several lines, and at times a component too far. Puddings are assemblies of classics like crème brûlée with apricot and ginger compote, and orange savarin with a citrus fromage frais sorbet. A lively, good-value wine list looks well beyond France but remains strongest in the traditional power-bases of Burgundy and Bordeaux. Modern vin de pays house wines are £13.50, or £4.50 for a 250ml glass.

CHEF: Mattias Karlsson PROPRIETORS: Norman Oley and Judy Caplin-Naake OPEN: Tue to Fri L 12 to 2, Tue to Sat D 7 to 10.30 CLOSED: first 2 weeks in Aug MEALS: alc (main courses £15.50 to £18.50). Set L £11.95 (2 courses) to £16.95, Set D Tue to Thur £16.95 (2 courses) to £20.95 SERVICE: 10% (optional) CARDS: Amex, Delta, MasterCard, Switch, Visa DETAILS: 40 seats. Private parties: 40 main room. Vegetarian meals. No children under 6. No-smoking area. Wheelchair access (also WC). Music. Air-conditioned (£5)

BERWICK-UPON-TWEED Northumberland **map 11**

▲ No. 1 Sallyport £ **NEW ENTRY**

1 Sallyport, Berwick-upon-Tweed TD15 1EZ
TEL/FAX: (01289) 308827 COOKING **3**
EMAIL: info@1sallyport-bedandbreakfast.com MODERN BRITISH
WEBSITE: www.1sallyport-bedandbreakfast.com £23–£27

Elizabeth Middlemiss's successful and upmarket B&B is back in the pages of the Guide because she is once again offering dinner to non-residents, albeit only on Friday and Saturday evenings thus far. Entered from a quiet, cobbled alley, the hall and dining room have a homely yet surprisingly modern look. You are likely to be seated next to other diners at one of the two large communal tables, and choice is limited to two dishes per course. Her consistently honest and straightforward cooking has produced a starter of tomato and basil soup, full-bodied and slightly sweet, then casseroled duck breast with shallots, sultanas and thyme, the juice successfully setting off the sweet sultanas. Finish with tarte Tatin, or crème caramel with 'dark caramel melting into an excellent cream'; cheeses are in good condition. There is no wine list but bring your own bottle (£1 per person corkage). This is a very personal operation and run with a passion for good food and hospitality.

CHEF/PROPRIETOR: Elizabeth Middlemiss OPEN: Fri and Sat D only 7 to 8 (all week for residents; booking essential for both residents and non-residents) MEALS: Set D £14.95 (2 courses) to £18.25 SERVICE: net prices, card slips closed CARDS: Amex, Delta, MasterCard, Switch, Visa DETAILS: 18 seats. Private parties: 18 main room, 6 to 18 private rooms. No smoking. Occasional music ACCOMMODATION: 3 rooms, all with bath/shower. TV. B&B £60 to £80 (*The Which? Guide to Good Hotels*) (£5)

BIDDENDEN Kent **map 3**

West House **NEW ENTRY**

28 High Street, Biddenden TN27 8AH COOKING **5**
TEL: (01580) 291341 FAX: (01580) 292501 MODERN BRITISH
£31–£43

Part of a terrace of lovely old tile-hung buildings, West House, which opened in the summer of 2002, is a strongly individual place run by a husband and wife. Graham Garrett's experience with Richard Corrigan in London (see entry Lindsay House) may explain a penchant for strong, earthy flavours on the daily-changing menu. Confident, technically assured cooking produces solid consistency – from salted mackerel with pink fir apple potato and beetroot dressing, to poached duck egg with celeriac purée and red wine sauce – with local, seasonal and rare-breed materials a feature.

Menu descriptions are short and crisp, presentation straightforward, flavours clear and contrasts strong: viz. a starter of three good-sized caramelised scallops with a couple of rashers of grilled bacon in a thin pool of creamy cauliflower purée. Other excellent raw materials have been pieces of Kentish Ranger chicken (thigh, wing and breast) surrounded by whole chestnuts and sprouts, plus a few sliced ceps, in a rich and creamy stock-based sauce. Poached pear, richly flavoured with cinnamon yet fresh and fruity, has come with a scoop of vanilla ice cream and a few streaks of vanilla custard. In-house bread is strikingly fresh, butter tastes 'as if churned that very morning', and value for money is considered 'outstanding' for food of this calibre. The only notes of discord concern out-of-character Muzak, and service that hasn't quite matched the kitchen's output. A short list of wines arranged by price (most under £20) starts with vin de pays at £10.95 (£2.95 a glass).

CHEF: Graham Garrett   PROPRIETORS: Graham Garrett and Jackie Hewitt   OPEN: Tue to Fri and Sun L 12 to 2, Tue to Sat D 7 to 10   MEALS: alc L (main courses £12 to £14). Set D £24.50   SERVICE: 10% (optional), card slips closed   CARDS: MasterCard, Switch, Visa   DETAILS: 35 seats. Private parties: 35 main room. Car park. Children's helpings. Wheelchair access (not WC). Music

---

BIRCH VALE Derbyshire   **map 8**

▲ Waltzing Weasel ₷✱

New Mills Road, Birch Vale SK22 1BT
TEL/FAX: (01663) 743402
EMAIL: w-weasel@zen.co.uk   COOKING 1
WEBSITE: www.w-weasel.co.uk   ANGLO-EUROPEAN
on A6015, ½m W of Hayfield   £28–£46

Just outside Hayfield, amid hilly countryside, the whimsically named Waltzing Weasel functions as a pub and a restaurant-with-rooms. The small, formal dining room has polished wooden tables, and windows overlooking an attractive stone terrace and garden. The menu offers a range of simple, gutsy dishes, many of which show an Italian influence. One such is a main-course selection of antipasti, which may include red onion crostini, baked fennel, fried aubergine with tomato and pork with dolcelatte cheese. Other main courses might include the Roman-inspired abbacchio, here straightforward leg of lamb, rather than the baby milk-fed variety, and served with a rather forceful anchovy and garlic sauce. Bread, baked on the premises, is crisp-crusted and springy, and service cheerful. Although some eyebrows have been raised at the menu pricing, most of the 36 wines listed cost less than £20, with house wine starting at £13.85.

CHEF: Tracy Young   PROPRIETORS: Michael and Linda Atkinson   OPEN: all week 12 to 2, 7 to 9   MEALS: alc L (bar food: main courses £8 to £14.50). Set D £23.50 (2 courses) to £27.50   SERVICE: not inc, card slips closed   CARDS: Delta, MasterCard, Switch, Visa   DETAILS: 80 seats. 20 seats outside. Private parties: 35 main room, 12 private room. Car park. Vegetarian meals. Children's helpings. No smoking. Wheelchair access (not WC). No music. No mobile phones. Air-conditioned   ACCOMMODATION: 8 rooms, all with bath/shower. TV. Phone. B&B £45 to £105 (*The Which? Guide to Good Hotels*)

Bank ♥

4 Brindleyplace, Birmingham B1 2JB

TEL: (0121) 633 4466   FAX: (0121) 633 4465   COOKING 2
EMAIL: bankbirmingham@bankrestaurants.com   MODERN EUROPEAN
WEBSITE: www.bankrestaurants.com   £25–£62

Over the canal from the Symphony Hall, Brindleyplace is the hub of Birmingham's restaurant, bar and culture scene. This branch of Bank has a large bar area for drinkers and nibblers, so it's a long walk to an open-plan eating area at the back, overlooking an open deck. Inside, the tables are quite close, so this is no place for a quiet tête-à-tête (and the decibels can mount up, too). The ambitiously long and eclectic carte is a something-for-everyone gambol through French-focused modern European cuisine. An inspector's starter of seared 'Thai' tuna came with chopsticks but without an overload of flavour, although a succeeding Scottish ribeye steak, with a first-class béarnaise sauce and crisp but fluffy chips, restored faith in the kitchen. Timings of meat are not as spot-on as they could be, but there are flashes of fine cooking. A pannacotta that came with a diced-fruit salsa was simple, refreshing and well made. Service is smiley but not always joined-up. The wine list here is briefer than at the original Bank in London, and suffers a little from the reduced options by the glass (five whites but just three reds from £2.90), but the concept is the same: tasty wine from modern producers, fairish prices (though never the cheapest in town), and a supplementary selection of smart bottles for special days.

CHEFS: David Colcombe and Stephen Woods   PROPRIETOR: Bank Restaurant Group   OPEN: Mon to Fri L 12 to 3, D 5.30 to 11, Sat brunch 11.30 to 3, D 5.30 to 11.30, Sun brunch 11.30 to 3.30, D 5 to 10   CLOSED: 1 Jan, 3 May   MEALS: alc (main courses £9.50 to £20). Set L £11.50 (2 courses) to £14, Set D 5/5.30 to 7 and 10 to 11/11.30 £11.50 (2 courses) to £14. Bar and Sat/Sun brunch menus available   SERVICE: 12.5% (optional), card slips closed   CARDS: Amex, Delta, Diners, MasterCard, Switch, Visa   DETAILS: 250 seats. 100 seats outside. Private parties: 350 main room, 16 to 100 private rooms. Vegetarian meals. Children's helpings. No-smoking area. Wheelchair access (also WC). No music. Air-conditioned (£5)

Chung Ying Garden £

117 Thorp Street, Birmingham B5 4AT

TEL: (0121) 666 6622   FAX: (0121) 622 5860   COOKING 2
EMAIL: chungyinggarden@aol.com   CHINESE
WEBSITE: www.chungying.co.uk   £26–£60

At the heart of Birmingham's Chinatown, within walking distance of New Street station and clearly flagged with huge red and silver banners, is this Birmingham stalwart. The large multi-level dining room is smartly decorated, the tables dressed with thick cloths. A larger than usual menu offers numerous banqueting options, and a wide selection of Hong Kong-style Cantonese dishes, beginning with nearly 60 dim sum. Among more unusual offerings are fried frogs' legs with bitter melon, braised fish head with belly pork and bean curd, and sizzling dishes of venison or lamb with ginger and spring onion. Seafood options use the freshest market produce, for dishes such as baked crab with green chilli in black bean sauce, or fried sliced eel, and there are all the usual crowd-pleasers in the way of sweet-and-sours, kung po dishes and the likes of deep-fried crispy shredded beef with vinegar-sharp OK sauce. Well-drilled, amiable service adds to the occasion, and there is a short but serviceable wine list opening with house red and white at £9.50 a bottle, or £11.50 a litre. The elder sibling, Chung Ying (just over the road), hasn't received the same plaudits.

CHEF/PROPRIETOR: Siu Chung Wong   OPEN: all week 12 to 11.30 (10.30 Sun)   CLOSED: 25 Dec
MEALS: alc (main courses £7 to £13). Set L and D £16 (min 2) to £80 (min 5)   SERVICE: not inc, card
slips closed   CARDS: Amex, Delta, Diners, MasterCard, Switch, Visa   DETAILS: 350 seats.
Private parties: 200 main room, 10 to 200 private rooms. Vegetarian meals. Wheelchair access
(also WC). Music. Air-conditioned (£5)

▲ Hotel du Vin & Bistro ▮

25 Church Street, Birmingham B3 2NR
TEL: (0121) 200 0600   FAX: (0121) 236 0889   COOKING 3
EMAIL: reservations@birmingham.hotelduvin.com   MODERN EUROPEAN
WEBSITE: www.hotelduvin.com   £36–£58

Thanks to sympathetic restoration this fine redbrick city centre building retains much of its character. There is a Bubble Bar for aperitifs, a courtyard open to the sky (save for a pigeon net) with a fountain, statues, plants and tables, and a dining room with trademark wooden tables, bare floorboards, and lots of vinous paraphernalia. If the setting is recognisably Hotel du Vin (see also entries in Bristol, Tunbridge Wells, Winchester and Brighton - and coming soon to Harrogate), so too is the style of food, with its broad European sweep from tomato soup with pesto, via ham hock and foie gras terrine, to a well-balanced Gruyère and leek tart made with good pastry, the plate streaked with lines of pesto and balsamic. It plays to the gallery in the shape of Black Angus ribeye steak (with pommes frites and green peppercorn sauce), and corned beef hash with a fried egg and HP sauce, but also turns out nuggets of deep-fried, breadcrumbed sweetbreads with a rémoulade-type sauce. Ice creams and tarts (chocolate, lemon and Bakewell among them) feature among desserts, although a trio of plum goodies comes highly commended.

Hotel du Vin wine lists are packed full of good ideas from around the world. Affordable basics draw you in, but as your eye strays over the page you start to wonder if today might not be the day for a treat, and before you know it you've traded up from a tasty modern Languedoc-Roussillon vin de pays at £15.50 to a 1990 Mas de Daumas Gassac at £105. Nine wines by the glass start at £3.55.

CHEF: Eddie Grey   PROPRIETOR: Hotel du Vin Ltd   OPEN: all week 12 to 2, 6.30 to 10   MEALS: alc
exc Sun L (main courses £14.50 to £17.50). Set L Sun £23.50   SERVICE: not inc   CARDS: Amex,
Delta, Diners, MasterCard, Switch, Visa   DETAILS: 85 seats. 30 seats outside. Private parties: 60
main room, 10 to 25 private rooms. Vegetarian meals. Children's helpings. No cigars/pipes in
dining room. Wheelchair access (also WC). No music   ACCOMMODATION: 66 rooms, all with bath/
shower. TV. Phone. Room only £115 to £395. Rooms for disabled. Baby facilities (*The Which?
Guide to Good Hotels*)

Metro Bar & Grill ☜

73 Cornwall Street, Birmingham B3 2DF	COOKING 2
TEL: (0121) 200 1911 FAX: (0121) 200 1611	MODERN EUROPEAN
WEBSITE: www.themetrobar.co.uk	£25–£56

Set in the business district and occupying the ground floor of what looked to one reporter like a tasteful redbrick office block, this is a smart dual-purpose bar and brasserie. On a Friday lunch the bar 'positively heaves' with suits, but proceed down the curved walkway to find the comparatively quieter split-level dining room with its wood floorboards, mirrored wall and clear view of the busy kitchen. A longish brasserie-type carte (and a set-price deal in the evening) is supplemented by a few fish dishes of the day – perhaps well-timed ('still bouncy') red mullet with pea, mint and asparagus risotto. First courses might include deep-fried squid with a brioche and lemon crust served with almond aïoli, or 'decently made' tomato, fennel and Roquefort tart set on a bed of well-dressed leaves. Main courses run from spit-roast ribeye with chestnut and celeriac mash and rosemary jus, to Moroccan marinated lamb pavé with fig, apricot and lime tabbouleh. Peach infused rice pudding with poached peaches might be one way to finish, or opt for blackberry cheesecake with biscotti. Service is 'pleasant and approachable', and the wine list covers all the usual bases, with house bottles £11.95 and half a dozen by the glass from £2. There are also some (youngish) upmarket Burgundies and ten champagnes.

CHEF: Mathew Knight   PROPRIETORS: Chris Kelly and David Cappendell   OPEN: Mon to Fri L 12 to 2.30, Mon to Sat D 6.30 to 9.30   CLOSED: 25 and 26 Dec, 1 Jan, bank hols   MEALS: alc (main courses £10.50 to £19). Set D £12 (2 courses) to £15. Bar menu available   SERVICE: not inc   CARDS: Amex, Delta, MasterCard, Switch, Visa   DETAILS: 120 seats. Private parties: 200 main room. Vegetarian meals. Wheelchair access (also WC). Music. Air-conditioned

La Toque d'Or

27 Warstone Lane, Hockley,	
Birmingham B18 6JQ	COOKING 4
TEL: (0121) 233 3655 FAX: (0156) 275 4957	FRENCH
WEBSITE: www.latoquedor.co.uk	£30–£62

In the city's rejuvenated jewellery quarter, between two such shops, is this comforting and relaxed dining room, quite Parisian-feeling, with bare brick walls and claret-coloured drapes at stained-glass windows. The strains of Nat King Cole evoked nostalgia at inspection, but Didier Philipot's cooking hasn't stood still. Landais boudin noir is teamed with a sweet/tart combination of beetroot and Cox's apple, while a main-course fillet of daurade (bream) might be confidently and skilfully matched with chorizo, ratte potatoes, black olives and capers, and roast cherry tomatoes dressed in basil. Caramelised Skye scallops are sensitively cooked, timed and seasoned well, and accompanied by asparagus and tomato confit for an early summer lunch starter.

Even in dishes that sound over-elaborate, commendable restraint is shown, so that a 'fragrant and impressive' lovage-scented jus, Cumbrian air-dried ham and morels managed to combine coherently with honey-roasted lamb's sweetbreads. Desserts are simple: maybe toffee soufflé with brandy-laced vanilla ice cream, or a salad of orange segments with gingerbread ice cream and a marmalade coulis. 'Welcoming and hospitable' French service enhances enjoyment, and a short and mostly French wine list is supplemented with a scattering of Italian and southern-hemisphere bottles. House French is £12.90 a bottle, £3.20 a glass.

CHEF: Didier Philipot   PROPRIETOR: SSPG Consulting Ltd   OPEN: Tue to Fri L 12.30 to 1.30, Tue to Sat D 7 to 9.30   CLOSED: 1 week Christmas, 1 week Easter, 2 weeks summer, post-bank-hol Tues   MEALS: Set L £15.50 (2 courses) to £18.50, Set D £24.50   SERVICE: not inc   CARDS: Amex, Delta, MasterCard, Switch, Visa   DETAILS: 32 seats. Private parties: 40 main room. Vegetarian meals. Children's helpings. Wheelchair access (also WC). Music. Air-conditioned

BISHOP'S WALTHAM Hampshire   map 2

Restaurant on the Square

The Square, Bishop's Waltham SO32 1AR	COOKING 4
TEL: (01489) 891515 FAX: (01489) 896928	FRENCH
EMAIL: lunch@therestaurantonthesquare.com	£25–£83

There have been some changes in the kitchen since the 2003 edition of the Guide, but the restaurant continues to shine in the capable hands of new chef Michael Smith. Set in a former bank, it is a very handsome building overlooking the town square (actually more of a widening of the street than a true square), and according to a first-time visitor 'the ambience is delightful'; the main dining area is cool, minimalist and very smart, with spacious tables and high-backed chairs.

'Adventurous but not pretentious' is how a reporter described the food on the plate. Crab salad with lemon and mint may comprise three oval mounds of green-flecked crab set round a graceful little sparkling-fresh salad. A well-timed fillet of beef could be accompanied by that dinner party standby of yore, duchesse potatoes, and roast rump of tender lamb with tarragon jus has been well received. For afters, cheeses are served with knowledge and style by the staff, while sweets might take in nectarine tarte Tatin (cooked to order) with honey-and-spice ice cream, or white chocolate cheesecake with blueberry sauce. Classical Europe dominates the wine list, but there are New World goodies too, especially from South Africa. Prices start at £13.50 and six come by the glass from £4 to £5.

CHEF: Michael Smith   PROPRIETOR: Maine Castle Ltd   OPEN: all week L 12 to 2.30 (4 Sun), Mon to Sat D 7 to 9.30   CLOSED: 25 Dec to 2 Jan, Sun and Mon Jul to Aug   MEALS: alc D only (main courses £12.50 to £27.50). Set L £9.95 (2 courses) to £12.95   SERVICE: 12.5% (optional), card slips closed   CARDS: Amex, Delta, Diners, MasterCard, Switch, Visa   DETAILS: 50 seats. Private parties: 35 main room, 4 to 20 private rooms. Vegetarian meals. Children's helpings. No smoking in 1 dining room. Wheelchair access (not WC). Music £5

£   *means that it is possible to have a three-course meal, including coffee, half a bottle of house wine and service for £30 or less per person, at any time the restaurant is open, i.e. at dinner as well as lunch. It may be possible to spend considerably more than this, but by choosing carefully you should find £30 or less achievable.*

BISPHAM GREEN Lancashire   map 8

Eagle & Child 🍴 £

Malt Kiln Lane, Bispham Green L40 3SG
TEL: (01257) 462297   FAX: (01257) 464718
from M6 junction 27 take A5209 over Parbold   COOKING 1
Hill, turn right on B5246, take fourth left   MODERN EUROPEAN
signposted Bispham Green; pub is ½m on right   £25–£37

The atmosphere might be typical English country pub – scrubbed wooden tables and assorted chairs, beams, brass and country scenes aplenty – but the food offers some interesting twists and turns in addition to more predictable dishes. The specials board is where most interest lies, listing starters such as fillet of grey mullet with Japanese salad, honey and soy; or smoked chicken with tomato with mascarpone penne. Good Lancashire produce can make an appearance in the form of breast of Goosnargh duck with cep purée and celeriac; or fillet of salmon with asparagus and Morecambe bay shrimps. Puds too show some ambition with a 'well-made' crème brûlée, or an 'intense' chocolate tart. Service is friendly and relaxed. A 30-strong wine list is very reasonably priced, with house wine kicking off the list at £10 (£1.75 glass)

CHEFS: Neil McKevitt and Sarah Hunt   PROPRIETOR: Bispham Green Brewery Co   OPEN: Mon to Sat 12 to 2, 6 to 8.30 (9 Fri and Sat), Sun 12 to 8.30   CLOSED: 25 Dec evening   MEALS: alc (main courses £6.50 to £12.50)   SERVICE: not inc, card slips closed   CARDS: Delta, MasterCard, Switch, Visa   DETAILS: 150 seats. 45 seats outside. Private parties: 70 main room, 10 to 50 private rooms. Car park. Vegetarian meals. Children's helpings. No smoking in 1 dining room. Music

BLACKPOOL Lancashire   map 8

Kwizeen £   **NEW ENTRY**

47–49 King Street, Blackpool FY1 3EJ   COOKING 2
TEL: (01253) 290045   MODERN EUROPEAN
WEBSITE: www.kwizeen.co.uk   £18–£41

'At last Blackpool has a consistently good restaurant with a chef who doesn't cut corners – and it's affordable' – we can even forgive them the jokey name (just). Occupying two former shops, Kwizeen has a strident pink and blue façade, but inside, walls are plain cream with large wooden effigies of cutlery. Bare floorboards, wrought-iron chairs and a wooden-topped bar make a bright, fashionable, if severe, interior. Bold, clever food features local ingredients, and Marco Calle-Calatayud is not afraid of flavours: venison in chocolate and chilli sauce, as well as veal sweetbreads and 'superb' rosemary-scented shortbread have won particular praise. Starters – be warned, portions are generous – might include a frothy cappuccino of wild mushroom soup, or Morecambe Bay shrimps with garlic served warm in a crisp Parmesan cheese basket. To follow, maybe fillet of sea bass with a 'particularly well-judged' ginger butter sauce, or crispy duck breast with a mushroom herb crumble, port sauce and a swirl of mashed potato. One couple would have preferred their glazed lime tart with a jot more sugar, but were impressed by thin, crispy strawberry pancakes with a delightful basil ice cream in a tuile basket. A compact bistro wine list has some decent bottles and reliable house Californians at £9.50

CHEF: Marco Calle-Calatayud   PROPRIETORS: Marco Calle-Calatayud and Tony Beswick   OPEN: Mon to Fri L 12 to 1.30, Mon to Sat D 6 to 9.30   CLOSED: 20 Feb to 7 Mar   MEALS: alc (main courses £10 to £20). Set L £5.95 (2 courses)   SERVICE: not inc   CARDS: Delta, MasterCard, Switch, Visa   DETAILS: 40 seats. Private parties: 40 private room. Vegetarian meals. No cigars/ pipes. Music. No mobile phones

BLAKENEY Norfolk   map 6

▲ White Horse Hotel ✴ £

4 High Street, Blakeney NR25 7AL
TEL: (01263) 740574   FAX: (01263) 741339
WEBSITE: www.blakeneywhitehorse.co.uk   COOKING 1
off A149 between Wells-next-the-Sea and   MODERN BRITISH-PLUS
Sheringham   £30–£51

'A lot of sky for your money here,' noted one visitor impressed by the coastal vistas and ample bird life. Beyond the pub's informal bars and sitting areas is a quiet, relaxed dining room – brick, flint and plaster painted bright yellow – where a wide-ranging menu might start with ham hock and Puy lentil salad, or grilled smoked salmon on aubergine salsa. Most fish is grilled – from sea bass, via red mullet, to halibut topped with Welsh rarebit – and ribeye steak gets equally straightforward treatment and a roast beef tomato; Roquefort polenta with creamy leeks and walnuts may be a vegetarian option. Local supplies include shellfish, asparagus, soft fruit and game, and desserts range from refreshing passion-fruit sorbet to comforting treacle tart, or rich chocolate mousse. Most wines on the varied Adnams list stay obligingly below £20, with prices starting at £11.95.

CHEFS: Chris Hyde and Peter Thorogate   PROPRIETORS: Daniel Rees and Sue Catt   OPEN: Tue to Sun D 7 to 9   CLOSED: 2nd/3rd weeks Jan   MEALS: alc (main courses £9 to £17). Bar menu available L and D all week   SERVICE: not inc   CARDS: Amex, Delta, MasterCard, Switch, Visa   DETAILS: 36 seats. Private parties: 36 main room. Car park. Vegetarian meals. Children's helpings. No smoking. Wheelchair access (not WC). Occasional music. No mobile phones   ACCOMMODATION: 10 rooms, all with bath/shower. TV. Phone. B&B £30 to £90   £5

BOLTON ABBEY North Yorkshire   map 9

▲ Devonshire Arms, Burlington Restaurant ▮ ✴

Bolton Abbey BD23 6AJ
TEL: (01756) 710441   FAX: (01756) 710564
EMAIL: reservations@thedevonshirearms.co.uk   COOKING 6
WEBSITE: www.devonshirehotels.co.uk   MODERN BRITISH
at junction of A59 and B6160, 5m NW of Ilkley   £38–£82

Originally built in the seventeenth century as a coaching inn, the Devonshire Arms is now a grand country-house hotel. Owned by successive Dukes of Devonshire since 1753, it sits in the heart of the Wharfedale countryside, with its woods, moors and River Wharfe. Beautiful flower displays and lit candelabra set the stage in the salmon pink-toned dining room, in which antique polished tables are immaculately set with sparkling cutlery and glassware. Service, from smartly dressed servers in black suits, is relaxed and professional.

A great deal of effort goes into the preparation of dishes, and each course is complemented by a small appetiser such as ham hock terrine wrapped in bacon, or pumpkin and Gruyère soup. Seasonal and locally sourced produce is evident in a pressing of game – from the estate – with sweet pickled vegetables on a carpaccio of figs; alternatively slices of lightly cooked seared foie gras come set on plump langoustines and well-made rösti. Main dishes that impressed at inspection were fillet of moist royal dourade, the skin nicely crisp, resting on crab tortellini and accented by white asparagus and cubes of red pepper and sauté potatoes and tender milk-fed veal layered with foie gras and spinach. Desserts, such as a deeply flavoursome warm bitter chocolate fondant with pistachio ice cream, or royal Tokaj jelly and rhubarb, are out of the top drawer.

The Devonshire Arms had to pay £5.45 postage to send us their wine list – a weighty tome indeed, and filed in a ring binder to allow weekly updates. Bordeaux is its chief passion, with vintage after vintage of first growths going back to 1900 and invariably hitting the great 1961 vintage. Burgundy shows similar depth and the Rhône and Italian reds continue in the same vein. In California trophy hunters can goggle at the ultra-rare Screaming Eagle – five vintages of it starting at £1,650. At the other end of the scale are 28 house wines under £20. Ten by the glass span a broad range (£4.25 to £17.75).

CHEF: Michael Wignall   PROPRIETORS: the Duke and Duchess of Devonshire   OPEN: Sun L 12 to 2, all week D 7 to 9.30   MEALS: Set L Sun £27.50, Set D £55   SERVICE: not inc, card slips closed CARDS: Amex, Delta, Diners, MasterCard, Switch, Visa   DETAILS: 60 seats. Private parties: 90 main room, 6 to 30 private rooms. Car park. Vegetarian meals. Children's helpings. No smoking. Wheelchair access (also WC). Occasional music   ACCOMMODATION: 41 rooms, all with bath/ shower. TV. Phone. B&B £150 to £200. Rooms for disabled. Baby facilities. Swimming pool. Fishing (*The Which? Guide to Good Hotels*)

BOROUGHBRIDGE   North Yorkshire   map 9

Dining Room ▼ ✕

20 St James's Square, Boroughbridge YO51 9AR   COOKING 4
TEL/FAX: (01423) 326426   MODERN BRITISH
                                                                   £27–£46

'A lovely place that adds up to more than the sum of its parts,' is how one reporter summed up a visit to the Dining Room. The house, set in Boroughbridge's Georgian main square (and entered via an alleyway at the side), has an air of luxury within: white-and-navy décor in the spacious dining room sets off a modern, blond-wood servery buffet and pale tall-backed dining chairs. Midweek (à la carte) lunches are reservations-only; dinners are two-/ three-course affairs, with five or six choices per course.

An ordinary-sounding roast tomato and red pepper soup has impressed with assertive flavours, accurate seasoning and quality ingredients, while well-reported main courses have included fried breast and thigh of guinea fowl sauced with port and wild mushrooms, and tender roast duck confit atop a slice of black pudding with roast apple and a Calvados-laced stock reduction. One diner (who feels Chris Astley's brûlées rival any he has tasted in France) recommends the chocolate soufflé: 'What's 15 minutes [wait] for something so delicious?' Or try Pontefract cake ice cream with a compote of rhubarb. Attentive service adds to the sense of comfort. The smartly presented wine list opens with eight by the glass (£3.20 to £5.70), and 13 house wines by the bottle start at £12.50. The main selection is overwhelmingly from France and the New World, and the more expensive bottles are well chosen.

CHEF: Christopher Astley   PROPRIETORS: Christopher and Lisa Astley   OPEN: Wed to Fri (reservations only) and Sun L 12 to 2, Tue to Sat D 7 to 9.30   CLOSED: 25 Dec, bank hols, 1 to 25 July   MEALS: alc L (main courses £8.50 to £14). Set D £19.95 (2 courses) to £26   SERVICE: not inc, card slips closed   CARDS: Delta, MasterCard, Switch, Visa   DETAILS: 30 seats. Private parties: 35 main room. Vegetarian meals. Children's helpings. No smoking in 1 dining room. Wheelchair access (not WC). Music. No mobile phones £5

BOUGHTON LEES Kent   map 3

▲ Eastwell Manor ⁵✳   NEW ENTRY

Eastwell Park, Boughton Lees TN25 4HR
TEL: (01233) 213000   FAX: (01233) 635530
EMAIL: eastwell@marstonhotels.com   COOKING 3
WEBSITE: www.eastwellmanor.co.uk   ANGLO-FRENCH
on A251, 3m N of Ashford   £28–£76

Eastwell, which appeared temporarily as a Round-up entry in last year's Guide following a change of chef, is now restored to the main listings with the arrival in August 2002 of Neil Wiggins. Few Home Counties venues make quite such an imposing backdrop for a chef's talents: a long sheep-lined drive, a flagstone courtyard, and then a vision of oak-panelled magnificence within.

The white linen and silver candelabra in the dining room set the tone for the classical style of country-hotel cooking that Eastwell plies. A slice of chicken and foie gras terrine with a toasted brioche and pear chutney, bound in streaky bacon, is as luxurious – and as balanced on the palate – as one hopes, and raw spring onion adds textural contrast to the tomato butter sauce that supports a well-made fishcake of smoked haddock. Loin of venison benefits from the sweetening presence of a gratin of beetroot and a port sauce, while a fillet of salmon is balanced on a tower of crushed ratte potatoes and accompanied by baby artichoke hearts and diced tomato. Much care is devoted to making you feel indulged at dessert stage, in the form of crisp-topped rice pudding brûlée garnished with fruit and a gingerbread biscuit, or of the 'superb, bitter and rich' chocolate tart with clotted cream enjoyed by an inspector. The wine list is in keeping with the setting, in terms of length and prices. Individual growers within each section are singled out for profiling, but the main business is in France. Turn to the back for the house wines, which run from £14 to £37.

CHEF: Neil Wiggins   PROPRIETOR: T. Parrett   OPEN: all week 12.30 to 2.30, 7 to 9.30   MEALS: alc (main courses £20.50 to £28.50). Set L £10 (2 courses) to £15, Set D £35. Bar menu available   SERVICE: not inc, card slips closed   CARDS: Amex, Delta, Diners, MasterCard, Switch, Visa   DETAILS: 90 seats. 30 seats outside. Private parties: 90 main room, 5 to 90 private rooms. Car park. Vegetarian meals. Children's helpings. No smoking. Wheelchair access (not WC). Music. No mobile phones   ACCOMMODATION: 62 rooms, all with bath/shower. TV. Phone. B&B £200 to £355. Rooms for disabled. Baby facilities. Swimming pool (*The Which? Guide to Good Hotels*)

▲ Linthwaite House 🍴

Crook Road, Bowness-on-Windermere LA23 3JA
TEL: (015394) 88600   FAX: (015394) 88601
EMAIL: admin@linthwaite.com
WEBSITE: www.linthwaite.com   COOKING 5
off B5284, ¾m S of Bowness, near Windermere   MODERN BRITISH
golf club   £31–£64

The hotel (built as a private house in 1900) is in a great position overlooking
Lake Windermere. Spacious, well upholstered and properly cared for, it has two
candlelit dining rooms: 'smart yet not formal' is how the style struck one visitor.
A standard three-course format becomes four at dinner thanks to an
intermediate soup course, such as pea and mint. The approach, though, is both
serious and professional without being stuffy, and among 'eminently choosable'
dishes might be red mullet escabèche or Lune Valley lamb with fondant potato
and black pudding. Good materials, combined with skill and confidence in the
cooking make for enjoyable and assured results: perhaps a light pithiviers pastry
case filled with delicately flavoured goats' cheese and pieces of soft pear, sitting
on truffle-spiked celeriac rémoulade and served with a nutty dressing. Tried and
tested combinations take in a tender and impressively timed venison fillet, with
a simple stock-based reduction, and a skinless Goosnargh chicken breast,
covered in a creamy sauce and served with mushrooms and rösti.

Results are consistently good across the board: an individual apple tart made
with first-class shortcrust pastry comes with a frothy crème anglaise and a rum
and raisin ice cream. Service is practised and well paced, and the wine list is
user-friendly, although prices tend to be high. Vina Carmen Chardonnay
(£16.50) and Cabernet Sauvignon (£17.95) from Chile are among half a dozen
house wines available in five measures – 125ml to 75cl.

CHEF: Andy Nicholson   PROPRIETOR: Mike Bevans   OPEN: all week 12.30 to 1.30, 7 to 9   MEALS:
alc (main courses £6.50 to £15). Set L Mon to Sat £13.50, Set L Sun £17.95, Set D £42 (4
courses). Light L menu available Mon to Sat   SERVICE: not inc, card slips closed   CARDS: Amex,
Delta, Diners, MasterCard, Switch, Visa   DETAILS: 60 seats. 20 seats outside. Private parties: 40
main room, 16 to 40 private rooms. Car park. Vegetarian meals. Children's helpings. No children
under 7 after 7pm. No smoking. Wheelchair access (also WC). Music. No mobile phones
ACCOMMODATION: 26 rooms, all with bath/shower. TV. Phone. B&B £94 to £286. Rooms for
disabled. Baby facilities. Fishing (The Which? Guide to Good Hotels) £5

Porthole Eating House 🍷 🍴

3 Ash Street, Bowness-on-
Windermere LA23 3EB
TEL: (015394) 42793   FAX: (015394) 88675   COOKING 4
EMAIL: gianni@porthole.fsworld.co.uk   ANGLO-ITALIAN
WEBSITE: www.porthole.fsworld.co.uk   £22–£57

Hospitality is a plus at this long-standing Bowness fixture, thanks to the warmth
of the Bertons (mother and daughter out front), who create a refreshingly
welcome feel. Chef Andy Fairchild was away for six months, but is now back at

the stoves. Cooking – served against a backdrop of dark wooden posts, a ship's wheel, a real fire, lacquered red ceilings, and various items of bric-à-brac – is honest and straightforward. If the menu sounds old-fashioned – with breadcrumbed scampi, Wiener schnitzel and prawn cocktail – there is skill underpinning it. A fine wild mushroom risotto (something not so often found) impressed one couple, and meaty, home-made beef and mustard sausages are recommended too, served with pumpkin and root vegetables. Walkers should get their exercise in first – the large portions might make it a struggle afterwards. Simple grills (Dover sole or fillet steak) come with buttery sauces, all the better to partner a fine bottle of wine, and desserts run from tiramisù to orange Positano.

The wine list is long and strong, with an exceptional range from Germany in particular. Prices are good, mature vintages abundant, and, under £20 or over, you're spoilt for choice. Allow time to study its pages, clearly signposted by country and region; dessert wines are tucked among the main selections.

CHEFS: Andy Fairchild and Gianni Berton   PROPRIETORS: Gianni and Judy Berton   OPEN: Thurs, Fri and Sun L 12 to 2, Wed to Mon D 6.30 to 10.30   MEALS: alc (main courses L £7 to £11, D £11 to £17). Set L £15   SERVICE: not inc, card slips closed   CARDS: Amex, Delta, Diners, MasterCard, Switch, Visa   DETAILS: 40 seats. 25 seats outside. Private parties: 20 main room, 20 to 40 private rooms. Vegetarian meals. No smoking in dining room; permitted in lounge, bar upstairs and patio. Music

BRADFORD West Yorkshire   map 8

Akbars ⚡✳ £

1276 Leeds Road, Thornbury, Bradford BD3 8LF	COOKING 2
TEL: (01274) 773311 FAX: (01274) 785760	INDIAN
WEBSITE: www.akbars.co.uk	£17–£36

Akbars may bill itself as an 'oriental restaurant,' but it's the food of northern India and Pakistan that attracts diners, plus the 'terrific value for money'. This is honest cooking with a few gimmicky flourishes – these extend to the interior, which boasts a glitter ball and faux-marble flooring (one room even has a ceiling done up in brightly coloured fabric to look like a tent). Good-quality naan breads are brought to tables suspended on curious metal frames. Spicing is 'fresh and distinctive' and there's a sizeable range of vegetarian dishes as well as meaty standbys such as dansak, korma and dopiaza, all available with the customer's choice of protein. Balti dishes abound and some interesting ones are found under 'chef's specialities' – tu-caseet, spring chicken with prawns and coriander, for instance. Service is super-efficient (not always easy with crowds this large). House wine sells for £7.95 a bottle. A second branch is located at 15 Eastgate, Leeds; tel: (0113) 245 6566.

CHEF: Talab Hussain   PROPRIETOR: Shabir Hussein   OPEN: Sun all day 1 to 12, all week D 5 to 12   MEALS: alc (main courses £5 to £9). Set D £10.95 (2 courses) to £22.95   SERVICE: not inc   CARDS: none   DETAILS: 270 seats. Private parties: 50 main room. Car park. Vegetarian meals. Children's helpings. No smoking in dining room. Wheelchair access (not WC). Music. Air-conditioned

BRAMPTON Cambridgeshire   map 6

▲ Grange Hotel ▮ ✳

115 High Street, Brampton PE28 4RA
TEL: (01480) 459516 FAX: (01480) 459391
EMAIL: nsteiger@grangehotelbrampton.com
WEBSITE: www.grangehotelbrampton.com

COOKING **2**
MODERN EUROPEAN
£28–£50

Behind the squarish red-brick façade of Nick and Susanna Steiger's Georgian hotel situated at one end of Brampton's meandering High Street, there's a homely atmosphere and some ambitious cooking. A blanquette of well-seared scallops and crisp young asparagus on a bed of sliced Jersey Royals has made a pleasant starter, while among main courses a decent fillet of beef with a tarragon and walnut crust was accompanied by a well-made tarragon and mushroom sauce, or there may be fillet of sea bass with vegetable tagliatelle and new potatoes. Pudding choices may take in peach soup with thyme baked Alaska – the latter a creamy peach ice inside a well-browned meringue – or chocolate tart with orange and Cointreau curd. Service is welcoming and efficient. Top-quality wines and enjoyable gluggers at well under £20 form a happy combination of deft choices and generous prices. House basics are £11.50 and 13 by the glass are £2.10 to £2.75.

CHEFS: Mark Caffrey and Nick Steiger PROPRIETORS: Nick and Susanna Steiger OPEN: all week L 12 to 2 (2.30 Sun), Mon to Sat D 6.30 to 9.30 MEALS: alc (main courses £8.50 to £17). Bar menu available SERVICE: not inc CARDS: Amex, Delta, MasterCard, Switch, Visa DETAILS: 38 seats. Private parties: 38 main room, 2 to 16 private rooms. Car park. Vegetarian meals. Children's helpings. No smoking. Wheelchair access (not WC). No music ACCOMMODATION: 7 rooms, all with bath/shower. TV. Phone. B&B £60 to £90. Baby facilities (£5)

BRAMPTON Cumbria   map 10

▲ Farlam Hall

Brampton CA8 2NG
TEL: (01697) 746234 FAX: (01697) 746683
EMAIL: farlamhall@dial.pipex.com
WEBSITE: www.farlamhall.co.uk
on A689, 2½m SE of Brampton (not at
Farlam village)

COOKING **3**
MODERN ENGLISH COUNTRY-HOUSE
£44–£55

The manor here dates back to Elizabethan times, but the present Farlam Hall, creeper-clad and set amid landscaped gardens, ornamental lake and stream, is predominantly Victorian. Spacious and relaxing lounges with open fires, and a blue and gold dining room, all sumptuously decorated and furnished, provide a suitable venue for Barry Quinion's English country-house cooking. On a busy Saturday night our inspector reported a house-party atmosphere and service 'with a swing'. The five-course menu is sensibly limited to three starters and mains, the latter typically encompassing seasonal poultry/game, a meat and a fish option. Start, perhaps, with watercress and pear soup, followed by a refreshing sorbet. Roast rack of local lamb comes with garlic and rosemary resting on a mound of good mashed potatoes surrounded by a lamb jus with roasted shallots, and tender boned Lancashire quail is filled with chicken mousseline. A well-made lemon tart with strawberry coulis, and pannacotta with stewed plums, have both been enjoyed. A straightforward wine list starts at £13.75 for house Chilean and Australian, then ranges the world, offering choice below £20 and above.

CHEFS: Barry Quinion and Martin Langford   PROPRIETORS: the Quinion and Stevenson families   OPEN: all week D only 8 to 8.30   CLOSED: 25 to 30 Dec   MEALS: Set D Sun to Fri £33.50, Set D Sat £34.50   SERVICE: not inc, card slips closed   CARDS: MasterCard, Switch, Visa   DETAILS: 40 seats. Private parties: 24 main room. Car park. No children under 5. No cigars/pipes. Wheelchair access (not WC). No music. No mobile phones   ACCOMMODATION: 12 rooms, all with bath/shower. TV. Phone. D,B&B £130 to £270. No children under 5 (*The Which? Guide to Good Hotels*)

BRAY Berkshire　　　　　　　　　　　　　　　　　　　　　　　　**map 3**

Fat Duck 🍷 ✳

High Street, Bray SL6 2AQ　　　　　　　　　　　　　　　COOKING **9**
TEL: (01628) 580333　FAX: (01628) 776188　　　　　MODERN EUROPEAN
WEBSITE: www.thefatduck.co.uk　　　　　　　　　　　　　**£48–£118**

Bray is a well-groomed village with a pretty church, a couple of pubs, and two world-class restaurants, one of them this unassuming, painted brick house on a bend. It looks old, with its low, beamed ceiling, but the modernisation is tasteful, with big abstract oil paintings and well-spaced, smartly set tables producing a calm and soothing effect. Pretty well everything else, though, is fireworks. 'Fantastic, stunning' is how the succession of dishes can appear. They are based around a three-course format but with many extras thrown in, and there is an 11-course tasting menu that comes in for unstinting praise.

There is a large element of fun involved – space dust in a chocolate pudding, bacon and egg ice cream, smoky bacon- and tobacco-flavoured petits fours – and dishes can appear 'bizarre in the extreme', taking in snail porridge, or cauliflower risotto with chocolate jelly. 'One item was served by the waitress into our mouths on a teaspoon,' reported one visitor. But the dynamism and energy are not just for show: in fact, the cooking is 'original and innovative without being precious or foolishly experimental', and is firmly embedded in sound culinary judgement.

Everything tastes 'clean and pure' – mussels in a popcorn sauce served with hake 'tasted like they went from sea to sauce within seconds' – and any experimentation is carried out well before dishes are allowed into the dining room, so what we experience is minutely considered. None more so than a small, carefully assembled tower based around a tranche of melting foie gras, the whole dish pervaded by the essence of the sea, thanks to its marinated ceviche-style salmon, its oyster vinaigrette, and its topping of crisp, flavour-packed crab biscuits: a dish whose flavours and textures combined complexity and power.

Slow cooking at low temperature may be controversial – there is no external caramelisation of meat, so no searing or brown crust to contrast with the interior - as in a saddle of lamb, pink outside as well as in, with 'excellent flavour', topped with a piece of thin, crisp, dry fat and served with cubes of lambs' tongues, a luscious and comforting onion purée, and a rich, intense, but not overly reduced sauce. The sheer consistency is impressive, too, from perfectly roast scallops with oloroso jelly, to a first-class piece of lightly bouncy veal sweetbread (salt-crusted, cooked in a bag with hay, and dusted with pollen), combined with salty-sweet cockles and a deep-flavoured stock-based sauce.

'Extras' are no mere fillers; rather, each is an adventure in itself: a frothy, gently sharp palate cleanser of lime and green tea foam; a thin, translucent, red pepper lollipop; and a grain mustard ice cream around which is poured a red cabbage 'gazpacho'. Most impressive of all is a glass layered with dense green pea purée, a clear, rich, intense quail jelly, and a langoustine cream. Desserts are no less fascinating, having produced an ethereally light lychee and mango bavarois, paired with a richly flavoured blackberry sorbet, the plate slicked with a bright yellow purée of mango and Douglas fir.

Bread, perhaps surprisingly, is a pleasantly simple, unfussy, straight-up choice of brown or white. Staff are attentive without being intrusive, service is friendly, helpful, knowledgeable, considerate, and inspires confidence, and, as to value, 'we were still smiling even after the hefty bill'. Wines are not cheap, but you get good quality for your money and £20 or so will buy some appealing South African whites, good reds from Bergerac and the south of France and an introduction to the excellent ranges from Alsace and the Loire. Bordeaux and Burgundy and leading Italians appear in their full magnificence and California and Australia also pull out the stops, but the list searches out less well-known regions too, like Austria and the Savoie. An exciting range is offered by the glass (£5 to £13.50), and an aperitif or dessert sherry is probably obligatory given the wonderful selection of 25 by the glass.

CHEF/PROPRIETOR: Heston Blumenthal   OPEN: Tue to Sun L 12 to 2.30 (3 Sat, 3.30 Sun), Tue to Sat D 7 to 9.30 (10 Fri and Sat)   CLOSED: 22 Dec to 5 Jan   MEALS: Set L £29.75, Set D £60, Set L and D tasting menu £75 (whole table)   SERVICE: 12.5%, card slips closed   CARDS: Amex, Delta, Diners, MasterCard, Switch, Visa   DETAILS: 50 seats. Private parties: 50 main room. Children's helpings. No smoking. No music

Riverside Brasserie ▼

Bray Marina, Monkey Island Lane, Bray SL6 2EB
TEL: (01628) 780553   FAX: (01628) 674 312

COOKING 6
MODERN EUROPEAN
£37–£54

The simple white building in Bray marina also functions as a pit stop for boats on the Thames, but the informal atmosphere of the small, dark wood-panelled dining room and tiny open-plan kitchen area hits the right note. And on fine days, tables are set outside under blue parasols by the river.

Though there are visible influences of co-owner Heston Blumenthal's style (see Fat Duck, above), this is not so much pushing boundaries as relaxing into a New World Order - chips are cooked three times, meat is cooked long and slow. Dishes range from the refined and sophisticated (chicken liver and foie gras mousse) to more rustic (brandade with fried onions, or lyonnaise sausages with choucroute and pommes purée). Among highlights of a recent inspection meal were 'thin but flavourful' fish soup with rouille, Gruyère and croûtons, piquillo peppers wittily presented with filo pastry sombreros and stuffed with marinated mackerel – an 'unexpected but most successful combination' – and 'meltingly soft' slow-cooked pork belly with celeriac two ways: an ultra-creamy roasted purée and a remoulade. The Blumenthal touch is most apparent in desserts such as apple crumble: 'a good version with reassuringly tart apples and a playful addition of space dust in such a dose that it felt like pixies were playing snooker on my back teeth.' The wine list is fairly short but covers a good range of prices and styles and offers a fair selection by the glass. Prices start at £13.50. Fourteen wines by the glass (£3 to £6.30) and a cherry-picking whizz around the world make for an ideal brasserie wine list. Prices start at £13.50, with a fair selection under £20 and a tempting line-up of smarter bottles.

CHEF: Simon Atridge PROPRIETOR: Bookdawn Ltd OPEN: all week L 12 to 3, Mon to Sat D 6.30 to 10 CLOSED: Sun D, all day Mon and Tue in winter MEALS: alc (main courses £12.50 to £15) SERVICE: 10% (optional), card slips closed CARDS: Amex, Delta, Diners, MasterCard, Switch, Visa DETAILS: 35 seats. 80 seats outside. Private parties: 40 main room. Car park. Vegetarian meals. Children's helpings. No cigars/pipes. Music

▲ Waterside Inn

Ferry Road, Bray SL6 2AT
TEL: (01628) 620691 FAX: (01628) 784710
EMAIL: reservations@waterside-inn.co.uk
WEBSITE: www.waterside-inn.co.uk

COOKING 9
FRENCH
£55–£184

The charming setting beside the Thames is best appreciated in summer, with drinks on the terrace beside the small pagoda, or from a table near a window, but the place is welcoming at any time of year. The chinoiserie (or japaneserie) extends inside, there is oodles of space between tables, angled mirrors ensure that everybody gets a view of what's going on, and the whole place feels plush and spacious yet quite intimate. It is not a place to come to for innovative food, but rather for a refined version of classic French cooking with a hefty price tag. What you get for the money, though, is effortless, refined and confident cooking.

Typical of the output has been a traditional, soft-textured quenelle de brochet, a light, bouncy and labour-intensive starter bathed in a first-class, creamy but lightly acidified shellfishy medium: 'French comfort food writ large.' Smoked haddock soufflé, roast scallops, and poached lobster might also turn up among seafood starters, while main courses have included a dish of a generously thick chunk of accurately timed John Dory, crisp-skinned, fresh-as-can-be, and supported by immaculately crafted fondant potato pillars, all in a deeply flavoured shellfish sauce. Throughout, main items remain centre stage, dishes are balanced and well conceived, and all the components are generally impeccably rendered. Slices of pale, just-cooked veal, for example, come in a clear but intensely flavoured stock juice, with a pair of thin-walled foie gras ravioli and a couple of slices of roasted marrowbone. Skill, assurance and precision lie behind everything from the deeply satisfying sauces to a faultlessly executed mirabelle soufflé, puffed invitingly above its metal mould, a cliché of the repertoire, perhaps, but 'immensely pleasing'. Indeed, no one could accuse the Waterside of being wildly original; one of the few signs of 'innovation' has been yet another way with truffles, this time in a crème brûlée with truffle ice cream, the former perfectly rendered, the latter 'decadently flavourful'.

Cheese is treated as seriously as everything else, and the set-lunch deal is a good one, not just because it includes a constant supply of mineral water and unlimited coffee, but also because it delivers the likes of pigeon and foie gras terrine en croûte, halibut with wild mushrooms, and blackberry bavarois and sorbet. Service, led by Diego Masciaga, is attentive and intelligent, staff are well drilled, and ladies are still given menus without prices. Wines include plenty of champagne, Burgundy, Rhône and claret in three figures, maybe four, some of it from venerable vintages, but precious little that most people would regard as affordable. Five house wines range from £19 to £40.

CHEFS: Michel and Alain Roux   PROPRIETOR: Michel Roux   OPEN: Wed to Sun 12 to 2 (2.30 Sat and Sun), 7 to 10; also Tue D 1 June to 31 Aug   CLOSED: 26 Dec to 29 Jan   MEALS: alc (main courses £31 to £49.50). Set L Wed to Sat £39.50 to £80, Set L Sun £54 to £80, Set D £80   SERVICE: 12.5% (optional), card slips closed   CARDS: Amex, Delta, Diners, MasterCard, Switch, Visa   DETAILS: 75 seats. Private parties: 80 main room, 6 to 10 private rooms. Car park. Vegetarian meals. Children's helpings. No children under 12. No cigars in dining room. Wheelchair access (not WC). No music. No mobile phones   ACCOMMODATION: 9 rooms, all with bath/shower. TV. Phone. B&B £165 to £300. No children under 12

BRIDGE Kent   **map 3**

White Horse Inn ✸ £   **NEW ENTRY**

53 High Street, Bridge CT4 5LA
TEL: (01227) 830249   FAX: (01227) 832814
EMAIL: thewaltons-thewhitehorse@hotmail.com
WEBSITE: www.kenttodo.com/
whitehorseinnbridge

(badge: KENT OF THE YEAR NEWCOMER)

COOKING **4**
MODERN BRITISH
£28–£57

As you drive through the sprawling village, you can't miss the White Horse, a white-painted building with a thatched roof and a traditional pub sign jutting out from the front. The setting might be a pub, but the dining room, all pale walls, a high ceiling and large windows, operates along formal restaurant lines. Visitors have had praise for the fresh ingredients and attractive presentation, and the proprietors set great stock in good-quality, local producers, with a page of the menu dedicated to all their main suppliers. French waiting staff, dressed in black and white, are on hand to deliver a full complement of hors d'oeuvres, appetisers, sorbets and petits fours in addition to the usual three courses.

An inspector was impressed by an appetiser of asparagus cream, which provided an intense hit of asparagus. A starter of marinated duck foie gras terrine and smoked duck breast with a blood orange and rocket salad delivered rich and powerful flavours, too, while a generous main course of citrus-crusted loin of pork with a sage and garlic sauce was expertly cooked, with layers of flavour. Those who still have room may be tempted by desserts such as pear clafoutis, with a rich, sweet, eggy batter, or raspberry soufflé with Kentish cobnut praline ice cream. The wine list is put together with value in mind, with plenty between £10 and £15.

CHEFS: Ben Walton, James Miles and Gary Rogers   PROPRIETOR: Alan Walton   OPEN: Wed to Sun L 12 to 2.15, Tue to Sat D 7 to 9.15   CLOSED: 26 Dec, 1 and 2 Jan   MEALS: alc (main courses £10.50 to £19.50). Set L and D £18.50   SERVICE: not inc, card slips closed   CARDS: Delta, MasterCard, Switch, Visa   DETAILS: 60 seats. 30 seats outside. Private parties: 35 main room, 10 to 20 private rooms. Car park. Vegetarian meals. Children's helpings. No smoking. Music. No mobile phones (£5)

London Round-ups listing additional restaurants that may be worth a visit can be found after the main London section.

Black Chapati

12 Circus Parade, New England Road,	COOKING **4**
Brighton BN1 4GW	GLOBAL
TEL: (01273) 699011	£32–£49

Since the Black Chapati started in 1987, appearances have softened, slightly, but the food has always been the main thing, and the surroundings secondary; they remain minimal but adequately comfortable. Steve Funnel uses British ingredients with ideas, techniques and spices from the Indian Subcontinent, and has gradually incorporated Far Eastern influences too (no need to jet exotic fresh ingredients around the world when you can create such zingy combinations with what is available at home). Timing of fish is accurate – witness scallops, seared and caramelised outside but moist inside, teamed with stir-fried noodles, bean sprouts and coriander to create a harmony of soft textures and warm and subtle flavours. A range of more assertive but complementary flavours are brought together in grilled duck breast (pink flesh, dark fried skin) with diced Chinese sausage and green and crisp mange-tout on soft, moist polenta. Accompaniments are important too; chutneys with Sri Lankan lamb patties, and Malaysian pickles with grilled chicken, are fresh and robust. Skills of a different kind bring exceptionally intense ices, such as blackberry-and-rosewater. Nine reds, nine whites and six good dessert bottles start at £10.50; most are under £20, all are European and the choices are both sound and individualistic.

CHEFS/PROPRIETORS: Stephen Funnell and Lauren Alker   OPEN: Tue to Sat D only 7 (6.30 Sat) to 10
MEALS: alc (main courses £11.80 to £15.50)   SERVICE: 10%, card slips closed   CARDS: Amex,
Delta, MasterCard, Switch, Visa   DETAILS: 32 seats. Private parties: 10 main room. Vegetarian
meals. Wheelchair access (not WC). Music

La Fourchette

101 Western Road, Brighton BN1 2AA	COOKING **2**
TEL/FAX: (01273) 722556	FRENCH
	£32–£39

At the time of going to press, La Fourchette was due to move to new premises a few doors down the road, which should solve the reported problem of lack of space. It is to be hoped that the move also sees an improvement in service, which has shown erratic form. What is unlikely to change is the French bistro-esque cooking style. One of the two menus is dedicated to fish, with starters ranging from classic fish soup with rouille and Gruyère to Thai-flavoured roast scallops with 'perfumed' mushrooms, and main courses of roast sea bream with remoulade and smoked bacon, or pan roast mullet and sardines with spicy, crispy potatoes. Non-fish dishes are likely to include veal sweetbread and foie gras terrine among starters, with roast breast of mallard on celeriac mash to follow. Desserts have featured chocolate and pear tart and Tia Maria mousse, and house wines on the short, exclusively French list are £9.75. Note that some of the information in the details below is incomplete or will change after the move to new premises.

CHEF/PROPRIETOR: Pascal Madjoudj   OPEN: Tue to Sat L 12 to 2.30, Mon to Sat D 7 to 10.30
MEALS: Set L and D £19 (2 courses) to £23   SERVICE: 10%, card slips closed   CARDS: Amex,
Delta, Diners, MasterCard, Switch, Visa   DETAILS: 35 seats. Vegetarian meals. No mobile
phones

Gingerman

21A Norfolk Square, Brighton BN1 2PD   COOKING 3
TEL/FAX: (01273) 326688   MODERN EUROPEAN
                                                                          £25–£55

A long, narrow room with bare wooden floors and tables neatly set with white
linen provide a calm, unfussy backdrop for Ben McKellar's commendably
'direct approach' to cooking. His menu is wide-ranging, while care goes into the
sourcing of ingredients. Brown crab meat appears on toast among starters, and
crispy pork belly is 'subtly' spiced and comes with wilted pak choi. Main
courses might include roasted fillet of cod with tomato tart and paprika dressing,
fillet of roast Buchan beef with oxtail, or wood pigeon breast with well-judged
cauliflower purée (the star dish at inspection). Desserts offer comfort or
adventure in the form of steamed lemon pudding with vanilla sauce, or Madjool
dates stuffed with mascarpone and lime syrup, and cheeses were considered
'spot-on in terms of condition'. The shortish wine list is predictable, although
the dessert wines, all offered by the glass, reveal a rare example from Gascony
that is worth investigating. House French is £10.95.

CHEF: Ben McKellar   PROPRIETORS: Ben McKellar and Pamela Abbott   OPEN: Tue to Sat 12 to
1.45, 7 to 10   CLOSED: 2 weeks winter, 2 weeks summer   MEALS: Set L £12.95 (2 courses) to
£14.95, Set D £22 (2 courses) to £25   SERVICE: not inc, 10% for parties of 6 or more   CARDS:
Amex, Delta, Diners, MasterCard, Switch, Visa   DETAILS: 36 seats. Private parties: 40 main
room. Children's helpings. No-smoking area. Music

▲ Hotel du Vin & Bistro ▮   [NEW ENTRY]

2–6 Ship Street, Brighton BN1 1AD
TEL: (01273) 718588   FAX: (01273) 718599   COOKING 3
EMAIL: reception@brighton.hotelduvin.com   MODERN EUROPEAN
WEBSITE: www.hotelduvin.com   £33–£58

This newest branch of the Hotel du Vin chain (see entries in Birmingham,
Bristol, Tunbridge Wells and Winchester, with Harrogate to follow) opened in
late 2002 in a side street just off the seafront. Once past the doorman and through
the white reception area, enter into a spacious galleried bar, which is reliably
packed with an affluent crowd who are wittily mirrored in a first-floor mural of a
crowded, trendy bar. The bistro is more brasserie, but is a lively, jumping,
invariably busy room where no carpet, curtains or tablecloths exist to absorb the
sound. First impressions have been somewhat inconsistent, but the kitchen has
turned out a fine dish of crisp-fried lambs' tongues on an earthy underlay of
peas, potato and mint, and good saddle of rabbit sparingly smeared with fennel
cream and served with lyonnaise potatoes. Cheaper cuts of meat and offal
supplement some accurate fish cookery (fillet of brill with gnocchi, French
beans, rocket and pesto makes an admirable lunch dish), but there have also
been tales of tough calves' kidneys and bland salmon terrine. Three diners

armed with a spoon each went at the prune and Armagnac tart with crème anglaise and were collectively satisfied, or there may be creamed vanilla rice with a compote of honey-roasted pineapple. Service does its best, but the kitchen can stutter when the place is full.

The wine list is a much friendlier beast than the 'Liste du Vin' tag and brass rivets on the outside might suggest, opening with sommelier Corinne Michot's changing selection of 20-odd wines by the glass (from £3.70 to £16), chosen to showcase a loose theme such as 'wines from the Old World'. Breadth, depth, length, strength and whatever else you might desire come as standard in all regions, but modest pricing and a huge selection under £20 make a welcome bonus.

CHEF: Graham Ball   PROPRIETOR: Hotel du Vin Ltd   OPEN: all week 12 to 2, 6.30 to 10   MEALS: alc (main courses £12.50 to £17.50). Set L Sun £23.50   SERVICE: not inc   CARDS: Amex, Delta, Diners, MasterCard, Switch, Visa   DETAILS: 85 seats. 25 seats outside. Private parties: 14 main room, 2 to 36 private rooms. Vegetarian meals. Children's helpings. No cigars/pipes in bistro. Wheelchair access (also WC). No music. Air-conditioned   ACCOMMODATION: 37 rooms, all with bath/shower. TV. Phone. Room only £115 to £350 (double room). Rooms for disabled. Baby facilities (*The Which? Guide to Good Hotels*)

La Marinade 🍴✷

NEW ENTRY

77 St George's Road, Kemp Town,
Brighton BN2 1EF
TEL: (01273) 600992
WEBSITE: www.lamarinade.co.uk

COOKING 1
MODERN EUROPEAN
£22–£48

Nick Lang took this place over in the summer of 2002 and has given it a new lease of life. The small but bright ground-floor dining room (plus one for smokers upstairs) is the setting for menus showing various Mediterranean and oriental influences. Shredded confit duck and celeriac salad dressed in rice-wine vinegar and sake; sea bass on a potato and Parmesan cake with salsa verde and tapenade; and lightly roast lamb with anchovy stuffing on piquillo peppers and artichoke hearts show the range. A vein of imagination and verve runs through the food, although a seafood starter lacked its promising-sounding fruity, spicy dressing at inspection. Not to be missed at dessert stage is the lemon and lime posset, coming as a generous glass of textured, tangy cream, or try the home-made ice creams, which include varieties made with amaretti biscuits or marshmallow. The short wine list offers choice enough to suit the food and opens with house Chileans at £10.95 (£2.95 a glass).

CHEF: Nick Lang   PROPRIETORS: Nick Lang and Kuldip Kaur   OPEN: Thur to Sat L 12 to 2.45, Tue to Sat D 6 to 11   CLOSED: 2 weeks Jan   MEALS: alc (main courses L £7.50, D £12.50 to £15.50). Set L £12.50, Set D 6 to 7.15 £12.50   SERVICE: not inc, 10% for parties of 6 or more   CARDS: Delta, Diners, MasterCard, Switch, Visa   DETAILS: 45 seats. Private parties: 25 main room, 20 private room. Vegetarian meals. Children's helpings. No smoking in 1 dining room. Wheelchair access (not WC). Music. Air-conditioned   £5

If customers are asked to switch off mobile phones while in a restaurant, this is noted in the details at the end of an entry.

One Paston Place

1 Paston Place, Brighton BN2 1HA
TEL: (01273) 606933   FAX: (01273) 675686
EMAIL: info@onepastonplace.co.uk
WEBSITE: www.onepastonplace.co.uk

COOKING 6
MODERN EUROPEAN
£30–£66

Yellow-washed walls, bare boards, starched white napery and well-spaced tables still make this place feel a touch more metropolitan than many Brighton siblings. 'It's relaxed,' commented a reporter, 'but one senses an underlying attitude of great seriousness towards the food.' The style is rooted in classical French mode, but not so inextricably as to preclude the odd foray into other styles.

Scallops are always worth a punt to start, perhaps with salsify and blood orange, or with a smoky aubergine coulis that is discreet enough not to overwhelm them. Foie gras adorned with rhubarb, beetroot and Szechuan peppercorns has become a speciality: textural contrasts cleverly conceived, flavours all working together. If main courses can be over-elaborate (witness a piece of turbot poached in milk, served with pancetta, bay leaves, red onion compote and a mixture of chips, some of regular, some of sweet potato), they involve outstanding ingredients. Milk-fed lamb with mint and rocket pesto and olive oil mash pleased once again at inspection, as did a creamily fresh coconut sorbet accompanying feather-light passion-fruit soufflé, and the grande assiette of five chocolate items is chocoholics' heaven. Home-made breads, appetisers like duck rillettes with fig compote, good coffee and petits fours are all worthy supporting acts, and Nicole Emmerson 'reigns with quiet authority' over all. The few New World wines on the list seem beside the point: trawl the French regions for Madiran and Menetou-Salon as much as for Bordeaux and Burgundy. Prices start at £16, and there are lots of halves.

CHEF: Mark Emmerson   PROPRIETORS: Mark and Nicole Emmerson   OPEN: Tue to Sat 12.30 to 1.45, 7.30 to 9.30   MEALS: alc (main courses £21 to £23). Set L £16.50 (2 courses) to £19   SERVICE: net prices, card slips closed   CARDS: Amex, Delta, Diners, MasterCard, Switch, Visa   DETAILS: 42 seats. Vegetarian menu on request. No children under 7 at D. No cigars/pipes. Wheelchair access (not WC). Music. No mobile phones. Air-conditioned

Sevendials

1–3 Buckingham Place, Brighton BN1 3TD
TEL: (01273) 885555   FAX: (01273) 888911
EMAIL: info@sevendialsrestaurant.co.uk
WEBSITE: www.sevendialsrestaurant.co.uk

COOKING 2
MODERN EUROPEAN
£23–£48

This useful place occupies a wedge-shaped site on the Sevendials roundabout, and the door (at the thin end) opens *Tardis*-like into a surprisingly capacious dining room, all burgundy and dark wood. A chicken and madeira consommé that includes chicken tortellini, and a stuffed quail with celeriac purée, show a willingness to cook, rather than merely assemble. For main courses grilled marinated neck fillet of lamb, and pan-fried duck breast with sweet potato and pea galette, on the same menu as pot roasted monkfish explore the challenges of fast and slow cooking. Puddings, too, seem to have developed: the range includes raspberry crème brûlée, hot chocolate and hazelnut fondant, and a citrus terrine. Lunch, with two choices at each course, looks good value. Cocktails head the drinks list (this *is* Brighton), but wine-bibbers have the choice of six house wines (£12.50 to £16 or £3/£4 a glass), a short international range up to £25, and a few European 'fine wines' on top.

CHEF/PROPRIETOR: Sam Metcalfe   OPEN: Tue to Sun 12 to 2.45, 7 to 10 (9.30 Sun)   CLOSED: 25 Dec to 5 Jan   MEALS: Set L £10 (2 courses) to £12.50, Set D £19.50 (2 courses) to £22.50. Summer Terrace menu available April to Sept 10.30 to 6   SERVICE: 12%, card slips closed CARDS: Amex, Delta, Diners, MasterCard, Switch, Visa   DETAILS: 55 seats. 55 seats outside. Private parties: 100 (standing) main room, 10 to 20 private rooms. Vegetarian meals. Children's helpings. No children under 12 after 7pm. Wheelchair access (also WC). Music

---

Terre à Terre

71 East Street, Brighton BN1 1HQ	COOKING **4**
TEL: (01273) 729051 FAX: (01273) 327561	GLOBAL VEGETARIAN
WEBSITE: www.terreaterre.co.uk	£30–£50

The remit here is delivery of classy vegetarian food (including plenty for vegans) with – in the words of the proprietors – 'enthusiasm, passion and humour'. Most reporters agree: 'it is somewhere I know I could take someone who would go "wow" after their meal.' The menu roves the world for influences, with South Indian, Japanese, Greek and Italian flavours coming to the fore. The lunchtime 'Bite' menu focuses on sandwiches, breads and salads, some of which also appear on the evening 'Savour' menu. Here they are joined by main courses such as oakie smokie soufflé (a twice-baked soufflé served with onion rings, minted potatoes, braised lettuce and pea parcels with sauce St-Germain), or yabba jabba beefy tea, a vegan dish based on miso and mushrooms enlivened with yuzu pesto and aubergine pickle. Puddings, such as rhubarb and rosehip sorbet, seem tame in comparison. The 'bright, clean, spacious' interior has been refurbished since the last edition of the Guide, and there's a heated decked patio. All the ciders and spirits, and most of the beers, are produced organically or biodynamically, as are the wines, which are a broad-ranging selection from Europe and the southern hemisphere. House red and white, from France, are £12.75 a bottle, £3.75 a glass.

CHEF: Lawrence Glass   PROPRIETORS: Amanda Powley and Philip Taylor   OPEN: Tue to Sun L 12 to 5.30, all week D 6 to 10.30   CLOSED: 24 to 26 Dec   MEALS: alc (main courses £8 to £12) SERVICE: not inc, card slips closed, 10% for parties of 6 or more   CARDS: Amex, Delta, Diners, MasterCard, Switch, Visa   DETAILS: 110 seats. 15 seats outside. Private parties: 30 main room. Vegetarian meals. Children's helpings. No-smoking area. Wheelchair access (also WC). Music. Air-conditioned

---

If customers are asked to switch off mobile phones while in a restaurant, this is noted in the details at the end of an entry.

Which? Online subscribers will find The Good Food Guide *online, along with other Which? guides and magazines, at* www.which.net. *See the website for information on how to become a subscriber.*

BRIMFIELD Herefordshire map 5

▲ Roebuck Inn ✳ £

Brimfield SY8 4NE
TEL: (01584) 711230 FAX: (01584) 711654
WEBSITE: www.theroebuckinn.com
just off A49, 5m S of Ludlow

COOKING 3
MODERN BRITISH
£24–£49

It may not look all that remarkable from the outside, but inside there is an appealing lounge – an old room with a fireplace and bar – and an interlinked pair of bright, airy dining rooms with parquet floors, deep orange walls, blue upholstery and tablecloths. The 'Country Pub and Dining' menu (as it is labelled) is a generous carte with some old-fashioned things on it (fillet steak stuffed with Stilton, for example) as well as modern ones (well-presented chicken boudin served with sweet potato and Madeira sauce). First-class raw materials are generally in evidence: witness tender roast rump of lamb ('really tasting of lamb') served pink on a bubble and squeak potato cake, or a moist, very fresh and well-timed piece of herb-crusted fillet of cod with a tomato and basil sauce. Although butterscotch tart has disappointed, a bread-and-butter pudding made with brioche, croissant, apricot sauce and vanilla crème anglaise has hit the spot. Forty-plus wines, from light aperitif whites to big reds, begin at £10 for Santa Rita Chardonnay or Duboeuf Merlot.

CHEF: Jonathan Waters PROPRIETOR: Peter Jenkins OPEN: all week 12 to 2.30, 7 to 9.30
CLOSED: 25 Dec MEALS: alc (main courses £7 to £19) SERVICE: not inc, card slips closed
CARDS: Delta, MasterCard, Switch, Visa DETAILS: 60 seats. Private parties: 50 main room. Car park. Children's helpings. No smoking. Wheelchair access (not WC). No music. No mobile phones ACCOMMODATION: 3 rooms, all with bath/shower. TV. Phone. B&B £45 to £70 (*The Which? Guide to Good Hotels*) £5

BRISTOL Bristol map 2

Bell's Diner ♥ ✳ £

1–3 York Road, Montpelier, Bristol BS6 5QB
TEL: (0117) 924 0357 FAX: (0117) 924 4280
EMAIL: info@bellsdiner.com
WEBSITE: www.bellsdiner.co.uk

COOKING 4
MODERN EUROPEAN-PLUS
£28–£53

Christopher Wicks continues to make improvements to his corner restaurant, and now alongside the original dining room, with its cast-iron fireplace and striped blinds, there is a more spacious, white-walled room replacing the courtyard. The cuisine has shifted its focus somewhat, and has yielded to an experimentalism that might team, for example, beetroot jelly with beef carpaccio; horseradish ice cream with smoked eel; and scallops with oloroso sherry jelly. Some innovations work, but it is the simpler dishes that please most. Pork rillettes – 'an uncompromisingly traditional slab of tender, shredded meat bound with plenty of flavoursome fat' – needed only the cornichons and toast it came with, while main courses like warm duck breast on a potato cake with courgette, asparagus and broad bean salad impress for the quality of their main ingredients. At dessert stage jasmine tea ice cream undermined a slice of fine mocha tart, while baked muscat custard was the highlight of the meal for another.

The wine list supports, rather than competes with, the food. After France, Italy and Spain show well, the New World taking a back seat; Domaine de Trévallon, Provence's star organic producer, appears in ten vintages. Prices are fair and there's interesting drinking under £20, plus 13 by the glass.

CHEFS: Christopher Wicks, Toby Gritton and Jake Platt PROPRIETOR: Christopher Wicks OPEN: Tue to Fri L 12 to 2.30, Mon to Sat D 7 to 10 CLOSED: 24 to 31 Dec, bank hol Mons MEALS: alc (main courses £12.50 to £18.50). Set L and D £18.50 SERVICE: not inc, 10% for parties of 6 or more CARDS: Amex, Delta, MasterCard, Switch, Visa DETAILS: 60 seats. Private parties: 30 main room. Vegetarian meals. Children's helpings. No smoking. Music (£5)

Brazz 🍽 ✳ £

85 Park Street, Bristol BS1 5PJ
TEL: (0117) 925 2000 FAX: (0117) 929 0225
WEBSITE: www.brazz.co.uk

COOKING 1
MODERN BRASSERIE
£24–£50

Located at the top of a steep hill close to the university, this noisy, smart, blue-themed and brightly lit open-all-hours brasserie is sociable and spacious. The daily-changing carte delivers straightforward modern British food based on well-sourced components. Though a starter of pan-fried duck served in a salad with Asian noodles failed to make the grade at inspection, a main course of warm skate salad with Jersey Royals, green beans and herb dressing was well executed and showed up its 'terrific ingredients', and navarin of lamb has been tender and flavourful. Puddings might include a 'classic' vanilla crème brûlée. Service is cheerful but can come under strain when things get busy. Wines start at £10.95, with a good range by the glass or 50ml carafe; most bottles are under £20.

CHEF: Nathan Muir PROPRIETOR: Brazz plc OPEN: all week 12 to 3, 6 to 10.30 (11 Fri and Sat). Breakfast menu available 9 to 12, reduced menu 3 to 6 MEALS: alc (main courses £7 to £16) SERVICE: 10% (optional), card slips closed CARDS: Amex, Delta, Diners, MasterCard, Switch, Visa DETAILS: 100 seats. Private parties: 100 main room. Vegetarian meals. Children's helpings. No smoking in 1 dining room. Wheelchair access (also WC). Music. Air-conditioned

---

Deason's ✳

43 Whiteladies Road, Clifton, Bristol BS8 2LS
TEL: (0117) 973 6230 FAX: (0117) 923 7394
EMAIL: enquiries@deasons.co.uk
WEBSITE: www.deasons.co.uk

COOKING 2
MODERN BRITISH
£25–£56

Clifton, for one reporter, is 'the Bristol equivalent of Chelsea'. It is certainly one of the more chic parts of the city, and this Victorian end-of-terrace restaurant does its best to fit in, with a bright, contemporary décor in neutral tones and calming modern artworks on the walls. The menus are 'cosmopolitan and bang up to date', offering bold flavours in audacious combinations: slow-cooked ox tongue and chorizo layered with creamed butternut squash is the sort of thing to expect for starters. Among main courses, tender, rare beef fillet has made a good impression, accompanied by walnut and foie gras ravioli, truffled blackberries and a bay-infused jus. Choices typically extend to roast chicken breast stuffed with black pudding and ox tongue on a potato and celeriac cake with port-glazed onions, and simpler dishes such as pan-fried skate with capers, lemon and parsley butter. Desserts don't always come off as intended, but on the whole this is a likeable restaurant with amenable service. A brief but well-rounded wine selection includes good sherries, a page of good-value 'wine promotions' and seven house options by the glass. House wines start at £12.75.

CHEF: Jason Deason   PROPRIETORS: Jason and Jodie Deason   OPEN: Sun to Fri L 12 to 2.30, Mon to Sat D 7 to 10.30   MEALS: alc D (main courses £13.50 to £20). Set L Mon to Fri £11.50 (2 courses) to £14.50, Set L Sun £12.50 (2 courses) to £15.50, Set D Mon to Fri £17.50 (2 courses) to £21.50   SERVICE: 10% (optional)   CARDS: Amex, Delta, Diners, MasterCard, Switch, Visa   DETAILS: 80 seats. 22 seats outside. Private parties: 40 main room, 12 to 40 private rooms. Vegetarian meals. Children's helpings. No smoking. Music. Air-conditioned (£5)

FishWorks ✖

128 Whiteladies Road, Clifton, Bristol BS8 2RS   COOKING 3
TEL: (0117) 974 4433   FAX: (0117) 974 4933   SEAFOOD
WEBSITE: www.fishworks.co.uk   £33–£61

Fishmonger plus a dining room is proving a popular combination in Bristol's busy, upmarket suburb of Clifton (branches in Bath, Christchurch and London offer the same formula – see entries). Fish is delivered daily from Newlyn Market in Cornwall, and the emphasis is on letting fresh ingredients speak for themselves. Customers can choose any fish or shellfish from the shop to be cooked to order, or they can mine the 'Classic' and the specials boards. Fruits de mer selections have proved popular, as have crevettes with tarragon mayonnaise, and combinations like chargrilled squid with lemon and chilli, or grey mullet with garlic dressing. Specials might include a 'well-made' appetiser of brandade of cod, or roast hake with chickpeas and salsa verde, plus vegetables (extra). Service is helpful and friendly in what is reported as a busy but informal dining experience. The wine list is predictably dominated by whites – offering lots of interest at reasonable prices. Three whites, three reds, a rosé and a Manzanilla are offered by the glass; prices start at £12.50 the bottle, £3.25 the glass.

CHEFS: Matthew Prowse, Dave Daly and Tom Hills   PROPRIETOR: FishWorks plc   OPEN: Tue to Sat 12 to 3, 6 to 10.30   CLOSED: Christmas, Tue after bank hol Mons   MEALS: alc (main courses £9 to £22)   SERVICE: not inc   CARDS: Amex, Delta, MasterCard, Switch, Visa   DETAILS: 54 seats. Vegetarian meals. Children's helpings. No smoking. Wheelchair access (not WC). Music. No mobile phones

▲ Hotel du Vin & Bistro ▮

The Sugar House, Narrow Lewins Mead,
Bristol BS1 2NU
TEL: 0117-925 5577   FAX: 0117-925 1199
EMAIL: reservations@bristol.hotelduvin.com   COOKING 3
WEBSITE: www.hotelduvin.com   MODERN EUROPEAN
                                                    £35–£60

A former sugar warehouse houses the Bristol branch of this gradually expanding hotel chain (see entries Brighton, Birmingham, Tunbridge Wells, Winchester, with Harrogate on the horizon). The bistro menu is as pan-European as the name implies, offering bresaola and celeriac rémoulade, or seared squid with chilli and spring onion, but also includes a section of 'simple classics' that appeals to reporters, who speak fondly of well-flavoured oxtail terrine with good shallot marmalade, or a generous portion of nicely textured split pea and ham hock soup. Challenging combinations like halibut with Puy lentils, lardons and red wine jus are produced with as much care as a simpler whole grilled Dover sole with a decent hollandaise. The latter's accompanying chips were less than crisp, though. Desserts are a fruity bunch and run to peach tart with raspberry sorbet, roast plums with vanilla ice cream, and rhubarb crumble.

Wine lists vary across the chain, but are all outstanding. In this one, all regions are brimming with good choices over a broad price range. For special occasions, focus on the three pages of 'prestige wines' or the 45 sparklers; novelty-seekers could try the Thai white (£14.50). Prices start at £11.95 with plentiful choice under £20 and ten or so by the glass from £3.20.

CHEF: Rob Carr   PROPRIETOR: Hotel du Vin Ltd   OPEN: all week 12 to 2, 6.30 to 10   MEALS: alc exc Sun L (main courses £14.50 to £17.50). Set L Sun £23.50   SERVICE: not inc   CARDS: Amex, Delta, Diners, MasterCard, Switch, Visa   DETAILS: 85 seats. Private parties: 60 main room, 10 to 30 private rooms. Car park. Vegetarian meals. Children's helpings. No pipes/cigars. Wheelchair access (also WC). No music   ACCOMMODATION: 40 rooms, all with bath/shower. TV. Phone. Room only £120 to £295. Rooms for disabled. Baby facilities (*The Which? Guide to Good Hotels*)

Lords ♥ ⅝※

43 Corn Street, Bristol BS1 1HT	COOKING **4**
TEL/FAX: (0117) 926 2658	ANGLO-FRENCH
WEBSITE: www.lordsrestaurant.com	£34–£65

NEW ENTRY

Lords offers a welcome retreat from the brashness of Corn Street. Inside, a masculine, clubby feel pervades thanks to the black and beige colour scheme and the touches of marble and expensive table settings, softened with fresh flowers and vibrant paintings. In fact, the setting hasn't really altered since Markwick's was installed here. The menu is similar, too. Ingredients are good quality – Glenarm salmon, organic chicken and vegetables – and, as with the restaurant's previous incarnation, the style of cooking remains hearty Anglo-French, and the separate fish menu is still available. A starter of salmon 'tartar,' a curious mix of tartare and ceviche, topped with smoked salmon and served with dressed cucumber 'sambal' may be followed by a complex, punchily-flavoured honey-glazed Trelough duck breast with chestnuts, smoked bacon and cabbage-and-beetroot Dauphinoise. 'Worth the 20-minute wait,' was one reporter's verdict on a dessert of warm apple and cinnamon tarte Tatin served with Calvados ice cream, which delivered 'a real kick'. Vegetarians have their own menu of imaginative dishes. Service is warm, enthusiastic and keen to please. Consistently good quality in a global round-up means stiff competition for the French classics on the friendly, informative wine list, but with such fair pricing even Burgundy and Bordeaux could tempt ordinary mortals here. Fifteen house wines are £14 to £18 and glass prices start at £2.90.

CHEF: Simon Searle   PROPRIETORS: Hardev and Gurdip Singh   OPEN: Mon to Fri L 12 to 2, Mon to Sat D 6 to 9.30   CLOSED: 1 week Christmas, 1 week Easter, second 2 weeks Aug, bank hols MEALS: alc (main courses L £11 to £13, D £16.50 to £20.50)   SERVICE: not inc   CARDS: Amex,

Delta, MasterCard, Switch, Visa DETAILS: 50 seats. Private parties: 28 main room, 2 to 20 private rooms. Vegetarian meals. Babes in arms and children over 6 welcome. Children's helpings. No smoking in 1 dining room. No music. No mobile phones. Air-conditioned

Quartier Vert ▼

85 Whiteladies Road, Bristol BS8 2NT	COOKING 3
TEL: (0117) 973 4482 FAX: (0117) 974 3913	MEDITERRANEAN
WEBSITE: www.quartiervert.co.uk	£28–£58

QV is a beacon of simplicity with white walls and oak floors, the succinct daily menus sourced from excellent local suppliers. An affection for Iberia pervades. A bar area offers tapas and more substantial Mediterranean-based salads, hams, grilled fish and soups; venture either upstairs or down to the two restaurant areas for greater complexity. Tiny broad beans added to a carefully flavoured risotto with pecorino provided 'bite', while poached mussels skilfully combined fresh sea taste with tomato and ginger. Main courses might feature sirloin steak from Carswell Farm 'tasting like beef ought to', served with a fine salsa verde; baked fillet of bass with mushroom risotto; or a 'classic fabada' of tender pork shoulder with pancetta, chorizo and planchada beans. An expertly made rhubarb tart seemed more custard than rhubarb but pleased nonetheless. The Spanish connection shows up too in the good range of sherries and fine reds on offer, including Priorato from Clos Martinet at £24.25, but the wine as a whole provides a well-balanced European selection with just a few New World wines. Fourteen wines come by the glass for around £2.50 (bottles from £12.50), and prices overall are fair with lots of options under £20.

CHEF: Barny Haughton PROPRIETORS: Barny Haughton and Connie Coombes OPEN: all week 12 to 3, 6 to 10.30 CLOSED: 1 week Christmas, Sun after 4 in winter MEALS: alc (main courses £10.50 to £18.50). Set L £14.50 (2 courses) to £17.50. 'Little dishes' available in bar area SERVICE: not inc, 10% for parties of 5 or more CARDS: Delta, MasterCard, Switch, Visa DETAILS: 80 seats. 25 seats outside. Private parties: 50 main room, 10 to 25 private rooms. Vegetarian meals. Children's helpings. Wheelchair access (not WC). Music

riverstation

The Grove, Bristol BS1 4RB	COOKING 3
TEL: (0117) 914 4434 FAX: (0117) 934 9990	MODERN BRITISH-PLUS
WEBSITE: www.riverstation.co.uk	£23–£53

Acres of glass and steel that seem to jut out on to the river ensure that this avant-garde conversion of a former police station makes a strong visual statement. On the ground floor is a casual deli-bar, which is ideal for a quick lunch (mixed meze have been recommended), while the informal first-floor dining room is a bright, colourful space with river views. It's an appropriate setting for the cosmopolitan, contemporary cooking – menus read like an inventory of high-impact flavours. Starters, for example, have included potted crab with mace and lemon, and mushroom and ginger soup with coconut cream. A main course of roast hake with butter beans, tomato, parsley and mussel dressing proved a well-balanced combination of fresh flavours at inspection. Indeed, fish appears to be a strength, though 'rosy' loin of lamb with a root vegetable gratin has also been favourably reported, and desserts receive good notices too: 'seriously wobbly and refreshing' elderflower jelly with a berry compote and thick cream, for example. Service is attentive and prompt, and wines are a well-chosen selection with lots of good drinking below £25. House wines start at £12.

CHEF: Peter Taylor   PROPRIETORS: Peter Taylor, John Payne and Shirley Anne Bell   OPEN: all week 12 (10.30 Sat) to 2.30 (3 Sun), 6 to 10.30 (11 Fri and Sat, 9 Sun)   CLOSED: 25 and 26 Dec, 1 Jan   MEALS: alc (main courses £11 to £17). Set L Mon to Fri £11.50 (2 courses) to £13.75, Set L Sun £14 (2 courses) to £16.50. Deli-bar menu available   SERVICE: not inc, 10% for parties of 8 or more   CARDS: Delta, Diners, MasterCard, Switch, Visa   DETAILS: 120 seats. Private parties: 120 main room. Vegetarian meals. Children's helpings. No-smoking area. Wheelchair access (also WC). No music

---

Severnshed 🍴✹ £

The Grove, Harbourside, Bristol BS1 4RB	
TEL: (0117) 925 1212 FAX: (0117) 925 1214	COOKING 3
EMAIL: info@severnshed.co.uk	MODERN BRITISH-PLUS
WEBSITE: www.severnshed.co.uk	£28–£46

Cool and contemporary, the stainless steel bar, large leather sofas and locally hand-made wooden tables sit comfortably in the huge expanse of this listed former boathouse. Brunel's gabled roof with wrought-iron beams and wooden ceiling could have been constructed with this twenty-first-century décor in mind. Dishes such as pan-fried sardines with beetroot and potato salad and herb focaccia, or tomato tortilla and Asian duck wrap with fries, can be selected from the 'Daytime Café Menu', while in summer the newly refurbished riverside terrace is a good place to sample seasonal additions to the menu (more fresh fish, lobster, salads) while surveying the quaysides crammed with houseboats, barges and dockland paraphernalia. From homely fish and chips with 'Yorkshire caviar' (mushy peas) to dishes with a variety of global influences – Thai green curry with deep-fried won tons, or crisp-coated goats' cheese with caramelised red onion marmalade and salsa verde – there's something to suit most tastes and pockets, and with seating for over a hundred there's a lively, cosmopolitan feel to the place. A dozen reds and fewer whites give global coverage; 'Shed red' and its white equivalent come in at £9.95.

CHEF: James Brown   PROPRIETOR: Organic Venturers Ltd   OPEN: all week 12 to 11   MEALS: alc (main courses £9 to £15.50). Set L (2 courses) Mon to Fri 12 to 7 £7.77. Café menu available 12 to 7   SERVICE: 10% (optional), card slips closed   CARDS: Amex, Delta, MasterCard, Switch, Visa   DETAILS: 120 seats. 100 seats outside. Vegetarian meals. Children's helpings. No smoking. Wheelchair access (also WC). Music. Air-conditioned (£5)

If 'vegetarian meals' is noted in the details at the end of an entry, this means that a restaurant routinely lists at least one vegetarian starter and main course on menus. Other restaurants, however, may offer good vegetarian choices if you let them know in advance, so it is worthwhile phoning to enquire.

If 'The Which? Guide to Good Hotels' is noted at the end of an entry, this means that the establishment is also in the 2004 edition of our sister guide, published in September 2003.

BRITWELL SALOME Oxfordshire   map 2

The Goose ⁵⁄✲

Britwell Salome OX9 5LG
TEL: (01491) 612304   FAX: (01491) 613945
on B4009, just outside Watlington, 5 min from
M40 junction 6

COOKING **4**
ENGLISH
£25–£54

Though unremarkable to look at from the outside, this 'dining room in pub's clothing' has light, modern interiors that give the place a 'rustic chic' tone, and an 'informal and relaxed but upmarket' atmosphere.

Compact menus limit choice to around half a dozen options per course, which gives chef-proprietor Michael North leeway to produce impressive incidentals, such as a 'rich, intense' appetiser cappuccino of wild mushroom with truffle oil. That this is not typical pub food should by now be apparent, more so when you consider starters of foie gras parfait with toasted brioche and fig chutney, or an earthy combination of well-made tagliatelle with wild mushrooms, broad beans and peas. Dishes are not over-elaborate but show sound technical skills with flavours shining through clearly, as in an inspector's colourful main course of crisp-skinned 'squeaky fresh' hake fillet with crushed new potatoes, braised fennel and sauce vierge, or braised lamb and potato torte with creamed spinach and lamb jus. To finish, a trio of apple tart Tatin, sticky toffee pudding and praline ice cream has proved well balanced. Service from a young team is efficient and attentive, and though fairly short, the wine list covers an impressive range, from humble vins de pays at £10.95 through to Louis Latour Corton at £67.50.

CHEF: Michael North   PROPRIETOR: The Goose Restaurant Ltd   OPEN: Tue to Sun L 12 to 2.30 (3 Sun), D 7 to 9.30   MEALS: alc (main courses £12 to £16.50). Set L Tue to Fri and Set D Tue to Thur and Sun £12 (2 courses) to £15   SERVICE: not inc   CARDS: Amex, Delta, MasterCard, Switch, Visa   DETAILS: 50 seats. 30 seats outside. Private parties: 30 main room, 20 to 30 private rooms. Car park. Children's helpings. No smoking in 1 dining room. Music ⓔ⑤

BROADHEMBURY Devon   map 2

Drewe Arms ⁵⁄✲

Broadhembury E14 3NF
TEL: (01404) 841267   FAX: (01404) 841118
off A373, between Cullompton and Honiton

COOKING **2**
SEAFOOD
£31–£52

Located in a picture-postcard, typical Devon village with lots of thatched cottages surrounding it, the Drewe Arms has found a winning formula and stuck to it. Fresh fish served simply is what it's about. There are meaty dishes, particularly game in season, but fish dominates the menu – and contributes to the décor: walls are covered in piscine prints. Swedish influence from co-owner Kirstin Burge can be spotted on the menu – gravlax with dill and mustard sauce, John Dory with capers and the classic Swedish 'Janson's Temptation', a baked dish of anchovies, potatoes, onions and cream. Daily specials, chalked up on a board, might offer griddled sardines with garlic and herbs, whole lobster with salad and new potatoes, and crab cakes with tomato salsa. Wind up with lemon posset or Swedish apple cake. Friendly, family-style service starts with a warm greeting. The well-annotated wine list sensibly sticks mostly to food-friendly whites. Bottle prices start at £14.50, or £2.95/£3.95 a glass.

CHEFS: Nigel and Andrew Burge   PROPRIETORS: Nigel, Kerstin and Andrew Burge   OPEN: all week L 12 to 2, Mon to Sat D 7 to 9.15   MEALS: alc (main courses £9 to £18.50). Bar menu available   SERVICE: not inc   CARDS: Delta, MasterCard, Switch, Visa   DETAILS: 40 seats. 50 seats outside. Private parties: 28 main room. Car park. Vegetarian meals. Children's helpings. No smoking in 1 dining room. Wheelchair access (also women's WC). No music

---

BROADWAY Worcestershire   **map 5**

▲ Dormy House, Tapestries Restaurant ▼ ⁵✻

Willersey Hill, Broadway WR12 7LF
TEL: (01386) 852711   FAX: (01386) 858636
EMAIL: reservations@dormyhouse.co.uk   COOKING 3
WEBSITE: www.dormyhouse.co.uk   MODERN EUROPEAN-PLUS
just off A44, 3m E of Broadway   £30–£62

Dormy House began as a seventeenth-century farmhouse, but conversions and extensions over the years have transformed it into a vision of country-house opulence. You may find yourself playing croquet with a jug of Sangria on hand, while leather armchairs, swagged curtains and a riot of patterned fabrics offer all the trappings of luxury – unless you prefer to sweat off postprandial guilt on the cardiovascular gym equipment. And Alan Cutler superintends some notable dinners from a range of menus: a daily-changing prix fixe and a six-course gourmet menu, plus a Sunday set lunch, not to mention a simpler bar menu. The rich and exuberant style tops a baked turbot fillet with shellfish mousse and crisp potato scallops, or adds a confit of blackberries to Barbary duckling breast in a reduction of orange and cloves. Some combinations seem to strive too consciously for novelty (a pistachio and Sauternes sauce with Dover sole), but the effect is cumulatively impressive, especially when you may begin a meal with frothed lobster and Armagnac soup, and end it with chocolate-sauced strawberry cheesecake. The service is properly observant, and if the atmosphere seems a little stiff, the champagne page of the wine list will help you unwind (at a price). Diners daunted by fat wine lists will appreciate the quick recommendations on the front page and the succeeding selection of ten house wines. The main focus is on France, including a sound selection of affordable red Bordeaux.

CHEF: Alan Cutler   PROPRIETOR: Mrs I.P. Sørensen   OPEN: Sun L 12 to 2, all week D 7 to 9.30 (9 Sun)   CLOSED: 25 to 27 Dec   MEALS: alc (main courses £17.50 to £23). Set L Sun £21, Set D £34 to £37.50. Bar menu also available   SERVICE: not inc   CARDS: Amex, Delta, MasterCard, Switch, Visa   DETAILS: 80 seats. 30 seats outside. Private parties: 160 main room. Car park. Vegetarian meals. Children's helpings. No children under 16 after 7pm. Jacket and tie. No smoking. Wheelchair access (also WC). No music. Air-conditioned   ACCOMMODATION: 48 rooms, all with bath/shower. TV. Phone. B&B £110 to £195. Rooms for disabled. Baby facilities (*The Which? Guide to Good Hotels*)

See inside the front cover for an explanation of the symbols used at the tops of entries.

BROCKENHURST Hampshire map 2

Simply Poussin ⚡✳

The Courtyard, Brookley Road,
Brockenhurst SO42 7RB
TEL: (01590) 623063   FAX: (01590) 623144
EMAIL: simply@lepoussin.co.uk
WEBSITE: www.simplypoussin.co.uk

COOKING 3
MODERN BRITISH
£26–£48

'A good regular' is how one reader describes this long-standing stalwart – the restaurant turns 21 in 2004. This poussin is the sibling (or is that chick?) restaurant to Le Poussin in Lyndhurst (see entry), and Alex Aitken ensures that high standards are maintained at both addresses. Choice in the daily menus has increased, and the idea of taking local produce (where possible) and cooking it 'simply' is a winning formula. Flavour combinations are enticing – witness soused mackerel with beetroot carpaccio, followed by honey-glazed duck breast with caramelised chicory, creamy mashed potatoes and redcurrant sauce, or roasted veal sweetbreads wrapped in prosciutto on a potato galette. A glass of dessert wine is suggested with each pudding: Monbazillac, for example, with spiced pineapple tarte Tatin and coconut sorbet. Elsewhere, the wine list has a decent number of bottles under £25, with prices starting at £12, or £4 by the glass.

CHEFS: Neil Duffett and Alex Aitken   PROPRIETORS: Alex and Caroline Aitken   OPEN: Tue to Sat 12 to 2, 7 to 10   MEALS: alc (main courses £12.50 to £15). Set L and D Tue to Fri £10 (2 courses) to £15   SERVICE: 10% (optional), card slips closed   CARDS: Amex, Delta, MasterCard, Switch, Visa   DETAILS: 34 seats. 4 seats outside. Private parties: 30 main room. Car park. Vegetarian meals. No children under 8 at D. Children's helpings. No smoking. Wheelchair access (not WC). Music

BROMSGROVE Worcestershire map 5

▲ Grafton Manor ⚡✳

Grafton Lane, Bromsgrove B61 7HA
TEL: (01527) 579007   FAX: (01527) 575221
EMAIL: steven@grafman.u-net.com
WEBSITE: www.graftonmanorhotel.co.uk
off B4091, 1½m SW of Bromsgrove

COOKING 4
MODERN INDIAN/EUROPEAN
£30–£54

Grafton Manor may be within earshot of the M5, but this beautiful, ancient red-brick manor takes you back to a pre-motorway era. Despite a grand staircase, intricate mouldings and rich, clearly defined colours, all golds, deep blues, reds and greens, this family-run hotel and restaurant holds a few surprises – most obviously on the menu, which combines classical country-house dishes with chef Simon Morris's gastronomic passion: Indian cooking. So while there are starters such as salmon and dill terrine, and main courses of parsley chicken with a smoked bacon and wild mushroom sauce, there are also the likes of Gujarati-style curd cheese curry with red lentil masala pakora, or tandoori monkfish with chickpea and coriander sauce. Desserts, too, cross international boundaries, with chocolate and Armagnac mousse accompanied by orange and cardamom biscuits. Although the Indian cooking has a few detractors, others believe that 'the more Morris concentrates on Indian food, the better', praising the 'amazing spicing' in a main course of grilled fillet of halibut with prawn korma and a laverbread oatcake. Service is young and committed. The wine list is heavy on classical France, but there's a smattering of New World bottles too. Prices, starting at around £10, are fair.

CHEF: Simon Morris PROPRIETORS: the Morris family OPEN: Sun to Fri L 12.30 to 1.45, Mon to Sat D 7.30 to 9.30 CLOSED: New Year, bank hols MEALS: Set L Mon to Fri £20.50, Set L Sun £18.50, Set D £27.85 to £32.75 SERVICE: not inc, card slips closed CARDS: Amex, Diners, MasterCard, Switch, Visa DETAILS: 60 seats. Private parties: 160 main room, 20 to 50 private rooms. Car park. Vegetarian meals. Children's helpings. No smoking. No music. No mobile phones ACCOMMODATION: 9 rooms, all with bath/shower. TV. Phone. B&B £85 to £165. Rooms for disabled (*The Which? Guide to Good Hotels*)

BRUTON Somerset   map 2

Truffles 🌟

95 High Street, Bruton BA10 0AR   COOKING 3
TEL/FAX: (01749) 812255   MODERN EUROPEAN
WEBSITE: www.trufflesbruton.co.uk   £38–£49

Denise Bottrill, a genuinely genial hostess, and chef Martin have overseen their homely restaurant since 1986. Culinary fashions have moved on since then, and so has this kitchen, and although some ideas are borrowed from far afield – 'Thai-inspired' seabass with a hot-and-sour sauce, for example – it is the Mediterranean that underpins the menus. Fish soup with rouille, Gruyère and croutons sits alongside fillet of smoked pork with an apple and thyme stuffing wrapped in Parma ham served with a Calvados sauce. Attention to quality, with top-class butter and meat, increasingly sourced from organic suppliers, is notable throughout. Seven New World house wines, around £14, are followed by a list which shows enthusiasm and knowledge, as evidenced in the page of Bordeaux second wines and a decent selection of half-bottles.

CHEF: Martin Bottrill PROPRIETORS: Denise and Martin Bottrill OPEN: Tue to Sat D only 7 to 10; also open L Easter Sun and Mothering Sun MEALS: Set D £25.95 SERVICE: not inc CARDS: MasterCard, Switch, Visa DETAILS: 30 seats. Private parties: 20 main room, 8 to 12 private rooms. Vegetarian meals. No children under 6. No smoking while others eat. Wheelchair access (not WC). No music. Air-conditioned £5

BUCKLAND Oxfordshire   map 2

▲ Lamb at Buckland 🌟 £

Lamb Lane, Buckland SN7 8QN   COOKING 2
TEL: (01367) 870484 FAX: (01367) 870675   MODERN BRITISH
off A420, 4m NE of Faringdon   £27–£59

This eighteenth-century stone pub set in a quiet Cotswold village has both a congenial bar with a 'village pub' feel and lamb motifs aplenty, plus a brighter, slightly more formal restaurant looking out over a flagstoned patio. One printed menu operates throughout, supplemented by specials and puddings on blackboards. The cooking reflects a range of international (and particularly European) influences; Britain's hearty simplicities seem to shine – Cullen skink, shepherd's pie, oxtail casserole, salmon and prawn kedgeree, and grouse pie – though there's brandade de morue, hasenpfeffer and Peruvian-style pot-roast pork for the adventurous. Alongside pavé au chocolat, or warm poached dates, puddings like junket, treacle tart and bread-and-butter pudding receive top-notch treatment. House wines at £12.95 (£3.25 a glass) anchor a list of three dozen bottles, the majority under £20; there is a generous range by the glass and a fair number of half-bottles.

CHEF: Paul Barnard   PROPRIETORS: Paul and Peta Barnard   OPEN: Tue to Sun L 12 to 2 (2.30 Sun), Tue to Sat D 6.30 to 9.30 (10 Fri and Sat)   CLOSED: 24 Dec D, 25 and 26 Dec   MEALS: alc (main courses £8 to £20). Set L Sun £19.95 (2 courses) to £22.95   SERVICE: not inc, card slips closed   CARDS: Delta, MasterCard, Switch, Visa   DETAILS: 60 seats. 12 seats outside. Private parties: 60 main room, 8 to 18 private rooms. Car park. Vegetarian meals. Children's helpings. No smoking in restaurant. Wheelchair access (not WC). Music. No mobile phones   ACCOMMODATION: 1 room with bath/shower. TV. Phone. D,B&B £95 to £145. Baby facilities (£5)

BUCKLERS HARD Hampshire   map 2

▲ Master Builder's House Hotel, Riverview Restaurant ♥

Bucklers Hard SO42 7XB
TEL: (01590) 616253   FAX: (01590) 616297   COOKING 3
EMAIL: res@themasterbuilders.co.uk   MODERN EUROPEAN
WEBSITE: www.themasterbuilders.co.uk   £31–£54

Steeped in maritime history, the eighteenth-century Master Builder's House is in a peaceful setting on the banks of the Beaulieu River on Lord Montagu's estate. The mood is relaxed, and both the lounge and the chic but informal dining room have river views – the latter also features a collection of David Bailey portraits of 1960s stars.

The menus aim to comfort rather than challenge, with a repertoire of unfussy modern British brasserie-style dishes, ranging from lamb cutlets with garlic purée and sea kale to lemon sole with prawn bisque. Results on the plate may lack a 'wow' factor, but fine ingredients are handled carefully to produce clear, well-balanced flavours, as in a generous starter of tagliatelle with wild mushrooms and Parmesan, a simple main course of 'top-quality, perfectly cooked' grilled halibut on steamed vegetables and baked tomatoes, and an attractive dessert of hot apple and cinnamon soufflé with cinnamon ice cream. A dozen house wines at £12.50 (or £3.95 a glass) make an eminently reasonable start to a solidly (if not masterfully) built short list that majors on France. Wines from the Beaulieu Estate and a focus on champagne add interest.

CHEF: Dennis Rhoden   PROPRIETORS: John Illsley and Jeremy Willcock   OPEN: all week 12 to 3, 7 to 10   MEALS: alc (main courses £10 to £17). Set L £19.95, Set D £29.50   SERVICE: not inc, card slips closed   CARDS: Delta, MasterCard, Switch, Visa   DETAILS: 70 seats. 40 seats outside. Private parties: 40 main room. Car park. Vegetarian meals. Children's helpings. No music   ACCOMMODATION: 25 rooms, all with bath/shower. TV. Phone. B&B £125 to £225

To find a restaurant in a particular area use the maps at the centre of the book.

▲ Jonathan's at the Angel

14 Witney Street, Burford OX18 4SN
TEL: (01993) 822714   FAX: (01993) 822069   COOKING 5
EMAIL: jo@theangel-uk.com   MODERN EUROPEAN/BRASSERIE
WEBSITE: www.theangel-uk.com   £30–£60

On a narrow lane off the main street, the Angel is a honey-coloured Cotswolds coaching inn (the owners describe it as a brasserie-with-rooms) dating from the Tudor period, with window boxes and lots of flowers and greenery outside. At the back is a pleasant courtyard for outside dining. Inside, there's a bar with the menu chalked above it. With beamed ceilings, an open fire, old oak floorboards and a cheerful ambience, the place oozes character.

It is to the menu above the bar that most eyes turn, to read the frequently changing specials. Starters might include rich vegetable soup accompanied by plump wild mushroom ravioli, or a moist truffle risotto with roast asparagus and rocket dressing. 'Tender and tasty' fore rib of Scottish beef, cooked rare, satisfied at inspection, as did its accompaniment of lighter-than-usual Yorkshire pudding. Care is taken with vegetables, too, which are cooked al dente. Ice creams and sorbets are made in-house, but, if in more indulgent mood, finish with a beautifully nutty and creamy iced praline and meringue parfait, served with a mini rum baba and mango coulis. 'At its best, a good to very good restaurant, with good ingredients and no short-cuts,' summed up a reporter, although service can be slow. The short wine list has eight house recommendations, from £13.75 to £16.50 a bottle (£4.50 to £4.95 a glass).

CHEFS: Jonathan Lewis and Greig Palmer   PROPRIETOR: Jonathan Lewis   OPEN: Tue to Sun L 12 to 2, Tue to Sat D 7 to 9.30   MEALS: alc (main courses £11 to £19.50). Set L £14.50 (2 courses) to £18.50. Light L menu available Tue to Sat   SERVICE: not inc, card slips closed   CARDS: MasterCard, Switch, Visa   DETAILS: 34 seats. 25 seats outside. Private parties: 40 main room. Vegetarian meals. Children's helpings. No-smoking area. Wheelchair access (not WC). Music. No mobile phones   ACCOMMODATION: 3 rooms, all with bath/shower. TV. Phone. B&B £70 to £98. No children under 9 (The Which? Guide to Good Hotels) £5

Fishes ⁵⁄✳

Market Place, Burnham Market PE31 8HE
TEL: (01328) 738588   FAX: (01328) 730534   COOKING 4
EMAIL: buzzmatt@eggconnect.net   SEAFOOD
WEBSITE: www.burnhammarket.co.uk   £25–£71

Big bay windows overlook the beautiful village green from this relaxed, fresh feeling restaurant, devoted to fish (book ahead if you want meat or vegetarian dishes). Much is delivered from local fishermen – the menu changes twice a day, to reflect what's available – and flour for the consistently praised breads comes from a nearby mill. Essentially simple combinations are executed in style: for example, Dublin Bay prawns with aïoli and lemon, a perfectly balanced intense red fish soup, or plaice with chips and tartare sauce. Underlying the cooking is a sharp intelligence that produces dishes from date-, almond- and feta-stuffed mackerel, via Norfolk smoked eel with foie gras and piquillo terrine, to tandoori monkfish with chana masala and kachumba. There are some interesting puddings (like compote of winter fruit and nuts with Pedro Ximenez ice cream) and decent pastry work. The set-price menus (you can also order all dishes individually) are good value. Good coffee and a generous willingness to discuss recipes contribute further to the atmosphere of relaxed and confident professionalism. Wines are a good modern mix at mostly very reasonable prices, with whites the major interest. Bottles start at £10.95, with six by the glass (£2.95 to £5.50).

CHEFS: Matthew Owsley-Brown and Nigel Coleman   PROPRIETORS: Matthew and Caroline Owsley-Brown   OPEN: Tue to Sun L 12 to 2, Tue to Sat D 7 to 9.30   CLOSED: 14 to 26 Dec, 4 to 31 Jan, 22 to 30 June   MEALS: alc (main courses L £8.50 to £12.50, D £13 to £28). Set L £15.50, Set D £20 (2 courses) to £25   SERVICE: not inc, card slips closed   CARDS: Delta, MasterCard, Switch, Visa   DETAILS: 42 seats. Private parties: 12 main room, 6 to 12 private rooms. Children's helpings. No children after 8.30pm. No smoking. Wheelchair access (not WC). Music

▲ Hoste Arms ♥ ⅝ £

The Green, Burnham Market PE31 8HD
TEL: (01328) 738777   FAX: (01328) 730103
EMAIL: reception@hostearms.co.uk
WEBSITE: www.hostearms.co.uk

COOKING 2
MODERN BRITISH
£30–£56

This buttercup-yellow inn in the heart of a pretty village has three dining rooms served by a hard-working kitchen that produces its own excellent granary bread and a lengthy brasserie-style menu. At inspection, three giant, beautifully fresh but insufficiently sealed scallops came with an 'excellent, intense' parsnip purée; other starters could be pan-fried veal sweetbreads, or tea-smoked trout chowder. One diner's main-course slab of tasty halibut had a creamy yet *al dente* pancetta risotto with it; meat eaters might fancy roast best end of lamb with pommes dauphinoise and roast vegetables. Puds range from ice creams and sorbets to liquorice crème brûlée or treacle tart, and friendly, responsive service draws the customers back. Scanning the short, to-the-point wine list or browsing the fuller, annotated version uncovers some bargains and hefty flavours. Australian, South African and Tuscan reds are well represented, and there are fine clarets and Burgundies too. Prices start at £10.75 with ten by the glass from £2.60 (175ml) or £3.70 (250ml).

CHEF: Andrew McPherson   PROPRIETOR: Paul Whittome   OPEN: all week 12 to 2, 7 to 9   CLOSED: 24 Dec D, 31 Dec L   MEALS: alc (main courses £9.50 to £16.50)   SERVICE: not inc, card slips closed   CARDS: Delta, MasterCard, Switch, Visa   DETAILS: 120 seats. 60 seats outside. Private parties: 70 main room, 15 to 25 private rooms. Car park. Vegetarian meals. Children's helpings. No smoking in 1 dining room. Wheelchair access (also WC). Occasional music. Air-conditioned ACCOMMODATION: 36 rooms, all with bath/shower. TV. Phone. B&B £71 to £200. Rooms for disabled (*The Which? Guide to Good Hotels*)

£ *means that it is possible to have a three-course meal, including coffee, half a bottle of house wine and service for £30 or less per person, at any time the restaurant is open, i.e. at dinner as well as lunch. It may be possible to spend considerably more than this, but by choosing carefully you should find £30 or less achievable.*

BURNSALL North Yorkshire   map 8

▲ Devonshire Fell

Burnsall BD23 6BT
TEL: (01756) 729000   FAX: (01756) 729009   COOKING **2**
EMAIL: reservations@thedevonshirearms.co.uk   MODERN BRITISH
WEBSITE: www.devonshirehotels.co.uk   £27–£50

Originally a club for 'gentlemen mill owners', this impressive, tall stone edifice is now a country hotel with colourful gardens and glorious views over the River Wharfe. You can eat in the central modern bar, with its glass, mirrors and light wooden floor, or settle for the plush surroundings of the conservatory dining room. One brasserie-style menu – livened up by daily specials – is served throughout, and it divides up into 'Simple' and 'Tapas' (spicy lamb kofta, chicken tikka, skewered anchovies and the like) before 'Considerable' roast duck breast with braised red cabbage, or fillet of sea bass with creamed leeks and mustard sauce. There are also a few meat and fish grills, plus puddings along the lines of blueberry macaroon, or Baileys cheesecake. Service is 'willing' if a little inexperienced. The well-chosen wine list is a broad selection arranged by price. House recommendations begin at £2.40 a glass, £11.95 a bottle.

CHEF: Neil Waterfield   PROPRIETOR: The Duke of Devonshire   OPEN: all week 11.30 to 2.30, 6.30 to 10 (9.30 Sun)   MEALS: alc (main courses £6 to £17)   SERVICE: not inc   CARDS: Amex, Delta, Diners, MasterCard, Switch, Visa   DETAILS: 50 seats. 12 seats outside. Private parties: 70 main room. Car park. Vegetarian meals. Children's helpings. No smoking in 1 dining room. Wheelchair access (also WC). Occasional music   ACCOMMODATION: 12 rooms, all with bath/shower. TV. Phone. B&B £70 to £160. Baby facilities (*The Which? Guide to Good Hotels*)

BURRINGTON Devon   map 1

▲ Northcote Manor

Burrington EX37 9LZ
TEL: (01769) 560501   FAX: (01769) 560770
EMAIL: rest@northcotemanor.co.uk
WEBSITE: www.northcotemanor.co.uk   COOKING **3**
on A377 between Umberleigh and Crediton, 4m   MODERN FRENCH
NW of Chulmleigh   £36–£62

Owners and chef changed in late 2002, but this fine, sprawling stone-built house in 20 acres of garden and woodland, encompassing within an inviting sofa-strewn lounge and calmly warm dining room, all remain well cared for. The modern European style of cooking now leans more distinctly towards France – in, for example, springtime starters of confit of duck and red cabbage, or chicken liver parfait, followed by sea bass with spinach and saffron beurre blanc, or lamb with cassis sauce. Greater consistency though is needed to justify the highish prices. At inspection provençale tart and a rabbit terrine were disappointments, but Dover sole had a suitably firm texture and the beurre blanc was nicely piquant, and moist chicken breast had a good depth of flavour and showed careful sourcing. Puddings are favourites such as pannacotta with raspberries, or chocolate brownie with orange sorbet. A list of good to grand bottles has scarcely anything below £20, but house wines start at £13.95.

CHEF: Christophe Lorillard   PROPRIETORS: Mr and Mrs J.P. Mifsud   OPEN: all week 12.30 to 2, 7 to 9   MEALS: Set L £18.50 (2 courses) to £25.50, Set D £35. Snack menu available   SERVICE: not inc, card slips closed   CARDS: Amex, Diners, MasterCard, Switch, Visa   DETAILS: 35 seats. Private parties: 80 main room, 2 to 20 private rooms. Car park. Vegetarian meals. Children's helpings. No smoking. Occasional music. No mobile phones   ACCOMMODATION: 11 rooms, all with bath/shower. TV. Phone. B&B £99 to £230. Baby facilities (*The Which? Guide to Good Hotels*) £5

BURTON ON THE WOLDS Leicestershire   map 5

Langs ⚡✻

Horse Leys Farm, 147 Melton Road, Burton on
the Wolds LE12 5TQ

TEL/FAX: (01509) 880980   COOKING **4**
EMAIL: langsrestaurant@amserve.net   MODERN EUROPEAN
WEBSITE: www.langsrestaurant.co.uk   £24–£50

The converted farmhouse that is now Langs is named on the Ordnance Survey Landranger map, indicating both its size and also its comparative isolation. Inside, terracotta and cream are the predominant colours, and stout ceiling beams add solidity. Gordon Lang's menus read simply and enticingly, and deliver the flavours they promise with creditable panache. A Sunday lunch for one party provided satisfaction in the form of crab terrine, smoked bacon and cherry tomato salad, fine roast beef with gratin dauphinois, real rice pudding, and a version of pavlova that seemed almost to eschew the meringue component but was still richly tasty. Sometimes presentation might appear to upset the applecart, as in gravad lax made into a gâteau and garnished with Parmesan crisps and avocado, but techniques are sound, matching crisp-roasted duck breast with bacon and Puy lentils, and adding apple to bread-and-butter pudding. Service is laudably attentive, and wines are a reasonably well-chosen, if pricey, bunch, fairly spread between France and the New World. House wines are £12.75 and £13.75 a bottle, £3.10 and £3.20 a glass.

CHEF: Gordon Lang   PROPRIETORS: Gordon Lang and Paul Simms   OPEN: Tue to Fri and Sun L 12 to 2 (2.30 Sun), Tue to Sat D 7.15 to 9.45 (10 Sat)   MEALS: alc exc Sun L (main courses £12 to £16.50). Set L Tue to Fri £12 (2 courses) to £14, Set L Sun £14.95, Set D Tue to Fri £16.50   SERVICE: not inc, card slips closed   CARDS: Delta, MasterCard, Switch, Visa   DETAILS: 50 seats. 20 seats outside. Car park. Vegetarian meals. Children's helpings. No smoking. Wheelchair access (also WC). No music. No mobile phones

---

BUSHEY Hertfordshire   map 3

St James ⚡✻

30 High Street, Bushey WD23 3HL   COOKING **2**
TEL: (020) 8950 2480   FAX: (020) 8950 4107   MODERN ENGLISH
                                                                                            £31–£57

A converted shop in a suburban shopping parade, St James's large glass frontage looks out on to the parish church, attractively floodlit at night. Though one diner thought brick walls and wooden floors not conducive to a quiet environment, another highlighted the very warm welcome and felt 'good furnishings and well-appointed tables make for a pleasing, relaxing setting'. Leek and potato soup or smooth chicken pâté and onion marmalade might feature among starters. To follow, calf's liver on bacon, slices of veal on rösti and spinach, and excellent tournedos, 'cooked to rare perfection with a mustard and herb crust', have all been enjoyed. Desserts receive a more lukewarm response, but lemon posset with ginger biscuits and balsamic berries pleased one reporter. A fairly basic list of mostly French and Italian wines is complemented by some serious Bordeaux and Burgundy. House wines are £11.95.

CHEF: Simon Trussel   PROPRIETORS: Simon Trussel and Alfonso la Cava   OPEN: Mon to Sat 12 to 2, 6.30 to 9.30   CLOSED: 25 Dec, bank hols   MEALS: alc (main courses £15 to £18). Set L and D £13.95 (2 courses)   SERVICE: 12.5%, card slips closed   CARDS: Amex, MasterCard, Switch, Visa   DETAILS: 80 seats. Private parties: 80 main room, 30 to 45 private rooms. Vegetarian meals. No smoking in 1 dining room. Wheelchair access (also WC). Music. No mobile phones. Air-conditioned

---

BUXTON Derbyshire   màp 5

Columbine ⅝ £   NEW ENTRY

7 Hall Bank, Buxton SK17 6EW
TEL: (01298) 78752   FAX: (01298) 71561   COOKING 2
EMAIL: www.columbine1@btinternet.com   MODERN BRITISH
WEBSITE: www.buxtononline.net/columbine   £24–£37

This popular restaurant up behind the King's Head Hotel may prove hard to find, so ring for directions. Portions here are large, but the cooking is simultaneously skilled, sensitive and robust. White fish soup (two shelled crab claws clinging to the rim, excellent fish stock liquor the texture of full-cream milk, chunky pieces of cod and haddock and floating fresh herbs) made a fine start for an inspector, preceding sweet, tender lamb, almost drowning in a good lamb stock infused strongly with rosemary. Or a large fillet each of moist yet springy sea bass and bream may come on leeks with elaborate decoration of flaky pastry crescents, radish, carrot and raw tomato. Finish, if you've room, with a large triangle of light, moist bread-and-butter pudding, scented delicately with nutmeg, in a sea of creamy vanilla custard. Wines rely on big producers; starting at £8.95 they continue the generosity, with virtually everything below £15.

CHEF: Steve McNally   PROPRIETOR: Kim and Steve McNally   OPEN: Wed to Sat and Mon (Mon to Sat May to Oct) D 7 to 9.45   CLOSED: 24 Dec to 1 Jan   MEALS: alc (main courses £9 to £13). Light L menu available Thur to Sat July to mid-Aug; pre- and post-theatre available (prior booking required)   SERVICE: not inc, card slips closed   CARDS: Delta, MasterCard, Switch, Visa DETAILS: 45 seats. Private parties: 20 main room, 10 to 20 private rooms. Vegetarian meals. Children's helpings. No smoking in 1 dining room. Music

---

All details are as accurate as possible at the time of going to press, but chefs and owners often change, and it is wise to check by telephone before making a special journey. Many readers have been disappointed when set-price bargain meals are no longer available. Ask when booking.

CAMBRIDGE Cambridgeshire map 6

▲ Hotel Felix `NEW ENTRY`

Whitehouse Lane, Huntingdon Road,
Cambridge CB3 0LX
TEL: (01223) 277977   FAX: (01223) 277973
EMAIL: help@hotelfelix.co.uk
WEBSITE: www.hotelfelix.co.uk

COOKING 2
MEDITERRANEAN
£35–£62

At this slick new hotel in a refurbished and extended Victorian mansion, opened in November 2002, some things were still settling down when the Guide inspected. The Graffiti restaurant, crisp, chic and contemporary, has shades of mushroom and grey, dark floorboards and a wire sculpture (male torso *sans* fig leaf) over the fireplace. Stuart Conibear previously worked at the Ivy and the Dorchester. His menu – big on ingredients like cavolo nero, amaretti, chorizo, smoked paprika and treviso – may open with fabulously tender home-smoked duck breast with shallot compote, potato rösti and cassis vinaigrette, or a goats' cheese and red onion tartlet with baby spinach and sautéed girolles. Trendy-sounding main courses might include marinated tuna loin with a pine kernel crust, or monkfish tail wrapped in Parma ham with squid-ink tagliatelle. Desserts, like panettone bread-and-butter pudding, or tarte Tatin, are more traditional. The wine list is cosmopolitan and the pricing fair, with house wines from £10.25.

CHEF: Stuart Conibear   PROPRIETORS: Jeremy and Vivien Cassel   OPEN: all week 12 to 2, 6.30 to 10 (10.30 Fri and Sat)   MEALS: alc (main courses £12 to £22). Café/bar menu available   SERVICE: not inc   CARDS: Amex, Delta, Diners, MasterCard, Switch, Visa   DETAILS: 50 seats. 40 seats outside. Private parties: 60 main room, 6 to 40 private rooms. Car park. Vegetarian meals. Children's helpings. Wheelchair access (also WC). Music   ACCOMMODATION: 52 rooms, all with bath/shower. TV. Phone. B&B £125 to £260. Rooms for disabled. Baby facilities (*The Which? Guide to Good Hotels*) £5

Midsummer House ✸✷

Midsummer Common, Cambridge CB4 1HA
TEL: (01223) 369299   FAX: (01223) 302672
EMAIL: reservations@midsummerhouse.co.uk
WEBSITE: www.midsummerhouse.co.uk

COOKING 6
FRENCH/MEDITERRANEAN
£41–£101

Reached by a footbridge over the Cam, and with the common stretching out in front, Midsummer House has bagged itself a prime spot. With its conservatory and yellow dining room walls hung with bright oil paintings for sale, it looks posh and feels romantic. The food is a clever mix of classical and avant-garde, with a strong French bias, offering, for example, pot-roast squab pigeon with pistachio nuts, cocoa nibs, caraway syrup and Valrhona sauce, or steamed sea bass with crab mousse, chilli syrup and vanilla froth.

Underlying all this are 'first-rate raw materials faultlessly handled', with fine judgement applied to timing and saucing: for example, a thick, de-boned salmon steak (pink, moist, lightly cooked) wrapped around a solid chunk of foie gras, the richness countered by a dribble of oystery dressing. Although quite busy (that dish also included tiny dice of cucumber and saffron potato with dabs of seaweed jelly), the food stops short of being fussy. Nevertheless, presentation is taken as seriously as anything, judging by a 'space potato' of crisply fried filaments hovering above the plate thanks to a central hole fitted around a cone of buttery spinach; chunks of pink, perfectly timed veal kidney lay around this, together with some snails and a sauce tasting of the 'essence of parsley'.

Gentle invention is also applied to desserts, which might turn up dark chocolate with banana ice cream, coconut bubbles and lime candyfloss. Incidentals might include a cucumber jelly with salmon dice and cauliflower froth, a range of painstakingly made and notably sweet pre-dessert bonbons, and 'row upon neat diagonal row' of chocolates with coffee. Service can be a bit 'bossy' (a visitors' book is presented for signing at the end), and reporters gasp in unison at the high prices. The excellent wine list, with plenty of interest in the New World as well as great depth in traditional regions, plus a fine range of dessert wines, is marred only by the prices, though just over 20 come by the glass, from £4 to £13.50.

CHEF: Daniel Clifford   PROPRIETOR: Midsummer House Ltd   OPEN: Tue to Sat 12 to 2, 7 to 10   MEALS: Set L £20 (2 courses) to £48, Set D £45 to £65   SERVICE: not inc, 12.5% for parties of 7 or more   CARDS: Amex, Delta, MasterCard, Switch, Visa   DETAILS: 60 seats. Private parties: 50 main room, 10 to 22 private rooms. Children's helpings. No smoking. Wheelchair access (not WC). No music. No mobile phones (£5)

Twenty Two Chesterton Road ⅝✶

22 Chesterton Road, Cambridge CB4 3AX
TEL: (01223) 351880   FAX: (01223) 323814
EMAIL: davidcarter@restaurant22.co.uk
WEBSITE: www.restaurant22.co.uk

COOKING 2
MODERN EUROPEAN
£34–£59

First park your car (leave plenty of time). Then enter what feels like an old-fashioned family living room, but for the closely packed tables and upholstered chairs. Here a three-course menu offers four choices at each, plus an intermediate salad and an optional extra fishy second course. A crisp-crusted fresh mackerel fillet, garnished with diced tomatoes and fennel, was a tasty starter, and a very good tarragon stock sauce accompanied roast guinea fowl. Otherwise, there might be French onion and cider soup to start, followed by beef bourguignonne with Parmesan tuiles and gremolata, and then a pudding like tiramisù with coffee bean sauce. Slow service has been reported, but one diner welcomed the staff's unpushy yet responsive approach. Interesting 'special parcels' supplement a French-oriented wine list that includes creditable short selections from elsewhere. Prices are fair all round, and four house wines start at £11.95.

CHEF: Martin Cullum   PROPRIETOR: David Carter   OPEN: Tue to Sat D only 7 to 9.45   CLOSED: 1 week Christmas to New Year   MEALS: Set D £24.50   SERVICE: not inc   CARDS: Amex, Delta, Diners, MasterCard, Switch, Visa   DETAILS: 40 seats. Private parties: 26 main room, 12 private room. Vegetarian meals. No children under 10. No smoking. Occasional music. No mobile phones. Air-conditioned

---

(£5) indicates that the restaurant has elected to participate in the Good Food Guide voucher scheme. For full details, see page 6.

CANTERBURY Kent
map 3

Goods Shed £

NEW ENTRY

Station Road West, Canterbury CT2 8AN
TEL: (01227) 459153

COOKING 3
MODERN BRITISH
£25–£48

The Goods Shed is not the sort of place you come across every day. A restaurant in a farmers' market (originally a Victorian railway shed) that serves cracking food cooked by a chef who has trained at places like Le Gavroche (see entry, London), using only produce from the market, is indeed trendsetting. The dining area is on a raised wooden platform along one wall, with the kitchen open to view at one end. In terms of cooking, everything is dead simple and entirely unpretentious but based on superb fresh produce. A starter of seared scallops with butter-bean purée, drizzled with a vivid green herby dressing, and main courses such as slow-cooked belly pork with apple, impress with their clarity of flavours and skilful execution. To round off, there may be cheeses, in fine condition, or puddings such as lemon meringue pie. Although some have been heard to mutter about 'London prices', the Goods Shed represents good value for food of this quality. A short list of wines is chalked up on a blackboard, most under £20; or BYO for a modest corkage charge of £3.

CHEF: Blaise Vasseur   PROPRIETOR: Susanna Atkins   OPEN: Tue to Sun L 12 to 2.30 (3 Sat and Sun), Tue to Sat D 6 to 9.30   MEALS: alc (main courses £7.50 to £16). Set L and D £25   SERVICE: not inc   CARDS: Delta, Diners, MasterCard, Switch, Visa   DETAILS: 75 seats. Car park. Vegetarian meals. Children's helpings. No-smoking area. No music

CARLISLE Cumbria
map 10

Number 10 ⅹ

10 Eden Mount, Stanwix, Carlisle CA3 9LY
TEL/FAX: (01228) 524183

COOKING 2
MODERN BRITISH
£28–£46

Number 10 is a charming Victorian town house that will take you back to the nursery, thanks to decorative features that include a doll's house and a rocking horse, and things like cruet sets in the shape of toy soldiers. The food is more sophisticated, dealing in the likes of feta cheese terrine with sunblush tomato dressing and rocket and olive salad, or spinach and smoked haddock tart for starters. Main courses, meanwhile, typically take in roast chicken breast with apricot and almond stuffing and a white port and cream sauce, Parmesan-crumbed pork fillet with lemon and crème fraîche sauce, or pan-fried venison steak with caramelised onions and Madeira sauce. To finish, there's grown-up chocolate brandy pot with a white chocolate and almond cake and chocolate sauce, or a childhood throwback in the shape of ginger sponge pudding with toffee sauce. Service is 'charming and helpful', and wines are priced from £10.75.

CHEF: Geoffrey Ferguson   PROPRIETORS: Geoffrey and Isabel Ferguson   OPEN: Tue to Sat D only 7 to 9.30   CLOSED: Feb, 1 week late Oct   MEALS: alc (main courses £11 to £17)   SERVICE: not inc, card slips closed   CARDS: Amex, Delta, MasterCard, Switch, Visa   DETAILS: 24 seats. Private parties: 24 main room. Vegetarian meals. No smoking while others eat. Wheelchair access (not WC). Music

CARTMEL Cumbria

map 8

▲ Aynsome Manor ⁵✳ £

Cartmel LA11 6HH
TEL: (01539) 536653   FAX: (01539) 536016
EMAIL: info@aynsomemanorhotel.co.uk
WEBSITE: www.aynsomemanorhotel.co.uk
off A590, 1m N of village

COOKING 2
COUNTRY-HOUSE
£25–£41

This eighteenth-century house with its redecorated Victorian dining room has a faintly old-fashioned feel, yet provides the backdrop for a cuisine that takes in such outré items as confit of Norfolk duckling with chorizo mash and Drambuie jus, or smoked haddock crème brûlée with endive and basil salad. Main courses might pair fried veal escalope with champ potatoes and mustard velouté, for example, or monkfish with ratatouille, fennel cream and tomato coulis. Much is satisfying – salmon with saffron and crab butter sauce, or a tempura of two kinds of melon with a fruit sorbet – although an inspector found some shortcomings in the timing and composition of dishes. Desserts may be the best part, judging by a sticky toffee pudding, and a properly cinnamon-poached pear with a first-rate sweet basil ice cream and chocolate sauce. Wines, from Europe and the New World, are well-chosen, varied and fairly priced; half a dozen house wines are £12.

CHEFS: Nicholas Stopford and Daniel Richards   PROPRIETORS: Tony, Margaret, Christopher and Andrea Varley   OPEN: Sun L 1, Mon to Sat D 7 to 8.30   CLOSED: 2 to 29 Jan   MEALS: Set L Sun £14.75, Set D £19.50 to £23.50   SERVICE: not inc   CARDS: Amex, Delta, MasterCard, Switch, Visa   DETAILS: 28 seats. Private parties: 28 main room. Car park. Vegetarian meals. No children under 5 at dinner. Children's helpings. No smoking. No music   ACCOMMODATION: 12 rooms, all with bath/shower. TV. Phone. D,B&B £56 to £152. Baby facilities (*The Which? Guide to Good Hotels*) £5

▲ L'Enclume ♥ ⁵✳

CUMBRIA
OF THE
YEAR
NEWCOMER

NEW ENTRY

Cavendish Street, Cartmel LA11 6PZ
TEL: (015395) 36362   FAX: (015395) 38907
EMAIL: info@lenclume.co.uk
WEBSITE: www.lenclume.co.uk

COOKING 6
MODERN EUROPEAN
£33–£143

The former smithy – in a narrow street near the priory – has been turned into a smart restaurant-with-rooms. It looks quite the most modern thing to have hit Cartmel for years, and is an embodiment of the chef/patron's ambition to put the village on the gastronomic map. Plate-glass doors lead to a light, open-plan dining room where rough-textured walls, flagstone floor, beamed ceiling and colourful modern artworks add up to a 'clean and tasteful' combination of rustic and contemporary. An anvil (enclume) is, of course, on display.

The cooking is creative and confident, with a sense of direction and purpose, and has made quite a splash in the Lakes. Presentation is a strong point, and dishes tend to arrive as tottering towers: for example, three identical ones built from fondant potato, pak choi, seared sea bass, and a 'knockout' lobster beignet; or a lamb version combining a disc of sweetly braised shoulder topped by a nugget of sweetbread wrapped in spinach, next to a fat cube of herb-thatched lamb fillet, all surrounded by a neat version of ratatouille, in a well-judged stock and balsamic sauce.

Sourcing and timing of materials are both admirable, with only the occasional stumble, and combinations are well considered, be they a line of roast scallops and fat, shelled langoustines with a slick of carrot and cardamom emulsion, or the more adventurous circular 'cake' of well-flavoured oxtail meat wrapped in caul and sandwiched between discs of turnip, topped with a sliver of grilled turbot fillet. That same sense of balance runs through into desserts. Three blobs of thick anise-infused custard, for example, accompany a sliced poached pear layered with 'something appealingly biscuity', while a four-part assiette of lemon makes the most of its textural contrasts: a tiny wedge of micro-thin pastry with a sharp-tasting filling, an ice cream wafer, a hot soufflé, and a blob of soft, creamy mousse.

The repertoire is an evolving one, with the promise of more in the way of local materials to come – including herbs, roots and tinctures – that may have fallen out of favour. Service is friendly and easy-going, without airs or graces, and yet polite and correct, while wines have an eye for quality without breaking the bank. France is the main wine interest, and that includes poking about for good bottles from odd corners like Arbois and the Côte Roannaise. Burgundy looks exciting and the Loire and the Rhône are well covered, but Bordeaux is a bit uneven, with a few gaps and some surprisingly young vintages. New World bottles are interesting. Nine by the glass start at £3.

CHEF/PROPRIETOR: Simon Rogan   OPEN: Tue to Sun 12 to 1.45, 7 to 9.30   MEALS: alc (main courses £19 to £26). Set L £19.50, Set D £75 (inc wine) to £95   SERVICE: not inc   CARDS: Amex, Delta, Diners, MasterCard, Switch, Visa   DETAILS: 50 seats. 20 seats outside. Private parties: 50 main room, 1 to 10 private rooms. Car park. No children under 10. No smoking. Wheelchair access (not WC). Occasional music. No mobile phones   ACCOMMODATION: 7 rooms, all with bath/shower. TV. Phone. B&B £120 to £200. Rooms for disabled. Baby facilities (*The Which? Guide to Good Hotels*)

▲ Uplands ⁵⁄✻

Haggs Lane, Cartmel LA11 6HD
TEL: (015395) 36248   FAX: (015395) 36848
EMAIL: uplands@kencomp.net
WEBSITE: www.uplands.uk.com
2½m SW of A590, 1m up road opposite Pig and
Whistle

COOKING **4**
BRITISH
£25–£48

Cartmel is an attractive low-lying village in a setting that is more reminiscent of the rolling Dales than the craggy peaks of Lakeland. The format at Uplands is set in stone, and the repertoire changes little, but the kitchen's skills have been finely honed over the years. Dinner starts at 8, perhaps with langoustines and crab with endive salad dressed with caper mayonnaise, or pan-fried calf's liver with bacon and an onion and kumquat sauce. Next comes soup – always a highlight – served in generous measure in a tureen for the table to share and accompanied by freshly baked bread. The Lakeland idiom is expressed to the full at main-course stage, where sea bass fillet with ginger and spring onions and chive sauce, or braised guinea fowl with bread sauce, game chips and port sauce, are served with the same selection of five elaborate vegetables. Strawberry and passion-fruit pavlova, and chocolate and Grand Marnier mousse are the sort of things to expect for dessert. The short wine list offers a good range of fairly priced wines, with plenty under £20, including six house wines at £12.50.

CHEF: Tom Peter   PROPRIETORS: Tom and Diana Peter   OPEN: Fri to Sun L 12.30 for 1 (1 sitting), Tue to Sun D 7.30 for 8 (1 sitting)   MEALS: Set L £16.50, Set D £30   SERVICE: not inc, card slips closed   CARDS: Amex, Delta, MasterCard, Switch, Visa   DETAILS: 28 seats. Private parties: 28 main room. Car park. Children's helpings. No children under 8. No smoking. No music ACCOMMODATION: 5 rooms, all with bath/shower. TV. Phone. D,B&B £142 to £162 (double room). No children under 8 (*The Which? Guide to Good Hotels*)

CASTLE COMBE Wiltshire   map 2

▲ Manor House, Bybrook Restaurant £✗

Castle Combe SN14 7HR
TEL: (01249) 782206   FAX: (01249) 782159
EMAIL: hmeager@manor-housecc.co.uk
WEBSITE: www.exclusivehotels.co.uk
on B4039, 3m NW of junction with A420

COOKING 3
ENGLISH
£37–£106

Manicured lawns and a stream are the 'idyllic' setting for this grand manor house. The Bybrook Restaurant has equally attractive views over the grounds, and its smart white-clothed tables set the scene for some serious eating. The menus might start with smoked haddock soup, guinea-fowl cake with port and lentils, or seared Irish scallops with caramelised chicory and a Sauternes emulsion. Main courses have taken in a 'perfectly timed' breast of guinea fowl with a 'daring combination' of turnip dauphinois and red onion with beetroot, and seared Shetland salmon with capers, sultanas and parsley. There is plenty to satisfy vegetarians, too, such as a warm tart of blue cheese and pears with rocket salad and walnut oil, and, in the evening, a seven-course gourmet menu alongside a more carnivorous one. Sunday lunch has produced 'utterly melt-in-the-mouth' roast beef, and desserts have not been short of praise either: warm chocolate tart with coffee ice cream, for example, or rich hazelnut parfait topped with raspberry sorbet. Service, from well-trained staff, is attentive and, despite steep prices on the comprehensive wine list, a good range of half-bottles and a six-strong house selection make it possible to select wines around £20.

CHEF: Mark Taylor   PROPRIETOR: Exclusive Hotels   OPEN: all week 12.30 to 2 (1.30 Sun), 7 to 9.30 MEALS: Set L Mon to Sat £16.95 (2 courses) to £18.95, Set L Sun £24.50, Set D Sun to Thur £35 to £65, Set D Fri and Sat £45 to £65. Bar menu available   SERVICE: not inc, card slips closed CARDS: Amex, MasterCard, Switch, Visa   DETAILS: 108 seats. Private parties: 108 main room, 4 to 12 private rooms. Car park. Vegetarian meals. Children's helpings. No smoking. Wheelchair access (also WC). No music. No mobile phones   ACCOMMODATION: 47 rooms, all with bath/ shower. TV. Phone. Room only £145 to £500. Rooms for disabled. Baby facilities. Swimming pool. Fishing (*The Which? Guide to Good Hotels*)

CAUNTON Nottinghamshire

map 5

Caunton Beck ⅄✳

Main Street, Caunton NG23 6AB
TEL: (01636) 636793   FAX: (01636) 636828

COOKING 2
MODERN EUROPEAN/PACIFIC RIM
£21–£47

This pub and restaurant is housed in a meticulously restored sixteenth-century cottage in the pretty village of Caunton. The bar area, with a low beamed ceiling and an open fireplace, leads to a comfortable dining room. Informality is the order of the day here, and a relaxed atmosphere pervades. Menus are short, with about seven first courses and seven mains. One reporter referred to a starter of cream of carrot and coriander soup as 'a winner', while main courses such as roast whole skate wing au poivre demonstrate the kitchen's ability to source good-quality produce and turn out satisfying dishes. Finish with warm blackberry and frangipane tart, or bitter chocolate ganache with vanilla ice cream. The set lunch and dinner menus offer limited choice but good value. Some fine producers show up on the wine list, and there is plenty of choice by the glass, including a well-chosen selection of dessert wines. Bottle prices start at £10.50.

CHEFS: Andrew Pickstock and Katie Crewe   PROPRIETOR: Wig & Mitre   OPEN: all week 8 to 11
MEALS: alc (main courses £8 to £17). Set L and D (exc Sun L and Sat D) £10 (2 courses) to £12.95. Breakfast and sandwich menu available   SERVICE: not inc   CARDS: Amex, Delta, Diners, MasterCard, Switch, Visa   DETAILS: 120 seats. 40 seats outside. Private parties: 55 main room, 30 private room. Car park. Vegetarian meals. Children's helpings. No smoking. Wheelchair access (also WC). No music   £5

CAVENDISH Suffolk

map 6

▲ George ⅄✳

NEW ENTRY

The Green, Cavendish CO10 8BA
TEL: (01787) 280248   FAX: (01787) 281703
EMAIL: reservations@georgecavendish.co.uk
WEBSITE: www.georgecavendish.co.uk

COOKING 4
MODERN BRITISH
£28–£57

Rural England barely gets more picture postcard than this. The timber-framed building that houses the George is around six centuries old, sits right on the village green with the church behind, and is more of a restaurant-with-rooms than a pub nowadays, although the small bar is open all day. The Nicholsons, who took over in 2002, have retained an understated feel to the place, with exposed beams and brickwork and solid wooden furniture. Eat indoors or out, and expect some high-flown modern British cooking, embellished with plenty of international touches. The fixed-price menu might see you journeying from crispy duck spring rolls with hoisin sauce and celeriac rémoulade, through poached finnan haddock with a poached egg, crushed new potatoes, sautéed spinach and grain mustard velouté, to arrive in satisfaction at hot caramelised banana with rum and raisin ice cream.

Ingredients are local when possible, and the meat cookery is a special draw, with accurately timed Aberdeen Angus sirloin with Yorkshire pudding and horseradish at Sunday lunchtime, or pot-roast honey-glazed lamb shank with parsnip mash, green beans and rosemary jus. Cosmopolitanism extends to bread-and-butter pudding made with panettone, and the European cheeses that are served with spiced pear. Relaxed, friendly service makes everyone feel at home, while a short but carefully chosen wine list opens with French country wines at £9.95 and ascends to a handful of pedigree Burgundies.

CHEF: Jonathan Nicholson   PROPRIETORS: Jonathan and Charlotte Nicholson   OPEN: all week 12 to 3, 6 to 10   CLOSED: 2 weeks Jan, Sun D Oct to Apr   MEALS: alc (main courses £8.50 to £20). Set D £12.95 (1 course) to £19.95. Light L menu available Mon to Sat   SERVICE: not inc   CARDS: Delta, MasterCard, Switch, Visa   DETAILS: 52 seats. 40 seats outside. Private parties: 24 main room, 10 to 22 private rooms. Vegetarian meals. Children's helpings. No smoking. Music   ACCOMMODATION: 4 rooms, all with bath/shower. TV. Phone. B&B £45 to £95. Baby facilities   (£5)

CHADDESLEY CORBETT Worcestershire   map 5

▲ Brockencote Hall ⅝✳

Chaddesley Corbett DY10 4PY
TEL: (01562) 777876   FAX: (01562) 777872
EMAIL: info@brockencotehall.com
WEBSITE: www.brockencotehall.com
on A448, Kidderminster to Bromsgrove road, just
outside village

COOKING 4
MODERN FRENCH
£27–£65

This French-owned country-house hotel, with a French chef and mostly French staff, is set in 70 acres of landscaped grounds. It is 'well cared for, in a French château style, with a beautiful garden and patio with wide views'. 'Modern French fusion cooking with Mediterranean and European influences' is how the owners describe the style. There are two menus, an à la carte and a table d'hôte, the former more expensive but 'well worth the difference', according to one visitor. On offer may be a signature dish of frogs' legs with organic shiitake mushroom mousse and garlic and celeriac cream, or grilled red mullet with plum tomato and olive tart for starters. Move on to, say, wild sea bass from Devon served with lemon linguine, or tournedos of Scottish beef with wild mushrooms and a truffle reduction, before choosing between baked banana cheesecake, or pineapple carpaccio and a pink pepper tuile. Ingredients are sourced with care, using local produce where possible. Service is professional but friendly, while the wine list concentrates on Bordeaux and Burgundy and pretty much ignores the world outside France. House wines are £12.80.

CHEF: Jérôme Barbançon   PROPRIETORS: Alison and Joseph Petitjean   OPEN: Sun to Fri L 12 to 1.30, all week D 7 to 9.30   MEALS: alc (main courses £13.50 to £22.50). Set L Mon to Fri £13 (2 courses) to £17, Set L Sun £22.50, Set D £27.50 to £42.50   SERVICE: net prices, card slips closed   CARDS: Amex, Diners, MasterCard, Switch, Visa   DETAILS: 60 seats. Private parties: 48 main room, 8 to 36 private rooms. Car park. Vegetarian meals. Children's helpings. No smoking. Wheelchair access (also WC). Music   ACCOMMODATION: 17 rooms, all with bath/shower. TV. Phone. B&B £96 to £180. Rooms for disabled. Baby facilities. Fishing (*The Which? Guide to Good Hotels*)   (£5)

New main entries are listed near the front of the book. Some may have appeared in earlier years (though not in the previous edition) or as a Round-up entry last year.

CHAGFORD Devon

map 1

▲ Gidleigh Park ▮ ⅚✼

Chagford TQ13 8HH
TEL: (01647) 432367   FAX: (01647) 432574
EMAIL: gidleighpark@gidleigh.co.uk
WEBSITE: www.gidleigh.com
from Chagford Square turn right at Lloyds Bank
into Mill Street, take right fork after 150 yards,
follow lane for 1½m

COOKING 8
MODERN EUROPEAN
£65–£111

The black-and-white building spreads lazily in grounds that accommodate *inter alia* a river splashing idly over big boulders. It is a house of character, solid, welcoming, informal and comfortable. And high gastronomic expectations are almost invariably met: 'one of the best meals we have ever had in a restaurant' testified one reporter.

The food seems now to have a clearer focus, whether a simple appetiser of crab fricassée (a pile of warm white meat surrounded by an impeccable shellfish stock) or a thin, friable pastry case filled with a lightly smoky and deeply flavoured onion confit, topped with tasty quail meat and poached quail eggs, flavours coalescing in 'a small piece of inspired cooking'. Dishes transcend their components, too – witness a ring of light, bouncy chicken mousse generously scattered with young asparagus and fresh morels, in a gentle yet lively froth.

If this is highly worked food, it is neither self-conscious nor over-elaborate. Main items claim the limelight, with accessories in support: perhaps roast best end of lamb (two well-trimmed rare chops), with a skewer of kidney and cubes of saddle, on an impressive mirepoix of vegetables, plus 'textbook' fondant potato. Fine judgement is also applied to desserts, which can often achieve a simplicity that belies the effort that created them, viz. a small tower of pain d'épice biscuits and ice cream, beside three cooked bananas in a lake of ginger-spiked butterscotch sauce.

With copious extras (including sole goujons and tartare sauce to begin, excellent bread, and petits fours to finish), plus fair-sized portions, there is much food to get through in the course of a meal. Prices are high, but 'for a once-in-a-while treat ... well worth it', and service is still charming, unobtrusive yet attentive. As for wines, there's no point in scouring the list for bottles under £20 (well, there's one at £19), but prices are nonetheless fair. The outstanding selections of European wines by no means dominate (California is notably strong), and there's strength in depth, with several vintages of many wines. Eight wines by the glass from £5 to £10 are representative of the list's overall quality. Michael Caines has taken on more responsibilities, this time in partnership with the Marriott hotel group, with his Michael Caines restaurant at the Bristol Marriott Royal, which opened in summer 2003.

CHEF: Michael Caines   PROPRIETORS: Paul and Kay Henderson   OPEN: all week 12.30 to 2, 7 to 9
MEALS: Set L £27 (2 courses) to £41. Set D £70 to £75. Light L menu available   SERVICE: not inc,
card slips closed   CARDS: Amex, MasterCard, Switch, Visa   DETAILS: 35 seats. Private parties:
28 main room. Car park. No children under 7. No smoking. No music   ACCOMMODATION: 15
rooms, all with bath/shower. TV. Phone. D,B&B £270 to £550. Baby facilities. Fishing

▲ 22 Mill Street

22 Mill Street, Chagford TQ13 8AW   COOKING 6
TEL: (01647) 432244   FAX: (01647) 433101   MODERN EUROPEAN
WEBSITE: www.22millstreetrestaurant.co.uk   £31–£51

The restaurant behind the cream and green shopfront, on a street of attractive old town houses, has an unusually relaxing, welcoming and unintimidating atmosphere: 'I always feel right at home there,' observed one visitor. It has a small lounge, a big friendly golden retriever, and an understated dining room with well-spaced tables. Dinner offers the option of six courses with no choice (for £36), or three with some choice (for £32), and most reporters reckon that the value is good.

Fresh materials lay a secure foundation, perhaps in the form of a neat set of green asparagus spears in May, with a well-judged hollandaise sauce, and clear flavours and attractive presentation are part of the deal, evident in a starter of first-class scallops in a highly flavoured broth of lime, coriander and ginger. Flavours can indeed be quite forceful, judging by a roast fillet of cod with crab ravioli in a pungent roast shellfish velouté, and by a moist, tender fillet of red mullet paired with robust anchovies, but there is contrast, too, provided in this case by crunchy, tasty green beans and soft, creamy quail's eggs.

Timing is impeccable, producing a pink-roast breast of Gressingham duck, the skin crusted to perfection, and a leg bursting with chopped meat, olives and thyme – 'a brilliant dish' – but there is also a lightness of touch: for example, in an unctuous, unmoulded crème brûlée topped with a translucent sugar crisp, served with strawberries and honeycomb. Minor details, from appetisers to petits fours, are well rendered, and service is notably friendly: as well as being a talented chef, Duncan Walker is also an affable presence, joining in the service, making polite enquiries and putting people at ease. The wide-ranging yet manageable wine list is serious enough, though most bottles come in under £25, including a Pierro LTC (Little Touch of Chardonnay) with Semillon and Sauvignon (from Margaret River) and a Slaley Merlot (from Stellenbosch).

CHEFS: Duncan Walker and Stephen Langston   PROPRIETOR: Duncan Walker   OPEN: Wed to Sat L 12.30 to 1.45, Mon to Sat D 7.30 to 9   CLOSED: 2 weeks Jan, 1 week June   MEALS: Set L £19.50 (2 courses) to £22, Set D £28 (2 courses) to £36   SERVICE: net prices, card slips closed   CARDS: Delta, MasterCard, Switch, Visa   DETAILS: 22 seats. No-smoking area. No music. No mobile phones   ACCOMMODATION: 2 rooms, both with bath/shower. TV. B&B £40 to £55

CHEESDEN   Greater Manchester   map 8

Nutters ⁵⁄₄✗

Edenfield Road, Cheesden OL12 7TY   COOKING 6
TEL/FAX: (01706) 650167   MODERN BRITISH
on A680 between Norden and Rochdale   £28–£50

Andrew Nutter has become something of a cult figure in the region. This converted country pub is merely the hub of a network of operations that have included books, a Channel 5 TV series and, perhaps most appreciated of all, a hands-on cookery master class on the first Thursday of each month, at which willing participants get to see the lunch dishes they are about to eat being prepared. A taste for strenuous self-promotion does not always bode well, but the truth is that he is a very good chef, and full of clever, successful ideas.

Discriminating use of local supply lines always helps, and these underpin the menus here. Dishes are painstakingly presented, but also quite substantial, and even though descriptions may bemuse, what turns up on your plate is impressive enough. Far Eastern technique is brought to bear on a starter of flash-seared salmon fillet with sweet leeks and fritters of king prawn and coconut, or there may be a populist Indian touch, as in the mango and cucumber raita that garnishes a roulade of goats' cheese, roasted red peppers and basil. Vegetarians have a separate menu to choose from, with perhaps five starters and four mains, the latter exemplified by shiitake and pak choi spring roll with 'lozenges' of gratinated fennel. For omnivores, fillet of brill with sautéed crab balls and a lobster and champagne sauce sounds reassuringly classical, or there could be poppy seed-crusted pork medallions with celeriac fondant and smoked bacon ravioli. A confectioner's shop of nursery treats awaits at dessert stage, but grown-ups might be drawn to miniature lemon curd and marshmallow bombes with what the menu describes as 'a gin and tonic explosion'. By comparison with the menus, the wine list might seem rather staid, with its roll calls of French classics, although Australia is given a fair outing. Those two countries provide the house wines at £11.80.

CHEF: Andrew Nutter   PROPRIETORS: Andrew, Jean and Rodney Nutter   OPEN: Wed to Mon 12 to 2 (4 Sun), 6.45 (6.30 Sat and Sun) to 9.30 (9 Sun)   CLOSED: first 2 weeks Aug   MEALS: alc exc Sun L (main courses £11 to £17). Set L Sun £19.95, Set D £32   SERVICE: not inc, 10% for parties of 10 or more   CARDS: Amex, Delta, MasterCard, Switch, Visa   DETAILS: 84 seats. Private parties: 40 main room. Car park. Vegetarian meals. Children's helpings. No smoking. Wheelchair access (also WC). Music

---

CHELTENHAM Gloucestershire   map 5

Le Champignon Sauvage ♥

24–26 Suffolk Road, Cheltenham GL50 2AQ   COOKING 8
TEL: (01242) 573449   FAX: (01242) 254365   FRENCH
                                                                £31–£82

On the edge of Cheltenham's busy centre, in an area that claims its own identity ('the Suffolks'), Le Champignon Sauvage is a smart and colourful haven of excellence. Taking up two shopfronts – one half is a bar, the other the dining room – it is small and intimate and has 'class written all over it'. If it already feels opulent and French, then the menu seems to confirm that impression, with its pressed bouillabaisse terrine, and duck foie gras with Maury syrup. But look a little more closely and the kitchen's wide-ranging inventiveness soon shows through: perhaps in the nougat sauce that accompanies seared scallops, or in a breast of pigeon with a samosa of its leg and pineapple chutney.

David Everitt-Matthias certainly 'knows how to put the "oo" in cooking'. Nearly every dish is presented on a differently styled plate, and the food is typically intricate, a combination of ingeniously conceived ideas and refined treatment: for example, in a 'satisfying and enticing' dish pairing tender, juicy slices of lamb with chewy razor clams and delicate sweetbreads. The food may sometimes sound elaborate, but flavour partnerships invariably work. A dish of tender, moist roe deer marinated in tea and spices shared the plate with braised belly pork given a Chinese spicing, the ensemble set off by simple mashed potatoes and a strewing of wild mushrooms.

Combinations vary from classical to novel, but none is contrived or attention-grabbingly outlandish. Thickly sliced wood pigeon, for example, comes on a bed of mixed leaves and chunks of beetroot, with a tangy yet mellow juniper-flavoured dressing, while fillets of red mullet are balanced on a neatly moulded round of crab couscous, surrounded by a dribble of melon and feta: altogether 'an inspired combination'. Vegetables arrive on a separate plate, the same for all (a conspicuously old-fashioned gesture), and vegetarians should note that 24 hours' notice is required for their special needs.

Desserts tend to be very sweet, taking in a liquorice and tangerine parfait with rhubarb, and a wedge of dense prune and date cake with a chunky ginger ice cream. Appetisers, such as truffle cream with flageolet beans and lardons, provide an auspicious start, and petits fours are 'not to be missed'. Care and attention to detail are second to none, and there is nothing lazy or complacent about the smooth-running operation, so it feels as much a labour of love as a business. Upbeat, helpful service from Helen Everitt-Matthias 'cannot be faulted', and of course there is nothing she doesn't know about the food. The wine list appropriately focuses on France, starting with house vin de table at £10.50, and sets out to offer good-value drinking rather than impressing with unaffordable bottles. Australia, New Zealand and California make up the balance. Just five wines come by the glass, but half-bottles are plentiful.

CHEF: David Everitt-Matthias PROPRIETORS: David and Helen Everitt-Matthias OPEN: Tue to Sat 12.30 to 1.30, 7.30 to 9 CLOSED: 10 days Christmas, 3 weeks June MEALS: Set L £16.50 (2 courses) to £48, Set D Tue to Fri £17.50 (2 courses) to £48, Set D Sat £35 (2 courses) to £48 SERVICE: not inc CARDS: Amex, Delta, Diners, MasterCard, Switch, Visa DETAILS: 28 seats. Private parties: 22 main room. Vegetarian meals. No smoking at D before 10pm. Wheelchair access (not WC). No music. No mobile phones (£5)

Chelsea Square Brasserie £

60 St Georges Place, Cheltenham GL50 3PN — COOKING **3**

TEL/FAX: (01242) 269926 — MODERN BRITISH

£24–£37

Large, modern, glass-ceilinged, with bright colours, tiny tables and decent chairs, this brasserie has found its way into the hearts of Cheltenham's youth. The menus allow flexibility: under-10s are introduced to sophistication with crostini, and the delights of home-made ice cream with hot chocolate sauce. Many of the starters, such as grilled squid on marinated crumbed feta and black olive salad with a confit lemon dressing, or mille-feuille of Jerusalem artichoke risotto with Parmesan tuile and a mushroom pecorino sauce, are also available as main courses, and invoke the flavours of the Med. Savouries, such as Welsh rarebit or Somerset Brie stuffed with figs, and a range of ports, bring a hint of English tradition, and desserts like bread-and-butter pudding or warm rhubarb and apple tart continue to keep the home fires burning. Wines are affordable: house at £6.95, glasses from £1.95, and the 30-plus wine list with many around £10. The Reserve List offers well-aged Burgundies, Sauternes and clarets at fair prices.

CHEF: Ryan Bell   PROPRIETOR: Tony Amos   OPEN: Mon to Sat 12 to 2 (2.30 Fri and Sat), 6 to 10 (10.30 Fri and Sat)   CLOSED: 25 and 26 Dec, 1 Jan, bank hol L   MEALS: alc (main courses £8 to £11)   SERVICE: not inc, 10% for parties of 6 or more   CARDS: Delta, MasterCard, Switch, Visa   DETAILS: 90 seats. Private parties: 100 main room. Vegetarian meals. Children's helpings. No smoking. Music

Daffodil £✳

18–20 Suffolk Parade, Montpellier,	COOKING 3
Cheltenham GL50 2AE	MODERN EUROPEAN
TEL: (01242) 700055 FAX: (01242) 700088	£23–£58

From its original use as a cinema, this Art Deco palace on the outskirts of town has become a smart restaurant. Colours and materials reflect the brashness of the earlier period, but the style of the food is fashionable European fusion. Flavourings can range from Dijon mustard to pesto or apple and pear chutney, while mushrooms, olives and sunblush tomatoes might accompany tagliatelle. Intelligent handling of bold combinations can result in a starter of warm crab and leek tart with curried herb butter sauce, leading on to monkfish in a coriander crust with chorizo and a salad of mango and chilli couscous. Skill and judgement shine out at dessert stage too: toffee, banana and pecan pudding with vanilla ice cream, say, or chocolate and cherry torte with honeycomb and passion-fruit sorbet. Service by smartly attired staff is on the ball. Prices on the short and eclectic wine list are generally under £20, with eight bottles, from around £13, plus two sparklers, also served by the glass.

CHEF: Andrew Palmer   PROPRIETOR: Marcel Frichot   OPEN: Mon to Sat 12 to 2.30, 6.30 to 10   CLOSED: 25 and 26 Dec, 1 Jan, Easter Mon   MEALS: alc (main courses £11.50 to £20). Set L £10 (2 courses) to £12.50   SERVICE: not inc, 10% for parties of 6 or more   CARDS: Amex, MasterCard, Switch, Visa   DETAILS: 150 seats. 10 seats outside. Private parties: 150 main room. Vegetarian meals. Children's helpings. No smoking in 1 dining room. Wheelchair access (also WC). Music

Lumière ♥ £✳

Clarence Parade, Cheltenham GL50 3PA	
TEL: (01242) 222200	COOKING 4
EMAIL: dinner@lumiere.cx	GLOBAL
WEBSITE: www.lumiere.cx	£39–£60

A cool, comfortably modern room and a straightforwardly presented fixed-price menu set the scene at Geoff and Lin Chapman's appealing restaurant. The cooking draws on a global template to partner salmon brochette with Asian noodles, spiced yam with a confit of Barbary duck, and chargrilled springbok fillet with thyme-roasted mushrooms and truffle-scented sauce. Memorable results have included foie gras wrapped in Parma ham; an appetiser cup of 'wonderfully flavoured shellfish soup'; and, accompanying carefully steamed and grilled asparagus spears, a tiny cup of asparagus soup with saffron. The dish aptly listed as 'one perfect cheese' (an unusual and brilliant formula) might bring exquisitely creamy Gorgonzola, or a close cousin of Vacherin, in peak condition. Puddings also please, including a nicely balanced and flavoursome tiramisù. Professional, informed and easy-going service is overseen by Lin Chapman.

The wine list, tasteful and modern (in both presentation and selection) has a penchant for Italy and California, but Burgundy is good too. Established wines have detailed tasting notes, while regularly changing 'guests' simply fall into regional lists. Quality is high and prices reasonable, although only four bottles beat £20.

CHEFS: Geoff Chapman and Tom Allen   PROPRIETORS: Lin and Geoff Chapman   OPEN: Tue to Sat D only 7 to 8.30   CLOSED: 1st 2 weeks Jan, 2 weeks late summer   MEALS: Set D Tue to Thur £26.50 (2 courses), Set D Fri and Sat £32   SERVICE: not inc   CARDS: MasterCard, Switch, Visa DETAILS: 28 seats. Private parties: 36 main room. No smoking. No music. No mobile phones. Air-conditioned

Mayflower

32–34 Clarence Street, Cheltenham GL50 3NX	COOKING 2
TEL: (01242) 522426 FAX: (01242) 251667	CHINESE
WEBSITE: www.themayflowerrestaurant.co.uk	£17–£60

'A place for all occasions,' observed one local devotee. The Kong family has been here for more than two decades, and their 'very reliable' restaurant has become something of a local institution. They continue to keep their customers satisfied with a long menu that eschews exotica and anatomical curiosities in favour of a well-tried assortment of Cantonese, Pekinese and Szechuan dishes based around familiar ingredients. Appetisers include mussels with black beans and chilli, and deep-fried crispy lamb with pancakes, while more substantial offerings take in sautéed king prawns with cashew nuts, chicken with oyster sauce, and sliced roast duck with ginger and pineapple. There's also plenty for vegetarians (shredded bamboo shoots with bean curd, for example). The value for money is excellent, and the 50-strong wine list is a notch above the provincial Chinese average. House French is £11.95.

CHEFS: Mrs M.M. and Mr C.F. Kong   PROPRIETORS: the Kong family   OPEN: all week 12 to 1.45, 5.45 to 10 (11 Fri and Sat)   CLOSED: 24 to 26 Dec   MEALS: alc (main courses £5.50 to £12.50). Set L £6.90, Set D £19.50 to £22 (all min 2 or more)   SERVICE: not inc   CARDS: Amex, Delta, MasterCard, Switch, Visa   DETAILS: 120 seats. Private parties: 80 main room, 20 to 45 private rooms. Vegetarian meals. Music. Air-conditioned £5

CHESTER Cheshire   **map 7**

▲ Chester Grosvenor, Arkle 🍾

Eastgate, Chester CH1 1LT	
TEL: (01244) 324024 FAX: (01244) 313068	COOKING 6
EMAIL: chesgrov@chestergrosvenor.co.uk	EUROPEAN
WEBSITE: www.chestergrosvenor.co.uk	£41–£94

The building (in Grosvenor hands since 1865) is a mix of red brick, stone, and faux half-timbering, sporting a glass-fronted brasserie on the ground floor, and the altogether separate Arkle restaurant, approached along a maze of corridors, replete with pillars, skylight, and paintings of horses. Simon Radley's menus make a bid for moneyed customers with their luxury ingredients – Devon crab and caviar, seared and poached foie gras with cabbage and Gewürztraminer, or turbot with a lobster sausage – but there is far more to his output than expensive materials. That crab and caviar starter, for instance, comes with fennel pollen, while seared scallops have turned up in the company of frogs' legs beignets and a garlic and parsley coulis.

Some of the pairings may raise a quizzical eyebrow, but all are done with a sound sense of culinary logic: grilled sea bass with sweet-and-sour beetroot and seared foie gras, perhaps, or a first course of Lancashire suckling pig with poached langoustines and white bean and mustard rémoulade. Vegetarians get their own enticing five-course menu, which might consist of a truffled egg croustade with roast pumpkin and artichoke tempura; celeriac lasagne with Puy lentils, tomato and asparagus; and a panaché of ceps and morels with a ravioli of goats' cheese, parsnip and truffle, followed by cheese and dessert.

Among desserts, chocolate is given prominence (perhaps a hot soufflé, or baked chocolate and almond génoise with liquid cherries and iced Kirsch), or there may be a banana tarte Tatin. The bread table offers around eight different kinds, sliced to order; service is of a high standard; and the heavyweight wine list is most assuredly of grand-hotel calibre, with prices from £12 to £5,000. A spectacular collection of premium Burgundies includes old vintages from Georges Roumier. California also stands out, topped by the showpiece flourish of Opus One listed in every vintage since the maiden 1979. Ostentatious, certainly, but there's much of interest, and every region is taken seriously. Just enough comes in under £20, and half-bottles are plentiful. House wines are around £14, and more than a dozen come by the glass from £2.75.

CHEF: Simon Radley   PROPRIETOR: Grosvenor Estate   OPEN: Tue to Sun L 12 to 2.30, Tue to Sat D 7 to 9.30   CLOSED: 25 Dec to 20 Jan exc 31 Dec   MEALS: Set L £30 to £52, Set D £45 (2 courses) to £60   SERVICE: not inc, 12.5% for parties of 6 or more   CARDS: Amex, Delta, Diners, MasterCard, Switch, Visa   DETAILS: 45 seats. Private parties: 45 main room, 18 to 240 private rooms. Vegetarian meals. Children's helpings. No infants at D. Jacket and tie. No-smoking area. Wheelchair access (not WC). Music. Air-conditioned   ACCOMMODATION: 80 rooms, all with bath/shower. TV. Phone. Room only £199.75 to £616.87. Rooms for disabled. Baby facilities

Brasserie 10/16 £

Brookdale Place, Chester CH1 3DY	COOKING 2
TEL: (01244) 322288 FAX: (01244) 322325	MODERN EUROPEAN
WEBSITE: www.brasserie1016.co.uk	£21–£50

This lively, modern brasserie-style venue is an offshoot of the Brasserie in Hawarden (see entry), just across the border in Wales. Informal and flexible, it opens from lunchtime through to late evening, although the main menu is not available between 2 and 6pm. Reporters have found that standards can be rather inconsistent, especially at times when the kitchen's 'A-team' is off duty – and service, too, has disappointed – but on the whole there is still plenty to recommend. An eclectic cooking style takes in everything from a tart of chorizo, dolcelatte and spinach with tapenade dressing to grilled coconut and coriander chicken with oriental noodles in satay sauce, and that's just for starters. Main courses have included grilled salmon with bubble and squeak – the high point of an inspection meal – and braised lamb shank with rosemary and garlic on Lancashire hotpot. The short wine list opens with six house selections from £9.95.

CHEFS: Mark Jones and Iain Derbyshire   PROPRIETORS: Neal Bates and Mark Jones   OPEN: all week 12 to 10   MEALS: alc (main courses £7 to £18). Set L £4.90 to £8.80 (both 2 courses), Set D exc Fri and Sat after 7pm £8.80 (2 courses) to £13.80 (2 courses, inc wine)   SERVICE: not inc CARDS: Amex, Delta, MasterCard, Switch, Visa   DETAILS: 160 seats. Private parties: 80 main room, 30 to 80 private rooms. Vegetarian meals. No-smoking area. Wheelchair access (also WC). Music

CHETTLE Dorset   map 2

▲ Castleman Hotel ♥ ⅚⋇ £

Blandford Forum, Chettle DT11 8DB
TEL: (01258) 830096   FAX: (01258) 830051
EMAIL: chettle@globalnet.co.uk
WEBSITE: www.castlemanhotel.co.uk
off A354, 7m NE of Blandford Forum

COOKING 2
ENGLISH
£24–£43

Aspirations here include being 'a neighbourhood restaurant ... not a chintzy house' – hard to achieve in an English Baroque house with panelled hall and what is virtually an art gallery on the walls. But shock and awe evaporate in the glow of friendliness emitted by staff and owners alike; a second aspiration, 'to offer guests an enjoyable experience', is easily achieved. Knowledgeable local sourcing of seasonal produce brings a neighbour's strawberries, roe venison, scallops dived by a friend at Kimmeridge, and meat from a butcher with 'a small slaughterhouse with its own field'. Refreshingly straightforward menus offer leek and watercress soup, venison and mushroom pie, or grilled John Dory with parsley and lemon butter. Desserts run to lemon sponge pudding with chilled vanilla custard, and almond meringues with apricot purée. A very strong wine list is gloriously unintimidating, and prices are commendable. Three house wines come by the glass or bottle (£2.50/£10), and they're flavoursome choices.

CHEFS: Barbara Garnsworthy and Richard Morris   PROPRIETORS: Edward Bourke and Barbara Garnsworthy   OPEN: Sun L only 12 to 2, all week D 7 to 9.30   MEALS: alc D (main courses £8.50 to £15.50). Set L Sun £17   SERVICE: not inc, card slips closed   CARDS: Delta, MasterCard, Switch, Visa   DETAILS: 40 seats. Private parties: 40 main room. Car park. Vegetarian meals. No smoking. Wheelchair access (also WC). No music   ACCOMMODATION: 8 rooms, all with bath/shower. TV. Phone. B&B £45 to £80 (*The Which? Guide to Good Hotels*)

CHIGWELL Essex   map 3

Bluebell   NEW ENTRY

117 High Road, Chigwell IG7 6QQ
TEL: (020) 8500 6282   FAX: (020) 8500 6942

COOKING 2
MODERN EUROPEAN
£29–£57

This whitewashed cottage with two sparely but comfortably decorated dining rooms and a vibrant feel has put Chigwell on the culinary map. Fresh breads signal seriousness, and ingredients are balanced skilfully in a first course of squid stuffed with crab, lemon and herbs with red pesto, or in a leek and pancetta filo tart with a tangy paprika and Parmesan crust. Successes at inspection included the squid, plus 'real chips' and their accompanying accurately chargrilled beef fillet with well-matched mustard sauce. Finally, in

March, Essex's secret microclimate has produced a brandy-snap basket of 'seasonal fruit sorbets' made with lemon, mango and blackberry; profiteroles with hot chocolate sauce make an any-time alternative. Waiters are efficient but busy, and wines starting at £11.95 offer a good range, some bottles at significant mark-ups. Reporters warn that the atmosphere can get very smoky.

CHEF: Paul Korton   PROPRIETOR: Gregory Molen   OPEN: Tue to Fri and Sun L 12 to 1.45 (3.30 Sun), Tue to Sat D 6.45 to 10   MEALS: alc D (main courses £14 to £19). Set L £11.95 (2 courses). Set L Sun £18.95   SERVICE: not inc, card slips closed   CARDS: Amex, Delta, Diners, MasterCard, Switch, Visa   DETAILS: 95 seats. Vegetarian meals. Children's helpings. No cigars/pipes. Occasional music. Air-conditioned

---

CHINNOR Oxfordshire   map 2

Sir Charles Napier 🍷 ✳

Spriggs Alley, Chinnor OX39 4BX
TEL: (01494) 483011   FAX: (01494) 485311
take B4009 to Chinnor from M40 junction 6, turn   COOKING 4
right at mini-roundabout and continue up hill for   ANGLO-FRENCH-PLUS
1½m to Spriggs Alley   £35–£74

After the two-mile climb up through beech woods from Chinnor village, you will find this assortment of ancient buildings tucked into a wooded fold, or you could go by car, of course. Lunch on the terrace overlooking the large lawn is a real summer treat. While high-cost, high-quality ingredients could push up à la carte bills, good-value two-course set menus include simpler dishes like pumpkin and garlic soup, or braised shank of lamb with winter vegetables. First courses on a spring carte ranged from seared pigeon breast with creamed salsify and truffles to tomato risotto with squid and Parmesan. Main courses such as baked halibut with mussel sauce and dill potatoes, and roast guinea fowl with confit of shallots, rösti and Madeira, show careful marriages of ingredients while avoiding flashy complexity. Desserts change according to the season; winter months may bring warming apple and blackberry crumble, and hot date cake with toffee sauce, while spring/summer may see a strawberry soup with basil ice cream or lemon meringue tart. Knowledgeable introductions to each region offer sound guidance through the lengthy and immaculately chosen wine list; there's something for all-comers in every region (including half-bottles), and diners on a budget can have a taste of the really good stuff via an adventurous by-the-glass selection (£3.50 to £6).

CHEF: Eric Devaux   PROPRIETOR: Julie Griffiths   OPEN: Tue to Sun L 12 to 2.30 (3.30 Sun), Tue to Sat D 7 to 10   CLOSED: 3 days at Christmas   MEALS: alc (main courses £15.50 to £19.50). Set L £15.50 (2 courses), Set D £16.50 (2 courses). Light L menu available Tue to Fri   SERVICE: 12.5% (optional), card slips closed   CARDS: Amex, Delta, Diners, MasterCard, Switch, Visa   DETAILS: 70 seats. 70 seats outside. Private parties: 45 main room, 6 to 20 private rooms. Car park. Vegetarian meals. Children's helpings. No children under 7 at D. No smoking in 1 dining room. Wheelchair access (not WC). Occasional music. No mobile phones. Air-conditioned

---

'The ground floor is rather like sitting in a cheerfully colourful, extensive set of country-style kitchen cupboards.' (On eating in the Midlands)

---

map 5

▲ Cotswold House ▼ ✷

The Square, Chipping Campden GL55 6AN
TEL: (01386) 840330   FAX: (01386) 840310   COOKING 5
EMAIL: reception@cotswoldhouse.com   MODERN BRITISH
WEBSITE: www.cotswoldhouse.com   £34–£61

This hotel looks diagonally across Chipping Campden's town square (which mainly functions as a car park) at the market hall, an open structure on ancient upright posts. Internally it has a glorious circular stairwell and, in the quite intimate-feeling Garden Room Restaurant, a trio of arched French windows giving lush views over the grounds.

Simon Hulstone's team delivers contemporary classical food with a patina of country-house sophistication: a warm salad of pigeon with wild mushrooms, shallots and truffled celeriac to start, or escabèche of red mullet with soused vegetables spiked with coriander. Presentation ensures that dishes look the part, whether a colourful vegetarian main course of artichokes and asparagus on open lasagne with a foamy pea sauce, or a meat-and-fish pairing like roast brill with seared foie gras, or pork belly with scallops, button onions and pancetta crisps. Desserts include the likes of chocolate crackle with mandarin ice cream and poached clementines, or iced strawberry parfait with hot banana spring rolls and fruit paysanne. Good nibbles, breads and butter add to the experience, and in summer a stroll around the grounds afterwards seems a must.

Cheaper, simpler dishes are to be had in Hicks Brasserie Bar, which shares the main restaurant's kitchen. Its wine list offers much tasty drinking under £20 and over a dozen by the glass for £3.50 to £5.50. The restaurant has a more serious list, packed with quality in all regions and mixing mature bottles with up-to-date finds like the Quincy from Domaine des Ballandors (£24).

CHEF: Simon Hulstone   PROPRIETORS: Ian and Christa Taylor   OPEN: Sun L 12 to 2.30, all week D 7 to 9.30   MEALS: alc (main courses £12 to £20). Set L £25, Set D £40. Brasserie menu available   SERVICE: not inc   CARDS: Amex, Delta, MasterCard, Switch, Visa   DETAILS: 40 seats. Private parties: 55 main room. Car park. Vegetarian meals. Children's helpings. No smoking. Music. No mobile phones   ACCOMMODATION: 20 rooms, all with bath/shower. TV. Phone. D,B&B £115 to £395. Baby facilities (The Which? Guide to Good Hotels) (£5)

map 2

FishWorks ✷

10 Church Street, Christchurch BH23 1BW   COOKING 3
TEL: (01202) 487000   SEAFOOD
WEBSITE: www.fishworks.co.uk   £33–£61

Surprisingly, in this successful group that combines seafood cafés with fishmongers, this is the only branch to have a coastal location; the other branches are in Bath (the original), Bristol and Chiswick (see entries). Décor in the two tiny dining areas on different floors is rather 'bare bones', but service is friendly and accommodating. The food follows the FishWorks formula: quality seafood sourced directly from the coast, whether British or foreign: perhaps Newlyn lemon sole, River Fowey mussels, Spanish anchovies, French oysters. Menus change seasonally and aim for simplicity that showcases the freshness of the fish; vegetables are extra. An extensive repertoire involves a 'classic' menu – perhaps including skate with black butter, spaghetti alle vongole, and grilled sea bass with rosemary, olive oil and sea salt – plus, for crustacea-lovers, everything from langoustines and clams to a lavish 'fruits de mer' platter. Daily blackboard specials may add in scallops with pancetta and basil, or grilled swordfish steak. Alternatively, two diners could choose a whole fish from the fishmonger's counter and have it prepared to their liking. Though cooking may suffer the odd lapse, it's generally on the ball. Desserts are secondary (perhaps a Sicilian lemon tart), while fish-friendly wines include nine by the glass and house from £12.50.

CHEFS: Nick Davies and Adam Stocker   PROPRIETOR: FishWorks plc   OPEN: Tue to Sat 12 to 3, 6 to 10.30   CLOSED: 25 Dec, and Tue after bank hols   MEALS: alc (main courses £9 to £22) SERVICE: not inc   CARDS: Amex, Delta, MasterCard, Switch, Visa   DETAILS: 42 seats. Vegetarian meals. Children's helpings. No smoking. Wheelchair access (not WC). Music. No mobile phones. Air-conditioned

---

CLAYGATE Surrey   map 3

Le Petit Pierrot

4 The Parade, Claygate KT10 0NU   COOKING 3
TEL: (01372) 465105   FAX: (01372) 467642   MODERN FRENCH
                                                                           £22–£49

In an inspector's words, this place 'remains impervious to fashionable trends'. The resolutely Francophile menu may start with a cream of mussel soup with saffron and diced vegetables ('satiny, creamy and highly satisfying') or a mille-feuille of snails and oyster mushrooms in a light garlic sauce. At inspection, fish dishes were accurately timed, including 'firm and springy' monkfish medallions in a creamy mushroom sauce. Foie de veau lyonnaise, or tender, slightly gamey roast duck with caramelised turnips and cardamom and chutney sauce, may be among meat dishes. Desserts tend to have plenty of sweetness: viz. vanilla bavarois with star anise and caramelised oranges, or a gratin of pears in Galliano. The cheaper of the two lunch menus looks particularly good value. The exclusively French wine selection covers the classic regions, especially Bordeaux and Burgundy, at reasonable prices and offers plenty of halves; house vins de pays cost £11.75.

CHEFS: Jean-Pierre Brichot and Eric Plantureux   PROPRIETORS: Jean-Pierre and Annie Brichot OPEN: Mon to Fri L 12.15 to 2, Mon to Sat D 7.15 to 9.30   CLOSED: 1 week Christmas, bank hols MEALS: Set L £12.25 (2 courses) to £21.75, Set D £25.50   SERVICE: not inc   CARDS: Amex, Diners, MasterCard, Visa   DETAILS: 32 seats. Private parties: 34 main room. No children under 9. Wheelchair access (not WC). Occasional music

---

Which? Online subscribers will find The Good Food Guide *online, along with other* Which? *guides and magazines, at* www.which.net. *See the website for information on how to become a subscriber.*

CLIFFORD'S MESNE Gloucestershire — map 5

▲ Yew Tree Inn ♟ — NEW ENTRY

Clifford's Mesne GL18 1JS
TEL: (01531) 820719
EMAIL: yewtreepaul@aol.com
WEBSITE: www.theyewtreeinn.co.uk

COOKING 3
MODERN EUROPEAN
£38–£45

Dating from the sixteenth century, the Yew Tree is now an upmarket country inn run by husband and wife team Paul and Anna Hackett. This is predominantly an eating place rather than a straightforward pub, and shows high ambitions. Meals get off to a good start with 'first-class' home-made breads and well-made appetisers – on one occasion a 'refreshing' cold soup of asparagus and broccoli. Among starters, sauté of Cornish scallops with shallots and leeks in a coriander cream sauce has made a favourable impression, not least for the 'fresh and bouncy, lightly cooked' scallops, while a creamy risotto of courgette, sun-dried tomato, spring onion and basil was equally well judged. Creamy sauces are also a common feature of main courses, such as 'brilliantly timed, translucent' escalope of cod with spring onion mash, the sauce this time flavoured with Chardonnay and basil. There might also be roasted breast of Hereford duck on potato rösti with a stock-based coriander-infused sauce, while desserts have featured a 'rich and decidedly lemony' tart with prune and Armagnac ice cream. Service is cheerful and accommodating. The wine list is, appropriately, an upmarket version of a pub list. It can barely contain its enthusiasm for the finer things, particularly from France, but never overcharges and manages to restrain itself long enough to assemble an international selection under £20. An impressive 30 options by the glass range from £3.25 to £5.25.

CHEF: Paul Hackett   PROPRIETORS: Paul and Anna Hackett   OPEN: Tue to Sun L 12.15 to 14, Tue to Sat D 7 to 9   CLOSED: 1 week Oct, 2 or 3 weeks Jan   MEALS: Set L and D £21.95 (2 courses) to £27   SERVICE: not inc, card slips closed   CARDS: MasterCard, Switch, Visa   DETAILS: 40 seats. 36 seats outside. Private parties: 30 main room. Car park. Children's helpings. Wheelchair access (not WC). Music   ACCOMMODATION: 2 rooms. TV. B&B £40 to £70

CLIPSHAM Rutland — map 6

Olive Branch ⚜✗

Main Street, Clipsham LE15 7SH
TEL: (01780) 410355
FAX: (01780) 410000

COOKING 3
MODERN AND TRADITIONAL BRITISH
£20–£48

Quirkiness and informality are what one expects to find in a successful country pub, and the Olive Branch has them to spare. Good home-made wholemeal bread served on a wooden board with olive butter sets the quality-conscious tone, and the menus back it up. Enthusiastic reports have come in for bresaola with a rocket salad dressed in white truffle oil, expertly timed chargrilled halibut, and properly textured pannacotta with a compote of mixed fruits. An innovative impulse shows up in tandoori monkfish with jasmine rice and pak choi, but classical things such as chargrilled ribeye steak with rösti, celeriac purée and a red wine sauce are proficiently done too. To finish, pedigree British farmhouse cheeses vie with well-crafted desserts such as hot chocolate soufflé with pistachio ice cream. Polite and willing service adds to the relaxed atmosphere. The short printed wine list is supplemented by a blackboard giving bin ends and wines by the glass. Prices start at £9.95 a bottle, or £2.50 a glass.

CHEF: Sean Hope   PROPRIETOR: Rutland Inn Company   OPEN: all week L 12 to 2 (3 Sun), Mon to Sat D 7 to 9.30   CLOSED: 26 Dec, 1 Jan   MEALS: alc (main courses £8 to £16.50). Set L £9.50 (2 courses) to £11.50. Bar menu available Mon to Sat L   SERVICE: not inc, card slips closed CARDS: Delta, MasterCard, Switch, Visa   DETAILS: 45 seats. 25 seats outside. Private parties: 20 main room, 14 to 20 private rooms. Car park. Vegetarian meals. Children's helpings. No smoking in 1 dining room. Wheelchair access (not WC). Occasional music

COCKERMOUTH Cumbria   map 10

Quince & Medlar ⚶✳

13 Castlegate, Cockermouth CA13 9EU
TEL: (01900) 823579

COOKING 2
VEGETARIAN
£30–£39

Toil upwards towards the castle and hard by it you will find Colin and Louisa Le Voi's refined vegetarian restaurant. Housed in a Georgian building retaining many original features, this is as idiosyncratic and interesting as one could wish for. Influences are drawn in from all over, from the East European-inspired solyanka (shredded Savoy cabbage cooked with caraway seeds and dill, layered with sweet potatoes and smoked Cumberland cheese) to basmati rice rings, formed of grated root vegetables and rice topped with glazed button onions and crème fraîche and finished with Madeira sauce. You can bookend these main courses with the likes of asparagus mousse with sour cream and chive sauce, or chickpea and apricot pâté with home-made oat biscuits, and sweet things such as compote of dried fruits, or lemon tart. The short list of organic wines keeps prices on a tight leash, with house French at £10.50.

CHEFS/PROPRIETORS: Colin and Louisa Le Voi   OPEN: Tue to Sat and bank hol Sun D only 7 to 9.30 CLOSED: 24 to 26 Dec, bank hols exc Sun   MEALS: alc (main courses £12)   SERVICE: not inc, card slips closed   CARDS: MasterCard, Switch, Visa   DETAILS: 26 seats. Private parties: 14 main room. No children under 5. No smoking. Music

COLCHESTER Essex   map 6

Lemon Tree

48 St Johns Street, Colchester CO2 7AD
TEL/FAX: (01206) 767337
EMAIL: reservations@the-lemon-tree.com
WEBSITE: www.the-lemon-tree.com

COOKING 1
MODERN BRITISH
£15–£41

Outside, there's an inviting terrace; inside, part of the Roman city wall forms the back of this fresh, airy and unpretentious place. Menus packed with modern influences bring us smack up to date. Decent smoked salmon on sun-dried tomato bread and a competent salad tested culinary ambition less than a successful cauliflower and curry soup, velvety smooth and with flavours combining well. Carefully timed salmon on a bed of leeks, and a well-marinated Barbary duck on a horseradish mash, made pleasant main courses. Puddings seemed to be a weak point at inspection. Service is accommodating, friendly and professional, and wines show equal regard for the customer. Mark-ups are generally low, with house wines starting at £10.95, and range and quality are appealingly adventurous.

CHEF: Patrik Minder   PROPRIETORS: Joanna and Patrik Minder   OPEN: Mon to Sat 12 to 9.30 (10 Sat)   MEALS: alc (main courses £8 to £14). Set L £5.95 (1 course) to £9.95, Set D £6.95 (1 course) to £12.95   SERVICE: not inc   CARDS: Amex, Delta, MasterCard, Switch, Visa   DETAILS: 90 seats. 40 seats outside. Private parties: 60 main room, 15 to 30 private rooms. Vegetarian meals. Children's helpings. Wheelchair access (also women's WC). Occasional music (£5)

COLWALL STONE Herefordshire   map 5

▲ Colwall Park ♀ ✳   NEW ENTRY

Walwyn Road, Colwall Stone, Colwall WR13 6QG
TEL: (01684) 540000   FAX: (01684) 540847
EMAIL: hotel@colwall.com
WEBSITE: www.colwall.com
on B4218 between Great Malvern and Ledbury

COOKING 2
MODERN BRITISH
£27–£57

Though it sounds like a country estate, Colwall Park is actually a village-centre mock-Tudor pile of Victorian vintage. The dining room is grand enough, with a high, beamed ceiling, red velvet curtains, panelling and chandeliers, and formal service reflects the lofty ambitions of the cooking. Dishes can be rather complex, as in a starter of asparagus tips with a salad of wild mushrooms, black truffle and soft quails' eggs. To follow, an 'assiette of Middle White pork' comes with black pudding, a fondant of Granny Smith apples and a sage and onion galette, while a reporter's 'montage of venison' presented the meat three ways – loin fillet, sausage and pithiviers – along with spiced red cabbage, glazed parsnips and griottines. A simpler menu is offered in the bar, mixing traditional and modern ideas, from cottage pie to Thai chicken sambal. The wine list works its way purposefully around the world, scooping up a fair number of budget bottles and lots under £20 without letting quality slip. Short fine wine selections add polish and a number of goodies not on the main list are corralled into the 'patron's choice'. Six house wines are £12.99 or £3.15 for a glass.

CHEF: Martin Lovell   PROPRIETORS: Iain and Sarah Nesbitt   OPEN: Sun L 12.30 to 2, all week D 7.30 to 9   MEALS: alc D (main courses £16 to £20). Set L Sun £13.95 (2 courses) to £15.95. Bar menu available all week L and D   SERVICE: 10% (optional), card slips closed   CARDS: MasterCard, Switch, Visa   DETAILS: 40 seats. Private parties: 40 main room, 4 to 100 private rooms. Car park. Vegetarian meals. Children's helpings. No smoking. Wheelchair access (also women's WC). Music. No mobile phones   ACCOMMODATION: 22 rooms, all with bath/shower. TV. Phone. B&B £65 to £150 (The Which? Guide to Good Hotels) (£5)

'There was just me, the head chef, and a single waiter, all evening, though the evening of course didn't last that long.' (On eating in Warwickshire)

COOKHAM Berkshire

map 3

Manzano's

19–21 Station Hill Parade, Cookham SL6 9BR
TEL: (01628) 525775

COOKING **4**
MEDITERRANEAN
£32–£61

Richard and Deena Manzano run their restaurant as if it were an extension of their own home, guided by the philosophy that 'our customers are the most important people in the world'. So a warm welcome can be taken as read. Given the track record for consistently high standards, it's also a fairly safe bet that the cooking will make a good impression too. Essentially Spanish, the cooking blends traditional and modern ideas seamlessly to come up with a lively menu. Roulade of suckling pig with chorizo, piquillo peppers and Serrano ham on redcurrant and chilli dressing is a typical starter, or there may be crab and langoustine ravioli with velvet crab sauce. Main courses have included salmon braised in red Rioja with seafood salpicon, while 'plank steak' adds a touch of theatre to a meal, served at table on the smouldering embers of the burning plank it is cooked on. To finish, hot apple charlotte comes with Calvados cream, and marbled white and dark chocolate marquise is served with raspberries in Cassis. Wines are well chosen and good value, the list opening with four house wines at £11.95 and £13.50.

CHEF: Richard Manzano   PROPRIETORS: Richard and Deena Manzano   OPEN: Mon to Fri L 12 to 2, Mon to Sat D 7 to 10   CLOSED: 2 weeks Aug, bank hols   MEALS: alc (main courses £15 to £18.50). Set L £10 (2 courses), Set D £20   SERVICE: 12.5% (optional), card slips closed   CARDS: Amex, Delta, Diners, MasterCard, Switch, Visa   DETAILS: 34 seats. 12 seats outside. Private parties: 34 main room. Car park. Vegetarian meals. Children's helpings. Wheelchair access (not WC). Occasional music. Air-conditioned   £5

COOKHAM DEAN Berkshire

map 3

▲ Inn on the Green

NEW ENTRY

The Old Cricket Common,
Cookham Dean SL6 9NZ
TEL: (01628) 482638   FAX: (01628) 487474
EMAIL: reception@theinnonthegreen.com
WEBSITE: www.theinnonthegreen.com
off A404, S of M40 junction 4; for more detailed
directions it is best to phone or check the inn's
website

COOKING **4**
MODERN BRITISH
£35–£79

Formerly a pub, this mock-Tudor inn opened after a sumptuous make-over under a new team in February 2003. Three dining areas (all smoking) with a mixture of ancient and modern trappings are part of what is now a slick and smart 'boutique' hotel and restaurant. Garry Hollihead (see Embassy, London) is the driving force behind the menu and his name is very much in evidence; head chef is Douglas Kerr. Among the repertoire of 'signature' and other dishes may be tuna tartare with peashoot salad, and steamed hake with chorizo and curly kale. Luxuries such as black truffle are liberally scattered about – in the appetiser, starter and main course for one visitor – but while materials are generally good they sometimes have to struggle to prove it: scallops, for example, have been topped with scallop mousse, breadcrumbs and salt, before being baked and accompanied by puddles of sweet, buttery pea purée.

Desserts might take in a perfectly executed and intensely flavoured hot blueberry soufflé with an equally powerful lemon curd ice cream. Bread is well made, prices are ambitiously high, music was loud during our visit, and service is hardly sharp enough to warrant the 12.5 per cent charge. There are some good and interesting wines on the list, which isn't designed for anybody who wants change from £20, although a couple of Vin de Pays d'Oc house recommendations (from Lurton) come in at £15.

CHEFS: Garry Hollihead and Douglas Kerr   PROPRIETOR: Sphere Restaurants   OPEN: all week 12 to 2.30 (3 Sun), 7 to 9.30 (10 Fri and Sat)   CLOSED: 1 week early Jan   MEALS: alc exc Sun and bank hol L (main courses £15 to £25). Set L Mon to Sat £14.95 (2 courses) to £19.95, Set L Sun £23.50, Set D Sun to Thur £19.95   SERVICE: 12.5%, card slips closed   CARDS: Amex, Delta, MasterCard, Switch, Visa   DETAILS: 60 seats. 100 seats outside. Private parties: 100 main room. Car park. Vegetarian meals. Children's helpings. Wheelchair access (also WC). Music. No mobile phones. Air-conditioned   ACCOMMODATION: 9 rooms, all with bath/shower. TV. Phone. B&B £90 to £160. Rooms for disabled

CORSCOMBE Dorset   map 2

▲ Fox Inn 🍴 £

Corscombe DT2 0NS
TEL/FAX: (01935) 891330
EMAIL: dine@fox-inn.co.uk
WEBSITE: www.fox-inn.co.uk
off A356, 6m SE of Crewkerne

COOKING 1
MODERN BRITISH
£24–£47

This long thatched building hidden in narrow, winding lanes just outside the village of Corscombe has a definite pub feel. The owners have changed, but George Marsh is still in the kitchen, the à la carte menu remains stable, and fish remains a speciality. Reports suggest that most interest lies in the lengthy, fish-dominated specials board. Starters might include salmon tartare with home-made garlic mayonnaise, or gratin of crab, monkfish and bacon, or a warm salad of pigeon breast and bacon. Main courses of whole roast bream with dill and sea salt, or pan-fried fillets of sea bass with chorizo and basil mash, are joined by meat options such as Boursin-stuffed, bacon-wrapped chicken breast. Vanilla cream terrine with fruit coulis wasn't a thrilling finish for one reporter. The wine list takes a trip around the world starting from £10.50, and five wines come by the glass from £2.75.

CHEFS: George Marsh and Sue Wheeler   PROPRIETORS: Clive Webb and Margaret Hannell   OPEN: all week 12 to 2, 7 to 9 (9.15 Fri and Sat)   CLOSED: 25 Dec   MEALS: alc (main courses £8.50 to £18.50)   SERVICE: not inc, card slips closed   CARDS: Amex, Delta, MasterCard, Switch, Visa   DETAILS: 65 seats. 24 seats outside. Private parties: 30 main room, 10 to 30 private rooms. Car park. Vegetarian meals. Children's helpings. No smoking in 1 dining room. No music. No mobile phones   ACCOMMODATION: 4 rooms, all with bath/shower. TV. B&B £55 to £100. No children under 16 (The Which? Guide to Good Hotels)

CORSE LAWN Gloucestershire

map 2

▲ Corse Lawn House ❦ ✱

Corse Lawn GL19 4LZ
TEL: (01452) 780771   FAX: (01452) 780840
EMAIL: enquiries@corselawn.com
WEBSITE: www.corselawn.com
on B4211, 5m SW of Tewkesbury

COOKING 2
ANGLO-FRENCH
£29–£64

Tables are set beside the old coach wash in summer, where ducks and moorhens entertain, and the main road goes by on the other side without intruding much. The bistro has its own entrance and menu, while the main dining room's pink and green décor feels old-fashioned yet calm and well cared for. A long carte is supplemented by a fair-value fixed-price menu, and a card on each table outlines the policy on fish: endangered species (including many familiar names) have been replaced by more sustainable sardines, sole and turbot, and by less-well-known pollack or megrim (perhaps roast with tartare sauce).

Early summer has produced English asparagus with hollandaise, while other starters might be spiced up with a chutney (apple for foie gras terrine) or a salsa (mango and cucumber with potted crab). Meat dishes run to haunch of venison with port sauce, and calf's liver with pancetta and horseradish mash, although accompanying vegetables could be improved. Another early-summer treat has presented elderflower three ways – sorbet, jelly and fritter – and cheeses are served in traditional style with biscuits, celery and fruit. France, with lots of top-notch mature Bordeaux and Burgundy plus a good range in the Loire, is the chief interest of a wine list that contrives to be both very serious and wholly approachable – due in large part to the reasonable prices, a good range under £20 and down-to-earth notes. Intelligent short selections from other regions, both European and New World, include top names from the Mosel and some smart choices from New Zealand. House wines start at £11.50 (£3 per glass), the half-bottle list is huge and good sherries and old ports add an extra dimension.

CHEFS: Baba Hine and Andrew Poole   PROPRIETORS: the Hine family   OPEN: all week 12 to 2, 7 to 9.30   CLOSED: 24 to 26 Dec   MEALS: alc (main courses £14 to £20). Set L £16.50 (2 courses) to £18.50, Set D £27.50   SERVICE: not inc, card slips closed   CARDS: Amex, Diners, MasterCard, Switch, Visa   DETAILS: 70 seats. 40 seats outside. Private parties: 80 main room, 18 to 36 private rooms. Car park. Vegetarian meals. Children's helpings. No smoking. Wheelchair access (also WC). No music. No mobile phones   ACCOMMODATION: 19 rooms, all with bath/shower. TV. Phone. B&B £85 to £130. Rooms for disabled. Baby facilities. Swimming pool

---

If 'vegetarian meals' is noted in the details at the end of an entry, this means that a restaurant routinely lists at least one vegetarian starter and main course on menus. Other restaurants, however, may offer good vegetarian choices if you let them know in advance, so it is worthwhile phoning to enquire.

'The chef is a showman . . ., never happier than when flaming something in a wok and attracting everybody's attention with huge flames. The fact that this produces a fug of smoke throughout the room does not seem to concern him.' (On eating in Herefordshire)

CORSLEY Wiltshire
map 2

Cross Keys £
NEW ENTRY

Lyes Green, Corsley BA12 7PB
TEL: (01373) 832406   FAX: (01373) 832934

COOKING 3
MODERN BRITISH
£28–£49

Set at right angles to the road, this large pub was taken over in April 2001 by Francis and Kate Green, who have transformed it into a respected food venue. A dedicated eating area is stylishly done up in warm earth tones and bare wooden tables with fat candles. An appealing monthly-changing menu, based on local produce where available, has been noted for its inclusion of first-class raw materials and the 'quite perfect' sauces which accompany dishes. Proceedings start with, perhaps, sea trout fishcakes and watercress salad, or ham hock terrine with truffle oil. An inspector was impressed by a main course of honey-roast duck breast served with Thai-spiced butternut squash and an oriental-spiced sauce, while alternatives might be pan-roast haunch of venison with celeriac purée and kümmel sauce, or poached fillet of Cornish brill with confit tomatoes and shrimp gravy. Lavender-scented chocolate mille-feuille, or peach and blueberry summer pudding with clotted cream round things off. Service is eager to please and pleasant, while the short wine list balances value and quality; bottle prices start at £9.50.

CHEF: Francis Green   PROPRIETORS: Francis and Kate Green   OPEN: all week 12 to 2.30, Tue to Sat 7 to 9.30   MEALS: alc (main courses £10 to £15.50)   SERVICE: not inc, card slips closed   CARDS: Amex, Delta, MasterCard, Switch, Visa   DETAILS: 50 seats. 20 seats outside. Private parties: 30 main room, 8 to 14 private rooms. Car park. Children's helpings. No-smoking area. Wheelchair access (not WC). Music £5

CRAYKE North Yorkshire
map 9

▲ Durham Ox
NEW CHEF

Westway, Crayke YO61 4TE
TEL: (01347) 821506   FAX: (01347) 823326
EMAIL: enquiries@thedurhamox.com
WEBSITE: www.thedurhamox.com

MODERN EUROPEAN
£24–£53

The pretty little village of Crayke is really on the map thanks to the Durham Ox – classy restaurant and traditional village pub, both. Reports have been consistently good, though the appointment of a new chef after our inspection has resulted in a no-score entry this year.

Supplementing the carte, a board over the fireplace lists restaurant-style (and -priced) specials. Previously, queen scallops came in two large shells, half a dozen in each, sprinkled with chives and tomatoes and oozing lemon juice, Cheddar and Gruyère, and 'fabulous' duck breast came thick, succulent and tender, with crispy skin coated in honey. The new chef's repertoire includes potted shrimps with fennel salad and toast, slow-cooked belly pork with couscous, and pecan tart with coconut ice cream. Wines are split into bands, with the £10.95 and £13.95 ranges also sold by the glass (£2.65 and £3.25), and there's a good selection at £15.95; pricier and smarter stuff is mostly French.

CHEF: Jason Plevey   PROPRIETORS: the Ibbotson family   OPEN: all week 12 to 2.30 (3 Sun), 6 to 9.30 (8.30 Sun)   CLOSED: 25 Dec   MEALS: alc (main courses £11 to £20). Set L Sun £10.95 (1 course) to £16.95, Set D Mon to Thur 6 to 7 (Sun 6 to 8.30) £9.95 (2 courses) to £13.50   SERVICE: not inc, card slips closed   CARDS: Amex, MasterCard, Switch, Visa   DETAILS: Car park. Vegetarian meals. No children. No smoking. Wheelchair access (not WC). Music   ACCOMMODATION: 8 rooms, all with bath/shower. TV. B&B £60 to £120 (*The Which? Guide to Good Hotels*) (£5)

CRAY'S POND Berkshire

White Lion ✱

NEW ENTRY

Goring Road, Goring Heath, Cray's
Pond RG8 7SH
TEL: (01491) 680471   FAX: (01491) 681654
EMAIL: reservations@innastew.com
WEBSITE: www.innastew.com

COOKING 2
GLOBAL
£25–£52

Stuart and Caroline Pierrepont have done a grand job in renovating and maintaining this village pub in pretty countryside a few miles from Reading. The interior, with its 'amazingly low ceilings', is still reminiscent of a traditional watering hole, although framed menus from famous restaurants suggest that the real emphasis is on things culinary. Beyond the bar are several dining areas – one partly glassed-in, another with lovely parquet flooring and oriental rugs – and the menu is perfectly pitched to suit both village locals and commuters with an appetite for big-city food; simple ideas like fish and chips or 'ground rump' burger with chilli jam line up alongside crispy fried duck and belly pork with bean shoots and spiced cabbage or a 'very fine' ragoût of monkfish, snapper and sole with wild mushrooms – which one reporter devoured with 'gusto'. Savoury dishes tend to win the day over mainly traditional sweets like cold lemon soufflé. The wine list is sensibly organised but bereft of vintages; house wine is £11.95.

CHEFS: Symon Reed and Robert Worham   PROPRIETORS: Stuart and Caroline Pierrepont   OPEN: Tue to Sun L 12 to 2, Tue to Sat D 6 to 9.30   MEALS: alc (main courses £8 to £18). Set L Sun £9.95 (1 course) to £15.95. Bar and light snack menu available   SERVICE: not inc   CARDS: MasterCard, Switch, Visa   DETAILS: 55 seats. 30 seats outside. Private parties: 30 main room. Car park. Vegetarian meals. Children's helpings. No smoking in 1 dining room. Music

CROSTHWAITE Cumbria

map 8

▲ Punch Bowl Inn ✱

Crosthwaite LA8 8HR
TEL: (015395) 68237   FAX: (015395) 68875
EMAIL: enquiries@punchbowl.fsnet.co.uk
WEBSITE: www.punchbowl.fsnet.co.uk
in village, next to church

COOKING 4
MODERN BRITISH
£24–£50

This is a whitewashed Lakeland country pub where the atmosphere isn't in the least bit stuffy and the approach to food and wine is serious - 'not quite a pub with food, nor a formal dining experience', summed up one visitor. Served amid log fires on undressed tables, the food is rich and sustaining, with carefully wrought dishes making optimal use of local produce. Fell-bred Cumbrian lamb might appear as chump cut, roasted and served on grain mustard mash with a red wine and thyme sauce and oyster mushrooms. The River Lune supplies salmon, which might appear as a three-way starter (smoked with horseradish sauce, gravad lax, and ceviche), and there are wild damsons from the Lyth valley, to go into a spicy chutney served with air-dried ham and melon. Other well-reported dishes have included chicken breast in Thai curry sauce, and a memorable dessert of poached fruits with lavender honey ice-cream, while the Tunisian orange cake drenched in honey has become something of a signature dish in readers' reports. British farmhouse cheeses come with oatcakes, celery and apple. Wines are a cut above the pub norm, too, with 20 options by the glass (£2.75 to £3.65) from a well-priced modern range.

CHEF: Steven Doherty   PROPRIETORS: Steven and Marjorie Doherty   OPEN: Tue to Sun L 12 to 2, Tue to Sat D 6 to 9   CLOSED: last week Nov, first week Dec, 25 Dec, 1 week Jan   MEALS: alc (main courses £9 to £14). Set L £9.95 (2 courses) to £12.95, Set L Sun £13.95 (2 courses) to £15.95. Set D 6 to 7 £15.95 (2 courses) to £17.95   SERVICE: not inc   CARDS: MasterCard, Switch, Visa   DETAILS: 60 seats. 20 seats outside. Private parties: 30 main room. Car park. Vegetarian meals. Children's helpings. No smoking in dining room, smoking permitted in bar. No music. No mobile phones   ACCOMMODATION: 3 rooms, all with bath/shower. TV. B&B £37.50 to £105 (*The Which? Guide to Good Hotels*)

CRUDWELL Wiltshire   map 2

▲ Old Rectory 🍴✳

Crudwell SN16 9EP
TEL: (01666) 577194   FAX: (01666) 577853
EMAIL: office@oldrectorycrudwell.co.uk
WEBSITE: www.oldrectorycrudwell.co.uk

COOKING 3
MODERN BRITISH
£29–£63

In a serene Cotswolds hamlet of grey-stone buildings, the Old Rectory is a picture of charm, especially the views from the wood-panelled dining room over formal gardens. Peter Fairclough cooks in a country-house style that – although occasionally quite complex – shows culinary good sense, blending modern and traditional ideas intelligently. The menus cover wide and varied territory but show a preference for fish and game, typically kicking off with pea soup with seared scallops, or roast squab pigeon breast with thyme mash, pearl barley and beetroot risotto. Main courses range from roast brill with saffron mash, spinach and clam chowder to roast Wiltshire venison with carrot and swede dauphinois, girolles and a blackberry jus. Vanilla crème brûlée with apple sorbet and Granny Smith jus is the sort of dessert to expect, although the cheeseboard is an enticing alternative. Five house wines from £12.95 open a good-value international list.

CHEF: Peter Fairclough   PROPRIETORS: Derek and Karen Woods   OPEN: all week 12 to 1.45, 7 to 9 (9.30 Sat)   MEALS: Set L Mon to Sat £15.95 (2 courses) to £18.95, Set L Sun £13.95 (2 courses) to £16.50, Set D £26.50   SERVICE: not inc   CARDS: Amex, Delta, Diners, MasterCard, Switch, Visa   DETAILS: 55 seats. 30 seats outside. Private parties: 40 main room, 6 to 30 private rooms. Car park. Vegetarian meals. Children's helpings. No children under 7 at D. No smoking. Wheelchair access (also WC). Music   ACCOMMODATION: 12 rooms, all with bath/shower. TV. Phone. B&B £75 to £165. Baby facilities (*The Which? Guide to Good Hotels*)

Mansfields ⁵⁄★

1 Broad Street, Cuckfield RH17 5LJ	COOKING 2
TEL: (01444) 410222 FAX: (01444) 410333	MODERN EUROPEAN
	£33–£50

This small black-and-white building near the centre of the village has idiosyncratic shutters on the outside. Inside, wheelback chairs with upholstered but slightly unyielding seats surround smallish tables clothed in layers of linen and enhanced by flowers and candles. The carte of around half a dozen starters and mains changes five or six times a year and has a modern European bent. Thus grilled goats' cheese on marinated sweet peppers with a balsamic and sun-dried tomato dressing could lead on to gourmet lamb medallions with ratatouille, or Somerset smoked eel might precede a veal escalope with creamed morels. Classic desserts include vanilla crème brûlée, lemon tart with a confit of oranges, and poached pears in a cinnamon and red wine punch accompanied by Cornish ice cream. Three dozen unexceptional wines include two dozen from Europe, and prices start at £10.50 for house French red or white.

CHEFS: Günther and Marc Schlender   PROPRIETORS: Günther and Patricia Schlender   OPEN: Tue to Sat D 7 to 10 (lunches for pre-booked parties only)   MEALS: alc D (main courses £10 to £15.50) SERVICE: not inc, 10% for parties of 6 or more, card slips closed   CARDS: Delta, MasterCard, Switch, Visa   DETAILS: 32 seats. Private parties: 12 main room, 8 to 12 private rooms. Vegetarian meals. Children's helpings. No smoking in 1 dining room. No smoking on Saturdays. Music (£5)

▲ Ockenden Manor ⁵⁄★

Ockenden Lane, Cuckfield RH17 5LD	
TEL: (01444) 416111 FAX: (01444) 415549	
EMAIL: ockenden@hshotels.co.uk	COOKING 5
WEBSITE: www.hshotels.co.uk	MODERN FRENCH
off A272, 2m W of Haywards Heath	£36–£90

The Manor is tucked away down its own little lane off the road that runs through the centre of this smart, moneyed village. It is a country-house hotel on a human scale, despite its nine acres of gardens, from the low-ceilinged hallway to the pair of dining rooms, which avoid excessive flounce in favour of comfort and good taste, with well-dressed tables and low lighting.

Inspection revealed plenty of conscientious effort evident in both the sourcing of materials and the flair with which they are cooked. A pair of fixed-price menus is offered: one mobilises such ingredients as beef fillet, duck and sea bass, while the other offers the more economical likes of pork, salmon or oxtail. Honey-roast quail on a galette of crisp potato with a restrained Sauternes sauce, as a first course, manages to combine richness and lightness in the one dish, while another diner enjoyed a pair of huge grilled scallops on onion cream with truffled baby leeks and a red wine sauce. As may be seen, there is no shyness in going for it, but the overall balance of dishes remains stable. A classic pairing of Roquefort and walnuts is the accompaniment for grilled beef fillet, and fish dishes might be more simply treated, teaming red mullet and cod with tapenade and green vegetables. A dull dessert of roasted pineapple with coconut ice cream was the only letdown at inspection, but hot chocolate tart with orange ice cream has been a better bet. Coffee comes with plentiful petits fours, breads are fine, but service could be sharpened up. The wine list is hit and miss: no problem if you want to splurge out on a prestige bottle, but the decent, affordable wines that most of us are after are sewn thinly among the showy names in Europe, and several selections, especially among the whites, fall a bit flat. House wines start at £16, and only three come by the glass.

CHEF: Steve Crane   PROPRIETORS: Sandy and Anne Goodman   OPEN: all week 12.30 to 2, 7 to 9.30 (7.15 to 9 Sun)   MEALS: Set L Mon to Fri £12.95 (2 courses) to £47, Set L Sat £15.50 to £47, Set L Sun £24.50, Set D £38 to £60. Bar menu available   SERVICE: not inc   CARDS: Amex, Delta, Diners, MasterCard, Switch, Visa   DETAILS: 45 seats. 20 seats outside. Private parties: 75 main room, 8 to 16 private rooms. Car park. Vegetarian meals. Children's helpings. No smoking. Wheelchair access (also WC). No music. No mobile phones   ACCOMMODATION: 22 rooms, all with bath/shower. TV. Phone. B&B £99 to £320 (*The Which? Guide to Good Hotels*)   (£5)

DARGATE Kent

map 3

Dove

Plum Pudding Lane, Dargate ME13 9HB
TEL/FAX: (01227) 751360

COOKING 3
FRENCH
£33–£48

The outside of this quaint-looking pub, in the picture-postcard village of Dargate, is decked with window boxes full of flowers. Inside, it's all bare floorboards, chunky wooden furniture and a hodgepodge of decorative jumble. Don't let the place fool you, though – it can do restaurant food as well as any 'proper' restaurant in the area. The menu offers up starters ranging from simply grilled sardines; spring onion and crab risotto flavoured with shallot and herb dressing to tomato and sweet pepper soup. Braised haunch of wild venison and oyster mushrooms, a confit duck leg with braised red cabbage and roasted black pudding, or fillet of tuna, grilled and served on crushed new potatoes, provide ample choice for mains, while desserts might take in apple and almond tart, or passion-fruit crème brûlée. The wine list is short yet interesting and good value, with almost all bottles priced under £25; house red and white start at £12.

CHEF: Nigel Morris   PROPRIETORS: Nigel and Bridget Morris   OPEN: Tue to Sun 12 to 2, Wed to Sat 7 to 9   MEALS: alc (main courses £14.50 to £17). Snack L menu also available   SERVICE: not inc, card slips closed   CARDS: Delta, MasterCard, Switch, Visa   DETAILS: 25 seats. 20 seats outside. Car park. Vegetarian meals. Children's helpings. No music

---

Some restaurants leave credit card slips open even though they also make a fixed (or 'optional') service charge. The Guide strongly disapproves of this practice as it may result in consumers unknowingly paying twice for service.

Several sharp operators have tried to extort money from restaurateurs on the promise of an entry in a guidebook that has never appeared. The Good Food Guide *makes no charge for inclusion.*

DARTMOUTH Devon   map 1

Carved Angel ▼ ◇ ⁙

2 South Embankment, Dartmouth TQ6 9BH
TEL: (01803) 832465   FAX: (01803) 835141   COOKING 5
EMAIL: enquiries@thecarvedangel.com   MODERN BRITISH-PLUS
WEBSITE: www.thecarvedangel.com   £36–£65

Dartmouth is a busy place, and the Angel's prime spot overlooking the water, and Kingswear on the opposite bank, gives visitors a ringside seat of all the touristy action. The dining room is bright and cheerful, full of light at lunchtime, with local artwork for sale on the pale rag-rolled walls; its open aspect is helped by a view of the kitchen, where three or four chefs work away. One of them is Roger Hawkshaw, who arrived at the beginning of 2003 and whose set-price meals are at once simple and enticing, offering perhaps a slab of terrine attractively partitioned into its constituents – gently smoky ham, white chicken meat and rich foie gras – served with a sugared roast fig, or a fresh-tasting fillet of sea bass served with crushed potatoes, baby gem lettuce and sauce vierge.

Materials are well sourced, the style is appealing without being flamboyant, and results have included a 'salad' combining four small, fat and juicy scallops, some sliced and sautéed ceps, and a caper-strewn beurre noisette, as well as a main course of pot-roast chicken breast with crisp and edible skin, accompanied by a first-class thin raviolo filled with creamy foie gras, and by a morel sauce. Seasonality is sometimes a bit askew, but technique is accomplished, producing, for example, a deep-pink, well-risen, properly made raspberry soufflé with a small sauceboat of (cold) raspberry cream and a gently flavoured stem ginger ice cream. Service has varied from 'coordinated' to 'shambolic'. France and the New World turn up wines to please all palates, but elsewhere the list is sketchy. Prices start at £12.25 but are mostly on the high side, and seven come by the glass for £2.50 to £6.50.

CHEF: Roger Hawkshaw   PROPRIETORS: Paul and Andie Roston, and Peter Gorton   OPEN: Tue to Sun L 12.30 to 2.30, Mon to Sat D 7 to 9   CLOSED: 3 days at Christmas   MEALS: Set L £18.50 (2 courses) to £23.50, Set D £25 to £39.50   SERVICE: not inc   CARDS: Delta, MasterCard, Switch, Visa   DETAILS: 50 seats. Private parties: 40 main room, 10 to 20 private rooms. Vegetarian meals. Children's helpings. No children under 10 at D. No smoking. Wheelchair access (not WC). Music. No mobile phones

DEDHAM Essex   map 6

▲ milsoms £

Stratford Road, Dedham CO7 6HW
TEL: (01206) 322795   FAX: (01206) 323689   COOKING 1
EMAIL: milsoms@talbooth.co.uk   GLOBAL
WEBSITE: www.talbooth.co.uk   £32–£55

'A constant happy cacophony' was how one reporter described the buzz at this busy Georgian country hotel. The dining room, which also doubles as a bar, is an attractive space done up in a modern style. Menus seem to offer something for everyone, from duck tacos with hoi sin sauce to organic salmon fillet with kedgeree and poached hen's egg; and then there's 'chef's mezedes': a collection of stuffed vine leaves, air-dried meats and deep-fried squid, among other things. Desserts such as chocolate brownie seem to be made to appeal to young palates (the place is popular with families). The short wine list is as eclectic as the cooking. Prices start at £10.95 a bottle, and there's a separate 'fine wine' list. milsoms (*sic*) does get busy; as no reservations are taken, would-be diners are advised to arrive early. Under the same ownership are nearby Le Talbooth and the Pier Hotel's Harbourside Restaurant at Harwich (see entries).

CHEF: Stas Anastasiades   PROPRIETORS: Gerald and Paul Milsom   OPEN: all week 12 to 2.15, 6 to 9.30 (10 Fri and Sat)   MEALS: alc exc Sun L (main courses £9 to £14). Sun L £16.50 (2 courses) to £21. Light L available   SERVICE: not inc   CARDS: Amex, Delta, Diners, MasterCard, Switch, Visa   DETAILS: 80 seats. 80 seats outside. Private parties: 6 to 16 private rooms. Car park. Vegetarian meals. Children's helpings. No-smoking area. Wheelchair access (also WC). Music. Air-conditioned   ACCOMMODATION: 14 rooms, all with bath/shower. TV. Phone. Room only £72.50 to £130. Rooms for disabled. Baby facilities (*The Which? Guide to Good Hotels*)

▲ Le Talbooth ▼ ⁵⁄✗

Gun Hill, Dedham CO7 6HP
TEL: (01206) 323150   FAX: (01206) 322309
EMAIL: itreception@talbooth.co.uk
WEBSITE: www.talbooth.com

COOKING **4**
MODERN EUROPEAN
£34–£72

Le Talbooth has been in existence since 1952 and one regular describes its setting, a lovely timber-framed house on the banks of the River Stour, as 'as attractive as ever.' Through the years, the original building has been extended and the family's restaurant and hotel holdings have increased to include milsoms (see above) and Pier Hotel, Harbourside Restaurant (see entry, Harwich). The menu is a mix of old favourites, such as lobster thermidor and Dover sole, and the more modern fricassee of monkfish and lobster, served with basmati rice, or loin of venison with haggis ravioli and vegetable gratin. For afters, there may be British farmhouse cheeses or comfort-style dishes such as apple crumble or blackberry and vanilla cheesecake. Service, from a young brigade, is 'relaxed and wholly professional'. A fitfully brilliant and reliably good-value wine list includes mature red Bordeaux and well-chosen Chablis from the traditional regions, while South Africa is championed with a passion from the New World. Elsewhere, total reliance on Hugel for Alsace and sketchy coverage of many regions let the side down a little. A dozen house wines start at £13.50 or £4 per glass.

CHEFS: Terry Barber and Ian Rhodes   PROPRIETORS: Paul and Gerald Milsom   OPEN: all week L 12 to 1.45, Mon to Sat D 7 to 8.45 (and Sun D May to Sept for barbecue)   MEALS: alc Mon to Sat (main courses £15.50 to £25). Set L Sun to Fri £18 (2 courses) to £21.50   SERVICE: 10%, card slips closed   CARDS: Amex, Delta, Diners, MasterCard, Switch, Visa   DETAILS: 75 seats. 40 seats outside. Private parties: 80 main room, 8 to 34 private rooms. Car park. Vegetarian meals. No smoking before 9pm. Wheelchair access (also WC). Music. No mobile phones   ACCOMMODATION: 10 rooms, all with bath/shower. TV. Phone. B&B £95 to £220. Rooms for disabled. Baby facilities (*The Which? Guide to Good Hotels*)

| NEW CHEF | is shown instead of a cooking mark where a change of chef occurred too late for a new assessment of the cooking.

DERBY Derbyshire

map 5

Darleys ⚡✳

Darley Abbey Mills, Darley Abbey,
Derby DE22 1DZ
TEL/FAX: (01332) 364987
WEBSITE: www.darleys.com
off A6 2m N of city centre

COOKING 3
MODERN BRITISH
£27–£64

This former mill has a picturesque setting overlooking the River Derwent.
Despite the historic context of the building, this is a restaurant with a
contemporary air (there is a deck terrace with tables overlooking the river,
where aperitifs and coffee can be served) in terms of both design and cooking.
An up-to-the-minute menu at lunch might offer starters such as Caesar salad
with pancetta and seared duck livers, and a main course of sautéed monkfish
with tomato and wild mushroom ragoût. At dinner the à la carte has produced
pan-roasted fillet of veal with dauphinois potatoes, stuffed morels and truffle
sauce, preceded by seared scallops with squid ink fettucine and cardamom
infused red pepper froth. Vegetarians are well looked after with a separate
menu. Desserts such as hot Toblerone soufflé with Baileys ice cream and
butterscotch sauce are built for comfort. A well-rounded international wine list
has plenty of options under £20, starting with a dozen house wines, mostly at
£14, or £3.50 a glass.

CHEFS: Kevin Stone and Nik Chappell PROPRIETORS: David and Gillian Pinchbeck OPEN: all
week L 12 to 2 (2.30 Sun), Mon to Sat D 6.30 to 10 CLOSED: bank hols MEALS: alc D (main
courses £17 to £20.50). Set L £13.50 (2 courses) to £17.50 SERVICE: 10% (optional), card slips
closed CARDS: Amex, Delta, Diners, MasterCard, Switch, Visa DETAILS: 70 seats. 16 seats
outside. Private parties: 70 main room. Car park. Vegetarian meals. Children's helpings. No
smoking. Wheelchair access (not WC). Music. No mobile phones. Air-conditioned £5

DINTON Buckinghamshire

map 3

La Chouette ♥ ⚡✳

Westlington Green, Dinton HP17 8UW
TEL: (01296) 747422
3½m SW of Aylesbury off A418, follow signs to
Westlington and Ford

COOKING 4
BELGIAN
£21–£61

This prosperous-looking, well-cared-for ancient building lies beside the green
in an out-of-the-way village between Aylesbury and Thame. Beams, low
ceilings and bare wooden floors are brightened up with wildlife photographs
and a toy owl (la chouette) dressed in chef's whites. The rows of empty Belgian
beer bottles indicate the chef/patron's origins, and the thrust of his cooking.
Duvel beer might crop up in a sauce for brill, a liking for chicory is evident (in a
long-standing partnership with Scottish scallops, for example) and rich sauces
are not unusual: béarnaise with Angus beef fillet perhaps. Other menus
(including a tasting one) are built directly from the carte, and meals usually end
with a 'surprise!' dessert, part of M Desmette's playfulness with his customers.
Wine is almost exclusively from France, and mostly top drawer. Several pages of
Bordeaux and Burgundy are complemented by an in-depth focus on a small

number of highly rated producers from other regions; the more affordable bottles are well chosen too. Just eight bottles come in under £20, with house white and red a mere £11.50 or £2.50 for a glass.

CHEF/PROPRIETOR: Frederic Desmette OPEN: Mon to Fri L 12 to 2, Mon to Sat D 7 to 9 MEALS: alc (main courses £14 to £16). Set L £11 to £37.50, Set D £29.50 to £37.50 SERVICE: 12.5% (optional), card slips closed CARDS: Delta, MasterCard, Visa DETAILS: 40 seats. 12 seats outside. Private parties: 40 main room. Car park. Children's helpings. No smoking in 1 dining room. No music. No mobile phones

DORRIDGE West Midlands   map 5

▲ Forest

25 Station Approach, Dorridge B93 8JA	COOKING 4
TEL: (01564) 772120 FAX: (01564) 732680	MODERN FRENCH
WEBSITE: www.forest-hotel.com	£25–£51

'Hansel and Gretel-like' on the outside, this conference centre and restaurant/ bar is all open-plan bare boards, red faux-leather chairs and neutral-toned walls on the inside. The Forest is very popular, especially with the city-slicker set (it's not far from Birmingham and the NEC), most of whom settle for the bar area rather than the restaurant area. Former sous-chef James Pye has taken over from Ian Mansfield; his cooking seems to be carrying on in a similar vein, and there tend to be more hits than misses. Singled out for applause was an intensely flavoured blackcurrant sorbet 'to die for', from the dessert menu. Before that, diners may plump for the likes of pan-fried mackerel with marinated vegetables, punctuated with little blobs of caviar. The raw materials in a main course of breast of Gressingham duck with thyme rösti, spring greens and blueberry jus received fulsome praise, particularly the bird. Everything takes place at a decent pace, and service is knowledgeable and on-the-ball. Prices are very reasonable, particularly on Tuesday evenings, when a prix-fixe is offered. Wines, arranged by style, are also fairly priced, with most bottles under £20.

CHEF: James Pye PROPRIETORS: Gary and Tracey Perkins OPEN: Tue to Sun L 12 to 2, Tue to Sat D 6.30 to 10 CLOSED: 25 Dec MEALS: alc (main courses £10 to £18.50). Set L £10 (2 courses) to £15, Set L Sun £17.50, Set D Tue £12.50 (2 courses) to £17 SERVICE: not inc CARDS: Amex, Delta, MasterCard, Switch, Visa DETAILS: 70 seats. 40 seats outside. Private parties: 70 main room, 12 to 150 private rooms. Car park. Vegetarian meals. Children's helpings. No smoking. Wheelchair access (also WC). Music. Air-conditioned ACCOMMODATION: 10 rooms, all with bath/shower. TV. Phone. B&B £62.50 to £95.50 (£5)

DORRINGTON Shropshire   map 5

▲ Country Friends

Dorrington SY5 7JD	
TEL: (01743) 718707	COOKING 6
EMAIL: countryfriends@ukonline.co.uk	MODERN BRITISH
on A49, 5m S of Shrewsbury	£42–£51

'Thank goodness for Country Friends' begins one fairly typical report on this black and white building on the A49 just south of Shrewsbury. It flies the flag for good eating hereabouts, starting with a warm welcome from Charles Whittaker, whose informal air echoes that of the house itself: a pubby lounge with faded gold banquettes, and a smarter dining room overlooking the garden, with well spaced tables, a bold abstract, and an inglenook fireplace. There is no fast footwork here, just a gentle interpretation of British food with all its varied input, taking in potato gnocchi with a creamed rabbit sauce, a twice-baked leek and Llanboidy cheese soufflé, or a pleasing and accurately cooked pea and lightly smoky bacon risotto, offered at the height of the English pea season in July.

Readers who prefer their food simple, rather than elaborate and showy, will find the Whittakers oblige by keeping theirs as straightforward as can be, for example in a dish of scallops – five large pieces of white muscle, translucent in the centre, surrounding a small pile of coral – all on a lake of tomato purée spiked with diced onion. There was nothing more to this dish than that, apart from a side plate of vegetables: crunchy, breadcrumbed cauliflower florets (a fixture), plus grilled courgette, aubergine and pepper. An open pastry case – correctly termed a flan – with a deep lemon-flavoured custardy filling, together with a well-made sauce of whizzed up and sieved raspberries, is also typical of the kitchen's output and made a good finish to an inspection meal. The wine list is just right: unassuming, reasonably priced and good quality, with a balance of traditional France and New World. Prices start at £12.75.

CHEF: Charles Whittaker   PROPRIETORS: Charles and Pauline Whittaker   OPEN: Wed to Sat 12 to 2, 7 to 9   CLOSED: 2 weeks mid-July, half-term Oct   MEALS: Set L and D £29.30 (2 courses) to £31.70. Light L menu available   SERVICE: not inc   CARDS: MasterCard, Switch, Visa   DETAILS: 45 seats. Private parties: 45 main room. Car park. Vegetarian meals. No smoking. Wheelchair access (not WC). No music   ACCOMMODATION: 1 room, with bath/shower. D,B&B £85 to £140. No children

DRYBROOK Gloucestershire   map 5

Cider Press ⅝✳

The Cross, Drybrook GL17 9EB
TEL: (01594) 544472   FAX: (01594) 544550   COOKING 2
EMAIL: info@ciderpress.org.uk   MODERN EUROPEAN
WEBSITE: www.ciderpress.org.uk   £25–£47

Set in a village on the edge of the Forest of Dean, an outpost of an older England, the Cider Press is very much a local restaurant. The dining area is crammed full of pictures and knick-knacks, creating a domestic atmosphere reinforced by the host Jon Whateley. Helen Short's cooking mixes local and Mediterranean influences in, say, ravioli with local smoked chicken on a tagliatelle of buttery leeks, or seared escalope of pork loin with bacon-wrapped sage forcemeat on an oaked cider sauce. Fish is supplied from Cornwall, the results of which appear on a daily-changing blackboard, listing perhaps sesame roasted sea bass and mixed seafood in tomato and saffron broth. Desserts show enthusiasm for darker, warmer flavours: chocolate and hazelnut bread-and-butter pudding perhaps, or baked orange tart with marmalade ice cream and muscovado pavlova with dark rum and bananas. House wines are £9.95 and a decent range of bottles rarely goes to £20.

CHEF: Helen Short   PROPRIETORS: Jon Whateley and Helen Short   OPEN: Sun L only 12 to 2, Wed to Sat D 7 to 9.30   MEALS: alc exc Sun (main courses £9.50 to £15.50). Set L Sun £12.95 (2 courses) to £15.95   SERVICE: not inc   CARDS: MasterCard, Switch, Visa   DETAILS: 24 seats. Private parties: 24 main room. Vegetarian meals. No smoking. Occasional music. No mobile phones

DURHAM Co Durham   map 10

Bistro 21 ✸

Aykley Heads House, Aykley Heads,	COOKING 3
Durham DH1 5TS	MEDITERRANEAN
TEL: (0191) 384 4354 FAX: (0191) 384 1149	£24–£52

Once the servants' wing of an eighteenth-century villa on the northern edge of the city, the building has taken well to sympathetic conversion, with painted rough-hewn stone walls, a glassed-in courtyard, and a quirkily decorated pink and grey dining room. The kitchen delivers consistently good quality from a generous and appealing carte that knows how to please the crowd with its ham knuckle terrine, foie gras sausage, duck spring rolls, and sirloin steak and chips. Ideas can also be imaginative without being complicated, and fine materials are exemplified by three prime, plump, translucent scallops sitting on a disc sliced from a first-rate mushroom 'sausage', with a smear of buttery sauce. Dishes are well judged too, taking in roast hake and watercress with deep-fried parsley, and pot-roast partridge with a scoop of polenta, a rasher of smoky bacon, and some onion rings in batter. Desserts aim for comfort, offering spotted dick, sticky toffee pudding, and an individual pear and blackcurrant crumble with a small jug of custard. Service can be 'dippy' but is also 'cheerful and friendly', and a short, to-the-point wine list stays mostly under £25, starting with house Duboeuf red and white at £11.50. See Newcastle and Ponteland for other restaurants in Terry Laybourne's group.

CHEF: Mark Anderson   PROPRIETOR: Terence Laybourne   OPEN: Mon to Sat 12 to 2, 7 (6 Sat) to 10.30   CLOSED: 25 Dec, bank hols   MEALS: alc (main courses £10.50 to £16.50). Set L £12 (2 courses) to £14.50   SERVICE: not inc   CARDS: Amex, Delta, Diners, MasterCard, Switch, Visa   DETAILS: 55 seats. 24 seats outside. Private parties: 55 main room, 5 to 30 private rooms. Car park. Vegetarian meals. Children's helpings. No smoking. Wheelchair access (also WC). Music

EASTBOURNE East Sussex   map 3

▲ Grand Hotel, Mirabelle ♥ ✸

King Edwards Parade, Eastbourne BN21 4EQ	COOKING 7
TEL: (01323) 435066 FAX: (01323) 412233	MODERN EUROPEAN
WEBSITE: www.grandeastbourne.com	£28–£76

The Mirabelle remains a plush and comfortable place where gentlemen are requested to wear either a jacket or a tie, but not necessarily both. Dinner offers a seven-course tasting menu and a choice of two three-course menus (note that prices include coffee and service), and although this is a rather grand hotel, Gerald Röser has put his own unshowy stamp on things.

His is a meticulous and quietly confident style of cooking, in which flavours are apparent without being overly assertive, so the food makes an impact without relying on gimmicks, as in a first course of tender, pink-cooked, lightly gamey wood pigeon breast, accompanied by a rasher of bacon and by lentils in a rich, wine-based sauce. The food achieves a rare balance in being 'strong yet gently refined': for example, in a well-hung, characterful rack of gently herby salt-marsh lamb, cut open to reveal its pink centre, served with vegetables 'snatched from the cradle'.

The cooking is not without a degree of individuality, evident in a firm, beetroot-flavoured 'custard' that accompanies thin slices of briefly fried scallops, fanned out on a flat cylinder of chive-strewn potato. What stands out, though, is that precise cooking of meat and fish results in maximum flavour and firm texture: at inspection, two generous fillets of briefly baked John Dory breaking into big, chunky flakes, served with fennel, spinach, and an 'exceptional' sauce made from stock, cream and saffron.

Presentation is attractive, while desserts are 'gloriously simple': chocolate fondant with pistachio, or a lime cream, essentially a freestanding, smoothly textured crème brûlée, served with a creamy butterscotch and bitter orange sauce. Staff are friendly and helpful, but wines have not escaped criticism on the grounds of both price and presentation. Nonetheless, this is an impressive list where the best bottles are appropriately matured, although less attention has been paid to the lower reaches. France and the rest of Europe are the chief interests; forays into the New World are most convincing in South Africa. Eighteen wines by the glass start at £3.70.

CHEFS: Keith Mitchell and Gerald Röser   PROPRIETOR: Elite Hotels   OPEN: Tue to Sat 12.30 to 2, 7 to 10   CLOSED: first 2 weeks Jan   MEALS: Set L £16.50 (2 courses) to £19, Set D £35 to £55 SERVICE: net prices, card slips closed   CARDS: Amex, Delta, Diners, MasterCard, Switch, Visa DETAILS: 48 seats. Private parties: 50 main room. Car park. Vegetarian meals. Children's helpings. Jacket or tie. No smoking. Wheelchair access (also WC). Music. No mobile phones. Air-conditioned   ACCOMMODATION: 152 rooms, all with bath/shower. TV. Phone. B&B £135 to £430. Rooms for disabled. Baby facilities. Swimming pool (*The Which? Guide to Good Hotels*) £5

EAST CHILTINGTON East Sussex   map 3

Jolly Sportsman ▼ 💥 £

Chapel Lane, East Chiltington BN7 3BA
TEL/FAX: (01273) 890400
EMAIL: jollysportsman@mistral.co.uk
WEBSITE: www.jollysportsman.com
from B2116 ½m E of Plumpton, turn N   COOKING **3**
(signposted East Chiltington), after 1½m turn left   MODERN EUROPEAN
(pub is signposted)   £24–£52

The Jolly Sportsman gets smarter year on year, and recent improvements to this yellow weather-boarded pub in a quiet Sussex lane include a terrace for alfresco eating. Outside are rustic wooden tables on the lawn, while inside is an appealing mix of rough stone walls, warm colours and contemporary art in the form of pictures and sculptures. The food is modern and direct: witness a simple but beautifully made starter of mackerel, fennel, anchovy and red pepper salad. A main-course haunch of venison with port and juniper, served rare with a 'superb, gorgeous, rich' gratin dauphinois, impressed one reporter. Desserts like

Bakewell tart with vanilla sauce, and chocolate tart with crème fraîche, may tempt the sweet-toothed. Presentation is spare and neat, flavour contrasts are well judged, and dishes are structured around fine raw materials. Although not cheap by pub standards, the place is undoubtedly popular and has a real atmosphere; one reporter found patrons 'having one hell of a ball' on a Saturday night. Service is smart, hard-working, relaxed and friendly. The wine list, opening modestly at £10.45 and offering eight by the glass (from £2.70 to £4.95), blossoms into something more ambitious. Italy is favoured, and Burgundies are exquisitely well chosen, although the New World has fewer highlights; there is a good selection of halves.

CHEFS: Richard Willis and Bruce Wass PROPRIETORS: Bruce and Gwyneth Wass OPEN: Tue to Sun (and bank hol Mons) L 12.30 to 2 (12.15 to 3 Sun), Tue to Sat D 7 to 9.30 (10 Fri and Sat) CLOSED: 4 days Christmas MEALS: alc (main courses £9 to £17). Set L £11 (2 courses) to £14.75 SERVICE: 10%, card slips closed CARDS: Delta, MasterCard, Switch, Visa DETAILS: 70 seats. 30 seats outside. Private parties: 60 main room, 12 to 20 private rooms. Car park. Vegetarian meals. Children's helpings. No smoking. Wheelchair access (also WC). No music

EAST END Hampshire — map 2

East End Arms

Main Road, East End SO41 5SY
TEL: (01590) 626223
EMAIL: jennie@eastendarms.co.uk
WEBSITE: www.eastendarms.co.uk
off B3054, 4m E of Lymington

COOKING 3
MODERN BRITISH/SEAFOOD
£28–£43

Close to Lymington, and approached through one of the prettiest parts of the New Forest, this thoroughly straightforward pub, with red patterned carpet, an unmatched assortment of tables and chairs, and walls in shiny nicotine yellow, is almost consciously ordinary. Such simplicity may or may not be post-modern irony, but when it comes to the food this is refreshingly and unselfconsciously plain and has a bias towards fish. Good ingredients are supported by solid skills and a sensibility that produces well-judged chips and a simple roast whole lemon sole – though the kitchen can spring surprises with a pairing of scallops and black pudding. The lunchtime menu starts with robustly filled baguettes at £5.50, moving on to main dishes like fish pie, rabbit casserole, braised venison hock or coquilles St Jacques. Puddings are staples like crème brûlée or rhubarb upside-down crumble. Four house wines are £12 (£3.25 a glass), and the short, mainly European list stays mostly under £20.

CHEF: Paul Sykes PROPRIETORS: Stuart Kitcher and Paul Sykes OPEN: Tue to Sun L 12 to 2, Tue to Sat D 7 to 9 CLOSED: 25 Dec and 1 Jan MEALS: alc (main courses L £7 to £12, D £10 to £15) SERVICE: not inc, card slips closed CARDS: Delta, MasterCard, Switch, Visa DETAILS: 34 seats. 60 seats outside. Car park. Children's helpings. Music

---

The cuisine styles noted at the tops of entries are only an approximation, often suggested to us by the restaurants themselves. Please read the entry itself to find out more about the cooking style.

EAST GRINSTEAD West Sussex   map 3

▲ Gravetye Manor ▐ ⁵⋇

Vowels Lane, East Grinstead RH19 4LJ
TEL: (01342) 810567   FAX: (01342) 810080
EMAIL: info@gravetyemanor.co.uk   COOKING 7
WEBSITE: www.gravetyemanor.co.uk   TRADITIONAL BRITISH/MODERN FRENCH
off the B2110, 2 miles SW of East Grinstead   £39–£77

Given the weather it is worth arriving early to enjoy the carefully tended garden (one such as you might normally expect to pay to perambulate) and also the house itself, a genuinely ancient pile with panelled rooms and old pictures. Expect a few recurring luxuries, such as truffles and foie gras, but the cooking doesn't rely on them too much for effect. Materials are scrupulously sourced and well handled by an ambitious kitchen that takes care over details without losing sight of the ensemble – and seems to have become even more assured over the past year.

Dishes can be complex, requiring a range of high-level skills to prepare, but what is promised is delivered – notably a pillow of perfectly timed sea bass fillet of 'outstanding flavour', a smooth, creamy but firm scallop mousseline forming an almost undetectable bond with it, surrounded by a light, caviar-flecked sauce. Main-course lamb impressed at inspection for its 'best-ever' maturity and quality: a neat pile of slices of pink yet dark colour and firm, even texture, served with small chunks of sweetbread, a few pieces of asparagus, richly flavoured morels, and a deeply flavoured stock-based sauce. Flavouring partnerships are well conceived, and dishes deftly executed. Among starters a rectangular slab of chunky yet smooth and 'incredibly rabbity' terrine (with a light crunch from hazelnuts) has come with a restrained apple and ginger compote, while a luxuriant and 'grown-up' pudding could take the form of a thin, sweet, crisp pastry tart well filled with a rich and unsweet chocolate mix, oozing in the centre, served with a pile of raspberries under a blob of vanilla-flavoured ice cream. Extras are on a par, from pastries and 'toasty things' with aperitifs, via good bread, to fine petits fours, while staff ('serious Euro twenty-somethings') are knowledgeable enthusiasts who tread with ease the boundary between familiarity and professionalism. Given that service is included, and spring water is free, value is considered fair.

The heavyweight wine list digs back a fair way into the history of Bordeaux and Burgundy, turning up plenty of treasures, but is equally in tune with the modern world, with good Australians, South Africans, Californians and more easily affordable South Americans. Alsace, the Rhône and Germany make rewarding reading too. Prices, taking the service into account, are fair for the quality, starting at £16 with six by the glass for £5 to £7.

CHEF: Mark Raffan   PROPRIETORS: Peter Herbert and family   OPEN: all week 12.30 to 1.45, 7 to 9.30   CLOSED: 25 Dec D residents only   MEALS: Set L £27 to £52, Set D £37 to £52. Bar and (seasonally) garden menus available   SERVICE: net prices, card slips closed   CARDS: MasterCard, Switch, Visa   DETAILS: 45 seats. 12 seats outside. Private parties: 20 main room. Car park. Vegetarian meals. No children under 7. No smoking. No music. No mobile phones ACCOMMODATION: 18 rooms, all with bath/shower. TV. Phone. Room only £100 to £310. No children under 7. Baby facilities. Fishing (The Which? Guide to Good Hotels)

EASTON GREY Wiltshire   map 2

▲ Whatley Manor ▼   NEW ENTRY

Easton Grey SN16 0RB
TEL: (01666) 822888   FAX: (01666) 826120
EMAIL: reservations@whatleymanor.com   COOKING 7
WEBSITE: www.whatleymanor.com   MODERN EUROPEAN
on B4040 3m W of Malmesbury   £76–£91

During three years of renovation, extension and refurbishment to this vast country house hotel (still ongoing as the Guide went to press) entire wings have been added, as well as tarmac drives and acres of Cotswold stone walling. To say that no expense has been spared would be an understatement. It is about the size of a small village (they employ five gardeners) and is the last word in opulence, with handmade wallpapers, expensive woods in the bar, and specially commissioned emerald green chandeliers made in Venice. It takes a confident and experienced chef to live up to all that, and Martin Burge (formerly head chef at John Burton-Race at the Landmark) seems to be the right man for the job.

Even on the small sample of dishes reported on so far, consistency appears to be a strength. There is lots of foam, but stock bases are first-class and modish combinations have included smoked belly pork with roast scallop and cauliflower purée, alongside steamed sea bass with grey shrimps and iced basil and langoustine cappuccino. The food is skilful, sophisticated (one of the hotel's watchwords) and cosmopolitan. Timing tends to be 'conventional', producing chunks of rather solid lamb sweetbreads, in an otherwise well-judged starter that also contained toasted hazelnuts, a jumble of seasonal vegetables and a 'superb' cep-flavoured foam.

Seafood is nevertheless well handled, judging by a dish of three large scallops with turned saffron potatoes, partnered by two red mullet fillets on a bed of mixed squid rings with diced sun-dried cherry tomatoes. The foam in this case was an intense and top class bouillabaisse, 'rich, yet clean-tasting'. Techniques are sound at dessert stage too: for example, in a layered soufflé with distinct stripes of chocolate and pistachio, served with a deep brown bitter chocolate sorbet speared by a pistachio-studded biscuit and with a pistachio ice cream with a filigree chocolate biscuit stuck into it. A 'huge team' of staff, nearly all male and French, are [intimidatingly] smart and self-assured, but equally professional and charming.

The wine list confounds expectations. Instead of a ponderous trawl through the finest bottles of France (present, of course, but they don't dominate), here is a fresh global selection, quite expensive but not excessively so. The Loire is good, Italy is strong, Austria and Switzerland add interest and there is plenty at £19, plus Indian house red at £18. Six by the glass are £5.50–£7.50.

CHEF: Martin Burge   PROPRIETOR: Mr C. Landolt   OPEN: Wed to Sun D only 7 to 10   MEALS: Set D £60   SERVICE: 10% (optional), card slips closed   CARDS: Amex, Delta, Diners, MasterCard, Switch, Visa   DETAILS: 55 seats. Private parties: 15 main room, 10 to 30 private rooms. Car park. Vegetarian meals. No children under 12. Wheelchair access (also WC). Occasional music. No mobile phones   ACCOMMODATION: 23 rooms, all with bath/shower. TV. Phone. B&B £325 to £1,125. Rooms for disabled. No children under 12. Swimming pool

EAST WITTON North Yorkshire   map 9

▲ Blue Lion £

East Witton DL8 4SN
TEL: (01969) 624273   FAX: (01969) 624189
EMAIL: bluelion@breathemail.net
WEBSITE: www.thebluelion.co.uk   COOKING 3
on A6108 Masham to Leyburn road, 2m SE of   MODERN BRITISH
Middleham   £25–£53

East Witton's trim, bucolic charm and architectural coherence would make a
good costume drama setting, and in the Blue Lion's long frontage beside the
main road, the arched entrance to the car park announces this former coaching
inn. The bar menu here subsumes crab and ginger fritters or blue-cheesed fillet
steak on rösti. But in the restaurant you might embark on roast medallions of
monkfish wrapped in Parma ham with brown shrimps and sauce vierge, before
perhaps tackling a lamb duo of confit rack and braised shoulder served with
olive oil mash, or slow-roast honey-glazed duckling, carved from a trolley, with
apple gravy. Vegetarians can choose from around seven dishes, and meals end
with warm treacle tart with vanilla ice cream and custard, or crème brûlée
embellished with raspberries. Service is helpful, and on the extensive, fairly
priced wine list (a model for others to follow) house French is £10.95 (£2.75 a
glass).

CHEF: John Dalby   PROPRIETORS: Paul and Helen Klein   OPEN: Sun L 12 to 2.15, all week D 7 to
9.30   MEALS: alc (main courses £8 to £16). Bar menu available, except Sun L   SERVICE: not inc
CARDS: Delta, MasterCard, Switch, Visa   DETAILS: 80 seats. 40 seats outside. Private parties: 40
main room, 6 to 20 private rooms. Car park. Vegetarian meals. Children's helpings. Wheelchair
access (also WC). No music   ACCOMMODATION: 12 rooms, all with bath/shower. TV. Phone. B&B
£53.50 to £89. Baby facilities (The Which? Guide to Good Hotels)

ELLAND West Yorkshire   map 8

La Cachette ♥ 🍞 £

31 Huddersfield Road, Elland HX5 9AW   COOKING 3
TEL: (01422) 378833   FAX: (01422) 327567   MODERN EUROPEAN
                                                         £25–£52

La Cachette looks and feels like a sophisticated bistro/brasserie. The owners
describe it as a restaurant and wine bar, and occasionally people do pop in just
for a drink, but generally they come to make full use of the dining room. In
summer 2003 Jonathan Nichols, formerly at Bradley's in Huddersfield (see
entry), joined as head chef. The menu has undergone a few tweaks, but no major
revolution, sticking mainly to tried and tested flavour combinations. Start,
perhaps, with fishcakes, golden-brown on the outside and packed with flakes of
salmon, white fish and parsley, with chunky tartare sauce on the side. Main
courses might include moist, tender chicken breast filled with mushrooms and
served with dauphinois potatoes and chive and truffle butter, or pan-fried pork
escalope with buttered tagliatelle and gazpacho sauce. For dessert, choose
between cheeses or traditional Eton mess, sticky toffee pudding with
butterscotch sauce, or crème brûlée, and finish with excellent espresso and

cinnamon biscuits. Front-of-house is professional and pleasant, and regular visitors report that 'the welcome is genuine'. The wine list hops around the world to gather an up-to-date collection of bottles, mostly at very good prices. Eight house wines, starting at £10.95 (£2.20 a glass), are identified by style.

CHEF: Jonathan Nichols   PROPRIETOR: CGL Partnership   OPEN: Mon to Sat 12 to 2.30, 6 to 9.30 (10 Fri and Sat)   CLOSED: 25 Dec to 4 Jan, 25 Aug to 8 Sep, bank hols   MEALS: alc (main courses £8 to £16). Set L £8.95 (2 courses), Set D Mon to Thur and 6 to 7 Fri and Sat £15.95 (inc wine)   SERVICE: not inc   CARDS: Delta, MasterCard, Switch, Visa   DETAILS: 85 seats. Vegetarian meals. Children's helpings. Music. Air-conditioned

ELY Cambridgeshire   map 6

Old Fire Engine House ⅝✳

25 St Mary's Street, Ely CB7 4ER   COOKING 1
TEL: (01353) 662582   FAX: (01353) 668364   TRADITIONAL ENGLISH FARMHOUSE
£30–£48

This appealingly homely restaurant has large wooden tables, pew seating and an old worn tile floor in a dining room that is reached via the kitchen. The populist, no-frills cooking style includes reliable soups such as ham and lentil, tasty herrings pickled in dill with yoghurt and cucumber, and trencherman portions of main courses like roast leg of lamb with herb stuffing. Second helpings are offered as standard, so nobody is likely to leave feeling hungry, especially when there may well be a temptation such as chocolate and Cointreau cheesecake to finish. Friendly, efficient service gets the job done. Michael Jarman has put together an unashamedly Francocentric wine list, with a good selection of wines by the glass (from £2.75), classy half-bottles, and some alluring mature vintages from Bordeaux, the Rhône and Burgundy. Chilean house wines are £9.

CHEF: Terri Baker   PROPRIETORS: Ann Ford and Michael Jarman   OPEN: all week L 12.15 to 2, Mon to Sat D 7.15 to 9   CLOSED: 24 Dec to 5 Jan, bank hols   MEALS: alc (main courses £12.50 to £16)   SERVICE: not inc   CARDS: Delta, MasterCard, Switch, Visa   DETAILS: 55 seats. 20 seats outside. Private parties: 35 main room, 10 to 22 private rooms. Car park. Vegetarian meals. Children's helpings. No smoking in 1 dining room. No music. No mobile phones

EMSWORTH Hampshire   map 2

▲ 36 on the Quay ♥ ⅝✳

47 South Street, Emsworth PO10 7EG
TEL: (01243) 375592 and 372257   COOKING 6
FAX: (01243) 375593   MODERN EUROPEAN
WEBSITE: www.36onthequay.co.uk   £35–£82

Smack on the quayside, with sights and sounds of the sea, this whitewashed seventeenth-century building now has four bedrooms to add to its appeal. Its small conservatory bar, courtyard garden, and soft pastel shades of yellow and pale blue lend it an intimate, sophisticated and comfortable atmosphere, while Ramon Farthing's menus yield plenty of attractive, contemporary dishes. Seafood understandably plays a starring role, perhaps appearing as diver-caught scallops with creamed and tempura cauliflower, or as a generous bowl of broth full of strips of root vegetable, pieces of well-timed John Dory and small pesto ravioli.

This is refined, ambitious cooking using well-sourced and first-rate ingredients, and despite their intricacy dishes are well balanced: two generous fillets of brill – 'fresh, top quality, flakingly tender, perfectly timed' – come on celeriac fondant, surrounded by langoustines and small piles of spinach, all in a fine roast chicken reduction. The 'wow' factor was present in an individual rabbit and leek pie made with first-class pastry, sitting on thin slices of rare and succulent rabbit, encircled by warm marinated prunes, shallots and mushrooms in a light grain mustard sauce. Desserts tend to be variations on themes: a 'stunningly executed' pineapple version incorporating zingy sorbet interlaced with pineapple crisps, together with a Tatin topped with coconut cream; or four ways with pear, including brûlée, parfait, frangipane with honey sauce, and a mille-feuille. Service is knowledgeable, attentive and efficient, and big names from Bordeaux and Burgundy on the wine list are another 'wow', although prices are more 'ouch'. Alsace, the Loire and the Rhône are quality packed, and the more affordable selection from southern France is spot-on. Otherwise a selection from California turns up some expensive thrills, but the house selection of a dozen wines under £20 is no great shakes.

CHEFS: Ramon Farthing and Steven Midgley   PROPRIETORS: Ramon and Karen Farthing   OPEN: Tue to Fri L 12 to 2, Mon to Sat D 7 to 9.45   MEALS: Set L £17.95 (2 courses) to £21.95, Set D £38 to £55   SERVICE: not inc   CARDS: Amex, Delta, Diners, MasterCard, Switch, Visa   DETAILS: 44 seats. 10 seats outside. Private parties: 45 main room, 8 to 11 private rooms. Car park. Children's helpings. No smoking. Wheelchair access (not WC). Occasional music. No mobile phones   ACCOMMODATION: 4 rooms, all with bath/shower. TV. B&B £60 to £100 (double rooms)

Fat Olives 🍴✳ | NEW ENTRY |

30 South Street, Emsworth PO10 7EH
TEL: (01243) 377914   COOKING 3
EMAIL: info@fatolives.co.uk   MODERN BRITISH
WEBSITE: www.fatolives.co.uk   £24–£46

Bare wood tables and whitewashed walls, damask napkins and polished glasses combine to create a smart minimalist interior in this tiny seventeenth-century former fisherman's cottage on the street running down to Emsworth harbour. Fat Olives has an attractive take on the Med-nosh theme. First courses like cockles, chorizo and dry sherry, or pigeon breast with mint pea purée and pancetta, exemplify Lawrence Murphy's robustly imaginative rifling of the traditions and larders of Europe. A successful main course combined pink bream with linguine and a good rich white wine cream sauce. Baked chocolate mousse 'with a wickedly gooey centre' came with a fresh orange sorbet, showing skill and simplicity in a satisfying synergy that avoided redundant ingredients; an alternative might be mango, lime and rosewater cheesecake. Julia Murphy takes efficient charge of greeting and all that goes with it. Starting at £11.75, the wine list canters quickly through all the major production areas, often relying on safe big names, but also offering a Godello white from Galicia.

CHEF: Lawrence Murphy   PROPRIETORS: Lawrence and Julia Murphy   OPEN: Tue to Sat 12 to 2, 7 to 10   CLOSED: 2 weeks from 24 Dec, 1 week Oct   MEALS: alc L and D (main courses £10.50 to £14.50). Set L £10 (1 course) to £16   SERVICE: not inc, card slips closed   CARDS: Delta, MasterCard, Switch, Visa   DETAILS: 28 seats. 10 seats outside. Private parties: 24 main room. Vegetarian meals. No children under 8. No smoking. Wheelchair access (also WC). Music £5

EPWORTH North Lincolnshire   map 9

Epworth Tap ▼ 🍷 ✳

9–11 Market Place, Epworth DN9 1EU
TEL: (01427) 873333   FAX: And fax
WEBSITE: www.epworthtap.co.uk   MODERN EUROPEAN
3m S of M180 junction 2   £27–£50

As the Guide went to press this restaurant closed.

CHEF: Stephanie Morrison   PROPRIETOR: Gail Perry   OPEN: Sun L 12 to 3, Wed to Sat D 6.30 to 9.30   CLOSED: 25 Dec to 1 Jan   MEALS: alc D (main courses £10 to £17). Set L Sun £9.95 (1 course) to £15.95   SERVICE: not inc, card slips closed   CARDS: Delta, MasterCard, Switch, Visa   DETAILS: 54 seats. Private parties: 26 main room. Vegetarian meals. No smoking. Music £5

ERMINGTON Devon   map 1

▲ Plantation House, Matisse ✳

Totnes Road, Ermington PL21 9NS
TEL: (01548) 831100   FAX: (01548) 831248
EMAIL: enquiries@plantationhousehotel.com   COOKING 5
WEBSITE: www.plantationhousehotel.com   MODERN EUROPEAN
on A3121, 10m E of Plymouth   £38–£80

A former rectory, Plantation House Hotel has a handsome cream-painted Georgian stucco façade and large windows overlooking surrounding farmland. Pale cream carpets and walls and blue upholstered chairs set off colourful Matisse reproductions on the restaurant walls.

Ashley Hatton's cooking is intricate but not fussy, with impeccable ingredients respectfully but imaginatively treated, and timing is exact. After canapés, an amuse-bouche and very good bread, there might be a delicate boudin of lobster and king prawn on a julienne of courgettes with a lobster velouté, or a 'faultless' ballottine of foie gras with prune purée 'teardrops'. A main course of tender duck with a raviolo of spinach and cabbage, plum compote and sherry vinegar sauce was a stellar dish for execution and balance. The signature dessert, apple Matisse, is two rounds of apple with a crispy thatch of apple shreds and a julienne of apple, piled up into a tower and served with a shot glass of cold dry cider. Lunch is a simpler affair, with the same integrity and high-quality ingredients; expect sunblush tomato risotto followed by pan-fried salmon.

Both Cobys – Alan deals with wine and Helen with front-of-house – are genuinely hospitable, and although waits can be long when the dining room is busy service has been commended. The wine list is divided into three ranges: Plantation (easy-going), New World Connoisseurs (trendy) and Classic (traditional). Prices are highish, and only the house basics come by the glass (£16 the bottle, £4 the glass).

CHEF: Ashley Hatton   PROPRIETOR: Helen Coby   OPEN: Mon to Fri L 12 to 2, Mon to Sat D 7 to 9   MEALS: alc (main courses £11.50 to £17.50). Set D £36   SERVICE: not inc, card slips closed   CARDS: Amex, Delta, MasterCard, Switch, Visa   DETAILS: 40 seats. 20 seats outside. Private parties: 40 main room, 8 to 20 private rooms. Car park. Vegetarian meals. Children's helpings. No smoking. Wheelchair access (not WC). Music   ACCOMMODATION: 10 rooms, all with bath/shower. TV. Phone. B&B £70 to £115. Baby facilities (*The Which? Guide to Good Hotels*) £5

EVESHAM Worcestershire   map 5

▲ Wood Norton Hall, Le Duc's | NEW ENTRY |

Le Duc Restaurant, Wood Norton,
Evesham WR11 4YB
TEL: (01386) 425780   FAX: (01386) 425781   COOKING 3
EMAIL: info@wnhall.co.uk   MODERN FRENCH
WEBSITE: www.wnhall.co.uk   £32–£64

Wood Norton Hall has, at various points in its history, been a private house for French nobility, a secret broadcasting centre for the BBC during the Second World War and the centre of the Corporation's broadcast training. It is now a conference venue, housing Le Duc's Fine Dining Restaurant. The linked dining rooms, in common with the Hall as a whole, have carved wood panelling everywhere, plus pillared fireplaces and shiny black chandeliers.

Good raw materials and consistency characterise the kitchen, which has turned out an open raviolo incorporating well-timed scallops and fresh-tasting mushrooms, enlivened by a creamy 'parsley cappuccino', and terrine of foie gras with dates and a grape compote. The quality and presentation of fillet of beef with fondant potatoes, crisp salsify and green beans impressed at inspection; alternatively opt for poached halibut with lemongrass and basil scented gnocchi, or venison fillet with red onion, parsley purée and port sauce. Desserts, such as Irish coffee mousse with chocolate 'sugar cubes' with orange and fennel seed biscuits, are ambitious constructions. There's an army of staff on hand and a fairly pricey global wine list. Chilean house wines are £15.75.

CHEF: Paul Napper   PROPRIETOR: National Real Estate   OPEN: Sun L 12 to 2, Mon to Sat D 7 to 9.30   MEALS: Set L Sun £21.50, Set D £37.50   SERVICE: not inc, card slips closed   CARDS: Amex, Delta, MasterCard, Switch, Visa   DETAILS: 60 seats. 25 seats outside. Private parties: 75 main room, 12 to 75 private rooms. Car park. Children's helpings. Wheelchair access (also WC). Music. No mobile phones   ACCOMMODATION: 45 rooms, all with bath/shower. TV. Phone. B&B £105 to £230. Rooms for disabled. Baby facilities. Fishing

EXETER Devon   map 1

Brazz 🍴 ⚡

10–12 Palace Gate, Exeter EX1 1JA	COOKING 2
TEL: (01392) 252525 FAX: (01392) 253045	BRITISH BRASSERIE
WEBSITE: www.brazz.co.uk	£27–£51

Brazz – all pale wood, stainless steel and sharp lighting – remains bright, stylish, zingy and very good fun, with a welcome by staff who seem to enjoy being here. There are siblings in Taunton and Bristol (see entries). Good-quality ingredients appear in well-thought-through assemblies such as chargrilled squid, chorizo, red pepper and olive salad. Accurately cooked steak with fine frites, and exciting contrasts in crispy salmon fishcakes with unctuous creamed leeks, demonstrated the 'simplest is best' axiom, though this does not preclude the elaborately constructed cathedral pudding, 'a sinfully rich concoction of cream, chocolate and sponge'. The no-nonsense, good wine list, with plenty to choose from, is fairly priced, starting with house French at £10.95, £2.75/£3.75 per small/large glass and £7.40 per half-bottle. Or choose one of the fruit or wheat beers.

CHEF: Dean Milner   PROPRIETOR: Brazz plc   OPEN: all week 12 to 3, 6 to 10.30 (11 Fri and Sat) CLOSED: 25 Dec   MEALS: alc (main courses £7 to £16). Reduced price menu 3 to 6   SERVICE: 10% (optional), card slips closed   CARDS: Amex, Delta, Diners, MasterCard, Switch, Visa   DETAILS: 150 seats. Private parties: 150 main room. Vegetarian meals. Children's helpings. No smoking in 1 dining room. Wheelchair access (also WC). Music. Air-conditioned

▲ Michael Caines at Royal Clarence 🍷 ⚡

Cathedral Yard, Exeter EX1 1HD	
TEL: (01392) 310031 FAX: (01392) 310032	COOKING 5
EMAIL: tables@michaelcaines.com	FRENCH
WEBSITE: www.michaelcaines.com	£33–£69

The spacious restaurant, with views from its front windows over the cathedral, is on the ground floor of the venerable, centrally located and well-known hotel. Large white-clothed tables, high-backed chairs smartly done out in blue and grey, modern artwork on white-cream walls, and attractive lighting give it a chic, minimalist feel, and provide the backdrop for the 'best food in Exeter city'.

Meat cooking excels, in a set-lunch menu's tender fillet of beef, cooked pink and served with a rich red wine sauce, glazed button onions, carrots and lardons, all sitting on smooth, light, creamy celeriac purée. Fish, too, is given no short shrift: grilled sea bass served with marinated vegetables and fennel cream sauce comes crispy-skinned yet moist and tender inside. Choice opens out on the carte with perhaps roast partridge with braised chicory, toasted walnuts and quince purée, or veal fillet with noodles, roasted parsnips, garlic and creamy Madeira sauce, while starters might take in crab and sweet potato cake with rocket and Thai-spiced sauce, or terrine of game and winter vegetables with truffle vinaigrette.

Desserts have varied from 'good' to 'outstanding': from slightly too-sweet mille-feuille of caramelised apples and vanilla parfait, to rhubarb trifle with marinated strawberries – which for an inspector was 'the best pud I have had in ages'. Service from smartly dressed staff is professional and efficient, while the varietally organised wine list makes tempting reading even if prices are on the high side. Those with less than £20 to spend are limited to the six house wines (£16 or £3.95 a glass), but that is no great hardship because they make up a tasty little range. Michael Caines has teamed up with the Marriott hotel group to open his Michael Caines restaurant at the Bristol Marriott Royal in summer 2003.

CHEF: Jean-Marc Zanetti   PROPRIETOR: Michael Caines   OPEN: all week: 12 to 2.30, 7 to 10
MEALS: alc (main courses £16.50 to £23). Set L £16.50 (2 courses) to £19.50   SERVICE: not inc
CARDS: Amex, Delta, Diners, MasterCard, Switch, Visa   DETAILS: 76 seats. Private parties: 76
main room, 12 to 100 private rooms. Vegetarian meals. Children's helpings. No smoking.
Wheelchair access (not WC). No music. Air-conditioned   ACCOMMODATION: 56 rooms, all with
bath/shower. TV. Phone. Room only £105 to £130. Baby facilities (£5)

EXFORD Somerset   map 2

▲ Crown Hotel ⁵⚹   NEW ENTRY

Park Street, Exford TA24 7PP
TEL: (01643) 831554   FAX: (01643) 831665
EMAIL: info@crownhotelexmoor.co.uk   COOKING 3
WEBSITE: www.crownhotelexmoor.co.uk   MODERN BRITISH
on B3224, 12m SW of Minehead   £46–£61

Exford is in the heart of Exmoor National Park, and in the middle of Exford is a large, many-gabled building: the Crown. Bar food offers somewhat traditional dishes in informal surroundings, while, at dinner only, those wanting something altogether different can turn to the restaurant for a no-choice table d'hôte gourmet menu of five courses. Reports suggest that the kitchen is clearly skilled, if at times inconsistent, and uses fine raw materials: in 'excellently timed' pan-fried foie gras with pea purée, escabèche of red mullet, or slow roast fillet of Exmoor beef with truffle mash. Vegetables could be improved. Though a dessert of strawberry jelly with basil cream has disappointed, a 'glorious, oozing' chocolate fondant with some excellent custard certainly did not. The wine list, starting with French house wines at £13.95, offers plenty of interest below £20.

CHEF: Scott Dickson   PROPRIETORS: Hugo and Pamela Jeune   OPEN: all week D only 7 to 9 (open
L for bar food)   MEALS: Set D £32.50. Bar L and D menu also available   SERVICE: 10% (optional)
CARDS: Amex, Delta, MasterCard, Switch, Visa   DETAILS: 38 seats. Private parties: 26 main
room, 8 to 14 private rooms. Car park. Children's helpings. No children under 7. No smoking.
Occasional music. No mobile phones   ACCOMMODATION: 16 rooms, all with bath/shower. TV.
Phone. B&B £55 to £110. Baby facilities. Fishing (£5)

FARNBOROUGH Kent   map 3

Chapter One

Farnborough Common, Locksbottom,
Farnborough BR6 8NF
TEL: (01689) 854848   FAX: (01689) 858439   COOKING 5
WEBSITE: www.chaptersrestaurants.co.uk   MODERN EUROPEAN
at junction of A21 and A232   £31–£65

You wouldn't take this for a former pub, surveying the spacious, open-plan
interior, where stripped-pine floor, pale walls and dark-blue upholstered chairs
combine to create a pleasingly expansive feel, although tables are close together.
Andrew McLeish sources with care and produces food with a high degree of
polish, in terms of both presentation and palate impact. Lobster ravioli with a
bisque-style lobster sauce fired up with cognac is given a new twist by
incorporating a purée of cauliflower, while a ballottine of organic chicken,
'singing with flavour', combined with foie gras parfait, fig chutney and roasted
hazelnuts to provide a superb contrast of textures and complementary flavours.
Confident pairing extends to root vegetable/fish compositions, perhaps roast
halibut with a beetroot tarte Tatin, and main courses often come with an
interesting pasta construction, like the cannelloni of shoulder meat accompanying rump of lamb and fondant potato. The dessert menu includes sweet
wine suggestions: a glass of Tuscan Aleatico perhaps to partner apple tart served
with a sorbet of apple, vodka, and thyme and almond nougatine. Staff, copious
in number, could be better drilled in the cheese and bread departments, but
otherwise do the job efficiently. The wine list favours France and southern
Europe over the New World. Mark-ups are high, and the quality not uniformly
inspiring; prices start at £13.50.

CHEF: Andrew McLeish   PROPRIETOR: Selective Restaurants Group   OPEN: all week 12 to 2.30
(2.45 Sun), 6.30 to 10.30 (9 Sun)   CLOSED: 1 to 4 Jan   MEALS: alc D (main courses £14.50). Set L
£16 (2 courses) to £19.50. Brasserie L menu available Mon to Sat   SERVICE: 12.5% (optional),
card slips closed   CARDS: Amex, Delta, Diners, MasterCard, Switch, Visa   DETAILS: 120 seats.
Private parties: 20 to 55 private rooms. Car park. Vegetarian meals. Children's helpings. No
cigars/pipes. Wheelchair access (not WC). Music. Air-conditioned

FARNHAM Dorset   map 2

▲ Museum Inn ⚡✶

Farnham DT11 8DE
TEL: (01725) 516261   FAX: (01725) 516988
EMAIL: enquiries@museuminn.co.uk   COOKING 5
WEBSITE: www.museuminn.co.uk   MODERN EUROPEAN
off A354, 8m NE of Blandford Forum   £31–£56

In a tiny village of thatched cottages, this is a seventeenth-century inn extended
by that Victorian 'modern Major General', archaeologist and anthropologist
Augustus Lane Fox Pitt-Rivers to accommodate visitors to his (now closed)
personal museum nearby. Today, upkeep of the premises inside and out is of a
high order, although not necessarily luxurious: 'we ate in the aptly named
Shed'.

The Shed restaurant is only open for two dinners a week, plus Sunday lunch, so most reporters eat bar food, which is a little less expensive, though still well worth the journey and has the same contemporary approach. Ideas are often lively, taking in roast scallops with chorizo and celeriac purée, for example, but keep their feet on the ground: there may be cauliflower and smoked haddock soup to start, or Welsh rarebit with rocket and chicory, followed by chargrilled chicken with tagliatelle, smoked bacon and tarragon. The European focus narrows slightly when it comes to desserts, which are as likely to include lemon posset or sticky toffee pudding as chilled pannacotta with caramel and rum. Service is welcoming, efficient and helpful, and a varied list of reasonably priced wines starts with house wines (three red, three white) at £11.

CHEF: Mark Treasure   PROPRIETORS: Mark Stephenson and Vicky Elliot   OPEN: restaurant Sun L 12 to 3, Fri and Sat D 7 to 9.30; bar open L and D all week   CLOSED: 25 Dec and 31 Dec   MEALS: alc (main courses £9.50 to £18.95). Bar menu L and D   SERVICE: not inc, card slips closed   CARDS: MasterCard, Switch, Visa   DETAILS: 40 seats. Private parties: 40 main room. Car park. Vegetarian meals. No children under 5. No smoking in dining room, smoking permitted in bar. Wheelchair access (also WC). No music. No mobile phones   ACCOMMODATION: 8 rooms, all with bath/shower. TV. Phone. B&B £65 to £120. Rooms for disabled. No children under 5 (*The Which? Guide to Good Hotels*)

FAVERSHAM Kent   map 3

▲ Read's ▮

Macknade Manor, Canterbury Road,
Faversham ME13 8XE
TEL: (01795) 535344   FAX: (01795) 591200   COOKING 6
WEBSITE: www.reads.com   MODERN BRITISH
on A2 Canterbury road, ½m E of Faversham   £33–£81

Although this is a substantial Georgian manor house, 'it feels very much like walking into someone's home, albeit a home on a grand scale'. Rona Pitchford greets and oversees the service, which can range from 'professional and friendly' to 'chatty and jolly', while starched white linen, heavy silver cutlery and elegant glassware all add to the upmarket feel. Seasonal and local materials contribute significantly to the output, including seafood from Whitstable, fruit from Brogdale, and Kentish spring lamb, perhaps served with Mediterranean vegetables. Other vegetables are home grown, particularly during the summer when the walled kitchen garden comes into its own.

Menus are anxious to divulge as much detail as possible – a hot soufflé of mature Montgomery Cheddar on a bed of glazed smoked haddock in a creamed sauce, for example – but behind them lies a comparatively straightforward repertoire, taking in ham hock terrine with home-made piccalilli, and roast chicken breast with morels, cream and Madeira. And there is sufficient scope in all this for traditional treatments (such as beef fillet served Rossini-style with foie gras) to share the billing with less usual ones: halibut fillet, for example, has come with an oxtail and macaroni 'bourguignonne' and red wine sauce.

Desserts tend to be quite busy, incorporating several elements into a whole, producing a lemon tart served with iced lime parfait and pink grapefruit marinated in tequila, and a seasonal compote of rhubarb layered with vanilla and ginger, served with a rhubarb shake. Fifty-plus 'best buys' from £16 to £26 make a welcoming start to the wine list, but clarets and Burgundy are the main focus, backed up well by the rest of France. Australia and New Zealand are best of the other countries. Prices are reasonable, and six come by the glass for £4.

CHEF: David Pitchford   PROPRIETORS: Rona and David Pitchford   OPEN: Tue to Sat 12 to 2, 7 to 9.30   CLOSED: bank hols   MEALS: Set L £19.50 to £42, Set D £42 to £45   SERVICE: not inc, card slips closed   CARDS: Amex, Delta, Diners, MasterCard, Switch, Visa   DETAILS: 40 seats. 12 seats outside. Private parties: 60 main room, 4 to 30 private rooms. Car park. Children's helpings. No cigars/pipes. Wheelchair access (also WC). No music. No mobile phones   ACCOMMODATION: 6 rooms, all with bath/shower. TV. Phone. B&B £95 to £150 (*The Which? Guide to Good Hotels*) (£5)

FAWSLEY Northamptonshire   map 5

▲ Fawsley Hall,
The Knightly Restaurant ♥ ✳ | NEW ENTRY |

Fawsley, Daventry NN11 3BA
TEL: (01327) 892000   FAX: (01327) 892001
EMAIL: reservations@fawsleyhall.com   COOKING 5
WEBSITE: www.fawsleyhall.com   MODERN EUROPEAN
1½m E of A361, 5½m S of Daventry   £38–£71

This ochre-stone Jacobean building, 'astoundingly beautiful and very grand indeed', may be ancient but it now houses a very modern operation, offering all the conference, wedding, health and beauty facilities you could possibly need, besides staging concerts and plays. Service is laid on thick and is 'thoroughly professional'.

Having worked at Lords of the Manor, Upper Slaughter (see entry), Philip Dixon is used to such a setting, and his classically inclined cooking shows confidence and expertise. First-rate raw materials are exploited in dishes as simple as they are skilful: a large raviolo of fresh pasta filled with white crabmeat and served on 'just warmed' samphire with a creamy bouillabaisse jus exemplifies starters, as does a pressed terrine of chicken, foie gras and baby leeks with truffle dressing. To follow, 'immaculately timed' (i.e. very pink) and flavoursome cannon of Cornish lamb has been layered with sliced lamb's tongue and accompanied by a 'luscious, beautifully wobbly' pea and mint mousse; or there might be seared bream fillet with marinated potatoes and a rocket and fennel salad. Desserts uphold the standard: perhaps 'technically perfect' and 'deeply flavoured' blackcurrant soufflé with intense fennel ice cream (an 'absolutely brilliant' flavour combination). In fact, the only disappointments at inspection were some poorly executed incidentals and scalding hot plates. An interesting wine list, arranged by style, pools good names from all over. Ten easy-drinkers at or under £20 (£3.30 to £4.90 a glass) set the ball rolling, while fine wines are heavily promoted as 'affordable excess'.

CHEF: Philip Dixon   PROPRIETOR: Simon Lowe   OPEN: all week 12 to 2.30, 7 to 9.30   MEALS: alc (main courses L £12 to £14, D £14 to £22). Set D £31 to £45   SERVICE: 12.5% (optional)   CARDS: Amex, Delta, MasterCard, Switch, Visa   DETAILS: 70 seats. 30 seats outside. Private parties: 8 to 150 private rooms. Car park. Vegetarian meals. Children's helpings. No smoking. Wheelchair access (also WC). Music   ACCOMMODATION: 43 rooms, all with bath/shower. TV. Phone. B&B £130 to £325

FERNHURST Surrey   map 3

King's Arms ✦✗ £ | NEW ENTRY |

Midhurst Road, Fernhurst GU27 3HA   COOKING 2
TEL/FAX: (01428) 652005   MODERN BRITISH
on A286, 1m S of Fernhurst on sharp bend   £30–£44

Low beams, lots of dark oak and an open fireplace give this cosy seventeenth-century inn, built of Sussex stone, a very traditional look. Simple bar food is available, but there is also a separate dining room with a more ambitious menu. Plenty of choice is offered, starters ranging from cream of woodland mushroom soup to bruschetta of provençale vegetables with feta cheese and tomato dressing, via smoked cod, mushroom and bacon fishcakes with herb mayonnaise. To follow, six tender seared scallops have been served on 'sticky, buttery' lobster and tarragon risotto with lobster sauce, while a generous portion of pink roast loin of lamb has come with a classic accompaniment of sautéed spinach, roast potatoes and mint oil. For dessert, 'irreproachable' lemon and raspberry crème brûlée with crunchy ginger snaps has been recommended. A straightforward, good-value wine list opens with house French at £10.

CHEF: Michael Hirst   PROPRIETORS: Michael and Annabel Hirst   OPEN: all week L 12 to 2.30, Mon to Sat D 7 to 9.30   CLOSED: 25 and 26 Dec   MEALS: alc (main courses £11.50 to £15)   SERVICE: not inc   CARDS: Delta, MasterCard, Switch, Visa   DETAILS: 50 seats. 60 seats outside. Private parties: 28 main room, 10 to 12 private rooms. Car park. Vegetarian meals. Children's helpings No children under 14 after 7pm. No smoking in 1 dining room. No music

FERRENSBY North Yorkshire   map 9

▲ General Tarleton ✦✗

Boroughbridge Road, Ferrensby HG5 0PZ
TEL: (01423) 340284   FAX: (01423) 340288   COOKING 4
EMAIL: gti@generaltarleton.co.uk   MODERN BRITISH
WEBSITE: www.generaltarleton.co.uk   £29–£55

In open countryside on the edge of the small village of Ferrensby, the General Tarleton is one of a pair of pub/restaurants owned and run by Denis Watkins and John Topham, the other being the Angel in Hetton (see entry). Over the years they have built up quite a reputation. Informal bar meals are just as popular as dinner in the more formal restaurant, which, despite being spread over two floors, can get very busy – Saturday evenings are particularly frenetic. Both service and food have occasionally suffered as a result, although some reporters have found the ambience 'peaceful' and service 'polite and efficient'.

But with John Topham himself in charge of the kitchen, there is no doubt that the inventive modern British cooking can be impressive. There are plenty of attention-grabbing ideas among the generous choice offered. Starters have included Nidderdale smoked salmon with red pepper and chilli ice cream, and a warm salad of duck confit with chorizo, lardons and walnut dressing, as well as simple asparagus with hollandaise. To follow, there may be chargrilled beef fillet with oxtail and horseradish risotto, and seared yellowfin tuna with butterbean and truffle purée. Desserts are a strong suit – 'wobbly' pannacotta 'redolent of vanilla' with rhubarb compote was the high point of one meal. The long wine list has a strong Burgundy contingent. Mark-ups throughout are not greedy, and there is a good choice by the glass. House Vins de Pays d'Oc are £12.95.

CHEFS: John Topham and Robert Ramsden PROPRIETORS: Denis Watkins and John Topham OPEN: Sun L 12 to 2.15, Tue to Sat D 6 to 9.30 CLOSED: 25 Dec MEALS: alc D (main courses £11 to £17.50). Set L £17.50, Set D Sat £29.50. Bar/brasserie menu available SERVICE: not inc CARDS: Amex, Delta, MasterCard, Switch, Visa DETAILS: 80 seats. 30 seats outside. Private parties: 40 main room, 2 to 40 private rooms. Car park. Vegetarian meals. Children's helpings. No smoking. Wheelchair access (also WC). Occasional music. No mobile phones ACCOMMODATION: 14 rooms, all with bath/shower. TV. Phone. B&B £74.95 to £99.90. Rooms for disabled. Baby facilities

FLETCHING East Sussex   map 3

▲ Griffin Inn ▼ £   NEW ENTRY

Fletching TN22 3SS
TEL: (01825) 722890 FAX: (01825) 722810
EMAIL: thegriffininn@hotmail.com
WEBSITE: www.thegriffininn.co.uk   COOKING 2
off A272, between Maresfield and Newick, 3m   MODERN EUROPEAN
NW of Uckfield   £29–£54

The Griffin has been Fletching's focal point since the sixteenth century. Every inch the traditional inn, it has separate bar and dining areas, each with its own menu, plus options for al fresco eating – pretty patio or extensive gardens. Cooking appropriately focuses on care and skill, rather than convoluted complexity, as demonstrated by a puff pastry tart of sweet red onion and red pepper with 'just melting' goats' cheese, or artichoke soup with croûtons and basil. The same goes for main courses of pan-seared bream with 'rather too highly flavoured' bouillabaisse, clams and mussels with minted aïoli; or for grilled marinated lamb fillet with roast sweet potatoes and red onion chutney. Dessert might include dark chocolate tart with mascarpone and mixed berries, or lemon and grappa pannacotta. A monthly-changing bunch of wines under £20 opens a list that offers variety, value and enthusiasm; Italy and Australia are favourite countries. A dozen house wines start at £10.50 (£2.70 a glass).

CHEFS: Russell Pavey and Andrew Billings PROPRIETORS: Nigel and Bridget Pullan OPEN: all week L 12 to 2.30, Mon to Sat (all week in summer) D 7 to 9.30 CLOSED: 25 Dec MEALS: alc (main courses £8.50 to £18.50). Set L Sun £22.50. Bar menu available SERVICE: not inc, card slips closed CARDS: Amex, Delta, Diners, MasterCard, Switch, Visa DETAILS: 65 seats. 30 seats outside. Private parties: 35 main room. Car park. Vegetarian meals. Children's helpings. Wheelchair access (also WC). No music. No mobile phones ACCOMMODATION: 8 rooms, all with bath/shower. TV. B&B £50 to £120. Rooms for disabled. Baby facilities (*The Which? Guide to Good Hotels*)

Restaurateurs justifiably resent no-shows. If you quote a credit card number when booking, you may be liable for the restaurant's lost profit margin if you don't turn up. Always phone to cancel.

FORTON Lancashire

map 8

Bay Horse Inn ✳ | NEW ENTRY |

Bay Horse, Forton LA2 0HR
TEL/FAX: (01524) 791204
EMAIL: cwilki5769@aol.com
WEBSITE: www.bayhorseinn.com   COOKING **3**
from M6 junction 33 take A6 towards Preston;   MODERN BRITISH
take second left-hand turn; pub is on right   £25–£53

At the foot of the Lancashire fells, the countryside around the hamlet of Bay Horse (which shares its name with the pub) is verdant and appealing. The pub is no ordinary village inn, however, being more a combination of pub and serious restaurant. Orders are taken in the bar, but meals are served in two dining rooms, done out in deep pink tones and dark wood.

Chef Craig Wilkinson's menus are well considered and built around good local ingredients, such as Bowland lamb, Morecambe Bay shrimps and Cumbrian venison sausages. The kitchen shows flair in presentation, and flavours are allowed to speak for themselves. One visitor was impressed by the intensely yellow, creamy, garlic-scented aïoli served with a starter of grilled langoustines; while matured, succulent fillet of beef was simply pan-fried with wild mushrooms and came with 'new potato chips' and Madeira sauce, allowing the quality of the meat to shine through. Puddings – such as Lancashire cheesecake topped with apple purée and served with home-made vanilla ice cream – have met with universal approval. Service is relaxed and informal, the kitchen's timing was faultless at inspection, and there is no sense of being rushed. There's a selection of draught beers, which may provide more excitement than the rather ordinary list of wines. Bottle prices start at £10.95.

CHEF: Craig Wilkinson   PROPRIETORS: Brian, Mae and Craig Wilkinson   OPEN: Tue to Sun L 12 to 1.45 (1 Sat, 3.30 Sun), Tue to Sat D 7 to 9.15   CLOSED: 1 week Jan, 1 week Aug   MEALS: alc (main courses £9 to £17). Set L Sun £13.95 (2 courses) to £15.50. Sandwich menu available L Tue to Sat   SERVICE: not inc, 10% for parties of 10 or more   CARDS: Amex, Delta, MasterCard, Switch, Visa   DETAILS: 50 seats. 20 seats outside. Private parties: 30 main room, 15 to 30 private rooms. Car park. Vegetarian meals. Children's helpings. No children under 14. No smoking in 1 dining room. Wheelchair access (not WC). Occasional music

FOTHERINGHAY Northamptonshire

map 6

Falcon ♟ ✳

Fotheringhay PE8 5HZ
TEL: (01832) 226254   FAX: (01832) 226046
WEBSITE: www.huntsbridge.co.uk   COOKING **3**
    MODERN EUROPEAN
N of A605, 4m NE of Oundle   £29–£54

There's not much left of the castle where Mary Queen of Scots was executed but this honey-coloured stone village still has a most unusual church (a cut-down abbey), plus the Falcon (where two reporters swear they saw a ghost in the car park). But Ray Smikle's cooking is not introspective; it is 'flavourful, fresh, unpretentious, colourful' and as good-humoured as he is. A terrine of gravad lax and grilled salmon varied with chunky chopped leeks made an enjoyable whole that exceeded the sum of its parts. And real skills showed in a generous fillet of beautifully grilled red snapper with roast aubergines and well-caramelised red and yellow peppers – Technicolor, yes, but no yawn, despite slightly tired sautéed potatoes. Extras like bread and butter could improve, but there are pleasing details like booze-soaked raisins and crispy toffee in a couple of assorted ice creams, or try chocolate truffle torte with orange compote. Service is young and helpful but a trifle inexperienced. Wines divide neatly into 'under £20' and 'top class' sections, both packed with exciting options that stray far beyond the mainstream and with annotations that actually help you choose. A baker's dozen by the glass (£2.95 to £6) has the same spirit of adventure. See Keyston, Madingley and Huntingdon for others in the inspirational Huntsbridge group.

CHEF: Ray Smikle   PROPRIETORS: Ray Smikle and John Hoskins   OPEN: all week 12 to 2.15, 6.30 to 9.30   MEALS: alc (main courses £10 to £18). Set L Mon to Sat £12 (2 courses). Bar snack menu available   SERVICE: not inc   CARDS: Amex, Diners, MasterCard, Switch, Visa   DETAILS: 65 seats. 35 seats outside. Private parties: 60 main room, 12 to 30 private rooms. Car park. Vegetarian meals. Children's helpings. No smoking. No music. No mobile phones

---

FOWEY Cornwall   **map 1**

▲ Marina Hotel,
Nick Fisher at the Waterside 🕌✸ | NEW ENTRY |

Esplanade, Fowey PL23 1HY
TEL: (01726) 833315   FAX: (01726) 832779   COOKING 4
EMAIL: marina.hotel@dial.pipex.com   SEAFOOD
WEBSITE: www.themarinahotel.co.uk   £41–£86

Having reached this peaceful spot on the Cornish south coast, drive carefully downhill towards the harbour, turn on to the Esplanade, and stop. If you are lucky, somebody from the hotel will park the car for you. A pale lemon-coloured, balconied building perched above the sea, the Marina was once the summer residence of successive Bishops of Truro. Decorative mouldings and marble pillars lend class to the interiors, and the dining room has a clean, nautical, 'on-board' feel, according to a reporter, with striped blinds, paintings for sale and good views over the estuary.

A restaurant named after its chef creates a certain *frisson* of anticipation, which in this instance is fully deserved. Nick Fisher, who has cooked his way through a fair few of London's top hotels, marries sound culinary concepts with impeccable technique. That may produce a first course of lobster on new potato salad dressed with truffles and champagne, or a simple but outstandingly flavoured and thickly textured soup combining pieces of langoustine tail in a sweet pepper and cherry tomato broth. Timing and general treatment of fish is particularly impressive – witness pan-fried halibut, perfectly moist and meaty, in a creamy lemon sauce containing morsels of lobster and langoustine – but meat main courses hit the mark too. This was the case with an inspection dish of sautéed breast of guinea fowl with violet potato (unusual vegetables are something of a trademark) and a well-reduced tarragon sauce. Frozen accompaniments are the norm in desserts such as chocolate fondant with pistachio ice cream, or a tian of raspberries and chocolate with mango sorbet, while a version of crème brûlée with almonds, served with caramel ice, rounded off a spring dinner in rich but subtle style. The highly polished, professional service complements the place well. Although it is presented on an A3 card, the wine list is quite short, with prices that are mostly on the painful side of £20. House wines start at £16.95.

CHEF: Nick Fisher   PROPRIETOR: Steve Westwell   OPEN: all week 12 to 2, 6.30 to 10   CLOSED: L Oct to Easter   MEALS: alc (main courses £13 to £29). Set D £34.50 to £48.50 (latter is tasting menu)   SERVICE: not inc, card slips closed   CARDS: Amex, Delta, MasterCard, Switch, Visa   DETAILS: 36 seats. 12 seats outside. Private parties: 45 main room, 70 to 100 private rooms. Vegetarian meals. Children's helpings. No smoking. Music   ACCOMMODATION: 16 rooms, all with bath/shower. TV. Phone. B&B £85 to £230. Rooms for disabled (*The Which? Guide to Good Hotels*)

FRAMPTON MANSELL Gloucestershire   map 2

White Horse £

Cirencester Road, Frampton Mansell GL6 8HZ
TEL: (01285) 760960
WEBSITE: www.cotswoldwhitehorse.com   COOKING 2
on A419 7m W of Cirencester, beside turning to   MODERN ENGLISH
Frampton Mansell   £26–£46

It may appear a pub on the outside, but the inside offers a restaurant look and feel with an open-plan dining area and lounge separated only by a bar counter. A little of the pub atmosphere is retained with exposed stonework and bare tables, and the menu offers a range of both the traditional and the more contemporary, such as starters of seared Cornish scallops or pan-fried lamb's kidneys, and main courses might include braised faggots and spring onion mash, or breast of pheasant with roast fig. Tender ribeye steak sourced from rare-breed cattle and first-class lemon sole have received praise. Finish perhaps with red wine poached pear with ginger biscuits and vanilla ice cream, or vanilla and cardamom rice pudding. The reasonably priced wine list is helpfully arranged in wine styles, with house wine starting at £10.75.

CHEF: Howard Matthews   PROPRIETORS: Emma and Shaun Davis   OPEN: all week L 12 to 2.30 (3 Sun), Mon to Sat D 7 to 9.45   CLOSED: 24 and 25 Dec   MEALS: alc (main courses £9.50 to £13.50). Snack L also available   SERVICE: not inc   CARDS: Delta, MasterCard, Switch, Visa   DETAILS: 50 seats. 40 seats outside. Private parties: 50 main room. Car park. Vegetarian meals. Children's helpings. No cigars/pipes. No music

FRITHSDEN Hertfordshire   map 3

Alford Arms £

Frithsden HP1 3DD   COOKING 2
TEL: (01442) 864480   FAX: (01442) 876893   MODERN BRITISH
                                                          £25–£45

Non-eaters get a small section to call their own in this pub in a rustic setting, but it is the business of eating that really sets the Alford Arms apart. This is a kitchen that provides 'way above' regular pub food. 'Small plates' (as opposed to starters), like crispy lamb with stir-fried noodles, or smoked chicken and bacon terrine with spicy tomato relish, suggest that eaters of single courses are welcome, while those wishing to go on to a main course could choose perhaps pan-fried sea bream on crushed new potatoes with watercress sauce, or chargrilled duck with rösti potatoes and roast beetroot. Subtle flavouring and technical skill are evident, as in an inspector's 'understated, not too sweet' rose, cardamom and almond ice cream, with a decided oriental taste, and sound pastry work in the lemon tart that accompanied it. Around 25 wines start at £10.25 for vin de pays, with the majority of bottles under £20. Around a dozen are served by the glass.

CHEF: Damien Ng   PROPRIETORS: David and Becky Salisbury   OPEN: all week 12 to 2.30 (3 Sun), 7 to 10   CLOSED: 25 and 26 Dec   MEALS: alc (main courses £9.25 to £13.50)   SERVICE: not inc   CARDS: Amex, Delta, MasterCard, Switch, Visa   DETAILS: 71 seats. 82 seats outside. Car park. Vegetarian meals. Children's helpings. Wheelchair access (not WC). Music

FUNTINGTON West Sussex   map 3

Hallidays ⅚⍇

Watery Lane, Funtington PO18 9LF	COOKING 2
TEL: (01243) 575331	MODERN BRITISH
on B2178, 4½m NW of Chichester	£26–£50

'A great little restaurant serving totally honest good food', was one reporter's verdict on this converted set of three 600-year-old, brick-and-flint thatched cottages. The cooking is modern British with an emphasis on local, seasonal produce, which has produced starters of Stilton, egg and avocado salad ('an enjoyable combination of flavours and textures'), spicy crab cakes, and a 'light and refreshing' salad of scallops with cucumber raita and chilli jam. Among main courses have been liver and kidneys on sage mash ('rather rich but enjoyable'), brill with a light, coriander-infused curried tartare sauce, and 'deliciously tender' roast partridge with good dauphinoise. Finish with blackcurrant crème brûlée with lavender shortbread, or Eton mess with 'plump and plentiful' raspberries. Most reporters consider service to be not only friendly but also attentive without being obtrusive. A good-value, wide-ranging wine list opens with house selections from £10.50.

CHEF: Andy Stephenson   PROPRIETORS: Andy Stephenson and Peter Creech   OPEN: Wed to Fri and Sun L 12 to 1.15, Wed to Sat D 7 to 9.15   CLOSED: 1st week Sept, 2 weeks early Mar   MEALS: alc Wed to Sat (main courses £15 to £16.50). Set L £13.50 (2 courses) to £15.50, Set L Sun £16.95   SERVICE: not inc, card slips closed   CARDS: Delta, MasterCard, Switch, Visa   DETAILS: 30 seats. Private parties: 30 main room. Car park. Vegetarian meals. No smoking in dining room, smoking permitted in bar. Wheelchair access (also women's WC). No music

All entries in the Guide are re-researched and rewritten every year, not least because restaurant standards fluctuate. Don't rely on an out-of-date Guide.

⅚⍇ *indicates that smoking is banned in all eating areas.*

GALPHAY North Yorkshire

map 9

Galphay Arms £

NEW ENTRY

Galphay HG4 3NJ
TEL/FAX: (01765) 650133
EMAIL: thegalphayinn@btopenworld.com
off B6265, 4½m W of Ripon

COOKING 4
MODERN BRITISH
£26–£47

A few years ago this was a run-down pub in fine countryside; the MacArthurs transformed it into a warmly welcoming place, and also shifted emphasis firmly to the food. Wide-ranging skills are apparent in accurately fried and tender calf's liver, careful vegetable cooking and decent baking. Local smoked salmon thrilled one reporter, smokiness combining with melt-in-the-mouth succulence; fine mixed salads, dressed lightly with olive oil, accompanied this and another starter of two slabs of moist, chunky terrine of pork, chicken and chorizo. The chargrilled liver, 'among the best ever eaten', had thick rashers of bacon wrapping caramelised onions, a high-class take on a domestic stand-by. An unassuming collection of vegetables cooked slightly crisp was served as a single portion, and adequate for two people. Crème brûlée was newly torched and flecked with vanilla seeds that made its good flavouring visible, while a show-stopping chocolate pudding – deeply flavoured, crisp at one end, oozing in the centre, and accompanied by a well-made crème anglaise – also showed essentially simple ideas executed well. Friendly service is knowledgeable, and a neatly selected 30-odd wines start fairly at £9.95; six are available by the glass.

CHEF: Kate Mainey PROPRIETORS: Robert and Sam MacArthur OPEN: Wed to Mon 12 to 2, 6.30 to 9.30 MEALS: alc (main courses from £5.50 L and £8.50 D to £15) SERVICE: not inc, card slips closed CARDS: Amex, Delta, Diners, MasterCard, Switch, Visa DETAILS: 34 seats. Private parties: 40 main room. Car park. Vegetarian meals. Children's helpings. Occasional music

GATESHEAD Tyne & Wear

map 10

▲ Eslington Villa ✳

8 Station Road, Low Fell, Gateshead NE9 6DR
TEL: (0191) 487 6017   FAX: (0191) 420 0667
leave A1(M) at Team Valley Trading Estate,
approach Gateshead along Team Valley; at top
of Eastern Avenue, turn left into Station Road

COOKING 3
ANGLO-FRENCH
£24–£50

This handsome nineteenth-century villa is in the most unlikely setting high above the Team Valley Trading Estate. The restaurant is one large Victorian-style room plus the clever addition of a conservatory overlooking the valley. Dave Kennedy and his team admit to a degree of eclecticism in their approach to food, and the menu accordingly might offer first courses of braised mussels with roasted butternut squash mousse, or roast courgette and Gorgonzola risotto, and a main course of, say, sautéed quail with salsify, button onions and Madeira sauce. More straightforward tastes might enjoy loin of lamb with Savoy cabbage and garlic croquettes, or chargrilled sirloin steak with chips and béarnaise. Finish with something like praline crêpe with tangerine salsa, vanilla ice cream and pistachios, or pear tarte Tatin with caramel sauce and gingerbread ice cream.

Service is attentive but unobtrusive. The well-selected wine list opens with half a dozen house bottles from £11.50.

CHEF: Dave Kennedy PROPRIETORS: Melanie and Nick Tulip OPEN: Sun to Fri L 12 to 1.45, Mon to Sat D 7 to 9.45 MEALS: alc (main courses £9.50 to £15.50). Set L £12.50 (2 courses) to £14.50, Set D Mon to Fri £18.50 SERVICE: not inc CARDS: Amex, Delta, Diners, MasterCard, Switch, Visa DETAILS: 86 seats. 20 seats outside. Private parties: 86 main room, 8 to 36 private rooms. Car park. Vegetarian meals. Children's helpings. No smoking. Music ACCOMMODATION: 18 rooms, all with bath/shower. TV. Phone. B&B £54.50 to £74.50. Baby facilities (*The Which? Guide to Good Hotels*)

McCoys at the Baltic, Rooftop Restaurant ?

| | NEW ENTRY |

Centre for Contemporary Arts, South Shore
Road, Gateshead NE8 3BA
TEL: (0191) 440 4949   FAX: (0191) 440 4950

COOKING 5
MODERN BRITISH
£31–£53

Towering over Gateshead's Millennium Bridge is this imposing brick-built flour mill converted into an art gallery, and both bridge and gallery are big on ambition and style. Its catering, run by the McCoys (see entry, Staddlebridge), includes ground-floor café, brasserie above and, up top, a glass-and-steel dining room with unrivalled views over Tyneside. An inspector's crisply seared scallops, translucent inside and notably fresh, came with a salmon spring roll, a won ton filled with minced prawn, and a lime and chilli dressing. After that came crisp-skinned halibut ('can't fault timing, or freshness') on a rough bundle of spinach, with al dente green asparagus spears (in October), a well-made potato galette, and excellent basil butter sauce. Seafood is well handled here. Carnivores might choose roast rabbit, or slow-cooked shoulder of pork, and a cheesy finale of whipped Brie de Meaux with a port reduction competes with, say, peanut butter pudding with banana and brown butter sauce. Service may be a bit disjointed, but gets things done. Wines come from a well-chosen modern list that doesn't dither in France, offers good flavours by the glass (£3.25 to £7.50), has decent basics at £12.95 and a sprinkling of star names, including Krug Grande Cuvée at £110.

CHEF: Tony Riches PROPRIETORS: Tom and Eugene McCoy and Marcos Bennet OPEN: all week L 12 to 2.30, Mon to Sat D 7 to 10 MEALS: Set L £16.95 (2 courses) to £19.95, Set D £19.95 (1 course) to £32 SERVICE: not inc, 10% for parties of 8 or more CARDS: Delta, Diners, MasterCard, Switch, Visa DETAILS: 80 seats. Private parties: 80 main room, 4 to 33 private rooms. Vegetarian meals. Wheelchair access (also WC). Music. No mobile phones. Air-conditioned

---

Subscribers to Which? Online can access The Good Food Guide *on www.which.net.*

Not inc *in the details at the end of an entry indicates that no service charge is made and any tipping is at the discretion of the customer.*

GILLINGHAM Dorset   map 2

▲ Stock Hill ⚡✗

Stock Hill, Gillingham SP8 5NR
TEL: (01747) 823626   FAX: (01747) 825628
EMAIL: reception@stockhillhouse.co.uk   COOKING 5
WEBSITE: www.stockhillhouse.co.uk   MODERN EUROPEAN
off B3081, 1m W of Gillingham   £36–£57

This large late-Victorian stone house, hidden away in wooded, well-manicured
grounds on the Dorset/Somerset border, has been painstakingly restored by the
Hausers. Halfway up the beech-lined drive the life-sized statue of a wild boar
may serve as a hint that game has its place on the menu. Interiors reflect both the
house's pedigree and the Hausers' individualistic taste – flamboyant
('sometimes quirky') but ultimately sensitive. Rooms are filled with antiques,
ornate mirrors, oils and objets d'art. In the dining room well-spaced tables
overlook the garden, their crisp white linen set off by powder-pink walls; here
Nita Hauser directs the formal service with practised efficiency.

  Set-price menus offer an appealing repertoire of full-flavoured dishes that can
include some unusual but accomplished combinations; perhaps a starter
ballottine of guinea fowl, spicy Viennese sausage and robust black pudding
with red onion and olive oil salsa. Mains could see a nicely presented paupiette
of veal filled with ham and sage, finished in Noilly Prat and cream with a chive
tagliatelle and tartare of broccoli; or there might be red sea bream tails fried in
Guinness batter and served on tomato cream. Some of the indulgent and
beautifully crafted puddings originate from Peter Hauser's native Austria – for
instance, Fürst Pückler Torte auf Beeren Saft (a gâteau featuring vanilla sponge,
meringue, chocolate cream and apricot jam). Dishes make use of home-grown
vegetables from the hotel garden alongside well-sourced produce from the
surrounding countryside's abundant larder. The wine list is predominantly
French, but there are bottles from around the globe, including three from
Austria. House French wines begin at £16.05.

CHEFS: Peter Hauser and Lorna Connor   PROPRIETORS: Peter and Nita Hauser   OPEN: Sun L
12.15 to 1.30 (booking essential), all week D 7.30 to 8.30   MEALS: Set L Sun £25, Set D £35
SERVICE: not inc, card slips closed   CARDS: MasterCard, Switch, Visa   DETAILS: 24 seats. 8 seats
outside. Private parties: 24 main room, 4 to 12 private rooms. Car park. Vegetarian meals. No
children under 7. Children's helpings. No smoking. No mobile phones   ACCOMMODATION: 8
rooms, all with bath/shower. TV. Phone. D,B&B £120 to £290. No children under 7 (The Which?
Guide to Good Hotels)

Occasional music *in the details at the end of an entry means live or recorded music is
played in the dining room only rarely or for special events.* No music *means it is never
played.*

The Guide relies on feedback from its readers. Especially welcome are reports on new
restaurants appearing in the book for the first time. All letters to the Guide are
acknowledged.

GITTISHAM Devon   map 2

▲ Combe House ▼ ✳

Gittisham EX14 3AD
EMAIL: stay@thishotel.com   COOKING **4**
WEBSITE: www.thishotel.com   MODERN BRITISH
1½m off A30, 2m SW of Honiton   £34–£74

This is a Grade I listed Elizabethan manor of honey-coloured stone, many a
gable, and stone-mullioned windows. Eschewing the fussiness often found in
country-house hotels, Combe House revels in an 'extremely relaxing
atmosphere'. The dining room sticks to neutral colours and the walls are hung
with botanical prints in gold frames. The kitchen is headed by Philip Leach, and
his menus deliver 'the full works' while maintaining the integrity of the core
ingredient in each dish.

The great strength here lies in the quality of the supplies, from meat and game
right down to the potatoes used to make mash (and including herbs from their
own kitchen garden), and the front page of the menu lists the provenance and
suppliers of the fish, meat, vegetables and dairy products. An inspector praised
the 'superb quality' of the fowl in a starter of pot-roast quail with wild
mushroom mousse and tarragon cream, as well as the 'excellence of raw
materials' in a main course of grilled fillet of John Dory with pan-seared scallops
and parsley sauce, a dish that featured good mash, 'the tiniest ever' baby leeks,
and 'excellently fresh' scallops. Desserts such as 'brilliant' baked chocolate
pudding with bitter chocolate ice cream keep chocaholics happy. Service is
'attentive and friendly without being familiar'. The wine list declares an
intention to please rather than impress and, with the occasional lapse such as
1982 Pétrus at £1,800, sticks admirably to the brief. France and Australia are the
main interests. Chablis is a particular love, with 26 examples from good
producers starting at £18. Prices overall are very fair considering the location,
starting at £14.50 with lots of choice under £20 and six by the glass for £3.60 to
£5.

CHEF: Philip Leach   PROPRIETORS: Ken and Ruth Hunt   OPEN: all week 12 to 2, 7 to 9.30
CLOSED: 4 to 18 Jan   MEALS: Set L Mon to Sat £15 (2 courses) to £32.50, Set L Sun £25, Set D
£32.50 to £44. Bar L menu available   SERVICE: not inc, card slips closed   CARDS: Amex, Delta,
Diners, MasterCard, Switch, Visa   DETAILS: 50 seats. 24 seats outside. Private parties: 40 main
room, 10 to 20 private rooms. Car park. Vegetarian meals. Children's helpings. No smoking.
Wheelchair access (also WC). No music. No mobile phones   ACCOMMODATION: 15 rooms, all with
bath/shower. TV. Phone. B&B £99 to £265. Fishing (The Which? Guide to Good Hotels)

GODALMING Surrey   map 3

La Luna ✳   NEW ENTRY

10–14 Wharf Street, Godalming GU7 1NN   COOKING **2**
TEL: (01483) 414155   FAX: (01483) 418286   ITALIAN
                                                                £31–£64

Located in the premises of what was once a Mongolian restaurant, La Luna has a
'very pleasant', 'very Italian' ambience: hotpots have been replaced by stockpots
– and pasta pots, and more besides. Despite the fact that this is an Italian

restaurant, Frenchman Erik Michel, formerly chef/proprietor of Michel's in nearby Ripley, is one of the chefs, and his influence can be felt. The restaurant itself features lots of glass, plain white walls and black leather seats, the minimalist effect relieved by some enormous plants. There's a modern Mediterranean/Italian feel to the menu. A starter of chargrilled prawns may be served with grapefruit and orange segments, with salad leaves and pine nuts, while pasta dishes might include garganelli in a swordfish, white wine, aubergine and mint sauce, and main courses could run to grilled ribeye steak with mushrooms and braised radicchio. Finish with apple tart with blackberries and raspberry sauce, or poached pear with Amaretto. The all-Italian wine list has some good producers, but best value is found on the page of house wines, from £11.75 to £17.50.

CHEFS: Giovanni Puglisi, Erik Michel and Orazio Primavera   PROPRIETORS: Daniele Draed and Orazio Primavera   OPEN: Tue to Sat 12 to 2, 7 to 10   CLOSED: first week Jan, 2 weeks Aug   MEALS: alc (main courses £10.50 to £20). Set L £10.95 (2 courses), Set D £22.50   SERVICE: not inc   CARDS: Delta, MasterCard, Switch, Visa   DETAILS: 58 seats. Private parties: 18 main room, 32 private room. Vegetarian meals. No smoking. Wheelchair access (not WC). Music. Air-conditioned (£5)

GOLCAR West Yorkshire   map 8

▲ Weavers Shed ▼ ⁵⁄✸

Knowl Road, Golcar HD7 4AN
TEL: (01484) 654284   FAX: (01484) 650980
EMAIL: info@weaversshed.co.uk
WEBSITE: www.weaversshed.co.uk
on B6111, 2m W of Huddersfield via A62

COOKING 5
MODERN BRITISH
£21–£61

Here on the outskirts of Huddersfield an old woollen mill has been artfully transformed into a restaurant with rooms. Exposed stone walls, soft cream shades and clever lighting create a welcoming feel in the lounge and flag-floored dining room. The professionalism here extends to poultry-keeping – producing chicken, duck and quail eggs – and running both a kitchen garden and a wild garden that contributes yarrow, meadowsweet, mugwort and coltsfoot to menus best characterised as modern British with a northern slant (a slant that includes 'substantial' helpings). One diner's tartlet of smoked squab and onion confit made an intensely flavoured winter starter, and a main course of bacon-wrapped roast monkfish with salsify and colcannon almost defeated another. Other mains might include old-breed pork with braised trotter and red cabbage, or Worsborough red deer: a loin cut, chargrilled and served with caramelised shallots and cheese-topped mash. In proper northern fashion, you can end on ale cake (containing Theakston's Old Peculier) with the cheeses, or try a warm Eccles cake with a wodge of Kirkham's Lancashire. Most desserts come with a home-made ice cream, perhaps a brandy butter version to complement a rich prune and Armagnac soufflé.

Visitors have praised the selection of six house wines (£11.95, or £3 a glass) that clearly signal the main list's interest in independent producers, especially from south-west France and the Languedoc (though it ranges far wider, too). While there are expensive bottles too, sticking below £20 here leads to intriguing new territory, not dull compromises.

CHEFS: Stephen Jackson, Ian McGunnigle, Robert Jones and Cath Sill PROPRIETORS: Stephen and Tracy Jackson OPEN: Tue to Fri L 12 to 1.45, Tue to Sat D 7 to 9 (10 Sat) CLOSED: 25 Dec to 1 Jan MEALS: alc (main courses £13 to £20). Set L £9.95 (2 courses) to £12.95 SERVICE: not inc CARDS: Amex, Delta, Diners, MasterCard, Switch, Visa DETAILS: 60 seats. Private parties: 40 main room, 26 private room. Car park. Vegetarian meals. No smoking. Music. No mobile phones ACCOMMODATION: 5 rooms, all with bath/shower. TV. Phone. B&B £50 to £80. (*The Which? Guide to Good Hotels*) £5

GORING Oxfordshire   map 2

Leatherne Bottel

The Bridleway, Goring RG8 0HS
TEL: (01491) 872667   FAX: (01491) 875308
EMAIL: leathernebottel@aol.com   COOKING 3
WEBSITE: www.leathernebottel.co.uk   MODERN EUROPEAN
off B4009 just N of Goring   £34–£67

In January 2003 this isolated Thamesbank former pub was badly hit by flooding, but it is now 'firing on all cylinders' again after refurbishment. The riverside terrace remains idyllic for summer lunches, and 'efficient, enthusiastic' service from young Antipodeans sets a relaxed, friendly tone. In some respects this is a fairly old-fashioned enterprise, particularly its cottagey décor and its smoking policy ('We are a cigar-friendly restaurant,' proclaims the wine list). Cooking is more up to date, with novel ideas – such as pan-fried monkfish with radishes, borlotti beans and sweet chilli jam, or sea trout on mushroom mousseline with asparagus and sliced baby fennel salad – as well as more traditional ones, including lamb loin on ratatouille with a strong-flavoured stock-based sauce, or pan-fried bream with spinach, Puy lentils and a saffron-infused mussel sauce. Home-made ice creams feature in several of the desserts, like the orange and cardamom version accompanying pink peppercorn meringue. The food is popular, though a tendency to over-season has been noted. A handful of relatively modest house wines from £14.75 opens a rather highfalutin' list – those with over £25 to spend will fare best.

CHEF: Julia Storey PROPRIETOR: Croftchase Ltd OPEN: Mon to Sat L 12.30 to 2 (2.30 Sat), Sun L 12 to 3.30, Mon to Sat D 7 to 9 (9.30 Fri and Sat) MEALS: alc (main courses £17.50 to £20). Set D £23.50. Light L menu available SERVICE: 10%, card slips closed CARDS: Amex, Delta, MasterCard, Switch, Visa DETAILS: 50 seats. 70 seats outside. Car park. Vegetarian meals. No pipes. No music. No mobile phones £5

GRANGE Cumbria   map 10

▲ Borrowdale Gates Hotel ▼ 🍴 ✳

Grange CA12 5UQ
TEL: (017687) 77204   FAX: (017687) 77254
EMAIL: hotel@borrowdale-gates.com   COOKING 3
WEBSITE: www.borrowdale-gates.com   MODERN BRITISH
off B5289, about 3m S of Keswick, ¼m N of Grange   £25–£71

The Borrowdale Gates Hotel has a wonderful location, just beyond the southern end of Derwent Water; a backdrop of towering peaks give the impression of 'being surrounded by an intense, changing watercolour'. Although new owners have taken over since last year's Guide, very little seems to have changed. Pale green and pink still dominate the interior, and the ambience is 'tremendously calm and settled'. The Monday to Saturday lunch menu is light and unfussy, with plenty of fish options: a thick, warming apple and celeriac soup may precede pan-fried cod on a wild mushroom and polenta base, with crisp chargrilled vegetables, for instance. Dinner is a more complicated four-course affair. There may be a salad of butternut squash and asparagus as a first course, followed by an intermediate soup or sorbet, and then perhaps a main course of Dover sole meunière, or roast haunch of venison. 'Melt-in-the-mouth' was how one reporter described a dessert of treacle tart with crème anglaise and mango sorbet. Service is well judged, and the wine list offers a sound global selection, with the emphasis on France. But good and interesting bottles crop up all over and at fair prices – Ceretto's Blangè Arneis in Italy or St Clair's Merlot from New Zealand, both at £19.75, for example. Six wines come by the glass from £3.25.

CHEF: Justin Howe   PROPRIETORS: Colin and Carol Slaney   OPEN: all week 12.15 to 1.30, 7 to 8.45   CLOSED: Jan   MEALS: alc L Mon to Sat (main courses £7.50 to £12). Set L Sun £15.75, Set D £32.50   SERVICE: not inc   CARDS: Amex, Delta, MasterCard, Switch, Visa   DETAILS: 60 seats. 15 seats outside. Private parties: 24 main room. Car park. Vegetarian meals. Children's helpings at L. No smoking. Wheelchair access (also WC). No music. No mobile phones   ACCOMMODATION: 29 rooms, all with bath/shower. TV. Phone. D,B&B £65 to £175. Rooms for disabled. Baby facilities (The Which? Guide to Good Hotels)   £5

GRASMERE Cumbria   map 8

▲ White Moss House ▮ ⁵✳

Rydal Water, Grasmere LA22 9SE
TEL: (015394) 35295   FAX: (015394) 35516
EMAIL: sue@whitemoss.com
WEBSITE: www.whitemoss.com
on A591, at W end of Rydal Water

COOKING 5
BRITISH
£44–£53

Close to Rydal Water, White Moss House has a restrained dining room with bare wooden tables and a formula unvaried over many years: no choice before dessert, and soup is followed by fish (often a soufflé), meat, then dessert and cheese. Materials are fresh, sometimes organic and often local – Mansergh Hall lamb (roast rack with a herb crust), Holker Hall venison (marinated fillet with cep and girolle sauce), and Coniston char (in a soufflé). Skills are evident, too, in a roast fillet of ale-marinated, Fell-bred beef cooked pink and rested ('absolutely ace'), with roast potatoes, baby beetroot and a truffled woodland mushroom sauce. And soups (maybe a smooth, well-judged celeriac and chive) are 'a real joy', simple yet deeply flavoured. If some dishes' parts don't inevitably make a ravishingly exciting whole, this may be partly due to the comparatively unchanging repertoire. While the world moves on, White Moss House serves old favourites like Eton Mess, and Guardsman's pudding: a fine steamed sponge served with an appealingly sharp raspberry coulis.

Reporters mention meanness with cheeses (you choose from a list, not by eye, and get 'exactly two biscuits'), but they are well kept. Wines, meanwhile, offer exciting choices, whether you stick below £20 or indulge in mature claret. The list is structured around French regions and their grapes, with New World counterparts featured after each, ending with interesting Spanish and Italian bottles that fit nowhere else. Prices are very fair and a good range by the glass starts at £2.75.

CHEF: Peter Dixon PROPRIETORS: Peter and Sue Dixon OPEN: Mon to Sat D only 8 (1 sitting) MEALS: Set D £34.50 SERVICE: not inc, card slips closed CARDS: MasterCard, Switch, Visa DETAILS: 18 seats. Private parties: 18 main room. Car park. Vegetarian meals (with prior notice). Children's helpings. No smoking. No music ACCOMMODATION: 6 rooms, all with bath/shower. TV. Phone. D,B&B £75 to £190. Baby facilities. Fishing (*The Which? Guide to Good Hotels*) (£5)

GREAT GONERBY Lincolnshire **map 6**

Harry's Place

17 High Street, Great Gonerby NG31 8JS
TEL: (01476) 561780
on B1174, 1m N of Grantham

COOKING **7**
MODERN FRENCH
£56–£84

The location may be unexpected – a blue-fronted Georgian house on a rather ordinary street – but everything about this operation is done with care and deliberation. It starts with the discreet way arrivals are anticipated by Caroline Hallam, a hostess who expertly balances friendliness with professionalism, and is evident in the tiny dining room with its deep-red walls, painted cornices, antique pine furniture and fresh flowers: in the circumstances (only three tables) it can feel like being at a dinner party in someone else's home. A lot of effort goes into servicing the maximum ten covers, which starts with a near-fanatical sourcing of raw materials. Fish is always wild, beef and lamb come from the Real Meat Company, poultry (guinea fowl or chicken) typically arrives twice weekly from France, and game is usually from Scotland or Cumbria.

Visitors are struck by the intensity of flavours right from the word go: for example, in soups such as a garlicky and sweetly pungent tomato version with pesto, or a deep, richly flavoured, truffle-oiled mushroom soup with a coarse, earthy texture and a refreshing lift of lemon. Accurate timing can be taken as read, producing lightly seared Orkney scallops in a spicy Chinese-style dressing, and pink loin of spring lamb with Madeira sauce and a few 'unexpected treats', including sliced kidney and a light, lemony, eggy, herby stuffing. Main courses are typically accompanied by potatoes and an enterprising salad: perhaps little gem hearts with local asparagus tips and green beans in a light dressing incorporating cream, sherry vinegar and lots of herbs. Indeed, a generous use of fresh herbs is another characteristic of the cooking, which might toss tarragon (along with Avruga caviar) into an hollandaise to accompany turbot fillet, or mix sage, tarragon and rosemary in a Madeira sauce for Lincolnshire grey partridge.

There may be a choice of only two items per course, but meals are invariably well balanced, ending perhaps with a wobbly cherry brandy jelly (with a 'rich, strong flavour reminiscent of Christmas past') served with creamy yoghurt and black pepper, or a textbook chocolate mousse that is light, smooth, glossy, and perfectly positioned on the bittersweet continuum. Although no money is wasted on staff or frills, such a small operation inevitably means that meals cannot be cheap; comments such as 'worth every penny' give some idea of perceived value, even though the short wine list might do more to help. But Louis Jadot red and white Burgundy (£26) are also available by the glass at £5.

CHEF: Harry Hallam   PROPRIETORS: Harry and Caroline Hallam   OPEN: Tue to Sat 12.30 to 2, 7 to 9.30   CLOSED: 25 and 26 Dec, bank hols   MEALS: alc (main courses £25 to £30)   SERVICE: not inc   CARDS: Delta, MasterCard, Switch, Visa   DETAILS: 10 seats. Private parties: 10 main room. Car park. Children's helpings. No children under 5. No smoking. Wheelchair access (not WC). No music   £5

GREAT MILTON Oxfordshire   map 2

▲ Le Manoir aux Quat' Saisons 🍾 ✳

Church Road, Great Milton OX44 7PD
TEL: (01844) 278881   FAX: (01844) 278847
EMAIL: lemanoir@blanc.co.uk   COOKING 9
WEBSITE: www.manoir.co.uk   MODERN FRENCH
off A329, 1½m from M40 junction 7   £66–£162

Given enough time (and the weather), a walk round the garden is recommended; this is a well-tended working garden that supplies vegetables, herbs and fruits in season. Otherwise the approach from the car park is 'magical', with lavender and lilac much in evidence in summer. Inside, where a calm, friendly atmosphere imbues rather sumptuous surroundings, it is like entering a special other world, where attentive and largely French staff provide generally unobtrusive and impeccable service, and the food can be a knockout: 'unquestionably one of the finest meals we have ever eaten'.

M Blanc's celebrated salad-making abilities are applied to good effect on the menu gourmand; for example, a 'superb' piece of translucent salmon fillet (cooked slowly in oil, lemon and dill), falling apart at a touch, decked out with a few flakes of firm salt cod, some blobs of caviar, thin ribbons of mouli and cucumber, bits of raw cauliflower, and a few streaks of horseradish sauce. The kitchen is equally at home with a refined quail-egg ravioli (with wild mushrooms, truffles and poultry jus) as with a simple, earthy, richly flavoured beetroot terrine 'of exemplary smoothness', accompanied by cubes of beetroot jelly, a tiny mound of Puy lentils and a sour-cream dressing.

Timing can sometimes be conservative; our inspector's veal kidneys were an example, but a lot of skill went into the first-class snails, jumble of vegetables, and top class wine-based sauce that accompanied them. Other meat dishes have included tender, tasty noisette of venison with an understated bitter cocoa 'grand veneur' sauce and braised chestnuts; and pink-cooked Trelough duck with a little foie gras and excellent gratin dauphinois potatoes. Among desserts, the old classic of an edible painter's palette of ice creams and sorbets remains a triumph, as does a bitter cocoa sorbet resting at the bottom of a hot pistachio souffle, both flavours 'seriously intense', and the dish 'brilliant in its stunning simplicity, and deeply impressive in its technical accomplishment'.

Portions may seem smallish to some, but the overall balance of a meal is appreciated, leaving reporters 'entirely satisfied'. Cost is a problem for some reporters though, who feel that a little more bang per buck is needed; quite a few express nostalgia for the value they might find in an equivalent restaurant in France, and more than one has highlighted the hefty £17 price of a plate of cheese. As a general observation, the seven-course menu gourmand costs little more than three courses from the carte.

Wines won't mitigate the total cost, but they rise majestically to the occasion. The sommelier's guidance has been applauded, and some help in steering through an encyclopaedic list that explores all corners of France will be welcome for many diners. In the wake of multiple vintages of the greatest Bordeaux, top bottles from other countries (including Uruguay and Romania) can look something of an afterthought. Just five come by the glass, from £6.50 to £8.

CHEFS: Raymond Blanc and Gary Jones   PROPRIETOR: Raymond Blanc   OPEN: all week 12.15 to 2.30, 7.15 to 10   MEALS: alc (main courses £32 to £37). Set L £45, Set D £95   SERVICE: not inc CARDS: Amex, Delta, Diners, MasterCard, Switch, Visa   DETAILS: 99 seats. Private parties: 50 main room, 50 private room. Car park. Vegetarian meals. Children's helpings. No smoking. Wheelchair access (also WC). No music. No mobile phones. Air-conditioned   ACCOMMODATION: 32 rooms. TV. Phone. B&B £245 to £1,200. Rooms for disabled. Baby facilities (*The Which? Guide to Good Hotels*)

GREAT MISSENDEN Buckinghamshire

map 3

La Petite Auberge

107 High Street, Great Missenden HP16 0BB
TEL: (01494) 865370

COOKING 4
FRENCH
£37–£51

This is an ordinary terrace building with lilac woodwork at the south end of the High Street. Its long, narrow interior is unremarkable, and the focus is firmly on food. The menus (French, with English subtitles) may look traditional, but skilful, accurately timed cooking and careful presentation demonstrate a creative hand. Classic combinations of excellent ingredients are arranged with the components separated, exposing flavours, textures and colours and letting the customer explore sequences, contrasts and complementarities; and thick sauces that obscure appearance and blanket tastes are avoided. Filet d'agneau à la grain de moutarde displayed potato rösti and mange-tout in adjacent segments of the plate, with thin sticks of chargrilled salsify in the third quarter, and the remainder occupied by the lamb, crusty outside but tenderly pink inside, thickly sliced and resting on its thin, intense stock-based sauce. Similar precision set the subtlety of cinnamon ice cream off against the slightly burnt taste of wafer-thin slices of baked apple. A succinct, exclusively French wine list, starting at £11.50 and with much below £20, is soundly chosen; high-quality digestifs include old Calvados and Armagnac. Mme Martel serves with formal, friendly charm.

CHEF: Hubert Martel   PROPRIETORS: Mr and Mrs H. Martel   OPEN: Mon to Fri D 7.30 to 10.30 CLOSED: 2 weeks Christmas, 2 weeks Easter   MEALS: alc D (main courses £16 to £17)   SERVICE: not inc   CARDS: Delta, Diners, MasterCard, Switch, Visa   DETAILS: 30 seats. Private parties: 30 main room. Children's helpings. Wheelchair access (also WC). No music

Report forms are at the back of the book; write a letter if you prefer; or email us at goodfoodguide@which.net

GREAT YELDHAM Essex   map 3

White Hart ♥ ⅝✕

Poole Street, Great Yeldham CO9 4HJ
TEL: (01787) 237250   FAX: (01787) 238044
EMAIL: reservations@whitehartyeldham.co.uk
WEBSITE: www.whitehartyeldham.co.uk

COOKING 2
ANGLO-FRENCH-PLUS
£23–£51

John Dicken's red-roofed, ochre-fronted pub/restaurant is nearing its half-millennium as a hostelry. Set back a little from the main road, it has been elegantly and comfortably decorated, boasting huge inglenook fireplaces. Vegetarian and children's menus supplement the main menu choice, which extends broadly across a range from game terrine with runner bean chutney to grilled Portland scallops with Puy lentils and pancetta to start, and from skate meunière with a sauté of oyster mushrooms, prawns and capers to braised oxtail with creamed leek mash and winter root vegetables to follow. The quality of principal ingredients is appreciably fine, and they are cooked with care. Puddings might be sticky toffee with fudge sauce, or perhaps traditional sherry trifle. Service makes everyone feel welcome. A delightfully straightforward wine list, arranged by style, is full of good ideas at all price levels. A baker's dozen come by the glass from £1.95 to £3.95, and at the upper end brief selections from classical regions mingle with their New World counterparts.

CHEF/PROPRIETOR: John Dicken   OPEN: all week 12 to 9.30   MEALS: alc (main courses £7 to £16.50). Set L Mon to Fri 12 to 2 £10.50 (2 courses) to £14.50   SERVICE: not inc   CARDS: Amex, Delta, Diners, MasterCard, Switch, Visa   DETAILS: 120 seats. 40 seats outside. Private parties: 80 main room, 8 to 36 private rooms. Car park. Vegetarian meals. Children's helpings. No smoking. Wheelchair access (also WC). Music. No mobile phones

GRIMSTHORPE Lincolnshire   map 6

▲ Black Horse Inn ♥ ⅝✕

Grimsthorpe PE10 0LY
TEL: (01778) 591247   FAX: (01778) 591373
EMAIL: dine@blackhorseinn.co.uk
WEBSITE: www.blackhorseinn.co.uk

COOKING 1
MODERN BRITISH
£23–£44

Sitting in the shadow of Grimsthorpe Castle, this is an eighteenth-century country inn with a gentrified feel, many treasures in its wine cellar and a growing reputation for food. You can eat chargrilled vegetable terrine or smoked haddock with bubble and squeak in the comfortable, upmarket bar, or opt for something more ambitious in the restaurant. Expect, say, watercress risotto with pan-fried chicken livers as a starter, followed by roast rump of lamb with ratatouille, or roast monkfish with an onion, bay and lemon compote and sauce nero. An extensive game menu is featured in season, with furred and feathered delights such as hare casseroled in red wine sauce, and teal with sautéed wild mushrooms, roast lentils and thyme jus. A short list of 16 wines concentrates on modern, fruity styles under £20, with an Alsace Pinot Blanc from Deiss and a classically styled budget Bordeaux (both £15.95) hinting at the greater depth and traditional leanings of an impressive and good-value restaurant list arranged by style. Five wines are £3 per glass, and bottles start at £8.95.

CHEF: Brian Rey   PROPRIETORS: Brian and Elaine Rey   OPEN: Tue to Sun L 12 to 2, Mon to Sat D 7 to 9.30   MEALS: alc (main courses £9.50 to £16). Bar menu available   SERVICE: not inc, card slips closed   CARDS: Amex, Delta, Diners, MasterCard, Switch, Visa   DETAILS: 74 seats. 40 seats outside. Private parties: 36 main room, 12 private room. Car park. Vegetarian meals. Children's helpings. No smoking. Occasional music   ACCOMMODATION: 6 rooms, 5 with bath/shower. TV. Phone. B&B £45 to £95

GRIMSTON Norfolk   map 6

▲ Congham Hall ▼ ✗

Lynn Road, Grimston PE32 1AH
TEL: (01485) 600250   FAX: (01485) 601191
EMAIL: info@conghamhallhotel.co.uk
WEBSITE: www.conghamhallhotel.co.uk   COOKING 5
off A148 or B1153, 6½m E of King's Lynn and at   MODERN BRITISH/FRENCH
W edge of Grimston   £28–£66

Congham offers the full country-house package, including parkland, tennis court, putting green and pool. The late Georgian house is stolidly imposing, decorated in the grand style, with plush sofas and an antique escritoire in the lounge, and dripping chandeliers in the dining room.

In the Orangery restaurant you could go for it and try the menu gourmand at lunch or dinner, but the ordinary prix fixe is enticing enough. Fraser Miller's bold and confident cooking doesn't deal in pastel-hued flavours. For some, his strong, concentrated sauces outgun the dishes' main ingredients; others welcome the forthrightness of, say, a ballottine of quail with artichoke purée and truffle dressing, or monkfish tail with parsley noodles, pancetta and a velouté of saffron and ginger. A separate vegetarian menu offers four dishes that can be permed as starters or mains. Otherwise, appreciate the artistry that goes into a terrine of ham hock and foie gras with apple chutney and toasted brioche, or the counterpoint of flavours in a sea bass papillote with crab and coriander mousse, boulangère potatoes and tomato beurre blanc. Hard-to-penetrate pastrywork in desserts has earned some criticism, so raspberry and champagne mousse with macerated strawberries may be a good bet. Service is pleasant, 'but a little lacking in finesse and knowledge', and the wine list – annotated, organised by style and definitely food-friendly – mixes the famous and less well-known in each category. Burgundies are well chosen and fairly priced, but elsewhere value is variable, and under £20 pickings are lean.

CHEF: Fraser Miller   PROPRIETOR: Von Essen Hotels   OPEN: all week 12 to 1.45, 7 to 9.15 CLOSED: Dec 25 D   MEALS: alc L (main courses £8 to £11.50). Set L £11.50 (2 courses) to £29.95, Set D £29.50 (2 courses) to £41.95. Bar menu available   SERVICE: not inc, card slips closed CARDS: Amex, Delta, Diners, MasterCard, Switch, Visa   DETAILS: 60 seats. 20 seats outside. Private parties: 60 main room, 4 to 20 private rooms. Car park. Vegetarian meals. Children's helpings. No children under 7 at D. No smoking. Wheelchair access (not WC). No music. No mobile phones   ACCOMMODATION: 14 rooms, all with bath/shower. TV. Phone. B&B £99 to £240. Swimming pool (The Which? Guide to Good Hotels)   £5

HALIFAX West Yorkshire

▲ Shibden Mill Inn

NEW ENTRY

Shibden Mill Fold, Shibden, Halifax HX3 7UL
TEL: (01422) 365840   FAX: (01422) 362971
EMAIL: shibdenmillinn@zoom.co.uk
WEBSITE: www.shibdenmillinn.com

COOKING 3
MODERN BRITISH
£29–£45

Downstairs there's a 'pubby' feel to this converted seventeenth-century mill tucked quietly away in the Shibden Valley, but upstairs the restaurant, with its high-vaulted ceiling, dark petrol-blue walls and heavy, tapestry-style drapes, is a different kettle of fish. Comfortably upholstered chairs, and tables clothed in white linen grace the room where an inspector enjoyed starters of chargrilled asparagus with a little mound of crayfish and miniature ramekin of 'tart' salad cream, and perfectly done roast quail with scrambled egg and truffle oil.

Each course has its own fixed price, and among main dishes you might choose braised pork with lentil vinaigrette and broad beans; tender slices of lamb fillet accompanied by a delicate confit of garlic cloves, aubergine and lime (all soft and caramelised); or roast cod with haddock and parsley mash. Rhubarb and custard tart with toasted marshmallow and ginger ice cream has failed to impress; otherwise, dessert choices might include strawberry cheesecake, coconut rice pudding or warm lardy cake. Service at weekends can be somewhat erratic. There are some 50-plus wines to chose from, on a list with offerings from around the world, including a dozen wines by the glass (£1.90 to £5.90) and house bottles from £9.90.

CHEF: Adrian Jones   PROPRIETOR: Mr S.D. Heaton   OPEN: all week 12 to 2, 6 to 9.30 (7.30 Sun) CLOSED: 25 and 26 Dec D, 1 Jan D   MEALS: alc (main courses £9 to £14.50). Bar menu also available   SERVICE: not inc, card slips closed   CARDS: Amex, Delta, MasterCard, Switch, Visa DETAILS: 60 seats. 20 seats outside. Private parties: 60 main room, 8 to 10 private rooms. Car park. Vegetarian meals. Children's helpings. Music   ACCOMMODATION: 12 rooms, all with bath/ shower. TV. Phone. B&B £60 to £115 (£5)

HAMPTON HILL Greater London

map 3

Monsieur Max ♥

133 High Street, Hampton Hill TW12 1NJ
TEL: (020) 8979 5546   FAX: (020) 8979 3747
EMAIL: monsieurmax@aol.com
WEBSITE: www.monsieurmax.co.uk

COOKING 6
FRENCH
£40–£68

Inside this squat, green-painted house on an unremarkable high street is an architectural and decorative hotchpotch of provincial French and 'wannabe Parisian' that coalesces into 'a late 20th-century budget interpretation' of Art Deco. The menu is long, and items are complex – perhaps smoked eel fillet on sliced ovals of ratte potato, accompanied by smoked salmon gateau with watercress fromage blanc, beetroot bavarois, and cucumber and apple vinaigrette – and at lunch about half the dishes carry supplements. But the style is hearty and notably generous. Pigeon (plump breasts and roast drumsticks) has a 'wondrous little minced sausage of garlicky pigeon offal', lentils and butter- and cream-rich mash; or August could bring grouse with reduced cooking juices and 'top-notch' red cabbage. Materials are first-class and the kitchen hugely competent, although dishes can feel heavy, with lots of butter and strong sauces (one couple fasted for 24 hours after lunch here). Even baked fillet of sea bass in a seaweed crust comes with sardines, foie gras, artichokes crushed with saffron, wild asparagus, and pine nut Choron.

The 'beautiful, lumbering wood-and-marble' cheese trolley keeps a massive selection in perfect condition, for serving simply with excellent bread. Alternatively, a citrus tart with rich, crumbly shortcrust pastry comes with a tuile filled with caramel crunch and chocolate ice cream. Attentive and charming service is supplied by largely French staff. House wines from £14.50 (£4 a glass) introduce a list whose focus is predominantly French and classical – diners on a budget should look south for affordable bottles.

CHEF: Alex Bentley   PROPRIETOR: Sunbow Ltd   OPEN: Sun to Fri L 12 to 2.30, all week D 7 to 9.30   CLOSED: 25 Dec   MEALS: Set L £20 (2 courses) to £25, Set D £37.50   SERVICE: 12.5% (optional), card slips closed   CARDS: Amex, Diners, MasterCard, Switch, Visa   DETAILS: 80 seats. Private parties: 90 main room. Children's helpings. No children under 8. Wheelchair access (not WC). No music. Air-conditioned

---

HAROME North Yorkshire   map 9

▲ Star Inn ✣ £

High Street, Harome YO62 5JE
TEL: (01439) 770397   FAX: (01439) 771833   COOKING 5
WEBSITE: www.thestaratharome.co.uk   MODERN BRITISH
off A170, 3m SE of Helmsley   £28–£57

This is the kind of rural picture that townies dream about: a fourteenth-century thatched inn with a flagstone floor, low beams, open fires and wonky walls, in a small farming village complete with duck pond and cricket pitch. But thanks to the diligence of the Perns, it is no backwater; rather it is a strongly rooted enterprise in which local suppliers of poultry, game and beef figure prominently, and eggs (hen, duck, quail and guinea fowl) all come from the village. In return, they have set up a corner shop across the road as a bakery/deli to sell some of the kitchen's output.

Andrew Pern dubs his style of cooking 'regional British with Yorkshire influences', which might translate into a pub classic such as bangers and mash, a duck liver faggot with pickled onion hash and Yorkshire relish, or a starter of grilled black pudding and pan-fried foie gras ('excellent in texture and appearance') served with apple and vanilla chutney and a scrumpy reduction. Other combinations that have impressed include lamb with goats' cheese mash, and belly pork with cabbage and noodles. Vegetables come separately, the same with all dishes, and desserts run from raspberry Bakewell tart with mulled cherries to steamed marmalade pudding with bitter chocolate sorbet. Service is well organised and efficient, and house wine is £11.95.

CHEF: Andrew Pern   PROPRIETORS: Andrew and Jacquie Pern   OPEN: Tue to Sat L 11.30 to 2, Sun L 12 to 6, Tue to Sat D 6.30 to 9.30 (10 Sat)   CLOSED: 25 Dec, 2 weeks spring, bank hols   MEALS: alc (main courses £8.50 to £18)   SERVICE: not inc, card slips closed   CARDS: Delta, MasterCard, Switch, Visa   DETAILS: 60 seats. 30 seats outside. Private parties: 34 main room. Car park.

Vegetarian meals. Children's helpings. No smoking. Occasional music ACCOMMODATION: 11 rooms, all with bath/shower. TV. Phone. B&B £90 to £195. Rooms for disabled (*The Which? Guide to Good Hotels*)

HARROGATE North Yorkshire   map 8

Attic

62A Union Street, Harrogate HG1 1BS
TEL: (01423) 524400   FAX: (01423) 523191
EMAIL: info@attic-harrogate.co.uk
WEBSITE: www.attic-harrogate.co.uk

NEW CHEF

MODERN EUROPEAN
£24–£48

Carved from what was once a warehouse, the Attic has a modern, sleek yet comfortable look and service that is friendly and professional. The downstairs room, with flagstone floors, houses a curved bar where guests can enjoy a drink before climbing to the pale grey- , navy- and black-toned dining room; the main feature here is the glass roof which, on sunny days, gives the place an al fresco feel. A new chef arrived too late for us to assess, although the sensibly short, seasonal menu – half a dozen starters, mains and desserts – still focuses on forthright flavours. The astute modern wine list is excellent value, with six tasty house wines at £11.50 or £2.85 a glass. The newly added 'premier' section offers good quality for the price on celebration days.

CHEF: Joe Horvath PROPRIETOR: Chris Patchett OPEN: Mon to Sat 12 to 2, 6.30 to 10 CLOSED: 26 Dec, 1 Jan MEALS: alc (main courses £5.50 to £14.50). Set L £11.50 (2 courses) to £14.50, Set D 6.30 to 7.30 £11.50 (2 courses) to £14.50. Snack L menu available SERVICE: not inc CARDS: Amex, Delta, MasterCard, Switch, Visa DETAILS: 56 seats. Private parties: 45 main room. Vegetarian meals. No cigars/pipes. Music £5

Drum and Monkey £

5 Montpellier Gardens, Harrogate HG1 2TF
TEL: (01423) 502650   FAX: (01423) 522469

COOKING 2
SEAFOOD
£20–£51

If you are looking to satisfy a craving for seafood, be warned that booking in advance at this popular, well-established restaurant is a better alternative than waiting in line in an orderly queue. A pub-like lower floor is complemented by an upstairs restaurant with closely packed tables and chairs and some banquette-style seating. Navigating a low-fat route through the menu is just possible, with curried king prawns showing Eastern promise, but 'popular fish only' (in the words of William Fuller) are the staple, generally delivered in a rich 1970s mode: hollandaise and Mornay sauces, scallops Normandy-style with Calvados, and salmon and watercress mousse set the nostalgic tone. Puddings, including vanilla ice cream with raisins soaked in Madeira – 'very boozy' – satisfy in a similarly old-fashioned way. Fairly priced and predictable, the wine list is dominated by white European bottles. Prices open at around £10.

CHEFS: Keith Penny and Selina Leamy PROPRIETOR: William Fuller OPEN: Mon to Sat 12 to 2.30, 6.30 to 10.15 CLOSED: D 24 Dec to 2 Jan MEALS: alc (main courses L £6 to £17, D £8 to £18) SERVICE: not inc CARDS: Delta, MasterCard, Switch, Visa DETAILS: 56 seats. Children's helpings. No music

map 3

Golden Palace £

146–150 Station Road, Harrow HA1 2RH   COOKING 4
TEL: (020) 8863 2333 and 8424 8899   CHINESE
FAX: (020) 8863 3388   £27–£58

Although a parade of shops on a busy main road in Harrow may seem an
unlikely setting for a top-class Chinese restaurant, the Golden Palace is doing its
bit to raise the gastronomic profile of the area with some seriously impressive
and great-value cooking. The dining room has a cheerful modern feel, lighting is
subtle, and tables are laid with good-quality linen and glassware, and those
more used to surly Chinatown waiters will be pleasantly surprised by the
friendly, helpful, clued-up and attentive service.

The long menu offers a fairly familiar range of dishes from the standard
repertoire of Cantonese, Pekinese and Szechuan cooking, but the shorter list of
specials is where the main interest lies, including such dishes as steamed eel in
black-bean sauce, veal ribs in spicy salt and chilli, and goose feet with shiitake
mushroom hotpot. Stir-fried cuttlefish with Chinese broccoli was a hit at
inspection, providing a well-balanced mix of textures and flavours, while
paper-wrapped chicken came with an intriguing and delicate sauce of black
beans and honey. Even the staples are done well, such as sweet-and-sour pork
featuring lean meat in light batter, and crisp-skinned charcoal-roast duck. Meals
begin with an appetiser soup, made with 'fantastic' stock and containing herbs,
nuts, fruit and strips of tender pork, and might end with a banana fritter or
pancakes with red-bean paste. Wine prices start at £10.50.

CHEF/PROPRIETOR: G. Ho   OPEN: Mon to Sat 12 to 11.30, Sun and bank hols 11am to 10.30pm
CLOSED: 25 Dec   MEALS: alc (main courses £5.50 to £20). Set L and D £14.50 to £22.50 (all min 2
or more)   SERVICE: 10%   CARDS: Amex, Delta, Diners, MasterCard, Switch, Visa   DETAILS: 150
seats. Private parties: 80 main room, 10 to 70 private rooms. Vegetarian meals. Wheelchair
access (also WC). Music. Air-conditioned

map 6

▲ Pier Hotel, Harbourside Restaurant ♟ ✳

The Quay, Harwich CO12 3HH
TEL: (01255) 241212   FAX: (01255) 551922   COOKING 2
EMAIL: lesley@pieratharwich.co.uk   SEAFOOD/ENGLISH
WEBSITE: www.milsomhotels.co.uk   £31–£68

The Pier Hotel is a colourful and characterful hotel looking out to the Stour
estuary with its busy traffic of large ferries; the upstairs Habourside is the
smarter of its two restaurants, with neat, clean and nautically themed décor and
good views. The menu focuses on seafood – they have their own lobster tanks –
and ingredients are fresh-tasting, sauces well made, and presentation attractive.
Shellfish bases intensify soups and may zip up a starter of fried red mullet with
tomato and herb sauce; while main-course poached halibut gets Mediterranean
touches from crisp Parma ham, tomato concassé and drizzled pesto; and grilled
lobster with herby, lemony melted butter and a delicate tarragon-flavoured

béarnaise is served in prime condition. For meat eaters jellied pork knuckle with a tangy onion jam is as dextrously handled as the fish, and a main course of suprême of chicken is braised with teriyaki sauce. Puddings have received fewer plaudits, though home-made ice creams may be just the ticket. Service is both professional and friendly. A soundly judged wine list, strongest on France and South Africa, includes excellent whites to complement the cuisine. Six house wines come by the glass for £2.20 to £3.60.

CHEF: Chris Oakley   PROPRIETOR: P. Milsom   OPEN: all week 12 to 2, 6 to 9.30   MEALS: alc (not Sun L; main courses £10 to £31.50). Set L £16 (2 courses) to £19. Bistro and bar snack menus available   SERVICE: 10%, card slips closed   CARDS: Amex, Delta, Diners, MasterCard, Switch, Visa   DETAILS: 140 seats. 30 seats outside. Private parties: 90 main room, 40 private rooms. Car park. Vegetarian meals. Children's helpings. No smoking. Music. No mobile phones   ACCOMMODATION: 14 rooms, all with bath/shower. TV. Phone. B&B £67.50 to £160. Baby facilities (*The Which? Guide to Good Hotels*)

HATHERSAGE Derbyshire   map 8

▲ George Hotel 🍴   NEW ENTRY

Hathersage S32 1BB
TEL: (01433) 650436   FAX: (01433) 650099   COOKING 3
EMAIL: info@george-hotel.net   GLOBAL
WEBSITE: www.george-hotel.net   £33–£63

From the outside the George exudes a sense of tradition, but grown-up chic is what you get the moment you walk through the doors. The smart bar area features vibrantly upholstered furnishings, while the restaurant has a cool, contemporary décor, the cream and white paintwork contrasting with dark beams and stone walls. The lunch menu is fairly simple, with a variety of sandwiches, soups and some heartier dishes, but the kitchen really comes into its own in the evening. Chef Ben Handley offers modern dishes of carefully chosen, well-matched ingredients, as in a 'precisely timed' starter of pan-roast monkfish accompanied by an oriental noodle salad and a sweet chilli dressing swirled into tiny puddles. A main course of noisettes of lamb, cooked pink, has been served with potato gnocchi, shiitake mushrooms, crispy leeks and Madeira sauce, while lightly seared tuna steak comes coated with strips of pancetta on a bed of wilted rocket, with anchovies adding good textural and salty contrast. Well-kept French and English cheeses, served with walnut and raisin bread, may tempt diners away from puddings such as a classic crème brûlée with a light, thin crust. The reasonably priced wine list is organised by style, with bottle prices starting at £13.50.

CHEF: Ben Handley   PROPRIETOR: Eric Marsh   OPEN: all week 12 to 2.30, 7 to 10   MEALS: alc (main courses £10 to £20). Set L Sun £18.95   SERVICE: not inc, card slips closed   CARDS: Amex, Delta, Diners, MasterCard, Switch, Visa   DETAILS: 55 seats. Private parties: 80 main room, 6 to 20 private rooms. Car park. Vegetarian meals. Children's helpings. No smoking. Wheelchair access (also WC). Music. No mobile phones   ACCOMMODATION: 19 rooms, all with bath/shower. TV. Phone. B&B £75 to £155

▲ *means accommodation is available.*

HAWORTH West Yorkshire   map 8

▲ Weavers ⅘✳

13–17 West Lane, Haworth BD22 8DU	COOKING 3
TEL: (01535) 643822 FAX: (01535) 644832	MODERN BRITISH
WEBSITE: www.weaversmallhotel.co.uk	£26–£49

The Brontë family parsonage is not the only lure in Haworth. Head for its car park, and Weavers rises before you. A restaurant-with-rooms, with a bar with a simple blackboard menu on the ground floor, it takes as its mainstay good northern supplies. A level of complexity in the cooking is usually brought off well. Rump of Dales-bred beef is smoked and cured in Yorkshire ale, and appears with the fillet served as carpaccio on a roasted beetroot and rocket salad with horseradish cream for starters. A mixed fish main course, such as sea bream, scallops and prawns in a broth of shellfish and star anise, is given textural contrast with a crisp risotto cake, and peppered breast of Gressingham duck comes with a confit duck spring roll, bubble and squeak rösti, and a sauce of Yorkshire rhubarb and ginger. Finish in style with a rich chocolate tart with Seville orange jelly and warm custard. Service is friendly and efficient, with Colin Rushworth singled out for his 'character and charm'. The jumbled, fairly priced wine list opens with southern French vins de pays at £10.95.

CHEFS: Jane, Colin and Tim Rushworth PROPRIETORS: Jane and Colin Rushworth OPEN: Wed to Fri and Sun L 12 to 2, Tue to Sat D 6.30 to 9 CLOSED: 10 days Christmas, last week June MEALS: alc (main courses £10 to £17). Set L £12.50 (2 courses) to £16, Set D Tue to Thur 6.30 to 7.30 £12.50 (2 courses) to £16. Bar menu available SERVICE: not inc CARDS: Amex, Delta, Diners, MasterCard, Switch, Visa DETAILS: 65 seats. Private parties: 14 main room, 10 to 14 private rooms. Vegetarian meals. Children's helpings. No smoking. Music. No mobile phones. Air-conditioned ACCOMMODATION: 3 rooms, all with bath/shower. TV. Phone. B&B £55 to £80 (The Which? Guide to Good Hotels) £5

HAYDON BRIDGE Northumberland   map 10

General Havelock Inn ⅘✳ £

9 Ratcliffe Road, Haydon Bridge NE47 6ER	
TEL: (01434) 684376 FAX: (01434) 684283	
EMAIL: generalhavelock@aol.com	
WEBSITE: www.northumberlandrestaurants.co.uk	COOKING 2
on A69, 6m W of Hexham, 100yds from junction	MODERN EUROPEAN
with B6319	£20–£40

An old roadside inn by the South Tyne, this is a warmly welcoming, popular and unpretentious place, its dining room a lovely converted barn. Ambition does not outrun culinary skills, which include a fine feel for flavour, and excellent local meat (including succulent lamb chops and pheasant) and vegetables prepared with a minimum of fuss. On the four-course prix fixe dinner menu (there's a carte as well) curried parsnip soup might precede potato and wild mushroom gnocchi, and then a main course of veal sweetbreads, or sea bass on a bed of ratatouille. A feuilleté of tender pear, soft pastry and a lightly caramelised sauce with excellent vanilla ice cream has been well received, or try well-kept northern cheeses – like Ribblesdale, Cuddys Cave and Swaledale – with home-produced oatcakes. The 20-odd wines are a good-value international selection starting at £9.50, with only champagne going over £20.

CHEF: Gary Thompson PROPRIETORS: Gary and Joanna Thompson OPEN: Tue to Sun L 12 to 2, Tue to Sat D 7 to 9 CLOSED: Tues during Jan MEALS: alc (not Sun L; main courses L £5.50 to £8, D £6.50 to £13). Set L £9.50 (2 courses) to £12.75, Set D £17.25 (2 courses) to £22. Light L menu available SERVICE: not inc, card slips closed CARDS: Delta, MasterCard, Switch, Visa DETAILS: 60 seats. 30 seats outside. Private parties: 60 main room. Children's helpings. No smoking in dining room, smoking area in bar. Wheelchair access (also WC). No music (£5)

HAYWARDS HEATH West Sussex   map 3

Jeremy's

Borde Hill, Balcombe Road, Haywards
Heath RH16 1XP
TEL: (01444) 441102   FAX: (01444) 443936   COOKING 5
EMAIL: jeremys.bordehill@btinternet.com   MODERN EUROPEAN
WEBSITE: www.homeofgoodfood.com   £32–£57

The drive into Borde Hill Gardens is one to lift the spirits, even if they drop a little on seeing the tea room adjacent to the restaurant. Once inside Jeremy's, though, order is restored in the smart and civilised dining room, with apricot-coloured walls and neatly set tables. Intensity of flavour abounds, often from less expensive ingredients, as in a vividly flavoured celery, parsley and lemon soup, and 'rich and delicious' chicken livers with Jerusalem artichoke in a Madeira reduction. 'Posh' ingredients, such as turbot served with soba noodles, are treated with equal imagination.

Main courses may include rack of Southdown lamb with saffron mash and roasted red pepper, while desserts run to such fashionable ensembles as rhubarb jelly with rosewater cream and a ginger tuile, or a crema catalana served with sherry-poached dried apricots and a 'light-as-a-snowflake' star-shaped biscuit. There is a terrace outside for summer eating with good views of the Sussex countryside. Staff are friendly, and the brief wine list has some good producers, particularly from California and Italy. Five house selections are around £13. The gardens of Borde Hill House are well worth exploration, but you'll have to pay for the privilege.

CHEF: Frederic Bodeau PROPRIETORS: Jeremy and Vera Ashpool OPEN: Tue to Sun L 12.30 to 2.30, Tue to Sat D 7.30 to 10 CLOSED: first week Jan MEALS: alc exc Sun L (main courses £13 to £19). Set L £16.50 (2 courses) to £20.50, Set D Tue to Thur £16.50 (2 courses) to £20.50 SERVICE: not inc, 10% for parties of 8 or more CARDS: Amex, Diners, MasterCard, Switch, Visa DETAILS: 50 seats. 120 seats outside. Private parties: 50 main room, 50 to 120 private rooms. Car park. Vegetarian meals. Children's helpings. No-smoking area. Wheelchair access (also WC). Music (£5)

The Guide office can quickly spot when a restaurateur is encouraging customers to write recommending inclusion. Such reports do not further a restaurant's cause. Please tell us if a restaurateur invites you to write to the Guide.

HELSTON Cornwall
map 1

Morley's ⁵⚹

NEW ENTRY

The Mews, 4 Wendron Street, Helston TR13 8PS
TEL: 01326 564433

COOKING 2
MODERN EUROPEAN
£36–£48

An alley off the main shopping street conceals Morley's. If the décor struck one couple as 'rather dated', with its grey carpet and dark wood furniture, there's nothing retro about Simon Morley-Smith's cooking. His menus change regularly, taking their cue from local ingredients – Newlyn fish, organic salads from the Lizard, meat from Cornish farms. Flavours are distinctive, and dishes look good on the plate too. Poached fish sausage with marinated mussels and piccalilli made an interesting and well-executed starter, likewise a combo of fried pork tenderloin, lamb's kidney with gnocchi and chive sauce. Mains are equally attractive, witness confit of lamb shredded between rösti potatoes with glazed artichoke, shallots and dark cassis gravy, or fried duck breast alongside a Parmesan basket of coriander risotto. To finish, an individual berry soufflé with blackberry sorbet was 'well worth the wait'. The well-spread wine list has house French at £9.95.

CHEF: Simon Morley-Smith PROPRIETORS: Simon and Joanne Morley-Smith OPEN: Mon to Sat D 7 to 9.30 CLOSED: Jan MEALS: Set D £17 (1 course) to £26 SERVICE: not inc, card slips closed CARDS: Delta, MasterCard, Switch, Visa DETAILS: 24 seats. Private parties: 26 main room. Vegetarian meals. No smoking. Music £5

HEMINGFORD GREY Cambridgeshire
map 6

Cock ⁵⚹ £

47 High Street, Hemingford Grey PE28 9BJ
TEL: (01480) 463609
EMAIL: oliver.thain@condorpubs.com

COOKING 2
MODERN BRITISH
£18–£41

The Cock consists of a duo of pub and restaurant side by side in a picturesque village. The restaurant interior, entered independently, has a contemporary feel, with pale colours and stripped wooden floors. The menu offers a range of dishes with a nod to our European partners in addition to well-turned-out English staples, along the lines of wild mushroom risotto with prosciutto and Parmesan, or beetroot and apple salad with walnuts and Stilton, and main courses of roast chicken breast with a red wine, onion and bacon sauce, or pan-fried calf's liver with sweet potato purée and lime butter. A blackboard lists a range of home-made sausages with mash, and desserts include sticky toffee pudding, or perhaps honey bavarois with vanilla sauce. Service has been described as warm and friendly. The wine list takes a short world tour, with prices starting at £8.95 for house French. Oliver Thain and Richard Bradley now also run the Crown and Punchbowl in Horningsea, just north of Cambridge, which is due to open as the Guide publishes.

CHEF: Chris Brading PROPRIETORS: Oliver Thain and Richard Bradley OPEN: all week L 12 to 2.30, Mon to Sat D 7 to 9.30 MEALS: alc L Mon to Sat and D (main courses £9 to £15). Set L Mon to Sat £7.95 (2 courses) to £10.95, Set L Sun £13.95 (2 courses) to £16.95 SERVICE: not inc

CARDS: Delta, MasterCard, Switch, Visa   DETAILS: 60 seats. 36 seats outside. Private parties: 40 main room. Car park. Vegetarian meals. No smoking. Wheelchair access (not WC). No music. No mobile phones (£5)

HENLEY-IN-ARDEN Warwickshire   map 5

Edmunds ✸✶

64 High Street, Henley-in-Arden B95 5BX   COOKING 5
TEL/FAX: (01564) 795666   MODERN BRITISH
                                                               £28–£42

Within easy reach of the M40 and with a rail link to Birmingham, Henley is an attractive dormitory town of linear construction. At its centre is Andy and Beverley Waters' Grade II listed sixteenth-century cottage restaurant. Steeply roofed and timbered, it has been knocked through within to create a spacious jumble of rooms decorated in smart country style, with flowers in abundance.

The cooking is very much in the modern British mould, with some artful combinations of ingredients wedded to deft technique. Reporters wax lyrical about dishes such as Thai-spiced prawn risotto, or 'beautifully sweet and tender' herb-crusted rack of Cornish lamb with an infusion of tomato and basil. Simple starters like glazed goats' cheese with grilled asparagus and a herb salad dressed in aged balsamic elicit the same degree of enthusiasm as the more complex main courses, which might include braised belly pork on cabbage confit with caramelised apples and sage. Timing of both meats and fish is impressively precise, and the show-stopping desserts have their followers too. Valrhona chocolate tart with raspberry cream was the star at a late-summer dinner, while crème brûlée with a compote of rhubarb and strawberries, garnished with almond tuiles, has also received approval. Service is young, friendly and full of cheer. The relatively modest wine list includes house wines from France (£10.95) and Chile (£11.50).

CHEF: Andy Waters   PROPRIETORS: Andy and Beverley Waters   OPEN: Tue to Fri L 12 to 1.45, Tue to Sat D 7 to 9.45   CLOSED: 1 week May, 1 week Aug, 1 week Sept, 1 week Nov, 1 week Dec MEALS: Set L £12 (2 courses) to £24.50, Set D £22.50 (2 courses) to £24.50   SERVICE: not inc, card slips closed, 10% for parties of 6 or more   CARDS: Delta, MasterCard, Switch, Visa   DETAILS: 44 seats. Vegetarian meals. Children's helpings. No smoking. Wheelchair access (not WC). Music (£5)

HEREFORD Herefordshire   map 5

▲ Castle House, La Rive ♟ ✸✶

Castle Street, Hereford HR1 2EE
TEL: (01432) 356321   FAX: (01432) 365909   COOKING 7
EMAIL: info@castlehse.co.uk   ANGLO-FRENCH
WEBSITE: www.castlehse.co.uk   £33–£64

With this edition, Castle House clocks up five years waving the flag for fine food in Hereford. Indeed the Heijns have made such an impact locally (their nearby 'Left Bank Village' combines restaurant, tapas bar, deli, wine cellar, flower shop, ice cream parlour, coffee house and more) that they have been granted the Freedom of the City. Castle House itself is a swanky hotel, yellow inside and out, with a slightly formal but well-kept dining room. The watery setting is a plus in fine weather, and lunch is considered 'ridiculously good value for money'.

The cooking is characterised by fine materials and evident skills, and the wordy menu is sprinkled with emulsions, jellies and pickles that appear as blobs, snippets and trickles ('dainty' and 'fussy' is how it can seem). But the workmanship is undeniably first-class, taking in for example an upmarket faggot – a sticky ball of braised oxtail spiked with truffle – resting on a disc of lightly crunchy celeriac, surrounded by a port sauce and tiny dice of root vegetables. Some items that get star billing on the menu may take only a minor role on the plate, although that does not diminish the impact of the food itself. A thick chunk of well hung and flavourful Hereford beef fillet, cooked rare, comes with a 'compression' of grated carrot and cheese, but sadly no obvious sign of the advertised roast sweetbread and braised tongue at inspection. Fish is equally well handled, judging by a fine piece of well-crusted Scottish halibut ('fresh as a daisy') centre stage, with a skinless lobster 'sausage', some artichoke purée, a smear of intense shellfish sauce (referred to as a 'casserole' on the menu), and a few dabs of lemon foam.

Desserts typically include a 'study' of some sort, in one case a refreshing citrus version incorporating a tiny, properly risen hot soufflé, a mound of ice cream, a blob of sorbet, and a circular tower of jelly atop a mousse. Chocolate has featured as a deeply flavoured fondant, with a white chocolate parfait and a dark chocolate ice cream. Service is well paced and friendly, and traditional France is the main concern of the wine list, with Bordeaux in particular enthusiastically launching into three-figure prices. Knowledgeable dabbling around the world satisfies all palates, but with a budget of £20 it is best to stick to the six house wines at £16.95.

CHEF: Stuart McLeod   PROPRIETORS: Dr and Mrs A. Heijn   OPEN: all week 12.30 to 1.30, 7 to 10 MEALS: Set L £18.95, Set D £36.95   SERVICE: not inc   CARDS: Amex, Delta, Diners, MasterCard, Switch, Visa   DETAILS: 32 seats. 50 seats outside. Private parties: 82 main room. Car park. Vegetarian meals. Children's helpings. No smoking. Wheelchair access (also WC). Music. Air-conditioned   ACCOMMODATION: 15 rooms, all with bath/shower. TV. Phone. B&B £95 to £250. Rooms for disabled. Baby facilities (*The Which? Guide to Good Hotels*)

HETTON North Yorkshire   map 8

▲ Angel Inn ✳ ▼

Hetton BD23 6LT
TEL: (01756) 730263   FAX: (01756) 730363
EMAIL: info@angelhetton.co.uk
WEBSITE: www.angelhetton.co.uk
off B6265, 5m N of Skipton

COOKING 5
MODERN BRITISH
£30–£57

The reputation of this 'gentrified country pub' spreads far beyond its immediate locale, a tiny village just outside Skipton – so book a table in the dining room or join the queues for a table in the bar. The latter offers an upmarket take on pub grub, with a regular menu offering the likes of roast breast of Goosnargh duckling on braised red cabbage with Agen prunes and red wine sauce, along with blackboard specials such as poached smoked haddock with spinach, slow-roast tomatoes and hollandaise.

Cooking in the dining room is only slightly more refined (some dishes appear on both menus), with starters taking in terrine of duck confit with a port reduction, or rustic fish soup with aïoli, followed by pan-seared sea bass on a crisp olive and tomato tart with salsa verde, or roast chump of lamb with thyme mash and confit vegetables. Desserts are sophisticated updates of nursery favourites like steamed ginger sponge with rhubarb and an orange and juniper compote. Service is generally well organised and friendly. The wine list is definitely more restaurant than pub, with top drops from Italy, Burgundy and Bordeaux looming largest but at fair prices. House wines are £11.95 to £19.70, with 15 by the glass for £2.15 to £3.75. Like its sibling establishment, the General Tarleton at Ferrensby (see entry), the Angel now offers guest accommodation.

CHEFS: Denis Watkins and Bruce Elsworth PROPRIETORS: Denis and Juliet Watkins OPEN: Sun L 12 to 2, Mon to Sat D 6 to 9 (9.30 Fri and Sat) CLOSED: 25 Dec, 1 week Jan MEALS: alc Mon to Fri D (main courses £11.50 to £18). Set L £21.50, Set D Mon to Fri 6 to 7 £16.50 (2 courses, inc wine), Set D Sat £32.50. Bar menu available SERVICE: not inc, card slips closed CARDS: Amex, MasterCard, Switch, Visa DETAILS: 56 seats. 40 seats outside. Private parties: 40 main room, 30 to 40 private rooms. Car park. Vegetarian meals. Children's helpings. No smoking in 1 dining room. Wheelchair access (not WC). No music. Air-conditioned ACCOMMODATION: 5 rooms, all with bath/shower. TV. B&B £105 to £150. Rooms for disabled

HINDON Wiltshire   map 2

▲ Angel Inn 🍴

Angel Lane, Hindon SP3 6DJ	COOKING 3
TEL: (01747) 820696 FAX: (01747) 820869	MODERN EUROPEAN
	£29–£49

The Angel Inn 'is rapidly making a name for itself in this rural outback', according to one fan. A B&B-cum-pub, it has 'comfortable but spare' rooms and an inviting long, narrow dining room, where the emphasis is on good food. In charge of the stoves is Matthew Laughton, whose extensive and eclectic menu features a number of Mediterranean influences that complement modern British dishes such as slow-roast shank of lamb on bubble and squeak with a Madeira jus, or pan-fried calf's liver with leek mash and crispy bacon. A hot crab galette met with approval, while other starters might be equally tempting: grilled sardines with black olives and tomatoes, or a salad of prosciutto with peppered mozzarella, rocket and a pomegranate dressing. Puddings range from crème brûlée to plums poached in balsamic syrup. The wine list is strong in the southern hemisphere but favours France, kicking off with vins de pays at £11.

CHEF: Matthew Laughton PROPRIETORS: Penny Simpson, Bill Laret and Jeff Fergus OPEN: all week L 12 to 2, Mon to Sat D 7 to 9 CLOSED: 26 Dec, 2 Jan MEALS: alc (main courses £7 to £14) SERVICE: not inc CARDS: Delta, MasterCard, Switch, Visa DETAILS: 52 seats. 36 seats outside. Private parties: 14 main room, 8 to 14 private rooms. Car park. Vegetarian meals. No smoking. Wheelchair access (not WC). No music ACCOMMODATION: 7 rooms, all with bath/shower. TV. Phone. B&B £45 to £95 (£5)

All entries, including Round-ups, are fully indexed at the back of the Guide.

▲ Homewood Park ⁵⁄⁴✳

Hinton Charterhouse BA2 7TB
TEL: (01225) 723731   FAX: (01225) 723820
EMAIL: res@homewoodpark.com   COOKING **5**
WEBSITE: www.homewoodpark.com   MODERN ENGLISH
off A36, 6m SE of Bath   £35–£69

Homewood is 'a very comfortable, well-maintained country-house hotel' a few miles outside Bath. A huge entrance hall and a pair of bay-windowed dining rooms are decorated in restrained chintz, and the views over the grounds make a tranquil backdrop for new chef Jean de la Rouzière's sure-footed, confident cooking. A lightness of touch distinguishes most dishes, so that nothing appears over-treated, and the seasonings lift the main ingredients rather than overshadow them.

That was certainly the case with an inspector's first course of seared Skye scallops, which were cleverly but delicately crusted with polenta and served on creamed celeriac and topped with crisp 'wafers' of Parma ham. More mainstream ideas might include fish soup with rouille, or a game and foie gras terrine with walnut vinaigrette. Star of the show among main courses one spring evening was rack of Wiltshire lamb of miraculous tenderness, accompanied by baked aubergine, garlic-marinated tomato, and apricot and raisin couscous. A generous serving of veal cutlet has been been partnered with girolles and creamed cabbage flavoured with caraway. A pre-dessert (such as intensely sweet apple sorbet) heralds the arrival of the real thing, which may be a texturally delightful espresso parfait studded with hazelnut and pecan nougatine, with a tangy crème anglaise scented with bergamot and whisky. Cheeses could do with a bit more looking after, but incidentals all come up to the mark. Service works hard to ensure all runs smoothly. The wine list leads with a roll call of French classics at uncomfortable prices, with more cursory selections from elsewhere, though there is just enough from the southern hemisphere to provide real choice. Four house wines (three French and one Chilean) are £17.

CHEF: Jean de la Rouzière   PROPRIETOR: Alan Moxon   OPEN: all week 12 to 2, 7 to 9.30   MEALS: Set L £19.50, Set D £39.50   SERVICE: not inc, card slips closed   CARDS: Amex, Delta, Diners, MasterCard, Switch, Visa   DETAILS: 85 seats. Private parties: 85 main room, 20 to 40 private rooms. Car park. Vegetarian meals. Children's helpings. No smoking. Wheelchair access (also WC). No music. No mobile phones   ACCOMMODATION: 19 rooms, all with bath/shower. TV. Phone. B&B £115 to £265. Rooms for disabled. Baby facilities. Swimming pool (*The Which? Guide to Good Hotels*)

The text of entries is based on unsolicited reports sent in by readers, backed up by inspections conducted anonymously. The factual details under the text are from questionnaires the Guide sends to all restaurants that feature in the book.

To find a restaurant in a particular area use the maps at the centre of the book.

HOLKHAM Norfolk   map 6

▲ Victoria 🍴

Park Road, Holkham NR23 1RG
TEL: (01328) 711008   FAX: (01328) 711009
EMAIL: victoria@holkham.co.uk
WEBSITE: www.victoriaatholkham.co.uk

COOKING 3
MODERN EUROPEAN
£28–£55

The Victoria is on the main coast road, on the edge of the huge estate owned by
Earls of Leicester since the eighteenth century, which includes Holkham Hall, a
deer park, almshouses and more besides. The brick and flint building is solid
and forceful-looking, which doesn't quite prepare one for the rather exotic
interior. Much of the furniture comes from Rajasthan; there is carving
everywhere, from the doors separating the lounge and the main dining room to
open stone partitions. Paintings of various styles abound on the walls. Since last
year a new chef has been brought on board, but the style of cooking hasn't
significantly changed. The raw materials are good and timings are as accurate for
vegetables as they are for fish and meat. Ideas, too, are generally well conceived.
A starter of seared scallops (perched atop raita) may be accompanied by
cauliflower purée and a contrasting spiced oil. The quality of meat in a main
course of new season's lamb with Jersey Royals, broad beans and tomato
impressed an inspector. A dessert of poached white peach with raspberries,
organic frozen yoghurt and a honey tuile may be served in a neat little tower,
offset by a sharp apricot coulis. The Victoria is a popular place that can get busy,
but staff are plentiful. A well-chosen wine list is organised by style, with prices
starting at £12.50.

CHEF: Neil Dawson   PROPRIETOR: Viscount Coke   OPEN: all week 12 to 2.30 (3 Sat and Sun), 7 to
9.30 (10 Fri and Sat)   MEALS: alc (main courses L £6 to £16, D £11 to £17)   SERVICE: not inc
CARDS: Delta, MasterCard, Switch, Visa   DETAILS: 60 seats. 100 seats outside. Private parties:
40 main room, 10 to 20 private rooms. Car park. Vegetarian meals. Children's helpings. No
smoking in 1 dining room. Wheelchair access (also women's WC). Music   ACCOMMODATION: 11
rooms, all with bath/shower. TV. Phone. B&B Sun to Thur £140, Fri and Sat £170. Rooms for
disabled. Baby facilities (The Which? Guide to Good Hotels)

HOLT Norfolk   map 6

Yetman's ❢

37 Norwich Road, Holt NR25 6SA
TEL: (01263) 713320
WEBSITE: www.yetmans.net

COOKING 5
MODERN BRITISH
£48–£64

This small, attractive house on the main road that skirts the village has a tiny
lounge, and two small dining rooms where yellow and grey predominate; space
is not wasted, yet it feels comfortable. This isn't a formal restaurant – Mr
Yetman's determinedly laid-back manner makes him 'an unusual host' – but
there is nothing slack about either service or food.

Alison Yetman's fresh and appealing modern cooking produces a tart of local
asparagus and Gruyère, or cockles poached in white wine with olive oil, chilli,
garlic and pasta. And you get what it says on the menu, without distraction:
perhaps a starter combining grilled aubergine (not bitter), globe artichokes

(very fresh), flavoursome tomatoes, marinated red and yellow peppers, and ewe's milk cheese; or duck breast (cooked medium-well, as requested by a nine-year-old) with spiced blackberries. And, given the local input, it is no surprise that the seasons are properly observed: in April, for example, wild sea trout with asparagus, then rhubarb and ginger bombe. Alternatively, perhaps, toasted cinnamon and apple pancakes, or the River Café's chocolate Nemesis with Seville orange curd.

When it comes to assembling a wine list, the Yetmans have rewritten the rules: no house wines, no ponderous pages of classic regions, in fact virtually nothing from France – just three dozen fairly priced 'wines that we like drinking' presented with meaningful tasting notes. New World Sauvignon Blancs are a particular favourite. Daily menus carry a selection of six wines by the glass (from £4.25) at the bottom.

CHEF: Alison Yetman   PROPRIETORS: Alison and Peter Yetman   OPEN: Sun L 12.30 to 2, Wed to Sat D 7 to 9.30 (Wed to Sun at bank hols and late Jul to end-Aug)   CLOSED: 25 to 31 Dec, 3 weeks Oct/Nov   MEALS: Set L Sun £26.50 (2 courses) to £36.75, Set D £26.50 (2 courses) to £36.75   SERVICE: not inc   CARDS: Amex, Delta, MasterCard, Switch, Visa   DETAILS: 32 seats. Private parties: 20 main room. Vegetarian meals. Wheelchair access (not WC), No music

HOLY CROSS Worcestershire   map 5

Bell & Cross ⁙ £

Holy Cross DY9 9QL   COOKING 1
TEL: (01562) 730319   FAX: (01562) 730733   MODERN EUROPEAN
off A491, SE of West Hagley   £26–£52

The Bell & Cross is a listed building (or an old pub, if you prefer) at the foot of the Clent Hills. Its owners are Roger and Jo Narbett; Roger is in charge of the kitchen, while Jo looks after front-of-house. Roger, incidentally, is the official chef of the England football team, so when he's away Paul Mohan mans the stoves. The Narbetts describe their style of cooking as 'modern, satisfying fare'. The menu tends toward the traditional, such as sautéed lambs' kidneys to start, with main courses of chargrilled Cotswolds lamb cutlets with black pudding, balsamic onions and port sauce, or pot-roast chicken breast with Savoy cabbage, peas and spicy sausage. A few trendier ideas make appearances, among them starters of Peking crispy duck salad, or mozzarella wrapped in Parma ham with smoked tomato chutney, and a main course of grilled fillet of sea bass with asparagus and saffron risotto and red pepper sauce, although it's back to comfort food at the pudding course, with the likes of treacle tart, and tarte Tatin with butterscotch sauce and Calvados crème fraîche. The wine list is short but well chosen, with house wines, from Chile, at £10.50.

CHEFS: Roger Narbett and Paul Mohan   PROPRIETORS: Roger and Jo Narbett   OPEN: all week L 12 to 2 (2.30 Sun), Mon to Sat D 6.30 to 9.15 (9.30 Fri and Sat)   MEALS: alc (main courses £9.50 to £16)   SERVICE: not inc, card slips closed   CARDS: MasterCard, Switch, Visa   DETAILS: 64 seats. 50 seats outside. Private parties: 28 main room, 14 to 28 private rooms. Car park. Vegetarian meals. Children's helpings. No smoking in 1 dining room. Wheelchair access (not WC). Music

Dining rooms where music, either live or recorded, is never played are signalled by No music in the details at the end of an entry.

HONLEY West Yorkshire   map 8

Mustard & Punch ▼ £

6 Westgate, Honley HD9 6AA
TEL: (01484) 662066   FAX: (01484) 660742

COOKING 4
ANGLO-FRENCH
£20–£50

On the main street in Honley is a restaurant whose décor and menu would be at home in smarter cosmopolitan surroundings. The imaginative menu might offer deep-fried Brie with oven-dried black figs, or pot-roast pork cheeks with Parmesan gnocchi and crackling. Main courses have some equally robust dishes, such as pot-roast honey-glazed pork shank with pancetta and baby onions, or roast rump of lamb with a fricassee of kidneys. The kitchen's ability to use good local ingredients imaginatively shows up in a trio of Yorkshire game – a small pastry case of pheasant, hare terrine, and sliced pigeon – which one visitor described as 'magnificent'. Fish lovers are not neglected, with the likes of pan-roast fillet of turbot with crayfish, girolles and a tomato and chive velouté, or grilled fillet of sea bass with five-spice and oriental vegetables. Desserts, too, show a kitchen that is innovative: a warm chocolate brownie is accompanied by vanilla clotted cream and cherry syrup, and espresso- and Armagnac-soaked Agen prune brûlée comes with acacia flower ice cream. Although service can seem inexperienced, it is enthusiastic. As for wines, one reporter has been so impressed with the Puglian house red at just £9.75 that he has ordered it on every visit. But the global list has plenty more good-value wines, and six come by the glass for £1.95 to £3.10. As the Guide went to press Chris Dunn, co-chef and co-proprietor with his brother Rick, sold his interest in the business, leaving Rick as the sole chef-patron.

CHEF/PROPRIETOR: Rick Dunn   OPEN: Mon to Fri L 12 to 2, Mon to Sat D 7 (6 Fri and Sat) to 10   MEALS: alc (main courses £8 to £16). Set L £10.50 (2 courses) to £13.50, Set D Mon to Thur £17.95 (2 courses) to £21.95 (inc wine)   SERVICE: not inc   CARDS: Amex, Delta, MasterCard, Switch, Visa   DETAILS: 63 seats. Private parties: 30 main room, 10 to 30 private rooms. Vegetarian meals. Wheelchair access (also WC). Music. Air-conditioned £5

HORNBY Lancashire   map 8

▲ Paul Reed's Dining Room, Castle Hotel ✺

NEW ENTRY

High Street, Hornby LA2 8JT
TEL: (015242) 21204   FAX: (015242) 22258
EMAIL: information@diningroomhornby.co.uk
WEBSITE: www.thecastlehotel.net
on A683 NE of Lancaster

COOKING 5
MODERN BRITISH-PLUS
£31–£71

Though situated in a small village outside Lancaster, the Castle is 'rather more than a village inn', oozing luxury and grandeur in its beamed dining room, with starched linen and vases of flowers on the tables. Paul Reed cooks in a modern British style that encompasses wider European and Asian influences. Dishes can be as simple as a goats' cheese fritter with wild mushroom salad and walnut pesto, or as complex as ballottine of rabbit saddle with foie gras, sweet fig and pear jam and rosemary brioche, while ambitious main courses have included thyme-marinated tuna steak with exotic fruit and green peppercorn salsa, red chard, herb salad and a coconut and lemongrass velouté, and roast pancetta-wrapped wood pigeon on a sweet beetroot risotto set off with a liquorice-infused jus. To finish, lemon tart comes with 'mouthwatering' elderflower ice cream and 'tangy' blackberry jam. Roughly half the wine list is given over to France, half to the rest of the world. Quality is generally high, but a few cheaper wines would be welcome – prices start at £22 for a Canadian Pinot Blanc.

The Castle Barns bar, in a converted outbuilding, offers a more informal mode of dining at lunch and dinner, with hearty, rustic cooking by the same kitchen team. Expect the likes of liver, mash and onion gravy, braised lamb shoulder with cabbage and bacon, and deep-fried cod with thin chips and mushy peas.

CHEFS: Paul Reed and Lee Stainthorpe   PROPRIETOR: Sean Collidge   OPEN: Sun L 12.30 to 2.30, Wed to Sat D 7 to 9.30   MEALS: Set L £15, Set D £39.95   SERVICE: 10%, card slips closed   CARDS: Diners, MasterCard, Switch, Visa   DETAILS: 50 seats. 16 seats outside. Private parties: 80 main room, 2 to 60 private rooms. Car park. Vegetarian meals. Children's helpings. No smoking. Wheelchair access (also WC). Music   ACCOMMODATION: 12 rooms, all with bath/shower. TV. Phone. B&B £80 to £140 (double room) £5

HORNCASTLE Lincolnshire   map 9

Magpies ✳

71–75 East Street, Horncastle LN9 6AA   COOKING 2
TEL: (01507) 527004   MODERN BRITISH
                                                                      £19–£41

'A delightful family-run establishment with a good ambience', judged one visitor to Magpies. Recent refurbishment has transformed the black and white exterior: now, cream stucco walls are set off by Caribbean-blue and white window frames. In the low-ceilinged interior pale lemon walls display framed modern prints, and white damask cloths add a touch of class. At inspection, frothy mushroom soup with truffle oil had a smooth, light consistency, and though a dish of mussels with white wine sauce pleased less, a main course of roast cod with smoked salmon and chive velouté demonstrated good-quality ingredients and a fine sauce. Suprême of 'perfectly roasted' guinea fowl with thyme jus, or pot-roasted belly pork with honey and cloves, could be other main-course contenders. The line-up for dessert might include prune and Armagnac sundae, or lemon tart. Lunch is good value, and house wine is sensibly priced at £12.

CHEF: Matthew Lee   PROPRIETORS: the Lee family   OPEN: Tue to Fri L 12.30 to 2, Tue to Sat D 7 to 10   CLOSED: Christmas, New Year   MEALS: Set L £8.50 (2 courses) to £9.95, Set D £24   SERVICE: not inc   CARDS: Delta, MasterCard, Switch, Visa   DETAILS: 40 seats. Private parties: 40 main room. Vegetarian meals. No smoking . Music. Air-conditioned

---

🍲 indicates that there has been a change of chef since last year's Guide, and the Editor has judged that the change is of sufficient interest to merit the reader's attention.

HORNDON ON THE HILL Essex   map 3

▲ Bell Inn ⅜✳

High Road, Horndon on the Hill SS17 8LD
TEL: (01375) 642463   FAX: (01375) 361611   COOKING **2**
EMAIL: info@bell-inn.co.uk   MODERN EUROPEAN
WEBSITE: www.bell-inn.co.uk   £25–£46

Set at the centre of a pretty village, the front of this ancient inn, with its well-tended hanging baskets, creates a good first impression, while inside it really looks the part of the 'olde worlde' country pub. Eat from a short simple bar menu that lists the likes of smoked haddock fishcakes with basil or grilled cod fillet with white beans and watercress, plus a selection of interesting sandwiches at lunchtime, or book a table in the restaurant. Here, the blackboard menu offers varied modern European cooking with starters ranging from oyster risotto with Camembert and pancetta to shrimp bisque with pork won ton and liquorice, while main courses might include poached halibut with sesame salt and cauliflower purée, grilled ribeye of beef with mustard and honey dressing, and beer-battered halibut fishcake with poached egg and truffle. Finish perhaps with lemon tart and poached figs. The wine list is fairly short but well chosen, with some smart bottles in France. Mark-ups are fair and transparent, as all bottles are also available for retail sale at sensible prices.

CHEF: Finlay Logan   PROPRIETORS: John and Christine Vereker   OPEN: all week 12 to 1.45 (2.15 Sun), 6.45 to 9.45   CLOSED: 25 and 26 Dec, bank hols   MEALS: alc (main courses £9.50 to £13.50). Set L £13.95 (2 courses) to £15.95. Bar and sandwich menu also available   SERVICE: not inc, card slips closed   CARDS: Amex, Delta, MasterCard, Switch, Visa   DETAILS: 80 seats. 36 seats outside. Private parties: 12 main room, 14 to 36 private rooms. Car park. Vegetarian meals. Children's helpings. No smoking . No music   ACCOMMODATION: 15 rooms, all with bath/shower. TV. Phone. Room only £50 to £100. Rooms for disabled. Baby facilities (*The Which? Guide to Good Hotels*)

HUDDERSFIELD West Yorkshire   map 9

Bradley's ⅜✳ £

84 Fitzwilliam Street, Huddersfield HD1 5BB   COOKING **2**
TEL: (01484) 516773   FAX: (01484) 538386   MEDITERRANEAN/MODERN BRITISH
EMAIL: andrewatbradleys-restaurant.co.uk   £15–£50

Andrew Bradley's restaurant has been a Huddersfield fixture for ten years and is going stronger than ever, judging by the busy calendar of events listed in the newsletter. The host's unremitting enthusiasm and the colourful décor combine to create a cheery bistro ambience, and there is plenty to be animated about on the food front too. The all-embracing menu offers everything from grilled Mexican chicken with peppers, gremolata and crème fraîche to ham hock terrine with Lancashire cheese and brown sauce for starters, while main courses take in seared beef fillet with slow-cooked rib and onion marmalade, and pan-fried venison with buttered greens, celeriac purée and chocolate oil, as well as plainer dishes such as grilled turbot. Finish perhaps with pear and apple pie with blackberry ice cream. The no-nonsense wine list offers plenty of choice for those with less than £15 to spend.

CHEF: Eric Paxman   PROPRIETOR: Andrew Bradley   OPEN: Mon to Fri L 12 to 2, Mon to Sat D 6 to 10 (10.30 Fri and Sat)   CLOSED: bank hols   MEALS: alc (main courses £10 to £17). Set L £5.50 (2 courses) to £7.50, Set D £15.50 (inc wine)   SERVICE: not inc   CARDS: MasterCard, Switch, Visa   DETAILS: 120 seats. Private parties: 120 main room, 20 to 60 private rooms. Car park (D only). Vegetarian meals. Children's helpings. No smoking in 1 dining room. Wheelchair access (also WC). Music. Air-conditioned

Dining Rooms at Strawberry Fair ✳ £ | NEW ENTRY |

14-18 West Gate, Huddersfield HD1 1NN
TEL: (01484) 513103   FAX: (01484) 428616
WEBSITE: www.strawberryfair.com

COOKING 2
MODERN EUROPEAN
£23–£40

Central Huddersfield needed this, and the Dining Rooms opened upstairs at 'posh crockery shop' Strawberry Fair in December 2002, are already popular; they offer breakfast, sandwiches and teas as well as serious lunches. Bare wooden floor and pale colour scheme give a cool, modern feel echoed in the regularly changing menus. To start there are salads (tomato and mozzarella, Caesar, chicken), soup, or maybe smoked salmon and scrambled eggs. Main dishes like salmon tempura with 'smoky-flavoured' tomato chutney and chunky home-made tartare sauce are approvingly reported, as is pink and tender wok-fried duck with Singapore noodles, water chestnuts, pickled pink ginger and hoi sin sauce. For the more traditional, there's local sausages with mash and onion gravy, or venison with sweetcorn rösti and cassis sauce. Desserts have included Baileys brûlée and lavender bavarois with Earl Grey and lemon syrup. Service at all times is 'helpful, polite and professional'. There are only eight wines, none above £12.50 and all available by the glass.

CHEF: Richard Greenway   PROPRIETOR: Phillip Harrison   OPEN: Mon to Sat L only 11.30 to 4.30   CLOSED: 25 Dec, 1 Jan, bank hols   MEALS: alc (main courses £7 to £11). Breakfast, sandwich and Afternoon Choice menus available   SERVICE: not inc, card slips closed   CARDS: Amex, Delta, MasterCard, Switch, Visa   DETAILS: 50 seats. Vegetarian meals. Children's helpings. No smoking. Wheelchair access (also WC). No music. No mobile phones. Air-conditioned

▲ Lodge Hotel ♥ ✳

48 Birkby Lodge Road, Birkby,
Huddersfield HD2 2BG
TEL: (01484) 431001   FAX: (01484) 421590
EMAIL: contact@birkbylodgehotel.com
WEBSITE: www.birkbylodgehotel.com

COOKING 3
MODERN EUROPEAN
£27–£52

Though new owners took over this large nineteenth-century house in early 2003, consistency from the kitchen, overseen by Richard Hanson since 1989, seems to be assured. Sound technique and unfussy presentation underpin the cooking, in perhaps a starter of roast squash cooked to a satisfying brown richness and served in a salad with prosciutto bacon and pecorino, or a main course of well-timed red snapper surrounded by a 'properly made' tomato sauce, or 'plump, moist' chicken breast with wild mushrooms, sage, smoked bacon and raisin jus. Desserts might include sticky toffee pudding, or Thai rice pudding with mango coulis. Good bread and decent coffee complete the picture, along with service that combines efficiency and warmth. The wine list gives good value and all regions are soundly represented, but it never quite hits the heights (though New Zealand reds offer unexpected excitement). Nine house wines start at £12.95 (£3.25 a glass).

CHEF: Richard Hanson PROPRIETOR: Ian Barton OPEN: Sun to Fri L 12 to 1.45, Mon to Sat D 7 to 9.45 CLOSED: 26 to 31 Dec and 26 May MEALS: alc (main courses £12.50 to £16). Set L £18.50, Set D £23.95 SERVICE: not inc, card slips closed CARDS: Amex, Delta, Diners, MasterCard, Switch, Visa DETAILS: 100 seats. Private parties: 64 main room, 8 to 22 private rooms. Car park. Vegetarian meals. Children's helpings. No smoking. Wheelchair access (also women's WC). Music. Air-conditioned ACCOMMODATION: 13 rooms, all with bath/shower. TV. Phone. Room only £40 to £55. Rooms for disabled. Baby facilities (*The Which? Guide to Good Hotels*) (£5)

Thorpe Grange Manor

Thorpe Lane, Almondbury, Huddersfield HD5 8TA
TEL: (01484) 425115 FAX: (01484) 359398
EMAIL: ron.neilson@ntlworld.com
WEBSITE: www.thorpegrangemanor.com
off A629, 3m E of Huddersfield

COOKING 3
ANGLO-FRENCH
£23–£62

Thorpe Grange is an eighteenth-century manor house set in two and a half acres of secluded grounds in the village of Almondbury, on the eastern edge of Huddersfield. Four members of the Neilson family run the show, with Jason Neilson taking care of the cooking. His is an ambitious, elaborate style, as demonstrated by a starter of guinea-fowl breast bound with caramelised apple and onion farce, wrapped in puff pastry and served on a Madeira sauce. Main courses might include suckling pig marinated in five-spice and sage, accompanied by black pudding and Madeira sauce, and roast sea bass, monkfish, langoustine and scallops in a red pepper and dill sauce, as well as simpler ideas such as beef fillet in black truffle sauce. Desserts are of the order of a white chocolate cup filled with rhubarb and strawberry compote and topped with brandy sabayon. Prices are fair and choice varied on the wine list, starting with six house selections at £11.50 and £12.50.

CHEF: Jason Neilson PROPRIETORS: Ronald, Gillian, Jason and Ruth Neilson OPEN: all week 12 to 1.45, 6 (7 Fri and Sat) to 9 MEALS: alc (main courses £14.50 to £22.50). Set L Mon to Sat £12.50 (2 courses) to £14.95, Set L Sun £14.95, D 6 to 7.30 £15.50, Set D £19.95 SERVICE: not inc CARDS: Delta, MasterCard, Switch, Visa DETAILS: 60 seats. 20 seats outside. Private parties: 40 to 50 private rooms. Car park. Vegetarian meals. Children's helpings. No children under 5 after 7.30pm Sat. No cigars/pipes. Wheelchair access (also WC). Music. Air-conditioned (£5)

£ *means that it is possible to have a three-course meal, including coffee, half a bottle of house wine and service for £30 or less per person, at any time the restaurant is open, i.e. at dinner as well as lunch. It may be possible to spend considerably more than this, but by choosing carefully you should find £30 or less achievable.*

▲ Hunstrete House, Terrace Restaurant ▯

Hunstrete, Pensford BS39 4NS
TEL: (01761) 490490   FAX: (01761) 490732
EMAIL: info@hunstretehouse.co.uk   COOKING 4
WEBSITE: www.hunstretehouse.co.uk   MODERN BRITISH
off A368, 7m W of Bath   £31–£66

In pastoral surroundings off the Bath to Wells road, a comfortable house of
mellow golden stone sits in grounds from which fallow deer can peer into the
Library. It has a choice of lounges and a wisteria-draped terrace for sitting, as
well as a dining room with tasselled curtains and pilasters. The walled kitchen
garden has been redesigned to provide Philip Hobson with even more fresh
fruits, vegetables and herbs (not to mention flowers for table settings). The
cooking style tends to gentle opulence, fitting in with the surroundings, so that a
package of langoustine and tomato comes wrapped in filo and with a citrus
dressing, sea bass is accompanied by buttery pasta, and roast beef fillet sits on
aubergine purée and is served with glazed baby onions and a Madeira jus. A
November dinner left one pair with happy memories of tenderly pink and
succulent venison, and of a generous portion of white chocolate crème brûlée.
Other desserts are equally comforting: a blueberry muffin, promoted from the
breakfast table, is imaginatively teamed with lemon curd ice cream. Service is
generally attentive and professional.

The substantial wine list majors on Bordeaux and Burgundy but delivers a
exciting mix of highly rated and good-value wines (Canet-Valette St-Chinian
for £25.50 is both) in short selections from the south of France and the New
World. Five house wines start at £15.95, or £3.75 for a glass.

CHEF: Philip Hobson   PROPRIETOR: Culloden House Associates   OPEN: all week L 12 to 2, Tue to
Sat D (all week, April to Oct) 7 to 9.30   MEALS: alc D (main courses £22.50 to £25). Set L £15.95 (2
courses) to £19.95   SERVICE: not inc, card slips closed   CARDS: Amex, Diners, MasterCard,
Switch, Visa   DETAILS: 50 seats. 16 seats outside. Private parties: 50 main room, 12 to 40 private
rooms. Car park. Vegetarian meals. Children's helpings. No smoking. Wheelchair access (not
WC). No music. No mobile phones   ACCOMMODATION: 25 rooms, all with bath/shower. TV.
Phone. B&B £135 to £350. Rooms for disabled. Baby facilities. Swimming pool (May to Oct) (The
Which? Guide to Good Hotels) £5

▲ Old Bridge Hotel ▮ ✳

1 High Street, Huntingdon PE29 3TQ
TEL: (01480) 424300   FAX: (01480) 411017   COOKING 4
EMAIL: oldbridge@huntsbridge.co.uk   MODERN BRITISH
WEBSITE: www.huntsbridge.co.uk   £26–£58

The building once housed a bank and retains that solid, worthy-looking
appearance in its manifestation as part of the Huntsbridge group (see entries in
Fotheringhay, Keyston and Madingley). Gain admittance around the back,
where a trim, tree-shaded garden leads down to the Great Ouse. There are two
eating areas, the Terrace and the Dining Room, with plans afoot for a major

refurbishment of the latter in the summer of 2003. The usual division of simpler cooking in one and grander in the other doesn't apply here, though: Martin Lee cooks the same menu for both.

Expect fresh, seasonal food of considerable panache and bold flavours. Scallops are seared and served with roasted artichoke and vegetables à la grecque, and black pudding appears as a starter with mashed potato, caramelised apple and red wine sauce. Simple salads come in three sizes (as a side dish, starter or main), but the more robust appetite is well catered for by the likes of squab pigeon with juniper, rosemary and butternut squash, or baked hake fillet with spiced couscous. Both seasoning and timing are accorded due consideration, and most dishes seem to deliver what they promise. Desserts contribute to the feeling of being looked after, with Valrhona chocolate fondant and Jersey cream among the runners, but the enterprising approach also finds room for something like carrot and cardamom pancakes with Cape gooseberry compote and vanilla ice cream. Good cheeses and coffee, as well as efficient service, complete the picture.

The wine list has been put together with something like evangelical glee. You like it by the glass? Here are 13 innovative choices from £2.95 to £6. Staying under £20? Choose from around 40 wines arranged by style. Splashing out? Then dive into the 'top-class' list of famous, rare and offbeat bottles. Mark-ups are geared to favour the more expensive wines.

CHEF: Martin Lee   PROPRIETORS: John Hoskins, and Martin and Jayne Lee   OPEN: all week 12 to 2.30, 6.30 to 10   MEALS: alc (main courses £9 to £19.50). Set L Mon to Sat and Set D Sun to Fri 6.30 to 7.30 £12 (2 courses) to £15.50   SERVICE: not inc   CARDS: Amex, Diners, MasterCard, Switch, Visa   DETAILS: 100 seats. 25 seats outside. Private parties: 90 main room, 5 to 50 private rooms. Car park. Vegetarian meals. Children's helpings. No smoking in 1 dining room. Wheelchair access (not WC). No music. No mobile phones. Air-conditioned   ACCOMMODATION: 23 rooms, all with bath/shower. TV. Phone. B&B £90 to £180. Baby facilities. Fishing

ILKLEY West Yorkshire
map 8

Farsyde ✱ £

1–3 Brook Street, Ilkley LS29 8DQ   COOKING 4
TEL: (01943) 602030   FAX: (01943) 602030   MODERN BRITISH
WEBSITE: www.thefarsyde.com   £19–£40

Farsyde moved premises within Ilkley as the Guide went to press. The new restaurant will be bigger, we know that, and will be non-smoking (smokers can repair to the bar area), but not much more as far as its appearance goes. The food, however, remains the same. The lunchtime menu satisfies a range of appetites economically with bagels and sandwiches from as little as £2, while the rest of the menu offers appetisers like salad niçoise, pasta, and risotto – in one instance a creamy mushroom and chorizo version, topped with crispy bacon and fried parsnip shavings, which had well-balanced flavours and bite. Main courses might include ribeye steak served on black pudding with caramelised apple, roast shallots, rocket leaf and Parmesan dressing, or a successful assembly of moist chicken breast atop a salad including warm livers. Raspberry brûlée, akin to a scented cheesecake adorned with small curly brandy-snaps, may be a good choice for pudding; another could be a generous but light slab of Bakewell tart. Fish night has been a fixture for Wednesdays. Service is friendly and

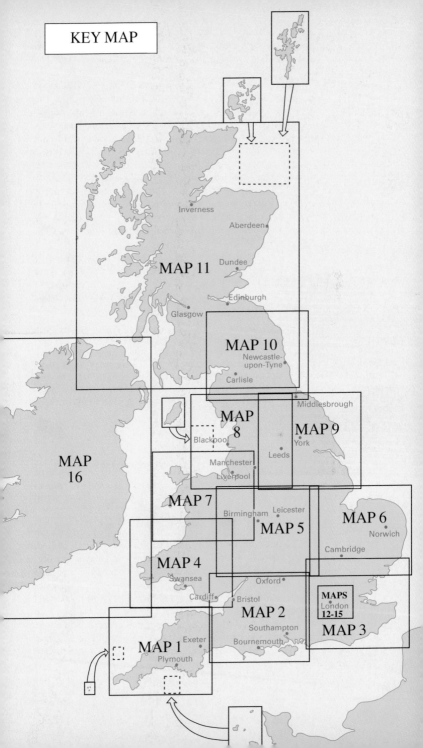

KEY MAP

MAP 16

MAP 11

Inverness
Aberdeen
Dundee
Edinburgh
Glasgow

MAP 10

Newcastle-upon-Tyne
Carlisle

Middlesbrough

MAP 8

MAP 9

Blackpool
York
Manchester
Leeds
Liverpool

MAP 7

Birmingham
Leicester

MAP 5

MAP 6

Norwich

Cambridge

MAP 4

Swansea
Oxford
Cardiff
Bristol

MAPS
London
12-15

MAP 2

MAP 3

Southampton
Bournemouth

MAP 1

Exeter
Plymouth

MAP 1

■ Restaurant
▲ Restaurant with accommodation
○ *Round-up entry*
□ Combined main and
△ round-up entries

0   5   10 miles
0   15 kms
© Copyright

Isles of Scilly
28 miles WSW of Land's End

New
Grimsby ● ▲ St Martin's
○ *Tresco*

Hugh Town ●

Lundy Island

*Bude
Bay*

*Port Isaac
Bay*

Bodm

▲ Padstow
St Merryn ■ Wadebridge
Bodmin
Coll

Watergate Bay

Newquay C O R N W A L

A392

Ligger Bay A30

A39
St Austell ▲ Fowey

St Austell Ba

Portreath ■ A390 □ Truro

St Ives □ *St Ives
Bay* Portloe ○

Treen ○ A30 *Veryan
Bay*

St Just ● St Mawes ▲ ▲ Portscatho

△ Penzance A394 *Constantine* Falmouth

▲ Lamorna Cove Porthleven ■ ■ Helston *Falmouth
Bay*

Lands *Mount's* ○ *Mawgan* ○ *Gillan*

End *Bay*

Lizard Point

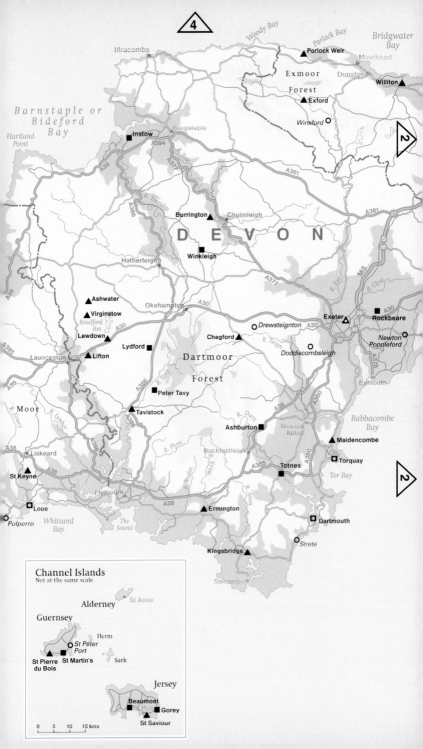

MAP 2

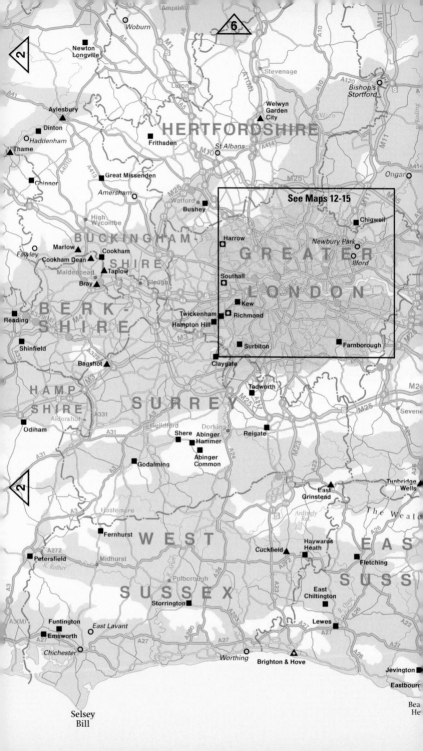

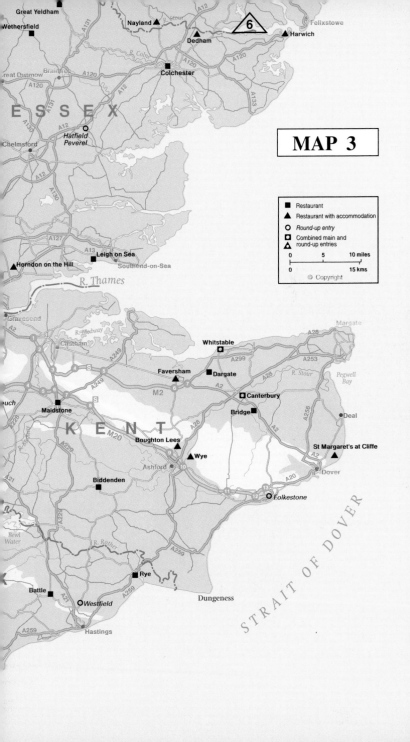

MAP 3

Great Yeldham
Wethersfield
Nayland
Dedham
Felixstowe
Harwich
6
R. Colne
R. Stour
Great Dunmow
Braintree
A120
A120
Colchester
A12
A131
A130
A12
A120
A133
E S S E X
Hatfield Peverel
Chelmsford
A12
A130
A127
A13
Leigh on Sea
Southend-on-Sea
Horndon on the Hill
R. Thames

■ Restaurant
▲ Restaurant with accommodation
○ *Round-up entry*
◧ Combined main and
△ round-up entries

0   5   10 miles
0   15 kms
© Copyright

Gravesend
Margate
A2
R. Medway
Chatham
A228
A253
A299
R. Stour
Whitstable
Pegwell Bay
Faversham
Dargate
A240
A2
M2
Canterbury
A256
Maidstone
K E N T
M20
Bridge
Deal
A28
A2
Boughton Lees
A28
St Margaret's at Cliffe
A2
A229
Wye
A20
A21
Ashford
Dover
Biddenden
Folkestone
A299
Bewl Water
R. Rother
A259
Battle
Rye
STRAIT OF DOVER
Westfield
Dungeness
A259
Hastings
A21

MAP 4

- ■ Restaurant
- ▲ Restaurant with accommodation
- ○ *Round-up entry*
- ☐ Combined main and
- △ round-up entries

0   5   10 miles

0   15 kms

© Copyright

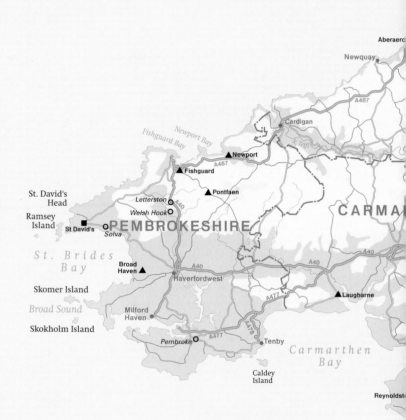

C A R D I G A N

B A Y

Aberaerc

Newquay

A487

Cardigan

Fishguard Bay   *Newport Bay*

▲ Newport

▲ Fishguard

A487

St. David's
Head

▲ Pontfaen

Letterston ○ *A40*

Ramsey
Island

Welsh Hook ○

■ St David's ○ **PEMBROKESHIRE**

Solva

CARMA

A40

*St. Brides
Bay*

Broad
Haven ▲

A40

Haverfordwest

Skomer Island

A477

▲ Laugharne

Broad Sound

Milford
Haven

Skokholm Island

A477

Pembroke ○

A478

Tenby

*Carmarthen
Bay*

Caldey
Island

Reynoldst

B R I S T O L

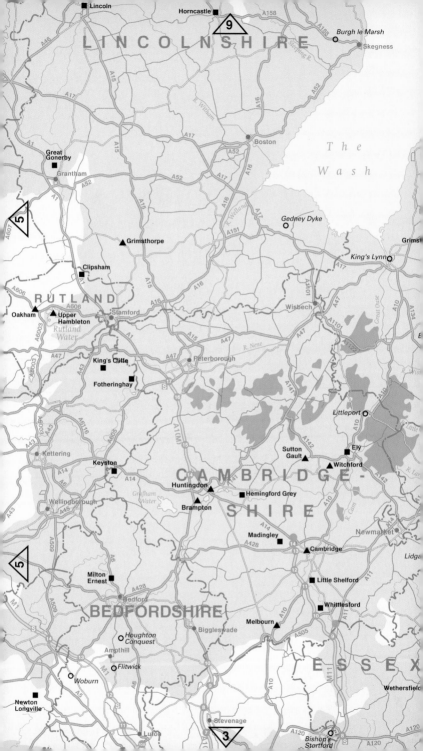

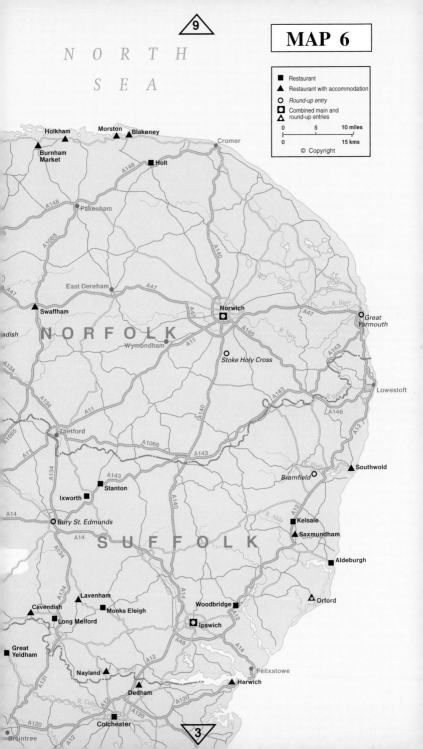

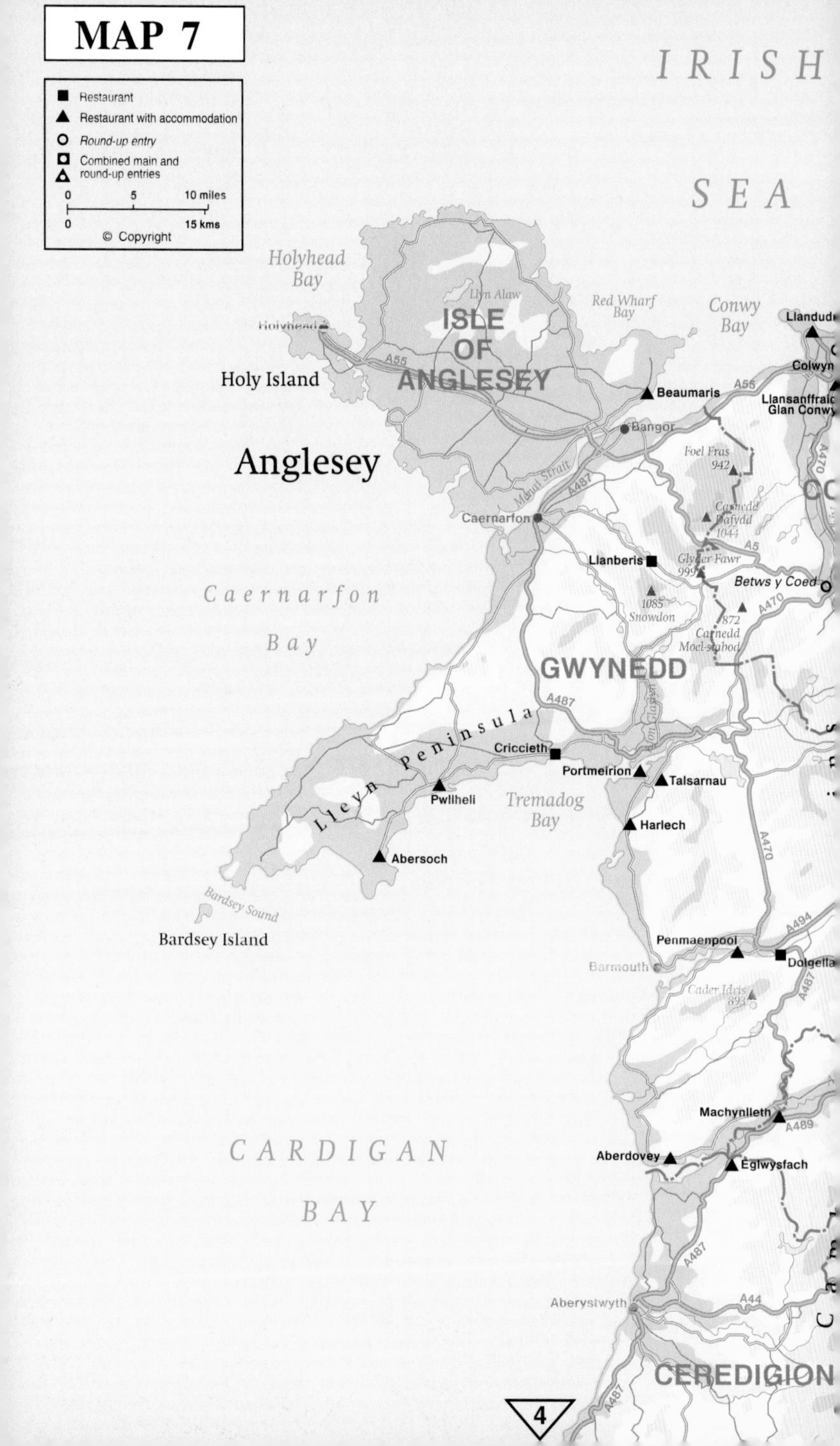

MAP 7

- ■ Restaurant
- ▲ Restaurant with accommodation
- ○ *Round-up entry*
- ◨ Combined main and
- △ round-up entries

| 0 | 5 | 10 miles |
| 0 | | 15 kms |

© Copyright

IRISH

SEA

Holyhead Bay

Llyn Alaw

Red Wharf Bay

Conwy Bay

Llandud

ISLE OF ANGLESEY

Holyhead

A55

Colwyn

Holy Island

▲ Beaumaris

A55

Llansanffraid Glan Conwy

Anglesey

Bangor

A487

A470

CC

Caernarfon

Foel Fras 942 ▲

A5

Carnedd Dafydd 1044 ▲

Caernarfon

Llanberis ■

Glyder Fawr 999 ▲

Betws y Coed ○

Bay

1085 *Snowdon*

872 *Carnedd Moel-siabod* ▲

GWYNEDD

A470

A487

Criccieth ◨

Portmeirion ▲

▲ Talsarnau

Pwllheli ▲

Tremadog Bay

▲ Harlech

A470

Lleyn Peninsula

▲ Abersoch

Bardsey Sound

Penmaenpool ▲

A494

Bardsey Island

Barmouth

Dolgellau

Cader Idris 893 ▲

A487

Machynlleth

A489

CARDIGAN

Aberdovey ▲

▲ Eglwysfach

BAY

A487

Aberystwyth

A44

CEREDIGION

△ 4

MAP 8

- ■ Restaurant
- ▲ Restaurant with accommodation
- ○ Round-up entry
- ⬚ Combined main and
- △ round-up entries

0 5 10 miles
0 15 kms
© Copyright

CUMBRIA

Whitehaven
Ennerdale Water
Ullswater
Grange in Borrowdale
10
Scafell Pike 977
Wast Water
Grasmere
Windermere
Ambleside
Windermere
Hawkshead
Bowness-on-Windermere
R. Esk
R. Duddon
Near Sawrey
Kend
Crosthwaite
A595
A5092
A590
Ulverston
Cartmel
Barrow-in-Furness
Isle of Walney
Morecambe
Heysham
Lancas
Morecambe Bay
Forton
Fleetwood
Point of Ayre
Ramsey Bay
Ramsey
Poulton-le-Fylde
R. Wyre
Kirk Michael
Isle of Man
Laxey Bay
Blackpool
Kirkham
M55
Glenmaye
Douglas
Preston
Lytham St Anne's
Port Erin
Port St Mary
Calf of Man
Southport
Wrightin
Bispham Green
Ormskirk
Skelmersdale
M58
MERSEYSIDE
Wallasey
St Hele
Liverpool
Birkenhead
Conwy Bay
Colwyn Bay
Prestatyn
Llandudno
Rhyl
Colwyn Bay
Runcorn
R. Mersey
M56
Llansanffraid Glan Conwy
A55
CHE
Pearl Fras
CONWY
Denbigh
7
FLINTSHIRE
Hawarden
Chester
Little Barrow

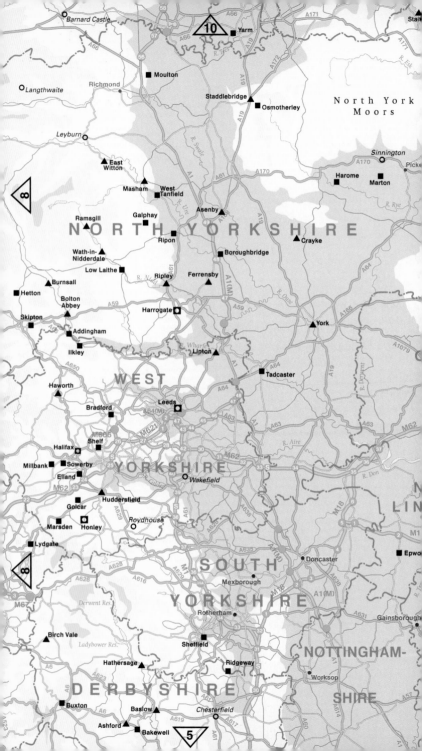

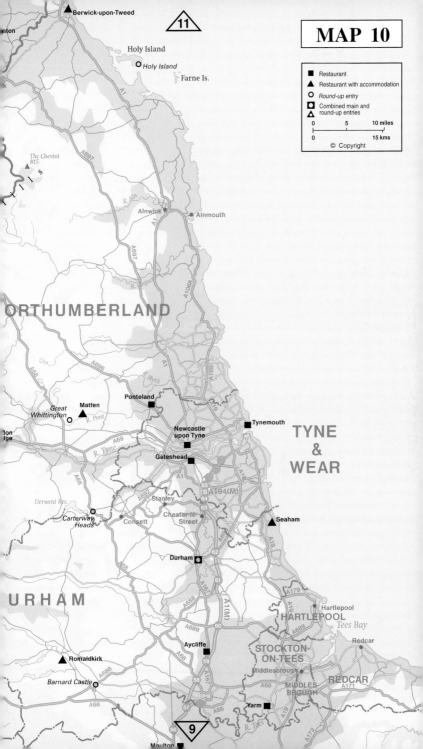

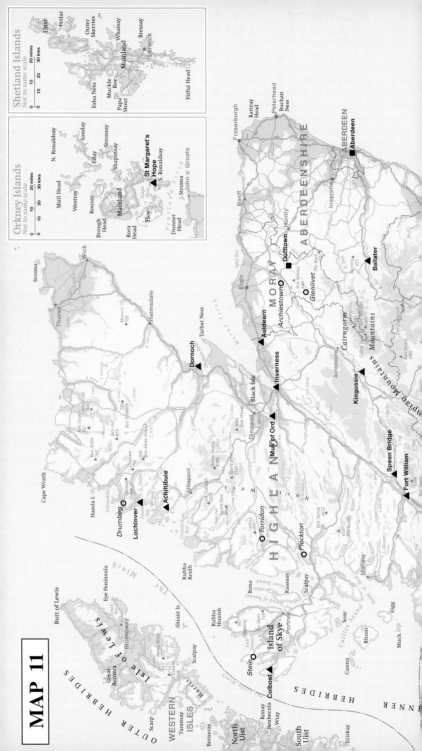

MAP 11

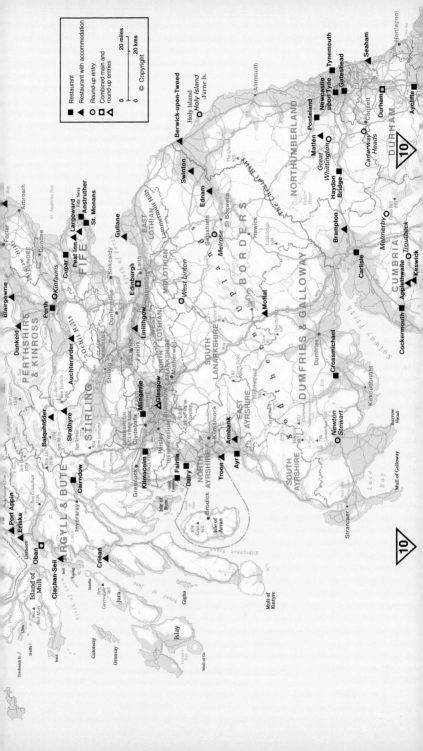

Greater London

BARNET

Stanmore

Finchley
Rani
Two Brothers

Vrisaki
Wood
Green

Mosaica

Hendon

HARROW

Bistro Aix

Café Japan

Parsee

WEMBLEY

See Map 13

Hampstead

CAMDEN

Willesden

Sushi-Say

Sabras

BRENT

A40(M)

William IV

See Map 15

HAMMERSMITH
AND
FULHAM

CITY OF
WEST-
MINSTER

Ealing

Acton

Gilbey's

Ealing Park
Tavern

Orsino

Anglesea
Arms

Havelock Tavern
Cotto

See Map 14

KENSINGTON
AND
CHELSEA

Adams Café

Chez Moi

Popeseye

FishWorks

Fish Hoek

Snows on
the Green

Azou

La Trompette

Thai Bistro

HAMMERSMITH

Reba

Brentford

Riva

Gate

River
Café

Ole Tapas

Blue Elephant

Ransome's Dock

Sonny's

Salisbury
Tavern

Chutney
Mary

Stepping
Stone

MVH

Fulham

Emile's

Mims

Tsunami

Redmonds

Phoenix

Putney Bridge

Enoteca Turi

*Del
Buongustai*

Brady's

The Victoria

Crowthers

Ditto

Thyme

RICHMOND

3 Monkey

Twickenham

WANDSWORTH

Sarkhel's

Chez Bruce

Kastoori

Radha Krishna
Bhavan

Wharf

Light House

Wimbledon

Streatham

Merton

Kingston upon
Thames

*Mirch
Masala*

Mitcham

KINGSTON
UPON
THAMES

Malden

MERTON

CHIGWELL

EDMONTON

A1010

A10

A112

Woodford

Hainault

A123

A1112

4

REDBRIDGE

A12

Walthamstow

A503

A10

WALTHAM
FOREST

A104

ILFORD

A124

Rasa
Rasa Travancore
Istanbul Iskembecisi

HACKNEY

A11

A118

NEWHAM

A406

A123

Barking

BARKING &
DAGENHAM

A13

Little
Georgia
Armadillo

Thai Garden

A102(M)

East Ham

A114

A11

TOWER
HAMLETS

New
Tayyabs

A13

Poplar

R. Thames

Thamesmead

Wapping Food

Ubon

Royal China
Moshi Moshi Sushi
Mem Saheb

Woolwich

A206

A2

A102(M)

Greenwich

Spread
Eagle

GREENWICH

A205

A209

A202

A2

Chapter Two

A20

A2

A210

LAMBETH

Lewisham

The Green

Le Chardon

Babur Brasserie

A205

Eltham

Dulwich

A20

Catford

A211

A222

LEWISHAM

Sidcup

midie

A2212

A208

Crystal Palace

A2212

A212

BROMLEY

A208

A224

Beckenham

A21

MAP 12

■ Restaurant
▲ Restaurant with accommodation
Round-up entry

0   5km
0   4 miles

© Copyright

BROMLEY

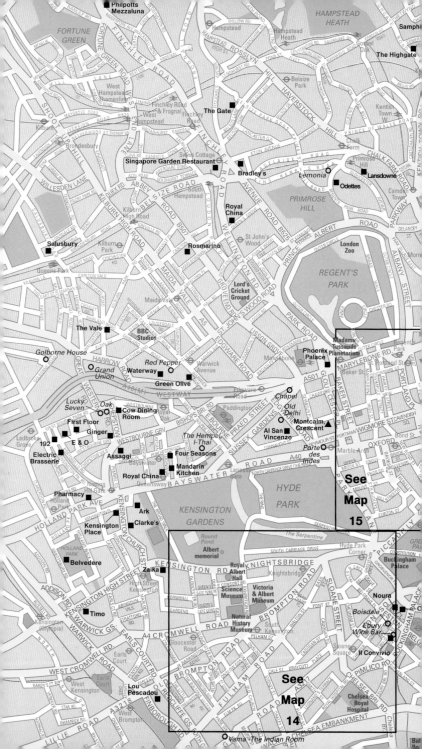

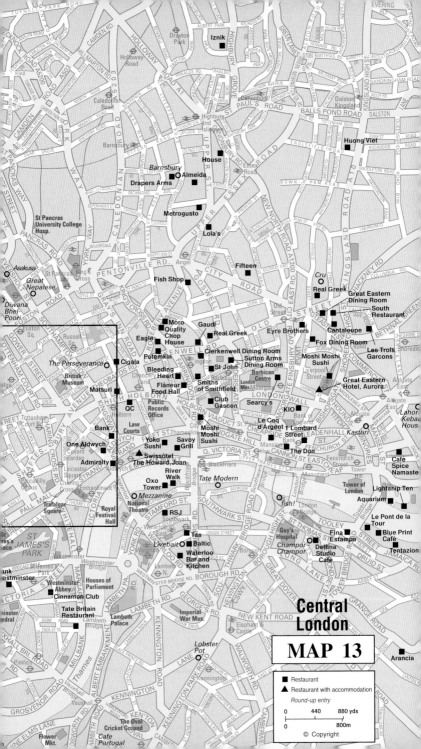

Iznik

Drayton
Park

Huong Viet

House

Barnsbury
Almeida
Drapers Arms

Metrogusto

Lola's

St Pancras
University College
Hosp.

Fifteen

Asakusa
Great
Nepalese
Cru
Real Greek
Great Eastern
Dining Room
South
Restaurant

Diwana
Bhel-
Poori

Fish Shop

Moro
Quality
Chop
House

Gaudi
Real Greek
Eyre Brothers
Cantaloupe
Fox Dining Room
Les Trois
Garcons

The Perseverance
Cigala
Eagle
Potemkin
Clerkenwell Dining Room
Sutton Arms
Dining Room
Moshi Moshi
Sushi

British
Museum

Bleeding
Heart
St John
Searcy's
Great Eastern
Hotel, Aurora

Matsuri
Flâneur
Food Hall
Smiths
of Smithfield

QC
Public
Records
Office
Club
Gascon
KIO

Bank
Moshi
Moshi
Sushi
Le Coq
d'Argent
Lombard
Street
Kasturi

One Aldwych
Law
Courts
Yoko
Sushi
Savoy
Grill
The Don

Lahor
Kebab
Hous

Admiralty
Swissôtel
The Howard, Joan
River
Walk
Café
Spice
Namaste

Trafalgar
Square
Oxo
Tower
Mezzanine
Tate Modern
Lightship Ten
Aquarium

Royal
Festival
Hall
National
Theatre
fish!
Le Pont de la
Tour

RSJ
Fina
Estampa
Blue Print
Café

ST
JAMES'S
PARK

Tas
Livebait
Baltic
Waterloo
Bar and
Kitchen

Champor
Champor
Delfina
Studio
Cafe
Tentazio

Westminster
Abbey
Cinnamon Club
Guy's
Hospital

Tate Britain
Restaurant

Houses of
Parliament

Lambeth
Palace
Imperial
War Mus.
NEW KENT ROAD

Arancia

Lobster
Pot

The Oval
Cricket Ground
Café
Portugal

Central
London

MAP 13

■ Restaurant
▲ Restaurant with accommodation
Round-up entry

0   440   880 yds
0   800m
© Copyright

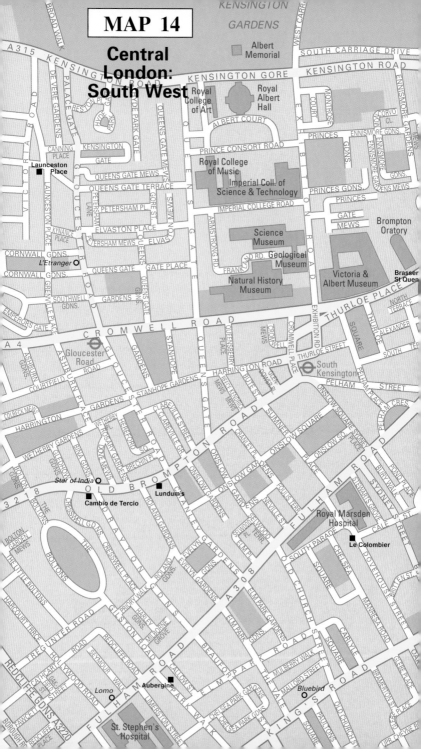

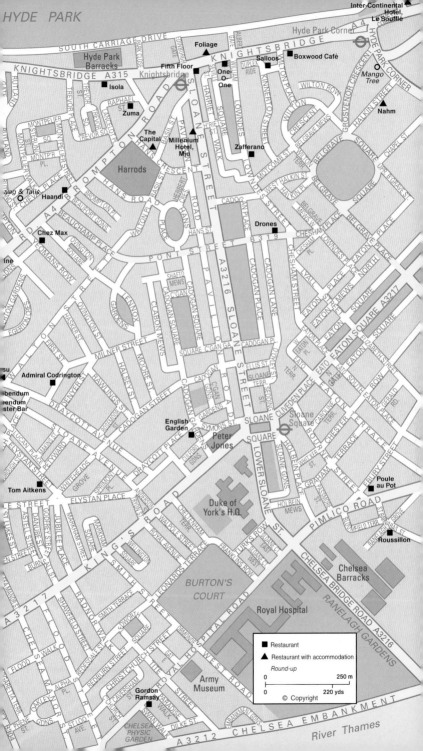

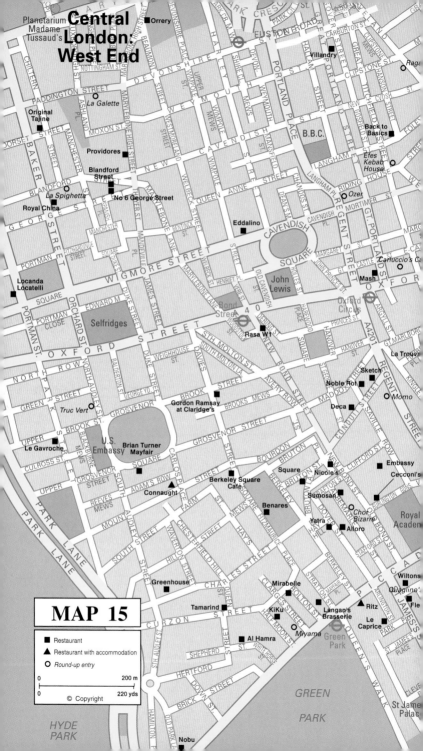

MAP 16

Restaurant
Restaurant with accommodation
Round-up entry
Combined main and round-up entries

| 0 | 40 | 80 miles |
| 0 | 40 | 80 | 120 Kms |

© Copyright

ATLANTIC

OCEAN

Rosapenna
Portstewart
Rathmullan
Coleraine
LONDONDERRY
Rathlin I.
Inishtrahull Sound
ANTRIM
DONEGAL
Ballyclare
Carrickfergus
Strabane
Donegal
TYRONE
Bangor
Antrim
Belfast
Lurgan
DOWN
Downpatrick
Donegal Bay
FERMANAGH
Enniskillen
Portadown
Armagh
Sligo
Blacklion
Monaghan
MONAGHAN
Crossmolina
Castlebaldwin
Fenagh
Cavan
IRISH
SLIGO
Carrick-on-Shannon
LEITRIM
CAVAN
LOUTH
SEA
Newport
MAYO
ROSCOMMON
LONGFORD
Drogheda
MEATH
IRELAND
Athlone
WESTMEATH
Dunshauglin
GALWAY
Oughterard
Dublin
Kilcolgan
Clarin Bridge
KILDARE
Dublin
OFFALY
Kildare
M7
Ballyvaughan
Birr
Portlaoise
Doolin
Lisdoonvarna
LAOIS
WICKLOW
Wicklow
CLARE
Arklow
Shannon
TIPPERARY
KILKENNY
CARLOW
LIMERICK
Gorey
Tipperary
Cashel
Listowel
LIMERICK
Kilmaganny
WEXFORD
Tralee
Kilmallock
Clonmel
Dingle
Kanturk
Mallow
WATERFORD
Wexford
KERRY
Waterford
Killorglin
CORK
Kenmare
Cork
Shanagarry
Ballylickey
Douglas
Cobh
Bantry
ST. GEORGE'S CHANNEL
Ballydehob

ATLANTIC

OCEAN

knowledgeable. Espresso is the real thing, and an interesting list of three dozen wines starting at £8.25 canters across the globe, with most bottles well below £15.

CHEF/PROPRIETOR: Gavin Beedham   OPEN: Tue to Sat 11.30 to 2, 6 to 10   MEALS: alc (main courses £4.50 to £15). Set L £11.95, Set D Tue to Thur 6 to 7.15 £11.95 (2 courses)   SERVICE: not inc   CARDS: Delta, MasterCard, Switch, Visa   DETAILS: 80 seats. Vegetarian meals. No smoking; smoking permitted in bar area. Music

INSTOW Devon   map 1

Decks ✦   NEW ENTRY

Hatton Croft House, Marine Parade,
Instow EX39 4JJ
TEL: (01271) 860671   FAX: (01271) 860820   COOKING 3
EMAIL: decks@instow.net   SEAFOOD
WEBSITE: www.decksrestaurant.co.uk   £20–£54

The dining areas in Decks capitalise on stunning views across the estuary to Appledore beyond, while the attractive modern décor in pale yellows, blues and white has as its centrepiece a huge mast from an old schooner, for one reporter completing the illusion of being on board a ship. There's a nod to carnivores and vegetarians, but fish dominates the menu. Velvet-textured lobster bisque is full of fresh flavour, while expertly prepared sole and salmon terrine, with contrasting rocket, has been described as 'a visual treat which also delivered to the taste-buds'. Main courses might include pan-fried scallops with crab and avocado, or a generous portion of 'juicy and succulent' black bream fillets on baby spinach bound in a tomato and pepper compote. Dishes are served under silver domes, followed by the ceremonial lifting of the lids. Puddings might run to white chocolate and blueberry crème brûlée, while rich home-made truffles with coffee left a reporter 'purring'. A wide-ranging wine list of around 50 bins offers good choice by the glass (from £3.10). House South African Chenin Blanc and Pinotage are £11.50 and £12.40 respectively.

CHEF/PROPRIETOR: Lee Timmins   OPEN: Tue to Sat 12 to 2.30, 7 to 9.30   CLOSED: 24 to 26 Dec   MEALS: alc (main courses L £6 to £18.50, D £12.50 to £18.50). Set L and D £21.50   SERVICE: not inc, card slips closed   CARDS: Amex, Delta, MasterCard, Switch, Visa   DETAILS: 50 seats. 32 seats outside. Private parties: 45 main room. Vegetarian meals. Children's helpings. No smoking in 1 dining room. Wheelchair access (also WC). Music. Air-conditioned

IPSWICH Suffolk   map 6

Bistro on the Quay ✦ £   NEW ENTRY

3 Wherry Quay, Ipswich IP4 1AS   COOKING 2
TEL/FAX: (01473) 286677   BISTRO
                                                                   £20–£45

With its high ceilings and polished wooden floors and tables, this is a bright, airy place, a large window overlooking the quay adding to the attraction. Unpretentious bistro it most certainly is, attracting a crowd for light lunches – dishes like mushroom omelette, fishcakes, or grilled Mediterranean vegetables – and a fixed-priced menu as well as the carte. Excellent home-made malty bread accompanies a timbale of Cromer crab with pickled cucumber, and, in season, asparagus comes with a poached egg and balsamic vinegar. Among main courses might be pink-roast loin of lamb in a red wine sauce with dauphinois potatoes, and grilled sea trout with crushed peas and a butter sauce. Finish with something like date and walnut pudding with toffee ice cream. Wines are a short selection from Europe and the southern hemisphere. Around half a dozen come by the glass, with bottle prices starting at £10.25.

CHEF: Anthony Brooks   PROPRIETORS: Anthony and Kathy Brooks   OPEN: all week L 12 to 2 (2.30 Sun), Mon to Sat D 6.30 to 9.30   CLOSED: 25 Dec to 4 Jan   MEALS: alc (main courses £8 to £14). Set L and D £9.50 (2 courses) to £11.95   SERVICE: not inc   CARDS: Amex, Delta, MasterCard, Switch, Visa   DETAILS: 90 seats. Private parties: 14 main room, 20 to 30 private rooms. Vegetarian meals. Children's helpings. No children after 9pm. No smoking in 1 dining room. Wheelchair access (also WC). No music (£5)

IXWORTH Suffolk   map 6

Theobalds ▼ ✄

68 High Street, Ixworth IP31 2HJ   COOKING 3
TEL/FAX: (01359) 231707   ANGLO-FRENCH
WEBSITE: www.theobaldsrestaurant.co.uk   £29–£51

Simon and Geraldine Theobald's abidingly popular restaurant has now been in the Guide for over 20 years. It is a heavily beamed, agreeably ancient place, parts dating from the fifteenth century, and all very easy on the eye. Confining himself (except by arrangement) to dinners and Sunday lunch, Simon cooks a wide-ranging menu that mixes English modes with hints of warmer climes. A robustly native roast breast and braised leg of Gressingham duckling sauced with port, redcurrants and ginger might be followed by creamed rice pudding with poached rhubarb. But there could also be a starter salad of shredded Serrano ham with Gruyère, apple and croûtons in mustard vinaigrette, and main courses like grilled sea bass on candied aubergines and vine tomatoes, dressed in olive oil and basil. Finish perhaps with a bouquet of home-made ice creams and sorbets in a brandy-snap basket, or nougat glacé with chocolate sauce. As would one expect from such well-versed practitioners, the approach is spot-on and the service cordial. Half the wines on the nicely balanced list are under £20; pricier bottles are mostly French classics with the benefit of some age. Four modern house wines also come by the glass for £2.95 and there are plenty of halves.

CHEF: Simon Theobald   PROPRIETORS: Simon and Geraldine Theobald   OPEN: Sun L 12.15 to 1.30, Tue to Sat D 7 to 9   MEALS: alc D (main courses £13 to £17.50). Set L Sun £19.95, Set D £22   SERVICE: not inc, card slips closed   CARDS: Delta, MasterCard, Switch, Visa   DETAILS: 42 seats. 12 seats outside. Private parties: 42 main room, 8 to 16 private rooms. Vegetarian meals. Children's helpings. No children under 8 at D. No smoking. Wheelchair access (not WC). No music

---

If a restaurant is new to the Guide this year (did not appear as a main entry in the last edition), NEW ENTRY *appears opposite its name.*

JEVINGTON East Sussex

map 3

Hungry Monk ⅚✳

Jevington BN26 5QF
TEL/FAX: (01323) 482178
WEBSITE: www.hungrymonk.co.uk
off A22, on road between Polegate and Friston

COOKING 2
ENGLISH/PROVINCIAL FRENCH
£39–£61

After 27 years, the Mackenzies' Monk has changed little: low doorways and antique furnishings add to the inviting, intimate atmosphere. The menu evolves sedately, keeping its distance from the cutting edge of culinary fashion yet delivering twice-baked spinach and Parmesan soufflé alongside versions of favourite '60s starters such as smoked salmon and prawn roulade. There are small twists to tradition, like caramelised leeks accompanying fillet of beef, and Feta crust on best end of lamb served with a red wine and orange sauce. Meat dishes are given most prominence, though fish eaters and vegetarians get a look-in too. Fans will be glad that house signature dessert – banoffi pie – still features, or try treacle tart with home-made vanilla ice cream. Some noteworthy, high-priced and well-aged French classics grace a wine list that starts at £12 and shows good sourcing and fair mark-ups.

CHEFS: Gary Fisher and Nick Sharman PROPRIETORS: Nigel and Susan Mackenzie OPEN: Sun L 12 to 2.30, all week D 6.45 to 9.30 CLOSED: bank hols except Good Friday MEALS: Set L £26.95, Set D £28.95 SERVICE: not inc, 12.5% for parties of 7 or more, card slips closed CARDS: Amex, MasterCard, Switch, Visa DETAILS: 40 seats. Private parties: 16 main room, 4 to 16 private rooms. Car park. Vegetarian meals. Children's helpings. No children under 5 in main dining room. No smoking in 1 dining room. Occasional music. No mobile phones. Air-conditioned (£5)

KELSALE Suffolk

map 6

Harrisons ⅚✳ £

Main Road, Kelsale IP17 2RF
TEL/FAX: (01728) 604444
on A12 outside village; going N look for sign for
Carlton Industrial Estate and then turn left at lay-
by after sharp bend

COOKING 5
MODERN BRITISH
£22–£45

The thatched and beamed cottage is beside a lay-by on the main road yet quite secluded: watch out for the chickens running around. It is an ancient building full of character, with a ground-floor dining room and another up a steep spiral staircase, neither boasting any straight lines or right angles. What powers the kitchen are local materials – many courtesy of the Suffolk Smallholders Society, some in very small quantities – which are woven into an ever-changing menu. Pheasant cock-a-leekie, pappardelle with field mushrooms, and pannacotta with blackberries are typical of Peter Harrison's style.

The cooking can be as characterful as the surroundings, often 'plain-speaking stuff', as in a jumbled mound of generous chunks of sautéed sweetbreads, big cubes of melting Saddleback pork confit with crisp crackling, and grilled chorizo, all well dressed with garlic mayonnaise. Meat tends to be sourced from butchers accredited by the Rare Breeds Survival Trust, and well hung too: for example, a 'magnificent' roast rack of Suffolk lamb – three fat cutlets, pink yet well crusted – on a pile of clearly spiced aubergine, with a scoop of hummus and streaks of yoghurt for a sauce. All this (especially the saucing) may be simple, but its very straightforwardness makes a powerful impact. At the same time there is a high degree of technical accomplishment, as in a big wedge of professionally made passion-fruit tart, with crisp pastry and an intensely flavoured, creamy custard filling topped with a thin layer of soft fruit jelly. Service is friendly and smiley, and good value is maintained thanks to a varied and sensibly chosen wine list that starts with house Inzolia from Sicily and Sangiovese from Puglia at £9.95.

CHEF: Peter Harrison   PROPRIETORS: Peter and Melanie Harrison   OPEN: Tue to Sat 12 to 2, 7 to 10   CLOSED: 2 weeks Christmas   MEALS: alc (main courses £10 to £14.50). Set L Mon to Fri £11.50 (2 courses) to £13.50   SERVICE: not inc, card slips closed   CARDS: Delta, MasterCard, Switch, Visa   DETAILS: 60 seats. 12 seats outside. Private parties: 24 main room, 10 to 24 private rooms. Car park. Vegetarian meals. Children's helpings. No children under 8. No smoking. Wheelchair access (not WC). No music. No mobile phones

---

KENDAL Cumbria   map 8

Bridge House ※⊹   NEW ENTRY

1 Bridge Street, Kendal LA9 7DD
TEL/FAX: (01539) 738855   COOKING 4
EMAIL: info@bridgehousekendal.co.uk   MODERN ENGLISH
WEBSITE: www.bridgehousekendal.co.uk   £27–£50

Last seen in the 1999 edition of the Guide at Roger's in Windermere, the Pergl-Wilsons have resurfaced at this attractive Georgian town house just outside the town centre. The quietly elegant building retains its period charm, and diners get a view over the River Kent from the first-floor dining room. Roger Pergl-Wilson's core Anglo-French repertoire is fleshed out with ideas from elsewhere, producing a lime, chilli and coriander mayonnaise to partner English asparagus, for example, although the bulk of the dishes tend to stay in familiar European territory: an admirable grainy-textured leek and potato soup is served with warm bread, and a wedge of well-flavoured spinach and Parmesan tart in crisp pastry is served with cold tomato confit.

Dishes are simple, fresh and uncluttered, taking in pink, tender, roast rack of lamb tasting of its fennel, rosemary and garlic marinade, and an old-fashioned but well-executed dish of lightly crisped, pink calf's liver with Dubonnet and oranges. Among regional items, Flookburgh shrimps might turn up alongside grilled halibut fillet, and the corn-fed chicken is from Goosnargh, served with a tarragon cream sauce. Chips come highly recommended. Textures are well handled, too, judging by a crisp meringue spiked with bits of walnut, served with a creamy coffee sauce. A short, French-dominated wine list offers fair value, starting with six house wines (three of each) at around £10 to £12.

CHEF: Roger Pergl-Wilson   PROPRIETORS: Roger and Alena Pergl-Wilson   OPEN: Tue to Sat 12.30 to 1.30, 6.30 to 9.30   MEALS: alc D (main courses £11.50 to £15). Set L £12.50 (2 courses) to £16.50, Set D Tue to Fri £17.90   SERVICE: not inc, card slips closed   CARDS: Delta, MasterCard, Switch, Visa   DETAILS: 36 seats. Private parties: 16 main room, 12 to 16 private rooms. Vegetarian meals. Children's helpings. No children under 10. No smoking in dining rooms, smoking permitted in bar. Music

Déjà-vu ✺ £

124 Stricklandgate, Kendal LA9 4QG

TEL/FAX: (01539) 724843

COOKING **2**
MEDITERRANEAN
£16–£47

On a corner site at the station end of the main street, Déjà-vu is a small, relaxed restaurant with, according to one reader, more than a hint of the 1970s bistro about it, which perhaps goes some way to explaining the name. Fabien Bellouère cooks a Mediterranean menu, encompassing sunny salads of artichoke, cherry tomatoes and smoked mozzarella, or seared tuna with salsa piccante. Daily specials are chalked up on a board, and supplement the likes of venison fillet with purple potato civet, and a vegetarian version of tagine made with baby vegetables and served with couscous. Theme evenings include Spanish and American nights. Finish with walnut tart served with rum and raisin ice cream, or chocolate and Tia Maria brûlée. Wines are largely French, though house selections are Spanish Viura (£9) and Tempranillo (£10.50).

CHEF: Fabien Bellouère   PROPRIETOR: Frances Wood   OPEN: Fri to Sat 12 to 2, Mon to Sat 5.30 to 9 (9.30 Fri, 9.45 Sat)   MEALS: alc Thur to Sat D (main courses £4.50 to £15). Set L Fri and Sat £5.95 (2 courses) to £8.25, Set D 5.30 to 7.30 £13.95 (2 courses) to £17.50. American-style menu Mon D (main courses £8 to £15), vegetarian menu Tue D (main courses £8.50 to £9.50), Spanish menu Wed D (main courses £10 to £13)   SERVICE: not inc, 10% for parties of 6 or more, card slips closed   CARDS: Amex, Delta, Diners, MasterCard, Switch, Visa   DETAILS: 44 seats. Private parties: 32 main room, 6 to 12 private rooms. Vegetarian meals. No smoking while others eat. Wheelchair access (not WC). Music £5

KENILWORTH Warwickshire   **map 5**

Restaurant Bosquet

97A Warwick Road, Kenilworth CV8 1HP

TEL/FAX: (01926) 852463

COOKING **5**
FRENCH
£41–£57

After refurbishment in autumn 2002 the décor here has a lighter, more modern touch. Even if the old domestic feel may have diminished, customers evidently approve, and the comfy leather chairs will certainly be welcomed. Unchanged, though, is Bernard Lignier's conscientious, quality-first approach to sourcing and cooking: 'The product,' he feels, 'is too important to be maltreated by fashion and fads.' Free-range poultry, Scottish beef and lamb, Brixham shellfish and fine French cheeses all play their parts in the enticing, classical menus, which are either à la carte or prix fixe.

A soup of celeriac and roast garlic with wild mushrooms makes an opulent starter – if foie gras, scallops or game terrine don't catch your eye. The truly ostentatious might go for oysters on asparagus purée topped with caviar and sauced with champagne, before addressing loin of veal with its sweetbreads in a rich Madeira sauce. The overtly French style adds bitter orange to a breast of duck, and bitter chocolate to saddle of venison, and when it comes to desserts, chocolate gâteau is paired with raspberry coulis, or strawberries with rosemary and lime sorbet. Jane Lignier runs the front-of-house with both restraint and panache. The exclusively French wine list pulls together famous names from the classic regions (including clarets in vintages that are drinking well) and a discerning selection from the south. This policy doesn't turn up much under £20, but house wines at £13.50 are good quality.

CHEF: Bernard Lignier   PROPRIETORS: Bernard and Jane Lignier   OPEN: Tue to Fri L (bookings only) 12 to 1.15, Tue to Sat D 7 to 9.15   CLOSED: 1 week Christmas, 3 weeks Aug   MEALS: alc L (main courses £18). Set L £27.50, Set D £27.50   SERVICE: not inc   CARDS: Amex, MasterCard, Switch, Visa   DETAILS: 26 seats. Private parties: 30 main room. Children's helpings. Wheelchair access (not WC). No music. No mobile phones

Simpson's ♥

101–103 Warwick Road, Kenilworth CV8 1HL
TEL: (01926) 864567   FAX: (01926) 864510
EMAIL: info@simpsonsrestaurant.co.uk
WEBSITE: www.simpsonsrestaurant.co.uk

COOKING 5
MODERN FRENCH
£32–£80

A simple yet elegant décor in pale neutral tones, abundant mirrors on the walls, lush displays of foliage and 'perfectly set tables with spotless glassware, cutlery and napery': for one reporter, this was the perfect setting for a celebratory family lunch. The cooking has a strong Gallic accent and, although the menus may not be the most innovative around, the results on the plate are accomplished and impressive.

Start perhaps with 'meltingly delicious' goats' cheese ravioli, 'unctuous' seared foie gras with poached fig, fig compote and port sauce, or a pressed ham hock and chicken terrine with celeriac rémoulade and mustard cream, then move on to roast rack of Cornish lamb with aubergine 'royale', aromatic couscous and a mint jus, monkfish with stuffed courgette flowers, or roast squab pigeon with braised cabbage, pleurotte mushrooms, wild rice, confit garlic and pigeon jus. Creativity is unleashed at dessert stage to come up with white chocolate mousse with aromatic Puy lentils and Kirsch sauce, or roast Muscavado pear with a cone of chocolate sorbet and chocolate sauce. If the carte prices seem out of reach, a pair of fixed-price menus offer a good-value alternative, and if you really want to push the boat out there is a six-course gourmet menu.

France is the focus of the extensive wine list, with a wealth of smart bottles, but finds itself in good company from its Italian and Spanish neighbours as well as the southern hemisphere. Prices are just a bit high, but 17 by the glass (£3.75 to £9) and a sound range from £15 to £20 provide more than enough budget options.

CHEF/PROPRIETOR: Andreas Antona   OPEN: Tue to Sat 12.30 to 2, 7 to 10   CLOSED: last 2 weeks Aug   MEALS: alc (main courses £21 to £25). Set L £15 (2 courses) to £49.50, Set D £29 (2 courses) to £49.50   SERVICE: not inc, 10% for parties of 6 or more   CARDS: Amex, Delta, Diners, MasterCard, Switch, Visa   DETAILS: 60 seats. Private parties: 14 main room, 15 to 40 private rooms. Car park. No-smoking area. No music. No mobile phones. Air-conditioned

---

The Guide's top-rated restaurants are listed near the front of the book.

KESWICK Cumbria   map 10

▲ Swinside Lodge ⁑   [NEW ENTRY]

Grange Road, Newlands, Keswick CA12 5UE
TEL/FAX: (01768) 772948
EMAIL: info@swinsidelodge-hotel.co.uk
WEBSITE: www.swinsidelodge-hotel.co.uk   COOKING 2
from A66 1m W of Keswick, turn S at Portinscale   MODERN BRITISH
and follow Grange road for 2m   £39–£47

This Victorian family house in a big landscape has a charming ex-academic for a
hostess and a kitchen that uses local supplies and produces everything from
bread to petits fours. A four-course dinner is a no-choice affair until dessert.
Twice-baked soufflé of local smoked cheese has been lauded for its appealing
flavour, light texture and a well-balanced dressing on the accompanying pear
and walnut salad, and the soup course might run to leek and broccoli, or cream of
asparagus, served with good home-made bread. Main dishes might include
roast lamb, roast guinea fowl, or pan-fried sea bream and, alongside vegetables,
have been accurately timed and carefully cooked. The choice of two puddings
might be between crème brûlée and chocolate mousse, or between treacle tart
(pastry a touch hard for one reporter) with Chantilly cream, and a tuile
overflowing with ripe fruits and a decent ice cream. Tasty breads and strong
coffee confirm a kitchen that knows its basics. A brief but adequate wine list
starts at £11.50.

CHEF: Clive Imber   PROPRIETORS: Kevin and Susan Kniveton   OPEN: all week D only 7.30 (1
sitting)   MEALS: Set D £29.50   SERVICE: not inc, card slips closed   CARDS: Delta, MasterCard,
Switch, Visa   DETAILS: 20 seats. Private parties: 20 main room. Car park. Vegetarian meals with
advance notice. Children's helpings. No children under 5. No smoking. Wheelchair access (not
WC). No music   ACCOMMODATION: 7 rooms, all with bath/shower. TV. B&B £63 to £140. No
children under 5 (*The Which? Guide to Good Hotels*)

KEW Greater London   map 3

Glasshouse ▮

14 Station Parade, Kew TW9 3PZ   COOKING 5
TEL: (020) 8940 6777   FAX: (020) 8940 3833   MODERN BRITISH
                                                            £30–£65

Despite refurbishment, this five-year old 'neighbourhood' restaurant near Kew
Gardens station looks much as before, with light and dark browns
predominating. Though hard surfaces and close-together tables can make it
difficult to have a conversation, Glasshouse represents the best in contemporary
eating: ambitious but not flashy, upmarket but not too expensive, and able to
deliver a sense of occasion without fawning or formality.

The food is as appealing as it is contemporary, with a gently innovative streak,
offering deep-fried lamb's tongue with sauce gribiche; venison and foie gras
haché with field mushrooms and celeriac; and pink bream with spinach and
ricotta pancakes, deep-fried capers and aïoli. One of the most warmly reported
starters has been fresh, crispy mackerel with sliced potatoes in a mustard
vinaigrette, but other successes have included the 'best ever' butternut squash

soup, and slow-roast belly pork with a choucroute tart and caramelised apple slices. There is a deal of comfort among desserts, which have delivered vanilla waffle (with a scoop of milk ice cream) and a richly flavoured lemon-curd crème brûlée with a thin hard topping. Service from mainly French staff has varied from 'detached' to 'friendly and helpful'. The wine list picks up modern trends, like sherry (six by the glass from £3.50) and Austria and Germany, while covering very thoroughly all corners of France, plus Italy, Australia, California, etc. There are not many bottles under £20, though they're interesting ones; 20 wines come by the glass, and there are good selections of halves and magnums.

CHEF: Anthony Boyd   PROPRIETOR: Larkbrace Ltd   OPEN: Mon to Sat 12 to 2.30, 7 (6.30 Fri and Sat) to 10.30, Sun 12.30 to 3, 7.30 to 10   CLOSED: 4 days at Christmas, 1 Jan   MEALS: Set L £17.50 to £25, Set D £30   SERVICE: 12.5% (optional), card slips closed   CARDS: Amex, Delta, MasterCard, Switch, Visa   DETAILS: 65 seats. Private parties: 70 main room. Vegetarian meals. Children's helpings at Sat and Sun L. Wheelchair access (not WC). No music. Air-conditioned

KEYSTON Cambridgeshire   map 6

Pheasant ▾ ✳ £

Village Loop Road, Keyston PE18 0RE
TEL: (01832) 710241   FAX: (01832) 710340   COOKING 5
on B663, 1m S of junction with A14 and 4m SE of   MODERN EUROPEAN
Thrapston   £28–£56

Keyston is in farming country, a picturesque and quiet village of whitewashed, thatched cottages. Charmingly cottagey inside, the Pheasant, like other members of the Huntsbridge group (see entries in Fotheringhay, Huntingdon and Madingley), serves fine food and wine in a relaxed pub-like setting with friendly service – and does it unpretentiously and with style. But if the approach is down to earth, it also has flair. Clive Dixon cooks in a style one reporter described as 'thoroughly enjoyable but a bit liquorice allsorts'. So starters range from deep-fried Brie with roast onion jam, via tataki of tuna with wasabi-dressed white radish, to a layered terrine of salmon and brill with Caesar salad. (The last – 'melting, luscious' fish layered in a soft, herby jelly – was the star of an inspection meal.) Among main courses have been Angus beef pudding with 'the lightest of suet crusts' covering a generous portion of tender beef; tasty fillet of Cornish spring lamb with crisp sautéed sweetbreads and spring vegetables; and unctuous pig's trotter in a sweet, rich glaze, stuffed with braised oxtail and served with woodland mushrooms, and a 'gorgeous, creamy' parsnip purée.

Finish with a selection of 'intensely fruity' ice creams and sorbets, or something more exotic like Tuscan honey, nut and candied fruit parfait with citrus salad and passion fruit. Huge wine glasses with space for swirling and sniffing do justice to the passionately chosen and annotated range. As on all Huntsbridge lists, the wines are divided into '£20 and under' and 'top class' selections, plus a stimulating range by the glass that includes sherries.

CHEF: Clive Dixon   PROPRIETOR: Huntsbridge Ltd   OPEN: all week 12 to 2, 6.30 to 9.30 (7 to 8.45 Sun)   CLOSED: D on 25 and 26 Dec and 1 Jan   MEALS: alc (main courses L £5, D £9 to £18.50). Snack menu available   SERVICE: not inc   CARDS: Amex, Delta, Diners, MasterCard, Switch, Visa   DETAILS: 80 seats. 20 seats outside. Private parties: 34 main room. Car park. Vegetarian meals. Children's helpings. No smoking. Occasional music

KIBWORTH BEAUCHAMP Leicestershire   map 5

Firenze

9 Station Street, Kibworth Beauchamp LE8 0LN
TEL: (0116) 279 6260   FAX: (0116) 279 3646   COOKING **3**
EMAIL: firenze@fish.co.uk   MODERN ITALIAN
WEBSITE: www.firenze.co.uk   **£25–£44**

Lino and Sarah Poli want you to know all about the treasures of Florence, not just its food but its art, architecture and la dolce vita too. Perched on a roundabout in the middle of Kibworth Beauchamp, they may be far from their source of inspiration, but they wipe away geographical distance by means of fine, sunny cooking and well-chosen wines. The menu follows the classic Italian structure, with antipasti, such as bruschetta with pan-fried chicken livers, followed by pasta dishes like garganelli with prawns, broccoli and toasted almonds, before getting on to the business of fish or meat. The kitchen keeps things simple, with fillets of sole teamed with deep-fried zucchini, and breast of duck roasted in honey and black pepper. Indeed, it's even possible to have a costolletta Milanese should you fancy one. The panache with which it is all brought off extends to puddings such as chocolate truffle cake with orange marmalade ice-cream, or pannacotta with passion fruit. A splendid 17 wines by the glass heads an all-Italian list that brings in many of the best new-wave producers. House wines are £11.50 for white and £12.50 for red.

CHEFS: Lino Poli and Stuart Batey PROPRIETORS: Lino and Sarah Poli OPEN: Tue to Fri L 12 to 2, Tue to Sat D 7 to 10 CLOSED: 1 week Christmas, 1 week Easter, 2 weeks Aug MEALS: alc (main courses £8.50 to £16.50). Set L £10 (1 course) SERVICE: not inc CARDS: Delta, MasterCard, Switch, Visa DETAILS: 70 seats. Private parties: 70 main room, 16 to 30 private rooms. Vegetarian meals. Children's helpings. No-smoking area . Wheelchair access (not WC). Music

KINGHAM Oxfordshire   map 5

▲ Mill House 🍴   **NEW ENTRY**

Kingham OX7 6UH
TEL: (01608) 658188   FAX: (01608) 658492
EMAIL: stay@millhousehotel.co.uk   COOKING **5**
WEBSITE: www.millhousehotel.co.uk   MODERN BRITISH-PLUS
off B4450 4½m SW of Chipping Norton   **£26–£67**

This rambling Cotswold stone building, more manor than mill, has modern extensions that blend in well. The inside feels 'middle-class English': lots of lounges, comfortable sofas, drapes, and two linked dining rooms.

If the cooking style seems slightly indeterminate, chef Paul Haywood – formerly with the Chavignol team and the Chav Brasserie in Chipping Norton – brings great technical skill to fine raw materials. A starter of hand-dived Cornish scallops (two giants, strongly crusted on top, the rest translucent) included a small stack of shredded skate dusted with brioche crumbs on a layer of silky fresh spinach, plus a tiny quantity of well-judged, buttery, shellfish stock sauce. Price supplements on the lengthy dinner menu make a mockery of its set price (half the dishes have supplements), but results are unquestionable. Pink, tasty, sliced roast chump of lamb, for example, comes on swede purée surrounded by a jumble of vegetables, a mozzarella variation of gratin dauphinois and a light, creamy-ish, super-fresh lamb stock sauce – 'the best I've had in years' thought one who ate a 'hugely enjoyable meal'.

Desserts (such as roast plum Tatin) may not match that standard, but extras include fresh and tasty co-joined loaves on a chopping board with a knife. Service has the personal touch, and staff 'ask how you are every half hour or so'. The wine list starts ominously (Mouton Cadet at over £20), but outside classic regions there are some serviceable wines at reasonable prices, including four house wines at £12.25 and £13.50.

CHEF: Paul Haywood   PROPRIETOR: John Parslow   OPEN: all week 12 to 2, 7 to 9.30   MEALS: alc (main courses L £7 to £15, D £15 to £20). Set L £15.75, Set D £26. Bar and light L menus available   SERVICE: not inc, card slips closed   CARDS: Amex, Delta, Diners, MasterCard, Switch, Visa   DETAILS: 80 seats. 24 seats outside. Private parties: 80 main room. Car park. Vegetarian meals. Children's helpings. No smoking. Wheelchair access (also WC). No music. No mobile phones   ACCOMMODATION: 23 rooms, all with bath/shower. TV. Phone. B&B £85 to £140. Rooms for disabled (The Which? Guide to Good Hotels) £5

KINGSBRIDGE Devon   map 1

▲ Ship to Shore ⅝✳

45 Church Street, Kingsbridge TQ7 1BT
TEL: (01548) 854076   FAX: (01548) 857890   COOKING 4
EMAIL: enquiries@ship-to-shore.co.uk   MODERN BRITISH
WEBSITE: www.ship-to-shore.co.uk   £33–£67

Diners – and dinner is what is offered – should not be deterred by the tea-shop-looking exterior. Inside, the Stanton family clicks impressively into gear: son Richard deploys considerable and serious talents in the kitchen, where his mother, Rosamund, works with him, and father, Roger, is a helpful but not intrusive host. Table linen, glass and crockery are straightforward and unfussy, like the menu's descriptions of dishes that draw on the range and quality provided by South Devon's fisheries and farms. Refreshingly blunt first courses like crab pot, halibut with creamed spinach, or garlic and pine kernel tartlet may be succeeded by plain grilled whole Dover sole, or hake with a caper and tomato vinaigrette. Appropriate but limited elaboration is applied, so black bream comes en papillote to preserve its moistness. Classic vanilla crème brûlée will be just that (and excellent), and home-produced bread and petits fours and good coffee show attention to detail as well as hard work. A fair selection of mainly European wines, with six house bottles at £10.50 (£3 a glass), and ungrasping mark-ups – Sancerre, a good yardstick, is a reasonable £17.95 – allow drinkers to treat themselves to range as well as quality.

CHEFS: Richard and Rosamund Stanton   PROPRIETORS: Richard, Rosamund and Roger Stanton   OPEN: Tue to Fri (Aug, Tue to Sun) D 7 to 9   MEALS: alc D (main courses £12 to £30)   SERVICE: not inc, card slips closed   CARDS: Delta, MasterCard, Switch, Visa   DETAILS: 36 seats. Private parties: 36 main room, 2 to 4 private rooms. Car park. Vegetarian meals. No smoking. Wheelchair access (not WC). Music   ACCOMMODATION: 2 rooms, all with bath/shower. TV. B&B £30 to £35. Baby facilities

KING'S CLIFFE Northamptonshire

map 6

King's Cliffe House ▼ ✳ £

31 West Street, King's Cliffe PE8 6XB
TEL: (01780) 470172   FAX: 0870 126 8588
EMAIL: kehr@onetel.net.uk
S of A47, 12m W of Peterborough

COOKING 4
MODERN EUROPEAN
£25–£44

The quality sourcing of ingredients – from free-range ducks and guinea fowl, local asparagus and mushrooms, local meat, even own-made bread based on flour specially ground at a local windmill – is a prime motivation for chef/proprietors Andrew and Emma Wilshaw. Gloucester Old Spot pork butchered at a small local abattoir may be turned into a terrine and spiked with pistachio spices and herbs. Main courses may feature grilled Cornish sea bass with parsley and caperberry sauce, or loin of local lamb with couscous and a rosemary jus, while desserts run to comforting clotted cream ice cream with brown sugar meringue and poached peach. A hand-picked selection of wines, many in half-bottles, is a knowledgeable mix of Old World and New, with mostly mature bottles. Prices are very fair, starting at £9.95 with four by the glass at around £2.

As regular customers will know, Andrew Wilshaw is unwell and the restaurant is temporarily closed as we go to press. We wish him well, and hope to see King's Cliffe House soon re-opened.

CHEFS/PROPRIETORS: Andrew and Emma Wilshaw   OPEN: Wed to Sat D only 7 to 9.15   CLOSED: 2 weeks autumn, Christmas, 1 Jan, 2 weeks spring   MEALS: alc (main courses £11 to £15.50) SERVICE: net prices   CARDS: none   DETAILS: 15 seats. Private parties: 15 main room. Car park. Vegetarian meals. Children's helpings. No smoking. No music. No mobile phones

KINGTON Herefordshire

map 5

▲ Penrhos Court ✳

Kington HR5 3LH
TEL: (01544) 230720   FAX: (01544) 230754
EMAIL: martin@penrhos.co.uk
WEBSITE: www.penrhos.co.uk
on A44, ½m E of Kington

COOKING 3
MEDITERRANEAN
£40–£52

Thirty years have elapsed since Martin Griffiths took over this fine complex of ancient buildings on the Welsh border. Daphne Lambert, 'green and organic' nutritionist and author, takes skilful care of her Soil Association-certified kitchen as well as its garden, which supplies, along with local dairies, chicken from a nearby farm and eco-friendly fish from Cornwall, the bulk of the restaurant's ingredients. A format that has remained much the same for many years now no longer offers a carte, but centres around a daily-changing, limited-choice menu. Unchanged, however, is the aim to match the palpable freshness of the ingredients to a robust approach to flavouring. The no-choice first course is generally soup (beetroot, say); then perhaps a salad or savoury mousse (celeriac with shitake mushroom and tomato sauce at one February dinner); then a choice of (usually) chicken, fish or vegetarian (maybe Thai marinated chicken, red mullet fillet with potato rösti and basil dressing, or leek tarte Tatin); and finally a trio of desserts to pick from (ginger yoghurt ice, for example). House wines starting over £14 and prices rising fairly steeply thereafter have to be set against a selection that shows good range and careful choices.

CHEF: Daphne Lambert   PROPRIETORS: Martin Griffiths and Daphne Lambert   OPEN: Mon to Sat D only 7.15 to 8.45   MEALS: Set D £29.50 to £32.50   SERVICE: not inc, card slips closed   CARDS: MasterCard, Switch, Visa   DETAILS: 30 seats. 12 seats outside. Private parties: 70 main room, 6 to 20 private rooms. Car park. Vegetarian meals. Children's helpings. No smoking. Wheelchair access (also WC). No music. No mobile phones   ACCOMMODATION: 15 rooms, all with bath/shower. TV. Phone. B&B £65 to £135. Rooms for disabled (*The Which? Guide to Good Hotels*)

KIRKHAM Lancashire   map 8

Cromwellian

16 Poulton Street, Kirkham PR4 2AB   COOKING 3
TEL/FAX: (01772) 685680   MODERN BRITISH
                                                                £29–£45

Behind the reticent, tiny exterior and equally self-effacing dining room (more like a tea room), the Fawcetts ensure unpretentious excellence – Josie cooks with measured accuracy while Peter welcomes with well-judged warmth. Menus change seasonally, though there are year-round favourites like warm potted shrimps with a delicately spiced brandy butter, and Aberdeen Angus fillet, impressive in size and flavour, with a nicely balanced port and Stilton sauce. Oven-baked breast of chicken with a rich brown gravy and bacon lardons is a straightforward dish but executed perfectly, showing that it makes perfect sense to play to one's strengths: using decent ingredients and preparing them simply. Cheeses (English), or 'the lightest, fluffiest, most perfect apple upside down pudding I have ever eaten' – it came with toffee fudge ice cream and a light butterscotch sauce – might round things off. The wine list has reliable flavours from around the world at fair prices; house bottles are £10.50 (£2.75 a glass).

CHEF: Josie Fawcett   PROPRIETORS: Peter and Josie Fawcett   OPEN: Tue to Sat D 7 to 9   MEALS: Set D £16 (2 courses) to £19.50   SERVICE: not inc, card slips closed   CARDS: Amex, Delta, MasterCard, Switch, Visa   DETAILS: 20 seats. Private parties: 10 main room, 10 to 12 private rooms. Vegetarian meals. No music

LAMORNA Cornwall   map 1

▲ Lamorna Cove Hotel ⅚✳ | NEW ENTRY |

Lamorna Cove, Lamorna TR19 6XH
TEL: (01736) 731411   FAX: (01736) 732316
EMAIL: reception@lamornacove.com   COOKING 4
WEBSITE: www.lamornacove.com   ANGLO-FRENCH
off 3315, 6m S of Penzance   £35–£76

Spectacularly sited overlooking Lamorna Cove, the Artist's Palette restaurant at the stylish Lamorna Cove Hotel is a conservatory-like beamed structure, with large windows designed to make the most of the marine views. Local supplies inform Robert Stirrup's carefully crafted, seasonal Anglo-French menus. A starter dish of seared red mullet on saffron risotto with a bouillabaisse sauce was timed to perfection, and a main-course 'taste of the sea' of turbot, scallops and more red mullet in a Gewürztraminer wine and cream sauce with finely diced vegetables was both accurately cooked and attractively presented. An old favourite like calf's liver and mash gains authority from the addition of bacon, onion and rosemary; sautéed kidneys were served in spring with poached new season's lamb, accompanied by garlic 'pannacotta' and a niçoise jus. Chocolate moelleux cake with hot, runny centre came with basil ice cream, or there could be poached strawberries with a rhubarb jelly. One slight niggle has been dishes that arrive a little cooler than expected, perhaps because of time spent arranging their components. The wine list succinctly covers the known vinous globe, including England, at reasonable mark-ups. Half a dozen house wines start at £12.95 a bottle.

CHEF: Robert Stirrup   PROPRIETORS: Tania and Peter Hopkinson   OPEN: all week 12 to 2.30, 7 to 9.30   CLOSED: Jan   MEALS: alc Mon to Sat (main courses £13.50 to £27). Set L Sun only £25, Set D £27.50. Breakfast 8 to 9.30, tea 2.30 to 5   SERVICE: not inc, card slips closed   CARDS: MasterCard, Switch, Visa   DETAILS: 45 seats. 27 seats outside. Private parties: 45 main room. Car park. Vegetarian meals. No children under 14 at D. No smoking. Wheelchair access (also WC). Music   ACCOMMODATION: 12 rooms, all with bath/shower. TV. Phone. Room only £60 to £175. Rooms for disabled. No children under 14

LANGAR Nottinghamshire   map 5

▲ Langar Hall ♥ ⚹⚹

Langar NG13 9HG
TEL: (01949) 860559   FAX: (01949) 861045
EMAIL: langarhall-hotel@ndirect.co.uk
WEBSITE: www.langarhall.com   COOKING 3
between A46 and A52, 4m S of Bingham, next to   ENGLISH
Langar church   £26–£68

At the end of a long drive, past a croquet lawn and magnificent old trees, stands the early Victorian house, with the village church rising behind. The striking burnt-orange façade gives some hint of the characterful décor within, which extends to faux-marble pillars and free-standing statuary in the dining room. The menu aims to catch the attention too, with some assured classical cooking. A soup of honey-roast parsnips might kick things off, to be succeeded by the old-school pleasure of a whole Dover sole with champagne sauce. Slightly less traditional are brill and mussel risotto, or guinea-fowl breast sauced with Pineau des Charentes, with maybe baked rhubarb cheesecake and ginger ice-cream to finish. Since this is Stilton country, it is as well not to miss a taste of the pace-setting Cropwell Bishop or Colston Basset versions on offer. Sensible selections of Bordeaux and Burgundy sit alongside New World offerings from the likes of Isabel Estate, Mulderbosch and Seresin that show a keen nose for exciting modern flavours. Five of the ten house wines are available at £4 per glass, and prices overall are admirably restrained.

CHEFS: Toby Garratt and Garry Booth   PROPRIETOR: Imogen Skirving   OPEN: all week 12 to 1.45, 7 to 10 (8 Sun)   MEALS: alc D (main courses £13.50 to £20). Set L £12.50 (2 courses) to £22.50, Set D £25 to £35   SERVICE: 5% (optional), card slips closed   CARDS: Amex, Delta, MasterCard, Switch, Visa   DETAILS: 30 seats. 20 seats outside. Private parties: 22 main room, 8 to 22 private rooms. Car park. Vegetarian meals. Children's helpings. No smoking. Wheelchair access (also WC). No music ACCOMMODATION: 10 rooms, all with bath/shower. TV. Phone. B&B £65 to £185. Baby facilities. Fishing (*The Which? Guide to Good Hotels*) £5

LANGFORD BUDVILLE Somerset   map 2

▲ Bindon Country House, Wellesley Restaurant ⚡✗

Langford Budville TA21 0RU
TEL: (01823) 400070 FAX: (01823) 400071   COOKING 3
EMAIL: stay@bindon.com   ANGLO-FRENCH COUNTRY-HOUSE
WEBSITE: www.bindon.com   £31–£62

This country house, now in its sixth year, offers a rural retreat with grand façades, seven acres of garden, and traditional décor. French chef Patrick Robert still presides over a largely traditional menu with contemporary twists and one which demonstrates that the kitchen is in safe hands. Goats' cheese roulade with aubergine pickle, and lobster, monkfish and vegetable terrine with a saffron dressing are typical starters. Reports in the main are positive: roast chump of lamb with pomme fondant and rosemary sauce was 'cooked to perfection', as was a 'nage' of seafood – the delicateness of the dish making an impression on one reporter. Extras abound such as a pre-dessert of apple jelly with lavender syrup and passion-fruit sorbet – 'an abstract work of art'. If you can, follow that with perhaps a lemon soufflé with lemongrass and champagne sorbet, or apple tart in caramel sauce. Service is knowledgeable and friendly. A well-chosen, relatively short wine list – by country-house standards – provides a dozen house wines, with six offered by the glass (£4). The remainder, arranged by grape variety, lean towards France.

CHEF: Patrick Robert PROPRIETORS: Lynn and Mark Jaffa OPEN: all week 12 to 1.30, 7.30 to 9
MEALS: Set L £12.95 (2 courses) to £16.95, Set D £29.95 (2 courses) to £36 SERVICE: not inc
CARDS: Amex, Delta, Diners, MasterCard, Switch, Visa DETAILS: 50 seats. 30 seats outside.
Private parties: 50 main room, 4 to 25 private rooms. Car park. Vegetarian meals. Children's helpings. No smoking. Wheelchair access (not WC). Occasional music. No mobile phones ACCOMMODATION: 12 rooms, all with bath/shower. TV. Phone. B&B £95 to £205. Rooms for disabled. Baby facilities. Swimming pool (*The Which? Guide to Good Hotels*) £5

LANGHO Lancashire   map 8

▲ Northcote Manor ⚐ ⚡✗

Northcote Road, Langho BB6 8BE
TEL: (01254) 240555 FAX: (01254) 246568
EMAIL: sales@northcotemanor.com   COOKING 6
WEBSITE: www.northcotemanor.com   MODERN BRITISH
on A59, 9m E of M6 junction 31   £28–£77

A lengthy refurbishment programme is underway at this large country house, but for now the pleasant, airy dining room overlooking Bleasedale Fell makes a fine setting for some up-to-the-minute cooking: perhaps oyster tempura with deep-fried seaweed and chilli aïoli to start, or a plate of organic charcuterie taking in wild boar pancetta, smoked Middle White ham and Old Spot speck, served with house pickles. Traditional dishes do appear – roast grouse with game chips and bread sauce for example – but the distinctive regional accent is what strikes most forcibly, in say a Mrs Kirkham's Lancashire cheese soufflé or the long-standing combination of black pudding and buttered pink trout served with mustard and nettle sauce. Local materials abound, in the form of Goosnargh chicken, and Bowland Forest beef and lamb, although their accompaniments might take inspiration from further afield – lemon marmalade with the beef, couscous with the lamb, for example. Desserts are mostly international: a wild berry tart soufflé with liquorice ice cream, or a mille-feuille of strawberries and pineapple with Kirsch cream and pineapple sorbet. The wine list is packed with good names in all regions, although Italy, Australia and the Spanish reds stand out. Prices are on the high side and have occasioned complaints from otherwise satisified reporters. Six house wines come by the glass for around £4.50 and the range of half-bottles is particularly broad.

CHEFS: Nigel Haworth and Warwick Dodds   PROPRIETORS: Craig Bancroft and Nigel Haworth   OPEN: Sun to Fri L 12 to 1.30 (2 Sun), all week D 7 to 9.30 (10 Sat)   CLOSED: 25 Dec, 1 Jan, bank hol Mons   MEALS: alc (main courses £18.50 to £25.50). Set L £17.50, Set D £50   SERVICE: 10% (optional)   CARDS: Amex, Delta, MasterCard, Switch, Visa   DETAILS: 70 seats. Private parties: 70 main room, 8 to 40 private rooms. Car park. Vegetarian meals. Children's helpings. Jacket and tie. No smoking. Wheelchair access (not WC). Music. No mobile phones   ACCOMMODATION: 14 rooms, all with bath/shower. TV. Phone. B&B £100 to £150. Rooms for disabled. Baby facilities (*The Which? Guide to Good Hotels*)

LAVENHAM Suffolk   map 6

▲ Great House ⁙✳

Market Place, Lavenham CO10 9QZ
TEL: (01787) 247431   FAX: (01787) 248007   COOKING 1
EMAIL: info@greathouse.co.uk   FRENCH
WEBSITE: www.greathouse.co.uk   £26–£62

Lavenham's market square holds a fabulous collection of ancient half-timbered houses but the Great House stands out for its stark, white-painted, symmetrical Georgian façade. It is older than it appears, as becomes apparent inside, where there are thick beams and a brick inglenook. Signs of the past are also evident in the food, the French menus dealing in the likes of truite aux amandes, and filet de sole farcie à la mousse de curry. The cream-laden cooking can seem a little rich for modern tastes, but it does have its supporters, and a carefully cooked roast saddle of venison with a clear-tasting, well-reduced red wine sauce, roasted pear and wobbly spinach mousse was a highlight at inspection. Service is willing but not always able. The wine list opens with eight house selections by the glass, half-litre or bottle, and prices start at £10.20.

CHEF: Regis Crépy   PROPRIETORS: Regis and Martine Crépy   OPEN: Tue to Sun L 12 to 2.30, Tue to Sat D 7 to 9.30 (10 Sat)   CLOSED: Jan   MEALS: alc excl Sun L (main courses £9 to £19). Set L £14.95 (2 courses) to £17.95, Set L Sun £21.95, Set D Tue to Fri £22.95. Light L menu available Tue to Sat   SERVICE: not inc   CARDS: Amex, Delta, MasterCard, Switch, Visa   DETAILS: 45 seats. 30 seats outside. Private parties: 60 main room. Children's helpings. No smoking in dining room; smoking permitted in lounge/bar area. Music   ACCOMMODATION: 5 rooms, all with bath/shower. TV. Phone. B&B £65 to £150. Baby facilities (*The Which? Guide to Good Hotels*)

LEAMINGTON SPA Warwickshire   map 5

Love's ✷✸

15 Dormer Place, Leamington Spa CV32 5AA	COOKING 5
TEL/FAX: (01926) 315522	MODERN EUROPEAN
EMAIL: lovesrestaurant@aol.com	£24–£61

The half-basement dining room at Love's looks onto a tiny flower-filled stone patio, and across the road is the green, with its legion of dog-walkers and playing children. The interior is simple: walls are hung with artworks from local artists, and tables are set with good white linen. Chef-patron Steve Love – a former Roux scholar – describes his cooking as 'classically French with a modern feel'. Fittingly, a five-course menu gourmand might feature tian of goats' cheese, poached pear and onion marmalade, perhaps crab and lemon rocket salad with sautéed squid and an assiette de viande. Alternatively a starter of seared hand-dived scallops with a quenelle of pike mousse, frogs' legs and sauce vert, might turn up on the dinner menu, along with braised belly of veal with langoustines. Dishes tend to include a number of textures and flavours, raw materials are top-class, and technical skills very much in evidence (good sauces, for example). Desserts hold a few surprises, such as iced sweetcorn parfait with dark chocolate and cumin sorbet, or an 'exceptional' trio of lemon (mousse, tartlet and sorbet). Love's partner, Claire Thorpe, runs front-of-house, providing 'service of a high order', and the well-rounded wine list covers Old and New Worlds, with plenty of choice under £25.

CHEF: Steve Love PROPRIETORS: Steve Love and Claire Thorpe OPEN: Tue to Sat 12 to 2, 7 to 9.45 CLOSED: Christmas, 1st 2 weeks Jan, last 2 weeks Aug MEALS: alc L (main dishes £8), Set L £13.50, Set D £23.50 (2 courses) to £37.50 (whole table only) SERVICE: 10% (optional) CARDS: Delta, MasterCard, Switch, Visa DETAILS: 32 seats. Private parties: 32 main room. Vegetarian meals. Children's helpings. No smoking. Music. No mobile phones (£5)

LEEDS West Yorkshire   map 8

Brasserie Forty Four

44 The Calls, Leeds LS2 7EW	COOKING 4
TEL: (0113) 234 3232 FAX: (0113) 234 3332	MODERN EUROPEAN
EMAIL: brasserie44@onetel.net.uk	£23–£63

A forerunner of Leeds' 1990s revival, this elegant but informal waterside brasserie epitomises how successful and enjoyable this genre can be in the right hands. The menu disregards geography, drawing on ideas from around the world, but everything manages to seem in place. A glance at dishes 'From Bill Rae's Whitby Smokehouse' will remind you that this is Yorkshire. A satisfied diner recommended the chef for the 'freedom of Yorkshire' for producing such main courses as 'unbelievably flavoursome' daube of ox cheek with dumplings, and 'moist and delicious' blanquette of rabbit. Equally successful have been starters of a pheasant and sage chipolata, and smoked chicken and leek tart in the lightest of pastry. From further afield come an Alsace-style salad of shredded pork, garlic sausage and choucroute, imam bayaldi, and well-reported crème brûlées – perhaps Armagnac and espresso, or white chocolate and Baileys.

Otherwise, desserts are along traditional lines: burnt rice pudding with poached pears, or spotted dick with cinnamon custard. Service is friendly and professional, and the wine list has lots of fruity, modern options under £20. Only the Australian white and Chilean red house wines come by the glass, but refreshingly these are not the most basic bottles on the list (£14.95/£3.65).

CHEF: Jeff Baker PROPRIETOR: Michael Gill OPEN: Mon to Fri L 12 to 2, Mon to Sat D 6 to 10.30 (11 Fri and Sat) CLOSED: bank hols MEALS: alc (main courses £10 to £16.50). Set L and D 6 to 7.15 £11.50 (2 courses) to £14 SERVICE: 10% (optional), card slips closed CARDS: Delta, Diners, MasterCard, Switch, Visa DETAILS: 110 seats. Private parties: 110 main room, 12 to 50 private rooms. Vegetarian meals. Children's helpings by arrangement. No cigars/pipes. Music. Air-conditioned

Fourth Floor

Harvey Nichols, 107–111 Briggate,
Leeds LS1 6AZ   COOKING 4
TEL: (0113) 204 8000   FAX: (0113) 204 8080   MODERN BRITISH
WEBSITE: www.harveynichols.com   £26–£58

Like its Knightsbridge sibling, the Leeds branch of Harvey Nichols has its restaurant on the top floor, reached via the deli, with a balcony affording superior views of the city. With a long bar to one side and the busy open-plan kitchen to the other, there is an agreeable sense of informality about it all. City-slick service dispenses food that is impeccably sourced and cheeringly seasonal, even if the ideas come from all over the place: salt-cod fritters with pea purée and tomato sauce might be followed by pumpkin and carrot pastilla with olive and lemon dressing, or 'pink, tasty and tender' chargrilled calf's liver with firm haricot beans in a Parmesan cream, the whole sauced with a dense and glossy reduction sharpened with Cabernet Sauvignon vinegar. Fish is ably cooked, as evidenced by a well-timed piece of roast halibut wrapped in Parma ham, accompanied by roasted chicory and a vivid green sauce ravigote. Vegetable side orders are charged extra (even though the chips are nothing special), but save room for one of the inventive desserts, which may take in lime and passion-fruit cheesecake, or a vibrantly flavoured parfait of white chocolate, stem ginger and coconut, served with fine chocolate biscotti. Good coffee and breads add lustre to the occasion, as do the imaginatively chosen, if expensive, wines, which open with house French at £13.50. Note that an 'optional' 10 per cent is added to the bill, though credit card slips are left open.

CHEFS: Richard Allen and Louise McCrimmon PROPRIETOR: Harvey Nichols OPEN: all week L 12 to 3 (4 Sat and Sun), Thur to Sat D 5.30 (7 Sat) to 10 CLOSED: 25 and 26 Dec, 1 Jan MEALS: alc (main courses £10.50 to £17). Set L £15 (2 courses) to £18, Set D £10.95 (2 courses) to £14.95. Bar menu available Mon to Wed 3 to 6, Thur and Fri 3 to 8, Sat 4 to 6; breakfast all week 10 to 12 SERVICE: 10% (optional) CARDS: Amex, Delta, Diners, MasterCard, Switch, Visa DETAILS: 80 seats. 12 seats outside. Private parties: 200 main room. Vegetarian meals. Children's helpings Sun L. Wheelchair access (also WC). Music. Air-conditioned

denotes an outstanding wine cellar; ♥ *denotes a good wine list, worth travelling for.*

Leodis ▼

Victoria Mill, 4 The Embankment, Sovereign
Street, Leeds LS1 4BJ   COOKING 3
TEL: (0113) 242 1010   FAX: (0113) 243 0432   BRASSERIE/MODERN BRITISH
WEBSITE: www.leodis.co.uk   £28–£65

At one time this converted riverside mill was a warehouse used for storing Yorkshire Relish. Nowadays you are likely to encounter a different kind of Yorkshire Relish, provided by a lively, enthusiastic crowd – indeed, it can get a bit too lively for some reporters, and there have been occasional slips in the usually slick, friendly service, but it is certainly a popular venue. The décor in the large, open-plan dining area is in modern brasserie style, with bare brick walls and stripped wooden floors, and menus follow suit, offering a wide range of comforting options such as moules marinière, warm poached egg and bacon salad, seared squid with garlic, chilli and rocket, roast cod with a tapenade crust, gammon shank with pea purée, and roast Gressingham duckling with tarte Tatin, with crème brûlée or chocolate marquise to finish. The wine list is packed with good bottles at reasonable prices and stretches to some prestigious offerings, including fine Italians and a page of mature clarets. Bottle prices start at £13.95, and nine by the glass are £3.75 to £6. A sister establishment, Paris, is at Calverley Lane, Rodley, Leeds, tel. (0113) 258 1885.

CHEF: Steve Kendal   PROPRIETORS: Martin Spalding, Steve Kendal and Phil Richardson   OPEN: Mon to Fri L 12 to 2, Mon to Sat D 6 to 10 (11 Sat)   MEALS: alc (main courses £8 to £17). Set L and D (exc after 7.15 Sat) £16.95   SERVICE: 10% (optional), card slips closed   CARDS: Amex, Delta, Diners, MasterCard, Switch, Visa   DETAILS: 180 seats. 60 seats outside. Car park (D only). Vegetarian meals. No cigars/pipes. Wheelchair access (also WC). Music. Air-conditioned

Livebait £

Shears Yard, The Calls, Leeds LS2 7EY
TEL: (0113) 244 4144   FAX: (0113) 243 7933   COOKING 3
EMAIL: gcg_lb_leeds@groupechezgerard.co.uk   SEAFOOD
WEBSITE: www.santeonline.co.uk   £24–£74

The main attraction of any restaurant called Livebait is likely to be the fish, and on that score this one comes up trumps (there are others in Manchester and London; see Round-up entries). The menu does not shy away from adventure, and may turn up a main course of Indian dry-rubbed tuna with green chilli chutney and red pepper raita, or a starter of pan-roast Cornish squid with chorizo and polenta. More traditional treatments are in evidence, too, with grills such as Dover sole, and salmon and cod fishcake, or fish pie. Desserts tend to be simple affairs such as lemon tart. Purposeful but 'polite and efficient' staff move quickly in this lively, bustling place. The wine list, mostly fish-friendly white wines, kicks off at £9.95, and the majority of bottles are below £20.

CHEF: Stuart Tattersal   PROPRIETOR: Groupe Chez Gérard   OPEN: Mon to Sat 12 to 3, 5.45 to 10.30 (11 Thur to Sat)   CLOSED: 25 Dec, 1 Jan, Aug bank hol   MEALS: alc (main courses £8 to £30). Set L £10.95 (2 courses) to £13.95, Set D Mon to Thur and Fri and Sat 5.45 to 7 £10.95 (2 courses) to £13.95. Bar menu available   SERVICE: 10% (optional), card slips closed   CARDS:

Amex, Diners, MasterCard, Switch, Visa DETAILS: 80 seats. 40 seats outside. Private parties: 90 main room. Vegetarian meals. Children's helpings. Wheelchair access (also WC). Music. Air-conditioned (£5)

No. 3 York Place

NEW ENTRY

3 York Place, Leeds LS1 2DR
TEL: (0113) 245 9922   FAX: (0113) 245 9965   COOKING 6
EMAIL: dine@no3yorkplace.co.uk   MODERN EUROPEAN
WEBSITE: www.no3yorkplace.co.uk   £31–£77

No. 3 York Place is on the site of what once was Guellers, and although the physical appearance is much the same, chef Martel Smith is making his mark. The long, narrow room is smartly furnished, with tables for two quite closely packed along both sides of a central 'spine', banquettes down each wall and well-designed leather seats. Service is polished 'while retaining a pleasing formality'. An appetiser of potato and pancetta 'cappuccino' may make an impressive entrée to proceedings, followed perhaps by a carefully made risotto of Cornish crab, offset by a quenelle of tomato sorbet. Fish is fresh and well timed, as in a main course of roast tranche of Whitby cod, a thick fillet with a crisp skin perched atop boned, braised oxtail and a red wine stock reduction. The selection of French and British cheeses impressed one visitor, particularly a seldom-found unpasteurised Wensleydale. The sweet-toothed, however, may find it difficult to pass up the likes of bitter chocolate fondant with smooth milk ice cream. The wine list explores France before offering some representation from most wine-producing countries. There are some expensive bottles, but prices start at around £14.

CHEF: Martel Smith   PROPRIETOR: FMC Ltd   OPEN: Mon to Fri L 12 to 2, Mon to Sat D 6.30 to 10   CLOSED: 25 to 30 Dec, bank hols   MEALS: alc (main courses £13 to £20). Set L and D Mon to Fri 6.30 to 7.30 £14.50 (2 courses) to £18, Set D £45   SERVICE: 10% (optional), card slips closed   CARDS: Amex, Delta, MasterCard, Switch, Visa   DETAILS: 48 seats. Private parties: 60 main room. No-smoking area. Music. Air-conditioned

Pool Court at 42 ⚡✲

44 The Calls, Leeds LS2 7EW   COOKING 7
TEL: (0113) 244 4242   FAX: (0113) 234 3332   CLASSIC FRENCH/MODERN BRITISH
EMAIL: poolcourt@onetel.net.uk   £42–£83

Restful greys and blues predominate in this sleek, calm, city-centre restaurant by the river. Lighting is pleasantly subdued, and strategically placed screens help to ensure a measure of privacy between tables. Prime-quality loaves are brought on a trolley and cut to order, and the menu offers some five or six choices per course, making the most of seasonal items such as roast grouse in autumn, pink cannon of Yorkshire lamb in spring (on a ragoût of globe artichoke, Puy lentils, garlic confit and almonds), or a summery 'pot-au-feu' of native shellfish with basil tortellini.

This is refined yet very appealing food, exemplified by a jokily named starter of 'Pool Court's Fish and Chips' consisting of four battered parcels – of salt-cod, scallop, oyster and Dublin Bay prawn – that were 'wonderfully fresh, accurately timed and crisply fried', and served with a bowl of chips and a lime-flavoured tartare sauce. Daily fish dishes are discussed at table: perhaps a large chunk of impeccably fresh boneless grilled halibut coated with lemony gremolata, served with an admirably sweet-sharp-sour vegetable pickle. Indeed, the kitchen is not afraid to innovate with oriental flavours when appropriate, producing a gently spiced ravioli of oxtail that 'couldn't be bettered', helped by the quality of its thin, silken pasta topped with a slice of black truffle, and by the powerful oxtail consommé in which it all floated.

There have been lapses, but most reports are enthusiastic, not least for desserts such as a large, light and well-risen savarin of wild strawberries, and for peach melba – 'old-fashioned and very impressive' – the fruit coated in a thin layer of raspberry coulis and served with a smooth vanilla ice cream in a thin pastry tart. Alternatively, the unpasteurised British and French cheeses are kept in excellent condition. Service is well drilled, friendly and informative, and the wine list offers plenty of interesting bottles at comparatively reasonable prices (especially whites). House Californian red and Chilean white are £15.50.

CHEF: Jeff Baker   PROPRIETOR: Michael Gill   OPEN: Mon to Fri L 12 to 2, Mon to Sat D 7 to 10 (8.30 Sat)   CLOSED: bank hols   MEALS: Set L and D £25 (2 courses) to £55   SERVICE: 10%, card slips closed   CARDS: Delta, MasterCard, Switch, Visa   DETAILS: 38 seats. 18 seats outside. Private parties: 38 main room. Vegetarian meals. Children's helpings by arrangement. No children under 3. No smoking. Wheelchair access (also WC). Music. No mobile phones. Air-conditioned

---

Room | NEW ENTRY |

Bond House, The Bourse Courtyard, Boar Lane,
Leeds LS1 5DE
TEL: (0113) 242 6161   FAX: (0113) 388 8688   COOKING 1
EMAIL: event@roomleeds.com   MODERN BRITISH
WEBSITE: www.roomleeds.com   £27–£51

Behind a gated courtyard near Leeds's shopping centre is this studiedly cool and decidedly sexy new venue. The name of the basement bar, which is kitted out in purple velvet, is the Bedroom (not to be taken too literally), and is for drinks only (bookings required), while the large ground-floor dining area is not without its own creature comforts, with squashy aubergine-coloured sofas, zinc bar, slate floor and abstract art all contributing to the 'exciting, casual and airy' ambience. Chris Tolson, who spent five years at the Fourth Floor restaurant of Harvey Nichols in Leeds (see entry), brings a sense of urban panache to the menus. What sounds like a drearily trad starter dish of prawn and avocado cocktail is given a clever new spin with crisp-battered prawns, an avocado timbale and lime-spiked coleslaw. A main-course option of lamb bourguignonne has delivered 'meltingly tender' pot-roast meat, full of 'lovely gelatinous bits', served with smooth potato purée, while a handsome tranche of halibut has been appealingly fresh and accompanied by tangy parsley sauce. A chocolate cookie and a scoop of banana ice cream have been the best items on a dessert assiette. Staff, dressed in T-shirts that expose their midriffs, are young and carefree, which feels right in such a 'chic, hip, funky and terrifically lively' place. A short but enterprising wine list includes an Italian Gewürztraminer and a Tunisian red. Prices start at £10, and a dozen are served by the glass.

CHEF: Chris Tolson   PROPRIETOR: Frontroom Restaurants   OPEN: Mon to Sat 12 to 2.30, 6 to 11 (10 Mon and Tue)   CLOSED: 25 and 26 Dec, bank hol Mons   MEALS: alc (main courses £12.50 to £17). Set L and D Mon to Fri £13.95 (2 courses) to £16.50. Bar menu available   SERVICE: 10% (optional)   CARDS: Amex, Delta, MasterCard, Switch, Visa   DETAILS: 120 seats. 52 seats outside. Private parties: 200 main room, 6 to 18 private rooms. Children's helpings. Wheelchair access (also WC). Music. Air-conditioned (£5)

Simply Heathcotes

Canal Wharf, Water Lane, Leeds LS11 5PS
TEL: (0113) 244 6611   FAX: (0113) 244 0736
EMAIL: leeds@simplyheathcotes.co.uk
WEBSITE: www.heathcotes.co.uk

COOKING **1**
MODERN BRITISH
£25–£54

Formerly Heathcotes at Rascasse, this converted riverside warehouse has been rebranded to bring it in line with the Simply Heathcotes philosophy. This hasn't brought about any significant alterations; it remains a pleasant venue, done out in wood, glass and chrome, and attractive river views are a bonus. Menus follow the now familiar Heathcote version of modern British cookery that produces chargrilled artichokes on brioche with hollandaise; risotto of sun-dried tomato and tapenade; roast suckling pig with sage stuffing, cider potato and apple sauce; and seared monkfish with curried cauliflower couscous and cucumber dressing. Vegetables are extra. Sweets include knickerbocker glory and bread-and-butter pudding, and service is smart and friendly but not very knowledgeable. Wines tend to be a little overpriced but offer a wide choice, starting with house French varietals from £12.

CHEF: Simon Peacock   PROPRIETOR: Paul Heathcote   OPEN: all week 12 to 2.30, 6 to 10 (11 Sat, 10.30 Sun)   CLOSED: Bank hols except Good Friday   MEALS: alc (main courses £9 to £15.50). Set L £9.50 (1 course to £15.50, Set D Mon to Sat 6 to 7, Sun 6 to 10.30 £13.50 (2 courses) to £15.50   SERVICE: 10% (optional)   CARDS: Amex, MasterCard, Switch, Visa   DETAILS: 150 seats. Private parties: 150 main room. Car park. Vegetarian meals. Children's helpings. No smoking. Wheelchair access (also WC). Music. Air-conditioned

Sous le Nez en Ville ▐ £

The Basement, Quebec House, Quebec Street,
Leeds LS1 2HA
TEL: (0113) 244 0108   FAX: (0113) 245 0240

COOKING **3**
MODERN EUROPEAN
£26–£55

This long-established Leeds favourite is a true individual. It may have fallen behind a little in the fashion stakes, but the casual yet professional style, helpful, knowledgeable French staff and appealing modern European cooking add up to a winning formula. Among starters, oriental influences appear in the form of pan-fried scallops with salt and pepper squid and pickled soy vegetables, while oak-roast salmon and prawn fishcake with good home-made tomato ketchup represents the domestic strand to the cooking. One menu is given over to fish, producing at inspection a simply presented main course of grilled sea bass on herb risotto, which showed off careful preparation and good-quality ingredients. Alternatives might include chargrilled tuna with 'green and gold' caponata, while non-fish options typically feature roast venison with caramelised apple and black pudding mash, or simply chargrilled sirloin with béarnaise, and desserts are things like steamed pineapple sponge with vanilla custard. Wines throughout the extensive list, from Bordeaux to Australia, are appropriately bottle-aged. Fair pricing and outstanding quality, from basic to premium to rare and special bottles, complement this admirable devotion to our drinking pleasure. Prices start at £10.95, and 15 by the glass are £2.20 to £5.95.

CHEFS: Andrew Carter and Andrew Lavender   PROPRIETOR: Sous le Nez Ltd   OPEN: Mon to Sat 12 to 2.30, 6 to 10 (11 Sat)   CLOSED: L Good Fri, bank hol Mons   MEALS: alc (main courses £9.25 to £17.50). Set L Sat 12 to 2 £18.95, Set D Mon to Fri 6 to 7.30, Sat 6 to 7 £18.95. Bar menu available   SERVICE: not inc   CARDS: Delta, Diners, MasterCard, Switch, Visa   DETAILS: 85 seats. Private parties: 4 to 20 private rooms. Vegetarian meals. Music. Air-conditioned (£5)

LEEK Staffordshire

▲ Number 64   NEW ENTRY

64 St Edward Street, Leek ST13 5DL   COOKING 2
TEL: (01538) 381900   FAX: (01538) 370918   BRITISH-PLUS
EMAIL: enquiries@number64.com   £20–£54

This impressive double-fronted Georgian building, home to a speciality food shop, pâtisserie, wine bar, restaurant and rooms, occupies a spot at the bottom of St Edward Street. Pre-dinner drinks can be taken in the fabulously decked-out cellar with its stone walls and modern wooden bar. Upstairs, the restaurant, which overlooks an attractive garden, combines soft apricot shades with bare oak tables and simple vases of flowers. Baked monkfish and chervil tart with curried yoghurt glaze comes with very light pastry and a creamy glaze, while home-smoking has produced a successful starter of wood pigeon with chestnut, tarragon and a cream vinaigrette. 'Substantial and delicious' saddle of rabbit with pan-fried gnocchi, peas and broad beans was the star dish at inspection. Rhubarb crumble with stem ginger ice cream and caramel pannacotta with kumquat compote and ginger biscuits give a flavour of desserts. A carefully selected wine list offers good value for money; ten house wines start at £9.95.

CHEF: Mark Walker   PROPRIETOR: Nigel Cope   OPEN: Tue to Sun L 12 to 2, Tue to Sat D 7 to 9 MEALS: alc (main courses L £6 to £9, D £14 to £20). Set D £39.95   SERVICE: not inc   CARDS: Amex, Delta, MasterCard, Switch, Visa   DETAILS: 46 seats. 20 seats outside. Private parties: 40 main room, 8 to 14 private rooms. Vegetarian meals. Children's helpings. Music ACCOMMODATION: 3 rooms, all with bath/shower. TV. Phone. B&B £65 to £95. No children. Baby facilities

LEIGH-ON-SEA Essex   map 3

Boatyard   NEW ENTRY

8–13 High Street, Leigh-on-Sea SS9 2EN   COOKING 2
TEL/FAX: (01702) 475588   MODERN EUROPEAN
WEBSITE: www.theboatyardrestaurant.co.uk   £27–£73

This former boatyard sits on the water's edge offering views of the Thames estuary. Inside is a large, contemporary dining space with a few nautical touches such as a boat-shaped bar. Dining, too, offers plenty that is modern, such as prawn tempura with an oriental salad, or chargrilled vegetables with marinated mozzarella. Scallops with petits pois, roast cod with sweet potato chips, or sea bass fillet with grilled artichoke all fit the theme, but meat eaters are well catered for with gutsy offerings such as crispy belly pork with black pudding, or pan-fried Irish ham sausages with buttered mash and mustard sauce. Finish perhaps with peach crème brûlée, or a sugar tart stuffed with caramel mascarpone and figs with sautéed mango. Service has been praised, as have regular live music slots. A short, straightforward wine list provides plenty of interest under £25, with five house wines at £12.95 and £13.50.

CHEF: Jonathan Luck   PROPRIETOR: John Cross   OPEN: Wed to Sun L 12 to 3 (4.30 Sun), Tue to Sat D 6.30 to 11   CLOSED: 25 and 26 Dec   MEALS: alc D (main courses £15 to £20). Set L £10.95 (2 courses) to £14.95. Cover £1.50   SERVICE: not inc   CARDS: Delta, MasterCard, Switch, Visa   DETAILS: 178 seats. Private parties: 200 main room. Car park. Vegetarian meals. Children's helpings. No-smoking area. Wheelchair access (also WC). Music. Air-conditioned

---

LEWDOWN Devon   **map 1**

▲ Lewtrenchard Manor 🍷 ✴

Lewdown EX20 4PN
TEL: (01566) 783256   FAX: (01566) 783332
EMAIL: stay@lewtrenchard.co.uk
WEBSITE: www.lewtrenchard.co.uk   COOKING **6**
off A30 Okehampton to Launceston road; turn   MODERN BRITISH
left at Lewdown   £25–£57

The house looks ancient and solid, with more than its fair share of gables, dark oak panelling, big fireplaces and old paintings. It is well looked after and feels welcoming, with a bar for aperitifs and nibbles, and well-spaced, smartly set tables in the candlelit dining room. Jason Hornbuckle's menus are full of interest, offering a terrine of smoked chicken and globe artichoke served with goats' cheese beignets, perhaps followed by slow-cooked salmon with smoked salmon won tons in a coriander and lemongrass sauce.

Results are characterised by both flavour and sound conception. This applies equally to a small tower of 'first-class' compressed oxtail with a strewing of frothy leeks and a red wine sauce as to a four-part plate of duck consisting of finely minced rillettes in a small cylindrical tower of leek; a 'tartare' made from breast meat briefly seared and then diced; a small disc of ballottine of foie gras; and a tiny crème brûlée dish of foie gras mixed with cream. Although gone in a few mouthfuls, this all added up to a 'delightful whole'. Fine materials are intelligently handled, notably in a dish of stuffed loin of lamb, cooked pink, accompanied by lightly gelatinous diced breast meat encased in breadcrumbs and deep-fried, this component a 'minor triumph' and only eclipsed by a splendid 'shepherd's pie' of thin pastry filled with cumin-flavoured minced lamb.

Such themes and variations are effective among desserts, too: for example, in an unmoulded crème brûlée of 'perfect consistency' resting on a thin slice of caramelised pineapple, surrounded by a caramel sauce flecked with passion-fruit seeds, accompanied by a slightly sharp passion-fruit sorbet: a harmonious dish in which all parts work effectively together. Service is willing and smiling, and if that doesn't win you over, the wine list ('a belter', according to one report) should do the trick. Most at home in France, this intelligent selection also makes special efforts in South Africa, but there are good choices everywhere and prices range from very fair to positive giveaways. Seven house wines are £12 a bottle, £2.75 a glass.

CHEF: Jason Hornbuckle   PROPRIETOR: Von Essen Hotels   OPEN: Tue to Sun L 12 to 1.30, all week D 7 to 9   MEALS: Set L £10 (2 courses) to £15, Set D £35   SERVICE: not inc, card slips closed   CARDS: Amex, Delta, Diners, MasterCard, Switch, Visa   DETAILS: 50 seats. Private parties: 30 main room, 10 to 50 private rooms. Car park. Children's helpings. No children under 8 at D. No smoking. Wheelchair access (also WC). Occasional music   ACCOMMODATION: 9 rooms, all with bath/shower. TV. Phone. B&B £95 to £195 (double room). No children under 8. Fishing (*The Which? Guide to Good Hotels*) (£5)

LEWES East Sussex   map 3

Circa ⚡✕

145 High Street, Lewes BN7 1XT
TEL: (01273) 471777   FAX: (01273) 488416   COOKING 3
EMAIL: eat@circacirca.com   FUSION
WEBSITE: www.circacirca.com   £36–£56

Spun candyfloss, garam masala dust, yam caramel, crying tortilla – culinarily speaking, 'we're definitely not in Kansas', as Dorothy might have said to the Cowardly Lion (or maybe it was the Tin Man). Whatever, the menu at Circa is certainly eye-catchingly inventive. While many restaurants have abandoned fusion cooking in favour of a more back-to-basics approach, chef Marc Bolger continues to go bravely where no chef has gone before. Vegetarians may like to try hot grass toast with summer truffle butter, girolles and ginger custard, while main-course seared New Zealand venison may be served with beets Anna, pomegranate greens and cumin jus, and grilled swordfish may be flavoured with fermented bean oil and accompanied by yellow curried spinach and chicken stock radish. Desserts (here called 'The End') may include white manuka honey parfait with baklava garnish and saffron croissants. Perhaps not surprisingly with such culinary callisthenics, perfect balance is not always struck within the dishes, but there is real skill in the kitchen and at least, says one reporter, 'the food is fun'. The surroundings, all curvy lines and copper-toned walls, are sophisticated and smart, while service is well drilled but relaxed. The short wine list starts at £11.95 and includes eight by the 250-millilitre glass from £4. The 'reserve' range of smart bottles was similarly short when reviewed but is set to expand.

CHEF: Marc Bolger   PROPRIETOR: Ann Renton Biles   OPEN: Tue to Sun L 12 to 3, Tue to Sat D 6 to 10   MEALS: alc (main courses L £12.50 to £15, D £17.50 to £20). Set L £12.50 (2 courses)   SERVICE: 10% (optional), card slips closed   CARDS: Amex, Delta, Diners, MasterCard, Switch, Visa   DETAILS: 90 seats. Private parties: 90 main room. Vegetarian meals. Children's helpings. No smoking in 1 dining room. Wheelchair access (also WC). Music. Air-conditioned

▲ Arundell Arms ♟ ✳

Lifton PL16 0AA
TEL: (01566) 784666   FAX: (01566) 784494
EMAIL: reservations@arundellarms.com
WEBSITE: www.arundellarms.com
just off A30, 4m E of Launceston

COOKING 5
MODERN BRITISH
£33–£61

It's hard to miss the Arundell Arms as you pass through Lifton on the old A30. The ivy-covered eighteenth-century coaching inn, a first-rate venue for shooting and fishing parties, is as grand as it is venerable. You could enjoy a simple meal from the all-day bar menu of snacks, sandwiches and dishes like smoked mackerel and horseradish fishcakes, or you could eat in the more formal dining room, where options include two- or three-course deals alongside an impressive five-course seasonal menu. Top-quality regional produce is at the heart of the cooking, which constructs dishes carefully and elaborately around simple but forthright flavour combinations. How about lemon sole fritters with green mayonnaise and caramelised lime, or perhaps venison and pork terrine with pistachios, honey toast and apricot chutney, for starters? Follow that with thyme-roasted rack of lamb with rhubarb compote and a piquant white wine and mint sauce, or Aylesbury duck fillet with puréed parsnips, celery flower fritters and a wood mushroom cream – or just stick to 'simply grilled' Devon Red Ruby fillet steak, or turbot cutlet with béarnaise. Marinated Agen prune fritters with cocoa sugar and cinnamon ice cream is a typically creative dessert. The wine list adeptly bridges the pub/restaurant divide with a faultless selection of traditional and modern flavours. Prices are reasonable, with plenty to choose from under £20, including the six high-quality house wines that start at £13 (£3.50 a glass), as well as a good range of half-bottles.

CHEFS: Philip Burgess and Nick Shopland   PROPRIETOR: Anne Voss-Bark   OPEN: all week 12.30 to 2, 7.30 to 9.30   CLOSED: 24 to 26 Dec D   MEALS: Set L £19 (2 courses) to £23.50, Set D £33 (2 courses) to £39.50. Bar menu available   SERVICE: not inc   CARDS: Amex, Delta, Diners, MasterCard, Switch, Visa   DETAILS: 70 seats. 25 seats outside. Private parties: 70 main room, 30 private room. Car park. Vegetarian meals. Children's helpings. No-smoking area. Wheelchair access (also WC). Music   ACCOMMODATION: 27 rooms, all with bath/shower. TV. Phone. B&B £49.50 to £130. Baby facilities. Fishing (*The Which? Guide to Good Hotels*) £5

Wig & Mitre ✳

30–32 Steep Hill, Lincoln LN2 1TL
TEL: (01522) 535190   FAX: (01522) 532402
WEBSITE: www.wigandmitre.com

NEW CHEF
MODERN BRITISH
£21–£51

If traditional mealtimes don't suit your schedule, then the Wig & Mitre can probably oblige. From 8am to around midnight, this pub/restaurant serves food: breakfast in the morning and afternoon, as well as sandwiches, a set-price lunch and a full carte. It's on two floors, with plenty of space and an informal, relaxed atmosphere. In the room upstairs, cartoons of famous judges preside over bare wooden tables with 'church window' chairs.

The departure of chef Peter Dodd after some 22 years is bound to ring some changes, although the enduring presence of Valerie Hope and the continuation of this tried-and-tested formula is reassuring. New man Saleem Ahmed's menu includes snail and parsley spring rolls alongside a more traditional-sounding chicken Caesar salad among starters, followed by, perhaps, roast cannon of lamb with basil and pine nut polenta and pecorino pesto. Gluten-free choices are highlighted, and desserts run to cherry Bakewell tart with bay leaf anglaise and cream Chantilly. Prices on the wine list of 50-plus bottles start at £10.50, and the majority remain below £20. Over 20 bottles are also sold by the glass from £2.60.

CHEF: Saleem Ahmed   PROPRIETORS: Michael and Valerie Hope, and Toby Hope   OPEN: all week 8 to 11   MEALS: alc (main courses £8.50 to £18). Set L £10 (2 courses) to £12.95   CARDS: Amex, Delta, Diners, MasterCard, Switch, Visa   DETAILS: 135 seats. Private parties: 65 main room, 20 private room. Vegetarian meals. Children's helpings. No smoking. No music   £5

LINTON West Yorkshire   map 8

▲ Wood Hall ✸✖

Trip Lane, Linton LS22 4JA
TEL: (01937) 587271   FAX: (01937) 584353
EMAIL: woodhall@arcadianhotels.co.uk
WEBSITE: www.arcadianhotels.co.uk
from Wetherby take A661 N for ½m, turn left for
Sicklinghall and Linton, then left to Linton and   COOKING 3
Wood Hall; turn right in Linton opposite Windmill   MODERN EUROPEAN
pub and continue 2m along single-track road   £26–£65

Wood Hall is a secluded grand hotel dating from 1750 and reached along an uneven, narrow road a little way out of the village of Linton. A suitably well-to-do feeling pervades the chandeliered dining room, which offers sweeping views over the gardens and a menu that deals in rich, classical cooking. Starters might include cream of salsify soup with black truffle, or a pressed terrine of foie gras, guinea fowl and leeks with black fig chutney. Dishes are often labour-intensive: a poached fillet of brill is accompanied by crab tortellini and a crab and ginger bisque sauce, while roast loin of lamb comes with aubergine compote, potato terrine, and a jus enriched with black olives and capers. Desserts make use of herbs and spices as well as the usual sweet things, partnering a poached pear with star anise parfait and a sesame tuile, or teaming a sharp-tasting lemon and lime tart with basil sorbet. A broadly based wine selection has many fine vintages, but mark-ups are on the stiff side. House varietals from La Serre, a Sauvignon Blanc and a Merlot, are £16.50, and there is a list of eight wines by the glass, priced between £4.50 and £5.

CHEF: Lee Parsons   PROPRIETOR: Hand Picked Hotels   OPEN: Sun to Fri L 12 to 2, all week D 7 to 10   MEALS: Set L £12.50 (2 courses) to £15, Set D £24 (2 courses) to £39. Bar menu available SERVICE: not inc, card slips closed   CARDS: Amex, Delta, Diners, MasterCard, Switch, Visa DETAILS: 35 seats. Private parties: 30 main room, 10 to 100 private rooms. Car park. Children's helpings. No smoking. Wheelchair access (also WC). Occasional music. No mobile phones ACCOMMODATION: 45 rooms, all with bath/shower. TV. Phone. B&B £95 to £150. Rooms for disabled. Baby facilities. Swimming pool. Fishing

Foxcote Inn £ ✳

Station Lane, Little Barrow CH3 7JN
TEL: (01244) 301343   FAX: (01244) 303287
WEBSITE: www.thefoxcote.com
off A56, 5½m NE of Chester

COOKING 2
SEAFOOD
£24–£51

Perhaps you can call in just for a drink at this pub/restaurant, but most people come to eat. Menus are chalked on a blackboard in the cottagey bar dining area, and dishes change daily. The kitchen's forte is seafood, which gets lively, contemporary treatments, as in starters of wok-tossed squid with lemongrass, chilli and coriander butter, or pan-fried king scallops with Bury black pudding and a chicory and orange chutney. Main courses might subsume poached salmon fillet on buttered linguine with crayfish and lobster bisque, or baked halibut on cherry tomato and leek risotto with minted pea purée. Among simpler alternatives might be grilled whole Dover sole with lemon and chive butter, and non-fish dishes could include beef fillet with horseradish mash and port jus. Five sweets range from banana bread-and-butter pudding to white chocolate crème brûlée (or an assiette of all five). Wines start at £9.95 and France receives most attention.

CHEFS: Leigh Parry and Kelvin Ward   PROPRIETORS: Leigh Parry and Cathy Goulding   OPEN: Tue to Sun L 12 to 2.15, Tue to Sat D 6 to 9.15   CLOSED: first 2 weeks Jan   MEALS: alc (main courses L £6 to £8, D £10 to £17). Set D Tue to Thur 6 to 7 £12 (2 courses) to £15   SERVICE: not inc, card slips closed   CARDS: Delta, MasterCard, Switch, Visa   DETAILS: 85 seats. Private parties: 25 main room. Car park. Vegetarian meals. Children's helpings. No smoking in 1 dining room. Wheelchair access (also WC). Music

Harrow ▮ ✳

Little Bedwyn SN8 3JP
TEL: (01672) 870871
EMAIL: dining@harrowinn.co.uk
WEBSITE: www.harrowinn.co.uk
off A4, 4m SW of Hungerford

COOKING 4
MODERN BRITISH
£30–£63

This serious but cheery-feeling restaurant is a simple brick building on the edge of an exceptionally pretty village. In deep middle England it may be, but food (and wines) show a cosmopolitan (especially Spanish) influence. Ingredients, though, are mainly British and carefully provenanced: not only is the Aberdeen Angus fillet described on the menu as 'pure bred', but the individual animal is also identified. Similarly, the turbot served with wild mushroom risotto is line-caught, and the 'beautifully fresh' Ibericised cod with chorizo, capers and anchovies actually came from Newlyn. A reporter has endorsed the quality of seafood including a tiger prawn timbale surmounted by avocado and seared yellowfin tuna flavoured with soy and wasabi sauce.

There is also commendation for desserts, notably 'sumptuous' coffee ice cream; alternatively try the mostly British selection of cheeses, some accompanied by sherries or wines (indeed, many dishes come with a wine recommendation). And there is no questioning the quality and commitment of the wine list, nor its individuality: sherries and Riojas are a strong feature, Australia and New Zealand a passion, prices are good, and Cloudy Bay Sauvignon is listed at an absurdly cheap £16 as if to prove a point. There are extended selections from a number of wineries and a healthy range by the glass from £4 (or £2.50 with the set lunch).

CHEFS: Roger Jones and John Brown   PROPRIETORS: Roger and Sue Jones   OPEN: Wed to Sun L 12 to 2, Wed to Sat D 7 to 9   CLOSED: 3 weeks Christmas, 3 weeks Aug   MEALS: alc (main courses £15 to £20). Set L £15 (2 courses) to £17.50, Set D £35   SERVICE: not inc, card slips closed   CARDS: Delta, MasterCard, Switch, Visa   DETAILS: 38 seats. 24 seats outside. Private parties: 38 main room. Vegetarian meals. Children's helpings. No smoking. Wheelchair access (not WC). No music. No mobile phones   £5

LITTLE SHELFORD Cambridgeshire   map 6

Sycamore House ♥ ⅹ

1 Church Street, Little Shelford CB2 5HG
TEL: (01223) 843396

COOKING 3
MODERN BRITISH
£34–£41

Ten years ago the Sharpes started their operation in this neat detached house in a village five miles south of Cambridge. A no-frills honesty runs through their four-evenings-a-week set-price dinners, from the spare interior and wooden chairs (sometimes a little hard on the less well padded), through Susan Sharpe's courteous, restrainedly friendly service, to the kitchen, where Michael cooks good ingredients in an engagingly straightforward style. Exotic touches – a duck pancake with hoisin sauce, maybe – are barely glimpsed amid the unpretentiously described repertoire of, say, roast partridge with redcurrant and port gravy (not jus, not even sauce, but gravy), a bolder escalope of trout with red-pepper crust, or a vegetarian risotto with goats' cheese, roast tomato and rocket. Menus are brief – a salad course sits between choices of four starters and mains (two meat, one fish and a vegetarian dish for the latter) – but they nevertheless offer real choices. Desserts are favourites like sticky toffee or a steamed Cambridge pudding served with clotted cream. Bread and coffee have been ordinary but adequate. Wines are thoughtfully chosen and very good value, and the appealing short list gives at least a nod to all regions. House red and white are quality French for under £11, or £2.50 a glass.

CHEF: Michael Sharpe   PROPRIETORS: Michael and Susan Sharpe   OPEN: Wed to Sat D 7.30 to 9 CLOSED: Christmas   MEALS: Set D £25   SERVICE: not inc, card slips closed   CARDS: Delta, MasterCard, Switch, Visa   DETAILS: 24 seats. Private parties (not Fri or Sat): 24 main room. Car park. Vegetarian meals. No children under 12. No smoking. No music   £5

Net prices *in the details at the end of an entry indicates that the prices given on a menu and on a bill are inclusive of VAT and service charge, and that this practice is clearly stated on menu and bill.*

A list of London restaurants by cuisine can be found near the front of the book.

Chung Ku £

Columbus Quay, Riverside Drive,
Liverpool L3 4DB   COOKING **4**
TEL: (0151) 726 8191   FAX: (0151) 726 8190   CHINESE
WEBSITE: www.chungkurestaurant.co.uk   £18–£66

Panoramic views of the Mersey from the windows on both floors of this design-conscious contemporary Columbus Quay restaurant are an obvious pull. So is the extensive menu, which trawls through a broad and often familiar, mainly Cantonese repertoire of meat, fish and vegetarian dishes. Among those recommended have been fresh and tasty shell-on mussels in a good satay sauce; crisp, moist and tender salt and pepper pork ribs; roast duck with creamy fat; and plump scallops served with seasonal vegetables. A separate Chinese-language menu lists a number of dishes not on the English-language version, although attempts to explore these can founder on language difficulties. Dim sum aficionados will be pleased with the large and excellent selection here, around 50, from deep-fried prawn dumplings and five-spice yam cakes to steamed baby squid balls. House French wines at £10.50 open a list that covers all major European and New World bases, not forgetting China itself. There is also a sister restaurant at East Lancashire Road, Carr Mill, St Helens tel: (01744) 609868.

CHEF: Au Tung   PROPRIETORS: Mr and Mrs Shum   OPEN: all week 12 to 11.30 (12 Fri and Sat, 10 Sun and bank hols)   CLOSED: 25 Dec   MEALS: alc (main courses £7.50 to £30). Set L £9.50, Set D £19 to £28 (all set meals min 2). Dim sum menu available all week 12 to 6   SERVICE: not inc
CARDS: Amex, Delta, MasterCard, Switch, Visa   DETAILS: 400 seats. Private parties: 200 main room, 30 to 200 private rooms. Car park. Vegetarian meals. Wheelchair access (also WC). Music. Air-conditioned

---

Other Place Bistro   [NEW ENTRY]

29A Hope Street, Liverpool L1 9BQ   COOKING **3**
TEL/FAX: (0151) 707 7888   MODERN EUROPEAN
                                                                       £20–£46

Just around the corner from the Philharmonic Hall, the Other Place offers good-value pre-performance dinners in addition to providing a quick, civilised and inexpensive lunchtime refuge. Spread over two floors, it has dark green walls and chunky wooden tables with paper cloths which contribute to an appropriately relaxed feel. An unpretentiousness can be found in the cooking, too, which has turned out sea bass with garlic mash, flavourful roast beef well partnered by parsnip and horseradish mash, and roast Goosnargh duck breast with banana fritters. Starters range from an 'extremely good' terrine of fresh and smoked salmon with scallops to pan-fried black pudding with mash and mustard cream, and puddings are along the lines of a soft, light ginger sponge with a matching sauce, or mocha pots. Friendly and helpful service fits the bill, and the short, modern wine list follows the menu's theme of well-chosen simplicity and is very good value; prices open at £10.95. The Other Place

Restaurant is at 141–143 Allerton Road, Liverpool, tel: (0151) 724 1234, and the Other Place Deli is at 121 Allerton Road, tel: (0151) 724 7718.

CHEF: Rhian Cradock   PROPRIETORS: David Thorneycroft, Sheila Benson, Sean Miller, Mark Benson and Philippa Feeney   OPEN: Tue to Fri L 11.30 to 2.30, Tue to Sat D 6 to 10   CLOSED: 24 Dec, bank hols   MEALS: alc exc Fri and Sat D (main courses L £5.50 to £8.50, D £9.50 to £14). Set D Tue to Fri 6 to 7 £11.95 (2 courses) to £13.95, Set D Fri and Sat £18.95 (2 courses) to £22.95   SERVICE: not inc, card slips closed   CARDS: Delta, MasterCard, Switch, Visa   DETAILS: 54 seats. Private parties: 34 main room, 12 to 20 private rooms. Vegetarian meals. Children's helpings. No cigars/pipes. Music

Simply Heathcotes £⅄ £

Beetham Plaza, 25 The Strand, Liverpool L2 0XL
TEL: (0151) 236 3536   FAX: (0151) 236 3534
EMAIL: liverpool@simplyheathcotes.co.uk
WEBSITE: www.heathcotes.co.uk

COOKING 3
MODERN ENGLISH
£25–£53

In a plaza of office buildings hard by the side of the Liver Building, this arm of Paul Heathcote's mini-empire is a masterpiece of quirky design. A curving wall of sheer plate glass might make things a little steamy if the sun is beating down, but the atmosphere within is cool enough to compensate, an attribute that extends to the practised approach of the staff. The food mixes the house style of determined northern regionalism with one or two Mediterranean touches: seared scallops (a brace, with roes intact) sit atop a heap of rocket and chopped black olives, garnished with a Parmesan crisp. A main course of roast suckling pig with pork and sage stuffing, a single majestically browned roast potato, and a sauce of cider and mashed apple returns us triumphantly to Lancashire. In between there may well be a properly timed piece of salmon fillet with crisped skin, served with soft polenta and peas, or sea bass on a risotto base with fritters of plum tomato and courgette. As well as bread-and-butter pudding with apricot compote and clotted cream, it is possible to evoke memories of childhood seaside holidays with a tall glass of authentic knickerbocker glory. The brasserie-style wine list plies most of its trade in France, Italy and the southern hemisphere. House wines are £12 to £13.50, and there are ten by the glass.

CHEF: Gavin Williams   PROPRIETOR: Paul Heathcote   OPEN: all week 12 to 2.30, 6 to 10 (11 Sat, 9.30 Sun)   CLOSED: 25 and 26 Dec, 1 Jan, bank hol Mons   MEALS: alc (main courses £9 to £15.50). Set L and D 12 to 2.30, 6 to 7 (9.30 Sun) £13.50 (2 courses) to £15.50   SERVICE: 10% (optional), card slips closed   CARDS: Amex, Delta, MasterCard, Switch, Visa   DETAILS: 72 seats. Private parties: 15 main room, 8 to 24 private rooms. Vegetarian meals. Children's helpings. No smoking. Wheelchair access (also WC). Music. Air-conditioned

---

If 'vegetarian meals' is noted in the details at the end of an entry, this means that a restaurant routinely lists at least one vegetarian starter and main course on menus. Other restaurants, however, may offer good vegetarian choices if you let them know in advance, so it is worthwhile phoning to enquire.

£5 *indicates that the restaurant has elected to participate in the* Good Food Guide *voucher scheme. For full details, see page 6.*

---

60 Hope Street ♥

60 Hope Street, Liverpool L1 9BZ
TEL: (0151) 707 6060   FAX: (0151) 707 6016   COOKING 4
EMAIL: info@60hopestreet.com   MODERN EUROPEAN
WEBSITE: www.60hopestreet.com   £26–£74

This end-terrace, double-fronted, classical Georgian house retains its domestic address in the name of the Manning brothers' restaurant. The main dining room is on the ground floor, with a slightly less formal café-bar in the basement, and a room for private bookings above.

Contemporary brasserie-style cooking is built around traditional ideas, some as close to home as roast lamb with bubble and squeak, others, such as Italian cheese and basil torta with tomato salad, or fried fillet of cod with baba ganoush, drawing on influences from both shores of the Mediterranean. Or there may be crab spring rolls with an Asian dipping sauce, or perhaps a superb assemblage of seared scallops on a bed of crushed Jersey Royals bound with rich mayonnaise, served with a high-intensity Bloody Mary sauce. Sea bass was a well-timed main course at inspection, the thick wedge of flavourful fish easily coping with Jerusalem artichokes, wild mushrooms, spinach and a rosemary beurre blanc to boot. If you feel you need them on top of all that, vegetable side dishes are charged extra (the chips are 'top-notch'). Desserts, however – sticky toffee pudding for example – have let the side down. Service is willing, but can lack polish. As for the wine, good names keep popping up on the list, with much that is food friendly – none more so than a 1996 Chinon from Joguet (£26.95). Fresh and interesting varietals start off at £12.95, and six wines come by the glass (£2.50–£3.50).

CHEF: Gary Manning   PROPRIETORS: Colin and Gary Manning   OPEN: Mon to Fri L 12 to 2.30, Mon to Sat D 7 to 10.30. Café-bar menu also available Mon to Sat noon to 10.30   CLOSED: bank hols   MEALS: alc (main courses £13.95 to £24.95). Set L £11.95 (2 courses) to £14.95   SERVICE: not inc, 10% for parties of 6 or more   CARDS: Delta, MasterCard, Switch, Visa   DETAILS: 90 seats. Private parties: 90 main room, 10 to 30 private rooms. Vegetarian meals. Children's helpings. No-smoking area. No music. Air-conditioned

Tai Pan £

W.H. Lung Building, Great Howard Street,   COOKING 4
Liverpool L5 9TZ   CHINESE
TEL: (0151) 207 3888   FAX: (0151) 207 0100   £16–£52

Don't be put off by the setting: despite being little more than a big space above a warehouse, this remains one of the best places in the north-west for authentic Chinese cooking, and at very reasonable prices. First-class dim sum are a feature – on Sunday lunchtimes, get here early or expect to queue, as crowds gather from far and wide for a slice of Hong Kong life. As well as a long standard menu of anglicised dishes, there is a 'Chinese-only' menu, which is by far the better bet for those who want to make the transition from sweet-and-sour pork to belly pork with yams. Among highlights are various roast meats and seafood dishes: deep-fried crispy oysters with salt and Worcester sauce for dipping, for example, or the signature dish of lobster with ginger and spring onions on a bed of noodles. The list of around three dozen wines constitutes a respectable selection at fair prices. House wines are £9.50.

CHEF: S.O. Chan   PROPRIETOR: Yatesbury Ltd   OPEN: all week 12 to 11 (9.30 Sun and bank hols)   MEALS: alc (main courses £5 to £14.50). Set L £5.45 (2 courses) to £8.45, Set D £16 to £26 (all min 2)   SERVICE: not inc   CARDS: Amex, Delta, MasterCard, Switch, Visa   DETAILS: 250 seats. Private parties: 280 main room, 10 to 80 private rooms. Car park. Vegetarian meals. Wheelchair access (also WC). Music. Air-conditioned

▲ Ziba at the Racquet Club ♥ £ | NEW ENTRY |

Hargreaves Building, 5 Chapel Street,   COOKING 4
Liverpool L3 9AG   MODERN BRITISH
TEL: (0151) 236 6676   FAX: (0151) 236 6870   £26–£54

Those who noticed Ziba's omission from last year's Guide will no doubt be pleased to see it return, this time in the Victorian splendour of the Racquet Club, opposite the Liver Building. Excellent use has been made of the vast space to create a classy-looking dining room, where a huge reproduction of an Italian Renaissance painting hangs on one wall, and large, ornate chandeliers fill the ceiling.

The cooking is 'remarkably similar' to the old Ziba, both in style and quality. Refinement and delicacy are the watchwords, chef Jon Valentine producing dishes with well-defined flavours that reflect the quality of the ingredients used: one reporter's starter of goats' cheese and celeriac gâteau 'with a lovely fluffy consistency' came with a complementary red pepper syrup, while cannelloni of quail with white haricot and broad beans and a chicken sauce showed a pleasing lightness of touch. Main courses range from simple classics such as grilled lemon sole with parsleyed new potatoes and tartare sauce to more innovative creations like duck breast with beetroot jam, pomme galette and cabbage farci, which proved a harmonious and well-executed combination for its reporter. The star among desserts is the 'assiette of lemon', comprising a delicate tart, a posset, a lemon cream sandwiched in discs of 'exquisite' shortbread, and a moist, tangy sponge cake. Wines are a modern mix arranged by style, with a good balance of budget and smarter bottles. Prices start at £11.50, and ten come by the glass for £3 to £5.

CHEF: Jon Valentine   PROPRIETORS: Martin and Helen Ainscough   OPEN: Mon to Fri L 12 to 2.30, Mon to Sat D 6 to 10 (11 Fri and Sat)   CLOSED: bank hols   MEALS: alc (main courses £9 to £16.50). Bar menu available 11 to 7   SERVICE: not inc   CARDS: Amex, Delta, MasterCard, Switch, Visa   DETAILS: 100 seats. Private parties: 20 to 130 private rooms. Vegetarian meals. No-smoking area. Music. Air-conditioned   ACCOMMODATION: 8 rooms, all with bath/shower. TV. Phone. Room only £95 (double room). Swimming pool

Card slips closed *in the details at the end of an entry indicates that the total on the slips of credit cards is closed when handed over for signature.*

London Round-ups listing additional restaurants that may be worth a visit can be found after the main London section.

▲ Waterdine ▼ ✸

Llanfair Waterdine LD7 1TU
TEL: (01547) 528214   FAX: (01547) 529992
WEBSITE: www.the-waterdine.co.uk
off B4355, 4m NW of Knighton

COOKING 5
MODERN BRITISH
£25–£48

The Waterdine is a sixteenth-century inn on a narrow country road just outside the village, close to the Offa's Dyke path. It still functions very much as a pub, with some good real ales for those just wanting a drink, plus decent bar food, ranging from Cumberland sausage with mash and mustard sauce to Cornish crab cake with ginger beurre blanc.

The separate dining room has its own more ambitious menu, with a modern cooking style in which top-quality local produce is to the fore (beef and lamb come from farms in the village) but influences come from all over. Expect starters such as Yorkshire blue cheese soufflé with poached pear, or loin of rabbit sliced and served on a mushroom tart with beetroot purée and hazelnut oil. Roast Trelough duck with sage sauce might follow, or a sea bass fillet served on braised leeks in a light butter sauce, or perhaps local Berkshire pork with black pudding served on onion mash and spinach with a Hereford cider sauce. Among desserts enjoyed by reporters have been Victoria plum soufflé, and a 'light and creamy' lemon curd tart. A dozen 'especially recommended' wines from £10.50 to £24.35 set the tone of a list that takes a healthy interest in good flavours at fair prices, regardless of geography, mixing reliable old stagers like Guigal's Côtes du Rhône (£18.10) with newer discoveries like Honig Sauvignon Blanc from California (£21.80). Six by the glass range from £2 to £5.

CHEF/PROPRIETOR: Ken Adams   OPEN: Tue to Sun L 12.15 to 1.45, Tue to Sat D 7.15 to 9   CLOSED: 1 week early Dec, 1 week Jan   MEALS: alc exc Sat D and Sun L (main courses £10.50 to £15.50). Set L Sun £15, Set D Sat £26. Bar menu available   SERVICE: not inc, card slips closed   CARDS: MasterCard, Switch, Visa   DETAILS: 34 seats. Private parties: 24 main room, 14 to 16 private rooms. Car park. Vegetarian meals. No children under 8. No smoking. No music ACCOMMODATION: 3 rooms, all with bath/shower. TV. B&B £50 to £80. No children under 12 (*The Which? Guide to Good Hotels*)

▲ Angel Restaurant ▼ ✸

LONG CRENDON Buckinghamshire   map 2

47 Bicester Road, Long Crendon HP18 9EE
TEL: (01844) 208268   FAX: (01844) 202497
WEBSITE: www.angelrestaurant.co.uk

COOKING 1
MODERN BRITISH
£30–£69

On a corner of the main road that runs through the village, the Angel is a fifteenth-century listed building with exposed beams, open fires, leather sofas and pine tables, although the mix of styles also embraces a traditional bar with blackboard specials (French onion soup, perhaps, or chargrilled swordfish steak) and a wrap-around conservatory in shades of yellow and green. The bistro cooking might take in a generous starter of fresh-tasting chargrilled squid and powerful salsa, accompanied by leaves and a 'salad cream' dressing, and while the kitchen might not aim to make everything in-house, the essentials are tasty and convincing enough, including rack of English lamb, served pink as requested, and a mango tarte Tatin with a first-class, creamy, vanilla-speckled ice cream. The wine list moves things up a gear with an international selection that's particularly strong on Australia. Eleven house wines are £14.25, or £3.55 a glass, and, while pricing isn't everything you could wish for, there's plenty under £20.

CHEFS: Trevor Bosch and Donny Joyce   PROPRIETORS: Trevor and Annie Bosch   OPEN: all week L 12 to 2.30, Mon to Sat D 7 to 9.30   MEALS: alc (main courses £12.50 to £27). Set L Mon to Sat £13.95 (2 courses) to £16.95   SERVICE: not inc   CARDS: Delta, MasterCard, Switch, Visa DETAILS: 75 seats. 30 seats outside. Private parties: 35 main room. Car park. Vegetarian meals. Children's helpings. No smoking in 1 dining room. Music. Air-conditioned   ACCOMMODATION: 3 rooms, all with bath/shower. TV. Phone. B&B £65 to £75. Baby facilities (*The Which? Guide to Good Hotels*) (£5)

LONG MELFORD Suffolk   map 6

Scutchers 💥

Westgate Street, Long Melford CO10 9DP   COOKING 3
TEL: (01787) 310200   FAX: (01787) 375700   MODERN BRITISH
WEBSITE: www.scutchers.com   £33–£56

Scutchers mixes smartness with simplicity in its ambience of pine furniture, bold primary colours and relatively formal service. The front is yellow-painted brick, and parts of the building date back to the fifteenth century; the inside, brightly lit in the evenings, is spacious and open-plan, divided up by different levels and standing timbers. Nick Barrett's food treads the tried-and-true bistro line, with smoked salmon, grilled asparagus en croûte, and seared scallops to start, and classics like grilled skate wing with brown butter, capers and shrimps among the mains. Even where some unexpected element appears in a dish, such as the black pudding added to the gravy with a roast duck breast on Puy lentils, the overall effect doesn't jar. The much-imitated iced berries with hot white chocolate sauce, which originated at the Ivy (see entry, London) is offered here too, or there may be American-style pancakes with caramel sauce and pecan ice-cream. The wine list is varietally arranged, and furnishes good choice in both glasses and half-bottles. Prices work upwards from £11.50.

CHEFS: Nicholas Barrett and Guy Alabaster   PROPRIETORS: Nicholas and Diane Barrett   OPEN: Tue to Sat 12 to 2, 7 to 9.30   MEALS: alc (main courses £12 to £18)   SERVICE: not inc   CARDS: Amex, Delta, MasterCard, Switch, Visa   DETAILS: 70 seats. Private parties: 70 main room. Car park. Vegetarian meals. No smoking. Wheelchair access (also WC). No music. Air-conditioned

---

The Guide always appreciates hearing about changes of chef or owner.

Prices quoted in the Guide are based on information supplied by restaurateurs. The prices quoted at the top of each entry represent a range, from the lowest price of a three-course meal with service and wine to the highest; the latter is inflated by 20 per cent to take account of likely price rises during the year of the Guide.

LONGRIDGE Lancashire

map 8

Longridge Restaurant ⚡✳

104–106 Higher Road, Longridge PR3 3SY
TEL: (01772) 784969   FAX: (01772) 785713
EMAIL: longridge@heathcotes.co.uk
WEBSITE: www.heathcotes.co.uk
from Preston, follow Town Centre signs, drive
uphill though centre of Longridge, then turn left,
following signs for Jeffery Hill

LANCASHIRE GFG 2004 COMMENDED

COOKING **6**
MODERN BRITISH
£28–£61

It cannot be easy to change the habits of a dozen years and start afresh, but the world and cooking move on, and sadly too few restaurants have the energy or drive to do what Paul Heathcote has just done. The stone cottage at the top of the hill has had a makeover 'and it's a big improvement'. Gone is the chintzy look and the dark panelling, in have come bright lights and colourful paintings, and a change of name confirms the new identity. In a bid for greater accessibility, prices have come down a bit, and the restaurant is now open all day on Sunday. Frills, including appetisers and petits fours have gone (but they 'always used to annoy us', confided one couple), and although the bread is no longer made in-house it is still first rate. A new carte is backed up by a fixed-price lunch and a few blackboard specials.

The resulting simplification is no mere dumbing down. Supplies are still carefully sourced, and results have included a May-time pea soup, 'sweet and full of fresh pea flavour', containing chunks of smoked haddock, and a marbled terrine of Goosnargh duck and foie gras bound in a light jelly, served with a brioche and wobbly cubes of apple jelly. The skill level remains high, typically combining simple, well-timed roasts with well-made stock-based sauces: perhaps pink duck breast with a small pie of shredded leg meat, in a sticky, dark, intensely flavoured reduction, or best end of sweet-flavoured, spring-like lamb sliced on to a cake of couscous mixed with peas and aubergine, with a light stock reduction.

Desserts show similar expertise, producing a mulled pear Tatin with spiced, flavour-packed, juicy fruit ('a triumph'), and a dish of raspberries three ways: a small trifle using 'booze-soaked sponge', a tart made with good pastry, and a strongly flavoured sorbet. Staff are more relaxed and less formal, but as pleasant and helpful as ever, and the 100-strong wine list includes some choice under £25 (including Ninth Island Pinot Noir from Tasmania), and four house wines from £13 to £14.50.

CHEFS: Paul Heathcote and David Aspin   PROPRIETOR: Paul Heathcote   OPEN: Tue to Fri L 12 to 2.30, Tue to Sat D 6 (5 Sat) to 10, Sun 12 to 9   CLOSED: 1 Jan   MEALS: alc (main courses £12 to £18.50). Set L £18.50   SERVICE: 10% (optional), card slips closed   CARDS: Amex, Delta, Diners, MasterCard, Switch, Visa   DETAILS: 70 seats. Private parties: 70 main room, 10 to 18 private rooms. Car park. Vegetarian meals. Children's helpings. No smoking in 1 dining room. Wheelchair access (not WC). Music (£5)

The Guide's longest-serving restaurants are listed near the front of the book.

Thyme ✦ £

1–3 Inglewhite Road, Longridge PR3 3JR   COOKING 3
TEL/FAX: (01772) 786888   MODERN EUROPEAN
WEBSITE: www.thyme-restaurant.co.uk   £26–£45

A thoroughly modern place from top to toe, Thyme has a smart, fresh appearance and a menu that draws inspiration from around the world alongside a commitment to using local produce and local suppliers. This is confirmed by the abundant mention of Lancashire cheese and black pudding – the two coming together in a starter with ham hock wrapped in Parma ham with parsley and potato salad – and other celebrations of local culinary tradition, brought up to date or given an innovative slant. Loch Fyne smoked salmon marinated with orange and aniseed is roasted and served with horseradish mash, and confit of shank of lamb comes 'Indian style' with a risotto of sultanas, apple and cucumber and a yoghurt dressing. Puddings have included chocolate tart with a matching sauce and ice cream. The short, good-value wine list is confidently chosen and packed with modern flavours and the odd classy touch from the Old World. House wines are £10.75 or £2.75 a glass. Near by in Preston a second branch recently opened, Thyme at the Sirloin Inn, Station Road, tel: (01254) 852293.

CHEF: Mike Law   PROPRIETOR: Alex Coward   OPEN: Tue to Sat 12 to 2.30, 6 to 9.30, Sun 1 to 8
CLOSED: bank hols   MEALS: alc (main courses £11 to £15). Set L £6.95 (2 courses), Set D 6 to 7.30
£6 to £6.50   SERVICE: not inc, card slips closed   CARDS: Amex, Delta, Diners, MasterCard,
Switch, Visa   DETAILS: 45 seats. Private parties: 45 main room. Vegetarian meals. No smoking in
1 dining room. Wheelchair access (also WC). Music. No mobile phones (£5)

LOOE Cornwall   map 1

Water Rail ✦

Lower Market Street, Looe PL13 1AX   COOKING 2
TEL: (01503) 262314   SEAFOOD
                                                           £28–£104

Right in the heart of old (East) Looe, the Water Rail is a cottage restaurant adorned with hanging baskets. A pair of small dining rooms with roughly plastered walls and a lobster tank is the setting for what can be a thoroughly retro experience, from the 1950s Muzak to the regular menu of old stalwarts such as deep-fried whitebait, prawn cocktails and profiteroles. Venture on to the specials menu though and things start to get interesting. A bowl of sweet-and-sour Thai soup replete with mussels, cuttlefish, prawns and crab was sensational at inspection, and a whole lobster fresh from the tank served with properly pungent garlic butter was 'firm, succulent, sweet and juicy'. Other seafood dishes might include chargrilled yellowfin tuna steak with a creamy mustard sauce, and meals end with decently rich Cornish crème brûlée or Cointreau-laced chocolate mousse. A short, unremarkable wine list opens with Concha y Toro Chardonnay and Cabernet Sauvignon at £9.95.

CHEF: Richard Maior-Barron PROPRIETORS: Richard and Denise Maior-Barron OPEN: Wed to Mon D only 7 to 9 (Oct to May), 7 to 10 (June to Sept) CLOSED: 25 Dec, 1 to 31 Jan MEALS: alc (main courses £9 to £60). SERVICE: not inc, card slips closed CARDS: Delta, MasterCard, Switch, Visa DETAILS: 40 seats. Private parties: 20 main room, 2 to 12 private rooms. Vegetarian meals. No children under 10. No smoking. Music. No mobile phones £5

LOW LAITHE North Yorkshire   map 9

Dusty Miller

Low Laithe, Summerbridge HG3 4BU   COOKING 5
TEL: (01423) 780837   ANGLO-FRENCH
on B6165, 2m SE of Pateley Bridge   £34–£59

This unassuming but attractive stone building sits beside the road north-west of Harrogate, on the way to Pateley Bridge. An open fire, and Liz Dennison and her staff, all contribute to a warm welcome, while Brian Dennison's hand-written, daily-changing menus concentrate on fairly traditional food, from a springtime dish of 'just past crunchy' asparagus with a rich hollandaise, via chicken liver parfait, to fillet steak with béarnaise sauce. It is the practised mastery of essential techniques that gives the food its edge, producing an intense scampi soup (with optional cream in a jug), and a 'brilliant', slow-cooked, grease-free, boneless duck, the flesh virtually shredded, the skin crisp. Part of the skill lies in sourcing: seafood takes in Whitby crab – perhaps in a salad, or maybe in lightly spiced crab cakes with a crisp rösti-type covering of potato, resting on thin rice noodles – while game, beef and lamb are all local.

First-rate pastrywork is applied to desserts of, for example, tarte Tatin with 'melting puff pastry', and firm, juicy blackcurrants baked in a biscuity, shortcrust pastry pie, both served with cream and ice cream in separate containers for ladling or spooning on as required. A short list of French wines (plus a couple from New Zealand) is supplemented by a few fine wines and a single house red and white at £12.90.

CHEF: Brian Dennison PROPRIETORS: Brian and Elizabeth Dennison OPEN: Tue to Sat 7 to 11 CLOSED: 24 to 27 Dec, 1 Jan, 1 week July MEALS: alc (main courses £18). Set D £24 SERVICE: not inc CARDS: Amex, Delta, MasterCard, Switch, Visa DETAILS: 45 seats. Private parties: 30 main room, 6 to 15 private rooms. Car park. Children's helpings. No children under 9. Wheelchair access (not WC). Occasional music

---

LUDLOW Shropshire   map 5

▲ Dinham Hall

Dinham, Ludlow SY8 1EJ
TEL: (01584) 876464   FAX: (01584) 876019   COOKING 4
EMAIL: info@dinhamhall.co.uk   MODERN EUROPEAN/FRENCH
WEBSITE: www.dinhamhall.co.uk   £40–£69

Custard yellow has replaced pink on the dining room walls, and stiff table linen and fresh flowers contribute to an air of comfort rather than high style. A new chef offers a repertoire less overtly French than his predecessor's, and he uses English for his reassuringly brief and good-value menus. A complex starter of seared scallops with ricotta cappelletti, spinach and Parma ham demonstrates that ambition is high. The same meal delivered earthy fragrances of wild mushrooms, red chard and Madeira and rosemary jus with a wild-tasting pigeon that impressed by its execution and its bold flavours. Equally punchy combinations like monkfish with capers, lemon and pancetta, or pistachio crème brûlée with mocha sorbet show genuine and successful experiment. This is an intelligent kitchen that clearly cares about ingredients, with only one or two slip-ups at inspection (hard pasta, disappointing ice cream). Service could be more knowledgeable. Wines, starting at £13.50, include 20 well-aged clarets and a fair worldwide range, with modest choice below £20.

CHEF: Peter James McGregor   PROPRIETORS: J.P. and J.E. Mifsud   OPEN: all week 12.30 to 1.45, 7 to 8.45 (9.45 Sat)   CLOSED: 25 Dec D   MEALS: Set L £19.75 (2 courses) to £25.75, Set D £32.50. Light L/bar menu available   SERVICE: not inc, card slips closed   CARDS: Amex, Delta, Diners, MasterCard, Switch, Visa   DETAILS: 22 seats. Private parties: 45 main room, 4 to 30 private rooms. Car park. Vegetarian meals with advance notice. Children's helpings. No children under 8. No smoking. Wheelchair access (not WC). No music   ACCOMMODATION: 15 rooms, all with bath/shower. TV. Phone. B&B £75 to £180. (*The Which? Guide to Good Hotels*)

Hibiscus ✤

17 Corve Street, Ludlow SY8 1DA
TEL: (01584) 872325   FAX: (01584) 874024
WEBSITE: www.hibiscusrestaurant.co.uk

COOKING **8**
FRENCH
£39–£78

The low-key blue-and-white sign, down the hill from The Feathers, marks a remarkably stylish restaurant. Old oak panelling and rough stone walls in the bar area and interconnecting dining rooms give a reassuring feel, and formal but plain table settings unobtrusively set off 'serious but not intimidating' cooking imbued with confidence and ease.

Exemplifying Bosi's creativity within a classical framework is a first course of unctuous foie gras ice cream surrounded by a thick, smooth foam of brioche emulsion, streaked with balsamic caramel. The 'hugely enjoyable' result is little short of sensational, evoking the luxurious taste and texture of foie gras, perfectly complemented by the pinpoint sweet/sharpness of balsamic caramel. Equally arresting was a slow-cooked but perfectly pink calf's kidney served with baby turnips drizzled with a gently sharp apple-based beurre blanc, accompanied by a streak of earthy kohlrabi purée. Such carefully considered and well-crafted cooking involves fine judgement to create interesting partnerships, yet keeps the main item always in focus, viz. a whole fillet of lamb, seared one side, pink the other, and properly rested, served with small and distinctive accompaniments: a powerful aubergine purée, sliced potato with anchovy, and a purée of goats' cheese.

Precisely prepared and presented, the food is rich without heaviness, so portions are not large but are satisfying – making desserts eminently manageable. A disc of iced gingerbread parfait comes with a scoop of carrot sorbet, well judged for sweetness, and a wafer-thin piece of see-through caramel tasting wonderfully of cumin, an inspired interaction. After this a Jerusalem artichoke pannacotta may not surprise, but its balance and partnership with caramel ice cream and pieces of lemon demonstrate not attention-seeking gimmickry but very remarkable cooking.

Incidentals are equally impressive, from light-as-air cheese puffs to an appetiser cocotte (an eggshell containing a nearly-raw yolk underneath a soup such as lentil and bacon), via three types of first-class bread. Claire Bosi manages front-of-house with efficiency, empathy and quiet confidence, her easy charm contributing to the warm atmosphere. Wines accommodate differing pockets and incorporate a range of styles from France and elsewhere.

CHEF: Claude Bosi   PROPRIETORS: Claude and Claire Bosi   OPEN: Wed to Sat L 12.30 to 1.30, Mon to Sat D 7 to 9.30   CLOSED: 25 Dec to 18 Jan, 10 days Aug   MEALS: Set L £19.50 (2 courses) to £25, Set D £35 to £42.50. Set D £50 (whole table only)   SERVICE: not inc, card slips closed CARDS: MasterCard, Switch, Visa   DETAILS: 28 seats. Private parties: 30 main room. Car park. Children's helpings. No smoking. Wheelchair access (not WC). No music. No mobile phones

Merchant House ✂

Lower Corve Street, Ludlow SY8 1DU
TEL: (01584) 875438
EMAIL: shaunhill@merchanthouse.co.uk
WEBSITE: www.merchanthouse.co.uk

COOKING **8**
MODERN BRITISH
£45–£66

Down the hill, half a mile from the town centre, lies the trigger of Ludlow's gastronomic rise. Simply furnished, soothingly decorated, bare wood floors and tables, a few bits of carpet and some wall hangings ... it feels restrained but not austere. And the friendly welcome and efficient, charming, straightforward service (and service-included pricing) all contribute to an understated approach that sees eating as about enjoying food and company. Most importantly, it delivers; 'one of the best all-round meals I've had for a long time' is a typical reaction.

Most reports praise the fish, accurately timed and often lifted by a lightly spicy accompaniment: say, monkfish with salsa-like skinned tomatoes infused with garlic and ginger ('you couldn't get much simpler, nor much better'). Freshness, timing and balance combine to give the food vitality. And meat dishes equally accomplished could include game, rack of lamb, or perhaps duck: 'not your usual slivers in arty-farty presentation' but four generous slices of breast and two plump legs, with just enough sauce (a stock reduction) to enhance the flavour. Similarly, a 'juicy and succulent' quail starter sets two boneless breasts and two legs on a small, gently creamy, herb-flecked risotto, with a puddle of reduced stock around the edge – 'not fussy or clever, just simple and good.' Fine, unflamboyant craftsmanship, unerringly applied, creates deep satisfaction, maybe via a squidgy, creamy and lightly cakey Samloi (a Hungarian version of trifle), or a pear poached in red wine, with a creamy rice pudding ice cream: accurate treatment and fine judgement turning simple into first-class.

They don't ask if the food is alright (they know it is), nor how you want the meat cooking (they know how to cook it) – 'give me this kind of service every time'. Likewise, after tasting, wine is left on the table for DIY pouring, as it should be. Shaun Hill has good bottles ('more artisan than blue chip' says the list) at an average mark up, so they are not cheap, but, from Vintage Tunina to Zind-Humbrecht Riesling, from Allegrini's La Grola to Cigare Volant, they are worth drinking. Prices start at £14.50.

CHEF: Shaun Hill   PROPRIETORS: Shaun and Anja Hill   OPEN: Fri and Sat L 12.30 to 1.45, Tue to Sat D 7 to 9   CLOSED: 1 week from 25 Dec, 1 week spring   MEALS: Set L £27.50, Set D £33   SERVICE: net prices, card slips closed   CARDS: Delta, MasterCard, Switch, Visa   DETAILS: 22 seats. Private parties: 8 main room. No smoking. Wheelchair access (not WC). No music

▲ Mr Underhill's ♥ £✳

Dinham Weir, Ludlow SY8 1EH	COOKING 7
TEL: (01584) 874431	MODERN EUROPEAN
WEBSITE: www.mr-underhills.co.uk	£42–£56

At the bottom of a steep hill below the castle right on the River Teme, with an attractive courtyard garden to one side, Mr Underhill's is a long, narrow, light and airy dining room with French windows and patio doors. It sports tubular-steel chairs and top-drawer stiff white napery, and offers a simple-sounding menu with no choice before dessert. Given the relatively limited repertoire that obtains (many similar dishes seem to recur in reports), life should be comparatively easy for the kitchen in terms of supplies, economics, preparation and organisation. Nevertheless, the food is up to date, raw materials are first class, and technical skills are exemplary.

The timing of fish, for example, is quite precise. A thick slab of poached brill, its centre still slightly translucent, its flesh firm, is served with creamy Savoy cabbage and a 'salsa' of chopped cucumber and lime cream, and a springy, steamed pavé of brill also comes on finely shredded cabbage, with a drizzle of cardamom and lime sauce. Meals generally start with fish and proceed to a seriously meaty main course, such as fillet of local (Mortimer Forest) venison gently infused with juniper, served with wild mushrooms, creamy celeriac, a cake of loosely assembled roasted diced root vegetables and, best of all, a bowl of 'superbly decadent' truffled potato purée. Marches lamb has also featured: as a roast rack (two rose-pink chops) and slow-cooked shoulder (neatly rolled and sliced), also served with creamy celeriac, along with potatoes baked in their jackets then mashed 'with lots of butter and cream'.

The comfort factor often figures prominently, especially in the colder months, perhaps in the form of a risotto 'made with patience and no short cuts', incorporating smoked haddock, skinned tomato, and wilted wild rocket leaves. It also runs through desserts of, perhaps, creamy rice pudding, a light Italian bread-and-butter pudding dusted with grated chocolate, or prune and Armagnac tart, more like a clafoutis or a twice-baked soufflé, with a clear marzipan taste, surrounded by a light, orange-flavoured whipped cream. Some (though not all) feel welcomed, and there are plenty of extras to fill in the gaps between courses (meals are not rushed): from cheese tartlets to a fine pre-dessert of banana cream with maple syrup.

The wine list sensibly concentrates on very drinkable bottles – wines have some bottle age where needed, and a good selection from California, for example, eschews earnest Cabernets in favour of venison-friendly Zinfandels. All regions get a look-in, and quality is consistently high. 'Special Selections' pluck out enticing options from across the range, and wines by the glass start at £2.50.

CHEF: Chris Bradley   PROPRIETORS: Chris and Judy Bradley   OPEN: Wed to Mon D only 7.15 to 8.30   MEALS: Set D £30 to £32   SERVICE: not inc   CARDS: MasterCard, Switch, Visa   DETAILS: 24 seats. 24 seats outside. Car park. Children's helpings. No 2- to 8-year-olds. No smoking. No music. No mobile phones   ACCOMMODATION: 6 rooms, all with bath/shower. TV. Phone. B&B £60 to £135. No 2- to 8-year-olds. Fishing (*The Which? Guide to Good Hotels*)

LUND East Riding of Yorkshire — map 9

Wellington Inn ▼

19 The Green, Lund YO25 9TE
TEL: (01377) 217294   FAX: (01377) 217192

COOKING **3**
MODERN BRITISH
£31–£53

Flagstone floors, a proper log fire, dishes chalked up on a blackboard in the bar – little wonder that 'homely' and 'traditional' are two of the adjectives that visitors have used to describe this lively pub-cum-restaurant. The menu in the tastefully decorated dining room lists what the management call 'unpretentious' dishes such as smoked and fresh salmon rösti cake with ginger and lime and a chilli dipping sauce to start, and, for mains, escalope of pork fillet stuffed with mozzarella, basil, smoked tomato and anchovies, with mushroom and Marsala sauce, or spiced monkfish with a lightly curried cream sauce. Desserts may include iced toffee and banana parfait, or vanilla cheesecake with 'boozy' morello cherries. Service can be stretched, and waits for food correspondingly lengthy, although the staff are friendly and knowledgeable. Real ales might be the drink of choice in the bar, but the restaurant wine list is well worth a look. Bubbling with enthusiastic tasting notes, it is a collection of intensely flavoured wines at very fair prices, starting at £10.95 for fruity Sicilian white or Australian red. Further up the list, South Africa is a favourite region. Five wines come by the glass for £2.75 to £3.75.

CHEFS: Sarah Jeffery and Toby Greensides   PROPRIETORS: Russell and Sarah Jeffery   OPEN: Tue to Sat D only 7 to 9.30   MEALS: alc (main courses £13 to £19). Bar menu available Tue to Sun L, Tue to Sat D   SERVICE: not inc, card slips closed   CARDS: Delta, MasterCard, Switch, Visa   DETAILS: 42 seats. Private parties: 42 main room. Car park. Vegetarian meals. No children under 16. Music. No mobile phones

LYDFORD Devon — map 1

Dartmoor Inn ✷ £

Lydford EX20 4AY
TEL: (01822) 820221   FAX: (01822) 820494
on A386 Tavistock to Okehampton Road

COOKING **4**
MODERN BRITISH-PLUS
£24–£52

The Burgesses' strong relationship with local suppliers gives them the clout to 'commission' small quantities of vegetables and meat which, in the hands of capable chefs, has transformed the Inn into a good restaurant. Unstuffy integrity pervades, from the front-of-house warmth generated by Karen Burgess to Philip's unpretentious approach that allows good-quality ingredients the uncluttered space to show their qualities. Good-value two- or three-course set lunches like leek and potato soup, and a main course of slowly cooked ribs of pork with grilled apples and a mustard mash, are augmented by such imaginative bar snacks as celeriac fritters with a blue cheese cream sauce. Evening menus bring slightly greater elaboration in fillets of John Dory, Dover sole and celery flowers deep-fried in saffron batter, and charcoal grilled fillet of beef marinated in garlic and thyme, served with béarnaise sauce. The nine house wines from £11.50, also available by the glass, introduce a compact and reliable list that draws on Europe, the Americas and Antipodes.

CHEFS: Philip Burgess and Andrew Honey   PROPRIETORS: Karen and Philip Burgess   OPEN: Tue to Sun L 12 to 2.15, Tue to Sat D 6.30 to 9.15   CLOSED: 25 and 26 Dec   MEALS: alc (main courses £10 to £18). Set L Tue to Sat £11.75 (2 courses) to £14.75, Set L Sun £15.75 (2 courses) to £18.75   SERVICE: not inc, card slips closed   CARDS: Delta, MasterCard, Switch, Visa   DETAILS: 85 seats. 25 seats outside. Private parties: 16 main room. Car park. Vegetarian meals. Children's helpings. No children under 5 at Fri and Sat D. No smoking. Occasional music. No mobile phones £5

LYDGATE Greater Manchester   map 8

▲ White Hart Inn ⚡✱

51 Stockport Road, Lydgate OL4 4JJ
TEL: (01457) 872566   FAX: (01457) 875190
EMAIL: booking@thewhitehart.co.uk
WEBSITE: www.thewhitehart.co.uk
on A6050, 3m E of Oldham

COOKING **4**
ANGLO-FRENCH
£25–£51

Bar, brasserie, restaurant, inn – the White Hart, sitting on the edge of the Pennines, covers all the bases. Simple three-course set lunch (Monday to Saturday) and early-evening dinner (Monday to Friday) menus might run to Saddleworth Sausage Company's pork and leek sausage with black pudding mash and onion gravy, and for dessert, sticky toffee apple pudding. A more extensive and more ambitious carte has seen roast red pepper mousse with aubergine crisps and chive and feta dressing, for instance, precede a dozen or so mains from braised shoulder of lamb with rocket mash, sun-dried tomato and basil pesto, to sea trout with dill potato cake and curried spinach. Whether you fancy finishing with a simple scoop of ice cream at £1.50, something more indulgent like chocolate fondant muffin with white chocolate ice cream and chocolate sauce, or a traditional sponge and custard, the dessert menu can sort you out. Some diners have reported slow or insouciant service at busy times. Plenty of half-bottles and wines by the glass feature on a global wine list starting at £14.25.

CHEF: John Rudden   PROPRIETORS: Charles Brierley and John Rudden   OPEN: Mon to Sat 12 to 2.30, 6 to 9.30, Sun 1 to 8.30   MEALS: alc (main courses £11 to £17.50). Set L Mon to Sat £14.25, Set L Sun £18.25, Set D Mon to Fri 6 to 6.45 and Sun £14.25   SERVICE: not inc, card slips closed   CARDS: MasterCard, Switch, Visa   DETAILS: 100 seats. 30 seats outside. Private parties: 60 main room, 12 to 60 private rooms. Car park. Vegetarian meals. Children's helpings. No smoking. Wheelchair access (also WC). Occasional music. Air-conditioned   ACCOMMODATION: 12 rooms, all with bath/shower. TV. Phone. B&B £68.50 to £98.50. Baby changing. Baby facilities (*The Which? Guide to Good Hotels*)

'When I asked what was in the lemon cream, the waiter said ''lemon and cream''. I guess I walked into that one.' (On eating in London)

LYMINGTON Hampshire   map 2

Egan's ⅚✳

24 Gosport Street, Lymington SO41 9BE   COOKING 2
TEL: (01590) 676165   MODERN BRITISH
                                                         £22–£50

A crowd-pleasing formula of generous and reliable food coupled with a relaxed
atmosphere proves a winning formula at this unpretentious, friendly bistro
close to the High Street of this popular resort and yachting haven. Quality local
ingredients, imaginatively handled and presented, draw on the fruits of sea and
forest; the evening carte offers plenty of fish and a wide choice of game in season.
Seafood certainly catches the eye: a starter of halibut fillet paired with a crab
samosa, vegetable 'spaghetti' and Thai-spiced sauce, for example. There are
more classical touches afoot too: smoked haddock thermidor, shellfish bisque,
and béarnaise to accompany beef fillet with rösti and a mushroom 'medley'.
Desserts roll out a little simpler: perhaps chocolate tart with Cointreau ice cream.
A lengthy, global wine list offers bags of drinking under £20, with four house
wines at £11.95.

CHEF: John Egan   PROPRIETORS: John and Deborah Egan   OPEN: Tue to Sat 12 to 2, 6.30 to 10
MEALS: alc D (main courses £12 to £17). Set L £8.95 (2 courses) to £11.95   SERVICE: not inc
CARDS: MasterCard, Switch, Visa   DETAILS: 50 seats. 12 seats outside. Private parties: 22 main
room, 18 to 24 private rooms. Vegetarian meals. Children's helpings. No smoking in 1 dining
room. Music

LYNDHURST Hampshire   map 2

▲ Le Poussin at Parkhill 🍷 ⅚✳

Beaulieu Road, Lyndhurst SO43 7FZ
TEL: (023) 8028 2944   FAX: (023) 8028 3268   COOKING 6
EMAIL: sales@lepoussin.co.uk   MODERN BRITISH
WEBSITE: www.lepoussin.co.uk   £31–£78

A new kitchen and total refurbishment was being planned in 2003, which
should answer the reservations of a couple of readers who have commented that
the place was beginning to feel a little worn. It is the sister establishment to
Simply Poussin (see entry, Brockenhurst), having once done service as a boys'
school. Alex Aitken offers a highly burnished style of country-house hotel
cooking but takes a few risks along the way – successful ones. A signature dish
consists, not surprisingly, of roast poussin fashioned into a terrine with foie gras
and prunes, 'a delicious mini-meal on its own', according to one reporter. Roast
quail is served on a chicory tart, its legs presented in a salad alongside a parfait of
quail liver. Main-course meats show up well, too, pink-roast breast of duck and
best end of lamb being singled out for praise. Clever presentations extend to
turbot served with a coat of potato scales on creamed leeks, while saddle of
rabbit might be given a liver stuffing, wrapped in prosciutto and served with
wild mushrooms, asparagus and creamy mash. Desserts take care not to overload
the system at the end of what might have been a fairly rich meal. Light and
refreshing citrus jelly with mango sorbet delighted one reporter, or there could

well be a hot passion-fruit soufflé with matching sauce and sorbet. Service has been criticised for being 'a little intrusive', while others have commended it as 'exemplary'.

The wine list does not seek to overawe – although the cellar has the bottles for it – choosing to open quietly with a 'sommelier's selection' of a dozen or so good-value wines under £20. The depth of the list gradually emerges through page after page of rather pricier fine French wines, complemented by interesting bottles winkled out of little-frequented backwaters. Selections elsewhere are brief but never less than interesting. Twenty-five wines come by the glass (£3.50 to £10.50).

CHEF: Alex Aitken   PROPRIETORS: Alex and Caroline Aitken   OPEN: all week 12 to 2, 7 to 10   MEALS: alc (main courses £17.50 to £21.50). Set L £15 (2 courses) to £20, Set D £35 to £50   SERVICE: 10% (optional), card slips closed   CARDS: Amex, Delta, MasterCard, Switch, Visa   DETAILS: 50 seats. 20 seats outside. Private parties: 100 main room, 4 to 40 private rooms. Car park. Children's helpings. No children under 10 at D. No smoking. Wheelchair access (also women's WC). No music. No mobile phones   ACCOMMODATION: 19 rooms, all with bath/shower. TV. Phone. B&B £75 to £250. Rooms for disabled. Baby facilities. Fishing (*The Which? Guide to Good Hotels*)

LYTHAM ST ANNE'S Lancashire   map 8

▲ Dalmeny Hotel, Atrium | NEW ENTRY |

19–33 South Promenade,
Lytham St Anne's FY8 1LX
TEL: (01253) 712236   FAX: (01253) 724447
EMAIL: reservations@dalmeny.demon.co.uk
WEBSITE: www.dalmenyhotel.com/atrium

COOKING 4
MODERN EUROPEAN
£25–£51

Lytham St Anne's may have something of the air of days gone by, but at the Dalmeny Hotel, on the seafront, 'smart, stark, modern' design has arrived. The Atrium is an expansive, towering glass conservatory with a mezzanine-level bar, a blond-wood floor and unclothed tables, plus a grand piano and palms adding an old-fashioned touch. Darren Pilling cooks in sophisticated, metropolitan fashion, producing an admirable risotto of king prawns, given a 'cheerful glow' from saffron and topped with mascarpone, or accompanying an aromatic duck pancake with stir-fried vegetables and teriyaki sauce. Ingredients show each other off: green beans and rösti for garlicky roast rack of lamb; mash, spinach and a shellfish broth for fillet of sea bass. Vegetarians might opt for a beetroot and shallot tarte Tatin, partnered with roast roots glazed with goats' cheese and a balsamic dressing. Desserts include roast figs with crème fraîche and a port and cinnamon syrup, and lemon tart with Grand Marnier whipped cream. Substantial waits between courses seem *de rigueur*, but reporters suggest that patience is amply rewarded. A short but inspired wine list equally bills Europe and the New World, with prices mostly pegged below £20. The baseline is £10.95.

CHEF: Darren Pilling   PROPRIETOR: Webb Hotels Ltd   OPEN: all week D only 6 to 9.30   CLOSED: 24 to 26 Dec   MEALS: alc exc Fri (main courses £12.50 to £18). Set D £15.50. Bar menu available   SERVICE: not inc   CARDS: Amex, Delta, Diners, MasterCard, Switch, Visa   DETAILS: 72 seats.

Private parties: 100 main room. Car park. Vegetarian meals. No cigars/pipes. Wheelchair access (also WC). Occasional music. Air-conditioned ACCOMMODATION: 128 rooms, all with bath/shower. TV. Phone. B&B £83 to £130. Rooms for disabled. Baby facilities. Swimming pool

MADINGLEY Cambridgeshire   map 6

Three Horseshoes 💲❋

High Street, Madingley CB3 8AB
TEL: (01954) 210221   FAX: (01954) 212043   COOKING 4
off A1303, 2m W of Cambridge, close to M11   MEDITERRANEAN/GLOBAL
junction 13   £30–£54

Madingley is a photogenic little village on the outskirts of Cambridge, in which you will find this heart-warming country pub by the side of a meadow. Run by the Huntsbridge group (which also takes in the Falcon at Fotheringhay, the Old Bridge at Huntingdon and the Pheasant Inn at Keyston; see entries), it is a cheering place, with small-paned windows and interesting prints on the walls. As well as the bar dining area, there is a separate restaurant behind the bar, which extends into a conservatory and a tree-shaded garden with trestle tables, so take your pick. Richard Stokes is an imaginative cook, drawing ideas primarily from Italy and producing well-made, agreeably creamy garlic and chive risotto with wild mushrooms and Parmesan, and carefully timed main courses such as spankingly fresh turbot with lemon, capers and chargrilled asparagus, and properly seared beef fillet with carrots and chickpeas, served with a roast chilli salsa to add punch. Appealing lightness characterises desserts such as pannacotta with figs and honey, and pear and almond tart with a subtly flavoured ice cream of Vin Santo. Good Italian coffee and quality appetisers add lustre to what is clearly a thoroughly professional operation, an impression that extends to the 'smart but informal' service. Although we were unable to see a wine list this year – it was being updated as we went to press and not even a 'preview' was available – bottles will have been chosen with characteristic flair by Master of Wine John Hoskins, and there is sure to be a good choice by the glass.

CHEF: Richard Stokes   PROPRIETOR: Huntsbridge Ltd   OPEN: all week L 12 to 2, Mon to Sat D 6.30 to 9.30   MEALS: alc (main courses £9.50 to £17.50)   SERVICE: not inc, card slips closed   CARDS: Amex, Delta, Diners, MasterCard, Switch, Visa   DETAILS: 90 seats. 40 seats outside. Private parties: 60 main room. Car park. Vegetarian meals. No smoking in 1 dining room. Wheelchair access (not WC). No music

MAIDENCOMBE Devon   map 1

▲ Orestone Manor 🍷 💲❋

Rockhouse Lane, Maidencombe TQ1 4SX
TEL: (01803) 328098   FAX: (01803) 328336
EMAIL: enquiries@orestone.co.uk   COOKING 4
WEBSITE: www.orestone.co.uk   MODERN ENGLISH
on A379 between Torquay and Teignmouth   £26–£61

Orestone Manor is set amid beautiful gardens that run down to Babbacombe Bay. The latest makeover, by new owners Rose and Mark Ashton, has resulted in a pleasing mish-mash of the colonial and oriental, with rugs, 'an abundance of elephants' and wickerwork helping to create the effect. There seems to be a new vibrancy in the cooking, too. This could be because of the involvement of chef Michael Caines of Gidleigh Park, Chagford (see entry), who has been working with Orestone Manor's Anthony Hetherington.

Food is cooked in a kitchen that is visible through glass to the diners, and the standard is high, displaying imagination tempered with skill in execution. The ambitious menu might begin with a light, fluffy, double-baked Stilton soufflé, or seared scallops served with tortellini made from the coral and a fashionable 'cappuccino' of cep. For main courses, Earl Grey-smoked duck has been pan-fried and served with crushed celeriac and Madeira jus, and fillet of South Devon beef paired with wild mushrooms, cherry tomatoes and béarnaise sauce. Finish, perhaps, with individual lemon meringue tarts with passion-fruit sorbet and thyme ice cream. Service is cheerful, friendly and efficient. A modern selection of wines arranged by style shows a keen nose for good flavours and restraint in pricing. House wines start at £13.75, with six options by the glass from £3.40.

CHEF: Anthony Hetherington   PROPRIETORS: Rose and Mark Ashton   OPEN: all week 12.30 to 2.30, 7 to 9 (9. 30 Sat)   MEALS: alc (main courses L £8 to £14, D £14.50 to £19.95). Set L £12.50 (2 courses) to £14.50, Set L Sun £18.50. Light L also available   SERVICE: not inc   CARDS: Amex, Delta, MasterCard, Switch, Visa   DETAILS: 65 seats. 30 seats outside. Private parties: 65 main room, 8 to 20 private rooms. Car park. Vegetarian meals. Children's helpings. No smoking. Wheelchair access (also WC). Music. No mobile phones   ACCOMMODATION: 12 rooms, all with bath/shower. TV. Phone. B&B £69 to £179. Rooms for disabled. Swimming pool (*The Which? Guide to Good Hotels*) (£5)

MAIDSTONE Kent   map 3

Soufflé

31 The Green, Bearsted, Maidstone ME14 4DN   COOKING 2
TEL/FAX: (01622) 737065   ANGLO-FRENCH
                                                               £28–£57

'The Restaurant on the Green' – the restaurant's self-appointed subtitle – is a fair description, as the Soufflé occupies one of a row of sixteenth-century cottages facing Bearsted village green. Take advantage of this popular spot by sitting out on the pergola-covered terrace for an aperitif – weather permitting. Inside, timber frames and exposed brickwork continue the old-world feel. Nick Evenden's innovative menu may kick off with a salad of wood pigeon with foie gras and beetroot, or a terrine of smoked and marinated salmon with mustard, tarragon and olive oil dressing, and go on to main courses of fillet of beef topped with celeriac and a white truffle oil gratin, or poached sea bass stuffed with mushroom and fennel purée. For dessert, liquorice mousse on spiced cake in caramel might appeal, while more conventional puddings such as a trio of crème brûlées are also on offer. France dominates the wine list; house Vin de Pays d'Oc is £12.50.

CHEF: Nick Evenden   PROPRIETORS: Nick and Karen Evenden   OPEN: Tue to Fri and Sun L 12 to 2, Tue to Sat D 7 to 9.30   MEALS: alc (main courses £16 to £18.50). Set L £13.50 (2 courses) to £16.50, Set D Tue to Fri £22.50   SERVICE: 10% (optional), card slips closed   CARDS: Amex, Delta, MasterCard, Switch, Visa   DETAILS: 40 seats. 25 seats outside. Private parties: 50 main room, 8 to 25 private rooms. Car park. Vegetarian meals. Children's helpings. No children under 8 D. No-smoking area. No cigars/pipes . Wheelchair access (also men's WC). Occasional music. No mobile phones £5

▲ Crowne Plaza Midland, French Restaurant ✳

Peter Street, Manchester M60 2DS
TEL: 0161 236 3333   FAX: 0161 932 4100
EMAIL: sales@ichotelsgroup.com
WEBSITE: www.manchester-themidland.crowneplaza.com

COOKING 4
MODERN FRENCH
£44–£86

One devotee of old ways considers the French Restaurant at the old Midland Hotel possibly 'the only proper dining room with proper service left in Manchester'. It has Regency-style décor, a formal tone (much flipping of napkins), and our devotee ('I do like a good bit of trolleying in a dining room') was delighted when the breads arrived that way.

The menu is bilingual (marked by eccentric spelling) but dishes are not exclusively Gallic – hot-and-sour soup with freshwater prawns, and wild mushroom risotto with vegetable crisps and smoked garlic point in another direction entirely. The fundamental tone, though, is modern French, leading to 'impeccably executed' beef fillet with a steamed boudin of pancetta and shallots, and gratin dauphinois, or perhaps macadamia-crusted cod fillet with rocket and Parmesan mash. At dessert stage mille-feuille of white chocolate and honeycomb with clementine coulis is one option, and one reporter admired the balance of sweet and sharp flavours in a summer fruit sablé containing discs of chocolate. Overall, 'this grand old Manchester barge maintains its stately course'. The wine list, arranged by style, is French-led but not half as monoglot as the setting might imply. French house wines are £14.50 (£2.90 a glass).

CHEFS: Simon Holling and Andre Matter   PROPRIETOR: InterContinental Hotels plc   OPEN: Mon to Sat D only 7 to 10.30 (11 Fri and Sat)   CLOSED: bank hols   MEALS: alc (main courses £21 to £30). Set D Fri and Sat £29 to £38   SERVICE: not inc, card slips closed   CARDS: Amex, Delta, Diners, MasterCard, Switch, Visa   DETAILS: 50 seats. 50 seats outside. Private parties: 50 main room. Vegetarian meals. Children's helpings. No smoking before 10. Wheelchair access (also WC). Music. No mobile phones. Air-conditioned   ACCOMMODATION: 303 rooms, all with bath/shower. TV. Phone. Room only £165 to £195. Rooms for disabled. Baby facilities. Swimming pool (The Which? Guide to Good Hotels) £5

Greens

43 Lapwing Lane, West Didsbury,
Manchester M20 2NT
TEL: (0161) 434 4259   FAX: (0161) 448 2098

COOKING 1
VEGETARIAN
£12–£31

A small green awning and a large front window advertise this vegetarian specialist. Its colourful décor is echoed in a wide-ranging menu that swings from an Italian bean casserole with pesto rice balls to a Malaysian laksa, from goats' cheese rolled in honey (with mango coulis) to a red Thai vegetable curry with sticky rice. The menu changes about five times a year, main-course portions are large, and the three-course set-price menu is a comparative bargain, perhaps offering soup of the day, cheese sausages with mash and onion gravy, and either lemon syllabub, or sticky toffee pudding with butterscotch sauce. They are not licensed, and mercifully there is no corkage charge.

CHEFS/PROPRIETORS: Simon Rimmer and Simon Connolly OPEN: Mon to Fri L 12 to 2, Sun L 12.30 to 3.30, all week D 5.30 to 10.30 CLOSED: bank hols MEALS: alc (main courses £10 to £10.50). Set L Tue to Fri £5.95 (1 course) to £10, Set L Sun £12.50, Set D Sun, Mon and 5.30 to 7 Tue to Sat £12.50. Unlicensed: BYO, no corkage SERVICE: not inc, card slips closed CARDS: Delta, MasterCard, Switch, Visa DETAILS: 30 seats. 10 seats outside. Private parties: 30 main room. Children's helpings. No cigars/pipes. Vegetarian meals

Koreana £

40A King Street West, Manchester M3 2WY
TEL: (0161) 832 4330 FAX: (0161) 832 2293
EMAIL: jonkoreana@aol.com
WEBSITE: www.koreana.co.uk

COOKING 1
KOREAN
£21–£51

'Welcome to our little family restaurant', begins the menu in this enduring Mancunian outpost of Korean cooking, where 'natural charm' abounds. Everyone out front has a genuine eagerness to please and staff are happy to guide customers through the intricacies of the menu, with its set meals, banquets and so forth. All the mainstays of the cuisine are in evidence, from gochi gui (skewers of marinated grilled chicken) and bulgogi (beef marinated in soy sauce, garlic, sesame, ginger, spring onions and pear) to highly rated yook hwae (a take on steak tartare prepared at the table) – not to mention that ever-present accompaniment, fiery kim-chee pickle. There are also a few interlopers from Japan in the shape of sushi and tempura. Korean saké, plum wine and spicy bek se ju are alternatives to the workaday wine list; house French is £8.95.

CHEFS: Mrs H. Kim and Cheung Hong PROPRIETOR: Koreana Ltd OPEN: Mon to Fri L 12 to 2.30, Mon to Sat D 6.30 (5.30 Sat) to 10.30 (11 Fri and Sat) CLOSED: 25 and 26 Dec, 1 Jan, bank hols L MEALS: alc (main courses £6.50 to £14). Set L £5.50 to £8 (2 courses), Set D £9.90 (2 courses) to £17.90. Business lunch menu also available SERVICE: not inc, 10% for parties of 8 or more, card slips closed CARDS: Amex, Delta, Diners, MasterCard, Switch, Visa DETAILS: 60 seats. Private parties: 60 main room. Vegetarian meals. Children's helpings. Occasional music (£5)

Lime Tree ♥ ⁵⁄✳

8 Lapwing Lane, West Didsbury,
Manchester M20 8WS
TEL: (0161) 445 1217 FAX: (0161) 434 0574
WEBSITE: www.thelimetreerestaurant.com

COOKING 2
GLOBAL
£22–£49

Housed in a corner building with very little parking nearby, this old Didsbury trouper has clocked up nearly 20 years. It still offers what can best be described as modern global cooking in a smart but casual pair of rooms, one a sort of conservatory addition. Scallops come with a dressing of sweet chilli and ginger, rocket and crème fraîche to start, or there might be grilled halloumi with a lime and caper vinaigrette. Performance can be a bit hit and miss, but dishes in the former category have included a straightforward bowl of moules marinière, pink-cooked roast loin of lamb, perhaps served with braised leeks wrapped in Parma ham, and a top-drawer apple crumble with vanilla ice cream, brilliantly combining hot and cold, sweet and sharp, and soft and crunchy elements in admirable balance. 'A speedy team of youngsters' makes it all happen. The wine list looks rather traditional by comparison – long on classical French wines, with some affordable options in Bordeaux and Burgundy – but takes in sprightlier selections from Spain, Italy and the New World, which are the main source of the dozen or so 'wines of the month'. Prices are good, with eight house wines starting at £10.95, or £2.75 a glass.

CHEFS: Jason Dickenson and Jason Parker PROPRIETOR: Patrick Hannity OPEN: Tue to Fri and Sun L 12 to 2.45, all week D 6 to 10.30 CLOSED: 25 and 26 Dec, 1 Jan MEALS: alc (main courses £10.50 to £15). Set L Tue to Fri £14.95, Set D 6 to 6.45 £14.95 SERVICE: not inc, 10% for parties of 6 or more CARDS: Amex, Delta, MasterCard, Switch, Visa DETAILS: 90 seats. 20 seats outside. Vegetarian meals. Children's helpings. No smoking in 1 dining room. Wheelchair access (not WC). Music

Lincoln 🍷

1 Lincoln Square, Manchester M2 5LN
TEL: (0161) 834 9000 FAX: (0161) 834 9555
EMAIL: mail@thelincolnrestaurant.com
WEBSITE: www.thelincolnrestaurant.com

COOKING 1
MODERN BRITISH
£24–£52

This stylish establishment close to the centre of Manchester offers internationally inspired cooking that 'gets the important things right' – seasoning, sourcing and timing. Begin with king prawns coated in Moroccan spices, a wild mushroom and truffle linguini or roast asparagus spears wrapped in Parma ham. At inspection, main-course sea bass and tempura of sea bream were both outstandingly fresh and perfectly timed; the bass came with noodles and rather mild hot-and-sour broth, while the bream had impressive lime-scented Thai sticky rice along with chilli oil and coconut and coriander pesto. Jam roly-poly with real custard was 'a welcome blast of nostalgia', and a rich chocolate cake laced with Cognac and drizzled with crème anglaise came with a smooth, creamy ice cream. Service is mostly efficient. The wine list covers all bases, starting with house bottles at £11.65 (£2.95 a glass).

CHEF: Ashley Clarke PROPRIETOR: Nicola Done OPEN: Sun to Fri L 12 to 2.30, Mon to Sat D 5.30 to 10.30 (11 Sat) MEALS: alc (not Sun L; main courses £10 to £16). Set L £12.50 (2 courses) to £14.50, Set D 5.30 to 7 £12.50 (2 courses) to £14.50 SERVICE: 10% (optional), card slips closed CARDS: Amex, Delta, MasterCard, Switch, Visa DETAILS: 120 seats. Private parties: 150 main room. Vegetarian meals. Children's helpings. No cigars/pipes. Wheelchair access (also WC). Music. Air-conditioned

Le Mont 🍴   NEW ENTRY

Levels 5 and 6, Urbis Centre, Cathedral Gardens,
Manchester M4 3BG
TEL: (0161) 605 8282 FAX: (0161) 605 8283
EMAIL: hostess@urbis.org.uk
WEBSITE: www.urbis.org.uk

GREATER MANCHESTER
GFG 2004
COMMENDED

COOKING 5
MODERN FRENCH
£39–£74

Opened just as the last edition of the Guide went to press, on the fifth and sixth floors of the Urbis Centre, and with a panoramic view of the city skyline, Le Mont is already making waves. The pale wood, exposed concrete and light grey colour scheme point to a contemporary approach, and the food is 'modern French cuisine with a Manchester influence', evident not least in the menu's tortured franglais. 'Les viandes de fellbred' is one section, which includes Galloway beef from the Borders, the carefully timed fillet, for example, served with béarnaise and Madeira sauces and on-plate vegetables. Herdwick lamb from Cumbria might appear in a dish of 'gigot d'agneau Lancashire Hot Pot', combining pink, flavourful rack with a pastry basket in which cubed lamb and sliced potatoes are underpinned by red cabbage.

There are soups and pasta dishes as well as fish that can be taken as a main or intermediate course: perhaps Dover sole fillet wrapped around lobster mousseline with trompette mushrooms. Meals might start with a tripartite dish of duck confit, smoked duck (with mango purée) and stuffed quail, or with a terrine of moist rabbit, firm foie gras and vegetables set in a Sauternes jelly. Portions tend to be generous, but those who make it to pudding might be rewarded with a plate of raspberry desserts accompanied by liquorice ice cream, or with a well-judged cinnamon-poached pear served with coffee ice cream and chocolate sauce. Staff come in for special mention for their ability to lift domes, refold napkins, and their general 'hovering', although they are also relaxed and casual. There isn't a lot under £20 on the lengthy and ambitious wine list (whose notes could be improved), but there is some good drinking. Six house wines are available from £16.95 (£4.50 to £6.80 a glass).

CHEF: Robert Kisby   PROPRIETOR: Operator Urban Experience   OPEN: Mon to Fri L 12 to 2.30, Mon to Sat D 7 to 10.30   CLOSED: 25 Dec to L 6 Jan, bank hols   MEALS: alc (main courses £11 to £27.50). Set L and D £18.95 (2 courses) to £28.95   SERVICE: not inc   CARDS: Amex, Diners, MasterCard, Switch, Visa   DETAILS: 74 seats. Private parties: 50 main room. Vegetarian meals. No smoking in 1 dining room. Wheelchair access (also WC). No music. Air-conditioned

Moss Nook

Ringway Road, Manchester M22 5WD	COOKING 5
TEL: (0161) 437 4778 FAX: (0161) 498 8089	MODERN BRITISH
on B5166, 1m from Manchester Airport	£29–£86

'Nothing much changes here,' commented one reader – the Harrisons have been at Moss Nook since 1973 and their chef since 1983 – and 'it is quite refreshing to be freed from the tyranny of cappuccinos and Jackson Pollocks'. The décor is plush and smart and sets the tone. Loyalty to older values shows in consistent mastery of well-tried techniques, and ingredients are selected according to quality, regardless of cost. Flavours are well accented, and contrasts are encouraged: a rich sauce accompanying a sautéed veal escalope is cut by olives and asparagus, and four fat scallops sit in a sharp beurre blanc with lime. Veal kidneys might come with a port wine sauce in a pastry nest among starters, and breast of duckling with potato gratin, Kirsch and cherry sauce is a typical main. Vegetables are consistently praised, and pastry work, as in a raspberry and cinnamon wafer, impresses. Service (complete with assiduously lifted domes) is led from the front by the long-serving 'skilful and nice' manageress. And just as the menu does not expect customers to economise, so it is no surprise to find the back of the wine list packed with carefully selected French grandees; the other European wines and the 'New World Selection' lower the average cost. Prices start at £13, and there is some choice under £20, though more above it.

CHEF: Kevin Lofthouse   PROPRIETORS: Pauline and Derek Harrison   OPEN: Tue to Fri L 12 to 1.30,
Tue to Sat D 7 to 9.30   CLOSED: 2 weeks Christmas   MEALS: alc (main courses £19.50 to £30).
Set L £19.50, Set D £36.50 (both whole tables only)   SERVICE: not inc, card slips closed   CARDS:
Amex, Delta, MasterCard, Switch, Visa   DETAILS: 65 seats. 20 seats outside. Private parties: 55
main room. Car park. No children under 12. No pipes. Occasional music. No mobile
phones (£5)

New Emperor £

52–56 George Street, Manchester M1 4HF
TEL: (0161) 228 2883   FAX: (0161) 228 6620   COOKING 1
EMAIL: info@newemperor.co.uk   HONG KONG CANTONESE
WEBSITE: www.newemperor.co.uk   £16–£56

Handy for 'a spur-of-the-moment Cantonese meal', is one verdict on this popular
Chinatown address (assuming you're in Manchester, of course). The big open-
plan dining room has a 'superficial gloss' enhanced by shiny wooden furniture,
wall panels and 'New Emperor' embossed into the carpet, and plenty of good
things show up on the menu. There's a regular assortment of dim sum such as
steamed beef balls, pan-fried dumplings with vinegar dip and spicily fragrant
parcels of glutinous rice in lotus leaves, although the most promising dishes are
listed elsewhere: stir-fried Dover sole with Chinese greens was the hit of one
meal, with the choice extending to sliced beef with preserved cabbage and pork
with winter bamboo shoots, in addition to roast meats, hotpots and one-plate
meals. Service is 'businesslike' and tea is free, but note the obligatory 10 per cent
'eat-in charge'. House wines start at £9.90.

CHEF: Mr Aung   PROPRIETOR: Andrew He   OPEN: all week noon to midnight (1am Sat)   MEALS:
alc (main courses £6.50 to £13). Set L £8 to £12, Set D £16.50 to £35.50 (all min 2)   SERVICE: 10%
CARDS: Amex, Diners, MasterCard, Switch, Visa   DETAILS: 200 seats. Private parties: 200 main
room, 5 to 15 private rooms. Vegetarian meals. Wheelchair access (also WC). Music. Air-
conditioned

Ocean Treasure £

Greenside Way, Middleton,
Manchester M24 1SW
TEL: (0161) 653 6688   FAX: (0161) 653 3388   COOKING 2
EMAIL: enquiry@oceantreasure.co.uk   CHINESE
WEBSITE: www.oceantreasure.co.uk   £16–£59

Once you have found your way to the trading estate on the outskirts of Oldham
(take a city map), this Chinese restaurant above an Oriental supermarket is
easily recognised with its brightly coloured, pagoda-like exterior. Daytime dim
sum are well up to the mark; visitors have appreciated char sui cheung fun,
scallop dumplings and 'absolutely first-rate' fried molly paste (turnip cakes), in
addition to the curiously titled 'shark's fin soup dumpling'. True to its name, the
place bills itself as a 'seafood restaurant', and there are tanks to keep the
maritime creatures alive. Elsewhere, the main menu majors in Cantonese dishes
along the lines of stir-fried pork in yellow bean sauce, or duck with green
pepper and black bean sauce. A quartet of house wines (from £2.30 a glass,

£10.90 a bottle) opens the list, which also features a 'connoisseur' selection of big-name Bordeaux and Burgundies.

CHEF: Wong Chi Keung PROPRIETORS: Stewart Yip and Jack Lui OPEN: all week 12 to 11 (noon to midnight Fri and Sat, 11 to 11 Sun) MEALS: alc (main courses £7.50 to £13). Set L £4.30 (1 course) to £7.80. Set D £18 to £38 (all min 2) SERVICE: not inc CARDS: Amex, Delta, Diners, MasterCard, Switch, Visa DETAILS: 250 seats. Private parties: 250 main room, 10 to 50 private rooms. Car park. Vegetarian meals. Wheelchair access (also WC). Occasional music. Air-conditioned

Pacific ❧✳

58–60 George Street, Manchester M1 4HF
TEL: (0161) 228 6668 FAX: (0161) 236 0191
EMAIL: enquiries@pacific-restaurant-manchester.co.uk
WEBSITE: www.pacific-restaurant-manchester.co.uk

COOKING 2
CHINESE/THAI
£29–£56

The unassuming entrance deep in Chinatown hides all manner of goings on, including a pair of 'Pacifics' (one Chinese, the other Thai); however, our summary – and rating – applies only to the Chinese part of the operation. Tables are well spaced in the airy, pleasingly decorated dining room, where the menu is geared towards English customers who are, perhaps, unsure of their ground: the idea is to select your own cooking method and match it with the sauce of your choice. Alternatively, there's a strong contingent of dim sum, including fried cuttlefish cakes and impeccable siu mai dumplings, each topped with a whole prawn. The kitchen can also deliver the goods in other departments: witness splendid roast duck 'with absolutely no compromise to European tastes', and scallop-stuffed prawns quickly fried in salt and pepper ('simply magic', according to one aficionado). Service is courteous, friendly and helpful. House wines range from £9.90 to £14.90.

CHEF: Tim Wong PROPRIETOR: Marshbanks Ltd OPEN: all week 12 to 11 MEALS: alc (main courses £7.50 to £12.50). Set L £5.50 (2 courses) to £9.50, Set D £20 to £35 SERVICE: 10% CARDS: Amex, Delta, Diners, MasterCard, Switch, Visa DETAILS: 250 seats. Vegetarian meals. Children's helpings. No smoking in 1 dining room. Wheelchair access (also WC). Music. Air-conditioned

Restaurant Bar & Grill ✑ £

14 John Dalton Street, Manchester M2 6JR
TEL: (0161) 839 1999 FAX: (0161) 835 1886

COOKING 2
MODERN EUROPEAN
£26–£53

'This is the sort of place I'd eat in all the time given the chance,' enthused one reporter, who was taken with pretty much everything about the trendy bar/restaurant: its stylish, minimalist décor, buzzing atmosphere (read: loud music), friendly and professional service, and good value for money, not to mention the eclectic bistro-style menu of dishes from the USA, the Mediterranean, and the Middle and Far East. Start perhaps with fried chilli squid with noodle salad, Caesar salad, or feta and spinach quesadilla with preserved lemon, before moving on to fusilli with prosciutto, peas and Parmesan, Thai green chicken curry with coconut rice, cod with roast parsnips, or roast rump of spring lamb with artichokes, broad beans, crispy gnocchi and salsa verde. Finish with raspberry crème brûlée or iced Malteser parfait. A short but lively wine list focuses on good-value drinking, starting with house South African at £10.95.

CHEF: Alan Earle   PROPRIETOR: Derek Lily   OPEN: Mon to Fri 12 to 3, 6 to 11, Sat and Sun and bank hols 12 to 11   MEALS: alc (main courses £9 to £15.50)   SERVICE: not inc, card slips closed, 10% for parties of 6 or more   CARDS: Amex, Delta, Diners, MasterCard, Switch, Visa   DETAILS: 170 seats. Private parties: 50 main room. Vegetarian meals. No-smoking area. Music. Air-conditioned

Simply Heathcotes 🍞 ✳

Jacksons Row, Manchester M2 5WD	COOKING 2
TEL: (0161) 835 3536 FAX: (0161) 835 3534	MODERN ENGLISH
WEBSITE: www.heathcotes.co.uk	£25–£53

A sweep of wooden and steel stairs leads up from the curvy, modern reception desk to the bar area, beyond which is the dining room. Warm earth colours keep the crisp, contemporary surroundings at this city-centre establishment from feeling stark. As with the other branches of Simply Heathcotes (see entries, Leeds, Liverpool and Preston), the aim is to offer fairly priced, brasserie-style cooking. Paul Heathcote made his name 'gentrifying' Lancashire staples such as fish, chips and mushy peas, and lamb hotpot, both of which may appear on the menu. A big hit at inspection was a starter of summer vegetable and herb risotto, the perfectly cooked vegetables and rice in a creamy herb-speckled sauce topped with shavings of Parmesan; also coming up trumps was a buttery pea and lettuce sauce in a main course of pan-fried haddock with crushed potatoes. Expect something like knickerbocker glory or bread-and-butter pudding to finish. There's value to be found on the wine list, which features some classy New World and French bottles. House selections are £12 to £13.50.

CHEF: Andy McGuinness   PROPRIETOR: Paul Heathcote   OPEN: Mon to Sat 12 to 2.30, 5.30 to 10 (11 Sat), Sun 12 to 2.30, 6 to 9.30   CLOSED: bank hols exc Good Fri   MEALS: alc (main courses £10 to £15.50). Set L and D 5.30 to 7 £13.50 (2 courses) to £15.50   SERVICE: 10% (optional), card slips closed   CARDS: Amex, Delta, Diners, MasterCard, Switch, Visa   DETAILS: 150 seats. Private parties: 120 main room, 20 to 65 private rooms. Vegetarian meals. Children's helpings. No smoking. Wheelchair access (also WC). Music. Air-conditioned

▲ Watersreach at the Golden Tulip   [NEW ENTRY]

Waters Reach, Trafford Park,	COOKING 4
Manchester M17 1WS	GLOBAL
TEL: (0161) 868 1900 FAX: (0161) 872 6556	£31–£58

Ian Morgan has remained chef at this former Rhodes & Co restaurant next to Manchester United's ground, and from all accounts – good raw materials, accurately timed dishes and attention to detail – it remains in the top flight. Although décor has stayed much the same – 'upmarket diner' is one description – the menu has gone more global. For starters, pressed ham and apricot terrine with mango salsa and curry mayonnaise sits alongside Thai pork hotpot with egg noodles and greens, or seared scallops on potato blinis with Bury black pudding. For mains, too, the scope is broad: deep-fried fish 'n chips, grilled calf's liver with chorizo sausage, or fillet of lamb rolled in sumac and cinnamon. For pudding try perhaps a Baileys crème brûlée, or a jasmine pannacotta with bitter chocolate sorbet and Indian almond milk. Service has also received praise, with the young staff hitting the right note of efficiency with enthusiasm. The wine list is equally global, offering around three dozen wines (eight by the glass) with enough of interest below £25.

CHEF: Ian Morgan   PROPRIETOR: Golden Tulip   OPEN: Mon to Fri L 12 to 2.30, all week D 6.30 to 10; advance booking essential for match days   CLOSED: L bank hols   MEALS: alc (main courses £8.50 to £16.50). Bar menu also available   SERVICE: 10% (optional)   CARDS: Amex, Delta, Diners, MasterCard, Switch, Visa   DETAILS: 90 seats. Private parties: 150 main room, 30 to 170 private rooms. Car park. Vegetarian meals. Children's helpings. Wheelchair access (also WC). Music. Air-conditioned   ACCOMMODATION: 168 rooms, all with bath/shower. TV. Phone. Room only £98 to £112. Rooms for disabled. Baby facilities   (£5)

Yang Sing ♟

34 Princess Street, Manchester M1 4JY	COOKING 5
TEL: (0161) 236 2200 FAX: (0161) 236 5934	CANTONESE
WEBSITE: www.yang-sing.com	£29–£57

With dining and private banqueting on two floors, supplied by three kitchens, Yang Sing is a sizeable operation. Closely packed tables in the basement ensure the place is cheerful and noisy, helped along by service that (when not too pressed) is generally benign. Yang Sing prides itself on meeting customers' needs and designing meals around preferences and requirements – for a banquet, to a budget, for an occasion, whatever – so it pays to make your wishes known, to bring all the permutations and combinations down to a manageable size. Alternatively there are some set dinners.

A large part of its enduring appeal is the dim sum menu, and not just because it offers what is claimed as 'possibly the widest range in Europe' at lunchtime, but because of the quality, from char siu and wind-dried oyster parcel to salt and pepper ribs, from scallop dumplings to steamed ox tripe, all 'well up to the standard I expect here', according to a regular. Seasonal items might appear in the form of sticky steamed pigs' feet with a sweet sauce at Chinese New Year for example. Good sourcing (not least of seafood) contributes to the clear and distinct flavours, and frying techniques are well understood. Vegetarians get a good deal too. Five house wines at £12.95 or £3.50 for a glass, and 16 special recommendations should be all the wine list anyone needs, but they're backed up by over 100 bottles ranging from Burgundy and Bordeaux, to the rest of France and beyond.

CHEF: Harry Yeung   PROPRIETOR: Yang Sing Ltd   OPEN: all week 12 to 11.45 (12.15 Fri and Sat, 10.45 Sun   MEALS: alc (main courses £5.50 to £12). Set D £17.50 (min 2 people). Banquets from £22 per person   CARDS: not inc   CARDS: Amex, Delta, MasterCard, Switch, Visa   DETAILS: 250 seats. Private parties: 250 main room, 20 to 250 private rooms. Vegetarian meals. Children's helpings. Wheelchair access (also WC). Music. Air-conditioned

---

Prices quoted in the Guide are based on information supplied by restaurateurs. The prices quoted at the top of each entry represent a range, from the lowest price of a three-course meal with service and wine to the highest; the latter is inflated by 20 per cent to take account of likely price rises during the year of the Guide.

▲ Danesfield House, Oak Room ⅝✳

Henley Road, Marlow SL7 2EY
TEL: (01628) 891010   FAX: (01628) 484115
EMAIL: sales@danesfieldhouse.co.uk   COOKING 4
WEBSITE: www.danesfieldhouse.co.uk   ANGLO-FRENCH
on A4155 between Marlow and Henley   £38–£86

Both the imposingly stately house and the grand topiary in the gardens date from
the late-Victorian era. That should give some indication of the dignified tone set
at Danesfield, and the panelled dining room (the Oak Room, indeed) comes
complete with a fine stone fireplace and fruity still lifes. Damian Broom cooks
with an eye on the seasons, adapting the carte and fixed-price menus
accordingly and drawing in fish from Cornwall, beef from Scotland and lamb
from Wales to lend lustre to the dishes. Cornish crab is poached, dressed in
vinaigrette and served with a 'crab biscuit', or you might choose to begin with
carpaccio of Aberdeen Angus with 'humanely reared' foie gras, truffles and
Madeira. Fish is treated fairly robustly in the modern way, with John Dory on a
spring menu being roasted, served with grilled asparagus and sauced with cep
cream, while meat dishes may turn up more wild mushrooms to accompany
cannon of lamb with white truffle butter. The sense of style that pervades it all
continues into desserts such as peanut parfait with bitter chocolate mousse, or an
assiette of fine English and Continental cheeses. The wine list picks out quality
names around the world, but even the basic bottles are expensive at £20. Ten by
the glass are £3.50 to £7.50.

CHEF: Damian Broom   OPEN: all week 12 to 1.45, 7 to 10   MEALS: Set L £18.50 (2 courses) to
£24.50, Set D £35.50 (2 courses) to £47.50   SERVICE: not inc, card slips closed   CARDS: Amex,
Delta, Diners, MasterCard, Switch, Visa   DETAILS: 39 seats. 20 seats outside. Private parties: 8
main room, 4 to 110 private rooms. Car park. Vegetarian meals. Children's helpings. No
smoking. Wheelchair access (also WC). No music. No mobile phones. Air-conditioned
ACCOMMODATION: 87 rooms, all with bath/shower. TV. Phone. B&B £185 to £300. Rooms for
disabled. Baby facilities. Swimming pool (£5)

Vanilla Pod ⅝✳ | NEW ENTRY |

31 West Street, Marlow SL7 2LS   COOKING 5
TEL: (01628) 898101   FAX: (01628) 898108   MODERN BRITISH
WEBSITE: www.thevanillapod.co.uk   £33–£67

The green-and-white vanilla pod and flower on the sign outside this small
brick-and-flint building hardly prepares you for the dining room's orange, red,
yellow and terracotta, and its warm Mediterranean feel. There are beams too,
crisply starched white tablecloths, and a menu of imaginative, well-flavoured
and attractively presented dishes. Its language can be a bit opaque: what, for
example, is a 'gastrique'?

Whatever it is, it accompanies two seared, diver-caught scallops 'as fresh as
the morning' in unlikely but effective combination with rhubarb. The
eponymous vanilla appears, for example, as a poaching agent for neatly carved
corn-fed chicken on a fine pea risotto with a delicate vanilla yoghurt sauce.

Flavours are emphatic but not overdone, witness a rosy roast squab pigeon, 'nicely hepatic, just gamey, and timed to a split-second', served with a savoury mille-feuille of potato slices and shiitake mushrooms. And careful treatment creates spot-on textures: for example, springy and yielding (but not soft) poached sea bass, plus fennel and firm spears of asparagus in a light creamy sauce. The vegetarian menu could feature impossibly thin pasta, filled to bursting with strongly flavoured creamed goats' cheese, on a raft of artichoke and other vegetables. Desserts have met with mixed success, but highlights have numbered a light and well-judged blueberry crème brûlée partnered by a creamy-textured lemon thyme sorbet. Service from formally dressed staff is unobtrusive, professional and friendly, and a short, mainly French wine list doesn't dip below £20 except for four Vin de Pays d'Oc house wines (£16.50), an Italian Pinot Grigio and an Argentinian Malbec.

CHEF/PROPRIETOR: Michael Macdonald   OPEN: Tue to Sat 12 to 2, 7 to 10   CLOSED: 24 Dec to 5 Jan, 1 week Easter, last week Aug, 1st week Sept, bank hols   MEALS: Set L £16.50 (2 courses) to £18.50, Set D £34.50 to £39.50   SERVICE: not inc   CARDS: Amex, Delta, MasterCard, Switch, Visa   DETAILS: 42 seats. Private parties: 34 main room, 8 private room. Vegetarian meals. Children's helpings. No smoking. Wheelchair access (not WC). No music

MARSDEN West Yorkshire   map 8

▲ Olive Branch

Manchester Road, Marsden HD7 6LU
TEL: (01484) 844487   COOKING 3
EMAIL: reservations@olivebranch.uk.com   MODERN ENGLISH
on A62, between Slaithwaite and Marsden   £30–£51

Despite refurbishments and extensions, the sturdy character of what started life as a pub is retained in its guise as a restaurant. When it is busy, which it invariably is, ordering at the bar can result in a good-natured scrum. The menu looks alarmingly long, but the kitchen seems able to deliver. A pigeon breast and a rabbit sausage, both sitting on celeriac mash, pleased at every level with fine timing, and the sauces – robust chocolate vinaigrette for the pigeon, subtle and creamy tarragon with the sausage – achieving their different effects admirably. Simplicity laced with innovation and the use of excellent ingredients also distinguishes main courses: venison medallions so succulent that reflective silence temporarily overpowered conversation, and 'perfectly cooked monkfish' whose expected-to-be-predictable chilli sauce was revitalised with fresh mint. An inspector finished with 'fine pannacotta'. Duboeuf house wines at £10.95 (£2.40 a glass) round out a wide and interesting selection, with plenty under £20 and some classy bottles above.

CHEF: Paul Kewley   PROPRIETORS: John and Ann Lister   OPEN: Sun L and D 1 to 8.30, Tue to Sat D 6.30 to 9.30   CLOSED: first 2 weeks Jan, 2nd week Aug   MEALS: alc (main courses £10 to £17). Set L £12.95, Set D Tue to Thur and Sun 6.30 to 7.30 £12.95 (2 courses)   SERVICE: not inc, card slips closed   CARDS: Delta, MasterCard, Switch, Visa   DETAILS: 65 seats. 12 seats outside. Private parties: 40 main room. Car park. Vegetarian meals. Children's helpings. No smoking area. Wheelchair access (not WC). Music   ACCOMMODATION: 3 rooms, all with bath/shower. TV. Phone. Room only £45 to £60 (The Which? Guide to Good Hotels) (£5)

MARSH BENHAM Berkshire   map 2

Red House

Marsh Benham RG20 8LY   COOKING **2**
TEL: (01635) 582017   FAX: (01635) 581621   MODERN BRITISH
                                                         £28–£56

In bygone days the Water Rat pub, this dapper thatched red-brick building still bears signs of its past but has been transformed with style, creating an upmarket impression while retaining an air of informal geniality. Menus live up to the setting, showing touches of class within an unassuming modern British framework: starters range from chicken terrine with mixed leaves to cream of watercress and white truffle oil with lobster ravioli, while main courses might be seared cod fillet on beetroot risotto with white wine and herb velouté, roasted rack of Welsh lamb with artichokes, baby onions, lardons and white truffle sauce, or simply pan-fried escalope of veal with garlic mash and mushroom sauce. Traditionally minded desserts take in coffee crème brûlée and pear Belle Hélène. The list of around 50 mostly French wines kicks off with four house choices at £12.95 a bottle, £3 a glass.

CHEF: Yves Girard   PROPRIETOR: Tricrane Ltd   OPEN: all week L 12 to 2, Tue to Sat D 7 to 10 CLOSED: 25 and 26 Dec, 1 Jan   MEALS: alc (main courses £11 to £16). Set L and D £13.75 (2 courses) to £16.95, Set L Sun £15.95 (2 courses) to £18.95   SERVICE: not inc   CARDS: Amex, Delta, MasterCard, Switch, Visa   DETAILS: 85 seats. 30 seats outside. Private parties: 60 main room. Car park. Vegetarian meals. Children's helpings. No-smoking area. Wheelchair access (also WC). Occasional music. No mobile phones (£5)

MARTEN Wiltshire   map 2

Windmill ♥ ⅝✕

Salisbury Road, Marten SN8 3SH   COOKING **5**
TEL: (01264) 731372   FAX: (01264) 731284   MODERN EUROPEAN
                                                         £31–£65

In the middle of nowhere, surrounded by fields, this is a spacious and comfortable, stylishly refurbished dining room with interesting artworks on the dusky-pink walls, and a new terrace for outside eating when weather permits. Service from the owner and staff is charming and courteous. It all makes a good first impression, which the cooking lives up to. The style is an updated version of classical French, 'deceptively simple rather than cutting-edge daring' but highly accomplished nonetheless. Bold and vibrant colours give the food strong visual appeal, as in a reporter's 'brilliantly orangey-red' sweet pepper purée to accompany prosciutto, while a saffron and champagne sauce to go with sea bass was a burst of sunshine on a dull day. The skill in the execution brings out the best in the 'fantastic quality' of materials to produce 'delicate and harmonious' flavours. The perfect timing and lightness of sesame-crusted monkfish strips wowed one reporter, while others have been impressed by golden beetroot risotto with pan-roast foie gras and a foie gras biscuit, and a 'tasting' of pork comprising trotter, loin and belly with apple sauce and sage potato, all of which showed skilful preparation and elegant presentation. To finish, there may be tarte Tatin with vanilla ice cream, or hot rice pudding with frozen banana parfait and red berry sauce. The wine list is arranged by style, deftly mixing Old World and New and offering plenty under £20, while some smart bottles appear on a 'fine and rare' list. Two dozen come by the glass for £3.60 to £6.50.

CHEF: Peter Brewer PROPRIETOR: Chris Ellis OPEN: Tue to Sun L 12 to 2, Tue to Sat D 6.45 to 9.15 MEALS: alc D (main courses £14.50 to £19). Set L £14.95 (2 courses) to £18.95, Set D £13.95 (1 course) to £19.95. Light L menu and £49.50 tasting menu available. SERVICE: not inc CARDS: Delta, MasterCard, Switch, Visa DETAILS: 40 seats. 28 seats outside. Private parties: 44 main room. Car park. Vegetarian meals. Children's helpings. No smoking in 1 dining room. Wheelchair access (not WC). Occasional music £5

MARTON North Yorkshire   map 9

Appletree ⚡✳

Marton, nr Pickering YO62 6RD
TEL: (01751) 431457 FAX: (01751) 430190   COOKING 3
EMAIL: appletreeinn@supanet.com   MODERN BRITISH
WEBSITE: www.appletreeinn.co.uk   £22–£48

You feel at home the moment you sink into any one of the settees in this old country inn, where the big fireplace and beamed ceilings are reassuringly rustic. Suitably robust dishes such as an Italian-style roast porchetta on black pudding with glazed apples and a Calvados jus, and beef and onion pie with rich gravy 'in a proper shortcrust pastry' have been endorsed by reporters. However, the menu pushes some way beyond that of the typical country pub with, for example, twice-baked Brie and roast chestnut soufflé to start, followed by chicken and mussels in a tarragon and Chardonnay cream sauce. Desserts maintain the balance, with blackberry and apple sponge with Calvados cream sitting alongside vanilla crème brûlée with brandied raisin fudge and a coconut tuile. Friendly service and value for money are mentioned in reports, and should the restaurant's home-made chutneys, bread, terrines or chocolates make an impression, they're stocked in a small shop on the premises. Four wines come by the glass from a list that efficiently caters for all tastes. Prices open at £11.

CHEFS: T.J. Drew and Iain McGrain PROPRIETORS: Melanie Thornton and T.J. Drew OPEN: Wed to Mon 12 to 2, 6.30 to 9.30 (7 to 9 Sun) CLOSED: 2 weeks Oct, 25 Dec, 1 Jan, 2 weeks Jan MEALS: alc (main courses L £6.50 to £13, D £11 to £16.50). Light L menu available Wed to Sat and Mon SERVICE: not inc, card slips closed CARDS: Delta, MasterCard, Switch, Visa DETAILS: 60 seats. 16 seats outside. Private parties: 26 main room, 8 to 10 private rooms. Car park. Vegetarian meals. Children's helpings. No smoking. Music

MARTON Shropshire   map 7

Sun Inn ⚡✳ £

Marton SY21 8JP   COOKING 4
TEL: (01938) 561211   MODERN BRITISH
                                                            £21–£46

An appropriately bright Mediterranean disposition radiates from the dining room of the Sun, done out in shades of yellow and pale green, which is otherwise a sombre, stone-built, unpretentious and simply fitted-out pub. Steve MacCallum attends to seasonal changes and buys soundly sourced produce, some of it locally. Lamb may come in a highly successful stew with tomatoes and chunks of carrot and swede, or as a herb-crusted rack with gratin potatoes and rosemary sauce. Starters are equally impressive, from pan-fried scallops on avocado and pesto sauce, to a simple dish of baked red pepper and tomato with air-dried ham and Parmesan. Among desserts singled out for praise have been a light date pudding with butterscotch sauce and vanilla ice cream, and 'impeccable' rhubarb crème brûleé. The set-price Sunday lunch is complemented by bar lunches served on other days. Wines are a sound selection, with prices starting at £10.25. Two big-hitters excepted, everything is below £20.

CHEF: Steve MacCallum   PROPRIETORS: Ian and Rosie MacCallum   OPEN: Wed to Sun L 12 to 2, Tue to Sat D 6 to 9   MEALS: alc exc Sun L (main courses £8.50 to £16). Set L Sun £9.50 (2 courses) to £12.50. Bar L menu available Wed to Sat   SERVICE: not inc, card slips closed CARDS: MasterCard, Switch, Visa   DETAILS: 20 seats. Private parties: 20 main room. Car park. Vegetarian meals. Children's helpings. No smoking. Music (£5)

MASHAM North Yorkshire   map 9

Floodlite £

7 Silver Street, Masham HG4 4DX   COOKING 5
TEL: (01765) 689000   ANGLO-FRENCH
                                                                        £22–£47

Run by a husband-and-wife team, Charles Flood in the kitchen and Christine Flood handling front-of-house, Floodlite is a place where tradition endures. Set in what was once a shop, the restaurant is busy with potted plants, display cases of crockery and pink cushions, all topped off by a large crystal chandelier. The menu is quite long, with more than a dozen starters, ten main courses and a dozen desserts. Here, too, tradition looms large, with dishes such as asparagus with hollandaise sauce, grilled Dover sole and lemon tart. That said, the chef is not afraid to take chances (witness a main course of chicken breast stuffed with banana, with mild curry sauce). A starter of Arbroath smokie soufflé may come with 'terrific' beurre blanc, and sautéed king scallops have found favour. Among main dishes, boiled or grilled lobster, or seared sea bass, might vie with roast saddle of Yorkshire lamb, or roast grouse. Desserts rely on tried-and-true combinations, such as chocolate parfait with cherries macerated in Kirsch, or warm apple and almond flan with praline ice cream and butterscotch sauce. The three-course lunch is 'one of the best bargains in the UK'. The wine list is moderately priced, with seven house wines at £10.95 and four sweeties to finish with.

CHEF: Charles Flood   PROPRIETORS: Charles and Christine Flood   OPEN: Fri to Sun L 12 to 2, Tue to Sat D 7 to 9   MEALS: alc (main courses £9.50 to £17.50). Set L £12.50 (2 courses) to £14.50, Set D £13.50 (2 courses) to £16   SERVICE: not inc, card slips closed   CARDS: Amex, MasterCard, Visa   DETAILS: 36 seats. Private parties: 28 main room, 10 private room. Children's helpings. No music (£5)

▲ Swinton Park, Samuel's ▮ ✂   NEW ENTRY

Masham HG4 4JH
TEL: (01765) 680900   FAX: (01765) 680901
EMAIL: enquiries@swintonpark.com
WEBSITE: www.swintonpark.com

COOKING 4
MODERN BRITISH
£25–£51

The 200 acres of parkland surrounding this seventeenth-century castle hotel does much to raise expectations, and the building can't help but leave an impression: it is big, it is grand, it has a 'proper' tower. The dining room is suitably spacious, with gold-leaf, large windows, heavy curtains, white linen-clad tables and upholstered high-backed chairs. Formally dressed staff, 'pleasant and attentive', help set the stage for David Spencer's cooking.

His modern menu might kick off with seared lamb loin, goats' cheese, red chard and rocket salad, or 'moist and tasty' rillettes of duck with orange and coriander salad. Main courses run the gamut from pasta layered with ceps and celeriac in a port and Madeira froth to Wensleydale wild boar wrapped in prosciutto, served with butternut squash and bubble and squeak. Reporters have also enjoyed 'superb' roast rib of beef, with traditional accompaniments, at Sunday lunch. 'Light and intense' sticky toffee pudding impressed a Yorkshireman, and passion-fruit tart with mango and white chocolate ice cream has also been singled out.

The wine list leans towards France and is well chosen, with Languedoc and the Loire adding depth to the major regions. Prices start at £13.50, and a dozen by the glass are £3.40 to £5.10, complemented by a good range of ports, sherries and pudding wines. Rosemary Shrager's cookery school is located at Swinton Park.

CHEF: David Spencer   PROPRIETORS: the Cunliffe-Lister family   OPEN: all week 12.30 to 2.30, 7 to 10   MEALS: Set L £12 (2 courses) to £16, Set D £32. Bar menu available   SERVICE: not inc
CARDS: Amex, Delta, Diners, MasterCard, Switch, Visa   DETAILS: 60 seats. 20 seats outside. Private parties: 90 main room, 2 to 80 private rooms. Car park. Vegetarian meals. Children's helpings. No children under 12 at D. No smoking. Wheelchair access (also WC). Music ACCOMMODATION: 30 rooms, all with bath/shower. TV. Phone. B&B £100 to £350. Rooms for disabled. Baby facilities. Fishing (*The Which? Guide to Good Hotels*)

MATFEN Northumberland   **map 10**

▲ Matfen Hall ✂

Matfen NE20 0RH
TEL: (01661) 886500   FAX: (01661) 886055
EMAIL: info@matfenhall.com
WEBSITE: www.matfenhall.com
off B6318, just S of Matfen village

COOKING 3
MODERN BRITISH
£28–£53

One of the Blackett ancestors, Sir Edward, built Matfen in its present form in 1830. It is a colossal baronial pile, full of majestically large rooms and sweeping staircases, and surrounded by acres of land that now does service as a golf course. The emphasis is on corporate entertainment, but the experience is an enjoyable one, not least because of the refreshing informality with which the place is run.

Craig McMeeken offers some unchallenging, but technically accomplished, cooking on both the fixed-price and à la carte menus. A pair of chargrilled sardines with chilli and lime butter kicked one meal off well, and was followed by impressive baked cannon of lamb with red wine sauce. Breast of guinea fowl has been served with a sauce of spiced plums and juniper berries, while fish options might take in seared halibut with tomatoes and beurre blanc. Finish with banana crème brûlée, lemon soufflé or good summer pudding. The unstuffy approach extends to the relatively compact wine list, which is particularly notable for New World whites and French reds. House French is £13.45 a bottle, or £3.25 for a standard glass.

CHEF: Craig McMeeken PROPRIETORS: Sir Hugh and Lady Blackett OPEN: Sun L 12 to 2.30, all week D 7 to 9.45 MEALS: alc D (main courses £9.50 to £18.50). Set L Sun £16.95, Set D £23.50. Light menu also available SERVICE: not inc CARDS: Amex, Diners, MasterCard, Switch, Visa DETAILS: 100 seats. Private parties: 120 main room, 15 to 120 private rooms. Car park. Vegetarian meals. Children's helpings. No smoking. Wheelchair access (also WC). Music. No mobile phones ACCOMMODATION: 31 rooms, all with bath/shower. TV. Phone. B&B £97.50 to £225. Rooms for disabled. Baby facilities (*The Which? Guide to Good Hotels*)

MELBOURN Cambridgeshire   map 6

Pink Geranium ▼ ✗

25 Station Road, Melbourn SG8 6DX
TEL: (01763) 260215 FAX: (01763) 262110   COOKING 5
EMAIL: bookings@pinkgeranium.co.uk   MODERN BRITISH
WEBSITE: www.pinkgeranium.co.uk   £33–£75

This pink painted house in a village of commuters and high-tech Cambridge whizz-kids sits in its own garden, complete with burbling stream and white picket fence. A profusion of stout beams means a lot of 'mind your head, sir', and the décor is relentlessly pink and flowery, but the cooking, although based on simple ideas and well-tried combinations, contrives to introduce new twists and original touches.

Salmon marinated in beetroot is a natural colour on one side and a fine, rich pink on the other, with flavour contrasts to match; a buttery orange sauce, classic partner to beetroot, and excellent salad rounds off a successful combination. But there are straightforward starters too, like asparagus, poached egg and Parma ham. Rump of tender, pink lamb has been double-sauced with a chunky pesto and reduced pan juices, all three working well together, and served with good fondant potato and roast vegetables to make an outstanding dish. Old-style simplicity might appear in seared salmon with new potatoes, fine beans and spinach. At inspection a mango and raspberry parfait with orange and raspberry syrup was frozen solid – it 'probably had good flavours, but it was impossible to tell' – whereas pear crumble with sauce anglaise shouldn't have the same problem. Service is old-fashioned and most attentive, with much topping up of glasses. The wine list does its traditional business in France very well, but also musters enthusiasm for the rest of Europe and the New World, especially Australia and New Zealand. Prices reflect the affluence of the locality to some extent, but there is plenty under £20 and a dozen come by the glass from £3.95 to £5.95.

CHEF: Gordon Campbell   PROPRIETOR: Lawrence Champion   OPEN: Tue to Sun L 12 to 2, Tue to Sat D 7 to 9.30   CLOSED: 25 and 26 Dec, 1 Jan   MEALS: alc exc Sun L (main courses £16.50 to £26). Set L Tue to Sat £15 (2 courses) to £19.50, Set L Sun £22.50, Set D Tue to Fri £19.50 (2 courses) to £25   SERVICE: 10% (optional), card slips closed   CARDS: Amex, Delta, MasterCard, Switch, Visa   DETAILS: 60 seats. Private parties: 50 main room, 4 to 14 private rooms. Car park. Vegetarian meals. Children's helpings. No smoking. No music (£5)

▲ Sheene Mill ⚡✳

Station Road, Melbourn SG8 6DX
TEL: (01763) 261393   FAX: (01763) 261376
EMAIL: info@sheenemill.co.uk
WEBSITE: www.sheenemill.co.uk

COOKING 3
GLOBAL
£26–£57

At this small hotel, converted from a water mill, Steven Saunders runs a bistro restaurant with a strong commitment to organic produce. Most vegetables, prepared and cooked to a very high standard, are supplied by the neighbouring nursery. An essential simplicity of individual dishes combines with a catholicity of influences that, on one winter menu, showed carbohydrates taking in sweet potato noodles (with terrine of confit duck and hoisin dressing), walnut mash (partnering braised shoulder of lamb), Parmesan polenta (with venison and ratatouille), lime-scented rice (with vegetable brochette and satay sauce) and fondant and rösti potatoes (with roast duck and ribeye steak, respectively). Far Eastern flavourings are omnipresent – for example in a Thai fish soufflé. French house wines from £11.50 are part of a polyglot list that has a decent range of half-bottles and about a dozen wines by the glass. Deeper pockets are indulged with Domaine de la Pousse d'Or Volnay and Corton Charlemagne.

CHEFS: Steven Saunders and Lee Scott   PROPRIETORS: Sally and Steven Saunders   OPEN: all week L 12 to 2.30, Mon to Sat D 7 to 10   CLOSED: D 25 Dec, 26 Dec, 1 Jan   MEALS: Set L Mon to Sat £12 (2 courses) to £16, Set L Sun £22.50, Set D Mon to Fri £30, Set D Sat £35. Snack menu available Mon to Fri 10.30 to 10   SERVICE: 10% (optional), card slips closed   CARDS: Amex, Delta, MasterCard, Switch, Visa   DETAILS: 120 seats. 30 seats outside. Private parties: 100 main room. Car park. Vegetarian meals. Children's helpings. No smoking. Wheelchair access (also WC). Music. Air-conditioned   ACCOMMODATION: 9 rooms, all with bath/shower. TV. Phone. B&B £75 to £120 (The Which? Guide to Good Hotels) (£5)

MELLOR BROOK Lancashire   map 8

▲ Feilden's Arms ⚡✳   [NEW ENTRY]

Whalley Road, Mellor Brook BB2 7PR
TEL: (01254) 812219   FAX: (01254) 769011
EMAIL: kostasnigel@feildens.fsnet.co.uk
WEBSITE: www.feildensarms.co.uk

COOKING 6
MODERN EUROPEAN
£22–£69

The Feilden's Arms is a genuine pub with a proper bar. As is the trend in recent years, it has been gutted and refurbished in modern style, but preserves a few nooks and crannies for drinkers and bar-food eaters; the restaurant is in a large conservatory-style extension. The kitchen, headed by chef/patron Nigel Smith with two appointed head chefs, shows a sense of self-belief, which translates as confidence on the plate: dishes are imaginative, sharply and skilfully executed and full of flavour.

This may be a pub, but ingredients such as sea bream, quail and foie gras are no strangers to the menu. The last may appear in a starter, pan-fried and delicately wrapped in potato, served with grape chutney. Other starters might include an intriguing-sounding smoked salmon jelly and a simple dish of beautifully made gnocchi with rocket salad. Tower formations contribute to eye appeal in main courses such as John Dory with buttered peas and – again – foie gras. Meatier options might include braised pig's cheek with offal and a gherkin jus, or smoked guinea fowl with Savoy cabbage and garlic sauce. After such earthy things, desserts such as a delightfully delicate champagne jelly – actually three miniature jellies separately encasing a strawberry, a blackberry and a raspberry – may come as a surprise. Service is friendly but professional. The wine list is a varied and interesting collection of bottles from Europe and the New World. Eight house wines are £9.95 to £11.25 (£2.60 to £2.90 a glass).

CHEFS: Michael Shaw and Steve Williams PROPRIETOR: Leehand Leisure OPEN: Wed to Sun L 12 to 2.30, Tue to Sat D 7 to 9 (9.45 Sat) CLOSED: 25 Dec MEALS: alc D (main courses £16 to £21). Set L £11.95 (2 courses) to £14.95, Set D £24.95 (2 courses) to £26.95. Bar menu available Mon to Sat L, Mon to Fri D, Sun 3 to 9 SERVICE: not inc, card slips closed CARDS: Amex, Delta, Diners, MasterCard, Switch, Visa DETAILS: 70 seats. 15 seats outside. Private parties: 70 main room. Car park. Vegetarian meals. Children's helpings. No smoking. Wheelchair access (also WC). Music. No mobile phones ACCOMMODATION: 4 rooms, all with bath/shower. TV. B&B £48 to £58 (£5)

MILFORD ON SEA Hampshire map 2

Rouille ⅝✖

69–71 High Street, Milford on Sea SO41 0QG
TEL: (01590) 642340
EMAIL: rouille@ukonline.co.uk
WEBSITE: www.rouille.co.uk

COOKING 4
MODERN FRENCH
£26–£51

The paprika-coloured front of this neighbourhood place enlivens the sleepy end of Milford's High Street. Unpretentiousness shines through the restrained, sophisticated décor. Dishes such as a perfectly timed goats' cheese and chive soufflé with walnut, almond and rocket salad, and duck confit samosas with a well-balanced black cherry sauce illustrate the kitchen's skills and sensitivity to flavour combinations. Main courses maintain the momentum: for example, top-quality fillets of John Dory with well-timed saffron rice surrounded by a rich, roast tomato and clam dressing, and less pricey ingredients are no less satisfying, as in chargrilled chicken breast resting on crushed cumin-spiced potatoes with coconut curry sauce dotted with vegetables. Finish with vanilla crème brûlée accompanied by 'excellent' raspberry sorbet, or perhaps pear and almond tart. A short list of fine wines complements two pages with some smart options from France and good-value gluggers from around the Mediterranean and the New World. Prices start around £13.

CHEF: Lui Hollomby PROPRIETORS: Nicky and Lui Hollomby OPEN: Wed and Thur L 12 to 2, Tue to Sat D 7 to 9.30 CLOSED: last 2 weeks Nov MEALS: Set L £16.95, Set D £16.95 to £31.50

SERVICE: not inc   CARDS: Delta, MasterCard, Switch, Visa   DETAILS: 24 seats. Private parties: 30 main room. Children's helpings. No smoking in 1 dining room. Wheelchair access (not WC). Occasional music. Air-conditioned

MILLBANK West Yorkshire   map 8

Millbank ⅛✗

Millbank, Nr Sowerby Bridge HX6 3DY
TEL: (01422) 825588   FAX: (01422) 822080   COOKING 5
EMAIL: millbankph@ukonline.co.uk   MODERN EUROPEAN
WEBSITE: www.themillbank.com   £29–£49

The Halseys' restaurant may feel as though it is in the middle of trendy Leeds, but the situation is pure rural Yorkshire. Turn up the hill in the centre of the village to find it, then park close against the walls of the narrow road, as there's no car park. In fine weather head for the decked area, which has stunning views across the valley.

Great pride is taken in the sourcing of materials: corn-fed poultry, Lancashire suckling pigs, smoked beef from the Dales, local game, and lobsters and crabs brought from Holy Island. Glen Futter brings to the operation a sharp city slickness that extends from imaginative bar snacks to the main menus. Besides appreciating the thoughtful and attentive service, one couple found a simple risotto of red peppers and tomatoes first-class, and main courses of venison sausages and calf's liver with green beans, both served with creamy mash, got the thumbs-up too. In the evenings, all the stops are pulled out for saddle of hare with potato pie and plum sauce, or a halibut fillet served with a poached egg and mushroom tartlet. Vegetables sides are extra, and include mashed carrot for those tired of the potato version. Then, if you've room, try banana and walnut sponge, or a house assiette of chocolate. Wines, stylistically listed, start from £9.90 (£2.50 a glass) for a Puglian red.

CHEF: Glen Futter   PROPRIETORS: Paul and Christine Halsey   OPEN: Wed to Sun L 12 to 2, Tue to Sat D 5.30 to 9.30 (6 to 10 Fri and Sat)   MEALS: alc (main courses £9 to £14). Bar menu available
SERVICE: not inc   CARDS: Delta, MasterCard, Switch, Visa   DETAILS: 46 seats. 38 seats outside. Vegetarian meals. No smoking. Wheelchair access (not WC). Music

MILTON ERNEST Bedfordshire   map 6

Strawberry Tree

3 Radwell Road, Milton Ernest MK44 1RY
TEL/FAX: (01234) 823633   COOKING 6
EMAIL: strawberrytree_restaurant@yahoo.co.uk   MODERN EUROPEAN
on A6, 5m north of Bedford   £39–£64

Inside this thatched former pub, the gigantic ceiling beams and original fireplace speak of great age. Two dining rooms, one each side of the bar/lounge, are smartly turned out and decorated with paintings, some of them for sale. The ticking of an old clock adds to the sense of unhurried tranquillity.

Andrew and Jason Bona use high-quality ingredients like Gloucester Old Spot pork, Dexter beef and organic eggs from just up the road and take care not to 'mess about' with their flavours too much. Immaculately neat presentation showcases deftly constructed terrines – of pigeon breasts and beetroot, perhaps, or trout with dried tomatoes, fennel and celeriac – as well as more mainstream pastas and risottos. The meat is well-handled, whether best end of Suffolk lamb, crusted with upliftingly fresh herbs and served with pea purée, braised lettuce and a tiny dauphinois of celeriac, or roast duck sauced with cherries, apple and cinnamon. Ices and sorbets figure in desserts such as cocoa biscuit ganache with espresso ice cream, or blackberry and lemon trifle with apple sorbet. The small portions and geometrically perfect designs create a slightly reverential atmosphere that the front-of-house approach does nothing to dispel, but the underpinning of sound technique and imaginative flair are indubitable. France, the southern hemisphere and one Rioja make up the short wine list, but the choices are mostly inspired. House vins de pays are £14.50 (Merlot-Syrah) and £15 (Viognier-Chardonnay).

CHEFS: Jason and Andrew Bona   PROPRIETORS: John and Wendy Bona   OPEN: Wed to Fri L 12 to 1.45, Wed to Sat D 7.30 to 8.30   CLOSED: 2 weeks Jan, 2 weeks summer   MEALS: alc L (main courses £14 to £18). Set D £38   SERVICE: not inc, 12.5% for parties of 6 or more, card slips closed   CARDS: Delta, MasterCard, Switch, Visa   DETAILS: 22 seats. Private parties: 18 main room, 4 to 10 private rooms. Car park. Vegetarian meals. Children's helpings. No-smoking area. Wheelchair access (also men's WC). No music

---

MONKS ELEIGH Suffolk   map 6

Swan Inn ❊ £ | NEW ENTRY |

The Street, Monks Eleigh IP7 7AU   COOKING 3
TEL/FAX: (01449) 741391   MODERN EUROPEAN
on B1115 between Sudbury and Stowmarket   £25–£46

The Swan commands a prime position on the corner of the main road that runs through the picturesque, medieval village of Monks Eleigh. Once inside the cream-painted, thatched building, expect to find exposed beams, cream walls and highly polished tables. The menus are chalked up on blackboards, pub-style, and the formula is simple and the ambience relaxing.

While some have spotted 'a distinctly Italian bias in the kitchen', there are other influences, too, more broadly European. Potted rillettes of pork may be accompanied by green tomato chutney, and, in season, local asparagus may be served simply with melted butter and lemon. Winning smiles of satisfaction at inspection was a main course of chargrilled chicken breast with a 'divine' compote of aubergine, tomato and basil in which the herb suffused through the other ingredients without overpowering them. At dessert, there might be 'memorable' and 'ultra-light' apple and ginger pudding with sticky toffee sauce, or strawberry crème brûlée. Front-of-house is overseen by Carol Ramsbottom with admirable warmth of character. Wines on the succinct list (supplied by Lay & Wheeler) start at £10 and almost all are under £20.

CHEF: Nigel Ramsbottom   PROPRIETORS: Carol and Nigel Ramsbottom   OPEN: Wed to Sun 12 to 2, 7 to 9.30   CLOSED: 25 and 26 Dec   MEALS: alc (main courses £9 to £16)   SERVICE: not inc, card slips closed   CARDS: Delta, MasterCard, Switch, Visa   DETAILS: 40 seats. Private parties: 40 main room, 12 to 40 private rooms. Car park. Vegetarian meals. Children's helpings. No smoking. No music £5

       map 6

▲ Morston Hall ▼ ⚡✖

Morston NR25 7AA
TEL: (01263) 741041   FAX: (01263) 740419
EMAIL: reception@morstonhall.com   COOKING **6**
WEBSITE: www.morstonhall.com   MODERN BRITISH
on A149, 2m W of Blakeney   £35–£63

Peaceful north Norfolk, a short walk from the Norfolk Coast Path, is the setting for this small hotel and restaurant. The local flint and brick house is softened by a big lawn, lots of well-stocked flowerbeds and a large pond. Print patterns abound in the interior, while the dining room walls are hung with paintings from a local gallery. Local produce figures large on the menu, from lobsters and crabs to strawberries. Four-course no-choice dinners, padded out with nibbles and appetisers, are served at a single sitting, with one frequent guest proclaiming that the daily-changing menu 'sparkles with imagination and skill'.

An appetiser of chargrilled scallop, its coral perched atop on a little bed of guacamole, has preceded a 'perfect in every way' starter of warm muffin with poached quail's egg, watercress, hollandaise and Parma ham. Main courses of roast breast of corn-fed chicken served with angel hair pasta (flecked with lots of herbs) and truffle jus, or lasagne of Morston lobster served with 'its own cappuccino' and samphire, featuring ultra-thin, elastic pasta and fresh lobster, are examples of Galton Blackiston's 'classically perfect' style. A summertime dessert of mille-feuille of summer berries with own-made mint ice cream and raspberry sabayon was put together with seasonality in mind. Overall, timings are mostly spot-on, and the large, all-male team of waiting staff is professional yet unstuffy. An appetising bunch of wines is arranged by grape variety, and it's worth turning to the 'other grapes' pages for some offbeat goodies. Prices are mostly fair, with plenty under £20, and a dozen by the glass (£3 to £7) include some stylish options.

CHEFS: Galton Blackiston and Samantha Wegg   PROPRIETORS: Tracy and Galton Blackiston OPEN: Sun L 12.30 for 1 (1 sitting), all week 7.30 for 8 (1 sitting)   CLOSED: 25 and 26 Dec, 1 Jan to 1 Feb   MEALS: Set L £24, Set D £40   SERVICE: not inc, card slips closed   CARDS: Amex, Delta, Diners, MasterCard, Switch, Visa   DETAILS: 40 seats. Private parties: 40 main room, 10 to 14 private rooms. Car park. Children's helpings. No smoking. Wheelchair access (also WC). No music. No mobile phones   ACCOMMODATION: 7 rooms, all with bath/shower. TV. Phone. D, B&B £110 to £240. Baby facilities (*The Which? Guide to Good Hotels*)

       map 2

▲ Beetle & Wedge Hotel, Dining Room ▼ ⚡✖

Ferry Lane, Moulsford OX10 9JF
TEL: (01491) 651381   FAX: (01491) 651376
EMAIL: kate@beetleandwedge.co.uk   COOKING **4**
WEBSITE: www.beetleandwedge.co.uk   ANGLO-FRENCH
off A329 4m S of Wallingford, down Ferry Lane to river   £49–£72

Standing proud on the banks of the Thames, this is a charming venue even out of season. Whether you go for the modern conservatory Dining Room, or the brick-built Boathouse alongside (which focuses on chargrilled dishes), both are comfortable and relaxing places in which to eat.

The Dining Room seeks to strike a balance in its menus between introducing new ideas and styles and meeting loyal regulars' long-held expectations. Thus old favourites like artichoke heart with wild mushroom and hollandaise sauce might be followed by spicy lamb shank and couscous. Other main courses have encompassed loin of English veal with kidneys, sweetbreads and wild mushroom sauce, and pan-fried fillet of sea bass with spinach and béarnaise sauce. Treacle sponge with custard and ice cream, and hot Cointreau soufflé with raspberry coulis are among mostly traditional desserts. Generous portions are reported, and service receives decent plaudits. France underpins the fairly traditional wine list, with meaty Bordeaux and Burgundy selections complemented by good choices from Rhône, Alsace and Loire. Otherwise there's Italy and a quick world tour. Six house wines are sold by the glass/bottle (£3.95/£16.50) or part-bottle, but no halves are listed.

CHEFS: Richard Smith and Olivier Bouet   PROPRIETORS: Richard and Kate Smith   OPEN: Wed to Sun 12 to 1.45, 7 to 9.45   MEALS: alc (main courses £17.50 to £22.50). Set L Sun and Set D £37.50   SERVICE: not inc   CARDS: Amex, Delta, Diners, MasterCard, Switch, Visa   DETAILS: 35 seats. 50 seats outside. Private parties: 64 main room, 8 to 64 private rooms. Car park. Vegetarian meals. Children's helpings. No smoking. Wheelchair access (also WC). Occasional live music. No mobile phones   ACCOMMODATION: 11 rooms, all with bath/shower. TV. Phone. B&B £99 to £175. Rooms for disabled. Baby facilities (*The Which? Guide to Good Hotels*)

MOULTON North Yorkshire   **map 9**

Black Bull Inn ♥

Moulton DL10 6QJ
TEL: (01325) 377289   FAX: (01325) 377422   COOKING 4
EMAIL: sarah@blackbullinn.demon.co.uk   SEAFOOD/MODERN BRITISH
1m SE of Scotch Corner   £27–£61

This pleasant old country inn near the A1 makes a useful alternative to the horrors of motorway catering, besides being deservedly popular in its own right. Eating is spread across the lively, casual bar and the more formal but still relaxed dining room (a converted Pullman railway carriage).

The bedrock of the cooking is seafood, often treated inventively. There might be sautéed squid with spring onion and mascarpone risotto and balsamic syrup, or tempura oysters with chilli jam, along with more conventional poached turbot with hollandaise, or bacon-wrapped monkfish on creamed spinach and bouillabaisse sauce. Meat eaters can enjoy starters like black pudding won tons on sweet potato purée, and mains such as roast lamb loin with flageolet beans, garlic, peas and parsley, or pan-fried duck breast with fennel fondue and Vin Santo sauce. Crêpes suzette is a popular dessert. This being a pub, there are draught beers, including Theakston Best, but the good-value wine list complements the food. Excellent seafood whites come from the Loire, Germany and Burgundy, in particular; reds include Burgundy, claret, and some good old Côte-Rôties from Guigal, and New World selections are brief but astute. Three come by the glass (£2.20), and house bottles start at £11.95.

CHEF: Paul Grundy   PROPRIETORS: A.M.C. and S.C. Pagendam   OPEN: Mon to Fri L 12 to 2, Mon to Sat D 6.45 to 10.15   CLOSED: 24 to 26 Dec   MEALS: alc (main courses £16 to £20). Set L £16.50. Bar L menu available   SERVICE: not inc   CARDS: Amex, Delta, Diners, MasterCard, Switch, Visa   DETAILS: 100 seats. 16 seats outside. Private parties: 10 main room, 10 to 30 private rooms. Car park. Vegetarian meals. No children under 7. Wheelchair access (not WC). No music

NAYLAND Suffolk   map 6

▲ White Hart

11 High Street, Nayland CO6 4JF
TEL: (01206) 263382   FAX: (01206) 263638   COOKING 3
EMAIL: nayhart@aol.com   MODERN EUROPEAN
WEBSITE: www.whitehart-nayland.co.uk   £25–£53

Excellent service (on most occasions) and smart table settings give all the signs that this outpost of the Roux empire aspires to the values of its founders. Extravagances, such as sea bass with a caviar and champagne sauce, sit alongside the bourgeois modesty of loin of pork on a cassoulet of white beans and home-smoked sausage: both dishes at £9.90 on the 'Lacarte' look good value, as do set-price lunch basics like whole grilled plaice with chips and a dill flavoured sauce. Starters of 'clear, tasty' Scotch broth with oxtail, and 'beautifully presented' smoked chicken salad have been endorsed by reporters, along with main courses of confit of duck leg with lentils, lardons and roasted turnips. For dessert, there may vanilla and apricot crème brûlée, or trio of excellent sorbets. Range and quality are evident on the main wine list, but prices rise steeply from the commendable dozen-plus wines on the lunchtime 'Menu Rapide', all available by the glass and for £11 the bottle.

CHEF: Carl Shillingford   PROPRIETOR: Michel Roux   OPEN: Tue to Sun 12 to 2.30 (3 Sun), 6.30 to 9.30 (10 Sat, 9 Sun)   CLOSED: 26 Dec to 9 Jan   MEALS: alc (main courses £9.90 to £16.30). Set L £9.95 (2 courses) to £12.95, Set D (not Sat) £16.50 (2 courses) to £21.50   SERVICE: 12.5% (optional), card slips closed   CARDS: Amex, Delta, Diners, MasterCard, Switch, Visa   DETAILS: 50 seats. 30 seats outside. Private parties: 70 main room, 10 to 36 private rooms. Car park. Vegetarian meals. Children's helpings. Wheelchair access (not WC). Music   ACCOMMODATION: 6 rooms, all with bath/shower. TV. Phone. B&B £69 to £95. Baby facilities (*The Which? Guide to Good Hotels*) £5

NEAR SAWREY Cumbria   map 8

▲ Ees Wyke

Near Sawrey LA22 0JZ
TEL/FAX: (015394) 36393
EMAIL: mail@eeswyke.co.uk   COOKING 2
WEBSITE: www.eeswyke.co.uk   BRITISH
on B5285 2m S of Hawkshead   £35–£42

The Lees took over Ees Wyke in February 2003 but have aimed to maintain the same tone of comforting, unfussy warmth at this small country hotel, which is situated between Hawkshead and the ferry across Windermere. Richard Lee has retained the five-course menu format of his predecessor, with an intermediate savoury course (such as a poached egg on a bed of spinach) following the starter choice, which might be a well-made puff pastry tartlet topped with goats' cheese, red onion, aubergine and peppers, flavoured with rosemary, thyme and garlic. Main courses keep things simple, with cubed chicken breast sautéed with tiny mushrooms and cream, or a grilled fillet of salmon with hollandaise, served with a plethora of vegetables. Fruity desserts might include pears poached in white wine and cinnamon, served with caramel sauce, before a concluding cheese course of British and French specimens. Service at inspection was marred by lapses and mix-ups, suggesting that a certain amount of bedding-in is still needed. An eminently fairly priced wine list gives about equal cracks of the whip to France and the southern hemisphere, with French and Australian house wines at £11.50.

CHEF: Richard Lee   PROPRIETORS: Richard and Margaret Lee   OPEN: all week D only 7.15 (1 sitting)   MEALS: Set D £26   SERVICE: not inc, card slips closed   CARDS: Delta, MasterCard, Switch, Visa   DETAILS: 25 seats. 25 seats outside. Private parties: 25 main room. Car park. No children under 10. No smoking. No music. Air-conditioned   ACCOMMODATION: 8 rooms, 6 with bath/shower. TV. B&B £52 to £104. No children under 10 (*The Which? Guide to Good Hotels*) (£5)

NETHER ALDERLEY Cheshire   map 8

Wizard ❧✳

Macclesfield Road, Nether Alderley SK10 4UB   COOKING 3
TEL: (01625) 584000   FAX: (01625) 585105   MODERN BRITISH
                                                                    £23–£51

'A classy old pub in an idyllic country setting' is the description offered by one visitor to this pub-turned-restaurant in an exclusive part of Cheshire. Although the Wizard has a small bar, the interior is geared up for eating, with two rooms casually decked out with wooden tables, and one more formal dining room. There is nothing casual about the menu, with around eight choices for each course, nor the service, which is professional, competent and friendly. Caesar salad, 'excellent in presentation and structure', and 'well-executed' goats' cheese with chorizo and mixed leaves, have been first-course dishes that have hit the right note. Main courses run to such modern and appealing pairings as hoisin-braised shank of lamb with red cabbage marmalade, or grilled baby halibut fillet with basil butter. Puddings that have received praise have come in the form of a 'classy' apple and almond sponge with a good crème anglaise, while the wide-ranging wine list has some top-notch stuff but also plenty of interest below £20. Eight house wines are £12 and £13.

CHEF: Paul Beattie   PROPRIETOR: Bispham Green Brewery   OPEN: Tue to Sun L 12 to 2, Tue to Sat D 7 to 9.30   MEALS: alc exc Sun L (main courses L £5 to £9.50, D £9.50 to £17). Set L Tue to Sat £11.50 (2 courses) to £14.50, Set L Sun £15.95 (2 courses) to £18.95   SERVICE: not inc L, 10% D, card slips closed   CARDS: Amex, Delta, MasterCard, Switch, Visa   DETAILS: 90 seats. 20 seats outside. Private parties: 40 main room, 40 to 120 private rooms. Car park. Vegetarian meals. Children's helpings. No smoking in 1 dining room. Wheelchair access (also men's WC). Music

See inside the front cover for an explanation of the symbols used at the tops of entries.

NETTLEBED Oxfordshire

map 2

▲ White Hart 🍴✳

High Street, Nettlebed RG9 5DD
TEL: (01491) 641245   FAX: (01491) 649018
EMAIL: info@whitehartnettlebed.com
WEBSITE: www.whitehartnettlebed.com

COOKING **4**
MODERN BRITISH
£40–£61

Chris Barber has sold the Goose in Britwell Salome (see entry), and his energies are now concentrated on this seventeenth-century brick and flint inn. His cooking style remains in the same modern British vein as previously, typically producing starters of grilled scallops with pea purée and home-dried tomatoes, and seared fillet of Cornish mullet with saffron-scented potato salad and crème fraîche, while main courses range from pan-fried salmon fillet with pea and herb risotto to roast breast of Gressingham duck with cannellini beans and a cider jus. Among desserts have been intriguing ideas such as chicory crème brûlée and more straightforward ones such as iced praline parfait.

The second dining option is the pub-like White Hart Bistro, which has a simpler, more traditional menu, offering the likes of roast pepper and goats' cheese tart, deep-fried spicy squid, lamb curry with rice, and grilled chicken with mushroom risotto and cep jus. Service throughout is 'quick and pleasant'. Wines are slightly cheaper in the bistro, but value on the full restaurant list is fair, with a generous handful of bottles below £20 as well as a good range of pricier clarets.

CHEF/PROPRIETOR: Chris Barber   OPEN: Tue to Sat; 12 to 2, 7 to 9   MEALS: Set L and D £25 to £50. Bistro menu available all week   SERVICE: 12.5% (optional), card slips closed   CARDS: Amex, Delta, MasterCard, Switch, Visa   DETAILS: 30 seats. Private parties: 40 main room, 6 to 20 private rooms. Car park. Vegetarian meals. No children under 14. No smoking. Wheelchair access (also WC). No music   ACCOMMODATION: 12 rooms, all with bath/shower. TV. Phone. B&B £105 to £145. Rooms for disabled (£5)

NEWBURY Berkshire

map 2

▲ Newbury Manor 🍷 🥯 🍴✳

The Restaurant, London Road,
Newbury RG14 2BY
TEL: (01635) 528838   FAX: (01635) 523406
EMAIL: therestaurant@newbury-manor-
hotel.co.uk
WEBSITE: www.newbury-manor-hotel.co.uk

COOKING **5**
MODERN EUROPEAN
£35–£65

Set in nine acres of woodland and water meadows, with the rivers Kennet and Lambourn flowing through the grounds, this one-time Georgian manor house (now predominantly a business and function hotel) proves quite an oasis on the fringes of town. The informal River Bar looks out over the waters, while the Piano Bar cuts a more traditional tone over aperitifs. New chef David Williams had only just arrived as we visited, and though the cuisine will doubtless evolve and develop, results were impressive nonetheless. The compact, modern carte is based on sound classical techniques and dotted with luxury items. Dishes are light, perfectly portioned, and cleverly constructed with sound combinations and some 'wow-factor' elements – the cromesquis of foie gras accompaniment to a main course of roast Anjou pigeon and port jus providing a memorable moment when eaten whole (as advised). Raw materials are typically first-class, again portrayed by new season rump of lamb with parsnip purée and an olive oil and lentil jus, while presentation shows imagination and finesse throughout. Among starters might be a risotto of smoked haddock and leeks with a delicately fried quail's egg, while desserts could run to banana tarte Tatin and pistachio ice cream or summer berries with champagne jelly.

The stylish cuisine deserves a better venue than the over-spill conservatory being used on our visit; the restaurant, with its bold décor of striking turquoise walls and parquet floor was in use for a function. Service, from the front-of-house manager, was knowledgeable, enthusiastic and professional. Wines are an astute international selection, mostly smart bottles at substantial prices. The Loire and the south-west complement the premium bottles from Bordeaux in France, while Italy and the USA are other favourite countries. Eight modern house wines start at £14.50, and 16 by the glass are £4.50 to £12.50.

CHEF: David Williams PROPRIETOR: Robert Rae OPEN: Sun to Fri L 12 to 2 (12.30 to 2.30 Sun), Mon to Sat D 7 to 9.30 CLOSED: bank hols MEALS: Set L £16.50 (2 courses) to £22.50, Set D £23.50 (1 course) to £39 SERVICE: not inc CARDS: Amex, Delta, Diners, MasterCard, Switch, Visa DETAILS: 60 seats. 15 seats outside. Private parties: 80 main room, 3 to 40 private rooms. Car park. Vegetarian meals. Children's helpings. No smoking. Wheelchair access (also WC). Music. No mobile phones. Air-conditioned ACCOMMODATION: 33 rooms, all with bath/shower. TV. Phone. B&B £115 to £200. Rooms for disabled. Baby facilities (£5)

▲ Donnington Valley Hotel, Wine Press ▮ ⅙✳ NEW ENTRY

Old Oxford Road, Donnington,
Newbury RG14 3AG   COOKING 2
TEL: (01635) 551199   MODERN BRITISH–PLUS
WEBSITE: www.donningtonvalley.co.uk   £28–£65

'A little piece of California in Berkshire' is how one visitor described this friendly hotel and restaurant, sibling to the more illustrious Vineyard at Stockcross (see entry), also owned by Sir Peter Michael. A striking modern structure, it is a 'great barn of an open space', with polished wooden floors, comfortable sofas, a grandfather clock and other bits of 'traditional English' memorabilia. In the Wine Press restaurant, with its huge vaulted timbered ceiling with chandeliers, and cream walls hung with pictures related to winemaking, the menu is an appealing modern British repertoire. For starters, seared scallops may be accompanied by a tower of robust black pudding, drizzled with a light veal jus, while a main course of crisp-skinned halibut may be enlivened by a tomato and green pepper salsa, and breast of duck by a spicy pineapple compote. Finish with something like treacle and apple tart with Calvados sorbet and cinnamon custard, or apple strudel with Chantilly cream. The wine list doesn't set out to match its sibling's magnificent range, and offers just a glimpse of its encyclopaedic collections of California's, France's and Italy's finest. Instead you'll find an extremely well balanced selection from all regions, including lots of bottles under £20 grouped into price bands at the front of the list. Sixteen by the glass start at just £2.50.

CHEF: Kelvin Johnstone   PROPRIETOR: Sir Peter Michael   OPEN: all week 12 to 2, 7 to 10   MEALS: alc (main courses L £7.50 to £12.50, D £14 to £22.50). Set L £16 (2 courses) to £19, Set D £22 (2 courses) to £26   SERVICE: not inc, card slips closed   CARDS: Amex, Delta, MasterCard, Switch, Visa   DETAILS: 90 seats. 28 seats outside. Private parties: 170 main room, 10 to 50 private rooms. Car park. Vegetarian meals. Children's helpings. No smoking. Wheelchair access (also WC). Music. No mobile phones. Air-conditioned   ACCOMMODATION: 58 rooms, all with bath/shower. TV. Phone. B&B £150 (double room). Rooms for disabled

NEWCASTLE UPON TYNE Tyne & Wear   map 10

Blackfriars Café Bar ✼ | NEW ENTRY |

Friars Street, Newcastle upon Tyne NE1 4XN
TEL: (0191) 261 5945   FAX: (0191) 213 0045   COOKING 2
EMAIL: bookings@sidneys.co.uk   GLOBAL
WEBSITE: www.blackfriarscafebar.co.uk   £18–£47

This café is housed in a group of medieval buildings (a former priory) set around a courtyard in the heart of the old city. The spacious interior features wooden tables, beamed ceilings and tiled floors, and in fine weather diners can eat al fresco in the courtyard. The owners describe their style as 'globally inspired, experimental', and the menu certainly touches down on most continents: in North Africa for Tunisian crab and harissa brik with yuzu labneh, and merguez sausages with an apricot and sultana couscous cake (which impressed at inspection), for example. Vegetarians are not overlooked on this global ingredient quest: twice-baked Gruyère soufflé with pear chutney, or an Italianate dish of linguine with truffle, Parmesan shavings and a basil and pear salad. Meats are carefully sourced (beef is from Castle Estates herds in the Welsh borders, free-range poultry is reared locally), perhaps turning up as fillet steak with cottage cheese dumplings and caramelised onion mash, or chicken breast and prawn laksa with quail's eggs and soba noodles. The cooking is doubtless ambitious, but 'not over-ambitious', and the combinations work more often than not. The wines on the short list have been carefully selected and are fairly priced from £10.50; suggested wines are listed beside dishes on the menu. The restaurant is under the same ownership as Sidney's in Tynemouth (see entry).

CHEF: Andy Drape   PROPRIETORS: Andy and Sam Hook   OPEN: Tue to Sun L 12 to 2.30, Tue to Sat D 6 to 10   CLOSED: bank hols exc Good Fri   MEALS: alc exc Sun L (main courses £10 to £16). Set L £7.90 (2 courses) to £9.90, Set D Tue to Fri 6 to 7 £9.90 (2 courses) to £12.90. Café menu available L   SERVICE: not inc, 10% for large parties   CARDS: Delta, MasterCard, Switch, Visa   DETAILS: 60 seats. 50 seats outside. Private parties: 110 main room, 20 to 60 private rooms. Vegetarian meals. Children's helpings. No smoking. Wheelchair access (not WC). Occasional music. Air-conditioned   (£5)

Café 21 ✼

19–21 Queen Street, Princes Wharf, Quayside,   COOKING 6
Newcastle upon Tyne NE1 3UG   BISTRO
TEL: (0191) 222 0755   FAX: (0191) 221 0761   £25–£59

This may be 'only' a café or bistro, but it is a fine example of its kind, being both functional (there is somewhere to hang your coat, in the style of French brasseries) and stylish, with gleaming glasses, white cloths and shining cutlery.

And if the food is not elaborate, that is much to its credit. Its appeal is evident from a wild mushroom and smoked bacon vol-au-vent, rare salmon spring rolls with lime and ginger dipping sauce, and an expertly made cheese and spinach soufflé.

Main courses have featured sirloin steak with herb butter and thin chips, lamb confit with a casserole of white beans and mint pesto, and light, crisp, flavourful fishcakes. The blackboard belies that well-known oxymoron 'vegetarian choice' by offering asparagus risotto topped with Parmesan and Cheddar cheese and spinach soufflé with Caesar salad, and the set lunches are 'an incredible bargain': perhaps chicken livers with balsamic sauce, followed by roast breast of mallard with red cabbage and wild berries. Farmhouse cheeses are kept in good condition, and desserts range from plum tart with lemongrass ice cream to chocolate 'samosas' with spiced pears. The welcome is warm, staff are courteous, pleasant and knowledgeable, and wines are user-friendly, offering good choice under £20. House Duboeuf is £11.50.

CHEF: Christopher Dobson PROPRIETORS: Terence and Susan Laybourne OPEN: Mon to Sat 12 to 2.30, 6 to 10.30 CLOSED: bank hols MEALS: alc (main courses £10.50 to £20.50). Set L £13 (2 courses) to £15.50 SERVICE: not inc CARDS: Amex, Delta, Diners, MasterCard, Switch, Visa DETAILS: 60 seats. Vegetarian meals. Children's helpings. No smoking in 1 dining room. Wheelchair access (not WC). Music

Fisherman's Lodge 🍷 $*

TYNE & WEAR GFG 2004 COMMENDED

Jesmond Dene, Jesmond, Newcastle upon Tyne NE7 7BQ
TEL: (0191) 281 3281 FAX: (0191) 281 6410
EMAIL: enquiries@fishermanslodge.co.uk
WEBSITE: www.fishermanslodge.co.uk

COOKING **6**
SEAFOOD/MODERN BRITISH
£33–£102

Like its sisters down the coast at Seaham and across the country at Windermere (see entries), the nineteenth-century Lodge provides high tech wizardry for its business customers (think video conferencing and plasma screens), without compromising the appeal of its quiet location. The décor too manages to be both dramatic and restful, combining dark browns throughout and white cloths on candle lit tables in the dining room. The kitchen also appears to have shifted up a notch or two, producing distinctive and skilfully managed meals with well-defined flavours.

Fish remains a strong suit, perhaps turning up as grilled cod with sweet potato purée, sea bream with langoustine tortellini, or triumphantly fresh monkfish wrapped in the thinnest piece of pancetta imaginable, sautéed, sliced, and served with a well-made risotto and a smear of meaty, stock-based sauce. Shellfish typically appears among starters – roast Orkney scallops with celeriac purée, or king prawn tempura with spicy mango chutney – although there is much to delight elsewhere too: 'absolutely ace' calf sweetbread, for instance, soft inside yet properly seared, served with artichokes, girolles and finely shredded celeriac rémoulade. The food is simply conceived and confidently executed, right through to desserts such as an accomplished lemon soufflé, partnered by a 'masterful' citrus tart, and by a well-judged sweet-sharp lime and lemongrass granita. Wines (which open with a sensibly short list of moderately priced recommendations) don't stint on quality. The full list is a well-rounded international selection that turns up a few star names, with Bordeaux and Burgundy covered in greater depth.

CHEF: Paul Amer PROPRIETORS: Tom and Jocelyn Maxfield OPEN: Mon to Sat 12 to 2, 7 to 10.30 CLOSED: 25 and 26 Dec, bank hols MEALS: alc (main courses £20 to £37). Set L £14.95 to £19.50 SERVICE: not inc CARDS: Amex, Delta, MasterCard, Switch, Visa DETAILS: 65 seats. 16 seats outside. Private parties: 60 main room, 4 to 40 private rooms. Car park. Vegetarian meals. Children's helpings. No smoking in dining room, smoking permitted in bar. Wheelchair access (also WC). Music

Treacle Moon ✳️   NEW ENTRY

5–7 The Side, Quayside, Newcastle upon
Tyne NE1 3JE   COOKING 4
TEL: (0191) 232 5537 FAX: (0191) 221 1745   MODERN BRITISH
WEBSITE: www.treaclemoonrestaurant.com   £43–£64

Extensive redevelopment of Newcastle's quayside area has seen it become one of the most fashionable parts of the city – local attractions include the Millennium Bridge and the Baltic Arts Centre. Treacle Moon finds itself at the heart of this boom, on a cobbled street that runs down to the quay. 'International cuisine with an oriental flavour' is how the restaurant describes its style, which is borne out by starters such as wok-seared wild mushrooms with sweet saké, coriander and soy, or a tian of tea-smoked salmon with vegetable noodles, toasted macadamia nuts and horseradish crème fraîche, and main courses of roast duck breast with spring onion mash, braised cabbage and a port jus, chargrilled beef fillet with lyonnaise potatoes, broad beans and truffle jus, or poached halibut with exotic mushrooms, new potatoes and white wine cream sauce. To finish there may be rhubarb and apple crumble with crème anglaise and vanilla ice cream, or rich chocolate and orange tart with clotted cream. Bottle prices on the short wine list start at around £15 and quickly rise beyond £20.

CHEF: Neil Howden PROPRIETORS: Tom and Jocelyn Maxfield OPEN: Mon to Sat D only 5.30 to 10 MEALS: alc (main courses £14 to £20) SERVICE: not inc CARDS: Amex, Delta, MasterCard, Switch, Visa DETAILS: 30 seats. Private parties: 40 main room. Vegetarian meals. No smoking in 1 dining room. Music. No mobile phones. Air-conditioned

Vermont Hotel, Blue Room   NEW ENTRY

Castle Garth, Newcastle upon Tyne NE1 1RQ
TEL: (0191) 2331010 FAX: (0191) 2331234   COOKING 6
EMAIL: info@vermont-hotel.co.uk   MODERN EUROPEAN
WEBSITE: www.vermont-hotel.co.uk   £51–£76

The Vermont is a grand city-centre hotel in an elevated position by the castle. Unusually, its entrance is on the sixth floor, which is actually ground level, while the Blue Room restaurant is downstairs on the third floor (it all makes sense when you get there). The restaurant name is appropriate: décor majors in dark petrol blue, relieved by cream banquettes, and generously spaced, smartly laid tables are lit with individual blue oil lamps.

The 'slightly sombre' atmosphere is reflected in some serious-minded and luxurious cooking. Presentation is a strong point of chef John Connell's approach, but his real flair is in careful handling of delicate flavours: witness starters of gently pan-fried scallops on neat rectangles of crisp, caramelised pork belly with creamed potato and white truffle shavings, or rich confit salmon set off with delicate summer vegetables in a lightly acidic truffle dressing. The highlight of an inspection meal was an impressively balanced main course of rare roe deer fillets with a dusting of gingerbread crumbs, accompanied by beetroot 'carpaccio' and a savoury chocolate sauce. Also receiving praise has been a generous fillet of Angus beef topped with foie gras in a surprisingly delicate red wine sauce alongside fondant potato, sweet shallots and girolle mushrooms, while desserts have featured inventive combinations such as a three-part dish of creamy cold saffron porridge, vanilla posset with red fruit jelly, and a red fruit juice with fennel seeds. An interesting list of around 200 wines – half French, half rest-of-the-world – keeps mark-ups in check; prices start at £17. The details below are approximate and some may be missing, as the restaurant did not return the Guide's questionnaire.

CHEF: John Connell   PROPRIETOR: Taz Group Ltd   OPEN: Tue to Sat D only 7 to 11   MEALS: alc (main courses £19.50 to £24). Set D £34 to £65 (whole table only)   SERVICE: not inc   CARDS: n/a   DETAILS: 40 seats. Car park. Other details n/a   ACCOMMODATION: 101 rooms, all with en suite bath/shower. Phone. Prices n/a

---

NEW MILTON Hampshire   map 2

▲ Chewton Glen 🍷 ⨂

Christchurch Road, New Milton BH25 6QS
TEL: (01425) 275341   FAX: (01425) 272310
EMAIL: reservations@chewtonglen.com
WEBSITE: www.chewtonglen.com | NEW CHEF |
from A35 follow signs to Walkford and Highcliffe; after   MODERN EUROPEAN
Walkford take 2nd left down Chewton Farm road   £37–£99

Since our last edition the bar area has been doubled, and the conservatory dining room refurbished. Reporters find this ultra-smooth operation, a byword for cosseting and indulgence, 'difficult to fault' for service and food. However, just as Pierre Chevillard clocked up 25 years at the stoves – an enviable record – he departed. The good news is that his replacement is Alan Murchison, formerly at L'Ortolan, Shinfield (see entry). New menus are unavailable as we go to press, although we've previously written about his 'supremely confident cooking'.

Service over this year has been 'hard to fault'. The wine list probably deserves a health warning: house wines start at £5.50 a glass, and four-figure prices aren't misprints. But it's a fine list for plump pockets, strong on the classics and including the smartest Australians and Californians. A few bottles under £20 rub shoulders with the superstars, but some usually good-value wines are heavily marked up.

CHEF: Alan Murchison   PROPRIETORS: Martin and Brigitte Skan   OPEN: all week 12.30 to 1.45, 7.30 to 9.30   MEALS: alc (main courses L £10.50 to £21.50, D £31 to £38.50). Set L £20, Set L Sun £36, Set D £55 to £95. Lounge and Pool Bar menus available   SERVICE: 10%, card slips closed   CARDS: Amex, Delta, Diners, MasterCard, Switch, Visa   DETAILS: 120 seats. 50 seats outside. Private parties: 80 main room, 4 to 110 private rooms. Car park. Vegetarian meals. Children's helpings. No children under 5. No smoking. Wheelchair access (also WC). Occasional music. No mobile phones. Air-conditioned ACCOMMODATION: 59 rooms, all with bath/shower. TV. Phone. Room only £260 to £745. Rooms for disabled. No children under 5. Swimming pool (*The Which? Guide to Good Hotels*)

NEWTON LONGVILLE Buckinghamshire   map 3

Crooked Billet 🍶 ✳

2 Westbrook End, Newton Longville MK17 0DF
TEL: (01908) 373936   FAX: (01908) 631979
WEBSITE: www.thebillet.co.uk
of A421, 4m SW of Milton Keynes

COOKING 3
MODERN BRITISH
£28–£50

This looks and feels like a proper local combined with a restaurant and takes both food and wine seriously. Bar lunch sandwiches are a cut above average, while the restaurant offers salads, pasta and calf's liver with maple cured bacon, grilled duck sausage, mash and onion gravy and the like. Elaboration may peak on the dinner menu with a 'study on rabbit' (roast fillet, confit leg, sautéed liver and kidney, rabbit and sage burger, accompanied respectively by fondant potato, wilted spinach, flat mushroom and braised carrot) and 'pear three ways': tart with almond, wine-poached and with whiskey ice cream. A small kitchen might be overstretched by such complexity, but 'self-sufficiency in herbs and salads' and credits for suppliers on the menu affirm its serious intent.

Wines, an immaculate collection of nearly 200, are listed first by region and then again by flavour. All are available by the glass, and the chance to compare several Zind-Humbrecht Alsace wines, say, or to see if Pesquera Ribera del Duero deserves its reputation, is rare and tempting. France is covered in depth; other selections are thinner. Prices start at £14.50 a bottle, but generally are high; glasses, at around a quarter of the bottle price, run up to a staggering £170.

CHEF: Emma Gilchrist   PROPRIETORS: John and Emma Gilchrist   OPEN: Tue to Sun L 12 to 2 (12.30 to 3.30 Sun), Tue to Sat D 7 to 10   CLOSED: 25 and 26 Dec, 2 weeks Jan   MEALS: alc (main courses L £9 to £14, D £10 to £20). Bar L menu available Mon to Fri   SERVICE: not inc, card slips closed   CARDS: Amex, Delta, MasterCard, Switch, Visa   DETAILS: 50 seats. 50 seats outside. Private parties: 8 main room. Car park. Vegetarian meals. Children's helpings. No smoking. No music. No mobile phones

NORTON Shropshire   map 5

▲ Hundred House Hotel ✳

Bridgnorth Road, Norton TF11 9EE
TEL: (01952) 730353   FAX: (01952) 730355
EMAIL: hundredhouse@lineone.net
WEBSITE: www.hundredhouse.co.uk
on A442, 6m S of Telford

COOKING 3
MODERN EUROPEAN
£29–£58

This place carries a lot of history: the main brick building is Georgian, while a half-timbered thatched barn in the courtyard dates from the fourteenth century and was once the local law court. There's also a herb garden and a flower garden. The warm, inviting interior is mostly pared back to bare brick, except for the dining area, which has very dark shiny wood panelling.

Stuart Phillips' menu is based on high-quality raw materials, and, although there can be a lot happening on the plate, timing and technique have been praised. Confit of Hereford duck legs could come with rocket, tomato and chorizo salad and white bean purée as a starter, while with a main course of pan-fried venison loin you might get caponata, braised cabbage, a goats' cheese tartlet and port and pepper sauce. Vegetarians might choose from hot potato cakes served with aïoli, mushroom sauce, tempura onion rings and rocket. Desserts are generally less ambitious: a simple summer pudding, say, or lemon tart with fresh cream. The most interesting bottles on the short, modern wine list are in the 'connoisseurs selection'. A dozen house wines (sold by the large or small glass) are £12.50 a bottle.

CHEF: Stuart Phillips PROPRIETORS: Henry, Sylvia, Stuart and David Phillips OPEN: all week 12 to 2.30, 6 to 9.30 CLOSED: 25 and 26 Dec D MEALS: alc (main courses £10 to £23). Bar menu available SERVICE: not inc, card slips closed CARDS: Delta, MasterCard, Switch, Visa DETAILS: 60 seats. 20 seats outside. Private parties: 30 main room. Car park. Vegetarian meals. Children's helpings. No smoking in 1 dining room. Wheelchair access (also WC). Occasional music ACCOMMODATION: 10 rooms, all with bath/shower. TV. Phone. B&B £75 to £125. Baby facilities (*The Which? Guide to Good Hotels*) £5

NORTON Wiltshire   map 2

Vine Tree   NEW ENTRY

Foxley Road, Norton SN16 0JP   COOKING 3
TEL: (01666) 837654 FAX: (01666) 838003   MODERN BRITISH
EMAIL: info@thevinetree.co.uk   £27–£58

Formerly a mill, the Vine Tree is now an inviting pub-restaurant with an olde-worlde feel, thanks to a wealth of old oak beams, flagstone floors, and a large central fireplace where a log fire burns in winter. As if that wasn't atmospheric enough, the building is reputedly haunted by two ghosts. Chef Steve Smith cooks a short, frequently changing menu in a simple style with a focus on direct, clear flavours. Another plus is that everything is made on the premises, from bread and pasta through to ice creams that go into desserts such as 'baby' baked Alaska, containing 'intensely fruity' strawberry ice cream under a crisp meringue crust. Before that you may have enjoyed starters of a classic bouillabaisse with garlic croûtons and rouille, or vine tomato cappuccino with poppy seed fleurons and basil oil, followed by seared tuna on a bed of sweet beetroot cubes and crisp roasted fennel with a balsamic vinegar and basil dressing, or 'perfectly timed' roast Gressingham duck breast with chunks of fresh pineapple, chilli, lime and coconut cream. A short, varied wine list opens with a dozen 'Vine Tree Favourites' priced from £10.75 and all available by the glass.

CHEF: Steve Smith PROPRIETORS: Charles Walker and Tiggi Wood OPEN: all week 12 to 2 (2.30 Sat), 6 to 9.30 (10 Fri and Sat) CLOSED: 25 Dec MEALS: alc (main courses £11 to £29.50). Set Sun L £12.95 (2 courses) to £16.50. Light menu also available exc Fri and Sat D SERVICE: not inc CARDS: Amex, Delta, Diners, MasterCard, Switch, Visa DETAILS: 75 seats. Car park. Vegetarian meals. Children's helpings. No-smoking area. Wheelchair access (not WC). Music

indicates there are some restrictions on smoking, though it is not banned altogether.

NORWICH Norfolk   map 6

Adlard's 🍴

79 Upper St Giles Street, Norwich NR2 1AB
TEL: (01603) 633522   COOKING **6**
EMAIL: bookings@adlards.co.uk   MODERN BRITISH
WEBSITE: www.adlards.co.uk   £32–£69

On the surface little seems to have changed at this Norwich fixture. It is a
compact dining room with a wooden floor, a colourful array of modern art on the
walls, and the affable presence of the proprietor greeting and odd-jobbing in his
blue apron. Control of the kitchen, however, has passed from Roger Hickman to
Tom Kerridge, who has worked in some fine restaurants, including Monsieur
Max and Odette's (see entries, Hampton Hill and London). He sets out his stall
with some skill, offering a pithiviers of braised Burgundy snails to start,
followed by sea bass with a seaweed crust.

Craftsmanship and attention to detail are evident: for example, in a precisely
formed and sliced loin of rabbit stuffed with langoustine and rosemary, served
with baby gem lettuce, shallot purée and an intense herby reduction. Simple in
presentation, yet complex in execution, the repertoire has included a successful
terrine of foie gras, pork belly and smoked eel. Contrasts also tend to be
pronounced, thanks to an artful relish here and there: in a tender, well-flavoured
fillet of Angus beef (cooked rare and accurately seasoned) with roast artichokes,
pickled turnip and oxtail crépinette; and in scallops paired with a sweet carrot
purée and pungent pickled ginger.

Dishes are well presented and carefully considered, and if portions seem on
the small side of average, one benefit is that desserts can be properly
appreciated, from 'spot-on' vanilla-flecked crème brûlée with slow-dried
strawberries and a matching sorbet, to a rich three-part chocolate dish consisting
of mousse, ice cream and fondant. Service is informal but helpful and efficient,
and the sometimes idiosyncratically annotated wine list contains some real
treats and much of interest, although not many bargains. House La Serre
Sauvignon Blanc and Chilean Carmenère are £14 (£3.75 a glass).

CHEF: Tom Kerridge   PROPRIETOR: David Adlard   OPEN: Tue to Sat L 12.30 to 1.30, Mon to Sat D
7.30 (7 Sat) to 10.30   CLOSED: 1 week Christmas   MEALS: alc (main courses £16 to £23). Set L
£15 (2 courses) to £19   SERVICE: not inc, card slips closed   CARDS: Amex, Delta, Diners,
MasterCard, Switch, Visa   DETAILS: 40 seats. Private parties: 40 main room. Vegetarian meals.
Children's helpings. Wheelchair access (not WC). No music. Air-conditioned

Tatlers 🍴 ⚡

21 Tombland, Norwich NR3 1RF
TEL: (01603) 766670   FAX: (01603) 766625   COOKING **3**
EMAIL: info@tatlers.com   MODERN BRITISH
WEBSITE: www.tatlers.com   £27–£59

Set over four rooms of a converted Georgian town house, near the main entrance
to the Norman cathedral, Tatlers delivers reliability and an unpretentious,
distinctive style to the city centre. So you'll find an upstairs bar and décor that
keeps things simple and honest, with chunky scrubbed tables, and modern art

(for sale) on the walls. Service follows suit, and is informal, relaxed and generally efficient. The modern, brasserie-style food sits well with its surroundings and features quality local produce: perhaps Cromer crab 'puffers' (beignets) with charred tomato salsa, or grilled Norfolk asparagus with Parma ham, aged balsamic and Parmesan to start. Chump of Norfolk lamb could be teamed with chargrilled courgettes, fondant potato and wilted spinach, while Blakeney samphire might accompany fillet of John Dory with crushed new potatoes. Desserts sound less localised: perhaps baked American cheesecake with poached cherries and a matching sauce. The French-led wine list is a well-thought-out selection of bottles, with eight house wines from around £12.

CHEFS: Duncan Philip and Roger Hickman   PROPRIETOR: Tatlers 2002 Ltd   OPEN: Mon to Sat 12 to 2, 6.30 to 10   CLOSED: 24 Dec to 2 Jan   MEALS: alc (main courses £10 to £18). Set L £14 (2 courses) to £17   SERVICE: not inc, card slips closed, 10% for parties of 10 or more   CARDS: Amex, Delta, MasterCard, Switch, Visa   DETAILS: 70 seats. Private parties: 30 main room, 6 to 70 private rooms. Vegetarian meals. No smoking in 1 dining room. Music

NOTTINGHAM Nottinghamshire   map 5

▲ Hart's ⅝✳

1 Standard Court, Park Row,
Nottingham NG1 6GN
TEL: (0115) 911 0666   FAX: (0115) 911 0611   COOKING 6
EMAIL: ask@hartsnottingham.co.uk   MODERN ENGLISH
WEBSITE: www.hartsnottingham.co.uk   £26–£64

This year has seen the opening of Hart's Hotel next door to the restaurant (see room details at foot of entry). The latter retains its relaxed, modern feel, which is very much in keeping with Mark Gough's classy yet unpretentious cooking. His approach is comparatively simple, but is of that kind of simplicity that requires a great deal of skill and plenty of culinary good sense. One reporter found a starter of sea bream on mashed potato with chorizo and roasted red peppers to be 'a picture of colour, with firm, sweet fish and lovely contrasting flavours', while another's marinated salmon with green peppercorns, lime and chives was simply 'stunning'. Main courses layer on flavours in equally impressive fashion, partnering baked hare loin with red cabbage and quince purée, pan-fried monkfish with wild mushrooms and turkey jus, and chicken breast with foie gras and truffle risotto. If ingredients are fine and ideas well conceived, technique is spot on too, with meat cooked precisely as requested: duck arrives impressively crisp-skinned, while venison is 'tender, sweet and melted in the mouth'. Meals might finish with mango Tatin for two, or perhaps iced honey parfait with coconut tuiles. Wines are an easygoing mix of classic and modern flavours, mostly under £20, supplemented by a Eurocentric list of finer bottles. The odd niggle has been caused by rushed and disorganised service, though this is by no means the consensus – other reports have found waiting staff to be attentive, prompt and efficient.

CHEF: Mark Gough   PROPRIETOR: Tim Hart   OPEN: all week 12 to 2, 7 to 10.30 (9 Sun)   CLOSED: 26 Dec, 1 Jan   MEALS: alc (main courses £8 (2 courses) to £20). Set L £11.95 (2 courses) to £14.95 Set L Sun £18, Set D Sun £11.95 (2 courses) to £14.95   SERVICE: 12% (optional), card slips closed   CARDS: Amex, Delta, Diners, MasterCard, Switch, Visa   DETAILS: 80 seats. 20

seats outside. Private parties: 80 main room, 6 to 110 private rooms. Car park. Vegetarian meals. Children's helpings. No smoking. Wheelchair access (also WC). No music ACCOMMODATION: 32 rooms, all with bath/shower. TV. Phone. Room only £112 to £225. Rooms for disabled

▲ Hotel des Clos, Restaurant Sat Bains ✳

Old Lenton Lane, Nottingham NG7 2SA

TEL: (0115) 986 6566   FAX: (0115) 986 0343

EMAIL: info@hoteldesclos.com

WEBSITE: www.hoteldesclos.com

COOKING 6

MODERN EUROPEAN

£36–£74

This restaurant-with-rooms, set in Victorian farm buildings, is in peaceful, pretty gardens a few steps from the Trent. The dining room – comfortably furnished, with cream walls and curtains and dark beams – is the setting for Sat Bains's modern and complex cooking. One reader admitted to being 'bowled over by the quality of the cuisine'. The pairing of unusual flavours and textures is clearly a passion and has seen a starter of roast scallops matched with peanut brittle, tartare of scallops, apple, sea salt and avocado purée, while a main course of vanilla-roast sea bass combines roast salsify, white beans, and fennel and vanilla with vanilla sauce. The kitchen can also deliver medium-rare Buccleuch beef with creamed morels, fondant potato and marrowbone and chicken gravy. Desserts may feature poached pear with rice pudding, Muscat jelly and Roquefort cream. The fixed price dinner includes three choices at each course, plus a stream of inter-courses included in the price – amuse bouche, caramelised skate, ceps risotto, cheese, pre-dessert and 'treats', all off one menu. Supplements might increase the price of a set lunch. Some reporters feel that the setting doesn't do justice to the food. House champagne from Gosset (£45) sets the style for an international wine list full of quality bottles that finally settles in Bordeaux. Six house wines are £14.50 to £16, starting at £3.75 a glass.

CHEF: Sat Bains PROPRIETORS: the Ralley family OPEN: Tue to Fri L 12 to 2, Tue to Sat D 7 to 9.30 (10 Sat) CLOSED: bank hols MEALS: Set L £17.95 (2 courses) to £32.50, Set D £45 SERVICE: 10% (optional), card slips closed CARDS: Amex, Delta, Diners, MasterCard, Switch, Visa DETAILS: 36 seats. 14 seats outside. Private parties: 40 main room, 6 to 14 private rooms. Car park. Vegetarian meals. Children's helpings. No children under 8. No smoking. Wheelchair access (also women's WC). Music. No mobile phones ACCOMMODATION: 9 rooms, all with bath/ shower. TV. Phone. B&B £95 to £139.50. Rooms for disabled. Fishing (*The Which? Guide to Good Hotels*)

Saltwater | NEW ENTRY

Corner House, Forman Street,

Nottingham NG1 4AA

TEL: (0115) 924 2664   FAX: (0115) 924 3221

EMAIL: saltwater-restaurant.com

WEBSITE: www.saltwater-restaurant.com

COOKING 2

MODERN ECLECTIC

£21–£50

Perched at the top of the Warner Brothers' cinema complex, Saltwater is a comfortable, modern eatery with two bar areas, lots of lounge seating and comfortable cushioned banquettes (there are also outside tables in good weather). The enormous floor-to-ceiling windows in the split-level dining room afford everyone a good view of the Nottingham skyline. Modish-style food ('modern eclectic' is what they call it) is served on square white plates: perhaps seared red mullet to start, served with citrus salad and mustard dressing, or a main course of fillet of roast beef, crisp and sizzled on the outside and pink inside, with crushed new potatoes. The lunch menu focuses more on sandwiches and lighter dishes, while puddings take in lemon tart, and Key lime pie with amaretto ice cream. The short wine list (which was about to be 'radically changed' as the Guide went to press) has decent offerings by the glass. Bottle prices start at £12 but move up quickly.

CHEF: Chris Hooton   PROPRIETOR: Andrew Bentley   OPEN: all week 12 to 2.30 (5 Sat and Sun), 6 to 10 (10.30 Fri and Sat, 9 Sun)   MEALS: alc (main courses L £6 to £14, D £12 to £16). Set L £9 (2 courses) to £12   SERVICE: 10% (optional)   CARDS: Amex, Delta, MasterCard, Switch, Visa   DETAILS: 85 seats. 50 seats outside. Private parties: 50 main room. Vegetarian meals. No children after 7pm. No-smoking area. Wheelchair access (also WC). Music. Air-conditioned

Sonny's 🦞

3 Carlton Street, Hockley, Nottingham NG1 1NL	COOKING 3
TEL: (0115) 947 3041 FAX: (0115) 950 7776	GLOBAL
	£24–£55

Plate-glass windows creating a light, airy feel and pillars painted a cool grey mark out this city-centre restaurant. The chefs may come and go, but the cooking steers a reliable course. The formula, based on a flexible aim to please, includes a children's menu at Sunday lunch, good-value set meals, and light lunches served in the café section. Fish and garlic soup with generous strips of fish may make an appearance among starters, along with, in season, English asparagus with truffled hollandaise and a poached egg. Among main courses, seared calf's liver, served pink as requested, shows spot-on accuracy, accompanied by crushed new potatoes and a 'tip-top vegetable liquor' containing asparagus, mange-tout, broad beans and peas. Among other options might be baked salmon with sautéed chorizo and a saffron and fish broth, or roast duck breast with fondant potato and braised lentils. Smooth vanilla pannacotta with caramelised orange segments and a subtle mint and orange syrup makes an accomplished finale. Ten decent wines by the glass (£2.85 to £4.85) make sensible lunchtime options, while the short list offers plenty under £20 but stretches to some world-class bottles.

CHEF: Bruce Theobald   PROPRIETORS: Rebecca Mascarenhas and James Harris   OPEN: all week 12 to 2.30 (3 Sun), 7 to 10.30   MEALS: alc (main courses £9.50 to £16.50). Set L Mon to Fri £12.95 (2 courses) to £15, Set L Sun £17.95, Set D Sun to Wed £15 (2 courses) to £19.50. Light L menu available   SERVICE: 10% (optional), card slips closed   CARDS: Amex, Delta, MasterCard, Switch, Visa   DETAILS: 90 seats. Vegetarian meals. Children's helpings. No-smoking area. Music. Air-conditioned (£5)

The Guide relies on feedback from its readers. Especially welcome are reports on new restaurants appearing in the book for the first time. All letters to the Guide are acknowledged.

World Service ![symbol]

Newdigate House, Castle Gate,
Nottingham NG1 6AF
TEL: (0115) 847 5587   FAX: (0115) 847 5584
WEBSITE: www.worldservicerestaurant.com

COOKING 3
MODERN BRITISH
£23–£62

Historical Newdigate House is the setting for this restaurant plus cocktail bar, hidden behind high walls in the city centre. It scores high in the atmosphere stakes: enter via an oriental garden into the opulently styled lounge. Though the building is typically Georgian and English, the décor throughout has an Indonesian theme, and the friendly, helpful waiters are dressed in traditional Indonesian costume.

The cooking tends not to be quite so exotic, sticking mainly to contemporary pan-European ideas, but nonetheless offers plenty of interest. Galantine of chicken with almonds and apricots and a Parma ham salad, or terrine of rabbit and root vegetables with prune and balsamic dressing, might be followed by 'sweet, tender' lamb chops with a caramelised onion tart and tomato tapenade, or 'firm, sweet, perfectly cooked' braised turbot with a buttery vermouth sauce. Desserts are a strong point: one reporter's rhubarb with crumble and custard soufflé was a 'sensation', comprising a small jug of rhubarb purée to pour into a feather-light soufflé. The wine list mixes up modestly priced basics with some heavy mark-ups on the better wines; alternatively, look at the range of sakés by the glass.

CHEFS: Chris Elson and Preston Walker   PROPRIETORS: Ashley Walter, Philip Morgan and Chris Elson   OPEN: all week 12 to 2.15 (3 Sun), 7 to 10 (9 Sun)   MEALS: alc (main courses £11.50 to £19). Set L Mon to Sat £10.50 (2 courses) to £14, Set D Sun £10.50 (2 courses) to £14   SERVICE: not inc, 10% for parties of 10 or more   CARDS: Amex, MasterCard, Switch, Visa   DETAILS: 70 seats. 30 seats outside. Private parties: 35 main room, 8 to 35 private rooms. Car park at D and weekends. Vegetarian meals. Children's helpings. No smoking in 1 dining room. Music £5

OAKHAM Rutland   map 5

▲ Nicks Restaurant, Lord Nelsons House ![symbol]

NEW ENTRY

11 Market Place, Oakham LE15 8HD
TEL/FAX: (01572) 723199

COOKING 4
MODERN BRITISH
£25–£62

Nick's can be found secreted away in a corner of Oakham's Market Place, in the Lord Nelsons House hotel, a medieval timber-framed building which, by the way, has no links with Britain's former sea hero. It has been under the present ownership since 1999, when Nick Healey (who counts the George V in Paris among former employers) took over as chef/patron; his wife, Amanda, runs front-of-house. Inside is a warren of narrow passages, where in the dining area – two linked rooms – red and magnolia colours dominate. Cooking technique and timing were spot on at inspection. Dishes are fairly traditional in concept: starters, for instance, might be as straightforward as grilled monkfish with asparagus hollandaise or a salad of small, succulent scallops, seared and served with asparagus and oven-dried tomatoes. Following on, roast rack of English lamb, cooked pink, may be served with Puy lentils and a well-flavoured reduced rosemary sauce, while poached pear on shortbread might come with ginger and mascarpone ice cream. Service is friendly and efficient, and the up-to-date globe-trotting wine list is crowned by a range of fine wines at non-barmy prices. Italian basics are £10.95 and 18 come by the glass from £2.95 to £5.50.

CHEF: Nick Healey   PROPRIETORS: Nick and Amanda Healey   OPEN: Tue to Sat L 12 to 2.30, Thur to Sat D 7 to 9.30   CLOSED: 2 weeks from 24 Dec, 2 weeks from 26 July   MEALS: alc (main courses L £7 to £15, D £11 to £20)   SERVICE: not inc   CARDS: Delta, MasterCard, Switch, Visa DETAILS: 40 seats. Private parties: 40 main room. Vegetarian meals. Children's helpings. No smoking. Wheelchair access (not WC). Music. No mobile phones   ACCOMMODATION: 4 rooms. TV. B&B £65 to £90

ODIHAM Hampshire   map 2

Grapevine

121 High Street, Odiham RG29 1LA   COOKING 3
TEL: (01256) 701122   ENGLISH/ITALIAN
WEBSITE: www.grapevine-gourmet.co.uk   £21–£45

A double-fronted property with bow windows, situated on the broad High Street of this attractive Georgian town, the Grapevine exudes warmth and hospitality. The bistro-style décor includes prints lining the rich-coloured walls, a wooden floor and well-spaced tables. Modern English cuisine is Mediterranean influenced – start, perhaps, with bruschetta of crab with bitter leaves and almond aïoli, then move on to, say, monkfish and red snapper with saké and Chinese five-spice vegetables. Alternatively, charred duck breast has been served with polenta-crusted fig and purple truffle potatoes, or pithiviers of vegetables with a chilli pesto. Puddings could take in blueberry pancake with maple syrup and amaretto ice cream, or walnut, almond and chocolate torte. Cheeses from the Grapevine Delicatessen are likely to feature, also. The 50-plus wine list is fairly priced. Six choices of house wine include Sauvignon and Merlot at £11.

CHEFS: David Bennett and Matthew Carroll   PROPRIETOR: Matthew Fleet   OPEN: Mon to Fri L 12 to 2, Mon to Sat D 6 to 10   CLOSED: 1 week Christmas   MEALS: alc (main courses £10 to £16). Set L £8.95 (2 courses) to £12.95, Set D 6 to 7 £12.95 (2 courses) to £14.95   SERVICE: not inc, 10% for parties of 8 or more   CARDS: Amex, Delta, Diners, MasterCard, Switch, Visa   DETAILS: 40 seats. Private parties: 50 main room. Vegetarian meals. Children's helpings. No cigars/pipes. Wheelchair access (not WC). Music. Air-conditioned

OLD BURGHCLERE Hampshire   map 2

Dew Pond ♥ ⅝✸

Old Burghclere RG20 9LH
TEL: (01635) 278408   FAX: (01635) 278580   COOKING 4
WEBSITE: www.dewpond.co.uk   ANGLO-FRENCH
off old A34, 3m W of Kingsclere   £40–£52

This country restaurant with superb views over Beacon Hill and Watership Down has been fashioned from a pair of sixteenth-century drovers' cottages. There is a split-level terrace for drinks on warm evenings (otherwise a couple of small lounges) and a two-part pastel-pink dining room whose candles, lamps and fireplaces help to give it a quiet, rural feel. Keith Marshall's well-balanced repertoire of modern dishes reads well, taking in a warm salad of seared scallops, a twice-baked savoury soufflé, calf's liver, and perhaps a saddle of roe deer sourced from a local estate, served with creamed parsnips and wild mushrooms.

The food is light and attractively presented, producing a puff pastry case of asparagus and wild mushrooms in a pool of hollandaise, and a fishcake with a French bean salad dressed with well-flavoured tomato compote. Peppered beef fillet (from Scotland) has been tender and well timed, and pan-fried loin of pork has come with wilted spinach, good red onion marmalade and crushed potatoes. Desserts have included caramelised lemon tart, apple and Calvados parfait, and a turned-out vanilla crème brûlée with raspberries. Service is attentive and helpful, and the well-judged wine list is arranged by styles with an appetising global selection in each category and plenty under £20. Brief selections of 'notably fine wines' live up to the hype. Four house wines are £11.95, or £3 a glass, and an expanded range by the glass is promised.

CHEF: Keith Marshall PROPRIETORS: Keith and Julie Marshall OPEN: Tue to Sat D only 7 to 9.30 CLOSED: 2 weeks Christmas, 2 weeks Aug MEALS: Set D £28 SERVICE: not inc, 10% for parties of 8 or more CARDS: Delta, MasterCard, Switch, Visa DETAILS: 50 seats. 100 seats outside. Private parties: 50 main room, 20 to 30 private rooms. Car park. Vegetarian meals. No smoking. Wheelchair access (also WC). No music. No mobile phones (£5)

OMBERSLEY Worcestershire   map 5

Venture In ⁵⁄✕

Main Road, Ombersley WR9 0EW   COOKING 3
TEL/FAX: (01905) 620552   MODERN BRITISH/FRENCH
                                                               £28–£52

The Worcester to Kidderminster road has long since bypassed Ombersley, leaving it a quiet village of considerable charm. The Venture In distinguishes itself with a mellow, attractive, low-ceilinged dining room and some pleasingly accomplished cooking. Many readers praise the presentation and accurate timing of dishes such as steamed asparagus with chive beurre blanc, seared salmon fillet with cucumber and dill 'laces' and tomato butter, and roast breast of Gressingham duck with sweet-pickled red cabbage, mashed potato and a sauce of port and sage. As well as the main lunch and dinner menus, an occasional gourmet fish menu might feature fried fillet of monkfish with roasted fennel and a bouillabaisse sauce. Desserts that receive the thumbs up include a memorable banana pannacotta with burnt sugar topping, and a chocolate brownie served with pistachio ice cream and cherries steeped in liqueur. Service is full of warmth and cheer. An imaginative selection of global wine starts with Chilean Sauvignon Blanc at £12 and a red Côtes du Rhône at £13. Five house selections are £11.

CHEF: Toby Fletcher PROPRIETORS: Toby and Alison Fletcher OPEN: Tue to Sun L 12 to 2, Tue to Sat D 7 to 9.30 MEALS: Set L £16.95 (2 courses) to £19.95, Set D £30.50. Gourmet fish L and D menu every second Wed £33 SERVICE: not inc, card slips closed CARDS: Delta, MasterCard, Switch, Visa DETAILS: 35 seats. Private parties: 35 main room. Car park. Vegetarian meals. No children under 10 D. No smoking. Music. No mobile phones. Air-conditioned

▲ Crown and Castle, Trinity

Orford IP12 2LJ
TEL: (01394) 450205   COOKING 4
EMAIL: info@crownandcastle.co.uk   MODERN BRITISH-PLUS
WEBSITE: www.crownandcastle.co.uk   £30–£49

Set at the heart of the quaintly idyllic and historic town of Orford, the Crown and
Castle is an attractive Victorian inn with a relaxed atmosphere. Its
'sophisticated' contemporary décor is reflected in a fashionably bright and
breezy menu, priced according to portion size. Starters tend to be simple ideas
like 'very fresh, meaty and sweet tasting' Scottish langoustines presented with a
bowl of sorrel mayonnaise, or 'rich, smooth and creamy' Spanish almond soup,
its mild flavour lifted with the addition of smoked paprika and crunchy toasted
almonds. Main courses might include 'well flavoured' slow-roasted Gloucester
Old Spot pork belly with clams and scallop corals in a shellfish broth, or
Moorish rump of lamb, the tender slices of meat set on a creamy sweet potato
cake containing whole cloves of garlic, along with a minted tomato salsa. To
finish, gooseberry fool made with Jersey cream was, at inspection, 'as good as
gooseberry fool could get' with a rich and creamy yet tart flavour. The extensive,
highly individual and interesting wine list runs to 143 bins, including a good
selection of half-bottles and a reasonable choice by the glass.

CHEF: Ruth Watson   PROPRIETORS: David and Ruth Watson   OPEN: all week 12 to 2, 7 to 9 (9.30
Sat), summer D 6.30–9.30   CLOSED: 24 to 26 Dec, 2nd week Jan, Sun D winter (exc Christmas
and school hols)   MEALS: alc D (main courses £9.50 to £16.50). Set L £14.50 (2 courses) to
£23.50. Snack menu Sun to Fri L   SERVICE: not inc   CARDS: MasterCard, Switch, Visa   DETAILS:
56 seats. 60 seats outside. Private parties: 12 main room, 8 to 14 private rooms. Car park.
Vegetarian meals. No children under 9. Children's helpings. Wheelchair access (not WC). No
music. No mobile phones   ACCOMMODATION: 18 rooms, all with bath/shower. TV. Phone. B&B
£60 to £135 (The Which? Guide to Good Hotels)

Golden Lion ⅝⋇ £

6 West End, Osmotherley DL6 3AA   COOKING 3
TEL: (01609) 883526   FAX: (01609) 884000   ENGLISH/FRENCH/ITALIAN
                                                                       £23–£44

In a village just inside the North York Moors National Park, the Golden Lion
offers hospitality to hikers and a melange of locals and townies from not-so-
distant Teesside. Once solely a pub, it now has a dual role as both bar and
restaurant. The kitchen works to a generalised cosmopolitanism, with chicken
Kiev, grilled sardines in olive oil, lasagne, and burgers with Mexican salsa
alongside pan-fried cod with chips and peas, steak and kidney pie in a suet
crust, and 'superb' calf's liver with fried onions, mash and peas. Whatever the
sources of inspiration, the kitchen knows its oignons: fish is accurately cooked,
casseroles are given time to tenderise and extract meaty essences, and flavour
combinations – for example salmon fishcake with spinach and creamy sorrel
sauce, or apple, prune and walnut cake – are well conceived. Service is speedy

and courteous, and the double-sided wine list includes four house selections at £12 and £14.50. Bottles are sourced largely from Europe and passed on at fair prices, with most under £20.

CHEF: Peter McCoy   PROPRIETORS: Christie Connelly, Peter McCoy and Belal Radwan   OPEN: all week 12 to 3.30, 6 to 10   CLOSED: 25 Dec   MEALS: alc (main courses £6.50 to £14)   SERVICE: not inc, card slips closed   CARDS: Delta, MasterCard, Switch, Visa   DETAILS: 90 seats. 20 seats outside. Private parties: 50 main room. Vegetarian meals. Children's helpings. No smoking in 1 dining room. Wheelchair access (not WC). Music

OSWESTRY Shropshire   map 7

▲ Sebastians 🌲✳

45 Willow Street, Oswestry SY11 1AQ
TEL: (01691) 655444   FAX: (01691) 653452   COOKING 3
EMAIL: sebastians.rest@virgin.net   FRENCH
WEBSITE: www.sebastians-hotel.co.uk   £41–£53

This triple-frontaged terrace establishment (owned by the Fishers since 1988) feels rather like a classic French bistro in a rather quaint English setting – viz. the menu: French with English subtitles. It goes in for some old provincial favourites: champignons au Roquefort, then a sorbet (granite à la citronelle) could be followed by filet d'agneau aux fèves, or maybe pavé de boeuf à l'estragon. Perky, piquant touches surface in dishes such as fillets of sea bass with a star anise sauce and apple chutney, or perhaps nougat parfait with a mango and mint salsa garnish. A two-choice vegetarian menu, which has included layers of herb pancake with mushroom, leek and carrots served on a sweet pepper cream acknowledges non-carnivores' desire for something above second-best. Chilean house red or white costs £12.95; there's a good range of halves between £6.45 and £12.50, and another 50-odd French and New World bottles provide plenty of choice.

CHEF: Mark Sebastian Fisher   PROPRIETORS: Mark Sebastian Fisher and Michelle Adrienne Fisher   OPEN: Tue to Sat D 6.45 to 9.30   CLOSED: 25 and 26 Dec, 1 Jan   MEALS: Set D £27.95   SERVICE: not inc, card slips closed   CARDS: Amex, Delta, MasterCard, Switch, Visa   DETAILS: 35 seats. 25 seats outside. Private parties: 40 main room. Car park. Vegetarian meals. Children's helpings. No smoking. Wheelchair access (not WC). Music   ACCOMMODATION: 8 rooms, all with bath/shower. TV. Phone. Room only £60 to £70. Rooms for disabled. Baby facilities £5

OXFORD Oxfordshire   map 2

▲ Al-Shami 🌲✳ £

25 Walton Crescent, Oxford OX1 2JG   COOKING 1
TEL: (01865) 310066   FAX: (01865) 311241   LEBANESE
WEBSITE: www.al-shami.co.uk   £19–£39

Since 1988 this popular venue in a Victorian terrace has been serving Lebanese food to a mixed crowd of university types and visitors to the city of spires. The culinary action takes place in a brightly decorated, buzzy dining room where meze are the undisputed stars of the show: on the impressive list of hot and cold appetisers you might encounter everything from hlaiwat (fried sweetbreads with lemon juice) and grilled halloumi cheese in bread to stuffed vine leaves, a salad of lambs' brains and even qray des (prawn cocktail to you and me). The remainder of the menu is a classic selection of grills, vegetarian options and fish dishes (baked cod with hot tomato sauce, for example), plus Lebanese sweets and Arabic ice creams. Almaza beer and arak stake their claim on the drinks list, which also includes a handful of vintage Ch. Musar. House Lebanese is £9.99.

CHEF: Mimo Mahfouz   PROPRIETOR: Al-Shami Oxford   OPEN: all week 12 to 11.45   MEALS: alc (main courses £7 to £12). Cover £1   SERVICE: not inc, 10% for parties of 6 or more   CARDS: MasterCard, Switch, Visa   DETAILS: 100 seats. Private parties: 50 main room, 50 private room. Vegetarian meals. No smoking in 1 dining room. Wheelchair access (also WC). Music ACCOMMODATION: 12 rooms, all with bath/shower. TV. Phone. B&B £35 to £45. Baby facilities ⓔ5⃝

Branca £

111 Walton Street, Oxford OX2 6AJ
TEL: (01865) 556111   FAX: (01865) 556501
EMAIL: info@branca-restaurants.com
WEBSITE: www.branca-restaurants.com

COOKING 2
MODERN ITALIAN
£26–£47

A buzzing and busy atmosphere, friendly service, all-day opening and good-value menus make this large, modern Italian brasserie and bar an understandably popular spot with the university crowds. The repertoire is wide ranging, taking in starters of buffalo mozzarella with roasted peppers, basil and capers, pumpkin soup with Taleggio crostini, or Jerusalem artichoke risotto with caramelised onions and truffle oil. Pizzas come with toppings such as smoked ham, Gorgonzola and spring onions, and main courses vary from pan-fried salmon with peas, pancetta and sage to duck confit with cannellini beans and salsa verde. Desserts are old favourites such as tiramisù or lemon tart. Wines number 12, all available by the bottle (from £10.45), glass or 500-millilitre 'pot'.

CHEF: Michael Macquire   PROPRIETORS: Paul Petrillo and Julian Rosser   OPEN: all week 12 to 11.30 (10.30 Sun)   CLOSED: 25 and 26 Dec   MEALS: alc (main courses £9 to £13). Set L £5 (1 course), Set D Mon to Fri 5 to 7 £10 (2 courses, inc wine)   SERVICE: not inc, card slips closed, 10% for parties of 5 or more   CARDS: Amex, Delta, MasterCard, Switch, Visa   DETAILS: 110 seats. Private parties: 30 main room. Vegetarian meals. Children's helpings. No-smoking area. Wheelchair access (also WC). Music. Air-conditioned

Cherwell Boathouse £

50 Bardwell Road, Oxford OX2 6ST
TEL: (01865) 552746   FAX: (01865) 553819
EMAIL: info@cherwellboathouse.co.uk
WEBSITE: www.cherwellboathouse.co.uk

COOKING 3
MODERN ENGLISH/FRENCH
£23–£40

It's thirty-five years since the Verdins first opened the Cherwell Boathouse and things go from strength to strength. The sight of a neat row of empty punts is redolent of pleasure, sunshine and relaxation. In summer especially it's a location to savour, although the comfortable interior, variously described as 'very much more than a conservatory', and 'quite a sophisticated restaurant', widens the appeal. Visitors have also praised the enthusiastic, knowledgeable staff, a varied menu and value for money.

As a starter, scallops have been 'beautifully cooked and presented', while, among main courses, slow-roast loin of pork has been described as 'falling apart with tenderness and bursting with flavour', and rack of lamb is accompanied by 'an attractive array of vegetables'. Desserts like lemon, parsley and gin sorbet, or rhubarb, walnut and sultana crumble maintain interest. The Verdins have amassed a fine collection of clarets during their long tenure and have the patience to list them only when they reach their peak, and the sense of fairness to do so at reasonable prices. The same goes for Burgundy, and there is good value with less grandeur in the rest of France, while well-chosen New World contributions, mostly from California, add a modern touch. House wines start at around £10.

CHEFS: Wayne Cullen and Mark Horton PROPRIETORS: Anthony and John Verdin OPEN: all week 12 to 2 (2.30 Sat and Sun), 6.30 to 10 CLOSED: 25 to 30 Dec MEALS: Set L Mon to Fri £12.50 (2 courses) to £19.50, Set L Sat and Sun £20.50, Set D £22.50 SERVICE: not inc CARDS: Amex, Delta, MasterCard, Switch, Visa DETAILS: 70 seats. 40 seats outside. Private parties: 120 main room, 10 to 50 private rooms. Car park. Vegetarian meals. Children's helpings. No smoking. Wheelchair access (also WC). No music (£5)

Chiang Mai Kitchen ⚞✳

Kemp Hall Passage, 130A High Street,
Oxford OX1 4DH
TEL: (01865) 202233 FAX: (01865) 250055
WEBSITE: www.chiangmaikitchen.co.uk

COOKING 2
THAI
£33–£56

This rickety-looking seventeenth-century timber-framed building in a tiny alley off the south of the High Street has age-warped floorboards and out-of-kilter doorways that blend well with the Thai wood-carvings on the walls, and the oil lamps on the tables. The place is popular, and the food largely authentic – tom yum poh tak soup, packed with squid, prawns and mussels, reminded one reporter of a dish enjoyed on a Thai express train. The lengthy menu covers most bases and incorporates a separate list of vegetarian dishes. From the non-veggie list, jungle curry can be made of venison or rabbit and Thai vegetables. A decent (though not cheap) version of pad thai was in turns sweet, peanutty, eggy, oily and hot. Desserts are a cut above average, and the short wine list is reasonably priced, with house wines starting at £10.50.

CHEF: Pun Bua-In PROPRIETOR: Helen O'Malley OPEN: all week 12 to 2.30, 6 to 10.30 CLOSED: Christmas, Easter, bank hols MEALS: alc (main courses £6.50 to £10.50) SERVICE: not inc, 10% for parties of 5 or more CARDS: Amex, Delta, Diners, MasterCard, Switch DETAILS: 80 seats. Private parties: 33 main room, 10 to 25 private rooms. Vegetarian meals. No smoking in 1 dining room. Wheelchair access (not WC). No music (£5)

Gee's ⚞✳

61 Banbury Road, Oxford OX2 6PE
TEL: (01865) 553540 FAX: (01865) 310308
EMAIL: info@gees-restaurant.co.uk
WEBSITE: www.gees-restaurant.co.uk

COOKING 2
MODERN EUROPEAN
£26–£66

Gee's is dramatically sited in the projecting conservatory of a late-Victorian house just off the main thoroughfare of St Giles. White-linen-dressed tables, cane chairs, slatted blinds and foliage fronds create an appealingly raffish atmosphere, and the courteous and proficient service reinforces it. A no-choice dinner menu supplements the main carte, which deals in homely cooking mostly brought off with polish. Spicy pumpkin soup adorned with coriandered yoghurt and parsnip crisps may be followed by fried calf's liver with creamed potatoes, onion marmalade and bacon. A hint of a Mediterranean influence comes in spaghettini with lemon, capers, rocket and tapenade, and a willing populist touch in a house burger served with smoked bacon, blue cheese, guacamole and hand-made chips. A baked apple filled with sultanas and Calvados and served with vanilla ice cream makes a comforting way to finish, or there's the selection of pedigree British and French cheeses. French house wines at £12.50 head up a short but carefully chosen list that offers eight wines and the house champagne by the glass.

CHEF: Michael Wright   PROPRIETOR: Jeremy Mogford   OPEN: all week 12 to 2.30, 6 to 11 CLOSED: 25 and 26 Dec   MEALS: alc (main courses £8 to £19). Set L £12.50 (2 courses) to £16, Set D £24.95   SERVICE: not inc, 10% for parties of 6 or more   CARDS: Amex, Delta, MasterCard, Switch, Visa   DETAILS: 85 seats. 25 seats outside. Private parties: 85 main room. Vegetarian meals. Children's helpings. No smoking. Wheelchair access (also WC). Music. Air-conditioned

---

PADSTOW Cornwall   map 1

The Ebb ✸   NEW ENTRY

1A The Strand, Padstow PL28 8B5   COOKING 4
TEL/FAX: (01841) 532565   SEAFOOD-PLUS
                                                                    £39–£47

The owners of this new restaurant with tapas bar last appeared in the Guide when they ran the No. 6 Café, just round the corner. The Ebb is 'delightfully light and airy', the white walls set off with modern paintings and 'tall, dramatic' flowers on the tables. Karen Scott's seafood-oriented cooking shows a few more adventurous flourishes than before, but is all handled with skill and confidence. 'Plump, juicy, just-seared' scallops with bright corals, served with a sweet chilli sauce and a salad of rocket and sorrel, or a tian of crab with guacamole and spiced cherry tomatoes kick off proceedings. Among main courses to receive enthusiastic responses from reporters have been monkfish and shrimps in a fragrant five-spice sauce with black rice, and succulent cod that 'fell into translucent flakes', topped with crisp pancetta and served on soft cannellini beans with chopped tomatoes and fennel – an 'ideal' balance of flavours and textures. Non-fish options have included roast chicken breast with herby mash, baby carrots and a tarragon and pastis sauce, and to finish there may be 'truly moreish' baby figs in rum syrup with vanilla ice cream. Prices on the short, straightforward wine list start at a very reasonable £12 and stay mostly below £20.

CHEF: Karen Scott   PROPRIETORS: Peter and Karen Scott   OPEN: Wed to Mon D only 6 to 10 CLOSED: Nov to Feb   MEALS: alc (main courses £17.50). Set D £24 (2 courses) to £28   SERVICE: not inc, card slips closed   CARDS: Delta, Switch, Visa   DETAILS: 76 seats. Private parties: 70 main room, 30 to 40 private rooms. Vegetarian meals. No children under 12. No smoking. Music. No mobile phones

Margot's �֍

11 Duke Street, Padstow PL28 8AB

TEL: (01841) 533441

EMAIL: enquiries@margots.co.uk

WEBSITE: www.margots.co.uk

COOKING **3**

MODERN BRITISH

£29–£46

Heading up from the harbour look out for the blue-and-white sign and the blue-painted window surrounds that pick out Margot's, a small and friendly, busy bistro with a genuinely warm welcome – and it has a single sitting, so you can linger long over your meal. Of course, seafood looms large on the menu; tartare of smoked salmon and trout with artichoke hearts and truffle oil might be one starter, Thai-spiced shark (exemplifying the upbeat approach) another. There are appealing combinations in meat and fish main courses, too: rack of lamb with herb crust, spring onion mash and rosemary jus, or a fried fillet of pink sea bream with linguini and tarragon fish cream sauce. The success rate is maintained in desserts like sticky toffee pudding with butterscotch sauce, or saffron poached pear with shortbread and jelly. House wines come by the glass, 40cl carafe or bottle from £9.95 for Pinot Grigio, with a wider selection – mainly French and Antipodean – staying largely under £20.

CHEFS: Adrian Oliver and David Amaglo PROPRIETORS: Adrian and Julie Oliver OPEN: Wed to Sun L 12 to 2, Wed to Mon D 7 to 9 CLOSED: 3 weeks Nov, 4 weeks Jan MEALS: alc L (main courses £11 to £15.50). Set D £22.95 (2 courses) to £25.95 SERVICE: not inc CARDS: Amex, Delta, MasterCard, Switch, Visa DETAILS: 20 seats. Private parties: 20 main room. Children's helpings. No smoking. Wheelchair access (not WC). Music (£5)

▲ Rick Stein's Café ✖

10 Middle Street, Padstow PL28 8AP

TEL: (01841) 532700 FAX: (01841) 532942

EMAIL: reservations@rickstein.com

WEBSITE: www.rickstein.com

COOKING **3**

GLOBAL/SEAFOOD

£31–£49

The café feels 'bright and welcoming, with the new bar looking particularly inviting'. The brief menu offers starters like 'green, creamy, subtly flavoured' parsley soup, or stir-fried salt-and-pepper prawns (huge and garlicky). Mains include devilled mackerel teamed with mint and tomato salad, or warm cod ('extremely fresh ... falling in flakes on to the fork') with a sharp caper-rich thinned mayonnaise; and there's a token sirloin steak for inveterate carnivores. This place tempers ambition with practicality and keeps a watchful eye on details: decent rolls, properly chunky chips (crisp outside, floury inside), and luscious cream detectable in a crème brûlée. The carte is the same all day, and in the evening there's also a good-value set-price dinner. The short, no-fuss wine list majors on seafood-friendly whites, starting at £14 (£3.50 a glass).

CHEFS: Paul Harwood and Roy Brett PROPRIETORS: Rick and Jill Stein OPEN: all week 12 to 3, 7 (6 summer) to 10 CLOSED: 24 to 26 Dec, 31 Dec D, 1 May MEALS: alc (main courses £8.50 to £15). Set D £19.50 SERVICE: not inc CARDS: Delta, MasterCard, Switch, Visa DETAILS: 40 seats. 10 seats outside. Vegetarian meals. Children's helpings. No smoking. Occasional music ACCOMMODATION: 3 rooms, all with bath/shower. TV. Phone. B&B £80 to £100. Baby facilities (*The Which? Guide to Good Hotels*)

▲ St Petroc's Bistro ⚡✗

4 New Street, Padstow PL28 8EA
TEL: (01841) 532700   FAX: (01841) 532942
EMAIL: reservations@rickstein.com
WEBSITE: www.rickstein.com

COOKING **3**
BISTRO
£35–£50

Up one of Padstow's narrow roads from the Seafood Restaurant (see following entry), this 'provides yet another dimension to the Rick Stein kaleidoscope of fishy treats'. The main hotel, painted off-white, has large sash windows, a portico entrance, and looks smart and inviting. In its Bistro the look is bright, airy and contemporary: no tablecloths, well-spaced tables and white walls hung with abstracts.

The menu (five choices per course) has plenty of fish – but, the management points out, there's more meat and poultry here than at the Seafood Restaurant. The keep-it-simple philosophy produces, for example, a good piece of correctly cooked and very fresh cod on creamy spring onion mash with a soy and butter sauce. A starter of tender, flavourful chargrilled squid comes with a marinade containing whole and crushed peppercorns and pieces of red chilli. Desserts are nothing fancy, perhaps a creamy pannacotta with steamed plums, or a baked chocolate mousse (made with good dark chocolate) served with lashings of clotted cream. Service is relaxed, informal and competent. On the wine list fish-friendly whites sensibly outnumber reds, with prices from £12.25 and plenty by the glass.

CHEFS: Alistair Clive and Roy Brett   PROPRIETORS: Rick and Jill Stein   OPEN: all week 12 to 1.30, 7 to 9.30 (10 in summer)   CLOSED: 21 to 26 and 31 Dec, 1 May   MEALS: alc (main courses £10 to £15.50)   SERVICE: not inc   CARDS: Delta, MasterCard, Switch, Visa   DETAILS: 54 seats. Car park. Vegetarian meals. Children's helpings. No smoking. Music. Air-conditioned ACCOMMODATION: 10 rooms, all with bath/shower. TV. Phone. B&B £105 to £170. Baby facilities (*The Which? Guide to Good Hotels*)

▲ Seafood Restaurant ▮

Riverside, Padstow PL28 8BY
TEL: (01841) 532700   FAX: (01841) 532942
EMAIL: reservations@rickstein.com
WEBSITE: www.rickstein.com

COOKING **6**
SEAFOOD
£50–£103

'A really wonderful meal, enhanced by knowledgeable and interested staff' is a typically enthusiastic endorsement of Rick Stein's flagship restaurant. It consists of a small conservatory at the front for drinks, and a modern, bright dining room with white walls and colourful abstracts of a foodie nature. Although sightings of the man himself are rarer these days, the food nevertheless bears the imprint of his 30 or more years of cooking and of his global travels, taking in anything from plain oysters via stir-fried mussels with black beans, to monkfish vindaloo with pilau rice.

Given the wide range of customers – including families with children hacking away at whole lobsters – the menu offers an obligingly broad spectrum of dishes, including a warm salad of tuna with cannellini beans, and deep-fried local cod – 'fresh as a daisy, with excellent batter' – served with big, well-made chips, proper mushy peas, and a dollop of good tartare sauce. Moist, steamed fillet of hake comes with an unctuous sauce verte and large, soft Spanish butter beans, while a simply presented spider and velvet crab risotto stole the show for one visitor: the flavour 'terrific', the whole beautifully balanced, indeed 'one of the best seafood risottos I can recall tasting'.

Desserts may not be quite on a par with main courses, but have delivered a pleasantly sticky meringue with banana and passion-fruit-infused custard, and a light, creamy, wobbly pannacotta with baked plums. Bread is first-class, staff are efficient and polite, and prices are high – 'deservedly so', some say. The extensive wine list is well matched to the cooking, notably in the 16-strong, quality-orientated house selection (£16.50 to £22 a bottle/£3.55 to £4.50 a glass). This is one of the rare venues where you can enjoy Australia's Tower Estate wines because Stein is one of the owners.

CHEFS: Stéphane Delourme and Roy Brett (executive chef)   PROPRIETORS: Rick and Jill Stein   OPEN: all week 12 to 2, 7 to 10   CLOSED: 21 to 26 and 31 Dec, 1 May   MEALS: alc (main courses £17.50 to £39.50). Set L and D £47.50 to £75 (inc wine)   SERVICE: not inc   CARDS: Delta, MasterCard, Switch, Visa   DETAILS: 104 seats. Vegetarian meals. Children's helpings. No children under 3. No music. Air-conditioned   ACCOMMODATION: 13 rooms, all with bath/shower. TV. Phone. B&B £105 to £220 (double room). Baby facilities (*The Which? Guide to Good Hotels*)

PAINSWICK Gloucestershire   map 2

▲ Painswick Hotel ♥ ⚶

Kemps Lane, Painswick GL6 6YB
TEL: (01452) 812160   FAX: (01452) 814059   COOKING 5
EMAIL: reservations@painswickhotel.com   BRITISH
WEBSITE: www.painswickhotel.com   £29–£67

This majestic former rectory was built in the Palladian style in 1790, and boasts a grand porticoed entrance and views over the village and countryside. The dining room, which is hung with oil portraits, is relaxing and comfortable, an ambience reinforced by the seamlessly professional French service. Kevin Barron's is a busy kitchen, producing lunches and dinners seven days a week, and working fine, locally sourced materials into some highly polished cooking. One reporter writes approvingly of a summer lunch that began with 'light, frothy and delicious' white bean cappuccino soup, and then proceeded to beautifully timed fillet of monkfish, wrapped in Parma ham and accompanied by delicately flavoured vanilla-spiced mash and a smooth lobster butter sauce, 'a perfectly judged combination of flavours and textures'. At dinner, things become more ambitious still, with Cornish turbot perhaps paired with oxtail mash, crispy bacon and truffle oil, or Woodchester pork served two ways: as braised belly and herb-roast loin, with fondant potatoes, baby onions and black pudding. Presentations place a premium on artistry, producing a dessert of raspberry parfait and vanilla ice cream that has been an architectural marvel, or orchestrating an array of flavours in hot chocolate fondant served with marmalade smoothie and a white chocolate and vodka sorbet.

The thoughtful wine list strikes a happy balance between the affordable and the covetable and is strongest in Bordeaux and Burgundy, with most of the bottles appropriately aged. Unusually, the same philosophy is extended to the brief (but good) selections from elsewhere in the world. Various shortlists ('cellarman's choice', 'wines of the month' and the six house wines by the glass) offer useful short-cuts to some satisfying flavours, and there is a good selection of half-bottles. A new proprietor took over as we went to press, with no changes planned in the kitchen.

CHEF: Kevin Barron   PROPRIETOR: Guus Thomas-Verweij   OPEN: all week 12 to 2, 7 to 9.30 MEALS: alc D (main courses £21.50 to £23). Set L £14 (2 courses) to £17, Set D £28 (2 courses) to £31. Light L available Mon to Sat   SERVICE: not inc, card slips closed   CARDS: Amex, Delta, MasterCard, Switch, Visa   DETAILS: 30 seats. 16 seats outside. Private parties: 60 main room, 2 to 18 private rooms. Car park. Children's helpings. No smoking. Occasional music ACCOMMODATION: 19 rooms, all with bath/shower. TV. Phone. B&B £75 to £200 (*The Which? Guide to Good Hotels*) £5

PAULERSPURY Northamptonshire   map 5

▲ Vine House Hotel ⅝✳

100 High Street, Paulerspury NN12 7NA
TEL: (01327) 811267   FAX: (01327) 811309   COOKING 3
WEBSITE: www.vinehousehotel.com   MODERN BRITISH
off A5, 2½m SE of Towcester   £43–£51

In this delightful stone-built house in its lovely garden, an 'oasis in the Milton Keynes area', a husband-and-wife team (she out front, he at the stoves) deal in excellent English produce on a daily-changing menu. A herby, spicy starter dumpling of finely minced Gloucester Old Spot pork with tangy Bramley apple sauce, and wafer-thin treacle cured salmon, give imaginative twists to tradition. Skilled sourcing of ingredients like Indian Sussex chicken – locally reared, succulently roast, served with intense mushroom sauce laced with tiny rosemary-scented shallots – or 'meltingly moist local venison' with Puy lentils and a wine and truffle sauce, combines with kitchen skill to transform the ordinary. Fish is well-handled, too, as in Cornish brill fillet with braised leeks and Parmesan sauce. Well-kept cheeses and desserts like pungent, tender rhubarb under a 'robustly crumbly' crumble, and apricot mousse with apricot coulis, are typical desserts. Relaxed and informed service can be tested when numbers pressure mounts. Wines are mostly French, with house bottles at £12.75 (£12.95 for Australian alternatives) and some affordable wines among the Bordeaux and Burgundy.

CHEF: Marcus Springett   PROPRIETORS: Marcus and Julie Springett   OPEN: Thur and Fri L 12.30 to 2, Tue to Sat D 7 to 9   CLOSED: 2 weeks at Christmas   MEALS: Set L and D £29.95   SERVICE: not inc   CARDS: MasterCard, Visa   DETAILS: 30 seats. Private parties: 30 main room. Car park. Children's helpings. No smoking. Wheelchair access (not WC). No music. No mobile phones ACCOMMODATION: 6 rooms, all with bath/shower. TV. Phone. B&B £59 to £85 (*The Which? Guide to Good Hotels*) £5

The text of entries is based on unsolicited reports sent in by readers, backed up by inspections conducted anonymously. The factual details under the text are from questionnaires the Guide sends to all restaurants that feature in the book.

▲ Churchill Arms £

Paxford GL55 6XH

TEL: (01386) 594000   FAX: (01386) 594005   COOKING **4**
EMAIL: mail@thechurchillarms.com   MODERN EUROPEAN
WEBSITE: www.thechurchillarms.com   £23–£45

This 'very welcoming Cotswolds pub' opposite the village church is the kind of place where you can expect to encounter a throng of drinkers enjoying real ales at the bar, although it enjoys quite a reputation for its food. Menus, listed on blackboards, show a fondness for robust, earthy flavours, as in starters of quail's breast on crisp bubble and squeak, game faggot with citrus sauce, and confit duck, 'which fell away from the bone', served on rösti with beetroot and fromage frais. To follow, sea bream has come with sweet-and-sour curry sauce and crunchy sweet potato fritters, and 'beautifully cooked' calf's liver with olive oil potatoes and courgettes, while pork tenderloin is partnered by carrot and ginger fondue with sherry and shallots. Among desserts, 'zingy' lemon cheesecake was the highlight of one reporter's meal, or there might be roly-poly pudding with custard. Around two dozen wines are also listed on blackboards, prices starting at £9.95.

CHEFS: Sonya Brooke-Little and Ivan Reid   PROPRIETORS: Leo and Sonya Brooke-Little   OPEN: all week 12 to 2, 7 to 9   MEALS: alc (main courses £8 to £14)   SERVICE: not inc   CARDS: Delta, MasterCard, Switch, Visa   DETAILS: 60 seats. 60 seats outside. Private parties: 20 main room. Children's helpings. No music   ACCOMMODATION: 4 rooms, all with bath/shower. TV. Phone. B&B £40 to £70 (double room) (*The Which? Guide to Good Hotels*)

Abbey Restaurant ⅝✳

Abbey Street, Penzance TR18 4AR

TEL/FAX: (01736) 330680   COOKING **5**
EMAIL: kinga@theabbeyonline.com   MODERN EUROPEAN
WEBSITE: www.theabbeyonline.com   £32–£56

As you walk down towards the harbour, besides taking in the view look out for the multicoloured flags – or the brilliant blue exterior of the Abbey Hotel, which is next door to the Tunnicliffes' restaurant. (Since last year's Guide, they have also taken on the management of the hotel on behalf of its owner, Jean Shrimpton.) The restaurant has a ground-floor bar (with a live video feed showing the kitchen at work) and a cream-walled, first-floor dining room with French windows and bay views.

Ben Tunnicliffe's cooking is fresh and modern, attractively presented and evenly balanced between fish and meat dishes. A starter of home-smoked goose with seared foie gras and caramelised apple had all the right textures and a nicely judged balance of flavours. Sliced chargrilled pork loin with a wedge of goats' cheese-studded polenta and cold peperonata made a fine spring lunch dish for one reporter, while the timing of crisp-fried squid with chilli jam was appreciated by another. Satisfying desserts have included a version of chocolate trifle with amaretto-soaked sponge, although a crème brûlée involving rhubarb, saffron and honey seemed overloaded. Service is unflaggingly polite and charming, and the concise and sound wine list, starting with house French at £10.50 (£2.75 a glass), includes a couple from Cornwall.

CHEFS: Ben Tunnicliffe and Scott Foy   PROPRIETORS: Ben and Kinga Tunnicliffe   OPEN: Fri and Sat L 12 to 2, Tue to Sat D 7 to 9.30 (10 April to Sept)   CLOSED: 3 weeks Jan   MEALS: alc (main courses L £10 to £17, D £12 to £21)   SERVICE: not inc   CARDS: Delta, MasterCard, Switch, Visa DETAILS: 30 seats. Private parties: 22 main room. Vegetarian meals. No children at D. No smoking. No music. No mobile phones. Air-conditioned (£5)

Harris's ✬✖

46 New Street, Penzance TR18 2LZ
TEL: (01736) 364408
EMAIL: harriss.restaurant@lineone.net
WEBSITE: www.harrissrestaurant.co.uk

COOKING 3
ANGLO-FRENCH/SEAFOOD
£39–£62

The rosy glow of the dining room at Harris's, open since 1972, is familiar to many loyal patrons, both locals and visitors. The restaurant's consistency through the years has been praised, but things have not stood still. Ingredients and techniques have moved with the times: a starter of grilled smoked duck breast may be served on endive and mizuna leaves, with walnut oil dressing. Seafood plays the lead here, with lobsters and wet fish coming from Newlyn fish market, while scallops are sourced from Falmouth Bay. Lamb and beef come from nearby farms, and in season 'tasty, tender, juicy' venison comes in from the West Country moors and game from local shoots. But, whether it's fish or meat, Roger Harris believes in 'letting the ingredients speak for themselves', without over-spicing or over-saucing. Own-made breads have also come in for praise, as have puddings that range from Apfelstrudel to fresh raspberries and strawberries with white chocolate ice cream in a biscuit basket. Service, headed by Anne Harris, is well-judged, and the mainly French wine list has six house wines at £12.50 a bottle (£3.15 a glass).

CHEF: Roger Harris   PROPRIETORS: Roger and Anne Harris   OPEN: Tue to Sat 12 to 2, Mon to Sat 7 to 10   CLOSED: 3 weeks Nov to Feb   MEALS: alc (main courses £14 to £22). Light L menu available   SERVICE: 10%, card slips closed   CARDS: Amex, MasterCard, Switch, Visa   DETAILS: 40 seats. Private parties: 20 main room, 8 to 20 private rooms. No smoking in 1 dining room. Occasional music. No mobile phones

▲ Summer House

Cornwall Terrace, Penzance TR18 4HL
TEL: (01736) 363744   FAX: (01736) 360959
EMAIL: reception@summerhouse-cornwall.com
WEBSITE: www.summerhouse-cornwall.com

COOKING 2
MEDITERRANEAN
£34–£41

Conceived as a seaside bolthole for jaded townies, this discreet Grade II listed hotel, run by a friendly couple, is in a quiet road close to the seafront and has a tropical walled garden for pre-dinner drinks and candlelit summer dining. The Regency architecture contrasts with the bold Mediterranean colour scheme of the small dining room, which reflects Ciro Zaino's cooking. Fixed-price menus offer three or four choices per course, starters perhaps taking in seared Newlyn scallops with fennel velouté, or poached chicken with marinated red peppers. To follow, there might be pan-roasted monkfish with rich red wine sauce, or suprême of guinea fowl with shiitake mushrooms and a creamy sauce made with sweet Recioto wine. Finish maybe with mascarpone ice cream with prunes and Armagnac, or amaretto-scented peaches. Around three dozen Italian wines are priced from £12.

CHEF: Ciro Zaino   PROPRIETORS: Ciro and Linda Zaino   OPEN: Thur to Sat D 7.30 to 9 (summer Tue to Sat)   CLOSED: Dec to Feb   MEALS: Set D £23.50   SERVICE: 10%, card slips closed   CARDS: Delta, MasterCard, Switch, Visa   DETAILS: 22 seats. 20 seats outside. Private parties: 25 main room. Vegetarian meals. No smoking before 10pm. Music. No mobile phones   ACCOMMODATION: 5 rooms, all with bath/shower. TV. B&B £70 to £95. No children under 13 (*The Which? Guide to Good Hotels*)

PETERSFIELD Hampshire   map 2

JSW ▮ ⅙✸

1 Heath Road, Petersfield GU31 4JE	COOKING **5**
TEL: (01730) 262030	MODERN BRITISH
	£35–£55

Petersfield is a pleasant market town, and JSW is sited on one corner of the large and dignified main square. The dining room is small and narrow but also cool and bright, thanks to large windows. Framed drawings of nudes on the walls will offend only the most delicate sensibilities (although one reader felt they could be positioned more sensitively!). Reporters are unanimously impressed with the cooking: a 'sublimely decadent' starter of rich, buttery cep and truffle risotto, or 'translucently pearly' smoked haddock topped with a slice of golden fried potato, an oozing poached egg and a foamy velouté swirled over a pea purée. Main courses have featured an 'assembly line' of a miniature oxtail pudding with feather-light suet crust and spicy, aromatic filling, with little piles of thinly sliced rare grilled steak, swede, carrot and cabbage. Equally successful has been honey and pepper glazed duck breast cooked very rare and served with rich, creamy truffle mash. Desserts tend to stick to a theme: apple crème brûlée, for example, comes with a sharp apple sorbet and diced stewed apples.

The ever-expanding wine list still offers plenty of good-value bottles. The major European and New World regions are all well attended to, but it is the less mainstream regions that are of particular interest, with a serious collection of ten German wines at £20 or under, and leading wines from Alsace and the Rhône. Dessert wines impress too. Eight table wines come by the glass for £4.50.

CHEFS: Jake Watkins and Mike Webber   PROPRIETOR: J.S. Watkins   OPEN: Tue to Sat 12 to 1.30, 7 to 9.30   CLOSED: last week Dec, first 2 weeks Jan, 2 weeks Jun   MEALS: Set L £17.50 (2 courses) to £22.50, Set D £27.50 (2 courses) to £32.50   SERVICE: not inc   CARDS: Delta, MasterCard, Switch, Visa   DETAILS: 22 seats. Private parties: 25 main room. Vegetarian meals. No children under 8. No smoking. Wheelchair access (not WC). No music. No mobile phones

---

All entries in the Guide are re-researched and rewritten every year, not least because restaurant standards fluctuate. Don't rely on an out-of-date Guide.

PETER TAVY Devon

map 1

Peter Tavy Inn 🍴 £

Peter Tavy PL19 9NN
TEL: (01822) 810348   FAX: (01822) 810835
EMAIL: peter.tavy@virgin.net
off A386, 3m NE of Tavistock

COOKING 1
MODERN EUROPEAN
£18–£43

This is an archetypal West Country pub on the edge of Dartmoor: an un-messed-about low, white-painted stone building that has escaped the attention of both modernisers and the self-consciously 'folksy'. Out front there are friendly and helpful staff, while those in the kitchen produce no-nonsense 'you get what you see' food, such as roast beef and Yorkshire pudding, or Cumberland sausage and mash, using local suppliers and ingredients. Classic pub grub like ploughman's with six Devon cheeses sits alongside less locally rooted cooking such as roasted vegetable and Brie filo parcels. Slightly grander dishes in the evening – say, roast duck breast with Peking sauce, or a whole lemon sole – are pricier but still good value. Alongside the real ales there is an annotated wine list of 30-odd bottles from across the world (nearly all under £20), including seven house wines between £7.95 and £12.95, all available by the glass.

CHEFS: Steve Byrne and Christine Kilfedder   PROPRIETORS: Graeme and Karen Sim   OPEN: all week 12 to 2, 6.30 to 9   CLOSED: 24 Dec D, 25 Dec, 26 Dec D   MEALS: alc (main courses L £5.50 to £11, D £7 to £19)   SERVICE: not inc, card slips closed   CARDS: Delta, MasterCard, Switch, Visa   DETAILS: 70 seats. 100 seats outside. Private parties: 45 main room. Car park. Vegetarian meals. Children's helpings. No smoking in 1 dining room. Music £5

PLYMOUTH Devon

map 1

Chez Nous 🍷

13 Frankfort Gate, Plymouth PL1 1QA
TEL/FAX: (01752) 266793

FRENCH
£48–£58

As the Guide went to press this restaurant was sold.

CHEF: Jacques Marchal   PROPRIETORS: Jacques and Suzanne Marchal   OPEN: Tue to Sat D only 7 to 10.30   CLOSED: first 3 weeks Feb, first 3 weeks Sep   MEALS: Set D £35   SERVICE: not inc CARDS: Amex, Delta, Diners, MasterCard, Switch, Visa   DETAILS: 28 seats. Private parties: 32 main room. No children under 10. No pipes. Wheelchair access (not WC). Music

PONTELAND Northumberland — map 10

Café 21 🍳 £

35 The Broadway, Darras Hall,
Ponteland NE20 9PW
TEL/FAX: (01661) 820357

COOKING 4
MODERN EUROPEAN
£23–£56

The setting may be a modern shopping parade in the middle of Darras Hall – Tyneside's stockbroker belt estate – but there's something distinctively French about the operation, one of three in Terence Laybourne's North Eastern empire (see also Durham and Newcastle upon Tyne). The young staff are dressed as if in a Parisian bistro (but have a warm Geordie style of service), good French bread generally kicks off a meal, and the menu is suitably 'bistro'. Moist, light mushroom fritters come as a starter, or perhaps nicely flavoured scallops, seared and served with black-bean vinaigrette. Timing is usually right on fish dishes such as pan-fried sea bass with couscous, red onion and mango salsa, and there are plenty of meaty options too (sirloin steak with chips, or duck confit with lyonnaise potatoes). Desserts such as sachertorte and lemon crumble cheesecake are a typical finish. The wine list is concise, with own-label Cuvée 21 (from Georges Duboeuf) starting the bidding at £11.50.

CHEF: Ian Lowrie   PROPRIETOR: Terence Laybourne   OPEN: Sat L 12 to 2.30, Mon to Sat D 5.30 to 10   CLOSED: bank hols   MEALS: alc (main courses £9.50 to £19.50). Set D Mon to Fri 5.30 to 7 £11.50 (2 courses) to £13.50   SERVICE: not inc   CARDS: Amex, Delta, Diners, MasterCard, Switch, Visa   DETAILS: 70 seats. Private parties: 70 main room. Vegetarian meals. Children's helpings. No-smoking area. Wheelchair access (also WC). Music

POOLE Dorset — map 2

▲ Mansion House 🍷 ✳

Thames Street, Poole BH15 1JN
TEL: (01202) 685666   FAX: (01202) 665709
EMAIL: dining@themansionhouse.co.uk
WEBSITE: www.themansionhouse.co.uk

COOKING 3
MODERN BRITISH
£28–£53

This Georgian town house in the centre of Poole may look the epitome of tradition, but culinary skills do not stand still here, as members of its 4,000-strong dining club might testify. A terrine of wild sea trout, rocket mash and pan-fried scallops, or lamb carpaccio with anchovy straws and olives, might kick off a wide-ranging menu. Main courses cater for all tastes with dishes such as roast monkfish with lentils, pancetta and mustard cream, or roast rack of Dorset lamb with peas, lettuce and bacon. Desserts keep up with the times too: coconut pannacotta with grilled bananas, say, or Baileys and praline parfait with warm chocolate tart. In contrast to the more formal surroundings, service is good-humoured and relaxed but helpful. Pleasant, too, to find an accessible wine list, with house recommendations starting at £12.95 (£3 a glass). Several pages of 'good value' whites and reds arranged by style offer a broad global survey, while the 'fine wine' list focuses on clarets, Burgundy and a few smart New World bottles at fair prices.

CHEF: Gerry Godden   PROPRIETORS: Jackie and Gerry Godden   OPEN: Sun to Fri L 12 to 2, Mon to Sat and Sun bank hol D 7 to 9.30   MEALS: Set L £17 (2 courses) to £19.25, Set D £20.95 (2 courses) to £26.45   SERVICE: not inc   CARDS: Amex, Delta, Diners, MasterCard, Switch, Visa DETAILS: 85 seats. Private parties: 100 main room, 14 to 36 private rooms. Car park. Vegetarian meals. Children's helpings. Under-5s must eat at 7pm at D. No smoking in 1 dining room. Occasional music. Air-conditioned   ACCOMMODATION: 32 rooms, all with bath/shower. TV. Phone. B&B £70 to £135. Baby facilities (*The Which? Guide to Good Hotels*) £5

PORLOCK WEIR Somerset   map 1

▲ Andrew's on the Weir 🌟

Porlock Weir TA24 8PB
TEL: (01643) 863300   FAX: (01643) 863311   COOKING 4
EMAIL: information@andrewsontheweir.co.uk   MODERN ENGLISH/EUROPEAN
WEBSITE: www.andrewsontheweir.co.uk   £25–£79

Sandwiched between Exmoor and the sea, Porlock Weir provides a haven for a few boats and hostelries, one of which is this yellow-painted hotel/restaurant with a small garden in front. It has big settees in the bar, and a two-part, brightly coloured dining room done out in terracotta, brown and yellow, with gold brocade fabrics and a view over such activity as there is down by the water. Seafood is a self-proclaimed highlight, menus include 'market' and vegetarian versions as well as the carte, and regional supplies are a strength, taking in a local fish soup as a main course, and a dish of milk-fed Exmoor lamb combining tender, flavourful loin and heavily seasoned minced shoulder in a cabbage leaf.

These are supplemented by items from further afield such as Loch Fyne langoustines – minced up with coriander, enclosed in fine pasta, and served with cubes of scallop and tomato flesh in a clear broth 'full of shellfish flavour' – and perhaps a luxurious-sounding pigeon breast stuffed with foie gras, ceps and truffles (in April). Desserts are variable, the better one at inspection being a first-class orange crème brûlée turned out of its mould and served with a gently sharp orange sorbet, fried orange segments and a well-made orange jus. The wine list is arranged by style, with decent choices at fair prices, plus a collection of vintages of Grange. Seven house wines are £10.25 to £19.95 (£3.45 to £5.50 a glass).

CHEF: Andrew Dixon   PROPRIETORS: Andrew Dixon and Rodney Sens   OPEN: Tue to Sun L 12 to 2.30, Tue to Sat D 7 to 9.30   CLOSED: Jan   MEALS: alc (main courses £18). Set L £11.50 (2 courses) to £15, Set L Sun £18. Set D £55   SERVICE: not inc, card slips closed   CARDS: Amex, Delta, MasterCard, Switch, Visa   DETAILS: 35 seats. Private parties: 25 main room, 10 private room. Car park. Vegetarian meals. No children under 12. No smoking. Music. No mobile phones ACCOMMODATION: 5 rooms, all with bath/shower. TV. B&B £45 to £100. No children under 12 (*The Which? Guide to Good Hotels*)

The text of entries is based on unsolicited reports sent in by readers, backed up by inspections conducted anonymously. The factual details under the text are from questionnaires the Guide sends to all restaurants that feature in the book.

PORTHLEVEN Cornwall

map 1

▲ Critchards 😼✳

Harbourside, Porthleven TR13 9JA	COOKING 1
TEL: (01326) 562407 FAX: (01326) 564444	SEAFOOD
WEBSITE: www.critchards.com	£30–£64

A seafood restaurant by the quayside is just the ticket in Cornwall. After close to a decade in the Guide, the Critchards keep up their lively succession of ideas, many with an Eastern slant, from a tempura of crab, mango and rocket, to a Thai-style, coconut-flavoured treatment of red gurnard, served with a crab and lemongrass filo roll. Supplies come from Newlyn, St Ives, and Porthleven itself, and the regularly changing menu responds to availability: how about fillet of trigger fish, a transatlantic visitor swept along by the Gulf Stream and caught in local lobster pots, served with lime and stem ginger butter? Desserts might take in vanilla pannacotta. Service is friendly and efficient, and wines include a number under £20. Among whites are Bonterra organic Chardonnay from California, a New Zealand Sauvignon Blanc or two, and a local medium-dry St Perran at £13.95.

CHEF: Jo Critchard   PROPRIETORS: Steve and Jo Critchard   OPEN: Mon to Sat D only 6.30 to 9.30 (10 in high season)   CLOSED: mid-Dec to mid-Jan   MEALS: alc (main courses £10 to £25)   SERVICE: not inc   CARDS: MasterCard, Switch, Visa   DETAILS: 44 seats. Private parties: 25 main room. Vegetarian meals. Children's helpings. No smoking. Occasional music   ACCOMMODATION: 2 rooms, both with bath/shower. TV. B&B £55 to £65 (double room). No children under 6 (£5)

PORTREATH Cornwall

map 1

Tabb's 😼✳

Tregea Terrace, Portreath TR16 4LD	COOKING 2
TEL: (01209) 842488	MODERN BRITISH-PLUS
	£24–£53

Cartwheels suspended from the ceiling and plain, unpainted granite walls contribute a degree of rusticity to this former blacksmith's. Dine in the main restaurant or front conservatory, where friendly, efficient and unstuffy service is the norm. Nigel and Melanie Tabb are committed to using increasing amounts of regional produce, ranging from organic vegetables and smoked Cornish goats' cheese to local meat, and fish fresh from Newlyn market. A successful starter has been scallops marinated in lime juice, English mustard and garden herbs. Main courses have seen roast breast of Gressingham duck, cooked slightly pink, on a bed of shredded beetroot and onions with cream and truffle oil, and pan-fried wild venison fillet, 'cooked to perfection' and successfully complemented by lentil purée and a red wine sauce with tomatoes, chilli and a little bitter chocolate. Chocoholics will find themselves well catered for – chocolate marquise with cardamom ice cream, or chocolate tart with caramelised bananas and rum cream – and hand-made chocolates accompany coffee; or go for home-made ice cream and sorbet. French house red or white at £9.95 starts a selection of 30 or so from around the world, with just a handful overstepping the £20 mark.

CHEF: Nigel Tabb   PROPRIETORS: Nigel and Melanie Tabb   OPEN: Sun L 12.15 to 1.45, Wed to Mon D 7 to 9   CLOSED: 1 week Oct, 1 week Jan   MEALS: alc D (main courses £11.50 to £20). Set L £15, Set D £18   SERVICE: not inc, card slips closed   CARDS: Delta, MasterCard, Switch, Visa   DETAILS: 30 seats. Private parties: 30 main room. Vegetarian meals. Children's helpings. No smoking. Wheelchair access (not WC). Music

PORTSCATHO Cornwall   map 1

▲ Driftwood ✸   NEW ENTRY

Rosevine, Portscatho TR2 5EW
TEL: (01872) 580644   FAX: (01872) 580801   COOKING 5
EMAIL: info@driftwoodhotel.co.uk   MODERN BRITISH
WEBSITE: www.driftwoodhotel.co.uk   £45–£54

Don't let the unprepossessing driveway put you off. The building may look ordinary, too, but the location is wonderful, perched high above the sea, with a panoramic view over the water – the dining room has a huge expanse of glass through which to make the most of it. What was once the Roseland Hotel has been renamed the Driftwood Hotel by its new owners, and a thorough makeover, playing on the driftwood theme, has resulted in a colour scheme of sand, sun-bleached driftwood and chalky white, offset by slatey-blue. The chef is Scot Mark Wishart, who oversees the short but well-conceived menu. Flavour combinations are clear and interesting, raw ingredients are good, and sauces are a high point.

At inspection, a main course of grilled cod with buttered cabbage, Umbrian lentils and grain mustard sauce centred on a very generous, thick wedge of crisp-skinned fish. Something fishy might turn up among starters too – perhaps escabèche of red mullet with coriander, saffron and carrots – alongside pea, rocket and ham risotto. Local Calenick pork is cooked in milk with rosemary and garlic and comes with a cider fondant, rosemary gravy and caramelised apple in a well-executed main course. Desserts tend to straightforward flavours, as in lemon tart with lime sorbet and raspberry sauce, or strawberry and almond tart. A stylish wine list favours New World wines, with prices kicking in at £13.

CHEF: Mark Wishart   PROPRIETORS: Paul and Fiona Robinson   OPEN: all week D only 7.30 to 9.30   CLOSED: Christmas, 3 to 31 Jan   MEALS: Set D £32   SERVICE: not inc, card slips closed   CARDS: Amex, MasterCard, Switch, Visa   DETAILS: 34 seats. 12 seats outside. Private parties: 54 main room. Car park. Children's helpings. No smoking. Music. No mobile phones   ACCOMMODATION: 11 rooms, all with bath/shower. TV. Phone. B&B £97.50 to £180

POULTON Gloucestershire   map 2

Falcon Inn ✸   NEW ENTRY

London Road, Poulton GL7 5HN
TEL: (01285) 850844   FAX: (01285) 850403
EMAIL: reservations@thefalconpoulton.co.uk
WEBSITE: www.thefalconpoulton.co.uk   COOKING 4
on A417 between Cirencester and Fairford   EUROPEAN
                                                             £25–£49

GLOUCESTERSHIRE
OF THE YEAR
NEWCOMER

Two friends from university decided to stop moaning about poor food and try to do something about it instead. That was the starting point, although experience at the Table in Torquay under Trevor Brooks (now at Kinnaird; see entry, Dunkeld, Scotland) and at the Carved Angel in Dartmouth (see entry) has obviously helped the project along. They bought this village pub and, by the time the Guide appears, expansion and refurbishment should have been completed. The menus change monthly, and the cooking is in predominantly European mode.

Some of it is pretty down to earth, too, including grilled gammon with fried egg and chips; indeed, materials in general are refreshingly free of luxury, offering perhaps a coarse country terrine, and grilled sardines. The food is uncluttered, simple and exactly as described: crisp-crusted confit duck leg with a salad of orange segments and watercress ('very good flavour and texture combinations'). Ambition is kept comfortably in check, and top-class raw materials include rare-breed meats and some ace seafood: for example, a fillet of crisp-skinned sea bass on a mound of freshly and properly prepared risotto mixed with chunks of young asparagus spears and Parmesan.

Desserts are equally straightforward without being clichés, and might run to gooseberries in honey and saffron custard, or a wobbly pannacotta-style coconut cream surrounded by mango wedges, pink grapefruit and lime segments: 'very simple, very fresh.' Service is slowly paced but 'positively thoughtful' (a bit of a rarity), and some 30-odd well-sourced wines are extensively but sensibly annotated. House Vin de Pays d'Oc is £10.50 (£2.50 a glass).

CHEFS: Robin Couling, Jeremy Lockley and Pete Miller   PROPRIETORS: Robin Couling and Jeremy Lockley   OPEN: Tue to Sun L 12 to 2.30, Tue to Sat D 7 to 9   MEALS: alc exc Sun L (main courses £8 to £16). Set L Sun £14.95 (2 courses) to £19.95   SERVICE: not inc   CARDS: Delta, MasterCard, Switch, Visa   DETAILS: 70 seats. 16 seats outside. Private parties: 25 main room, 16 to 25 private rooms. Car park. Vegetarian meals. Children's helpings. No smoking in 1 dining room. Wheelchair access (also WC). Music (£5)

POULTON-LE-FYLDE Lancashire   map 8

▲ River House

Skippool Creek, Thornton-Le-Fylde, Poulton-Le-
Fylde FY5 5LF
TEL: (01253) 883497   FAX: (01253) 892083
EMAIL: enquiries@theriverhouse.org.uk
WEBSITE: www.theriverhouse.org.uk   COOKING 4
from roundabout junction of A585 and B5412   FRENCH-PLUS
follow signs to Skippool Creek   £35–£59

The journey may be 'down a bumpy track half-hidden by trees, facing crumbling jetties and beached boats', but once you arrive, you will find a 'full of character' interior and a welcoming charm about the place. 'The River House does not change, it evolves,' says chef/proprietor Bill Scott – the evolution since the last entry being that lunch is no longer served – and respondents continue their enthusiasm for Scott's cuisine – 'classic dishes done honestly, but with no pretentious waffle', as one reader put it. Chestnut soup or plump, firm queen scallops poached in a creamy mustard and dill sauce might open proceedings, followed perhaps by 'first-rate' chateaubriand with béarnaise sauce, or baked seafood special – scallops, prawns, white fish and salmon in a herb sauce. Portions are reportedly generous, so pace yourself to leave room for warm rhubarb timbale or ticky tacky pudding, the latter apparently first served here in 1958. The wine list gives few clues as to the producers in many regions, but where it does it reveals good names, as well as unfamiliar but affordable options in Bordeaux. Prices look good value.

CHEF/PROPRIETOR: Bill Scott   OPEN: Mon to Sat D only 7.30 to 9.30   CLOSED: 25 and 26 Dec, 1 Jan   MEALS: alc (main courses £16 to £22). Set D £25   SERVICE: not inc   CARDS: Delta, MasterCard, Switch, Visa   DETAILS: 40 seats. Private parties: 40 main room. Car park. Vegetarian meals. No children under 7. Music   ACCOMMODATION: 4 rooms, all with bath/shower. TV. Phone. B&B £70 to £90 (*The Which? Guide to Good Hotels*)   £5

PRESTBURY Cheshire   map 8

▲ White House

New Road, Prestbury SK10 4HP
TEL: (01625) 829376   FAX: (01625) 828627
EMAIL: info@thewhitehouse.uk.com   COOKING 2
WEBSITE: www.thewhitehouse.uk.com   MODERN BRITISH
on A538, 4m N of Macclesfield   £26–£72

Alcoves and fixed screens in etched glass, a fireplace, and limed wood beams fit tastefully into a blue and brown colour scheme at this restaurant entering its twentieth year. Changing three times annually, the menu supports north-western suppliers; thus Cumbrian fell-bred meats, cheese from Chester and fresh seafood should be strong bets on an ambitious and eclectic carte showcasing contemporary British cuisine. Start perhaps with steamed Welsh mussels with tomato, saffron and coriander and continue with one of ten or more main-course options: half a crispy duckling with spiced burnt orange sauce and confit sweet potatoes, or 'beautifully pink' roast rack of lamb on a light jus of tomato, thyme and stock served with a shallot tarte Tatin. Pastry has been commended, too. so hot apple filo croustade with tarragon and crème fraîche might make a good finish. Beginning at £13.95 (£3.50 a glass), 50 or so wines cross four continents.

CHEFS: Ryland Wakeham and Mark Cunniffe   PROPRIETORS: Mr and Mrs Ryland Wakeham, and Judith Wakeham   OPEN: Tue to Sun L 12 to 2, Mon to Sat D 7 to 10   CLOSED: 25 Dec   MEALS: alc exc Sun L (main courses £12 to £19). Set L £14.95, Set D Mon to Fri £15.50 (2 courses) to £18.50. Bar L menu available Tue to Sat   SERVICE: not inc, card slips closed   CARDS: Amex, Delta, MasterCard, Switch, Visa   DETAILS: 75 seats. 12 seats outside. Private parties: 40 main room, 12 to 40 private rooms. Car park. Vegetarian meals. Children's helpings. No smoking before 2pm and 10pm. Wheelchair access (not WC). Music   ACCOMMODATION: 11 rooms, all with bath/shower. TV. Phone. Room only £80 to £130. No children under 10 (*The Which? Guide to Good Hotels*)

Restaurateurs justifiably resent no-shows. If you quote a credit card number when booking, you may be liable for the restaurant's lost profit margin if you don't turn up. Always phone to cancel.

Simply Heathcotes ✦

23 Winckley Square, Preston PR1 3JJ
TEL: (01772) 252732   FAX: (01772) 203433
EMAIL: preston@simplyheathcotes.co.uk
WEBSITE: www.heathcotes.co.uk

COOKING 3
BRASSERIE
£26–£49

This converted town-centre Georgian terraced house combines a ground-floor restaurant and a basement bistro/café, and offers a menu of spit-roasts, fish 'n chips, sandwiches, and drinks ranging from organic beer to hot chocolate. Seasonally changing menus in the relaxed, comfortable main dining room offer the kind of innovative modern British cookery for which Paul Heathcote has become famous (see Leeds, Liverpool, Longridge and Manchester for others in the stable). Plenty of choice is offered, with starters ranging from potted crab and salmon with cucumber, tomato and tarragon to warm spiced duck pancakes with mango relish. The informal, flexible mood is emphasised by a selection of dual-priced pasta and rice dishes, such as Cheddar cheese risotto with pickled onion marmalade, while main courses typically feature roast suckling pig with fondant potato and apple sauce, and seared sea bass fillet with braised fennel. Innovative desserts have included red wine and basil jelly with vanilla cream. Wines offer ample variety and fair value, with house selections from £12.50. The Heathcote empire has recently expanded into the next-door premises in the shape of the Olive Press, an informal, family-friendly pizzeria.

CHEF: Matt Nugent   PROPRIETOR: Paul Heathcote   OPEN: all week 12 to 2.30, 7 to 10 (Fri 6 to 10, Sat 6 to 11)   CLOSED: 25 and 26 Dec, bank hols, 1 and 2 Jan   MEALS: alc (main courses £9 to £15). Set L and D Mon to Thur 6 to 7.45, Fri and Sat 6 to 7 £13.50 (2 courses) to £15.50. Light L menu also available   SERVICE: 10% (optional), card slips closed   CARDS: Amex, Delta, Diners, MasterCard, Switch, Visa   DETAILS: 80 seats. Private parties: 70 main room brasserie, 80 bistro. Vegetarian meals. Children's helpings. No smoking. Wheelchair access (also WC). Music. Air-conditioned

Ramsons ▼ ✦ £

18 Market Place, Ramsbottom BL0 9HT
TEL: (01706) 825070   FAX: (01706) 822005
off A56/M66, 4m N of Bury

COOKING 4
ITALIAN
£23–£60

The end-of-terrace property, in a now trendy village, has changed a few times since Chris Johnson and Ros Hunter started here in 1985. The basement is now a café, the ground floor a restaurant with designer fabrics, good lighting, and a mix of wooden pews and upholstered chairs. Although it doesn't have the fiercely regional focus of a typical restaurant in Italy, Ramsons does capture the feel of eating there, and Abdulla Naseem (from the Maldives) has a real understanding of the Italian way of cooking. Chris Johnson has identified growers and farmers – some local, some in Italy – who provide materials that honestly reflect their origins. And, not for the first time, he has reinvented the business, now offering a range of menus including a carte, a budget version, a tasting menu, and a list of bar snacks. Among successes from the carte have been three accurately seared

Shetland scallops on a heap of fennel purée with a creamy saffron sauce, and pink, juicy nuggets of lamb fillet, arranged around a mound of flavourful mashed potato, generously scattered with meaty, braised cremini mushrooms. Desserts move closer to British territory, with sticky toffee pudding, and lemon tart – although vanilla-flavoured pannacotta is appropriately soothing. As with the food, so with the wine: Johnson has scoured Italy in person to find the wines for a list packed with colour, information and prices that encourage experimentation. A broad range is listed from each of his selected producers. Ten or so come by the glass starting at around £2.

CHEFS: Abdulla Naseem and Amy Bicknell   PROPRIETORS: Ros Hunter and Chris Johnson   OPEN: Tue to Sun L 12 to 2.30 (1 to 3.30 Sun), Tue to Sat D 6 to 10   CLOSED: 2 weeks May   MEALS: alc exc Sun L (main courses £8.50 to £17.50). Set L and D 6 to 7 £11 (2 courses) to £17   SERVICE: not inc, card slips closed   CARDS: Delta, MasterCard, Switch, Visa   DETAILS: 44 seats. Vegetarian meals. No smoking. Music. No mobile phones (£5)

RAMSGILL North Yorkshire   map 8

▲ Yorke Arms 🌟

Ramsgill HG3 5RL
TEL: (01423) 755243   FAX: (01423) 755330   COOKING 7
EMAIL: enquiries@yorke-arms.co.uk   MODERN BRITISH
WEBSITE: www.yorke-arms.co.uk   £40–£95

Several buildings seem to have been amalgamated to produce this combination of pub, bar and dining room beside the village green. And it is not short on character, sporting a stripped-wood floor in the dining room, a dark carved oak dresser, and tapestry wall hangings; pewter jugs and plates abound, and the bare wooden tables are well spaced. It is what most people might hope to find in a Dales village, and the kitchen is equally integrated with its surroundings. Local produce features, from lamb and beef to grouse and pheasant, and the tasting menu of six courses at £55 a head is one way in which to sample some of these: a terrine of Yorkshire potted beef with ham hock and foie gras, Nidderdale lamb pie (including faggots and braised shank), and braised leg and saddle of Dales hare.

Luxury materials also find a home – lobster ravioli with shellfish broth, or fillet of beef with foie gras, landaise potatoes and wild mushrooms – but they are deployed sensibly. Roast wood pigeon comes with pineapple relish as well as foie gras, and roast brill is partnered by tarragon and goats' cheese. This bright seam of gentle invention runs through much of the menu, producing artichoke and lemon soup, black pudding cooked in brioche, and tempura of vegetables with aubergine chilli pickle. Fish, meanwhile, comes from Fleetwood and Whitby, maybe turning up as roast turbot in a turnip and sweetcorn chowder.

Although full of ideas, Frances Atkins keeps her feet on the ground. Desserts, for example, might take in grapefruit and mango terrine, or marinated cherry tart with white chocolate ice cream. And talking of feet on the ground, walkers can call in for a light lunchtime snack: a chicken, bacon and egg club sandwich, perhaps, or sirloin steak with chips and aïoli. A sound collection of wines balances traditional French regions against the southern hemisphere, with an emphasis on quality throughout. Those who want change from a £20 note might consider the eight French house wines under £15.

CHEFS: Frances Atkins and Roger Olive   PROPRIETORS: Gerald and Frances Atkins   OPEN: all week 12 to 2 (2.30 Sun), 7 to 9 (9.30 Sat); Sun D residents only   MEALS: alc (main courses £17.50 to £21.50). Set L Sun £23 (2 courses) to £31, Set D (min 2) £45 to £85 (inc wine). Light L menu available   SERVICE: not inc   CARDS: Amex, Delta, Diners, MasterCard, Switch, Visa   DETAILS: 75 seats. 20 seats outside. Private parties: 45 main room, 4 to 20 private rooms. Car park. Vegetarian meals. No children under 12. No smoking. Wheelchair access (not WC). Music. No mobile phones   ACCOMMODATION: 14 rooms, all with bath/shower. TV. Phone. D,B&B £100 to £320. No children under 12 (*The Which? Guide to Good Hotels*) (£5)

READING Berkshire   map 2

London Street Brasserie   [NEW ENTRY]

2–4 London Street, Reading RG4 8DL   COOKING 2
TEL: (0118) 950 5036   FAX: (0118) 950 5028   MODERN EUROPEAN
WEBSITE: www.londonstbrasserie.co.uk   £34–£72

London Street Brasserie overlooks the River Kennet, which wends its way through Reading town centre. The sympathetically restored eighteenth-century building has a striking contemporary interior sporting lots of blond wood and white walls hung with artwork. There's a small bar area and a decked terrace overlooking the river. The menu is a lengthy affair and fairly ambitious in its aims; well-presented dishes are based on good-quality fresh produce and demonstrate skill. Starters such as well-timed pan-fried Scottish scallops may be served with a spicy tamarind dressing. To follow there might be roast rump of lamb 'Orvieto', served rare, with Tuscan vegetables, broad beans, fennel and a vigorous red wine jus, or a generous escalope of halibut on Savoy cabbage with smoked salmon and a chive beurre blanc. Caramelised lemon tart with pink grapefruit sorbet delivers a good combination of flavours. Service, by young staff, is attentive, bright and breezy. The wine list balances interest and good value, with house wines starting at £13.50.

CHEF: Paul Brotherton   PROPRIETOR: Paul Clerehugh   OPEN: all week 12 to 10.30 (11 Fri and Sat) CLOSED: 25, 26 and 31 Dec   MEALS: alc (main courses £11 to £20). Set L and D Mon to Sat 12 to 7 £12.95 (2 courses)   SERVICE: not inc, 10% for parties of 6 or more   CARDS: Amex, Delta, MasterCard, Switch, Visa   DETAILS: 70 seats. 12 seats outside. Private parties: 70 main room. Vegetarian meals. No cigars/pipes. Music

REIGATE Surrey   map 3

Dining Room ⁵⋇

59A High Street, Reigate RH2 9AE   COOKING 5
TEL/FAX: (01737) 226650   MODERN BRITISH
WEBSITE: www.tonytobinrestaurants.co.uk   £34–£65

TV chef Tony Tobin's restaurant is a slick operation. The first-floor dining room is done out in warm tones, complemented by mirrors, giving the place a fairly cosmopolitan air. Fixed-price menus include a number of intriguing-sounding international ingredients, which invite scrutiny. For instance, a first course of pan-seared red mullet fillets served with shaved fennel and fennel oil, or shredded duck salad with sweet-and-sour beets and beetroot relish.

Main dishes are perhaps a bit less adventurous and tend toward meaty options, say, pot-roast best end of veal with Jerusalem artichoke purée and braised shallots, and seared fillet of beef with foie gras, fondant potato, chard and truffle dressing. The fish options are just as interesting and might include Szechuan-spiced tuna with Asian-scented cucumber noodles and tomato and potato crisps. Desserts range from the inventive (apricot tarte Tatin with Thai basil ice cream) to the traditional (sticky toffee pudding). Plates tend towards the decorative, service towards the formal. Some good producers show up on the short wine list, particularly in the 'Library List'. Four house wines are served by the glass (£3.95) and bottle (£14.95).

CHEFS: Tony Tobin and Josh Clarke   PROPRIETOR: Tony Tobin   OPEN: Sun to Fri L 12 to 2 (12.30 to 2.30 Sun), Mon to Sat D 7 to 10   CLOSED: 24 Dec to 6 Jan, bank hols   MEALS: Set L Mon to Fri £19.50, Set L Sun £28.50, Set D Mon to Thur £22.50 (2 courses) to £29, Set D Fri and Sat £28.50 (2 courses) to £35   SERVICE: 12.5% (optional), card slips closed   CARDS: Amex, Delta, MasterCard, Switch, Visa   DETAILS: 70 seats. Private parties: 50 main room. Children's helpings. No smoking. Music. Air-conditioned

---

RICHMOND Surrey   map 3

Burnt Chair ▼

5 Duke Street, Richmond TW9 1HP
TEL: (020) 8940 9488   COOKING 3
EMAIL: connect1@burntchair.com   GLOBAL
WEBSITE: www.burntchair.com   £34–£61

'Another delightful meal, thoughtfully hosted by the ever-courteous Mr Oo', concluded a local devotee of this neighbourhood restaurant in a high-ceilinged converted shop. There have been changes in the kitchen since the last edition of the Guide, but the current brigade seems to have settled in well. A fixed-price menu is now offered midweek, there are pre-theatre options, and prices on the carte have been reduced to make them 'more competitive'. The dedication to eclectic ideas remains, flavours are acutely gauged and the results are harmonious: 'wafer-thin' ravioli filled with delicately spiced lamb comes with a thick 'steak' of grilled aubergine splashed with a garlic-laced yoghurt sauce, while fillet of butterfish (a type of pomfret) sits on a 'nage' of green beans and tagliatelle topped with curls of coconut and fried shallots. Cheeses are served 'au naturel' or worked into savouries like grilled Crottin de Chavignol with walnut and apple salad; otherwise finish sweetly with white chocolate and vanilla parfait, or pear tarte Tatin.

'Of the various wine-producing regions in the world, it is California which most captures my heart and imagination,' impassions Mr Oo, who goes on to prove it with a lengthy Californian list. France, especially Burgundy, seems to get him going too. Californian house wines are £14.75 (£3.75 a glass), but prices are not cheap and very little else is under £20.

CHEFS: John Barry, Ivo Manni and Sami Gruda   PROPRIETOR: Weenson Andrew Oo   OPEN: Tue to Sat D only 6 to 11   CLOSED: 10 days Christmas   MEALS: alc Fri and Sat (main courses £12 to £19). Set D Tue to Thur £18 (2 courses) to £20, Set D 6 to 7 £15 (2 courses). Cover £1   SERVICE: not inc, 12.5% for parties of 5 or more   CARDS: Delta, MasterCard, Switch, Visa   DETAILS: 36 seats. Private parties: 36 main room. Vegetarian meals. Children's helpings. No smoking. No music

RIDGEWAY Derbyshire
map 9

Old Vicarage ▼ ⅝✳

Ridgeway Moor, Ridgeway S12 3XW
TEL: (0114) 247 5814
EMAIL: eat@theoldvicarage.co.uk
WEBSITE: www.theoldvicarage.co.uk
from A616, ¾m NW of Mosborough, turn W on
B6054/B6388; in Ridgeway, turn S; restaurant is
½m on left, nearly opposite village church

COOKING **6**
MODERN BRITISH-PLUS
£40–£76

Back in 1846, when this large stone house was built, vicars obviously lived on a far grander scale than their present-day counterparts. Set in well-maintained formal gardens, it overlooks the Moss Valley conservation area. Chef/proprietor Tessa Bramley keeps herself busy with writing cookery books and appearing on TV but still devotes plenty of attention to making sure everything runs smoothly here at the Old Vicarage.

Her cooking is led by local produce, which she uses to create a simple yet sophisticated repertoire of dishes with a predominantly British flavour but taking in wider influences. Thus, starters might feature baked fillet of Bridlington cod with garlic and pancetta and a roast tomato and basil dressing, cumin-spiced potato cake with a poached egg, chervil sabayon and Gruyère soldiers, or rustic Thai-style mussel soup with chilli and coconut milk. Main courses are similarly varied, taking in cardamom- and balsamic-glazed roast squab pigeon with fondant potatoes and pan-fried foie gras, alongside roast red mullet on butternut squash risotto with anchovy tempura and chervil cream, and chargrilled Aberdeen Angus fillet on spiced red cabbage with parsnip and thyme purée and buttered greens. An impressive selection of British cheeses provides a savoury alternative to desserts such as passion-fruit soufflé with glazed lemon cream and mango sorbet, or baked chocolate pudding with chocolate fudge sauce and custard. The wine list is arranged by style and packed with good bottles, running from sprightly New Worlders to some very smart French classics. Prices are not the cheapest and just four wines come by the glass at £4.50.

CHEFS: Tessa Bramley, Nathan Smith and Andrew Gilbert   PROPRIETOR: Tessa Bramley   OPEN: Tue to Fri and Sun L 12.30 to 2.30, Tue to Sat D 7 to 10   CLOSED: 26 and 31 Dec, 1 Jan   MEALS: Set L £25 to £46, Set D £46   SERVICE: not inc, card slips closed   CARDS: Amex, Delta, MasterCard, Switch, Visa   DETAILS: 50 seats. 20 seats outside. Private parties: 50 main room, 10 to 20 private rooms. Car park. Vegetarian meals. No smoking. Wheelchair access (also WC). Occasional music. No mobile phones

---

If a restaurant is new to the Guide this year (did not appear as a main entry in the last edition), NEW ENTRY *appears opposite its name.*

RIPLEY North Yorkshire
map 9

▲ Boar's Head ▼ ✳

Ripley Castle Estate, Ripley HG3 3AY
TEL: (01423) 771888 FAX: (01423) 771509
EMAIL: reservations@boarsheadripley.co.uk
WEBSITE: www.boarsheadripley.co.uk

COOKING **3**
MODERN BRITISH
£21–£43

This stone hotel surveying the village square has restrained grandeur and a welcoming, smartly professional but relaxing atmosphere. Details like freshly baked breads, smoked salmon tart with light pastry and decent petits fours show genuine skills. The brasserie offers robust dishes – Cumberland sausage and mash is typical – while the restaurant goes as far as vanilla-marinated monkfish, or terrine of cured salmon, wild mushroom and goats' cheese (and pulls them off), the richness in the latter just tamed by a sharp lime and lemongrass salsa. In a well-judged trio of lamb (loin, liver and cabbage-wrapped mince patty) with a lightly reduced sauce, each component impressed, as did 'good, matured, textured' fillet of beef with a finely made watercress and wild mushroom mousse. Ice creams and fruit sauces with puddings are firmly flavoured: chocolate, cardamom and blueberry soufflé, and a rich, soft brownie with Kirsch-soaked cherries have both come with raspberry sauce and excellent vanilla ice cream. Burgundy and the Loire stand out amid the extensive French coverage in a world-spanning wine list that mixes affordable easy drinking from £12.25 with weightier classics. Seven wines come by the glass (£2.75 to £3.95), and there are lots of half-bottles.

CHEF: Jason Main PROPRIETORS: Sir Thomas and Lady Ingilby OPEN: all week 12 to 2, 6.30 to 9.30 MEALS: alc (main courses £9 to £14). Set L £11 (2 courses) to £15, Set L Sun £15.95, Set D £18.50 to £32.50 SERVICE: not inc CARDS: Amex, Delta, Diners, MasterCard, Switch, Visa DETAILS: 80 seats. 80 seats outside. Private parties: 40 main room. Car park. Vegetarian meals. Children's helpings. No smoking. Wheelchair access (also WC). Music ACCOMMODATION: 25 rooms, all with bath/shower. TV. Phone. B&B £99 to £140. Rooms for disabled. Baby facilities. Fishing (*The Which? Guide to Good Hotels*)

RIPON North Yorkshire
map 9

Restaurant Twenty Seven ✳
NEW ENTRY

27 Kirkgate, Ripon HG4 1PB
TEL: (01765) 608688

COOKING **6**
MODERN EUROPEAN
£20–£60

Once through the bar of what looks from outside like a shop in an old terrace, just a few steps from the cathedral, this opens out into a spacious, airy dining room with a stone floor, bare brick walls, and some timber and plaster, all of which lend it a clean and simple feel. The menu doesn't take long to read, with just four choices per course, although some dishes may need a second glance. Did it really say smoked eel soup with scrambled eggs and cider apples? Or Bresse pigeon with langoustine, cauliflower and iced Valrhona? It certainly did. This is obviously a chef with a highly developed sense of humour. But can he cook? The answer is again, thankfully, yes. John Lyons last appeared in the

Guide (in the 2002 edition) at Rascasse in Leeds, then opened here at the beginning of 2002.

Only a few chefs (notably Heston Blumenthal at the Fat Duck, Bray, and Paul Kitching at Juniper, Altrincham; see entries) manage successfully to pull off the trick of exciting us with what at first sight appear outlandish combinations, but John Lyons certainly makes a decent fist of it. Pineapple topped with beetroot foam, and deep-fried frog's leg with a 'fabulous' lime and garlic risotto are merely amuse-bouches. Once he gets going, there is no stopping the Lyons steamroller. 'A truly amazing combination' could apply to many things on the menu but was used to describe a starter of sweet, roast, hot-smoked salmon, accompanied by a cylinder of white chocolate filled with cucumber sorbet. Meat and fish combinations are of course nothing new, but here they seem to explore that relationship a little more thoroughly than usual. Turbot, for example, comes braised in red wine with pear Tatin and country ham, while a moist, cumin-spiced tranche of brill is served with a pile of thoroughly braised lamb and a powerful harissa sauce.

Desserts tend to steer clear of the fruit end of the spectrum, instead preferring four ways with vanilla (pannacotta, crème brûlée, steamed sponge and ice cream), and a sweetshop terrine (containing Crunchie, Turkish Delight and mint Aero), served with a powerful menthol sorbet and a Cadbury's Creme egg. Service is keen to please, and wines stay mostly under £20 apart from a page of special bottles. House Vin de Pays d'Oc is £10.99.

CHEF: John Lyons   PROPRIETORS: John and B. Lyons   OPEN: Wed to Sat L 12 to 2, Tue to Sat D 6.45 to 9 (9.30 Sat)   MEALS: Set L £8.95 (2 courses) to £10.95, Set D Tue to Thur 7 to 8 £16.95, Set D Tue to Sat £22 (2 courses) to £40   SERVICE: not inc, card slips closed   CARDS: Delta, MasterCard, Switch, Visa   DETAILS: 30 seats. Private parties: 36 main room. Vegetarian meals. Children's helpings. No smoking. Music £5

ROADE Northamptonshire   map 5

▲ Roade House ⅝✳

16 High Street, Roade NN7 2NW
TEL: (01604) 863372   FAX: (01604) 862421
EMAIL: info@roadehousehotel.co.uk   COOKING 4
WEBSITE: www.roadehousehotel.co.uk   MODERN BRITISH
off A508, 5m S of Northampton   £30–£61

The original pub, right on the road, is pebbledash painted brick red, with later extensions in stone and brick behind. Inside, the sky-lit bar area has the same cane chairs with woven backs and seating as the dining room, whose décor combines green, ochre and red, along with curtains depicting the Battle of Hastings. Despite a few reservations – notably uninspiring bread and problems with timing of some of the cooking at inspection – most respondents are well pleased. Typical dishes from the six-choice carte could include baked salmon fillet with celeriac purée and basil and lime sauce, or pan-fried fillet steak with wild mushroom risotto. There is praise for a tartlet of smoked haddock with poached egg and a tomato and cheese sauce, 'elegant on the plate, oozing with very rich cheese sauce – very French in conception and execution'. Particularly good pheasant, 'an above average vegetarian meal', and a creamy rhubarb ice cream subtly spiced with nutmeg also have met with approval. For one reporter this is an example of the 'perfect combination of restaurant with rooms'. Australia is the highlight of the good-value wine list, and France has plenty of reliable names. Four house bottles are £12, or £3.50 per glass.

CHEFS: Chris Kewley and Steve Barnes   PROPRIETORS: Chris and Sue Kewley   OPEN: Tue to Fri and Sun L 12.15 to 2, Mon to Sat D 6.45 to 9.45   CLOSED: 1 week at Christmas   MEALS: alc exc Sun L (main courses £15 to £23). Set L £16 (2 courses) to £19, Set L Sun £21   SERVICE: not inc   CARDS: Amex, Delta, MasterCard, Switch, Visa   DETAILS: 50 seats. Private parties: 58 main room. Car park. Children's helpings. No babes in arms at weekend D. No smoking. Wheelchair access (also WC). Occasional music. Air-conditioned   ACCOMMODATION: 10 rooms, all with bath/shower. TV. Phone. B&B £58 to £80. Rooms for disabled. Baby facilities

ROCHDALE Greater Manchester   map 8

After Eight ⅚✳

2 Edenfield Road, Rochdale OL11 5AA
TEL/FAX: (01706) 646432   COOKING 3
EMAIL: ataylor@aftereight.uk.com   MODERN BRITISH
WEBSITE: www.aftereight.uk.com   £29–£45

On the outskirts of Rochdale, this classically inspired 1820s stone house, its name in restrained gold letters on the front, is homely and welcoming behind the bourgeois splendour of its façade. It's 15 years since the Taylors started up here, and Geoff cooks to a Modern British formula 'with all its international influences'. Ingredients are first-rate; much comes direct from northern farms, with cheeses (including Swaledale and a traditional Lancashire) a speciality, while items like olives are carefully sourced. A well-balanced à la carte menu with five choices at each course (and three more on the vegetarian menu) is complemented by no-choice and limited-choice prix fixes. Dishes that sound pedestrian when described, like a fishcake with shredded cabbage and a curried sauce, have impressed in reality. Guinea fowl might be accompanied by black pudding, celeriac and chickpeas, and well-made reductions or fruit-based sauces crop up, as in duck with a rich plum sauce. Puddings tend to childhood favourites like steamed ginger with a grown-up crème anglaise, or exotica like Italian cheesecake of ricotta and marsala. House wines at £11.50 head a very good-value list with tempting bottles from all regions.

CHEF: Geoff Taylor   PROPRIETORS: Geoff and Anne Taylor   OPEN: Tue to Sat D only 12 to 3, 7 to 9.30 (L party bookings only)   CLOSED: 25 Dec, 1 Jan, 6 to 12 May   MEALS: alc (main courses £12 to £16). Set D Tue to Fri £18 to £24   SERVICE: not inc, 10% for parties of 10 or more   CARDS: Amex, Delta, Diners, MasterCard, Switch, Visa   DETAILS: 45 seats. Private parties: 30 main room, 10 to 20 private rooms. Vegetarian meals. Children's helpings. No smoking in 1 dining room. Wheelchair access (not WC). Music (£5)

£ *means that it is possible to have a three-course meal, including coffee, half a bottle of house wine and service for £30 or less per person, at any time the restaurant is open, i.e. at dinner as well as lunch. It may be possible to spend considerably more than this, but by choosing carefully you should find £30 or less achievable.*

ROCKBEARE Devon
map 1

Jack in the Green ♪※
NEW ENTRY

London Road, Rockbeare EX5 2EE
TEL: (01404) 822240   FAX: (01404) 823445
EMAIL: info@jackinthegreen.uk.com
WEBSITE: www.jackinthegreen.uk.com
off A30, 3m NE of Exeter

COOKING 2
GLOBAL
£27–£38

'Unpretentious' is a word that neatly sums up this inn, a white pebbledash building set in four acres. Inside, the rooms are a bit of a rabbit warren, abounding in hunting prints and horse brasses. Service is swift, efficient and intelligent, and what's on the plate is freshly prepared, well timed and based on good raw materials. The restaurant menu is commendably short, usually with six starters and six main courses (there is also a separate vegetarian menu). On offer might be starters such as 'confit' of Thai-style chicken flavoured with lemongrass and coriander, or chicken liver and foie gras parfait, with an 'honest and delicate' flavour. Among main courses, duck breast, sourced from nearby Creedy Farm near Tiverton, may be served on a bed of noodles stir-fried with vegetable strips in sesame oil and then dunked in plum sauce. Desserts, such as sticky toffee pudding and Bakewell tart, tend to be hefty affairs. The rather lengthy wine list is strong on Australia and France. It, like the restaurant, offers good value for money, with house French starting at £9.95.

CHEFS: Mr M. Mason and Mr C. Sampson   PROPRIETOR: Paul Parnell   OPEN: Mon to Sat 12 to 2, 6 to 9.30, Sun 12 to 9.30   CLOSED: 25 Dec to 3 Jan   MEALS: Set L and D Mon to Sat £18 (2 courses) to £22.25, Set L and D Sun £14.25 (2 courses) to £18. Bar menu available   SERVICE: not inc   CARDS: Delta, MasterCard, Switch, Visa   DETAILS: 140 seats. 20 seats outside. Private parties: 70 main room, 16 to 70 private rooms. Car park. Vegetarian meals. Children's helpings. No smoking in 1 dining room. Wheelchair access (also WC). Music. Air-conditioned

ROMALDKIRK Co Durham
map 10

▲ Rose and Crown ♪※

Romaldkirk DL12 9EB
TEL: (01833) 650213   FAX: (01833) 650828
EMAIL: hotel@rose-and-crown.co.uk
WEBSITE: www.rose-and-crown.co.uk
on B6277, 6m NW of Barnard Castle

NEW CHEF
TRADITIONAL ENGLISH
£24–£48

For nearly 15 years this generously proportioned three-storey pub next to the equally solidly stone-built village church has been base for Christopher and Alison Davy's intelligent approach to food and wine. A certain elegance prevails in the dining room, with its oak panelling, muted lighting and crisp white table cloths. In the summer of 2003, Andrew Lee – a long-standing member of the kitchen team – became head chef. The hands-on approach of the owners will not change, and a strong emphasis on local and seasonal ingredients will continue to bring Cotherstone and Ribblesdale cheeses and Teesdale fell lamb, as well as home-made breads and chutneys. Dishes are treated, in their own words, 'with modern variations' – which has applied to pan-fried breasts of wood pigeon with a parsnip tartlet, juniper berry sauce and grilled pancetta, or three-cheese tagliatelle with honey-roast walnuts. Simpler dishes are available in the bar at lunchtime and in the evening every day. Service comes in for praise, and the well-annotated wine list, arranged by grape variety, combines a rich assortment of Antipodeans with European classics. Chilean red and white house wines are £11.95, and ten wines come by the glass.

CHEF: Andrew Lee PROPRIETORS: Christopher and Alison Davy OPEN: Sun L 12 to 1.30, all week D 7.30 to 9 CLOSED: 24 to 26 Dec MEALS: Set L £15.95, Set D £26. Bar menu available SERVICE: not inc, card slips closed CARDS: MasterCard, Switch, Visa DETAILS: 24 seats. 24 seats outside. Private parties: 20 main room. Car park. Vegetarian meals. Children's helpings. No children under 6 . No smoking. Wheelchair access (not WC). No music. No mobile phones ACCOMMODATION: 12 rooms, all with bath/shower. TV. Phone. B&B £70 to £110. Rooms for disabled. Baby facilities (The Which? Guide to Good Hotels) (£5)

ROMSEY Hampshire   map 2

▲ Bertie's

80 The Hundred, Romsey SO51 8BX   COOKING **1**
TEL: (01794) 830708   FAX: (01794) 507507   MODERN EUROPEAN
WEBSITE: www.berties.co.uk   £28–£54

Like its brother in Winchester (see Round-up entry), this branch of Bertie's (once a coaching inn) is festooned with Jenny Muncaster's colourful paintings – although the interior is, perhaps, darker and more intimate. Former sous-chef Gavin Frampton has been promoted to top man in the kitchen, and he makes a genuine attempt to source good raw materials, including fish: pan-fried black bream with red wine butter, samphire and black olives is a typical example from the daily specials board. Otherwise, the monthly-changing carte is a dressed-up bistro selection running from pork tenderloin in a leek, apple and Calvados chowder to 'well-presented' teriyaki duck with rice noodles and oriental vegetables. Ice creams are home-made, and reporters have also enjoyed crème brûlée with cardamom shortbread. Service is 'unpretentious, friendly and courteous'. Ten house wines (from £3 a glass, £11.50 a bottle) head the wide-ranging, fairly priced list.

CHEF: Gavin Frampton PROPRIETOR: David Birmingham OPEN: Mon to Sat 12 to 2, 6.30 to 10 MEALS: alc (main courses L £7 to £16, D £11 to £19). Set L £9.95 (2 courses), Set D Mon to Fri £17.95 SERVICE: not inc, 10% for parties of 6 or more CARDS: Amex, Delta, Diners, MasterCard, Switch, Visa DETAILS: 66 seats. 25 seats outside. Car park. Vegetarian meals. No smoking in 1 dining room. Music ACCOMMODATION: 7 rooms, all with bath/shower. TV. B&B £45 to £75 (£5)

Three Tuns ⁂ | NEW ENTRY |

58 Middlebridge Street, Romsey SO51 8HL   COOKING **3**
TEL: (01794) 512639   FAX: (01794) 514524   MODERN BRITISH
                                                                      £32–£45

Not long ago the 'local' in these parts, the Three Tuns has eschewed beams, horse brasses and pub carpets for a clean, minimalist interior of grey-green Welsh slate, unadorned white walls, and low, 'dramatic'-looking pub tables: just the right setting for its new gastro-pub credentials. On the menu might be starters of black pudding with a poached egg, potato purée and devilled sauce, or beetroot carpaccio with crumbled goats' cheese, while a main course ribeye of beef has come perfectly rare as requested, accompanied by peppercorn sauce, comforting cauliflower cheese and nicely judged fondant potatoes. Otherwise there might be slow-cooked confit shoulder of lamb, subtly flavoured with cumin, served with stewed leeks and dauphinois potatoes, or pan-fried Scotch salmon in a red wine and shallot jus with minted pea purée and rösti. To finish, go for crème brûlée with mango sorbet. Service is friendly and informal, and the short, moderately priced wine list starts at £12 and rarely exceeds £20.

CHEF: Damian Brown   PROPRIETOR: Nick Geaney   OPEN: all week L 12 to 2.30, Mon to Sat D 6.30 to 9.30   MEALS: alc (main courses £12). Set L and D £17 (2 courses) to £22. Bar L menu available Mon to Sat   SERVICE: not inc, card slips closed   CARDS: Amex, Delta, MasterCard, Switch, Visa   DETAILS: 60 seats. 50 seats outside. Private parties: 60 main room. Car park. Vegetarian meals. Children's helpings. No smoking in 1 dining room. Music (£5)

ROSS-ON-WYE Herefordshire   map 5

Pheasant at Ross ▮ ⁵⁄✳

52 Edde Cross Street, Ross-on-Wye HR9 7BZ   COOKING 2
TEL: (01989) 565751   COUNTRY COOKING
WEBSITE: www.pheasants-at-ross.co.uk   £40–£48

The strongly held values at this converted sixteenth-century inn have not diminished over the ten years it has appeared in the Guide: notably dedication to local produce, including rare-breeds meat, and a pioneering approach to wines by the glass. Ingredients all come from within a 30-mile radius, though in terms of culinary inspiration, there are no limits. But don't expect experiments in exotic fusion – the style is more grounded. Starters might feature spiced crab with prawns and mace butter, or pan-seared scallops with bacon, pea purée and cider vinegar-flavoured potato crisps, while main courses take in roast rack of Welsh Marches lamb with caponata and basil oil, chicken breast with black pudding and 'King Offa' brandy sauce. Desserts range from classic bread-and-butter pudding to preserved figs poached in port and lavender honey. Wines are another matter. The fascinating, utterly individual list opens with three dozen 'starter partners' and sherries by the glass, then an adventurous list of 20 table wines also by the glass from £3.10 to £5. Next come the lists by food partners and styles before varietals take the stage, with generally out-of-favour Riesling and Semillon leading the way. Prices are unstressful, with loads of options under £20.

CHEF/PROPRIETOR: Eileen Brunnarius   OPEN: Thur to Sat D 7 to 9.30 (other evenings for booked groups of 8 or more)   CLOSED: 22 Dec to 2 Jan   MEALS: Set D £21.50 (2 courses) to £26   SERVICE: not inc   CARDS: Amex, Delta, Diners, MasterCard, Switch, Visa   DETAILS: 20 seats. Private parties: 30 main room. Vegetarian meals. Children's helpings. No smoking. Wheelchair access (not WC). Occasional music (£5)

If customers are asked to switch off mobile phones while in a restaurant, this is noted in the details at the end of an entry.

ROWDE Wiltshire   map 2

George & Dragon ⅓⁜ £

High Street, Rowde SN10 2PN   COOKING 3
TEL: (01380) 723053   FAX: (08712) 422964   SEAFOOD
EMAIL: gdrowde@tiscali.co.uk   £21–£55

This long pebbledash pub, with a pretty walled garden at the rear, is geared up for diners, especially the fish-loving variety, and does a roaring trade. Reports continue to indicate some inconsistency in the kitchen, ranging from 'fantastically tender and succulent' roast razor clams and 'perfect' langoustines with mayonnaise to less successful fish terrine. Although skate wing with capers and black butter was not up to scratch at inspection, roast monkfish and Thai fish curry have received praise. Non-fish eaters are catered for, too: perhaps Denhay air-dried ham with figs and mascarpone to start, followed by wild rabbit risotto. Puddings end on a high note: 'rich and luscious' chocolate mousse cake with coffee ice cream, perhaps, or prune and Armagnac tart. Service by young staff is friendly and well paced, and the well-chosen wine list has plenty of interest, with most wines under £25. Nine house wines are £10 or £12 (£2.50 or £3 a glass).

CHEFS: Tim Withers and Kate Patterson   PROPRIETORS: Mr and Mrs Tim Withers   OPEN: Tue to Sat 12 to 2, 7 to 10   CLOSED: 25 Dec, 1 Jan   MEALS: alc (main courses £7 to £20). Set L £10 (2 courses) to £12.50   SERVICE: not inc   CARDS: Delta, MasterCard, Switch, Visa   DETAILS: 40 seats. 16 seats outside. Car park. Vegetarian meals. Children's helpings. No smoking. No music. No mobile phones

RYE East Sussex   map 3

Landgate Bistro ⅓⁜ £

5–6 Landgate, Rye TN31 7LH   COOKING 4
TEL: (01797) 222829   MODERN BRITISH
WEBSITE: www.landgatebistro.co.uk   £23–£39

Just outside the walls of this now landlocked medieval port (its ancient street plan still intact) sits the Landgate: two adjacent properties linked together to house the bar and restaurant. Pot plants screen the plate glass window from the street and the warm bare brick walls display Fay Godwin photographs and framed posters.

The Landgate punches a bit above 'bistro' weight, and its prices are net: no service charge is added or expected. A Tuesday to Thursday set price menu is a reduced subset of the carte. The latter starts with, say, leek and Roquefort tart, or salmon and salt cod fishcakes, and then offers over a dozen mains, from scallops and brill with orange and vermouth sauce, to fillet of beef in pastry with rosemary béarnaise, or griddled noisettes of Sika venison. Gratin potatoes and vegetable side dishes at just £1 each have been well received. Desserts might include walnut and treacle tart, Jamaican chocolate cream and a highly rated lemon and sherry syllabub. There are seven wines by the glass and a good sprinkling of half-bottles; house wine is just under £10, prices rise to £35 (1990 Ch. Potensac), and 20-odd varied bins come in under £15.

CHEF: Toni Ferguson-Lees   PROPRIETORS: Nick Parkin and Toni Ferguson-Lees   OPEN: Tue to Sat D 7 to 9.30 (10 Sat)   CLOSED: 2 weeks Christmas, 1 week summer   MEALS: alc (main courses £10 to £13.50). Set D Tue to Thur £17.90   SERVICE: net prices, card slips closed   CARDS: Delta, MasterCard, Switch, Visa   DETAILS: 30 seats. Vegetarian meals. Children's helpings. No smoking. Music £5

ST IVES Cornwall   map 1

Alba ⅚✗

Old Lifeboat House, Wharf Road,	COOKING 2
St Ives TR26 1LF	MODERN EUROPEAN
TEL: (01736) 797222 FAX: (01736) 798937	£28–£52

This tasteful conversion of the lifeboat house commands great views straight across St Ives Harbour. Tables near the huge picture windows at the upstairs restaurant are favoured, but the décor, too, is worthy of a good look: fresh and light, with pale wood and white walls hung with modern paintings. Although the proprietors call the style of cooking 'modern European', there's a certain Italian influence resonating through the menu. Classic Italian dishes such as aquacotta ('cooked water' – soup, in other words – here based on tomatoes and wild mushrooms) can be found on the vegetarian menu or, for desserts, grappa pannacotta served with roast strawberries. Being this close to the sea, it's hardly surprising that fish, sourced straight from the boats in the harbour, makes a frequent appearance. 'Haven't tasted better' was the verdict delivered by one visitor on a dish of sea bass (line-caught locally), which may come with baby fennel, girolles and a langoustine broth. Otherwise go for a main course of poached free-range Cornish chicken breast with an asparagus and morel velouté. Service has been deemed 'friendly, professional and efficient'. There are some interesting bottles on the wine list, with prices starting at £11.50.

CHEF: Grant Nethercott   PROPRIETOR: Harbour Kitchen Co Ltd   OPEN: all week 12 to 3, 6 to 10   CLOSED: 25 Dec   MEALS: alc (main courses L £8 to £14, D £12 to £17.50). Set L £14.50 (2 courses) to £17.50, Set D £18 (2 courses) to £21   SERVICE: not inc   CARDS: Amex, Delta, MasterCard, Switch, Visa   DETAILS: 40 seats. Private parties: 45 main room. Vegetarian meals. Children's helpings. No smoking. Music. Air-conditioned

Pickled Fish | NEW ENTRY |

3 Chapel Street, St Ives TR26 2LR	COOKING 3
TEL: (01736) 795100	MODERN BRITISH
	£18–£44

This addition in a town that is rapidly becoming the foodie, as well as arty, capital of the South West offers cooking from excellent local ingredients that is sound and good value. In a tucked-away location, but close to the action, this pale-blue-painted room has wooden floor and chairs, decent cutlery and white tablecloths – and good food. Fresh wholemeal rolls, ice creams and petits fours are all home-made. Starters come in interesting, imaginative combinations – confit cod, poached in duck fat, pickled Savoy cabbage and saffron aïoli, say, or the clean simplicity of velvety cream of white crabmeat and potato soup, cleverly spiced with paprika croûtons. Main courses, served with a selection of vegetables, sensibly maintain a simple-is-best approach, exemplified in accurately grilled sea bass fillets with lemon-braised celery (robust acidifying is a favourite with Ben Reeve) and a well-made vanilla velouté, or perhaps fried Cornish beef with black pudding and chicken livers as well as an intriguing and successful thyme and pearl barley reduction. Classic desserts get twists: perhaps creamy rice pudding flavoured with orange and cardamom, or a white chocolate crème brûlée delicately scented with star anise. And – hurrah – this is a BYO restaurant; the unprepared are directed to a nearby off-licence.

CHEF: Ben Reeve   PROPRIETORS: Ben and Jennifer Reeve   OPEN: Tue to Sat (and Mon in July/Aug) D 7 to 10   CLOSED: 2 weeks Jan   MEALS: alc (main courses £12 to £17). Set D £14.50   SERVICE: not inc, card slips closed   CARDS: Delta, MasterCard, Switch, Visa   DETAILS: 30 seats. Private parties: 30 main room. Vegetarian meals. Children's helpings. Music. Air-conditioned (£5)

Porthminster Beach Café ✸ 📖

Porthminster Beach, St Ives TR26 2EB
TEL/FAX: (01736) 795352   COOKING 4
EMAIL: p.minster@btopenworld.com   GLOBAL
WEBSITE: www.porthminstercafe.co.uk   £26–£50

'Café' is no affectation at this beach-side venue: the opening hours allow the pleasures of morning coffee and afternoon tea as well as lunch and dinner. Heaters on the terrace extend its use beyond warm weather only, although the setting (inside or out) is unbeatable on a sunny day. Lobsters come from a local boat, other fish daily via Matthew Stevens from Newlyn. Robust and sensitive methods and pairings receive equal praise, in perfectly gauged first courses such as squid fried with smoky chorizo, balanced with lemon and watercress, and prawn risotto lightened with crème fraîche (not the usual butter), or a main course of John Dory in the testing company of black olive crushed potatoes, wilted spinach and lemon caper salad. Meat is in the minority here, but is carefully sourced and treated with similar imagination. Bread, charged for but worth it, and pastry, are consistent – witness a crispy base for a rich chocolate tart, cut with a serious espresso ice cream, or rustic apple pie with clotted cream. The wine list is short and to the point, starting at £10.95. Many are by the glass.

CHEFS: Michael Smith, Fabian Christoph, Benjamin Day and Samuel Oakley   PROPRIETORS: James Woolcock, David Fox, and Roger and Timothy Symons   OPEN: all week 12 to 4, 6 to 10. Light menu also available   CLOSED: 1 Nov to 2 weeks before Easter   MEALS: alc (main courses L £8 to £13, D £9.50 to £18)   SERVICE: not inc   CARDS: Delta, MasterCard, Switch, Visa   DETAILS: 52 seats. 60 seats outside. Vegetarian meals. No smoking. Music. No mobile phones

Occasional music *in the details at the end of an entry means live or recorded music is played in the dining room only rarely or for special events.* No music *means it is never played.*

New main entries are listed near the front of the book. Some may have appeared in earlier years (though not in the previous edition) or as a Round-up entry last year.

ST KEYNE Cornwall   map 1

▲ Well House ▼ ⁵✳

St Keyne PL14 4RN
TEL: (01579) 342001 FAX: (01579) 343891
EMAIL: enquiries@wellhouse.co.uk
WEBSITE: www.wellhouse.co.uk   COOKING 4
on B3254, 3m S of Liskeard; at end of village near   MODERN BRITISH
church, follow sign to St Keyne Well   £35–£57

Set in three acres of grounds in the Looe Valley, Well House takes its name from
the fact that it stands on the site of St Keyne's Well. It's a plain Victorian house
built of grey stone, and owner Nick Wainford takes a laid-back approach that
gives the place a relaxed atmosphere. But a lot of work goes into making it seem
this way, not least in the kitchen, where Matthew Corner creates an ambitious
menu of bright, modern dishes. Seared scallops with lemon and thyme risotto,
and duck confit with roast Comice pear and star anise jus are typically lively-
sounding starters, while main courses have featured breast of guinea fowl with
tomato and basil jus, pan-fried red mullet with buttered pak choi and coriander
velouté, and roast pork tenderloin with Savoy cabbage and caramelised shallots
in a jus. For dessert, there might be lemon posset with grilled figs, or rhubarb tart
with elderflower sorbet.

The wine list starts out all earnest with strong collections of Bordeaux and
Burgundy but soon lightens up and delivers a good global range at fair prices –
even in those classical French regions. Options under £20 are plentiful, but only
three house wines come by the glass (£2.75).

CHEF: Matthew Corner PROPRIETORS: Nick Wainford and Ione Nurdin OPEN: all week 12.30 to
1.30, 7 to 9.30 MEALS: Set L £18.50 (2 courses) to £23.50, Set D £32.50 SERVICE: not inc, card
slips closed CARDS: Delta, MasterCard, Switch, Visa DETAILS: 32 seats. 18 seats outside.
Private parties: 32 main room. Car park. Vegetarian meals. No children under 8 at D. Jacket and
tie. No smoking. Wheelchair access (also WC). No music. No mobile phones ACCOMMODATION:
9 rooms, all with bath/shower. TV. Phone. B&B £115 to £170 (double room). Swimming pool (The
Which? Guide to Good Hotels)

ST MARGARET'S AT CLIFFE Kent   map 3

▲ Wallett's Court ⁵✳

Westcliffe, St Margaret's at Cliffe CT15 6EW
TEL: (01304) 852424 FAX: (01304) 853430
EMAIL: wc@wallettscourt.com   COOKING 3
WEBSITE: www.wallettscourt.com   ANGLO-FRENCH
on B2058, off A258 Dover to Deal road, 3m NE of Dover   £30–£73

Although the estate figures in the Domesday Book, the present building is a
stripling of a seventeenth-century former farmhouse perched picturesquely near
Dover's white cliffs. Rescued and restored since the 1970s by the Oakleys, it is
now a country hotel with a historic but twee-free ambience. Locally reared lamb,
fish from Kent boats and Aberdeen Angus beef from distant Speyside inform
Stephen Harvey's accomplished and original cooking. Menu choice is generous,
and might encompass a rock oyster trio to start (with cucumber and dill cream,

with chorizo, and with raspberry and shallot vinaigrette), and main courses that run the gamut from sea bream and salsify with vanilla risotto, to squab pigeon breasts with Puy lentil casserole and a truffled Madeira sauce. Inventive vegetarian dishes include roast pepper and olive tart with oregano pesto and pine nuts. A European cheese selection offers a savoury alternative to desserts such as peanut parfait with brazil nut tuile and Belgian chocolate sauce. Wines are a cheerily jumbled international assortment, with plenty by the glass and half-bottle, and very fair prices. House selections are Guigal's benchmark red Côtes du Rhône and Torres' citrus-fresh Santa Digna Sauvignon Blanc from Chile, both £14.95.

CHEF: Stephen Harvey   PROPRIETORS: the Oakley family   OPEN: Tue to Fri and Sun L 12 to 2, all week D 7 to 9   MEALS: Set L £15 (2 courses) to £17.50, Set D £35 to £45. Bar menu available   SERVICE: not inc   CARDS: Amex, Delta, Diners, MasterCard, Switch, Visa   DETAILS: 70 seats. Private parties: 40 main room, 6 to 40 private rooms. Car park. Vegetarian meals. No children under 8 after 8. No smoking. Occasional music. No mobile phones   ACCOMMODATION: 16 rooms, all with bath/shower. TV. Phone. B&B £75 to £150. Baby facilities. Swimming pool (*The Which? Guide to Good Hotels*) £5

ST MARTIN'S Isles of Scilly   map 1

▲ St Martin's on the Isle ⁵⁺*

Lower Town, St Martin's TR25 0QW
TEL: (01720) 422090   FAX: (01720) 422298   COOKING 5
EMAIL: stay@stmartinshotel.co.uk   MODERN EUROPEAN
WEBSITE: www.stmartinshotel.co.uk   £52–£70

It takes a plane, helicopter or boat, followed by and inter-island hop to get from the mainland to unspoilt, tranquil St Martin's but, weather permitting, it is no great ordeal and well worth it for the rewards that await you. The island's one hotel achieves high standards in all quarters, with comfortable rooms and cheery, attentive staff. Dinner is enhanced by stunning views from the dining room, although the food surmounts even this distraction.

Local and seasonal produce are naturally the lynchpins of the cooking; the set menu is often partly based on local fishermen's catches, and the shellfish menu (ordered 24 hours ahead and operating via supplements to the set menu) is wholly Scillonian-sourced. The refined, elegant cooking style aims for a light, fresh feel, so starters might feature salad of crab, fennel and avocado with lemon purée and salsa verde, or beef carpaccio with a tian of tomato and basil, and salad of artichokes and green beans. Follow perhaps with rosemary-scented poussin with a boudin of herbs, foie gras and spring vegetable bouillon with Madeira; or maybe monkfish on herb purée with asparagus and hollandaise. Desserts range from simple, classic crème brûlée to gratin of red-wine-poached plums and spiced orange cake with crème fraîche ice cream. Wines are mostly easy-drinking, with a few smarter bottles. Prices reflect the location, so interesting options are over £20, but £25 opens the door to the majority of the list. Ten come by the glass from £2.70.

CHEF: Stewart Eddy   PROPRIETORS: Peter and Penny Sykes   OPEN: all week D only 7 to 9.30 CLOSED: Nov to Feb   MEALS: Set D £39.50. Bar menu available   SERVICE: not inc, card slips closed   CARDS: Amex, Delta, Diners, MasterCard, Switch, Visa   DETAILS: 80 seats. Private parties: 100 main room, 2 to 25 private rooms. Car park. Vegetarian meals. Children's helpings.

No children under 12. No smoking. No music. No mobile phones ACCOMMODATION: 30 rooms, all with bath/shower. TV. Phone. Rooms for disabled. Baby facilities. Swimming pool. Fishing (*The Which? Guide to Good Hotels*)

ST MAWES Cornwall
map 1

Green Lantern

NEW ENTRY

Marine Parade, Saint Mawes TR2 5DW
TEL: (01326) 270878   FAX: (01326) 270594
EMAIL: info@thegreenlantern.uk.com
WEBSITE: www.thegreenlantern.uk.com

COOKING **4**
MODERN EUROPEAN
£37–£54

Reporters have been quick to spot this small, friendly restaurant that opened in July 2002 and to praise Andy Mason's fusion-tinged cooking and the unpretentious hospitality of owners Chris and Carolyn Waite. Look for a custard-coloured terrace overlooking a small shingle beach beside the harbour wall, then for the green-glazed lantern outside. Inside, amid plain but artistic seaside-themed décor and modern black-and-white photographs, nine tables clothed in stiff white linen stand on wide, bare oak boards. Our inspector felt the dishes needed paring down for sharper focus, but attractively presented food was drawing appreciative 'oohs and aahs' all around. Superb local butter and crisp-crusted home-baked bread were praised, and the fusion of flavours in a crab, avocado, mango and cucumber starter with rocket and oven-dried tomatoes has impressed several diners. Good raw materials make their mark in dishes like roast monkfish with garlic-butter-poached escargots, rösti and other trimmings, or gamey, 'beautifully cooked' pheasant, and venison, 'so tender it melted in the mouth'. Desserts could range from pannacotta with bilberries and an almond biscuit, to crystallised ginger and molasses cake. Over 60 bins offer good choice, with a dozen by the glass (plus pre- and post-prandials) and house wines from £12.50.

CHEF: Andy Mason   PROPRIETORS: Chris and Carolyn Waite   OPEN: Tue to Sat D 7 to 9 (in July/ Aug Mon to Sat D 6 to 9.30)   CLOSED: Nov 15 to 30, Dec 25 and 26, Jan 8 to Feb 7   MEALS: alc (main courses £14.50 to £17.50)   SERVICE: not inc   CARDS: Delta, MasterCard, Switch, Visa   DETAILS: 24 seats. Private parties: 24 main room. Vegetarian meals. Children's helpings. No children under 7. No Smoking. Music £5

▲ Rising Sun

The Square, St Mawes TR2 5DJ
TEL: (01326) 270233   FAX: (01326) 270198
EMAIL: therisingsun@btclick.com
WEBSITE: www.innsofcornwall.co.uk

COOKING **3**
MODERN ENGLISH
£30–£46

The Rising Sun is a small, friendly hotel with sea views from its elegant conservatory dining room, where tables are attractively set with candles and flowers. Ann Long's accomplished and inventive cooking and attractive presentation of dishes bring the best out of high-quality local ingredients. Among starters, reporters have praised a 'very light' crab, mackerel and smoked salmon terrine served with two sauces, one of melon and mint, the other of melon and strawberry, and 'mouthwateringly good' seared scallops and sliced chorizo with hot chilli mayonnaise and a green pepper and ginger salsa. To follow, options have included lamb with Madeira sauce, redcurrants and spicy red cabbage, game pie with an impressively light suet crust and a thick, rich sauce, and Dover sole fillets in lobster sauce. Finish with 'subtle' vanilla pannacotta with a red wine and raspberry jelly, or raspberry oatmeal meringue. The wine list opens with 10 house selections at £11 a bottle, £2.75 a glass, and value is good throughout the well-chosen list.

CHEF: Ann Long   PROPRIETOR: John Milan   OPEN: Sun L 12 to 2, all week D 7 to 9   MEALS: alc L Sun (main courses £8 to £18), Set D £26 (2 courses) to £29. Bar menu available   SERVICE: not inc, card slips closed   CARDS: Delta, MasterCard, Switch, Visa   DETAILS: 50 seats. 50 seats outside. Private parties: 50 main room. Car park. Children's helpings. No smoking. Wheelchair access (also WC). No music   ACCOMMODATION: 8 rooms, all with bath/shower. TV. Phone. B&B £40 to £100. Baby facilities (*The Which? Guide to Good Hotels*)

▲ Hotel Tresanton

Lower Castle Road, St Mawes TR2 5DR
TEL: (01326) 270055   FAX: (01326) 270053   COOKING **4**
EMAIL: info@tresanton.com   MODERN EUROPEAN
WEBSITE: www.tresanton.com   £38–£58

A laid-back air suited to cutting a dash on the prow-like terrace overlooking the sea pervades the smart affluence ('nautique' rather than seriously nautical) likely to be found at the Tresanton. Olga Polizzi has created a smart and extremely fashionable hotel, with a bright and cosmopolitan restaurant benefiting from views across the water. English tradition mingles with modern Med as the kitchen seeks to create combinations familiar to migrants from metropolitan brasseries. Gnocchi with coppa di Parma, wild mushrooms and garlic, or a chorizo and white bean casserole with spinach, or seared scallops with leeks and keta caviar – typical first courses from the set menus – sit alongside main dishes of roast best end of lamb with dauphine potatoes and green beans, or polenta with tomato, basil and spinach Parmesan. Rhubarb and apple crumble with vanilla ice cream, or warm chocolate pudding with Chantilly cream, draw inspiration from our own north European dairy-based cooking. A lunchtime snack menu or cream tea on the terrace complement the grander main meals. Wines starting at £13.50 are a canny range running from modest but good up to mature and pricey. Ch. Doisy-Védrines Sauternes at £5 (admittedly in a fun-size 75cl glass), or a 5-putt Tokay at £8, are treats to be grateful for.

CHEF: Paul Wadham   PROPRIETOR: Olga Polizzi   OPEN: all week 12.30 to 2.30, 7 to 9.30   MEALS: Set L £20 (2 courses) to £25, Set D £34. Light L menu available   SERVICE: not inc, card slips closed   CARDS: Amex, MasterCard, Switch, Visa   DETAILS: 50 seats. 60 seats outside. Private parties: 40 main room. Car park. Vegetarian meals. Children's helpings. Wheelchair access (not WC). No music   ACCOMMODATION: 29 rooms, all with bath/shower. TV. Phone. B&B £166 to £265. Baby facilities (*The Which? Guide to Good Hotels*)

If 'The Which? Guide to Good Hotels' is noted at the end of an entry, this means that the establishment is also in the 2004 edition of our sister guide, published in September 2003.

ST MERRYN Cornwall

map 1

Ripley's

NEW ENTRY

St Merryn PL28 8NQ
TEL: (01841) 520179   FAX: (01841) 521641

COOKING **5**
MODERN BRITISH
£35–£51

This small restaurant stands out from its neighbours in a small terrace thanks to its custard-yellow pebbledash façade and its white, modern-looking sign. White is the theme inside, too, relieved by a slate floor and bright contemporary paintings, all very spruce and uncluttered. The talented Mr Ripley, who used to cook at the Seafood Restaurant just down the road in Padstow (see entry), offers a seasonal carte (with a choice of just four items at each stage) and a weekly-changing set-price menu, in which local produce features, and in which meat has equal billing with fish.

Among the 'stunning' raw materials have been 'out-of-this-world' scallops (corals attached) sprinkled with sesame seeds and accurately seared, sitting on a thin, sweet and gingery dressing made with hazelnut oil and soy, attended by a Thai-style salad spiked with coriander: 'it couldn't have been fresher, more interesting or better balanced.' The style is reassuringly straightforward, with nothing too exotic or adventurous, and presentation is plain and simple: for example, a generous slab of 'fabulous', well-hung Scottish beef fillet – still attached to the bone, and cooked blue as requested – topped with bone marrow butter flecked with chilli and chives, accompanied by a clear, classical sauce of red wine and port full of chopped shallot. Vegetables (including Jersey Royals, broad beans and asparagus at a May meal) arrive on a separate serving dish and 'couldn't have been tastier'.

Desserts run from queen of puddings to Cornish strawberries with clotted cream ice cream, and although the one at inspection (a wedge of baked egg custard tart with creamy nutmeg ice cream and intense blackcurrant sauce) was slightly less thrilling than the rest, it was still good. Bread is first class, service is smart and professional yet friendly, and a short, sharply chosen and fairly priced wine list starts with a clutch of French house wines around £12.

CHEF/PROPRIETOR: Paul Ripley   OPEN: Tue to Sat D only 7 to 9.30   CLOSED: 2 weeks Christmas, last 2 weeks Jan   MEALS: alc (main courses £17.50 to £18). Set D £23.50   SERVICE: not inc, card slips closed   CARDS: Amex, Delta, MasterCard, Switch, Visa   DETAILS: 32 seats. Private parties: 20 main room. No smoking. Music

SALE Greater Manchester

map 8

Hanni's £

4 Brooklands Road, Sale M33 3SQ
TEL: (0161) 973 6606   FAX: (0161) 972 0469

COOKING **2**
EASTERN MEDITERRANEAN
£30–£51

This successful neighbourhood restaurant occupies a converted shop, handily placed adjacent to Brooklands Metrolink Station. It continues to attract a loyal band of followers, who come to enjoy satisfying food steeped in the flavours of the eastern Mediterranean. Meze are mostly familiar items such as falafel, börek (fried filo pastries) and hummus with fried aubergines. Lamb is king when it comes to main courses such as kleftiko, stifado and – even – a variation on osso buco; assorted kebabs include chicken tikka; couscous comes in several guises; while desserts are predictable stuff such as baklava, Turkish delight and savoury fried halloumi cheese in pastry. The two-course 'happy hour menu' is a good deal. Greece, Israel, Lebanon and Turkey, along with a few goodies from more mainstream regions, show up on the modestly priced international wine list; house wine is £11.95 (£2.85 a glass).

CHEF: Mr Hooninian PROPRIETORS: Mohamed Hanni and Jennifer Al-Taraboulsy OPEN: Mon to Sat D only 6 to 10.30 (11 Fri and Sat) CLOSED: 25 and 26 Dec, 1 Jan, Good Fri, Easter Mon MEALS: alc (main courses £10.50 to £14). Set D Mon to Fri 6 to 7 £10 (2 courses), Set D £11 (2 courses) SERVICE: not inc CARDS: Amex, Delta, MasterCard, Switch, Visa DETAILS: 50 seats. Private parties: 50 main room. Vegetarian meals. Children's helpings. Wheelchair access (not WC). Music. Air-conditioned

SALFORD Greater Manchester   map 8

▲ Lowry Hotel, River Room, Marco Pierre White

50 Dearmans Place, Chapel Wharf,
Salford M3 5LH   NEW CHEF
TEL: (0161) 827 4041   FAX: (0161) 827 4001   FRENCH
WEBSITE: www.thelowryhotel.com   £32–£76

You would expect the 'very chic, very minimalist' Lowry Hotel in the Salford Quays to have a suitably trendy restaurant, and the River Room, Marco Pierre White fits the bill. The air of restrained extravagance and the cool stylishness of the venue raise expectations of something special on the food front, so let's hope that new chef Steve McCloughlin, promoted from sous-chef, delivers. The repertoire of Marco-inspired dishes is set to continue, which has seen pig's trotter with black pudding and piquant salsa verde alongside a fluffy omelette topped with pieces of lobster and sauce américaine among hors d'oeuvres. Main dishes might see Aberdeen Angus fillet with a Madeira jus and sweet roasted shallots. Wines are a classy selection starting at £16, though only a handful cost under £25, and service is competent if a little edgy. Reports on the new team, please.

CHEF: Steve McCloughlin PROPRIETOR: Rocco Forte OPEN: all week 12 to 2.30 (12.30 to 2.30 Sat, 12.30 to 4.30 Sun), 6 to 10.30 (10 Sun) MEALS: alc exc Sun L (main courses £13.50 to £19). Set L £15 (2 courses) to £18, Set D 6 to 7 £15 (2 courses) to £18 SERVICE: 10% (optional) CARDS: Amex, Delta, Diners, MasterCard, Switch, Visa DETAILS: 120 seats. 12 seats outside. Private parties: 8 to 20 private rooms. Car park. Vegetarian meals. Children's helpings. No children under 13. Wheelchair access (also WC). Music. No mobile phones. Air-conditioned ACCOMMODATION: 165 rooms, all with bath/shower. TV. Phone. Room only £204 to £1050. Rooms for disabled. Baby facilities

The cuisine styles noted at the tops of entries are only an approximation, often suggested to us by the restaurants themselves. Please read the entry itself to find out more about the cooking style.

SAPPERTON Gloucestershire   map 2

Bell at Sapperton ⅝✴

Sapperton GL7 6LE
TEL: (01285) 760298   FAX: (01285) 760761   COOKING **1**
EMAIL: thebell@sapperton66.freeserve.co.uk   MODERN EUROPEAN
WEBSITE: www.foodatthebell.co.uk   £30–£49

This stone pub in a beautiful Cotswold village certainly makes an impression.
The interior is no less impressive – flagstones, exposed walls, open fires, and a
'very civilised atmosphere'. Menus change weekly (and blackboard fish specials
change daily, with 'the best fish 'n chips in the district' perhaps alongside a
highly rated lobster risotto). Dishes can range from pubby (chargrilled spicy
lamb, and cheese burger with French fries) to modish (Mediterranean tagliolini
with tomatoes, artichokes and olives), and there's always roast beef at Sunday
lunch. Desserts include banana fritters with sesame syrup and ice cream, or
maybe sherry berry trifle. Since last year the wine list has been expanded and
arranged by style, but still offers fair value and now has 17 by the 175ml or
250ml glass; an eclectic global selection includes interesting dessert wines and
is topped off by some pricier big names.

CHEF: Alyson McKenzie   PROPRIETORS: Paul Davidson and Pat Le Jeune   OPEN: all week 12 to 2,
7 to 9.30   CLOSED: 25 Dec, evenings of 26 and 31 Dec and 1 Jan   MEALS: alc (main courses
£10.50 to £16.50)   SERVICE: not inc, card slips closed   CARDS: MasterCard, Switch, Visa
DETAILS: 80 seats. 50 seats outside. Private parties: 10 main room. Car park. Vegetarian meals.
Children's helpings. No children under 10 after 6.30. No smoking in 1 dining room. No music. No
mobile phones

SAWLEY Lancashire   map 8

Spread Eagle ⅝✴ £

Sawley BB7 4NH
TEL: (01200) 441202   FAX: (01200) 441973   COOKING **3**
WEBSITE: www.the-spreadeagle.co.uk   MODERN BRITISH
off A59, 3½m NE of Clitheroe   £20–£45

This well-patronised inn, dating back to the seventeenth century, sits on the
edge of the Forest of Bowland, and the huge windows of its three dining rooms
have magnificent views of the River Ribble and Pendle Hill. Inside, tables have
starched white tablecloths, waitresses wear black and white, and background
music to one visitor seemed faintly 'hymnal'. The menu is fairly brief, and
simplicity plays a strong part in dishes such as rich and creamy split pea velouté
soup, or another starter of grilled medallion of black pudding with braised
lentils and honey-mustard sauce. Main courses may feature firm-fleshed seared
fillet of sea bass, or slow-cooked boneless lamb shank with lemon, caper and
parsley sauce. Desserts such as 'substantial, gutsy' warm date and ginger
sponge, or orange and cardamom crème brûlée display a good variety of flavours.
For savoury-lovers, the cheeseboard might include local Lancashire creamy,
Garstang blue or Ribblesdale buffalo cheeses. On the fairly priced, eclectic wine
list California, Italy and France loom large, but there's also a Canadian Pinot
Gris; prices start at £9.95 for house French.

CHEF: Greig Barnes PROPRIETORS: Nigel and Ysanne Williams OPEN: Tue to Sun L 12 to 2, Tue to Sat D 6 to 8.45 MEALS: alc exc Sun L (main courses £8.50 to £16). Set L Sun £12.50 (2 courses) to £14.95. Set L and D Tue to Fri £9.25 (2 courses) to £12.20 SERVICE: not inc CARDS: Amex, MasterCard, Switch, Visa DETAILS: 180 seats. Private parties: 180 main room, 10 to 50 private rooms. Car park. Vegetarian meals. Children's helpings. No smoking. Wheelchair access (also WC). Music £5

SAXMUNDHAM Suffolk   map 6

▲ Bell Hotel 🌤 £   NEW ENTRY

31 High Street, Saxmundham IP17 1AF   COOKING 4
TEL/FAX: (01728) 602331   ANGLO-FRENCH
                                                              £22–£45

Since taking over this seventeenth-century coaching inn in autumn 2002, Andrew and Caroline Blackburn have smartened up the dining room and modernised the menu. The former now sports a green and white colour scheme, tables are topped with crisp white damask, and cutlery sparkles. And, while the bar area remains 'unreformed', the modern European menu is bang up to date. There have been a number of positive reports since the change of hands, with lots of praise for the 'real quality and refinement' of the cooking. Ingredients are good, and the menu is not so long on ingredients that it loses focus. Starters such as a salad of pan-fried scallops and pancetta feature smallish, 'meltingly tender' scallops, while a salad of asparagus is trimmed with sunblush tomatoes and brioche croûtons. A main course of roast poussin with asparagus and fondant potato came with a sauce so delicious that a spoon was required to consume every last drop. Desserts may feature the likes of cinnamon parfait with clementines, or a 'brilliant' passion-fruit tart with raspberry sauce. Service is pleasant, if not particularly slick. Prices indicate that value for money is a priority, a policy that extends to the wine list, where most of the bottles are under £20. Eight house wines start at £9.50 a bottle, £2.30 a glass.

CHEF/PROPRIETOR: Andrew Blackburn OPEN: Tue to Sun L 12 to 2, Tue to Sat D 6.30 to 9 CLOSED: D 25 Dec, 26 Dec, 1 week autumn, 1 week Feb MEALS: alc (main courses £9 to £16). Set L £10.50 (2 courses) to £13.50, Set D £16 SERVICE: not inc, card slips closed CARDS: MasterCard, Switch, Visa DETAILS: 30 seats. 15 seats outside. Private parties: 30 main room, 20 to 40 private rooms. Vegetarian meals. No children under 8 after 7.30pm. No smoking. No music ACCOMMODATION: 10 rooms, all with bath/shower. TV. B&B £35 to £80. Baby facilities

SCARBOROUGH North Yorkshire   map 9

Lanterna

33 Queen Street, Scarborough YO11 1HQ   COOKING 3
TEL/FAX: (01723) 363616   ITALIAN
WEBSITE: www.lanterna-ristorante.co.uk   £31–£55

This classic, defiantly not modern, Italian restaurant is as much part of Scarborough as the nearby Boyes department store. In its two small rooms, the walls are lined with press cuttings and testimonials from satisfied diners, some long departed. Two extant, faithful customers, though, enjoyed their tonno e fagioli and sirloin steak with mushroom Barolo sauce just as much as those of 30 years earlier. And yet there is no self-satisfied stasis. Daily specials, including fish that Giorgio selects daily at the harbour, and vegetables religiously *di stagione*, keep it lively. Italian produce – including wine, the remarkable prosciutto San Daniele, oils and truffles – is imported direct, and menus are Italian, in language and structure. A section of dishes including the revered white truffle, and two pages (one of hand-made pasti, another of risotti using Carnaroli rice) show how they are put to good use. Puddings include tiramisù, pannacotta, zabaglione and more, and service, by Rachel, is well informed and cheerful. Wines are almost all Italian, with house bottles at £13, many good things below £15, and wines from Italy's classic regions available in several vintages.

CHEF: Giorgio Alessio   PROPRIETORS: Giorgio and Rachel Alessio   OPEN: Mon to Sat D only 7 to 10   CLOSED: 2 weeks Oct, 25 to 26 Dec, 1 Jan   MEALS: alc D (main courses £12 to £30) SERVICE: not inc, card slips closed   CARDS: Delta, MasterCard, Switch, Visa   DETAILS: 30 seats. Private parties: 30 main room. Vegetarian meals. No children under 2. Wheelchair access (not WC). Music. Air-conditioned

SEAHAM Co Durham   map 10

▲ Seaham Hall Hotel ♥ 🍽 🕏

Lord Byron's Walk, Seaham SR7 7AG
TEL: (0191) 516 1400   FAX: (0191) 516 1410   COOKING 5
EMAIL: reservations@seaham-hall.com   MODERN EUROPEAN
WEBSITE: www.seaham-hall.com   £34–£87

The setting is wild, rugged and nothing less than 'beautiful': a Georgian mansion, much extended over the years, sitting amid fine gardens on a headland looking over the North Sea, not far south of Sunderland. A colour scheme of muted neutrals and contemporary sculptures sets a rather rarefied tone in the interior. Its first chef, under whom it shot into the Guide last year, has now departed (see Vermont Hotel, Newcastle upon Tyne), to be replaced by Matthew Weedon, who seems content to continue with the mix of familiar and gently inventive culinary styles set by his predecessor. A designer's sensibility is brought to bear on presentation, as witness a tian of Mediterranean vegetables – actually fashioned from aspic-set tomato containing a kind of ratatouille preserve – topped with a herbed raviolo of goats' cheese, the whole assemblage surrounded by cherry tomatoes, olives, red onion strips and blobs of tapenade. Roast scallops are fashionably teamed with a cauliflower purée, with shreds of pancetta completing the seasoning. These are well-judged dishes, admirable in their restraint and balance, and that sense of acuity is sustained into main courses such as pink-roast duck breast accompanied by sautéed foie gras, a ring of potato gratin, shredded Savoy cabbage and a few tiny turnips, or fillet of sea bass with a fricassee of baby leeks and morels in a Madeira jus. To finish, there may be oozy chocolate fondant, perfectly counterpointed by Guinness ice cream, or a well-made tarte Tatin of pineapple offset by smooth, intense coconut sorbet. The fixed-price menu of three courses plus coffee represents a good introduction to the style for those on a budget. Once again, readers suggest that the staff could lighten up a little.

The wine list gets its teeth into most regions while keeping the overall length under control, and prices are better value than you might expect, with a number of options under £20. The smartest bottles, including some vintage ports, are in 'private cellar' selections – perhaps they don't really want to sell them.

CHEF: Matthew Weedon   PROPRIETORS: Tom and Jocelyn Maxfield   OPEN: all week 12 to 2.30, 7 to 9.30   MEALS: alc (main courses £24 to £28). Set L £14.95 (2 courses) to £19.75, Set D £34. Light L menu available   SERVICE: not inc   CARDS: Amex, Delta, Diners, MasterCard, Switch, Visa DETAILS: 60 seats. 20 seats outside. Private parties: 12 main room, 12 to 120 private rooms. Car park. Vegetarian meals. Children's helpings. No smoking. Wheelchair access (also WC). Music. No mobile phones. Air-conditioned   ACCOMMODATION: 19 rooms, all with bath/shower. TV. Phone. B&B £165 to £500. Rooms for disabled. Baby facilities. Swimming pool (*The Which? Guide to Good Hotels*)

SEAVIEW Isle of Wight   map 2

▲ Seaview Hotel ⸬✳

High Street, Seaview PO34 5EX
TEL: (01983) 612711   FAX: (01983) 613729   COOKING **3**
EMAIL: reception@seaviewhotel.co.uk   ANGLO-FRENCH
WEBSITE: www.seaviewhotel.co.uk   £26–£47

The Seaview is a handsome double-fronted building on the town's high street, which leads directly down to the sea. A tall flagpole outside flies the Union Jack and St George's Cross, while, inside, lots of wood and sea-related artefacts enliven the bar and restaurant areas: a ship's wheel, a ship's mast across the ceiling, pictures of boats and various other bits maintaining the theme. The two dining rooms of contrasting styles – one bright and sunny, the other slightly more formal – offer the same menu. Chefs Michael Green and Mavis Barry make an effort to source as much local produce as possible, such as free-range chicken, served with oak-smoked garlic and rosemary risotto, and the fillet of beef served, perhaps, with hollandaise périgourdine and fondant potato. Chutney from the Garlic Farm may accompany a starter of chicken liver and mushroom pâté, with an apricot and garlic version served with a selection of English cheeses, and Mr Minghella's vanilla ice cream comes with caramelised apple and sultana suet pudding. Corney & Barrow house wines, at £10.95, start the bidding on the wine list, which puts an emphasis on France. The hotel is still run by Nick and Nicky Hayward despite the company name listed below.

CHEFS: Michael Green and Mavis Barry   PROPRIETORS: Techaid Ltd   OPEN: all week L 12 to 1.30, Mon to Sat D 7.30 to 9.30 (residents only Sun D)   MEALS: alc exc Sun L (main courses £11 to £17). Set L Sun £16.95   SERVICE: not inc, card slips closed   CARDS: Amex, Delta, Diners, MasterCard, Switch, Visa   DETAILS: 70 seats. 50 seats outside. Private parties: 40 main room. Car park. Vegetarian meals. Children's helpings. No children under 5 at D. No smoking in 1 dining room. Wheelchair access (not WC). No music. No mobile phones. Air-conditioned ACCOMMODATION: 16 rooms, all with bath/shower. TV. Phone. B&B £55 to £140. Baby facilities (*The Which? Guide to Good Hotels*) (£5)

Which? Online subscribers will find The Good Food Guide *online, along with other Which? guides and magazines, at* www.which.net. *See the website for information on how to become a subscriber.*

SELLACK Herefordshire   map 5

Lough Pool Inn 🍴 ✳ £

Sellack HR9 6LX   COOKING **4**
TEL: (01989) 730236   FAX: (01989) 730462   MODERN EUROPEAN
off A49, 3m NW of Ross-on-Wye   £28–£48

'Delightfully remote in feel but easily accessible,' is how one visitor described
this pub-cum-restaurant owned by Stephen Bull, himself a chef of some
renown, although he doesn't man the stoves these days. The black, white and
brick building, with its mustard-toned dining room, still functions as a pub,
although the cooking style is more in keeping with that of a restaurant. Chris
Leebon is now in charge of the kitchen, but the food remains in the Stephen Bull
vein. Old favourites such as haggis fritters and Hereford ribeye steak are still on
the menu, and North African/Eastern Mediterranean influences run through
some dishes, such as well-rendered mint and garlic chicken breast served with
chickpea purée, aubergine and olive purée and a 'terrific' smoked paprika sauce.
Fresh, accurately timed sea bass may be served with orange and saffron sauce,
while a first-class starter of crab mousse with cucumber relish comes topped
with a 'brilliant' golden-yellow jelly tasting of fish stock and saffron. Desserts
tend to be cakey: warm ginger cake with treacle toffee cream, perhaps, or
cranberry and frangipane tart. At busy times the staff may have difficulty in
keeping up with the pace; otherwise, service has been described as 'attentive
and professional'. Pub pricing means that most bottles on the well-chosen wine
list are under £20, starting at £11 (£2.75 a glass).

CHEF: Chris Leebon   PROPRIETOR: Stephen Bull   OPEN: Tue to Sun L 12 to 2, Tue to Sat D 7 to
9.15 (open all week Apr to late Sept)   CLOSED: 25 Dec, Sun D Nov to Mar   MEALS: alc (main
courses £10 to £16)   SERVICE: not inc, card slips closed   CARDS: Delta, MasterCard, Switch,
Visa   DETAILS: 80 seats. 40 seats outside. Private parties: 35 main room, 6 to 11 private rooms.
Car park. Vegetarian meals. Children's helpings. No smoking. Wheelchair access (not WC). No
music

SHAFTESBURY Dorset   map 2

▲ Wayfarers

Sherborne Causeway, Shaftesbury SP7 9PX   COOKING **4**
TEL/FAX: (01747) 852821   MODERN EUROPEAN
on A30, 2m W of Shaftesbury   £27–£51

The clematis-clad exterior of this large, prosperous-looking white-painted old
inn gives way to a low-ceilinged interior with a huge hearth (with a real log fire
when the weather calls for it) and stone walls. The décor is rather busy, with
sprays of dried flowers and lots of bric-à-brac. Equally, many of the dishes are
quite labour-intensive: for example, pan-seared duck foie gras comes in a puff
pastry tart with pear and quince purée and Calvados syrup, and crab, potato and
coriander mousseline is baked en croûte and accompanied by seared king
scallops, air-dried ham and roasted pepper purée. Seared fillets of lemon sole
with roasted prawns and pineapple cream might be among main courses, along
with fillet of lamb tortellini stuffed with haggis on a cream of butternut squash
and roasted tomatoes. For dessert, English and Continental cheeses are

alternatives to puddings of iced amaretto and espresso tiramisù. Raw materials are good, and freshness seems to be a top priority in Mark Newton's kitchen. The weekday set-price Bistrot menu is particularly good value, as is the mainly French wine list, which includes six by the glass from £2.20.

CHEF: Mark Newton   PROPRIETORS: Clare and Mark Newton   OPEN: Tue to Fri and Sun L 12 to 1.30, Tue to Sat D 7 to 9.15   CLOSED: 3 weeks after Christmas, approx 1 week June/July   MEALS: alc (main courses £16 to £17). Set L and D Mon to Fri £16.95   SERVICE: not inc, card slips closed   CARDS: Amex, Delta, MasterCard, Switch, Visa   DETAILS: 34 seats. 8 seats outside. Private parties: 34 main room. Car park. Vegetarian meals. No children under 8 at D. No smoking before 10.15pm at D. Wheelchair access (also women's WC). No music   ACCOMMODATION: 1 room, with bath/shower. B&B £55 to £70. No children under 12 (£5)

SHEDFIELD Hampshire   map 2

Wickham Vineyard ♥ ✳

Botley Road, Shedfield SO32 2HL
TEL: (01329) 832985   COOKING 5
EMAIL: erica@wickhamvineyard.co.uk   MODERN EUROPEAN
WEBSITE: www.wickhamvineyard.co.uk   £31–£71

It isn't often that one gets to look out over a vineyard when dining in Britain, yet that is the view from the picture window of this comfortably appointed restaurant, whose walls of pale custard and burgundy are covered in an array of modern artwork, all for sale. James Graham's cooking is strong on visual presentation. The menu changes with the seasons, with winter providing lambs' kidneys and sweetbreads in a puff pastry case with sauce diable, or sea bass with braised lettuce and caviar for starters. These may be followed by braised rabbit with a consommé of rabbit and ceps, or chump of lamb with white beans and tarragon. The simple descriptions belie the technical skills of the chef but help to underline the quality of the raw materials. For dessert there may be a selection of British and European cheeses, or puddings such as praline parfait, and bananas and caramel, each with a suggested glass of sweet wine. Service, headed by Erica Graham, is obliging, pleasant and knowledgeable. The vineyard's own wines, by the glass or bottle, open a characterful international list that stretches from £13 basics to interesting producers like Planeta and rarities such as the white Nuits-St-Georges from Dom. de l'Arlot.

CHEF: James Graham   PROPRIETORS: Gordon and Angela Channon   OPEN: Wed to Sun 12 to 2, 7 to 9 (6 to 8 Sun)   MEALS: Set L Wed to Sat £19.50, Set L Sun £17.50 (2 courses) to £19.50, Set D Wed to Sat £32.50 to £45, Set D Sun £25 to £45   SERVICE: not inc, card slips closed, 10% for parties of 7 or more   CARDS: Delta, MasterCard, Switch, Visa   DETAILS: 40 seats. 15 seats outside. Private parties: 50 main room. Car park. Vegetarian meals. Children's helpings. No smoking. Wheelchair access (also WC). Music. No mobile phones (£5)

(£5) *indicates that the restaurant has elected to participate in the* Good Food Guide *voucher scheme. For full details, see page 6.*

Blue Room Brasserie £

798 Chesterfield Road, Woodseats,
Sheffield S8 0SF   COOKING **4**
TEL: (0114) 255 2004   FAX: (0114) 255 1635   MODERN EUROPEAN-PLUS
WEBSITE: www.blueroombrasserie.co.uk   £26–£55

'Modern European with an Asian influence' is how the proprietors of the Blue Room sum up the style of cooking undertaken at this bright and cheery suburban eatery. So, if fish is your thing, that may mean choosing between Scottish smoked salmon with capers and half a lemon, or salmon sashimi with ginger, wasabi and hot soy dressing. For main courses, there are simple grills (steaks and chicken) as well as a variety of traditional and trendy dishes: among the former, perhaps pan-fried calf's liver and black pudding with shallot mash and a sage jus; among the latter, five-spice roast breast of duck with egg noodles, pak choi, spring onions, black-bean dressing, sweet chilli sauce and crisp won tons. Since last year, the wine list has been expanded and is now almost equally divided into Old and New World selections. Four house wines are £11.95 and £12.95 (£2.95 and £3.25 a glass).

CHEF: Christian Kent   PROPRIETORS: Christian, Scott and Lindsay Kent   OPEN: Sun L 12 to 3, Tue to Sat D 6 to 10 (10.30 Sat)   CLOSED: bank hols   MEALS: alc (main courses £8 to £17)   SERVICE: not inc   CARDS: Delta, Diners, MasterCard, Switch, Visa   DETAILS: 130 seats. Private parties: 120 main room, 12 to 40 private rooms. Car park. Vegetarian meals. Children's helpings. No cigars/pipes in dining room. Wheelchair access (also WC). Music. Air-conditioned

Carriages

289 Abbeydale Road South, Dore,
Sheffield S17 3LB   COOKING **3**
TEL: (0114) 235 0101   MODERN ENGLISH
WEBSITE: www.carriagesrestaurant.co.uk   £27–£51

Out of town on the Abbeydale Road South sits Carriages, a square building with large picture windows. Tastefully converted, with an attractive décor, the modern restaurant was originally a shop. Inside is a bit cramped, but there's nevertheless a light, airy feel. Main courses range from modish pan-seared sea bass with pancetta and prawn risotto to more traditional roast saddle of lamb with herb mash and sauce vierge. Starters might take in a terrine of ham hock and Gruyère with poached foie gras, or pan-seared scallops with asparagus in filo, and a meal could conclude with cinnamon crème brûlée, or baked chocolate tart with coconut ice cream. The carefully chosen wine list includes some good choices from all regions. House Merlot and Sauvignon Blanc are £11.90 the bottle, £2.75 the glass.

CHEF: James Riley   PROPRIETOR: Cary Brown   OPEN: Sun L 12 to 3, Wed to Sat D 7 to 10 CLOSED: first 2 weeks Jan   MEALS: alc Sat D (main courses £10 to £16). Set L Sun £18.95, Set D Wed to Fri £22   SERVICE: not inc   CARDS: MasterCard, Switch, Visa   DETAILS: 60 seats. Private parties: 60 main room. Car park. Children's helpings. No-smoking area. Wheelchair access (also WC). Music

Greenhead House ✗

84 Burncross Road, Chapeltown,
Sheffield S35 1SF
TEL/FAX: (0114) 246 9004

COOKING 2
MODERN EUROPEAN
£30–£59

To get to the entrance one goes to the back of the house, via the attractive, well-tended garden, and readers talk of a warm welcome on arrival. The dining room has rustic red and green curtains and yellow walls, and tables are set with starched white linen. Four-course dinners are priced according to the main dish chosen. Start perhaps with mushroom soup with ceps (soups are a strength, enhanced by own-made brown bread), then choose between home-made sorbet, a fruit dish (melon and Parma ham, say), or maybe poached salmon. Some main dishes rely on time-honoured combinations like beef fillet medallions with horseradish sauce, although grilled lemon sole fillets can come with a roast pepper and a rocket and lobster salad. Desserts have included ginger shortbread with rhubarb and clotted cream, or a compote of cherries and blackcurrant with elderflower cream. This is not daring cooking, but for 20 years now the Allens have been providing Sheffield with good food and warm and relaxed service. A short, good-value wine list spans the world and rounds off with an interesting 'fine wines' list. House wines are £13.50.

CHEF: Neil Allen   PROPRIETORS: Neil and Anne Allen   OPEN: Thur to Fri L 12 to 1, Wed to Sat D 7 to 9   CLOSED: 25 Dec to 1 Jan, 2 weeks Easter, 2 weeks Aug   MEALS: alc L (main courses £9.50). Set D £33 to £38. Light L menu available   SERVICE: not inc, card slips closed   CARDS: Amex, Delta, MasterCard, Switch, Visa   DETAILS: 32 seats. 10 seats outside. Private parties: 36 main room. Car park. Children's helpings. No children under 5. No smoking. Wheelchair access (not WC). No music. No mobile phones

Rafters

220 Oakbrook Road, Nether Green,
Sheffield S11 7ED
TEL: (0114) 230 4819

COOKING 4
MODERN BRITISH
£37–£48

Although the setting remains much as before – an octagonal dining room with a high-pitched ceiling above a shop – there have been changes here since the last edition of the Guide, with head chef Marcus Lane now joint chef/proprietor with Michael Sabin. At inspection, their wide-ranging, modern European style produced a well-balanced starter of steamed asparagus between slices of lightly toasted brioche laced with truffle oil, served with a lemon and herb hollandaise, while 'mille-feuille' of crab featured white crabmeat mixed with finely diced cucumber between deep-fried won ton pastry leaves with sauce gribiche. Among main courses have been artistically presented rosemary-roast cannon of lamb, the 'pink, lean and tender' meat sliced and set on a tartlet of parsnip purée, surrounded by baby spring vegetables and finished with a sherry vinegar jus. Other choices might include caramelised pork loin with wild mushroom mousseline and a Puy lentil sauce with mustard and Madeira, or roast cod fillet in a pistachio and herb crust with roast peppers stuffed with black pudding in a red wine sauce. Finish perhaps with white chocolate mousse with wild berry compote and milk chocolate sauce. Wines are arranged by style with helpful tasting notes. Prices throughout the list are pitched low, starting at £11.50 for house French.

CHEFS/PROPRIETORS: Marcus Lane and Michael Sabin   OPEN: Mon and Wed to Sat D only 7 to 9.30 (10 Fri and Sat)   CLOSED: 1 to 10 Jan   MEALS: Set D £24.95   SERVICE: not inc, card slips closed   CARDS: Amex, Delta, MasterCard, Switch, Visa   DETAILS: 40 seats. Private parties: 40 main room. Vegetarian meals. Children's helpings. No children under 5. Music. No mobile phones. Air-conditioned

Richard Smith at Thyme ▼ £

32–34 Sandygate Road, Crosspool,
Sheffield S10 5RY
TEL: (01142) 666096
WEBSITE: www.thymeforfood.com

COOKING 5
MODERN BRITISH/MEDITERRANEAN
£17–£58

The western outskirts of Sheffield are home to this popular restaurant, where a small porch with faux orange trees in terracotta pots leads to a very modern bar lounge with French windows. Beyond is the contemporary dining room, the blue/grey walls of which give a cool, minimalist cast. Despite the sophisticated look, 'one feels welcome just stepping inside the door', according to one visitor, although others have found the 'bistro-like atmosphere' noisy. 'Robust, gutsy flavours, hearty portions and direct and simple food' is how the proprietors describe their style of cooking. This manifests itself in regional dishes such as Yorkshire fish and chips and breast of Gressingham duck with 'posh duck pastie', but the menu is more southern Mediterranean than northern England: Moroccan-style spiced lamb 'spring roll' with aubergine, feta, chickpeas, mint and cucumber may be followed by a colourful, tasty bowlful of Tuscan salad comprising mushrooms, buffalo mozzarella and pesto wafers, or a casserole of lamb, merguez sausage, white beans, sherry, peppers and saffron mash. Well-made desserts might include rhubarb jelly with bavarois or crème brûlée with raspberries and shortbread biscuit. Reports on service vary from 'alert and friendly' to overzealous. Wines are mostly well-priced bistro gluggers under £20, but astutely picked; the small selection of fine wines shows the same eye for quality. Bottles start at £12.50.

CHEFS: Simon Wild and Tim Vincent   PROPRIETORS: Richard and Victoria Smith   OPEN: all week 12 to 2, 6 to 10   CLOSED: 26 Dec and 1 Jan   MEALS: alc (main courses £9.50 to £18.50). Set L £5 (2 courses) to £7.50, Set D £15 to £22.50   SERVICE: not inc   CARDS: Amex, MasterCard, Switch, Visa   DETAILS: 90 seats. Private parties: 70 main room, 8 to 30 private rooms. Vegetarian meals. Children's helpings. No-smoking area. Wheelchair access (also WC). Music. Air-conditioned (£5)

Slammers

| NEW ENTRY |

625A Eccleshall Road, Sheffield S11 8PT
TEL: (0114) 268 0999
WEBSITE: www.slammersseafood.co.uk

COOKING 3
SEAFOOD
£31–£50

Slammers is named after the glass vessels in which the house speciality is served: six small glasses each containing a different type of cold seafood, including a large shell-on king prawn, rings of squid lightly fried in tempura, a portion of smoked salmon, and crumbed, fried salmon with a hot chilli sauce.

There's much more in the way of fishy things, from dressed crab to grilled monkfish with a choice of sauces. Pan-fried sea bass accompanied by new potatoes crushed with sunblush tomatoes and basil has demonstrated pinpoint timing, while a half-lobster with mayonnaise may be simply cooked and presented with mustard mayonnaise and sweet pickle. Raspberries with mascarpone make a simple but satisfying end to the meal. A couple of vegetarian options and one meat main course complete the picture. There is a reasonable wine list (nothing exotic), with the majority of bottles costing under £12.

CHEF: Gareth Nutter   PROPRIETOR: Cary Brown   OPEN: Tue to Sat L 12 to 2, Mon to Sat D 6.30 to 10   MEALS: alc (main courses £11 to £16)   SERVICE: not inc, 10% for parties of 8 or more   CARDS: MasterCard, Switch, Visa   DETAILS: 70 seats. Private parties: 80 main room. Vegetarian meals. No-smoking area. Wheelchair access (also WC). Music

SHELF West Yorkshire   map 8

Bentley's 🍴✕

12 Wade House Road, Shelf HX3 7PB
TEL: (01274) 690992   FAX: (01274) 690011   COOKING 4
EMAIL: bentleys@btinternet.com   MODERN BRITISH
WEBSITE: www.bentleys-foodandwine.co.uk   £18–£45

Visitors have recalled the Tardis on discovery of the larger-than-seems-possible basement dining area of this modest terraced house. A customer returning after 18 months found the same 'terrific value' and the food 'probably even better!' Bread and petits fours made on the premises demonstrate a commitment that is backed up by sound technical skills and good produce. An early spring set lunch menu majoring on reassuring comfort included leek and potato soup, and mussels in wine and cream, then haddock and prawn Mornay on spinach with mashed potato, along with duck breast with black pudding and cassis juice, and wound up with rhubarb crumble with brandy cream, and caramelised rice pudding with red berries. More complex alliances appear on the evening menu: Lune Valley duck pan-roasted and served on a lime, ginger and apricot sauce with baby pak choi. House wines – there are four, all available by the glass – start at £9.95 and are followed by 30 or so decently selected bottles, most of them under £20.

CHEFS: Paul Bentley and Anthony Bickers   PROPRIETORS: Paul and Pam Bentley   OPEN: Tue to Fri L 12 to 2, Tue to Sat D 6.30 to 9   MEALS: alc (main courses £10 to £16.50). Set L £5.95 (1 course) to £10.25   SERVICE: not inc, card slips closed   CARDS: Delta, MasterCard, Switch, Visa   DETAILS: 68 seats. Private parties: 24 main room, 10 to 24 private rooms. Vegetarian meals. Children's helpings. No smoking. Music. Air-conditioned

---

If 'vegetarian meals' is noted in the details at the end of an entry, this means that a restaurant routinely lists at least one vegetarian starter and main course on menus. Other restaurants, however, may offer good vegetarian choices if you let them know in advance, so it is worthwhile phoning to enquire.

▲ Charlton House Hotel, Mulberry Restaurant ▼ ✣

Charlton Road, Shepton Mallet BA4 4PR
TEL: (01749) 342008   FAX: (01749) 346362
EMAIL: enquiry@charltonhouse.com   COOKING 5
WEBSITE: www.charltonhouse.com   MODERN BRITISH
1m E of Shepton Mallet on A361 towards Frome   £32–£86

If you get a certain sense of *déjà vu* when you walk through Charlton House's rather grand portals, fear not. It's because Roger and Monty Saul, founders of Mulberry (purveyors of fabrics and home furnishings) are also the owners of this country-house hotel, which incorporates a conference centre and restaurant. The company's trademark-burnished red and gold 'autumn leaf' colour palette sets the tone for the interior décor, which carries over to the dining room.

The kitchen's ambitions are high, and those ambitions are generally met. One visitor was pleased with the 'very fresh and tantalising' flavours of a springtime lunch, while another saluted the 'excellent flavours', which 'made the best of high-class ingredients'. To start, a terrine of lamb and chargrilled Mediterranean vegetables with fennel and olive salad and warm focaccia expertly combines discrete ingredients, flavours and textures. Organic salmon with morels, asparagus, broad beans and home-made garganelli pasta may be enlivened by an impressive, intense, chive-flecked sauce for a main course. Look out for seasonally inspired desserts such as poached rhubarb with pannacotta and a shortbread biscuit with basil sorbet, or red berry crème brûlée with tarragon sorbet. Service is very smooth, very professional, very French, and the wine list is engagingly modern, well chosen and arranged by style, matching New World against Old all the way. If your budget's tight, it's probably best to stick to the good range of wines by the glass (19 at £3 to £7.75), as prices are on the high side and very few bottles come in under £20.

CHEF: Adam Fellows   PROPRIETORS: Mr and Mrs R.J. Saul   OPEN: all week 12.30 to 2, 7.30 to 9.30 (10 Fri and Sat)   MEALS: Set L £14.50 (2 courses) to £45, Set D £45 to £54. Light L menu available   SERVICE: not inc, 5% for parties of 8 or more   CARDS: Amex, Delta, Diners, MasterCard, Switch, Visa   DETAILS: 90 seats. 16 seats outside. Private parties: 100 main room, 12 to 70 private rooms. Car park. Vegetarian meals. Children's helpings. No smoking. Wheelchair access (also WC). Music. No mobile phones   ACCOMMODATION: 17 rooms, all with bath/shower. TV. Phone. B&B £112 to £315. Baby facilities. Swimming pool. Fishing (*The Which? Guide to Good Hotels*)

A list of London restaurants by cuisine can be found near the front of the book.

Some restaurants leave credit card slips open even though they also make a fixed (or 'optional') service charge. The Guide strongly disapproves of this practice as it may result in consumers unknowingly paying twice for service.

SHERE Surrey   map 3

Kinghams ✤

Gomshall Lane, Shere GU5 9HE
TEL: (01483) 202168   COOKING 3
WEBSITE: www.kinghams-restaurant.co.uk   MODERN ENGLISH
just off A25 Dorking to Guildford road   £33–£60

Low ceilings and beams, coupled with small rooms centred around a hearth, give a distinctly olde-worlde feel to Kinghams. The menu, however, has a more contemporary feel. You are invited 'to begin' with perhaps pan-fried medallion of venison on celeriac fondant, or thinly sliced scallops marinated in a sharp lime, spring onion and tomato dressing. Main courses offer a twist to some traditional staples, such as breast of Gressingham duck in a citrus marinade with braised pak choi, or roast partridge with caramelised parsnips and sweet onion chutney. A daily-changing fish board extends choice with, perhaps, steamed mussels with shallots, or fillet of halibut topped with bell peppers. Puddings include dark chocolate bavarois on a coffee sauce, or iced Grand Marnier parfait, and for the indecisive a trio of apple desserts may appeal: sorbet, mini-tarte Tatin and baked apple stuffed with mascarpone, walnuts and praline. Anecdotal information about the producers adds spice to a well-balanced, mostly European wine list, which also highlights organic wines. South America is a force in the house range (£11.95 to £15.95). Five by the glass start at £3.

CHEF/PROPRIETOR: Paul Baker   OPEN: Tue to Sun L 12.15 to 2, Tue to Sat D 7 to 9   CLOSED: 25 Dec to 4 Jan   MEALS: alc (main courses £11 to £22). Set L £13.95 (2 courses), Set L Sun and Set D Tue to Thur £15.95 (2 courses)   SERVICE: not inc   CARDS: Amex, Delta, Diners, MasterCard, Switch, Visa   DETAILS: 50 seats. 20 seats outside. Private parties: 50 main room, 20 to 30 private rooms. Car park. Vegetarian meals. No smoking. Wheelchair access (not WC). No music. No mobile phones (£5)

SHINFIELD Berkshire   map 2

L'Ortolan ▾ ✤

Church Lane, Shinfield RG2 9BY
TEL: (0118) 988 8500   FAX: (0118) 988 9338 | NEW CHEF |
EMAIL: info@lortolan.com   MODERN FRENCH
WEBSITE: www.lortolan.com   £42–£110

Given the view from outside – an old, square-shaped, red-brick vicarage with a battlemented roof line – the 'mildly oriental minimalist' interior can come as a bit of a surprise. It feels sophisticated, moneyed, and has an air of 'posh anonymity' about it. There is a fairly traditional bar, a conservatory with natural-coloured blinds and generous sofas, and a dining room in brown, beige and white with suede-covered chairs and tall glass vases filled with sprouting bamboo.

Chef Alan Murchison has departed for Chewton Glen, New Milton (see entry), and has been replaced here by Daniel Galmiche, formerly at Harveys in Bristol (now regrettably closed). The restaurant was unable to furnish us with new menus before we went to press, nor can we confirm the prices below, but if the chef's past performance is anything to go by, first-class ingredients, considerable cooking skills and vivid presentation are to be expected. Staff are plentiful and attentive, and the wine list has real verve. New World selections are short but smart, and European countries include cutting-edge wines such as southern Italians from Maffini and Planeta alongside top-notch traditional bottles. Eight house wines range from £15 to £23 (£4.50 to £6 a glass), and there are more worth trying under £20, plus a goodly number of half-bottles.

CHEF: Daniel Galmiche PROPRIETOR: Peter Newman OPEN: all week L 11.45 to 2, Mon to Sat D 6.30 to 10 CLOSED: 27 to 30 Dec, bank hols MEALS: alc (main courses £25 to £32). Set L Mon to Sat £27 to £49, Set L Sun £30 to £40, Set D £49 SERVICE: not inc CARDS: Amex, Delta, Diners, MasterCard, Switch, Visa DETAILS: 64 seats. 30 seats outside. Private parties: 44 main room, 8 to 20 private rooms. Car park. Vegetarian meals. Children's helpings. No smoking. Wheelchair access (not WC). No music. No mobile phones

---

SHIPHAM Somerset
map 2

▲ Daneswood House 🍴 ✳

Cuck Hill, Shipham BS25 1RD
TEL: (01934) 843145   FAX: (01934) 843824
EMAIL: info@daneswoodhotel.co.uk
WEBSITE: www.daneswoodhotel.co.uk
S of Bristol off A38 towards Cheddar; hotel is on left as you leave the village

COOKING 2
MODERN BRITISH
£32–£66

Having negotiated three steep hairpin bends to arrive at this many-gabled Edwardian house, you are rewarded with stunning views. New chef Ross Duncan offers an ambitious carte and gourmet menu, but simplicity seems to have won favour with most diners. A 'simple, very effective' salad of pickled squid and marinated mackerel with hazelnut dressing, and 'excellent' lightly smoked mussels with coriander have been good starters. 'Succulent' roast cod on onion mash gets the thumbs up, while pan-fried leg of English lamb with dauphinois potatoes showed variable execution. To finish there might be deep-fried strawberries with well-made clotted cream ice cream and strawberry coulis. Service is unpretentious and welcoming. France dominates the wine list, which has a good range of half-bottles and a selection of 15 house wines priced from £10.95 to £17.95.

CHEF: Ross Duncan PROPRIETORS: David and Elise Hodges OPEN: Sun to Fri L 12 to 2, all week D 7 to 9.30 MEALS: alc D (main courses £14 to £22). Set L £17.95 (2 courses) to £19.95. Bar menu available SERVICE: not inc CARDS: Amex, Delta, Diners, MasterCard, Switch, Visa DETAILS: 50 seats. Private parties: 35 main room, 10 to 14 private rooms. Car park. Vegetarian meals. Children's helpings. No smoking. Wheelchair access (also WC). Occasional music. No mobile phones ACCOMMODATION: 17 rooms, all with bath/shower. TV. Phone. B&B £79.50 to £150. Baby facilities (*The Which? Guide to Good Hotels*) £5

The Guide is totally independent, accepts no free hospitality, and survives on the number of copies sold each year.

London Round-ups listing additional restaurants that may be worth a visit can be found after the main London section.

SHREWSBURY Shropshire   map 5

Sol Brasserie 🗇 £ 🛠

82 Wyle Cop, Shrewsbury SY1 1UT
TEL: (01743) 340560
EMAIL: solbrasserie@btopenworld.com

COOKING 2
BRASSERIE
£26–£44

The narrow frontage here zings with royal blue and marigold. In November 2002 the previous owners sold to members of their kitchen team, and now Toby Leech remains as chef/proprietor. He has sought to continue the easy-on-the-palate style of brasserie cooking. A crispy duck salad in a tiny bowl with red onion, cucumber and coriander dressed in soy juggled 'strong flavours that were a match for each other', while a main course of excellent, carefully timed lamb confit came with buttered mash and a stock sauce pungent with garlic and rosemary. Some menu items seem to tease ('beans on toast' is white haricots on ciabatta), but vegetarians are properly catered for, and a good selection of desserts embraces coffee and walnut parfait, or roast pineapple served on glass noodles with a syrup of vanilla and lime. A simpler lunch menu brings smoked haddock topped with Welsh rarebit, dishes of tagliatelle or penne (with pea and bacon, say), and ribeye steaks and home-made burgers. Service is laid-back but efficient, and the short wine list opens with French Chardonnay and Montepulciano d'Abruzzo at £10.95.

CHEF/PROPRIETOR: Toby Leech   OPEN: Tue to Sat 12 to 2.30, 6.30 to 9.30   MEALS: alc (main courses £6.50 to £13)   SERVICE: not inc   CARDS: Switch, Visa   DETAILS: 40 seats. Private parties: 26 main room, 8 to 20 private rooms. Vegetarian meals. Children's helpings. No smoking. Music. No mobile phones

SHURDINGTON Gloucestershire   map 2

▲ Greenway 🛠 | NEW ENTRY |

Shurdington GL51 4UG
TEL: (01242) 862352   FAX: (01242) 862780
EMAIL: greenway@btconnect.com
WEBSITE: www.the-greenway.co.uk

COOKING 7
MODERN FRENCH
£35–£129

Last in the Guide as a main entry four years ago, Greenway returns with a big splash. The beautiful and imposing old Cotswold manor house ('hairy with creepers') has been conservatively modernised, aiming for posh rather than exciting, with deep sofas in the lounges, and a dining room in the conservatory extension at the back. Adam Simmonds, who has worked at Le Manoir and Paul Heathcote's (see entries, Great Milton and Longridge) comes up with plenty of interesting-sounding ideas: tortellini of oysters and foie gras with watercress bouillon, perhaps, or a salad of sautéed langoustines with artichoke purée and rhubarb sorbet.

Impeccable raw materials have combined with 'fabulous workmanship' to produce, for example, a starter of confit pork belly and home-made black pudding, alternating with tiny slices of scallop, surrounded by a pool of clear, warmly flavoured oil. Although the food may be a little short on individual character and personality, the kitchen's skills are not in question. Along with a few of his distinguished colleagues, Adam Simmonds produces slow-cooked rare meat: for example, an 'impressive and luscious' cannon of lamb, served on tomato couscous with a few dice of bright green mint jelly, an aubergine purée and an artistic swirl of cream-coloured froth. Also 'technically perfect' has been a caramel soufflé – 'deeply, intensely flavoured' – served with a prune ice cream.

Presentation is a serious matter, dishes are quite elaborate, and meals come with a host of extras: a jellied oyster in the lounge, a deep-fried quail's egg at table, and pineapple 'choucroute' and sorbet before dessert (all of which disjointed the meal for one reader). Service from a mix of nationalities is formal, professional, assiduous and knowledgeable. Wine prices on the stylistically arranged list tend to be high (£62 for an albeit excellent Californian sparkler, Quartet), although range and variety are good. Half a dozen house wines sell for between £15 and £22.50.

CHEF: Adam Simmonds   PROPRIETOR: Grandiose Management   OPEN: all week 12 to 2.30, 7 to 9.30   MEALS: alc exc Sun L (main courses £14.50 to £26.50). Set L Mon to Sat £21 to £90, Set L Sun £25, Set D £32 to £90   SERVICE: not inc   CARDS: Amex, Delta, Diners, MasterCard, Switch, Visa   DETAILS: 40 seats. 24 seats outside. Private parties: 56 main room, 6 to 20 private rooms. Car park. Vegetarian meals. Children's helpings. No smoking. Wheelchair access (also WC). Music. No mobile phones   ACCOMMODATION: 21 rooms, all with bath/shower. TV. Phone. B&B £99 to £280. Rooms for disabled (£5)

SKIPTON North Yorkshire   map 8

Le Caveau ![smoking banned] £

86 High Street, Skipton BD23 1JJ   COOKING 2
TEL: (01756) 794274   ANGLO-FRENCH
                                                               £24–£45

This pint-sized restaurant in the centre of this unspoilt market town is reached by careful descent of a flight of very steep steps. Inside, the napery is all stiffly starched, but the staff are just the opposite, marshalling visitors around the confined space with friendly efficiency. Richard Barker uses as much local produce as he can lay his hands on, turning it into successful dishes such as plump and well-timed scallops with a timbale of Savoy cabbage and tarragon sauce, followed perhaps by a very fresh, generous serving of sea bass with lemon butter sauce. Other reference points have included spicy Moroccan vegetable tagine, lamb shank sauced with white port and mint, and indulgences such as Tia Maria cheesecake with Baileys crème anglaise to finish. The English and Continental cheeses have included a blue goats' cheese from Croatia, which must surely be a first for Skipton. Exemplary value distinguishes the wine list, which darts about the globe in search of interesting flavours and kicks off with house wines from Georges Duboeuf at £9.95.

CHEF: Richard Barker   PROPRIETORS: Brian Womersley and Richard Barker   OPEN: Tue to Sat 12 to 1.45, 7 to 9.30   CLOSED: first week Jan, 30 May to 8 June, 5 to 21 Sept   MEALS: alc (main courses L £8 to £16, D £10 to £16.50)   SERVICE: not inc   CARDS: Amex, Delta, MasterCard, Switch, Visa   DETAILS: 28 seats. Private parties: 30 main room, 10 to 18 private rooms. Vegetarian meals. No smoking. Music (£5)

---

 indicates that smoking is banned in all eating areas.

Brilliant ✳ £

72–76 Western Road, Southall UB2 5DZ
TEL: (020) 8574 1928   FAX: (020) 8574 0276
EMAIL: brilliantrestaurant@hotmail.com
WEBSITE: www.brilliantrestaurant.com

COOKING 3
NORTH INDIAN
£27–£63

Every August, this seminal Southall Indian closes its doors and takes a holiday: the time-out 'gives our customers a chance to try other restaurants', say the Anand brothers. Come September, the regulars start to return and – judging by reports – standards seldom falter. The menu still has a sprinkling of East African specialities reflecting the owners' native Kenya (deep-fried cassava chips and tandoori tilapia fish, for example) as well as ever-reliable aloo tikki (vegetable patties with 'rich tamarind sauce and excellent chickpeas'). Distinctive, freshly ground spices are the key to perennial favourites like methi chicken and king prawn masala, while bowls of keema peas or palak lamb with spinach are ideally suited to large groups. Mattar paneer and channa masala have shone out among the choice of vegetables along with superlative bhindis (okra), which are lightly cooked to preserve their texture. Rice never disappoints, while chapattis are reckoned to be a better bet than naan in the bread department. House wine is £9, although beer and lassi are probably more suitable partners for the food.

CHEF: D.K. Anand   PROPRIETORS: K.K. and D.K. Anand   OPEN: Tue to Fri 12 to 2.30, Tue to Sun 6 to 11   MEALS: alc (main courses £4.50 to £13). Set L and D £17.50 (min 10)   SERVICE: net prices, card slips closed   CARDS: Amex, Delta, Diners, MasterCard, Switch, Visa   DETAILS: 250 seats. Private parties: 120 main room, 80 to 120 private rooms. Car park. Vegetarian meals. Children's helpings. No smoking in 1 dining room. Wheelchair access (also WC). Music. Air-conditioned (£5)

Madhu's   [NEW ENTRY]

39 South Road, Southall UB1 1SW
TEL: (020) 8574 1897   FAX: (020) 8813 8639
EMAIL: info@madusonline.com
WEBSITE: www.madhusonline.com

COOKING 3
NORTH INDIAN
£24–£57

After a fire destroyed the original premises, a new Madhu's rose in its place in 2003, with upmarket décor, new ideas and a glossy, modern-sounding menu – although plenty of Sanjay Anand's old favourites are still in evidence. You now walk over a glass display containing water, whose colour changes in a repeated pattern, in fact the whole place looks – and feels – chic, smart and distinctly cosmopolitan. Two new chefs have been flown over from Delhi and it shows in specialities such as tandoori prawns marinated in achari (pickle) spices, as well as re-workings of stalwarts like aloo tikki with sambal and methi chicken. Masala fish is tilapia cooked in a 'lively' sauce, while dhal makhani is based on black lentils 'stirred for many hours', says the menu. Details such as pilau rice, well-made breads and coffee from an Italian espresso machine flesh out the picture, and neatly uniformed staff are keenly attentive. The revamped wine list is a knowledgeably assembled slate, kicking off with house Bordeaux at £2.50 a glass, £8 a bottle.

CHEFS: H. Bhanot and J.P. Singh   PROPRIETORS: Sanjay and Sanjeev Anand   OPEN: Mon and Wed to Fri L 12 to 3, Wed to Mon D 6 to 11.30   CLOSED: 25 Dec, bank hols L   MEALS: alc (main courses £6 to £12). Set L £17.50, Set D £20. Bar menu available   SERVICE: not inc, card slips closed   CARDS: Amex, Delta, Diners, MasterCard, Switch, Visa   DETAILS: 102 seats. Private parties: 45 main room, 20 to 30 private rooms. Vegetarian meals. Wheelchair access (also WC). Music. Air-conditioned £5

SOUTHAMPTON Hampshire   map 2

Oxfords   NEW ENTRY

35–36 Oxford Street, Southampton SO14 3DS
TEL: (023) 8022 4444   FAX: (023) 8022 2284   COOKING 2
EMAIL: bookings@oxfordsrestaurant.com   MODERN EUROPEAN
WEBSITE: www.oxfordsrestaurant.com   £25–£56

This smart, contemporary brasserie, with pavement seating, is airy, with a wooden floor and bare tables providing the backdrop for an equally contemporary menu. Brasserie stalwarts like caramelised red onion and goats' cheese tart have found favour among starters, along with a salad of wild mushrooms and new potatoes with spinach and rocket and a basil and sun-blush tomato dressing. Fish is a speciality: perhaps baked suprême of cod topped with crisp pancetta on parsley mash surrounded by mushy peas, or grilled halibut on pappardelle with creamed spinach. The kitchen does a bit of a globetrot, too, coming up with Mexican-style chicken wrap with guacamole and mango salsa, and Thai-marinated strips of beef with water chestnuts, baby corn, pak choi and rice noodles. Desserts are more predictable, among them sticky toffee pudding and chocolate brownie. Service, by young staff, is efficient and attentive. The global wine list of around 50 wines offers 16 by the glass. A French duo starts the bidding at £11.50 (£3.30 a glass).

CHEF: Rob Galbraith   PROPRIETORS: Simon Foderingham and Jimmy Hajiantoni   OPEN: all week L 12 to 2.30 (6 Sun), Mon to Sat D 6 to 10.30   MEALS: alc (main courses L £6 to £15, D £10.50 to £15.50)   SERVICE: not inc   CARDS: Amex, Delta, MasterCard, Switch, Visa   DETAILS: 110 seats. 36 seats outside. Private parties: 100 main room. Vegetarian meals. No-smoking area. Wheelchair access (also WC). Music. Air-conditioned

SOUTHPORT Merseyside   map 7

Warehouse Brasserie £

30 West Street, Southport PR8 1QN
TEL: (01704) 544662   FAX: (01704) 500074   COOKING 3
EMAIL: info@warehousebrasserie.co.uk   GLOBAL
WEBSITE: www.warehousebrasserie.co.uk   £19–£52

A smart and luxurious brasserie fashioned out of an old clothes warehouse, the fittingly named Warehouse Brasserie attracts a clientele that extends upwards to the well-heeled glamorous young types you get around these parts. The dinner menu, divided up into small dishes – buttered pink trout with Bury black pudding and mustard cream, say – salads, large dishes and side dishes, is wide ranging, offering pasta, oriental-inspired flavours such as satay and teriyaki, as well as modern European dishes such as excellent tilapia served with jerk tomatoes and ratatouille. There is also more straightforward stuff such as fillet steak and fish 'n chips. Ingredients are of good quality, and cooking is sound. The short wine list reflects the varied clientele, with French house wine starting at £10.95 and finishing with California's Opus One 1998 at £195. The atmosphere can get noisy, but service manages to keep up with the heady pace.

CHEF: Marc Vérité PROPRIETOR: Paul Adams OPEN: Mon to Sat 12 to 1.45, 5.30 to 10 MEALS: alc (main courses £7 to £16). Set L £7.95 (2 courses) to £9.95, Set D Mon to Thur £10.95 (2 courses) to £13.95 SERVICE: not inc, 10% for parties of 8 or more CARDS: Amex, Delta, MasterCard, Switch, Visa DETAILS: 110 seats. Private parties: 74 main room, 40 to 50 private rooms. Vegetarian meals. Children's helpings. No cigars/pipes. Music. Air-conditioned

SOUTHSEA Hampshire   map 2

Bistro Montparnasse

103 Palmerston Road, Southsea PO5 3PS   COOKING 2
TEL: (023) 9281 6754   MODERN EUROPEAN
WEBSITE: www.bistromontparnasse.co.uk   £26–£45

Originally a private house on one of Southsea's main thoroughfares close to the seafront, this pleasingly decorated neighbourhood restaurant serves its town well. Fixed-price lunch and dinner menus change regularly, supplies are local where possible, and the kitchen takes on board flavours and influences from around the globe. A filo basket of crispy duck with glazed pineapple tips its hat to the orient, while noisettes of lamb with calves' sweetbreads and a sweet wine and truffle jus, and ribeye steak with potato and onion confit and port sauce bring matters closer to home. Each day there's also a fish special, while the list of straightforward desserts might run to hot chocolate pudding, or lime and tequila mousse. Seasonal gourmet menus are a feature, and the wine list is a well-chosen slate offering quality and fair value. Eight house selections kick off at £12 a bottle, £2.40 a glass.

CHEFS: Kevin Bingham and Andrew Blakeledge PROPRIETORS: John Saunders and Kevin Bingham OPEN: Tue to Sat 12 to 2, 7 to 9.30 CLOSED: 25 and 26 Dec, first 2 weeks Mar, first 2 weeks Oct MEALS: Set L £12 (2 courses) to £15, Set D £18.50 (2 courses) to £23.50. Light L menu available SERVICE: not inc CARDS: Delta, MasterCard, Switch, Visa DETAILS: 36 seats. Private parties: 36 main room, 10 to 30 private rooms. Vegetarian meals. Wheelchair access (not WC). Music

SOUTHWOLD Suffolk   map 6

▲ Crown Hotel

90 High Street, Southwold IP18 6DP
TEL: (01502) 722275 FAX: (01502) 727263   COOKING 2
EMAIL: crown.reception@adnams.co.uk   MODERN BRITISH-PLUS
WEBSITE: www.adnams.co.uk   £32–£45

A relaxed airy dining room makes a good contrast to the snug bar of this popular East Anglian fixture, set on the High Street of the picturesque seaside town. Rufus Wickham, who took over the stoves in early 2003, offers up two- and three-course menus that might begin with aromatic and creamy mussel and saffron soup, or a salad of 'tender and succulent' rare beef fillet and gherkin, carrot and onion in a light vinaigrette. Sautéed guinea fowl with braised parsnip, turnip, swede and wild mushrooms and wonderfully buttery mash has been a main course pointing to some good ingredients handled deftly, while a pot-au-feu of cod, brill, mussels and clams had an excellent broth. Delicately vanilla flavoured pannacotta alongside firm, tangy rhubarb, and a blood-orange and mango jelly rounded off an early summer meal. Service is well trained and intelligent. At the time of going to press, a full wine list was not available to the Guide, but we note an interesting spread of 20 house and 'classic' wines, all except one under £20 and all available by the glass, from £2 to £5.

CHEF: Rufus Wickham PROPRIETOR: Adnams Sole Bay Brewery OPEN: all week 12.30 to 1.30, 7.30 to 8.45 MEALS: Set L £18.50 (2 courses) to £21.50, Set D £24 (2 courses) to £29. Bar menu available all day from 12 to 10. SERVICE: not inc CARDS: Delta, MasterCard, Switch, Visa DETAILS: 24 seats restaurant, 60 bar. 15 seats outside. Car park. Vegetarian meals. No children under 5 in restaurant after 8pm. No smoking in restaurant, no-smoking area in bar. Wheelchair access (also WC). No music. No mobile phones ACCOMMODATION: 14 rooms, all with bath/shower. TV. Phone. B&B £75 to £130. Baby facilities (*The Which? Guide to Good Hotels*) £5

SOWERBY West Yorkshire   map 8

Travellers Rest ⅙✳   NEW ENTRY

Steep Lane, Sowerby HX6 1PE   COOKING **3**
TEL: (01422) 832124 FAX: (01422) 831365   MODERN BRITISH PLUS
                                                              £30–£52

Steep Lane, accurately named, takes you high on to the moors to the Travellers Rest, where the isolated and unpretentious exterior belies a contemporary interior – 'a country pub with a city edge', they call it. Darren Collinson does interesting and lively mixing and matching, and errs towards complexity. A starter of a salad of Lancashire cheese, chilli beetroot, fresh asparagus and balsamic dressing may be followed by breast of chicken stuffed with black pudding with Stilton mash, or fillet of lamb, potato and carrot à la dauphinoise, with aubergine and tomato salad. Portions are generous. Light and moist cheesecakes – orange and ginger, say, or rhubarb – demonstrate deft baking skills. Service by the young (and enthusiastic) team is overseen with charm and efficiency by Caroline Lumley. Twenty or so carefully chosen wines – modestly marked up – start at £9.25.

CHEF: Darren Collinson PROPRIETOR: Caroline Lumley OPEN: Sat and Sun L 1 to 3.30, Wed to Sun D 6 to 9.30 (8 Sun) MEALS: alc (main courses £10.50 to £17). Bar menu available SERVICE: not inc CARDS: Delta, MasterCard, Switch, Visa DETAILS: 50 seats. 30 seats outside. Private parties: 100 main room. Car park. Vegetarian meals. No children under 11 after 7pm. No smoking. Wheelchair access (not WC). Music

---

🍲 indicates that there has been a change of chef since last year's Guide, and the Editor has judged that the change is of sufficient interest to merit the reader's attention.

Subscribers to Which? Online can access **The Good Food Guide** *on www.which.net.*

▲ McCoy's

The Cleveland Tontine, Staddlebridge DL6 3JB
TEL: (01609) 882671   FAX: (01609) 882660   COOKING **5**
WEBSITE: www.mccoysatthetontine.co.uk   BISTRO
6m NE of Northallerton, at junction of A19 and A172   £26–£54

The Cleveland Tontine Inn, a little over two centuries old, stands on a major junction of the A19. It is a 'rambling and delightfully shabby, but warm and comfortable' old pile, with McCoy's Bistro in the basement. Now extended, improbably enough, with a conservatory, this is a stone-floored, homely place, illuminated by dim wall lights. A mixture of fixed-price and à la carte menus, together with a separate vegetarian listing, offers a variety of ways of trying Marcus Bennett's lively, imaginative cooking. The tendency to pile flavours one on top of another is still evident, and if a dish is not necessarily thereby made greater than the sum of its parts, at least those parts are all interesting: a starter of black pudding with sweet-and-sour beetroot, horseradish cream, chorizo and mustard tortellini and apple purée proved that at inspection. Equally, however, a dish of lightly seared, tiny scallops with balsamic-dressed herby leaves and a sprinkling of diced bacon has been appreciated precisely for its straight-forwardness. Many of the main courses are given a pair of superimposed sauces of contrasting textures, so that sea bass with noodles might come with green curry cream and sweet soy (as well as grilled fennel and tomato confit), while thick-sliced, perfectly timed venison fillet is accompanied by bread sauce and mustard cream, as well as an enliveningly spicy sausage of the meat. After all this experimentation, desserts are surprisingly quite traditional, with chocolate marquise and sticky toffee pudding on offer, but perhaps also 'an unfeasibly deep torte' of Tia Maria truffle with orange and Cointreau compote. 'Unfailingly friendly and helpful' service contributes to making this one of the region's most alluring venues. The wine list is a short but knowledgeable selection that spans the major producing countries. A little more choice under £20 would make it more democratic, but house wines from southern France are £13.95.

CHEF: Marcus Bennett   PROPRIETORS: the McCoy brothers   OPEN: all week 12 to 2, 7 to 9.30 CLOSED: 25 and 26 Dec   MEALS: alc (main courses £10 to £18). Set L £12.95 (2 courses) to £14.95, Set D Sun to Thur 6.30 to 7.45 £16.95 (2 courses) to £19.95   SERVICE: not inc   CARDS: Amex, Diners, MasterCard, Switch, Visa   DETAILS: 70 seats. Private parties: 40 main room, 12 to 30 private rooms. Car park. Vegetarian meals. Children's helpings. Music. Air-conditioned ACCOMMODATION: 6 rooms, all with bath/shower. TV. Phone. B&B £80 to £100. Baby facilities

All entries, including Round-ups, are fully indexed at the back of the Guide.

Net prices *in the details at the end of an entry indicates that the prices given on a menu and on a bill are inclusive of VAT and service charge, and that this practice is clearly stated on menu and bill.*

STAITHES North Yorkshire
map 9

▲ Endeavour | **NEW ENTRY**

1 High Street, Staithes TS13 5BH
TEL: (01947) 840825
EMAIL: theendeavour@ntlworld.com
WEBSITE: www.endeavour-restaurant.co.uk

COOKING 3
MODERN BRITISH/SEAFOOD
£37–£57

Down a steep incline from the cliff-top main road, Staithes is a village consisting of a single narrow street leading to the sea. Endeavour (named after local hero Captain Cook's ship) is a small restaurant with rooms and a menu focusing on fresh, locally-caught fish – a passion of Brian Kay's. His scallop mousse with watercress sauce features a first-class mousse, light and freshly made and tasting wonderfully of scallop. For main courses, the likes of hake in a herb crust may feature, or pan-fried medallions of monkfish with rosemary and smoked bacon sauce, and there are meat dishes too: braised rabbit with black olives, say, or fillet steak with basil mustard. To finish, there may be regional cheeses, or bread-and-butter pudding, or maybe chocolate and rum terrine, could tempt the sweet-toothed. Service, by the chefs/proprietors is 'delightful' and friendly, and the wine list is modest, with a few interesting bottles, sold at fair prices starting from £10.50.

CHEFS/PROPRIETORS: Brian Kay and Charlotte Willoughby OPEN: Tue to Sat (and bank hol Sun) D only 7 to 9 CLOSED: 25 and 26 Dec MEALS: alc D (main courses £11 to £20) SERVICE: not inc, 10% for parties of 8 or more CARDS: Amex, Delta, MasterCard, Switch, Visa DETAILS: 36 seats. Private parties: 16 main room, 16 private room. Car park. Vegetarian meals. No smoking. Music. No mobile phones ACCOMMODATION: 3 rooms, all with bath/shower. TV. B&B £60 to £70 (*The Which? Guide to Good Hotels*) £5

STANTON Suffolk
map 6

Leaping Hare 🍽

Wyken Vineyards, Stanton IP31 2DW
TEL: (01359) 250287 FAX: (01359) 252372
at Ixworth, turn E off A143 and follow signs for
Wyken Vineyards

COOKING 2
MODERN BRITISH
£29–£50

This 400-year-old timbered barn on the charmingly English Wyken Hall Estate is a pleasing blend of historic and artistic, housing country store, café and restaurant. Modern British cuisine, executed with confidence and skill and served on simple white crockery, uses quality local ingredients, which are 'allowed to shine without being overpowered by too much fussing around'. After perhaps a fresh and elegant carpaccio of tuna with marinated peppers and basil dressing, a generous portion of pork tenderloin might follow, served in thick ovals with a splurge of soft, creamy colcannon, a large parcel of tender baby leeks wrapped in bacon and a light cider sauce. Desserts have included baked vanilla cheesecake with poached rhubarb, or pannacotta with English strawberries. Friendly staff, smartly turned out in lilac and purple, deliver professional service. Two dozen reasonably priced wines (which include five from the Wyken Vineyards) start at £12.75.

CHEF: Alex Turner   PROPRIETORS: Sir Kenneth and Lady Carlisle   OPEN: all week L 12 to 2, Fri to Sat D 7 to 9   CLOSED: 24 Dec to 5 Jan   MEALS: alc (main courses £10 to £16). Café L menu available   SERVICE: not inc   CARDS: Delta, MasterCard, Switch, Visa   DETAILS: 50 seats. 20 seats outside. Private parties: 70 main room. Car park. Vegetarian meals. Children's helpings. No smoking. Wheelchair access (also WC). No music. No mobile phones

STATHERN Leicestershire   map 5

Red Lion Inn ✼   NEW ENTRY

2 Red Lion Street, Stathern LE14 4HS   COOKING 2
TEL: (01949) 860868   FAX: (01949) 861579   MODERN AND TRADITIONAL
                                                               £21–£49

The gang of three who own the Olive Branch, Clipsham (see entry) now have this revitalised village pub in the Vale of Belvoir under their wing. Beyond the flagstoned bar and lounge with its sofas and newspapers is the 'homely' beamed restaurant filled with paintings and artefacts – many of which are for sale. The back of the regularly changing menus proudly maps out the precise locations of its regional producers and suppliers (Mrs King's Melton Mowbray pork pie; cheeses, fruit and meat from nearby farms). That said, the kitchen takes a global view, witness Thai steamed mussels, sauté lambs' sweetbreads with morels, and pan-fried bream with red pepper mash, olives, saffron shallots and chorizo. Desserts include bread-and-butter pudding with crème anglaise. Local beers are on handpump, and the wine list of well-chosen youthful bottles is bolstered by some 'classic' vintages; prices begin at £10.95.

CHEF: Phil Lowe   PROPRIETORS: Ben Jones, Sean Hope and Marcus Welford   OPEN: all week L 12 to 2 (3 Sun), D 7 to 9.30   CLOSED: 1 Jan   MEALS: alc (main courses L £7.50 to £15.50, D £9 to £15.50). Set L £9.50 (2 courses) to £11.50, Set L Sun £14.50. Snack menu also available SERVICE: not inc, card slips closed   CARDS: Delta, MasterCard, Switch, Visa   DETAILS: 60 seats. 30 seats outside. Private parties: 20 main room. Car park. Vegetarian meals. Children's helpings. No smoking. Wheelchair access (not WC). Occasional music

STOCKBRIDGE Hampshire   map 2

Greyhound ♟ 🍴 ✼

31 High Street, Stockbridge SO20 6EY   COOKING 4
TEL: (01264) 810833   FAX: (01264) 811656   MODERN EUROPEAN
                                                               £29–£61

According to the owner, the philosophy behind the Greyhound is 'London food without pretension', and this it brings to the charming village of Stockbridge, famous as a fly-fishing centre because of the Test running through. The old colour-washed pub has been remodelled with a degree of style to offer a comfortable, rustic-chic tone. There's room for a few locals at the bar, but basically this is a food-centred place, the atmosphere informal but upmarket. There are fireplaces, beams, polished-wood floors and leaded-light windows; the dining area wraps around the bar and continues the theme with high-backed chairs at wooden tables. Chef Darren Bunn takes a modern approach, compiling a compact but enticing seasonal menu and utilising well-sourced local produce, particularly meat and game but first-rate fish too. A signature starter of fishcake with a poached egg and chive beurre blanc makes a regular appearance, while fillet of Buchan beef with herbed pomme purée, seared foie gras and a port and lentil jus, and pan-fried fillet of turbot in a creamy mushroom sauce with a leek and truffle oil gratin prove to be draw cards. Service is informal and efficient, although some reporters have found it under-performing. For all the modern styling, Bordeaux and Burgundy loom largest on the wine list, and even Australia and New Zealand lean towards expensive classics in the reds, topped by six vintages of Grange for £200 upwards. Look to South America or southern France for budget options and don't forget to sample one of the nine sherries by the glass from £2.50 to £3.

CHEF: Darren Bunn   PROPRIETOR: Barry Skarin   OPEN: all week L 12 to 2.30, Mon to Sat D 6 to 10 CLOSED: D 24 Dec, 25 Dec, D 31 Dec, 1 Jan   MEALS: alc (main courses £9 to £19.50)   SERVICE: 10% (optional), card slips closed   CARDS: Delta, MasterCard, Switch, Visa   DETAILS: 45 seats. 30 seats outside. Private parties: 40 main room. Car park. Children's helpings. No smoking. Wheelchair access (also WC). Occasional music. Air-conditioned

STOCKCROSS Berkshire   map 2

▲ Vineyard at Stockcross 🍶

Stockcross RG20 8JU
TEL: (01635) 528770   FAX: (01635) 528398
EMAIL: general@the-vineyard.co.uk   COOKING 8
WEBSITE: www.the-vineyard.co.uk   ANGLO-FRENCH
just off A4, 2m W of Newbury on B4000   £38–£78

The impact of the flames rising from a small lake (or large pond) on arrival cannot be over-stressed, although the reasons for it go beyond mere visual appeal. When Sir Peter Michael's house full of artworks caught fire, the water used to put out the flames apparently caused almost as much damage – hence the two intertwined elements. Other sculptures – of stone and metal – also decorate the outside of this plush, modern hotel that 'could have sprung up almost anywhere, possibly in Dallas'. Floral displays are impressive, and the split-level dining room has been cleverly divided up to feel both intimate and spacious. John Campbell is 'a bit of a dynamo', whose energy is apparent in an appealing and luxury-strewn modern menu that might take in wild mushroom risotto with truffle jelly, tournedos of organic salmon with spiced lentils and foie gras, or saddle of lamb with Venezuelan chocolate and bacon and hazelnut vinaigrette. If you want fillet steak, you will find it slowly cooked yet served rare, perhaps with horseradish mash.

Among the more exceptional items have been a pneumatically bouncy boudin of foie gras 'with wonderful depth of flavour', accompanied by a mix of flageolet and small white haricot beans, and by an artfully presented, crisp yet soft-centred quail's egg that had been breadcrumbed and deep-fried (all right then, you try it). The sense of indulgence provided by such carefully managed flavours and textures is considerable, all part of the 'immense amount of trouble' that goes into the cooking. It is controlled and disciplined, showing easy mastery of technique and extremely sound judgement, as in a pair of juicy, flavourful, pink squab pigeon breasts, served with a raviolo of chopped wild mushrooms bound in an eggy medium, together with al dente lentils and a fine stock-based sauce.

John Campbell may sometimes take an innovative approach, but he keeps his feet on the ground, is scrupulous about combinations of taste and texture, and doesn't mess up a good idea with too many frills or other gestures. A frivolous-sounding 'toffee-apple' dessert, for example, redolent of the fairground, consists of a small, lightly caramelised apple tart made with thin puff pastry, accompanied by a scoop of 'gentle but divine-tasting' goats' cheese ice cream and a tall glass combining candyfloss (the genuine article) with 'a moreish toffee-ish gunge'. To invest in a candyfloss machine just to make this one dessert gives some idea of the kitchen's dedication.

Incidentals and appetisers are up to the mark, and hierarchically organised staff are generally courteous, pleasant, efficient and knowledgeable, although a few glitches have been noted. As to value, especially at lunchtime, 'we were left rubbing our eyes in wonder', although the vegetarian menu at £49 is on the pricey side. The astonishing wine list is so big that it has to be split into two volumes – one for what is surely the UK's finest range from California, including Sir Peter Michael's own winery, and the other for the rest of the world, which for the most part means reams of France and Italy's finest. But everywhere gets a look-in, and the list is by no means all pitched at Millionaires' Row. Hats off to the Vineyard for offering a £12 Verdicchio that will just sit back and let the food do the talking.

CHEF: John Campbell   PROPRIETOR: Sir Peter Michael   OPEN: all week 12 to 2, 7 to 10   MEALS: Set L £19 (2 courses) to £49, Set D Sun to Thur £25 (2 courses) to £49, Set D Fri and Sat £39 (2 courses) to £49   SERVICE: not inc   CARDS: Amex, Delta, Diners, MasterCard, Switch, Visa   DETAILS: 70 seats. 20 seats outside. Private parties: 120 main room, 40 to 64 private rooms. Car park. Vegetarian meals. Children's helpings. No-smoking area. No smoking Fri and Sat D. Music. No mobile phones. Air-conditioned   ACCOMMODATION: 31 rooms, all with bath/shower. TV. Phone. B&B £160 to £600. Rooms for disabled. Swimming pool. Fishing (*The Which? Guide to Good Hotels*) £5

STORRINGTON West Sussex   map 3

Fleur de Sel ❧✗

Manleys Hill, Storrington RH20 4BT	COOKING 6
TEL: (01903) 742331 FAX: (01903) 740649	FRENCH
	£32–£64

The original sixteenth-century cottage has been 'amply added on to in the same cottage style', producing a small bar and a comfortable, spacious and formal dining room with ruched and floral curtains, its walls decorated with pleasantly avant-garde paintings. That sense of formality pervades the high-calibre, technically accomplished cooking too. The kitchen revels in foie gras (perhaps with a ginger jus), serves up asparagus in March (with a citrus butter sauce), and offers plenty of seafood, from a terrine of lobster mousse to roast monkfish with bacon and red wine sauce.

Michel Perraud seems keen on duos and medleys, which are impressively handled: a first course, for example, that combines tender, caramelised scallops with accurately timed salmon and slivers of moist John Dory, sitting on well-drained spinach and covered in a light and well-judged Roquefort sauce. Careful sourcing is evident throughout: for example, in a faultless, meaty venison and guinea-fowl terrine with a dense, jammy fruit chutney, and in a breast and leg of corn-fed chicken, cooked with exemplary timing, served with a thinnish port sauce 'thankfully not reduced to a glaze'.

Vegetables are turned and sculpted, cheeses come in first-class condition with customary British accompaniments, and desserts have included a gossamer-thin tuile basket containing warm, rum-soaked bananas covered in a just-melting tutti-frutti ice cream, the plate dressed with a Jackson Pollock riot of lines and dashes. Peripherals such as bread, appetisers, napery and flowers get full marks, and service is attentive, knowledgeable and professional, 'though I wish they would leave us to fill up our own glasses'. The largely French wine list combines affordable bottles (mainly from the south and west) with aristocratic ones from the classic regions. House vin de pays is £12.50.

CHEF: Michel Perraud   PROPRIETORS: Bernadette and Michel Perraud   OPEN: Tue to Fri and Sun L 12 to 1.30, Tue to Sat D 7 to 9.30   CLOSED: first 2 weeks Sept   MEALS: Set L and D Tue to Fri £15.50 (2 courses) to £34, Set L Sun £19.50 (2 courses) to £23.50   SERVICE: 12.5% (optional), card slips closed   CARDS: Amex, Delta, MasterCard, Switch, Visa   DETAILS: 54 seats. Private parties: 22 main room. Car park. No children under 12. No smoking. Wheelchair access (not WC). Music. No mobile phones

STOW-ON-THE-WOLD Gloucestershire   map 5

▲ Kings Arms £

The Square, Stow-on-the-Wold GL54 1AF
TEL: (01451) 830364   FAX: (01451) 830602   COOKING 2
EMAIL: info@kingsarms.stowonthewold.co.uk   MODERN EUROPEAN
WEBSITE: www.kingsarms-stowonthewold.co.uk   £25–£44

Right in the central square, the Kings Arms occupies two floors, the upstairs room sporting a large table set about with Rennie Mackintosh chairs, a wall of bottles that acts as a walk-in wine list, and a blackboard menu. The style is direct, flavours are often robust, and the cooking retains an air of integrity and lack of fuss: there are no fancy sauces or elaborate accompaniments. The daily-changing fare might offer an Andalucian garlic and egg soup, grilled razor clams, or a doorstep steak sandwich in thick, rustic, toasted bread. Meats are local (perhaps roast belly of Gloucester Old Spot pork), and fish, coming direct from Devon and Cornwall, gets plain treatment, as in a fresh-tasting, moist, firm-textured sea bream (minus its head, the skin scored) with a pile of fresh herbs and capers forming a salsa on top. Finish, maybe, with pannacotta or chocolate tart. The global selection of wines takes in plenty of choice under £20 as well as a few grander bottles. House Chardonnay is £12, Cabernet Sauvignon £11.

CHEF: Peter Robinson   PROPRIETORS: Louise and Peter Robinson   OPEN: Mon to Sat 12 to 2.30, 6 to 9.30 (10 Fri and Sat), Sun 12 to 2.30, 7 to 9   CLOSED: 4 days mid-May, 4 days late Oct MEALS: alc (main courses £8 to £13)   SERVICE: not inc   CARDS: Delta, MasterCard, Switch, Visa DETAILS: 60 seats. Car park. Vegetarian meals. Children's helpings. Music   ACCOMMODATION: 10 rooms, all with bath/shower. TV. Phone. B&B £55 to £120

Card slips closed *in the details at the end of an entry indicates that the total on the slips of credit cards is closed when handed over for signature.*

▲ Royalist Hotel ✗

Digbeth Street, Stow-on-the-Wold GL54 1BN
TEL: (01451) 830670   FAX: (01451) 870048
EMAIL: info@theroyalisthotel.co.uk
WEBSITE: www.theroyalisthotel.co.uk

COOKING 3
MODERN BRITISH
£26–£54

England's oldest inn (it dates from 947) successfully combines ancient beams and crooked walls with a smartly attired dining room, its fine napery, crockery and glassware adding 'a touch of class'. The food is stylish, too, ranging from a starter of seared scallops (with black pudding, risotto and an apple beignet), to a main course of braised Gloucester Old Spot trotter with morels and truffle purée. Fine materials have included a flavourful and 'clearly aged' roast fillet of local beef cooked as requested, served with a rich meaty sauce and some rather salty accompaniments, and braised shank of lamb with a neat disc of potato gratin and a superior rosemary-infused sauce. Vegetarians also get a look in, perhaps in the form of a flat dish of finely puréed potato spiked with truffle and blue cheese, or a goats' cheese beignet served with spinach and spicy tomato sauce. Finish perhaps with a pear Tatin, or chocolate fondant tart. Extras run to an appetiser and pre-dessert, service is considerate, and the wine list, while it runs to pricey bottles, is less intimidating than the heavy binding first suggests.

CHEF: Alan Thompson   PROPRIETORS: Alan and Georgina Thompson   OPEN: Mon to Fri L 12 to 2, Mon to Sat D 7 to 9   MEALS: Set L £12.50 (2 courses) to £15, Set D £27 (2 courses) to £32 SERVICE: 10% (optional), card slips closed   CARDS: Amex, Delta, MasterCard, Switch, Visa DETAILS: 30 seats. Private parties: 50 main room, 12 to 16 private rooms. Car park. Vegetarian meals. Children's helpings. No smoking. Wheelchair access (not WC). Music. No mobile phones ACCOMMODATION: 8 rooms, all with bath/shower. TV. Phone. B&B £50 to £170 (*The Which? Guide to Good Hotels*) (£5)

Margaux ✗

6 Union Street, Stratford-upon-Avon CV37 6QT
TEL/FAX: (01789) 269106
WEBSITE: www.restaurantmargaux.co.uk

COOKING 3
ENGLISH/MEDITERRANEAN
£29–£51

There's nothing shy or retiring about this small restaurant tucked away in a side street off the main road through Stratford town centre. Behind the cream façade is a long, narrow, bistro-style restaurant on two levels. The ground floor has been freshly repainted in apple green, the modern wood panelling remains as do the lovely wrought-iron railings leading down to the white room, which is non-smoking. All this is the backdrop for what owner Maggie Bretner refers to as her 'front-of-house performance' – luvvie-style welcoming of her patrons. But those more concerned with nephew Shaun's performance in the kitchen will find plenty to impress, with starters like seared scallops with lemon, cinnamon and sauce vierge, or duck terrine with confit leg and balsamic dressing. Main courses might include braised collar of pork with potato purée and mustard sauce, or chargrilled tuna with crab beignet and saffron dressing. Conclude perhaps by sampling steamed coconut and lime pudding or vanilla and white chocolate brûlée. Cooking is generally well conceived and executed, service 'friendly and efficient'. The wine list, with just 20 bottles (from £12.50) has six by the glass and is stronger on whites.

CHEF: Shaun Bretner   PROPRIETOR: Maggie Bretner   OPEN: Tue to Sat 12 to 2, 6 to 10   CLOSED: 25 and 26 Dec, 1 Jan, bank hols   MEALS: alc (main courses £9 to £18)   SERVICE: not inc, 10% for parties of 10 or more   CARDS: Amex, Delta, MasterCard, Switch, Visa   DETAILS: 50 seats. Private parties: 30 main room, 10 to 18 private rooms. Vegetarian meals. No smoking in 1 dining room. Music

Russons ✸✶ £

8 Church Street, Stratford-upon-Avon CV37 6HB   COOKING 1
TEL: (01789) 268822   MODERN BRITISH
£27–£46

In a terraced red brick building in the town centre, Russons makes the most of its ancient interior, with shiny flagstone floors, beamed ceiling and irregular plastered walls painted a sunny yellow. It feels like a neighbourhood bistro, pleasantly simple and uncluttered, with an ambience that is 'warm and relaxing', as one reporter put it. Presentation of the food is unfussy, and dishes tend toward simple bistro-style offerings, such as moules marinière or salade niçoise for starters, and roast rump of English lamb, or perhaps grilled sea bass with Greek salad, for mains. Desserts may feature banoffi pie or own-made ice creams. Sauces are a strength. Service, headed by David and Sarah Russon, is very relaxed, friendly, genuine and unpretentious. A shortish but wide-ranging wine list kicks off at £10.50 for Chilean house red and white, and four are served by the glass.

CHEFS: Nick Watson and Paul Short   PROPRIETORS: David and Sarah Russon   OPEN: Tue to Sat 11.30 to 1.30, 5.30 to 9.30   CLOSED: 1 week at Christmas, 1 week at Easter, 2 weeks end-Aug MEALS: alc (main courses £9.50 to £16)   SERVICE: not inc, card slips closed   CARDS: Amex, Delta, MasterCard, Switch, Visa   DETAILS: 46 seats. Vegetarian meals. No children under 5 after 7. No smoking in 1 dining room. Music. Air-conditioned

STUCKTON Hampshire   map 2

▲ Three Lions ♥ ✸✶

Stuckton SP6 2HF
TEL: (01425) 652489   FAX: (01425) 656144
EMAIL: the3lions@btinternet.com   COOKING 6
WEBSITE: www.thethreelionsrestaurant.co.uk   ANGLO-FRENCH
off B3078 1m SE of Fordingbridge   £35–£61

Though it looks utterly unremarkable – a two-storey, red-brick detached house in a community that is hardly more than a dot on the map – this it is a supremely polished country restaurant with rooms. The polish doesn't quite extend to the dining room décor, with little china animals crowding dressers, and tatty old books heaped on shelves (even so, a relief from the chrome froideur of over-designed city eateries).

Reporters praise Mike Womersley's cooking and the consistent quality they find here. Fungi from the New Forest, fish from day-boats and locally shot game appear on menus that are simplicity itself in their descriptions. Galette of smoked haddock, seared scallops and langoustines, free-range pork and crackling, even loin of lamb with 'crispy bits', tell you without fanfare exactly what you're going to get, and what turns up on the plate then speaks eloquently for itself. Partridge in grape sauce and pan-fried sweetbreads were main courses to remember for one couple, while a two-year-old who pilfered parents' asparagus and leek soup, a dish of prawns, and a runny-centred hot chocolate pudding, emerged a satisfied customer. Praline pancake, or poached pears with verbena ice-cream, might be alternative endings, or continental cheeses. Front-of-house staff are 'young, efficient and keen', coping admirably with the bustle. After an enticing selection of house bottles from £12.75 (£2.60 a glass), the wine list sweeps straightforwardly through France, though oddities like a 1996 Salitage Chardonnay (£24) from Western Australia pep up the rest of the world. A good range of half-bottles rounds things off.

CHEF: Mike Womersley   PROPRIETORS: Mike and Jayne Womersley   OPEN: Tue to Sun L 12 to 2, Tues to Sat D 7 to 9.30   CLOSED: 2 weeks Feb   MEALS: alc (main courses £13.50 to £18). Set L Tue to Fri £15.75 (2 courses)   SERVICE: not inc   CARDS: Delta, MasterCard, Switch, Visa DETAILS: 60 seats. 10 seats outside. Private parties: 32 main room, 10 to 35 private rooms. Car park. Vegetarian meals. Children's helpings. No smoking. Wheelchair access (not WC). No music. No mobile phones   ACCOMMODATION: 4 rooms, all with bath/shower. TV. B&B £59 to £85. Rooms for disabled. Baby facilities (*The Which? Guide to Good Hotels*) £5

STURMINSTER NEWTON Dorset   **map 2**

▲ Plumber Manor ⚡✕

Sturminster Newton DT10 2AF
TEL: (01258) 472507   FAX: (01258) 473370
EMAIL: book@plumbermanor.com
WEBSITE: www.plumbermanor.com

1½m south west of Sturminster Newton on the	COOKING **2**
Hazlebury Bryan road; at brown tourist sign turn off the	ANGLO-FRENCH
A357 to Hazlebury Bryan; manor two miles down road	£30–£53

This solid, grey-stone manor house is at the end of a curving drive lined with chestnut trees. In the grounds are stables and a barn, converted into guest accommodation, plus formal gardens and a little orchard. It's the home of the Prideaux Brune family, who have occupied this ancestral home for the last 300 years, and four family members oversee the cooking and front-of-house. One visitor writes: 'It is exactly the same as it was 25 years ago. No new ideas, no gimmicks, just very good, honest food.' There is evidence of very sound techniques: for example, carpaccio of beef, served with watercress and Parmesan, is 'positively silky in texture'. Main courses might include traditional pairings such as pheasant with red wine and mushrooms, or salmon with a creamy green pepper sauce. Vegetables are served in gargantuan portions, which, added to the fact that butter and cream figure largely, means that not every diner will make it to pudding. Those who do might encounter a light and airy mango mousse with strawberry coulis. The wine list is mostly French, but there's a short New World section and a good selection of half-bottles. House wines start at £12.50.

CHEF: Brian Prideaux Brune   PROPRIETOR: Richard Prideaux Brune   OPEN: Sun L 12 to 1.30, all week D 7.30 to 9   CLOSED: Feb   MEALS: Set L £19, Set D £25   SERVICE: not inc   CARDS: Amex, Diners, MasterCard, Switch, Visa   DETAILS: 65 seats. Private parties: 45 main room, 12 to 25 private rooms. Car park. Vegetarian meals. Children's helpings. No smoking. Wheelchair access (also WC). No music   ACCOMMODATION: 16 rooms, all with bath/shower. TV. Phone. B&B £90 to £160. Rooms for disabled. Baby facilities (*The Which? Guide to Good Hotels*)

SURBITON Surrey   map 3

French Table

85 Maple Road, Surbiton KT6 4AW   COOKING 4
TEL: (020) 8399 2365   FAX: (020) 8390 5353   FRENCH/MEDITERRANEAN
                                                                  £26–£54

In 'an area not overloaded with good restaurants', the French Table is much appreciated. Looking bright, neat and clean, it has a friendly and informal atmosphere, efficient service, and close-together tables (conversation may be difficult) laid with white linen cloths. The carte, which changes every six weeks, is supplemented by daily specials such as milk-fed lamb from the Pyrenees, while the lunch menu changes weekly. Grilled salmon might come on a bed of new potatoes with a few langoustines for company, or a risotto with duck confit parked on top (presentational 'towers' are par for the course).

Combinations can be novel – for example, calf's liver with sweet potato, crispy wild mushroom ravioli and black peppercorn sauce – but there may also be more straightforward medallions of veal with sun-dried tomatoes, or Scottish beef fillet with roasted shallots and a foie gras froth. Although not all reporters have been ecstatic, one writes that 'I have eaten here several times and never had a poor experience'. A small but first-rate cheeseboard is sourced from La Fromagerie, and desserts might include coconut mousse with coconut crumble and pineapple. A lively and reasonably priced wine list starts with vin de pays red and white at £11.75.

CHEF: Eric Guignard   PROPRIETORS: Eric and Sarah Guignard   OPEN: Wed to Fri and Sun L 12 to 2.30, Tue to Sat D 6 to 10.30   CLOSED: 25 and 26 Dec, first week Jan, last 2 weeks Aug   MEALS: alc D (main courses £10.50 to £15). Set L Wed to Fri £12.50 (2 courses) to £15.50, Set L Sun £16.50   SERVICE: 12.5% (optional), card slips closed   CARDS: Delta, MasterCard, Switch, Visa   DETAILS: 48 seats. Vegetarian meals. Children's helpings. No-smoking area. No cigars/pipes in dining room. Wheelchair access (not WC). Music. No mobile phones. Air-conditioned

SUTTON GAULT Cambridgeshire   map 6

▲ Anchor Inn ♥ ✳ £

Sutton Gault CB6 2BD
TEL: (01353) 778537   FAX: (01353) 776180
EMAIL: anchorinnsg@aol.com   COOKING 3
WEBSITE: www.anchor-inn-restaurant.co.uk   MODERN BRITISH
off B1381 Sutton to Earith road, just S of Sutton, 6m W of Ely   £28–£51

The Anchor stands next to the New Bedford River in a setting that is just as you would expect of the Fens – flat, rural and peaceful. The well-stated aims – to avoid too much eclecticism, to provide 'fresh simple food...with bags of flavour', and to use locally sourced ingredients – have resulted in a meal that started with 'good and fresh' grilled king scallops with charred Mediterranean vegetables, sweet chilli sauce and crème fraîche, going on to a main course of 'very tasty' roast saddle of wild rabbit wrapped in Bayonne ham, with confit leg, soft polenta and cider sauce, and finishing with French apple tart with Calvados ice cream. Otherwise, the menu may not stray too far from a ramekin of baked smoked haddock with spinach, egg, mash and saffron cream sauce to start, and main courses of chargrilled calf's liver and bacon with mushroom mash and creamy onion sauce, or fillets of gilt-head bream with basil and olive mash and lemon butter sauce. The wine list is perceptively chosen with lots of interesting drinking below and around £20. Eight by the glass are £3.10 to £4.75.

CHEF: David Tumber   PROPRIETORS: Robin and Heather Moore   OPEN: all week 12 to 2 (2.30 Sun), 7 to 9 (9.30 Thur to Sat)   CLOSED: 26 Dec   MEALS: alc exc Sun L (main courses £10 to £16). Set L Sun £16.50 (2 courses) to £19.50. Light L menu available Mon to Fri   SERVICE: not inc   CARDS: Amex, Delta, MasterCard, Switch, Visa   DETAILS: 70 seats. 30 seats outside. Private parties: 30 main room. Car park. Vegetarian meals. Children's helpings. No smoking in 1 dining room. Wheelchair access (also WC). No music. No mobile phones   ACCOMMODATION: 2 rooms, both with bath/shower. TV. Phone. B&B £50 to £95 (*The Which? Guide to Good Hotels*)

SWAFFHAM Norfolk

map 6

▲ Strattons ⁵⚡

4 Ash Close, Swaffham PE37 7NH
TEL: (01760) 723845   FAX: (01760) 720458   COOKING 4
EMAIL: strattonshotel@btinternet.com   MODERN EUROPEAN
WEBSITE: www.strattons-hotel.co.uk   £48–£58

Swaffham is an attractive market town in the heart of the Norfolk Breckland, and although Strattons is not far off the market place, it might as well be in a world of its own. The handsome and immaculately maintained Palladian-style villa stands in secluded grounds, and interiors have an exotic feel, with a mix of antique and modern furnishings and artworks.

The cooking is rather more wholesome and down-to-earth than the setting may lead you to expect, and reflects Les and Vanessa Scott's passion for all things environmentally friendly – they are zealous about using local, seasonal ingredients, and are fortunate to have some first-rate suppliers within their self-imposed 25-mile limit. But their culinary inspirations are not so parochial, taking in starters of creamy radicchio and wild mushroom lasagne, and artfully presented Lebanese-style mixed meze. Among main courses might be a simple, homely suet pudding of roast chicken with sage gravy and mash, as well as more elaborate ideas like plum tomato tart with haddock, lemon mash and Stilton sauce. The cheese course – included in the set price – is a first-class selection and comes with 'amazingly good' home-made biscuits. Finish perhaps with an oaty, nutty plum crumble with custard. Service, overseen by Les Scott, is caring and attentive. Wines start at £14.90, with organic bottles clearly identified, and ten available by the glass. The accommodation is, like the rest of the house, stylish, creative and conscious of high ecological values.

CHEFS: Vanessa Scott and Margaret Cooper   PROPRIETORS: Les and Vanessa Scott   OPEN: Mon to Sat D only 7 to 9   CLOSED: 24 to 26 Dec   MEALS: Set D £35   SERVICE: not inc, card slips closed   CARDS: Amex, MasterCard, Switch, Visa   DETAILS: 22 seats. 6 seats outside. Private parties: 12

main room. Car park. Vegetarian meals. Children's helpings. No smoking. Music. No mobile phones ACCOMMODATION: 8 rooms, all with bath/shower. TV. Phone. B&B £75 to £180. Baby facilities (*The Which? Guide to Good Hotels*)

TADCASTER North Yorkshire

map 9

Singers ✳

16 Westgate, Tadcaster LS24 9AB	COOKING 3
TEL: (01937) 835121	MODERN EUROPEAN
WEBSITE: www.singersrestaurant.co.uk	£21–£37

Space is at a premium, the décor orange, and musical motifs and themes cover just about everything. There's no fancy menu-speak, with the broadly contemporary menu speaking for itself. A starter of a pile of tiny sweet scallops on a layer of wilted spinach in a thin filo case sprinkled with Parmesan has been declared 'a revelation', while red onion and tarragon tarte Tatin is another good example of the style. Main courses maintain a modern European focus, from authentically French sliced rump of lamb with gratin potatoes and redcurrant and rosemary jus – 'quality ingredients not messed about with' – to pork rolled into cylinders, wrapped in pancetta, with a prune at the centre, served with chestnuts and a light apple cream. Desserts of perhaps brioche-and-butter pudding, or chocolate and orange tart, keep up standards. Service is efficient and helpful, and value for money extends to wine prices starting at £9.95, with only champagne exceeding the £20 mark.

CHEFS: David Lockwood and Jonathan Wilson PROPRIETORS: Philip Taylor and Guy Vicari OPEN: Tue to Sat D only 6 to 9.30 CLOSED: 25 and 26 Dec MEALS: Set D Tue to Fri 6 to 7 £13.95, Set D Tue to Thur £15.95 (2 courses) to £19.95, Set D Fri and Sat £19.95 SERVICE: not inc, card slips closed CARDS: Delta, MasterCard, Switch, Visa DETAILS: 38 seats. Private parties: 38 main room. Vegetarian meals. No smoking. Wheelchair access (not WC). Music

TADWORTH Surrey

map 3

Gemini ✳

28 Station Approach, Tadworth KT20 5AH	COOKING 3
TEL/FAX: (01737) 812179	MODERN EUROPEAN
WEBSITE: www.gemini-restaurant.com	£27–£56

Gemini, in one of the wealthiest areas of the wealthy South-east, is a rare gem in this culinary desert, and provides efficient and accommodating service in fresh, warm and comforting surroundings. The repertoire works mostly within European conventions. Interesting and sound combinations such as noisettes of free-range pork topped with porcini mushroom mousse served with chorizo mash and cider bacon sauce might sound like an ingredient too far, yet for all the complexity flavours are usually deftly handled. Vegetarians are well cared for, with up to six mostly Mediterranean-influenced dishes that can be ordered as first or main courses. The briefer, simpler set-price menus provide particularly good value, including starters such as crispy sweetbreads and pancetta on a herb salad, followed by salmon and mullet fillets in a seafood cassoulet, or confit duck leg with wild mushroom risotto. Europe dominates a shortish, gently priced wine list that starts with an interesting eightsome of house bottles around £12 (five available by the glass) and ends with three sweeties (by glass or bottle) and half a dozen halves.

CHEF/PROPRIETOR: Robert Foster OPEN: Tue to Fri and Sun L 12 to 2, Tue to Sat D 7 to 9.30 CLOSED: 2 weeks from 25 Dec MEALS: alc Tue to Fri (main courses £15 to £17). Set L Tue to Fri £10.50 (1 course) to £16.50, Set L Sun £16.95 (2 courses) to £19.95, Set D Tue to Fri £14 (2 courses) to £17, set D Sat £34.50 SERVICE: not inc CARDS: Amex, Delta, Diners, MasterCard, Switch, Visa DETAILS: 50 seats. 12 seats outside. Private parties: 56 main room. Vegetarian meals. No children under 12 at D. No smoking. Wheelchair access (not WC). Music £5

TAPLOW Berkshire   map 3

▲ Cliveden, Waldo's ⚡✳

Taplow SL6 0JF
TEL: (01628) 668561 FAX: (01628) 661837
EMAIL: reservations@clivedenhouse.co.uk   COOKING 7
WEBSITE: www.clivedenhouse.co.uk   MODERN EUROPEAN
off A4, 2m N of Taplow on Cliveden road   £95–£132

Cliveden is a grand, imposing, National-Trust owned mansion, with formal gardens and woods sloping down to the Thames. Views from the Terrace Restaurant are splendid, over the gardens to the river beyond. By contrast, and for reasons best known to the management, the flagship Waldo's is consigned to the basement, where gentlemen are required to dress formally, even in hot weather. Fake books adorn the waiting area, abundant art hangs on the walls of the small dining room, and all effort is concentrated into two menus, which are available only five sessions a week. Three seems to be the chef's lucky number, judging by a trio of foie gras (ballottine, parfait and warm) with citrus sauce, and by a partnership of John Dory coated in onion and potato (on a bed of fine ratatouille), a plump, lightly cooked scallop (on a julienne of honey-flavoured carrot) and flavourful wild salmon (on potato purée).

The food involves a lot of workmanship, materials are generally first-rate, and techniques are sound, producing a starter of small slices of lightly seared, pepper-coated tuna, accompanied by excellent langoustine beignets and a sweet poppy seed and sesame tuile. Luxuries are conspicuous by their presence – in two pink fillets of Bresse pigeon, each combined with foie gras and wrapped in Savoy cabbage, in a sauce of broad beans flavoured with foie gras – and sweet and savoury flavours sometimes appear alongside each other: for example, in three generous slabs of warm home-smoked salmon with a strongly vanilla-flavoured apple dressing. Cheeses are well kept: after a selection is made, the items are taken away and arranged on a plate in strength order, with the addition of a goats' cheese soufflé.

Short menu descriptions, especially for desserts, don't convey the full impact. Peach melba, for this kitchen, consists of a raspberry and custard tart, rice pudding, a poached peach with raspberry sorbet, and vanilla pannacotta with a raspberry tuile. One of the highlights of an inspection meal was a chocolate medley incorporating a fine, deeply flavoured tart, white chocolate with a vermouth ganache, a fondant, an intense orange marquise, a macaroon and a brownie with vanilla ice cream. Coffee is first class too. The 'cellar team', ebulliently presented on the front page of the vast 'cellar file', doesn't miss a trick in terms of selection. Such sustained quality in all countries and regions, even rarely explored Austria, is quite overwhelming, but prices are high – 'outrageously' so in the view of one reporter – and for all the hype, comments on the service have been less than complimentary.

CHEF: Mark Dodson   PROPRIETOR: Von Essen Hotels   OPEN: Tue to Sat D only 7 to 9.30   CLOSED: Dec   MEALS: Set D £75 to £89   SERVICE: not inc   CARDS: Amex, Delta, Diners, MasterCard, Switch, Visa   DETAILS: 24 seats. Car park. Children's helpings. No children under 12. Jacket and tie. No smoking. Wheelchair access (not WC). Music. No mobile phones. Air-conditioned   ACCOMMODATION: 39 rooms, all with bath/shower. TV. Phone. B&B £250 to £850 (double room). Baby facilities. Swimming pool

TAUNTON Somerset   map 2

Brazz 🍴✻ £

Castle Bow, Taunton TA1 1NF	NEW CHEF
TEL: (01823) 252000 FAX: (01823) 336066	MODERN BRITISH
EMAIL: taunton@brazz.co.uk	£27–£53

Sleek, modern, bright and colourful, Brazz continues to impress reporters by its stylish good looks, while 'prompt, friendly and non-pushy' service puts diners at their ease. The menus have a retro feel, aiming for comfort rather than innovation: expect garlic mushrooms on toast, Caesar salad, omelette Arnold Bennett, ribeye steak with béarnaise, calf's liver with mash and onion gravy, salmon fishcakes, and skate wing with capers and black butter. We were notified about the arrival of a new chef too late to respond with an inspection, but there are unlikely to be changes to this tried-and-tested formula. Most of the wines on the short list are available by the large or small glass, or by the 500ml pitcher. Value throughout the list is excellent, with French red and white opening proceedings at £10.95.

CHEF: Raphael Rabillier   PROPRIETOR: English Brasserie Company   OPEN: all week 12 (12.30 Sun) to 3, 6 to 10.30 (11 Fri and Sat, 10 Sun)   MEALS: alc (main courses £8 to £16)   SERVICE: 10% (optional), card slips closed   CARDS: Amex, Delta, Diners, MasterCard, Switch, Visa   DETAILS: 80 seats. 4 seats outside. Private parties: 50 main room. Car park. Vegetarian meals. Children's helpings. No smoking. Wheelchair access (also WC). Music. Air-conditioned

▲ Castle Hotel ▐ ✻

Castle Green, Taunton TA1 1NF	
TEL: (01823) 272671 FAX: (01823) 336066	COOKING 7
EMAIL: reception@the-castle-hotel.com	MODERN BRITISH
WEBSITE: www.the-castle-hotel.com	£37–£70

Despite being hemmed in by chain retailers, pubs and car parks, the old fortress-like building, on a site dating from Norman times, still manages to look imposing: even the wisteria covering the façade is 150 years old. By contrast, the recent restyling of the dining room has produced 'eye-popping' results: shocking pink vies for attention with deep aquamarine, while gilt chandeliers and exuberantly carved mirrors give it all a baroque feel.

There is nothing ornate or rococo about the food, though. Aside from signature dishes such as scrambled duck egg with smoked eel and spiced oil, or the 'celebration of British beef' (which 'takes you on a grand tour of the beast'), the style is low-key and undemonstrative, offering Brixham crab cake with marinated cauliflower, and roast saddle of rabbit with young vegetables and potato gratin. But combinations are interesting, and the quality of raw materials (many of them local or regional) is first class, right from the organic flour used for bread (try the wholemeal) to three small stacked fillets of 'beautifully fresh' red mullet, accompanied by diced tomato, tiny cucumber balls, herbs and some excellent olive oil.

Flavours are well balanced, and techniques are admirable: for example, in a roughly shredded duck confit packed into a casing of duck skin and turned into a short fat sausage, then baked until crisp. This came with a 'breadcrumb box' containing the stock-based sauce – thin, clear, gelatinous – which oozed out when the box was sliced open, and with a summery collation of minted greens and beans. Vegetarian dishes are as well received as the rest, and recommended desserts have included a frothy mango custard ('brilliant' consistency) in a large brandy glass, with some DIY accompaniments of orange powder (dried and finely ground zest) and amaretti-flavoured crumbs to sprinkle over. Smart, all-male service is courteous, intelligent and intelligible. The extensive and earnest wine list credits the wine merchants as well as the producers, and a fine, upstanding bunch they are. French classics dominate but shorter selections elsewhere are bristling with quality. Prices are high but there is a fair range under £20 (especially in South America and southern France) and 11 by the glass for £4–£7.50 are joined by a page of sherries.

CHEF: Richard Guest PROPRIETOR: Kit Chapman OPEN: all week L 12.30 to 2.15, Mon to Sat D 7 to 10 MEALS: Set L £18.50 (2 courses) to £22.50, Set D £33 (2 courses) to £39. Bar L menu available SERVICE: 12.5% (optional), card slips closed CARDS: Amex, Delta, Diners, MasterCard, Switch, Visa DETAILS: 70 seats. Private parties: 80 main room, 12 to 30 private rooms. Car park. Vegetarian meals. Children's helpings. No smoking. Wheelchair access (not WC). Occasional music. No mobile phones ACCOMMODATION: 44 rooms, all with bath/shower. TV. Phone. B&B £108 to £185. Rooms for disabled. Baby facilities

Willow Tree 🍴✶

NEW ENTRY

3 Tower Lane, off Tower Street, Taunton TA1 4AR
TEL: (01823) 352835

SOMERSET OF THE YEAR NEWCOMER

COOKING 6
MODERN BRITISH
£24–£49

The small restaurant, down an alley off Tower Street, occupies a tall, gabled, seventeenth-century building. It has been done up with a degree of individuality, sporting exposed beams, an inglenook fireplace, natural colours and bright paintings – and opened just as the last edition of the Guide was published. Darren Sherlock has worked in a number of Roux enterprises in London, 'and does it ever show'. Although there are some oddities (the place operates as a tea room during the day, and noodles are made on the premises but not bread or ice cream), this is a thoroughly professional operation, where ideas tend to be restrained modern versions of classical combinations.

What brings dishes to life is the combination of first-rate raw materials and exquisite timing. Sharp technical skills include the pastry in a 'fabulously tasty' dish of gamey, sautéed pigeon breast (cooked blue, as requested), which came in a little pastry saucepan filled with lardons and chestnut mushrooms in a red wine sauce. Saucing, too, is a strength, helping to produce some 'fabulous combinations'. Results are subtle yet clear: for example, in half a dozen nicely crusted and accurately timed medallions of meaty, fresh and tasty monkfish, surrounding a central cone of thin noodles and similarly shaped celeriac and carrot, with a 'superb' sauce of cream, fish stock and fragrant caviar. Painstaking effort goes into each dish, although results don't appear laboured or overworked, and prices are extremely fair.

Well-defined flavours are also characteristic of desserts, such as a hot and evenly textured mango soufflé with a creamed apricot sauce. Cheeses, mostly English, are kept in peak condition. The place is minimally staffed, but Rita Rambellas epitomises the unpretentious yet committed nature of the place, running front-of-house capably and knowledgeably. A short wine list offers choice under £20 and a few smarter bottles too. Four house wines are £10.95 and £11.50.

CHEF: Darren Sherlock PROPRIETORS: Darren Sherlock and Rita Rambellas OPEN: Sun L 12 to 2, Tue to Sat D 6.30 to 9.30 CLOSED: Jan MEALS: alc D (main courses £12 to £17). Set L £11.95 (2 courses) to £14.95 SERVICE: not inc CARDS: Amex, Delta, MasterCard, Switch, Visa DETAILS: 40 seats. 10 seats outside. Private parties: 25 main room, 2 to 15 private rooms. Vegetarian meals. No smoking. Music. No mobile phones (£5)

TAVISTOCK Devon   map 1

▲ Horn of Plenty ⁵⁄✗

Gulworthy, Tavistock PL19 8JD
TEL/FAX: (01822) 832528
EMAIL: enquiries@thehornofplenty.co.uk   COOKING **6**
WEBSITE: www.thehornofplenty.co.uk   GLOBAL
3m W of Tavistock on A390, turn right at Gulworthy Cross   £29–£65

One of the more immediately obvious pleasures of eating at the Horn of Plenty is the panoramic view from the dining room's conservatory extension. Dartmoor is nearby, the River Tamar even closer, and if appetites are not already whetted by fresh air and exercise, they surely will be by Peter Gorton's set-price menus. These range from the least expensive – a no-choice version at lunch of perhaps mushroom soup with pesto, grilled salmon with a flavoured butter, and rice pudding fritters with passion-fruit jelly – to a rather more expensive and ambitious one at dinner.

Although ingredients come from north and south, east and west, they are marshalled with sound culinary judgement into dishes such as duck confit on a wild rice pancake with orange oil and shiitake butter sauce, or fried, truffle-crusted goats' cheese served on couscous. Main-course partnerships tend to be in more traditional vein, along the lines of roast venison loin with caramelised apples and Calvados sauce, or grilled sea bass with a lobster-flavoured sauce. There is a degree of comfort, too (this is, after all, a country-house hotel), evident in figs with a honey mousse, and even in the cheese option: a mixture of Stilton, egg yolk and brandy grilled on a croûton, with an apple and celery salad. Service is 'caring, fairly mature', and the wine list lingers awhile in the traditional regions of France, before taking a quick canter round the rest of the world. Ten house wines from £15-£22 make a fair range of affordable drinking, also served by the glass starting at £3.

CHEF: Peter Gorton PROPRIETORS: Paul Roston and Peter Gorton OPEN: Tue to Sun L 12 to 2, all week D 7 to 9 CLOSED: 24 to 26 Dec MEALS: Set L £18.50 to £23.50, Set D £25 to £39.50 SERVICE: not inc, 10% for parties of 10 or more CARDS: Delta, MasterCard, Switch, Visa DETAILS: 60 seats. 15 seats outside. Private parties: 70 main room, 2 to 15 private rooms. Car park. Vegetarian meals. Children's helpings. No smoking. Wheelchair access (also WC). Occasional music. No mobile phones ACCOMMODATION: 10 rooms, all with bath/shower. TV. Phone. B&B £105 to £200. Rooms for disabled. Baby facilities (*The Which? Guide to Good Hotels*) £5

TEDDINGTON Surrey — map 12

Wharf — NEW ENTRY

22 Manor Road, TW11 8BG
TEL: (020) 8977 6333 FAX: (020) 8977 9444
EMAIL: thewharf@walk-on-water.co.uk
WEBSITE: www.walk-on-water.co.uk

COOKING 2
MODERN EUROPEAN/SEAFOOD
£26–£56

Now run by Ray Neve (who has worked at Anton Mosimann's private club), this converted boathouse overlooking Teddington Lock has good views of the Thames. There's a large indoor restaurant plus a covered (and heated) terrace. The menu runs to dressed crab, young spinach with herb crostini and mango salsa, and oriental duck and noodle salad with hoi sin, sitting alongside more traditional moules marinière. The inclination towards seafood continues in main courses like seared loin of yellowfin tuna 'teriyaki style', or poached salmon and asparagus salad with hollandaise (though carnivores can get their fix with chargrilled entrecôte and sauce béarnaise, or a Wharf steak burger with fries). Desserts have been uneven, and service a little unsure. The short global wine list is more sure-footed, with around 40 wines starting at £11.95 (and plenty under £20), over a dozen of them available in two sizes of glass from £2.50.

CHEF: Nick Marfe PROPRIETOR: Ray Neve OPEN: all week 12 to 4, 6.30 to 10 (9.30 Sun) CLOSED: 25 and 26 Dec, 1 Jan MEALS: alc (main courses £9 to £16.50). Set L Mon to Sat £13 (2 courses) to £16, Set D Mon to Thur £17 (2 courses) to £20. Bar menu available SERVICE: 12.5% (optional), card slips closed CARDS: Amex, Delta, MasterCard, Switch, Visa DETAILS: 120 seats. Private parties: 60 private room. Car park. Vegetarian meals. Children's helpings. Wheelchair access (also WC). Music. Air-conditioned

TEFFONT EVIAS Wiltshire — map 2

▲ Howard's House ⁵✳

Teffont Evias SP3 5RJ
TEL: (01722) 716392 FAX: (01722) 716820
EMAIL: enq@howardshousehotel.com
WEBSITE: www.howardshousehotel.com
off B3089, W of Dinton and 9½m W of Salisbury, signposted Chicksgrove

NEW CHEF
MODERN BRITISH-PLUS
£41–£70

Anyone looking for a typical English village could do worse than nominate this one. A stream helps the impression, as does this comfortably appointed and colourfully furnished seventeenth-century dower house. A new chef arrived from the Chesil Rectory in Winchester (see entry) in August 2003, and his new

527

menus are not available as we go to press. Previously the repertoire has extended to Cornish crab bisque with white truffle oil, or smoked quail breasts in puff pastry with a wild mushroom ballottine, followed by roast mallard with braised Puy lentils, or seared beef fillet with dauphinois potatoes and Madeira jus, with careful sourcing providing a solid foundation. Desserts have included hazelnut and caramel crème brûlée, and wines come from a traditionally structured list led by France. Little comes in under £20, although choice up to £30 is fair and, thanks to vin de pays, Languedoc, Chile, Australia and Spain, seven house wines make it comfortably under £15.

CHEF: Nick Wentworth   PROPRIETORS: Bill and Noele Thompson   OPEN: all week 12.30 to 2, 7 to 9
MEALS: alc (main courses £14 to £24)   SERVICE: not inc   CARDS: Amex, Delta, MasterCard,
Switch, Visa   DETAILS: 40 seats. 18 seats outside. Private parties: 40 main room. Car park.
Vegetarian meals. Children's helpings. No smoking. Wheelchair access (not WC). Occasional
music   ACCOMMODATION: 9 rooms, all with bath/shower. TV. Phone. B&B £95 to £165. Baby
facilities (*The Which? Guide to Good Hotels*)

TETBURY Gloucestershire   map 2

Trouble House ⅝✳

Cirencester Road, Tetbury GL8 8SG
TEL: (01666) 502206   FAX: (01666) 504508
EMAIL: enquiries@troublehouse.co.uk   COOKING 5
WEBSITE: www.troublehouse.co.uk   MODERN EUROPEAN
on A433 1½m NE of Tetbury   £30–£48

These 'Troubles' were seventeenth-century, some Civil War commotion; apart from its location on a busy road, all is now calm and measured at this long, low cream-washed pub. The ordinary exterior reflects basic-but-smart internal decor. A salad of green beans and chicken livers with a mustard dressing exemplifies the aspirations of the kitchen: precise cooking (livers pinkish, beans crunchy, but not too much so, and creamy dressing), good raw materials and consideration of texture. Just-cooked, moist, roast black bream has been as successful as ox cheeks braised to a black, tender succulence with concentrated earthy flavours. A subtle pistachio cream was rendered almost redundant by very chocolatey hot chocolate cake with perfectly melting centre and rich coffee ice cream. Eight house wines (£10.25 to £12.85) also come in two sizes of glass, and the 40 or so other bottles provide fair range, many below £20, with hardly anything very posh.

CHEF: Michael Bedford   PROPRIETORS: Michael and Sarah Bedford   OPEN: Tue to Sun L 12 to
2.30, Tue to Sat D 7 to 9.30   CLOSED: bank hols, 2 weeks from 25 Dec, 1 week Sept   MEALS: alc
(main courses £11 to £14.50)   SERVICE: not inc   CARDS: Amex, Delta, MasterCard, Switch, Visa
DETAILS: 52 seats. 30 seats outside. Car park. No children under 14 in bar. No smoking in 1 dining
room. Music

The Guide relies on feedback from its readers. Especially welcome are reports on new restaurants appearing in the book for the first time. All letters to the Guide are acknowledged.

TETSWORTH Oxfordshire
map 2

Swan at Tetsworth

High Street, Tetsworth OX9 7AB
TEL: (01844) 281182   FAX: (01844) 281770
WEBSITE: www.theswan.co.uk

COOKING **4**
MODERN EUROPEAN
£32–£52

The Swan is a red-brick and partly white-plastered Elizabethan building, once a coaching inn and now a combined restaurant and antiques centre. It's a moot point whether the best way to enjoy the Swan is to spend a couple of hours wandering the labyrinthine stairs and cubbyholes of the antiques centre before falling into your seat for lunch, or to spend two hours over lunch before slowly exploring the antiques. Whichever way you choose, don't let the slightly ramshackle look of the dining room fool you – the cooking here is sharply focused and modern, based on Italian, French and modern British styles. To start, melt-in-the-mouth chicken liver crostini may be topped with tapenade and lightly dressed with rocket. Moist, juicy rump of lamb, a main course, may be offset by a herby jus and creamed baby leeks. For dessert, go for something like lemon and vanilla cheesecake, tiramisù, or a selection of English cheeses. Service is observant, knowledgeable and efficient, and the short wine list is carefully put together, organised by style and reasonably priced. Four house wines start the bidding at £12.50.

CHEF: Naseem Salam   PROPRIETOR: Swan Holdings Ltd   OPEN: all week L 12 to 2.15 (3.30 Sun), Tue to Sat D 7 to 9.15 (9.45 Sat)   CLOSED: 25 and 26 Dec   MEALS: alc (main courses £11 to £16.50)   SERVICE: not inc   CARDS: Delta, MasterCard, Switch, Visa   DETAILS: 55 seats. 20 seats outside. Private parties: 55 main room, 14 private room. Car park. Vegetarian meals. No-smoking area. Wheelchair access (also WC). Music £5

THORNBURY South Gloucestershire
map 2

▲ Thornbury Castle ⁵⚔
NEW ENTRY

Castle Street, Thornbury BS35 1HH
TEL: (01454) 281182   FAX: (01454) 416188
EMAIL: info@thornburycastle.co.uk
WEBSITE: www.thornburycastle.co.uk
off B4061, at N end of town

COOKING **6**
MODERN EUROPEAN
£56–£67

This grand Tudor castle-palace has an appropriately baronial feel, with suits of armour, a massive stone fireplace, tapestries and masses of candelabra throughout the building. Tables in the hexagonal tower dining room are set with silver platters and menus are presented in tasselled covers.

The contents of those menus, however, 'defy the expectations raised by the setting', chef Nicholas Evans showing a high degree of originality and ambition in his repertoire. As one reporter put it: 'Each dish takes an ingredient, and runs with it – often in unexpected directions.' Thus chicken and mushroom tortellini is partnered with foie gras, asparagus and roast chicken sauce, seared scallops come with cauliflower fritters and creamed cauliflower, crab risotto is finished with roast prawns and crab foam, and loin of lamb is presented on a shepherd's pie.

There is a sense of freshness and excitement, which is achieved without forgetting that flavour is the main priority: witness a starter that deconstructs traditional fish and chips to give 'succulent' pan-fried cod with crisp potatoes (three fat, brown chips) and pea purée ('about as refined as mushy peas can get') plus a confit tomato filled with gribiche sauce in place of ketchup and tartare sauce. The highlight of an inspection meal was a crisp-skinned duck breast with rich, gamey flavour, paired with a raviolo filled with a rillettes-like duck mixture, a 'fabulously rich' jus flavoured subtly with star anise, and an earthy potato purée. Desserts have let the side down a little: rhubarb cream with hazelnut biscuit, mascarpone and red wine syrup was well crafted but underwhelming. The wine list stretches well beyond France, turning up surprises like house label English Müller-Thurgau (£16) among a small selection under £20.

CHEF: Nick Evans   PROPRIETOR: Von Essen Hotels   OPEN: all week 12 to 2, 7 to 9.30   MEALS: Set L £22.50, Set D £42.50   SERVICE: not inc   CARDS: Amex, Delta, Diners, MasterCard, Switch, Visa   DETAILS: 46 seats. Private parties: 30 main room, 10 to 30 private rooms. Car park. Vegetarian meals. Children's helpings. No smoking. Wheelchair access (also WC). Music. No mobile phones   ACCOMMODATION: 25 rooms, all with bath/shower. TV. Phone. B&B £98 to £370. Rooms for disabled. Baby facilities

---

TITLEY Herefordshire   map 5

▲ Stagg Inn ▼ ⚒✳

Titley, Nr Kington HR5 3RL
TEL: (01544) 230221   FAX: (01544) 231390
EMAIL: reservations@thestagg.co.uk   COOKING 5
WEBSITE: www.thestagg.co.uk   MODERN BRITISH
on B4355 between Kington and Presteigne   £24–£54

The Stagg Inn, an old brick and stone, custard-painted building, still functions as the village local, with a warm and friendly feel. It is still very much a family concern: chef/co-proprietor Steve Reynolds mans the stoves while Nicola Reynolds runs front-of-house with unpretentious friendliness and unflappable common sense. Children, dogs – all are made to feel welcome.

'Focused simplicity' is how one visitor described the approach at the Stagg. The kitchen's technical skills are impressive, as are the quality of ingredients. Almost all of the food served here is local, much of it organic. The present-day owners of Titley Court supply the inn with vegetables, herbs and fruit while, in season, 'exceptionally supple and well-hung' venison, culled from the many local herds, is likely to feature on the menu – perhaps in the form of saddle of venison with port-marinated prunes and potato fondant. Ideas are straightforward and well conceived, and dishes can be 'dead simple', say a starter of pollock with calamari risotto complemented by 'perfect' squid ink sauce. Desserts such as spiced rhubarb with cinnamon pannacotta don't let the side down, while the cheeseboard features more than a dozen (local, of course) – maybe Ragstone goat, Stinking Bishop and True Bloo Ewe (bad name, nice cheese). The focus on quality sourcing carries on to the drinks list, where a host of good producers mingle under the banners of Europe (mostly France) and the New World. Prices are very fair and the bantering annotations entertain. Eight house wines are around £12 or £2 a glass.

CHEF: Steve Reynolds   PROPRIETORS: Nicola and Steve Reynolds   OPEN: Tue to Sun 12 to 2, Tue to Sat 6.45 to 10   CLOSED: first 2 weeks Nov, 25 and 26 Dec, 1 Jan, 1 week Feb, Tue after bank hols, May Day Mon bank hol   MEALS: alc exc Sun L (main courses £11.50 to £18.50). Set L Sun £13.90. Bar menu also available   SERVICE: not inc, card slips closed   CARDS: MasterCard, Switch, Visa   DETAILS: 40 seats. 16 seats outside. Private parties: 30 main room. Car park. Vegetarian meals on request. Children's helpings. No smoking. No music   ACCOMMODATION: 2 rooms, both with bath/shower. TV. B&B £40 to £70

TODMORDEN West Yorkshire   map 8

Old Hall ⅙✳

Hall Street, Todmorden OL14 7AD	COOKING 3
TEL: (01706) 815998 FAX: (01706) 810669	MODERN BRITISH
	£20–£53

Easily found in the centre of Todmorden, the Old Hall is precisely that, and mightily impressive it is too, with parts of the building dating back to the thirteenth century. The interior is a clever mixture of old and new: pale colours and creative use of furnishings and fabrics provide a contemporary, comfortable, uncluttered backdrop in the two dining rooms. The food offers as much local produce as the kitchen can muster, with some interesting twists and turns. Pan-fried Goosnargh duck livers on toasted ciabatta, or fillet of Calder Valley trout with horseradish and watercress mash are two examples of starters or 'lighter meals'. Main courses extend to smoked haddock Lancashire rarebit with smoked bacon, shoulder of Pendle lamb with parsnip mash, or Asian blackened monkfish with pickled vegetables and mint labneh. Puddings, too, twist and turn from Yorkshire parkin with stem ginger and custard to cranachan. A well-organised and varied wine list offers some real gems at very fair prices, with half a dozen house wines starting with a French Sauvignon Blanc at £10.95.

CHEF: Chris Roberts   PROPRIETORS: Nick and Madeleine Hoyle   OPEN: Tue to Sun L 12 to 2 (2.30 Sun), Tue to Sat D 7 to 9.30   CLOSED: first week Jan   MEALS: alc exc Sun L (main courses £11.50 to £16). Set L Tue to Sat £7.95 (2 courses), Set L Sun £10.95 (2 courses) to £13.95   SERVICE: not inc, 10% for parties of 10 or more   CARDS: Delta, Diners, MasterCard, Switch, Visa   DETAILS: 70 seats. 20 seats outside. Private parties: 60 main room, 8 to 24 private rooms. Vegetarian meals. Children's helpings. No smoking. Occasional music. No mobile phones

TORQUAY Devon   map 1

No 7 Fish Bistro £

7 Beacon Terrace, Torquay TQ1 2BH	COOKING 1
TEL: (01803) 295055	FISH
WEBSITE: www.no7-fish.com	£27–£50

The philosophy could not be simpler: procure the freshest fish from the boats, cook it without too much embellishment and ensure that any accompanying sauces are, according to a reporter, 'appropriate, uncomplicated and balanced'. Little wonder that this family-run bistro close to the harbour gets packed with tourists as well as locals. Blackboard specials make up the lion's share of the haul, and the choice depends on the catch, but you can expect, say, oysters, whole Brixham plaice, Dover sole and – of course – fish 'n chips. Elsewhere, seafood broth ('full of delicious goodies'), a skillet of mussels, prawns and scallops in 'very garlicky' oil, and grilled turbot have all passed muster. Occasionally the kitchen drifts into more exotic territory (salmon baked with mild Moroccan spices, for example), while almond ice cream with Amaretto makes a refreshing finale. Whites dominate the affordable wine list, which includes eight by the glass. Bottle prices start at £10.

CHEFS: Oliver and Paul Stacey   PROPRIETORS: Graham and Jill Stacey   OPEN: Wed to Sat L 12.45 to 1.45, Tue to Sat D 6 to 10.15 (7 to 9.45 winter); also open Mon D June and Oct, Sun and Mon D July to Sept   CLOSED: 1 week Nov, Christmas and New Year, 2 weeks Feb   MEALS: alc (main courses £10 to £17.50)   SERVICE: not inc   CARDS: Amex, Delta, MasterCard, Switch, Visa DETAILS: 38 seats. Private parties: 20 main room. Vegetarian meals. Children's helpings. Wheelchair access (not WC). Music. No mobile phones. Air-conditioned (£5)

TOTNES Devon   map 1

Effings ⁵⁄✳ £

50 Fore Street, Totnes TQ9 5RP   COOKING **4**
TEL: (01803) 863435   MODERN EUROPEAN
                                                                      £25–£48

Banks and boutiques surround this hybrid emporium run by people who know and care about food. Their efforts include supplying the excellent deli, cooking vacuum-packed ready meals and providing meals and snacks on the premises. Five modest tables benefit from the attention of a skilled kitchen, which at lunchtime shifts into top gear, generating main courses with a southern European accent, using local supplies when appropriate, including fish from Brixham and Dartmoor venison. Powerful combinations are common, as in a tartlet of black pudding and apple purée with beetroot, or jamón pata negra with grilled chicory and artichokes, although lasagne verde might also feature. The Fine deli-counter sets out antipasti, assiette gourmet and tapas, the last including Serrano ham, marinated figs and pequillo peppers, along with sourdough bread, savoury tarts and salads. Snacks, including their own ice creams, are served in the eating area mornings and afternoons. Quality runs throughout the short wine list, where the house selections are £13.95 (£3.50 a glass). A half-bottle of Ch. Doisy-Daëne 1981 at £19.95 (£5.75 a glass) and three Lustau sherries by the glass show that expertise and enthusiasm are not confined to food. Every town should have a place like this.

CHEFS: Nigel Marriage and Karl Rasmussen   PROPRIETORS: Jacqueline Williams and Michael Kann   OPEN: Mon to Sat L only 12 to 2.30   CLOSED: bank hols   MEALS: alc (main courses £8 to £18). Snacks and other menus available 9.30 to 12, 2.30 to 5   SERVICE: net prices, card slips closed   CARDS: Amex, Delta, MasterCard, Switch, Visa   DETAILS: 14 seats. Private parties: 14 main room. Children's helpings. No smoking. Wheelchair access (also WC). No music. No mobile phones. Air-conditioned

---

The Guide office can quickly spot when a restaurateur is encouraging customers to write recommending inclusion. Such reports do not further a restaurant's cause. Please tell us if a restaurateur invites you to write to the Guide.

Wills Restaurant ℁

3 The Plains, Totnes TQ9 5DR
TEL: 01803 865192   FAX: 01803 865192
EMAIL: info@www.eiaddio.com
WEBSITE: www.eiaddio.com

COOKING 2
MODERN EUROPEAN
£26–£63

This handsome Regency house was the birthplace of the Egyptologist and explorer William Wills, which goes some way to explain the serendipity of a décor that juxtaposes an ancient Egyptian head and an old polo helmet. The inspiration of the menu, however, is Europe, mainly France, with ingredients often from much closer to home ('lamb, beef, pork and venison lived within a 5-mile radius'). Oven-baked quenelle de Lyon with a creamy sauce, or black bream fillet with pommes écrasés and star anise sauce are overtly French, although a creamy risotto might accompany boudin of pork tenderloin with a Devon cider reduction. Puddings might include honey-roast tropical fruits with rum-and-raisin ice cream. House bottles from £11 are French; otherwise catholicity reigns: the 'Cabernet Sauvignon' category covers Portugal, Spain and Australia, ending with a cru bourgeois St Estèphe at a reasonable £28. Wills Café next door offers a cheerful alternative.

CHEF: Dominique Prandi   PROPRIETORS: Philip Silvester and Jenny Priest   OPEN: Tue to Sat D 7 to 10   CLOSED: Jan   MEALS: alc D (£15 to £23). Café menu available L (main courses £9 to £13)   SERVICE: not inc   CARDS: Amex, Delta, MasterCard, Switch, Visa   DETAILS: 26 seats. Private parties: 14 main room, 14 to 30 private rooms. Vegetarian meals. No smoking. Wheelchair access (also WC). Occasional music ⓔ5

TRURO Cornwall

map 1

Sevens ℁

NEW ENTRY

77 Lemon Street, Truro TR1 2PN
TEL: (01872) 275767   FAX: (01872) 274145
EMAIL: mail@sevenstruro.co.uk
WEBSITE: www.sevenstruro.co.uk

COOKING 4
MODERN EUROPEAN
£42–£70

Sevens opened in early 2003 with the kitchen under the direction of local culinary hero Kevin Viner. He has since departed, but the kitchen team continues to deliver the goods. A stone's throw from Truro's largely pedestrianised town centre, Sevens adjoins sister restaurant Café Citron (see entry, Round-ups), and its altogether more discreet entrance can be difficult to pick out among the honey-coloured stone façades. The interior makes a bright, light, modern impression, with pale colours offset by the warm, rich tones of the upholstery, and lots of glass. A large window into the kitchen allows diners to see dishes being prepared and cooked. Chefs Gavin Young and Colin Hankin preside over a sensibly short, modern menu (five choices at each course). Fish, such as a starter of John Dory served with crisp, thinly sliced peppers and drizzled with a sweetish plum and soy sauce, figures largely, but seared foie gras with a shallot and Muscat sauce might be an equally contemporary alternative. Tender roast loin of Cornish lamb has come with rosemary jus, borlotti beans, fondant potatoes and asparagus; breast of guinea fowl with a wild mushroom mousseline; and poached halibut with a shellfish nage. Summertime desserts included lemon crème brûlée with marinated berries, and poached peaches with honey ice cream and raspberry coulis. Wines are chosen with food-compatibility in mind; New World selections, like the excellent Glen Carlou Chardonnay from South Africa (£22) are particularly strong.

CHEFS: Gavin Young and Colin Hankin   PROPRIETORS: David and Jane White   OPEN: Wed to Fri L 12 to 2.30, Tue to Sat D 6.30 to 9.30   CLOSED: 25 and 26 Dec   MEALS: alc (main courses £16 to £20)   SERVICE: not inc   CARDS: MasterCard, Switch, Visa   DETAILS: 40 seats. Private parties: 40 main room. Children's helpings. No smoking. Wheelchair access (also WC). Music. Air-conditioned ⓔ5

TUNBRIDGE WELLS Kent   map 3

▲ Hotel du Vin & Bistro ❙

Crescent Road, Tunbridge Wells TN1 2LY
TEL: (01892) 526455   FAX: (01892) 512044   COOKING 4
EMAIL: reservations@tunbridgewells.hotelduvin.com   BISTRO
WEBSITE: www.hotelduvin.com   £36–£58

Little changes from year to year at this elegant Georgian townhouse hotel in the heart of genteel Tunbridge Wells – well, if it ain't broke… There's an air of clubby exclusivity and luxury throughout, and service is as slick and smooth as you might expect from a place that is 'dripping with well-trained staff'. Menus take a modern bistro line, concentrating on 'robust flavours, simple ingredients and yet sensational results' – traits that were evident at inspection in a starter of smoked chicken, spinach and walnut salad with lightly poached egg and crisp pancetta in a 'basket' of crisp Lebanese flat bread. Among main courses, grilled (but very rare) tuna loin on green olive relish with balsamic dressing has proved a 'decadent mix cooked with perfect timing'. Choice typically extends to roast halibut on chorizo risotto with salsa verde, and roast rump and confit shoulder of lamb with spring cabbage and rosemary sauce, and 'simple classics' include oxtail soup, chateaubriand (for two) with béarnaise, and even corned beef hash with HP sauce. Dessert might be wobbly pannacotta with poached rhubarb.

The chain continues to expand: see entries in Winchester, Bristol, Birmingham and Brighton, with Harrogate next in their sights. The wine lists are by no means identical. This one does not play up wines by the glass and perhaps has a smaller range of bottles under £20 than some, but these are minor gripes against an outstanding global range with fair prices and knowledgeable Gallic service on hand for advice.

CHEF: Chris Moore   PROPRIETOR: Hotel du Vin Ltd   OPEN: all week 12 to 1.45, 7 to 9.45   MEALS: alc exc Sun L (main courses £14.50 to £17.50). Set L Sun £23.50   SERVICE: not inc   CARDS: Amex, Delta, Diners, MasterCard, Switch, Visa   DETAILS: 85 seats. 20 seats outside. Private parties: 70 main room, 10 to 16 private rooms. Car park. Vegetarian meals. Children's helpings. No cigars/pipes in dining room. Wheelchair access (also WC). No music   ACCOMMODATION: 36 rooms, all with bath/shower. TV. Phone. Room only £95 to £145. Rooms for disabled. Baby facilities (*The Which? Guide to Good Hotels*)

Report forms are at the back of the book; write a letter if you prefer; or email us at goodfoodguide@which.net

---

Thackeray's ✸

85 London Road, Tunbridge Wells TN1 1EA
TEL: (01892) 511921   FAX: (01892) 527561
EMAIL: reservations@thackeraysrestaurant.co.uk
WEBSITE: www.thackeraysrestaurant.com

COOKING 5
MODERN FRENCH
£28–£71

Once through the front door of this white clapboard house, perched at one corner of Tunbridge Wells Common, you get toning shades of brown, with grey and white predominating – very stylish is the consensus. Walls are enlivened by huge abstract paintings, and linen-clad tables sport sparkling wine glasses, silver 'dress' plates and flowers. Servers are 'clad in black from top to toe,' says a visitor, who described their style as 'brisk' ('willing and welcoming', for another).

In keeping with the sleek surroundings, the food is French done in a modern style. There are a few classic dishes, such as a starter of marinated ham and parsley terrine, here served with a poached quail's egg and toasted Poilâne bread, but less traditional pairings are much in evidence. A main course of beautifully cooked roast Icelandic cod, for example, might be served with a frothy red wine sauce and steamed pak choi topped with a roast garlic clove. Presentation skills are high, with sauces and ingredients arranged artistically. A dessert of crème brûlée with white chocolate sorbet may come on a rectangular plate festooned with mint leaves and tuile spirals. A well-turned-out selection of wines is presented on a large white sheet of paper. Best value is found in 'Thackeray's selection', a dozen bottles priced between £11.50 and £20.

CHEFS: Richard Phillips and Kieren Steinbourne-Busse   PROPRIETORS: Richard Phillips and Paul Smith   OPEN: Tue to Sun L 12 to 2.30, Tue to Sat D 6.30 to 10.30   MEALS: alc exc Sun L (main courses £14.50 to £20). Set L £14.95 (2 courses) to £48, Set L Sun £22.50, Set D £48   SERVICE: 12.5% (optional), card slips closed   CARDS: Amex, Delta, MasterCard, Switch, Visa   DETAILS: 85 seats. 30 seats outside. Private parties: 60 main room, 6 to 16 private rooms. Vegetarian meals. Children's helpings. No smoking. Wheelchair access (not WC). Music. Air-conditioned

TWICKENHAM Greater London

map 3

A Cena ▼

NEW ENTRY

148 Richmond Road, Twickenham TW1 1PE
TEL/FAX: (020) 8288 0108

COOKING 2
ITALIAN
£22–£57

A Cena's presence on the busy Richmond Road is discreetly communicated with the name picked out in cream against a black background. The interior has a friendly, informal feel, with bare dark floorboards, wooden church chairs and a few well-placed touches of swagger in the form of oversized gilt mirrors. The food is good, imaginatively prepared Italian. Chunky slices of nutty brown and white bread may get the taste-buds in gear for starters such as crab salad with roasted almond aïoli or a pasta dish like ricotta, pine nut and lemon ravioli ('eye-opening taste sensation'). Simple good-quality ingredients are evident in capacollo (cured pork shoulder) with fennel bruschetta. Main courses may include breast of duck with cherry tomatoes, black olives and olive oil mash, while puddings tend towards the indulgent, such as coffee zabaglione torta with lashings of espresso-flavoured cream and chocolate shavings. The mostly Italian wine list is impeccably chosen, with top-rank producers throughout. Prices start at £12.50 but move up quickly. Eight come by the glass for £2.95 to £5.65.

CHEF: Nicola Parsons PROPRIETORS: Tim and Camilla Healy OPEN: Tue to Sun L 12 to 2.30, Tue to Sat D 7 to 10.30 MEALS: alc (main courses £8.50 to £20.50). Set L Tue to Sat £10 (2 courses) to £12, Set L Sun £18 (2 courses) to £22 SERVICE: not inc CARDS: Amex, Delta, MasterCard, Switch, Visa DETAILS: 51 seats. Private parties: 51 main room. Vegetarian meals. Children's helpings. Wheelchair access (not WC). Music. Air-conditioned

Brula
NEW ENTRY

43 Crown Road, St Margaret's,
Twickenham TW1 3EJ
TEL: (020) 8892 0602 COOKING **2**
EMAIL: (020) 8892 7727 FRENCH
WEBSITE: www.brula.com £20–£46

An inspector was enchanted when stepping into the stylish but unpretentious atmosphere of this neighbourhood restaurant, with its paper cloths over linen, stained glass window and dark wood fittings. Commendably simple dishes such as a salad of leeks, soft egg and creamed anchovies, and tarte fine of onion and thyme, are typical of the output. Carefully fried scallops on a bed of crisp bacon with endives braised in butter showed good judgement, and the thin, delicate pastry of a powerfully flavoured and smooth lemon tart was of high quality. The lunch menu, £9 for one or two courses (go for two, maybe?), looks good value, but vegetables and an initial dish of olives or almonds are charged for. Good wine merchants are used, with house bottles at £11.00 and several others sensibly available in 50cl carafe.

CHEF: Bruce Duckett PROPRIETORS: Lawrence Hartley and Bruce Duckett OPEN: Mon to Sat 12.30 to 2.30, 7 to 10.30 CLOSED: one week at Christmas, bank hols MEALS: alc (main courses £9.50 to £13.50). Set L £9 (2 courses) to £11 SERVICE: not inc, card slips closed CARDS: Delta, MasterCard, Switch, Visa DETAILS: 40 seats. 12 seats outside. Private parties: 10 main room, 10 private room. Vegetarian meals. No cigars/pipes. Wheelchair access (not WC). No music. No mobile phones

McClements

2 Whitton Road, Twickenham TW1 1BJ COOKING **7**
TEL: (020) 8744 9610 FAX: (020) 8744 9598 FRENCH
WEBSITE: www.mcclementsrestaurant.com £34–£110

Since the last edition of the Guide, this restaurant has made a determined effort to raise its game a notch higher than its previous admirable standard. John McClements has hired Barry Tonks as head chef (John McClements is now cooking at his new, second restaurant, Ma Cuisine; see entry below). The décor, too, has had a bit of a reassessment. The maroon velvet curtains have been retired, replaced by a soothing cream and beige colour scheme. Tables are well spaced, covered with soft white cloths and napkins to match. The restaurant may have lost some of its quirky charm, but has done so in an attempt to join the select ranks of London's restaurant elite. Diners now get not one pre-starter but four, and a plate of four pre-desserts. The menu fairly wallows in luxury ingredients, such as lobster, foie gras, truffles and langoustines.

Every dish proclaims imagination, diligence and integrity. While there's no doubting the artistry in the kitchen, it is applied in ways that enhance rather than mask the natural qualities of the ingredients. Menu descriptions swing between the lovingly catalogued and the flirtatiously opaque. 'A tasting of lamb', for example, centres on some slices of top-quality medium-rare neck fillet, which are stuffed with basil mousse, complemented by a deep-fried sweetbread and a pan-fried kidney, plus various accompaniments. Sauces are a strength here, as in a starter of ravioli of langoustine tails with truffle-scented potato, asparagus, baby leeks and a Madeira bouillon. Desserts are perhaps less ambitious than the other courses but are nonetheless well executed. The recipient of a raspberry soufflé with white chocolate ice cream declared it 'exemplary, towering and light'. Service, mostly French, is impeccably professional and discreet.

The wine list has had an upgrade, too, and now runs to more than 1,000 bottles, split into separate booklets for reds and whites. France is favoured, but other countries are all explored in some detail. Bottles under £20 do surface from time to time (there are more than in the round-up at the front), but mark-ups tend to be steep. House wines are £15, or £4.50 a glass, and ten 'sommelier's choice' come by the glass for £5.50 to £8 as well as a range of sherries.

CHEF: Barry Tonks   PROPRIETOR: John McClements   OPEN: Mon to Fri L 12 to 2.30, Mon to Sat D 7 to 10.30   MEALS: Set L £17.50 (2 courses) to £50, Set D Mon to Thur £25 to £50, Set D Fri and Sat £35 (2 courses) to £50   SERVICE: 10% (optional), card slips closed   CARDS: Amex, Delta, MasterCard, Switch, Visa   DETAILS: 50 seats. Private parties: 60 main room, 15 to 60 private rooms. Car park. Vegetarian meals. No smoking in 1 dining room. Wheelchair access (also WC). No music. Air-conditioned   (£5)

Ma Cuisine £   NEW ENTRY

6 Whitton Road, Twickenham TW1 1BJ
TEL: (020) 8607 9849   COOKING 3
EMAIL: johnmac21@aol.com   FRENCH REGIONAL
WEBSITE: www.mcclementsrestaurant.com   £19–£35

A sibling to McClements (see entry above) a couple of doors away, this authentic French neighbourhood bistro demonstrates John McClements's versatility beyond haute cuisine. Past the jolly, purple-painted façade is a tiny dining room with 'no concessions to modernity'; the décor, as well as the cuisine, is timelessly bourgeois, complete with plastic gingham table covers and friendly, unobtrusive service. Affordable prices combine with a convivial atmosphere and 'absolutely authentic execution' to produce a winning formula.

The menu is strewn with Gallic classics: bouillabaisse with rouille, salade niçoise, coq au vin, cassoulet (confit duck, Toulouse sausage and beans), and crème brûlée and crêpes suzette. Taking its lead from the French regional cooking, the wine list offers an appropriate short spread of Francophile options from £11 to £29. Buzzy but relaxed, with pine-wood banquettes, a black and white tiled floor and tightly packed tables, Ma Cuisine has hit the ground running.

CHEF/PROPRIETOR: John McClements   OPEN: all week L 12 to 2, Mon to Sat D 6.30 to 11   MEALS: alc (main courses £8 to £10.50). Set L £10.50, Set D £15   SERVICE: not inc, card slips closed   CARDS: Amex, Delta, Diners, MasterCard, Switch, Visa   DETAILS: 40 seats. 4 seats outside. Private parties: 40 main room. Vegetarian meals. Children's helpings. Wheelchair access (not WC). Music

TYNEMOUTH Tyne & Wear   map 10

Sidney's ❄

3–5 Percy Park Road, Tynemouth NE30 4LZ
TEL: (0191) 257 8500   FAX: (0191) 257 9800   COOKING 3
EMAIL: bookings@sidneys.co.uk   MODERN BRITISH-PLUS
WEBSITE: www.sidneys.co.uk   £18–£47

Sidney's is in the pretty coastal town of Tynemouth, described as a 'film location' setting by one visitor, with its Georgian and Victorian houses. The restaurant's décor, though, is bang up to date, with a colour scheme of crimson and purple, polished wooden floors and a brushed stainless-steel bar. The wide-ranging menu shows that this is a place with a serious attitude to food and wine. Fish comes from nearby North Shields, and steaks are from traceable Scottish herds. There's plenty for vegetarians, too: goats' cheese and hazelnut cheesecake with redcurrant compote, or perhaps chargrilled vegetable and tapenade mille-feuille with mint salsa verde. Otherwise, salt-cod fritters with a fiery tomato sauce might precede prune-stuffed guinea fowl; or seared duck liver and saffron-poached pear bruschetta set the scene before tandoori-style turbot fillets with coconut rice and pineapple chaat. Finish with chocolate, chestnut and fig tart. Each dish on the menu is helpfully annotated with a suggested wine accompaniment, many available by the glass. The short, well-chosen list kicks off with Georges Duboeuf at £10.50 a bottle, £2.95 a glass. Andy Hook also runs the Blackfriars Café Bar, Newcastle upon Tyne (see entry).

CHEF: Samantha Mowbray   PROPRIETORS: Andy Hook and Hooked-On Group   OPEN: Mon to Sat 12 to 2.30, 6 to 10   CLOSED: most bank hols exc Good Fri   MEALS: alc (main courses £10.50 to £16). Set L £5 (1 course, inc wine) to £9.95, Set D Mon to Fri 6 to 7 £9.95 (2 courses) to £12.95   SERVICE: not inc, 10% for parties of 6 or more   CARDS: Amex, Delta, MasterCard, Switch, Visa   DETAILS: 50 seats. Private parties: 30 main room, 15 to 22 private rooms. Vegetarian meals. Children's helpings. No smoking. Wheelchair access (not WC). Music. Air-conditioned   £5

ULLINGSWICK Herefordshire   map 5

Three Crowns

Bleak Acre, Ullingswick HR1 3JQ
TEL: (01432) 820279
EMAIL: info@threecrownsinn.com
WEBSITE: www.threecrownsinn.com   COOKING 4
from A417 turn E (signposted Ullingswick), then   MODERN BRITISH
straight on for 1½m   £24–£43

The proprietor of the Three Crowns describes the place as 'a small, rustic country pub', and you can't argue with that. Inside are two simply furnished dining rooms as well as a small bar: think exposed beams and a wood-burning stove, as well as some tables outside, which prove popular in good weather. Since the last edition of the Guide, when Brent Castle manned the stoves single-handedly, a second chef, Jon Howe, has been brought on board. The menu remains straightforward and lively. Witness the likes of grilled mackerel with dhal, or smoked salmon sausage with cucumber, mustard and crème fraîche for starters, or a main course of roast rack of Marches lamb with a white-bean and chorizo cassolette. The kitchen seems keen to point out the provenance of meat and cheeses, while desserts such as steamed lemon sponge with custard ice cream, or rhubarb crumble brûlée with ginger shortbread strike a traditional note. The lunchtime set-price menus are particularly good value. The wine list runs to around 30 bottles and has some interesting, food-friendly choices. Six house wines start at £13.75 a bottle, £3.50 a glass.

CHEFS: Jon Howe and Brent Castle   PROPRIETOR: Brent Castle   OPEN: Tue to Sun 12 to 2 (2.30 Sun), 7 to 9.30   CLOSED: 2 weeks Christmas   MEALS: alc (main courses £14). Set L £10.50 (2 courses) to £12.50   SERVICE: not inc, card slips closed   CARDS: Delta, MasterCard, Switch, Visa DETAILS: 45 seats. 24 seats outside. Private parties: 45 main room. Car park. Children's helpings. No-smoking area. Wheelchair access (also WC). No music £5

ULLSWATER Cumbria   map 10

▲ Sharrow Bay ❦ ✳

Ullswater CA10 2LZ
TEL: (01768) 486301   FAX: (01768) 486349
EMAIL: enquiries@sharrow-bay.com
WEBSITE: www.sharrow-bay.com   COOKING 6
2m from Pooley Bridge on E side of lake, on road   ENGLISH
signposted Howtown and Martindale   £45–£80

Sharrow Bay 'seems to have a gilt complex' according to a visitor who noted the musical icons, cherubs and fruits sculpted in gold on the walls and woven into the pink carpet. The place is devoted to pampering, which starts with a drink in the conservatory or one of the lounges. The vestigial 'dinner party' idea of all sitting down together remains in the 8pm dinner call.

The food is varied and attractive: in a light, flavourful, whizzed up mousse of crab and scallops with chunks of seafood embedded, or in a small, skinless fillet of brill, crisp outside, moist inside, served with lightly spiced aubergine. Combinations of different cuts and cooking methods are a trademark: for example a medallion of pink veal fillet covered in a creamy mushroom sauce, partnered by an equally generous portion of calf's liver and some smoked bacon. Cheese, which can be taken before or after dessert, offers a fair choice of mostly British examples, cut to order, while desserts themselves might include a refreshing, pyramid-shaped, clear framboise jelly filled with a mix of seasonal berries, or a dark chocolate tart with a creamy raspberry sorbet. Staff are polite and deferential but not obsequious. A fine selection of Bordeaux and Burgundy is augmented by other regions of the world, with a good selection of wines under £20. The 17 wines in the Sharrow Selection (from £16.95 to £34) are chosen to match the food and are all available by the glass.

CHEFS: Juan Martin and Colin Akrigg   PROPRIETOR: Nigel Lightburn   OPEN: all week 1 for 1.30, 8 for 8.30   CLOSED: mid Dec to end Feb   MEALS: Set L £30 to £38.25, Set D £49.25   SERVICE: 8%, card slips closed   CARDS: Amex, Delta, MasterCard, Switch, Visa   DETAILS: 65 seats. Private parties: 35 main room. Car park. Vegetarian meals. No children under 13. Jacket and tie. No smoking. Wheelchair access (also WC). No music. No mobile phones. Air-conditioned ACCOMMODATION: 25 rooms, all with bath/shower. TV. Phone. D, B&B £140 to £225. Rooms for disabled. No children under 13 (*The Which? Guide to Good Hotels*)

ULVERSTON Cumbria   map 8

▲ Bay Horse ⭐✗

Canal Foot, Ulverston LA12 9EL
TEL: (01229) 583972   FAX: (01229) 580502
EMAIL: reservations@thebayhorsehotel.co.uk
WEBSITE: www.thebayhorsehotel.co.uk   COOKING 4
off A590; just NE of Ulverston centre, turn SE and   COUNTRY-HOUSE
follow signs to Canal Foot   £28–£62

Situated at the end of a long cul-de-sac, after some unprepossessing industrial landscape, this pub used to mark the start or finish of a coach stage that ran across Morecambe Bay at low tide. Complementing its homely atmosphere are sweeping views over Cartmel Sands (so good from the conservatory dining room that they can initially distract attention from the menu). A serious, hard-working kitchen makes its own bread and the chutneys that accompany bar snacks. Dishes on the two menus (carnivore and vegetarian), plus a new weekly-changing set-price dinner, range from prawn and avocado cocktail, or smoked duck breast and fresh mango to start, to pan-fried lamb's liver and kidneys with smoked bacon, or roast cod with Dijon mustard and fresh herb crust on creamed spinach as main courses. The monthly-changing carte could show mushroom and marsala soup, or local potted shrimps with hot buttered toast, preceding poached halibut with asparagus, or roast guinea fowl. Typical puddings are coconut meringue with mango and kiwi fruit, or raspberry cheesecake with passion-fruit custard. The wine list emphasises likeable southern-hemisphere bottles – South African especially; £20 buys a fair choice, but prices soon push higher.

CHEF: Robert Lyons   PROPRIETORS: John Tovey and Robert Lyons   OPEN: Tue to Sun L 12 to 1.30, all week D 7.30 for 8 (1 sitting)   MEALS: alc (main courses £22.50 to £24). Set L £17.95, Set D £27.50. Bar L menu available   SERVICE: not inc, card slips closed   CARDS: Amex, Delta, MasterCard, Switch, Visa   DETAILS: 50 seats. Private parties: 50 main room, 20 to 30 private rooms. Car park. Vegetarian meals. No children under 12. No smoking. Wheelchair access (also WC). Music   ACCOMMODATION: 9 rooms, all with bath/shower. TV. Phone. B&B £77.50 to £145. No children under 12 (*The Which? Guide to Good Hotels*)

▲ *means accommodation is available.*

All details are as accurate as possible at the time of going to press, but chefs and owners often change, and it is wise to check by telephone before making a special journey. Many readers have been disappointed when set-price bargain meals are no longer available. Ask when booking.

▲ Hambleton Hall ▾ ✖

Upper Hambleton LE15 8TH
TEL: (01572) 756991   FAX: (01572) 724721
EMAIL: hotel@hambletonhall.com
WEBSITE: www.hambleton.hall.com
off A606, 3m SE of Oakham

COOKING **7**
MODERN BRITISH
£37–£121

A narrow tree-lined drive leads to a Victorian country house set among pines and cedars, with views over Rutland Water, as fine a location as one might find in these parts. A bright dining room with yellow walls and white napery, and a generally pampering atmosphere, add to the enjoyable ethos of the place. The carte changes twice a year, set menus daily, and luxury materials abound, including lobster, foie gras and particularly mushrooms.

Freshness and quality of ingredients provide a firm foundation, evident in a first-course salad tower of crab, avocado and green beans with a moat of gazpacho-like tomato sauce, but the kitchen's sure hand and judgement also make a strong impression. This is country-house cooking of a high order and serious purpose, and there is much more to it than simply technical prowess, although pasta is 'probably the best I've had in this country', judging by a lasagne of chanterelles with pea purée and chicken mousse, and by a raviolo filled with creamy, frothy foie gras sauce that accompanies Bresse pigeon. There is also 'knockout' depth and clarity of flavour in some dishes: for example, in a light starter of clear tomato essence with poached langoustine tail, offering 'a refreshing crossfire of intense flavours'. Partnerships are generally well considered, from a starter of sweet roast scallops paired with refreshing de-pithed oranges and gently bitter endive, to a fine tian of Mediterranean vegetables that accompanies a main-course loin of lamb. Main courses tend to be complex, beautifully presented and quite rich, taking in, for example, pink, moist, well-flavoured, honey-roast breast of Goosnargh duck, accompanied by confit leg, strips of plum, braised chicory, braised cabbage with lardons, and a stock reduction flavoured with orange and ginger.

Vegetarians are well served, French and British cheeses, unpasteurised for the most part, are kept in good condition, and desserts have included three ways with pineapple, incorporating small dice topped by an unctuous pannacotta-type cream, a small Tatin, and best of all a mille-feuille of sorbet between slices of dried fruit set in a caramel coating. Prices appear to be creeping up, a point that concerns reporters, although service is generally assiduous and professional. The wine list is well suited to its environment, with extensive listings of top names from Bordeaux, Burgundy, the Rhône and the USA. Prices are generally high, but a few wines are pitched under £20 and rather more up to £30 – many of them listed on the page of 'Wines of the Moment'. An extensive range by the glass starts at £4.50, and there's a notable selection of dessert wines.

CHEF: Aaron Patterson   PROPRIETORS: Tim and Stefa Hart   OPEN: all week 12.30 to 1.30, 7.30 to 9.30   MEALS: alc (main courses £30 to £38.50). Set L Mon to Sat £17.50 (2 courses) to £23, Set L Sun £36, Set D £29.50 (2 courses) to £35   SERVICE: not inc   CARDS: Amex, Delta, Diners, MasterCard, Switch, Visa   DETAILS: 50 seats. Private parties: 60 main room, 6 to 20 private rooms. Car park. Vegetarian meals. No smoking. No music. No mobile phones ACCOMMODATION: 17 rooms, all with bath/shower. TV. Phone. B&B £155 to £345. Rooms for disabled. Baby facilities. Swimming pool (*The Which? Guide to Good Hotels*)

UPPER SLAUGHTER Gloucestershire   map 5

▲ Lords of the Manor ♥ ⅚✳

Upper Slaughter GL54 2JD
TEL: (01451) 820243   FAX: (01451) 820696
EMAIL: lordsofthemanor@btinternet.com   COOKING 6
WEBSITE: www.lordsofthemanor.com   MODERN FRENCH
turn W off A429, 2½m S of Stow-on-the-Wold   £36–£99

Although the house has been added to over the course of centuries, the architectural blend is all but seamless, with a modern accommodation wing, high-ceilinged Victorian reception rooms, and a dining room smartly kitted out with subdued furnishings. Toby Hill's food fits the place to a T. His style is indulgent without being too rich, taking in beetroot risotto with duck confit, a mosaic of pork, chicken and foie gras with apple chutney and Cumberland sauce, and a saffroned consommé of red mullet with ratatouille tortellini.

First-class materials are generally impeccably handled, and there is an air of consummate professionalism about the cooking. Fish options range from light-sounding roast sea bass with sauce vierge to John Dory with crushed potatoes and foie gras velouté, but most dishes operate within a reassuringly classical framework. Stuffed saddle of rabbit comes with tagliatelle and tarragon jus, for example, and slow-roast but rare fillet of Angus beef is served with horseradish mash and bordelaise sauce.

The repertoire may hold few surprises but certainly doesn't lack interest. There might be roast scallops with tomato sorbet to start, and lemongrass crème brûlée with thyme ice cream to finish, or else an iced nougat parfait with a compote of spring rhubarb. Service is 'proper' (with trays held by one staff member, from which plates are delivered by another), although it has not been without mishaps. A couple of reports have also mentioned small portion sizes. High prices slightly sour the appeal of a very good wine list – not so much in the realms of fine Burgundy, Bordeaux and premium Italians, but there are no real concessions to budget-conscious diners in the good Australian selection either. Nonetheless, it's good to see a champion for the best of English wine. Ten 'sommelier's favourites' come by the glass from £5.50, by the bottle from £24.

CHEF: Toby Hill   PROPRIETOR: Empire Ventures   OPEN: all week 12.30 to 2, 7 to 9.15   MEALS: alc (main courses £23 to £28). Set L Mon to Sat £16.95 (2 courses) to £19.95, Set L Sun £23.50, Set D £40 to £65   SERVICE: 12.5% (optional), card slips closed   CARDS: Amex, Delta, Diners, MasterCard, Switch, Visa   DETAILS: 50 seats. 25 seats outside. Private parties: 50 main room, 8 to 30 private rooms. Car park. Vegetarian meals. Children's helpings. No children under 7. No smoking. Wheelchair access (not WC). No music   ACCOMMODATION: 27 rooms, all with bath/shower. TV. Phone. B&B £99 to £305. Rooms for disabled. Baby facilities (*The Which? Guide to Good Hotels*)

Dining rooms where music, either live or recorded, is never played are signalled by No music *in the details at the end of an entry.*

▲ Percy's 🍴

Virginstow EX21 5EA
TEL: (01409) 211236 FAX: (01409) 211460
EMAIL: relax@percys.co.uk
WEBSITE: www.percys.co.uk   COOKING 4
follow signs to Percy's at Coombeshead from Gridley corner   MODERN BRITISH
on A388, or from B3218 at Metherell Cross junction   £39–£69

Much of the 130-acre estate on which this 400-year-old custard-coloured house
stands is given over to producing supplies for the kitchen. There are trout ponds,
a kitchen garden, and sheep, geese and chickens roam freely through the
grounds. The 60-acre forest has been planted with fruit- and nut-bearing trees
and shrubs, and this year the Bricknell-Webbs have also opened a chefs' school –
lunchtime guests will be able to test the talents of their prodigies.

Whether you visit for lunch or dinner (and lunch is reckoned to be up to
scratch), the style, in theory, is simple home-cooking. In practice, a tendency to
dress dishes up with abundant herbs can make things seem more complex, as in
a reporter's starter of first-rate, lightly seared scallops, liberally scattered with
dill and served on a salad with a strong mustard dressing. To follow, choices
might include pan-fried monkfish with julienne of vegetables and ginger in
saffron sauce, or lavender-roast loin of lamb with a rosemary jus and mash
flavoured pungently with lovage. Well-made desserts have run to 'fresh, tangy'
lemon tart with rosemary ice cream and raspberries, or you could opt for the
selection of West Country cheeses. Around a dozen wines of each colour provide
good variety. Bottle prices start at £15, and there are six by the glass from £4.50.

CHEF: Tina Bricknell-Webb PROPRIETORS: Tony and Tina Bricknell-Webb OPEN: all week 12 to
1.30, 6.30 to 9 MEALS: Set L £20 (2 courses) to £25.50, Set D £40 to £45 SERVICE: not inc, card
slips closed CARDS: Amex, Delta, MasterCard, Switch, Visa DETAILS: 32 seats. Private parties:
28 main room, 12 to 40 private rooms. Car park. No children under 12. No smoking. Wheelchair
access (also WC). Music ACCOMMODATION: 8 rooms, all with bath/shower. TV. Phone. D,B&B
£155 to £290. Rooms for disabled. No children under 12. Fishing (*The Which? Guide to Good
Hotels*)

▲ Best Beech Inn 🍴   [NEW ENTRY]

Mayfield Lane, Best Beech Hill, Wadhurst TN5 6JH
TEL: (01892) 782046 FAX: (01892) 785092   COOKING 3
WEBSITE: www.bestbeechinn.co.uk   MODERN EUROPEAN
on B2100, midway between Mark Cross and Wadhurst   £24–£49

An original Cyclists' Touring Club badge on a chimney marks out this, part-
tiled, roadside Wealden pub. Walk through the wooden-floored bistro and bar
and into a richly decorated restaurant at the back. The kitchen makes the most of
good (and local) ingredients, and has really made an impact with a repertoire
that kicks off with an excellent creamy risotto of peas and broad beans crusted
with Parmesan flakes and decorated with truffle oil, and a well-made ham hock
and baby leek terrine with truffle and chorizo oils. Tender calf's liver, albeit

cooked through, a rich gravy scented subtly with sage, plus fine spinach and mash was a simple but well-executed dish, and careful timing showed in duck breast with young parsnips and carrots, served with a vanilla mash. A 'plate of chocolate' trio consisted of excellent milk chocolate ice, a crisp, deeply flavoured tart, and a warm fondant with crisp exterior and runny centre. Rhubarb and raspberry pannacotta with lightly poached compote of berries is a colourful alternative ending. One-plate dishes (pork, beer and hop sausages with mash and onion gravy) and sandwiches are offered at lunchtimes. Young staff are willing and efficient. Wines are a brief, reasonable set of 30, starting at £9.95 and offering plenty under £20.

CHEF: Michael Weir   PROPRIETOR: Roger Felstead   OPEN: all week L 12 to 2, Tue to Sat D 7 to 9
MEALS: alc (main courses L £7 to £11.50, D £15 to £17.50). Set D Mon to Thur £12.95 (2 courses)
to £14.95   SERVICE: not inc   CARDS: MasterCard, Switch, Visa   DETAILS: 65 seats. 21 seats
outside. Private parties: 32 main room. Car park. Vegetarian meals. No children in restaurant; no
children under 10 in bistro. No smoking in 1 dining room. Wheelchair access (not WC). Music
ACCOMMODATION: 7 rooms. TV. Phone. B&B £39.90 to £79.90 (£5)

WALKINGTON East Riding of Yorkshire   **map 9**

▲ Manor House ⅝✳

Northlands, Newbold Road,
Walkington HU17 8RU
TEL: (01482) 881645   FAX: (01482) 866501   COOKING **1**
WEBSITE: www.the-manor-house.co.uk   MODERN BRITISH
off B1230 towards Beverley from Walkington   £25–£63

This pleasant country-house hotel some way off the beaten track has an expensively draped conservatory dining room, and a modest three acres of grounds with stabling, should you happen to turn up on horseback. Derek Baugh offers an extensive, fixed-price dinner menu, built around local fish and meats, with lobsters and scallops from Bridlington when available. The modern British approach brings on a fashionable 'pan-fried stack' constructed of foie gras, celeriac and olive oil mash with a fruity fumet of sloe gin. A nerveless striving after novelty might see shredded rabbit confit teamed with grape chutney and a Thai dipping sauce, but main courses ply a distinctly more mainstream line: witness pork cutlet with glazed apple, sea bass with beurre noisette, and lobster thermidor. 'A tour of the cheeseboard' is the alternative to the tarts, sponges and puddings of the dessert menu. No wine list was supplied; house is £14.95.

CHEF: Derek Baugh   PROPRIETORS: Derek and Lee Baugh   OPEN: Mon to Sat D only 7 to 9.15
CLOSED: 25 Dec to 4 Jan   MEALS: Set D £15 (Mon to Fri) to £32.50   SERVICE: not inc, card slips
closed   CARDS: Delta, MasterCard, Switch, Visa   DETAILS: 50 seats. Private parties: 70 main
room, 8 to 20 private rooms. Car park. Vegetarian meals. No smoking. Children by arrangement.
Wheelchair access (not WC). Occasional music. No mobile phones   ACCOMMODATION: 7 rooms,
all with bath/shower. TV. Phone. Room only £70 to £110. Rooms for disabled

---

| NEW CHEF | *is shown instead of a cooking mark where a change of chef occurred too late for a new assessment of the cooking.*

---

map 2

▲ Bishopstrow House ✶✷

Warminster BA12 9HH
TEL: (01985) 212312   FAX: (01985) 216769
EMAIL: enquiries@bishopstrow.co.uk
WEBSITE: www.bishopstrow.co.uk
on B3414, 1m E of Warminster

| NEW CHEF |

MODERN COUNTRY-HOUSE
£32–£62

This Georgian country house is surrounded by acres of English gardens through which runs the River Wylye (good for trout fishing). Close to Bath, the hotel is host to those seeking rejuvenation of all kinds including the culinary variety. Chef Chris Suter departed in summer 2003 after some 15 years at the stoves to be replaced by his former sous-chef, Steve Bywater. This happened too late for an inspection, though we understand the style will remain the same. Previously, grilled asparagus has come with roast red peppers, tapenade and shaved Parmesan, tiger prawns as marinière with scallops, mussels, coconut lime and lemongrass. Roast sea bass with braised Puy lentils, pancetta and thyme is a typical main course, while desserts run to orange crème brûlée and tangerine sorbet, or melting chocolate sponge with exotic fruit and vanilla ice cream. A French duo kicks off the wine list at £14, and there is some interest below the £20 mark.

CHEF: Steve Bywater   PROPRIETOR: Von Essen Hotels   OPEN: all week 12.30 to 2, 7.30 to 9.30   MEALS: Set L Mon to Fri £12 (2 courses), Set D £38. Bar menu also available L and D exc Sat. Snack menu available 2 to 6   SERVICE: 15% (optional)   CARDS: Amex, Delta, Diners, MasterCard, Switch, Visa   DETAILS: 50 seats. 30 seats outside. Private parties: 70 main room, 10 to 30 private rooms. Car park. Vegetarian meals. Children's helpings. No smoking. Wheelchair access (also WC). Music. No mobile phones   ACCOMMODATION: 32 rooms, all with bath/shower. TV. Phone. B&B £99 to £375. Baby facilities. Swimming pool (*The Which? Guide to Good Hotels*) (£5)

map 5

Findons ✶✷

7 Old Square, Warwick CV34 4RA
TEL: (01926) 411755   FAX: (01926) 400453
EMAIL: rosemary@findons-restaurant.co.uk
WEBSITE: www.findons-restaurant.co.uk

COOKING 2
MODERN BRITISH
£36–£60

If the one-way system confuses, head in the direction of St Mary's Church to find Findons. Once there, you will be greeted by a lemon and blue colour scheme, interspersed with ornately framed prints of Art History's greatest hits from Caravaggio to Picasso. The cooking, praised by reporters for its precision and thoughtful presentation, covers a fair amount of ground too, running the gamut from bouillabaisse, or seared king scallops in a broth of lobster and Sambuca with caramelised chicory, to beef fillet on bubble and squeak with a basil jus. French-style desserts might involve making bread-and-butter pudding with brioche, or applying a rum and raisin anglaise sauce to a warm mousse of chocolate and black cherries. Service from French staff is conscientious and attentive. A short slate of limited-quantity mature clarets adds depth to the evenly mixed European and New World wine list. House French is £3.50 a glass, £12.95 the bottle. The restaurant is no longer open for lunch.

CHEF: Michael Findon   PROPRIETOR: Findon & Williams Ltd   OPEN: Mon to Sat D only 6.30 to 9.30   CLOSED: 26 Dec to 3 Jan   MEALS: alc (main courses £13 to £19)   SERVICE: not inc, 10% for parties of 6 or more   CARDS: Delta, Diners, MasterCard, Switch, Visa   DETAILS: 40 seats. 25 seats outside. Private parties: 30 main room, 8 to 14 private rooms. Vegetarian meals. No children under 11. No smoking in 1 dining room. Wheelchair access (not WC). Music   £5

WATERMILLOCK Cumbria   map 10

▲ Rampsbeck Country House Hotel ♀ 💥

Watermillock on Ullswater CA11 0LP
TEL: (017684) 86442   FAX: (017684) 86688
EMAIL: enquiries@rampsbeck.fsnet.co.uk
WEBSITE: www.rampsbeck.fsnet.co.uk   COOKING 4
on A592 Penrith to Windermere road 1½m from N   ANGLO-FRENCH
end of Ullswater   £37–£64

This eighteenth-century house overlooks Ullswater from 18 acres of grounds. For aperitifs you sit in one of two lounges on a comfy armchair, sofa or even a chaise longue, before moving to the relaxing pink-clothed dining room. It seems Andrew McGeorge's kitchen is on an upswing, showing panache in dishes like seared queen scallops in a salad, given texture by sautéed potatoes and leeks and flavoured by a spicy shallot dressing. At the four-course, fixed-price dinner (soup follows the starter) main courses balance richness and complexity with clear, fresh-tasting flavours: Dover sole en papillote is stuffed with carrot, leeks and parsnip, then finished with lush lobster sauce. If pig's cheek with roast roots and truffled mash bursts the usual bounds of country-house cooking, sumptuously creamy desserts respect them. Prune and Armagnac pudding with its own ice cream and butterscotch sauce resembles upmarket sticky toffee, while loose-textured crème brûlée laced with bourbon comes with a gutsy compote of rhubarb and ginger. Service is friendly and unintrusive. Wines are arranged by style, with France, Italy and Australia the major elements in an enterprising selection. Prices are fair, and most styles include both everyday and special-occasion bottles; ten house wines start at £11.25, and five come by the glass (£2.40).

CHEF: Andrew McGeorge   PROPRIETORS: Tom and Marion Gibb   OPEN: all week 12 to 1.15 (bookings only), 7 to 8.30   CLOSED: early Jan to mid-Feb   MEALS: alc (main courses £9 to £11). Set L £28, Set D £36 to £42.50. Light bar L menu available   SERVICE: not inc, card slips closed   CARDS: Delta, MasterCard, Switch, Visa   DETAILS: 40 seats. Private parties: 65 main room, 8 to 15 private rooms. Car park. Children's helpings. No smoking. No music. No mobile phones   ACCOMMODATION: 20 rooms, all with bath/shower. TV. Phone. B&B £60 to £210. Fishing (The Which? Guide to Good Hotels)

💥 indicates there are some restrictions on smoking, though it is not banned altogether.

All entries in the Guide are re-researched and rewritten every year, not least because restaurant standards fluctuate. Don't rely on an out-of-date Guide.

WATH-IN-NIDDERDALE North Yorkshire map 8

▲ Sportsman's Arms ▼ ⅍

Wath-in-Nidderdale, Pateley Bridge HG3 5PP	COOKING 4
TEL: (01423) 711306 FAX: (01423) 712524	ANGLO-FRENCH
off B6265, 2m NW of Pateley Bridge	£29–£51

The delightful Dales village of Wath-in-Nidderdale, with its old stone buildings, is the setting for this seventeenth-century hotel and restaurant. The surrounding grouse moors and trout streams couldn't be more English, but there's something distinctly French about the dining room, with its collection of antique clocks, mirrors and crisp linen-covered tables. The menu makes good use of local produce, as in a starter of pan-fried Nidderdale trout with beurre noisette, capers and almonds, or a main-course fillet of Pateley Bridge lamb with asparagus and a roasted garlic and tomato jus. Fish, delivered daily from Whitby, is a real strength, and among accomplished desserts might be crème brûlée, or summer pudding, which, according to the owners, is the 'most popular dessert over the past 23 years'. Service is friendly and professional. Presentation is crisp and prices are good on a wine list that looks modern but favours France. Burgundy is strong, and a fresh approach to Bordeaux turns up a number of bottles under £20. Other countries are sound but less of a thrill. House wines start at £12.90, and a dozen come by the glass from £2.50.

CHEFS: Ray and Jamie Carter, and Seth Marsland   PROPRIETORS: Ray and Jane Carter   OPEN: Sun L 12 to 2, Mon to Sat D 6.45 to 9   CLOSED: 25 Dec   MEALS: alc D (main courses £10.50 to £16). Set L £20. Bar menu available   SERVICE: not inc, card slips closed   CARDS: Delta, MasterCard, Switch, Visa   DETAILS: 80 seats. 30 seats outside. Private parties: 50 main room, 8 to 14 private rooms. Car park. Children's helpings. No smoking. Wheelchair access (not WC). No music. No mobile phones   ACCOMMODATION: 13 rooms, 12 with bath/shower. TV. Phone. B&B £60 to £105. Fishing (The Which? Guide to Good Hotels)

WELLS Somerset map 2

Ritcher's

5 Sadler Street, Wells BA5 2RR	COOKING 2
TEL: (01749) 679085 FAX: (01749) 673866	MODERN BRITISH
WEBSITE: www.ritchers.co.uk	£19–£40

Down an alley off the town square, this modest restaurant avoids anything remotely flashy or metropolitan. Ingredients, we're pleased to say, take centre stage, and this brings meat from independent farms, live lobsters and cheeses from a decent supplier. Menus have a faint air of nostalgia, but, especially in skilled hands, duck liver and foie gras pâté and standards like duck confit with roast cabbage and red wine and onion gravy are *ipso facto* to be appreciated. Simple dishes like smoked salmon with tarragon cream, and a main course of chicken with pea purée, have received praise. Dessert brings a 'very fruity' raspberry parfait, although apple tart has been reported as on the heavy side. Wines are taken seriously, and nine house bottles from £9.95 to £13.75, all available in two sizes of glass, head a fair international selection, ending with a notable range of vintage ports.

CHEF: Nick Hart PROPRIETORS: Nick Hart and Kate Ritcher OPEN: Tue to Sat 12 to 2, 7 to 9.30 (6.30 to 10 Sat) CLOSED: 26 Dec, 1 Jan MEALS: Set L £6.95 (1 course) to £10.95, Set D £19.50 (2 courses) to £23.50 SERVICE: not inc, card slips closed CARDS: MasterCard, Switch, Visa DETAILS: 40 seats. 12 seats outside. Private parties: 20 main room. Vegetarian meals. No children under 10 at D. No cigars/pipes when others are eating. Wheelchair access (not WC). Music

WELWYN GARDEN CITY Hertfordshire map 3

▲ Auberge du Lac

Brocket Hall, Lemsford, Welwyn Garden
City AL8 7XG
TEL: (01707) 368888 FAX: (01707) 368898
EMAIL: auberge@brocket-hall.co.uk
WEBSITE: www.brockethall.co.uk

COOKING **6**
MODERN FRENCH
£42–£95

After a taste of success followed by failure as a restaurant entrepreneur, Jean-Christophe Novelli has returned to what he does best, having been appointed head chef at this eighteenth-century hunting lodge in the grounds of Brocket Hall. As the Guide goes to press, however, we hear that Novelli is to overhaul the company's London property, to create Novelli in the City. The Auberge remains his priority, we are told. The conservatory dining area enjoys views over the Arcadian splendour of the park, and there's a slightly more sombre room with a brick-built, curved roof structure.

The confidence and verve exhibited in an inspection meal suggest that Novelli has been given the freedom to express his enthusiasm and talents to the full. Starters at that meal included an impressively light pan-fried goats' cheese terrine, wrapped in strips of marinated aubergine with red peppers and olive salsa on the side, and grilled deep-sea scallops and black pudding – three mini-towers with sweet scallops complementing spicy black pudding, sandwiching an apple crisp and dusted with coral powder, garnished with caviar and horseradish sauce.

Though Novelli works within an essentially classical French framework, he does so with great panache, and the results can be pretty exciting: witness roast turbot with a gently garlicky and creamy dauphinois topping, accompanied by six mussels stuffed with diced tomato and asparagus tips, roast garlic and a delicate cep sauce. Also impressive has been a pair of pink-roast lamb cutlets topped with a Stilton soufflé and served on green lentils with baby turnips, thyme flowers and roast garlic. Desserts, which come garnished with trademark sugar spirals, are exercises in contrast: hot bitter chocolate cake, for example, with a runny chocolate sauce centre, paired with white chocolate ice cream, or glazed lemon tart with lemon and thyme sorbet. Bordeaux and Burgundy are the chief interests of the mainly French wine list, including some vastly expensive special old vintages. Prices start at £20, but the list doesn't really get going below £30, so diners on a budget are best served by the appealing selection of 16 by the glass for £7 to £17.

CHEF: Jean-Christophe Novelli PROPRIETOR: CCA OPEN: Tue to Sun L 12 to 3, Tue to Sat D 7 to 10.30 MEALS: alc (main courses £13.50 to £30). Set L Mon to Fri £28 (inc wine), Set L Sat and Sun £35 SERVICE: 10% (optional), card slips closed CARDS: Amex, Delta, Diners, MasterCard, Switch, Visa DETAILS: 75 seats. 30 seats outside. Private parties: 60 main room, 4 to 18 private rooms. Car park. Vegetarian meals. Children's helpings. No cigars/pipes in dining room.

Wheelchair access (not WC). Music. No mobile phones. Air-conditioned   ACCOMMODATION: 16 rooms, all with bath/shower. TV. Phone. B&B £160 to £185. Rooms for disabled. No children under 2. Fishing

WEST BAY Dorset   map 2

Riverside Restaurant ♀ ✶

West Bay DT6 4EZ
TEL: (01308) 422011   FAX: (01308) 458808
WEBSITE: www.riverside-restaurant.co.uk
off A35, 1m S of Bridport

COOKING 3
SEAFOOD
£24–£73

Little changes at this unpretentious place seemingly marooned in the sea and approached by a footbridge. Barring a few meat and veggie dishes (two each), the menu is just fresh fish, served simply (vegetables are extra) in plain, uncluttered surroundings – all white except for a bare wood floor, blue chair seats, and art for sale on one wall. But in 2002 a talented former chef returned, bringing consistency and improving both cooking and presentation. Risotto was spot on this year: langoustines, spinach and proper rice transformed into an unctuous, not over-cheesy dish. Chilli and ginger with sea bass was brought off with subtlety and success. Vegetables can still be dull, chips have been poor, but puddings are generally fine: a nutty, creamy pistachio ice cream accompanied a crumbly shortcrust fig tart; alternatives could be gooseberry crème brûlée, or even Knickerbocker Glory. The mainly white wine list is excellent value and doesn't skimp on range or quality. We've heard the arguments but still wonder why so many other restaurants can't (or won't) sell, say, Jackson Estate Sauvignon at £17.50, Pieropan's Soave at £15.50 or fabled benchmark Cloudy Bay Sauvignon at £24.75. House basics and seven classier options come by the glass for £3.50 to £4.75.

CHEFS: Chris Ansell, Nic Larcombe and Will Watson   PROPRIETORS: Arthur and Janet Watson   OPEN: Tue to Sun L 12 to 2.15, Tue to Sat D 6.30 to 9 (phone to check; open Sun D and Mon L and D at bank hols)   CLOSED: 1 Dec to 14 Feb   MEALS: alc (main courses £9.50 to £25). Set L £12.50 (2 courses) to £15.50   SERVICE: not inc, card slips closed   CARDS: Delta, MasterCard, Switch, Visa   DETAILS: 90 seats. 20 seats outside. Private parties: 100 main room, 6 to 22 private rooms. Vegetarian meals. Children's helpings. No smoking. Wheelchair access (also women's WC). Occasional music

WEST TANFIELD North Yorkshire   map 9

▲ Bruce Arms ✶ £

Main Street, West Tanfield HG4 5JJ
TEL: (01677) 470325   FAX: (01677) 470796
EMAIL: geoffsmith@brucearms.com
WEBSITE: www.brucearms.com

COOKING 4
MODERN ENGLISH
£29–£47

Behind its vine-clad stone exterior lies the self-styled 'bistro with bedrooms'. A low-beamed bar with two main dining areas, with a third space towards the rear, is where the 'very personable' Jan Smith works with smiling efficiency, while husband, chef/patron Geoff, takes the helm in the kitchen. Starters might include twice-baked cheese soufflé or gravad lax with warm roast onion tart and crème fraîche. Ingredients for the half-dozen dishes at each course rely on local suppliers where possible, and roast rack of Dales lamb with fresh tarragon, or breast of chicken with field mushrooms, roast red onions and red wine gravy, show their quality. One reader was inspired by a main course combination of red snapper with avocado, prawn and mango salad. Desserts include coffee crème brûlée, or caramelised rice pudding with black cherry compote. House Duboeuf is £2.95 a glass or £10.95 a bottle, with a half-bottle option. Beyond this, the helpfully annotated list encompasses around 20 each of reds and whites, mostly under £20.

CHEF: Geoff Smith   PROPRIETORS: Geoff and Jan Smith   OPEN: Sun L 12 to 2 (also open L Wed to Sat Apr to Oct), Wed to Sun D 6.30 to 9.30   CLOSED: 2 weeks Feb   MEALS: alc (main courses £10.50 to £16.50)   SERVICE: not inc, card slips closed   CARDS: MasterCard, Switch, Visa DETAILS: 50 seats. 16 seats outside. Private parties: 26 main room. Car park. Vegetarian meals. No smoking in 1 dining room. Music   ACCOMMODATION: 3 rooms, all with bath/shower. TV. B&B £40 to £60

WETHERSFIELD Essex   map 6

Dicken's Brasserie ✂ £

The Green, Wethersfield CM7 4BS
TEL: (01371) 850723   FAX: (01371) 850727   COOKING 2
EMAIL: reservations@dickensbrasserie.co.uk   MODERN BRITISH
WEBSITE: www.dickensbrasserie.co.uk   £25–£44

Overlooking the small village green in a quiet corner of Essex, this neat, three-storey deep-blue-painted building with pleasant flower tubs around the front door houses two attractive yet informal dining rooms. The timbered main room at the back has an olde-worlde feel and comes complete with minstrel's gallery, while the smaller front room is done out in more modern style, with bright paintings of food on vivid blue walls. The winning formula continues to be unfussy, well-cooked and mostly traditional food, with many dishes offered both as starters or main courses. There are some international touches, too, and Thai salmon fishcakes, lamb kofta, or Mediterranean tart might sit alongside prawn cocktail, sausage and mash, and various grills. Deceptively simple duck liver salad with goats' cheese topped with a poached egg got all the elements spot on, and a light lemon brûlée with a fresh citrus salad has made a pleasant finish. Besides 20 or so wines on the list at £15 the bottle (£2.50/£3.75 the small/large glass), a few 'vintage' bottles are offered, plus house wines at £9.95.

CHEF/PROPRIETOR: John Dicken   OPEN: all week 12 to 2, 6.30 to 9.30   MEALS: alc (main courses £10 to £15.50). Set L Sun £12 (2 courses) to £16   SERVICE: not inc   CARDS: Delta, MasterCard, Switch, Visa   DETAILS: 40 seats. Private parties: 48 main room, 20 private room. Car park. Children's helpings. No smoking. Wheelchair access (not WC). Music. No mobile phones

---

▌ *denotes an outstanding wine cellar;* ♟ *denotes a good wine list, worth travelling for.*

Not inc *in the details at the end of an entry indicates that no service charge is made and any tipping is at the discretion of the customer.*

WHITBY North Yorkshire   map 9

Magpie Café ✹ £

14 Pier Road, Whitby YO21 3PU
TEL: (01947) 602058   FAX: (01947) 601801   COOKING 2
EMAIL: ian@magpiecafe.co.uk   SEAFOOD
WEBSITE: www.magpiecafe.co.uk   £19–£57

Waiting in the inevitable queue for a table at this bustling harbourside restaurant just opposite the fish market is 'an entertaining experience', thanks to the pleasant company of waiting diners: one visitor suggested that 'it's worth the wait' should become the restaurant's motto. Dishes of the day are chalked on a board, and there is a range of menus depending on the time of day, with most consideration given to 'all things fishy'. Whitby cod and chips is always on the menu, but you may be drawn to skate wing in black butter, lobster thermidor, or halibut 'de luxe' (cooked in butter and lemon juice with grapes). The wine list favours crisp whites and, like the restaurant as a whole, represents good value, with prices starting at £8.95.

CHEFS: Ian Robson and Paul Gildroy   PROPRIETORS: Ian and Alison McKenzie Robson   OPEN: all week 11.30 to 9 (6.30 Sun Nov to Mar)   CLOSED: 24 and 25 Dec, 5 Jan to 6 Feb   MEALS: alc (main courses £5.50 to £18)   SERVICE: not inc, card slips closed   CARDS: Delta, MasterCard, Switch, Visa   DETAILS: 100 seats. Private parties: 50 main room. Vegetarian meals. Children's helpings. No smoking. Occasional music. Air-conditioned £5

WHITCHURCH Hampshire   map 2

Red House ✹ £

21 London Street, Whitchurch RG28 7LH   COOKING 3
TEL: (01256) 895558   GLOBAL
                                                                          £25–£45

The Red House is actually white-walled, though its doors are red. It's an authentic pub, complete with public bar, plus an extensive terraced garden behind with children's play area and barbecue. The atmosphere is relaxed and the staff friendly, but what most impressed an inspector was the cooking, despite its unassuming air. Dishes are colourful and attractively presented and use quality ingredients with lots of flavour – qualities that were abundant in roast chump of lamb with a sausage of Parmesan- and rosemary-flavoured polenta and Madeira jus, as well as in monkfish with chive mash and foie gras butter. Starters have included chicken, artichoke and feta ravioli with cep sauce, and smoked halibut and red onion tart with roast pepper coulis and quails' eggs, and to finish there may be lemon tart and vanilla ice cream, or roughish-textured, clear-flavoured sorbets. Ten house wines are available by the bottle from £9.95, or the glass from £2.50. The full list runs to nearly 30 bins from across the world, the majority under £20.

CHEFS: Shannon Wells and Pete Nash   PROPRIETORS: Shannon and Caroline Wells   OPEN: all week 12 to 2, 6.30 (7 Sun) to 9.30   MEALS: alc (main courses £5 to £16)   SERVICE: not inc, 10% for parties of 8 or more, card slips closed   CARDS: MasterCard, Switch, Visa   DETAILS: 36 seats. 30 seats outside. Private parties: 30 main room. Car park. Vegetarian meals. No smoking. No music. No mobile phones

WHITSTABLE Kent

map 3

Sportsman ✳

Faversham Road, Seasalter, Whitstable CT5 4BP

COOKING **4**

TEL: (01227) 273370   FAX: (01227) 262314

MODERN EUROPEAN

£28–£48

The Sportsman stands in the shelter of sea defences in an isolated spot, with only ramshackle beach huts and marsh-grazing sheep for neighbours. Inside, the large central bar counter dominates, and plain décor and huge old pine tables laid with cutlery wrapped in paper napkins make sure you don't forget that this is still a pub at heart. Some love the unadorned simplicity; others find it uninspiring. Stephen Harris's cooking is similarly understated, occasionally leaving reporters underwhelmed. But for others it 'epitomises the perfection that can be found in simple treatment of fine ingredients', as in asparagus soup with the flavour of 'pure essence of asparagus', accompanied by a soft-boiled duck egg and asparagus 'soldiers'. Main courses have included lightly cooked cod fillet with a fresh, herby cockle pistou and silky-smooth mash, and roast rump of lamb cooked pink and served with 'sublime' boulangère potatoes and a rich yet delicate jus. Tricksy desserts have included a pairing of coffee parfait (made to look like a cappuccino) and Earl Grey granita with a 'refreshing citrusy zing'. The short blackboard wine list packs in quality – especially from the antipodes – and prices are good, starting with New Wave English house wine at £9.95 or £2.50 a glass.

CHEFS: Stephen Harris, Dan Flavell and Jim Shave   PROPRIETORS: Stephen, Philip and Damian Harris   OPEN: Tue to Sun L 12 to 2 (2.30 Sun), Tue to Sat D 7 to 9   CLOSED: 25 and 26 Dec   MEALS: alc (main courses £10 to £17)   SERVICE: not inc, card slips closed, 10% for parties of 6 or more   CARDS: Delta, MasterCard, Switch, Visa   DETAILS: 50 seats. Private parties: 45 main room. Car park. Vegetarian meals. Children's helpings. No smoking in 1 dining room. Music

Wheelers Oyster Bar

NEW ENTRY

8 High Street, Whitstable CT5 1BQ

COOKING **1**

TEL: (01227) 273311

SEAFOOD

£25–£44

'Established 1856' reads the legend outside this quaint-looking blue and pink shop. Inside is a small cluttered area with a seafood counter and a few stools, where fans 'pop in for oysters' and smoked salmon sandwiches. Beyond is a tiny 16-seater parlour used for 'proper sit-down meals': there's precious little elbow room, but it's all very jolly and informal. 'Stick to the simpler stuff' is sound advice as regards food: smoked haddock and cheese flan is a good choice from the 'light menu', otherwise consider something more substantial like grilled Dover sole. The kitchen also tackles a few ambitious-sounding ideas like caramelised scallops on asparagus, pea and mint risotto, and it's right on target with desserts such as lemon posset and strawberry crème brûlée. Book well in advance and bring your own drink (there's an off-licence across the road).

CHEF: Mark Stubbs PROPRIETOR: Delia Fitt OPEN: Tue and Thur to Sun 1 to 7.30 (7 Sun). Light L menu also available CLOSED: 25 Dec, two and a half weeks Jan MEALS: alc (main courses £12.50 to £18). Unlicensed, BYO (no corkage) SERVICE: not inc CARDS: none DETAILS: 16 seats. 4 seats outside. Private parties: 16 main room. Vegetarian meals. Wheelchair access (also WC). No music £5

WHITTLESFORD Cambridgeshire   map 6

Tickell Arms ✱   NEW ENTRY

1 North Road, Whittlesford CB2 4NZ   COOKING 5
TEL: (01223) 833128 FAX: (01223) 835907   MODERN FRENCH
just off A505 from M11 junction 10   £29–£67

The Tickell Arms looks intriguing from the outside, set back from the road behind shrubbery, its frontage painted 'the brightest blue ever', with stone lions guarding the front door. The quirkiness continues inside: pink and emerald green are the dominant colours, while the conservatory extension is filled with plants, some ceiling-height.

In the same way that the building resembles no other country pub, the food is about as far from pub grub as it is possible to be. Chef Spencer Patrick shows high ambition and a taste for luxuries in his cooking, which is not entirely surprising when you consider that his 'very cosmopolitan pedigree' includes stints as chef at various Marco Pierre White-owned restaurants in London. Raw materials are first-class and technique is finely honed, producing starters such as a subtle terrine of smoked guinea fowl, sweetbreads and foie gras, studded with pistachios and truffle and served with intensely flavoured glazed figs, or tortellini of Scottish lobster and scallops with coriander and coconut foam. Main courses have featured confit halibut with ventrèche and scallops on pea velouté ('more a clever collection of top-class ingredients than a thrilling new whole'), roast Barbary duck with cabbage stuffed with potato purée and a spicy sauce, and to finish there might be crème vanille with candied rhubarb. Bread failed to impress at inspection, and service could have been more on the ball. The short wine list offers house French white and Italian red at £15.

CHEF: Spencer Patrick PROPRIETOR: Tickell Arms Management OPEN: Tue to Sun L 12 to 2, Tue to Sat D 7 to 9 CLOSED: 24 to 26 Dec, 31 Dec, 1 Jan MEALS: alc (main courses L £8 to £17, D £12.50 to £25). Set L £16.50, Set D £34.50 SERVICE: not inc, card slips closed CARDS: Amex, Delta, Diners, MasterCard, Switch, Visa DETAILS: 45 seats. 20 seats outside. Private parties: 40 to 80. Car park. No smoking. Music. No mobile phones

WILLITON Somerset   map 2

▲ White House ▮ ✱

11 Long Street, Williton TA4 4QW   COOKING 6
TEL: (01984) 632306 and 632777   ENGLISH/MEDITERRANEAN
                                                                        £51–£61

The White House has for a long time been regarded as a haven of good taste, offering a civilised setting in a splendid Georgian mansion with a walled garden that can be viewed from the dining room. The fact that it is open for dinner only for just five months of the year serves to enhance the aura of exclusivity.

Menus radiate unpretentious Mediterranean vibes, offering attractively straightforward dishes such as thinly sliced grilled breast of local wood pigeon, served rare, on hot shredded beetroot, a polenta-crust tart filled with sliced tomatoes, goats' cheese, pesto and pine kernels, or a pancake filled with prawns, mussels and mushrooms and given a creamy cheese gratin topping. And that's just for starters. To follow, perhaps, there might be pork tenderloin stuffed with green olives and garlic, wrapped in bacon and herbs and served on a red pepper sauce, or pan-fried red mullet fillets on honey- and wine-marinated aubergine with a tomato coulis, while dessert could take in praline and chocolate marquise, or pannacotta with grappa-infused berries. Finely honed cooking skills are underpinned by excellent raw materials from local suppliers, and all herbs are home-grown. Tempting monthly selections open a wine list that holds to the traditional values of offering mature bottles at fair prices. Traditional regions dominate too – Bordeaux, the Rhône and Germany stand out – but more rustic regions of France are also explored and the few New World bottles are well chosen. Prices start at £13, or £3.20 a glass.

CHEFS/PROPRIETORS: Dick and Kay Smith OPEN: all week D only 7 to 8.30 CLOSED: end Oct to end May MEALS: Set D £38 SERVICE: not inc CARDS: none DETAILS: 22 seats. Private parties: 6 main room. Car park. Children's helpings. No smoking. Wheelchair access (not WC). No music ACCOMMODATION: 10 rooms, 9 with bath/shower. TV. Phone. B&B £50 to £112. Baby facilities

WINCANTON Somerset   map 2

▲ Holbrook House, Cedar Restaurant 🍴✗

Wincanton BA9 8BS
TEL: (01963) 32377   FAX: (01963) 32681
EMAIL: enquiries@holbrookhouse.co.uk   COOKING 4
WEBSITE: www.holbrookhouse.co.uk   MODERN EUROPEAN
on A371, about 1m N of A303   £27–£75

Holbrook House Hotel, a huge old manor house in 17 acres, has leisure and conference facilities, as well as the Cedar Restaurant. 'Granny's-attic' domesticity marks the décor – fringed lampshades and deep sofas by the fireplace - and the dining room has brocade wallpaper and patterned curtains, cushions and carpets. There's a tendency to over-embellish some dishes too, though underlying the complexity and flourishes are very good cooking and raw materials.

Brett Sutton's seven-course tasting menu may include seared pigeon with artichoke and baby spinach, followed by saffron lasagne with asparagus tips and scallops. And a late spring main menu might bring a warm salad of seared chicken livers with charlotte potatoes and poached egg to start, then roast loin of lamb with smoked chicken mousse, pease pudding and caper and basil sauce. If cheeses from the substantial trolley don't tempt, then vodka-marinated berries with orange sabayon and lemon and basil sorbet might. The personal touch does count for something here, and staff are genuinely courteous and friendly. Outside the major French regions the wine list has more breadth than depth; eight wines come by the glass from £3.50 to £5.50, and around 15 half-bottles are listed.

CHEF: Brett Sutton PROPRIETORS: Pat and John McGinley OPEN: Sun L 12.30 to 2, all week D 7.30 to 9.30 MEALS: Set L £12.95, Set D £28 (2 courses) to £42. Light L menu available SERVICE: 10% (optional), card slips closed CARDS: Amex, Delta, MasterCard, Switch, Visa DETAILS: 60 seats. 40 seats outside. Private parties: 60 main room, 20 to 200 private rooms. Car park. Vegetarian meals. Children's helpings. No smoking. Wheelchair access (not WC). Music. No mobile phones ACCOMMODATION: 21 rooms, all with bath/shower. TV. Phone. B&B £135 to £245. Rooms for disabled. Baby facilities. Swimming pool (*The Which? Guide to Good Hotels*)

WINCHCOMBE Gloucestershire   map 5

5 North Street ✸   NEW ENTRY

5 North Street, Winchcombe GL54 5LH   COOKING 5
TEL: (01242) 604566   FAX: (01242) 603788   MODERN EUROPEAN
EMAIL: marcusashenford@yahoo.co.uk   £31–£64

Smack in the middle of the village in an ancient, terraced, half-timbered building is 5 North Street. The two tiny, linked dining rooms, all beamed ceilings and polished tables, are plainly furnished, with deep red walls and a small fireplace. This is chef/proprietor Marcus Ashenford's first venture on his own, although he is no stranger to the Guide. His style of cooking sees lots of classical Mediterranean items such as ratatouille and pesto, and home-made pasta, alongside his trademark beignets and little 'Siamese twin' loaves of bread. Following nibbles (cheese beignets) and an appetiser of perhaps mushroom and smoked bacon soup, diners may move smoothly into a starter salad of home-cured salmon with grilled scallops dressed with bright, grassy-green puddles of pure-tasting chive 'essence' and streaked with reduced balsamic vinegar. Main courses such as fillet of beef topped with an oxtail and tarragon raviolo with celeriac and horseradish purée and an intense oxtail reduction combine strong and interesting flavours. Clever workmanship is evident throughout, not least in a beautifully made dessert of nougatine parfait with fennel sorbet, which features crisp hazelnuts and creamy parfait. Service – 'good, observant and well informed' – is overseen by Kate Ashenford. The wine list is not of the same calibre as the cooking, but prices, at least, are sane, starting at £11.95.

CHEF: Marcus Ashenford PROPRIETORS: Marcus and Kate Ashenford OPEN: Wed to Sun L 12 to 2.30, Tue to Sat D 7 to 9.30 CLOSED: first 2 weeks Jan MEALS: alc L (main courses £9.50 to £12.50). Set D £19.50 to £42.50 SERVICE: not inc CARDS: Delta, MasterCard, Switch, Visa DETAILS: 26 seats. Private parties: 26 main room. Vegetarian meals. Children's helpings. No smoking. Wheelchair access (not WC). Music. No mobile phones

▲ Wesley House ✸

High Street, Winchcombe GL54 5LJ
TEL: (01242) 602366   FAX: (01242) 609046   NEW CHEF
EMAIL: reservations@wesleyhouse.co.uk   MODERN BRITISH
WEBSITE: www.wesleyhouse.co.uk   £26–£75

This ancient half-timbered building has an olde-worlde feel on the inside too, with a long, narrow room providing a bar and two eating areas; décor is eclectic but aims for comfort. Chef Martin Dunn, with experience in some good London kitchens, arrived in the summer of 2003. His menus offer broad appeal, with baked crottin goats' cheese, truffle honey, tomato confit and mesclun salad, or sweet potato and vanilla velouté among starters. Main courses are equally cosmopolitan, with Moroccan spiced fillet of lamb with tomato and olive couscous and a vegetable ragoût, alongside pepper crusted halibut with samphire and mussel dressing. Finish with pineapple and coconut parfait with exotic fruit salad. There is also a bar menu with soup, salads, and some fancy sounding sandwiches. House wines (£12) hail from Italy but the real interest is in South Africa, with quality bottles from the likes of Morgenhof and Veenwouden. Ten by the glass are £3.50-£5.50.

CHEF: Martin Dunn PROPRIETOR: Matthew Brown OPEN: all week L 12 to 2, Mon to Sat D 7 to 9 (10 Sat) CLOSED: 25 and 26 Dec MEALS: alc L and Sun brunch (main courses £9.50 to £25). Set L Mon to Sat £12.50 (2 courses) to £15, Set D £29.50 (2 courses) to £35. Bar menu available SERVICE: not inc CARDS: Amex, Delta, MasterCard, Switch, Visa DETAILS: 50 seats. 16 seats outside. Private parties: 60 main room. Vegetarian meals. Children's helpings. No smoking in 1 dining room. Music ACCOMMODATION: 6 rooms, all with bath/shower. TV. Phone. B&B £40 to £80. Baby facilities (The Which? Guide to Good Hotels) £5

WINCHESTER Hampshire   map 2

Chesil Rectory ¦✳

1 Chesil Street, Winchester SO23 0HU   COOKING 6
TEL: (01962) 851555 FAX: (01962) 869704   MODERN BRITISH
                                                                   £47–£76

This handsome timber-framed building dating from the mid-fifteenth century is 'a real gem', thanks not least to its cobblestones, leaded windows, dark wood beams, big brick fireplace and low ceilings. The interior – two small dining rooms on the ground floor, one upstairs – is 'truly romantic', yet with large tables and plenty of elbow room. A change to the format this year means that lunch is available only on Saturday, and dinner is now six courses (with three choices per course), which are perfectly judged in terms of quantity. Even rich dishes – a version of tournedos Rossini, consisting of tender pink beef paired with foie gras and crisp rösti – are approached with a light touch. Fine raw materials provide a solid foundation, and combine with a high degree of skill and craftsmanship to produce, for example, a tranche of Newlyn cod 'correctly translucent' topped with equally fresh brown shrimps, a generously endowed mushroom risotto, and a duck ravioli sitting in an expertly made mushroom consommé with spring onions and baby broad beans.

Even the cheese course offers three options: a plate of three British cheeses, a salad with Colston Basset Stilton, or a twice baked Roquefort soufflé 'in fine fettle'. Desserts may not be quite up to the standard of the rest, but might take in a warm chocolate fondant with coconut sorbet, or a plate of light passion-fruit soufflé with mango sorbet. The interesting but 'rather pricey' wine list has comparatively little under £25; start with the house selection if you're drinking to a budget.

CHEF: Philip Storey PROPRIETORS: Philip and Catherine Storey OPEN: Sat only 12 to 2, Tue to Sat 7 to 9.30 CLOSED: 24 Dec to 1st week Jan MEALS: Set L £30 to £45, Set D £45 SERVICE: not inc CARDS: Amex, Delta, Diners, MasterCard, Switch, Visa DETAILS: 45 seats. Private parties: 45 main room, 8 to 45 private rooms. Vegetarian meals. Children's helpings. No smoking. Wheelchair access (not WC). Music

▲ Hotel du Vin & Bistro ▮ 🍞

Southgate Street, Winchester SO23 9EF
TEL: (01962) 841414   FAX: (01962) 842458
EMAIL: reservations@winchester.hotelduvin.com
WEBSITE: www.hotelduvin.com

NEW CHEF
MODERN EUROPEAN
£36–£59

This burgeoning chain began by opening here and in Tunbridge Wells, before heading off into the urban hubs of Bristol, Birmingham and Brighton (see entries), plus Harrogate opening in autumn 2003. The ambience is more brasserie than bistro, with polished wood floors and a muted colour scheme, and attentive staff. Eddie Grey, listed in the 2003 Guide at the Birmingham branch, is now cooking here, and arrived too close to publication for a visit. The menus will continue to offer top-notch roast beef and Yorkshires for a Sunday lunch, or perhaps slow-roast belly pork with caramelised shallots and apple sauce. Before that, there may be scallops grilled in the shell and dressed with toasted hazelnuts and coriander butter, or chargrilled polenta with wild mushrooms, herbs and truffle oil. Vegetarian choices are pretty run-of-the-mill; there is a separate slate of vegetable side-dishes; plus 'simple classics', which extend to fillet of sea bass with fennel salad and olive oil. Lovers of sticky toffee or chocolate will usually find something to satisfy. The magnificent wine list pays attention to the lower end as well as the top-class wines. France is strongest, and Italy, Australia and the USA are particularly well covered. Spain, Germany and Austria are worth a look, too. House wines start at £12.95, by the glass from £3.

CHEF: Eddie Grey   PROPRIETOR: Hotel du Vin Ltd   OPEN: all week 12 to 1.45, 7 to 9.45   MEALS: alc (main courses £14.50 to £17.50). Set L Sun £23.50   SERVICE: not inc   CARDS: Amex, Delta, Diners, MasterCard, Switch, Visa   DETAILS: 65 seats. 20 seats outside. Private parties: 48 main room, 8 to 48 private rooms. Car park. Vegetarian meals. Children's helpings. No cigars/pipes in dining room. Wheelchair access (also WC). No music   ACCOMMODATION: 23 rooms, all with bath/shower. TV. Phone. Room only £105 to £185. Rooms for disabled. Baby facilities (*The Which? Guide to Good Hotels*)

▲ Wykeham Arms 🍴

75 Kingsgate Street, Winchester SO23 9PE
TEL: (01962) 853834   FAX: (01962) 868441
EMAIL: thewykehamarms@accommodatinginns.co.uk
WEBSITE: www.gales.co.uk

COOKING 2
INTERNATIONAL
£22–£46

The 'Wyk' is a 'true neighbourhood local', brimming with atmosphere, and abundant in what can only be described as 'character'. Culinary eclecticism may also be expected, and menus (plus lunchtime sandwiches and simple salads, and full-on Sunday lunch) show British tradition with some global gatherings. You could try gravad lax with mozzarella, then marlin with cocotte potatoes, feta couscous and a coriander and lime salsa – effortlessly encompassing much of the world's cuisine in a single meal, and that's before dessert. Equally, though, you could stick to game, apple and apricot terrine, followed by roast rack of lamb with a port and rosemary sauce. Finish with raspberry and elderflower jelly accompanying a fresh tropical fruit salad. Combinations don't always convince, but decent ingredients 'sought locally as much as possible' are honestly treated.

An 80-strong wine list has house wines at £11.45, 20 others by the glass, and very fair prices.

CHEFS: James Tea and Alex Jones PROPRIETOR: George Gale & Co. OPEN: all week L 12 to 2.30 (1.30 Sun), Mon to Sat D 6.30 to 8.45 CLOSED: 25 Dec MEALS: alc (main courses L £6 to £15, D £11 to £16.50), Set L Sun £14.50 (2 courses) to £18.50 SERVICE: not inc, card slips closed CARDS: Amex, Delta, Diners, MasterCard, Switch, Visa DETAILS: 95 seats. 60 seats outside. Private parties: 8 main room. Car park. Vegetarian meals. No children under 14. No smoking in dining room, smoking permitted in bar area. Wheelchair access (not WC). No music. No mobile phones ACCOMMODATION: 14 rooms, all with bath/shower. TV. Phone. B&B £50 to £120. No children under 14 (*The Which? Guide to Good Hotels*)

WINDERMERE Cumbria   map 8

▲ Gilpin Lodge ▼ ✳

Crook Road, Windermere LA23 3NE
TEL: (015394) 88818 FAX: (015394) 88058
EMAIL: hotel@gilpin-lodge.co.uk   COOKING 5
WEBSITE: www.gilpin-lodge.co.uk   MODERN BRITISH
on B5284, 2m SE of Windermere   £31–£65

Luxury and comfort abound at this late-Victorian country-house hotel, which is halfway between Bowness-on-Windermere and Kendal, making it well placed for Lakeland explorers. The 14 bedrooms are as comfortably appointed as the plush dining room, which has views over a verdant, well-kept cottage garden. Food is as elegantly refined as the setting, the style an educated take on the modern British idiom, producing starters such as ravioli of Morecambe Bay shrimps with carrot linguini and a cappuccino of red mullet, or Galia melon with summer berries and pink champagne sabayon. Dinner runs to five courses, following the starter with vodka-cured salmon with dill and grain mustard, perhaps, then a sorbet. Main courses take earthy flavours and give them artful twists, as in the pheasant leg pie to accompany roast pheasant with sauerkraut, fondant potato and grain mustard sauce, or the braised stuffed oxtail to partner pan-fried tournedos with spinach and red wine jus. Dinner might typically be rounded off with vanilla pannacotta with soft berry syrup, or hot sticky toffee pudding with crème Chantilly and toffee sauce. Lunches are a simpler version of the same style and, for those that stay, breakfast looks fit for royalty. The wine lists offers enjoyable drinking in both Europe and the New World, with a particularly good short range from Italy. Plentiful options at or under £20 include six house wines starting at £14.50 and there are ten wines by the glass from £4.

CHEF: Mark Jordan PROPRIETORS: John and Christine Cunliffe OPEN: all week 12 to 2.30, 6.45 to 9.15 MEALS: alc L Mon to Sat (main courses £8.50 to £13). Set L £14.75 (2 courses) to £19.50, Set D £38.50. Light lunch available Mon to Sat SERVICE: not inc CARDS: Amex, Delta, Diners, MasterCard, Switch, Visa DETAILS: 60 seats. 20 seats outside. Private parties: 10 to 20 private rooms. Car park. Vegetarian meals. No children under 7. No smoking. Wheelchair access (not WC). Music. No mobile phones ACCOMMODATION: 14 rooms, all with bath/shower. TV. Phone. D, B&B £150 to £270. No children under 7 (*The Which? Guide to Good Hotels*)

The Guide always appreciates hearing about changes of chef or owner.

▲ Holbeck Ghyll ⁵✱

Holbeck Lane, Windermere LA23 1LU
TEL: (015394) 32375   FAX: (015394) 34743
EMAIL: stay@holbeckghyll.com
WEBSITE: www.holbeckghyll.com   COOKING 5
from A591, 3m N of Windermere, turn E (Holbeck   MODERN FRENCH
Lane, signposted Troutbeck); hotel is ½m on left   £38–£82

A nineteenth-century stone-built house overlooking Windermere, Holbeck
Ghyll was once used as a hunting lodge by Lord Lonsdale. These days, it's a
country-house hotel incorporating a restaurant and a health spa. The oak-
panelled dining room has spectacular views of lake and fells, while the daily-
changing menu has its roots in France. This being a country-house hotel, an
amuse-bouche (such as a cup of vichyssoise) and a selection of appetisers are all
part of the stately progress of dinner. First courses may involve a terrine of rabbit
with foie gras and corn-fed chicken, attractively arranged in a mosaic pattern,
with sauce gribiche. The tendency to classical French technique is evident in
another starter, a salad of warm langoustines with lobster, served atop celeriac
rémoulade. Dinner may proceed to a main course of tender, pink best end of
lamb with shallot purée and rosemary jus, or roast brill with a ragoût of bacon,
celery and girolles. Vegetarians have their own menu (a galette of asparagus and
baby gem lettuce might be among the choices), and a separate menu lists a
selection of English cheeses from respected producers, plus a couple from
France. Desserts may include the likes of a light-textured pear and praline
parfait with nougat glace, trickled with crème anglaise. Service is helpful and
professional. A stylish line-up of six house wines (£18.50 to £23) gives fair
warning that this list doesn't offer much at everyday prices. Quality is good, but
the list leans heavily towards the premium end. New Zealand and South Africa
are better balanced.

CHEF: David McLaughlin   PROPRIETORS: David and Patricia Nicholson   OPEN: all week 12.30 to
2, 7 to 9.30   MEALS: Set L £25, Set D £45. Light L menu available   SERVICE: not inc, card slips
closed   CARDS: Amex, Delta, Diners, MasterCard, Switch, Visa   DETAILS: 50 seats. 20 seats
outside. Private parties: 20 main room, 1 to 20 private rooms. Car park. Vegetarian meals.
Children's helpings. No children under 8. No smoking. Wheelchair access (not WC). Occasional
music   ACCOMMODATION: 20 rooms, all with bath/shower. TV. Phone. B&B £120 to £240. Rooms
for disabled. Baby facilities (*The Which? Guide to Good Hotels*) £5

Jerichos ⁵✱

Birch Street, Windermere LA23 1EG   COOKING 5
TEL/FAX: (015394) 42522   ENGLISH
EMAIL: enquiries@jerichos.co.uk   £34–£50

The purple frontage, which makes Jerichos stand out from its neighbours, is a
colour theme continued into both dining rooms, where a mix of modern prints
contributes to the bright and warm atmosphere. Jo Blaydes is a personable and
friendly hostess out front; husband Chris and his team can be seen working
calmly and confidently in the kitchen. The menu is short, descriptions long-
winded, and results largely successful. Sound skills underpin the operation,
producing for example a dark coffee-coloured risotto infused with dried ceps,

spiked with chorizo, and lifted by its mustard dressing, and chicken stuffed with goats' cheese and sage and wrapped in pancetta (well timed, if slightly salty). Regional materials extend to Bury black pudding and Lune Valley lamb, and the vegetarian main course has been notably well rendered, judging by one reporter's dish of pepper stuffed with shallots and served with al dente chickpeas, noodles, a sweet-and-sour sauce and feta.

Desserts tend to be indulgent, perhaps taking in layers of shortbread sandwiched with coffee ice cream and 'a thick chocolate goo of great intensity', or discs of banana topped with liquorice parfait, surrounded by drizzles of butterscotch sauce and cream. The menu offers a couple of wine suggestions; the varied list itself is arranged according to its ability to partner seafood, lamb and so forth, with fair prices starting at £12.50 a bottle (£3.35 a large glass).

CHEF: Chris Blaydes PROPRIETORS: Chris and Jo Blaydes OPEN: Tue to Sun D only 6.45 to 9.30 CLOSED: last 2 weeks Nov, first week Dec, 25 and 26 Dec, 1 Jan MEALS: alc (main courses £13.50 to £17) SERVICE: not inc CARDS: Delta, MasterCard, Switch, Visa DETAILS: 36 seats. Private parties: 26 main room. Vegetarian meals. No children under 12. No smoking. Music

▲ Miller Howe

Rayrigg Road, Windermere LA23 1EY
TEL: (015394) 42536 FAX: (015394) 45664
EMAIL: lakeview@millerhowe.com — COOKING **5**
WEBSITE: www.millerhowe.com — ENGLISH COUNTRY-HOUSE
on A592, between Windermere and Bowness — £29–£64

Set in landscaped gardens, with views taking in water and peaks, Miller Howe tries to match the splendour of its surroundings with ornate decorative touches such as gilt cherubs suspended from the ceilings. Although reporters still have plenty of positive comments, there is a sense that the restaurant has lost some of its gloss, and service over the last year has not been up to previous standards.

Five-course dinner starts at eight, portions are generous, and the style is elaborate classical French. To start, there may be chicken liver parfait with home-baked brioche and endive and spiced date chutney, while the second course offers the choice between fish – pan-seared Oban scallops with celeriac purée, fish velouté and basil oil, for example – and soup, which might be cream of curried parsnip and banana. Sorbet comes next, before the main course: perhaps seared Périgord duck breast with Savoy cabbage, braised root vegetables, red wine and cinnamon sauce and seared foie gras, or roast loin of suckling pig on bubble and squeak with caramelised root vegetables and a port reduction. To finish there may be tarte Tatin with vanilla ice cream. New World wines take precedence over Europe, with solid names throughout: Cape Mentelle in Australia, Vavasour in New Zealand, Jordan in South Africa and Casa Lapostolle in Chile. House wines are £17.50, and ten come by the glass for £3.50 to £6.

CHEF: Paul Webster PROPRIETOR: Charles Garside OPEN: all week 12.30 to 2, 8 (1 sitting) MEALS: Set L Mon to Sat £17.50, Set L Sun £19.95, Set D £39.50 SERVICE: 10%, card slips closed CARDS: Amex, Delta, MasterCard, Switch, Visa DETAILS: 64 seats. Car park. Vegetarian meals. No children under 8. Jacket and tie. No smoking. Wheelchair access (also

WC). Music. No mobile phones. Air-conditioned   ACCOMMODATION: 15 rooms, all with bath/shower. TV. Phone. D,B&B £100 to £350. Rooms for disabled. No children under 8 (*The Which? Guide to Good Hotels*) £5

▲ Samling ⅍

Ambleside Road, Windermere LA23 1LR

TEL: (015394) 31922   FAX: (015394) 30400

EMAIL: info@thesamling.com

WEBSITE: www.thesamling.com

COOKING **5**

MODERN BRITISH

£41–£106

The Samling is a country-house hotel cast in a contemporary mode. The house itself, up a very steep drive from a narrow, winding road, is set above Lake Windermere. Inside, the sitting room feels like a modern take on the gentleman's club: comfortable and luxurious, with voluminous tobacco-brown draperies, wood panelling and plenty of comfortable sofas and armchairs. The relatively simple dining room aims for restraint, with subdued lighting, plain wooden floors and beige walls. The seven or eight tables are well spaced enough to keep dinner a private affair.

The cuisine is decidedly ambitious yet not pretentious, and the main menu, though short, has many inventive pairings. Roasted breast of quail, for instance, may come with oven-dried grapes and sautéed wild mushrooms. Main courses might include an assiette of pig's head with braised root vegetables, or a less challenging turbot poached in langoustine stock with morels and white asparagus. The eight-course menu gourmand is 'prepared with the precision of a true craftsperson', according to one reporter, who found that 'the courses are exceptionally well judged and finely balanced'. On this menu, a salad of Iberico ham may precede roasted sea bass with a bouillon of red peppers and saffron potatoes, followed by fillet of veal with a ragoût of knuckle and roasted sweetbreads. Desserts, along the lines of tarte Tatin with vanilla ice cream, or pineapple savarin with Szechuan pepper, are beautifully presented.

Quality control on the new wine list is impressive, so we'll excuse slightly high prices. Seven appealing house wines come by the glass for £5 to £6, then it's straight into a fine international list arranged by region and grape variety. The most imaginative choices come from outside France, and a separate 'Something Different' selection rounds up oddities like South African Touriga Nacional.

CHEF: Chris Meredith   PROPRIETOR: Tom Maxfield   OPEN: Sun L 12 to 1.30, all week D 7 to 10   MEALS: Set L £27.50, Set D £45 to £60   SERVICE: not inc   CARDS: Amex, MasterCard, Switch, Visa   DETAILS: 20 seats. Private parties: 20 main room. Car park. Vegetarian meals. Children's helpings. No children under 12. No smoking. Music. No mobile phones   ACCOMMODATION: 10 rooms, all with bath/shower. TV. Phone. D,B&B £180 to £415. Baby facilities (*The Which? Guide to Good Hotels*) £5

Prices quoted in the Guide are based on information supplied by restaurateurs. The prices quoted at the top of each entry represent a range, from the lowest price of a three-course meal with service and wine to the highest; the latter is inflated by 20 per cent to take account of likely price rises during the year of the Guide.

WINKLEIGH Devon   map 1

Pophams ⁵✳

Castle Street, Winkleigh EX19 8HQ   COOKING **5**
TEL: (01837) 83767   MODERN BRITISH
£31–£44

Extremely limited opening hours and a tiny dining room mean that it may take several attempts to coordinate a convenient occasion for a visit to Pophams and an available table. Chef/proprietor Melvyn Popham sticks to a limited but finely honed repertoire – menus don't change very often, and even the few choices offered sometimes run out. For all that, the cooking is regarded as first class, although it tends towards richness, and three courses may leave you rather full. Expect butternut squash soup with Parmesan, or warm crab tart, followed by chicken breast stuffed with smoked ham, basil and mozzarella with a creamy Noilly-Prat sauce, or boned best end of lamb in puff pastry with spinach and mushroom stuffing and Madeira sauce, with rhubarb tart and strawberry sauce to finish. Service is friendly and enthusiastic (a little too friendly for some), and the restaurant is unlicensed, so bring your own wine.

CHEF: Melvyn Popham PROPRIETORS: Melvyn Popham and Dennis Hawkes OPEN: Thur and Fri L only 11.45 to 2.30 CLOSED: Feb MEALS: alc (main courses £16 to £17.50). Unlicensed, BYO (no corkage) SERVICE: not inc CARDS: none DETAILS: 10 seats. No children under 14. No smoking. Occasional music. No mobile phones. Air-conditioned

WINTERINGHAM North Lincolnshire   map 9

▲ Winteringham Fields ♥ ⁵✳

Winteringham DN15 9PF
TEL: (01724) 733096 FAX: (01724) 733898   COOKING **9**
EMAIL: wintfields@aol.com   PROVINCIAL FRENCH/SWISS
WEBSITE: www.winteringhamfields.com   £46–£111

Is this 'the finest food in the UK outside London'? A number of reporters seem to think so. Is it the oddest location for such an enterprise? Probably. In an old, much-decorated and extended farmhouse in a small village near the Humber, a flowery jungle of greenery fills the conservatory, a couple of other lounges are kitted out 'like old drawing rooms', and the dining room is 'classic', with large, well-spaced tables (each sporting a painted ostrich egg), starched cloths and gleaming glasses. The Schwabs put the place on the market for a while but found no takers, and have now established a modus vivendi that keeps Germain in the kitchen and Annie supervising out front. Has any of this affected standards? Not a bit of it.

The list of ingredients reads like *Larousse Gastronomique* – sturgeon, caviar, sea bass, sweetbreads, truffles, baby turbot, Lincolnshire lamb, Bresse chicken, veal, suckling pig, langoustines, ceps, morels, crab apples, candied aubergine – all adding up to 'mouthfuls of pleasure and delight' from beginning to end. The cooking, too, is classically based, taking in pink, tender, gamey, pan-fried breasts of squab pigeon, together with stuffed confit leg topped with a crisp coil of garlic fritter. But the kitchen looks further afield for inspiration, turning up a fresh, moist fillet of sea bass and a silky tortellino of crab and lightly sharp lemongrass, helped along by a coconut milk 'laksa' spiked with slicks of pungent coriander pesto.

Dishes are honed to perfection: for example, luxurious ravioli of poached egg yolk (a variation perhaps on North Africa's brik à l'oeuf) sitting on veal sweetbreads, in a deeply flavoured chicken stock and Madeira sauce. But new dishes, such as an 'incredibly flavourful' modern take on bouillabaisse, also appear, combining pieces of utterly fresh fish (bream and monkfish among them) timed to the second, sitting in a small quantity of heady provençale broth, topped by a piece of squid looking like a yolk sack and containing a pungent saffron-infused rouille.

Plates may look like still-life paintings, but employ only what is necessary for culinary purposes, with no decorative extras. Desserts have a tendency not so much to melt in the mouth as simply to dissolve or disappear, among them a meringue 'tennis ball' enclosing soft caramelly ice cream, and a 'glorious' dark brown liquorice soufflé coated in orange powder, served with a clementine sorbet. Cheeses provide stiff competition, variously soft, gooey, smelly, hard, goats', ewes' and lots of blues; and the trolley 'driver' is praised for his knowledge, consideration and enthusiasm. Indeed, all the staff are professional and knowledgeable, but also friendly and not averse to a laugh if the occasion presents itself. 'Even for a lone diner they made it an occasion.'

It is not cheap, so the question inevitably arises 'is it worth it?' If you have the money, definitely. As one reporter put it, 'if ever proof were needed that you get what you pay for, Winteringham Fields provides the evidence'. Certainly, to enjoy the best of the wine list you will have to gloss over the prices, which are heavily marked up. Burgundy is impressive, and a number of fine Bordeaux châteaux are listed in several vintages; elsewhere, the ranges are sketchier, but Italy, South Africa, New Zealand and Switzerland might tempt, and the dessert wine list, with eight by the glass, merits a final splurge. Four basic table wines come by the glass for £4.25.

CHEF: Germain Schwab   PROPRIETORS: Annie and Germain Schwab   OPEN: Tue to Sat 12 to 1.30, 7 to 9.30   CLOSED: 2 weeks Christmas, last week Mar, first week Aug   MEALS: alc (main courses £28 to £32). Set L £25 (2 courses) to £29, Set D £38 to £68   SERVICE: not inc, card slips closed   CARDS: Amex, Delta, MasterCard, Switch, Visa   DETAILS: 42 seats. Private parties: 8 main room, 6 to 10 private rooms. Car park. No smoking. Wheelchair access (not WC). No music. No mobile phones   ACCOMMODATION: 10 rooms, all with bath/shower. TV. Phone. B&B £80 to £195. Rooms for disabled. No children under 8 exc babes in arms (*The Which? Guide to Good Hotels*)

WITCHFORD Cambridgeshire   map 6

▲ Needhams 🍴 £

186 Main Street, Witchford CB6 2HT	COOKING **2**
TEL/FAX: (01353) 661405	GLOBAL
off A142, 3m W of Ely	£23–£49

A rather modest sign marks this brick former farmhouse at the west end of the village. Inside flower-and-fruit prints, ruches, gathers and tassels are interposed with printed wallpaper, but young and enthusiastic Luke Pearson's cooking is cleaner-cut. Some Asian influences show in starters like ginger-spiced crab cakes with Thai coleslaw, or lemongrass and garlic sautéed prawns. A more European warm salad of queen scallops with pancetta and walnut and orange dressing may feature good, fresh, nicely timed scallops. A main-course chump of lamb could come with provençale vegetable couscous and aubergine 'caviar', or champ and crispy onions might partner a roast partridge. One visitor thought the bread unimpressive, but the desserts were better conceived: nicely creamy hazelnut frozen parfait with mango and mint salsa, or chocolate and ginger ice cream with a lemongrass-and-chilli-poached pear. Some find the background music irritating, but prices are ungrasping, service relaxed. House wines start at £9.95.

CHEF: Luke Pearson PROPRIETORS: Luke and Verity Pearson OPEN: Tue to Sun L 12 to 2, Tue to Sat D 7 to 9 (6.30 to 9.30 Sat) CLOSED: 26 Dec, first 2 weeks Jan MEALS: alc (main courses £11 to £16.50). Set L £16.25 SERVICE: not inc CARDS: Amex, Delta, MasterCard, Switch, Visa DETAILS: 50 seats. Private parties: 90 main room, 8 to 22 private rooms. Car park. Vegetarian meals. Children's helpings. No smoking. Wheelchair access (also WC). Music ACCOMMODATION: 2 rooms. B&B £35 to £50 (Fri and Sat only)

WOODBRIDGE Suffolk
map 6

Captain's Table ⚡✳

3 Quay Street, Woodbridge IP12 1BX
TEL: (01394) 383145 FAX: (01394) 388508
WEBSITE: www.captainstable.co.uk

COOKING 3
MODERN EUROPEAN
£25–£42

There is nothing nautical about the setting of the Pommier's simply decorated restaurant. The unprepossessing location and the 'workaday' décor is witness to some deft handling of good ingredients, often local. Menus offer widely diverse choice, which is interpreted by some as a lack of direction, and the style is somewhat quaint. However, the unfussy approach deserves praise and what makes it work is the fine local produce used, such as Cromer crab with lemon mayonnaise: the 'finest, freshest dressed crab I've ever had' said one seasoned reporter. Other starter options typically range from melon with ginger sorbet to deep-fried tiger prawns with red Thai curry dip, while main courses veer from spaghetti alla bolognese, to Scotch beef fillet à la bordelaise, to lamb kleftiko with onions, tomatoes and herbs. Finish perhaps with pink grapefruit and orange segments in jelly with passion-fruit coulis. A simple wine list opens with house French at £9.95.

CHEF: Pascal Pommier PROPRIETORS: Pascal and Jo Pommier OPEN: Tue to Sun and bank hol M L 12 to 2 (3 Sun high season and bank hols), Tue to Sat D and bank hol Sun and Mon 6.30 to 9.30 (10 Fri and Sat) CLOSED: first 2 weeks Jan MEALS: alc (main courses £7 to £15.50) SERVICE: not inc, card slips closed CARDS: Delta, MasterCard, Switch, Visa DETAILS: 50 seats. 30 seats outside. Private parties: 34 main room, 19 to 34 private rooms. Car park. Vegetarian meals. Children's helpings. No smoking. No music

If a restaurant is new to the Guide this year (did not appear as a main entry in the last edition), NEW ENTRY *appears opposite its name.*

WORCESTER Worcestershire   map 5

Brown's ⁵⁄✳

24 Quay Street, Worcester WR1 2JJ	COOKING 3
TEL: (01905) 26263 FAX: (01905) 25768	ANGLO-FRENCH
	£28–£54

It might look forbidding enough from the outside on a dark night: a hulking red-brick former grain mill by the River Severn, built in the late eighteenth century, towering over its surroundings. Inside, though, the conversion comes as quite a surprise, with a mezzanine gallery overlooking a bright, primrose-painted interior, mirrors used to maximise the sense of space, and good linen on the tables. The cooking has a nicely old-fashioned bent to it, which brings on asparagus hollandaise with Parmesan crisps, orange-dressed smoked chicken salad, and main courses such as a salmis of guinea fowl sauced with red wine, brandy and mushrooms. There is always a vegetarian main dish (perhaps spinach roulade with celery and walnuts) and fresh fish of the day, and meals end satisfyingly with the likes of lemon soufflé cheesecake, or sticky banana pudding with toffee sauce. The wine list makes a fair attempt to span the globe, picking up a couple of Canadian bottles along the way, with prices starting at £12.95.

CHEFS: W.R. Tansley and Gary Phipps   PROPRIETORS: W.R. and P.M. Tansley   OPEN: Tue to Fri and Sun L 12.30 to 1.45, Tue to Sat D 7.30 to 9.45   CLOSED: 24 to 31 Dec   MEALS: Set L £21.50, Set D £38.50   SERVICE: net prices, card slips closed   CARDS: Amex, Delta, MasterCard, Switch, Visa   DETAILS: 100 seats. Vegetarian meals. No children under 8. No smoking. Wheelchair access (also WC). No music

WORLESTON Cheshire   map 5

▲ Rookery Hall ⁵⁄✳

Worleston CW5 6DQ	
TEL: (01270) 610016 FAX: (01270) 626027	
EMAIL: if@arcadianhotels.co.uk	COOKING 3
WEBSITE: www.rookeryhallhotel.com	MODERN EUROPEAN
on B5074, 2½m N of Nantwich	£30–£76

Built in 1816, Rookery Hall, in 38 acres of gardens and wooded parkland, is a peaceful setting for what is today a 45-bedroom country-house hotel. In the elegant dining room, a heavily ornamented plaster ceiling and carved mahogany-panelled walls are lightened by floor-to-ceiling windows, which overlook lawns bordered by huge old trees. The kitchen has demonstrated technical skill in starters such as warm potato and goats' cheese terrine with plum and cinnamon syrup appearing alongside roast scallops with confit tomato salad and béarnaise. Modern ideas, often with a classical bent, can be seen in loin of venison with parsnip and potato purée and a blueberry sauce, or in fillet of roast halibut with tagliarini and a Sauternes and pistachio sauce. And, if it's interesting combinations that appeal, desserts have ranged from spiced apple won tons with coconut sorbet to lime leaf pannacotta with both strawberry and basil jus. The wine list is sensibly arranged by style, with prices from £16 and eight by the glass from £4.50 to £6. A couple of pages of 'fine and rare' bottles add distinction.

CHEF: Craig Malone   PROPRIETOR: Hand Picked Hotels   OPEN: Sun to Fri L 12 to 2, all week D 7 to 9.30   MEALS: alc (main courses L £10 to £15, D £17.50 to £25.50). Set L £15.95, Set D Mon to Thur £32.50. Bar menu available   SERVICE: not inc   CARDS: Amex, Delta, Diners, MasterCard, Switch, Visa   DETAILS: 35 seats. Private parties: 60 main room, 6 to 60 private rooms. Car park. Vegetarian meals. Children's helpings. No smoking. Wheelchair access (also WC). No music. No mobile phones   ACCOMMODATION: 45 rooms, all with bath/shower. TV. Phone. B&B £80 to £200. Rooms for disabled. Fishing (£5)

WRIGHTINGTON Lancashire   map 8

Mulberry Tree ❦ £

9 Wrightington Bar, Wrightington WN6 9SE
TEL/FAX: (01257) 451400   COOKING **4**
take Parbold exit from M6 junction 27 then first   MODERN BRITISH
right down Mossy Lea road   £28–£53

Wrightington-born Mark Prescott and James Moore started here in 2000 and have established a thriving business at this former pub. Light-handed decoration gives a 'light, airy' feel to an open-plan bar/dining area and two more formal dining rooms. The menu, changed every five weeks or so, is complemented by daily specials. Influences from Prescott's world-wide travels and classical training (including 16 years in Roux brothers' restaurants) are distilled into a 'very posh pub' style of modern British cuisine. Thus the bar menu includes some pub standards (rump steak and chips, or 'traditional ploughman's'), and good Northern ingredients appear in the dining room alongside some costlier items: lobster, sevruga caviar, foie gras. Portion sizes are generous, whether in a Northern-inspired terrine of ham, Lancashire cheese and black pudding, or in a main course of roast sea bass with Mediterranean vegetables, and a fruit and cream-packed pavlova has been named 'the star of the show'. The quality of ingredients is high, flavour combinations work, and execution is assured and professional; service is helpful and friendly, too. Prices on the wine list, split evenly between Old and New Worlds, are fair, with a few bargain bottles of champagne. House wines start at £12.25.

CHEF: Mark Prescott   PROPRIETORS: James Moore and Mark Prescott   OPEN: all week 12 to 2 (2.30 Sun), 6 to 9 (10 Fri and Sat)   CLOSED: 26 Dec, 1 Jan   MEALS: alc (main courses £10 to £18). Set L Sun £17.95. Bar menu available   SERVICE: not inc   CARDS: Delta, MasterCard, Switch, Visa   DETAILS: 140 seats. Private parties: 100 main room. Car park. Vegetarian meals. Children's helpings. No smoking. Wheelchair access (not WC). Music

---

🦢 *indicates that there has been a change of chef since last year's Guide, and the Editor has judged that the change is of sufficient interest to merit the reader's attention.*

If customers are asked to switch off mobile phones while in a restaurant, this is noted in the details at the end of an entry.

WYE Kent   map 3

▲ Wife of Bath ⚡✕

4 Upper Bridge Street, Wye TN25 5AF
TEL: (01233) 812232   FAX: (01233) 813630
EMAIL: reservations@wifeofbath.com
WEBSITE: www.wifeofbath.com

COOKING **2**
MODERN EUROPEAN
£27–£51

The Wife of Bath is easy to find on the main route through the quaint old village of Wye. The pleasant décor features well-spaced tables, heavy cutlery and off-white walls adorned with château- and vineyard-themed watercolours. Service is charmingly good-humoured and efficient. The cooking style is hard to pin down: 'eclectic, modern European with Asian influences' was one reporter's best stab at describing it, although Asian influences seem to be an occasional, rather than a regular, theme. Diners may start with warm smoked haddock mousse enlivened with crunchy, noodle-like ribbons of pickled cucumber, and follow it perhaps by succulent breast of local duckling with a spring roll of confit duck with soy and ginger, or seared tuna with tagliatelle and red pepper and shrimp salsa. For dessert, expect the likes of raspberry crème brûlée, or sticky toffee pudding with vanilla ice cream and a deliciously sweet, sticky sauce. The short wine list lines up France against 'The Rest of the World', which wins on points. French house wines are £13.75, Australian £14.50.

CHEF: Robert Hymers PROPRIETORS: Andrew and Nicola Fraser OPEN: Tue to Sat 12 to 1.30, 7 to 9.30 MEALS: alc L (main courses £14 to £17). Set L £11.75 (2 courses) to £15.75, Set D £26.75 SERVICE: not inc CARDS: Amex, Delta, MasterCard, Switch, Visa DETAILS: 52 seats. Private parties: 52 main room. Car park. Vegetarian meals. No smoking. Wheelchair access (not WC). No music ACCOMMODATION: 5 rooms, all with bath/shower. TV. Phone. B&B £45 to £95. Rooms for disabled (*The Which? Guide to Good Hotels*) (£5)

YARM Stockton-on-Tees   map 10

Chadwick's ⚡✕ £

104B High Street, Yarm TS16 0DT
TEL: (01642) 788558   FAX: (01642) 788344
WEBSITE: www.chadwicksrestaurant.com

COOKING **4**
GLOBAL
£21–£50

Yarm gives the lie to the notion that the north-east is all industrial muscle. The village is strung along a single broad main street, with this modern, self-styled 'Continental' restaurant at one end of it. Big windows, helped by mirrors and artwork, contribute to the clean and pleasantly light feel, and it affects a casual yet well-kept air. Pizzas, and sandwiches from the deli, are served throughout the day, lunches are appropriately light affairs, and there is breakfast too.

The kitchen works capably within its limits, delivering wholesome food without fuss: perhaps a simple upbeat salad of warm waxy potato, piquant chorizo and grilled tomato sprinkled with coriander; or a generous chunk of undyed smoked haddock served with a properly poached egg, a creamy and well-judged mustard sauce, and well-made bubble and squeak. Chocolate fondant with pistachio ice cream may be everywhere nowadays, but a skilfully made one, as here, still satisfies. Service is on the ball – personable without being intrusive – and value (especially at lunchtime) is remarkably good. Most wines stay obligingly under the £20 barrier, although a few more expensive fine wines provide balance. Duboeuf house red and white are £10.95.

CHEFS: David Brownless and Stephen Conyard   PROPRIETORS: David Brownless and D. Beattie   OPEN: Mon to Sat 11.30 to 2.30, 5.30 to 9.30   CLOSED: bank hols, second week Oct   MEALS: alc (main courses L £6 to £9.50, D £12 to £17.50)   SERVICE: not inc   CARDS: Delta, MasterCard, Switch, Visa   DETAILS: 70 seats. Private parties: 70 main room. Children's helpings. No smoking in 1 dining room. Music

---

YARMOUTH Isle of Wight   map 2

▲ George, Brasserie ▼

Quay Street, Yarmouth PO41 0PE
TEL: (01983) 760331   FAX: (01983) 760425   COOKING 3
EMAIL: res@thegeorge.co.uk   MODERN BRITISH
WEBSITE: www.thegeorge.co.uk   £33–£57

This seventeenth-century building is right by the water's edge – yachting fans can sit in the waterside garden and watch the boats, while those more interested in food can choose between an elegant restaurant and a more informal brasserie. Although both are under the guidance of chef Kevin Mangeolles, the brasserie elicits most feedback and the score relates only to this sunny and bright eating area.

Gutsy flavour combinations are the kitchen's preference, starters taking in tuna carpaccio with tomato and coriander salsa, white bean and truffle oil soup, and braised oxtail with chorizo and polenta. Among main courses, meat options range from corned beef hash with Savoy cabbage to braised milk-fed lamb with diced vegetables and rösti, while fish eaters might opt for red mullet with ratatouille and tapenade on tomato sauce. The restaurant menus run along similar lines, although dishes tend to be more refined and intricate, typically producing crab and vanilla soup with tomato and crab salad, followed by braised pork belly with seared scallops and carrot purée. A page each of whites and reds conduct the main business of the wine list, with a mostly French mix of reliable names set out in price bands. Fourteen house bottles at £12.50 (£3.95 a glass) and separate celebratory lists of champagne and mature clarets make up the balance.

CHEF: Kevin Mangeolles   PROPRIETORS: John Illsley, and Jeremy and Amy Willcock   OPEN: Brasserie: all week 12 to 3, 7 to 10; Restaurant: Tue to Sat D only 7 to 9.30   MEALS: Brasserie: alc (main courses £10 to £17); Restaurant: Set D £45   SERVICE: not inc, card slips closed   CARDS: Delta, MasterCard, Switch, Visa   DETAILS: Brasserie: 90 seats. 80 seats outside. Private parties: 40 main room. Vegetarian meals. Children's helpings. Wheelchair access (not WC). No music. Air-conditioned; Restaurant: 40 seats. Private parties: 20 main room. No children under 10. No music. Air-conditioned   ACCOMMODATION: 17 rooms, all with bath/shower. TV. Phone. B&B £125 to £215. No children under 10 (*The Which? Guide to Good Hotels*)

(£5) *indicates that the restaurant has elected to participate in the* Good Food Guide *voucher scheme. For full details, see page 6.*

YATTENDON Berkshire

map 2

▲ Royal Oak ⅝✻

The Square, Yattendon RG18 0UG
TEL: (01635) 201325   FAX: (01635) 201926
EMAIL: royaloak@corushotels.com
off B4009, 5m W of Pangbourne

COOKING 3
MODERN BRITISH
£30–£62

Overlooking the village square, the Royal Oak is a long red-brick inn partly covered in wisteria. Inside is a warren of rooms, including a comfortable dining room with honey-coloured walls hung with botanical prints, plants in pots, and posies on linen-clothed tables. The same long menu serves both here and the more informal bar/brasserie.

Italian influences prevail in the cooking, but the kitchen also finds inspiration elsewhere, including the Far East. Starters range from goats' cheese ravioli with tomato fondue to Thai-style mussels, while busy main courses typically take in honey and ginger marinated lamb chump with pak choi, oyster mushrooms and sweet chilli sauce, and roast halibut on celeriac cream with rösti, salsify, a red wine glaze and parsley oil. An inspector found much to praise, including 'superbly fresh' seared scallops with 'luscious' black and white puddings and an orange reduction, and a well-made orange and lemon soufflé with chocolate ice cream. Some dishes need to be more sharply focused, but technique is mostly sound and meals create a good overall impression. The international wine list has a fair selection under £20, starting with house white at £12, but reds in particular have plenty to tempt bigger spenders.

CHEF: Jason Gladwin   PROPRIETOR: Corinne MacRae   OPEN: all week 12 to 2.30, 7 to 9.30 (10 Fri and Sat)   MEALS: alc (main courses £10 to £20)   SERVICE: 10% (optional), card slips closed   CARDS: Amex, Delta, Diners, MasterCard, Switch, Visa   DETAILS: 80 seats. 60 seats outside. Private parties: 100 main room. Car park. Vegetarian meals. No children under 7. No smoking in 1 dining room. Music. No mobile phones   ACCOMMODATION: 5 rooms, all with bath/shower. TV. Phone. B&B £75 to £140. Baby facilities (*The Which? Guide to Good Hotels*)

YORK North Yorkshire

map 9

Blue Bicycle ☗ ⅝✻

34 Fossgate, York YO1 9TA
TEL: (01904) 673990   FAX: (01904) 677688
WEBSITE: www.bluebicyclerestaurant.com

COOKING 4
MODERN BRITISH
£32–£60

York is not short of historical buildings, but the shady history of this particular establishment, on the bank of the River Foss, is intriguing even by local standards. However, although staff are 'delightful, warm and welcoming', don't expect the kind of personal attentions received by patrons in earlier times (the place was a brothel at the turn of the last century). There are two dining rooms: one in the atmospheric basement with tables in the discreet candlelit alcoves that used to house beds, while the upstairs room enjoys views over the river and has a balcony where pre-dinner drinks may be taken. The same menus are served throughout, the lunchtime carte being a lighter version of the dinner menu, and the style is an updated take on traditional brasserie fare. Start perhaps with seared scallops on pea purée with pancetta and mint stock syrup, pan-fried smoked duck with Cajun-spiced Savoy cabbage and a citrus-flavoured vodka 'frappé', or even a retro classic like prawn cocktail, before moving on to halibut on seafood and black truffle couscous with shellfish sauce, chicken breast on pak choi and green beans with roast cashew nuts and a curry dressing, or spiced monkfish with crab and prawn boulangère and sautéed cabbage. Recommended desserts have included berry pudding with banana and vanilla, and quirky affectations, such as serving bread in plant pots, all add to the atmosphere. Australia and New Zealand provide good bottles at all levels on the savvy international list, while smart French names top the bill. House wines start at £13, with a dozen by the glass for £3.50 to £5.70.

CHEF: Kenny Noble   PROPRIETOR: Anthony Stephenson   OPEN: all week 12 to 2.30, 6 to 10 (9 Sun)   CLOSED: 26 Dec, 1 Jan   MEALS: alc (main courses L £11.50 to £16, D £13 to £20)   SERVICE: 10% (optional)   CARDS: MasterCard, Switch, Visa   DETAILS: 73 seats. Private parties: 20 to 35 private rooms. Vegetarian meals. No children under 12. No smoking. Occasional music. No mobile phones

Melton's ♥ ✳

7 Scarcroft Road, York YO23 1ND	COOKING 5
TEL: (01904) 634341 FAX: (01904) 635115	MODERN EUROPEAN
WEBSITE: www.meltonsrestaurant.co.uk	£26–£57

Situated in what was once a terraced house on a road leading into York city centre, Melton's is very much a local restaurant, with murals of the area and pictures of regular diners enhancing the neighbourhood feel of the place. Undressed dark wood tables give the restaurant a serious air, but the welcome is friendly and genuine. Food-wise, chef Michael Hjort and his team (John Coates joining after we go to press) have stated their commitment to using local, seasonal produce and 'concentrating on flavour'. These ingredients, whether local or not, and vegetables in particular, are treated with respect. For starters, risotto cake may come with wild mushroom salad, while a main course of roast butternut squash may be offset with a herby mascarpone mousse. Some dishes eschew simplicity in favour of something altogether more complex: on inspection, for example, a starter of ballotine of foie gras and duck with herb dressing impressed. A dessert of rhubarb and vanilla baked Alaska got all the flavours perfectly balanced and produced a 'wow' from the diner.

Waiting staff are mainly young but nonetheless professional, friendly, efficient and obviously well trained. Drinks are given a good deal of consideration too, and Melton's clearly wants you to enjoy your wine, with its carefully reasoned recommendations to match the menu. Seven house wines come by the bottle, carafe or glass (£12.50/£9/£3), and the wide-ranging list (with more wines by the carafe) is chosen with care and an eye for progressive producers.

CHEFS: Michael Hjort and John Coates   PROPRIETORS: Michael and Lucy Hjort   OPEN: Tue to Sat L 12 to 2, Mon to Sat D 5.30 to 10   CLOSED: 3 weeks at Christmas, 1 week Aug   MEALS: alc (main courses £12 to £18.50). Set L £17   SERVICE: not inc   CARDS: Delta, MasterCard, Switch, Visa   DETAILS: 40 seats. Private parties: 36 main room, 14 to 18 private rooms. Vegetarian meals. Children's helpings. No smoking in 1 dining room. Wheelchair access (not WC). Music. Air-conditioned (£5)

Melton's Too ⁵⅄

25 Walmgate, York YO1 9TX
TEL: (01904) 629222   FAX: (01904) 636677
WEBSITE: www.meltonstoo.co.uk

NEW CHEF
MODERN EUROPEAN
£24–£43

In York's café area, in a bare-boarded former saddler's, the plainer, simpler offshoot of Melton's (see entry above) serves straightforward cooking. We learned of a chef change too late for an inspection. Previously, however, we have had good reports of hearty main courses – such as salmon fishcakes with tartare sauce, and steak and kidney pie. Otherwise, expect the likes of duck and red onion pâté with onion marmalade, followed by three different sausages with red cabbage and pears (or maybe mustard-sauced smoked haddock with a poached egg), before ending in 'Chocolate Oblivion'. Service is relaxed, but sound. A list of international real ales complements the short wine slate, which opens with house Italians at £10.80.

CHEF: Steve Holding   PROPRIETORS: Michael and Lucy Hjort   OPEN: all week 10.30 to 10.30 (9.30 Sun)   CLOSED: 2 days at Christmas, 31 Dec evening, 1 Jan evening   MEALS: alc (main courses £7 to £12). Brunch and sandwich menu also available   SERVICE: not inc   CARDS: Delta, MasterCard, Switch, Visa   DETAILS: 120 seats. Private parties: 40 main room, 20 to 40 private rooms. Vegetarian meals. Children's helpings. No smoking in 1 dining room. Wheelchair access (also WC). Music. Air-conditioned £5

▲ Middlethorpe Hall ⁵⅄

Bishopthorpe Road, York YO23 2GB
TEL: (01904) 641241   FAX: (01904) 620176
EMAIL: info@middlethorpe.com
WEBSITE: www.middlethorpe.com

COOKING 3
MODERN ENGLISH
£31–£549

The Hall is an imposing three-storey edifice awash with Palladian grandeur. Within the oak-panelled dining room, Martin Barker's cooking plies an inventive, modern line, with some arresting ideas on show. Seared scallops come with artichokes, crisp pig's trotter and a chervil velouté, while powdered morels, apple purée and green lentils are the chosen accompaniments to a main course of roast sweetbreads. Vegetarian options are rather more mainstream than this, but may take in well-conceived goats' cheese ravioli with pumpkin mash and sauce verte. A dessert of a tower of chocolate discs interspersed with griottine cherries was highly rated by one reporter, or there might well be roasted baby pineapple served with coconut cream and Malibu, pineapple sorbet and passion-fruit juice. Both the dress code and the elaborately formal style of service suggest there is a way to go before Middlethorpe will feel ready to enter the same era as its cooking belongs to. The wine list is serious about France and pays more than lip service to the rest of the world. A service charge is included in the prices and reports suggest this is on the high side. Only the house wines (£14.50) and half-bottles come in under £20.

CHEF: Martin Barker   PROPRIETOR: Historic House Hotels   OPEN: all week 12.30 to 1.45, 7 to 9.45 CLOSED: residents only 25 and 31 Dec   MEALS: Set L £16.50 (2 courses) to £19.50, Set L Sun £23.50, Set D £37.95   SERVICE: net prices, card slips closed   CARDS: MasterCard, Switch, Visa DETAILS: 60 seats. Private parties: 50 main room, 6 to 50 private rooms. Car park. Vegetarian meals. No children under 8. Jacket. No smoking. Wheelchair access (not WC). No music. No mobile phones ACCOMMODATION: 30 rooms, all with bath/shower. TV. Phone. Room only £109 to £360. No children under 8. Swimming pool (*The Which? Guide to Good Hotels*)

Rish ✳️

NEW ENTRY

7 Fossgate, York YO1 9TA	COOKING 2
TEL: (01904) 622688 FAX: (01904) 671931	MODERN BRITISH
WEBSITE: www.rish-york.co.uk	£29–£62

This 'classy modern joint' attracts a smart young crowd who are wooed by ultra-stylish décor – all dark wood and chrome – comfortable fittings, and efficient, professional service. The upmarket, modern European cooking also aims to make an impact. Highlights at an inspection meal were pan-fried scallops – just seared on the outside – on minted pea purée with crisp pancetta and deep-fried onions; crisp-skinned roast Gressingham duck with pink peppercorn sauce; and chargrilled rump of lamb – almost burnt on the outside but pink and succulent in the middle – with crisp sweet potato dauphinois, purple-sprouting broccoli, garlic confit and a rosemary and lemon sauce. Desserts have included espresso pannacotta with dark chocolate and brandy sauce, and bread-and-butter pudding with apricot chutney and custard. This is ambitious cooking that doesn't always deliver, and it isn't cheap. A page of wines by the glass opens a list that offers broad scope and fair value. House selections start at £12.

CHEF: Michael Cushing   PROPRIETORS: Sam and Maria Abu Rish   OPEN: all week 12 to 2, 6 to 10 CLOSED: 25 to 27 Dec, 1 and 2 Jan   MEALS: alc (main courses £11 to £19.50). Set L and D Sun to Fri 6 to 7 £15 (2 courses) to £18.50   SERVICE: not inc, 10% for parties of 8 or more   CARDS: Amex, Delta, MasterCard, Switch, Visa   DETAILS: 70 seats. Private parties: 12 to 20 private rooms. Vegetarian meals. Children's helpings. No smoking in dining room, smoking permitted in bar and lounge. Wheelchair access (also WC). Music £5

Scotland

Silver Darling ✁

Pocra Quay, North Pier, Aberdeen AB11 5DQ
TEL: (01224) 576229   FAX: (01224) 588119

COOKING **6**
SEAFOOD
£30–£67

Full-height windows on all sides of this quayside restaurant ensure that light floods in and give great views out across the sea. You may catch sight of trawlers returning to port, and even porpoises at play. But if the setting or the highly polished service don't bowl you over, the cooking certainly will.

It helps that the fish and seafood are so fresh that they 'taste as if they had practically sprung out of the sea', and although Didier Dejean's cooking is complex, the various elements of dishes sing in perfect harmony. Such was the case at inspection in a delicately balanced ballottine of fresh and smoked salmon wrapped in a cabbage leaf, served with an 'impeccable' beurre blanc with lardons and Avruga caviar. Equally impressive has been a 'duo d'huîtres', an exercise in contrasting but complementary textures and flavours: three raw oysters with cucumber 'spaghetti' in dill, pickled samphire and a Thai dressing, plus three grilled under a crust of garlic, pecans, parsley and brioche crumbs. Among main courses, artfully presented lemon sole has come with crayfish tails, an 'ethereal' quenelle of Tomme de Savoie cheese, Avruga caviar and a 'refreshingly sharp' oyster and scallop coral reduction, while 'impeccably timed' pan-roast North Sea turbot has been topped with a delicate Comté cheese crust, placed on a bed of mushroom and celeriac mash with confit shallots and finished with a 'richly satisfying' red wine reduction. Desserts maintain the same level of technique and presentation: petits pots de crème en cassonade, for example, comprising five small portions of rich, wobbly, primrose-yellow crème brûlée with a light, crisp cassonade topping and flavoured with mango, chocolate, strawberry, rosemary and vanilla. Wines are almost exclusively French and mostly above £20, although a handful of 'vins du patron' start at £14.50.

CHEF: Didier Dejean   PROPRIETORS: Didier Dejean and Ms K. Murray   OPEN: Mon to Fri L 12 to 1.30, Mon to Sat D 7 to 9.30   MEALS: alc (main courses L £9.50 to £11.50, D £17.50 to £19.50) SERVICE: not inc, card slips closed   CARDS: Amex, Delta, Diners, MasterCard, Switch, Visa DETAILS: 54 seats. Private parties: 54 main room, 10 to 15 private rooms. No smoking. Music

▲ *denotes an outstanding wine cellar;* ♥ *denotes a good wine list, worth travelling for.*

ACHILTIBUIE Highland map 11

▲ Summer Isles Hotel ▮ ✳

Achiltibuie IV26 2YG
TEL: (01854) 622282   FAX: (01854) 622251
EMAIL: info@summerisleshotel.co.uk
WEBSITE: www.summerisleshotel.co.uk

take A835 to Drumrunie, 10m N of Ullapool; turn
W on single-track road for 15m; hotel is 1m past
Achiltibuie on L

COOKING 5
MODERN EUROPEAN
£31–£60

Fifteen or more miles from anywhere sits this white, slate-roofed, dormer-windowed house whose built-on conservatory, decked with coach lamps and window boxes, commands majestic views of ocean and islands. Unfussy comfort pervades. The food is a major draw, and the kitchen, overseen since 1986 by Chris Firth-Bernard, uses produce from sea and stream, hill, garden and the local smokehouse. Fish and shellfish dominate at lunchtime, with platters of unadorned oysters and lobster, smoked salmon and pickled herrings, all straightforwardly presented but bursting with flavour. Dinner brings a five-course set menu with no choice before the pudding. After perhaps a warm leek and asparagus flan demonstrating the kitchen's pastry skills, or a grilled halibut fillet with caper, lime and butter sauce, meat gets a look in: maybe wood-pigeon breast and oyster mushrooms as a second course, or rib of Aberdeen Angus with braised chicory and roast garlic for the third (fishy dishes occupy the other spaces). Ingredients as good as these need no fashionable enhancement, and balsamic vinegar and lemongrass are passed over in favour of more established (in British cooking) flavourings like vermouth and wine, or the preserved intensity of capers and anchovies. Uncomplicated classics like sticky toffee pudding, a meringue case with summer fruit, or chocolate fudge cake, precede the cheese.

Reporters praise the wine list. It's an international, if French-dominated, selection with reams of affordable bottles from Bordeaux and Burgundy alongside their namelier (and pricier) brethren, and a notable array of post-prandials.

CHEF: Chris Firth-Bernard   PROPRIETORS: Mark and Gerry Irvine   OPEN: all week 12.30 to 2, 8 (1 sitting)   CLOSED: 18 Oct to 31 Mar   MEALS: alc L (main courses £11 to £30). Set D £45. Bar menu available   SERVICE: net prices, card slips closed   CARDS: MasterCard, Switch, Visa   DETAILS: 28 seats. Private parties: 16 main room, 8 private room. Car park. Children's helpings. No children under 8. No smoking. No music. No mobile phones   ACCOMMODATION: 13 rooms, all with bath/shower. Phone. B&B £73 to £230. No children under 8 (*The Which? Guide to Good Hotels*)

'This [salmon] had not been a happy fish. Bland and flabby, it was obviously the product of an overcrowded fish farm. What a pity it wasn't alive to enjoy swimming about in the vegetable nage, which was copious enough to fill a good-sized goldfish bowl.'
(On eating in Wiltshire)

▲ Enterkine House 🍸✲

Annbank KA6 5AL
TEL: (01292) 521608/520580
FAX: (01292) 521582
EMAIL: mail@enterkine.com   COOKING 3
WEBSITE: www.enterkine.com   MODERN EUROPEAN
on B742, 5m E of Ayr   £31–£67

Reached via a long, twisting avenue lined with mature trees, through which one glimpses eventually the handsome, white-fronted 1930s house, this hotel sits in over 300 acres of undulating Ayrshire. Here Douglas Smith offers a repertoire of country-house cooking of noticeable flair, served in the evenings as a fixed-price menu of four courses plus coffee. Smoked trout served warm with a tartlet of baby leeks might be followed by seared scallops with linguini, spring vegetables and pesto as one route through the menu. Bolder appetites might begin with chargrilled lamb fillet with Stornoway black pudding and kidney mustard sauce, before going on to roast duck breast with a croustade of duck confit, and a sauce combining wild mushrooms, prunes and thyme. In between may have come a lightly aromatic, East Asian-style chicken noodle broth, while meals end with the likes of chocolate and orange pots with chocolate chip ice cream, or raspberry and vanilla shortcake with raspberry sauce. Vegetarians have their own equally enticing menu. Coffee comes with profiteroles. Prices on the French-led wine list reflect the opulence of the place. Half-a-dozen house selections at £18.95 hail from France, South Africa, Argentina and Chile. Note a jacket and tie is a requirement at dinner, and preferred at lunch.

CHEF: Douglas Smith PROPRIETOR: Oswald Browne OPEN: Sun to Fri L 12 to 2, all week D 7 to 9 MEALS: Set L £18.50, Set D £37.50 SERVICE: not inc CARDS: Amex, Delta, Diners, MasterCard, Switch, Visa DETAILS: 50 seats. Private parties: 60 main room, 2 to 14 private rooms. Car park. Vegetarian meals. Children's helpings. Jacket and tie. No smoking. Wheelchair access (also WC). Occasional music ACCOMMODATION: 8 rooms, all with bath/shower. TV. Phone. B&B £60 to £100. Rooms for disabled. Fishing (The Which? Guide to Good Hotels)

Cellar 🍷 ✲

24 East Green, Anstruther KY10 3AA   COOKING 6
TEL: (01333) 310378   FAX: (01333) 312544   MODERN SEAFOOD
                                                        £29–£59

'I'm still working, aided by really dedicated staff,' proclaims chef-proprietor Peter Jukes, who's been at the helm here for over 20 years. Despite this length of tenure he has not let grass grow under his feet: the Cellar has recently been refurbished and extended, and now has a classier look. The warm ambience remains, however, and no radical departures from tradition show on the menu – still as dedicated as ever to good ingredients and seasonality.

Herring and dill with sweet mustard dressing is a simple starter, though fine ingredients and a nicely matched dressing create a whole that exceeds the sum of its parts. Combinations are well considered and perfectly balanced, as in a main course of pesto-roast cod with greens, pine nuts and smoky bacon. At an inspection meal, lobster quiche was rich but light, with excellent pastry and nice chunks of lobster. For dessert, an iced hazelnut praline parfait with fruits and a berry and cassis sauce may round things off nicely. The wine list casually throws together some of the world's great bottles and seems equally at ease in Australia or Chile as it does in the traditional regions of France, where fine ranges of Bordeaux and Burgundy are complemented by unusually good coverage of Alsace. Prices, starting at £15, are mostly fair, and seven by the glass are £3.75 to £5.50.

CHEF/PROPRIETOR: Peter Jukes OPEN: Wed to Sat (and Sun in summer) L 1 to 1.30, Tue to Sat (all week in summer) D 7 to 9.30 MEALS: Set L £16 (2 courses) to £18.50, Set D £25 (2 courses) to £35 SERVICE: not inc, card slips closed CARDS: Amex, Delta, Diners, MasterCard, Switch DETAILS: 42 seats. Private parties: 42 main room. Children's helpings. No smoking. Occasional music

AUCHTERARDER Perthshire & Kinross   map 11

▲ Andrew Fairlie at Gleneagles ⁵⁂

Auchterarder PH3 1NF   COOKING 6
WEBSITE: www.gleneagles.com   MODERN FRENCH
                                                                  £79–£121

Though within the famous golfing hotel, Andrew Fairlie's restaurant is a separate business – be careful not to get it mixed up with the hotel's own dining room. It inspires widely varying reports, suggesting that it's the kind of place you either love or hate, but either way it is an experience reserved for high rollers. Whether or not you get value for money is a question of perspective, but Andrew Fairlie's cooking is undoubtedly classy. His resolutely classical French approach shows a well-disciplined sense of restraint, but while dishes are on the whole conceptually simple there is also an intelligently creative streak. So alongside straightforward ideas like pan-fried langoustines on crab risotto, starters also feature Skye scallops with braised pig's cheek and celeriac purée, and roast foie gras with caramelised chicory and ginger froth.

Main courses include some genuinely unusual ideas, notably with fish: pan-fried tronçon of turbot with beetroot jus, for example, and roast sea bass with anchovy beignets and another froth, this time of garlic. Meanwhile, veal sweetbreads are pot-roasted with salsify and asparagus, and rack of lamb comes with chèvre dauphinoise, and to finish there may be iced praline parfait with apple compote, or passion-fruit ravioli with a tropical fruit soup. The wine list is an exciting global selection of classics, modern stars and new finds, all at peak drinking age. But even reporters who are happy to pay the price of dinner find it offputtingly expensive. Only a couple of bottles are under £25, although there are 16 wines by the glass, from £7 to £16.

CHEF/PROPRIETOR: Andrew Fairlie OPEN: Mon to Sat D only 7 to 10 CLOSED: Jan MEALS: Set D £55 to £75 SERVICE: not inc CARDS: Amex, Diners, MasterCard, Switch, Visa DETAILS: 40 seats. Car park. Vegetarian meals. No children under 14. No smoking. Music. No mobile phones. Air-conditioned ACCOMMODATION: 273 rooms, all with bath/shower. TV. Phone. B&B £320 to £1,450. Rooms for disabled. Baby facilities. Swimming pool. Fishing (*The Which? Guide to Good Hotels*)

▲ Boath House ✸

Auldearn IV12 5TE
TEL: (01667) 454896 FAX: (01667) 455469
EMAIL: wendy@boath-house.demon.co.uk   COOKING 5
WEBSITE: www.boath-house.com   FRANCO-SCOTTISH
on A96, 2m E of Nairn   £42–£62

In 20 splendid acres of gardens, woodland, streams and a lake, Boath House is a lovingly restored listed Georgian mansion. The classically restrained style of the exterior is reflected in elegant interior décor, though the welcome from Wendy Matheson and her smartly attired staff is warm and friendly, and despite the grandeur the place has a lived-in, homely feel.

The dining room is a high-ceilinged space with terracotta walls, polished floorboards and tables with damask cloths and thick white candles – an appropriate setting for Charles Lockley's grown-up but uncomplicated cooking, in which local produce is to the fore, including fruit and vegetables from the kitchen garden. The five-course dinner menus offer limited choice but plenty of incidentals. Following elaborate appetizers and home-baked bread comes soup – maybe a smooth, understated celeriac and lemon potage topped with truffle slices – then a fish course: perhaps a trio of salmon (smoked with star anise, citrus-cured, and ballottine). Main course might be crisp-skinned Gressingham duck on subtly spiced oriental cabbage with a light, fruity sauce, or whole Dover sole with a creamy cep sauce, smoky-flavoured artichoke hearts and crushed potatoes. Before desserts of 'smooth, creamy' rum pannacotta with pineapple sorbet, or chocolate tart with clementine ice cream, comes a single cheese – ripe and creamy Howgate Camembert, for example. The well-composed Francophile wine list offers some classic bottles at classic prices, though there is also a good choice of more attainable house wines from £13.50.

CHEF: Charles Lockley PROPRIETORS: Don and Wendy Matheson OPEN: Thur to Sun L 12.30 to 1.45, all week D 7 to 8.45 MEALS: Set L £28.50, Set D £38 SERVICE: not inc CARDS: Amex, Delta, MasterCard, Switch, Visa DETAILS: 28 seats. Private parties: 20 main room, 8 private room. Car park. Children's helpings. No smoking. Wheelchair access (also WC). Occasional music. No mobile phones ACCOMMODATION: 6 rooms, all with bath/shower. TV. Phone. B&B £95 to £200. Rooms for disabled. Baby facilities (*The Which? Guide to Good Hotels*) (£5)

Fouters Bistro ✸ £

2A Academy Street, Ayr KA7 1HS
TEL: (01292) 261391 FAX: (01292) 619323   COOKING 2
EMAIL: eat@fouters.co.uk   MODERN SCOTTISH
WEBSITE: www.fouters.co.uk   £21–£48

Fouters occupies the vaults of a former bank, built in 1756 and used as such until 1973, when it traded its coffers for scoffers. The restaurant may be 'on the sombre side', as one visitor put it, but the *raison d'être* is the food, which is generally 'good and interesting', and based on organic produce where possible. At lunchtime, simple dishes dominate: perhaps oysters from the island of Seil, pasta with garlic, bacon, mushrooms and cream, or chargrilled steaks. The evening menu has a few more bells and whistles, producing a starter of Stornoway black pudding and game sausages with mango dressing, and main courses of a 'medley of local seafoods' featuring Hebridean salmon, Atlantic cod and West Coast scampi, or pheasant and Gressingham duck breasts with gratin dauphinois and a redcurrant and wine jus. Puddings are of the bread-and-butter and sticky toffee variety. France dominates the wine list, although Switzerland and Canada get a look in among the rest of the world. House wines are £11.95 and £15.50.

CHEFS: Laurie Black and Lewis Pringle   PROPRIETORS: Laurie and Fran Black   OPEN: Mon to Sat 12 to 2, 5 to 10   CLOSED: 25 and 26 Dec, 1 to 3 Jan   MEALS: alc (main courses L £5 to £12, D £9 to £16). Set L £5 (2 courses), Set D (exc after 7pm Sat) £9.50 (2 courses)   SERVICE: not inc   CARDS: Amex, Delta, Diners, MasterCard, Switch, Visa   DETAILS: 38 seats. Private parties: 24 main room, 10 to 14 private rooms. Vegetarian meals. Children's helpings. No smoking. Occasional music. No mobile phones. Air-conditioned   (£5)

BALLATER Aberdeenshire   map 11

▲ Balgonie Country House ⁵⁺✱

Braemar Place, Ballater AB35 5NQ
TEL/FAX: (013397) 55482   COOKING 3
EMAIL: balgoniech@aol.com   MODERN SCOTTISH
WEBSITE: www.royaldeesidehotels.com   £31–£54

Set in four acres of gardens with plenty of room for croquet and within easy striking distance of the Malt Whisky Trail and golf courses, Balgonie Country House – praised for its 'warm hospitality, comfort and attention to detail' – is a peaceful place to cool one's heels and relax. Although the house itself is Edwardian in style, the dining room has a more contemporary feel; the menu, too, is rather more modish than traditional, with ingredients such as curry oil appearing in a starter of artichoke soup with chargrilled artichokes. The menu, three or four courses depending on whether diners opt for the fish course (which may be, say, a gâteau of crab and cucumber), is brief, with just three or four choices per stage. Main courses may include medallion of venison with rösti potatoes, braised red cabbage and port jus, or honey-roast breast of duck with stir-fried vegetables and lemongrass jus. For afters, the sweet-toothed may be tempted by sticky toffee pudding or berry tartlet with blackcurrant sorbet; otherwise opt for a selection of Scottish and Irish cheeses. The wine list favours France over the New World and is strongest in Burgundy and Bordeaux. Most bottles cost more than £20, with prices starting at £15.75 for Beaujolais-Villages.

CHEFS/PROPRIETORS: John and Priscilla Finnie   OPEN: all week 12.30 to 2 (by reservation only), 7 to 9   CLOSED: 6 Jan to 12 Feb   MEALS: Set L £18.50, Set D £31.50   SERVICE: not inc, card slips closed   CARDS: Amex, Delta, Diners, MasterCard, Switch, Visa   DETAILS: 30 seats. Car park. Vegetarian menu can be requested when booking. Children's helpings. No smoking. Wheelchair access (also WC). Occasional music   ACCOMMODATION: 9 rooms, all with bath/shower. TV. Phone. B&B £55 to £140. Baby facilities (The Which? Guide to Good Hotels)   (£5)

⁵⁺✱ *indicates there are some restrictions on smoking, though it is not banned altogether.*

▲ Darroch Learg 🍷 ⅝✳

Braemar Road, Ballater AB35 5UX
TEL: (013397) 55443   FAX: (013397) 55252
EMAIL: info@darrochlearg.co.uk
off A93 Ballater to Braemar Road at W edge of
village

COOKING 6
MODERN SCOTTISH
£29–£62

According to one couple, this is 'our favourite restaurant, for its welcome, wonderful food, the experience and the view'. Built in late Victorian times, not far from the monarch's Scottish home at Balmoral, it sports gables, turrets, and an elegant conservatory dining room where the food exhibits a clear focus and sense of simplicity despite its accomplished workmanship. Among the 'beautifully plated' dishes are exceptionally fine hand-dived Loch Fyne scallops, just seared and served with black pudding, a dish that has appeared on the newly introduced five-course taster menu (along with pan-fried foie gras, saddle of roe deer, chocolate fondant, and cheese). Other shellfish options might run to a ravioli of langoustine and crab, while red-blooded Highland meats have included venison fillet ('never tasted any better'), and beef fillet with braised oxtail and tarragon sauce. Among desserts might be classic lemon tart, white chocolate mousse, or fresh berries with a champagne sabayon and mascarpone ice cream.

Great efforts are made on the wine list to present the affordable faces of Bordeaux and Burgundy, with astute choices like Ghislaine Barthod's Bourgogne Rouge (£22.30). The rest of France, especially the Loire, is good, Italy is quite grand, Spain modern and the New World solid. Five wines are £4.50 by the glass.

CHEF: David Mutter   PROPRIETORS: the Franks family   OPEN: all week 12.30 to 2, 7 to 9   CLOSED: Christmas, last 3 weeks Jan   MEALS: Set L £19.50, Set D £36 to £42.50   SERVICE: net prices, card slips closed   CARDS: Amex, Delta, Diners, MasterCard, Switch, Visa   DETAILS: 48 seats. 8 seats outside. Private parties: 62 main room. Car park. Children's helpings. No smoking. Wheelchair access (not WC). No music   ACCOMMODATION: 18 rooms, all with bath/shower. TV. Phone. B&B £42 to £155. Rooms for disabled. Baby facilities (*The Which? Guide to Good Hotels*)

BALQUHIDDER Stirling

map 11

▲ Monachyle Mhor 🍷 ⅝✳

Balquhidder FK19 8PQ
TEL: (01877) 384622   FAX: (01877) 384305
EMAIL: info@monachylemhor.com
WEBSITE: www.monachylemhor.com
from A84 NW of Callander, turn W at Kinghouse
for Balquhidder; hotel is 6m up glen

COOKING 5
MODERN SCOTTISH
£26–£54

Six miles up a single-track road in Rob Roy country, Tom Lewis produces some stylish food. Most ingredients are local, including fur and feather from the hotel's own ground or neighbouring estates, but the Lewises also gather wild mushrooms and produce hams and sausages from their own pigs. Results: home-cured bresaola and Parma ham with smoked aubergine tapenade, or pan-fried grouse breast with a pearl barley risotto incorporating mushrooms and white truffle oil. One reporter found the fat on untrimmed best end of local lamb contributed an 'out of this world' flavour.

Accurate timing produces moist yet crispy sweetbreads (with kohlrabi), and sensible yet lively partnerships link pan-fried loin of Comrie rabbit with pumpkin and thyme rösti, warm pickled pear and carrot relish, and partner West Coast scallops with smoked haddock and wild rice kedgeree spiked with wasabi and cracked peppercorn butter. Desserts have included a simple, effective trio of pots (chocolate mocha, caramel, and iced amaretto), and an 'exemplary' dark chocolate fondant with liquorice ice cream. The neat wine list shows a sure nose for quality and is sensibly priced, whether offering modern New Zealand Riesling from Palliser at £18 or top-class Condrieu from Georges Vernay at £45. House wines start at £12 or £2.50 a glass.

CHEF: Tom Lewis   PROPRIETORS: Rob, Jean, Tom and Angela Lewis   OPEN: all week 12 to 1.45, 7 to 8.45   MEALS: alc L Mon to Sat (main courses £8.50 to £15.50). Set L Sun £20, Set D £35 SERVICE: not inc   CARDS: MasterCard, Switch, Visa   DETAILS: 40 seats. 20 seats outside. Private parties: 24 main room, 6 to 12 private rooms. Car park. Vegetarian meals. Children's helpings. No children under 12. No smoking. Wheelchair access (also WC). No music. No mobile phones ACCOMMODATION: 10 rooms, all with bath/shower. TV. Phone. B&B £60 to £150. No children under 12. Baby facilities. Fishing (*The Which? Guide to Good Hotels*)

BLAIRGOWRIE   Perthshire & Kinross   map 11

▲ Kinloch House Hotel ♥ ⅚✳

Blairgowrie PH10 6SG
TEL: (01250) 884237   FAX: (01250) 884333
EMAIL: reception@kinlochhouse.com   COOKING 5
WEBSITE: www.kinlochhouse.com   SCOTTISH
on A923, 3m W of Blairgowrie towards Dunkeld   £27–£65

After 25 years running Airds in Port Appin (see entry), the Allen family decided on a change and have moved from small harbourside hotel to grand, ivy-clad country house. Refurbishment is ongoing, but for one reporter the Allens' touch is 'very evident', and the 'fantastic' views don't change. Bill McNicoll is still at the stove, his cooking using native produce (including vegetables from the restored Victorian kitchen garden) in an imaginative and distinctively Scottish style. Starters range from strongly flavoured Highland salmon marinated in whisky, to 'bloody but tender' pigeon breast with foie gras and onion chutney. A soup precedes the main course – perhaps smooth-textured honey, ginger and red pepper. Then 'very big' steaks are a menu fixture, served with a choice of sauces; other options might include 'very rare' lamb with its sweetbreads, or grilled halibut fillet with tarragon and foie gras ravioli on roast-garlic mash and a mussel sauce. Among accomplished desserts have been blueberry tart with excellent pastry, accompanied by cinnamon ice cream, and a 'glorious' prune and Armagnac soufflé. Impressive clarets arranged by vintage and some top-class Burgundies set a traditional tone for the wine list; non-French wines show less flair. Prices are highish, and 11 house wines, from £16.95 (£3.75 a glass), are a lucky dip, identified by region only.

CHEF: Bill McNicoll   PROPRIETORS: the Allen family   OPEN: all week 12 to 2, 7 to 9   CLOSED: 18 to 30 Dec   MEALS: Set L £16.50, Set D £35. Light L menu available   SERVICE: not inc, card slips closed   CARDS: MasterCard, Switch, Visa   DETAILS: 45 seats. 20 seats outside. Private parties:

45 main room, 4 to 18 private rooms. Car park. Vegetarian meals with prior notice. Children's helpings. No smoking. Wheelchair access (also men's WC). No music. No mobile phones ACCOMMODATION: 18 rooms, all with bath/shower. TV. Phone. D,B&B £95 to £330. Rooms for disabled. Baby facilities. Swimming pool (*The Which? Guide to Good Hotels*)

CAIRNDOW Argyll & Bute   map 11

Loch Fyne Oyster Bar ✾ £

Clachan, Cairndow PA26 8BL
TEL: (01499) 600236   FAX: (01499) 600234   COOKING 2
WEBSITE: www.loch-fyne.com   TRADITIONAL SEAFOOD
on A83, at head of Loch Fyne   £21–£73

Stunning scenery and the guarantee of excellent freshly caught shellfish draws crowds to the head of the loch, regardless of season. The restaurant is tourist-oriented, with an atmospheric buzz in the main dining area and the conservatory, and service can be hectic at times, although cheerful and informal. Fresh raw materials – there is ribeye steak or venison for carnivores – are treated simply and complex saucing is avoided. Three wonderfully fresh oysters with a lemon wedge and six queen scallops baked with garlic butter, followed by a generous lemon sole part baked and then grilled to bubble and brown the skin, have proved that simple can be best. There are no-frills salads and basic puddings such as lemon tart or crème caramel, and an affordable wine list that complements the food well. Prices start at £9.95 (£3.50 a glass). This is the senior member of the Loch Fyne chain, with ever-increasing numbers of branches dotted around the country.

CHEF: Tracy Wyatt   PROPRIETOR: Loch Fyne Oysters Ltd   OPEN: all week 9 to 8.30   CLOSED: 26 and 27 Dec, 1 and 2 Jan   MEALS: alc (main courses £5 to £34.50)   SERVICE: not inc   CARDS: Amex, MasterCard, Switch, Visa   DETAILS: 120 seats. 20 seats outside. Private parties: 40 main room. Car park. Vegetarian meals. Children's helpings. No smoking . Wheelchair access (also WC). Occasional music. No mobile phones (£5)

CLACHAN-SEIL Argyll & Bute   map 11

▲ Willowburn Hotel ✾

Clachan-Seil, by Oban PA34 4TJ
TEL: (01852) 300276   FAX: (01852) 300597
EMAIL: willowburn.hotel@virgin.net
WEBSITE: www.willowburn.co.uk
from Oban take A816 S for 8m; then take B844,
following signs for Seil Island and Luing, for 7m;   COOKING 3
after hump-backed bridge Willowburn is approx   MODERN SCOTTISH/FRENCH
¼m on left   £40–£49

In idyllic West Coast scenery, this long low white building is more a restaurant-with-rooms than a hotel, with a homely, unstuffy atmosphere. The set dinner is based mainly on local Scottish produce; herbs and soft fruit from the garden, fish delivered direct (some is smoked on the premises), lamb from nearby hills and game from further afield. Delicate pancakes with wild mushrooms and herbs and warm oysters with basil, lemon and wine may be followed by pea soup, sweetened lightly with pear and a touch of mint. Main courses, such as venison flavoured with herbs and a decent reduction, are equally straightforward and can achieve excellence: as in a subtle creamy sauce with rosemary and garlic accompanying well-judged roast loin of pork. Vegetables can be less accurately timed. Service can be slow, but is polite and friendly. Starting at £12.50, wines include many decent bottles on the modestly priced list.

CHEF: Chris Wolfe   PROPRIETORS: Jan and Chris Wolfe   OPEN: all week D only 7 for 7.30 CLOSED: Dec, Jan and Feb   MEALS: Set D £30   SERVICE: not inc, card slips closed   CARDS: Delta, MasterCard, Switch, Visa   DETAILS: 20 seats. Private parties: 10 main room. Car park. Vegetarian meals. Children's helpings. No smoking. Music. No mobile phones ACCOMMODATION: 7 rooms, all with bath/shower. TV. D, B&B £70 to £140. Baby facilities (*The Which? Guide to Good Hotels*)

COLBOST Highland   map 11

▲ Three Chimneys � ✻

Colbost, Dunvegan, Isle of Skye IV55 8ZT
TEL: (01470) 511258   FAX: (01470) 511358
EMAIL: eatandstay@threechimneys.co.uk   COOKING 5
WEBSITE: www.threechimneys.co.uk   MODERN SCOTTISH
on B884, 4m W of Dunvegan   £34–£88

Three Chimneys is as remote as it gets. Colbost is hardly what any mainlander would recognise as a village, and the Spears' restaurant-with-rooms in a former crofter's cottage sits beside the single-track road along tranquil Loch Dunvegan. Inside is a small dining room with low ceiling and little windows looking out on the loch.

Shirley Spear brings a high level of sophistication to Skye's pre-eminent kitchen. Fixed-price menus focus strongly on local produce. Bracadale crab is fashioned into a timbale bound with lime mayonnaise and served on a bed of chunky potato salad, its freshness and sharpness faultless in a first course. Unusual tiny leaves, nasturtium petals and dabs of good olive oil – a favoured garnish – appear again with local langoustines. A succeeding intermediate course might involve a simple seafood dish, a textbook Cullen skink, or a leek and fennel soup with both advertised flavours standing out proud and true. Fish (the strong suit here) extends into main courses, such as one reporter's poached halibut with an orange cream sauce and a giant raviolo of lobster resembling a mob-cap on top. Meat eaters might find, in season, Highland red grouse with a bramble and bitter chocolate game gravy, though inaccurate timing and poor seasoning of beef fillet let the side down for one reporter. Top-notch desserts have included the signature hot marmalade pudding with Drambuie custard, and a slice of chocolate tart with pistachio ice cream. The stylish wine list pulls no punches, kicking off with six house bottles from £16.25 to £19.95 (£3.95 to £4.95 a glass). Impressive Alsace, Bordeaux and Burgundy are matched by fine selections from Australia and New Zealand.

CHEFS: Shirley Spear and Isobel Tomlin   PROPRIETORS: Eddie and Shirley Spear   OPEN: Mon to Sat L 12.30 to 2, all week D 6.30 to 9.30   CLOSED: 5 to 30 Jan   MEALS: Set L £15 (2 courses) to £21, Set D £40 to £45   SERVICE: not inc   CARDS: Amex, Delta, MasterCard, Switch, Visa DETAILS: 40 seats. 6 seats outside. Private parties: 20 main room. Car park. Vegetarian meals.

Children's helpings. No children under 8 at D. No smoking. Wheelchair access (not WC). No music   ACCOMMODATION: 6 rooms, all with bath/shower. TV. Phone. B&B £155 to £190. Rooms for disabled. Baby facilities (*The Which? Guide to Good Hotels*)

CRINAN Argyll & Bute   map 11

▲ Crinan Hotel, Westward Restaurant 🍴

Crinan PA31 8SR
TEL: (01546) 830261   FAX: (01546) 830292
EMAIL: nryan@crinanhotel.com   COOKING 5
WEBSITE: www.crinanhotel.com   MODERN EUROPEAN
off A816, 6m NW of Lochgilphead   £56–£67

The white-painted, 200-year-old hotel is at the heart of this tiny fishing village (pop. 58), sandwiched between cliff and sea. Views towards Jura, Scarba and Mull are stunning: best from the Rooftop Restaurant, but not bad from the ground-floor Westward Restaurant either. The place is decorated with some of Frances Macdonald Ryan's bold and arresting seascapes, and the 'classically restrained' dining room is done up with wicker chairs and crisp damask tablecloths, all looking appropriately 'suitable for stylish eating'.

Menus change daily, and scallops typically appear in some form: at one meal a well-judged dish of plump, juicy specimens, timed to be translucent inside, accompanied by celeriac, carrots and leeks in a sweet-and-sour sauce with a light vanilla foam. The four-course dinner format takes in a no-choice intermediate dish, perhaps locally smoked rainbow trout with a caper and raisin vinaigrette, adding up to 'more than the sum of its parts'. Despite some inconsistencies (notably among meat dishes at inspection), the cooking shows a degree of skill and flair: perhaps robust monkfish tail with a smooth and creamy brandade, surrounded by peas in a light yet velvety truffled sauce. Among desserts, a smooth, 'blissfully creamy' and wobbly pannacotta is highly rated. There are no appetisers or petits fours (indeed coffee is a disappointing help-yourself Cona), but bread is freshly baked. Service can be a bit 'hit and miss', but there is something to suit most pockets on the knowledgeably annotated wine list, starting with house Côtes de Gascogne white (£16.50) and Coteaux du Languedoc red (£16).

CHEF: Ben Tish   PROPRIETORS: Nicolas and Frances Ryan   OPEN: all week D only 7 to 9 (8.30 winter)   CLOSED: Christmas and New Year   MEALS: Set D £42.50. Bar menu available   SERVICE: not inc, card slips closed   CARDS: Amex, MasterCard, Switch, Visa   DETAILS: 30 seats. 20 seats outside. Private parties: 60 main room, 20 to 45 private rooms. Car park. Children's helpings. No smoking. Wheelchair access (also WC). Occasional music   ACCOMMODATION: 20 rooms, all with bath/shower. TV. Phone. B&B £95 to £190. Rooms for disabled. Baby facilities. Fishing (£5)

Restaurateurs justifiably resent no-shows. If you quote a credit card number when booking, you may be liable for the restaurant's lost profit margin if you don't turn up. Always phone to cancel.

Plumed Horse ⚜✳

Main Street, Crossmichael DG7 3AU
TEL: (01556) 670333   COOKING **6**
EMAIL: plumedhorse@aol.com   MODERN EUROPEAN
WEBSITE: www.plumed-horse.co.uk   £28–£56

'A plumed horse in a one-horse hamlet!' joked one visitor to this edge-of-village restaurant resembling a white-washed barn. Surprise at reporters' good fortune in finding it is widely shared: 'it is remarkable to find a restaurant of this quality in such a small town', volunteered one, while another summed it all up as 'excellent food at reasonable prices'. The predominantly yellow dining room feels domestic in scale, although it is smart, too, and luxuries are conspicuous by their presence on the menu, notably among first courses: a parfait and ballottine of foie gras, no fewer than two caviars to accompany marinated salmon with sour cream, and a strongly herb-flavoured risotto imbued with truffle oil and decorated with truffled green beans and a thick scraping of Parmesan.

But even when materials are more conventional, quality is still high. Roast breast of free-range chicken has come with root vegetables and a mild rosemary sauce, and Gressingham duck breast with a well-balanced honey and black pepper dressing. Locally landed fish and shellfish are among the stars, including 'the sweetest scallops ever' in an assiette of seafood. Choice may be limited, especially on the set-price menus, but nobody seems to mind, not when there are desserts such as rhubarb crumble with clotted cream ice cream, or an 'immensely enjoyable' crisp pastry tart filled with fine dark chocolate, served with a pool of crème anglaise and a bulb of smooth, powerfully flavoured coffee ice cream. A short wine list doesn't seem quite to do justice to the food, but starts with house French at £12.50.

CHEFS: Tony Borthwick and James Pearce   PROPRIETOR: Tony Borthwick   OPEN: Tue to Fri and Sun L 12.30 to 1, Tue to Sat D 7 to 9   CLOSED: Christmas, 2 weeks Jan, 2 weeks Sept   MEALS: alc exc Sun L (main courses £17 to £19). Set L Tue to Fri £16.95, Set L Sun £18.95, Set D Tue to Fri £25   SERVICE: not inc, card slips closed   CARDS: Delta, MasterCard, Switch, Visa   DETAILS: 28 seats. Private parties: 20 main room, 10 to 20 private rooms. No smoking. Wheelchair access (also WC). No music. No mobile phones. Air-conditioned

Ostlers Close ▼ ✳

25 Bonnygate, Cupar KY15 4BU   COOKING **5**
TEL: (01334) 655574   MODERN SCOTTISH
WEBSITE: www.ostlersclose.co.uk   £30–£54

This informal, friendly little restaurant is hidden away off the high street of a small market town. Jimmy and Amanda Graham put great effort into sourcing their supplies – including growing herbs and vegetables and foraging for wild produce, especially mushrooms – and, according to a regular visitor, they 'continue to maintain very high standards of really good food'.

Pride in native produce shines through a menu where the ingredients' provenance is frequently included in dish descriptions. Perthshire grouse comes with its slow-cooked legs on wild mushrooms and a red wine sauce; roast fillet of Pittenweem turbot is served on lobster risotto with an asparagus sauce; and hand-dived Mull scallops are teamed with Glamis seakale and a pesto-flavoured olive oil. Jimmy Graham likes mixing and matching ideas from different cuisines, so a starter of pan-fried confit duck leg might be set off with potatoes and piccalilli, and a main-course duck breast could come with Bombay potatoes and a plum sauce. But there are straight-down-the-line classics too, such as roast saddle of venison with wild mushrooms, brown lentils and a game sauce. Dessert choices have included warm pear Tatin with toasted almond ice cream and blackcurrant sauce, or panettone bread-and-butter pudding with custard and raspberry ripple ice cream. The cellar must be disproportionately large to enable a small restaurant to house such a substantial collection of wines that thoughtfully covers all regions and is consistently reasonably priced. House wines from familiar Chilean names are £13 or £14 and £3.50 a glass.

CHEF: Jimmy Graham   PROPRIETORS: Jimmy and Amanda Graham   OPEN: Sat L 12.15 to 1.30, Tue to Sat D 7 to 9.30   CLOSED: 25 and 26 Dec, 1 and 2 Jan, 2 weeks Oct   MEALS: alc (main courses £10 to £18.50). Set D £22.50 (available Nov to May Tue to Fri only and must be pre-booked)   SERVICE: not inc, card slips closed   CARDS: Amex, Delta, MasterCard, Switch, Visa   DETAILS: 28 seats. Private parties: 22 main room. Children's helpings. No children under 6 at D. No smoking. No music. No mobile phones

DALRY North Ayrshire   map 11

Braidwoods ⚞✳

Drumastle Mill Cottage, Dalry KA24 4LN
TEL: (01294) 833544   FAX: (01294) 833553
EMAIL: keithbraidwood@btconnect.com
WEBSITE: www.braidwoods.co.uk
1m off A737 on Dalry to Saltcoats road

COOKING 6
MODERN SCOTTISH
£30–£63

After a decade at their secluded Ayrshire haven, Keith and Nicola Braidwood are still impressing visitors with the quality and consistency of their output. The setting is simple and understated – a couple of cottagey rooms in white stonewash with scenic paintings, white napery and fresh flowers – and an air of confidence pervades: 'you can sit back and relax in the expectation of assured professional cuisine of the highest standard.' Local and seasonal produce forms a bedrock, taking in hand-dived scallops from Mull, seared in nut-brown butter with precision timing, loin of Highland red deer with Jerusalem artichoke purée, and (in spring) a wobbly, pale-green timbale of young asparagus with chervil butter.

This is clear-flavoured food cooked with finesse, producing, for example, moist, pink-roast loin of Duchal Moor lamb 'exuding rich juices', on a bed of spinach with a fine wild mushroom jus, and a roast boneless quail stuffed with sturdy, crumbly black pudding, served with finely shredded Savoy cabbage briefly braised in the bird's juices. Such straightforward yet accomplished cooking has also yielded a luscious yet light-textured Valrhona chocolate tart with crisp pastry, served lukewarm with banana ice cream. An intermediate course at dinner typically offers a soup (perhaps cauliflower and smoked Cheddar) or a slice of Parmesan tart ('one of their great successes'). Coffee could be improved, but portions are well judged, and service is unobtrusive, attentive, courteous and skilled. A varied wine list, incorporating a decent spread of half-bottles, starts with house Jurançon Sec and Côtes d'Oakley from Cline Cellars in California at £16.95.

CHEFS/PROPRIETORS: Keith and Nicola Braidwood OPEN: Wed to Sun L 12 to 1.45, Tue to Sat D 7 to 9 CLOSED: 25 Dec, first 3 weeks Jan, first 2 weeks Sept MEALS: Set L Wed to Sat £16 (2 courses) to £19, Set L Sun £25, Set D £31 to £35 SERVICE: not inc, card slips closed CARDS: Amex, Delta, Diners, MasterCard, Switch, Visa DETAILS: 24 seats. Private parties: 16 main room. Car park. Vegetarian meals. No children under 12. No smoking. No music. No mobile phones

DORNOCH Highland   map 11

▲ 2 Quail 🍴

Castle Street, Dornoch IV25 3SN
TEL: (01862) 811811   COOKING 4
EMAIL: goodfood@2quail.com   MODERN EUROPEAN-PLUS
WEBSITE: www.2quail.com   £46–£55

Seemingly not many reporters to the Guide make it as far north as this historical cathedral town, but those who do tell us that the experience is most agreeable, particularly when it comes to dinner at this small, homely restaurant run by 'welcoming and friendly' Michael and Kerensa Carr. The weekly-changing menus offer three choices per course and reveal a pleasingly straightforward approach, taking in a broad range of influences, contemporary and traditional. Starters of smoked salmon kedgeree with watercress sauce, and Maryland-style crab cake with salsa verde have found favour with reporters, as has a main course of 'sensationally good' loin of venison with brandied cherries, walnuts and thyme. Alternatives have included halibut with courgettes, sorrel and a thyme butter sauce, roast duck breast with creamed cabbage, roasted shallots and red wine sauce, and fillet steak with pea purée, garlic-roast potatoes and shallots, and to finish there might be layered mango and coconut mousse with lime syrup. The wine list is fairly short but well chosen, offering good variety and fair value. Prices start at £13. Note the limited opening and that booking is essential.

CHEF: Michael Carr PROPRIETORS: Michael and Kerensa Carr OPEN: Tue to Sat D only 7.30 to 9.30; days and times may vary in winter CLOSED: 2 weeks Feb/Mar, bank hols MEALS: Set D £32.50 SERVICE: not inc CARDS: Amex, Delta, MasterCard, Switch, Visa DETAILS: 14 seats. Private parties: 10 main room. Children's helpings. No smoking. Occasional music. No mobile phones ACCOMMODATION: 3 rooms, all with bath/shower. TV. Phone. B&B £65 to £105. No children under 8 exc babes in arms. Baby facilities (The Which? Guide to Good Hotels)

All entries, including Round-ups, are fully indexed at the back of the Guide.

Which? Online subscribers will find The Good Food Guide *online, along with other Which? guides and magazines, at* www.which.net. *See the website for information on how to become a subscriber.*

DUFFTOWN Moray   map 11

La Faisanderie | NEW ENTRY |

2 Balvenie Street, Dufftown AB55 4AD
TEL: (01340) 821273   COOKING 2
EMAIL: chtiroastbeef@aol.com   FRANCO-SCOTTISH
WEBSITE: www.dufftown.co.uk/lafaisanderie.htm   £22–£49

This Anglo-French partnership makes an interesting blend in a town famous for
its distilleries. Situated in the central square, the stone-built restaurant offers a
'relaxing, unfussy atmosphere': décor is pleasant and unobtrusive, as is the
service provided by Mandy (English), while Eric (French) runs the kitchen. The
menu is described as French with a Scottish twist. Dishes such as cassoulet of
mussels and oysters with a Noilly Prat sabayon, and pan-fried medallions of
venison with roasted peach and sweet muscat cream bear this out. Also winning
praise have been asparagus with orange hollandaise, and baked sea trout with
lime and dill sauce. Puddings, too, follow the Scots-French theme: profiteroles
with Glenfiddich Solera chocolate sauce, or tropical fruit and coconut crème
brûlée with shortbread biscuit. The short, French wine list starts at £9.90 (£2.70
per glass).

CHEF: Eric Obry   PROPRIETORS: Mandy Bestwick and Eric Obry   OPEN: Thur to Mon L 12 to 1.30,
Wed to Mon D 6.30 (7 Fri and Sat) to 8.30 (9 summer)   CLOSED: 3 to 13 Oct, 22 Dec to 2 Jan, 15 to
28 Feb   MEALS: alc (main courses L £9 to £17, D £13.50 to £17). Set L £10.90 (2 courses) to
£13.90, Set D £21   SERVICE: not inc, card slips closed   CARDS: Delta, MasterCard, Switch, Visa
DETAILS: 30 seats. Private parties: 14 main room. Vegetarian meals. Children's helpings.
Wheelchair access (also WC). Music

DUNKELD Perthshire & Kinross   map 11

▲ Kinnaird 🍸

Kinnaird Estate, by Dunkeld PH8 0LB
TEL: (01796) 482440   FAX: (01796) 482289
EMAIL: enquiry@kinnairdestate.com
WEBSITE: www.kinnairdestate.com   COOKING 6
from A9 2m N of Dunkeld, take B898, signposted   MODERN EUROPEAN
Kinnaird, for 4½m   £44–£79

Even visitors who have been before are struck by the beautiful location of this
fine Edwardian mansion at the heart of a 9,000-acre estate in the wooded Tay
valley. Despite the grandeur, the atmosphere is more like a house than a hotel,
and the décor takes in everything from a trompe l'oeil mural in the splendid
dining room to 'my granny's lounge carpet'. Jacket and tie are expected to be
worn at dinner, which seems an excessive formality.

Great care is taken over all aspects of presentation – even the menus look
attractive, printed on iridescent paper – which especially goes for the food.
Trevor Brooks puts a contemporary spin on classical French cooking, taking in
ideas picked up from stints working abroad. Thus, a homely dish such as lamb
fricassee with asparagus and morels might appear as a starter next to a 'mosaic' of
foie gras, veal sweetbreads and chicken, or a crisp tart of oven-dried tomatoes
with pesto, creamed goats' cheese and anchovy beignet. Main courses tend to be

even more layered and highly crafted: an assiette of suckling pig comes with a tarte Tatin made of trotter, plus turnips and asparagus, while braised escalope of turbot is partnered with clams, dauphine potatoes and a chive-scented sauce, and venison is accompanied by beetroot, Savoy cabbage, salsify and celeriac fondant. To finish, there might be white chocolate and vanilla bavarois, or hot apricot soufflé with tamarind and passion-fruit sorbet. The wine list is a hefty volume of classy numbers, including a huge choice of fine wines from Bordeaux, Burgundy and California. Unfortunately, choice at the humbler end of the scale is somewhat limited: prices start at £20 and quickly escalate.

CHEF: Trevor Brooks   PROPRIETOR: Constance Ward   OPEN: all week 12.30 to 1.45, 7.15 to 9.30   MEALS: Set L £30, Set D £50. Light L menu available   SERVICE: not inc, card slips closed   CARDS: Amex, Delta, MasterCard, Switch, Visa   DETAILS: 36 seats. Car park. No children under 12. Jacket and tie at D. No smoking. Wheelchair access (also WC). No music. No mobile phones   ACCOMMODATION: 9 rooms, all with bath/shower. TV. Phone. D,B&B £225 to £375. Rooms for disabled. No children under 12. Fishing (*The Which? Guide to Good Hotels*)

EDINBURGH Edinburgh   map 11

Atrium ▼

10 Cambridge Street, Edinburgh EH1 2ED	COOKING 3
TEL: (0131) 228 8882 FAX: (0131) 228 8808	MODERN EUROPEAN
WEBSITE: www.atriumrestaurant.co.uk	£29–£65

Cheek-by-jowl with theatres, and with the Usher Hall round the corner, this stylish place is at the heart of Edinburgh life. Its subdued lighting, solid wood tables and linen-covered chairs are at the opposite end of the smart-dining spectrum from 'blue', its flashier sister upstairs (see entry). A mix of culinary influences can be seen in starters of vitello tonnato, pork and duck rillette with confit onions and seared foie gras, and terrine of wood pigeon and wild rabbit. At inspection the home-made linguine with wild mushrooms was a success, and another diner encountered 'scallops seared to perfection' with sauce Antiboise. The set dinner (£25, plus £15 extra for an interesting glass of wine matching each course) might include chicken stewed with aubergine, ham and tomato, the carte trumping it with halibut with cod brandade and asparagus. Puddings have included 'divine' combinations like chocolate and rhubarb mille-feuille with coffee anglaise displaying bold flavours and good pastry-work, or may be tiramisù with hazelnut ice cream, or else custard tart and roast figs. Sherries and some bold choices among the 14 wines by the glass (£4 to £9) open a pricey list of quality finds from all regions. House wines are £14 and one or two others stay under £20.

CHEF: Neil Forbes   PROPRIETORS: Andrew and Lisa Radford   OPEN: Mon to Fri L 12 to 2, Mon to Sat D 6 to 10 (all week L and D during Festival)   MEALS: alc (main courses £15.50 to £21). Set L £9.50 (1 course) to £17.50, Set D £25   SERVICE: not inc, 10% for parties of 6 or more   CARDS: Amex, Delta, Diners, MasterCard, Switch, Visa   DETAILS: 100 seats. 100 seats outside. Private parties: 100 main room. Vegetarian meals. Children's helpings. Wheelchair access (also WC). No music. Air-conditioned

The Guide's top-rated restaurants are listed near the front of the book.

▲ Balmoral, Number One

1 Princes Street, Edinburgh EH2 2EQ
TEL: (0131) 557 6727   FAX: (0131) 557 8740
EMAIL: numberone@thebalmoralhotel.com
WEBSITE: www.roccofortehotels.com

SCOTLAND GFG 2004 COMMENDED

COOKING 6
MODERN EUROPEAN
£40–£123

A large basement bar and dining room, done out in creams and browns, forms the backdrop for Jeff Bland's appealing contemporary food. His indebtedness to the Scottish larder – perhaps West Coast scallops with leeks and bacon, or Perthshire venison in a herb crust – is balanced by imports, mostly from France: a terrine of foie gras comes with Puy lentils, and Bresse duck is given a honey and black pepper treatment. Indeed, it is the European component that gives many of the dishes their character, as in a grilled fillet of Scottish beef served with truffle gnocchi and something called a tarragon foie gras café au lait.

Luxury materials are the order of the day, from langoustines to Dover sole; even the potatoes in a woodland mushroom soup are ratte, and a starter of humble pig's trotter comes with truffled Madeira sauce. But this is not mere luxury for the sake of it. Dishes are carefully constructed and well balanced, saucing is spot-on and the whole effect is of a polished and skilful brigade turning out dishes that are both simple and captivating.

As well as the carte there is a Market Menu, a Tasting Menu and one called Gourmet's Delights that takes in a selection of seafood, a plate of meat and game, and a platter of five desserts. Among the last might be nougat parfait with candied fruits and nuts, whisky jelly with oranges and Drambuie, and dark chocolate soufflé with ivory ice cream. The wine list is a cracker, with quality high throughout, but nothing much happens below £20, even in Chile and Argentina. A handful of wines by the glass at £5.50 each is about the only sop to those on a budget.

CHEF: Jeff Bland   PROPRIETOR: Rocco Forte Hotels   OPEN: Mon to Fri L 12 to 2, all week D 7 to 10   MEALS: alc (main courses £20 to £24). Set L £14.50 (2 courses) to £17.50, Set D £41 to £85 (inc wine)   SERVICE: not inc, 12.5% for parties of 6 or more   CARDS: Amex, Delta, Diners, MasterCard, Switch, Visa   DETAILS: 45 seats. Private parties: 100 main room. Children's helpings. No-smoking area. Wheelchair access (also WC). Music. No mobile phones. Air-conditioned   ACCOMMODATION: 188 rooms, all with bath/shower. TV. Phone. Room only £95 to £170. Rooms for disabled. Baby facilities. Swimming pool (£5)

blue

10 Cambridge Street, Edinburgh EH1 2ED
TEL: (0131) 221 1222   FAX: (0131) 228 8808
WEBSITE: www.bluebarcafe.com

COOKING 2
MODERN BRITISH
£27–£53

Situated above the Traverse theatre, this smart brasserie with pale wood floors, much stainless steel and black and transparent chairs still retains its pull. Dishes are generously portioned; set-price meals and the 'light blue' and vegetable side dishes are bargains. Finely textured chicken liver parfait served unfussily with pear chutney, carefully sourced duck with bubble and squeak, and fish – such as moist, flaky cod with a herby crust – with a mash or gratin or wilted vegetables result in shining flavours. Distinctive breads, simply dressed salads and excellent espresso show attention to detail. Puddings seem to command less attention but ice creams are particularly good. Some have found the music too loud, so try the sister restaurant on the same site (see Atrium) if you want something a little more restrained. The bistro-basic wine list is short, sweet and mostly under £20, with six by the glass from £3.25 to £3.85.

CHEF: David Haetzman   PROPRIETORS: Andrew and Lisa Radford   OPEN: Mon to Sat 12 to 3, 6 to 11 (open Sun during Festival)   CLOSED: 25 and 26 Dec, 1 Jan   MEALS: alc (main courses £11 to £15). Set L £8.45 (1 course) to £14.45, Set D exc Fri and Sat £9.45 (1 course) to £16.45   SERVICE: not inc, 10% (optional) for parties of 6 or more   CARDS: Amex, Delta, Diners, MasterCard, Switch, Visa   DETAILS: 120 seats. Private parties: 120 main room. Vegetarian meals. Children's helpings. No-smoking area. Wheelchair access (also WC). Music. Air-conditioned

▲ The Bonham ⁵⁄×

35 Drumsheugh Gardens, Edinburgh EH3 7RN
TEL: (0131) 623 9319   FAX: (0131) 226 6080
EMAIL: restaurant@thebonham.com
WEBSITE: www.thebonham.com

COOKING 3
MODERN EUROPEAN
£26–£63

Although it has been around for a few years now, the Bonham retains a sense of chic and shows no signs of falling out of fashion – perhaps because the Victorian town house setting and sympathetic décor have such a timeless appeal, while 'confident, well-trained and attentive' service keeps diners at their ease. The cooking is adventurous. Starters might be as simple as lightly spiced butternut squash soup or as elaborate as a fricassee of langoustine and scallops with a cauliflower flan and shellfish cappuccino, while interesting main-course ideas have included pavé of halibut poached in Cabernet Sauvignon with parsnip and nutmeg purée and gravad lax sauce, and confit rabbit leg with roasted root vegetables, chorizo and a thyme jus. More straightforward options might include pan-fried Scottish beef fillet with fondant potato, truffled white pudding and a Puy lentil jus, and to finish there's hot milk chocolate soufflé with a matching sorbet. Lunches are simpler and lighter and feature a 'healthy living' menu. The wine list is neatly compact and helpfully annotated, opening with eight house selections by the bottle from £13.50, or by the glass from £3.50.

CHEF: Michel Bouyer   PROPRIETOR: Peter Taylor   OPEN: all week 12 to 2.30 (12.30 to 3 Sun), 6.30 to 10   MEALS: alc D (main courses £15 to £19). Set L Mon to Sat £12.50 (2 courses) to £15, Set L Sun £15 (min 2, inc wine). Snack menu available   SERVICE: not inc, card slips closed   CARDS: Amex, Delta, Diners, MasterCard, Switch, Visa   DETAILS: 52 seats. Private parties: 60 main room, 1 to 70 private rooms. Vegetarian meals. No smoking. Wheelchair access (also WC). Music   ACCOMMODATION: 48 rooms, all with bath/shower. TV. Phone. B&B £140 to £325. Rooms for disabled. Baby facilities (The Which? Guide to Good Hotels) £5

Café St Honoré ⁵⁄×

34 NW Thistle Street Lane, Edinburgh EH2 1EA
TEL: (0131) 226 2211
WEBSITE: www.cafesthonore.com

COOKING 2
MODERN BISTRO
£25–£51

Tucked away on one of Edinburgh's cobbled lanes, St Honoré is pretty much everything you'd imagine when trying to conjure up an image of a traditional French bistro. On entering, you might even be tempted to pull up a bar stool and order a croque-monsieur. In fact, you won't find that dish on the menu, but you will find bright, modern ideas such as a warm salad of scallops, chorizo, spring onions and tomatoes, or roast stuffed quail with spinach, orange and cashew nuts for starters. Main courses range from baked halibut with clams, leeks and mushrooms to duck breast with beetroot, grapes and walnuts, via veal escalope with sweetbreads, asparagus and port. To finish there might be warm chocolate and orange fondant with berries and candied walnuts. Seven house wines at £10.50 a bottle, also available by the glass, open a concise, accessible and reasonably priced list.

CHEFS: Chris Colverson and Garrett O'Hanlon   PROPRIETORS: Chris and Gill Colverson   OPEN: Mon to Fri 12 to 2.15, 5.30 (6 Sat) to 10   CLOSED: 3 days Christmas, 3 days New Year, Apr and May bank hol Mons   MEALS: alc (main courses L £8.50 to £13.75, D £14 to £19.75). Set D Mon to Fri 5.30 to 7 £13.50 (2 courses) to £18   SERVICE: not inc, 10% for parties of 8 or more   CARDS: Amex, Delta, Diners, MasterCard, Switch, Visa   DETAILS: 56 seats. Private parties: 40 main room, 8 to 18 private rooms. Vegetarian meals. Children's helpings. No smoking in 1 dining room. Wheelchair access (also women's WC). Music

▲ Channings 🍳 ⁵⭐

15 South Learmonth Gardens,
Edinburgh EH4 1EZ
TEL: (0131) 315 2225   FAX: (0131) 332 9631
EMAIL: restaurant@channings.co.uk
WEBSITE: www.channings.co.uk

COOKING 2
MODERN SCOTTISH
£32–£66

An elegant Victorian ambience brings warmth to the dining room, and very proper hushed, discreet, smartly dressed service adds a professional touch. Chef Hubert Lamort delivers complex assemblies of towers and tuiles topped with herb sprigs, which are beautiful to the eye. The range of breads – second to none – good pastrywork and careful sourcing of ingredients (with scallops coming in for repeated praise) all demonstrate skill and care. Aubergine and tomato confit at inspection had a swirl of cream that looked pretty but blanketed flavours, though timing for meat and fish has been finely judged. Interesting-sounding marriages (such as a galette of confit garlic, basil milk and potato tuile accompanying monkfish) have demonstrated assured technical expertise, but again, flavours can sometimes be less intense than desired. Excellent desserts might include a fine mille-feuille of pistachio parfait with a tangy mango and lime sauce, or the inventive temperature and texture contrasts of a crushed strawberry compote comprising vanilla fromage frais, crispy puffed rice and warm plum clafoutis. The short wine list, arranged by grape variety, has just six bottles under £20. There is a wine bar, Ochre Vita, also on the site.

CHEF: Hubert Lamort   PROPRIETOR: Peter Taylor   OPEN: Tue to Sat 12.30 to 2, 7 to 10   MEALS: alc D (main courses £10.50 to £23). Set L £16 (2 courses) to £19. Bar menu available   SERVICE: not inc   CARDS: Amex, Delta, Diners, MasterCard, Switch, Visa   DETAILS: 34 seats. 24 seats outside. Private parties: 8 main room, 10 to 20 private rooms. Vegetarian meals. Children's helpings. No smoking. Music   ACCOMMODATION: 46 rooms, all with bath/shower. TV. Phone. B&B £105 to £260. Baby facilities

The Guide always appreciates hearing about changes of chef or owner.

First Coast £

NEW ENTRY

99–101 Dalry Road, Edinburgh EH11 2AB
TEL/FAX: (0131) 313 4404
EMAIL: info@first-coast.co.uk
WEBSITE: www.first-coast.co.uk

COOKING **1**
MODERN SCOTTISH
£21–£42

Trendily Spartan décor and a relaxed atmosphere characterise this neighbourhood bistro close to the Haymarket station. Cooking is fairly fashion-conscious too, aiming for a simple style with a focus on big flavours over elaborate presentation. Start perhaps with a salad of sticky pork ribs with mango and a mustardy dressing, or fishcakes with a refreshingly sharp chilli and coriander dip. To follow there may be roast chicken breast with chorizo and white bean stew, lamb and mussel pie, or grilled sea bass with pickled fennel, oven-dried tomatoes and lime butter sauce, and for dessert, choices typically include sticky toffee pudding with butterscotch sauce, or almond macaroon with strawberries and cream. Prices are pitched low to encourage return visits, and the set lunch and early-dinner menu – offering one, two or three courses – looks particularly good value. This goes for wines too, with half of the dozen bottles sneaking below the £10 barrier.

CHEF: Hector MacRae PROPRIETORS: Hector and Alan MacRae OPEN: Wed to Sat L 12 to 2, Mon to Sat D 5 to 11 CLOSED: 25 and 26 Dec, 1 Jan MEALS: alc (main courses £6 to £13). Set L and D 5 to 6.30 £5.95 (1 course) to £12.50 SERVICE: not inc CARDS: MasterCard, Switch, Visa
DETAILS: 55 seats. Private parties: 55 main room. Vegetarian meals. Wheelchair access (not WC). Music. Air-conditioned (£5)

Fishers in the City ▼ ✸ £

Thistle Street, Edinburgh EH2 1EN
TEL: (0131) 225 5109   FAX: (0131) 225 5434
WEBSITE: www.fishersbistros.co.uk

COOKING **3**
SEAFOOD
£22–£59

The atmosphere buzzes with happy chatter at busy times at Fishers in the City, younger sister to the Round-up entry in Leith. Like its sibling, it is a piscophile's dream, offering a daily-changing menu featuring the likes of yellow-tailed snapper, rainbow trout and Arbroath smokies. But carnivores are catered for too, with perhaps a main course of fillet steak with brandy and peppercorn sauce, or roast magret of duck. There is also a vegetarian menu. Dishes such as queen scallops with pancetta, and a main course of whole baby turbot with a lobster, celery and orange sauce, have met with approval. Flavour combinations can be unusual – viz. pan-fried Indian Ocean prawns marinated in Malaysian spices and Goan yoghurt dressing with a timbale of pecan, basil and lavender basmati rice. Nonetheless, those who like things simple can gain comfort with dishes like Loch Fyne oysters, and steamed West Coast mussels. Desserts include lemon tart with chocolate syrup, and sticky toffee pudding. The enthusiastic wine list offers stacks of good-value options under £20, plus a fine wine selection and a page devoted to the Dry River estate in New Zealand. Prices start at £10.95, and 15 by the glass are £2.95 to £4.85.

CHEFS: Dan Sugars and Andy Bird   PROPRIETORS: James Millar and Graeme Lumsden   OPEN: all week 12 to 10.30   CLOSED: 25 and 26 Dec, 1 Jan   MEALS: alc (main courses £8.50 to £24)   SERVICE: not inc   CARDS: Amex, Delta, Diners, MasterCard, Switch, Visa   DETAILS: 75 seats. Private parties: 50 main room. Vegetarian meals. No smoking in 1 dining room. Wheelchair access (also WC). Music. Air-conditioned

Forth Floor 🍷

NEW ENTRY

Harvey Nichols, 30–34 St Andrews Square,
Edinburgh EH2 2AD
TEL: (0131) 524 8350   FAX: (0131) 524 8351
WEBSITE: www.harveynichols.com

COOKING 4
MODERN BRITISH
£39–£70

The newest outpost of Harvey Nichols follows the format of other branches by naming the restaurant after the floor it occupies. But this being Edinburgh, they call it the Forth Floor, and though the view doesn't actually take in the water it is nothing short of 'magnificent', looking across the city to the castle. There are two parts to the operation: a lively bar/brasserie with a wide range of cocktails and a menu of things like smoked rainbow trout with piccalilli and potato salad, and braised lamb shank with Parmesan polenta and rosemary jus.

The restaurant, meanwhile, takes a more formal approach, its well-spaced tables set with white cloths and proper napkins. 'Mystical' piano music plays softly in the background and waiters don't walk, they 'glide'. Menus introduce some fashionable ideas to an otherwise straightforwardly classical style that produces starters of 'pink, tender and tasty' seared pigeon breast with crisp deep-fried celeriac and creamy, garlicky dauphinoise potatoes alongside seared scallops with courgette and chilli chutney and red pepper syrup. Among main courses have been 'assiette of beef' comprising fillet, tongue and a 'soft, sticky and light' ballottine of oxtail and chicken, and well flavoured rack of lamb with sautéed truffled potatoes, lamb's sweetbreads and mint sauce. To finish, hot chocolate fondant has been a good version, with a light texture and intense flavour, served with pistachio ice cream.

A glossy range of fashionable New World bottles falls into whimsical style categories like 'Bordeauxesque reds' or 'exotics', while Europe is treated more formally by country and region. Either way, the wine list makes exciting reading. Choices under £20 are plentiful and a dozen come by the glass (£3.50 to £5.50). Wine fans drooling for the better bottles should fight for a table on Tuesday evenings, when all wines are sold at retail prices (minimum £13.50). In the bar/brasserie a shorter list just about holds its own against the cocktails.

CHEF: Stuart Muir   PROPRIETOR: Harvey Nichols   OPEN: all week L 12 to 3 (3.30 Sat and Sun), Tue to Sat D 6 to 10 (all week D in Aug)   CLOSED: 25 Dec and 1 Jan   MEALS: alc (main courses £12.50 to £23)   SERVICE: 10%, card slips closed   CARDS: Amex, Delta, Diners, MasterCard, Switch, Visa   DETAILS: 90 seats. 32 seats outside. Private parties: 140 main room. Children's helpings. No-smoking area. Wheelchair access (also WC). Occasional music. Air-conditioned

The Guide relies on feedback from its readers. Especially welcome are reports on new restaurants appearing in the book for the first time. All letters to the Guide are acknowledged.

Haldanes ▼ ⁵⭑

39A Albany Street, Edinburgh EH1 3QY
TEL: (0131) 556 8407   FAX: (0131) 556 2662
EMAIL: dinehaldanes@aol.com
WEBSITE: www.haldanesrestaurant.com

COOKING **3**
MODERN SCOTTISH
£24–£65

'An old favourite to which we return each time we visit Edinburgh, and we are never disappointed,' say two experienced eaters-out. Maybe it is the comfortable, 'unostentatiously elegant' basement setting or the monthly-changing menu's adventurous permutations on best Scottish staples of fish, beef and venison. George Kelso accompanies venison with honey-glazed figs and roasted beetroots, tops Shetland salmon with crab and couscous crumble, or teams guinea fowl with a parsnip compote and light curry cream sauce. A starter of scallops with a crab and avocado salad has come in for praise, as has braised lamb shank with a well-judged cassoulet of root vegetables and baby broad beans. On the dessert menu, sweet wines by the glass are recommended to partner an already boozy banoffi pie served with a light rum syrup, or an old favourite like hot pear and apple crumble with ice cream. In between its jokey quotations the global wine list is quietly serious (and includes a handy guide to food and wine pairings). Nine house wines come by bottle or glass from £12/£3.25 to £14/£4.75, and there are two dozen half-bottle options.

CHEF: George Kelso   PROPRIETORS: George and Michelle Kelso   OPEN: Mon to Fri L 12 to 1.45, all week D 5.45 to 9.30   MEALS: alc (main courses L £6.25 to £11.50, D £17.50 to £22.50)   SERVICE: not inc   CARDS: Delta, Diners, MasterCard, Switch, Visa   DETAILS: 50 seats. Private parties: 50 main room, 10 to 20 private rooms. Vegetarian meals. Children's helpings. No smoking. No music. No mobile phones (£5)

Kalpna ⁵⭑ £

2–3 St Patrick Square, Edinburgh EH8 9EZ
TEL: (0131) 667 9890

COOKING **3**
INDIAN VEGETARIAN
£15–£36

'An old warhorse on the Edinburgh dining scene' is how one correspondent described Ajay Bhardwaj's long-serving bastion of Indian vegetarian cooking. The décor may be functional – although there have been some cosmetic improvements of late – but it's the 'really interesting, well-seasoned' food that matters. The menus range far and wide, from pakoras and dosas to more intriguing specialities: khoya kaju from Rajasthan includes cashews, reduced cream, sultanas and nutmeg, while diwani handi is mushrooms, paneer and spinach garnished with pickled ginger. Home-made kulfi is a pleasing way to finish. Otherwise opt for one of the Gujarati thalis. Accompaniments such as chutneys, rice and breads have all received the thumbs up. Wednesday night brings a three-course set menu and there are cut-price buffets at lunchtime. Indian wines from go-ahead Grover Vineyards feature prominently on a simple but good-value list of mostly New World wines. House red and white are £9.95.

CHEF/PROPRIETOR: Ajay Bhardwaj   OPEN: Mon to Sat L 12 to 2.30, all week D 5.30 to 10.30   MEALS: alc D exc Wed (main courses £4.50 to £7.50). Set L £5.50 (2 courses), Set D Wed £10   SERVICE: 10%, card slips closed   CARDS: Visa   DETAILS: 70 seats. Private parties: 30 main room. Vegetarian meals. No smoking. Wheelchair access (not WC). Occasional music

Martins ♥ ✲

70 Rose Street North Lane, Edinburgh EH4 3DX	COOKING 3
TEL: (0131) 225 3106	MODERN BRITISH
EMAIL: martinirons@fsbdial.co.uk	£30–£64

Martin and Gay Irons have for 20 years presided over this civilised restaurant, where everything is smart and neat and just so, and music and smoking are not allowed to sully the atmosphere. Menus support organic and local suppliers and a Mediterranean style prevails. A set price two-course lunch and no-choice three-course dinner are backed up by a short lunchtime and longer evening carte. Pan-fried haddock with a potato scone and pea purée, followed by shallot, honey and rosemary tarte Tatin, make an appealing lunch, and dinner has produced beautifully cooked halibut and seasonal lamb, 'succulent and wonderfully tender, with an excellent red wine reduction'. The board of unpasteurised Scottish and Irish cheeses at their peak remains a menu highlight, though it may compete for attention with desserts such as mini rhubarb crumble with a rhubarb and elderflower sherbet and crème anglaise. Some unusual house wines at £14 (£2.30 a glass) head up an interesting list with plenty from France, including a model selection from the Loire and goodies from the south. Elsewhere, brief selections hit the mark often enough, although value for money is variable.

CHEFS: Jason Gallagher, Neil Mackenzie and Raymond Sutherland   PROPRIETORS: Martin and Gay Irons   OPEN: Tue to Fri L 12 to 1.45, Tue to Sat D 7 to 9.45 (Mon to Sat D 6.30 to 11 during Festival)   CLOSED: 23 Dec to 22 Jan, 10 days May/June, 10 days start of Oct   MEALS: alc (main courses £17 to £23). Set L £13.50 (2 courses) excl 1 week before Christmas, Set D £25   SERVICE: not incl, 10% (optional) for parties of 6 or more   CARDS: Amex, Delta, Diners, MasterCard, Switch, Visa   DETAILS: 58 seats. Private parties: 30 main room, 2 to 20 private rooms. Vegetarian meals. No children under 8. No smoking. No music. No mobile phones

Off the Wall

105 High Street, Edinburgh EH1 1SG	
TEL/FAX: (0131) 558 1497	COOKING 4
EMAIL: otwedinburgh@aol.com	MODERN SCOTTISH
WEBSITE: www.off-the-wall.co.uk	£29–£63

Since its move from small premises near the university, David Anderson's restaurant seems to have grown in both stature and personality. This isn't some shouty modern brasserie, though; instead, the atmosphere is relaxed, quiet and calm ('with a buzz of people enjoying themselves'), with a new colour scheme of warm terracotta and oatmeal and the addition of a wood-burning stove; arched leaded-glass windows look over the Royal Mile. Scottish produce is celebrated in the shape of beef, rare-breed meats and seafood, but there is some out-sourcing to France and Italy too. It is all cooked with care and panache, starting with first courses that often sound like mains but are nicely judged: saddle of rabbit with black truffle risotto, perhaps, or feuilleté of roast halibut and crab with foie gras jus. Memorable dishes mentioned in readers' reports include monkfish with a light sauce combining olive oil, tomato and cream, and the famous beef, which is served with roast root vegetables and perhaps a cep cream sauce. Be sure to ask whether any scallops have been caught that day, as they are invariably excellent. Finish with honey and lemon parfait with a poached pear, or chocolate terrine with glazed oranges and a minted chocolate sauce. Wines offer a concise and unerringly fine selection, but mark-ups soon get into their stride. Prices open at £13.95 a bottle, or £3.75 a glass.

CHEF: David Anderson   PROPRIETORS: David Anderson and Aileen Wilson   OPEN: Mon to Sat 12 to 2, 6 to 10   CLOSED: 25 and 26 Dec, 1 and 2 Jan   MEALS: alc D (main courses £15 to £20). Set L £13.95 (2 courses) to £17.50   SERVICE: not inc   CARDS: Amex, Delta, MasterCard, Switch, Visa   DETAILS: 44 seats. Private parties: 44 main room. Children's helpings. No-smoking area. Occasional music (£5)

Restaurant Martin Wishart

54 The Shore, Leith, Edinburgh EH6 6RA
TEL: (0131) 553 3557   FAX: (0131) 467 7091   COOKING **6**
EMAIL: info@martin-wishart.co.uk   MODERN FRENCH
WEBSITE: www.martin-wishart.co.uk   £43–£74

A modest extension has been added to Martin Wishart's operation, but although it has increased the restaurant's capacity by half as much again, that only translates as an extra 15 covers. Booking early is still advised. Cream-colour décor and modest floral adornments allow diners to concentrate on the classy, formidably accomplished style of cooking for which Wishart has established one of the Scottish capital's most elevated reputations.

Ingredients are of the best, with an organic grower supplying fruit and vegetables, and meats such as Ronaldsay lamb from Orkney distinguishing the main-course choices. A reporter who enjoyed a late-summer lunch spoke highly of a bowl of impeccable gazpacho, in which all the elements registered loud and clear, right down to the spoonful of green pepper mousse and cheese straw with which it was garnished. That was followed by a technically unimpeachable fricassee of guinea fowl, 'the skin golden and a little crisp, the interior moist and succulent', served with new potatoes. The dinner menus show a willingness to take on a certain level of complexity, whether for a starter of sautéed foie gras and langoustine tails with pomme croustillant, braised fennel and a jus of raisins and Sauternes, or in a main course of poached turbot with scallops and an oyster in a vegetable and horseradish nage, with tagliatelle of saffron and cucumber. To finish, there may be omelette Rothschild with a soufflé and sorbet of apricot, or a plate of fine cheeses with oatcakes. Staff are 'attentive, agreeable and always ready to help', and the wine list has loads of interesting bottles, but mark-ups are steep and just a couple of wines dip below the £20 barrier.

CHEF/PROPRIETOR: Martin Wishart   OPEN: Tue to Fri L 12 to 2, Tue to Sat D 7 to 10   CLOSED: 25 and 26 Dec, 1 Jan   MEALS: alc (main courses £18 to £25). Set L £18.50 to £45, Set D £45 SERVICE: not inc   CARDS: Amex, MasterCard, Switch, Visa   DETAILS: 45 seats. Private parties: 50 main room. Vegetarian meals. Children's helpings. No smoking before 2pm and 10pm. Wheelchair access (also WC). Music

'Dining-room service grapples unsuccessfully with words like "water" and "bread".'
(On eating in Lincolnshire)

Rogue

NEW ENTRY

67 Morrison Street, Edinburgh EH3 8HH
TEL: (0131) 228 2700   FAX: (0131) 228 3299
WEBSITE: www.rogues.uk.com

COOKING **3**
MODERN EUROPEAN
£24–£66

On the ground floor of the old Scottish Widows building, Rogue goes in for a modern, minimalist style of white walls, white linen and white light setting off the black of the surrounding banquette seating. Food is contemporary and quite unminimal, as reports testify. Ham hock and haricot blanc broth, and pan-fried sweetbreads with asparagus offer satisfying ways to start. Mains are split into lighter courses – such as seared tuna with rocket, or pumpkin and goats' cheese pizza – and heartier dishes like seared halibut on mashed potato with prawn, caper and parsley butter, or fillet of beef with tagliatelle, spinach and foie gras butter. Puddings run to rhubarb crumble with stem ginger ice cream, or apple sponge with spiced syrup.

A three-course (£13.50) 'austerity' menu at lunch and weekday dinners includes not-so-austere-sounding beef carpaccio, or lamb neck with lemon and dried-fruit couscous. While the kitchen shows flair, service though a little inhibited is unobtrusively attentive. Wine prices will not shrink the wallet unduly, with plenty of interest under £20. Only four wines are available by the glass, with an Argentine Merlot starting the list at £14 (£3.50 the glass).

CHEF: Wyatt Shevloff   PROPRIETOR: David Ramsden   OPEN: Mon to Sat 12 to 3, 6 to 11   MEALS: alc (main courses £9 to £24). Set L £10 (2 courses) to £13.50, Set D Mon to Thur £10 (2 courses) to £13.50   SERVICE: not inc   CARDS: Amex, Delta, MasterCard, Switch, Visa   DETAILS: 90 seats. Private parties: 80 main room, 12 private room. Vegetarian meals. Wheelchair access (also WC). Music. Air-conditioned

Shore ⁵✳

3 The Shore, Leith, Edinburgh EH6 6QW
TEL/FAX: (0131) 553 5080
EMAIL: enquiries@the.shore.ukf.net
WEBSITE: www.edinburghrestaurants.co.uk

COOKING **2**
SEAFOOD
£27–£46

This atmospheric eighteenth-century waterside pub/restaurant has a welcoming feel, thanks to fresh flowers, gleaming glassware and an open fire. The short menus concentrate on fish and seafood prepared in an eclectic style that encompasses everything from smoked haddock and leek soup to mussels in tomato, garlic and vodka sauce for starters, with roast salmon on ratatouille with herb oil, or whole mackerel stuffed with feta and chives to follow. A main course of five perfectly seared scallops with little chunks of black pudding in a paprika sauce with spinach and parsley made the right impression at an inspection meal, and for dessert there may be 'light, moist' sticky toffee pudding, or cherry and brandy ice cream. The wine list is short and to the point, with virtually every bottle below £20. House French is £11.

CHEFS: Dan Styles, Alison Bryant, Robin Gray and Keith Czarnota   PROPRIETOR: Stuart Linsley   OPEN: all week 12 to 2.30 (12.30 to 3 Sat and Sun), 6.30 to 10   CLOSED: 25 and 26 Dec, 1 and 2 Jan   MEALS: alc (main courses L £8 to £10, D £12 to £15). Set L £15.95 (2 courses) to £17.95, Set D £18.95 (2 courses) to £22.95   SERVICE: not inc, 10% for parties of 8 or more   CARDS: Amex,

Delta, Diners, MasterCard, Switch, Visa DETAILS: 36 seats. 12 seats outside. Private parties: 36 main room, 25 to 36 private rooms. Vegetarian meals. Children's helpings. No smoking in 1 dining room. Wheelchair access (not WC). Music £5

Skippers £

1A Dock Place, Leith, Edinburgh EH6 6LU
TEL: (0131) 554 1018 FAX: (0131) 553 5988
WEBSITE: www.skippers.co.uk

COOKING 2
SEAFOOD
£23–£54

Nautical bric-a-brac, wood-panelled walls and red painted low ceilings give this fish bistro a cosy air. High-quality ingredients – mussels from Shetland, Loch Etive oysters, Mallaig langoustines and Arbroath smokies – create a gazetteer of Scottish seafood. Cullen skink maintains the national theme, but most recipes range more widely: Finnan haddie with roast tomatoes and brie and bacon lardons, oysters grilled with Parmesan cream, and a generous portion of plump mussels steamed with well-balanced Thai spices introduce a mix-and-match approach. There are token dishes for meat-eaters (ribeye steak, confit of duck), and at lunch 'light dishes' and starters (some come in two sizes) cover all appetites. Sensibly, the wine list is two-thirds white. Producers are not identified for French and 'fine' wines, but New World offerings are good and seven house selections start at £10.50.

CHEFS: Mary Walker and Matt Flitney PROPRIETORS: Gavin and Karen Ferguson OPEN: all week 12.30 to 2 (2.30 Sun), 7 to 10 CLOSED: 24 to 26 Dec, 31 Dec to 1 Jan MEALS: alc (main courses £7 to £21) SERVICE: not inc, 10% for parties of 6 or more CARDS: Amex, Delta, MasterCard, Switch, Visa DETAILS: 55 seats. Private parties: 35 main room, 15 to 25 private rooms. No cigars/pipes before 10pm. Wheelchair access (also WC). Music. No mobile phones

Tower Restaurant ▼ ⅍

Museum of Scotland, Chambers Street,
Edinburgh EH1 1JF
TEL: (0131) 225 3003 FAX: (0131) 247 4220
EMAIL: mail@tower-restaurant.com
WEBSITE: www.tower-restaurant.com

COOKING 2
SEAFOOD/MODERN BRITISH
£33–£78

Edinburgh star-spotters (of the celebrity kind) will not go far wrong in aiming for the Tower. Not only is it a designer paradise frequented by household names – a rooftop restaurant set above the sandstone-clad Museum of Scotland – but the cooking has drawn plaudits too. Buckie crab served in the shell with citrus mayonnaise and potato salad continues to win praise, as do the accomplished desserts, which take in the likes of sticky ginger pudding with lime sorbet and a particularly enjoyable selection of three different kinds of crème brûlée. In between, you might opt for braised pheasant breast with a confit of the leg, a black pudding and truffle parcel, and mash, although the smoked haddock risotto signally failed to impress. Vegetarian dishes show imagination. A crisply presented and thoroughly modern wine selection is structured in price bands and opens with 12 offerings by the glass for £3.50 to £6.50. Mark-ups are high and trophy hunters are well served at the top end.

CHEF: Steven Adair   PROPRIETOR: James Thomson   OPEN: all week 12 to 5, 5 to 11 '   CLOSED: 25 and 26 Dec   MEALS: alc (main courses L £9 to £18, D £13 to £24.50). Set L and D 5 to 6.30 £9.95 (2 courses)   SERVICE: not inc, 10% (optional) for parties of 8 or more   CARDS: Amex, Delta, Diners, MasterCard, Switch, Visa   DETAILS: 85 seats. 45 seats outside. Private parties: 85 main room. Vegetarian meals. No smoking. Wheelchair access (also WC). Music. Air-conditioned

Valvona & Crolla Caffè Bar 🍾 ⚡ £

19 Elm Row, Edinburgh EH7 4AA   COOKING 3
TEL: (0131) 556 6066   FAX: (0131) 556 1668   ITALIAN
WEBSITE: www.valvonacrolla.com   £27–£48

For some proper Italian food head north to this outpost of Italy that in 2004 celebrates 70 years of feeding Edinburgh. Behind the reticent frontage are deli, cookery shop, award-winning wine merchants, and the café, which – Festival time apart, when it also opens in the evening – runs from breakfast to tea, with lunch as the main event. Among close-set tables the atmosphere is a busy buzz, and, while service is polite and willing, you need to be prepared to wait. Drawing from excellent Scottish sources as well as Italian ones, the cooking for the most part receives enthusiastic response – from 'best-tasting lasagne ever', via praise for a moist, deeply flavoured chocolate tart with a scoop of crème fraîche, to small things like the quality of the waxy potatoes, and the bruschetta. A menu 'Per I Bambini' shows a properly Italian regard for children, offering soup, salami, pizzas and pasta with fresh ingredients – not a chip in sight. A short list of 'recommended wines' offers around a dozen by glass (£3.15 to £4.75) or bottle, but a £4 corkage charge gives access to the entire range of bottles from the shop at retail prices – perhaps the most exciting list of Italian wines in Britain and, these days, no slouch in other regions either.

CHEF: Mary Contini   PROPRIETORS: Philip and Mary Contini   OPEN: all week 8 to 6 (L 11.45 to 3) and D during Festival   CLOSED: 25 and 26 Dec, 1 and 2 Jan   MEALS: alc (main courses £9 to £12) SERVICE: not inc   CARDS: Amex, Delta, MasterCard, Switch, Visa   DETAILS: 80 seats. Private parties: 60 main room. Vegetarian meals. Children's helpings. No smoking. Wheelchair access (not WC). Music. Air-conditioned

▲ Witchery by the Castle   `NEW ENTRY`

Castlehill, Royal Mile, Edinburgh EH1 2NF
TEL: (0131) 225 5613   FAX: (0131) 220 4392   COOKING 4
EMAIL: mail@thewitchery.com   MODERN SCOTTISH
WEBSITE: www.thewitchery.com   £27–£74

Occupying a sixteenth-century building by the castle, the Witchery – under the same ownership as the nearby Tower (see entry) – has a richly atmospheric setting, full of history. There are two sumptuous dining rooms: the Witchery itself, which has oak panelling and tapestries on the walls, and the Secret Garden, which is reached by a stone staircase and has a splendid painted ceiling.

When you have to compete for attention with bagpipe-playing gilt cherubs, it seems wise to play it safe on the cooking side by covering all bases: simple and complex, traditional and modern, domestic and exotic. To start, there might be classic steak tartare with a fried quail egg alongside home-smoked Gressingham duckling with beetroot sorbet and greens. Main courses, meanwhile, have featured baked cod spread with a delicately flavoured tarragon mousse and wrapped in pancetta, served with white haricot beans and spinach; and a decent sized fillet of 'tasty, tender' Aberdeen Angus beef accompanied by soft chunks of braised shin in a rich celeriac and tomato broth. Creamy, garlicky gratin dauphinoise has been recommended as a side order, and for dessert, warm bitter chocolate torte has impressed for its pastry case, light texture and intense chocolate flavour.

We have only been able to see a small sample of the 900-strong wine list, so will have to defer judgement on an award, but it promises to be extremely impressive, particularly in the classic regions. Sommelier John Power is on hand to offer advice, and doesn't forget diners on a budget, with some good options under £20 and 14 wines by the glass (£3.45 to £7.25).

CHEF: Douglas Roberts   PROPRIETOR: James Thomson   OPEN: all week 12 to 4, 5.30 to 11.30
CLOSED: 25 and 26 Dec   MEALS: alc (main courses £14 to £20). Set L and Set D 5.30 to 6.30 and 10.30 to 11.30 £9.95 (2 courses)   SERVICE: not inc, card slips closed   CARDS: Amex, Delta, Diners, MasterCard, Switch, Visa   DETAILS: 120 seats. 20 seats outside. Private parties: 60 main room, 60 to 120 private rooms. Vegetarian meals. Music   ACCOMMODATION: 7 suites, all with bath/shower. TV. Phone. B&B £225 to £250

EDNAM Borders   map 11

▲ Edenwater House 🌟

Ednam TD5 7QL
TEL: (01573) 224070   FAX: (01573) 226615
EMAIL: relax@edenwaterhouse.co.uk   COOKING 4
WEBSITE: www.edenwaterhouse.co.uk   MODERN BRITISH
on B6461, 2m N of Kelso   £39–£47

A warm welcome awaits visitors to this former manse by the village church. Large picture windows give views over the attractive garden, and across fields towards the river, from the comfortable dining room.

The Kellys keep the atmosphere relaxed. Jeff is the genial and attentive but unobtrusive host, while Jacqui cooks. Her style is light, creative and modern, and the four-course, no-choice menus are well balanced to leave you 'blissfully satisfied but not bloated'. Meals typically open with Eyemouth langoustines on herb tagliolini with a dill and langoustine salsa. Next might come breast of Barbary duck with glazed radish, purple sprouting broccoli, sautéed new potatoes and a mandarin and ginger sauce, or maybe new season lamb with tarragon mousseline, a ragoût of peas and beans in filo pastry and dauphinoise potatoes. Third course is a savoury, perhaps goats' cheese fondant with whipped Brie, Parmesan crackling, plums and balsamic vinaigrette, and meals end with desserts such as strawberry and champagne jelly with mixed berries and vanilla cream. House French wines are £12.80 a bottle, £3.50 a glass.

CHEF: Jacqui Kelly   PROPRIETORS: Jeff and Jacqui Kelly   OPEN: Fri and Sat D only 7.30 to 8 (all week for residents)   CLOSED: 2 weeks Oct, Dec 25, first 2 weeks Jan   MEALS: Set D £32.50
SERVICE: net prices, card slips closed   CARDS: Delta, MasterCard, Switch, Visa   DETAILS: 16 seats. Private parties: 16 main room. Car park. No children under 10. No smoking. No music. No mobile phones   ACCOMMODATION: 4 rooms, all with bath/shower. TV. B&B £50 to £95. No children under 10. Fishing

ERISKA Argyll & Bute   map 11

▲ Isle of Eriska 💱✳

Ledaig, Eriska PA37 1SD
TEL: (01631) 720371   FAX: (01631) 720531
EMAIL: office@eriska-hotel.co.uk   COOKING **6**
WEBSITE: www.eriska-hotel.co.uk   SCOTTISH
off A828, 12m N of Oban   £48–£57

Eriska is a 'magical' island reached by a bridge from the mainland and privately owned by the Buchanan-Smith family. It is a haven of tranquillity, and offers plenty to suit all-comers, whether you are interested in observing wildlife, taking part in various sporting activities – ranging from golf to croquet – or being pampered in the hotel's spa. The house, a majestic Victorian pile, has a warm, homely atmosphere and attentive hosts – at least one member of the family is always around.

Dinners are as sumptuous and luxurious as the setting, running to six courses (sensibly limited to a couple of options at each), including a savoury and a selection from the cheese trolley to follow dessert. Though native produce is at the heart of the cooking, the scope of the kitchen's culinary thinking is broad, so the alternative to a starter of wild venison and courgette charlotte with globe artichokes and mustard jus might be a gâteau of brown crab layered with guacamole, mango salsa and soured cream with a cucumber salad and chilli dressing. Next comes a soup – perhaps celery and Stilton – before main courses of roast cod with spinach, white-bean purée and seared squid, or roast rib of Aberdeen Angus beef, carved at table and served with traditional accompaniments. The wine list ranges far and wide but sticks stubbornly to individual producers: Burgundy is basically all Latour and every thread of the Rothschild global web seems to be here. Nonetheless, prices are very good (£15 goes a long way here) and there are some New World treats. House wines are £9.60, or £3 per glass.

CHEF: Robert MacPherson   PROPRIETORS: the Buchanan-Smith family   OPEN: all week D only 8 to 9   CLOSED: Jan   MEALS: Set D £38.50   SERVICE: not inc, card slips closed   CARDS: Amex, Delta, MasterCard, Switch, Visa   DETAILS: 40 seats. Private parties: 20 main room, 6 to 20 private rooms. Car park. Vegetarian meals. Children's helpings. No smoking. Wheelchair access (also WC). No music. No mobile phones   ACCOMMODATION: 19 rooms, all with bath/shower. TV. Phone. B&B £130 to £290. Rooms for disabled. Baby facilities. Swimming pool (*The Which? Guide to Good Hotels*)

FAIRLIE North Ayrshire   map 11

Fins 💱✳

Fencefoot Farm, Fairlie KA29 0EG
TEL: (01475) 568989   FAX: (01475) 568921   COOKING **2**
EMAIL: fencebay@aol.com   SEAFOOD
WEBSITE: www.fencebay.co.uk   £25–£60

The addition of a neat and flower-bedecked conservatory extension has increased the space at Fins, the place to come for a wide range of fish and crustacea (you can buy it at their farm shop too). Lunch and dinner menus are similar but differently priced. Starters include hot- or cold-smoked salmon, herring marinated in ginger and lime, or perhaps baked oysters. Mains cover, say, salmon fishcakes and lemon butter, a cold seafood platter of fresh and cured fish and shellfish, or trout fillet with a walnut and Stilton crust. There are a few concessions to non-fish-eating companions: a soup of the day, grilled goats' cheese salad with roast vegetables, smoked duck salad or – in the evening – fillet steak with brandy cream sauce. Puddings include sticky toffee or apple flan, and there's local cheese and oatcakes too. White wines dominate a well-chosen and affordable list, with house Pays d'Oc blends at £10.80.

CHEFS: Jill Thain, Jane Burns and Gary Brown   PROPRIETORS: Bernard and Jill Thain   OPEN: Tue to Sun L 12 to 2.30, Tue to Sat D 7 (Sat 6.30) to 9.30   CLOSED: 25 and 26 Dec, 1 and 2 Jan, 1 week Jan   MEALS: alc (main courses L £8 to £14, D £13 to £25). Set L Tue to Thur £10 (2 courses), Set D Tue to Thur £12.50 (2 courses)   SERVICE: not inc, card slips closed   CARDS: Delta, MasterCard, Switch, Visa   DETAILS: 50 seats. Private parties: 32 main room. Car park. Children's helpings. Children at D by arrangement. No smoking. Wheelchair access (also WC). Music. No mobile phones (£5)

FORT WILLIAM Highland   map 11

Crannog ⚹

Town Pier, Fort William PH33 6PD
TEL: (01397) 705589   FAX: (01397) 705026   COOKING 2
EMAIL: bookings@crannog.net   SEAFOOD
WEBSITE: www.crannog.net   £27–£57

It would be hard for any restaurant to get much closer to the source of its supplies than Crannog, which stands on the edge of the harbour overlooking Loch Linnhe. Fish and seafood come straight off the restaurant's own boats, although some of it passes through the smokehouse as well. A mainly traditional approach characterises the cooking, with starters taking in Cullen skink, and langoustines in garlic butter, plus a few more adventurous ideas such as gratinated oysters with a chilli and herb crust. Main courses range from pistachio-crusted halibut with risotto and pink peppercorn sauce to grilled Loch Awe trout with crisped oats, lemon and hollandaise, and a few meat and vegetarian options ensure that everyone is kept happy. To finish, tipsy laird is a distinctively Scottish version of trifle made with Drambuie and raspberries. Prices on the short, mostly white, wine list start at £12.95.

CHEF: Gary Dobbie   PROPRIETOR: Finlay Finlayson   OPEN: all week 12 to 2.30 (3 summer), 6 to 9.30 (10 summer)   CLOSED: 25 Dec, 1 Jan   MEALS: alc (main courses £9 to £23)   SERVICE: not inc, card slips closed   CARDS: MasterCard, Switch, Visa   DETAILS: 65 seats. 20 seats outside. Private parties: 40 main room. Car park. Vegetarian meals. No smoking in 1 dining room. Wheelchair access (also WC). Occasional music

'The sommelier was hoping that I would order foie gras as he said that he had opened a bottle of 1989 Château d'Yqem Sauternes and I wouldn't regret trying a glass of it. I looked at the price of the bottle – £149 – and ordered a soufflé. He sulked rather.'
(On eating in the Lake District)

▲ Inverlochy Castle 🍴

Torlundy, Fort William PH33 6SN
TEL: (01397) 702177   FAX: (01397) 702953
EMAIL: info@inverlochy.co.uk
WEBSITE: www.inverlochy.co.uk
on A82, 4m N of Fort William

COOKING **6**
MODERN EUROPEAN
£45–£86

A castle fit for royalty – Queen Victoria stayed here – sitting in acres of rhododendrons. The Great Hall has a frescoed ceiling and Venetian crystal chandeliers, and three well-appointed dining rooms are furnished with gifts from the King of Norway. The food has a convincing pedigree too, with scallops from Skye, local game, some items from the walled kitchen garden, and a few luxuries from further afield. This is a highly professional kitchen, producing for example a single, round, plump raviolo, filled with a mix of scallop and white crab meat, with a trickle of velvety sauce and lightly gingered tomatoes and chopped spring onions. Individual elements are faultless, and although the demanding presentational requirements can seem to reduce the flavour impact of some dishes, there is no doubt about the excellence of, for example, two pieces of lightly cooked, crisp-skinned sea bream served on four asparagus tips with wafer-thin deep-fried fennel, roast artichoke heart, pesto oil and a lightly frothy fish velouté.

Flavour combinations are generally well judged, taking in a roast fillet of Angus beef crowned with a slice of fried foie gras, surrounded by halves of cherry tomato, broad beans, whole garlic cloves and shallots, and an eye-catching mascarpone semi-freddo with a fragile cinnamon biscuit, strawberry coulis and strawberries marinated in balsamic vinegar. Service is formal and precise, and guests are expected to be formal as well – jacket and tie are required. The wine list centres on France; short selections from Italy, Australia, New Zealand and the USA are well chosen. Prices start high – with nothing under £25 a bottle – which took the shine off the evening for one of our reporters. Half-bottles are plentiful but only the house wines come by the glass (£4.50).

CHEF: Matthew Gray   PROPRIETOR: Inverlochy Castle Hotel Ltd   OPEN: all week 12.30 to 2, 7 to 9.15   CLOSED: 6 Jan to 12 Feb   MEALS: Set L £28, Set D £52.50. Light L available   SERVICE: not inc, card slips closed   CARDS: Amex, MasterCard, Switch, Visa   DETAILS: 40 seats. Private parties: 30 main room, 2 to 50 private rooms. Car park. Vegetarian meals. Children's helpings. Jacket and tie. No smoking. Wheelchair access (not WC). Music. No mobile phones   ACCOMMODATION: 17 rooms, all with bath/shower. TV. Phone. B&B £205 to £395. Baby facilities. (*The Which? Guide to Good Hotels*)

Card slips closed *in the details at the end of an entry indicates that the total on the slips of credit cards is closed when handed over for signature.*

'[There were] huge arrangements of artificial flowers tipping menacingly out of elevated alcoves, one of which is shaped like a faux portico. After my experience with the stone bust I might be inclined to favour a table in the centre of the room, where the only danger could come from the elaborate central chandelier hanging from the moulded plasterwork.'
(On eating in London)

Amaryllis 🍴 £

1 Devonshire Gardens, Glasgow G12 0UX

TEL: (0141) 337 3434   FAX: (0141) 339 0047   COOKING 5
EMAIL: amaryllis@gordonramsay.com   MODERN EUROPEAN
WEBSITE: www.gordonramsay.com   £26–£79

With a new chef comes a different approach at Gordon Ramsay's most northerly
outpost. The interior makes good use of the Victorian penchant for light and
space – large windows and high ceilings – and is assuredly civilised, with
smartly set tables and burgundy colour chairs in both dining rooms. In the
Dining Room a carte offers the flexibility of just one or two courses (a welcome
option at lunchtime particularly) and comes up with rather more brasserie-style
dishes: lightly battered black pudding tempura with poached egg, for example,
or crisp spring rolls filled with duck confit, enlivened by peppery watercress and
a soy sauce to cut through the fattiness. Dishes are well constructed and
balanced, and pastrywork shows up well, for example in the leek and potato tart
that comes with good smoked haddock and a sharp Pommery mustard sauce.
Main dishes are self-contained – well-hung and well-flavoured ribeye steak
with meat juices, watercress purée and some fine fries – so there is generally no
need to order extra vegetables from the carte. The set menu in the Drawing
Room, meanwhile, is more ambitious, offering wild mushroom ravioli with
roasted ceps, truffles and a thyme velouté, followed perhaps by sea bream fillets
with brandade, salsify, courgette and a civet sauce.

A similar divide marks out desserts: rice pudding, or fruit jelly with sour
cream on the carte, and pineapple parfait with matching compote and chocolate
sorbet from the set-price menu. While service has ranged from 'stiff and formal'
to 'flawless' and 'unobtrusive', the wine list has been trimmed to a single sheet
of good-quality drinking arranged by style, but with few options under £20. A
dozen by the glass are £4 to £12.

CHEF: Colin Buchan   PROPRIETOR: Gordon Ramsay   OPEN: Wed to Fri and Sun L 12 to 2.30, Wed
to Sun D 6.45 (6 Sat) to 10.30   MEALS: alc (main courses £9 to £14). Set L and D £35 to £45
SERVICE: not inc   CARDS: Amex, Delta, MasterCard, Switch, Visa   DETAILS: 70 seats. Private
parties: 45 main room, 12 to 45 private rooms. Car park. Vegetarian meals. Children's helpings.
No cigars. No music

Brian Maule at Chardon d'Or ✳

176 West Regent Street, Glasgow G2 4RL

TEL: (0141) 248 3801   FAX: (0141) 248 3901   COOKING 5
EMAIL: info@lechardondor.com   FRENCH/MEDITERRANEAN
WEBSITE: www.lechardondor.com   £33–£66

The use of a BM logo in a repeating pattern on the menu paper marks this
restrainedly modern restaurant above an art gallery as a 'chef-driven'
establishment. Brian Maule returned to his Scottish roots from London's Le
Gavroche (see entry) after stints in France, and is something of a culinary meteor
– although, as his occasional appearances after dinner attest, he has nothing of

the media chef's *amour propre*. Indeed this is an unstuffy place, and professionalism and cheerfulness mark the service.

Not surprisingly, the cuisine is identifiably French, but in the modern idiom, emphasising sound technique without undue ostentation. A robust first course of warm duck confit is served with bacon and raisin salad and pine nuts, and there may well be pasta among the starters too, perhaps penne with scallops in a ginger butter sauce. Dishes are thoughtfully composed, the supporting ingredients well matched to their stars: hence a salmon steak is teamed with fennel, baby girolles and vermicelli, while gratin dauphinoise and leek fondue accompany roast rack of lamb. A six-course, no-choice 'Celebration Menu' (whole table only) proceeds from two preliminary courses and soup, through main-course meat and cheeses (Scottish and French), to arrive at a light dessert such as blackcurrant délice with a crisp honey tuile. The French-led wine list has bottles to delight lovers of mature Burgundy and claret, and there is also a reasonable showing of non-European wines and half-bottles. Unless money is no object, though, prices will pinch, for there's not much under £20; non-vintage house French is £13.75.

CHEF/PROPRIETOR: Brian Maule   OPEN: Mon to Fri L 12 to 2, Mon to Sat D 6 to 10   CLOSED: 2 weeks Jan, bank hols and during Glasgow Fair   MEALS: alc (main courses £17 to £19.50), Set L and D 6 to 7 £17.50, Set L and D £38 (whole table)   SERVICE: not inc, 10% for parties of 9 or more   CARDS: Amex, Delta, MasterCard, Switch, Visa   DETAILS: 100 seats. Private parties: 100 main room. Children's helpings. Vegetarian meals. No smoking in dining room; smoking permitted in bar only. Music. No mobile phones

Gamba ✱

225A West George Street, Glasgow G2 2ND
TEL: (0141) 572 0899   FAX: (0141) 572 0896
EMAIL: info@gamba.co.uk
WEBSITE: www.gamba.co.uk

COOKING 3
SEAFOOD
£29–£65

Under the sign of the metal fish outside, enjoyment pervades this smart and welcoming lower ground floor in the heart of the city. And the pleasure is reliably maintained by the simplicity of the fish cooking, epitomised by the commendably 'pared down austerity' of precisely timed grilled lemon sole fillets. Intelligence, imagination and cosmopolitan influences are apparent, and careful attention to robust flavouring – as in black bean salsa with sea bream fillets, and lemongrass with scallops. Though vegetables have come in for criticism, a proper Caesar salad dressing ('one of the best') has accompanied a seared swordfish starter, and a crayfish cocktail with malt whisky asserts the virtues of Scottish materials. There are a couple of dishes each for vegetarians and carnivores (good Aberdeen Angus fillet) and generously portioned desserts. An intriguing and well-selected wine list amplifies the expected with Valdespino sherries (including Palo Cortado) and a Canadian late-harvest Riesling; house wines start at £14.95 but almost everything else is over £20.

CHEF: Derek Marshall   PROPRIETORS: Derek Marshall and Alan Tompkins   OPEN: Mon to Sat 12 to 2.30, 5 to 10.30   CLOSED: 25 and 26 Dec, 1 and 2 Jan   MEALS: alc (main courses £11 to £22). Set L £13.95 (2 courses) to £16.95, Set D 5 to 6.30 £13.95 (2 courses) to £16.95   SERVICE: not inc, 10% for parties of 6 or more   CARDS: Amex, Delta, MasterCard, Switch, Visa   DETAILS: 66 seats. Private parties: 70 main room. Vegetarian meals. No children under 14. No smoking until after 2 (L) and 10 (D). Music. No mobile phones. Air-conditioned

Gordon Yuill

257 West Campbell Street, Glasgow G2 4SQ
TEL: (0141) 572 4052   FAX: (0141) 572 4050
WEBSITE: www.gordonyuillandcompany.co.uk

NEW CHEF

MODERN EUROPEAN
£37–£58

'The décor is "designer" and very well done. I liked the huge dripping church candles – very Miss Havisham', though at lunchtime the ambience veers to the bright and airy. The big change is in the kitchen, which welcomed Alan Winning too late for us to inspect the results of his work. His menus, however, reveal a brisk run through the a modern European repertoire with more than a nod to Italian influences. Starters might include cappuccino of woodland mushrooms and tarragon with garlic paillettes, or terrine of potatoes with baby spinach and roasted aubergines, while main courses might deliver pan-fried calf's liver with sage mash, red onion jam, prosciutto crisp and jus of thyme, or seared fillet of sea bass served with crushed potatoes and casserole of fennel and mussels. Puddings meanwhile bring forth relatively ambitious combinations such as passion-fruit parfait with consommé of peaches. The short wine list drops anchor briefly around Old and New Worlds; around ten wines are offered by the glass, and house bottles are £14.95.

CHEF: Alan Winning   PROPRIETOR: Gordon Yuill   OPEN: Mon to Sat; 12 to 2.30, 6 to 10   CLOSED: Dec 25, Jan 1 and 2   MEALS: alc (main courses £10.50 to £20)   SERVICE: not inc   CARDS: Amex, Delta, Diners, MasterCard, Switch, Visa   DETAILS: 80 seats. Private parties: 80 main room. Vegetarian meals. Wheelchair access (also WC). Music. Air-conditioned (£5)

▲ Hilton Glasgow, Camerons ⚡✗

1 William Street, Glasgow G3 8XY
TEL: (0141) 204 5555   FAX: (0141) 204 5004
WEBSITE: www.hilton.com

COOKING 4
MODERN EUROPEAN
£34–£71

Camerons is one of the restaurants at the Hilton Glasgow (as opposed to Hilton Glasgow Grosvenor, a mile north-west) from whose marbled, anonymous foyer one steps – as through a looking-glass – into a designer vision of a Scottish lodge, with tartans, swagged drapes and framed shooting scenes. Here James Murphy handles fine Scots produce with gentle assurance. Mussels and queenies in a lush caviar cream sauce overflow a puff-pastry 'tray', with braised al dente leeks for counterpoint. Or a haggis-stuffed spring roll may arrive with spaghetti of neeps, crispy potatoes and whisky sauce. 'Meltingly soft' Borders lamb 'somehow tasting of fresh fields' has come with vegetable ribbons, a sticky bean 'cassoulet' and mint salsa, while Rannoch Moor venison, 'just off-rare', may be partnered by parsnip dauphinois, Savoy cabbage, lentils and smoked bacon. Each ingredient contributes to a dish's impact, down to balsamic vinegar in the wild berry coulis with a strawberry tartlet. Celtic and French cheeses are in trim condition, and service is polished and knowledgeable. A lengthy wine list offers good choice in most regions and includes some enticingly mature bottles. Prices are mostly above £25, but there are plenty of half-bottles, and the Michel Laroche house varietals are £18 (£5.95 a large glass).

CHEF: James Murphy   PROPRIETOR: Hilton Group plc   OPEN: Mon to Fri L 12 to 1.45, Mon to Sat D 7 to 9.45   CLOSED: bank hols   MEALS: Set L £15.50 (2 courses) to £19.50, Set D £28 (2 courses) to £33   SERVICE: not inc   CARDS: Amex, Delta, Diners, MasterCard, Switch, Visa
DETAILS: 50 seats. Private parties: 70 main room, 2 to 6 private rooms. Vegetarian meals. Children's helpings. No smoking. Wheelchair access (also WC). Music. Air-conditioned
ACCOMMODATION: 319 rooms, all with bath/shower. TV. Phone. B&B £120 to £180. Rooms for disabled. Swimming pool

Rogano ⁵✴

11 Exchange Place, Glasgow G1 3AN	COOKING 4
TEL: (0141) 248 4055 FAX: (0141) 248 2608	SEAFOOD
WEBSITE: www.rogano.co.uk	£28–£82

Its Art Deco stylishness is not the least reason for Rogano's enduring popularity over the years; but the cooking pulls in the crowds, too. A pair who dined here in the autumn were full of praise for classics such as fish soup with rouille and Parmesan croûtons, 'strongly gamey' pheasant terrine, well-executed main courses, and the copious cheeseboard choice. Among the diverting contemporary offerings on the menus have been cumin-spiced monkfish with kedgeree and curry oil, and venison loin with haggis mousse, roasted shallots and a jus of Laphroaig whisky, but they take their place among such mainstream items as grilled lobster with béarnaise, and Aberdeen Angus fillet with Madeira sauce. Downstairs, in Café Rogano, a simpler menu takes in honey-glazed goats' cheese salad with chilli jam, and braised lamb shank with vegetable Scotch broth. Banana tarte Tatin with cinnamon and plum ice cream might be one way to finish. One would expect France to dominate the wine list in such a setting, and so it does. Prices are puzzlingly high on the main list, but four house wines are £15 or £3.20 a glass.

CHEF: Andrew Cummings   PROPRIETOR: Spirit Group   OPEN: all week 12 to 2.30, 6.30 to 10.30
CLOSED: 25 and 31 Dec, 1 and 2 Jan   MEALS: alc (main courses £18 to £33.50). Set L £16.95
SERVICE: 12.5% (optional), card slips closed   CARDS: Amex, Delta, Diners, MasterCard, Switch, Visa   DETAILS: 60 seats. Private parties: 80 main room, 8 to 24 private rooms. Vegetarian meals. No smoking before 2pm L, 10pm D. Wheelchair access (not WC). Music. No mobile phones. Air-conditioned (£5)

▲ Saint Jude's

190 Bath Street, Glasgow G2 4HG	
TEL: (0141) 352 8800 FAX: (0141) 352 8801	NEW CHEF
EMAIL: reservations@saintjudes.com	GLOBAL
WEBSITE: www.saintjudes.com	£23–£57

This 'boutique' hotel is situated in a Victorian townhouse in Glasgow's business district. Minimalism extends to the upstairs dining room, with wooden floors, banquette seating and lots of natural light. St Jude's has replaced one head with two – David Sherry and Nick Brock – to lead up the kitchen team, arriving too close to publication for an official visit. A carte operating alongside a good-value fixed-price deal lunchtimes and early evenings offers a global repertoire. Expect, perhaps, star anise pork belly with chilli plum dipping sauce, or smoked mackeral pâté with home-made piccalilli and brioche toast, followed by tiger prawn linguini, or gremolata marinated chicken with olive butter and vine ripened tomatoes. Finish with chocolate mousse with berry compote. A short wine list offers a good balance between Old World and New with plenty under £20; house wine is £12.50

CHEFS: David Sherry and Nick Brock   PROPRIETORS: Robert Paterson and Paul Wingate   OPEN: Sun to Fri L 12 to 3, all week D 6 to 10.30   CLOSED: 25 Dec, 1 Jan   MEALS: alc (main courses L £5.50 to £10.50, D £10.50 to £18.50). Set L and D 6 to 7.15 £11.50 (2 courses) to £14.50. Bar L and Tapas menus available   SERVICE: not inc   CARDS: Amex, Delta, Diners, MasterCard, Switch, Visa   DETAILS: 60 seats. Private parties: 60 main room, 10 to 25 private rooms. Vegetarian meals. Children's helpings. No cigars/pipes. Music. Air-conditioned ACCOMMODATION: 6 rooms, all with bath/shower. TV. Phone. Room only £90 to £185

78 St Vincent

NEW ENTRY

78 St Vincent Street, Glasgow G2 5UB
TEL: (0141) 248 7878   FAX: (0141) 221 1874
EMAIL: frontdesk@78stvincent.com
WEBSITE: www.78stvincent.com

COOKING 2
MODERN SCOTTISH
£26–£49

Housed in a former bank, with lofty ceilings, original mouldings and a white marble staircase, 78 St Vincent is styled like a French brasserie, with intimate dining booths and lots of dark wood. Duncan McKay, who arrived just after the last edition of the Guide went to press, has introduced a fashionable fusion twist to Scottish staples. Traditional dishes, such as a full-flavoured terrine of smoked ham hock wrapped in Savoy cabbage with butter beans and sauce gribiche, rub shoulders with more trendy-sounding items, such as seared king scallops with an orange and cardamom reduction. The restaurant aims to use Scottish produce as far as possible, as in loin of Rannoch venison topped with wild mushrooms accompanied by braised celeriac and a zesty bittersweet jus. Cheeses are supplied by Arran dairies; otherwise, to finish there might be lemon and poppy seed parfait with poached strawberries, or cherry and almond tart with Kirsch and mascarpone ice cream. Service is smooth, and the absence of Muzak came as 'a blessed relief' to one reporter. The wine list has some appealing selections and around ten by the glass. House wines start at £13.95 a bottle (£3.50 a glass).

CHEF: Duncan McKay   PROPRIETORS: Michael Conyers and Julie Williams   OPEN: all week 12 to 3, 5 to 10 (10.30 Fri and Sat)   CLOSED: 25 Dec, 1 and 2 Jan   MEALS: Set L £11.50 (2 courses) to £14.50, Set D £22.95 (2 courses) to £27.95   SERVICE: not inc, 10% for parties of 7 or more CARDS: Amex, Delta, Diners, MasterCard, Switch, Visa   DETAILS: 100 seats. Private parties: 100 main room, 8 to 14 private rooms. Vegetarian meals. Children's helpings. No-smoking area. Wheelchair access (also WC). No music. No mobile phones (£5)

'I rather think [the sommelier] had modelled his wine-pouring performance on that of those Spanish men you see in sherry advertisements. From a great height, and holding the bottle under its bottom; it's no wonder his face bore this permanent look of mute apprehension.' (On eating in Devon)

Stravaigin ▼ �

28 Gibson Street, Glasgow G12 8NX
TEL: (0141) 334 2665   FAX: (0141) 334 4099
EMAIL: bookings@stravaigin.com
WEBSITE: www.stravaigin.com

COOKING 4
GLOBAL
£24–£47

In the heart of Glasgow's West End, Stravaigin (and its sister establishment – see entry below) have positioned themselves at the very forefront of metropolitan restaurant fashion. Expect a loud ambience in the basement dining room, where tables are packed fairly close and where service is urbane and efficient. Striving for daring, exciting combinations and obscure ingredients, the menu mingles influences that include Greek and North African. Start with hare carpaccio and ox tongue, served with anise-poached pear and salsa verde, before proceeding to roast hake in a stew of spiced Tuscan sausage, with a salt cod fritter and roast pimento sauce. A more familiar dish might be the Aberdeen Angus sirloin that comes with 'mustard custard and a Merlot reduction'. Blink again at dessert stage: beetroot and chocolate cake comes adorned with squash and black pepper ice cream and rosemary caramel. Reassuringly, there may well be a warm apple and pecan tart with fig and blueberry ice-cream and a syrup of red wine and pomegranate. Less of a sense of adventure has gone into the wine list, but it's modern, quality is good and it suits the food. Just four house wines come by the glass.

CHEF: Alan Doig   PROPRIETOR: Colin Clydesdale   OPEN: Tue to Sun 12 to 2.30, 5 to 11   MEALS: Set L £18.95 (2 courses) to £21.95, Set D 5 to 7.30 (7 Sat) £12.95 (2 courses) to £14.95 (3 courses), Set D (2 courses) £23 to £29. Café bar menu also available   SERVICE: not inc   CARDS: Amex, Diners, MasterCard, Switch, Visa   DETAILS: 70 seats. Private parties: 70 main room. Vegetarian meals. Children's helpings. No smoking before 10pm. Occasional music. Air-conditioned (£5)

Stravaigin 2 � £

8 Ruthven Lane, Glasgow G12 9BG
TEL: (0141) 334 7165   FAX: (0141) 357 4785
EMAIL: mailbox@stravaigin2.com
WEBSITE: www.stravaigin.com

COOKING 3
GLOBAL
£22–£52

Located in an alley off the main road, the second of Colin Clydesdale's Glasgow restaurant duo (see entry above) has a bright and breezy, informal atmosphere within, with yellow-painted brick walls, wood floors and blond wood tables, newspapers for lone eaters and lively taped music. 'Think global, eat local' is the strap line here, and a variety of menus (from burgers 'made to our own 23-year-old recipe' via pre-theatre to the main carte, and – on weekends – all-day breakfast) offers a globe-trotting culinary journey that might begin with Mediterranean platter (olives, focaccia, dukka and hummus) and proceed to Vietnamese sticky pork belly with Hanoi orange, toasted peanut and crispy shallot salad. Through the flair and imagination, the kitchen shows an assuredness too: for example in twice-cooked confit duck served with mango and sweet lime, pickled choi sum, mint orange dressing and candied chilli – a dish that an inspector praised both for artful presentation and for its vibrant combination of flavours. Smooth and robust-tasting fennel and leek soup served with good Italian bread might be an excellent way to start, and to end there are carefully fused puddings: perhaps firm, subtly scented lemongrass pannacotta sprinkled with coconut and poppy seeds and served with an intense passion-fruit vanilla syrup. Wines start at £12.95, with around five by the glass, and everything on the short list stays under £20 barring a few sparklers and dessert wines.

CHEF/PROPRIETOR: Colin Clydesdale OPEN: all week 12 (11 Sat and Sun) to 11 CLOSED: 25 Dec, 1 Jan MEALS: alc (main courses £8 to £16). Set D 5 to 7 £10.95 (2 courses) to £12.95. All-day breakfast Sat and Sun 11 to 5; burger menus also available SERVICE: not inc CARDS: Amex, Delta, Diners, MasterCard, Switch, Visa DETAILS: 72 seats. Private parties: 40 main room, 25 to 40 private rooms. Vegetarian meals. Children's helpings. No smoking 12 to 2 and 5 to 10. Wheelchair access (also WC). Music. Air-conditioned £5

Ubiquitous Chip 🍶

12 Ashton Lane, Glasgow G12 8SJ
TEL: (0141) 334 5007   FAX: (0141) 337 1302
EMAIL: mail@ubiquitouschip.co.uk
WEBSITE: www.ubiquitouschip.co.uk

COOKING 4
SCOTTISH
£28–£71

Tucked behind Hillhead underground, the Chip is a long-time component of Glasgow gastronomy; it remains popular with the local academic/media crowd, and its warm welcome extends to children. In the main restaurant's quaintly bistro-like main dining room and lushly verdant covered courtyard Ronnie Clydesdale's proud advocacy of regional produce gives his menus a strong national identity. They also show a tendency to tricksy embellishments – such as a red onion tart Tatin to accompany roast duck breast – and some ideas can seem outré: viz. a starter of crispy custard of Ayrshire ham, lardons, watercress sauce and mushroom butter. But these mingle with less adventurous (but not less interesting) options, say, confit of Orkney salmon with pak choi salad, chargrilled potatoes and lime vinaigrette, or perhaps heather-fed lamb with lamb and apricot stovies, minted peas and shallots. To finish, there might be strawberry steamed pudding with white chocolate custard.

More informal is 'Upstairs at the Chip', where the menu offers things like collar of bacon with Malmsey sauce and black pudding mash, or basil and garlic marinated chicken with couscous. There is also the pubby, drinks-only 'Wee Chip' with its own entrance on Byres Road. The wine list takes its Bordeaux seriously; in fact it takes pretty much everywhere seriously and this is one of those rare places with a worthwhile range from Germany. Most regions kick off with a bottle or two under £20 and five house wines are £14.95 or £3.75 for a glass.

CHEF/PROPRIETOR: Ronald Clydesdale OPEN: Mon to Sat 12 to 2.30, 5.30 to 11, Sun 12.30 to 3, 6 to 11 CLOSED: 25 Dec, 1 Jan MEALS: Set L £21.50 to £26.50, Set L Sun £17.95, Set D £32.50 to £37.50 SERVICE: not inc CARDS: Amex, Delta, Diners, MasterCard, Switch, Visa DETAILS: 120 seats. Private parties: 60 main room, 20 to 60 private rooms. Vegetarian meals. Children's helpings. Wheelchair access (also WC). No music. No mobile phones. Air-conditioned

The Guide's longest-serving restaurants are listed near the front of the book.

GULLANE East Lothian

map 11

▲ Greywalls Hotel 🍷 ※

Muirfield, Gullane EH31 2EG
TEL: (01620) 842144   FAX: (01620) 842241
EMAIL: hotel@greywalls.co.uk
WEBSITE: www.greywalls.co.uk
off A198, at E end of Gullane

COOKING **4**
MODERN BRITISH
£53–£63

The house was built in 1901 for the Hon Alfred Lyttelton, who wanted to spend his days no more than a long putt's distance from the 18th green of Muirfield golf course. It has been in the ownership of the Weaver family since the 1920s, and retains the feel of a country home, with comfortable furnishings throughout, and immaculately set tables and jacket-and-tie order in the dining room.

Simon Burns calls on fish and meat supplies from Mallaig and Blairgowrie respectively, for preparations that are essentially quite simple, though main-course dishes often contain an unexpected element. Seared saddle of hare comes with celeriac purée and chocolate oil, while a piece of braised oxtail might be the enterprising accompaniment for a fillet of turbot with lemon dressing. Seasonings and combinations are impressively well judged. Starters are more mainstream – pressed ham hock with pease pudding, or peat-smoked Shetland salmon dressed in lemon and dill, for example – while puddings offer the likes of tiramisù with cappuccino sauce, or a tart of garden rhubarb and sour cream. Home-made oatcakes are served with the British and Irish cheeses. Despite a fondness for, and masterful selections of, fine Burgundy, mature Bordeaux and ribald doggerel verse, the wine list also moves with the times. 'Greywalls selection' embraces vins de pays as well as the New World, the finer points of which are well attended to in the full list. There's plenty of choice under £20 but not much on offer by the glass.

CHEF: Simon Burns   PROPRIETORS: Giles and Ros Weaver   OPEN: all week D only 7.15 to 9
CLOSED: Nov to Mar   MEALS: Set D £40   SERVICE: not inc, card slips closed   CARDS: Amex,
Delta, Diners, MasterCard, Switch, Visa   DETAILS: 50 seats. Private parties: 50 main room, 2 to
20 private rooms. Car park. Vegetarian meals. Children's helpings. Jacket and tie. No smoking.
Wheelchair access (not WC). No music   ACCOMMODATION: 23 rooms, all with bath/shower. TV.
Phone. B&B £120 to £240. Rooms for disabled. Baby facilities (*The Which? Guide to Good
Hotels*) ⓔ⑤

La Potinière ※

Main Street, Gullane EH31 2AA
TEL/FAX: (01620) 843214

NEW ENTRY

COOKING **6**
MODERN BRITISH
£28–£56

A long-time East Lothian resident wrote in to express pleasure when La Potinère reopened in July 2002 under new owners. Before it closed at the end of 2000, La Potinière had been a legend for a quarter of a century. Keeping the same name is bound to beg comparisons with the previous incarnation, but the new owners have not tried to imitate their predecessors. The interior is brighter and more airy, which is welcome given just how small the place is. In terms of cooking, 'execution is skilled and presentation is of a high standard'. 'Bringing out the best of Scotland's natural larder' is the stated aim of the owners, who use local suppliers and seasonal produce.

The menus offer just a couple of choices at each course, the lunchtime version kicking off perhaps with 'superb' butternut squash soup with ginger cream, followed by 'well-seasoned, perfectly cooked' pork fillet with Calvados sauce, mustard mash and honey-glazed vegetables, or seared trout accompanied by a flavourful basil sauce and sunblush tomato mash. In the evening, Arbroath smokies may appear in the form of a mousse with cucumber and dill as an intermediate course between a starter of, say, a light puff pastry tart of goats' cheese and roast vegetables dressed with pesto and a main course of baked breast of guinea fowl with Puy lentils, pancetta, button mushrooms and a herb sauce. The 'simply outstanding' cheeseboard is a stiff competitor to desserts of 'wonderful' coconut and banana frangipane tart with raspberry compote. Service is affable, and the wine list of around 30 bottles, mostly French with a smattering from the New World, starts off with four house wines from £15.50 to £18 (£3 to £4 a glass).

CHEFS/PROPRIETORS: Mary Runciman and Keith Marley   OPEN: Wed to Fri and Sun L 12.30 to 2, Wed to Sun D 7.30 to 9   CLOSED: 22 to 30 Dec   MEALS: Set L £15.50 (2 courses) to £18, Set D £35   SERVICE: not inc, card slips closed   CARDS: MasterCard, Switch, Visa   DETAILS: 28 seats. Private parties: 30 main room. Car park. Children's helpings. No smoking. Wheelchair access (not WC). No music

INVERKEILOR Angus   map 11

▲ Gordon's

32 Main Street, Inverkeilor DD11 5RN
TEL/FAX: (01241) 830364   COOKING 4
WEBSITE: www.gordonsrestaurant.co.uk   MODERN SCOTTISH
off A92 from Arbroath to Montrose   £27–£51

A beamed ceiling, exposed-stone walls, bare wooden floorboards and an open fireplace may add up to the kind of features you'd expect in an old pub, but this is a handsome restaurant with tables laid with white cloths, cream napkins and gleaming glassware. Dinner is three or four courses, and the cooking is decidedly Scottish in flavour, albeit an ambitious and inventive interpretation of Scottish cooking, in which traditional ideas are given some very untraditional treatments: such as starters of Arbroath smokie in a tian with crushed avocado and gazpacho sauce, or pan-fried squab pigeon with chanterelle risotto, Arran mustard and chorizo dressing.

The intermediary stage might offer a choice between citrus fruit terrine with Earl Grey sorbet and lemongrass syrup, or cappuccino of artichoke, cauliflower and white truffle velouté with herb scones, while main courses typically range from pan-fried monkfish, sea bass and scallops with pipérade and chive butter fondue to loin of Perthshire venison with braised kohlrabi, red cabbage and bitter chocolate jus. Finish with a selection of Scottish farmhouse cheeses or perhaps something like banana tarte Tatin with rum and raisin ice cream and caramel sauce. Prices on the compact, well-annotated wine list start at £10.95 and mostly stay below £20.

CHEFS: Gordon and Garry Watson   PROPRIETORS: Gordon and Maria Watson   OPEN: Wed to Fri and Sun L 12 to 1.45, Tue to Sat D 7 to 9   CLOSED: first 3 weeks Jan   MEALS: Set L £16.50 (2 courses) to £18.95, Set D £30.50 to £33.50   SERVICE: not inc   CARDS: Delta, MasterCard, Switch, Visa   DETAILS: 24 seats. Private parties: 20 main room, 10 private room. Car park. Children's helpings. No children under 12. No-smoking area. Wheelchair access (also WC). No music. No mobile phones   ACCOMMODATION: 3 rooms, 2 with bath/shower. TV. B&B £47 to £90. No children under 12

INVERNESS Highland   map 11

▲ Culloden House Hotel, Adams Dining Room ⚞✳

Milton of Culloden, Inverness IV2 7BZ
TEL: (01463) 790461   FAX: (01463) 792181
EMAIL: info@cullodenhouse.co.uk
WEBSITE: www.cullodenhouse.co.uk   COOKING 2
from Inverness take A96 to Nairn, turn right after   INTERNATIONAL
1m, then left at Culloden House Avenue   £36–£62

Faded Georgian grandeur and the proximity of the battlefield create historical appeal at this creeper-clad mansion where Michael Simpson manages a skilled team producing carefully constructed dishes. An authentic red lentil soup including diced vegetables and ham reminded a returning diner of how straightforwardly good the food is here. Red pepper in a stuffing mousse for chicken, a good gravy, pesto-flavoured noodles and decent vegetables deftly brought together complementary flavours, while accurately grilled lemon sole fillets on a mound of baked vegetables and fine mustard sauce showed sensitive control of tricky ingredients. To round things off, a richly smooth chocolate torte was given zest with fresh raspberries and an intense raspberry sorbet: another marriage of quiet skill and honest ingredients. The mainly French list of relatively young wines has only one bottle under £20, and prices rise steeply (the cheapest red is £24.95).

CHEF: Michael Simpson   PROPRIETOR: North American Country Inns   OPEN: all week 12.30 to 2, 7 to 9   CLOSED: 24 to 28 Dec   MEALS: alc (main courses £12.50 to £18). Set D £38   SERVICE: not inc   CARDS: Amex, Diners, MasterCard, Switch, Visa   DETAILS: 60 seats. Private parties: 60 main room, 2 to 60 private rooms. Car park. Vegetarian meals. Children's helpings. No children under 10. No smoking. Occasional music. No mobile phones   ACCOMMODATION: 28 rooms, all with bath/shower. TV. Phone. B&B £85 to £279. Baby facilities (£5)

▲ Dunain Park ▼ ⚞✳

Inverness IV3 8JN
TEL: (01463) 230512   FAX: (01463) 224532
EMAIL: dunainparkhotel@btinternet.com   COOKING 2
WEBSITE: www.dunainparkhotel.co.uk   MODERN SCOTTISH
on A82 towards Fort William, 1m from town   £38–£59

'I didn't want to leave,' was the plaintive conclusion of one reporter captivated by the charming setting of this impressively grand Georgian mansion in extensive grounds just outside Inverness. The elegance and splendour extend to the dining room too, but owners Edward and Ann Nicoll add a homely note with their friendly, personal approach to service. Some elaborate touches are also evident in the cooking, though the style is essentially simple, dealing in multi-layered but sensibly restrained combinations: chicken breast with wild mushroom risotto and a Madeira sauce, for example, or pastry-wrapped loin of lamb with nutmeg-flavoured duxelles, served with mint béarnaise. Four-course meals might start with turnip soup garnished with toasted pine kernels, followed by a John Dory fillet with Puy lentils and balsamic vinegar; desserts, served buffet style on a sideboard, might be lemon cheesecake or pecan pie. The wine list sidesteps the temptation to match the setting with unattainable grand bottles, choosing instead to seek out affordable options in the classic regions and a mix of gluggers and better bottles in the New World, with plenty under £20; house wines start at £14.50.

CHEF: Ann Nicoll   PROPRIETORS: Edward and Ann Nicoll   OPEN: all week, D only 7 to 9   MEALS: alc (main courses £16 to £19)   SERVICE: not inc, card slips closed   CARDS: Amex, Delta, Diners, MasterCard, Switch, Visa   DETAILS: 36 seats. Car park. Vegetarian meals. Children's helpings. No smoking. Wheelchair access (not WC). No music   ACCOMMODATION: 13 rooms, all with bath/shower. TV. Phone. B&B £178 to £220. Rooms for disabled. Baby facilities. Swimming pool (*The Which? Guide to Good Hotels*) £5

Rocpool £   NEW ENTRY

1 Ness Walk, Inverness IV3 5NE   COOKING 3
TEL: (01463) 717274   FAX: (01463) 798503   MODERN EUROPEAN
WEBSITE: www.rocpool.com   £22–£53

This fashionable venue on the west bank of the Ness has a stylish yet casual feel, with a bright, colourful décor, loud pop music and a cooking style that might be summed up as 'anything goes'. Crisp tempura chicken with a sweet mint, chilli and spring onion relish, tender braised pork in sweet-and-sour sauce, and 'zingy' coriander, carrot and ginger soup are typical of starters, while among main courses might be honey- and sesame-glazed chicken salad with Thai coleslaw and coconut cream dressing, and 'Asian risotto' with wild mushrooms, soy and ginger, topped with Parmesan and deep-fried slivers of sweet potato. If some of the ideas sound a bit wild, rest assured that chef Steven Devlin has the skill to carry them off – flavours shine through but are carefully controlled. As well as the main menu, a list of smaller tapas-style dishes is offered to encourage informality and sociability. House wines are £11.95.

CHEF: Steven Devlin   PROPRIETORS: Adrian Pieraccini and Steven Devlin   OPEN: Mon to Sat L 12 to 2.30, all week D 6 to 10   CLOSED: 25 Dec, 1 Jan   MEALS: alc (main courses L £6 to £8, D £9 to £17). Set L £6.95 (2 courses). Tapas menu available Sun to Fri 12 to 10, Sat 12 to 6   SERVICE: not inc, card slips closed   CARDS: Delta, Diners, MasterCard, Switch, Visa   DETAILS: 60 seats. Vegetarian meals. Children's helpings. Wheelchair access (also WC). Music. Air-conditioned £5

The Guide office can quickly spot when a restaurateur is encouraging customers to write recommending inclusion. Such reports do not further a restaurant's cause. Please tell us if a restaurateur invites you to write to the Guide.

▲ Killiecrankie House Hotel 🍷 ⁛

Killiecrankie PH16 5LG
TEL: (01796) 473220   FAX: (01796) 472451
EMAIL: enquiries@killiecrankiehotel.co.uk
WEBSITE: www.killiecrankiehotel.co.uk
off A9, 3m N of Pitlochry

COOKING 3
GLOBAL
£44–£53

Killiecrankie House is a Victorian dower house set above the River Garry in its wooded valley and surrounded by splendid gardens that provide a relaxing view from the dining room. Mark Easton is strongly committed to local produce – some of the fruit, veg and herbs come from the hotel's kitchen garden – but when he cooks it, his outlook is much broader. Starters take in traditional ideas such as grilled scallops wrapped in bacon with salad leaves and orange dressing, but also more contemporary themes like warm ricotta and lemon flan with sunblush tomato salad and basil oil. Among main courses, pan-fried venison fillet might come with baked potato cake and a date and port sauce, while grilled Atlantic char is partnered with a tomato and lemon cream sauce. There are always cold options too, like poached salmon with mayonnaise and new potatoes, and, to finish, perhaps glazed lemon tart with Chantilly cream. For more informal dining, the conservatory bar menu is just the ticket. Tim Waters's wine trade experience has gone into a stimulating and decent-value list. Australia and New Zealand stand out, while the Languedoc is the place for budget bottles from £13.90. Eight by the glass are £3.65 to £5.25.

CHEF: Mark Easton   PROPRIETOR: Tim and Maillie Waters   OPEN: all week D only 7 to 8.30   CLOSED: 3 Jan to 13 Feb   MEALS: Set D £33. Bar L and D menu available   SERVICE: not inc, card slips closed   CARDS: Delta, MasterCard, Switch, Visa   DETAILS: 32 seats. Private parties: 16 main room, 6 to 12 private rooms. Car park. Vegetarian meals. Children's helpings. No smoking. Wheelchair access (not WC). No music. No mobile phones   ACCOMMODATION: 10 rooms, all with bath/shower. TV. Phone. D,B&B £79 to £198. Baby facilities (£5)

Café Zola £

NEW ENTRY

12 St James Terrace, Lochwinnoch Road,
Kilmacolm PA13 4HB
TEL: (01505) 871999

COOKING 2
MODERN SCOTTISH
£29–£46

Ferrier Richardson, who last appeared in the Guide at his now defunct Eurasia in Glasgow, has resurfaced in this picturesque village with a new, pared-down bistro-style restaurant with a 'jolly' atmosphere. Menus offer plenty of choice, mostly in a traditional, comforting vein, and tending towards elaborate constructions and complex flavour combinations. Among starters might be truckle Cheddar and smoked salmon soufflé with hollandaise sauce, or haggis, neeps and tatties with whisky butter sauce, while main courses range from roast quail with ratatouille gâteau, parisienne potatoes and tarragon essence to roast cod fillet with Parma ham, courgette and asparagus risotto and basil butter sauce. Desserts are modern staples such as lemon tart with crisp glazed topping, and to finish, coffee comes with home-made tablet. The wine list is well selected and keenly priced; house wines are £14, and four come by the glass.

CHEF: Ferrier Richardson   PROPRIETOR: Andrew Currie   OPEN: Tue to Sat 12 to 2.30, 7 to 9.30   CLOSED: 25 and 26 Dec, 1 and 2 Jan   MEALS: alc (main courses £9 to £15). Set D £19.95   SERVICE: 10% (optional)   CARDS: Delta, MasterCard, Switch, Visa   DETAILS: 42 seats. Vegetarian meals. Children's helpings. Wheelchair access (also WC). Music

KINGUSSIE Highland

map 11

▲ The Cross ♥ ⅝✳

Tweed Mill Brae, Ardbroilach Road,
Kingussie PH21 1LB
TEL: (01540) 661166   FAX: (01540) 661080
EMAIL: fabulousfood@thecross.co.uk
WEBSITE: www.thecross.co.uk

COOKING 5
MODERN BRITISH
£46–£62

This former water-powered tweed mill, beside the tumbling burn, is under new management. Becca Henderson, who worked with previous owners the Hadleys for a number of years, provides continuity, but David and Katie Young are no strangers to restaurants, since he used to be an AA chief inspector. The brave move from poacher to gamekeeper has been achieved with minimum disruption to The Cross; it still has a homely, informal feel to it, and instead of five courses with little or no choice, the menu now offers anything from two to four courses, with a modest choice of three items per course.

The food is enjoyable because it is cooked with considerable skill, and flavour combinations are well considered. 'Cooking without fuss' is how one visitor summed it up after eating a brittle, buttery, shortcrust pastry case filled with goats' cheese and sweet-tasting tomato, with an oil and balsamic dressing, followed by pink, tender rack of lamb accompanied by good dauphinoise potatoes, diced aubergine and a minty gravy. Well-sourced raw materials (many of them local or regional) are treated with respect: three succulent, diver-caught scallops from Skye, for example, are served on a creamy cauliflower purée with basil oil. Desserts have included rum pannacotta with rhubarb, and an 'exemplary' cheesecake made with a chocolate digestive base, lemony filling, and a dressing of lemon and passion-fruit coulis and cream. Service is informal, and Katie Young is amiable and efficient. The wine list takes an even-handed approach with plenty under £20. France, Spain (including sherries), Chile and South Africa are strongest and the range of dessert wines is unusually good. Only two wines come by the glass, but they are selected daily to suit the food.

CHEFS: Becca Henderson and David Young   PROPRIETORS: David and Katie Young   OPEN: Tue to Sat D only 7 to 8.30   CLOSED: 25 and 31 Dec, Jan   MEALS: Set D £28.50 (2 courses) to £38.50   SERVICE: net prices, card slips closed   CARDS: Amex, Delta, MasterCard, Switch, Visa   DETAILS: 28 seats. Private parties: 24 main room. Car park. Vegetarian meals. Children's helpings. No smoking. Wheelchair access (also WC). No music. No mobile phones   ACCOMMODATION: 8 rooms, all with bath/shower. Phone. B&B from £100 per room; D,B&B £80 to £220. Baby facilities (*The Which? Guide to Good Hotels*)

▲ *means accommodation is available.*

LARGOWARD Fife   map 11

▲ Inn at Lathones ⁵⅄   NEW ENTRY

by Largoward, nr St Andrews KY9 1JE
TEL: (01334) 840494   FAX: (01334) 840694
EMAIL: lathones@theinn.co.uk   COOKING 2
WEBSITE: www.theinn.co.uk   MODERN EUROPEAN
on A915, 5m SW of St Andrews   £22–£57

Behind this 400-year-old inn's simple white exterior is a colourful blue-and-yellow dining room. An assortment of menus includes exceptional-value two- and three-course set lunches, plus other prix-fixes and a couple of cartes. Breton chef Marc Guibert cooks the local produce in straightforward modern style. A starter of langoustines in tempura batter has come with pickled fennel, and a herby pancake wrapping pink-cooked pigeon breast and excellent foie gras mousseline is partnered by an assertive salad. Braised haunch of venison with a truffle sauce, and moist sea bass with oil-griddled peppers, courgettes and aubergines make successful partnerships. Sauces are good, and puddings – such as crisp-topped, delicately star-anise-scented crème brûlée with powerfully marinated raspberries – show clever control of flavouring. The wine list includes exceptional finds but is rather confusingly arranged with regions and prices jumbled up under catch-all Old and New World headings. Prices range from £11.50 to £350, but there's choice under £20.

CHEF: Marc Guibert   PROPRIETOR: Nick White   OPEN: all week 12 to 2.30, 6 to 9.30   CLOSED: 25 and 26 Dec, 6 to 22 Jan   MEALS: alc (main courses £11.50 to £19). Set L £10.50 (2 courses) to £14.50. Set D £20 to £28.50, 8-course Set D £37.50 (usually for whole table). Snack L menu available Mon to Sat   SERVICE: not inc   CARDS: Amex, Delta, Diners, MasterCard, Switch, Visa   DETAILS: 34 seats. Private parties: 45 main room, 10 to 70 private rooms. Car park. Vegetarian meals. Children's helpings. No smoking. Music. No mobile phones   ACCOMMODATION: 14 rooms, all with bath/shower. TV. Phone. B&B £75 to £160. Baby facilities (£5)

LINLITHGOW West Lothian   map 11

▲ Champany Inn ▮

Champany Corner, Linlithgow EH49 7LU
TEL: (01506) 834532   FAX: (01506) 834302
EMAIL: reception@champany.com   COOKING 5
WEBSITE: www.champany.com   SCOTTISH
2m NE of Linlithgow at junction of A904 and A803   £50–£86

This Scottish landmark, 20 years old in 2003, incorporates a Chop and Ale House across a converted farmyard from the main restaurant, where baskets of immaculate fresh vegetables in the reception tempt you into an octagonal dining room with a steeply sloped, tent-like wooden ceiling, oil paintings on the walls and fine glassware on polished mahogany tables.

The chefs, too, have been here 20 years, serving fine Scots beef in a variety of cuts. Alongside the hefty steaks of yore there are now smaller cuts, 10oz sirloin and 8oz fillet, and a lighter two-course set lunch. Cooking specifications are scrupulously followed, and the meat (brilliantly flavoured and enticingly textured) is well served by sauces such as black pepper, or Stilton and port.

Among accompaniments are bubbling-hot, garlicky dauphinois and crisp-fried onion rings. There are also a few non-steak mains, such as bacon- and tarragon-stuffed chicken, or lamb loin chops. Starters may include chilli-spiced prawns with shredded pickled cucumber, or smoked salmon, while among the puddings are a runny-centred baked chocolate moelleux, partnered with fast-melting coffee ice-cream. (And one reporter rejoiced at crème brûlée as nature intended: 'without chocolate or raspberries or nuts or anything extraneous'.) On the vast, crisply presented wine list South Africa accounts for over 100 bins, plus the six house wines (from £14.50/£3.75 a glass), and surfaces again on a strong dessert wine section. Bordeaux, Burgundy and Rhône are tops in Europe, though Spain is covered in rare depth too. But such quality costs, and little beyond the house selection is under £20.

CHEFS: Clive Davidson, David Gibson and Kevin Hope   PROPRIETORS: Clive and Anne Davidson
OPEN: Mon to Fri L 12.30 to 2, Mon to Sat D 7 to 10   CLOSED: 25–26 Dec, 1–2 Jan   MEALS: alc
(main courses £17.50 to £32.50). Set L £16.75 (2 courses). Chop and Ale House menu available
SERVICE: 10%, card slips closed   CARDS: Amex, Delta, Diners, MasterCard, Switch, Visa
DETAILS: 60 seats. 30 seats outside. Private parties: 30 main room. Car park. No children under 8.
Wheelchair access (also WC). No music   ACCOMMODATION: 16 rooms, all with bath/shower. TV.
Phone. B&B £95 to £125. Rooms for disabled (*The Which? Guide to Good Hotels*)

LOCHINVER Highland   map 11

▲ Albannach ▼ ⁵⁄✳

Baddidarroch, Lochinver IV27 4LP
TEL: (01571) 844407   FAX: (01571) 844285   COOKING 5
EMAIL: the.albannach@virgin.net   MODERN SCOTTISH
WEBSITE: www.thealbannach.co.uk   £50–£60

Spectacular views can be enjoyed from the panelled conservatory, for taking tea and pre- and post-meal drinks, while the candlelit dining room, with its French-style oak dining chairs, has a more sedate feel. Climate and geology inform the realism of the cooking, based as it is on the produce of local land, loch and sea. Dishes on the no-choice, five-course menu could start with breast of guinea fowl with loin of wild rabbit on juniper cabbage with guinea-fowl ravioli and cider sauce, or a rich, smooth bisque of languoustine, crab and lobster with burnt hollandaise and langoustine, followed by a courgette soufflé with red onion marmalade, or dill crêpes stuffed with goats' cheese and basil. Main courses push out the boat for, perhaps, seared local scallops with roast monkfish tails on saffron and seaweed rice, or pan-fried Gressingham duck breast on braised red cabbage, served with croft vegetables, potato and thyme galette and Madeira sauce. A selection of cheese follows – Cooleeney and Cashel Blue, say – and then dessert: lime torte with orange and ginger sauce and rhubarb poached in Sauternes, or chocolate tartlet with orange pannacotta and pears poached in red wine.

The wine list fizzes with enthusiasm, especially for France, with traditional regions bolstered by a range of value bins from St Chinian. The New World selections are packed with quality and value, and there's a huge list of half-bottles. House wines at £11 and £12 have plenty of company under £15.

MOFFAT

CHEFS/PROPRIETORS: Colin Craig and Lesley Crosfield   OPEN: Tue to Sun D only 8 (1 sitting)
CLOSED: mid-Nov to mid-Mar   MEALS: Set D £40   SERVICE: not inc   CARDS: MasterCard, Switch,
Visa   DETAILS: 16 seats. Car park. No children under 12. No smoking. No music. No mobile
phones   ACCOMMODATION: 5 rooms, all with bath/shower. Phone. D,B&B £115 to £250. Rooms
for disabled. No children under 12 (*The Which? Guide to Good Hotels*)

MILNGAVIE East Dunbartonshire   map 11

Gavin's Mill ✸

NEW ENTRY

3 Gavin's Mill Road, Milngavie G62 6NB   COOKING 2
TEL: (0141) 956 2255   MODERN SCOTTISH
                                                       £22–£46

The restaurant can be accessed via the Tesco car park but is perhaps more
picturesquely described as being on Allander Water, close to the start of the West
Highland Way. A ground-floor bar offers contemporary snack dishes, such as
smoked salmon fishcake with spicy avocado relish, or sliced stuffed quail with
niçoise salad, while the main dining goes on in an airy room upstairs. The daily-
changing menu deals in bright, modern cooking, delivering spinach and ricotta
gnocchi of concentrated flavour, set off with a buttery sage sauce and a Parmesan
crisp, or perhaps a contemporary classic pairing of scallops with pea purée,
garnished with pancetta and a mint vinaigrette. An inspector's main course of
sautéed sea bass was 'splendidly fresh and perfectly timed', supported by
marinated aubergine and plum tomatoes and a mellow yellow pepper coulis,
and other options might run to pan-fried saddle of rabbit stuffed with herbs and
currants and wrapped in Parma ham. The one constant on the menu is sticky
toffee pudding, 'because we face too many complaints if we try to take it off', but
a softly creamy chocolate tart with a fragile crust is also suitably luscious. Service
could smile a bit more, but the stylistically arranged wine list is a happy
conjunction of good value and upmarket bottles, starting at £11.50 with eight by
the glass (£3.25 to £3.90).

CHEFS: Rupert Staniforth and Jamie Donald   PROPRIETORS: Rupert and Aisla Staniforth   OPEN:
Mon to Sat 12 to 2.30, 6 to 10   CLOSED: 25 and 26 Dec, 1 and 2 Jan   MEALS: alc (main courses L
£5 to £7.50, D £10 to £15). Set L and D 6 to 7 £10.50 (2 courses) to £12.50. Bar menu available
SERVICE: not inc, card slips closed, 10% for parties of 8 or more   CARDS: Delta, MasterCard,
Switch, Visa   DETAILS: 70 seats. Private parties: 50 main room, 14 to 20 private rooms.
Vegetarian meals. Children's helpings. No smoking in 1 dining room. No music. No mobile
phones. Air-conditioned (£5)

MOFFAT Dumfries & Galloway   map 11

Limetree ✸

High Street, Moffat DG10 9HG   COOKING 3
TEL: (01683) 221654   FAX: (01683) 221721   MODERN BRITISH
WEBSITE: www.limetree-restaurant.co.uk   £25–£35

At the top of the High Street sits a two-storey house of random stonework, one of
Moffat's oldest, dwarfed by the three-storey buildings around. The bistro-style
interior is light and airy, with pale wooden tables and simple pictures on
roughly plastered walls. The effect is minimalist, but not severe.

Dinner is a three-choice, fixed-price affair, and Matt Seddon's practice of selecting the best and freshest in season from the kitchen garden of nearby Craigieburn House might account for diners' comments on robust flavours and interesting combinations. Starters have included smoked haddock risotto with peas and spring onions, and bruschetta of chicken livers, mushroom and bacon with a mustard cream dressing. After a main course of maybe sea bass with fennel and olive salad, or duck breast glazed with honey and ginger, served with roast parsnip and curried Puy lentils, there might be the unfussy simplicity of roast peaches with vanilla ice cream and summer berry sauce, or a more indulgent chocolate toffee pudding. With representatives from Old and New Worlds, the list of 18 wines starts at £10.50 for Corney & Barrow house wines, and mostly stays under £20.

CHEF: Matt Seddon PROPRIETORS: Matt and Artemis Seddon OPEN: Sun L 12.30 to 2.30, Tue to Sat D 6.30 to 9.30 MEALS: Set L £12.50 (2 courses) to £15.75, Set D £15.75 (2 courses) to £19.50 SERVICE: not inc, card slips closed CARDS: Delta, MasterCard, Switch, Visa DETAILS: 25 seats. Private parties: 16 main room. Children's helpings. No smoking. Wheelchair access (not WC). Music

▲ Well View $\mathbf{\xi}$✖

Ballplay Road, Moffat DG10 9JU
TEL: (01683) 220184   FAX: (01683) 220088
EMAIL: info@wellview.co.uk
WEBSITE: www.wellview.co.uk

COOKING 4
FRANCO-SCOTTISH
£23–£46

In 2004 the Schuckardts (Janet and daughter Lina cook; John welcomes unintrusively) celebrate 20 years at their comfortable Victorian country house. The no-choice dinner (though four puddings are offered) starts with appetisers showing a mastery of many skills – perhaps tiny sausage rolls, strong-tasting crab pâté or deep-fried cheese puffs – and breads, too, reinforce the impression of robustly straightforward cooking playing to its own strengths. Soups, such as a 'velvety carrot and apricot in which flavours blended imperceptibly', or maybe unfussy salads with imaginative marriages of ingredients, precede a second course, often of fish. A fowl of some sort – duck breast or maybe guinea fowl – will be complemented by powerful sauces (plum and sesame with the duck) and vegetables prepared and cooked attentively. Puddings tend to be cream-based: classic crème brûlée or rhubarb fool, or, just as likely, tiramisù, lemon mousse or pannacotta are all guaranteed to provide 'a perfect full stop'. The wine list favours France, with a number of good bottles. House wines are £13 a bottle or £3 a glass.

CHEFS: Janet Schuckardt and Lina Schuckardt PROPRIETORS: Janet and John Schuckardt OPEN: Sun L 12.15 to 1.15, all week D 7 to 8.30 MEALS: Set L £16, Set D £32 SERVICE: none, card slips closed CARDS: Amex, Delta, MasterCard, Switch, Visa DETAILS: 24 seats. Private parties: 20 main room, 6 private room. Car park. No children under 5 at D. No smoking. No music. No mobile phones ACCOMMODATION: 6 rooms, all with bath/shower. TV. B&B £60 to £102. Baby facilities (*The Which? Guide to Good Hotels*) (£5)

---

 indicates that smoking is banned in all eating areas.

MUIR OF ORD Highland   map 11

▲ Dower House ⚡✗

Highfield, Muir of Ord IV6 7XN
TEL/FAX: (01463) 870090   COOKING 2
EMAIL: goodfood@thedowerhouse.co.uk   MODERN BRITISH
WEBSITE: www.thedowerhouse.co.uk   £47–£57

The Dower House, built in the eighteenth century, is set in five acres of mature
woodland and gardens. The one-storey building is spacious and refreshingly
un-twee; its long dining room has a log fire at one end and polished wood tables.
This is very much a husband and wife operation, with Mena Aitchison looking
after front-of-house while Robyn puts his skills to work in the kitchen. Sourcing
local seafood, game, meat, bread and herbs is part of the game plan, and the
three-course, no choice menu changes daily. Begin perhaps with oriental-spiced
fish soup, or marinated red gurnard on sautéed cod roe, and follow with breast of
wood pigeon with Puy lentils, or fillet of beef with a herb relish. Desserts may
run to tarte Tatin, or hot chocolate soufflé. 'There are no gimmicks here, and the
food tastes as it should do,' concluded a reporter. Highlights of the half-French,
half-New World wine list are quality house wines from the Languedoc (£16, or
£4.50 a glass) and some smart choices from Australia and New Zealand.

CHEF: Robyn Aitchison PROPRIETORS: Robyn and Mena Aitchison OPEN: all week D only 7.30 to
9 (L by arrangement) CLOSED: 2 weeks Nov, Christmas MEALS: Set D £35 SERVICE: not inc,
card slips closed CARDS: MasterCard, Switch, Visa DETAILS: 25 seats. 6 seats outside. Private
parties: 25 main room. Car park. Children's helpings. No babies in dining room at D. No smoking.
Wheelchair access (also WC). No music ACCOMMODATION: 5 rooms, all with bath/shower. TV.
Phone. B&B £55 to £150. Rooms for disabled. Baby facilities (*The Which? Guide to Good Hotels*)

OBAN Argyll & Bute   map 11

Ee-Usk £

104 George Street, Oban PA34 5NS   COOKING 2
TEL: (01631) 565666   FAX: (01631) 570282   SEAFOOD
EMAIL: eeusk.fishcafe@virgin.net   £24–£49

Ee-Usk (a transliteration of the Scots Gaelic for 'fish', in case you wondered) has
moved from its former centre-of-town location to the North Pier, though
otherwise all continues much as usual, with seafood the focus. Expect local
oysters and mussels from Loch Etive, Inverawe salmon, Loch Linnhe prawns,
and much more besides. Autumn visitors from south of the border were
impressed by the precision and freshness of it all, enjoying langoustines with
chilli and ginger, a main-course mixed fish and shellfish platter with savoury
mash and parsley sauce, and seared scallops with a Mornay sauce. If you've set
your heart on a fillet steak or piri-piri chicken, you can be accommodated, but
from Thai fishcakes, via seafood pasta to breadcrumbed haddock, the meat of the
menu comes from the sea. Finish with satisfyingly rich crème brûlée. A short,
imaginative list of Oddbins wines is fairly priced; house selections are £9.95.

CHEFS: Sheila MacLeod and Marian McDonald PROPRIETORS: the MacLeod family OPEN: all week 12 to 3, 6 to 10 CLOSED: 25 and 26 Dec, 1 Jan MEALS: alc (main courses £8 to £17) SERVICE: not inc CARDS: Delta, MasterCard, Switch, Visa DETAILS: 54 seats. Children's helpings. No-smoking area. Music

PEAT INN Fife

map 11

▲ Peat Inn 🍷 ✴

Peat Inn KY15 5LH
TEL: (01334) 840206 FAX: (01334) 840530
EMAIL: reception@thepeatinn.co.uk
WEBSITE: www.thepeatinn.co.uk
at junction of B940 and B941, 6m SW of St
Andrews

COOKING 4
SCOTTISH
£30–£70

There aren't many restaurants that have appeared in the Guide for more than 30 consecutive years, and still fewer that have remained under the guidance of the same chef/proprietor for all that time. For this feat of tenacity and consistency of standards, David Wilson deserves approbation. The former coaching inn at the village centre that he runs with wife Patricia changes little from year to year: it is as warm and welcoming as ever, and service is polished, professional and pleasant.

A blend of French and domestic ideas characterises the cooking, with a focus on Scottish produce. At inspection, a starter of roast scallops on leeks and potatoes with bacon and pea purée featured lightly cooked shellfish of impressive freshness and flavour, while tender, pink venison liver and carefully cooked kidneys came with a sweet confit of onions and a well-reduced red wine sauce. Main courses are similarly full-bodied combinations, such as cassoulet of lamb, pork and duck, halibut fillet on vegetable risotto with lobster sauce, and beef fillet in Madeira sauce with roast shallots and a potato cake. More contemporary ideas appear at dessert stage, such as rhubarb soup with star anise and ginger, or chocolate pot with rosemary. The wine selection is emphatically food-oriented, though dismissive of the fuss made about precise food and wine pairings. It is structured around French regions, with honest vintage assessments to aid selection, supplemented by global round-ups of comparable/contrastable wines and a stand-alone German section. Very little costs under £20 but prices are mostly good for the quality and maturity of the wines on offer. House wines are £16 or £3.50 a glass.

CHEF: David Wilson PROPRIETORS: David and Patricia Wilson OPEN: Tue to Sat 1 (1 sitting), 7 to 9.30 CLOSED: 25 Dec, 1 Jan MEALS: alc D (main courses £16 to £21). Set L £19.50, Set D £32 to £45 (whole table only) SERVICE: not inc, card slips closed CARDS: Amex, Delta, MasterCard, Switch, Visa DETAILS: 48 seats. Private parties: 24 main room, 10 to 14 private rooms. Car park. Vegetarian meals. Children's helpings. No smoking. Wheelchair access (also WC). No music. No mobile phones ACCOMMODATION: 8 rooms, all with bath/shower. TV. Phone. B&B £75 to £155. Rooms for disabled (*The Which? Guide to Good Hotels*)

Subscribers to Which? Online can access **The Good Food Guide** *on www.which.net.*

Let's Eat ✢ £

77 Kinnoull Street, Perth PH1 5EZ
TEL: (01738) 643377   FAX: (01738) 621464   COOKING 4
EMAIL: enquiries@letseatperth.co.uk   MODERN EUROPEAN
WEBSITE: www.letseatperth.co.uk   £25–£50

For some living in the Perth area, Let's Eat is considered the benchmark by
which other restaurants are judged, and Tony Heath continues to seek out good
local produce, from organic salad leaves and vegetables to organic pork from
nearby Almondbank. Fillet of Inverurie beef may be served with a spinach and
herb potato cake, braised shallots and a Madeira and red wine sauce, while a
starter of angel hair pasta with herbs and asparagus may have Skye crab as its
centrepiece. Fish might make an appearance as seared fillet of Uist salmon on
crushed potatoes with a tomato and saffron sauce, or, more exotically, as grilled
brochette of monkfish and king prawns with a Thai-style coriander sauce and
coconut rice. Desserts can be quite homely, as in an apple, pear, rhubarb and
plum crumble, or steamed spiced apple and ginger pudding with cinnamon ice
cream. Service is overseen by Shona Drysdale, described by one fan as 'the
maîtresse d' of dreams, calm and immensely competent'. There are plenty of
interesting bottles on the wide-ranging wine list, with much to choose under
£20. House wines start at £11.

CHEF: Tony Heath, Graeme Pallister and Tomi Burns   PROPRIETORS: Tony Heath and Shona
Drysdale   OPEN: Tue to Sat 12 to 2, 6.30 to 9.45   CLOSED: 25 and 26 Dec, 1 and 2 Jan, 2 weeks
Jan, 2 weeks July   MEALS: alc (main courses L £9 to £12.50, D £11 to £17.50)   SERVICE: not inc,
card slips closed   CARDS: Amex, Delta, MasterCard, Switch, Visa   DETAILS: 70 seats. Private
parties: 70 main room. Vegetarian meals. Children's helpings. No smoking. Wheelchair access
(also WC). Music. No mobile phones (£5)

63 Tay Street ♥ ✢

63 Tay Street, Perth PH2 8NN   COOKING 4
TEL: (01738) 441451   FAX: (01738) 441461   MODERN SCOTTISH
WEBSITE: www.63taystreet.co.uk   £26–£49

On the embankment across the road from the Tay (and looking out over the
river), the small dining room here is quite plain but pleasant, with colour
provided by red upholstered chairs and lively paintings (variously described as
'amazing' and 'rather modern'). This place 'continues to impress', perhaps
because of good value – with few exceptions, there's one price for all dishes at
each course – or perhaps because welcoming service 'makes you feel happy'.

The weekly-changing menu focuses on local, seasonal produce: game from
the Cairngorms, asparagus from the Carse of Gowrie, beef and lamb from local
farms. There are influences from further afield, too: witness a starter spaghetti of
Skye prawns with chilli, coriander and ginger. While one frequent visitor
singled out a main-course sweetbread and pea risotto as 'a real highlight',
another enthused over a dish of sole on a 'sort of ratatouille' with mashed potato.
Sweet-toothed souls may finish with steamed ginger pudding and custard, or
banana crème brûlée with ice cream. The wine list, arranged by styles, has an eye

for fashion and delivers good flavours from all over. Prices are reasonable, with eight house bottles at £10.95 to £15.50 (£3.25 to £4.25 a glass).

CHEF: Jeremy Wares   PROPRIETORS: Jeremy and Shona Wares   OPEN: Tue to Sat 12 to 2, 6.30 to 9   CLOSED: 25 Dec, first 2 weeks Jan, last week June, first week July   MEALS: alc (main courses L £8, D £15 to £18)   SERVICE: not inc, card slips closed   CARDS: Amex, Delta, MasterCard, Switch, Visa   DETAILS: 32 seats. Private parties: 32 main room. Vegetarian meals. No children under 12. No smoking. Wheelchair access (also WC). No music (£5)

PITLOCHRY Perthshire & Kinross   map 11

Port-na-Craig Inn ⚡✶ £   NEW ENTRY

Port-na-Craig, Pitlochry PH16 5ND	COOKING 2
TEL: (01796) 472777 FAX: (01796) 481259	MODERN BRITISH
WEBSITE: www.portnacraig.com	£24–£43

Situated on the River Tummel, just below the Festival Theatre, this attractive set of stone buildings dating from 1650 has white-painted simplicity internally. Local supplies, some from the Thewes' family garden and varieties of wild mushrooms picked by them, plus notably wide ranges of game and shellfish, supply an able kitchen. Among starters, a generous portion of excellent scallops comes with understated garlic butter, and thickly sliced beef carpaccio, finely flavoured, is accompanied by good tapenade. Typical of main courses are 'flavoursome' loin of lamb with lentils and parsnip purée, and turbot, 'cooked perfectly', with hollandaise. Desserts can be well-judged combinations, as a dish of honey ice cream with hazelnuts and toffee sauce. Details like bread and coffee maintain standards, and service is affable and informal. A short, well-documented and carefully selected wine list starts at £10.50 and few bottles rise above £20.

CHEFS: Jamie Thewes and Fiona Harris   PROPRIETORS: the Thewes family   OPEN: Tue to Sun L 12.30 to 2 (2.30 Sun), Tue to Sat D 6 to 9   CLOSED: 24 Dec to mid-Mar   MEALS: alc (main courses £8 to £14.50). Bar menu available   SERVICE: not inc   CARDS: Delta, MasterCard, Switch, Visa   DETAILS: 38 seats. 70 seats outside. Private parties: 38 main room. Car park. Vegetarian meals. Children's helpings. No smoking. Wheelchair access (also WC). No music

PORT APPIN Argyll & Bute   map 11

▲ Airds Hotel ♥ ⚡✶

Port Appin PA38 4DF	
TEL: (01631) 730236 FAX: (01631) 730535	
EMAIL: airds@airds-hotel.com	COOKING 4
WEBSITE: www.airds-hotel.com	MODERN BRITISH
2m off A828, on E shore of Loch Linnhe	£35–£73

Soaring mountains, majestic lochs and eighteenth-century inns are pretty impressive sights individually, but when the three are together the result can be breathtaking. Such is the case with Airds, which stands on the shore of Loch Linnhe with views across the water to Mull and Lismore.

Just after the last Guide was published, the Allen family left to take over Kinloch House in Blairgowrie (see entry) and Shaun and Jenny McKivragan took over here. Wisely, they don't plan to make any major changes and have retained the services of chef Paul Burns. His is an elaborate, luxurious and fairly conservative style of cooking: breast of squab pigeon with foie gras, wild mushrooms and truffle, or roast langoustines with cucumber and tomato salad and herb mayonnaise to start, followed by braised turbot and scallops with spinach, asparagus and Vermouth velouté, or roast loin of lamb with potato gratin, braised cabbage, baby onions and garlic. The quality of ingredients is generally high, and cooking technique is sound. John Dory with foie gras and sun-dried tomatoes, however, failed to impress at a conceptual level, though turbot with scallops, squat lobsters and crayfish in beurre blanc proved a well-balanced combination, and puddings have been 'outstanding', including a sharply flavoured prune and Armagnac soufflé. 'House wine' here means a range of 18 quality bottles from £13 to £34, although only four wines come by the glass (£6). The main feature of the list is a good range of Burgundies from a small number of well-chosen producers. Other French regions are brief and the rest of the world briefer still, but some interesting bottles from Western Australia stand out.

CHEF: Paul Burns   PROPRIETORS: Shaun and Jenny McKivragan   OPEN: all week; 12 to 2, 7.30 to 8.30   CLOSED: 24 to 28 Nov, 5 to 23 Jan   MEALS: Set L £17.95 (2 courses) to £21.95, Set D £45. Light lunch also available   SERVICE: not inc, card slips closed   CARDS: Delta, MasterCard, Switch, Visa   DETAILS: 40 seats. Private parties: 40 main room. Car park. Vegetarian meals. Children's helpings. No children under 10 at D. No smoking. Wheelchair access (not WC). No music. No mobile phones   ACCOMMODATION: 12 rooms, all with bath/shower. TV. Phone. D,B&B £150 to £336 (B&B also available upon application). Rooms for disabled. Baby facilities (*The Which? Guide to Good Hotels*)

▲ Pierhouse 🍽 ⚡

Port Appin PA38 4DE
TEL: (01631) 730302   FAX: (01631) 730400
EMAIL: pierhouse@btinternet.com
WEBSITE: www.pierhouse.co.uk

COOKING 3
SEAFOOD
£21–£65

The busiest place in Port Appin is near the short pier, where boats land their catches, ferries cross to Lismore, and cars and lorries compete for parking space at peak times. Occupying what was the pier master's house, this no-nonsense seafood restaurant majors on stalwarts of the repertoire, from clam chowder and deep-fried whitebait, through Lismore oysters and chargrilled scallops, to lobster or langoustine thermidor. Platters of shellfish are served with crusty bread, mayonnaise and garlic dips. It may not be cutting edge (given deep-fried Camembert and mushroom stroganoff among supporting options) but those who stick to plain and simple seafood usually come away happiest. Finish perhaps with lemon tart, or sticky toffee pudding, and drink from a global wine list that stays mostly under £25. Four white and three red house wines are priced between £11 and £13.50.

CHEF: Ernie Jaffray   PROPRIETORS: Liz and David Hamblin   OPEN: all week 12.30 to 2.30, 6.30 to 9.30   CLOSED: 25 and 26 Dec   MEALS: alc (main courses L £7.50 to £20, D £10.50 to £30) SERVICE: not inc   CARDS: Delta, MasterCard, Switch, Visa   DETAILS: 70 seats. 30 seats outside. Private parties: 70 main room, 12 private rooms. Car park. Vegetarian meals. Children's helpings. No smoking. Wheelchair access (also WC). Music. No mobile phones ACCOMMODATION: 12 rooms, all with bath/shower. TV. Phone. B&B £45 to £100. Baby facilities (£5)

▲ The Creel ⅚✸

Front Road, St Margaret's Hope KW17 2SL
TEL: (01856) 831311
EMAIL: alan@thecreel.freeserve.co.uk
WEBSITE: www.thecreel.co.uk   COOKING **7**
off A961, 13m S of Kirkwall, on South Ronaldsay   MODERN SCOTTISH
                                                     £41–£53

Only ten yards from the sea wall, in a sheltered bay in Scapa Flow, this three-storey building houses a two-room restaurant that sets the standard for the whole of Scotland. 'Alan Craigie is a very special chef' whose strength is seafood. He doesn't try anything too fancy, but then he doesn't need to when his simple dishes use excellent local materials, exhibit an eye for successful combinations, and are the beneficiaries of a high degree of dedication. Soups are variously described as 'superlative' or 'world class', typically crammed with chunks of fish or shellfish: a rich, white-bean version with folded fillets of ling and sea witch; velvet crab with squid and lemon sole; exquisite partan bree; and rustic smoked haddock that was 'more like a meal than a soup'. Alternatives might range from old-fashioned queen scallops with garlic butter to a more eye-catching langoustine and megrim timbale with a watercress dressing and pesto.

Fish and shellfish are varied (one couple counted 17 kinds of fish and 10 of shellfish over the course of a week's stay), utterly fresh, 'cooked to perfection' and beautifully presented. This is not just now and again, or even most of the time; it is the conclusion of every reporter, about every dish in every meal. Main courses tend to pair fish together: for example, pan-fried monkfish with steamed lemon sole; skinless, hake-like torsk and lightly seared salmon fillets (with aubergine 'caviar'); or 'extraordinarily fresh' hake and barely cooked yet tender squid, served with a chorizo cassoulet in a little pastry case, with butter-bean and yellow pepper sauce.

Scallops are hand-dived, of course, vegetables organic, and lamb is from North Ronaldsay, perhaps fashioned into a chunky yet tender terrine and served with rhubarb chutney. Dishes look good without being fussy, and puddings have included an intense lemon tart with marmalade ice cream, and a pleasingly varied trio of rhubarb desserts: a gently flavoured creamy ice cream, a silky, tasty jelly, and a sophisticated, light, tartlet-style crumble. 'Irresistible' beremeal bannocks are made in-house, and the pocket-sized wine list is good value, with house wines £12.50 and £12.90.

CHEF: Alan Craigie PROPRIETORS: Alan and Joyce Craigie OPEN: all week D only 7 to 9 CLOSED: mid-Oct to end Mar MEALS: alc (main courses £16.50 to £18.50) SERVICE: not inc, card slips closed CARDS: Switch, Visa DETAILS: 40 seats. Private parties: 40 main room, 10 to 14 private rooms. Car park. Children's helpings. No smoking. Wheelchair access (also WC). No music ACCOMMODATION: 3 rooms, all with bath/shower. TV. B&B £45 to £80 (*The Which? Guide to Good Hotels*)

NEW CHEF *is shown instead of a cooking mark where a change of chef occurred too late for a new assessment of the cooking.*

Seafood Restaurant ✣

16 West End, St Monans KY10 2BX
TEL: (01333) 730327   FAX: (01333) 730508   COOKING 5
EMAIL: info@theseafoodrestaurant.com   SEAFOOD
WEBSITE: www.theseafoodrestaurant.com   £33–£59

The setting is spectacular, with fine views over the harbour and across the Firth
of Forth, while the dining room is given an arty touch with Charles Rennie
Mackintosh-style chairs. A second branch opened in St Andrews (tel (01334)
479475) as the Guide went to press, and we hope standards can be maintained
here. Modern seafood cookery with influences from home and abroad is the
name of the game, and the restaurant tells us that the kitchen refuses to use
frozen fish and that most of their supplies come from smaller inshore boats.

Start simply with half a dozen Kilbrandon oysters (they reckon theirs are the
best oysters in Scotland), or something more exotic such as peppered tuna
carpaccio with hoi sin, a dish that at inspection had a light texture but good
depth of flavour; follow perhaps with 'succulent' baked salmon on Savoy
cabbage with pine nuts and sultanas, or roasted cod on mash with bacon and
sauce vierge, or perhaps hake in a light Sauternes sauce. To finish, there might be
pannacotta with tart mango coulis, lemon tart 'with fine pastry' and orange
yoghurt sorbet, or cheeses with oatcakes. Wines are chosen to partner seafood
and represent a fairly wide spectrum of styles and prices, with France
dominating the list. Ten house wines, most of which are also available by the
glass, are priced from £12.

CHEF: Craig Millar   PROPRIETOR: Roybridge Ltd   OPEN: all week 12 (12.30 Sun) to 2.30 (3 Sun),
6.30 to 9.30   MEALS: Set L £16 (2 courses) to £20, Set D £25 (2 courses) to £35   SERVICE: not inc,
card slips closed   CARDS: Amex, Delta, MasterCard, Switch, Visa   DETAILS: 44 seats. 32 seats
outside. Private parties: 50 main room. Car park. Children's helpings. No smoking in 1 dining
room. Wheelchair access (also WC). No music. No mobile phones

▲ Old Pines ♟ ✣

Spean Bridge, by Fort William PH34 4EG
TEL: (01397) 712324   FAX: (01397) 712433
EMAIL: goodfood@oldpines.co.uk
WEBSITE: www.oldpines.co.uk
on A82 1m N of Spean Bridge at Commando   COOKING 4
Memorial take B8004 signposted Gairlochy; Old   MODERN SCOTTISH
Pines 300 metres on right   £41–£49

Just outside the village in 30 acres of wooded grounds, Old Pines enjoys views
across the Great Glen and Glen Spean towards Aonach Mor and Ben Nevis. It is
the family home of Bill and Sukie Barber, and accordingly has a warm, informal
family atmosphere. The Barbers are industrious producers of everything from
smoked fish to ice cream, and what they don't make or grow themselves comes
from first-rate suppliers. No choice is offered on the five-course dinner menus

and meals always start with a soup, perhaps a broth of mussels, fennel and leeks. Then comes fish: Isle of Muck langoustine with home-smoked mackerel pâté, for example. Main courses can be quite elaborate, with complex flavour combinations: roast venison fillet with spiced red cabbage and a wild mushroom and thyme sauce, accompanied by potatoes in cream, garlic and nutmeg, or duck breast with fried parsnips and a Seville orange, garlic and coriander sauce, mash and cauliflower in whole-grain mustard sauce. Brown sugar meringue with gooseberries, elderflower ice cream and a gooseberry and elderflower sauce is a typical dessert creation, and meals end with a selection of Scottish farmhouse cheeses and oatcakes. Wines, arranged by grape variety, are excellent value. Josmeyer in Alsace and New Zealanders Jackson Estate and Palliser, all with several bottles on the list, are worth looking out for. The selection of wines by the glass, usually six, varies from night to night, starting at £2.50.

CHEF: Sukie Barber   PROPRIETORS: Bill and Sukie Barber   OPEN: Tue to Sat D only 8 (1 sitting) (residents only Sun D)   CLOSED: 2 weeks Nov to Dec, 3 days Christmas   MEALS: Set D £26.50 to £32. Light L menu available Tue to Sun   SERVICE: not inc, card slips closed   CARDS: MasterCard, Switch, Visa   DETAILS: 24 seats. 8 seats outside. Private parties: 30 main room. Car park. Children's helpings. No smoking. Wheelchair access (also WC). No music ACCOMMODATION: 8 rooms, all with bath/shower. D,B&B £80 to £180. Rooms for disabled. Baby facilities (*The Which? Guide to Good Hotels*) (£5)

STRATHYRE Stirling   map 11

▲ Creagan House ✸

Strathyre FK18 8ND
TEL: (01877) 384638   FAX: (01877) 384319   COOKING 4
EMAIL: eatandstay@creaganhouse.co.uk   FRENCH/SCOTTISH
WEBSITE: www.creaganhouse.co.uk   £31–£43

Creagan is a wayside restaurant-with-rooms, and what a way! The A84 north of Callander runs alongside deep lakes and crags, the kind of setting that looks good whatever the weather. Set a little back from the road, the white-painted, seventeenth-century former farmhouse is run with practised efficiency and charm by Cherry Gunn out front, with husband Gordon at the stoves. Proceedings begin with drinks in the bar before guests are seated at around 8 o'clock, though late arrivals can be accommodated. His dinner menus are built around impeccable Scottish produce, such as scallops caught off Skye and presented on puff pastry with a shellfish sauce; saddle of venison served with juniper sauce accompanied by more of the meat and orange in a ragoût, or, of course, Aberdeen Angus, which comes as a steak 'served in your favourite way'. A selection of four imaginatively presented vegetables arrives with main courses. Meals end in fine style either with sophisticated desserts, such as a rhubarb crumble cake with ginger crème anglaise, or a plate of Scottish cheeses. It is all served with 'grace and humour' and the ready dispensing of wine advice if required. The house selections open at £9.90 on a list that does France thoroughly, before embarking on a whistle-stop tour of the other major producers.

CHEF: Gordon Gunn PROPRIETORS: Gordon and Cherry Gunn OPEN: all week D only 7.30 for 8 (1 sitting) CLOSED: 1 week Oct, 25 Jan to 5 Mar MEALS: Set D £21.50 to £25.75 SERVICE: not inc, card slips closed CARDS: Amex, MasterCard, Visa DETAILS: 14 seats. Private parties: 35 main room. Car park. Children's helpings. No children under 10. No smoking. Wheelchair access (not WC). No music. No mobile phones ACCOMMODATION: 5 rooms, all with bath/shower. B&B £57.50 to £95. Rooms for disabled. Baby facilities (£5)

STRONTIAN Highland

map 11

▲ Kilcamb Lodge 🍷 ⚡

Strontian PH36 4HY

TEL: (01967) 402257 FAX: (01967) 402041

EMAIL: enquiries@kilcamblodge.com

WEBSITE: www.kilcamblodge.com

on A861, near head of Loch Sunart

COOKING 4

SCOTTISH-FRENCH

£46–£55

Set in 20 acres of woodland, with a private shoreline on Loch Sunart and the Strontian river, Kilcamb Lodge is a grand stone-built country house with an impressive history that includes a stint as barracks for the Argyll militia during the 1745 uprising. Nowadays, it is a well-appointed hotel, run by Ian and Jenny Grant, who are reported to be 'courteous, efficient and friendly' hosts.

Their chef, Neil Mellis, provides four-course dinners with a markedly Scottish flavour, thanks to the use of mainly regional produce. Menus limit choice to a couple of options per course, starting perhaps with confit duck leg with orange and a spinach and Parma ham salad, or warm crab beignets with a mussel and cucumber casserole and salsa verde. Next comes soup or a salad, then main courses of chargrilled Aberdeen Angus fillet with mushroom and leek duxelles, turnip purée and a red wine jus, or maybe fillets of Mallaig monkfish wrapped in peppers and courgettes with spring onion mash and lemon butter sauce. Finish with a selection of Scottish cheeses and oatcakes, or tarte Tatin with vanilla ice cream. The chattily informative wine list offers good value on an international selection arranged by grape variety. Prices start at £10.50, with lots of options under £20, and eight by the glass are £3.50 to £4.75.

CHEF: Neil Mellis PROPRIETORS: Ian and Jenny Grant OPEN: all week D only 7.30 (1 sitting) MEALS: Set D £25 (2 courses) to £35. Bar L available SERVICE: not inc, card slips closed CARDS: MasterCard, Switch, Visa DETAILS: 25 seats. 10 seats outside. Private parties: 45 main room. Car park. No children under 12. No smoking. No music. No mobile phones ACCOMMODATION: 11 rooms, all with bath/shower. TV. Phone. B&B £70 to £155. Baby facilities. Fishing (*The Which? Guide to Good Hotels*)

Several sharp operators have tried to extort money from restaurateurs on the promise of an entry in a guidebook that has never appeared. The Good Food Guide *makes no charge for inclusion.*

If a restaurant is new to the Guide this year (did not appear as a main entry in the last edition), NEW ENTRY *appears opposite its name.*

▲ Wheatsheaf ⅝✳

Main Street, Swinton TD11 3JJ
TEL: (01890) 860257   FAX: (01890) 860688
EMAIL: reception@wheatsheaf-swinton.co.uk   COOKING 3
WEBSITE: www.wheatsheaf-swinton.co.uk   MODERN SCOTTISH
on A6112, 6m N of Coldstream   £24–£53

After 17 years, Alan and Julie Reid have left their restaurant-with-rooms
opposite the village green to set up a consultancy business. New owners Chris
and Jan Wilson took over just as the Guide was going to press, but have told us
that no major changes are planned; John Keir remains in the kitchen to ensure
continuity, along with other staff.

Menus, as before, are likely to be in a modern, rustic style led by the good-
quality produce that comes from local suppliers. Plenty of choice is offered –
around eight options per course – with starters ranging from grilled langoustines
in garlic butter to breast of wood pigeon with black pudding in Madeira sauce.
Main courses are similarly varied, taking in basil- and Parmesan-crusted baked
haddock, Serrano ham-wrapped chicken breast stuffed with duxelles and
served with tarragon cream sauce, and roast venison loin in sloe gin and juniper
sauce. To finish, there might be sticky ginger and pear pudding with vanilla
cream sauce. Six house wines at £11.75 a bottle, £2.85 a glass, open a good-value
list.

CHEF: John Keir   PROPRIETORS: Chris and Jan Wilson   OPEN: Tue to Sun L 12 to 2.15, Tue to Sat
D (also Sun in summer) 6.30 to 9.30   CLOSED: 25 and 26 Dec, 3 weeks Jan, 1 week July   MEALS:
alc (main courses L £5 to £12, D £12 to £18). Light L menu available   SERVICE: not inc, card slips
closed   CARDS: Delta, MasterCard, Switch, Visa   DETAILS: 45 seats. 16 seats outside. Private
parties: 26 main room, 12 to 18 private rooms. Car park. Vegetarian meals. Children's helpings.
No smoking. No music   ACCOMMODATION: 7 rooms, all with bath/shower. TV. Phone. B&B £58 to
£110. Baby facilities (The Which? Guide to Good Hotels)

▲ Lochgreen House ♟ ⅝✳

Monktonhill Road, Southwood, Troon KA10 7EN
TEL: (01292) 313343   FAX: (01292) 318861   COOKING 5
EMAIL: lochgreen@costleyhotels.co.uk   FRANCO-SCOTTISH
WEBSITE: www.costleyhotels.co.uk   £30–£52

Lochgreen House is part of the Costley Hotels group, which, fortunately, is not a
reflection of the price of dinner but actually the name of the owners and chef.
However, it certainly looks a well-heeled place, being a grand Edwardian
mansion set majestically at the end of a sweeping driveway in 30 acres of
grounds.

Andrew Costley's cooking lives up to the grandeur of the setting and features
plenty of bright ideas, some traditional, others more modern and innovative.
Four-course dinners might open with fillet of sea bream on couscous with
roasted cashew nuts, crapaudine of quail with Roquefort and walnut salad, or
maybe smoked salmon with Caesar salad and a red onion chutney. Next, there's

a choice of soup or sorbet – maybe cream of cauliflower versus cassis with champagne – while main course choices typically range from marinated lamb with aubergine caviar, crushed potatoes and provençale vegetables to curried cod with caramelised onion and coriander mash, via medallion of beef with pearl barley risotto, caramelised parsnips and red wine. To finish, lemon and ginger tart with coconut ice cream is an interesting update of a classic idea, as is hot chocolate pudding with malted Baileys ice cream. A solid wine list places the emphasis on France but patiently stacks up good bottles all around the world, with rare stars like Alphonse Mellot's Sancerre Cuvée Edmond (£55.95) adding an occasional burst of brilliance. Nine house wines range from £14.50 to £19.95 and come by the glass from £3.50.

CHEF: Andrew Costley   PROPRIETOR: Costley and Costley Hoteliers Ltd   OPEN: Sun L 12 to 2.15, all week D 7 to 9.30   MEALS: alc L (main courses £7.50 to £12). Set L Sun £19.95, Set D £32.50   SERVICE: not inc, card slips closed   CARDS: Amex, Delta, MasterCard, Switch, Visa   DETAILS: 120 seats. 50 seats outside. Private parties: 120 main room, 12 to 80 private rooms. Car park. Vegetarian meals. No smoking . Wheelchair access (also WC). Music. No mobile phones. Air-conditioned   ACCOMMODATION: 40 rooms 15 with bath/shower. TV. Phone. B&B £85 to £70. Rooms for disabled. Baby facilities (*The Guide to Good Hotels*)

MacCallums' Oyster Bar

The Harbour, Troon KA10 6DH
TEL: (01292) 319339
WEBSITE: www.maccallums.co.uk

COOKING **3**
SEAFOOD
£26–£48

Down by Troon harbour, where the fishing boats tie up (don't head for the marina), the MacCallums' seafood restaurant is housed in a sympathetically refurbished building that has an appealingly informal but businesslike air. The business, of course, is the freshest of fresh fish and crustaceans, delivered daily and cooked with simplicity and skill. There is usually one meat dish as a concession to those dragged along by fish-eating friends (chicken brochettes, perhaps, or roast duck breast with Arran mustard sauce), but the menu focuses firmly on the likes of oysters (of course), whole grilled sardines with tapenade, steamed mussels in garlic cream and Chardonnay, and gloriously under-adorned main courses such as simple grilled white fish with parsley butter. Note that vegetables are extra. Those seeking greater complexity may find their wishes answered by black bream with shellfish risotto and herb dressing, or chargrilled shark with polenta and sweet peppers, and everyone finishes with something like lemon and vanilla parfait with wild berry coulis. Wines are, naturally, mostly white; they are also mostly under £20, starting at £10.50 for the house selections.

CHEFS: Scott Keenan and Stephen Smith   PROPRIETORS: John and James MacCallum   OPEN: Tue to Sun L 12 to 2.30 (3.30 Sun), Tue to Sat D 7 to 9.30   MEALS: alc (main courses £8 to £14.50)   SERVICE: not inc, card slips closed   CARDS: Delta, MasterCard, Switch, Visa   DETAILS: 43 seats. Private parties: 43 main room. Car park. No-smoking area. Wheelchair access (not WC). Music

Wales

▲ Harbourmaster Hotel 🍴 £ | NEW ENTRY |

The Quay, Aberaeron SA46 0BA
TEL: (01545) 570755   FAX: (01545) 570762   COOKING 2
EMAIL: info@harbour-master.com   MODERN WELSH
WEBSITE: www.harbour-master.com   £23–£51

The Heulyns' refurbishment of this Grade II listed building brings a striking cobalt blue to Aberaeron's multi-coloured Georgian quayside, and the smart, cool bar (with a relaxing fire in winter) and tongue-and-groove panelled dining room an informal note. The ambitious kitchen majors on seafood, for the most part skilfully handled: for example, a starter of two juicy king scallops in crisp tempura batter served on a slice of good black pudding with fresh leaves and a sweet mango purée, followed by well-presented grilled seabass with Cardigan Bay lobster and smoked salmon risotto. Non-fish eaters have endorsed pan-fried duck breast with a mustard and honey glaze, and well-timed chargrilled fillet steak. Effort goes into sourcing fine ingredients – from Pembrokeshire potatoes to Welsh Black beef and local cheeses. Well-flavoured breads, moist risotto, fine potato mash and good vegetables have received the thumbs-up, and to finish there might be caramelised nectarine and lemon tart, or Celtic cheese platter with fruit, oatcakes and red onion marmalade. Wines are picked with flair and sold at very friendly prices, from £10.50. Ten by the glass are £2.50 to £4.50.

CHEF: Geraint Morgan   PROPRIETORS: Glyn and Menna Heulyn   OPEN: Tue to Sun L 12 to 2, Mon to Sat D 6.30 to 8.45   CLOSED: 24 Dec to 16 Jan   MEALS: alc (main courses £7.50 to £16.50)   SERVICE: not inc, card slips closed   CARDS: Delta, MasterCard, Switch, Visa   DETAILS: 40 seats. Vegetarian meals. No smoking. Wheelchair access (also WC). Music   ACCOMMODATION: 7 rooms, all with bath/shower. TV. Phone. B&B £45 to £105. No children under 5 (*The Which? Guide to Good Hotels*)

'So rock hard was the pasta that I could insert a fork in the middle and lift the [entire] pile entirely off the plate in a single lump. On demonstrating this feat, the restaurant manager looked sheepish and apologised, though the waiter didn't seem to see what the problem was. I did not venture on to dessert, though perhaps I should have since I have never sent all three courses of a meal back before, and on the basis of the first two courses I had a good chance of getting this prize.' (On eating in London)

▲ Penhelig Arms Hotel ▌ ✸

Terrace Road, Aberdovey LL35 0LT
TEL: (01654) 767215   FAX: (01654) 767690
EMAIL: info@penheligarms.com
WEBSITE: www.penheligarms.com   COOKING 2
on A493 Tywyn to Machynlleth road, opposite   BRITISH
Penhelig station   £25–£56

This seaside inn overlooking the Dovey estuary is praised by reporters for its consistency and as a 'reliable place for quality food and wine'. Proprietor Robert Hughes, though, says that they have sought to 'lighten' the food recently – apparent in a salad of smoked chicken and avocado with a fresh lime vinaigrette, or in main-course chargrilled tuna with roast peppers and rouille. But for 'damn-the-doctors' eaters, or those blessed with a whippet's metabolism, there's still sirloin steak with béarnaise, swordfish with hollandaise, and roast cod fillet with anchovy and garlic mayonnaise. Puddings range from white chocolate cheesecake through stalwarts like bread-and-butter pudding, to pineapple in Kirsch. The wine list – a passionately chosen range with real depth in all regions and a broad selection available by the glass – deserves not just our 'bottle' award but also a halo for offering outstanding value for money. Other restaurants please take note. Seventeen house wines range from £10 to £13.40.

CHEF: Jane Howkins   PROPRIETORS: Robert and Sally Hughes   OPEN: all week 12 to 2, 7 to 9.30
CLOSED: 25 and 26 Dec   MEALS: alc (main courses £9 to £12.50). Set L Sun £12.50 (2 courses),
Set D £25   SERVICE: not inc, card slips closed   CARDS: Delta, MasterCard, Switch, Visa
DETAILS: 36 seats. Private parties: 24 main room. Car park. Children's helpings. No smoking. No
music. Air-conditioned   ACCOMMODATION: 14 rooms, all with bath/shower. TV. Phone. B&B £35
to £90 (The Which? Guide to Good Hotels)

▲ Porth Tocyn Hotel ✸

Bwlch Tocyn, Abersoch LL53 7BU
TEL: (01758) 713303   FAX: (01758) 713538
EMAIL: porthtocyn.hotel@virgin.net
WEBSITE: www.porth-tocyn-hotel.co.uk   COOKING 4
on minor road 2m S of Abersoch through hamlets   MODERN EUROPEAN
of Sarn Bach and Bwlch Tocyn   £45–£54

The Fletcher-Brewers preside genially over their legacy of a row of former lead-miners' cottages converted into a hotel with magnificent views over Cardigan Bay and Snowdonia. An understanding, family-centred approach shows in the child-friendliness of staff, proprietors and even menus, and in imaginative sensitivity to the needs of children and parents alike. Concern for guests' physical and mental comfort is matched by an unfussy approach in the kitchen. Ingredients, many sourced locally, are handled skilfully, and marriages like mussel and white wine chowder with herb rouille, or a main course of Welsh lamb, garlic and thyme rösti and port jus with caramelised shallots, make the most of them. The cuisine is mostly rooted in British tradition (including savouries like devils on horseback offered alongside the puddings and before cheese) and familiar French cooking with tentative Italianate touches (poached plaice filled with spinach and saffron risotto and with a languoustine and brandy beurre blanc and poached crab ravioli, for example). Puddings may include pavlovas, port and claret jelly, or raspberry Athollbrose. The wine list puts a foot down in France and then takes a brisk trot around the world, offering many decent bottles below £20; six house wines start at £12.50. Note the restaurant is closed winters.

CHEFS: David Carney and Louise Fletcher-Brewer PROPRIETORS: the Fletcher-Brewer family OPEN: Sun L 12.15 to 1.55, all week D 7.15 to 9 (9.30 in 'peak season') CLOSED: mid-Nov to mid-Mar MEALS: Buffet L Sun £19.50, Set D £28.50 (2 courses) to £35. Bar L menu available Mon to Sat SERVICE: not inc, card slips closed CARDS: MasterCard, Switch, Visa DETAILS: 50 seats. 40 seats outside. Private parties: 40 main room, 15 private room. Car park. Vegetarian meals. Children's helpings. No children under 7 at D. No smoking. Wheelchair access (not WC). No music. No mobile phones ACCOMMODATION: 17 rooms, all with bath/shower. TV. Phone. B&B £58.50 to £143. Rooms for disabled. Baby facilities. Swimming pool (*The Which? Guide to Good Hotels*)

BASSALEG Newport map 4

Junction 28 ▼

Station Approach, Bassaleg NP10 8LD
TEL: (01633) 891891 FAX: (01633) 895978
from M4 junction 28 take A468 towards   COOKING 2
Caerphilly, turn right at Tredegar Arms and take   MODERN BRITISH
first left   £19–£47

One reporter rapped our knuckles – this bustling restaurant overlooks the Ebbw not the Usk as suggested in last year's Guide – then endorsed the food enthusiastically. The place is a medley of bamboo chairs, oriental statuary, palm trees, and classic and modern prints. The cooking offers 'homely dishes with a twist', including home-baked bread and local produce from cockles to venison. An inspection first course of light puff pastry with mushroom, smoked salmon and poached egg, and a main of calf's liver with smoked bacon parcel of black pudding and apple, were both well received. A chocolate marquise, and accompanying coffee sauce, was exactly right. Three enjoyable house wines (£10.95 to £2.50 a glass) set the tone for a short global list that unpretentiously offers good quality at fair prices, including a baker's dozen of half-bottles. The occasional star name adds a touch of glamour and better bottles are appropriately mature.

CHEF: Jon West PROPRIETORS: Richard Wallace and Jon West OPEN: all week L 12 to 2 (4 Sun), Mon to Sat D 5.30 to 9.30 MEALS: alc exc Sun (main courses £8 to £16). Set L £6.95 (1 course) to £10.45, Set L Sun £10.95 (2 courses) to £12.95, Set D Mon to Sat 5.30 to 7 £12.95, Set D £15.95 SERVICE: not inc, card slips closed CARDS: Amex, Delta, MasterCard, Switch, Visa DETAILS: 165 seats. Private parties: 60 main room. Car park. Vegetarian meals. No cigars/pipes. Wheelchair access (also WC). Music. Air-conditioned

All entries in the Guide are re-researched and rewritten every year, not least because restaurant standards fluctuate. Don't rely on an out-of-date Guide.

BEAUMARIS Isle of Anglesey   map 7

▲ Ye Olde Bulls Head ♥ ✸

Castle Street, Beaumaris LL58 8AP
TEL: (01248) 810329   FAX: (01248) 811294   COOKING **4**
EMAIL: info@bullsheadinn.co.uk   MODERN EUROPEAN
WEBSITE: www.bullsheadinn.co.uk   £43–£52

Originally built in the fifteenth century (and rebuilt in the seventeenth), Ye Olde
Bulls Head was the base for one of Oliver Cromwell's generals while his men
were laying siege to the nearby castle of Edward I. Despite its history, the place
is not set in aspic; indeed, it is 'bustling with life'. On the ground floor is a bar,
with old wooden beams and a fireplace, and a brasserie, while upstairs houses
the comfortable and stylish formal dining room. The two restaurants have
separate menus and different chefs. Upstairs, where tables are set with white
cloths and flowers, the menu shows influences from across Europe, as in an
escabèche of red mullet with cider and orange, and main courses of pan-fried
Hereford duck breast with borlotti beans, garlic and morels, or asparagus and
wild garlic flan with pine kernels. The emphasis is on allowing natural flavours
to shine through, enhanced by some clever combinations of ingredients. It is a
well-polished operation, with friendly, efficient service. The perky brasserie
drinks list offers two dozen wines at bargain prices, with ten by the glass from
£2.50. That pricing policy continues pretty much unabated on a delightful
restaurant list that targets France first and foremost but insists on excellence in
all regions. House wines – two French, two New World – are £14.25, or £3.75 a
glass.

CHEF: Ernst Van Halderen   PROPRIETOR: Rothwell and Robertson Ltd   OPEN: Mon to Sat D only 7
to 9.30   CLOSED: 25 and 26 Dec, 1 Jan   MEALS: Set D £30. Brasserie menu available all week 12
to 2, 6 to 9   SERVICE: not inc   CARDS: Amex, Delta, MasterCard, Switch, Visa   DETAILS: 45 seats.
Private parties: 25 main room, 6 to 15 private rooms. Car park. Vegetarian meals. No children
under 7 in dining room. No smoking. No music. No mobile phones   ACCOMMODATION: 13 rooms,
all with bath/shower. TV. Phone. B&B £65 to £120. Baby facilities (*The Which? Guide to Good
Hotels*)

BROAD HAVEN Pembrokeshire   map 4

▲ Druidstone ✸ £

Druidston Haven, Broad Haven SA62 3NE
TEL: (01437) 781221   FAX: (01437) 781133
EMAIL: jane@druidstone.co.uk
WEBSITE: www.druidstone.co.uk
6m W of Haverfordwest, from B4341 at Broad   COOKING **2**
Haven, turn right at sea; after 1½m turn left to   GLOBAL
Druidston Haven; hotel ¾m on left   £22–£41

Druidstone, a large stone cliff-top house with numerous converted out-
buildings, is one of the Guide's older entries, and one of the more individual – it
now has a room entirely powered by renewable energy. The dining room is laid
out for the exact number of diners, with dark green tablecloths and fresh
wildflowers, while the menu avoids florid descriptions and simply tells you

what you get on your plate. That might be king prawns with garlic mayonnaise, or a sweet potato and aubergine curry, or new season's lamb chops with red onion marmalade. Desserts strike a retro note with profiteroles and butterscotch sauce, say, or apple pie, or 'Druimisù' (the house take on tiramisù). And house wines, from a reasonably priced list, start at a refreshingly retro £7.50. The child – and environmental – friendliness of this operation bodes well for the future of the hospitality industry, of Wales, and of the planet.

CHEFS: Rod, Jane and Angus Bell and Jon Woodhouse   PROPRIETORS: Rod, Jane and Angus Bell
OPEN: Sun L 12.30 to 2, Mon to Sat D 7.30 to 9.30   MEALS: alc (main courses £9 to £16). Bar menu available   SERVICE: not inc, card slips closed   CARDS: Amex, Delta, MasterCard, Switch, Visa
DETAILS: 36 seats. 20 seats outside. Private parties: 36 main room, 6 to 12 private rooms. Car park. Vegetarian meals. Children's helpings. No smoking. Wheelchair access (also WC). No music   ACCOMMODATION: 11 rooms, 5 with bath/shower. B&B £35 to £116. Baby facilities

---

CAPEL GARMON Conwy   map 7

▲ Tan-y-Foel ⁙

Capel Garmon, Betws-y-Coed LL26 0RE
TEL: (01690) 710507   FAX: (01690) 710681
EMAIL: enquiries@tyfhotel.co.uk
WEBSITE: www.tyfhotel.co.uk

take turning marked Capel Garmon and Nebo   COOKING 5
from A470 about halfway between Betws-y-   MODERN BRITISH-PLUS
Coed and Llanrwst   £49–£57

The location is little short of 'fantastic': set up a narrow lane with the Conwy Valley and Llanrwst laid out all around, as well as the great mountainous spectre of Snowdonia. It may look like an old stone-built house from outside, but inside the smart and uncompromisingly modern décor is evident in the tasteful shades of brown, with hessian-covered walls in the lounge, in the simple but striking wooden wall sculpture in the dining room, and in the TYF logo seemingly written by a Japanese calligrapher.

Like everything else, the food has an air of confidence about it – 'bold and ambitious', one reporter called it – and it certainly revels in a wide variety of ingredients and flavours. Roast tilapia comes on a basil and chèvre couscous, and duck magret is given a salsa of leek, cumin, paprika, coriander and mint. But there are more homely items, too, such as a lightly peppery sausage incorporating corn-fed chicken, wild rabbit, and locally made faggot, set against a background of butter-bean purée. Presentation is as elegant as the surroundings. Choice extends to only a couple of items per course, but that suits the scale of the enterprise. Desserts might offer a red fruit terrine with spiced fruit tea and lime froth, or a light-textured yet eggy and rich-tasting panettone bread-and-butter pudding. Service is graceful, calm and unrushed, and the wine list is an appealing and fairly priced collection from around the world, starting with eight house selections from £15 to £18.

CHEF: Janet Pitman   PROPRIETORS: Mr and Mrs P.K. Pitman   OPEN: all week D only 7.30 to 8.15; booking essential   CLOSED: Dec, limited opening Jan   MEALS: Set D £33   SERVICE: not inc
CARDS: Delta, MasterCard, Switch, Visa   DETAILS: 12 seats. No children under 7. No smoking. No music   ACCOMMODATION: 6 rooms, all with bath/shower. TV. Phone. D,B&B £100 to £195. No children under 7 (*The Which? Guide to Good Hotels*)

CARDIFF Cardiff   map 4

Armless Dragon ✸ £

97 Wyeverne Road, Cathays, Cardiff CF24 4BG   COOKING 1
TEL: (029) 2038 2357   FAX: (029) 2038 2055   MODERN WELSH
WEBSITE: www.thearmlessdragon.co.uk   £17–£47

Unpretentious outside and sparsely adorned inside, the Armless Dragon has an unassuming appeal, enhanced by friendly service, crisp white tablecloths and discreet lighting. Modern Welsh cuisine, which seeks to support local suppliers, is highlighted in house specialities such as laver balls with ginger pickled vegetables or a main-course cannon of Brecon lamb with a faggot, spring cabbage, red lentil purée and rosemary oil. Other culinary influences show in braised belly pork flavoured with Chinese spices, or sea bream with a prawn and sweet chilli sauce. Winter desserts have encompassed warm boozy fruits with bara brith ice cream, and sharp lemon tart with clotted cream. A substantial and global wine list includes a couple of Welsh whites, and house 'wines for every day' begin at £8.90; generally prices fall below £20, many considerably below.

CHEF: Paul Lane   PROPRIETORS: Paul and Martine Lane   OPEN: Tue to Fri L 12 to 2, Tue to Sat D 7 to 9 (9.30 Fri and Sat)   MEALS: alc (main courses £10 to £16.50). Set L £8 (2 courses) to £10 SERVICE: not inc, card slips closed   CARDS: Delta, MasterCard, Switch, Visa   DETAILS: 45 seats. Private parties: 45 main room. Vegetarian meals. Children's helpings. No smoking. Wheelchair access (not WC). Music £5

Da Castaldo
NEW ENTRY

5 Romilly Crescent, Canton, Cardiff CF11 9NP   COOKING 2
TEL: (029) 2022 1905   FAX: (029) 2022 1920   MODERN ITALIAN
WEBSITE: www.dacastaldo.com   £22–£50

Terracotta walls and cherry-wood floors create the warmly relaxed, stylish setting for Antonio Castaldo's twenty-first-century Italian food – a 'stunning salad of prawns, bergamot and caramelised lime' and a carpaccio of beef with thinly sliced mushroom and Parmesan shavings laced with lemon juice and truffle oil, to give just a taster. The response to a request to change an advertised dish – it had a sauce similar to that of a first course – resulted in a tangy lemon and butter wine sauce with the pan-fried halibut, a combination which impressed as much as one comprising fillet of beef medallions in a green peppercorn, wild mushroom and brandy sauce. Desserts tend to be more conservative: tiramisù, or vanilla pannacotta with raspberries and redcurrants for example. Attention to detail includes excellent bread, fine cappuccino and convivially efficient service. The range of Italian wines is good and affordable, while France aspires to something grander, and the rest of the world is mostly ignored. Five house wines start at £10.95, or £2.50 a glass.

CHEF: Antonio Castaldo   PROPRIETORS: Antonio and Cheryl Castaldo   OPEN: Tue to Sat 12 to 2, 7 to 10 (10.30 Sat)   CLOSED: 25 Dec, 3 weeks Aug, bank hols   MEALS: alc (main courses £8 to £15). Set L £9.95 (2 courses) to £12.50   SERVICE: not inc   CARDS: Delta, MasterCard, Switch, Visa   DETAILS: 45 seats. Private parties: 45 main room. Vegetarian meals. Music. Air-conditioned £5

Da Venditto

7–8 Park Place, Cardiff CF10 3DP
TEL: (029) 2023 0781   FAX: (029) 2039 9949
EMAIL: sherry@vendittogroup.co.uk
WEBSITE: www.vendittogroup.co.uk

COOKING **4**
MODERN ITALIAN
£31–£66

Thanks to its large window and mirrors, its wooden floor and stainless steel, Da Venditto is spacious and well lit, with a light, modern feel to it. The cooking is quite bright and contemporary too, with a carte that might feature a velouté of cannellini beans and foie gras, or bruschetta with salt-cod, cherry tomatoes and rocket. 'Well-presented' food with some 'innovative ingredients' is how one visitor saw it.

Risotto is something of a speciality, either as an accompaniment (to baked cod for one reporter), or as a dish in its own right, with spring onion and saffron. Otherwise the menu might devote as much space to game as to more conventional lamb and beef: venison loin with red cabbage, perhaps, or partridge with Savoy cabbage and braised lentils. Seafood dishes, meanwhile, take in casserole of assorted fish and shellfish spiked with chilli and saffron. Wind up with balsamic crème brûlée, or something from their 'extensive collection' of cigars. Knowledgeable staff are pleasant, helpful and attentive, offering detailed explanations in response to queries. The all-Italian (plus champagne) wine list is organised by region, with a good showing of Super-Tuscans as well as a few more affordable wines. House red and white from Campania are £14.50 (£4 a glass).

CHEFS: Mark Freeman and Carl Hammett   PROPRIETOR: Toni Venditto   OPEN: Mon to Sat 12 to 2.30, 6 to 10.45   CLOSED: bank hols   MEALS: Set L £14.50 (2 courses) to £22.50, Set D £27.50 (2 courses) to £37.50   SERVICE: not inc   CARDS: Amex, Delta, MasterCard, Switch, Visa   DETAILS: 55 seats. Private parties: 55 main room. Car park. Vegetarian meals. No-smoking area. Wheelchair access (also WC). Music. No mobile phones. Air-conditioned

Le Gallois £

6–10 Romilly Crescent, Canton, Cardiff CF11 9NR
TEL: (029) 2034 1264   FAX: (029) 2023 7911
EMAIL: info@legallois-ycymro.com
WEBSITE: www.legallois-ycymro.com

COOKING **4**
MODERN FRENCH-PLUS
£27–£75

Le Gallois has an upbeat feel, from the light and bright setting, and from the bustling atmosphere. In the dining area, tables laid with mustard-yellow cloths and blue napkins echo the blue and yellow colour scheme of the walls. As the name suggests, the cooking is fundamentally French, but not of the predictably traditional sort. For instance, a starter of vine tomato tartare 'with its own consommé' is served with a seaweed sorbet. Flavoured oils may feature in several dishes, as in main courses of roast cod, with a fricassee of cockles, mussels and clams with fennel cream, enlivened with curry oil, or saddle of venison, with fondant potato, cauliflower purée, honey-roast parsnips and claret sauce, with chocolate oil. Such inventiveness has won chef Padrig Jones plaudits: 'outstanding' pot-roast pork and 'sublime' caramel pudding, while another endorsed the 'innovative' cooking and the quality of ingredients. Although not everyone has been happy with the wait at the bar, service otherwise has been described as 'attentive without ever being fussy'. Wines are mostly French, starting at £13.50, with ten by the glass from £2.50.

CHEF: Padrig Jones   PROPRIETORS: the Jones and Dupuy families   OPEN: Tue to Sat 12 to 2.30, 6.30 to 10.30   CLOSED: 1 week Christmas/New Year, 2 weeks Aug   MEALS: Set L £12.95 (2 courses) to £15.95, Set D £27 (2 courses) to £37   SERVICE: not inc, 10% for parties of 6 or more, card slips closed   CARDS: Amex, Delta, MasterCard, Switch, Visa   DETAILS: 60 seats. Private parties: 60 main room. Car park. Vegetarian meals. Children's helpings. No cigars/pipes. No-smoking area available. Wheelchair access (also WC). Occasional music. Air-conditioned

Izakaya Japanese Tavern 🍴 £

Mermaid Quay, Cardiff Bay, Cardiff CF10 5BW

TEL/FAX: (029) 2049 2939

EMAIL: ayakazi@aol.com

WEBSITE: www.izakaya-japanese-tavern.com

COOKING 4
JAPANESE
£20–£47

In the middle of Mermaid Quay looking over Cardiff Bay, this traditional Japanese tavern aims to produce the kind of cheerily informal, everyday eating out the Japanese themselves love. Bamboo screens, paper lanterns and plenty of illuminated signs create the right atmosphere in which to order a selection of appetisers, take your time, and order a little more as and when you feel like it.

The good things could well begin with salted edamame soy beans in their pods, served with sharply piquant kimuchi pickles – 'excellent savoury nibbles and very moreish' – and then go on to richly spicy miso soup with ramen egg noodles. The second part of hotate bata at least should be self-explanatory: it denotes the butter in which a single fresh, meaty scallop is cooked, along with some saké. Full-flavoured, stir-fried noodle dishes such as yaki soba, with pork and vegetables, are satisfying and full of interesting textures, and a chalkboard lists specialities and more unusual dishes, such as kawa shioage (deep-fried, salted chicken skin). Finish with subtly flavoured green tea ice cream or, as a Western concession, 'particularly good' creamy cheesecake. Accompany the food with saké or Japanese beer for the real experience, or there are house French Sauvignon Blanc and Merlot at £9.80.

CHEFS: Yoshiko Evans and Peter Mansbridge   PROPRIETORS: Iestyn and Yoshiko Evans   OPEN: Mon to Sat 12 to 2, 6 to 10.30, Sun 1 to 9.30   MEALS: alc (individual dishes £2 to £13.50). Set L and D £15 to £25   SERVICE: not inc   CARDS: Amex, Delta, Diners, MasterCard, Switch, Visa   DETAILS: 94 seats. 4 seats outside. Private parties: 50 main room, 12 to 30 private rooms. Vegetarian meals. No smoking in 1 dining room. Wheelchair access (also WC). Music

▲ St David's Hotel & Spa, Tides Restaurant 🍴

Havannah Street, Cardiff CF10 5SD

TEL: (029) 2045 4045   FAX: (029) 2031 3075

EMAIL: reservations@thestdavidshotel.com

WEBSITE: www.thestdavidshotel.com

NEW CHEF
MODERN EUROPEAN
£37–£78

Rocco Forte's 'unmistakable' hotel on the edge of Cardiff Bay is a minimalist's dream, with glass and stainless steel aplenty and impressive views across the Bay. Chef Daniel James's menu in the Tides Restaurant is set out on a page with neat sections: Fish and Shellfish sees, for example, turbot, either grilled or poached, with leaf spinach and hollandaise; while flying the Welsh flag under

Roasts and Grills is local Black beef with turmeric crust and red wine jus. Hors d'oeuvres include modern stalwarts like tuna carpaccio, and risotto with summer vegetables. Under the Vegetarian heading are three dishes (there's also a separate vegetarian menu that expands choice further), and Side Orders and Vegetables can raise the final bill. Finish (under Desserts and Savouries) with honey and lemon tart, or local cheeses with walnut bread. Optional service is added at 10 per cent, but the credit card slip is not closed, so commit that to memory. The 20 or so wines under £20 are left in the blocks by the rest of the list; just over a dozen are available by the glass.

CHEF: Daniel James   PROPRIETOR: Rocco Forte Hotels   OPEN: all week 12.30 to 2.15 (2.30 Sun), 6.30 to 10.15   MEALS: alc D (main courses £15.50 to £25). Set L £17.50 (2 courses) to £22.50, Set D £27.50 (2 courses) to £32. Bar menu also available   SERVICE: 10% (optional)   CARDS: Amex, Delta, Diners, MasterCard, Switch, Visa   DETAILS: 100 seats. 24 seats outside. Private parties: 12 to 220 private rooms. Vegetarian meals. Children's helpings. No smoking. Wheelchair access (also WC). Music. Air-conditioned   ACCOMMODATION: 132 rooms, all with bath/shower. TV. Phone. Room only £99 to £200. Rooms for disabled. Baby facilities. Swimming pool

Woods Brasserie

The Pilotage Building, Stuart Street, Cardiff Bay,	COOKING 4
Cardiff CF10 5BW	MODERN EUROPEAN
TEL: (029) 2049 2400 FAX: (029) 2048 1998	£33–£59

Occupying a nineteenth-century stone pilotage building, Woods is a lively brasserie with a convivial ambience and bright, airy décor. Ask for a table in the upstairs dining room if you want to enjoy the view over Cardiff Bay. After ten years at the helm, Martyn and Deborah Peters are no longer running Woods, although standards have been maintained: reporters unanimously praise the 'slick, amiable and competent' service, and still express high opinions of the cooking. The menu focuses on Europe, making forays into the Far East for spiced tuna with sesame marinated salad, or 'tender, lightly spiced' chicken in a sweet soy and sesame reduction. From closer to home, expect confit chicken and foie gras terrine with spiced pear marmalade, or 'refreshing' potato and leek soup with herbs Chantilly, followed perhaps by braised lamb shank with a rich jus and roasted vegetables, or roasted brill with creamed leeks and Madeira jus. Aniseed parfait with sesame and nougatine has been a memorable dessert. The short wine list matches the menu well. Prices start at £12.50, and ten wines come by the glass.

CHEF: Sean Murphy   PROPRIETOR: Choice Produce Ltd   OPEN: Mon to Sat 12 to 2, 7 to 10 CLOSED: 25 and 26 Dec, 1 Jan   MEALS: alc (main courses £10 to £18)   SERVICE: not inc, 10% (optional) for parties of 6 or more   CARDS: Amex, Delta, Diners, MasterCard, Switch, Visa DETAILS: 90 seats. 30 seats outside. Private parties: 60 main room, 30 private room. Vegetarian meals. Children's helpings. Wheelchair access (also WC). Music. Air-conditioned

---

Prices quoted in the Guide are based on information supplied by restaurateurs. The prices quoted at the top of each entry represent a range, from the lowest price of a three-course meal with service and wine to the highest; the latter is inflated by 20 per cent to take account of likely price rises during the year of the Guide.

CLYTHA Monmouthshire

map 2

▲ Clytha Arms ♥ ⁵⁄₊ £

Clytha NP7 9BW
TEL: (01873) 840206   FAX: (01873) 840209
EMAIL: clythaarms@tirlali.co.uk
off B4598, S of A40, 6m SE of Abergavenny

COOKING **3**
MODERN WELSH
£28–£51

This isolated house in wooded country has a country-pub feel, with locals playing darts and good real ales served, though it only became a pub 50 years ago. In the last ten the present owners have established a useful mix of pub snacks and ambitious restaurant dishes along with serious attention to wine. Local suppliers fuel an interestingly eclectic kitchen that produces wild mushroom ragoût, or rabbit and hazelnut terrine with beetroot chutney, followed by brodetto, or perhaps monkfish and scallops with balsamic sauce. A St David's day menu – all laverbread and lamb – confirms the strong Welsh allegiance. The long list of desserts range from Atholl brose to Welsh rarebit, by way of raspberry and Chianti sorbet with meringue. Ambition (in the range) and restraint (in pricing) run through a wine list packed with interesting and affordable drinking as well as top bottles at (mostly) very sensible prices. A tasty modern quintet come by the glass for £2.20 (£11.95 a bottle) and there's a good selection of half-bottles and dessert wines.

CHEFS: Andrew and Sarah Canning   PROPRIETORS: Andrew and Beverley Canning   OPEN: Tue to Sun L 12.30 to 2.15, Tue to Sat D 7 to 9.30   MEALS: alc (main courses £12 to £17.50). Set L and D £15.95 (2 courses) to £17.95. Bar snacks available   SERVICE: not inc, card slips closed   CARDS: Amex, Delta, Diners, MasterCard, Switch, Visa   DETAILS: 60 seats. Private parties: 50 main room, 20 private room. Car park. Vegetarian meals. Children's helpings. No smoking. No music   ACCOMMODATION: 4 rooms, all with bath/shower. TV. B&B £50 to £90 (£5)

COLWYN BAY Conwy

map 7

Café Niçoise

124 Abergele Road, Colwyn Bay LL29 7PS
TEL/FAX: (01492) 531555

COOKING **3**
MODERN EUROPEAN
£25–£45

Although it may not be readily apparent from its modest setting, inside is a friendly, inviting place where white linen and warm terracotta walls set the scene for some good cooking. At inspection fish dishes impressed the most: cod in a Parmesan crust, and halibut in fine condition, both cooked accurately, their respective sauces (butter and chive, and dill and green peppercorn) working well. For meat eaters there might be marinated roast loin of venison with celeriac purée and juniper berry scented jus, or cannon of Welsh lamb served with spiced courgettes. Vegetarians are pampered: first courses might include wild mushroom tagliatelle, or carrot and ginger soup, with Mediterranean vegetable samosas and tomato coulis to follow. Vanilla ice cream ('not to be missed') is made on the premises – as are bread and pasta – and served in a brandy-snap basket with chopped strawberries and raspberries; or choose sticky toffee pudding or crème brûlée. The short wine list has some quality bottles at reasonable prices, and a decent sprinkling of half-bottles. Six house recommendations starting at £9.95 come by the glass for £2.25. New owners took over after our inspection with assurances that they intend to keep changes minimal, and chef Chris Jackson remains to assure continuity. Reports please.

CHEF: Chris Jackson   PROPRIETORS: Colin and Aileen Kershaw   OPEN: Wed to Sun L 12 to 2, Tue to Sat D 7 to 10   CLOSED: Christmas   MEALS: alc (main courses £8 to £15). Set L Wed to Sat and D Tue to Fri £13.95 (2 courses) to £16.95, Set L Sun £12.75 (2 courses) to £15. Light lunch menu also available   SERVICE: not inc, card slips closed   CARDS: Amex, Delta, MasterCard, Switch, Visa   DETAILS: 32 seats. Private parties: 32 main room. Vegetarian meals. Children's helpings. No-smoking area. Music

CRICCIETH Gwynedd   map 7

Tir-a-Môr ♦ ✳ £

1–3 Mona Terrace, Criccieth LL52 0HG   COOKING 4
TEL: (01766) 523084   MODERN WELSH/SEAFOOD
                                                               £29–£46

'Just a short trot down the road to the sea', as one diner put it, Clare and Martin Vowell's corner-shop bistro with its tantalising tastes has long been a highlight of this sleepy North Wales resort. Chunky pine tables and chairs seat a couple of dozen diners, and individual oil lamps provide a discreet glow to enhance the experience of the highly regarded cuisine.

Tir-a-Môr means 'land and sea' and dishes are sourced locally from both. Seven or eight starters and mains on the menu are supplemented by around five more of each on the fish specials blackboards. The latter, reflecting daily and seasonal availability, could include clam chowder or sea trout and asparagus salad, baked lemon sole and a ragoût of turbot and king scallops. Alternatively, a duck confit starter, roast rump of local lamb, or Llyn beef tortellini with a rich mushroom, brandy and cream sauce might be on offer. Familiar desserts – pannacotta or lemon cheesecake, maybe – sit alongside the innovative twice-baked cheese mousseline served with pickled walnut salad and melba toast. Your patience is requested on busy nights, and slow service has been noted, but all agree the food's worth waiting for. Wines are a positive give-away on a list that mixes well-chosen basics with some top-quality bottles. Even prestige names like Cloudy Bay are fairly priced (£19.95). Interesting options under £20 include a range of Alsace Grand Crus from the Cave de Turckheim. Six or so wines come by the glass for £2.95 to £6.

CHEFS/PROPRIETORS: Clare and Martin Vowell   OPEN: Mon to Sat D only 7 to 9.30   CLOSED: Jan, and Fri and Sat Nov to Mar   MEALS: alc (main courses £11 to £17)   SERVICE: not inc   CARDS: MasterCard, Switch, Visa   DETAILS: 35 seats. Private parties: 25 main room. Vegetarian meals. No children under 7. No smoking till food service has ended. Wheelchair access (not WC). Occasional music. No mobile phones

The Guide office can quickly spot when a restaurateur is encouraging customers to write recommending inclusion. Such reports do not further a restaurant's cause. Please tell us if a restaurateur invites you to write to the Guide.

▲ Bear Hotel

High Street, Crickhowell NP8 1BW
TEL: (01873) 810408   FAX: (01873) 811696   COOKING 2
EMAIL: bearhotel@aol.com   MODERN WELSH
WEBSITE: www.bearhotel.com   £34–£48

The Bear looks every inch the fifteenth-century coaching inn – black-and-white exterior, archway for the coaches (well, cars these days), and enough hanging baskets to restock a garden centre. Once you are inside, the restaurant isn't the easiest place to locate (through the bar and past the reception via an unmarked door), but a warm welcome awaits when you get there. Good materials, many of them local, are handled deftly. An inspector enjoyed perfectly pan-roasted scallops and chicken livers, respectively with mashed potatoes flavoured 'amazingly' with vanilla, and mushroom and sage. Chump of Welsh lamb and slow-roast belly of pork were dishes that both achieved melting tenderness. To conclude, bread pudding made with brioche, and set in an exceptionally flavoured egg custard, included the contrasting bitterness of Bramley apple plus a crisp sugary coating and creamy vanilla ice. A good-value wine list, arranged by grape variety, has some tempting options at the top end. House wines, two French and one German, start at £8.95

CHEF: Brian Simmons   PROPRIETORS: Judy and Stephen Hindmarsh   OPEN: Sun L only 12 to 2, Tue to Sat D 7 to 9.30   MEALS: alc (main courses £14 to £18). Bar menu available all week 12 to 3, 6 to 10   SERVICE: not inc, card slips closed   CARDS: Amex, Delta, MasterCard, Switch, Visa
DETAILS: 60 seats. 30 seats outside. Private parties: 60 main room, 20 to 40 private rooms. Car park. Vegetarian meals. No-smoking area. Wheelchair access (also WC). No music
ACCOMMODATION: 34 rooms, all with bath/shower. TV. Phone. B&B £54 to £130. Rooms for disabled. Baby facilities (*The Which? Guide to Good Hotels*)

▲ Nantyffin Cider Mill Inn ♀ ✳

Brecon Road, Crickhowell NP8 1SG
TEL: (01873) 810775   FAX: (01873) 812127
EMAIL: info@cidermill.co.uk
WEBSITE: www.cidermill.co.uk   COOKING 2
1½m W of Crickhowell at junction of A40 and   MODERN WELSH-PLUS
A479   £24–£57

This pink-washed sixteenth-century inn may strike the stranger as an archetypal country pub, and indeed the place has a 'good feel' about it, helped by friendly service. The owners' long-established dedication to local ingredients, lent credibility by the Welsh mountain lamb, chicken, guinea fowl and other meats supplied by their own farm at Llangynidr, reflects the serious intention of the kitchen. Other local products on the brief, well-balanced menu might include Black Mountain oak-smoked salmon, accompanied by buttermilk blinis and dill crème fraîche, free-range duck breast, with pear and apricot chutney and a rich sauce, and Welsh cheeses. The style also extends to ravioli stuffed with goats' cheese, sweet potato and spring onions in a saffron and tomato sauce, and grilled fillets of red mullet with a casserole of potatoes, leeks and saffron with red pepper rouille. Desserts might take in poached figs in mulled wine jelly with raspberry compote. Despite the long preamble, the premise of the wine list seems admirably simple: lots of well-chosen, good-value drinking under £20, then some more over £20 – and bargain bin ends to round it off. Eight wines come by the glass from £2.85.

CHEF: Sean Gerrard   PROPRIETORS: Sean Gerrard, and Glyn and Jess Bridgeman   OPEN: all week 12 to 2.30, 6.30 to 9.30   CLOSED: 1 week Jan, Tue, Sun D Sept to Apr   MEALS: alc (main courses £10.50 to £16.50). Set Mon to Fri L and Sun to Thur D £10 (2 courses)   SERVICE: not inc, card slips closed   CARDS: Amex, Delta, MasterCard, Switch, Visa   DETAILS: 100 seats. 50 seats outside. Private parties: 60 main room. Car park. Vegetarian meals. Children's helpings. No smoking in 1 dining room. Wheelchair access (also WC). No music   ACCOMMODATION: 23 rooms, all with bath/shower. TV. Phone. B&B £40 to £115. Swimming pool. Fishing

---

DOLGELLAU Gwynedd   map 7

Dylanwad Da ▼ ✳ £

2 Ffôs-y-Felin, Dolgellau LL40 1BS	COOKING 2
TEL: (01341) 422870	BISTRO
WEBSITE: www.dylanwad.co.uk	£24–£42

A warm interior with bare wooden tables and chairs lies behind the red door and unassuming double-fronted fascia. While taking ideas from far afield, the cooking is based on decent ingredients from local hills and waters. Controlled but interesting flavours show in tender braised lamb with an unthickened red-wine sauce perfumed with thyme, and in sole fillets in a lightly-textured sesame batter lifted with a sweet plum sauce. Vegetables are 'properly timed', and in springtime Pembrokeshire potatoes 'really did taste like new'. Rather ordinary shortcrust didn't do justice to a tart's deftly flavoured rhubarb and ginger filling, though a rich, smooth chocolate cheesecake succeeded admirably. Details like bread and coffee can disappoint but, overall, this is straightforwardly intelligent and enthusiastic cooking that rates taste above appearance. Similar enthusiasm pervades the wine list, with its range of good-value modern and traditional flavours, including some mature clarets. House wines are just £10.80 (£2 a glass) and tasty with it.

CHEF/PROPRIETOR: Dylan Rowlands   OPEN: Thur to Sat D only 7 to 9 (Tue to Sat in summer, all week Easter, Whitsun and Aug bank hols)   MEALS: alc D (main courses £9.50 to £14.50). Set D £16.50   SERVICE: not inc   CARDS: none   DETAILS: 28 seats. Private parties: 28 main room. Vegetarian meals. Children's helpings. No smoking. Wheelchair access (not WC). Music. No mobile phones (£5)

'The waitress was very strange – it was as if she was a robot going through the motions. This impression was emphasised when I tried to ask her a question about the food – the cogs inside her head started groaning, her eyes popped out and she spewed ticker-tape out of her mouth, printed over and over with the message ''ERROR! DOES NOT COMPUTE!'' before collapsing in a smouldering heap of burned-out electronics. Well I exaggerate slightly. . . .'
(On eating in Kent)

EGLWYSFACH Powys   map 7

▲ Ynyshir Hall ♥ ⅚✳

Eglwysfach SY20 8TA
TEL: (01654) 781209   FAX: (01654) 781366
EMAIL: info@ynyshir-hall.co.uk   COOKING 7
WEBSITE: www.ynyshir-hall.co.uk   MODERN BRITISH
off A487, 6m SW of Machynlleth   £41–£85

'Sensational' is, apparently, the only word to describe this country retreat, with its rugged scenery, clipped and manicured parkland setting, plumped sofas, and the dramatic paintings on its brightly coloured walls: 'it's a scene from a colour supplement'. The Reens (who have been here 15 years now) are a hands-on team who create a happy and relaxed atmosphere, and after four years Les Rennie seems well into his stride too.

His carte offers only around three options per course, but there are vegetarian and tasting menus as well, so plenty for the kitchen to do. 'Exemplary' technical skills and vibrant flavours are evident everywhere, from a 'stunning dish' of chicken ballottine served with lightly seared foie gras plus pickled cauliflower (think piccalilli) to cut the richness, to roast fillet of Welsh beef topped with pan-fried foie gras and a drizzle of meat juices. Local rabbit and game feature, and much of the seafood comes from a fisherman who works Cardigan Bay; among highlights have been moist, full-flavoured gilt-head bream with pesto-filled aubergine, a creamy smoked-haddock risotto, and paper-thin cannelloni enclosing a mousseline of fresh prawns from nearby Borth, sharing the plate with aubergine purée, Avruga caviar and a mound of prawns lightly tossed in hot butter. Soups are 'full of flavour, with a velvety texture', for example a wonderfully rich wild mushroom velouté served with a spinach won ton and crème fraîche, and dishes show a fine sense of balance, not least such desserts as a tiny moulded jelly of mulled fruits with cinnamon and clove ice cream, or a light, refreshing Sauternes jelly served with fruit consommé and Greek yoghurt sorbet.

The house wine selection – a dozen serious bottles priced between £19 and £32 (£3.50 to £6.50 a glass) – makes it abundantly clear that quality rules the list and highlights its major strength: France. Old Bordeaux vintages, tip-top Burgundies and good short selections from the South, the Rhône, the Loire and Alsace add real depth. Italy and Australia are best covered of the other regions, but all are well chosen. The only downside is the prices.

CHEF: Les Rennie   PROPRIETORS: Rob and Joan Reen   OPEN: all week 12.30 to 1.30, 7 to 8.45 CLOSED: Jan   MEALS: Set L £29, Set D £42 to £56. Light L menu available   SERVICE: not inc, card slips closed   CARDS: Amex, Delta, Diners, MasterCard, Switch, Visa   DETAILS: 30 seats. Private parties: 25 main room, 14 to 16 private rooms. Car park. Vegetarian meals. No children under 9. No smoking. Wheelchair access (not WC). Occasional music. No mobile phones ACCOMMODATION: 9 rooms, all with bath/shower. TV. Phone. B&B £95 to £315. No children under 9 (The Which? Guide to Good Hotels)

Net prices *in the details at the end of an entry indicates that the prices given on a menu and on a bill are inclusive of VAT and service charge, and that this practice is clearly stated on menu and bill.*

FELINFACH Powys — map 4

▲ Felin Fach Griffin 🌟

Felinfach LD4 4DW
TEL: (01874) 620111   FAX: (01874) 620120
EMAIL: info@eatdrinksleep.ltd.uk
WEBSITE: www.eatdrinksleep.ltd.uk

COOKING 3
MODERN BRITISH
£29–£47

A big stone building, set back from the main road in the middle of rolling countryside, the Griffin radiates an upmarket smartness that nearly lifts it out of the country-pub category. That said, there are solid wooden beams and pillars, log fires, and any undue standing on ceremony is avoided. The menus steer a path between English country cooking and the cosmopolitan influences a chic urban clientele might expect, so there will very likely be mussels in coconut milk and coriander, or a risotto of butternut squash and red onions with asparagus and Parmesan, among locally shot pheasant with creamed mash and parsnips, and ribeye of local beef with béarnaise and chips. Reporters praise the attention to detail in what appears before them, and the sense of culinary daring, which continues through to desserts such as figs with amaretti praline, mascarpone and a honey and almond tuile. Some cannily chosen wines make up a list that might feel a little expensive in the circumstances. Sicilian house wines are £10.75.

CHEF: Ricardo van Ede   PROPRIETOR: Charles Inkin   OPEN: Tue to Sun L 12.30 to 2.30, all week D 6.30 to 9.30   CLOSED: 24 to 26 Dec, last 2 weeks Jan   MEALS: alc (main courses L £9.50 to £12, D £10 to £15). Set D £19.50 (2 courses) to £25   SERVICE: not inc, card slips closed   CARDS: MasterCard, Switch, Visa   DETAILS: 60 seats. 30 seats outside. Private parties: 50 main room, 10 to 20 private rooms. Car park. Vegetarian meals. Children's helpings. No smoking in 1 dining room. Wheelchair access (also WC). Music   ACCOMMODATION: 7 rooms, all with bath/shower. Phone. B&B £57.50 to £92.50 (The Which? Guide to Good Hotels) £5

FISHGUARD Pembrokeshire — map 4

▲ Three Main Street 🌟

3 Main Street, Fishguard SA65 9HG
TEL: (01348) 874275   FAX: (01348) 874017

COOKING 5
MODERN EUROPEAN
£42–£51

A Georgian townhouse in the centre of Fishguard is home to Inez Ford's and Marion Evans's relaxed and unpretentious restaurant-with-rooms. Comfortable sofas might well entice you into the bar area, while the pair of wood-floored dining rooms are brightly decorated, the rear one offering a view over the water. The abundance of reports received indicates the popularity of the place, which is owing, in no small measure, to the enviable consistency of what the kitchen produces. 'I never eat beef anywhere but here,' was the comment of one reporter, who went on to praise a 'beautifully flavoured', accurately timed piece of fillet with lightly peppered sauce. Other dishes that have pleased include Thai-spiced monkfish soup with lemongrass, ginger and coconut milk, and a thoughtfully composed main course of turbot, given strong support from broad beans, new season's asparagus and a dry vermouth sauce. The attention to detail extends to home-made pasta, perhaps layered with wild mushrooms and sprinkled with grated Parmesan and truffle oil, to the sourcing of ingredients such as Maes-y-Felin organic duck breast (served with apple purée, onions and sage), and to vegetarian main courses like a watercress and toasted almond tart with crème fraîche and sweet pepper purée. Desserts seem designed with a conscious effort not to overload, offering Seville orange and Grand Marnier jelly with stem ginger ice cream, or vanilla-speckled pannacotta with roasted apricots. An air of calm, authoritative assurance pervades the front-of-house approach. A cheery jumble of disparate wines opens with a house selection from four countries, starting at £12.95.

CHEFS/PROPRIETORS: Marion Evans and Inez Ford   OPEN: Tue to Sat L 12 to 2 (bookings only), D 6.30 to 9   CLOSED: Tue in winter, Feb   MEALS: Set D £24 (2 courses) to £30   SERVICE: not inc CARDS: none   DETAILS: 35 seats. Private parties: 20 main room, 15 private room. Vegetarian meals. Children's helpings. No smoking. Wheelchair access (not WC). No music. No mobile phones   ACCOMMODATION: 3 rooms, all with bath/shower. TV. B&B £50 to £80 (*The Which? Guide to Good Hotels*)

HARLECH Gwynedd   map 7

▲ Castle Cottage ⅜✳

Y Llech, Harlech LL46 2YL	COOKING 2
TEL: (01766) 780479 FAX: (01766) 781251	MODERN WELSH
WEBSITE: www.castlecottageharlech.co.uk	£34–£41

Compared to thirteenth-century Harlech Castle, the Cottage is a newcomer, dating from 1585. A piggy theme pervades bar and lounge (and bedrooms have names after breeds such as Berkshire and British Lop). In the simply furnished dining room contemporary paintings make a calm and colourful backdrop for Glyn Roberts's meaty, satisfying food. He majors on boned and rolled suckling pig, Welsh Black ribeye steak, and tender, pink-roast cannon of lamb in a well-made wine and stock sauce. Regional materials abound: Carmarthen ham, eggs Harlech (baked with laverbread and smoked Welsh cheese), grilled fillets of Conwy lemon sole, or impressively fresh potted shrimps from 'just down there' (Jacqueline Roberts points out of the window towards the sea). Finish perhaps with lemon posset, or Megan's double chocolate mousse. Service is casual and friendly. Wines of the week, two pages of good-value recommendations, and a short, well-chosen main list ensure good choice at reasonable prices, starting around £12.

CHEF: Glyn Roberts   PROPRIETORS: Glyn and Jacqueline Roberts   OPEN: all week D only 7 to 9.30 CLOSED: 3 weeks Jan   MEALS: Set D £22.50 (2 courses) to £24.50   SERVICE: not inc, card slips closed   CARDS: Delta, MasterCard, Switch, Visa   DETAILS: 45 seats. Private parties: 45 main room. Vegetarian meals. Children's helpings. No smoking. Wheelchair access (not WC). Occasional music. No mobile phones   ACCOMMODATION: 6 rooms, 4 with bath/shower. B&B £52 to £110. Baby facilities (*The Which? Guide to Good Hotels*) (£5)

£ *means that it is possible to have a three-course meal, including coffee, half a bottle of house wine and service for £30 or less per person, at any time the restaurant is open, i.e. at dinner as well as lunch. It may be possible to spend considerably more than this, but by choosing carefully you should find £30 or less achievable.*

The Brasserie £

68 The Highway, Hawarden CH5 3DH
TEL: (01244) 536353   FAX: (01244) 520888

COOKING **2**
MODERN EUROPEAN
£19–£47

Tables are set close but the feeling is stylish, not 'brasserie-brash'. Food has a Mediterranean slant with first courses such as goats' cheese with fine beans, sun-dried tomatoes and walnuts; while Thai cucumber salad with smoked salmon shows wider influences. Roasted loin of pork, penne pasta with sweet-and-sour sauce, and spinach and ricotta cannelloni have appeared as main courses on the good-value set-price menu, followed by classic puds such as raspberry pavlova or baked lemon tart. Similar dishes on the 'express lunch menu' can be chosen individually. The carte shows a touch more elaboration: a rich mix of Welsh fillet of beef, dolcelatte and baby spinach risotto, balsamic baked garlic and shallot confit. The 30 or so decently chosen wines are presented on an admirably clear list. House bottles start at £9.95, also offered in two sizes of glass, with most other wines well below £15. The same team run Brasserie 10/16 in Chester (see entry).

CHEF: Mark Jones   PROPRIETORS: Neal Bates and Mark Jones   OPEN: Tue to Fri and Sun L 12 to 2, all week D 6 to 9.15 (9.30 Fri and Sat)   CLOSED: 26 Dec, 1 Jan   MEALS: alc exc Sun L (main courses £9 to £17). Set L £9.95 (2 courses), Set D Mon to Fri and Sun £9.95 (2 courses). Light L menu also available Mon to Fri   SERVICE: not inc   CARDS: Amex, Delta, MasterCard, Switch, Visa   DETAILS: 60 seats. Private parties: 35 main room, 25 private room. Car park. Vegetarian meals. Children's helpings. No-smoking area. Wheelchair access (not WC). Music (£5)

Pear Tree ⁵✳

NEW ENTRY

6 Church Street, Hay-on-Wye HR3 5DQ
TEL: (01497) 820777
EMAIL: info@peartreeathay.co.uk
WEBSITE: www.peartreeathay.co.uk

COOKING **4**
GLOBAL
£28–£46

Rod and Penny Lewis opened in Hay-on-Wye – home of the famous literary festival every summer – in February 2003, Rod having previously been listed in the Guide as chef at an address in Llanfrynach. Standing on the main road through town, the Pear Tree is a three-storeyed, grey-stone Georgian building; inside, the two linked dining rooms are done out in dark boarded floors, tomato-coloured walls and 'romantic' lighting.

Sourcing quality meats locally (venison from Bwlch and ducks from Hereford, for example) and organic vegetables from just outside Hay, Rod Lewis cooks an imaginative menu of vivid, modern flavours. Fish shows up well, whether in a starter of sautéed monkfish accompanied by a forceful hot pepper marmalade, or in a fine main course of seared salmon wrapped in Parma ham with sour-cream-and-chive crushed potatoes and a warmly spicy slick of Puy lentils. Horizons are widened further with Vietnamese chicken noodle soup, or Moroccan-spiced and honey-glazed lamb shank. A pleasingly old-fashioned dessert has been a wedge of chocolate, almond, fig and orange meringue cake, served with Jersey cream streaked with caramel ('absolutely gorgeous'), or there may be glazed lemon tart. Home-made bread comes with olive oil. With service at inspection by a knowledgeable local woman, 'an impeccable ambassador for the kitchen', this is a confident and impressive start. Wines number just 21, but prices are mostly under £20, starting with house wines – a French Sauvignon and a Chilean Merlot – at £11.95.

CHEF: Rod Lewis   PROPRIETORS: Rod and Penny Lewis   OPEN: Thur to Sat L 12 to 2, Tue to Sat D 7 to 9   CLOSED: Dec 25 and 26, Jan 1   MEALS: alc (main courses L £7 to £9, D £11 to £15) SERVICE: not inc, card slips closed   CARDS: Delta, MasterCard, Switch, Visa   DETAILS: 32 seats. 24 seats outside. Private parties: 32 main room. Vegetarian meals. Children's helpings. No smoking. Music (£5)

LAUGHARNE Carmarthenshire   map 4

▲ The Cors ⅙✻

Newbridge Road, Laugharne SA33 4SH   COOKING 2
TEL: (01994) 427219   MODERN WELSH
                                                         £33–£48

The Cors occupies the front rooms of an impressive Victorian villa set in four acres of pre-Raphaelite-style gardens. Inside, Victorian and modern touches tastefully co-exist, so that antique furniture is set against stripped wood floors, large abstract oils hang on walls, and wood-burning stoves and fairy lights add to the atmospheric feel. Nick Priestland – whose home this is – sticks to a short menu that incorporates excellent local ingredients where possible, though will venture further afield too. Reporters have praised a starter of roasted figs with Gorgonzola and honey vinegar sauce – 'an inspired combination' – or a satisfying smoked haddock crème brûlée (flaked haddock in a creamy sauce and with a cheesy crust), while tender fillet of organic Welsh Black beef with green peppercorns and red wine jus impressed at inspection, as did well-executed, 'succulent' pan-fried fillet of sea bass on pak choi. Desserts, too, have satisfied: individual strawberry pavlova, and dense, rich chocolate nut torte. At busy sessions service can be slow. Although short, the wine list is well chosen and offers interest and value. A duo of French house wines start at £10.95 (£2.50 per glass).

CHEF/PROPRIETOR: Nick Priestland   OPEN: Thur to Fri D only 7 to 9.30   CLOSED: 25 and 26 Dec, last 2 weeks Oct   MEALS: alc (main courses £13.50 to £17.50)   SERVICE: not inc   CARDS: none DETAILS: 30 seats. 12 seats outside. Private parties: 24 main room. Car park. Vegetarian meals. No children under 12. No smoking in 1 dining room. Wheelchair access (not WC). Music. No mobile phones   ACCOMMODATION: 2 rooms, both with bath/shower. B&B £30 to £70 (The Which? Guide to Good Hotels) (£5)

🎨 indicates that there has been a change of chef since last year's Guide, and the Editor has judged that the change is of sufficient interest to merit the reader's attention.

Dining rooms where music, either live or recorded, is never played are signalled by No music in the details at the end of an entry.

LLANBERIS Gwynedd

map 7

Y Bistro ✦

43–45 High Street, Llanberis LL55 4EU
TEL/FAX: (01286) 871278
EMAIL: ybistro@fsbdial.co.uk
WEBSITE: www.ybistro.co.uk
off A4086, at foot of Snowdon, in centre of village

COOKING 2
MODERN WELSH
£32–£53

Sitting in stunning scenery at the foot of Snowdon, Y Bistro's shopfront exterior opens on to a typically Welsh front parlour of yesteryear. The dining room is dominated by pictures of local crags and waterfalls, and though the décor to one visitor looked a little '1950s', the good home-cooked food is not. Nerys Roberts draws on excellent local produce (Welsh Black beef, mountain lamb, locally reared pork) and 25 years' experience of feeding hungry walkers, and she is also a dab hand at vegetarian cooking. Warm chicken livers with bacon salad as a starter has been 'cooked to perfection with just a hint of pink', while a main course of a crisp seed and nut croustade comes with a ragoût of leeks, squash, tomatoes and artichoke hearts – 'a wonderful combination' – and lamb's liver is accompanied by braised peppers and rösti. Puddings have run to lemon and honey cheesecake, chocolate roulade, and pear and almond tart, while a fairly priced wine list, including Welsh bottles, kicks off at £10.50.

CHEF: Nerys Roberts   PROPRIETORS: Danny and Nerys Roberts   OPEN: Mon to Sat D only 7.30 to 10   CLOSED: Mon winter   MEALS: alc (main courses £13 to £18)   SERVICE: not inc, card slips closed   CARDS: Delta, MasterCard, Switch, Visa   DETAILS: 35 seats. Private parties: 40 main room. Vegetarian meals. Children's helpings. No smoking. Wheelchair access (not WC). No music (£5)

LLANDEWI SKIRRID Monmouthshire

map 4

Walnut Tree Inn ♨

Llandewi Skirrid NP7 8AW
TEL: (01873) 852797   FAX: (01873) 859764
WEBSITE: www.thewalnuttreeinn.com
on B4521, 3m NE of Abergavenny

COOKING 4
MEDITERRANEAN/ITALIAN
£31–£69

The black and white pebble-dashed building by the roadside looks much as it always has, with a flag-floored bar, and two interlinked dining rooms with bare wooden tables; and it remains completely unpretentious and matter-of-fact. A generous carte (supplemented by a set-price option at lunch) retains a few dishes from Taruschio days, such as Lady Llanover's salt duck, and vincisgrassi (porcini and Parma ham lasagne), and many of the starters keep last minute preparation down to a minimum: salads, oysters, terrines, bresaola, dressed crab, smoked salmon, or perhaps a full-flavoured soup of Jerusalem artichoke and potato sprinkled with bits of crunchy, salty pancetta.

The kitchen has also turned out a first-class dish of grilled Scottish scallops 'brilliantly fresh and sweetly sticky', accompanied by wafer-thin slices of viola aubergine, grilled asparagus and yet more salty pancetta convincingly pointing up the sweetness of the scallops. Pasta options might include gnocchi with braised wild rabbit sauce, meat dishes have taken in grilled ribeye of Usk beef, and the laudably simple approach is exemplified by a piece of juicy, fresh, pan-fried wild seabass accompanied by flavourful, semi-dried plum tomatoes. Among desserts, the hot chocolate fondant with pistachio ice cream is a fine example of its kind, service is 'as mildly idiosyncratic as ever' but friendly and knowledgeable, and wines include a tempting Italian range with plenty of top bottles but few budget options. House wines are £13.50 or £3.50 a glass.

CHEF: Stefano Lodi-Rizzini PROPRIETOR: Francesco Matioli OPEN: Tue to Sun and bank hol Mon L 12 to 2.30, Tue to Sat D 7 to 10.30 CLOSED: 24 Dec to 4 Jan MEALS: alc (main courses £9.75 to £25). Set L £16.50 to £19.50 SERVICE: not inc CARDS: Delta, MasterCard, Switch, Visa DETAILS: 70 seats. 15 seats outside. Private parties: 25 main room. Car park. Vegetarian meals. No-smoking area. Wheelchair access (not WC). No music

LLANDRILLO Denbighshire — map 7

▲ Tyddyn Llan

WALES OF THE YEAR RESTAURANT

Llandrillo LL21 0ST
TEL: (01490) 440264 FAX: (01490) 440414
EMAIL: tyddynllanhotel@compuserve.com
WEBSITE: www.tyddynllan.co.uk
on B4401, 4½m S of Corwen

COOKING 7
MODERN BRITISH
£30–£54

The Kindreds retired after 20 years at this former hunting lodge, and Bryan and Susan Webb, last seen in the 2001 edition of the Guide at Hilaire in London, took over at the end of 2002. Having exchanged a busy metropolis for no end of fields, hills and fresh air, their aim is, modestly, a restaurant-with-rooms. The stone-built house is set back from the road (look for the blue sign on the edge of the village), a veranda provides shade for pre-meal drinks in summer, and a kitchen garden yields a few seasonal vegetables and herbs. It is a well-kept house, with plenty of comfortable lounge space, and a couple of dining rooms where soft lighting and well-spaced tables can make it feel 'quite romantic'.

A clearly written menu points to the kitchen's straightforward approach, as it offers a potato pancake with smoked salmon and horseradish cream, or breast of chicken with wild mushroom risotto. The food is characterised by a clear focus on the main item, by first-class materials (some local), and by expert handling. 'Brilliantly fresh' Scottish scallops, for example, are accurately seared and translucent in the middle, their sweetness pointed up by the gentle sourness of finely diced, lightly pickled vegetables, and tempered by the peppery bite of rocket in a piquant dressing. This is cooking without frills or distractions, making a virtue of chunks of seared lamb sweetbreads, served with young artichokes and ceps in a first-class stock reduction, or a prime piece of firm, skinless turbot 'impeccably treated', in a perfectly judged herb butter sauce.

Desserts might range from pannacotta with rhubarb to a more elaborate tripartite chocolate dish consisting of a wedge of excellent 'cheesecake' (a mousse of immaculately smooth texture on a light, crumbly, biscuity base), a light puff pastry pithiviers with a dark molten filling, and an expertly made ice cream, each component flawlessly done, and between them offering clear contrasts of texture and temperature. Susan Webb is an 'ace' hostess, whose 'customary charm and efficiency' is at the heart of the well-paced service. The wine list is arranged by style, but with a stream of fine Californian offerings running through it, reflecting the expertise of its compiler, Neville Blech. Bordeaux, Burgundy and Italy also show up well in this innovative range and fair prices, including over 50 under £20, ensure a broad choice for all pockets. 'Smooth and mature' reds feature numerous classics in their prime. Sixteen come by the glass (£3 to £6.65) and the short selection of halves should grow over the coming year.

CHEF: Bryan Webb   PROPRIETORS: Bryan and Susan Webb   OPEN: Tue to Sun L 12.30 to 2.15 (2.30 Sun), all week D 7 to 9 (10 Fri and Sat). Hours may vary between Nov and Mar; phone to check   CLOSED: last 2 weeks Jan, first week Feb   MEALS: Set L £14.50 (2 courses) to £18.50, Set D £32. Light L menu available   SERVICE: not inc   CARDS: Delta, MasterCard, Switch, Visa   DETAILS: 50 seats. 18 seats outside. Private parties: 65 main room, 10 to 30 private rooms. Car park. Children's helpings. No smoking. Wheelchair access (also WC). Occasional music. No mobile phones   ACCOMMODATION: 13 rooms, 12 with bath/shower. TV. Phone. B&B £85 to £180. Rooms for disabled. Baby facilities (*The Which? Guide to Good Hotels*)

LLANDUDNO Conwy   map 7

▲ Bodysgallen Hall ♥ ⅗✕

Llandudno LL30 1RS
TEL: (01492) 584466   FAX: (01492) 582519
EMAIL: info@bodysgallen.com
WEBSITE: www.bodysgallen.com
off A470, 2m SE of Llandudno

COOKING 2
MODERN BRITISH
£30–£65

Bodysgallen feels venerable though not stuffy. The ancient wooden front door leads into a dark, beamed hall-cum-lounge, thence to a pinky-orange dining room with a big fireplace, chandeliers, and a splendid view over well-kept gardens. Much is familiar: wild mushroom risotto, a goats' cheese soufflé with sweet chilli dressing, and a slab of lightly glazed chicken and veal terrine with a blob of dark chutney and a well-dressed, gently minty salad. But less usual items include loin of Welsh lamb with a devilled kidney and lentil tartlet, or three small carp fillets laid along lines of mashed potato, with peas and bacon, and a shellfishy sauce full of diced vegetables. Welsh rarebit offers an alternative to desserts like tiramisù, or rhubarb and apple crumble. Not all the skills one expects of such an establishment are successfully deployed (pastry was a shortcoming at inspection) but service is capable, observant and friendly. The wine list covers the world from Australia to Wales. Six 'house recommendations' run from £14.50 to £21.50 and a 'cellarman's choice' adds eight more; eight by the glass start at £3.50.

CHEF: David Thompson   PROPRIETOR: Historic House Hotels   OPEN: all week 12.30 to 1.45, 7 to 9.30   MEALS: Set L £17 (2 courses) to £19, Set D £36   SERVICE: net prices, card slips closed CARDS: Delta, MasterCard, Switch, Visa   DETAILS: 60 seats. Private parties: 50 main room, 12 to 40 private rooms. Car park. Vegetarian meals. No children under 9. Jacket. No smoking. Wheelchair access (also WC). Occasional music. No mobile phones. Air-conditioned ACCOMMODATION: 35 rooms, all with bath/shower. TV. Phone. Room only £115 to £290. Rooms for disabled. No children under 9. Swimming pool (*The Which? Guide to Good Hotels*)

Subscribers to Which? Online can access The Good Food Guide *on www.which.net.*

▲ St Tudno Hotel, Garden Room Restaurant ▮ ✲

Promenade, Llandudno LL30 2LP

TEL: (01492) 874411   FAX: (01492) 860407

EMAIL: sttudnohotel@btinternet.com

WEBSITE: www.st-tudno.co.uk

COOKING **4**

MODERN EUROPEAN

£25–£58

Set discreetly in a terrace of Victorian houses overlooking the promenade and sea, the hotel to one reporter is a 'true Tardis', seeming far more spacious once one is inside. Hanging baskets and flower displays, crisp yellow napery, white antique style lamps, classic cutlery and bamboo and wicker chairs with deep, comfortable cushions provide the setting for some flamboyant cooking that celebrates local ingredients while drawing from further afield too. A starter of foie gras with a crisp beignet studded with truffle shavings on balsamic jelly and a mini brioche got full marks at inspection for presentation and taste, and spicy Great Orme crab cake has been praised for its freshness and contrasting textures. Well-timed fricassee of lobster and scallops (which 'bounced with freshness') has made a satisfying main course, while saddle of tender, pink Welsh lamb served with Chester potato cake and a casserole of French beans, olives and tomatoes has an intense garlic flavour. Portions tend to be generous. Finish perhaps with a raspberry trio consisting of perfect fresh fruit, a refreshing mousse, and a tartlet with sabayon topped by slightly caramelised fruit flashed under the grill. All is presided over by the inappropriately named Mrs Bland, who is a skilled, vivacious and amiable hostess. Extended selections from some of the Blands' favourite producers head up an enthusiastic and quality-packed wine list. Prices are mostly reasonable, and the short 'specially recommended' sections neatly summarise the list, starting at £12.50 and with a dozen by the glass (£3.30 to £6.20).

CHEFS: David Harding and Stephen Duffy   PROPRIETORS: Martin and Janette Bland   OPEN: all week 12.30 to 1.45, 7 to 9.30 (9 Sun and bank hol Mon). Early theatre dinner by arrangement Sun   MEALS: alc D (main courses £16.50 to £19). Set L Sun £17.50, Set L Mon to Sat £16.50   SERVICE: not inc, card slips closed   CARDS: Amex, Delta, Diners, MasterCard, Switch, Visa   DETAILS: 60 seats. Private parties (L only): 50 main room. Car park. Vegetarian meals. No children under 5 at D; children's helpings at L. No smoking. Wheelchair access (not WC). Music. No mobile phones. Air-conditioned   ACCOMMODATION: 18 rooms, all with bath/shower. TV. Phone. B&B £60 to £280. Baby facilities. Swimming pool (£5)

Occasional music *in the details at the end of an entry means live or recorded music is played in the dining room only rarely or for special events.* No music *means it is never played.*

If 'vegetarian meals' *is noted in the details at the end of an entry, this means that a restaurant routinely lists at least one vegetarian starter and main course on menus. Other restaurants, however, may offer good vegetarian choices if you let them know in advance, so it is worthwhile phoning to enquire.*

▲ Lake Country House ♥ ⅋

Llangammarch Wells LD4 4BS
TEL: (01591) 620202   FAX: (01591) 620457
EMAIL: info@lakecountryhouse.co.uk
WEBSITE: www.lakecountryhouse.co.uk   COOKING 4
at Garth, 6m W of Builth Wells, turn off B483 on to   MODERN BRITISH
B4519, then take first right   £35–£60

The house and its extensive grounds offer a vision of fine living: large comfortable sofas, a dining room spacious enough to double as a ballroom in a period costume drama, and service that is both 'attentive and restrained' all play their parts. Sean Cullingford's cooking style is very much in keeping with its surroundings, with gentle flavours and combinations that will do nothing to frighten the horses, but achieve a high degree of polish nonetheless.

The fixed-price dinner starts with a set soup – perhaps leek and potato topped with fried leek strips – before proceeding to a choice of four each of second courses and mains. Caramelised scallops have been accurately cooked, served on a bed of creamed leeks with a saffron beurre blanc, or there may be a ragoût of shellfish. Main courses have included pork tenderloin with vegetable 'tagliatelle', or, for those wishing to stick with the fish route, perhaps fillets of John Dory on orange-flavoured potato purée. There has been the odd comment that meats have not been quite as expressively flavourful as should be expected, but confidence is restored at dessert stage with the appearance of fine raspberry crème brûlée with shortbread biscuits, or maybe chocolate mousse imaginatively paired with a sorbet made of Orange Muscat wine.

The wine list comes in two halves. A well-rounded, modern selection opens with canny choices from the South of France and turns up some low prices in Bordeaux and Burgundy. The heart of the list, however, is far more in keeping with the tenor of the establishment – five unannotated pages of fine wines, mostly French classics with good producers and mature vintages to the fore. Just four house wines (from £15) come by the glass.

CHEF: Sean Cullingford   PROPRIETORS: Mr and Mrs J.P. Mifsud   OPEN: all week 12.15 to 1.45, 7.15 to 9   MEALS: Set L £21.50, Set D £35   SERVICE: not inc, card slips closed   CARDS: Amex, Delta, Diners, MasterCard, Switch, Visa   DETAILS: 50 seats. Private parties: 85 main room, 10 to 40 private rooms. Car park. Vegetarian meals. Children's helpings. No children under 7 in dining room after 7pm. Jacket and tie. No smoking. Wheelchair access (also WC). No music. No mobile phones   ACCOMMODATION: 19 rooms, all with bath/shower. TV. Phone. B&B £99 to £230. Rooms for disabled. Baby facilities. Fishing (*The Which? Guide to Good Hotels*) (£5)

All details are as accurate as possible at the time of going to press, but chefs and owners often change, and it is wise to check by telephone before making a special journey. Many readers have been disappointed when set-price bargain meals are no longer available. Ask when booking.

Report forms are at the back of the book; write a letter if you prefer; or email us at goodfoodguide@which.net

LLANRHIDIAN Swansea   map 4

Welcome to Town ✱

Llanrhidian SA3 1EH
TEL/FAX: (01792) 390015   COOKING **3**
EMAIL: enquiries@thewelcometotown.co.uk   CLASSICAL/MODERN WELSH
WEBSITE: www.thewelcometotown.co.uk   £24–£54

The Gower Peninsula provides the setting for this self-styled country bistro, though 'more restaurant than bistro', according to one visitor. Service is friendly and attentive, and 'The Welcome', as it is becoming known, offers a fixed-price lunch menu; although it may be limited in choice, salad niçoise with chargrilled yellowfin tuna, or leek risotto with aged Parmesan, might just hit the spot. The evening carte may well remind you where you are with braised shank of Welsh lamb with buttered carrots, or pan-fried fillet of turbot with leeks. Dishes have been praised for their integrity and consistency, as have the accompanying vegetables that 'enhance and complement' the main dishes – for example a 'gratifying' celeriac mash. Desserts getting the thumbs-up have notably included nougat parfait; or choose Welsh farmhouse cheeses, accompanied by oatcakes and walnut bread. The wine list offers good variety at affordable prices, kicking off with house French at £10.50.

CHEFS: Ian Bennett and Helen Farmer   PROPRIETORS: Ian and Jay Bennett   OPEN: Tue to Sun L 12 to 2, Tue to Sat D 7 to 9.30   CLOSED: first 2 weeks Feb   MEALS: alc (main courses £11 to £17.50). Set L £10.50 (2 courses) to £13.95   SERVICE: not inc, card slips closed   CARDS: MasterCard, Switch, Visa   DETAILS: 40 seats. 15 seats outside. Car park. Vegetarian meals. Children's helpings. No smoking. Music   (£5)

LLANSANFFRAID GLAN CONWY Conwy   map 7

▲ Old Rectory Country House ♛ ✱

Llanrwst Road, Llansanffraid Glan
Conwy LL28 5LF
TEL: (01492) 580611   FAX: (01492) 584555
EMAIL: info@oldrectorycountryhouse.co.uk   COOKING **6**
WEBSITE: www.oldrectorycountryhouse.co.uk   MODERN FRENCH/BRITISH
on A470, 1m S of junction with A55   £51–£70

Comfort and opulence are the watchwords at Michael and Wendy Vaughan's Victorian country house hotel, where they have been offering good food and quality accommodation for 20 years. Views from the house take in the Conwy estuary, the Norman castle and Snowdon, while the theme of interior décor is defined by fine antiques, oil paintings and pine panelling.

Arrive by 7.30 for aperitifs and sit down with everyone else at 8.15 for a no-choice menu (preferences and requirements are discussed when booking) cooked by Wendy. Her style is based on classic French cuisine but she updates it with some strikingly contemporary ideas. Roast spiced monkfish, for example, is served on vanilla risotto with red wine sauce for a starter, or there may be poached pear on a garlic croûton with spinach and balsamic-flavoured pulses and hollandaise sauce. Main courses tend to be conceptually straightforward but are often fairly elaborate in the construction: duck might be prepared three ways – roasted, poached and confit – and served with lentil casserole and a celeriac and parsnip mousse, while loin of Welsh mountain lamb comes with cabbage parcels and olive potatoes. Simpler ideas have included steamed turbot fillet with chargrilled asparagus and tomato butter sauce. Dessert is the one stage where a choice is offered – perhaps between lemon and raspberry bavarois and chocolate cake with chocolate fudge sauce – or try the selection of Welsh cheeses. The wine list is full of good, food-friendly ideas and nicely balanced between value and premium offerings. France includes Alsace wines from the excellent co-op at Turckheim, while the New World is a mix of cooler-climate styles and big monsters – with annotations that spell out what's what. Prices are very good, although the baseline level is quite high at £15.90.

CHEFS: Wendy Vaughan and Christopher Jones   PROPRIETORS: Michael and Wendy Vaughan
OPEN: Tue to Sat D only 7.30 for 8.15 (1 sitting)   MEALS: Set D £34.90   SERVICE: not inc, card slips
closed   CARDS: Delta, MasterCard, Switch, Visa   DETAILS: 14 seats. Car park. Children's
helpings. No children under 5 in dining room. No smoking. No music   ACCOMMODATION: 6 rooms,
all with bath/shower. TV. Phone. B&B £79 to £169. No children over 9 months and under 5 years
(*The Which? Guide to Good Hotels*)

LLANWRTYD WELLS Powys   map 4

▲ Carlton House ⁵✕

Dol-y-coed Road, Llanwrtyd Wells LD5 4RA
TEL: (01591) 610248   FAX: (01591) 610242   COOKING 6
EMAIL: info@carltonrestaurant.co.uk   MODERN BRITISH
WEBSITE: www.carltonrestaurant.co.uk   £39–£60

A relaxed and friendly atmosphere maintains at this three-storey town house in a Victorian spa town, and the small dining room has a bright and sunny feel. The Gilchrists, who have run Carlton House since 1991, 'have a generosity about them' and a personal touch much valued by their customers. Fixed-price meals are available to residents only (those for 'Gourmet Breaks' include wine), so non-residents are offered a short carte whose brevity (three options at each stage) is more than made up for by fine supplies, many of them local, which provide a solid foundation for the cooking. There is usually a soup (leek and potato with a poached egg, perhaps), and flavours are bright without being exotic: Carmarthen ham comes with celeriac rémoulade, and seared scallops might be given a lime and caper vinaigrette. Brill has featured among main-course fish (with black rice and leeks in a shellfish velouté), and the beef is local: perhaps pan-fried fillet with buttered cabbage and a sauce combining oxtail, truffle and Madeira.

The Carlton House take on chocolate fondant is to serve it with oranges in caramel and Grand Marnier, or there might be a lime posset with raspberry coulis and amaretti. Alan Gilchrist is 'attentive and humorous front-of-house', and the wide-ranging wine list offers good value, as well as a fair choice of half-bottles. Four Chilean house varietals cost from £11 to £12.50.

CHEF: Mary Ann Gilchrist PROPRIETORS: Alan and Mary Ann Gilchrist OPEN: Mon to Sat D only 7 to 8.30 CLOSED: 10 to 30 Dec MEALS: alc (main courses £20 to £25) SERVICE: not inc, card slips closed CARDS: Delta, MasterCard, Switch, Visa DETAILS: 14 seats. No smoking. Wheelchair access (not WC). No music. No mobile phones ACCOMMODATION: 6 rooms, all with bath/shower. TV. B&B £50 to £80. Baby facilities (*The Which? Guide to Good Hotels*) (£5)

MACHYNLLETH Powys
map 4

▲ Wynnstay ⅄✳

Maengwyn Street, Machynlleth SY20 8AE

TEL: (01654) 702941 FAX: (01654) 703884

EMAIL: info@wynnstay-hotel.com

WEBSITE: www.wynnstay-hotel.com

COOKING 3
MODERN WELSH
£19–£40

Refurbishment of this imposing coaching inn continues, but its air of amiability is intact. The kitchen emphasises local produce: sea bass, salmon and sea trout from nearby waters, partridge, pheasant and wild mushrooms from the countryside and beef, lamb and pork from the farms. Tradition meets modern techniques in a laverbread velouté with turbot, or Llanboidy cheese polenta with Welsh lamb and lentils, and two starters (a duo of robust game terrines, and pink-cooked wood pigeon) at inspection had excellent onion and apple chutney and walnut-oil-dressed leaves. Incidentals have disappointed – poor mint sauce spoiling good Jacob's lamb, and unimpressive bread – but unfussy vegetables are honest, and desserts like mango and passion-fruit délice with lime sorbet handle powerful flavours delicately. Service, though willing, can lack professionalism. The usefully annotated wine list starts at £10.75 and covers a wide range at fair prices.

CHEF: Gareth Johns PROPRIETORS: Charles and Sheila Dark OPEN: Sun L only 12 to 2, all week D 7 to 9 MEALS: Set L £6.95 (1 course) to £10.95, Set L Sun £7.75 (1 course) to £12.95, Set D £21 (2 courses) to £25. Bar menu available SERVICE: not inc CARDS: Amex, Delta, Diners, MasterCard, Switch, Visa DETAILS: 60 seats. Private parties: 60 main room, 8 to 14 private rooms. Car park. Vegetarian meals. Children's helpings. No smoking. Wheelchair access (also WC). Occasional music ACCOMMODATION: 23 rooms, all with bath/shower. TV. Phone. B&B £45 to £100. Baby facilities (£5)

NANTGAREDIG Carmarthenshire
map 4

▲ Four Seasons ⅄✳

Nantgaredig SA32 7NY

TEL: (01267) 290238 FAX: (01267) 290808

EMAIL: jen4seas@aol.com

WEBSITE: www.fourseasonswales.co.uk

on B4310, ½m N of Nantgaredig

COOKING 2
MODERN BRITISH
£37–£49

Set amid rolling farmland, this is a restaurant-with-rooms where visitors can enjoy a drink in the lounge before eating in the spacious restaurant, made more so by the addition of a conservatory. A four-course fixed-price menu is on offer, with a focus on local produce. A wide choice of starters might take in Black Mountain smoked salmon with warm laverbread tart, or Carmarthen ham, tomato and red onion salad. Main courses, too, have a distinctly Welsh feel, with leek and Caerphilly cheese pancakes with tomato and basil sauce, fillet of Welsh Black beef with mustard butter, or shank of Welsh lamb with peppers, tomatoes and red wine. Puddings are on the more conventional side, although the wine list offers more adventure, starting with five house wines all at £12.50.

CHEFS/PROPRIETORS: Maryann Wright and Charlotte Pasetti   OPEN: Tue to Sat D only 7.30 to 9.30   CLOSED: Christmas   MEALS: Set D £27.50   SERVICE: not inc, card slips closed   CARDS: Delta, MasterCard, Switch, Visa   DETAILS: 45 seats. 8 seats outside. Private parties: 50 main room. Car park. Vegetarian meals. Children's helpings. No smoking. Wheelchair access (not WC). Occasional music   ACCOMMODATION: 6 rooms, all with bath/shower. TV. B&B £50 to £100. Rooms for disabled. Baby facilities. Swimming pool (*The Which? Guide to Good Hotels*)

NANT-Y-DERRY Monmouthshire   map 2

Foxhunter ⅚✳

Nant-y-derry NP7 9DN	COOKING 4
TEL: (01873) 881101 FAX: (01873) 881377	MODERN EUROPEAN
E of A4042, 6m S of Abergavenny	£32–£61

Finding this tiny village and its former station-master's house can be tricky, but the effort is worth it. In the smart, uncluttered interior, where a big chimney-piece in the same rough stone as the exterior recalls the past, relaxed, very well-trained staff are equally ready to serve a single drink as the full-blown dinner-time carte. The kitchen does the lot (including superb bread), mixing technical skill with a robust, straightforward approach. Menus rely on local ingredients, but nevertheless are touched by a broad sweep of Italian influences. A winter lunch included Tuscan chestnut soup, an open lasagne with bolognaise, and a pannacotta with Seville orange marmalade; a dinner main course of local woodcock, cavolo nero, white beans and bruschetta exemplified the intelligently contained fusion. Either side of this might be starters like mild garlic soup with croûtons, or marinated salmon with cockles and crème fraîche, and such sweets as lemon posset with rhubarb and lychees. A shortish but nicely rounded wine list starts at £12.95 (four come by the glass); prices are fair, with plenty under £20, but also the wherewithal to celebrate special occasions – and there's vin Santo to partner the pannacotta.

CHEF: Matt Tebbutt   PROPRIETORS: Matt and Lisa Tebbutt   OPEN: Tue to Sat 12 to 2.30, 7 to 10   CLOSED: 25 Dec, 1 Jan, 2 weeks Feb   MEALS: alc (main courses £11 to £17). Set L £16.95 (2 courses) to £19.95   SERVICE: not inc, 10% for parties of 8 or more   CARDS: Delta, MasterCard, Switch, Visa   DETAILS: 65 seats. Private parties: 65 main room, 10 to 30 private rooms. Car park. Vegetarian meals. Children's helpings. No smoking. Wheelchair access (also WC). Music

---

The Guide is totally independent, accepts no free hospitality, and survives on the number of copies sold each year.

The text of entries is based on unsolicited reports sent in by readers, backed up by inspections conducted anonymously. The factual details under the text are from questionnaires the Guide sends to all restaurants that feature in the book.

NEWPORT Pembrokeshire   map 4

▲ Cnapan ⁵⅟✹

East Street, Newport SA42 0SY   COOKING 2
TEL: (01239) 820575   BRITISH
WEBSITE: www.online-holidays.net/cnapan   £20–£46

This pink pebble-dashed listed townhouse is the home of a family foursome
who for two decades have offered hospitality for visitors to this part of the
Pembrokeshire coast not far from Fishguard. The cooking tends towards the
traditional, with an imaginative twist or unusual ingredient providing added
interest. Smoked salmon and crab tartlet with anchovy mayonnaise found
favour with one visitor, and bruschetta topped with a 'satisfyingly creamy' mix
of mushroom and Cashel Blue cheese was a success. Main courses demonstrate a
desire to use good local ingredients: marinated pan-fried fillet of local lamb on
pea and spinach purée, or fillet of Welsh beef with a cracked peppercorn sauce,
the latter a 'perfectly executed classic'. Desserts, too, tend to the classic, taking in
crème brûlée with ginger, or rich rum and chocolate torte. Grilled slices of home-
made bread with cheese and herbs are from a secret recipe, by all accounts, and
worth the journey alone. Service is friendly, professional and attentive, and the
short, very reasonably priced wine list offers interest with a French regional duo
kicking off at £9.75.

CHEF: Judith Cooper   PROPRIETORS: Eluned and John Lloyd, and Michael and Judith Cooper
OPEN: Mon and Wed to Sat L 12 to 2, Mon and Wed to Sun D 6.45 to 8.45   CLOSED: Christmas,
Jan, Feb   MEALS: alc (main courses L £6.50 to £9.75, D £13.50 to £19.50)   SERVICE: not inc, card
slips closed   CARDS: MasterCard, Switch, Visa   DETAILS: 36 seats. Car park. Vegetarian meals.
Children's helpings. No smoking. Wheelchair access (not WC). Music. No mobile phones
ACCOMMODATION: 5 rooms, all with bath/shower. TV. B&B £40 to £66. Baby facilities (*The Which?
Guide to Good Hotels*)

NEWPORT Newport   map 2

Chandlery £ | NEW ENTRY |

77–78 Lower Dock Street, Newport NP20 1EH   COOKING 3
TEL: 01633 256622   FAX: 01633 256633   MODERN EUROPEAN
WEBSITE: www.chandleryrestaurant.co.uk   £22–£59

Opening a restaurant in a regeneration area might be considered brave, and in
resuscitating this elegant Georgian commercial building, Simon Newcombe has
shown (seemingly well-founded) confidence in both the locality and his own
abilities. The interior is light and airy, and the service welcoming and well
informed. Menus that change with the seasons show local ingredients treated
with a mostly European eclecticism that stops short of excess. A single raviolo
stuffed with tangy goats' cheese and tomato with buttery, lemony sauce
epitomises bold, feasible partnerships, and scallops with chilli, ginger, spring
onion and soy produces harmonising but still individual flavours. Pork with
black pudding, garlic mash and flageolets is a robust brasserie-like dish handled
sensitively, as are 'very classy' lamb torte (layers of slowly braised Welsh lamb
with potatoes dense enough to serve in a slice), and grilled halibut on creamed
leeks with truffled mash and a sharp lemon sauce. A trio of hot, rich bread

pudding, a cold, strong chocolate marquise and creamy ice cream maintained standards to the end. The annotated wine list is interesting and succinct, and six house bottles from £10.50 (£2.70 a glass) show pricing as fair as the food's.

CHEF/PROPRIETOR: Simon Newcombe OPEN: Tue to Fri L 12 to 2, Tue to Sat D 7 to 10 CLOSED: 1 to 2 weeks Christmas, 2 weeks end Aug MEALS: alc (main courses £9.50 to £17). Set L £9.95 (2 courses) to £12.95, Set D Tue to Thur £37.50. Light L menu available SERVICE: not inc, 10% for parties of 11 or more CARDS: Amex, Delta, MasterCard, Switch, Visa DETAILS: 80 seats. Private parties: 40 main room, 10 to 40 private rooms. Car park. Vegetarian meals. Children's helpings. Wheelchair access (also WC). Music. Air-conditioned

PENMAENPOOL Gwynedd

map 7

▲ Penmaenuchaf Hall ♟ ✦

NEW ENTRY

Penmaenpool LL40 1YB
TEL: (01341) 422129 FAX: (01341) 422787
EMAIL: relax@penhall.co.uk
WEBSITE: www.penhall.co.uk
off A493, 2m W of Dolgellau

COOKING 2
MODERN BRITISH
£27–£67

Elegant Victorian interiors overlooking the Mawddach estuary, a welcoming hostess in Lorraine Fielding, and a professional team set the scene for some ambitious cooking which may not always hit the mark, but at its best produces fine – especially fish – dishes that show skill and accuracy in timing and flavouring. Although at inspection neither a first-course goats' cheese tart nor a dessert of raspberry bavarois impressed, another starter of perfectly seared scallops with a coriander risotto did, along with two main-course fish dishes: brilliant roast fillet cod with a bold sultana purée, spiced sausage, couscous and spinach; and fine pan-fried turbot with a subtle lobster and basil cream sauce and crushed peas. Excellent petits fours and 'the best cappuccino in a long time' can end meals on a high note, and the wine list should please all palates and pockets. Nine house wines come in at £15 or under; there are some go-getting wines of the month, and an international range covers both the affordable and wish-list bottles from classic France. Well-chosen non-Champenois sparklers and sherries by the glass are bonuses.

CHEFS: Justin Pilkington, Anthony and Timothy Reeve PROPRIETORS: Mark Watson and Lorraine Fielding OPEN: all week 12 to 2, 7 to 9.30 (9 Sun) CLOSED: 4 to 15 Jan MEALS: alc D (main courses £22 to £24.50). Set L £14.95 (2 courses) to £15.95, Set D £32.50. Light L menu available Mon to Sat SERVICE: not inc, card slips closed CARDS: Delta, Diners, MasterCard, Switch, Visa DETAILS: 34 seats. 8 seats outside. Private parties: 20 main room, 8 to 16 private rooms. Car park. Vegetarian meals. Children's helpings. No children under 6. No smoking. Wheelchair access (also WC). Music ACCOMMODATION: 14 rooms, all with bath/shower. TV. Phone. B&B £75 to £176. Rooms for disabled. No children under 6 exc babes in arms. Baby facilities (*The Which? Guide to Good Hotels*) (£5)

The cuisine styles noted at the tops of entries are only an approximation, often suggested to us by the restaurants themselves. Please read the entry itself to find out more about the cooking style.

▲ Talkhouse 🍷 ✳

Pontdolgoch SY17 5JE
TEL: (01686) 688919　FAX: (01686) 689134
EMAIL: info@talkhouse.co.uk
WEBSITE: www.talkhouse.co.uk
on A470, about 1½m NW of Caersws

COOKING 3
MODERN BRITISH
£34–£47

The Talkhouse is a country pub with ambition and an emphasis on good food; it is a popular eating place for visitors to rural Wales and for dedicated locals. The simply furnished dining room looks out on to the garden. New owners have taken over since last year, installing a South African brigade in the kitchen, led by husband-and-wife team Peter and Elsie Innes. According to one regular, the food 'is even better now'. The menu is short, with four starters, mains and desserts: smoked haddock and saffron risotto topped with a poached egg and curried coconut sauce may be followed by tender honey-glazed Barbary duck breast with caramelised apple and a date and balsamic-scented sauce, or herb-roasted monkfish with sweet-and-sour pepper sauce, served with new potatoes. A dessert of orange blossom pannacotta with citrus and champagne salad and yoghurt sorbet has impressed, as did a dark chocolate mousse with chocolate syrup and coffee ice cream. The only quibble has been with vegetables, which at inspection tended to lack flavour. Staff are formal and courteous and the wine list well chosen, with South African selections particularly strong. Six 'wines of the month' are offered by the glass; bottle prices start at £12.

CHEFS: Peter and Elsie Innes　PROPRIETORS: Mark and Stephen Garratt　OPEN: Tue to Sun L 12 to 2, Tue to Sat D 7 to 9 (9.30 Fri and Sat)　MEALS: Set L and D £21.50 (2 courses) to £26. Set business L £21.50. Light lunch menu also available　SERVICE: not inc　CARDS: MasterCard, Switch, Visa　DETAILS: 35 seats. 10 seats outside. Private parties: 50 main room. Car park. Vegetarian meals. No children under 14 at D. No smoking. Wheelchair access (not WC). Music. No mobile phones　ACCOMMODATION: 3 rooms, all with bath/shower. TV. B&B £70 to £95
£5

▲ Tregynon Farmhouse ✳

Gwaun Valley, Pontfaen SA65 9TU
TEL: (01239) 820531　FAX: (01239) 820808
EMAIL: tregynon@online-holidays.net
WEBSITE: www.online-holidays.net/tregynon
at junction of B4313 Narberth to Fishguard road
and B4329, take B4313 towards Fishguard, then
first right and first right again

COOKING 1
MODERN BRITISH
£34–£46

This is a 600-year-old farmhouse where rough stone walls, black beams, a walk-in inglenook and neatly laid tables combine to produce a stylish atmosphere that is both rustic and refined. In order to accommodate visitors who stay for a week, the menu rotates day-to-day to ensure that guests staying for a full week won't face the same dish twice, or even a vegetable cooked the same way. The set-up is a set-price deal with a few supplements, and menus are nothing if not varied, taking in anything from mulligatawny soup to a toasted croissant filled with lambs' kidneys, from seafood choux puffs to chickpea noisettes (with a cider, cream and mushroom sauce). Pembrokeshire lamb is typically herb-crusted and roasted, a speciality sausage is made by a local butcher to the Heards' own recipe (with pork, cheese, laverbread, mustard seed and ale), and gammon and bacon are oak-smoked on the premises. Finish perhaps with home-made ice creams, or chilled lemon and banoffi flan. The short but lengthily annotated wine list is not without interest, but the 'special selection' of good-value wines is worth particular attention. Prices start at £11.50.

CHEFS: Peter and Jane Heard, and Gemma Cox   PROPRIETORS: Peter and Jane Heard   OPEN: Mon to Wed, Fri and Sat D only 7.30 to 8.30; booking essential   CLOSED: 31 Dec   MEALS: Set D £25.50 to £29   SERVICE: not inc   CARDS: Delta, MasterCard, Switch, Visa   DETAILS: 20 seats. Private parties: 14 main room, 2 to 6 private rooms. Car park. Vegetarian meals. No children under 8. No smoking. Wheelchair access (also WC). Music   ACCOMMODATION: 3 rooms, all with bath/shower. TV. Phone. B&B £75 to £85

PORTMEIRION Gwynedd   map 7

▲ Hotel Portmeirion ♥ ✸

Portmeirion LL48 6ET
TEL: (01766) 770000   FAX: (01766) 771331
EMAIL: hotel@portmeirion-village.com
WEBSITE: www.portmeirion-village.com
off A487, signposted from Minffordd

WALES
GFG
2004
COMMENDED

COOKING 4
MODERN WELSH-PLUS
£21–£53

Clough Williams-Ellis built Portmeirion in the 1920s quasi una fantasia, an Italianate gem on the side of a Welsh estuary. At its centre is the splendid hotel, a masterpiece of rococo design that boasts a discreetly lit dining room with a great bow-window, from which you may watch the tide roll in.

The kitchen shows an assured understanding of how to build up a dish – there is no straining after novelty for its own sake – so that a first course that pairs an escalope of oak-smoked salmon with Abergavenny ham and quails' eggs hangs together very successfully, and a fashionable salad of poached pear, avocado and feta dressed in balsamic pleased an inspector. Timing of main courses impresses for accuracy, whether the principal element is a piece of grilled halibut with a seafood fricassée combining cockles, mussels and scallops, or a fillet of Welsh beef accompanied by a tartlet of honey-roasted vegetables. Presentations belong to another era, but are artfully done, down to the tying of a bundle of green beans with a strip of pancetta. Head-turning desserts have included chocolate fondant with apricots and raisins, and iced rhubarb parfait with a well-made eggy sabayon. Expertly drilled service ensures everything proceeds smoothly, and the wine list, focused on France, offers commendable value, with a wealth of options under £15. Over a dozen clarets under £30 alongside a similar number of their grander siblings give an indication of the approach. Shorter selections elsewhere are packed with good names but shy away from premium bottles. Six house wines are £11, or £2.80 a glass.

Castell Deudraeth, a more austere greystone battlemented building nearby, is under the same ownership as the hotel, and serves a simpler style of brasserie food.

CHEFS: Colin Pritchard and Billy Taylor PROPRIETOR: Portmeirion Ltd OPEN: all week 12 to 2, 6.30 to 9.30 CLOSED: Jan 4 to 16 MEALS: Set L £13 to £16.50, Set D £35 SERVICE: not inc, card slips closed CARDS: Amex, Delta, Diners, MasterCard, Switch, Visa DETAILS: 100 seats. Private parties: 100 main room, 20 to 30 private rooms. Car park. Vegetarian meals. Children's helpings. No smoking . No music. No mobile phones ACCOMMODATION: 51 rooms, all with bath/ shower. TV. Phone. Room only £110 to £195. Rooms for disabled. Baby facilities. Swimming pool (*The Which? Guide to Good Hotels*)

PWLLHELI Gwynedd   map 7

▲ Plas Bodegroes 🍷 ✳

Nefyn Road, Pwllheli LL53 5TH
TEL: (01758) 612363   FAX: (01758) 701247
EMAIL: gunna@bodegroes.co.uk
WEBSITE: www.bodegroes.co.uk
on A497, 1m W of Pwllheli

COOKING **6**
MODERN WELSH
£28–£60

From the wisteria-covered veranda of the cream-coloured house, a woodland path (bluebell-strewn in spring) disappears along an avenue of tall and ancient beech trees. The house (built in 1780) looks and feels old, but the dining room is quite modern, painted deep, duck-egg blue, with bare wooden floorboards, small spotlights, and some appealing modern art on the walls. Chris Chown's food is contemporary, too, although it doesn't lose sight of its roots. Some items are evocatively native – cutlets of mountain lamb with a Welsh onion cake, or grilled fillet of Welsh beef – while others simply make the most of local materials, including fish and shellfish: perhaps seared scallops with tomato and artichoke confit, a warm salad of monkfish with Carmarthen ham, or a thickish fillet of steamed sea bass smeared with crabmeat.

The foundation is plain and honest cooking, and if reports this year suggest that the wow factor has been in rather short supply, there is still plenty to enjoy: from a starter of finely sliced lamb's liver served with cannellini beans in tomato sauce, to a dessert of rhubarb and apple sandwiched between heart-shaped cinnamon biscuits served with elderflower custard. Staff are pleasant and smiley, and little escapes Gunna Chown's attention. The wine list gives a good account of all regions, with particular strengths in Bordeaux, Burgundy, Alsace and Italy, and prices are very fair throughout, with over 80 bottles to choose from under £20. Half-bottles are available for many of the wines but just four come by the glass.

CHEF: Chris Chown PROPRIETORS: Chris and Gunna Chown OPEN: Sun L only 12 to 2.30, Tue to Sat D 7 to 9 (9.30 Sat and summer) CLOSED: Dec to Feb inc MEALS: Set L Sun £16.50, Set D £35 SERVICE: not inc CARDS: Delta, MasterCard, Switch, Visa DETAILS: 40 seats. Private parties: 40 main room, 12 to 16 private rooms. Car park. No smoking. Wheelchair access (also WC). Occasional music. No mobile phones ACCOMMODATION: 11 rooms, all with bath/shower. TV. Phone. B&B £40 to £150. Baby facilities (*The Which? Guide to Good Hotels*)

Some restaurants leave credit card slips open even though they also make a fixed (or 'optional') service charge. The Guide strongly disapproves of this practice as it may result in consumers unknowingly paying twice for service.

REYNOLDSTON Swansea   map 4

▲ Fairyhill ▮ ⁵⁄✖

Reynoldston SA3 1BS
TEL: (01792) 390139   FAX: (01792) 391358
EMAIL: postbox@fairyhill.net   COOKING **4**
WEBSITE: www.fairyhill.net   MODERN WELSH
Off A4118, 1½m NW of Reynoldston   £33–£64

The Gower peninsula's sandy beaches and sheltered coves are worth visiting any time, but knowing this eighteenth-century house, with its lake and woodland, is on hand for lunches and dinners every day of the week can only add to the allure. A diverting mixture of styles distinguishes the interiors, and, although there has been the odd report of slack service, the place is generally well-run.

Fixed-price menus without supplements, plus a simple carte at lunchtime, bring French touches to bear on many traditional local ingredients. A sausage of griddled chicken is accompanied by Llanboidy cheese and laverbread and sauced with mustard, while the famous Welsh Black beef might come with boulangère potatoes and juices infused with truffle. Seafood is well represented, whether in a gratin of salmon and scampi, or in a main-course pairing of skate and scallops with black and white tagliatelle. Save some room for desserts; hot items, like steamed treacle sponge with orange ice-cream, need to be ordered in advance, but, if you can't wait, go for something like praline glacé with mocha sauce. Be prepared to give the 40-page wine list lengthy consideration: three-figure prices abound – for Coche-Dury's burgundies, first-growth clarets, Pesquera Janus and the like – but, although prices are generally on the high side, you'll also find a couple of pages of bottles under £20 (seven of them available by the glass from £3.50); French country wines, the Rhône, Austria and Australia are good hunting grounds.

CHEFS: Paul Davies and Bryony Jones   PROPRIETORS: Paul Davies and Andrew Hetherington   OPEN: all week 12.30 to 2, 7.30 to 9   CLOSED: 26 Dec, 1–15 Jan   MEALS: alc L (main courses £15 to £18.50). Set L £14.95 (2 courses) to £18.95, Set D £29.50 (2 courses) to £37.50   SERVICE: not inc, card slips closed   CARDS: Amex, Delta, MasterCard, Switch, Visa   DETAILS: 60 seats. 20 seats outside. Private parties: 40 main room, 4 to 26 private rooms. Car park. Vegetarian meals. Children's helpings at L. No children under 8 in evening. No smoking. Music   ACCOMMODATION: 8 rooms, all with bath/shower. TV. Phone. B&B £120 to £245. No children under 8 (*The Which? Guide to Good Hotels*) (£5)

ST DAVID'S Pembrokeshire   map 4

Morgan's Brasserie ⁵⁄✖

20 Nun Street, St David's SA62 6NT
TEL: (01437) 720508   COOKING **2**
EMAIL: morgans@stdavids.co.uk   SEAFOOD/MODERN WELSH
WEBSITE: www.morgans-in-stdavids.co.uk   £31–£51

Morgan's is on the lower floor of a small Victorian terraced house. Cosy tea room domesticity dominates, from bentwood chairs and fresh flowers to rough stone walls, though tables are smartly and formally set. Vegetarian and meat dishes appear on the short printed menu, and (typically five) fish dishes are listed on a blackboard. Starters have included tomato and coconut soup, or a duck terrine described as 'a bit of a classic'. One diner's whole Dover sole from Milford Haven in a lemon and dill sauce was 'very plain and delicious', and roast monkfish in a bouillabaise sauce had 'bags of flavour'; but there might also be slow-cooked confit of Welsh lamb for confirmed carnivores. Desserts tend to richness – say, banana Bavarois, or chocolate, coffee and cardamom mousse – and France and South Africa lead a fairly priced wine list that starts at £12 (£2.50 a glass). Service is friendly but can be uneven, and tends to slow under pressure.

CHEF: Ceri Morgan   PROPRIETORS: Ceri and Elaine Morgan   OPEN: Mon to Sat D only 6.30 to 9 (days may vary in low season)   CLOSED: Jan and Feb   MEALS: alc (main courses £10 to £18.50) SERVICE: not inc, card slips closed   CARDS: MasterCard, Visa   DETAILS: 32 seats. Private parties: 20 main room. Vegetarian meals. Children's helpings. No smoking in dining room but permitted in bar. Music. No mobile phones

ST FAGANS Cardiff   map 4

▲ Old Post Office ⅝   NEW ENTRY

Greenwood Lane, St Fagans, nr Cardiff CF5 6EL   COOKING 4
TEL: (029) 20565 400   FAX: (029) 20563 400   MODERN EUROPEAN
EMAIL: heiditheoldpost@aol.com   £30–£61

If the name and the cottage-like outward appearance of the building conjure up 'olde worlde' expectations, the modern, minimalist, Scandinavian style of the interior décor may come as something of a surprise. But the effect is relaxed and informal, helped by 'efficient and amiable hosts' Ian and Heidi Urquhart. Fashionable flavours also dominate the cooking. At inspection, starters included a trio of salmon ('trios' and 'duos' are a recurring theme) comprising crisp-skinned, moist-fleshed roast salmon with spinach and plum sauce, gravadlax with sweet cucumber, and a ballottine with lumpfish roe. Main courses can seem a bit busy – witness roast pork tenderloin wrapped in crisp pancetta, with braised belly pork, black pudding mash, apple purée and pork jus, or roast halibut fillet on 'mellow, creamy' leeks and crisp rösti potatoes, with spinach purée and a frothy jus flavoured with oysters and truffles – but results are on the whole successful and presentation is strong throughout. This is especially true of desserts, such as a 'mille-feuille' of thin chocolate leaves layered with fresh strawberries, cream and redcurrants served with pistachio ice cream. The brief wine list hits the spot for all palates and most budgets, starting at £14.95. The Old Post Office is under the same ownership as Woods Brasserie (see entry).

CHEF: Tony Jenkins   PROPRIETOR: Choice Produce Ltd   OPEN: Thurs to Sun L 12 to 2, Wed to Sun D 7 to 9.30   MEALS: Set L £12.50 (2 courses) to £15.95, Set D £27.50 (2 courses) to £32.50 SERVICE: not inc, 10% (optional) for parties of 8 or more   CARDS: Amex, Delta, Diners, MasterCard, Switch, Visa   DETAILS: 24 seats. Private parties: 28 main room. Car park. Vegetarian meals. Children's menu Sun L. No smoking. Wheelchair access (also WC). Music. Air-conditioned   ACCOMMODATION: 6 rooms, all with bath/shower. TV. Phone. B&B £60 to £75. Rooms for disabled (£5)

A list of London restaurants by cuisine can be found near the front of the book.

SALEM Carmarthenshire

Angel ✷

NEW ENTRY

Salem, nr Llandeilo SA19 7LY
TEL: (01558) 823394

COOKING **2**
MODERN BRITISH
£30–£48

This rambling pub – next door to the independent chapel that gives the village its name – was recently taken over by Rod Peterson, who used to cook at the Cawdor Arms in nearby Llandeilo. Refurbishment is due but everything looks shipshape on the cooking side. Menus are a hotch-potch of global ideas, but always based on fine Welsh ingredients. The short carte – five starters and mains – might yield salmon ravioli with asparagus and fennel fondue, or Chinese-style crispy beef with sesame salad, followed by crisp-skinned wild Towy sewin on a creamy risotto of prawns and leeks, or 'pink, tender' roast best end of lamb on ratatouille with crushed potatoes and tapénade. To finish, one reporter's tiramisù was 'simply the best we have ever tasted'. A simple globe-trotting list with brief tasting notes stays mostly under £20; three house wines are £9.45 for the bottle, £1.75 per large glass.

CHEF: Rod Peterson   PROPRIETORS: Rod Peterson and Elizabeth Smith   OPEN: Wed to Fri and Sun L 12 to 2, Tue to Sat D 7 to 9   MEALS: alc (main courses £12 to £17)   SERVICE: not inc, card slips closed   CARDS: Delta, MasterCard, Switch, Visa   DETAILS: 60 seats. Private parties: 80 main room. Car park. Vegetarian meals. Children's helpings. No smoking. Music

SKENFRITH Monmouthshire

map 2

▲ Bell at Skenfrith ✷

Skenfrith NP7 8UH
TEL: (01600) 750235   FAX: (01600) 750525
EMAIL: enquiries@skenfrith.com
WEBSITE: www.skenfrith.com
on B4521 between Abergavenny and Ross-on-
Wye

NEW CHEF
MODERN BRITISH
£32–£57

This white-painted, slate-roofed stone building beside a hump-backed bridge over the River Monnow is simple and stylish inside with flagstone floors and an open-plan layout. The decent beers, ciders and games of a country pub co-exist with the white cloths, candles and fresh flowers of a formal restaurant. We were alerted to the arrival of a new chef too late for an inspection, but expect starters like lamb and foie gras terrine with orange onion marmalade and aubergine caviar dressing, followed by halibut with crab and spring onion risotto. Desserts might include vanilla and mint pannacotta. Service is by friendly, relaxed, 'delightful' staff. The ambitious wine list has some 100 bottles to chose from and offers a mix of regions and styles arranged in ascending price order, from £10 Spanish white to Bordeaux first growths; there are lots of good half-bottles and dessert wines.

CHEF: Denis Guillemin   PROPRIETORS: William and Janet Hutchings   OPEN: Tue to Sun (all week Apr to Oct) 12 to 2.30, 7 to 9.30 (9 Sun)   MEALS: alc exc Sun L (main courses L £7 to £15, D £12.50 to £17.50). Set L Sun £13.50 (2 courses) to £17.50. Bar L menu available   SERVICE: not inc, card slips closed   CARDS: Amex, Delta, MasterCard, Switch, Visa   DETAILS: 60 seats. 30 seats outside. Private parties: 40 main room, 40 to 100 private rooms. Car park. Vegetarian meals. Children's helpings. No smoking in 1 dining room. Wheelchair access (also WC). Music. ACCOMMODATION: 8 rooms, all with bath/shower. TV. Phone. B&B £65 to £150. Baby facilities (*The Which? Guide to Good Hotels*)

SWANSEA Swansea   map 4

La Braseria £

28 Wind Street, Swansea SA1 1DZ	COOKING 1
TEL: (01792) 469683 FAX: (01792) 456334	SPANISH
WEBSITE: www.labraseria.com	£23–£53

Situated as it is among many of the city's eateries, La Braseria offers a rather different experience. Two large tile-clad bodega-style rooms display meats and fish that are cooked to order. Once you have found a table, note the all-important table number then order your food at one of the bars; when the food is ready it is brought to you. The menu offers a wide range including traditional suckling pig, fish and shellfish – 'moist' and flavoursome halibut and 'soft, fresh scallops' to name but two. Note that some of the fish is sold by weight. Dishes include baked potato or French fries, though side orders of salad or bread are charged extra. Among desserts might be crème caramel or raspberry cheesecake. Service and atmosphere are 'friendly' and the wine list has some gems if you know where to look. House wine, Spanish of course, is £10.25.

CHEF: Ian Wing   PROPRIETOR: Manuel Tercero   OPEN: Mon to Sat 12 to 2.30, 7 to 11.30   CLOSED: 25 and 26 Dec   MEALS: alc (main courses £6.45 to £21.95). Set L £7.50 (2 courses)   SERVICE: not inc, card slips closed   CARDS: Amex, Delta, Diners, MasterCard, Switch, Visa   DETAILS: 170 seats. Private parties: 100 main room. Vegetarian meals. No prams or pushchairs. Wheelchair access (also WC). Music. Air-conditioned

Didier & Stephanie's

56 St Helens Road, Swansea SA1 4BE	COOKING 3
TEL: (01792) 655603 FAX: (01792) 470563	FRENCH
	£21–£42

The eponymous chefs-patrons have been serving regional French cooking at their town-centre restaurant since 2000. There are two dining rooms, a bay-windowed room up a few steps from the street, with a basement room taking the overspill at weekends. Simple pine décor and oatmeal-coloured walls establish a homely feel. Meaty starters have included crumbly, moist boudin noir served in chunks encased in filo, dressed in mustard sauce, and – also in filo – a serving of earthy, tender snails topped with herbs and surrounded by a green herb sauce and diced peppers (a refreshing change from the usual garlic butter). Well-reported main courses have included sea bass with tomatoes and black olives, memorably rich boeuf en daube, and duck leg confit with Puy lentils. A fine inspection dish of lamb shank, slow-braised so that it fell gently from the bone, was served with a distinctively herb-scented jus, and given a further novel twist of flavour with a few green olives. The green dappling in the crème brûlée comes from pistachios, while a plate of cheeses brought forth a chèvre, Brie, Pont l'Evêque, Bleu d'Auvergne and Reblochon, all in prime condition and accompanied by raisins and walnuts. 'Courteous, prompt and discreet' service gets its job done with a minimum of fuss. If you've a hankering for live accordion music, make a date for the second Thursday of every month. A short, French-led wine list is mostly reasonably priced, starting from £9.90 for the house wines.

CHEFS/PROPRIETORS: Stephanie Danvel and Didier Suvé   OPEN: Tue to Sat 12 to 2, 7 to 9 (9.30 Sat) CLOSED: Christmas and New Year, bank hols   MEALS: alc (main courses £11 to £13). Set L £7.20 (1 course) to £12.20   SERVICE: not inc, card slips closed   CARDS: Amex, Delta, MasterCard, Switch, Visa   DETAILS: 52 seats. Private parties: 28 main room, 15 to 22 private rooms. Children's helpings. Vegetarian meals. Music

Hanson's

Pilot House Wharf, Trawler Road,	COOKING 3
Swansea SA1 1UN	MODERN BRITISH/SEAFOOD
TEL: (01792) 466200 FAX: (01792) 203570	£24–£51

Above a fishing tackle shop, up a spiral stair, this restaurant is warm and informal. Pilot House Wharf is in Swansea Marina, where the trawlers now dock, so a strong emphasis on fish is not surprising. Fresh catches are shown on a blackboard, and no-frills, essentially traditional cookery brings starters such as smoked haddock fish cakes with tartare sauce, or smoked salmon, melon and prawns, followed perhaps by Cornish turbot with smoked bacon, or lemon sole. Meat eaters are not neglected, and might be offered chump of Welsh lamb with gratin of garlic potatoes, or duck breast with rösti, forest mushrooms and béarnaise. Alcohol features in some desserts, such as lemon tart with Cointreau, or prune and Armagnac bread-and-butter pudding. Wines are priced kindly; house bottles are £10.95, little is above £20 and most, whites especially, are drawn from Europe with genuine care.

CHEFS: Andrew Hanson and Gareth Bagley   PROPRIETORS: Andrew Hanson and Helen Tennant OPEN: all week L 12 to 2, Mon to Sat D 6.30 to 9.30   CLOSED: 24 to 26 Dec   MEALS: alc (main courses £10 to £19). Set L £10.95 (2 courses) to £13.95   SERVICE: not inc   CARDS: Delta, MasterCard, Visa   DETAILS: 46 seats. Private parties: 46 main room. Vegetarian meals. Children's helpings. Music   £5

TALSARNAU Gwynedd   map 7

▲ Maes-y-Neuadd ♥ ✳

Talsarnau LL47 6YA	
TEL: (01766) 780200 FAX: (01766) 780211	
EMAIL: maes@neuadd.com	COOKING 4
WEBSITE: www.neuadd.com	MODERN WELSH
off B4573, 1m S of Talsarnau	£24–£55

Set amid lawns where pink hydrangeas bloom, the house is a grey-stone building in the mountains overlooking Cardigan Bay. Inside is a warren of low-ceilinged rooms leading to a muted dining room with damask napkins and oil paintings of nearby Harlech Castle. The sense of gracious living is backed up by the cooking, which makes use of produce from the hotel's own vegetable gardens as well as a range of fine local materials. The format is a fixed-price dinner menu, beginning with a choice of two starters, one of which might be air-dried venison with onion confit, olive oil and Parmesan shavings, then a set fish dish, such as trout roulade with spring cabbage sauerkraut, followed by your pick of two main-course meats: perhaps breast and confit of duck with a potato galette and marmalade sauce, or roast loin of pork with mustard mash, apple and shallot compote and peppercorn sauce.

It is the fish dishes that draw particular praise, one reporter praising rillettes of smoked fish with herb yoghurt, and local sea bream with braised fennel. The final course seems to be the full works, with glazed seasonal fruits, white chocolate mousse, a selection of ice creams and sorbets, and Welsh cheeses all appearing on the same menu. The set-menu idea has also been applied to the wines, with three glasses selected to accompany the meal on offer for £14.50. House wines and local Glyndwr white make up other options by the glass, but the full list digs deeper, with sound ranges from France, some star names from Spain and a quick trot around the rest of the world.

CHEFS: Peter Jackson and John Owen Jones   PROPRIETORS: Peter and Lynn Jackson, and Peter and Doreen Payne   OPEN: all week L 12 to 1.45 (Mon to Sat bar lunches only), 7 to 8.45 D   MEALS: Set L Sun £15.25, Set D £31 to £35.   SERVICE: not inc   CARDS: Amex, Delta, Diners, MasterCard, Switch, Visa   DETAILS: 60 seats. 20 seats outside. Private parties: 50 main room, 2 to 15 private rooms. Car park. Children's helpings. No children under 7 at D. No smoking. Wheelchair access (also WC). Occasional music. No mobile phones   ACCOMMODATION: 16 rooms, all with bath/shower. TV. Phone. D,B&B £73 to £255. Rooms for disabled. Baby facilities (*The Which? Guide to Good Hotels*) £5

TREDUNNOCK Monmouthshire   map 2

▲ The Newbridge

Tredunnock NP15 1LY
TEL: (01633) 451000   FAX: (01633) 451001
EMAIL: thenewbridge@tinyonline.co.uk
WEBSITE: www.thenewbridge.co.uk
from Caerleon take Llangibby/Usk road; after
approx 3m turn right opposite hotel; go   NEW CHEF
through village of Tredunnock and down hill   MODERN WELSH/MEDITERRANEAN
to banks of River Usk   £22–£58

A beautiful location by a stone bridge over the River Usk is one of the principal charms of this rural restaurant with rooms. The dining room is light and airy with modern artworks on the walls that give the room a slightly art gallery feel. New chef Iain Sampson was still finding his feet when our inspector visited, but early signs bode well. His professed aim is to use local produce in a 'fine country dining' style, with 'fresh, clean, simple flavours'. This typically translates into starters of Mediterranean vegetable roulade with goats' cheese on rocket salad with balsamic vinaigrette, or duck and black pudding terrine with toasted brioche and plum chutney, followed by main courses ranging from simple pan-fried chicken leg on pesto tagliatelle to more involved dishes such as beef fillet with pomme fondant, spinach purée, mushroom pudding and Stilton sauce. A wine list was not available to the Guide as we went to press, but if it is similar to last year's, mark-ups will be low and there will be good choice under £20. House bottles start at £11.50.

CHEF: Iain Sampson   PROPRIETOR: Glen Rick Court   OPEN: all week L 12 to 2.30 (4 Sat, 3 Sun June to Aug), Mon to Sat D 6.45 to 9.30   CLOSED: 26 Dec, 1 Jan   MEALS: alc (main courses £6 to £20). Set L Sun £10.95 (2 courses) to £12.95   SERVICE: not inc   CARDS: Amex, Delta, Diners, MasterCard, Switch, Visa   DETAILS: 80 seats. 25 seats outside. Private parties: 70 main room, 8 to 16 private rooms. Car park. Vegetarian meals. Children's helpings. Wheelchair access (also WC). Music. Air-conditioned   ACCOMMODATION: 6 rooms, all with bath/shower. TV. Phone. B&B £70 to £145 (£5)

WHITEBROOK Monmouthshire   map 2

▲ Crown at Whitebrook ♥ ⁵⁄✳

Whitebrook NP25 4TX
TEL: (01600) 860254   FAX: (01600) 860607
EMAIL: crown@whitebrook.demon.co.uk
WEBSITE: www.crownatwhitebrook.co.uk
leave A466 at Bigsweir bridge, 6m S of   NEW CHEF
Monmouth; follow signs to Whitebrook; hotel is   MODERN EUROPEAN
2m on left   £28–£50

The Crown calls itself a 'romantic auberge', and its setting in a wooded valley between Monmouth and Tintern is romantic indeed. Chef Mark Turton departed as the Guide was going to press, to be replaced by his right-hand man, sous-chef James Sommerin. We are told the new man will continue the style he helped to create, so expect fortnightly-changing menus (more elaborate at dinner) offering dishes constructed with a designer's eye for detail, and using fine raw materials. Previously an assiette of duck (ballottine, a tartlet of rillettes and a parfait of foie gras) has been followed by smoked monkfish and king scallops accompanied by roast artichoke, orange and cardamom; and quince, chestnuts and vanilla have supported chargrilled loin of Scottish mountain hare.

Desserts have included clootie dumpling, clotted cream and a syrup of red wine and port; otherwise, there's a selection of Welsh and Continental cheeses. Matching wines to accompany such adventurous and contrasting flavours could be tricky, but the Crown's diverse cellar of around 100 bottles is up to it. Sixteen recommended wines start with straightforward vins de pays at £11.95 (£3.50 a glass), and overall prices are sensible, with plenty of choice under £20 and a large selection of half-bottles.

CHEF: James Sommerin   PROPRIETORS: Angela and Elizabeth Barbara   OPEN: Tue to Sun L 12 to 1.45, all week D 7 to 8.45   CLOSED: 22 Dec to 9 Jan   MEALS: alc L (main courses £9.50 to £12). Set L Sun £17.50, Set D £29.95   SERVICE: not inc, 10% for parties of 6 or more   CARDS: Amex, Delta, Diners, MasterCard, Switch, Visa   DETAILS: 32 seats. Private parties: 20 main room, 10 to 12 private rooms. Car park. Vegetarian meals. No children under 12. No smoking. No music   ACCOMMODATION: 10 rooms, all with bath/shower. TV. Phone. D,B&B £55 to £90. No children under 12 (£5)

Channel Islands

BEAUMONT Jersey   map 1

Bistro Soleil

La Route de la Haule, Beaumont JE3 7BA	COOKING **4**
TEL: (01534) 720249 FAX: (01534) 625621	BISTRO/SEAFOOD
EMAIL: katep@localdial.com	£21–£45

Large windows look out across the wide expanse of beach to the sea, while the
sound of seagulls, and the tinkling of the bell aboard Le Petit Train carrying
tourists from St Aubin to St Helier, add to the sense of atmosphere. This close to
the seashore, it is perhaps no surprise that fish has an important role to play on
the menu. Local diver-caught scallops, oysters, crab and lobster are likely to
make their appearance, the latter perhaps as a main course served grilled with
garlic and herb butter, thermidor, or simply steamed. For starters, Royal
Grouville Bay oysters are served with red wine vinegar, shallots and lemon.
Simplicity is the name of the game in many dishes, from grilled steaks (a choice
of five) served with béarnaise sauce, to pan-fried lemon sole with home-made
chips and tartare sauce. At lunch, baguettes and salads, such as Parma ham,
mozzarella and sunblush tomato, make up most of the running, while a set-price
dinner menu could be good value. Ditto the short, well-chosen wine list.

CHEF: Ian Jones   PROPRIETOR: Chris Power   OPEN: Tue to Sun L 12.15 to 2, Tue to Sat D 6.45 to
9.30   CLOSED: 25 and 26 Dec   MEALS: alc (main courses L £12 to £15, D £11 to £15.50). Set L
£12.50, Set D £25. Light L menu also available   SERVICE: not inc, 10% for parties of 10 or more
CARDS: Amex, Delta, MasterCard, Switch, Visa   DETAILS: 60 seats. 40 seats outside. Private
parties: 60 main room. Car park. Vegetarian meals. Children's helpings. No cigars/pipes.
Wheelchair access (not WC). Music. Air-conditioned

GOREY Jersey   map 1

Jersey Pottery, Garden Restaurant

Gorey JE3 9EP	
TEL: (01534) 851119 FAX: (01534) 856403	COOKING **2**
EMAIL: admin@jerseypottery.com	MODERN BRITISH/SEAFOOD
WEBSITE: www.jerseypottery.com	£28–£68

The name does not hark back to some forgotten craft workshop. This is the
restaurant of a fully operational pottery, with a ready stream of tourists to keep it
occupied. Seating is under a glass roof, with luxuriant greenery and fresh
flowers abounding, or on a patio extension with garden furniture, sunshades
and weeping willows. This is the closest the UK gets to the Mediterranean, and

there is plenty of that influence on the menus, with seafood aplenty (from seared scallops with pea and mint purée, to chargrilled fillet of brill on crab and potato salad) and a greater leaning of late towards classical dishes: whole grilled Dover sole with hazelnut and thyme butter, for example. Desserts, presented buffet-style, might include vanilla-poached pears with saffron yoghurt and raspberry compote. The wine list is divided democratically between Old and New Worlds, with house wines starting at £11.95.

CHEFS: Tony Dorris and Roger White PROPRIETORS: the Jones family OPEN: Wed to Sun L 12 to 2.30 (3 Sun), Wed to Sat D 7 to 9.30 CLOSED: 21 Dec to 14 Feb MEALS: Set L £15.50 (2 courses) to £19.50, Set D £20 (2 courses) to £25 SERVICE: not inc, card slips closed CARDS: Amex, Delta, Diners, MasterCard, Switch, Visa DETAILS: 180 seats. 50 seats outside. Private parties: 180 main room, 20 to 100 private rooms. Car park. Vegetarian meals. Children's helpings. No-smoking area. No pipes. Wheelchair access (also WC). Music £5

Suma's

Gorey Hill, St Martin, Gorey JE3 6ET	COOKING 5
TEL: (01534) 853291 FAX: (01534) 851913	MODERN EUROPEAN
	£19–£51

This modern restaurant, sister establishment to Longueville Manor in St Saviour (see entry), is done out in cool, pale wood and fresh, white tones, and the windows look out over Gorey Harbour to Mont Orgueil Castle in the distance. From the terrace (blankets provided when it's chilly) or a table by the windows, you can while away the time, eating some of Jersey's best food as you watch the fishing boats bob in the distance. In January 2003 a new chef, Daniel Ward, took over. 'Luxury' ingredients are less in evidence than before, and some dishes show an Asian influence, as in a starter of linguine with Eastern spice, spider crab, wok-fried greens and coriander. Others are more modern British – pan-fried calf's liver with dry-cured bacon, onion marmalade and champ, for instance – and there is plenty of seafood, too, from Royal Bay oysters to a brill and Jersey crab gratin with scallions and pickled ginger, or even a red mullet pizza with Mediterranean vegetables and aïoli verdi. Service (included in the dish prices) is swift and friendly, and wines favour the New World, with bottle prices from a very fair £8.50.

CHEF: Daniel Ward PROPRIETORS: Malcolm Lewis and Sue Dufty OPEN: all week 12 to 2.30, 6.30 to 9.30 CLOSED: 23 Dec to 10 Jan MEALS: alc (main courses £8.50 to £17). Set L £14 (2 courses) to £18 SERVICE: net prices, card slips closed CARDS: Amex, Delta, Diners, MasterCard, Switch, Visa DETAILS: 45 seats. 16 seats outside. Private parties: 40 main room. Vegetarian meals. Children's helpings. Music. No mobile phones. Air-conditioned

ST MARTIN'S Guernsey   map 1

Auberge   NEW ENTRY

Jerbourg Road, St Martin's GY4 6BH	
TEL: (01481) 238485 FAX: (01481) 727051	COOKING 4
EMAIL: theauberge@cwgsy.net	MODERN BRITISH
WEBSITE: www.theauberge.gg	£33–£50

This cliff-top building, on a narrow road leading to Jerbourg Point, was skilfully redesigned three years ago. It is modern, bright and minimalist, with floor-to-ceiling windows overlooking Le Pied du Mur Bay, and outside tables taking in the views. Inside, a wooden floor, smart bar and blond-wood tables give the space a contemporary feel. Chef Paul Olliver plays interesting tunes with styles and ingredients, and his modish carte may feature starters like Thai glass noodle soup with chilli, calamari and mussels, or a salad of chorizo, piquillo peppers and sweet potato with a poached egg. Top-quality fish and shellfish (scallops, crab, sea bass, mullet) are a feature of the menu, augmented by meat dishes such as calf's liver and bacon with buttery, well-seasoned crushed new potatoes, leeks and red wine jus, or loin of venison with fig tart, creamed spinach and a vanilla-scented jus. Vegetarians are well served, with the likes of potato and leek tartlet, or pea, onion and fennel risotto. Desserts range from classic peach Melba to daringly deep-fried lemongrass ice cream with peach and Malibu salad. The short wine list has some good bottles at fair prices, with weekly-changing house wines starting at £10.95. Service is professional and friendly.

CHEF: Paul Olliver   PROPRIETOR: Ian Irving-Walker   OPEN: all week L 12 to 2.30, Mon to Sat D (all week D June to Sept) 6.30 to 10   MEALS: alc (main courses £9 to £14). Set L £11.95 (2 courses) to £13.95   SERVICE: not inc   CARDS: Amex, Delta, Diners, MasterCard, Switch, Visa   DETAILS: 80 seats. 50 seats outside. Private parties: 120 main room. Vegetarian meals. Children's helpings. No smoking in 1 dining room before 9.30. Music. Air-conditioned

---

ST PIERRE DU BOIS Guernsey   map 1

▲ Café du Moulin ✸ | NEW ENTRY |

Rue de Quanteraine, St Pierre du Bois GY7 9DP
TEL: (01481) 265944   FAX: (01481) 267343
EMAIL: vincentfam@guernsey.net
WEBSITE: www.cafedumoulin.com
drive through St Pierre, pass Le Riche
supermarket on right, turn left at filter junction,   COOKING 5
pass church, drive to incline, take immediate   MODERN EUROPEAN
right (small fork) into country lane, follow to end   £36–£63

In this old converted granary building – with terrace, gardens and a view of an old but still functioning watermill – is a charming beamed dining room, done out in shades of beige, cream and white, with a real fireplace and a tiny bar. The cooking style of Christophe Vincent, who trained under Albert Roux, is richly founded on the classical luxuries, and his take on modern Continental cuisine makes much use of organic produce, on a seasonally changing menu. Special dishes are chalked on a board, and might include a single raviolo stuffed with lobster in tarragon cream, dressed in lobster oil – 'a wonderfully concentrated triumph'. Otherwise, the main menu offers asparagus soup with pea and mint mousse, seared sea bass on parsnip and vanilla purée, or a fashionable pairing of meat and seafood, as in veal fillet and langoustines sauced with champagne. Oriental-style rabbit pot au feu has come with wasabi ravioli, and fish 'n chips 'my way' is there for those who like a surprise. Singular dessert ideas have included sweet potato and praline tart with Grand Marnier nougat glace. Good home-made breads, coffee that is 'simply the best', and the top-drawer professionalism of the staff help to make the faintly arduous journey here more than worthwhile. An imaginatively chosen wine list avoids giving automatic predominance to France, and mark-ups are reasonable. Glass (125ml) prices start at £2.50, bottles at £11.50.

CHEF/PROPRIETOR: Christophe Vincent   OPEN: Wed to Sun L 12 to 2, Tue to Sat D 7 to 9   MEALS: alc (main courses £15 to £18). Set D £35 (£50 inc wine)   SERVICE: not inc   CARDS: Delta, Diners, MasterCard, Switch, Visa   DETAILS: 37 seats. 25 seats outside. Private parties: 37 main room. Car park. Vegetarian meals. Children's helpings. No children under 8. No smoking. Wheelchair access (not WC). Music   ACCOMMODATION: 3 apartments, all with bath/shower. TV. Apartment only £200 to £650. Apartments for disabled. No children under 8

ST SAVIOUR Jersey   map 1

▲ Longueville Manor

St Saviour JE2 7WF
TEL: (01534) 725501   FAX: (01534) 731613   COOKING 6
EMAIL: info@longuevillemanor.com   MODERN EUROPEAN
WEBSITE: www.longuevillemanor.com   £33–£75

Longueville Manor is a family-run thirteenth-century Norman manor house with all the indulgent trappings of a country-house hotel. Start the meal in one of the many comfortable lounges, complete with comfy sofas and open log fires; amuse-bouches are served here before diners go through to the dining room. With such a range of dishes, making a choice from among the four menus – the menu du jour, à la carte, and (both for the whole table) a 'taste of Jersey' menu and the gourmet menu – can be difficult, though definitely rewarding. From the gourmet version, oven-roast Gressingham duck may be served with glazed apples and cranberries, while the 'taste of Jersey' centres on fish: grilled scallop with truffled French beans, or grilled turbot with vine tomatoes and new season's peas, for example. Grand Marnier soufflé and pear baked in brioche set the tone for comfort-food afters. Service, technique and quality of ingredients are of high standards. Although the atmosphere is formal, there's an elegant charm about the place that puts diners at ease. The classical wine list is long on Burgundy and Bordeaux with reasonable ranges from elsewhere in France – and a wealth of vintage champagnes – but also gives dutifully thorough coverage of the rest of Europe and the New World. Prices start at £14, and 29 come by the glass for £3.50–£13.25.

CHEF: Andrew Baird   PROPRIETORS: Malcolm Lewis and Sue Dufty   OPEN: all week 12.30 to 2, 7 to 9.30   MEALS: alc (main courses £26.50 to £29). Set L £13.50 (2 courses) to £22.50, Set D £37.50 to £80 (inc wine, whole table). Snack menu also available   SERVICE: net prices, card slips closed   CARDS: Amex, Delta, Diners, MasterCard, Switch, Visa   DETAILS: 70 seats. 40 seats outside. Private parties: 70 main room, 2 to 24 private rooms. Car park. Vegetarian meals. Children's helpings. No smoking in 1 dining room. Wheelchair access (not WC). No music. No mobile phones   ACCOMMODATION: 30 rooms, all with bath/shower. TV. Phone. B&B £160 to £200. Rooms for disabled. Baby facilities. Swimming pool

Northern Ireland

 map 16

Ginger Tree

29 Ballyrobert Road, Ballyclare BT39 9RY	COOKING **3**
TEL: (028) 9084 8176 FAX: (028) 9084 4077	JAPANESE
	£23–£59

The restaurant is done out in fitting shades of red, black and white, and most of the tables look out over a soothing Japanese garden. For those unfamiliar with Japanese food, six different set menus offer a range of flavours and cooking techniques. For those willing to go 'off-piste', the à la carte offers a fairly wide range, from gyoza (steamed and fried meat and vegetable dumplings) and tonkatsu (deep-fried pork loin coated with breadcrumbs) to a variety of noodle dishes, including zaru soba (cold buckwheat noodles served with wasabi and a dipping sauce) and fish dishes involving salmon, eel or prawns. Dishes, if not always strictly 100 per cent authentic, are elegantly presented, and service is charming. The sizeable wine list roves the globe, with house wines starting at £11.50.

CHEF: Shotaro Obana   PROPRIETORS: Shotaro Obana and Elizabeth Wylie   OPEN: Mon to Fri L 12 to 2, Mon to Sat D 6 to 8.30   CLOSED: 24 to 26 Dec, 11 to 13 Jul   MEALS: alc (main courses £8.50 to £13.50). Set L £13.95, Set D £16 (Mon to Fri) to £35   SERVICE: 10% (optional)   CARDS: Amex, Delta, Diners, MasterCard, Switch, Visa   DETAILS: 60 seats. Private parties: 70 main room. Car park. Vegetarian meals. No children after 9pm. Children's helpings. No cigars. Wheelchair access (also WC). Occasional music. Air-conditioned

 map 16

Shanks ▼

The Blackwood Golf Centre, 150 Crawfordsburn	
Road, Bangor BT19 1GB	COOKING **5**
TEL: (028) 9185 3313 FAX: (028) 9185 2493	MODERN EUROPEAN
WEBSITE: www.shanksrestaurant.com	£34–£80

Set on a golf course within the Clandeboye Estate, a mile or so outside Bangor, Shanks is a stylish, upmarket restaurant, its dining room decked out with Hockney illustrations. Chef Robbie Millar makes a point of sourcing local, preferably organic ingredients, including game from the estate, though when it comes to culinary inspiration his outlook is broad-minded and free-range, picking up ideas from across Europe and beyond. Thus, among starters, there may be an expertly made classic onion soup with ham and cheese croûtons alongside spiced tuna tartare with a salad of quails' eggs and toasted brioche. Main courses meanwhile run from wild sea bass with roasted peppers, basil couscous and saffron butter vinaigrette to crispy pork belly with oats, honey and chilli, cauliflower purée and sweet raisin jus. Venison from the estate is a fixture on the menu, served perhaps with glazed beetroot, apple and celeriac and a Sauternes and truffle cream, and to finish there may be amaretti stuffed pear with honey anglaise. The stylish presentation of the wine list is backed up by plenty of substance. A modern approach sees France reined in to manageable proportions to make room for Italy, Spain, Australia and the USA. Sensible prices start at £13 and take in a broad range under £20, with six by the glass at £3.50–£4.50.

CHEF: Robbie Millar   PROPRIETORS: Robbie and Shirley Millar   OPEN: Tue to Fri L 12.30 to 2.30, Tue to Sat D 7 to 10   CLOSED: 24 to 26, 30 and 31 Dec, 1 Jan, 3 weeks July   MEALS: Set L £17 (2 courses) to £21, Set D £38   SERVICE: not inc, 10% for parties of 6 or more   CARDS: Amex, MasterCard, Switch, Visa   DETAILS: 65 seats. Private parties: 50 main room, 12 to 36 private rooms. Car park. Vegetarian meals. Children's helpings. No-smoking area. No cigars/pipes. Wheelchair access (also WC). Music. Air-conditioned

---

BELFAST Co Antrim   map 16

Alden's ♟

229 Upper Newtownards Road, Belfast BT4 3JF
TEL: (028) 9065 0079   FAX: (028) 9065 0032   COOKING 4
EMAIL: info@aldensrestaurant.com   MODERN IRISH
WEBSITE: www.aldensrestaurant.com   £23–£50

The smart, modern exterior (etched glass, restrained colours) raises expectations that are confirmed once you are inside: service is attentive and knowledgeable, the setting contemporary and stylish, and the cooking serious. Details such as the clear and succinct menu show a desire to set the customer at ease. Bold flavours are wrought from an impressive range of locally sourced ingredients, including shellfish, smoked salmon and game. Three slices of venison from the Finnebrogue estate on a bed of mashed potato surrounded by an intensely rich, slightly fruity sauce exemplify the approach: reliance on fine ingredients and accurate timing. Duck breast and rhubarb jus comes with just-cooked small carrots and asparagus, and banana crème brûlée with fresh raspberries. The mid-week set dinner, two courses for £15.95, looks good value.

An individual and food-friendly wine selection collects treats from around the world, often balanced by budget alternatives – a fine £35 Condrieu followed by a vin de pays Viognier at £12.50, for example. Fifteen house wines from £13.15 push far beyond the usual range of bubblegum modern flavours; six come by the glass from £3.25. Half-bottles include stylish sherries from Lustau.

CHEF: Cath Gradwell   PROPRIETOR: Jonathan Davis   OPEN: Mon to Fri L 12 to 2.30, Mon to Sat D 6 to 10 (11 Fri and Sat)   CLOSED: bank hols, 2 weeks July   MEALS: alc (main courses £5.50 to £17). Set D Mon to Thur and Fri 6 to 6.45 £16.95 (2 courses)   SERVICE: not inc   CARDS: Amex, Delta, Diners, MasterCard, Switch, Visa   DETAILS: 70 seats. Private parties: 80 main room. Vegetarian meals. Wheelchair access (also WC). Music. Air-conditioned

---

♦ *denotes an outstanding wine cellar;* ♟ *denotes a good wine list, worth travelling for.*

Cayenne ▼

7 Ascot House, Shaftsbury Square,
Belfast BT2 7DB
TEL: (028) 9033 1532   FAX: (028) 9026 1575
EMAIL: reservations@cayennerestaurant.com
WEBSITE: www.cayennerestaurant.com

COOKING **4**
FUSION
£26–£52

Behind a small illuminated sign, this city-centre establishment serves 'hot and funky food in a cool urban atmosphere'. Theatrical lighting, chunky typography and food that bounds around the globe create a buzzy atmosphere, underpinned by knowledgeable and welcoming staff. Fusion occurs across the menu rather than within the dish: one evening menu included two soups – potato, bean and chorizo; and cream of two celeries with blue-cheese croûtons – plus spinach and ricotta ravioli alongside fillet of hake with ginger citrus broth, pak choi and sesame prawn toast. 'High skill in the kitchen' showed in a peppered rump of venison with a hash brown, beetroot and juniper chutney, carrots and turnips – contrasting the meat's 'melting tenderness', with crunchy fried potato, al dente vegetables and nutty fragments of juniper berry. Desserts include date and walnut steamed pudding with roast bananas and toffee sauce, and, for one reader, a too freddo semi-freddo. An appropriately modern, varietally organised wine list offers good breadth of choice. Prices are mostly fair, with plenty of interest under £20 (turn to the fine wines page at the back for anything over £30). Eight wines come by the glass (£3.50–£4).

CHEFS: Andy Rea and Adam Miller   PROPRIETORS: Paul and Jeanne Rankin   OPEN: Mon to Fri L 12 to 2.15, Mon to Sat D 6 to 10.15 (11.15 Fri and Sat), Sun L and D 1 to 9   CLOSED: 25 and 26 Dec, Easter Mon, 12 July,   MEALS: alc (main courses £8.50 to £16). Set L £12 (2 courses) to £15.50, Set D 6 to 6.45 £12 (2 courses) to £15.50   SERVICE: not inc, 10% for parties of 6 or more, card slips closed   CARDS: Amex, Delta, Diners, MasterCard, Switch, Visa   DETAILS: 80 seats. Private parties: 70 main room. Vegetarian meals. Wheelchair access (also WC). Music. Air-conditioned

▲ Metro Brasserie

13 Lower Crescent, Belfast BT7 1NR
TEL: (028) 9032 3349   FAX: (028) 9032 0646
EMAIL: info@crescenttownhouse.com
WEBSITE: www.crescenttownhouse.com

COOKING **2**
MODERN EUROPEAN
£23–£46

Along with its sister establishment Bar Twelve, Metro is situated in the Crescent Townhouse hotel. A long room with stripped floors, it serves the evening trade with a two- or three-course early bird menu that may include home-made black pudding with pear and walnut chutney, or breast of chicken with fragrant rice, steamed greens and Thai red curry. Alongside a vegetarian carte offering, say, roast beetroot and rocket risotto, a 'fashionable fusion of Mediterranean and Thai' creeps in with crispy chilli beef with garlic and chilli mayonnaise, or perhaps pork fillet with chargrilled aubergines and pak choi. Desserts range from old favourites like sticky toffee pudding to chocolate and orange bavarois with caramelised mango. A short wine list offers a good-value world tour, starting with an Australian duo at £12.

CHEF: Stephen Taylor-Winter PROPRIETOR: Wine Inns Ltd OPEN: Mon to Sat D 5.30 to 10
CLOSED: 25 and 26 Dec, 11 and 12 Jul MEALS: alc D (main courses £10 to £16). Set D 5.30 to 7
£11.95 (2 courses) to £13.95. Bar L menu available SERVICE: not inc, card slips closed CARDS:
Amex, Delta, MasterCard, Switch, Visa DETAILS: 70 seats. Vegetarian meals. Music. Air-
conditioned ACCOMMODATION: 11 rooms, all with bath/shower. TV. Phone. B&B £50 to £125.
Baby facilities

Nick's Warehouse £

35 Hill Street, Belfast BT1 2LB   COOKING 5
TEL: (028) 9043 9690 FAX: (028) 9023 0514   MODERN IRISH
WEBSITE: www.nickswarehouse.co.uk   £23–£49

Built originally as a warehouse for the Bushmills Whiskey Company, the
building today houses a restaurant upstairs (bookings are taken, though it may
sometimes be busy with private functions), while downstairs is the lively Anix,
a large, utilitarian, space with an open-plan kitchen and a no-bookings policy –
turn up and join the throng.

Produce, from organic lettuce to wild boar, is sourced from a network of local
suppliers. Fried spiced squid on a pickled vegetable salad and a satay dressing,
or broccoli and cauliflower soup, might kick off dinner in either the restaurant or
the Anix, moving on to spiced brill with pulao rice and curry beurre blanc, or
loin of lamb with couscous and a smoked paprika sauce. For one diner, a
generous portion of scallops was accompanied by good bacon, nicely cooked
green beans and sunblush tomatoes. Lunch in the Anix and wine bar is an
equally globetrotting experience, with, perhaps a hummus and red onion
toasted panini, or more substantial roast gammon on champ with choucroute
and pineapple salsa. Lunch in the restaurant runs to Thai mussel broth and
fillets of sea bass with shiitake mushrooms, noodles and pak choi. Puddings
have been disappointing, but coffee is very good. Wines are mostly standard
bistro fare at reasonable prices, with eight by the glass at £2.95, but the list
stretches a bit further with a focus on Spain and a short collection of good-value
fine wines.

CHEFS: Nick Price, Gerrard Sands and Sean Craig PROPRIETORS: Nick and Kathy Price OPEN:
Mon to Fri L 12 to 3, Tue to Sat D 6 to 9.30 (10 Fri and Sat) CLOSED: 25 to 27 Dec, 1 Jan, 21 and
22 Apr, 6 May, 14 July MEALS: alc (main courses £8 to £16) SERVICE: not inc, 10% for parties of
5 or more CARDS: Amex, Delta, Diners, MasterCard, Switch, Visa DETAILS: 180 seats. Private
parties: 90 main room, 10 to 50 private rooms. Vegetarian meals. Children's helpings.
Wheelchair access (also WC). Music. Air-conditioned

Rain City £   **NEW ENTRY**

33–35 Malone Road, Belfast BT9 6RU   COOKING 3
TEL: (028) 9068 2929 FAX: (028) 9068 2060   ECLECTIC
                                                             £20–£48

Paul and Jeanne Rankin's latest venture (see Cayenne, also in the city) finds
them 'continuing to move away from fine dining towards a much more populist
and youth-orientated market'. So writes a reporter about this casual, 'retro chic'
diner close to Queen's University in Belfast's bedsit land. The menu aims to
please all-comers – including families with children (kids apparently get

unlimited top-ups on their drinks and the burgers are 'actually very good'). Breakfast kick-starts the day, and there's brunch at weekends, as well as lunch and dinner. Choose anything you like from a menu that intermingles snacks and more substantial dishes: expect an all-day output from the bakery, plus sandwiches, meze, salads and specials such as vegetable burrito with guacamole and sour cream, or loin of pork with Mediterranean vegetables. In the evening, grills (ribeye with whiskey peppercorn cream, perhaps) and pizzas (spicy shrimp, leeks, sun-dried tomatoes and basil) figure large and – to finish – there are some pleasing desserts, including vanilla cheesecake, and sticky toffee pudding. House wines from £10.95 head the short, affordable list.

CHEF: Andrew Rea   PROPRIETORS: Paul and Jeanne Rankin   OPEN: Mon to Wed 12 to 10, Thur to Sat 12 to 11.15, Sun brunch 8 to 3, 5 to 10   CLOSED: 25 and 26 Dec   MEALS: alc (main courses £5.50 to £12.50)   SERVICE: not inc   CARDS: Amex, Delta, Diners, MasterCard, Switch, Visa DETAILS: 140 seats. 20 seats outside. Private parties: 20 to 50 private rooms. Vegetarian meals. Children's helpings. No-smoking area. Wheelchair access (also WC). Music. Air-conditioned

Restaurant Michael Deane

36–40 Howard Street, Belfast BT1 6PF   COOKING **6**
TEL: (028) 9033 1134   FAX: (028) 9056 0001   MODERN EUROPEAN-PLUS
EMAIL: liz@deanesbelfast.com   £56–£79

Michael Deane's eponymous restaurant offers two modes of dining. On the ground floor is a spacious, lively and informal brasserie with a menu that offers a wide range of comforting dishes from traditional fish and potato pie, or roast chicken with spring onion mash, grilled pancetta and balsamic, to more novel ideas such as duck breast with spaghetti and chorizo carbonara.

Upstairs is the restaurant, where Michael Deane gets to show off the full extent of his considerable talents with a sophisticated modern European menu. As with the brasserie, the cooking blends classic and contemporary ideas, starting perhaps with spiced squab pigeon with cucumber, sticky rice and curry; brill lasagne with cabbage, foie gras and green vegetable salad; or brandade of salt cod with baby leeks, smoked salmon and potatoes. To follow, there might be roast halibut with a velouté of scallops, shiitakes and peas, ballottine of chicken and mushroom with roast sweetbreads and shallots, or beef fillet with cinnamon carrot confit, haggis and roast potatoes, while desserts have included steamed ginger pudding with apple and cinnamon ice cream, and dark chocolate mousse with passion-fruit jelly. The wine list opens with a page of wines in the £15–£18 price bracket. The rest of the extensive cellar is mostly given over to big French names with big prices, plus a fair choice from other countries.

CHEF/PROPRIETOR: Michael Deane   OPEN: Wed to Sat D only 7 to 9.30   CLOSED: Christmas, bank hols, first 2 weeks July   MEALS: Set D £33 (2 courses)   SERVICE: not inc, 10% for parties of 6 or more   CARDS: Amex, Delta, MasterCard, Switch, Visa   DETAILS: 30 seats. Private parties: 30 main room. Vegetarian meals. Music. No mobile phones. Air-conditioned

All entries in the Guide are re-researched and rewritten every year, not least because restaurant standards fluctuate. Don't rely on an out-of-date Guide.

Ta Tu

701 Lisburn Road, Belfast BT9 7GU
TEL: (028) 9038 0818   FAX: (028) 9038 0828
EMAIL: info@ta-tu.com
WEBSITE: www.ta-tu.com

COOKING **2**
MODERN EUROPEAN
£25–£47

An architectural 'surprise' in the Belfast suburbs beyond the university: what was once part of a parade of shops is now 'a concrete box' with minimalist Ta Tu tucked onto one side. Noisy crowds often pack the bar during the day and the decibel level is cranked up several notches in the evening; eat and drink amid the hubbub or retreat to the relative peace of the dining room. Either way, the food is an in-vogue cocktail of fusion, Asian and Mediterranean ideas ranging from duck confit and foie gras spring rolls with Indian mango salsa to ribeye steak with crunchy polenta, red onion marmalade and pesto butter. 'Clear defined tastes and contrasting textures' also define simpler lunch dishes like chargrilled chicken Caesar salad and pan-fried salmon with couscous. Service keeps pace with the action and the creditable worldwide wine list promises 12 by the glass.

CHEF: David Harding   PROPRIETOR: Bill Wolsey   OPEN: all week 12 to 6, 6 to 9.45 (8.45 Sun)
CLOSED: 25 and 26 Dec, 12 July   MEALS: alc (main courses L £7 to £10, £11 to £14). Set D Mon to
Thur and Sun £12.95 (2 courses) to £15.95. Bar and bistro menu also available   SERVICE: 10%
for parties of 6 or more   CARDS: Amex, Delta, MasterCard, Switch, Visa   DETAILS: 50 seats. 24
seats outside. Private parties: 50 main room. Vegetarian meals. Children's helpings. Wheelchair
access (also WC). Music. Air-conditioned

PORTSTEWART Co Londonderry   **map 16**

Smyths

| NEW ENTRY |

2–4 Lever Road, Portstewart BT55 7EF
TEL: (028) 7083 3564   FAX: (028) 7083 5551

COOKING **3**
MODERN EUROPEAN-PLUS
£26–£48

In a coastal resort a few miles from the Giant's Causeway, Smyths has an unassuming exterior that belies the bright, airy, intimate atmosphere of its upstairs bar and downstairs restaurant. Local fishermen supply lobster and crab, and nearby cheese-makers and Finnebrogue venison contribute to the short menu that uses fresh produce in due season. Alison Smyth describes the food as 'rustic with a sophisticated edge'. Some dishes, like starters of crunchy chilli-flavoured batter in tempura of tender squid, or mushroom stuffed with sun-dried tomatoes, olives and excellent goats' cheese, seem more cosmopolitan than country-cousin, but, whatever the culinary idiom, robust simplicity prevails. Richly creamy chicken liver pâté, served with excellent chargrilled bread, main courses of succulent lamb shank in a deeply flavoured liquor with detectable spicy notes, or tagliatelle verde with finely judged monkfish and salmon in well-balanced garlic cream sauce, all provide satisfaction. The local cheeses are interesting, desserts range from frangipane tart to espresso ice cream float with home-made panforte, and coffee is good. The upstairs bar serves simpler dishes like Irish stew, fresh mussels, and pork char siu with noodles. A neat, short wine list carries low mark-ups; prices range from £9 to £18.

CHEFS: Alison Smyth, Brian McGuinness and Derek Kennedy   PROPRIETORS: Alison and Al Smyth
OPEN: Tue to Sun D only 5.30 to 10 (Tue to Sun L 12 to 3 Easter, bank hols and June to Aug)
CLOSED: 25 Dec to 1 Jan   MEALS: alc D (main courses £10.50 to £16). Set L and D Sun £14 (2
courses) to £17. Bar menu available Tue to Sun L, Tue to Fri and Sun D 5.30 to 8.30   SERVICE: not
inc   CARDS: Delta, MasterCard, Switch, Visa   DETAILS: 50 seats. 8 seats outside. Private parties:
50 main room, 20 to 30 private rooms. Vegetarian meals. No-smoking area. Wheelchair access
(not WC). Music (£5)

Republic of Ireland

We have not given marks for cooking for the Republic of Ireland entries because of a shortage of reports; please do give us feedback should you visit. To telephone the Republic from mainland Britain, dial 00 353 followed by the number listed, but dropping the initial 0. Prices are quoted in euros.

BALLYDEHOB Co Cork   map 16

Annie's

Main Street, Ballydehob
TEL: (028) 37292   EUROPEAN
                                                                      €51–€67

'An excellent little place', thought one reporter after a meal at Dano and Anne Barry's friendly restaurant. Since opening in 1983, its great strengths have been honest cooking without fancy gestures and a 'sensible pricing policy'. Dinner runs to four courses, opening with straight-and-true ideas like local smoked salmon on creamy warm tagliatelle or duck liver pâté with Cumberland sauce; next comes a soup or sorbet, before the main event – which might be sirloin steak with garlic butter or scallops in white wine sauce. For dessert you could try blackberry and apple sponge. The 'adequate' wine list kicks off with half a dozen house selections at €16.

CHEFS/PROPRIETORS: Dano and Anne Barry OPEN: Tue to Sat D only 6.30 to 10 CLOSED: Nov, 24 to 26 Dec, bank hols MEALS: alc (main courses €24 to €25). Set D €38 to €42 SERVICE: not inc CARDS: MasterCard, Visa DETAILS: 44 seats. Vegetarian meals. Children's helpings. No smoking in 1 dining room. Wheelchair access (also WC). Occasional music. No mobile phones. Air-conditioned

---

BALLYLICKEY Co Cork   map 16

▲ Ballylickey House

Ballylickey, Bantry Bay
TEL: (027) 50071 FAX: (027) 50124
EMAIL: ballymh@circom.net   FRENCH
WEBSITE: www.ballylickeymanorhouse.com   €72–€86

The house stands on the Bantry to Glengariff road, set in beautifully tended gardens, with gasp-worthy views across Bantry Bay to the mountains in the distance. George Graves oversees a kitchen that cooks in the classical French idiom, as is suggested by the bilingual menu. Start with either tartare of brown crab, or a casserole of local mussels with chives, before proceeding to roast shank of lamb with an olive crust, grilled turbot with fresh sorrel, or pan-fried Ray wings with a noisette sauce. Remember to leave space at the end for a creamy dessert such as pistachio crème brûlée. The wine list is almost entirely French, with a handful of Italians bringing up the rear. House wines from Bordeaux are €29.

CHEF: Cèline Poux   PROPRIETORS: George and Christiane Graves   OPEN: all week D only 7.15 to 9.15   CLOSED: Nov to Mar   MEALS: Set D €43 (2 courses) to €50   SERVICE: not inc, card slips closed   CARDS: Amex, Diners, MasterCard, Visa   DETAILS: 40 seats. Private parties: 20 main room. Car park. No children under 4. Jacket and tie. No smoking. Occasional music ACCOMMODATION: 10 rooms, all with bath/shower. TV. Phone. B&B €220 to €£340. Baby facilities. Swimming pool

BALLYVAUGHAN Co Clare   map 16

▲ Gregans Castle Hotel ♥ ⬥ ⁵⁄✳

Ballyvaughan
TEL: (065) 7077 005   FAX: (065) 7077 111
EMAIL: res@gregans.ie
WEBSITE: www.gregans.ie   MODERN IRISH/EUROPEAN
on N67, 3½m S of Ballyvaughan   €62–€86

On the south of Galway Bay, at its back the fascinating limestone pavement country of the Burren, this is a base for hearty eating and energetic exploring. The kitchen draws on local riches from land and sea: braised Burren lamb with a comforting celeriac and potato mash, or poached lobster, served simply with lemon butter, are typical. Since arriving in spring 2003, chef Norman Mueller has introduced Eastern influences in such dishes as prawn and ginger won tons with sautéed pak choi and 'zesty' Asian sauce, or crispy duck on bean sprouts with rice noodles. Slightly more European sweets include sticky date and walnut pudding, or éclairs filled with crème chibouste. The wine list combines smart ranges from Europe and knowing Antipodean selections; prices start at €23.50 and rise quite steeply.

CHEF: Norman Mueller   PROPRIETORS: the Haden family   OPEN: all week D only 7 to 8.30 CLOSED: late Oct to mid-Mar   MEALS: alc D (main courses €26). Set D (2 courses) €35.50 to €49. Bar L menu available   SERVICE: not inc, card slips closed   CARDS: Amex, MasterCard, Visa DETAILS: 75 seats. Private parties: 75 main room, 20 to 30 private rooms. Car park. Vegetarian meals. Children's helpings. No smoking. Wheelchair access (not WC). Occasional music. No mobile phones   ACCOMMODATION: 21 rooms, all with bath/shower. Phone. B&B €95 to €198. Rooms for disabled. Baby facilities

BANTRY Co Cork   map 16

▲ Larchwood House ⁵⁄✳

Pearsons Bridge, Bantry
TEL: (027) 66181   MODERN IRISH
                                                              €56–€67

Ask one of the Vaughans to show you around their luxuriant gardens teeming with exotic flora. That should set you up majestically for Sheila's cooking, which is presented in the form of a fixed-price dinner menu of five courses, with a wide range of choice and a fondness for bright fruit flavours. Begin with a smoked salmon and citrus salad, or goats' cheese and pesto crostini, before gliding through soup (maybe carrot, peach and paprika), and then a fruity assemblage like pear and melon cocktail before a main course, perhaps one as light as scallops with basil and lemon, or as robust as breast of duckling with plum sauce. There will be something like a passion-fruit and mango ice cream terrine to finish. The wine list deals concisely with the world's main regions, kicking off with house French at €20.

CHEF/PROPRIETOR: Sheila Vaughan   OPEN: Mon to Sat D 7 to 9.30   CLOSED: 1 week at Christmas   MEALS: Set D €40   SERVICE: not inc   CARDS: Amex, Diners, MasterCard, Visa   DETAILS: 25 seats. Car park. No smoking in 1 dining room. Wheelchair access (not WC). Music   ACCOMMODATION: 3 rooms, all with bath/shower. B&B €40 to €80. Fishing

BLACKLION Co Westmeath   map 16

▲ MacNean Bistro ⁵✳

Main Street, Blacklion
TEL: (072) 53022   FAX: (072) 53404   MODERN IRISH
                                                        €36–€69

Ancient monuments dot the landscape of the wild North-west, but Neven Maguire's restaurant in this small-town Victorian hotel is bubbling with modern ideas. A starter of roast sea scallop with cabbage, Chinese five-spice and crispy noodles typifies the approach of taking local ingredients on a tour of the world's cooking styles. A rich main course might be sirloin of beef with truffle cream potatoes and Madeira jus, or opt for a lighter fillet of sea bass with potato purée, baby leeks and lobster cream. Baked raspberry shortcake with raspberry pannacotta and lemon curd ice cream is one of a trio of dessert specials requiring a 20-minute wait; alternatively choose chocolate delight with vanilla bean ice cream and coffee crème anglaise. Ten wines by the glass feature on a mainly French list.

CHEF/PROPRIETOR: Neven Maguire   OPEN: Sun L 12.30 to 3.30, Thur to Sun D 6 to 9 (9.15 Sat, 7.30 Sun)   CLOSED: 1 week Christmas, Good Friday   MEALS: alc D (main courses €10.50 to €23). Set L Sun €25, Set D €35 to €55   SERVICE: not inc, 10% for parties of 10 or more   CARDS: MasterCard, Visa   DETAILS: 31 seats. Private parties: 40 main room, 10 to 15 private rooms. Vegetarian meals. Children's helpings. No smoking in dining room. Music. No mobile phones. Air-conditioned   ACCOMMODATION: 5 rooms, all with bath/shower. TV. Phone. B&B €35. Baby facilities

CASHEL Co Tipperary   map 16

Chez Hans

Moor Lane, Cashel
TEL: (062) 61177   MODERN EUROPEAN
                                                        €50–€87

Cashel, once capital of the kingdom of Munster and now centre of Blue Cashel cheese production, sits amid the dairy country of Tipperary's Golden Vale. This family restaurant has a large menu, underpinned with good local ingredients. A starter tasting plate of Irish and Mediterranean appetisers might be followed by baked salmon with a Viennoise crust, ragoût of prawns, mussels and lobster, or roast pheasant with a shallot Tatin, or Dover sole simply with nut brown butter and parsley. Desserts run to pannacotta with fresh raspberries or a selection of Chez Hans' own ice creams. Three different six-course tasting menus look good value for larger groups. Service is prompt, and the wine list is a neat compendium of modest to grand, starting at €22.50.

CHEF: Jason Matthiä PROPRIETORS: Hans-Peter and Jason Matthiä OPEN: Tue to Sat D only 6 to 9.30 CLOSED: last 2 weeks Jan, first week Sept MEALS: alc (main courses €17 to €28). Set D Tue to Fri 6 to 7.30 €22 (2 courses) to €29, Set D €40 to €50 (all min 10) SERVICE: not inc CARDS: MasterCard, Visa DETAILS: 80 seats. Private parties: 80 main room. Car park. Vegetarian meals. No-smoking area. No cigars/pipes. Children's helpings. Wheelchair access (not WC). Music

CASTLEBALDWIN Co Sligo   map 16

▲ Cromleach Lodge 🍴✳

Castlebaldwin, Via Boyle
TEL: (071) 9165155   FAX: (071) 9165455
EMAIL: info@cromleach.com
WEBSITE: www.cromleach.com   MODERN IRISH
Signposted from Castle Baldwin on the N4   €74–€88

Views over Lough Arrow to Carrowkeel Cairns add to the attraction of Christy and Moira Tighe's country-house hotel. Organic and free-range ingredients make their presence felt on Moira's nightly fixed-price menus: loin of rabbit is wrapped in pancetta and served with truffle oil and rabbit jus as a starter, then comes a sorbet before Atlantic turbot on creamed spinach scented with nutmeg, or fillet of veal with Puy lentils and a whiskey and grain-mustard sauce. Finish with desserts such as warm pecan tart with vanilla ice cream. A heavyweight collection of fine vintages from France and the New World supplements the standard wine list; prices from €22.95.

CHEF: Moira Tighe PROPRIETORS: Christy and Moira Tighe OPEN: all week D only 6.30 to 8.30 MEALS: Set D €55 SERVICE: not inc CARDS: Amex, MasterCard, Visa DETAILS: 50 seats. Private parties: 24 main room, 4 to 24 private rooms. Car park. Vegetarian meals. Children's helpings. No children under 7. No smoking. Wheelchair access (not WC). Occasional music ACCOMMODATION: 10 rooms, all with bath/shower. TV. Phone. B&B €132 to €358. Rooms for disabled. Baby facilities

CORK Co Cork   map 16

Crawford Gallery Café 🍴✳

Emmet Place, Cork
TEL: (021) 4274415   IRISH/BRITISH
                                                      €29–447

A self-styled 'modern Irish bistro' (aka café) attached to the art gallery in Cork's old Custom House. Chef/proprietor Isaac Allen is from the family that owns Ballymaloe House in Shanagarry (see entry) and the same commitment to home-grown, local and organic produce (including meat) marks his approach to things. The set-up couldn't be simpler: breakfast and afternoon tea (2.30 to 4) frame the weekly lunch menu, which is a modest assortment including, perhaps, Tuscan chicken liver pâté or spicy fishcakes with olive and anchovy butter before steak, pasta, fish and puddings such as banoffi pie or chocolate and pear tart. The short wine list starts at €16.50 for the house wines.

CHEFS: Isaac Allen and Keith Woods   PROPRIETOR: Isaac Allen   OPEN: Mon to Sat L only 12.30 to 2.30   CLOSED: 24 Dec to 8 Jan   MEALS: alc (main courses €11 to €12). Set L €18. Breakfast 10 to 11.30   SERVICE: not inc, card slips closed   CARDS: MasterCard, Switch, Visa   DETAILS: 60 seats. Private parties: 80 main room, 80 to 200 private rooms. Vegetarian meals. No smoking in 1 dining room. Wheelchair access (also WC). No music.

DINGLE Co Kerry   map 16

Half Door ▼ ⚒

3 John Street, Dingle
TEL: (066) 9151600   FAX: (066) 9151297
EMAIL: halfdoor@iol.ie   MODERN IRISH/SEAFOOD
WEBSITE: www.halfdoor@iol.ie   €50–€112

The O'Connors' welcoming restaurant in Dingle town centre makes the most of its position on an Atlantic peninsula. Seafood is the first love, reflected in starter choices that range from oysters served au naturel, through seafood chowder, to spiced fishcakes with saffron sauce. Lobsters may be chosen from a tank in the old-fashioned way, and a platter of mixed seafood comes with garlic butter for dipping. Otherwise, the choice extends to roast rack of lamb with redcurrant sauce, and chargrilled Irish Angus fillet with red wine sauce. There are crumbles and cheesecakes to finish, or Irish farmhouse cheeses. Whether you follow the red meat or seafood route, the wine list has lots of good choices at fair prices. France dominates, but Australia is particularly worth a look among the reds. The 17-strong house selection is mostly under €22, and five by the glass are €5.40.

CHEF: Teresa O'Connor   PROPRIETORS: Denis and Teresa O'Connor   OPEN: Mon to Sat 12.30 to 2.30, 6 to 10   MEALS: alc (main courses €20 to €45). Set L €32, Set D €35   SERVICE: not inc   CARDS: Amex, MasterCard, Visa   DETAILS: 55 seats. Private parties: 25 main room. Vegetarian meals. Children's helpings. No smoking in 1 dining room. Wheelchair access (not WC). Occasional music. Air-conditioned

DONEGAL Co Donegal   map 16

▲ Harvey's Point ⚒

Lough Eske, Donegal
TEL: (074) 9722208   FAX: (074) 9722352
EMAIL: info@harveyspoint.com   MODERN EUROPEAN
WEBSITE: www.harveyspoint.com   €39–€75

Paintings from the proprietor's family in Switzerland grace the dining room of this chalet-style country-house hotel on the shores of Lough Eske. Chef Martin Lynch's four-course dinners might open with warm crab and sorrel tart with Romesco sauce, before a soup or sorbet; main courses bring together a mélange of components, as in baked hake with ratatouille risotto, chorizo, mussels and coriander cream or duo of roast Donegal lamb with crispy sweetbreads, fondant potato, spinach and mint béarnaise. Desserts are a little less complicated: iced nougat with strawberry coulis, for example. Reliable European names dominate the wine list, which has around two dozen house selections from €19.50.

CHEF: Martin Lynch PROPRIETORS: Marc Gysling and Deirdre McGlone OPEN: all week 12.30 to 2.30, 6.30 to 9.30 CLOSED: Mon and Tue from Nov to Apr MEALS: Set L €25, Set D €47. Bar snacks also available to 5.30 SERVICE: not inc, card slips closed CARDS: Amex, MasterCard, Visa DETAILS: 120 seats. Private parties: 30 to 350 private rooms. Car park. Vegetarian meals. No children under 12. No smoking. Wheelchair access (also WC). Music. Air-conditioned ACCOMMODATION: 20 rooms, all with bath/shower. TV. Phone. B&B €79 to €198. No children under 12

DOOLIN Co Clare map 16

▲ Ballinalacken Castle ⚘

Coast Road, Doolin
TEL/FAX: (065) 707 4025
EMAIL: ballinalackencastle@eircom.net   MODERN IRISH
WEBSITE: www.ballinalackencastle.com   €46–€87

This Victorian mansion, a little way out of Doolin on the Ballyvaghan road, boasts not just 100 acres of grounds but its own ruined medieval castle. Marion O'Callaghan runs a friendly and welcoming front-of-house, and son-in-law Frank Sheedy offers some well-thought-out modern cooking. Celeriac and apple soup on a good stock base, accurately cooked fish such as turbot on sun-dried tomato risotto with buttered leeks and an orange and thyme sauce, and good meats such as confit leg and five-spice breast of duck, accompanied by apple and parsnip mash and sauced with honey, ginger and cloves, are typical of the output. Desserts like caramelised plums with ginger ice cream are the alternatives to a plate of up-to-the-minute Irish cheeses. The French-led wine list gets as far as Lebanon's Ch. Musar as well as the New World and opens with house wines (Burgundies and Australian blends) at €19.

CHEF: Frank Sheedy PROPRIETORS: Mr and Mrs Denis O'Callaghan OPEN: Wed to Mon D only 6.45 to 9 CLOSED: end Oct to mid-Apr MEALS: alc (main courses €19 to €35) SERVICE: not inc CARDS: Amex, MasterCard, Visa DETAILS: 40 seats. Car park. Vegetarian meals. No smoking. Music. No mobile phones ACCOMMODATION: 12 rooms, all with bath/shower. TV. Phone. B&B €80 to €172. Baby facilities

DOUGLAS Co Cork map 16

Lovetts ▼ ⚘

Churchyard Lane, Well Road, Douglas
TEL: (021) 4294909, 4293604   MODERN EUROPEAN
€42–€89

Marie Harding is very proud, and justly so, of all her local suppliers, giving them star billing on the menus. The cornucopia of seasonal shellfish, free-range chickens, venison and farmhouse cheeses is bolstered by an industrious kitchen that makes its own breads, chutneys and pasta. All is turned into some fine cooking, in which cod is wrapped in prosciutto and served with roasted asparagus and courgettes, crab and brown bread are fashioned into a gâteau and served with a vinaigrette of leeks and cherry tomatoes, and a breast of duck might be paired with honey-roast celeriac and sauced with apples and port. Vegetarians don't miss out, the set menu including the likes of wild mushrooms with cashew nut crust and ricotta and spinach gnocchi. To finish, there might be caramelised banana bavarois. Southern France and Spain are favoured sources for wines, but this well-rounded list, in its own words, 'reflects many things'. Prices are fair, starting at €17.75.

CHEF: Marie Harding   PROPRIETORS: Niamh Lovett and Marie Harding   OPEN: Tue to Sat D only 6.30 to 9.30   CLOSED: 1 week Christmas, 1 week Aug, bank hols   MEALS: alc (main courses €18 to €33). Vegetarian set D €20 (2 courses). Brasserie menu also available   SERVICE: not inc, 10% for parties of 5 or more, card slips closed   CARDS: Amex, Diners, MasterCard, Visa   DETAILS: 48 seats. Private parties: 48 main room, 12 to 24 private rooms. Car park. Vegetarian meals. Children's helpings. No smoking. Wheelchair access (not WC). Music. No mobile phones

DUBLIN Co Dublin   map 16

Bleu ✻   NEW ENTRY

Joshua House, Dawson Street, Dublin 2
TEL: (01) 676 7015   FAX: (01) 676 7027   BISTRO
                                                                    €39–€72

Occupying a bright corner site in a modern building, Bleu is the latest offshoot to Eamonn O'Reilly's One Pico (see entry). The brown-and-cream colour scheme lends a contemporary air to what is one of the more cutting-edge establishments in town. The menu follows suit, with a repertoire of modern bistro fare. Pressed terrine of rabbit and chicken with soft boiled quails' eggs, or a tian of crab and tomato tartare could feature in the starting line up, while mains might roll out rump of lamb with herb crushed potatoes and grilled sea trout accompanied by fennel and apple salad. Strawberry crème brûlée and 'A plate of chocolate' round things off. Service is 'engagingly charming', if on occasions a little chaotic, but it's early days yet. House wine kicks in at €18, with 12 by the glass from €4.95.

CHEF: Jaime Farrugia   PROPRIETOR: Eamonn O'Reilly   OPEN: all week 12 to 3, 6 to 11   CLOSED: bank hols   MEALS: alc (main courses L €9.50 to €15, D €15 to €22)   SERVICE: not inc, card slips closed   CARDS: Amex, Diners, MasterCard, Visa   DETAILS: 58 seats. Private parties: 60 main room, 10 to 14 private rooms. Vegetarian meals. No smoking in 1 dining room (from Jan no smoking throughout). Wheelchair access (also WC). Music. Air-conditioned

▲ Browne's Brasserie 🍞

22 St Stephen's Green, Dublin 2
TEL: (01) 638 3939   FAX: (01) 638 3900
EMAIL: info@brownesdublin.com   MODERN EUROPEAN
WEBSITE: www.brownesdublin.com   €44–£87

Billed as a 'brasserie and townhouse', this handsome, high-ceilinged building occupies a prime site with a view over historic St Stephen's Green. A new chef arrived as the Guide went to press, so the kitchen that has previously produced foie gras terrine with peppered pears and lamb's lettuce and home-smoked salmon with spring onion mash, red wine and black mustard seed sauce, will bear the new man's mark. The menu has previously picked from the global melting pot, producing carpaccio of beef with wild mushroom and chestnut vinaigrette, duck spring rolls with Thai-spiced red cabbage, and desserts such as caramelised pineapple with Szechuan pepper and coconut ice cream. Note the time limit on tables at weekends. House wines start at €19.50.

CHEF: Stephen O'Connor PROPRIETOR: Barry Canny OPEN: Sun to Fri L 12.30 to 2.30, all week D 6.30 to 10.30 CLOSED: D 24 Dec to L 3 Jan MEALS: alc (main courses L €13.50 to €19, D €19.50 to €27). Set L €35, Set L Sun €28.50, Set D €52.50 SERVICE: not inc, 12.5% for parties of 6 or more CARDS: Amex, Delta, Diners, MasterCard, Visa DETAILS: 70 seats. Private parties: 70 main room, 30 private room. Vegetarian meals. Children's helpings. Music. Air-conditioned ACCOMMODATION: 11 rooms, all with bath/shower. TV. Phone. B&B €166 to €255. Baby facilities

Chapter One ❦ ✴

18/19 Parnell Square, Dublin 1, Dublin
TEL: (01) 873 2266 FAX: (01) 873 2266
EMAIL: info@chapteronerestaurant.com
WEBSITE: www.chapteronerestaurant.com

MODERN IRISH/EUROPEAN
€41–€96

Occupying a couple of generously proportioned basement rooms beneath the Writers' Museum, Chapter One has an aura of exclusivity. Ring the bell for admission to a fairly sombre dining room where large tables are widely spaced and a pianist plays quietly. Beneath an elegant veneer, menus display down-to-earth gastronomic good sense, blending flavours boldly but wisely. Among starters might be ham ravioli with white beans and spring onions, or glazed oysters with smoked bacon and sauerkraut, to be followed perhaps by rabbit fillet wrapped in black pudding and Bayonne ham, with purée potato, roasted garlic and confit rabbit leg; or slow-roasted duck with cassoulet, Savoy cabbage and an apple and horseradish compote. To finish, there's a fine-looking cheese board or desserts such as iced nougat with chocolate sauce. Wines are a global mix grouped by style, covering a fair price spread. Mature and magnificent bottles top the range, but prices start at a modest €20.

CHEF: Ross Lewis PROPRIETORS: Ross Lewis and Martin Corbett OPEN: Tue to Fri L 12.30 to 2.30, Tue to Sat D 6 to 10.45 CLOSED: 24 Dec to 7 Jan MEALS: alc (main courses €24.50 to €32). Set L €24.50 (2 courses) to €27.50, Set D 6 to 7 €28.50 SERVICE: 10% CARDS: Amex, Diners, MasterCard, Visa DETAILS: 90 seats. Private parties: 120 main room, 14 to 20 private rooms. Vegetarian meals. Children's helpings. No smoking in 1 dining room. Music. No mobile phones. Air-conditioned

▲ Clarence Hotel, Tea Room ❦

6–8 Wellington Quay, Dublin 2
TEL: (01) 407 0813 FAX: (01) 407 0818
EMAIL: reservations@theclarence.ie
WEBSITE: www.theclarence.ie

MODERN IRISH
€50–€128

This former Victorian hotel ballroom has latterly had an Arts and Crafts-style makeover. The set lunch, in particular, seems good value, while for unhurried diners an interesting eight-course menu might feature roast pigeon with celeriac purée, Toulouse sausage, Savoy cabbage and lentil jus, then caramelised monkfish, glazed shallots, trompettes and salsify balsamic and caper juice. A lunchtime 'study in bacon, cabbage and potato' plays to Irish tradition, with other dishes applying French methods to materials local (Bere Island scallops, Wicklow rabbit, Carlingford oysters) and foreign (mozzarella, gazpacho, pasta). Finish with homely pud (cookies and cream) or posh dessert (tarte Tatin of pineapple and star anise with peppered goats' cheese ice cream). Precise wine selection produces some stellar Bordeaux and Burgundy, plus serious stuff from other regions and countries – especially the USA and Australia. South America and South Africa provide cheaper options, but look also at the two dozen wines available in 175ml glass (from €6.10) or 350ml pichet.

CHEF: Anthony Ely PROPRIETORS: Bono and The Edge OPEN: Sun to Fri L 12.30 to 2.30 (12 to 3 Sun), all week D 6.30 to 10.30 CLOSED: 25 and 26 Dec MEALS: Set L €26 (2 courses) to €28.50, Set D €41.50 (2 courses) to €80 (whole table only). Bar menu available 11 to 5.30 SERVICE: not inc, 12.5% for parties of 8 or more CARDS: Amex, Delta, Diners, MasterCard, Visa DETAILS: 70 seats. Private parties: 16 main room, 10 to 70 private rooms. Vegetarian meals. No-smoking area. Wheelchair access (also WC). Music ACCOMMODATION: 48 rooms, all with bath/shower. TV. Phone. Room only €200 to €1,410. Rooms for disabled

Dish

NEW ENTRY

146 Upper Leeson St, Dublin 4
TEL: (01) 664 2135 FAX: (01) 664 2719

MODERN IRISH
€33–€74

Six years down the line, this restaurant in a well-heeled part of town still puts on a fashionable show. Lunch and early evening menus (6 to 7.30, Mon to Thur) take a global trip from Dish burgers to chargrilled Asian chicken breast with couscous, and it's the same story for dinner. Basque fish soup or goats' cheese parfait with roast beetroot tartar might open the show, and there is support from delightfully assembled salads, pasta and noodles. Successful main courses have included faultless chargrilled lamb cutlets with minted pea purée, while desserts such as rhubarb and strawberry crème brûlée and a 'fab' chocolate and pecan brownie have also 'hit the spot'. Service is generally 'keen' and the short wine list includes house recommendations at €7.95.

CHEF: Gerard Foote PROPRIETORS: Trevor Browne and Gerard Foote OPEN: all week 12 to 4, 6 to 11; Sat and Sun brunch CLOSED: 25 Dec and 31 Dec D MEALS: alc (main courses L and D Mon to Thur 6 to 7.30 €11 to €18, D €9.50 to €30) SERVICE: 10% for parties of 6 or more CARDS: Amex, Diners, MasterCard, Visa DETAILS: 65 seats. Private parties: 70 main room. Vegetarian meals. Children's helpings. No-smoking area. Music. Air-conditioned

L'Ecrivain 🍴

109A Lower Baggot Street, Dublin 2
TEL: (01) 661 1919 FAX: (01) 661 0617
WEBSITE: www.lecrivain.com

MODERN IRISH/FRENCH
€51–€129

Derry Clarke has been here since 1989, working to updated classic formulae and applying French techniques (plus influences from further afield) to fine Irish produce. The good-value set lunch might start with rabbit loin with Clonakilty black pudding and garlic fried potatoes, moving on to cod with a fricassee of mussels and clams, saffron and onion purée, and star anise froth. Among similarly multi-partite desserts, île flottante has a bittersweet chocolate salad, and espresso crème brûlée comes with mascarpone ice and chocolate tuile. There are also six- or seven-course tasting menus and cartes for carnivores (think seared scallops with crab spring roll, then pan-roast veal steak with goats' cheese and sage farce) and vegetarians. The wine list specialises in smart bottles at breathtaking prices. House Chileans at €25 and a range of 25 by the glass at €6.25–€12.50 are the affordable options.

CHEF: Derry Clarke   PROPRIETORS: Derry and Sallyanne Clarke   OPEN: Mon to Fri L 12.30 to 2, Mon to Sat D 7 to 11   CLOSED: 22 Dec to 4 Jan   MEALS: alc D (main courses €34 to €40). Set L €27 (2 courses) to €60 (whole table only), Set D €50 to €85 (whole table only)   SERVICE: 10% (on food only)   CARDS: Amex, MasterCard, Visa   DETAILS: 108 seats. 20 seats outside. Private parties: 33 main room, 10 to 20 private rooms. Vegetarian meals. Children to be supervised. No smoking in 1 dining room. Wheelchair access (also WC). Occasional music. No mobile phones. Air-conditioned

Eden

NEW ENTRY

Meeting House Square, Temple Bar, Dublin 2
TEL: (01) 670 5372
EMAIL: enquiries@edenrestaurant.ie
WEBSITE: www.edenrestaurant.ie

MODERN IRISH
€38–€73

In the often-boisterous Temple Bar, Eden's mosaic-tiled interior includes a greeting area with a mirrored ceiling, and a strange collection of wooden curves for a bar. Somehow it all works. The fittingly eclectic menu swings easily from Thai mussel broth, to smokies (cheesy smoked haddock –'incredibly moreish'), to seared peppered beef salad – all served at clothless white tables. 'Panache on a plate', said one inspector of a baked tomato salad with Parma ham, buffalo mozzarella and basil dressing. Roast magret of duck with celeriac bake, rhubarb balsamic jus and game chips delivered plenty of flavour, and a dessert of macerated strawberries with strawberry and raspberry ice cream, schnapps sabayon and sablés proved a 'concoction of indulgence'. Staff are young, enthusiastic and well-trained. France and Australia dominate a list of young wines that starts at €21.

CHEFS: Eleanor Walsh and Mick Durcan   PROPRIETORS: Jay Bourke and Eoin Foyle   OPEN: all week 12.30 to 3, 6 to 10.30   CLOSED: bank hols   MEALS: alc D (main courses €16 to €26). Set L €19 (2 courses) to €22, Set D Mon to Fri 6 to 7 €19 (2 courses) to €22   SERVICE: not inc, 12% for parties of 6 or more   CARDS: Amex, MasterCard, Visa   DETAILS: 52 seats. 44 seats outside. Private parties: 14 to 36 private rooms. Vegetarian meals. Children's helpings. Wheelchair access (not WC). Occasional music. No mobile phones. Air-conditioned

Les Freres Jacques ⁵✳

74 Dame Street, Dublin 2
TEL: (01) 679 4555   FAX: (01) 679 4725
EMAIL: info@lesfreresjacques.com
WEBSITE: www.lesfreresjacques.com

FRENCH
€36–€106

In a prime site opposite Dublin Castle and next to the Mermaid Theatre, this long serving city-centre restaurant continues to offer traditional French cooking based on carefully sourced Irish produce. Lobsters are kept in tanks, lamb is from Wicklow and there is game in season. This translates into a short evening carte that runs along the lines of marinated salmon with potato and chive salad, grilled fillet of beef with potato 'paillason' and provençale juices, then baked chocolate fondant with white chocolate sauce and crushed hazelnuts. The kitchen also has a fondness for pairing meat with fish, as in roast monkfish on a bed of braised oxtail and forest mushrooms. House French is €18.

CHEF: Richard Reau   PROPRIETOR: Jean-Jacques Caillabet   OPEN: Mon to Fri 12.30 to 2.30, Mon to Sat D 7.15 to 10.30 (11 Fri and Sat)   MEALS: alc D (main courses €27 to €38). Set L €20, Set D €34   SERVICE: 12.5%   CARDS: Amex, Delta, MasterCard, Switch, Visa   DETAILS: 65 seats. Private parties: 40 main room, 10 to 40 private rooms. Vegetarian meals. No smoking in 1 dining room. Music

Jacob's Ladder ✳

4–5 Nassau Street, Dublin 2
TEL: (01) 670 3865   FAX: (01) 670 3868
EMAIL: dinning@jacobsladder.ie
WEBSITE: www.jacobsladder.ie

MODERN IRISH
€43–€89

The Roches' restaurant is housed in a first-floor room with views over the Trinity College playing fields, so at the right time of day, you might just be treated to a spot of rugby union. What you will certainly be treated to is Adrian Roche's inventive cooking, which mixes and matches Eastern and Western modes, producing mussel and clam chowder scented with lemongrass and coconut, followed perhaps by roast rump of lamb with a purée of turnips and cumin, potatoes à la lyonnaise and a dressing of coriander and soy. An original vegetarian option might be leek and asparagus parcel with ginger couscous, shiitake mushroom gratin and celery pesto, and meals end with the likes of iced Baileys parfait with a coffee-poached pear and espresso syrup. The wine list opens with six house selections at €19.50 a bottle, or €4.75 a glass.

CHEF: Adrian Roche   PROPRIETORS: Adrian and Bernie Roche   OPEN: Tue to Sat 12.30 to 2.30 (2 Sat), 6 (7 Sat) to 10   CLOSED: 1 week Christmas, Good Friday, 17 Mar, 1 week from Aug bank hol   MEALS: alc (main courses L €13.50 to €14.50, D €28.50 to €30). Set D €31.74. Tasting menu available D €70 (min 2)   SERVICE: not inc   CARDS: Amex, Diners, MasterCard, Visa   DETAILS: 80 seats. Private parties: 50 main room, 20 to 50 private rooms. Vegetarian meals. Children's helpings. No smoking in 1 dining room. Music. No mobile phones

Mermaid Café

69–70 Dame Street, Dublin 2
TEL: (01) 670 8236   FAX: (01) 670 8205
EMAIL: info@mermaid.ie
WEBSITE: www.mermaid.ie

MODERN EUROPEAN
€39–€89

Conveniently placed opposite Dublin Castle and close to the Mermaid Theatre, this contemporary-style café does the business for locals, tourists and culture vultures alike. The food also has a modern flavour, and weekly-changing menus offer the likes of New England crab cakes or feta, grilled sweet potato and cashew nut salad before roast hake fillet with Jerusalem artichoke gratin, red chard and horseradish or chargrilled chicken breast with chorizo, mussel shrimp and saffron rice paella. To finish, the choice includes the day's ice cream, pear and frangipane tart or a brace of Irish cheeses. Sunday brunch is another option. Five house wines (from €18.95) top the good-value list.

CHEF: Benedict Gorman   PROPRIETORS: Mark Harrell and Ben Gorman   OPEN: all week 12.30 to 3.30, 6.30 to 11 (9 Sun), Sun brunch 12.30 to 3.30   CLOSED: 24 to 26 and 31 Dec, 1 Jan, Good Fri   MEALS: alc (main courses L €15, D €19 to €30). Set L €18.95 (2 courses) to €22.95. Sun brunch €9.50 to €15.50   SERVICE: not inc, 10% Sun brunch, 12.5% for parties of 5 or more, card slips closed   CARDS: MasterCard, Visa   DETAILS: 60 seats. Private parties: 45 main room, 1 to 24 private rooms. Vegetarian meals. No-smoking area. Wheelchair access (also WC). Music. Air-conditioned

One Pico

5–6 Molesworth Place, Dublin 2
TEL: (01) 676 0300   FAX: (01) 676 0411
WEBSITE: www.onepico.com

MODERN IRISH-PLUS
€47–€104

Located not far from the city centre, One Pico is a stylish, contemporary restaurant, with tables running along either side and down the middle of a wooden-floored room. Modern Irish and New World cuisine is the stated aim, presented on square plates in the form of complex dishes that usually manage to impress. Pumpkin and rosemary soup with truffled gnocchi is one way to start; another is a fashionable pairing of black pudding and scallops, served with pomme mousseline and horseradish. Meats dominate the main-course choice, and might offer something like rack of venison with celeriac purée, chargrilled pear, buttered kale and a blackcurrant-flavoured sauce. Vegetables are extra. Desserts stretch the imagination too, perhaps with frozen blackcurrant and lychee terrine with coconut carpaccio. The wine list zips enterprisingly around the world, but prices are high, opening at €25.

CHEFS: Eamonn O'Reilly and Maurice Fitzgerald   PROPRIETOR: Eamonn O'Reilly   OPEN: Mon to Sat 12.30 to 2.30, 6 to 10.30   MEALS: alc D (main courses €19 to €29). Set L €23 (2 courses) to €26   SERVICE: 10%   CARDS: Amex, Delta, Diners, MasterCard, Switch, Visa   DETAILS: 100 seats. Private parties: 80 main room, 10 to 48 private rooms. Vegetarian meals. No-smoking area. Music. Air-conditioned

Restaurant Patrick Guilbaud

21 Upper Merrion Street, Dublin 2
TEL: (01) 676 4192   FAX: (01) 661 0052
EMAIL: restaurantpatrickguilbaud@eircom.net

MODERN IRISH/FRENCH
€48–€176

The décor at Restaurant Patrick Guilbaud, one of Dublin's top dining establishments, may be simple but the cooking is complex. Housed next door to (and part of) the Merrion Hotel, the profusion of glass, the modern paintings and the hanging baskets of greenery are vaguely institutional, but nonetheless tasteful. Dinner here comes with 'all the extras' – that means amuse-gueules (aubergine 'caviar', perhaps, served on a silver spoon) before one moves on to starters such as lobster ravioli with coconut-scented lobster cream, toasted almonds and egg pasta, or duck foie gras and black fig with liquorice pain d'épice crumble and herb salad. For main courses, game might appear as red leg partridge with glazed and caramelised salsify, chestnuts and sultanas with foie gras cream sauce. The whole operation is slick and impressive. Wines, from the good-sized cellar, are a well-selected lot, with plenty from France.

CHEF: Guillame Lebrun   PROPRIETOR: Patrick Guilbaud   OPEN: Tue to Sat 12.30 to 2.15, 7 to 10.15   CLOSED: first week Jan, Good Friday, St Patrick's Day   MEALS: alc (main courses €36 to €54). Set L €30, Set D Tue to Thur €65   SERVICE: not inc   CARDS: Amex, Diners, MasterCard, Visa   DETAILS: 80 seats. 20 seats outside. Private parties: 80 main room, 2to 25 private rooms. Vegetarian meals. No music. No mobile phones. Air-conditioned

Roly's Bistro

7 Ballsbridge Terrace, Dublin 4
TEL: (01) 668 2611   FAX: (01) 660 8535
EMAIL: ireland@rolysbistro.ie   IRISH
WEBSITE: www.rolybistro.ie   €31–€87

The word 'bistro' conjures up images of close-packed tables and gingham cloths, but Roly's is a sizeable set-up capable of seating 200 with a kitchen brigade outnumbering a rugby team. Dublin Bay prawn cocktail, Kerry lamb and vegetable pie with roast parsnips, and fish 'n chips with mushy peas show that the old guard is doggedly supported, although the kitchen also produces spicy crab won ton with avocado and sweet chilli mayonnaise as well as roast chicken breast stuffed with Clonakilty black pudding and wild mushroom risotto with mascarpone. Breads are baked in-house and desserts might run to caramelised pistachio rice pots with poached pear and pistachio ice cream. The wine list is wide ranging, with ten house selections priced at €19.75.

CHEFS: Paul Cartwright and Colin O'Daly   PROPRIETORS: John and Angela O'Sullivan, Colin O'Daly and Paul Cartwright   OPEN: all week 12 to 3, 6 to 10   CLOSED: 25 to 27 Dec   MEALS: alc (main courses L €11 to €19, D €18 to €26.50). Set L €17.95, Set D Mon to Thu 6 to 6.45 €19.95 (2 courses) to €21.95   SERVICE: 10%   CARDS: Amex, Diners, MasterCard, Visa   DETAILS: 200 seats. Private parties: 14 to 100 private rooms. Vegetarian meals. Children's helpings. No pipes. Wheelchair access (also WC). Music. Air-conditioned

Shanahan's on the Green ♥ ⅜

119 St Stephen's Green, Dublin 2
TEL: (01) 407 0939   FAX: (01) 407 0940   STEAK AND SEAFOOD
WEBSITE: www.shanahans.ie   €67–€144

Situated in a grand Georgian house on the west side of St Stephen's Green, next to the College of Surgeons, Shanahan's is a vibrant, modern city restaurant. Centrepiece of the menu is a listing of cuts from certified Irish Angus beef, but you are by no means limited to that. Seafood starters take in oysters Rockefeller, sautéed garlic shrimp with white wine and capers, and crab salad with mustard and tarragon aïoli, and if you aren't in the mood for a spot of New York-style strip steak, there are also pancetta-wrapped loin of lamb with a red onion tarte Tatin, or olive-crusted sea bass. Rhubarb and orange crème brûlée should round things off in stimulating fashion. France and the USA are key players in an exciting but rather expensive wine list, while Italy and Spain come to the fore in a range of 'interesting reds'. Nine serious contenders line up by the glass for €7.50–€10.

CHEF: Leo Small   PROPRIETOR: John Shanahan   OPEN: Fri L only 12.30 to 2.15, all week D 6 to 10.30 (11 Fri and Sat). Bar menu also available   CLOSED: 1 week Christmas, Good Fri, bank hols   MEALS: alc D (main courses €36 to €45). Set L Fri €45   SERVICE: not inc, 15% for parties of 6 or more, card slips closed   CARDS: Amex, Delta, Diners, MasterCard, Visa   DETAILS: 100 seats. Private parties: 60 main room, 60 to 120 private rooms. Vegetarian meals. No smoking in 1 dining room. No cigars/pipes. Music. No mobile phones. Air-conditioned

Thornton's ▼ ⁵⁄✳

128 St Stephen's Green, Dublin 2
TEL: (01) 478 7008   FAX: (01) 478 7009
EMAIL: thornton.k@isite.ie   MODERN IRISH
WEBSITE: www.thorntons.com   €69–€172

The move to the former city centre site of Peacock Alley in the Fitzwilliam Hotel has resulted in a modern dining room, with superb views over St Stephen's Green. The T-shirted staff are professional and willing. The kitchen's ambitions are evident in plain-speaking dishes of braised pig with shallot purée and thyme sauce, or in an earthy, rich terrine of foie gras and rabbit, with tiny leek and truffle 'sandwiches'. Balance in the food is characterised in a frothy starter of sautéed prawns and prawn bisque with a truffle sabayon, and in a main course of turbot accompanied by a light mushroom purée and a sweet pea sauce 'full of summer flavours'. First-class deserts have yielded a warm chocolate tart, an intense pool of just-set chocolate inside a crisp, buttery shell, with raspberries in crème anglaise. The wine list concentrates on smart bottles, mostly from major regions, many with bottle age, and with accordingly high prices. Budget alternatives are thin on the ground. House wines start at €23.

CHEF: Kevin Thornton   PROPRIETORS: Kevin Thornton and Muriel O'Connor   OPEN: Tue to Sat 12.30 to 2, 6.30 to 10.30   CLOSED: 24 Dec to 6 Jan, bank hols   MEALS: alc (main courses €48 to €49). Set L €30 (2 courses) to €47, Set D €125   SERVICE: not inc   CARDS: Amex, Delta, Diners, MasterCard, Visa   DETAILS: 70 seats. Private parties: 50 to 100 private rooms. Vegetarian meals. Children's helpings. No smoking in 1 dining room. Music. No mobile phones. Air-conditioned

GOREY Co Wexford   map 16

▲ Marlfield House ⁵⁄✳

Courtown Road, Gorey
TEL: (055) 21124   FAX: (055) 21572
EMAIL: info@marlfieldhouse.ie   MODERN FRENCH
WEBSITE: www.marlfieldhouse.com   €56–€96

This imposing, impeccably maintained country house a mile outside the town has a fully operational kitchen garden, from which organically grown produce flows freely into Henry Stone's kitchen. Settle into the frescoed conservatory dining room, and prepare for a four-course menu that may well begin with salted duck breast wrapped in pastry with roast pepper and red onion, or oak-smoked salmon with herbed potato salad and horseradish cream. After a pause for soup, salad or sorbet, it's on to grilled hake with fennel, orange-scented aubergine and mussels, or perhaps roast pork belly with cabbage, pear and fig chutney, and crab apple jus. Rhubarb tart might provide a bracing finish in the spring, or else there could be orange pannacotta, or your selection from the Irish cheeseboard. Francophiles will appreciate the wine list, but there is a reasonable choice from the southern hemisphere too. Seven house wines come in at €24.

CHEF: Henry Stone   PROPRIETORS: Mary and Ray Bowe   OPEN: Sun L 12.30 to 1.45, all week D 7 to 9 (9.30 Sat)   MEALS: Set Sun L €38, Set D €60. Bar menu also available   SERVICE: not inc   CARDS: Amex, Diners, MasterCard, Visa   DETAILS: 65 seats. Private parties: 20 main room, 20 to 30 private rooms. Car park. Vegetarian meals. No children under 10 at D. Jacket and tie. No smoking. Wheelchair access (also WC). No music. No mobile phones. Air-conditioned   ACCOMMODATION: 20 rooms, all with bath/shower. TV. Phone. B&B €130 to €750. Rooms for disabled. Baby facilities

KANTURK Co Cork   map 16

▲ Assolas Country House ✤

Kanturk
TEL: (029) 50015   FAX: (029) 50795
EMAIL: assolas@eircom.net
WEBSITE: www.assolas.com
signposted from N72, NE of Kanturk, 8m W of   MODERN IRISH
Mallow   €59–€71

This beautifully located seventeenth-century, creeper-covered manor house has been home to successive generations of the Bourke family, with the present incumbents maintaining a particularly high standard. Hazel Bourke's kitchen is well supplied with local beef and lamb, and seafood comes from a supplier in Kenmare who, come the autumn, doubles as mushroom-gatherer. She keeps the preparations simple, serving hot tomato 'Tatin' to start, or maybe soup made with spinach from the garden, and following them with monkfish tail baked in a herb crust, or chicken breast stuffed with courgettes, cream cheese and herbs. Vegetables come as three separate dishes, and meals are rounded off with homely puddings, or a selection of the best Irish farmhouse cheeses. A concise, all-European wine list majors in French classics, with Guigal's red and white Côtes du Rhône as house wines at €22, or €6 a glass.

CHEF: Hazel Bourke   PROPRIETORS: the Bourke family   OPEN: all week D only 7 to 8   CLOSED: 1 Nov to 15 Mar   MEALS: Set D €48   SERVICE: none, card slips closed   CARDS: MasterCard, Visa   DETAILS: 18 seats. Private parties: 18 main room. Car park. Children's helpings. No children under 7 at D. No smoking. No music. No mobile phones   ACCOMMODATION: 6 rooms, all with bath/shower. Phone. B&B €170 to €252. Baby facilities

KENMARE Co Kerry   map 16

▲ Park Hotel Kenmare ▯ ✤

Kenmare
TEL: (064) 41200   FAX: (064) 41402
EMAIL: info@parkkenmare.com   MODERN IRISH
WEBSITE: www.parkkenmare.com   €36–€116

Plans are afoot to open a new spa at this majestic site overlooking Kenmare Bay in October 2003, with a health-conscious menu to boot. One sight of the elegant greystone building and its sumptuous setting are in themselves enough to restore one's zest for life, and Joe Ryan's cooking has always had one eye on those who are counting their calories. Wild mushroom ravioli with aubergine caviar and cardamom and coriander coulis, followed by carrot sorbet, and then a Mediterranean vegetable casserole, should help with this, but there are indulgences aplenty for those that want them. Pigeon breast with apple compote on honey 'pain perdu', glazed monkfish with sautéed artichokes, baby onions and lardons, and grenadine of veal with buttered leeks in a light cream sauce are there to tempt. If your conscience is clear, finish with warm chocolate fondant with vanilla ice cream. The imposing wine list gives pride of place to Bordeaux and Burgundy, but big names turn up elsewhere in France, and Australia and California show their upmarket faces. Diners on a budget can skip straight to the 'limited' list for options under €30.

CHEF: Joe Ryan   PROPRIETOR: Francis Brennan   OPEN: all week 11 to 6, 7 to 9   CLOSED: 1 to 23 Dec, 2 Jan to mid Feb   MEALS: alc (main courses L €11 to €16, D €26 to €35). Set D €49 (2 courses) to €64. Lounge menu available to 6   SERVICE: not inc, card slips closed   CARDS: Amex, Diners, MasterCard, Visa   DETAILS: 120 seats. 20 seats outside. Private parties: 120 main room, 20 to 60 private rooms. Car park. Vegetarian meals. Children's helpings. No children under 6 after 8pm. No smoking. Wheelchair access (not WC). Occasional music. No mobile phones   ACCOMMODATION: 46 rooms, all with bath/shower. TV. Phone. B&B €206 to €726. Rooms for disabled. Baby facilities

▲ Sheen Falls Lodge, La Cascade 🍾

Kenmare
TEL: (064) 41600   FAX: (064) 41386
EMAIL: info@sheenfallslodge.ie
WEBSITE: www.sheenfallslodge.ie
follow signs for Glengariff from Kenmare; hotel is   MODERN IRISH
down first left after suspension bridge   €92–€110

The airy, split-level dining-room here overlooks the Sheen Falls (illuminated at night), and the set dinner draws on local waters and farms, though native oysters can be teamed with champagne sabayon and beluga caviar from further afield. Main courses have seen roast chicken breast paired with organic beans, a purée of watercress, and a caper and raisin jus, and saddle of rabbit with a confit of leg and rabbit consommé. Seared scallops might come with a clam and oyster risotto ravioli. Desserts range from hot caramel soufflé with malt milk ice cream to whole poached clementine with lemongrass sorbet. An impressive wine list is strong in Bordeaux and Burgundy, covers the Rhône and southern appellations well, and the Loire and Alsace better than most. There are shorter selections from other countries, a dozen by the glass (€6.50–€9.50) and a fair range at or under €30 a bottle.

CHEF: Chris Farrell   PROPRIETOR: Bent Hoyer   OPEN: all week D only 7.15 to 9.30   CLOSED: first 3 weeks Dec, 3 Jan to 1 Feb   MEALS: Set D €65   SERVICE: not inc, card slips closed   CARDS: Amex, Diners, MasterCard, Visa   DETAILS: 120 seats. Private parties: 120 main room, 2 to 20 private rooms. Car park. Vegetarian meals. Children's helpings. No cigars/pipes. Wheelchair access (also WC). Music. No mobile phones   ACCOMMODATION: 66 rooms, all with bath/shower. TV. Phone. Room only €250 to €1,500. Rooms for disabled. Baby facilities. Swimming pool. Fishing

 indicates that smoking is banned in all eating areas.

KILCOLGAN Co Galway   map 16

Moran's Oyster Cottage | NEW ENTRY |

The Weir, Kilcolgan
TEL: (091) 796113   FAX: (091) 796503
EMAIL: moranseneweir@eircom.net   SEAFOOD
WEBSITE: www.moransoystercottage.com   €38–€99

'Simple seafood on the edge of Galway Bay' sums up this friendly little all-day
venue. 'Locally grown' oysters naturally show up on the menu, along with other
cold delicacies such as Dingle Bay smoked salmon, crab claws and prawn salad –
all of which are served with home-made brown bread. If you are looking for
something hot, the possibilities extend to seafood chowder, steamed mussels or
lobster with boiled potatoes and garlic butter. A couple of non-fish alternatives,
plus sandwiches, cheeses and a few sweets such as apple pie complete the
picture, along with 'excellent service' and wines from €13.90.

CHEFS: Paul McCarthy and Geraldine Jallon   PROPRIETOR: William Moran   OPEN: all week 12 to
10   CLOSED: 3 days at Christmas, Good Fri   MEALS: alc (main courses £13.20 to £40)   SERVICE:
not inc   CARDS: Amex, Diners, MasterCard, Visa   DETAILS: 100 seats. 30 seats outside. Private
parties: 40 main room, 6 to 15 private rooms. Car park. Children's helpings. Wheelchair access
(also WC). Music. Air-conditioned

LISDOONVARNA Co Clare   map 16

▲ Sheedy's ⁵⁄✳

Lisdoonvarna
TEL: (065) 7074026   FAX: (065) 7074555
EMAIL: info@sheedys.com   MODERN IRISH
WEBSITE: www.sheedys.com   €47–€77

John and Martina Sheedy run this converted Georgian residence as a country
house hotel – complete with an organic vegetable and herb garden in the
grounds. The kitchen makes productive use of the harvest in, say, roast rump of
lamb with root vegetables and thyme gravy or seared salmon on a herb risotto
with mustard cream sauce, while other supplies are from local producers.
Influences from far and wide surface on the menu: prawn spring rolls are served
with tomato and chilli jam, while grilled fillet steak with colcannon, black
pudding and a red wine and garlic sauce brings it all back home to Ireland. Old-
school favourites such as lemon meringue pie are typical desserts. House wine is
€18.50.

CHEF: John Sheedy   PROPRIETORS: John and Martina Sheedy   OPEN: all week D only 6.45 to
8.30   CLOSED: 15 Oct to 17 Mar   MEALS: alc (main courses €18 to €25). Bar menu available
SERVICE: not inc, card slips closed   CARDS: MasterCard, Visa   DETAILS: 28 seats. Private parties:
28 main room. Car park. Vegetarian meals. No children under 7 after 7.30. No smoking.
Wheelchair access (also WC). Music. No mobile phones. Air-conditioned   ACCOMMODATION: 11
rooms, all with bath/shower. TV. Phone. B&B €90 to €180. Rooms for disabled

🍳 *indicates that there has been a change of chef since last year's Guide, and the Editor
has judged that the change is of sufficient interest to merit the reader's attention.*

MALLOW Co Cork   map 16

▲ Longueville House 🍴

Mallow
TEL: (022) 47156   FAX: (022) 47459
EMAIL: info@longuevillehouse.ie
WEBSITE: www.longuevillehouse.ie
3m W of Mallow on N72 Killarney road turn right   MODERN IRISH/FRENCH
on to Ballyclough road   €69–€83

In this elegant Georgian manor house, with porticoed entrance, meals are taken either in the Presidents' Restaurant or in a grand Victorian conservatory extension, the Turner Room. William O'Callaghan's French/Irish cooking style is given to some complexity. Thin slices of dry-cured ham are served with toasted walnut and beer bread, a poached egg, béarnaise sauce and purple sprouting broccoli, while main courses bring on quail stuffed with chicken and mushroom mousse, an onion and bacon croûte and parsley sauce, or roast spiced loin of wild red deer with braised red cabbage, parsnip purée and a bitter chocolate jus. Desserts might take in a tartlet of fruits from the garden glazed with Kirsch sabayon and served with elderflower ice cream. The French-led wine list also accommodates Italian reds and New Zealand whites. House wines from southern France, imported directly by the proprietors, are €25.

CHEF: William O'Callaghan   PROPRIETORS: the O'Callaghan family   OPEN: all week D only 6.30 to 9   MEALS: Set D €50. Tasting menu €65 (whole table). Bar menu available 12.30 to 5   SERVICE: not inc, card slips closed   CARDS: Amex, MasterCard, Visa   DETAILS: 120 seats. Private parties: 60 main room, 18 to 30 private rooms. Car park. Vegetarian meals. Children's helpings. No smoking. Wheelchair access (not WC). Occasional music. No mobile phones   ACCOMMODATION: 20 rooms, all with bath/shower. TV. Phone. B&B €90 to €340. Baby facilities

NEWPORT Co Mayo   map 16

▲ Newport House 🍷 🍴

Newport
TEL: (098) 41222   FAX: (098) 41613
EMAIL: info@newporthouse.ie   IRISH/FRENCH
WEBSITE: www.newporthouse.ie   €74–€106

The prospect of salmon fishing attracts enthusiasts to Thelma and Kieran Thompson's Georgian country mansion. If salmon appears on the menu it is exclusively the 'wild' kind, and the kitchen also taps into plentiful supplies of local and regional produce. Dinner is a six-course affair, which might begin with carpaccio and whole-grain mustard salad before a plate of Clew Bay oysters. Next comes a soup or sorbet followed by, say, poached salmon (of course) with garden spinach, champagne and oyster sauce or chargrilled medallions of beef and veal with red wine and shallot sauce. Irish cheeses precede desserts such as Baileys soufflé with chocolate sauce. French classics dominate the extremely serious wine list, where clarets are offered by vintage all the way back to 1961, including a raft of 1982s. Burgundy and the Rhône follow suit and a few bottles from the rest of the world round things off. Prices are fair, with five house wines at €21–€30 or €4.50–€5.50 a glass.

CHEF: John Gavin PROPRIETORS: Thelma and Kieran Thompson OPEN: all week D only 7 to 9.30 CLOSED: 6 Oct to 18 Mar MEALS: Set D €55 SERVICE: not inc, card slips closed CARDS: Amex, Diners, MasterCard, Visa DETAILS: 35 seats. Private parties: 12 main room. Car park. Vegetarian meals. Children's helpings. No smoking. No music. No mobile phones ACCOMMODATION: 18 rooms, 16 with bath/shower. TV. Phone. B&B €128 to €302. Rooms for disabled. Baby facilities

OUGHTERARD Co Galway   map 16

▲ Currarevagh House

Oughterard, Connemara
TEL: (091) 552312   FAX: (091) 552731
EMAIL: mail@carrarevagh.com
WEBSITE: www.currarevagh.com
4m NW of Oughterard on Hill of Doon Lakeshore road

IRISH COUNTRY-HOUSE
€46–€56

One recent returnee was amazed to find the hotel unchanged since his last visit – back in 1978! – declaring the hotel 'a gem which should have a preservation order on it'. Dinner at Harry and June Hodgson's Connemara hotel is at 8, seven nights a week; choose from a set menu of five courses plus coffee. After an appetiser such as olive and onion pastry, a fish course is served, perhaps fillet of monkfish with a red pepper sauce, or mille-feuille of Loch Corrib trout. The centrepiece of the meal is usually a roast such as guinea fowl with a sausage meat stuffing, accompanied by bread sauce, duchesse potatoes and provençale vegetables. Desserts might include treacle tart with lime sorbet, and are followed by a finishing plate of usually Irish cheeses. A quintet of house wines from €15 heads up a list that majors on France.

CHEFS: June and Henry Hodgson PROPRIETORS: Harry and June Hodgson OPEN: all week, D only 8pm (1 sitting) CLOSED: 20 Oct to Mar MEALS: Set D €35 SERVICE: 10%, card slips closed CARDS: MasterCard, Visa DETAILS: 30 seats. Private parties: 15 main room. Car park. Vegetarian meals by request. Children's helpings. No non-resident children. No smoking. No music. No mobile phones ACCOMMODATION: 15 rooms, all with bath/shower. B&B €85 to €195. Baby facilities

RATHMULLAN Co Donegal   map 16

▲ Rathmullan House

Rathmullan
TEL: (074) 91 58188   FAX: (074) 91 58200
EMAIL: info@rathmullanhouse.com
WEBSITE: www.rathmullanhouse.com

MODERN IRISH
€48–€81

The Wheeler family grow their own organic fruits, herbs and vegetables in the walled garden here on Lough Swilly. Guests can take a drink in the beamed, high-ceilinged lounge before getting down to Peter Cheesman's cooking. Tian of crab with cardamom and citrus fruits and a carrot sauce makes a light but stimulating first course, and might be followed by roast fillet of turbot on grilled baby fennel with crushed potatoes and a five-spice sauce, or loin of local lamb served with aubergine purée and a courgette and pepper ragoût. Desserts include pistachio parfait and dark chocolate sauce, or treacle tart with vanilla ice cream and crème anglaise. For simpler fare for lunch or early (5 to 8pm) dinner try the Cellar Bar, where there is also a children's menu. A cosmopolitan wine list includes plenty of halves, some speciality bottles for the splashers-out, and New World house wines from €17.50.

CHEF: Peter Cheesman   PROPRIETORS: the Wheeler family   OPEN: all week D only 7.15 to 8.45 (9.15 Sat)   CLOSED: 1 Jan to 9 Apr 2004 (for renovation)   MEALS: Set D €35 (2 courses) to €45. Bar L and early D menu also available   SERVICE: 10%, card slips closed   CARDS: Amex, Diners, MasterCard, Visa   DETAILS: 100 seats. Private parties: 130 main room, 30 to 50 private rooms. Car park. Vegetarian meals. Children's helpings. Jacket and tie. No smoking. No music. No mobile phones. Air-conditioned   ACCOMMODATION: 24 rooms, all with bath/shower. TV. Phone. B&B €66 to €253. Rooms for disabled. Baby facilities. Swimming pool

SHANAGARRY Co Cork   map 16

▲ Ballymaloe House

Shanagarry
TEL: 353 21 4652531   FAX: 353 21 4652021
EMAIL: res@ballymaloe.ie
WEBSITE: www.ballymaloe.com   MODERN IRISH
2m outside Cloyne on Ballycotton road   €54–€98

The Allen family's hotel helped to put Cork on the gastronomic map a generation ago, and is fast approaching its fortieth anniversary. It is still run in the homeliest fashion, with much of the kitchen's provender grown within the grounds, and fine fish bought from the nearby Ballycotton catch. Choose from the laden hors-d'oeuvres table, before relaxing with a good soup such as spiced carrot and tomato, and then an entrée, which could be roast skate with a dressing of caramelised garlic and sherry vinegar. Main courses cast the net wide to take in Madras lamb curry with basmati, baked brill with orange-flavoured sauce maltaise, and bacon-stuffed guinea fowl with parsnip crisps and a pair of sauces. Irish farmhouse cheeses precede the heavily laden dessert trolley. Mature clarets and Burgundies head the wine list, but it soon expands to cover the New World too. House wines start at €19 for a Val d'Adige Pinot Grigio.

CHEF: Rory O'Connell   PROPRIETORS: the Allen family   OPEN: all week 1 to 1.30, 7 to 9.30 (7.30 to 8.30 Sun buffet D)   CLOSED: 23 to 26 Dec   MEALS: Set L €30, Set D (inc buffet) €55   SERVICE: not inc, card slips closed   CARDS: Amex, Diners, MasterCard, Visa   DETAILS: 100 seats. Private parties: 25 main room, 8 to 20 private rooms. Car park. Vegetarian meals. No children under 12 at D; children's portions L only. No music. No mobile phones   ACCOMMODATION: 33 rooms, all with bath/shower. Phone. B&B €110 to €282. Rooms for disabled. Swimming pool

---

Prices quoted in the Guide are based on information supplied by restaurateurs. The prices quoted at the top of each entry represent a range, from the lowest price of a three-course meal with service and wine to the highest; the latter is inflated by 20 per cent to take account of likely price rises during the year of the Guide.

WATERFORD Co Waterford **map 16**

Dwyers ✤

8 Mary Street, Waterford
TEL: (051) 877478   FAX: (051) 877480
EMAIL: info@dwyersrestaurant.com   FRENCH/MODERN IRISH
WEBSITE: www.dwyersrestaurant.com   €40–€74

Martin Dwyer tells us that he is still committed to the 'Euro-toque Charter' and continues to source ingredients from the pick of local suppliers. After some 15 years cooking in this converted police barracks, he is as enthusiastic as ever. Starters like chicken kofta on a bed of browned onions, or risotto of forest mushrooms set the global tone, before seared salmon fillet with Escoffier's walnut and horseradish relish, or roast duckling 'à la chinoise'. To finish, a nip of home-made sloe gin might hit the spot with desserts such as passion-fruit meringues. Fixed-price 'early-bird' menus are served, and the list of around three dozen wines includes house recommendations from €14.

CHEFS: Martin Dwyer and Declan Coughlan   PROPRIETORS: Martin and Sile Dwyer   OPEN: Mon to Sat D only 6 to 10   CLOSED: 1 week Christmas, bank hols   MEALS: alc (main courses €20.50 to €29). Set D 6 to 7 €27.50   SERVICE: not inc   CARDS: Amex, Diners, MasterCard, Visa   DETAILS: 32 seats. Private parties: 20 main room, 6 to 8 private rooms. Vegetarian meals. Children's helpings. No smoking in 1 dining room. No cigars/pipes. Wheelchair access (also WC). Music

WEXFORD Co Wexford **map 16**

La Riva

2 Henrietta Street, Wexford
TEL/FAX: (053) 24330   MODERN IRISH
EMAIL: warrengillen@aol.ie   €35–€64

Surveying the Slaney estuary from the windows here, one recalls that Wexford began as a Viking port, and the cooking here also reflects some pillaging in foreign parts. Good local ingredients married with Mediterranean- and Asian-influenced ideas please both the eyes and taste buds. Start with crab risotto with coriander, chilli and ginger; celeriac and roast garlic soup with Granny Smiths and Parma ham; or chicken spring roll with Asian greens, noodle salad and pineapple salsa. Roast marinated chicken breast on a black pudding ravioli with shiitake mushroom and sage velouté might follow, or homely sirloin steak with sautéed mushrooms and shallots. Apple and pecan crumble with vanilla ice cream is one of the more straightforward desserts. Service remains excellent, and a 'good, sensible' wine list starts at €16.

CHEF/PROPRIETOR: Warren Gillen   OPEN: Mon to Sat L 12.30 to 2.30, Mon to Sat D 6 to 10.30 (11 Fri and Sat), Sun (April to Oct and Dec) open 12.30 to 9   CLOSED: 25 and 26 Dec, Sundays from Jan to Mar and Nov   MEALS: alc D (main courses €18 to €22.50). Set L €22, Set L Sun €20, Set D Mon to Fri 6 to 7 €22.50, Set D €35   SERVICE: not inc, card slips closed   CARDS: Delta, MasterCard, Visa   DETAILS: 55 seats. Private parties: 40 main room. Vegetarian meals. Children's helpings. No children after 8pm. Music. No mobile phones. Air-conditioned

Round-ups

Looking for a suitable place to eat can be a lottery, especially if you are travelling around the country with no set plans in mind. The Round-up section is intended to provide some interesting gastronomic possibilities, whether you find yourself in an unfamiliar city centre or a rural outpost. Pubs are becoming increasingly valuable as sources of high-quality food, but the listings below also include modest family-run enterprises in country towns, racy café/bars and ethnic restaurants in big cities, and a sprinkling of hotel dining rooms in all parts of the land. Dip into this section and you are almost bound to find somewhere that suits your needs and pocket. Entries are based mainly on readers' recommendations, supported where appropriate by inspectors' reports. Sometimes restaurants appear in the Round-ups instead of the main entry section because seasonal closures or weekly openings limit their usefulness, or because late changes in the kitchen or to ownership have occurred, or because feedback this year has been thin on the ground. Reports on these are especially welcome, as they help to broaden our coverage of good eating places in Britain. Round-up entries (outside London) are arranged alphabetically by locality within England, Scotland, Wales, Channel Islands and Northern Ireland.

England

● **ALTON** (Hampshire)
Alton Grange Hotel, Truffles Brasserie
London Road, (01420) 86565. A 'decidedly quirky' country hotel and a 'local institution of undoubted charm', observed one reporter who ate well in its 'chintzy' restaurant. The kitchen dips its spoon into the 'world fusion' pot, as well as taking on the European classics: crab spring rolls wrapped in nori line up alongside 'silky smooth' fish and saffron soup. Away from the sea, Gressingham duck with a mushroom boudin and cep jus has also impressed, while desserts such as hazelnut praline parfait with raspberry coulis conclude events on a high note. Main courses £15–£20. Prices on the wine list zoom skywards from £13. Open all week L and D.

● **AMBLESIDE** (Cumbria)
Drunken Duck Inn Barngates, (01539) 436347. A favourite haunt of walkers and real ale buffs (the inn has its own brewery), this Lakeland hot-spot combines tradition with a touch of class. Don't expect 'pub grub' here: instead, the menu is a full-blown affair listing such elaborate dishes as liquorice-marinated

pigeon breast on Agen prunes and Parmesan risotto (£5.95) and seared scallops on roast beetroot and mustard purée with sultana and caper dressing (£13.95). To finish, consider the exotic delights contained in the assiette of tropical fruits (£5.95). Simpler lunch dishes, and a wide-ranging wine list from £11.25. Accommodation available. Open all week.

● **AMERSHAM** (Buckinghamshire)
Gilbey's 1 Market Square, (01494) 727242. Two courses for £10.95 is the attractive lunchtime deal in this Home Counties wine bar/bistro; otherwise dip into the main menu, which embraces tuna carpaccio with pomegranate dressing (£6.95), pan-roasted duck breast with baby vegetables (£13.95) and rhubarb mousse with chilled summer fruit 'soup' (£4.75). Eat in the courtyard when the weather allows. Gilbey's are wine merchants/importers and many of their French wines are offered at well below the market price (house wines are from £10.45). There's a second branch in Ealing (see entry, London Round-up). Open all week.

Kings Arms 30 High Street, (01494)
726333. Standing proud in Old
Amersham's main street, this centuries-
old timbered inn still boasts beams and log
fires – although its food isn't rooted in the
past. Fixed-price lunches (£12.50–£15.50)
are worth a punt: reporters have
applauded sauté rabbit with mustard,
wine and herbs as well as iced apple
soufflé. More ambitious dishes appear on
the evening carte, where main courses
(around £16) might include braised lamb
shank with minted couscous and fillet of
sea bass with scallop mousse in puff pastry.
The 70-strong wine list has house
recommendations from £11.90. Closed all
day Mon and Sun D.

● **ASHBOURNE** (Derbyshire)
The Dining Room 33 St Johns Street,
(01335) 300666. The setting is a converted
sixteenth-century building with a
courtyard, but this very promising
restaurant looks 'tastefully contemporary'
– with a menu to match. 'Pale pink' goats'
cheese ravioli with beetroot has been
'outstanding'; otherwise dinner might
begin with curried Shetland scallops, raita
and lime jelly (£8.50). Organic Ashbourne
lamb with summer vegetable and
butterbean casserole and vanilla jus
(£16.50) is a possible main course, before
hot cherry and chocolate brownie with
cherry and lime purée (£5.95). There's a
seasonal set menu (£19) at lunchtime.
Thoughtfully chosen wines from £11.95.
More reports please. Open Tue to Sat L
and D.

● **ATHERSTONE** (Warwickshire)
Chapel House Friar's Gate, (01827)
718949. Originally a dower house, now a
fairly secluded hotel tucked into one
corner of the market square. A new
kitchen team was settling in as the Guide
went to press, but the menu remains
ambitious and complex: 'plump' sea
scallops with a wild rocket saladette,
finished with Scottish smoked salmon
drapes (£11.95) is a typical first course,
which might be followed by calves' liver
and pancetta 'crowned with a red onion
confit and thyme Bordeaux glace' (£16),
while desserts (£4.50) could take in

poached pears in saffron and cardamom
syrup. House French is £10.75. Reports,
please. Open Mon to Sat D only.

● **AYMESTREY** Herefordshire
Riverside Inn Aymestrey, (01568)
708440. The Riverside is a combination of
inn and restaurant with a few guest rooms
attached. Dining goes on upstairs and
down, amid pewter mugs and glazed
earthenware. One-dish meals from the
bar menu include fresh fillets of pan-fried
Lugg trout sautéed with butter and
almonds (£7.25), while the more full-
dress approach of the restaurant menus
brings crisped confit duck leg on a bed of
Puy lentils (£11.95) and Marches lamb
accompanied by rosemary jus (£14.50).
Leave room, say, for three-chocolate torte
with blackcurrant coulis, or a light orange
mousse doused in Grand Marnier syrup.
Service is friendly enough and wines are a
well-selected bunch opening with house
red and white at £10.50. Open Tue to Sun
L and D.

● **BARNARD CASTLE** (Co Durham)
Blagraves House 30 The Bank, (01833)
637668. The Morley family have been
operating a restaurant out of this Grade I
listed house for 15 years. Their menus
don't dwell on the past, though, preferring
to look forward and outward for starters
like roast seafood with lemongrass and
coconut followed by chargrilled tuna fillet
with tapenade dressing. Grilled loin of
lamb with minted gravy strikes a more
classical note. The monthly-changing
menu includes a fixed-price option at £17
(Tue to Fri) and a carte with mains at £10–
£16. Open Tue to Sat D.

● **BARTON BENDISH** (Norfolk)
Spread Eagle Church Road, (01366)
347995. In a quiet West Norfolk
backwater, this village pub has been given
a new lease of life by owners Marjorie and
Jessica Ives. There's an upbeat and
decidedly upmarket feel to their menus:
home-smoked duck breast with celeriac
remoulade and curry oil (£5.25) and
seared hake with buttered cucumber and
Pernod sauce (£12.95) show the
prevailing style, while desserts could run
to iced coconut parfait with air-dried

pineapple (£4.95). Lighter options like penne with smoked haddock are also available at lunchtime. France gets top billing on the wine list; prices from £9.95. Accommodation available. Closed Mon.

● **BARTON UPON HUMBER** (North Lincolnshire)

Elio's 11 Market Place, (01652) 635147. A luxuriant covered courtyard now provides extra space for visitors to this long-running Humberside 'oasis'. Elio Grossi still fronts the place and has back-up from an attentive, all-Italian brigade. The cooking stays close to its roots, with plentiful pizzas and other trattoria staples showing up on the regular menu, but the real stars are the seafood specials: fish soup continues to get good reviews, along with 'meaty' baby halibut with lemon and capers, Dover sole and monkfish with peppercorn sauce. Desserts are workmanlike versions of tiramisù and so on. The wine list has an Italian bias. Accommodation available. Open Tue to Fri L (by arrangement only), Mon to Sat D.

● **BATCOMBE** (Somerset)

Three Horseshoes Batcombe, (01749) 850359. It's devilish to find (look for the village church), but this roomy Somerset stone pub is worth the trek. The restaurant – in a converted barn off the bar – boasts a promising menu including top-quality fish from Brixham (grilled plaice with tomato, basil and spring onion butter, for example). Otherwise, expect spiced smoked sausage in paprika sauce (£5.25) and roast duck breast with grapefruit and pear compote (£13.95) followed by wholesome puddings like Madeira, pineapple and treacle sponge (£4.25). West Country real ales and a slate of affordable wines from £10.95. Open all week.

● **BATH** (Bath & N E Somerset)

Firehouse Rotisserie 2 John Street, (01225) 482070. As its name suggests, the main action in this lively city-centre destination centres around the rotisserie and grill: choose anything from Creole blackened fillet of salmon (£12.50) to slow-roast shoulder of lamb with gremolata, white bean cassoulet and

ancho Cabernet gravy. Otherwise, turn your attention to the brick-fired oven, where vividly topped pizzas might include Gorgonzola with smoked bacon, Parmesan and sage (£10.50). Some quaffable young bloods show up on the short, modern list: house wines from £11.95. Closed Sun D. A second branch is in Anchor Square, Bristol, tel: (0117) 915 7323.

Woods 9–13 Alfred Street, (01225) 314812. This long-established brasserie behind the Assembly Rooms stretches through the ground floors of five adjacent Georgian townhouses. Fish and seafood figure large, often served simply with a flavoured butter, but with occasional flights of fancy, as in seared scallops with asparagus, crab oil and avruga. Bangers and mash, steaks and roast lamb accompanied by various boozy sauces satisfy the meat lovers. Set meals offer good value during the week (two courses at L £9.50, D £13.50), but the price racks up to £24.95 for three courses on Saturday night. Short wine list with 11 by the glass. Closed Sun D.

● **BIRKENHEAD** (Merseyside)

The Station 24–28 Hamilton Street, (0151) 647 1047. Perfectly placed for business or pleasure, this multi-purpose venture opposite the station comprises a small hotel, food store and deli, lunchtime bistro and evening restaurant. Meals are served in a large airy room with plate glass windows, and the dinner menu reads well: reporters have singled out clam chowder (£3.50), terrine of foie gras, lentils and sweet potato (a special), and corn-fed chicken breast with chorizo and Parmentier potatoes (£10). Desserts (£3.50) have included an enjoyable sticky toffee pudding, and the wine list features plenty of carefully selected bottles: prices start at £12. Open Mon to Sat L, Wed to Sat D. It is part of the group that includes Ziba at the Racquet Club in Liverpool (see main entry).

● **BIRMINGHAM** (West Midlands)

Café Ikon Ikon Gallery, (0121) 248 3226. The Ikon Gallery, in the fashionable Brindley Place canalside development, is where to go if you're looking for the very latest in contemporary art. The ground-floor café, however, is grounded in reality. A bright and suitably minimalist room is the setting for some lively cooking. The menu is based on tapas and the larger raciones. Expect dishes such as bieras y de gambas (scallops and prawns) £6.95, bacalao con lentejas (pan-fried cod cheeks with lentils and tomatoes) £4.75, or havas a la montañesa (baby broad beans and artichoke with goats' cheese) £4.35. Desserts could be apple pancakes, or traditional crema Catalana. Wines are sourced by a local wine merchant, with many coming from the Astardi Vinyard; prices start at £10.95. They also stock the whole Lustau range of sherries. Open all day Tue to Sun.

Hyatt Regency Hotel Court Café, (0121) 643 1234. Competing for attention with nearby Symphony Hall and the International Convention Centre, this monolithic glass tower is geared largely to the business/conference trade, but the ground-floor Court Café is a useful destination for all-comers. Call in for a bowl of pasta (around £11) or a large Caesar salad, otherwise consider main courses like fillet of sea bass with chorizo mash and basil oil (£14) or chargrilled Scotch sirloin with frites and red wine jus. Desserts such as banana cake with cappuccino iced yoghurt and butterscotch sauce (£5) complete the picture. Open all week D only.

Lasan 3–4 Dakota Buildings, (0121) 212 3664. This self-consciously modern Indian restaurant, all cream walls, bare tables and sculptural white chairs, is making waves in Birmingham, striking some as chic, others as 'a tad spartan'. No such dissent over the food, from one reporter's 'best ever' chicken tikka to innovative options like braised sea bass tenga in sour mango sauce with mushroom rice. Mains are £8–£12 with a tempting range of cheaper vegetarian options – perhaps koyful dansak (green papaya in a lentil purée). Thirty wines, including six by the glass. Reports please. Open Mon to Sat D only.

Maharaja 23–25 Hurst Street, (0121) 622 2641. Handily placed a few doors from the Hippodrome, this long-runner remains one of Birmingham's most reliable Indian restaurants. The short menu eschews current trends and 'balti' gestures in favour of classic dishes rooted in the Punjabi/Moghlai tradition. Tandoori specialities hold their place alongside a contingent of familiar-sounding curries (around £7.50) including chicken bhuna masala, keema matter (minced lamb with peas) and king prawn masala. Aloo tikkian (£2.45) is a noteworthy starter and there's a promising line up of vegetable dishes (around £5.25). House wines are £8.90. Closed Sun.

Le Petit Blanc 9 Brindley Place, (0121) 633 7333. Raymond Blanc's group of four high-profile brasseries (including this branch in Birmingham's cosmopolitan canalside development) is now being run in partnership with the Loch Fyne group. No doubt the flexible brasserie concept will remain, although precise information was not available at the time of writing. For more details, see Round-up entry, Oxford. Open all week.

San Carlo 4 Temple Street, (0121) 633 0251. Close to New Street station, down a side street, this modern-looking Italian has always been a step up from the usual pizza/pasta joint. Whatever your definition of quintessential Italian dining – be it seafood fritto misto, bistecca alla Romana or a wide range of pizzas and pasta – the large menu is bound to satisfy. Bruschetta and focaccia plug any gaps and daily fish specials are chalked up on a blackboard. Open all week.

Zinc The Pavilion, (0121) 200 0620. The Midlands branch of this Conran mini-chain occupies a prime site overlooking Birmingham's rejuvenated Canal Basin. Striking design features are used to telling effect: note the long zinc bar, sculpted spiral staircase and open-air terrace: it's a 'wonderful social place', observed one visitor. The bar menu (mains £5.50–£9) is tailored to grazing and snacking – panini, chorizo Caesar salad, chilli squid and the like – while the restaurant specialises in ingredients-led dishes such as gnocchi with courgettes, mushrooms and Parmesan, and lamb brochette with couscous and harissa (mains £13.50). The short, fairly priced wine list has plenty by the glass. Open Mon to Sat.

● **BISHOP'S STORTFORD** (Hertfordshire)
The Lemon Tree Water Lane, (01279) 757788. Lunchtime deals (£12–£15) provide great value in the Fishpool's amenable restaurant – and you don't have to commit to three courses. In the evening there's an equally affordable bistro-style menu promising, say, chargrilled asparagus before grilled halibut with fennel, new potato and crisp Parma ham (£14), or breast of chicken with roasted peppers and salsa verde (£12). Panettone bread-and-butter pudding and warm chocolate fondant with iced espresso parfait are typical sweets. Around 50 well-chosen wines including ten by the glass. Closed all day Mon and Sun D.

● **BOURNEMOUTH** (Dorset)
Bistro on the Beach Southbourne Coast Road, (01202) 431473. On summer days it's a beach-side café keeping the bucket-and-spade brigade happy with snacks and drinks, but Wednesday to Saturday evenings (and Tue in summer) the candles come out on the plastic-topped tables and it blossoms into a buzzing bistro. Regularly changing menus offer maybe Atlantic prawn and Poole Bay crab Caesar salad followed by leg of lamb steak with curried apricot sauce and couscous (£11.95). Set meals are £13.95 for two courses, £15.95 for three. Friendly service and a straightforward wine list from £10.95. Open Wed to Sat D winter, Tue to Sat D summer.

Westbeach Pier Approach, (01202) 587785. Just a few metres from the pier, this bright, young venue offers both a beachfront deck and a buzzing minimalist dining room. Fish with a spark of modern flavour is the main focus of the open-plan kitchen, as in roasted cod fillet with grilled aubergine and anchovy butter. Fixed price menus are £14 for two courses at lunch, £20 at dinner, with daily specials such as

whole crab salad (£20) as an alternative. Fifty-odd wines include ten by the glass. Reporters have praised food and service equally: more reports please. Open all week.

● **BRAMFIELD** (Suffolk)
Queen's Head The Street, (01986) 784214. Organic produce and local supplies are vigorously championed in this village pub with a garden overlooking the church. The owners' commitment translates into a menu with lots of home-grown touches: Wakelyn's Farm squash soup (£3.50) followed by Stonehouse Organic Farm chicken, leek and bacon crumble (£10.95), for example. But the kitchen is also given free-rein to conjure up pan-fried chorizo and pancetta salad or whole sea bass with pepper and onion dressing. Home-made ice creams continue the theme, along with puddings like pecan and maple tart (£3.95). Beers and wines are from Adnams. Open all week.

● **BRIGHTON & HOVE** (East Sussex)
Moshi Moshi Sushi Bartholomew Square, (01273) 719195. The South Coast branch of a ground-breaking 'kaiten' (conveyor belt) restaurant chain (see Main entry, London). Sit at the counter or tables, watch and take your pick from the colour-coded plates that pass by. Nigiri, maki and sashimi are the mainstays, but the menu also features made-to-order temaki handrolls, 'double-decker' bento boxes (£14.50), Japanese 'tapas' and more substantial hot dishes like salmon teriyaki donburi. Prices remain low: plates from £1.20–£3.50, sushi sets £7.50–£10, but note there's a minimum spend of £15 per head from the à la carte menu in the evening. Drink beer, saké or wine (from £11.50). Closed Mon.

● **BRISTOL** (Bristol)
The Glassboat (0117) 929 0704. Cast an eye over the waterside developments or watch the swans go by from this barge moored in a historic dock, 'the most consistent and pleasant' restaurant in Bristol according to one reporter, whether dining alone or with a group of 40. Lunchtime sees marinated calamari salad and other French/Mediterranean dishes

served in starter or main size, while mains proper include guinea fowl with braised fennel and orange (£12). Dinners have included duck mole (£16). Impressive wine list. A new chef took charge in July 2003: reports please. Closed Sat L and Sun.

● **BROADWAY** (Worcestershire)
Lygon Arms (01386) 852255. The sense of occasion and history seldom fails to impress visitors to this venerable Cotswold hotel. As the Guide went to press, it became part of the Furlong Group and chef Stephen Whitney was recruited from The Montcalm (see main entry, London). His menu has strong French/Mediterranean leanings, witness red mullet escabèche with its own brandade (£13), loin of herb-crusted Costwold lamb with provençale ratatouille (£21) and exotic sounding pineapple carpaccio with aniseed pannacotta, coconut sorbet and lemon-grass syrup (£6.50). Classic French vintages dominate the wine list; house wine is £15.95. Open Sat and Sun L, all week D.

● **BROMFIELD** (Shropshire)
Cookhouse Bromfield, (01584) 856565. A Georgian roadside inn that has been given a contemporary makeover as a family-friendly café bar/restaurant. Up-to-the-minute salads, open sandwiches, pizzas and the like are quick options, otherwise you can plump for the full works in the restaurant. Begin with, say, timbale of Cornish crab with saffron and crème fraîche before breast of free-range duck with plum sauce and red cabbage or herb-crusted noisettes of Shropshire lamb (mains £7.95–£15.95), then lime and ginger cheesecake to finish. Plenty of quaffable wines for around £15, including eight by the glass. Accommodation scheduled to open for 2004. Open all week L and D.

● **BROXTON** (Cheshire)
Frogg Manor Nantwich Road, (01829) 782629. 'Engaging (and unique)', is how one traveller summed up the special appeal of John Sykes' idiosyncratically run Georgian manor house. He also praised the 'interesting and rewarding' food: the long menu leaps from familiar to wackily titled creations, taking in toad 'not in the hole' and roast rack of lamb as well as Long John Silver's Jamaican Gunpowder beef with Navy rum and cream of Zanzibar (spiced bouillabaisse served with penne). Table d'hôte £16 and set D £30. A brace of house recommendations opens the list of 65 wines. Accommodation available. Open all week by reservation.

● **BURFORD** (Oxfordshire)
Lamb Inn Sheep Street, (01993) 823155. This centuries-old Cotswold inn wears its history well – with thick stone walls, flagstones and ancient timberwork in abundance – although the kitchen caters for twenty-first- century palates. New chef Ashley James arrived shortly before our deadline, but the cooking seems likely to retain a 'modern British' slant with dishes such as roast chump of Cornish lamb with beetroot and rosemary potatoes, chargrilled fillet steak or wild mushroom rocket tart (£14.95–£19.95), followed by desserts such as warm chocolate cappuccino with baby doughnuts (£5.75). Lunches and bar meals are simpler affairs. The lengthy wine list opens with recommendations from £13.50. Reports please. Open all week.

● **BURGH lE MARSH** (Lincolnshire)
Windmill 46 High Street, (01754) 810281. Named after the Grade I listed windmill that provides flour for its bread, this family-run restaurant is a likeable and reliable oasis a few miles from Skegness. Local produce including Lincoln Red beef and seasonal game share the billing with French imports and ideas such as pâté de foie gras, black pudding with bacon on flageolet beans and apple sorbet laced with Calvados. Set Sun L £13.95, Set D £19–£22.95. Eighty wines from £10.95 and a decent selection of ports. Open Sun L and Tue to Sat D.

● **BURY ST EDMUNDS** (Suffolk)
Maison Bleue at Mortimer's 30/31 Churchgate Street, (01284) 760623. A likeable place offering seafood cookery with a French. There are few surprises on the menu, which promises the likes of Mediterranean fish soup, seared tuna with

béarnaise sauce and skate meunière, plus carnivorous alternatives including gâteau of duck foie gras or medallions of pork with oregano (main dishes from £9.95), followed by desserts such as warm pear and almond tart. 'Attentive yet discreet staff and very reasonable prices'. Seventy keenly priced wines, with seven house selections. Closed Mon and Sun.

Angel Hotel Angel Hill, (01284) 714000. An imposing fifteenth-century, creeper-clad hotel across the square from the town's historic 'Abbeygate'. Fixed-price dinners (three courses £26.50) are served in the restaurant, where menus follow the European route for dishes like mushroom and spinach risotto, rump of lamb with Lyonnaise potatoes and mint pesto, and loin of monkfish with cabbage, chorizo and lentils, although there are detours for, say, courgette soup with 'Thai infusions' or Moroccan lemon chicken. Staff may seem 'flustered' under pressure. Open all week, L and D.

● **CANTERBURY** (Kent)
Lloyd's 89–90 St Dunstan's Street, (01227) 768222. Standing right by the Westgate medieval stone arch, this attractive modern venue aims for a touch of cosmopolitan sophistication. The cooking has a prominent French accent (with 'a contemporary twang') and fish gets a decent airing. Otherwise, starters (around £6.50) could include warm salad of calf's liver with raspberry vinaigrette, while braised wild boar with juniper berries, red wine and woodland mushrooms (£13.50) might show up among main courses. Vanilla pannacotta with rhubarb is a recommended dessert, and the wine list is a shortish, workmanlike slate. Open all week L and D.

● **CARTERWAY HEADS** (Northumberland)
Manor House Inn Carterway Heads, (01207) 255268. Chris and Moira Brown's stone-built pub overlooking the Derwent Valley is a rough-hewn, unpretentious place with real ales in the bar and a dining room hung with jugs. One regular menu (plus blackboard specials) is served

throughout. Reporters have endorsed 'honest' chicken liver pâté with onion marmalade (£4.40), sweet-cured herrings with crème fraîche (£8.25) and venison with red wine and chocolate sauce, while Moira Brown's desserts (from £3.60) are reckoned to be top of the 'school pud' class. The sensibly priced wine list kicks off with house French at £9.50. Accommodation available. Open all week L and D.

● **CASTLE DONINGTON** (Leicestershire)
Nags Head Inn Hill Top, (01332) 850652. From the outside, this looks like an unremarkable out-of-town roadside pub (handy for East Midlands Airport), but the food tells a very different story. Classy dishes like rare tuna with roast peppers and balsamic dressing or pork fillet with chorizo and tomato ragoût (main courses £13–16) give the blackboard menu a contemporary European edge. Elsewhere, expect starters like grilled goats' cheese with cranberry dressing (£5.95) and homespun sweets like treacle oat tart (£3.60). Snacks and ciabatta sandwiches also served at lunchtime and early evening. Well-kept real ales and affordable wines from £10. Open Mon to Sat L and D.

● **CHELTENHAM** (Gloucestershire)
Le Petit Blanc The Queens Hotel, (01242) 266800. Raymond Blanc's mini-chain of cosmopolitan brasseries is now being run in partnership with the Loch Fyne group. This branch, on the ground floor of the rather grand Queen's Hotel, will continue with its flexible brasserie concept, although precise information is not currently available. For more details see Round-up entry, Oxford. Open all week.

● **CHESTERFIELD** (Derbyshire)
Old Post Restaurant 43 Holywell Street, (01246) 279479. Hugh Cocker was chef at Perkins, Plumtree (a Guide entry for many years - see Round-up) before moving to this 'wonderfully relaxing' beamed restaurant in one of Chesterfield's oldest buildings. Early reports suggest he is doing well in his new premises. Cullen skink (£4.50) and asparagus with poached duck and Parmesan are good ways to start,

while approved main courses (around £15) have included steamed fillet of wild sea bass with fennel and garlic farce and pickled ginger butter. 'Satisfyingly tasty' pear and almond frangipane makes an enjoyable finale. Reports please.

● **CHICHELEY** (Buckinghamshire)
The Chester Arms Bedford Road, (01234) 391214. Set in lush Buckinghamshire countryside only 4 miles from the M1, this handsome old village pub seems to do a roaring trade. Chargrilled steaks (priced by weight from £9.80) are one of the star turns, supported by other dishes posted on a chalkboard. Here you might find starters like avocado and smoked chicken salad (£4.55), followed by mains such as grilled cod fillet with garlic butter (£9.55); puddings such as tiramisù and treacle tart (£3.25) are 'home-made by Clare and Mary'. Around 30 creditable wines from £10.40. Closed all day Mon and Sun D.

● **CHICHESTER** (West Sussex)
Comme Ça 67 Broyle Road, (01243) 788724. On Sundays, the prospect of a 'French family lunch' (£15.95–£18.95) woos customers to this staunchly Gallic restaurant in a converted pub. At other times, there's an elaborate French menu with florid English sub-titles that might begin with venison and Armagnac terrine with apple and grape chutney (£5.25) and move on to baked cod fillet with caramelised apples and Normandy cider velouté (£12.95) or 'boneless' rack of lamb scented with thyme. Finish in true style with French cheeses and typically Gallic desserts (£5.25). Useful for pre- and post-theatre dinners. Closed Mon all day and Sun D.

● **CONSTANTINE** (Cornwall)
Trengilly Wartha Nancenoy, (01326) 340332. Pub, restaurant, hotel, wine merchant all rolled into one, and 'worth the journey' whatever you go for it would seem. Check directions before setting out, as the delightful location in a wooded valley is remote. The wine list is fascinating, good value and highly individual. Set meals (£21.50 for two courses, £27 for three) offer plenty of options and concentrate on local

ingredients, maybe seared scallops on ratatouille with rocket and Parmesan followed by roast loin of Cornish venison on a celeriac potato cake with walnut stuffing and redcurrant sauce. Top-quality bar meals are a popular alternative. Open all week.

● **CROUCH** (Kent)
Chequers Inn Basted Lane, (01732) 884829. Blink and you might miss Crouch altogether: the tiny hamlet is tucked away in the Kent countryside south of the A25, and the charmingly run Chequers is at the centre of things. Typical starters from the upbeat menu might be game terrine with spiced plum chutney (£4.95), while mains have included roast guinea fowl with deep-fried beans and sweet potato mash (£12.95) and brochette of scallops and king prawns. 'Modest' desserts (all £4.25) are familiar items like chocolate truffle cheesecake. Traditional roasts draw the crowds for Sunday lunch. House wine from £9.95. Closed all day Mon and Sun D.

● **DARTMOUTH** (Devon)
Carved Angel Café 7 Foss Street, (01803) 834842. Rough white-painted walls, pine tables and an open kitchen set the tone in the junior sibling of the famous Carved Angel (see main entry). This relaxed café in a pedestrianised street is open all day for breakfasts, lunches of baguettes and omelettes and cream teas, with a popular children's menu. In the evenings a full dinner menu comes into play (two courses £15, three for £20) – twice-baked mushroom and goats' cheese soufflé followed by braised lamb shank with creamed potato and a red wine sauce, with sticky toffee pudding and local vanilla ice cream to finish. Open Mon to Sat L, Wed to Sat D.

● **DENMEAD** (Hampshire)
Barnard's Hambledon Road, (023) 9225 7788. David and Sandie Barnard share the duties in their eponymous restaurant in a shopping parade: he holds sway at the stoves, while she oversees proceedings out front. Their dinner menus change regularly, although you might begin with braised chorizo and poached egg salad (£4.95) before pan-fried sea bass on

sweet-and-sour peppers (£13.95) or grilled fillet of beef with oven-baked wild mushrooms and garlic confit; desserts like passion fruit and lemon brûlée (£4.50) round things off. Prices are lower at lunchtime, when main courses such as chicken breast with orange and Madeira sauce are around £7. Open Tue to Fri L, Tue to Sat D.

● **DODDISCOMBSLEIGH** (Devon)
Nobody Inn Doddiscombsleigh, (01647) 252394. Renowned for its awesome selection of West Country cheeses and a truly monumental wine list that runs to 800 bins (including around 25 by the glass), this thatched fifteenth-century country inn also boasts a wonderfully peaceful setting. Eat, say, sweet potato and chickpea soup or chicken breast with leek and ham sauce in the bar; otherwise opt for the restaurant, where the options might include pan-fried halibut with a sauce containing green peppercorns, tomatoes, peppers and coriander, followed by raspberry ripple crème brûlée (mains around £12, desserts £5). Accommodation available. Open Tue to Sat D only.

● **DREWSTEIGNTON** (Devon)
Drewe Arms Drewsteignton, (01647) 281224. The past lives on in this quintessential thatched Devon pub, although the food on offer now has a decidedly modern complexion. Judging by reports, the kitchen can still deliver a 'fine' steak and kidney pie, but much of the daily-changing blackboard menu has moved with the times. Other high points from recent meals have included confit of duck with hoisin sauce, scallop and cod crêpes and 'one of the best crème brûlées in a long time' (main courses £7.95–£12, desserts £3.95). Ploughman's and light dishes satisfy smaller appetites at lunchtime. Real ales, local cider and a dozen house wines start at £2.60 a glass. Accommodation available. Open all week L and D.

● **DURHAM** (Co Durham)
Pump House Farm Road, (0191) 386 9189. A converted Victorian pump house on the outskirts of Durham is indeed the setting for this 'seafood and steak restaurant', which is impressively decorated with 'huge branches covering the wall from floor to ceiling'. Fish shows up in starters like baked scallops with Gruyère and chive sauce (£7.50) and mains such as grilled Dover sole in parley butter. Steaks are from hung Northumbrian beef and other carnivorous options might include roast rump of Moroccan-spiced lamb with vegetable ragoût (£14). Lemon tart is a typical dessert; house wines are £12.50. Open all week.

● **EAST LAVANT** (West Sussex)
Royal Oak Pooks Lane, (01243) 527434. Surrounded by Downland a stone's throw from Goodwood, this cottagey pub has been given a few designer touches by its current owners. They have also cranked up the emphasis on food. Bar snacks are still served at lunchtime although the main thrust is now the full menu, which lists sophisticated starters (around £6) such as risotto of asparagus and sunblush tomatoes with truffle oil. Main courses are more robust: corn-fed chicken breast wrapped in pancetta with peperonata sauce (£12.50), for example. Puddings are recited by efficient staff. Sussex ales and some decent wines from £9.95. Accommodation available. Open all week.

● **EMSWORTH** (Hampshire)
Spencers 36/38 North Street, (01243) 372744. This Emsworth fixture sits on a busy street in the older, cottagey part of the town, away from the water. The downstairs brasserie and upstairs restaurant serve the same versatile bistro menu, with salads, pastas and mains like braised Moroccan shank of lamb (£12), complemented by a card of fish specials (£11.50–£14.50) – perhaps grilled plaice in roast red pepper, lemon juice, garlic and oregano dressing or deep-fried skate wing in smoked paprika and beer batter. Set two-course lunch and early dinner £7.45. Second branch in nearby Petersfield. Closed Sun.

● **EVESHAM** (Worcestershire)
Evesham Hotel Coopers Lane, (01386) 765566. 'We cannot change!' observes

John Jenkinson, whose family has been running this likeable Cotswold country hotel since 1975. 'Fresh as a Daisy' specials reflect the seasons – fillet of turbot with lemon butter and pickled samphire, for example – otherwise their idiosyncratic menus read like the pickings from a cook's tour complete with jokey names and comments in abundance: Trama prawns with courgettes and tomato purée (£5.25), Korean quail (£13.75) and Abulita's 'flan de coco' with banana cream (£4.50) have all put in an appearance. The gargantuan wine list of over 700 bins is housed in three massive photograph albums. Open all week L and D.

Riverside The Parks, (01386) 446200. A stone's throw from the River Avon in Evesham Abbey's historic Deer Park, this little hotel makes a pleasantly out-of-the-way retreat. Well-reported dishes from the fixed-priced, four-course dinner menu (£29.95) have included smoked haddock mousse and roast rack of lamb (perhaps served with crisp roast parsnips and home-made jelly). Other unfussy ideas based on carefully chosen ingredients might be Evesham asparagus with hollandaise, Hereford ribeye steak with hand-cut chips and béarnaise sauce, plus desserts like garden rhubarb fool with home-made biscuits. Simpler two-course lunches (£15.95). Over sixty wines, with house selections from £11.95. Open Tue to Sun L and Tue to Sat D.

● **EXETER** (Devon)

Carved Angel Café 21A Cathedral Yard, (01392) 210303. Breakfast (until noon) opens the innings at this informal, handily placed café facing the cathedral green. Light lunches take over until 3pm and the crowds flock in for baguettes (create your own fillings), sandwiches and a few more substantial items like oriental duck confit pizza with spicy coleslaw (£7.50). Dinner heralds ratatouille risotto with rocket and Parmesan, Moroccan-style lamb shank with couscous and profiteroles with pistachio ice cream (main courses £10.50–£12.95). Smoothies, juices and a handful of drinkable wines. Related to the Carved

Angel, Dartmouth (see main entry). Closed Sun D.

Galley 41 Fore Street, (01392) 876078. Paul Da-Costa-Greaves describes his converted 300-year-old cottage overlooking the Exe estuary as a 'restaurant-with-cabins' (for those wanting to stay overnight). Fish cookery is the kitchen's main business, supplies arrive daily and organic produce is vigorously endorsed. The effusively worded menu trawls its way through deep-fried squid marinated in Szechuan spices (£5.95), grilled fillets of sea bass with crushed potatoes and pesto liquor wrapped in a banana leaf (£18.95), and desserts like rhubarb crème brûlée. The drinks list is peppered with organic names; house wines are £12.95. Open Tue to Sat L and D.

St Olaves Hotel Mary Arches Street, (01392) 217736. Originally a Georgian merchant's house, complete with a walled garden, St Olaves is an intimate hotel handy for the city centre. Here, fixed-priced dinner menus (£24–£27.50) promise the likes of Brixham crab tart, then well-judged roast rump of lamb with boulangère potatoes and spring greens followed by, say, caramelised apple mille-feuille. Lunchtime set menus are £14 to £18.50. France dominates the wine list, which kicks off with six house selections. Open all week L and D.

● **FAWLEY** (Buckinghamshire)

Walnut Tree Fawley, (01491) 638360. Great views on to 'an amphitheatre of tall trees' are an eye-catching bonus at this well-heeled country pub/restaurant down a leafy Chiltern lane. Bar and restaurant menus overlap and the kitchen turns its hand to grilled salmon on pappardelle with provençale sauce, roast pumpkin and vodka risotto, and calves' liver on grain mustard mash. Vanilla and chocolate cheesecake is a typical dessert. Main courses £8.95 to £15.95. 'Genuinely friendly' licencees, Brakspear ales and a short wine list with 12 by the glass. Accommodation. Closed Sun and Mon D.

● **FLITWICK** (Bedfordshire)
Flitwick Manor Church Road, (01525) 712242. Croquet lawns, wooded parkland and four-poster beds set the tone at this grand country hotel in a historic manor, and cooking is naturally enough in the luxurious country-house mould. Expect expensive ingredients – perhaps pan-fried scallops with a salad of potato and asparagus and a summer truffle vinaigrette, then tournedos of Scotch beef with seared foie gras and roasted ceps – and expect to pay handsomely for them, with the main dinner menu at £49.50, simpler menus at £27.50 and the gastronomic option £55. Open all week, L and D.

● **FOLKESTONE** (Kent)
Pauls 2A Bouverie Road West, (01303) 259697. This long-established bistro is as popular as ever and booking remains (capital letters, underlined) essential for the Sunday carvery (£11.95). Other good-value options during the week are the lunch and supper 'clubs', i.e. set menus at £11.95 and £13.95. The evening menu leans towards France, perhaps corn-fed chicken breast with dauphinoise potatoes, celeriac purée and chive sauce (£11.95), with a spicier global approach at lunch, such as marinated tuna steak with lime and Cajun spices (£5.95). Sixty-odd wines, mostly under £20. Closed Sun D.

● **FORTON** (Lancashire)
El Nido Whinney Brow Lane, (01524) 791254. Early arrivals (6 to 7pm exc Sat) can take advantage of a special fixed-price menu (£10.95) in René Mollinga's enduring North Country restaurant; otherwise the table d'hôte is also an affordable prospect (£14.95). On offer is a mixed bag of Continental and Spanish favourites untouched by fashion: baked eggs with spinach, rack of lamb, cerdo a la Sevillana (fillet of pork with wine and herb sauce), and so forth. Gazpacho, paella and pollo con jamon hold their own on the carte. Thirty wines, including three by the glass. Open Sun L and Tue to Sun D.

● **FOWEY** (Cornwall)
Fowey Hall Hotel & Restaurant Hanson Drive, (01726) 833866. 'An imposing pile set high above the estuary, with the best views in town', observed one visitor to this grand hotel, where dinner is served in a lovely room with ornamental plaster ceilings. The fixed-price, three-course menu (£32.50) is an elaborate affair – witness poached fillet of Cornish rabbit with confit of the leg and a vanilla seed reduction or seared sea bass with smoked haddock risotto and aubergine relish – although there are also 'simple' alternatives like chargrilled beef fillet with mushrooms and slow-baked tomatoes. Glazed lemon tart with marinated cherries is a typical dessert. House wine is priced at £15 a bottle, £3.50 by the glass. Open all week L and D.

● **GEDNEY DYKE** (Lincolnshire)
Chequers Main Street, (01406) 362666. Steaks from Lincoln Red Beef, sausages courtesy of Gloucester Old Spot pigs and herb-crumbed pike with coriander oil are proof that this Fenland country pub takes its cue from thoughtfully procured ingredients. The kitchen also delivers wild mushroom and bacon soup, Roquefort-stuffed chicken breast with tomato, basil and Chardonnay sauce, and whole grilled plaice served simply with lemon and herb butter followed by desserts like lemon and caraway crème brûlée (£3.95). The 30-strong Adnams wine list has house selections from £7.95. Open all week.

● **GILLAN** (Cornwall)
Tregildry Hotel Gillan, (01326) 231378. The views are a big selling point at this family-run hotel high on the cliffs overlooking Falmouth Bay. Guests can also enjoy dinner in the Herra Restaurant, where the menu is fixed-price for four courses (£25); chargrilled ribeye steak with fries is a fixture, but everything else changes daily. Start, perhaps, with Thai chicken and coconut soup or pissaladière before baked salmon in a saffron couscous or citrus-crusted rack of lamb on green pea guacamole; next come puddings, while proceedings conclude with West Country cheeses. House wines are £12.50. Accommodation available. Open all week D only Mar to Oct.

● **GLEWSTONE** (Herefordshire)
Glewstone Court Glewstone, (01989)
770367. Christine and Bill Reeve-Tucker
are the personable owners of this country
house hotel in a glorious position
overlooking the Wye Valley. Guests can
enjoy dinner in the 'gracious, high-
ceilinged' Georgian Restaurant: one
favourably reported meal (three courses
£27) began with smoked chicken and
avocado salad with Caesar dressing, before
fillet of Hereford beef with mushroom and
shallot sauce. As a finale, there's a choice
between desserts like passion-fruit
cheesecake with mango sauce and a
selection of local and Welsh cheeses.
Lighter meals are available in the Bar
Bistro. House wines are £10. Open all
week.

● **GOOSNARGH** (Lancashire)
Solo Goosnargh, (01772) 865206.
According to one Lancastrian regular, this
'delicately decorated' and 'extremely
comfortable' eighteenth-century cottage
has become 'one of the better restaurants
in the area' since opening in 1986. The
evening carte is a broadly based affair: to
begin, Welsh goats' cheese with piccalilli
toast sits alongside Italian turkey tonnato
(£5.20), while mains might feature sauté
king prawns with a couscous timbale, and
pork fillets with caramelised apple and
piri-piri sauce (mains £12.80 to £17.90);
there's also a 'fish of the day'. House wine
is £11.90. Open Sun L and Tue to Sat D.

● **GREAT HINTON** (Wiltshire)
The Linnet Great Hinton, (01380)
870354. A serious makeover has turned
this remote country pub into 'a haven of
smart modernity', according to one
reporter, although the place still retains
remnants of its past. On the food front,
reporters have praised the 'top class'
home-baked bread and vibrant, globally
inclined dishes such as mussels in tomato
and garlic broth with pesto, and
tenderloin of pork stuffed with stir-fried
Thai vegetables wrapped in filo pastry. The
workmanlike wine list includes eight by
the glass. Open Tue to Sun L and D.

● **GREAT WHITTINGTON**
(Northumberland)
Queens Head Great Whittington,
(01434) 672267. Breast of wood pigeon on
black pudding mash with tomato salsa,
roast garlic and Burgundy sauce (£14.95)
is typical of the chef's specials in this
seventeenth-century village inn. The
regular menu also features plenty of
modern 'pub food' ideas like smoked
chicken on mango and nut salad (£6.50),
seared salmon with ratatouille and tomato
and herb coulis (£10.95) and – for
vegetarians – roast vegetable kebabs on
spiced noodles with sweet-and-sour
sauce. Two-course lunches £9.95; three
dozen international wines from £12.50.
Closed all day Mon and Sun D.

● **GREAT YARMOUTH** (Norfolk)
Seafood Restaurant 85 North Quay,
(01493) 856009. Since 1979, the Kikis
family has been delivering their own
version of classical fish cookery in a
converted pub by Yarmouth quay.
'Absolutely fresh' seafood is still the main
attraction, although it may receive plain
or elaborately creamy treatment. Expect
oysters, Mediterranean prawns (£7.95)
and lobsters hot or cold (£24.95), as well as
lemon sole with blue cheese sauce and a
few specials such as monkfish satay from
further afield. Service remains attentive
and welcoming. The long, fish-friendly
wine list includes house French at £11.50.
Closed Sat L and all day Sun.

● **HADDENHAM** (Buckinghamshire)
Green Dragon Church Way, (01844)
291403. Once a local watering hole, now a
fully blown country restaurant. Owners
Peter and Sue Moffat aim high on the food
front, and their menus promise ambitious
starters like goats' cheese parcel on red
pepper and sun-dried tomato risotto (£6)
before, duck breast with roasted rhubarb
and a cider and vanilla sauce (£14).
Desserts range from sticky toffee pudding
to cappuccino crème brûlée (£4.95). A
good 'selling point' is the fixed-price deal
on Tue and Thur evenings (two courses
£10.95), while the 50-strong wine list has
eight house selections from £11.50.
Closed Sun D.

● **HALIFAX** (West Yorkshire)
Design House Dean Clough, (01422) 383242. This contemporary restaurant in the vast Dean Clough Mills complex has seen a series of changes in the kitchen and ownership over the last few years. The current incarnation takes it into more relaxed brasserie territory, with chef Mark Mattock turning out pastas and risottos as well as several vegetarian options in starter or main course sizes. Starters proper (£3.75–£6) might be grilled goats' cheese tart or seared ostrich fillet, while steaks, again in various sizes, kick off a list of meaty mains (£9.50–£16) such as chargrilled venison strip loin with porcini and red wine sauce. Snappy global wine list. Reports please. Open Mon to Fri L and Tue to Sat D.

● **HARROGATE** (North Yorkshire)
Bettys 1 Parliament Street, (01423) 502746. Opened by a Swiss confectioner in 1919, this is the original branch of a quartet of renowned and immensely popular tea rooms that provide an invaluable service for footsore tourists and shoppers. Breads, cakes and pastries (£1.20–£7) are the main lifelines, but there are also savouries ranging from North Country stalwarts like Yorkshire rarebit (£6.75) to Alpine macaroni (£8.25) and rösti in various guises. Teas and coffees of every description, plus juices, organic beers and a pair of Swiss house wines (£13.75). Open all week. There are branches in Ilkley and Northallerton plus two outlets in York (one known as Little Bettys).

Quantro 3 Royal Parade, (01423) 503034. Philip Bowen (ex-Heathcotes at Rascasse, Leeds) is the gastro-guru behind this new venture and its sister in Leeds itself. The Harrogate branch has been glossily made-over and the contemporary menu touts vegetarian sushi alongside steak and pasta. Crab spring rolls with sweet chilli jam (£5.40) is a typical opener, while main courses could be anything from loin of lamb with piperade and saffron potatoes (£14.95) to grilled cod with celeriac purée; desserts (£4.50) might include 'posh' peach melba. One-course lunches cost around £6 and vin de pays is £12.45. Open Mon to Sat L and D. The Leeds outlet is at 62 Street Lane, tel: (0113) 288 8063. Reports on both branches, please.

● **HARROW** (Greater London)
Ram's 203 Kenton Road, (020) 8907 2022. Ram's Pure Vegetarian Surti Cuisine, to give it its full name, specialises in Gujarati food from the town of Surat. The bright, simple décor is more cafeteria than restaurant, but 'brilliant... interesting...wonderful' food makes this 'a real find in a difficult eating area,' as one reporter enthused. Flavours span a broad range: karela na raviya is bitter gourd with Surti masala while stuffed banana bhajia adds a sweet note. Fascinating breads and comforting dhals also feature. Prices are amazingly cheap, with much around £3 and nothing over a fiver. Try Surti lemon soda or play safe with wine or beer. Closed Mon.

● **HATFIELD PEVEREL** (Essex)
Blue Strawberry The Street, (01245) 381333. An old timbered building is the setting for this intimate village 'bistrot' three miles from Chelmsford. The main dining room is a 'modern version of Victoriana' and there's an enclosed terrace for fine-weather meals. 'Anglo-French with modern additions' sums up the menu, which might include seared tuna on pesto mash with baked cherry tomatoes (£5.50), roast duck breast with a gratin of turnip and potato plus a 'boozey-flavoured' cherry sauce (£14.95) and caramel crème brûlée with sesame brittle and butterscotch sauce (£4.75). Portions are extremely generous. Fixed-price weekday lunches from £9.50; house wine £9.95. Closed Sun D.

● **HEREFORD** (Herefordshire)
Café @ All Saints All Saints Church, (01432) 370415. A fund raising sideline for the listed Medieval church in which it stands, this enterprising café is also a godsend for shoppers and tourists. The menu changes daily and visitors have singled out its 'interesting variety' of meatless hot dishes (say, lentil, leek and Parmesan gâteau) and 'substantial'

desserts (orange syrup cake, New York Times nectarine torte). Soup, quiche, salads and sandwiches are also on offer. There are a couple of Chilean wines by the glass, otherwise quench your thirst with home-made lemonade, Dunkerton's cider or Dorothy Goodbody's Ale. Open Mon to Sat 8.30am to 5pm.

● **HEYTESBURY** (Wiltshire)
Angel High Street, (01985) 840330. Travellers call in at this seventeenth-century coaching inn for good value, hospitality and food that now shows plenty of flair. Whole baked Wylye trout, roast Longleat partridge and fillet of Wiltshire pork stuffed with pistachios and apricots fly the flag for local produce; the seasonal restaurant menu also runs to queen scallop and Jerusalem artichoke salad (£6.95) and canon of lamb with compote of peppers and rosemary-scented jus (£12.95), with desserts such as chocolate tart and cinnamon ice cream (£4.95) bringing up the rear. Creditable real ales and a short list of affordable wines (from £11.50). Accommodation available. Open all week.

● **HOLY ISLAND** (Northumberland)
Crown and Anchor Hotel Market Place, (01289) 389215. A valuable local resource and an agreeable stopover for visitors to tidal Holy Island (aka Lindisfarne). Dinner in the restaurant is the main focus of attention and reporters have endorsed a warm salad of black and white pudding with chorizo (£7.40), baked Tweed salmon with 'sunshine mayonnaise', and spaghetti with tomato and mascarpone (£11.40) along with desserts like pannacotta with blueberries (£4.50). Snacks and light meals are available at lunchtime. Wines (including ten by the glass) are listed on a blackboard above the drinkers' bar. Accommodation available. Open Mon to Sun L, Tue to Sat D.

● **HONLEY** (West Yorkshire)
Trattoria 6–13 Church Street, (01484) 660004. An old stone building on a cobbled street houses this brainchild of local chef Scott Hessel – a modern take on the rustic trattoria with fast-moving service and a buzzy atmosphere. The main

menu, supplemented by blackboard specials, combines basic crowd-pleasers with some serious but witty cooking: partridge salad (garnished with pear) or fillet steak given an Italian twist with dolcelatte, Parma ham and red wine sauce. Main course £3.95–£5.95. Wines are Italian or New World. Take-away pizza and pasta. Open all week D only.

● **HOUGHTON CONQUEST** (Bedfordshire)
Knife & Cleaver The Grove, (01234) 740387. A courtyard and orchard garden are eye-catching additions to this historic country inn, which now operates largely as a restaurant-with-rooms. Restored Jacobean panelling graces the bar, but the food offered in the conservatory dining room takes a more modern view of things. Daily fish specials are worth noting, otherwise the menu might run to spiced duck confit cakes (£6.25) and veal chop with gremolata, sage and mash (£14.50), before banana ice cream parfait with crème de Caçao sauce (£4.50). Up to 30 wines by the glass head a prestigious list: prices from £11. Closed Sat L and Sun D.

● **ILMINGTON** (Warwickshire)
Howard Arms Lower Green, (01608) 682226. The very model of a sprucely turned out and enthusiastically run Cotswold-stone pub: outside is the village green, and the whole place oozes gentrified prosperity. Menus are chalked on blackboards and the line-up changes weekly: plaice with lemon and chive dressing, beef, ale and mustard pie, and top-drawer summer pudding with clotted cream have all found favour with traditionalists, while seared squid with cannellini beans, red onion and chilli strikes a more adventurous note. Main dishes £9–£15. Around a dozen house wines by the glass bolster the 30-strong slate. Accommodation available. Open all week L and D.

● **IPSWICH** (Suffolk)
Galley 25 St Nicholas Street, (01473) 281131. Bustling, bistro-style restaurant run by 'talkative Turk', Ugur Vata. The menu shows some imaginative touches and it spreads its net far and wide, from

Tuddenham Hall asparagus with lemon butter (£6.95) and ribeye steak with chips to Middle Eastern soup with bulgur wheat and chargrilled pork loin dusted with North African spices (£14.95). Finish with Ipswich almond pudding made to an ancient recipe (£5.95). The international wine list includes seven by the glass. Closed Sun.

Il Punto Neptune Quay, (01473) 289748. The setting for this floating brasserie is a former Belgian gunboat and hospital ship now moored next to the old Customs House. Pasta, omelettes and light dishes (all £4.95) are served on the 'top deck' bar, while more serious French food is on offer in the restaurant. Typical offerings from the carte might be lobster and prawn ravioli with sorrel sauce (£5.95), roast rack of lamb with garlic and herb crust (£14.75) and Dover sole meunière. To finish, choose between home-made desserts and French cheeses with chutneys. Open Tue to Fri L, Tue to Sat D.

● **IRONBRIDGE** (Shropshire)
Malthouse The Wharfage, (01952) 433712. Museum buffs should find plenty of distractions in this self-styled 'country pub, restaurant and bar with rooms' facing the river. Earthy colours now define the interior, modern paintings are everywhere and the place even has regular live jazz. Sample Moroccan beef stew or Thai fishcakes in the bar, otherwise opt for the restaurant, where the menu is cranked up for duck confit and piquillo pepper terrine (£5.25), and pan-fried fillet of salmon on carrot and potato rösti with crab and tomato butter (£9.95). Desserts (£3.95) sound enticing, and house wine is £9.75. Open all week.

● **KING'S LYNN** (Norfolk)
Riverside 27 King Street, (01553) 773134. Views of the River Ouse are a major plus at this thriving and dedicated restaurant attached to the Arts Centre. Lunch is an ever-popular prospect: expect anything from moules marinière (£5.25) to lamb's liver with mash and gravy (£13.25). Dinner is now a seasonal fixed-price deal (£20–£25) – plus specials – and there's abundant choice from olive-crusted fillet of sea bass with red pepper and basil coulis and chargrilled leg of lamb steak to aubergine lasagne. Desserts range from home-made ice creams to banana and toffee tart. The wine list is tweaked each month; prices from £11.50. Closed Sun.

● **KINTBURY** (Berkshire)
Dundas Arms 53 Station Road, (01488) 658263. Renowned for its gorgeous setting on a little island between the River Kennet and the canal, David Dalzell-Piper's pub/restaurant is also an absolute godsend for wine lovers: his cellar holds some 200 bins, from house selections (£13.50 upwards) to serious French vintages with three-figure price tags. The menu follows a traditional path, taking in home-potted shrimps (£6.60), baked cod with chips and peas (£12) and bread-and-butter pudding (£4.95), but it also makes a few detours for meze and grilled sea bass with saffron and fennel beurre blanc. Top-notch real ales; accommodation available. Open Mon to Sat L and Tue to Sat D.

● **KNIGHTWICK** (Worcestershire)
The Talbot Knightwick, (01886) 821235. Home-brewed beers and home-made black pudding set the tone in this fourteenth-century roadside inn by the banks of the Teme. The Clift family grow their own vegetables, support local produce, and their kitchen bristles with 'honest endeavour'. Eat nettle soup (£4) and fried pig's liver with dry-cured bacon (£12) in the hop-festooned bar or try 'luscious' poached scallops with red chilli pickle and spaghetti carbonara in the blue dining room (set menus £15.95–£22.95). Finish with old-school sweets like chocolate puddle pudding. The keenly priced wine list features 10 by the glass. Accommodation available. Open all week L and D.

● **LANGTHWAITE** (North Yorkshire)
Charles Bathurst Inn Arkengarthdale, (01748) 884567. Dubbed the 'CB Inn', this substantial eighteenth-century village hostelry is enviably situated on the fringes of the Pennine Way. Dales craftsmen have applied their skills to the refurbished interior and the kitchen produces a decent

range of modern pub food. The daily menu (written on a huge mirror) takes in starters like Thai spare ribs (£4.65) and main courses including shank of lamb on a lentil and potato cake with juniper jus (£10.50) or grilled sea bass with garlic and herb butter. There's also game in season and puddings such as raspberry Eton Mess (£3.50). House wine £8.75. Accommodation available. Open all week.

● **LEEDS** (West Yorkshire)

Bryans 9 Weetwood Lane, (0113) 278 5679. This classic chippy has expanded into an air-conditioned sit-down restaurant and celebrates 70 years at the fryer this year. Haddock (with or without skin) comes in four sizes from £6.80 to £12.50 for the 'jumbo' portion including chips, and healthy eaters can choose to have their fish grilled. Drink wine (mostly white), tea or John Smith's Extra Smooth and fill any remaining space with no-nonsense desserts like apple pie and cream plus speciality coffees. Walking distance from the Headingley cricket ground and the Royal Armouries Museum. Open all week.

Cactus Lounge St Peter's Square, (0113) 243 6553. Bang in the middle of the arts district of Leeds city centre, this modern Mexican – bright, spacious and slickly branded with a funky minimalist cactus design – serves up a short menu of nachos, burritos, enchiladas and other stalwarts alongside more intriguing options like rich lamb and olive sonoran. Mains are mostly £7–£10, with a two-course pre-theatre option at £9.95 ideal for visitors to the West Yorkshire Playhouse or the Yorkshire Dance Centre immediately upstairs. Drink beers or the handful of good-value wines. Open Mon to Fri L, Mon to Sat D.

Little Tokyo 24 Central Road, (0113) 243 09090 'Useful, quite fun and fairly inexpensive' sums up this Japanese newcomer, with its healthy-sounding café food, speedy service and 'charming, knowledgeable' staff. Mainstays on the menu are bento boxes ('a stylish feast for the eye' from £9.65) plus variations on ramen, soba and udon noodles – not to mention mild Japanese curries. Saké-steamed mussels have also been well received and it might be worth investing £7 in the 'mushroom collection'. Drink beer, saké or tea. Closed Sun.

Olive Tree Oaklands, (0113) 256 9283. High-profile restaurateur George Psarias is rarely out of the limelight and his converted Victorian house in the suburbs is a Leeds landmark. Everyone seems to know the place and it gets 'full to the rafters' – although service somehow manages to cope. 'Absolutely vast' meze set the tone and the kitchen's fondness for trencherman helpings of Greek-Cypriot food continues with filo parcels stuffed feta cheese and mint, 'very tender' slow-cooked lamb, souvlaki and other classics, plus a few less familiar specials. Look for the Greek names on the wine list, which opens at £11.95. Closed Sun D.

Salvo's 115 Otley Road, (0113) 275 5017. Headingley's long-standing Italian favourite continues to offer excellent value to a packed room at lunchtimes with the 'rapido' menu, just £5 for two courses. On the full version pizzas and pastas (around £7.50) go beyond the predictable and are complemented by substantial mains (£11.50–£13.50) like roasted medallions of suckling pig with balsamic red pepper compote and caramelised apple crisps, and numerous specials, perhaps red snapper with pepper and olive tart. Wines stay mostly under £20. Closed Sun.

● **LEICESTER** (Leicestershire)

Opera House 10 Guildhall Lane, (0116) 223 6666. Over the centuries, this building close to the Cathedral served as an inn, hotel and antique shop before its transformation into restaurant. The kitchen supports local producers (one menu is purely organic) and the carte has pleased reporters: seared scallops with tomato salsa and basil oil (£9.75) and fillet of Scotch beef with a Stilton crust and rösti potato (£18.95) have been recommended; the assiette of 'beautifully presented' miniature desserts is a fine way to finish. The good-value wine list has house wines from £11.25. Closed Sun.

● **LEYBURN** (North Yorkshire)
Sandpiper Inn Market Place, (01969) 622206. There's a genuine family feel to the Harrison's substantial stone-built pub in the town's market place. Dishes old and new rub shoulders on the dinner menu: fishcakes with parsley and chive sauce (£5) and loin of lamb with cranberries and mint (£12.85) share the billing with caramelised belly pork with braised lentils and aged balsamic, and grilled sea bass with celeriac purée and roast garlic. Finish with, say, sticky toffee pudding (£3.95) or mango vacherin with passion-fruit sauce. Lighter dishes are offered at lunchtime. Around three dozen wines from £10.50. Accommodation available. Open Tue to Sun.

● **LICHFIELD** (Staffordshire)
Chandlers Corn Exchange, (01543) 416688. Vaulted ceilings and stained-glass windows lend a church-like feel in some parts of this former corn exchange, but elsewhere the wooden floorboards, panel ceilings and Venetian blinds bring it closer to a colonial club. Mostly vegetable-based starters include beef tomato with buffalo mozzarella salad with avocado and red pesto, while slow roast shoulder of lamb, shallots, rosemary and garlic is a typically hearty main course. A separate list of fish specials might include roast baby halibut with asparagus and wild mushroom fricassee. Set menus offer value, from £5.75 for one course at lunch to £15 for a three-course dinner. Open all week.

● **LIDGATE** (Suffolk)
Star Inn The Street, (01638) 500275. It looks like a traditional English country pub – complete with an inglenook and bar billiards table – but the food in this atmospheric hostelry is emphatically Mediterranean. Maria-Teresa Axon hails from Catalonia and her Spanish specialities have earned the place a good reputation. Boquerones (£5.90), hake à la Vasca and – of course – paella (£12.50) stand out on the daily menu, although other countries have their say: carpaccio of salmon and even sirloin steak with Stilton sauce, for example. Desserts (£4) are mostly old English favourites like apple pie. Spain is the main player on the wine list; house selections are £12. Closed Sun D.

● **LITTLEPORT** (Cambridgeshire)
Fen House 2 Lynn Road, (01353) 860645. A 'peaceful, friendly and comfortable' atmosphere pervades this smart white Georgian house on the northern edge of Littleport. Pause on a sofa in the cosy lounge for appetisers and pre-dinner drinks before moving on to the formal dining room for a French-influenced four-course dinner (£31.75). Five choices for starters and mains might include 'a wonderful flavoursome smooth pumpkin soup' (to quote the menu) then saffron-baked monkfish with ham and flageolet beans. Booking is essential as the restaurant seats just 18 people and is currently serving on Friday and Saturday evenings only. Around 50 wines start at £13.50.

● **LIVERPOOL** (Merseyside)
L'Alouette 2 Lark Lane, (0151) 727 2142. Merseyside bastion of all things Gallic for 20 years, L'Alouette's name is a French translation of its address. The menu comes with translations back into English, offering perhaps terrine of beetroot, asparagus and goats' cheese (£5.95) to start, while mains (£14.50–£17) may be fish such as pan-fried sea bass with a Dijon mustard and herb crust, or 'specialities' like breast of pheasant filled with a cep and herb mousse. Desserts are made on the premises daily. Good-value all-French wine list. Closed Mon and Sat L.

Shangri-La Ashcroft Buildings, (0151) 227 2707. Liverpool's long-established player on Chinese scene, this tiered dining room provides a staple diet of mainly familiar dishes. 'Stimulants to your amicable conversation' (aka appetisers) range from spare ribs in spicy salt (£5.80) to deep-fried scallops in yam pastry, while the remainder of the menu takes in grilled aromatic duck with minced prawn stuffing in straw mushroom sauce (£10), Cantonese hotpots (roast eel in garlic sauce, for example) and Szechuan chicken, plus sizzlers and one-plate dishes. Banquet menus are popular, service is 'courteous' and house wine costs £9.80. Open all week.

● **LONGSTOCK** (Hampshire)
Peat Spade Inn Longstock, (01264) 810612. Sarah Hinman and Bernard Startup fly the organic flag in their eminently civilised village pub. All vegetables and meat are from sustainable sources, and the kitchen makes good use of these ingredients for dishes like Crown Prince squash and almond soup (£4.25), Hereford beef and red wine casserole (£9.95) or duck and chorizo tagliatelle. The short menu also highlights supplies of top-class fish (bourride of salmon, escolar and mussels, for example), while straightforward desserts could run to baked lemon cheesecake (£4.50). Service is polite. A few organic wines appear on the list (prices from £9.95). No credit cards. Open Tue to Sun L and Tue to Sat D.

● **LOOE** (Cornwall)
Trawlers Bullers Quay, (01503) 263593. Park in the main village car park and walk past the fish market to find this quayside seafood restaurant. New owners arrived in summer 2003, but Todd Varnedoe remains at the stove. His cooking is an eclectic mix of modern European with a few Far Eastern flourishes and some input from his native Louisiana. The results might be warm salad of smoked duck with beetroot vinaigrette, crispy-skinned sea bass and stir-fried green beans with saffron sauce, followed by iced chocolate and Tia Maria torte with white chocolate sauce. House French is £11.75. Tue to Sat D only.

● **LOWER ODDINGTON**
(Gloucestershire)
Fox Inn Lower Oddington, (01451) 870555. New licensees are keeping things right on track in this quintessential, sympathetically improved Cotswold-stone pub with several eating areas and cottage garden at the back. Reliable hands in the kitchen conjure up robust, full-flavoured dishes like smoked chicken and leek risotto (£5.50), pesto-crusted cod with tomato and fennel (£9.75) and slow-cooked lamb shank with rosemary and garlic, in addition to desserts such as

poached pears with sticky gingerbread (£4.50). Well-kept real ales and an extended wine list of around 80 bins; prices from £11.25. Accommodation available. Open all week.

● **LYTHAM ST ANNE'S** (Lancashire)
Chicory 5–7 Henry's Street, (01253) 737111. Local residents have taken a shine to this smart new restaurant serving up a global mix of dishes. High-backed banquette seats in warm orange tones make a comfortable setting for dinner, starting with faggots of duck on gingered sweet potato purée (£5.95), or just a classic Caesar salad, followed by roast saddle of lamb stuffed with spinach, mushroom and sun-dried tomato (£15.95). Lunch is a cheaper and simpler affair. Reporters have praised flavourful home-made soups and breads as well as the cocktails, which are a speciality of owner and manager Bevan Middleton. Good global round-up of wines, too. Open all week.

● **MAIDEN NEWTON** (Dorset)
Le Petit Canard Dorchester Road, (01300) 320536. Pastel shades and candlelight set the scene for dinner in the Craigs' cottage restaurant. Their fixed-price menu (£22.50 and £26) is a mainly Anglo-French affair with a few oriental intrusions, backed up by daily specials. A typical meal might run along the lines of grilled goats' cheese salad, fillet of salmon on saffron risotto or rack of lamb with wilted spinach and a garlic and lemon reduction, followed by iced caramelised banana parfait or British cheeses. Around 40 fairly priced wines from £12.95. Open Tue to Sat D, and occasional Sun L

● **MALMESBURY** (Wiltshire)
Old Bell Abbey Row, (01666) 822344. The creeper-covered façade and mullioned windows attest to the 800-year history of this hotel. The fixed-price 'market menu' (£23) has five options for mains, and as many again appear on a carte (£13.50–£18.50), where you might choose queenie scallops with raisin dressing and honey and parsnip purée followed by roast loin of Welsh lamb with Kalamata olive and rosemary soubise. Well-trained, friendly service, and an

interesting, globetrotting wine list. Open all week.

● **MALVERN WELLS** (Worcestershire)
Planters 191–193 Wells Road, (01684) 575065. Sandra Pegg and chef Chandra de Alwis continue to provide a taste of South-east Asian cooking in their unlikely Worcestershire home-from-home, although they are beginning to scale down their activities. On Friday and Saturday evenings, however, you can sample authentic specialities such as Sri Lankan pancake rolls, Singapore sweet-and-sour duck breast (£9.50) and Thai red beef curry, plus rice, noodles and murtaba bread. Alternatively, the five-course 'rijstaffel' (rice table) brings everything together for £18.50 per head. House wine at £10 opens the affordable list. Open Fri and Sat D.

● **MANCHESTER** (Greater Manchester)
Bridgewater Hall, The Charles Halle Room Lower Mosley Street, (0161) 950 0000. Catering for concert evenings only, the Charles Hallé Room offers both pre- and post-performance sessions; chef Robert Kisby whizzes back to his regular kitchen at Le Mont in between. The set menu (£16.95 for two courses, £21.50 for three) features four starters, including regular fixture potage 'Yehudi Menuhin', and four or five substantial-sounding mains, perhaps medallion of veal with Spanish-style cassoulet or osso buco with lemon saffron rice and fresh spinach. Cheeses from independent producers are the stars at dessert time. Wines stay mostly under £20.

Little Yang Sing 17 George Street, (0161) 228 7722. The focus is on popular dishes done well at this reliable city centre Cantonese restaurant, regarded by one reporter as the 'pleasantest in Chinatown'. Meaty soft-shell crab (£3.50), tender fried beef with ginger and spring onion (£7.50) and fresh-tasting assorted seafood in XO sauce (£12.50) have made 'very satisfactory' eating. Concessions to English habits, like offering dim sum as evening starters as well as at lunchtime have been well received by reporters. Open all week.

Livebait 22 Lloyd Street, (0161) 817 4110. Green and white colour schemes set the tone in this vaulted Victorian building that now plies its trade as part of the London-based seafood chain (see Main entry, Leeds, Round-up entry London). The atmosphere is congenial and fish is generally of good quality: some applaud its 'clean fresh tastes', while others think the kitchen 'could do better'. Showpiece seafood platters, grills and straightforward dishes work best, although the repertoire also extends to Indian dry-rubbed tuna with green chilli chutney and red pepper raita. Main courses £9.95 to £29.75. Reasonably priced whites, starting at £10.50, are the main contenders on the wide-ranging list. Closed Sun.

Lounge 10 Tib Street, (0161) 834 1331. 'A runaway success' since it opened, this 'wildly over-the-top' venue is as much theatre as restaurant, with live music, equally lively murals and menus on glossy smart cards. Successes from the shortish repertoire have spanned everything from luxurious terrine of foie gras with port wine 'chewing gum' to re-invented peasant classics like straw-baked ham with cloves, mustard and heather blossom sauce, while apricot tart with cracked pepper ice cream has been a creditable dessert. Steer clear of caviar and side orders to keep prices in check, and note that the global wine list climbs steeply from £11.95. Open all week L and D.

Market Restaurant Edge Street/104 High Street, (0161) 834 3743. The owners have a 'fascination with the anthropology of cooking', according to loyal fans of this 'lovely jewel of a restaurant' just off Piccadilly. Their interest in the subject translates into an eclectic, monthly changing menu based around knowledgeably sourced ingredients: Thai fishcakes with cucumber relish (£5.95) could open the show with, say, Lebanese 'fattoush' (a mixed herb salad), before breast of corn-fed chicken with Cheshire air-dried ham, Taleggio and roasted pepper sauce (£15.95), and there might be apricot amaretti ice to finish (£4.75). Open Wed to Fri L, Wed to Sat D.

Palmiro 197 Upper Chorlton Road, (0161) 860 7330. A twenty-first-century trattoria inhabiting the shell of a defunct end-of-terrace shop. The short contemporary menu changes regularly to accommodate seasonal trends, and the kitchen works confidently with local and imported ingredients. In spring you might begin with courgettes and mint frittata (£3.95), then move on to red mullet saltimbocca (£11.50) before concluding with chocolate torte and 'true' vanilla sauce. Good humoured chef/proprietor Stefan Bagnoli 'never has an off-day', according to one regular. The all-Italian wine list is reckoned to be remarkable value; house wine is £9.25. Open Sun L and all week D.

Le Petit Blanc 55 King Street, (0161) 832 1000. Like other restaurants in Raymond Blanc's mini-chain, this outlet on the ground floor of a renovated '60s bank is now being run in partnership with the Loch Fyne group. No doubt the principles and flexible brasserie concept will remain. For more details see Round-up entry, Oxford. Open all week.

Stock Norfolk Street, 0161 839 6644. The opulence of the Stock Exchange Hall – complete with marble pillars and a huge domed ceiling – makes an impressive backdrop for this contemporary rendezvous. Italy rules on the menu, where the best bets are authentic pasta and well-handled fish. Seafood linguine is a good version, likewise home-made gnocchi; cod fishcakes with a sauce of spinach, green chillies and olive oil, grilled Dover sole and sea bass have also received the thumbs-up. Main courses £11–£27. Reds dominate the Italian wine list (prices from £15). Open all week L and D.

Tai Pan Brunswick House, (0161) 273 2798. Beyond the fringes of Manchester's Chinatown, this spacious restaurant above an oriental supermarket is a useful destination away from the hubbub of the city centre. Dim sum such as salt and pepper spare ribs continue to receive sound reports and there are some worthwhile dishes on the full menu, including duck with prawn meat stuffing.

Otherwise expect a familiar assortment of roast meats, one-plate rice and noodle dishes. Banquet menus (including a seafood extravaganza) are also popular. Open all week.

That Café 1031–1033 Stockport Road, (0161) 432 4672. Alison Eason and her team continue to feed Levenshulme locals and in-comers in this converted terrace house. Their monthly-changing dinner menus promise some enticing dishes with modern overtones: pan-seared scallops with celeriac purée and deep-fried leeks is a typical starter, while mains might include breast of Barbary duck with roast rhubarb and beetroot gravy. Desserts could feature mango kulfi with passion-fruit sauce. Main dishes around £14.50, early evening menus Tue to Fri (two courses £10.95), live jazz on the first Wednesday of each month and house wine at £9.95. Open Sun L and Tue to Sat D.

Zinc The Triangle, Hanging Ditch (0161) 827 4200. A lifesaver if you are in central Manchester and 'hunger strikes'. This branch of the Conran mini-chain faces the Triangle with a dining terrace in the Corn Exchange mall. The menu homes in on simple grills including Loch Duart salmon, pasta, true Brit favourites like fish 'n chips (£9.50) plus a few French-inspired staples such as confit of duck on mash; vanilla pannacotta with strawberry coulis (£4) is a typical dessert. House vin de pays is £12.50. Chef Nick Male was about to leave as the Guide went to press: reports on his successor, please. Open all week.

● **MAWGAN** (Cornwall)

New Yard Trelowarren, (01326) 221595. A converted coach house on Trelowarren Estate makes an unlikely but 'handsome' setting for this emphatically Gallic family restaurant. A new chef arrived in April 2003 but the French accent remains. Fish is landed on Bishop's Quay, lobsters are kept in a tank, and local farms supply organic vegetables and cheeses. Dishes from the current repertoire could include crab ravioli with Indian spices (£5.95), home-smoked Cornish beef on a potato rösti with red wine jus (£15.25), and gooseberry clafoutis with rose sorbet (£4.95). House wines at £10.95 open the global list. Reports please. Closed Mon and Sun D.

● **MELMERBY** (Cumbria)
Village Bakery Melmerby, (01768) 881811. In the vanguard of organically minded ventures and still thriving after more than 25 years, Andrew Whitley's bakery (and more besides) is now a national frontrunner with a well-respected reputation. You can taste the results of his crusading efforts in the restaurant, where much depends on the output of the wood-fired oven. Breakfast is a heartwarming treat that doesn't shy away from full fry-ups, while lunch is a crowd-pleasing mix of carnivorous, piscine and vegetarian options, say, lasagne, tuna with lemon and coriander or spinach and hazelnut tart. Beers, ciders and organic wines. Open all week.

● **MINCHINHAMPTON** (Gloucestershire)
Sophie's High Street, (01453) 885188. French country cooking is the theme in Sophie Dominique Craddock's Grade II listed Georgian building. At present the focus is on light meals and lunches based around a short menu that trots through pork and Armagnac terrine (£4.95), sirloin steak with roasted shallots and melted Roquefort (£10.95) and 'excellent' lemon tart (£4.50). Book well ahead for Sophie's Saturday evening extravaganzas, when the centrepieces might be cassoulet de Castelnaudary or guinea fowl with pruneaux d'Agen and broad beans. The all-French wine list includes bottles imported directly from selected vineyards; prices from £9.95. Open Tue to Fri L and Sat D.

● **NAILSWORTH** (Gloucestershire)
Mad Hatters Cossack Sqaure, (01453) 832615. 'We support local craftsmen, suppliers and artisans' runs the handout from this enthusiastically run neighbourhood restaurant-with-rooms. The owners also fly the flag for organic produce and their handwritten menus offer a line-up of well-tried seasonal dishes along the lines of tomato tartlet with fresh basil pesto (£4.50), escalope of

salmon with sorrel, and roast leg of venison with sour cherry and port sauce (£16.50). Puddings (£4.95) are comforting creations like chocolate and ginger mousse cake. Organic soft drinks and beers, plus a short wine list from £10 a bottle. Open Wed to Sun L, Wed to Sat D.

● **NEWARK** (Nottinghamshire)
Café Bleu 14 Castle Gate, (01636) 610141. Huge abstracts grace the artfully distressed walls, an ornate gilt mirror hangs over an Art Nouveau fireplace and live music is featured most evenings at this self-consciously trendy bistro by the river and next to the castle ruins. Imaginative menus might offer mosaic of roast chicken livers and foie gras with orange chutney and toasted brioche (£5.95) then crisp confit of duck with a risotto of spring onions, wild rocket and black foot chorizo (£12.95). 'Perfectly cooked' chicken and 'slightly pink' tuna pleased one couple. Modern wine list priced from £9.95. Closed Sun D.

● **NEWBURY PARK** (Essex)
Curry Special 2 Greengate Parade, (020) 8518 3005. Just off the A12, this glass-fronted restaurant is rightly popular, and a dressed-up mostly Asian clientele dine in two colourful rooms linked by a spiral staircase. Bollywood movies play on a screen downstairs and a party-like atmosphere prevails on busy nights, helped along by friendly service. Fresh, vibrant methi chicken and rich, spicy vegetarian paneer curry were complemented by perfectly cooked plain rice, fresh-tasting bhindi and a 'sublime' cheese nan on one visit. Mains mostly £5–£7. Very basic wine list and well-received Kenyan beers. Open Tue to Sat L and Tue to Sun D.

● **NEWTON POPPLEFORD** (Devon)
Dawsons Restaurant 6 Greenbank, (01395) 568100. Chris Dawson was head chef at Northcote Manor, Burrington (see main entry), and his latest venture, with wife Karen, is this appealing village restaurant. Fish is a big player on the monthly menu – risotto of baby clams and herbs (£6.50) and fillets of sea bream with sweet marinated vegetables and olive

potato (£14), for example. Alternatives might include confit of duck with sautéed foie gras and herb-crusted roast rib of veal, while desserts are the likes of apricot tarte Tatin with praline ice cream (£5.50). The keenly chosen list has house wines from £14.30. Reports please. Closed Sun and Mon.

● **NOMANSLAND** (Wiltshire)
Les Mirabelles Forest Edge Row, (01794) 390205. Overlooking a quiet corner of the New Forest, this elegant French bistro is a popular destination for those in the know, even in the depths of winter. Pleasant service and a substantial wine list contribute to a 'rather special' ambience. Brandade of salmon with dill might precede lamb fillet with kidney and fresh herbs on a wide-ranging French menu that also takes in Italian standards such as osso buco. Starters are mostly £5–£6, mains £11–£15. Classic desserts of sorbets, crème brûlée or unpasteurised cheeses start at £4.20. Closed Mon and Sun D.

● **NORWICH** (Norfolk)
Delia's Restaurant and Bar Norwich City Football Club, (01603) 218705. The nation's best-known cook turned football supremo is the driving force behind this pristine modern dining room attached to her adopted club. Dishes on the fixed-price menu (£25) are – not surprisingly – gleaned from her books and the signs are promising: potted Cromer Crab with Billingford Mill bread and roast Bressingham duck with sage, apple and onion forcemeat have been well received, likewise an impressive bitter chocolate and crème fraîche tart. Neal's Yard supplies a 'cheese of the week' and the short wine list is bolstered by a couple of weekly specials. The restaurant is currently open only for Sat D; booking essential.

● **NOTTINGHAM** (Nottinghamshire)
Bees Make Honey 12 Alfreton Road, (0115) 978 0109. Named after a '70s rock group (apparently), this no-frills venue really looks the part: beehives are painted on the windows, and the colour schemes are blue and peppermint green. Artwork shares the wall-space with blackboards

advertising a mixed bag of unpretentious dishes. Grilled halloumi and artichoke salad (£4.70) rubs shoulders with spring rolls, while mains have included monkfish and king prawns with chive beurre blanc (£16.95) as well as breast of duck with cranberry jus. Desserts (around £4.50) are something of an afterthought. Unlicensed, but you can BYO. No credit cards. Open Tue to Sat D.

● **ONGAR** (Essex)
Smiths Brasserie Fyfield Road, (01277) 365578. 'Famous for fish' runs the motto of this slick modern restaurant, owned by a family that has Billingsgate in the blood. The name stands out in bold metallic letters on the main road through an otherwise unremarkable residential area. Large marine-themed paintings adorn the plain cream walls and fish – traditionally fried or with a modern twist as in honey and soya crusted sea bass – shares the honours 50/50 with crustaceans on the menu (although incorrigible meat-eaters are also catered for). Mains are £11.50–£17, or £22 for lobster. Smart, attentive service. Decent short wine list. Open all week.

● **ORFORD** (Suffolk)
Butley-Orford Oysterage Market Hill, (01394) 450277. Renowned for its locally bred oysters and incomparable oak-smoked fish, this loyally supported 'fish café' is clearly on good form – judging by recent reports. The chairs may be uncomfortable and the tables closely packed, but that's part of the appeal. Oysters are served au naturel, they also appear in a soup and form a 'cocktail' with tomato juice (£4.50); smoked cod's roe on toast gets the thumbs-up, while specials like griddled squid (£6.90) and skate with capers have also pleased reporters. House wine is £10.95. Expect crowds and queues in the summer – especially during the Aldeburgh Festival. Open all week, winter closed Sun to Thur D.

● **OXFORD** (Oxfordshire)
Fishers 36 St Clements, (01865) 243003. The name across the bright red frontage just off Magdalen Bridge says it all. Fish and seafood are the specialities of this busy

bistro-restaurant, with menus changing daily according to what the market brings. Stay traditional with haddock and chips (£9.50) or go for chargrilled marlin steak with a salsa of pink peppercorn, spring onion and dill (£13.50). Special deals lunch and early dinner. Car park. Closed Mon and Tue L.

Le Petit Blanc 71–72 Walton Street, (01865) 510999. Shortly before the Guide was due to go to press, Raymond Blanc's Petit Blanc chain came out of receivership and went into partnership with the Loch Fyne Seafood Restaurant group. It seems likely that M. Blanc will continue to oversee menu development and that the flexible brasserie concept will remain: speedy meals, fixed-price menus, good deals for children and all-day patisserie, backed up by well-chosen wines from France and the New World. This all happened as we were going to press, leaving us no chance to report back on any improvements. There are currently branches in Birmingham, Cheltenham and Manchester (see Round up entries). Open all week.

White House 2 Botley Road, (01865) 242823. 'Lovely people, lovely place, brightening up a depressing area' was how one reporter summed up this bar and restaurant with an attractive walled garden near the station. Hot buttered breads open a long menu with a meaty focus and steaks to the fore (from £10.95), complemented by additional specials. Fish includes fillet of cod with gazpacho sauce (£10.95) and vegetarians can go for pastas such as wild mushroom ravioli with basil and tomato sauce (£9.95). Chips were 'a revelation' according to an enthusiastic report. Service can become disjointed when busy. Affordable wine list from £10.

● **PENZANCE** (Cornwall)
Mount Prospect Hotel The Bay Restaurant, (01736) 363117. There's a fine prospect of Mount's Bay and Penzance harbour from the terrace of this privately run hotel. Food is served in the Bay Restaurant/Café with its polished granite tables and ever-changing displays of artwork. Local produce is used

purposefully in dishes like grilled St Anthony's goats' cheese with aubergine and pepper salad (£5.50), and Cornish brill fillet with a crab and brioche crust and asparagus velouté (£14.95), while desserts might include chocolate and chestnut torte (£4.50). Service is 'prompt and cordial', and the wines are priced from £11.25. Accommodation available. Open all week.

● **PLUMTREE** (Nottinghamshire)
Perkins Old Railway Station, (0115) 937 3695. Wendy Perkins' two sons now conduct proceedings in this converted Victorian railway station, which is noted for its 'charming surroundings' and warm, courteous service. Menus change every few weeks and the good-value, bistro-style repertoire covers everything from spinach and feta cheese roulade (£8.95) to pan-fried red mullet with Mediterranean vegetables and coriander oil (£11.75). Two-course lunches (£9.75) are a snip for dishes like braised paupiettes of venison and banana sticky toffee pudding; Sunday roasts have also been commended. Keenly priced wines from £10.75. Reports please. Closed all day Mon and Sun D.

● **POLPERRO** (Cornwall)
Kitchen The Coombes, (01503) 272780. Ian and Vanessa Bateson's likeable restaurant caters admirably for visitors who make the seasonal trek to this Cornish village. Sustenance comes in the shape of globetrotting dishes including 'veggie' spring rolls with home-made mango and apricot chutney (£3.90), Moroccan lamb tagine (£11.90) and desserts such as pannacotta with summer fruit compote (£4.20). Fish 'extras' (John Dory with crab sauce, for example) are worth exploring and – if you really want to splash out – £80 will pay for a feast of 'fruits de mer' for two. Three dozen wines from £12.50. Note: no cheques. Open Tue to Sun, Easter to Sept D.

● **PORTH-Y-WAEN** (Shropshire)
The Lime Kiln Porth-y-Waen, (01691) 831550. Families are well catered for in Ian and Jayne Whyte's roadside free house on the A495. Menus are tailored to all tastes and the blackboard advertises

starters like pan-seared halloumi with hot-and-sour beetroot (£3.95) before grilled sea bass fillets on crispy noodles with roasted red pepper purée (£9.75) or chargrilled medallions of fillet steak with rosemary and horseradish sauce. The line-up of home-made desserts (£3.95) could include chocolate, brandy and meringue parfait. Baguettes are also served at lunchtime (not Sun). House wines from £7.75. Open Tue to Sun L and Tue to Sat D.

● **PORTLOE** (Cornwall)
The Lugger Portloe, (01872) 501322. A 'stunning' location in a tiny Cornish fishing village plus a cliffside terrace overlooking the sea are plus points for visitors to this intimate little hotel. Fixed-price, three-course dinners (£35) get a 'five-star build up' although the results on the plate can seem more straightforward: lettuce and watercress soup is a 'no-frills' affair, 'moist' pan-fried wild sea trout comes with a drizzle of basil and lime butter and, to finish, there might be spotted dick with vanilla sauce. Service is 'professionally laid back' and the well-chosen wine list has a decent selection by the glass. Open all week L and D.

● **RICHMOND** (Surrey)
Chez Lindsay 11 Hill Rise, (020) 8948 7473. Lindsay Wotton's passion for Breton cooking shows no sign of fading as the years pass. Her star turns are galettes made from organic buckwheat flour, with fillings from egg and cheese to chitterling sausage with onions and mustard sauce (prices £3–£8.50). There's also seafood in abundance – whelks with aïoli, warm rock oysters, plus more elaborate 'grand plats' (from £10.95) including grilled sea bass with mixed pepper butter. Sweet crêpes (from £2.75) round things off. Breton ciders, esoteric bières and Loire wines stand out on the drinks list; vin de pays is £10.95. Open all week L and D.

Petersham Hotel Nightingale Lane, (020) 8939 1090. Come for the views over Petersham Meadows to a lazy bend in the River Thames and for formal dining with crisp service in the luxurious surroundings of a 60-bedroom Victorian folly. New chef Russell Williams' set

dinners offer the full carte (£28 for three courses), a mix of pure classics with modern British twists – pan-fried baby Dover sole with tartare sauce, then seared fillet of beef with bone marrow tart and roasted ceps – while two-course lunches (£14.50) leave space for maybe warm bitter chocolate mousse with pistachio (£5.50 supplement). Serious, mainly French wine list. Reports please. Open all week, Sun D residents only.

● **ROYDHOUSE** (West Yorkshire)
Three Acres Inn Roydhouse, (01484) 602606. Combining the virtues of a country inn, hotel, restaurant and delicatessen, this huge set-up stands in glorious Yorkshire countryside only five miles from Huddersfield. Everything here is on a grand scale, including the menus. The world tour might begin with potted shrimps and buttered 'soldiers' (£6.95), before moving on to tandoori chicken with methi and seafood tagine with couscous (£14.95); finally there are desserts like mocha chocolate tart with praline ice cream (£5.50). The reasonably priced list of around 80 wines includes ten by the glass; house wines from £12.95. Open all week.

● **ST ALBANS** (Hertfordshire)
Sukiyaki 6 Spencer Street, (01727) 865009. Mr and Mrs Wakui's charming little restaurant just off the market place is a perfect spot for those hankering after a taste of domestic-style Japanese food. The menu doesn't change much and you won't find any raw fish, but take your pick from the modest selection of appetisers like chicken yakitori (£4.20) and gyoza (minced pork and vegetable dumplings) before salmon teriyaki (£9.50), tempura moriawase (deep-fried prawns and vegetables) or beef sukiyaki. There are also set dinners (from £18.50) and some affordable lunchtime deals. Drink green tea, beer or saké; house wine is £10.50. Open Tue to Sat L and D.

● **ST IVES** (Cornwall)
Tides Café 6 The Digey, (01736) 799600. It's worth exploring St Ives's many characterful little streets to find this informal modern café-restaurant with

slate floors, locally made mosaic tables and driftwood-framed mirrors. The blackboard menu may offer pan-fried squid with garlic, lemon and parsley zest and a rocket and mizuma salad at lunch (£8.50) or a more substantial dinner of John Dory fillets with black turtle bean, roasted red pepper and basil sauce (£14.95). Fat Italian anchovies on a starter of crostini opened 'the best meal of the week' for one holidaying couple. Short wine list from £11.95. Open Mon to Sat L and D.

● **SALISBURY** (Wiltshire)
LXIX 69 New Street, (01722) 340000. Modern artwork lightens the tone in this airy, cathedral-town 'bar and bistro'. Monthly specials add to the choice on the menu, but there are always appetite-sharpening snacks plus starters like goats' cheese crostini with sunblush tomato salad (£5.90). Follow on with pasta, noodles (perhaps topped with salmon, chilli and coriander), venison sausages with mash and roasted red onions (£7.50) or polenta with roast Mediterranean vegetables and chilli salsa. Desserts are stalwarts like chocolate bread-and-butter pudding. Thirty wines from £8.95. Closed Sun.

● **SHAFTESBURY** (Dorset)
Fleur De Lys 25 Salisbury Street, (01747) 853717. There are views over the Blackmore Vale from this 'extremely welcoming and cosy' dining room above a former coaching inn. The kitchen looks across the Channel for inspiration, so expect starters like pan-fried sweetbreads on celeriac purée with baked garlic and sherry sauce (£7.50), and mains such as roast saddle of venison with shallots, pears, ginger and raspberries in a raspberry sauce (£18), along with desserts including praline crème brûlée (£6). Staff are caring and friendly, and 'some good bargains' are to be found on the lengthy wine list; prices from £12.50. Closed Mon L and Sun D.

● **SHEPTON MALLET** (Somerset)
Blostin's 29–33 Waterloo Road, (01749) 343648. Nick and Lynne Reed's long-serving West Country restaurant

continues to tick over dependably as the years go by. Dinner is still fixed price (£15.95 or £17.95) and the well-tried repertoire (melon with fresh figs, skate with capers and prawns) is brightened up by seasonal specialities such as grilled scallops with gazpacho dressing (£4.95) and veal with portobello mushrooms and chive sauce (£14.50). Vegetarians have their own menu, while desserts might run to white chocolate crème brûlée. The wine list has plenty of sound drinking at low prices: house wines from £9.95. Open Tue to Sat D only.

● **SINNINGTON** (North Yorkshire)
Fox and Hounds Sinnington, (01751) 431577. Blackboard specials are the star turns in this roadside village inn on the edge of the North Yorks Moors: marinated pheasant breast might be served as a starter with sweet potato and pepper mash (£6.25), while grilled fillet of plaice could be paired with seared scallops and a tarragon and tomato salsa (£12.45). Regular lunch and dinner menus also tip their North Country flat cap to braised beef and potato pie or haddock and chips with mushy peas. Desserts range from sweet vanilla crêpes (£4.25) to a 'stack' of sorbets. House wine £11.50; accommodation available. Open all week.

● **SOUTHALL** (Greater London)
Gifto's Lahore Karahi 162–164 The Broadway, (020) 8813 8669. Expect crowds, noise and action in this vast ground-floor eating house on Southall's Broadway. Pakistani cooking is the order of the day and it's the real thing: in the snack department (from £1.20–£2.50) you will find bhel puri, papri chat and other nibbles, although the tandoor holds centre stage. The menu also lists tawa specials cooked on a hotplate and a challenging selection of curries (£6.50) including karela gosht (bitter gourd with lamb), quails masala and magaz (brains), as well as chicken korma. Unlicensed, but you can BYO. Open all week.

● **SOUTHAMPTON** (Hampshire)
White Star Tavern 28 Oxford Street, (023) 8082 1990. Formerly a seafarer's hotel, now transformed into

contemporary city bar-cum-bistro with first-rate, sympathetic comforts. Food in the 'Dining Rooms' befits the style of the place: tuna carpaccio and wild rocket salad (£5.25) is a typically in-tune starter, while mains might run to lobster linguine (£12) and crispy pork with potato rösti and Calvados sauce, with desserts like caramelised apple tart (£5) rounding things off. Brunch at weekends and food from noon to nine on Sunday. Service is switched on and there are champagnes aplenty on the carefully chosen wine list. Closed Mon L.

● **SOUTHPORT** (Merseyside)
Tyndall's 23 Hoghton Street, (01704) 500002. Converted town-house with some promising French-influenced cooking, especially sensitively handled meat and seafood. Downstairs is a relaxed bar and lounge area with bare floorboards, while the restaurant smartens up with carpets and swag curtains. Extensive fixed-price menu (£24.95 for three courses) includes good fish soups and full-flavoured honey-roasted duck breast with black cherry sauce. Similar but much pricier options offered à la carte. Open Tue to Sat D.

● **STOKE BRUERNE** (Northamptonshire)
Bruerne's Lock 5 The Canalside, (01604) 863654. Since last year's edition, Nicholas Woodward (whose family run the Boat Inn, across the Grand Union Canal) and Rachel Tapp have taken over this red-brick Georgian building and former sous-chef Simon Addison is now in charge of the stoves. No change to the menu though, where baked brioche of snails and frogs' legs with carrot dressing (£5.95) might precede pesto-marinated chicken with polenta, black pudding and mango sauce (£14.95), and there are five vegetarian options in small or large portions. Snack lunches are served on the canalside patio. Good value wine list with some smart bottles. Closed Mon, Sat L and Sun D.

● **STOKE HOLY CROSS** (Norfolk)
Wildebeest Arms 82–86 Norwich Road, (01508) 492497. Models of jungle beasts add to the 'safari lodge' image of this pub/restaurant south of Norwich. New chef Daniel Smith worked at Morston Hall and his style is overtly complex. Chargrilled chump of lamb with roast chorizo, butternut squash and courgette tagliatelle (£15.75) has impressed, and fish is given similar treatment: fillet of sea trout on crushed Jersey Royals with sauce Nero and buttered samphire, for example. Start with warm salad of squid and Alsace lardon (£5.95) and finish with one of the ever-so-pretty desserts (£5.25). Extensive, good-value wine list; prices from £11.50. Reports please. Open all week L and D. A sister pub, The Mad Moose Arms, is at Warwick Street, Norwich, tel: (01603) 627687.

● **STOKE PRIOR** (Worcestershire)
Epic' Bar Brasserie 68 Hanbury Road, (01527) 871929. An abbreviation of Epicurean, this was the first of Patrick McDonald's chain of brasseries bringing a splash of colourful urban chic to rural locations. The modern bistro menu offers chilled gazpacho crème fraîche, small or large chicken bang-bang salad, pastas, risottos and slow-roasted belly pork with caramelised apple and honey (starters £4.25–£6.50; mains £9–£15). Desserts include 'organic and grown up' ice creams. Short wine list mostly under £20. Convenient for the Avoncroft Museum and the famous Webbs of Wychbold garden centre. Closed Sun D. The other branches are in Whitacre Heath, tel: (01675) 462181, and Dunhampton, tel: (01905) 620000.

● **STOKE ROW** (Oxfordshire)
Crooked Billet Newlands Lane, (01491) 681048. Regular TV appearances have helped to put this remote Oxfordshire hostelry on the map. It's horrendously difficult to find, yet crowds pack in for the atmosphere, regular live music and – above all – food. The handwritten menu says it all in elaborate detail: pan-fried squid with chorizo, chilli, garlic, rocket and chilli oil (£6.90) is a typical starter, while mains could include venison fillet with McSween's haggis, baby spinach, roast fig, port, juniper and redcurrant sauce (£18). Desserts sound a touch

simpler: Bakewell tart and custard sauce
(£4.95), for example. The wine list roams
far and wide, with prices from £13.50.
Open all week.

● **STOW ON THE WOLD** (Gloucestershire)
Hamiltons Brasserie Park Street, (01451)
831700. There's a touch of sophistication
about this 'attractively done up' place,
with its marble floor, modern paintings
and 'style-conscious silverware'. The
kitchen brings a lot of ingredients into play
and there are some 'inventive combos'
such as tandoori collops of monkfish with
green pea and mint risotto (£13.25).
Starters raid the larder for lavender and
bay-infused duck confit, sticky black rice
and sweet-and-sour apricot chutney
(£6.50) while desserts might include bitter
orange tart with Campari and orange
posset (£4.50). Friendly service and a
well-spread wine list from £11.50. Open
all week.

● **STRETE** (Devon)
Laughing Monk Totnes Road, (01803)
770639. David Rothwell cooks while wife
Trudy serves in this converted Devon
schoolhouse. Little seems to change here:
a red theme dominates the dining room
and the extensive menu majors in tried-
and-tested favourites. Scallops with
seafood risotto is a pleasing starter, while
approved main courses have included
medallions of venison with seasonal
berries and a garlic and roasted onion
mash. To finish, the pudding trolley is
loaded with offerings like apricot sponge
and apple bake laced with Calvados. Main
courses £11.25–£15.25. The wine list is a
newly compiled, interesting slate with
house wines from £10.95. Open Tue to
Sat D.

● **SWANAGE** (Dorset)
Cauldron Bistro 5 High Street, (01929)
422671. Daily deliveries of local fish
explain why punters make a beeline for
the Flenley's seaside bistro. Specials
depend on the catch, but you might
encounter crab and prawns with Thai
coconut and lime sauce (£6.95), lobsters
cooked to order and grilled Dover sole
with fresh herbs, olive oil and lemon juice.
Otherwise, the handwritten menu lists

king scallops cooked in the wok and – for
meat eaters – honey-roast confit of duck
(£13.95). Finish with stem ginger ice
cream or Irish coffee crème brûlée (£4.50).
Light lunches are served Thur to Sun.
House wines from £10.95. Open Thur to
Sun L and Wed to Sun D.

● **TADPOLE BRIDGE** (Oxfordshire)
Trout Tadpole Bridge, (01367) 870382. A
pretty Thameside garden adds to the allure
of this cheery 'well heeled' pub in a tiny
Oxfordshire hamlet. Food plays a key role
in proceedings and the kitchen is capable
of delivering 'seriously good' dishes along
the lines of cured duck breast with soy,
ginger and melon (£5.95) and wild
mushroom risotto, as well as pan-fried
pork loin with apple Tatin, black pudding
and whole grain mustard sauce (£12.95)
and chargrilled Aberdeen Angus sirloin.
Puddings (£4.95) are mostly sponges, pies
and tarts. The wide-ranging wine list has
10 by the glass. Breakfast is a treat for
guests staying overnight. Closed Sun D.

● **TAUNTON** (Somerset)
Carved Angel Café Riverside Place,
(01823) 352033. The latest addition to the
Carved Angel group (see also entries in
Dartmouth and Exeter) occupies one of
the most picturesque sites in Taunton,
down by the River Tone. It follows the
same formula of simple daytime food to
refresh weary shoppers, stepping up into
restaurant gear in the evening. Simple
décor and bare tables are the order of the
day, while the bistro menu might offer
pan-fried pigeon breast on a spinach and
sunblush tomato risotto with pesto
(£5.50), then grilled fillet of black bream
with a leek and potato tart and herb
sauce (£11.95). Open Mon to Sun L, Thur
to Sat D.

The Sanctuary Middle Street, (01823)
257788. On two floors of a Taunton town
house (one for non-smokers), this
promising venue doubles as a wine bar
and restaurant: the decor is 'tranquil',
service is excellent and the food hits all the
right notes. Regulars rave about the salad
of rare roast beef with garlic potatoes, but
the weekly menu scours the globe for
mushroom and spinach risotto, Thai

fishcakes and tempura chicken with macadamia satay (main courses £10.95–£14.95). Daily seafood specials might include whole sea bass with rosemary, thyme and vanilla oil. Sweets and cheeses are recommended, and the house wines are 'very drinkable'. Open Mon to Fri L, Mon to Sat D.

● **TETBURY** (Gloucestershire)
Calcot Manor Tetbury, (01666) 890391. More brasserie than pub, the junior eating place (The Gumstar Inn) at this slick country hotel complex has a cottagey look described by one reporter as 'conservatively modern'. Numerous specials complement the regular menu, with 'ample' (£3.50–£6.50) or 'generous' (£7.50–£11.50) portions to suit your appetite and as few or as many courses as you wish. A full meal could be baked smoked applewood Cheddar cheese soufflé then salmon and herb fishcakes with dill butter and Calcot bread-and-butter pudding to finish. Helpful staff ensure rapid service. Short, modern wine list from £10.50. Open all week.
Close Hotel 10 Long Street, (01666) 502272. The hotel is a secluded sixteenth-century Cotswold stone building with an 'elegant' restaurant at the rear overlooking a 'lovely quiet garden'. A new chef donned his whites in 2003, and the evening 'Market Menu' (£28.50 for three courses) shows his modern French-inspired style: start with cauliflower and truffle cappuccino, before roast Gressingham duck breast on vanilla mash with rosemary jus or tournedos of monkfish with spiced lentils, wild mushrooms and foie gras. Finish with, say, hot chocolate fondant with Baileys ice cream or plump for the 'particularly good' cheeses. 'Decent' wines from £14.50. Reports please. Open all week.

● **TORQUAY** (Devon)
Mulberry House 1 Scarborough Road, (01803) 213639. Lesley Cooper's irrepressible one-woman show is now into its twentieth year and her immaculate Victorian terrace house is still a favourite with visitors. Distinctive home cooking based on sound local ingredients

is her trademark and the menu changes daily – three courses £15–£17.50. Start with gazpacho or provençale-style fish tart, before organic pork chop in cider with Bramley apples or grilled fillets of Torbay sole with savoury mayonnaise. Finish with strawberry pots or plum and almond crumble. Thirty well-chosen wines from £10. Booking essential for food and accommodation. Open Fri to Sun L, Wed to Sat D (residents only Mon and Tue D).

● **TREEN** (Cornwall)
Gurnard's Head Treen, (01736) 796928. The name refers to the great rocky promontory of Gurnard's Head which stands close to this Cornish inn. Given the location, it's no surprise that there's seafood on the menu: the eponymous gurnard puts in an appearance alongside specials like baked hake with cockles and samphire. Otherwise, expect starters like rillettes of pork with cornichons (£4.75) and mains such as seared pigeon breasts with a red wine reduction (£12.50). Bread-and-butter pudding with clotted cream (£3.95) is the pub's signature dessert. Six wines by the glass (from £2.40) head the short list. Accommodation available. Open all week.

● **TRESCO** (Isles of Scilly)
Island Hotel Tresco, (01720) 422883. A glorious setting and enviable views make this delightful hotel a real treasure on the sub-tropical 'Island of Flowers': admire the scene from one of the new balconies and terraces. Seasonal ingredients and exotic flavours form the backbone of the fixed-price dinner menu (£37.50), which might list chargrilled swordfish with papaya and mango salsa, and maple-baked pork loin with black pudding, spinach and Calvados, before baked chocolate truffle cake and pistachio ice cream. The 100-strong wine list has house selections from £16. Open all week.

● **TROUTBECK** (Cumbria)
Queens Head Hotel Townhead, (015394) 32174. For centuries this venerable coaching inn has been serving the needs of Lakeland travellers and tourists who come to admire the views over the Troutbeck Valley. These days, the kitchen feeds

visitors with restaurant dishes like cured salmon and crab rillette (£5.25), marinated haunch of local venison with braised red cabbage (£14.25) and seared tuna on a warm crushed potato and onion salad, followed by chocolate and Tia Maria torte (£3.75). A bar menu is also available lunch and evening. Real ales are alternatives to the sensibly priced wine list (vin de pays is £9.95). Accommodation available. Open all week.

● **TRURO** (Cornwall)
Café Citron 76 Lemon Street, (01872) 274144. Brasher, blue-fronted neighbour to more formal sister restaurant Sevens (see main entry), this all-day brasserie near the town centre has a relaxed Mediterranean feel. Menus are printed together on one laminated sheet offering salads and grills at lunch (£6–£7), more substantial dinners (£11–£16) like slow-roast rack of Cornish lamb in a basil, mint and rosemary crumb, plus all-day tapas/starters (£3–£5) that span the Med. 'Very fresh' fish impressed one visitor, and service is efficient. Opposite Hall for Cornwall, so useful for a pre-show meal. Short, good-value wine list. Closed Sun.

● **TWICKENHAM** (Greater London)
Loch Fyne Restaurant 175 Hampton Road, (020) 8255 6222. The Loch Fyne seafood empire continues to grow (see main entry, Cairndow) and its branches across the land provide a useful local service. This outlet in a converted pub sports clean-cut lines, well-spaced wooden tables and a menu that pleases piscophiles and carnivores alike. Gravlax and smoked haddock chowder (£4.95) have opened proceedings well, before grills and mains (£8–£15) such as dressed Cromer crab, smoked Islay sausages and whole bream with slow-roast tomatoes and olives. Two-course set lunches are £11.95. Around 20 wines make up the wine list. House wines are £10.95. Open all week.

● **UPTON SCUDAMORE** (Wiltshire)
Angel Inn 34b Upton Scudamore, (01985) 213225. 'A class act', concluded one reporter on this large, neat-looking, white-painted brick pub in a tiny village on the edge of the Wiltshire Downs. As pub and restaurant it's a proper all-rounder. Bare boards run throughout the popular bar where drinkers congregate and the 'thoroughly civilised' dining area with well-spaced pine tables set with flowers. Outstanding freshness and quality of raw materials have characterised the kitchen, but a new chef took over as we were going to press, so please send reports. Open all week.

● **WAKEFIELD** (West Yorkshire)
On The Edge 671 Barnsley Road, Newmillerdam, (01924) 253310. Rita Sutton's stone cottage overlooking the lake next to Newmillerdam Country Park makes a cosy setting for good-value evening meals and Sunday lunch. Many dishes on the menu are jazzed up with colourful accompaniments: duck breast with fig and ginger relish (£4.95), and seared tuna with chilli-spiced mango sauce (£12.25), for example. To finish, there might be toffee and pecan mousse with caramel sauce. 'Limited Edition' fixed-price menus (Tue to Fri from 6) offer a fair deal, and the modest wine list includes five by the glass. Open Sun L and Tues to Sun D.

Wolski's Monarch House, (01924) 381252. Spread over three floors of a splendid old wine warehouse, Wolski's combines an informal bar/brasserie, a smarter restaurant and a 'banqueting suite' for office parties and the like. Simple lunchtime fare gives way to a long evening menu with an emphasis on fish and seafood – perhaps seared baby squid with coriander chilli (£6) then plain grilled Dover sole (£13). Meat eaters could go for rosemary roasted lamb with spiced couscous, while beef tomato stuffed with mushroom ragoût is one of five vegetarian options. Set menu £13 for three courses before 7pm. Short wine list mostly under £20. Closed Sun D.

● **WARWICK** (Warwickshire)
The Rose and Crown 30 Market Place, (01926) 411117. 'We could eat here every week' raved a convert after three visits to this revitalised town-centre inn. It's now a fully-fledged gastro-pub-with-rooms

complete with breakfast and a flexible all-day menu until 6.30: sandwiches are served with chips or soup, and the 'deli plate' invites you to choose from cheeses, charcuterie and other provisions (£1.35 per item). Extra dishes surface for conventional lunch and dinner – perhaps chargrilled halloumi with baba ganoush (£4.50), specials like minted pea and feta risotto, and desserts including treacle and orange tart (£4.25). Around two dozen affordable wines from £10.50. Open all week.

● **WESTFIELD** (East Sussex)

Wild Mushroom Westfield Lane, (01424) 751137. 'Native lobster, wild mushroom, asparagus and rocket risotto' is typical of the extensive dinner menu in this family-run Victorian house. Other complex ideas might include foie gras and guinea fowl terrine with red onion marmalade and 'haricot vert' salad (£6.95), while main courses could include entrecôte of veal with tomato and basil jus and borlotti bean panache (£14). Finish with British cheeses or iced poppyseed parfait with poached apricots (£4.75). Fixed-price lunches (2 courses £13.95) remain a great favourite with regulars. Service is 'fine' and the 'sensible' wine list has house recommendations from £10.95. Open Tue to Fri and Sun L, Tue to Sat D.

● **WEYMOUTH** (Dorset)

Abbotsbury Seafood Bar Abbotsbury Oyster Farm, (01305) 788867. The setting – on the Fleet Lagoon – is a bonus for visitors to this casual seafood restaurant attached to Abbotsbury Oyster Farm. The celebrated bivalves play a starring role and other items come from a local fisherman with his own 'day boat'. Bad weather can mean no supplies, but – fingers crossed – there might be anything from whole Portland crab (£10) to grilled scallops. Begin with pan-fried octopus with garlic (£3.95) or prawn cocktail and ask about the local ice cream to finish. Steaks and gammon are non-piscine alternatives. Oyster Stout suits the food, otherwise opt for tea, coffee or wine. Open Tue to Sat L and Thur to Sat D.

Perry's 4 Trinity Road, (01305) 785799. 'Book early and ask for the window', advises a regular, who reckons this restaurant by the harbour is 'bliss'. The Hodder family have been in residence for more than a decade and they continue to specialise in fresh fish (although there are meat and vegetarian alternatives). Start the ball rolling with grilled scallops with lemon and garlic (£6.95), before roast fillet of turbot with warm citrus and cucumber dressing (£16.95) or lobster salad. Chocolate mousse cake with orange crème anglaise (£4.50) might conclude events. 'Exemplary service' and a decent selection of wines from £10.50. Closed Mon and Sat L, and Sun D in winter.

● **WHITSTABLE** (Kent)

Whitstable Oyster Fishery Co Royal Native Oyster Stores, (01227) 276856. Right on the beach, this Victorian brick warehouse (a former oyster store) packs out with visitors in high season. Simple décor of bare brick walls, checked tablecloths and a blackboard menu set the scene for unfussy fish and seafood – perhaps scallops with balsamic vinegar (£9.50) followed by grilled local cod with tartare sauce (£15.50), and of course oysters of 'unimpeachable freshness'. However, reporters concur in their unhappiness at the 'metropolitan' prices. Other ventures under the same ownership include the cafeteria-like East Quay Restaurant, the Hotel Continental and the Whitstable Brewery, whose wares can be sampled here. Open Tue to Sun L and D.

● **WICKHAM** (Hampshire)

Old House The Square, (01329) 833049. Grand eighteenth-century town-house, now a hotel combining the best of the original features with subtle modern touches. New chef James Dickson juggles modern dishes like barracuda and Indian spiced risotto with yoghurt and cilantro dressing with more established pot-roast lamb shank with garlic and rosemary creamed potato and doesn't overlook vegetarians (main courses £10–£16). Flavour-filled desserts are £5.95. Reasonable, mainly European wine list. Good peripherals like bread and olives and friendly, enthusiastic service. Closed Sun D

● **WINCHESTER** (Hampshire)
Bertie's 5 Jewry Street, (01962) 860006. There is a new chef at this popular, buzzy and unpretentious neighbourhood bistro, but it would appear to be business as usual. Usual being a slice of the Med behind a Winchester blue façade with tiled floor, pastel walls and bare tables. Modern British pan-fried calf's liver with crispy bacon, mustard mash, fine beans and redcurrant jus mixes with firmly Mediterranean saffron tagliatelle with goats' cheese, black olives, rocket, roast tomatoes and balsamic vinegar. Starters £4–£8, mains £9–£11 and set menus from £11.95. Friendly, entertaining service and good incidentals. Wine mostly under £20. Open Tue to Sat L and D.

● **WINSFORD** (Somerset)
Royal Oak Inn Winsford, (01643) 851455. In a village on the fringes of Exmoor National Park, this looks like every tourist's dream of a thatched West Country pub with centuries of history under its belt. Sustenance comes in the shape of praiseworthy bar meals (venison steak on braised red cabbage) and a short restaurant menu. Dinner might begin with warm salad of confit of duck with balsamic dressing (£5.50) before fillet of salmon with a pesto and Parmesan crust (£15.50); West Country cheeses and puddings like rhubarb crumble (£4.75) finish the show. House wine is £10.95. Accommodation available. Open all week.

● **WINTERTON** (North Lincolnshire)
George Market Street, (01724) 732270. You'll have to go upstairs for the restaurant – down below it's a traditional oak-beamed pub catering to the locals of this small town outside Scunthorpe. The dining room is more smart country inn, with bare boards, pine tables and dado railed green walls. Food aims far beyond pub grub, maybe a starter of blinis topped with smoked halibut, pickled cucumber and beetroot sorbet (£4.75), then for mains ragoût of turbot and scallops with fennel risotto and Noilly Prat sauce (£16.50), but also features comfort food like Lincolnshire sausage (£11.75) and traditional Sunday lunches. Open Sun L and Wed to Sat D.

● **WITNEY** (Oxfordshire)
Three Horseshoes 78 Corn Street, (01993) 703086. Handily placed close to the Butter Cross, this town pub has a rising reputation for food thanks to the presence of chef Lee Groves. He has worked in some pedigree kitchens and it shows in his up-beat menu. Start, perhaps, with grilled asparagus, orange mousseline and chive oil (£4.95) before best end of Oxford Downs lamb with roast fennel mash, olives, tomato and basil gravy (£13.50), and finish off with sixteenth-century English posset (£4.25). You can also lunch in the bar from a lighter menu of baguettes, omelettes and the like. The short, eclectic wine list starts at £10.25 (£2.60 the glass). Reports please. Closed Sun D.

● **WOBURN** (Bedfordshire)
Paris House Woburn Park, (01525) 290692. Since 1983, this fascinating black-and-white timbered house in the grounds of Woburn Park has been home to Peter Chandler's sophisticated restaurant. Appropriately, classic French cooking is the order of the day – whether you opt for set lunch (£30), the menu gastronomique or the fixed-price evening 'carte' (£52). Typical offerings from the latter might be chicken 'boudin blanc' with truffle sauce, loin of venison with pears and port wine sauce, and hot raspberry soufflé. The expense-account wine list kicks off with house vin de pays at £16. Open Tue to Sun L and Tue to Sat D.

● **WOLVERHAMPTON** (West Midlands)
Bilash Tandoori 2 Cheapside, (01902) 427762. Celebrating its 20th anniversary in 2003 with a full refurbishment and a new menu, this town-centre tandoori opposite the Civic Centre stays ahead of the pack with freshly made pickles and detailed spicing. Main dish prices run from £8.90 for vegetarian options and up to £22.90 for the house special Goan tiger prawn masala. Reporters have enjoyed shorisha maach (sea bass in a 'refreshing' mix of herbs and spices) and a 'very fresh'

spinach side dish. Attentive service and good modern wine list. Open Mon to Sat.

● **WORTHING** (West Sussex)
The Pepper Tree Montague Place, (01903) 823823. Close to the pier and the seafront, this restaurant/wine bar certainly lights up the Worthing scene. Brilliant yellow and bright orange are the colours in the open-plan dining rooms, where the menu promises 'fine cuisine from around the world'. Marinated baby artichokes on celeriac remoulade with baked goats' cheese and red onion confit (£6.95) is a decent combo, while mains are the likes of pigeon breast 'artfully arranged' with a slice of potato rösti, buttered cabbage and thyme jus (£15.50). To finish, warm molten chocolate pudding with vanilla ice cream (£5.50) has hit the button. Around thirty wines from £11.50,

four of which are sold by the glass (£2.95). Closed all day Mon and Sun D.

● **WYTHAM** (Oxfordshire)
White Hart Inn Wytham, (01865) 244372. A favourite with Oxford types wanting a break from the city, this traditionally rustic village pub can also surprise first-timers. The interior is bright, open and full of colour, and the kitchen deals in fashionable ingredients from the world larder. Expect anything from hot foccacia sandwiches (£7.25) and antipasti to salmon and ginger fishcakes with soy and wasabi dressing and mango salsa (£11.95) or confit of duck with sesame pak choi and hoisin sauce. Desserts (£4.95) might include summer pudding with clotted cream, and the wide-ranging wine list opens with twelve by the glass. Open all week, L and D.

Scotland

● **ARCHIESTOWN** (Moray)
Archiestown Hotel Archiestown, (01340) 810218. Dominating the village square, this eighteenth-century reddish-stone building has been revitalised by its current owners. Much of the hotel still feels like an old fashioned country house, although the terracotta-walled bistro strikes a more modern note. Starters such as tartlet of lambs' kidneys with spinach and green peppercorn sauce (£6) and desserts including crème brûlée with blueberries have been well received; elsewhere, the Scottish flag flies with Loch Etive mussels, locally gathered chanterelles, Angus-cross beef, and roast venison with red cabbage (£14). House wines are priced at £12.50 a bottle. Open all week L and D.

● **DRUMBEG** (Highland)
Drumbeg Hotel Drumbeg, (01571) 833236. Lovely views of Loch Drumbeg are just one alluring feature of this charming hotel close to the harbour. Fish is a key player in the kitchen, but the whole enterprise puts its faith in supplies from home and abroad. France dominates the menu, although it's tempered with English and Italian flourishes. The results sound irresistible: Scottish oysters with

free-range pork sausages from Lochinver (£7.90) or bowls of flageolet beans with wild thyme to start, then platters of locally landed 'fruits de mer' (£14.95) and dishes like monkfish roasted with bacon and puttanesca sauce – as well as coq au vin. To finish, pineapple roasted with spicy banana caramel (£4.50) could be a winner. Wines from £11.90. More reports, please. Closed Wed L.

● **EDINBURGH** (Edinburgh)
Fishers 1 Shore, (0131) 554 5666. Once a pub, this thriving venue on the Leith shoreline now combines a packed bar with a sedate dining room overlooking the water. Fresh fish is the focus and the menu reads well. Starters are particularly impressive – witness 'queenies' with rocket and Parmesan (£5.25) and impeccable langoustines with home-made mayonnaise. Elsewhere, the daily menu promises fillets of sea bass on citrus-marinated fennel (£14.50), grilled cod with Mediterranean couscous and – for meat eaters – Aberdeen Angus steaks. Staff are 'very pleasant' and the wine list is worth exploring; house French is £9.75. Open all week. There is also a branch 'in the city' (see main entry).

Suruchi Too 121 Constitution Street, (0131) 554 3268. Sari meets kilt in this unusual Indian restaurant, where flickering lights and a giant wooden elephant are familiar features. The menu promotes the cooking of the sub-continent with a broad Edinburgh accent: samosas are described as 'a licht pastry stappit, servit a flavourfu dookin sauce', venison, salmon and vegetable haggis fritters reinforce the Scottish allegiance. Butter chicken has passed with flying colours, puréed chickpeas with paneer is a pleasing combination and naan bread is 'rich and flavoursome'. Main course dishes £5 to £15. Service is 'very affable' and the wine list has house French at £10.50. Closed Sun L. The sister restaurant, Suruchi, is at 14A Nicholson Street; tel: (0131) 822 7227.

● **GLASGOW** (Glasgow)

Air Organic 36 Kelvingrove Street, (0141) 564 5200. For the organic element look to the list of ingredients, from the beef fillet to the greens; for air sit out on the paved area of this first-floor restaurant. Japan is the major influence, bringing sushi, saké, glass noodles with shiitake mushrooms and miso broth, and bento boxes from £12 to £16. Thai and Italian dishes also feature – watermelon Thai curry; prawn and lemon linguine with basil, chilli and garlic – while Med-Asian fusions produce the likes of peanut fried Thai salmon fishcakes with tzatziki and sweet chilli. Dishes range from £6.50 to £14. Open all week.

Café Gandolfi 64 Albion Street, (0141) 552 6813. Since the '80s this Glasgow landmark has been renowned for its bold designer furniture, stained glass and trendy buzz. Visitors also relish its all-day approach to food: say 'good morning' with eggs en cocotte on toast (£3.60), call in later for something Scottish (perhaps cullen skink or Stornaway black pudding with mushrooms and pancakes) or go Italian with a plate of linguine (£7.50). Seasonal specials bump up the menu and to finish there's lemon tart or apple pie (£3.60). Refresh yourself with Gandolfi lemonade, beer or one of the eminently quaffable wines (from £11.20). Open all week.

Rococo 202 West George Street, (0141) 221 5004. Revel in opulent surroundings at this fashion-conscious basement café-bar. A roving contemporary menu often looks to Italy or the East but also puts home-grown ingredients at the heart of many dishes, as in Perthshire venison with potato and thyme rösti, tomato compote and wilted greens. Three-course meals range from £18 to £36.50, with further choices on the carte. Two hundred wines climb from £17.95 to the sky. Closed Sun.

● **GLENLIVET** (Moray)

Minmore House Glenlivet, (01807) 590378. Well-travelled restaurateurs Victor and Lynne Janssen are at the helm of this elegant country house on the Glenlivet Crown Estate. They don't offer a written menu, so chef Victor describes and discusses each dish verbally. The choice varies daily, but a typical fixed-price dinner (£35) might run along the lines of minted pea soup with Lynne's home-baked 'health' bread, hot-smoked wild salmon on a horseradish hollandaise, and desserts such as hot apple and Calvados soufflé to round things off. The extensive wine list has a strong South African presence; prices from £15.95. Open all week.

● **KINFAUNS** (Perthshire & Kinross)

Kinfauns Castle Hotel nr Perth, (01738) 620777. Heritage and grandeur loom large in this baronial hotel, with its stained-glass coats-of-arms, tartans and panelling. Meals are served in the ornate Library Restaurant, where fixed-price menus (lunch from £14.50, dinner from £35) show plenty of Scottish touches. Start with a salad of Skye crab with quails' eggs and dill dressing before, say, fillet of Angus beef with strudel potatoes, braised French beans and port wine reduction. Desserts are intricate creations like apple and cinnamon spring rolls with a pot of toffee sauce and caramelised bananas. House wines from £17.50 head the huge 300-bin list. Open all week.

● **MELROSE** (Borders)

Burt's Hotel Market Square, (01896) 822285. This well-established, family-run hotel dating from the eighteenth century presents a fresh white frontage to Melrose's market square, brightened further by overflowing window boxes. Bar suppers of liver or lamb shank have been well received (though be aware the bar is packed out by traders and rugby fans on market and match days), while the formal restaurant offers set meals (three-course dinner £29.75) pairing traditional Scottish ingredients with a sense of adventure in medallion of Scotch beef fillet with a wild mushroom and roast garlic ragoût and Barolo and basil scented jus. Good service and a serious wine list, prices from £12.25. Open all week.

● **NEWTON STEWART** (Dumfries & Galloway)

Kirroughtree Hotel (01671) 402141. 'A lovely place – if you can find it', warns a traveller. This luxurious country mansion stands imposingly in its own grounds, with only a 'discreet' sign to signal its presence. Dinner is based around a formal four-course menu (£32.50) of solidly reliable fare: bang-bang chicken might set the ball rolling, before vichyssoise or duck confit with Puy lentil sauce. You might continue with plump loin of Kirroughtree venison with braised red cabbage and grain mustard sauce before concluding with 'fine' apple tart with cinnamon ice cream or Scottish cheeses. House wines £14.50. Open all week.

● **OBAN** (Argyll & Bute)

Waterfront 1 The Pier, (01631) 563110. 'Better than ever' enthused a visitor returning to this one-time seamen's mission within sight of the pier. Locally landed fish is the culinary inspiration, specials are 'dictated by the weather and the season', and the kitchen turns its hand to dishes like plentiful seafood chowder (£5.95) or cod fillet on chive mash with Thermidor sauce (£13.50). Venison and a few novelties like haggis spring rolls satisfy the carnivorous brigade, while Orkney ice creams make a refreshing alternative to desserts like sticky toffee pudding (£4.25).

Light dishes also available; house wine £11.95. Open all week.

● **PLOCKTON** (Highland)

Plockton Inn Innes Street, (01599) 544222. Set only 100 yards from the harbour, this family-run village inn naturally gives seafood top billing – and even has its own smokehouse. The haul from the boats generally yields local Plockton prawns (aka langoustines), which are served hot or cold (£5.95); also expect lemon sole, scallops and dishes like cod fillet with tomatoes, olives and parsley (£10.50). Meat-lovers and vegetarians might be offered Aberdeen Angus beefburgers, haggis and whole Camembert baked in its box and – to finish – there's brown bread ice cream. House wines are £9.50. Accommodation available. Open all week.

● **STEIN** (Highland)

Loch Bay 1–2 Macleod Terrace, (01470) 592235. A cottage by the shore is the atmospheric setting for this modest seasonal restaurant, where fresh simply cooked seafood is the business of the day. The owners procure organic salmon from Uist or Orkney, while lobsters and oysters are selected from the kitchen's own tanks; added to this, the menu might list sea bass, megrim or hake – depending on the catch. Start with steamed mussels or seared marinated squid and finish with, say, rhubarb Pavlova. Mains £8–£16.50. Three dozen wines suit the food, and there are seven by the glass. Accommodation. Closed Sat L and all day Sun.

● **TORRIDON** (Highland)

Loch Torridon Hotel Loch Torridon, (01445) 791242. Kilted out in full baronial garb, this grand Scottish country house stands proud in wild country at the head of Upper Loch Torridon. The hotel changed ownership during 2002, although chef Kevin Broome is still in the kitchen. Home-grown vegetables, Highland meat and daily supplies of shellfish dictate proceedings on his seasonal fixed-price menu (£39): pan-roast scallops with confit of young leeks and fennel pulp might precede long-braised shoulder of Black Isle lamb with Puy lentil casserole, before crème caramel 'scented' with heather honey and golden raisins. Ten house wines from £14. More reports please. Open all week D.

● **WEST LINTON** (Borders)
Old Bakehouse Main Street, (01968) 660830. Charmingly located in an old bakery with the original ovens still built into the walls, this restaurant highlights Scottish ingredients throughout, even when served Danish-style on open rye-bread sandwiches or given a fusion makeover, as in Anstruther crab cakes with lime, chilli, ginger and wasabi mayo. Similarly Gressingham duck comes with five spice, plum and ginger sauce and pak choi, while for traditionalists there's Aberdeen Angus sirloin with peppered sauce. Starters £3–£5.50; mains £10–£16. Open Wed to Sun L, Wed to Sat D.

Wales

● **BETWS-Y-COED** (Conwy)
Ty Gwyn Hotel Betws-y-Coed, (01690) 710383. Once a pit-stop on the old Holyhead-London road, this centuries-old coaching inn still delivers the goods for travellers and locals alike. The interior is deeply chintzy, but there's plenty to liven things up on the menu. Fish has been enthusiastically received: red snapper in a cream sauce with mussels and chives; and whole sea bass on a turmeric sauce dotted with crayfish, for example. The menu also lists grilled goats' cheese en croûte (£3.95), chargrilled steak with garlic mushroom velouté (£12.95) and specials like Welsh lamb with marmalade jus. House wine is £11. Accommodation available. Open all week.

● **BRECON** (Powys)
Tipple'n Tiffin Theatr Brychieniog, Canal Wharf, (01874) 611866. Relocating from Hay-on-Wye to a new home in the Brecon Theatre, the Gudsells's have taken both the relaxed café-bar look and informal, tapas-style menu of 'plates to share' with them. Expect local ingredients and an international style, perhaps slow roast ribs of Tamworth pork in hoisin marinade on chilli noodles or fondue-like Tiffin shards to dip in molten Welsh cheese with laver bread, and 'best ever' salads according to one self-styled 'aficionado'. Dishes are £6–£8, with no differentiation between starters and mains. Twenty good-value wines are all under £20. Closed Sun.

● **CARDIFF** (Cardiff)
Buffs 8 Mount Stuart Square, (029) 2046 4628. Handy for a wine bar lunch or a relaxed repast after work, this venue on the fringes of trendy 'Cardiff Bay' has something of the feel of a 'gentleman's club'. The kitchen delivers a fistful of 'round the world' standards, backed up by a few Welsh stalwarts: expect Thai fishcakes with tomato and chilli, lamb chops with blackcurrants and raspberries, and chargrilled fillet steak with butter and garlic sauce. Generous, comforting home-made puddings and around 40 very reasonably priced wines. Main courses £5 to £7 for L, and £11 to £15 for D. Open all week L and D.

Le Monde 60 St Mary Street, (029) 2038 7376. The procedure here is to queue (there are no bookings, except for large parties), choose from the displays of meat and fish, check out the salad bar and find a table. Chargrilling is the favoured cooking method in this vibrant city-centre venue and it's used for everything from halibut steaks to beef kebabs; alternatively there's sea bass in rock salt or deep-fried hake (main courses from £10–£14). Start with gravlax (£4.95) and finish with tarte Tatin. Two-course lunches are a snip (£9.95 Mon–Fri, and only £6.95 Sat). Wines, from £9.95, are listed on blackboards. Closed Sun. Under the same roof and run along similar lines are La Brasserie, tel: (0209) 2023 4134; and Champers, tel: (0209) 2037 3363.

● **GLANWYDDEN** (Conwy)
Queen's Head Glanwydden, (01492) 546570. For more than 20 years, Robert and Sally Cureton have been feeding all-comers in their pristine village pub/ restaurant. They run an extensive

monthly menu, which is backed up by specials like fillet of sea bass with sun-dried tomato and dill butter. Crispy duck leg on a bed of sticky onions (£4.95) is a typical starter, before pot-roast pheasant with orange and cranberry jus (£11.50), while puddings could include cherry Bakewell tart (£3.50). There are also open sandwiches at lunchtime and grills in the evening. Around 40 wines feature on the list, which kicks off at £11.95 a bottle, £2.40/£3.40 per small/large glass. Open all week.

● **LETTERSTON** (Pembrokeshire)
Something's Cooking The Square, (01348) 840621. 'A fish and chip shop with a difference' and 'a value-for-money oasis for hungry families on holiday', sum up the appeal of this green-tiled establishment on the Fishguard-Haverfordwest road. The stars of the show are spanking fresh fish from Milford Haven (line-cut haddock, 'moist, juicy' plaice, etc.) and hand-cut chips fried in palm oil, although there's support from crab cakes, cockles with laverbread and cold desserts. Take away or sit at one of the wooden tables in the restaurant. Main courses £5–£10.85. 'Delightful service', and a 'good simple wine list'. Open Tue to Sat, and Mon (in July and August only) L and D.

● **LLANARMON DYFFRYN CEIRIOG** (Wrexham)
West Arms Llanarmon Dyffryn Ceiriog, (01691) 600665. Once a pit-stop for drovers from the Welsh hills, this remote hostelry in the Ceiriog Valley is now a hotel with all mod cons. Straightforward grub is served in the beamed bar, while more ambitious offerings appear on the restaurant menu. Fixed-price dinners (£27.95 and £32) are built round centrepieces like fillet of organic Welsh lamb in puff pastry with a port and Cumberland sauce or roast hake with anchovies, tomatoes and saffron potatoes; start with local duck on an orange and walnut salad, and finish with dark chocolate and kumquat truffle. House wine is £13.50. Open all week.

● **LLANFRYNACH** (Powys)
White Swan Llanfrynach, (01874) 665276. The Brecon Beacons provide an awesome backdrop to this renovated rough-stone pub opposite the village church. Food rather than beer drinking is now the focus, and the kitchen supports small-scale local producers. Fish specials (perhaps monkfish with bacon, crushed potatoes and saffron sauce) bolster the menu, which shows a liking for worldwide flavours: grilled polenta with spiced aubergines and pecorino (£5.45) might precede Welsh lamb shank with Moroccan spices and couscous (£12.95) or mallard breast with sweet potato mash and red onion marmalade. Desserts are mostly homespun offerings like treacle tart (£3.95). Chilean house wines £11.95. Open Wed to Sat L and D.

● **LLANFYLLIN** (Powys)
Seeds 5 Penybryn Cottages, (01691) 648604. One visitor was bowled over by the 'proprietor cooking and wife up-front' approach in Mark and Felicity Seager's modest restaurant. There are no grand gestures, but the cooking is sound and prices are 'very reasonable'. Evening meals are fixed price (£20.50 or £22.50) and the short menu makes its way through grilled sardines with basil butter, and rack of lamb with Dijon and herb crust, before desserts like crème brûlée or lemon posset with blackcurrant sauce. The wine list stretches to 150 bins (including seven by the glass); prices from £11. Open Wed to Sun L and Wed to Sat D.

● **LLANWRTYD WELLS** (Powys)
Lasswade Country House Station Road, (01591) 610515. Roger and Emma Stevens are finding their feet in this Edwardian house near Llanwrtyd Wells' station and early signs are most encouraging. He cooks, she copes 'efficiently and genially' with front-of-house. The kitchen champions local and organic ingredients and there are no gimmicks. Visitors have heartily applauded smoked salmon terrine with seasonal Evesham asparagus, and baked monkfish with chilli jam and minted couscous, as well as dark chocolate and

honey tart with mulled orange compote and crème fraiche. Fixed-price dinners are £24.95 and the keenly priced wine list starts at £9.95. Accommodation available. Reports please. Open all week D only.

● **PEMBROKE** (Pembrokeshire)

Old Kings Arms Main Street, (01646) 683611. The restaurant of this old hotel close to Pembroke Castle is housed in the fifteenth-century kitchen with dark beams and copper pans much in evidence. Local ingredients are key to the success of the cooking whether for straightforward fresh fish or sturdy modern mains such as breast of local corn-fed chicken filled with Carmarthen ham and black pudding mousse (£13). Light bar meals are available. Fair range of wines under £20. Open all week.

● **ROCKFIELD** (Monmouthshire)

Stone Mill Rockfield, (01600) 716273. A converted sixteenth-century cider mill (complete with landscaped gardens) is the delightfully bucolic setting for this country restaurant. Chef Simon Kealy's cooking is a mix of home-grown with Italian flourishes: steamed black pudding with mustard sauce (£4.50) and roast rib of Welsh beef with horseradish cream and oxtail sauce (£14.50) share the billing with confit of duck calzone and brodetto. Lemon ricotta and almond cake is a straightforward dessert. Daily fixed-price menus are reckoned to be 'excellent value', likewise the wine list – house wine £11. Accommodation in adjoining cottages. Reports please. Closed Mon all day and Sun D.

● **SOLVA** (Pembrokeshire)

The Old Pharmacy 5 Main Street, (01437) 720005. Martin Lawton now runs the show in this 'very convivial' bistro on the ground floor of a former chemist's. Fish from Milford Haven and the local boats has been well received: 'the famous Solva crab' might be served in filo baskets (£6.90); lobster and bouillabaisse have been commended and there are also specials like grilled sea bass with jasmine rice and vanilla butter sauce. Choose anything from a bowl of pasta to a four-course meal from a menu that also

promises navarin of Welsh lamb (£16) and desserts like praline semi-freddo (£4.90). Good-value wines from £11.60. Open all week D only.

● **SWANSEA** (Swansea)

Knights 614–616 Mumbles Road, (01792) 363184. A panoramic view of the bay makes an appropriate backdrop to this stylish bistro, as locally caught fish and seafood is a major feature here – dressed crab and lobster thermidor, for example – complemented by more exotic barracuda and kingfish. The main menu takes in reliable favourites such as 'very nice' aromatic duck with plum sauce alongside ambitious options like sautéed loin of wild boar with a spicy avocado sauce (£13.25). Closed Sun D and Mon L.

P.A.'s 95 Newton Road, (01792) 367723. A cheerful buzz of conversation generally fills this relaxed Mumbles restaurant and wine bar. An extensive daily fish menu might offer baked sea bass with ginger and spinach sauce (£14.95), while choices for the economical two-course lunch (£9.50) could be grilled mackerel and trout with chilli, tomato and herb sauce then pan-fried duck breast with a redcurrant, rosemary and red wine jus. Weightier dinner mains run to marinated wild boar steak roasted with sun-dried tomatoes and olive tapenade (£12.70). Cheerful, helpful service ensures a loyal local following. Closed Sun D.

● **WELSH HOOK** (Pembrokeshire)

Stone Hall Welsh Hook, (01348) 840212. The restaurant of this country hotel is located in the oldest part of the building, a 600-year-old Pembrokeshire manor with stone flagged floors and rough oak beams. France is the inspiration and the food, from local produce, is traditional French with occasional modern twists – perhaps snails in garlic butter followed by duck breast marinated in honey, soy and ginger (£15.90) or fillet of beef on a pan-fried crust with creamy thyme and mushrooms sauce (£16.60), and a classic crème brûlée to finish. A four-course menu at £22.50 is an economical alternative to the carte. Mainly French wine list from £12.90. Open Tue to Sat D only.

Channel Islands

● **ST PETER PORT** (Guernsey)
La Frégate Les Cotils, (01481) 724624.
The popular restaurant of this luxurious
hotel enjoys a magical view over the
harbour, even if it has been tarnished a
little by construction of a municipal car
park. Muted cream chairs and paintwork,
stiff white linen tablecloths and rich blue
coastal landscapes on the walls add up to a
modernised formal look. Food remains
traditional, with various set menus
(£15.95–£24.95) and a carte that focuses
on local seafood for starters, then moves
on to mains along the lines of peppered
duck breast with wild mushrooms and
spinach in a cream and brandy sauce.
Smart, mainly French wine list. Open all
week L and D.

The Good Food Club 2003

Many thanks to all the following people who contributed to the 2004 Guide. . .

R. Abbott
Juliana Abell
Dr A.H. Abrahams
Dr Sidney Abrahams
Andrew Adams
Robert Adams
Peter Adcock
Mrs R. Ainscough
John and Leslie Aird
Sarah Akhtar
Lawrence and Dorothy Alexander
Mr and Mrs M. and S. Alexander
Mrs A. Allam
Robert Allon
Mr S. Amey
Mr and Mrs A.D. Amstell
A.S. Anderson
E.S. Anfilogoff
Sir Michael Angus
Mr T. Appleton
Cynthia Archer
Mrs G. Arnold
Aileen Arnot
Mrs A.K. Ashton
V. Ashworth
Mr C. Aspin
Hazel Astley
Margaret and Don Avery
H.L.K. Avis
Janet Awty
Michael Awty
C. Ayres
Mrs M.A. Bache
Mr R.J. Baglin
Mr and Mrs R.W. Bagnall
Nicholas Bailey
Mr W.H. Baily
Jo-Ann Baines
Mrs M. Baker
Mr R.W. Baker
John Bamforth
Prof Stephen Bann
Sue Barclay
John Barker

Barbara Barnard
Cheryl Barnes
Penny Barr
T.I.G. Barrasford
Janet Barron
Mr and Mrs B.J. Barry
Peter and Amanda Bartlett
Charles Bartley
Mr D.R. Bass
S. Batcup
Mr Bates
Jeremy Bath
Peter Bayley
Conrad Bayliss
T.H. Beale
Nigel Beardsley
Mr E. Beckett
Mr F.R. Beckett
Mrs J. Beddoe
Mr P. Bell
Dr and Mrs L. Bell-Perkins
David and Glynis Bellamy
John Bence
T. Benjamin
Gabrielle Bennett
P. Bennett
Paul Bentley
W.M. Bentsen
Lucy Beresford
Gabriele Berneck
Colin Berry
Mr W.J. Best
Tim Bevan
L. Bilimoria
Roger Bingham
Mrs V.A. Bingham
Betty and Chris Birch
Mr R.G. Birt
Carole Bisset
Alan Blacic
Mr C.T. Blackburn
Mrs Blackburn
Trevor and Ann Blackburn
Mrs J.A. Blanks
Edward Blincoe

Mr and Mrs S. Bliss
Jane Bloomfield
Mr K.W. Blyth
Christopher Bolton
Christine and Neil Bonsall
Dr Ben Booth
Mr and Mrs W.H. Booth
Dr and Mrs Borrows
Canon and Mrs M.A. Bourdeaux
Mr A.J. Bowen
John Boynton
Maggie Bracher
Anthony Bradbury
Mr M. Brady
Barry Brahams
Hugo Brailsford
Roger Braithwaite
Mr and Mrs Frank Branney
Elizabeth Brannigan
Mr B. Brears
Roisin Bresnihan
B. Breton
Mr and Mrs John Brierley
Mrs B. Briggs
Jane Bristow
Mr R.W. Broadhurst
Patrick Bromley
Alan Brooker
Douglas Brooks
Grahame Brooks
Tony Brooks
Col J.M. Browell
Dr and Mrs D.G. Brown
Graham Brown
Dr William Brown
Linda Browrigg
Lesley Bruin
William Bruton
Mr and Mrs Edgar Bryant
Gillian Buckenham
R.W. Buckle
Mrs F.A. Buckley
Mr M.H. Buckley

Mr P.M.A. Buckman
Michael Bunce
P.K. Buntin
Mr and Mrs A.G.M. Burge
Mr E. Burgess
Carol Burns
Mr M.H. Burr
A.W. Burton
Richard Bush
Mr Butler
R. Butler
Peter Byworth
Dr Denis Cahill
Nicholas Caiger
Peter Caley
Roger Calverley
Dr Brian Campbell
A. Campton
Peter Carr
Mrs J. Carrera
Dr John Carroll
Catherine Carter
Mrs S. Cartlidge
Mr and Mrs Richard Cartwright
Ms S.C. Cassells
Dr R.E. Catlow
Mrs J. Cave
Christopher Stephen Challener
Dr Anne-Carole Chamier
E.M. Chapman
Mr S.W. Chinn
Paddy and Kate Chronnell
Mr Churcher
Geoffrey and Pamela Clark
John Clark
Patricia Clark
D. Clarke
Mr C.L. Clarkson
Keith Clayton
Derek Clegg
John Clegg
K. Cleveland
Doug and Ruth Clunie

Roger Cockbill
Nigel Cockburn
Peter Cockerill
Prof and Dr Cohen
Shirley Coker
Mr and Mrs Cole
K.J. Coleman
Lady Coleridge
Janet Collett
Dr Joe Collier
Mr Collins
D.W.F. Collins
Hannah Colton
Mr R.T. Combe
Mrs V. Condron
Juliann and Linda Cooke
Anne Cooper
Catherine Cooper
Mrs J. Cooper
Dame Joyanne Copeland
G. Coppen
Rachel Cordes
Nick Cosin
Mr and Mrs A. Cotcher
Hannah Cotton
June Coubrough
Peter and Mary Coulson
Mr T.S. Couzens
Mr R.J. Cox
Sally Cox
Christine Cramb
R.I. Crawford-Smith
Mrs J.M. Crewe
Rodney Cross
G.C. Crossley
Mr and Mrs John Cunliffe
Mrs R.A. Currie
Jenny Curtis
Dr Stan da Prato
Peter Daines
Rosemary Dainty
Mr and Mrs P.F. Dakin
Mr K.W. Daley
Andrew Dalmahoy
Mr A. Daly
Mr and Mrs J.O. Dalzell
David Davey
Mr and Mrs D.W.M. Davidson
Beatrix Davies
Colin Davies
Duncan Davies

Mrs G. Davies
Dr J.M.P. Davies
Lynda Davies
Lynette Davies
Tony Davies
Mrs M. Davison
Dr and Mrs R.P.R. Dawber
Diane Day
Mr M.J. Day
John de Carle
Anthony de Kerdrel
Nigel Deacon
Nicola Dean
R.N. Dean
Mrs P.A. Debenham
Ms N.C. Dee
M. Denchfield
Daniel Denibas
Charles Dewhurst
Mark Dickinson
Ian Dingwall
K.H. Dinsley
M.L. Dodd
Colin Donald
Liz and Phil Donnelly
Mr and Mrs James Douglas
Dr Colin Dourish
Mrs V. Downes
Tony Downs
Mr D.R. Drucquer
John Ducker
Ian Duckworth
Mr N. Dudenby
Dr Andrew Dunn
Francis Durham
Chris Dyson
Dr R.J. Eaglen
Colin Eastaugh
Dr D.G. Easterby
Dr and Mrs Lindsay and Marion Easton
Dr S. Eden
Miss A. Edgar-Walters
Mr P. Edmondson
Aileen Edwards
Gary Edwards
Mr J. Edwards
K.H. Edwards
John Elder
Mr G. Elflett
Mrs C.M. Elkington
W.P. Elliott
Martin Ellis
Robert Ellis
Edith Elmy

Lt Col D.C.J. Emmett
Eddie and Henrietta English
Mrs H. Etherington
John and Rosy Ette
J.S. Evans
Caroline Faircliff
Richard Fairclough
Jed Falby
Jacquie Faller
Ann Farrow
Mr G.A. Fenn
A.B.X. Fenwick
Elizabeth Fergusson
Neville Filar
Prof L. Fine
Allson Flath
Mrs A. Fletcher
Mr A.T.R. Fletcher
Clare Fletcher
G.E. Fletcher
Penelope Fletcher
Ernst Floate
Jason Folley
Irene Footitt
Anne and Peter Foreman
Christopher Forman
Mrs P.L. Forrest
Christina Forster
Mr A. Foster
M.J. Fountain
Dr Rosslynne Freeman
Dr D.J. Frost
G.E. Frost
Derek Fry
Mrs B.M. Furnell
Mrs K. Garden
R.J. Garlick
Anthony Garrett
Mrs M. Gash
Dr Ian Gavin
Janet Gayler
Mr D.M. Gaythwaite
Dr P. Giangrande
Lady D. Gibbs
Richard Gibson
John Gilks
Mrs S. Gillespie
John Glaze
B. Glover
Mrs P.M. Glover
Roger Glover
Stephen and Pauline Glover
Mrs J. Godfrey
Matt Godfrey

Simon Godfrey
Mr and Mrs Goldfarb
D.L. Goldie
Mr B. Golding
Joy and Raymond Goldman
Linda and Susie Goldschmidt
Mrs A.E. Goodwin
Geoffrey and Diana Goodwin
John Goodwin
David Gordon
Mr M. Gordon-Russell
Terry Gorman
Robert Goudy
Mr and Mrs A. Gough
Dr P.E. Gower
Michelle Graham
Ronnie Graham
B.E. Gray
Mr and Mrs W.A. Gray
Dr M.J. Grayson
Mr and Mrs B.H. Green
Richard Green
Mr T.G. Green
Jim Greenwood
Mr W.N. Greenwood
P.A. Gregg
Conal Gregory
Mrs C. Grey
Mr R.F. Grieve
Edward Griffin
Mr R.F.B. Grimble
Lieut K.R. Groves
Russ Gunter
Pamela and Raymond Guy
Paul Halford
Dr Bryan Hall
C.J. Hall
Hazel Hall
Robert Hall
Tom Halsall
Mr A.D. Hamilton
Dr B. Hamilton
Matthew Hamlyn
John Hammond
Gordon Hands
Joseph Hanlon
Mr J.G. Hanson
David Harcus
D. Harding
Andrew Hardy
Mr J. Harison

Tim Harper
G.G. Harris
Mr J.H. Harris
Raymond Harris
Dr B.D.W. Harrison
Howard Harrison
Jenny Harrison
Ms P.M. Harrison
John Harrop
Ian Hart
Stan and Eileen Hart
Dr Peter Harvey
Molly Hattersley
Richard Hawkins
Carenza Hayhoe
Mr S.P. Hayward
Dr O. Heathcote
Rev Canon Neil
  Heavisides
T.P. Heavisides
Dr Ann Henderson
Mr N.F. Henshaw
Roger Hepher
Drs Geoffrey and
  Joselen Heron
Dr Andrew
  Herxheimer
Mary Jo Hewitt
Mrs L. Hibbert
Jennifer Hicks
Chris and Susan
  Higgins
Mrs J. Higgins
Mr F.R. Hilborne
Allen Hill
Angus and Annette
  Hill
Brian Hill
Jennifer Hill
Dr Jonathan Hill
Robert Hill
Rupert and Nicola
  Hill
Wendy Hillary
Eric Hinds
Mr and Mrs R. Hinds
Hubert Hirst
Mr and Mrs P.A.
  Hoare
Michael Hocking
Jenny Hogan
Malcolm Holliday
Debi Hollingworth
Geoff Holman
David and Heather
  Holmes
Victoria Hood Sandy
Betty Hooper
Mrs J. Hope

Derek Hopes
Sarah Hopkin
Amelia Hornblow
Mr and Mrs R.H.
  Horncastle
Andrew Horsler
Keith Hotten
Simon Houghton
Mr E.F. Housam
Mr D.P. Howell
Alison Hudson
Joan Hughes
Leonard Hughes
Mrs H. Hulme
Mr R.S. Humphries
Dr Tim Hunt
D.E. Hunter
Mr C.J. Hurd
Mrs M. Hurry
Mr T.J. Hypher
Rosemary Inge
K.G. Isaacson
Mr W. Jaeger
Ronald Jaffa
Ellen Jakubiel
Bruce Jamieson
Brenda Jeeves
M.F. Jeeves
Sir Elgar Jenkins
Valerie Jenkins
Col F.G. Jennings
Richard and Janet
  Jennings
Paul Jerome
Elspeth Jervie
David Jervois
Barbara Jiskoot
Ailsa Jobson
Mr B.M. Joce
Mr R.M. Jolly
Mr and Mrs A.G. and
  S.J. Jones
Douglas Jones
Ian Jones
Dr Mel Jones
Neil Jones
Paul Joslin
Vernon and Deirdre
  Jotcham
Mr M.R. Judd
Dina Kaufman
Dr Leon Kaufman
Mr A. Kellett-Long
Geoffrey Kemp
Louise Kemp
Ralph Kenber
Roger Kenber
Jane Kendrick
David Kenny

Mr J.D.B. Kerby
Mr J.D.R. Kewley
Elizabeth Key
Geoff Key
Sheila Keynton
Donald Kiddle
Mrs W. Kielbinska
Mr and Mrs J.H.
  Kilby
W.M. Kingston
Dr B.W. Kington
Mr and Mrs Michael
  Kirk
Eddie Kirkpatrick
John Kleeman
Patricia Kleinman
Robin Knapp
R.G.A. Knott
Peter Knowles
Dr and Mrs I. Koppel
Peter Krook
Mr I. Laidlaw-
  Dickson
Christine Lakic
Anthony Land
Mr P. Lane
Dr Kathy Lang
D. Lapthorne
Mr and Mrs Kevan
  Lavender
Mrs M.E. Lawrence
Richard Lawrence
Janita and Maurice
  Lay
Mr D.M. Lee
Geoffrey Lee
Mark Lee
Mr and Mrs W.M.
  Lee
Mrs C. Leedham
Mrs J. Leeke
Lt Col M.I. Leese
Mrs K. Leeson
James Lethem
Lionel Leventhal
Adrian Levine
Mr and Mrs Lewis
D.E. Lewis
Mr L.H. Lewis
Leonard Lewis
Philip Lewis
Richard Lewis
Roy Lewis
Mr B.N. Liddiard
Mr and Mrs R.G.
  Lightwood
Keith and Katherine
  Lindop
D.R. Linnell

Bob Lloyd
Dr David Lloyd
Brigitta Lock
Janet Lockett
D.M. Loten
Mary Louden
Mr G.M. Lough
Mr and Mrs P.A.
  Lowater
Jan Lowy
Jeremy Lucas
J. Lupton
Alan Lyster
Alasdair MacDonald
G.M. Macdonald
Dr I.S. Macdonald
Jean Macdonald
M.W.B.
  MacEacharn
Mr A.J. Macintosh
A.C. Mackesy
Irene Mackie
Mrs A. Mackinnon
Helen Maclennan
Brian Madderson
Mr C.B. Madderson
Alison Maddock
C. Maggs
John Mainwaring
Bridget Manley
Paul Manners
Susan Mansfield
Jacques Marchal
Dr Charles Markus
Mrs E. Marshall
Francois Marshall
Mr R.F.D. Marshall
Mr and Mrs Roger
  Marshall
Mr and Mrs G.D.
  Martin
Hugh Martin
Mr and Mrs Martin
Pauline Martin
Roger and Joan
  Martin
Mr and Mrs E.J.H.
  Mason
Mr and Mrs Roy
  Mathias
Paul Mathieu
Mrs S. Matthews
Stephen Matthews
Ian May
J.R. Maybank
Mrs E. Mcallister
G.J. Mcallister
Kevin and Margaret
  Mcbrien

Mr and Mrs G.A. McConnell
Mr E.S. McConway
Mr and Mrs I. McCutcheon
Kate McDowall
Cynthia McDowell
Michael Mcevoy
Mr McFeeters
M. Mcgarrigle
Colin and Lilian McGhee
Mr K.N. Mcilwrick
Peter Mckenna
Dr and Mrs J.G. McLaggan
Ian McLaren
Duncan Mclean
Marianne Mcmillan
N.J. Mcmullan
Mrs J. Mears
Mr H.C. Medcalf
Dr and Mrs C.P. Mellor
Mr and Mrs Malcolm Menzies
Anna Merton
Jenny Metcalf
Caroline Midmore
Milo Mighell
Mr T.W. Miller-Jones
Mrs S.B. Milne
Timothy Milward
Mr K.S. Mingle
Gillian Minogue
Mr A. Mitchell
G. Mitcheson
Wendy Montague
S.R. Montgomery
Mrs L. Moores
Jo Morgan
Michael Morgan
Jan Morris
Prof Norman Morris
Mr A.J. Morton
Peter Moss
Sam Muir
Sandy and Lorna Muir
Dr P.K. Mukherjee
John and Sue Mulready
Braham Murray
Mr P.J. Murrin
Mr and Mrs Natton
Mr C.H. Naylor
Mr Charles Naylor
Mr and Mrs Chris and Vicki Naylor

Dr S. Neidle
Mrs S. Nestor
Richard Newby
Adrian and Maggie Newell
Jamie Newman
Alan Nicholas
M. Nicholson
Mr I.S. Nixon
E. Norman
Dr J.R. Norman
J.G. Norris
T.J. Norris
Brian and Janice Nott
Dr Ian Nussey
David Nutt
Mr G.H. Nuttall
Michael O'Neill
Gregg O'Reilly
Charles Oatwig-Thain
John Oddey
Anthony Ogden
Prof Anthony Ogus
Miss H. Oram
Bill Orchard
Prof Orledge
Stuart Orr
Mr and Mrs R.E. Osborne
Suzi and Sean Ottewell
Mrs T.A. Owen
Meriel Packman
Amanda Page
Mr S.C. Palmer
Don Parker
Martin Parker
Mr D.J. Parry
John Patrick
Ruth Perkins
Keith Perry
Mr and Mrs A. Peryer
Dr E. Petrit
Mr and Mrs C. Philbin
Joanna Phillips
Mrs D.T. Pick
A.M. Pickup
T. Piedsall
Richard Pierce
David Pilling
George Pincus
Michael Pitel
Roger Plant
Roger and Angela Plastow

Jeremy Plewes
Anne Plummer
Mr and Mrs J. and M. Pockinhorn
Jim and Kit Polga
Dan Pollins
David Poole
Mr and Mrs R.J.M. Pope
Mr and Mrs J.S. Porter
Jacqueline Potter
Nigel Powis
Dr P.L. Pratt
Edward Presley
D.V. Price
Hugh Price
Robert Pullar
R.G. Pursey
Andrew Putnam
Dr and Mrs D.R.J. Quickenden
Tony Radevsky
Jack Raeburn
Ian Ramage
Alan Randall
William Rankin
Ronald Rankine
Caroline Raphael
Mrs S. Rasmussen
Peter Ratzer
Mrs K.E. Rawes
Mr B.S. Read
Mrs A. Redfern
Angela Redfern
Mr and Mrs Frank Redfern
Prof W.D. Redfern
Shirley Redpath
Jeffrey Reed
Herve Regent
Anne Rhodes
Clive and Gail Rhodes
Mr and Mrs G. Rhodes
Peter Richards
Mr C.J. Richardson
Ian Richardson
Carol Riddick
Dr M.G. Ridley
Mr and Mrs R. Ring
Gordon Ringrose
B.J. Ripley
Mr G. Roberts
Miss J. Roberts
Lynne Roberts
Maureen Robertson

Mr and Mrs Ivor Robinson
Mr J. Rochelle
Barry Rogers
Margaret Rogers
Larry Rolland
Mr H.D. Rose
Joyce Rose
Alexander Ross
Margaret Ross
J.E. Rowe
Michael Rowland
Miss J. Roy
Mr and Mrs Ian Royle
J.A. Rumble
John Rumsey
Robert Running
Mr D. Russell
Mr J.S. Rutter
Helen Rycroft
Ilse Ryder
Prof J.R. Rydzewski
David Rymer
Lady Sachs
Keith Salway
S.D. Samuels
Philip Sanders
Dr M.A. Sansbury
Michael Saunders
Anne Savage
Mary Sawyer
A.A. Schiff
Michael Schofield
K.H. Scollay
Esme Scott
Stella Scott
Mr and Mrs W.P. Scott
Martin and Genevieve Searle
Jessica Seaton
G.D. Sedgley
J.E.R. Seegor
Derek Seel
David Sefton
Paul Sellers
Louisa Service
Richard Sewell
Mr R.W. Seymour
Mr and Mrs P. Sha-darevian
Norbert Sharland
Carl Shavitz
Dr Mark Shaw
Olivia Shelley
Peter Shotts
Giles Sim
Mrs D. Siminson

Audrey and David Simpson
Peter Skinnard
Jenny Skinner
Andrew Slater
Fred Slegg
David Sleight
Rev R.C. Smail
John and Kate Smallwood
Margaret Smart
Mark Smee
Dai and Norette Smith
Frances Smith
Dr Linda Smith
Mrs P.M. Smith
Dr and Mrs R.W. Smith
Sue Smith
Andrew Smyth
Dr and Mrs B.A. Snowdon
Mrs B. Somerset Jones
Paula Somerville
Alan Spedding
Dr Seymour Spencer
Digby Squires
Jeremy Stanley-Smith
John and Vivien Steadman
Sheila Steafel
Mrs G.M. Stein
Anthony Stern
Alan Stevens
Alison Stevenson
John Stevenson
Tom Stevenson
Capt and Mrs J.S. Stewart
Dr John Stewart
Freddie Stockdale
Mrs B. Stokes
John Stott
Alan Strong
Mr and Mrs N. Stupple
Mr A.B. Suckling
M. Sullivan
Adele Summers

Roger Summers
Ian Sutcliffe
Ms A.M. Sutcliffe
John Sutcliffe
A.M. Sutton-Scott-Tucker
Mrs L. Swan
Dr M.T. Syddell
Colin and Irene Sykes
Brenda Symes
Mrs E.M. Talbot
Mr and Mrs Tate
A. Taylor
Mrs A.C. Taylor
George Taylor
J.D. Taylor
Mrs J. Taylor
Robert Taylor
Margaret Teager
Andrew Teather
G. Templeton
Paul Tendleman
Dr Diana Terry
Russell Thersby
Alan Thomas
Bernice Thomas
Dudley Thomas
Mr R.J. Thomas
N.J. Thompson
Mrs D.M. Thomson
John Thornburn
Jennifer Thornely
Mr D. Thornton
Mr and Mrs G.N. Thornton
Dr C. Thorogood
Howard Thrift
Mr R. Thurlon
Mr and Mrs Thurlow
Graham Thwaites
Judge David Ticehurst
David Tilehurst
Nigel Todd
Catherine Tomas
Michael Tomlinson
Philip Tordoff
John Tovey
Mrs C. Town
Tom Treadwell
Mr D.R. Trimmer
Mr J.D. Tromlett

J. Tross
Mrs M Tucker
Beryl and Dick Tudhope
D. Tunstall
Mr B.W.B. Turner
Col B.S. Turner
David Turner
R.L. Turner
Gavin Udall
Mr I.D. Usher
Annemieke Van-denberg
Mrs M. Vanlint
Louise Verrill
Mr P.H. Wainman
J.H. Waite
Mrs A.M. Walden
Mrs S.E. Walden
Judith Walker
Richard Walker
Stephen John Walker
Dr Robert Waller
Adrian Walsh
Capt P.J. Walsh
Mr G. Walton
Derek Ward
Mr A.J. Wardrop
Sir Gerald Warner
Mr R.A. Wartnaby
Paul Warwick-Munday
Mr and Mrs J.S. Waters
Mr and Mrs Watkins
A. Webb
John Webb
Mr and Mrs D.J. Weddle
Mr M.J. Weeds
Joanne Welch
Bridget Wells
Mr J.F.M. West
M.J. West
Mrs M. Weston-Smith
Stacey Whatling
Dr G.T. Whitaker
Mr M.J. White
C.R. Whitham
John Whiting
Paul Whittaker

Paul Whittard
Mr and Mrs S. Whittle
Martin Whitworth
D. Wilcock
Mr K. Wildbore
R.C. Wiles
John Wilkinson
Prof Wilks
Mr P. Willer
Anthony Williams
D. Williams
Gill Williamson
Michael Williamson
Sarah Wills
Drs A. and C. Wilson
Mr D.G. Wilson
Mr and Mrs Ian Wilson
Prof P.N. Wilson
Gerry and Roo Wilton
Anthony Winder
June Wise
Mr and Mrs T. Withers
Dr Philip Woodward
Barbara Wooldridge
Geoffrey Wooldridge
Mrs A. Wormersley
Alan Worsdale
Kay Worsley-Cox
Alan Wright
Angela Wright
Mr and Mrs E. and P. Wright
Keith Wright
Peter Wrobbel
Mr and Mrs John Wyatt
Andrew and Philippa Wyer
Richard Wyld
Mrs J. Wynter
Ellen Yahuda
Shirley Yarwood
Mrs M.J. Yates
B. Yoakes
George Yorke
Dr R.C. Young
Dr P.L. Zacharias

Index of entries

Index of entries

Names in bold are main entries. Names in italics are Round-ups.

Report Form

To the Editor *The Good Food Guide*
FREEPOST, 2 Marylebone Road, London NW1 4DF

Or send your report by electronic mail to: *goodfoodguide@which.net*

From my personal experience the following establishment should/should not be included in the Guide (please print in BLOCK CAPITALS):

_____

_____

Telephone_____

I had lunch/dinner/stayed there on (date) _____

I would rate this establishment _____ out of ten.

please continue overleaf

My meal for ___ people cost £_____ *attach bill where possible*

☐ Please tick if you would like more report forms

I am not connected in any way with management or proprietors, and have not been asked by them to write to the Guide.
Name and address (BLOCK CAPITALS, please)

_____

_____

Signed _____

As a result of your sending us this report form, we may send you information on *The Good Food Guide* and *The Which? Guide to Good Hotels* in the future. If you would prefer not to receive such information, please tick this box ☐.

To the Editor *The Good Food Guide*
FREEPOST, 2 Marylebone Road, London NW1 4DF

Or send your report by electronic mail to: *goodfoodguide@which.net*

From my personal experience the following establishment should/should not be included in the Guide (please print in BLOCK CAPITALS):

_____

_____

Telephone_____

I had lunch/dinner/stayed there on (date) _____

I would rate this establishment _____ out of ten.

please continue overleaf

My meal for ___ people cost £_____ *attach bill where possible*

☐ Please tick if you would like more report forms

I am not connected in any way with management or proprietors, and
have not been asked by them to write to the Guide.
Name and address (BLOCK CAPITALS, please)

_____

_____

Signed _____

To the Editor *The Good Food Guide*
FREEPOST, 2 Marylebone Road, London NW1 4DF

Or send your report by electronic mail to: *goodfoodguide@which.net*

From my personal experience the following establishment should/should not be included in the Guide (please print in BLOCK CAPITALS):

_____

_____

Telephone_____

I had lunch/dinner/stayed there on (date) _____

I would rate this establishment _____ out of ten.

please continue overleaf

My meal for ___ people cost £_____ *attach bill where possible*

☐ Please tick if you would like more report forms

I am not connected in any way with management or proprietors, and
have not been asked by them to write to the Guide.
Name and address (BLOCK CAPITALS, please)

_____

_____

Signed _____

As a result of your sending us this report form, we may send you
information on *The Good Food Guide* and *The Which? Guide to Good Hotels* in the
future. If you would prefer not to receive such information, please tick
this box☐.

Report Form

To the Editor *The Good Food Guide*
FREEPOST, 2 Marylebone Road, London NW1 4DF

Or send your report by electronic mail to: *goodfoodguide@which.net*

From my personal experience the following establishment should/should not be included in the Guide (please print in BLOCK CAPITALS):

_____

_____

Telephone_____

I had lunch/dinner/stayed there on (date) _____

I would rate this establishment _____ out of ten.

please continue overleaf

My meal for ___ people cost £_____ *attach bill where possible*

☐ Please tick if you would like more report forms

I am not connected in any way with management or proprietors, and have not been asked by them to write to the Guide.
Name and address (BLOCK CAPITALS, please)

Signed _____

Report Form

To the Editor *The Good Food Guide*
FREEPOST, 2 Marylebone Road, London NW1 4DF

Or send your report by electronic mail to: *goodfoodguide@which.net*

From my personal experience the following establishment should/should not be included in the Guide (please print in **BLOCK CAPITALS**):

_____

_____

Telephone_____

I had lunch/dinner/stayed there on (date) _____

I would rate this establishment _____ out of ten.

please continue overleaf

My meal for ___ people cost £_____ *attach bill where possible*

☐ Please tick if you would like more report forms

I am not connected in any way with management or proprietors, and have not been asked by them to write to the Guide.
Name and address (BLOCK CAPITALS, please)

_____

_____

Signed _____

To the Editor *The Good Food Guide*
FREEPOST, 2 Marylebone Road, London NW1 4DF

Or send your report by electronic mail to: *goodfoodguide@which.net*

From my personal experience the following establishment should/should not be included in the Guide (please print in BLOCK CAPITALS):

_____

_____

                              Telephone_____

I had lunch/dinner/stayed there on (date) _____

I would rate this establishment _____ out of ten.

please continue overleaf

My meal for ___ people cost £_____ *attach bill where possible*

☐ Please tick if you would like more report forms

I am not connected in any way with management or proprietors, and have not been asked by them to write to the Guide.
Name and address (BLOCK CAPITALS, please)

_____

_____

Signed _____

As a result of your sending us this report form, we may send you information on *The Good Food Guide* and *The Which? Guide to Good Hotels* in the future. If you would prefer not to receive such information, please tick this box ☐.

Report Form

To the Editor *The Good Food Guide*
FREEPOST, 2 Marylebone Road, London NW1 4DF

Or send your report by electronic mail to: *goodfoodguide@which.net*

From my personal experience the following establishment should/should not be included in the Guide (please print in BLOCK CAPITALS):

_____

_____

Telephone_____

I had lunch/dinner/stayed there on (date) _____

I would rate this establishment _____ out of ten.

please continue overleaf

My meal for ___ people cost £_____ *attach bill where possible*

☐ Please tick if you would like more report forms

I am not connected in any way with management or proprietors, and have not been asked by them to write to the Guide.
Name and address (BLOCK CAPITALS, please)

_____

_____

Signed _____

To the Editor *The Good Food Guide*
FREEPOST, 2 Marylebone Road, London NW1 4DF

Or send your report by electronic mail to: *goodfoodguide@which.net*

From my personal experience the following establishment should/should not be included in the Guide (please print in BLOCK CAPITALS):

_____

_____

Telephone_____

I had lunch/dinner/stayed there on (date) _____

I would rate this establishment _____ out of ten.

please continue overleaf

My meal for ___ people cost £_____ *attach bill where possible*

☐ Please tick if you would like more report forms

I am not connected in any way with management or proprietors, and have not been asked by them to write to the Guide.
Name and address (BLOCK CAPITALS, please)

_____

_____

Signed _____